A
B
C
D
E
F
G
H
I
J
K
L
M
N
O
P
Q
R
S
T
U
V
W
X
Y
Z

The University of Chicago Spanish Dictionary

Universidad de Chicago

Diccionario
Inglés-Español *y* Español-Inglés

Tercera Edicion, Revisada y Ampliada

Un Diccionario Manual Nuevo y Conciso que
Contiene las Voces y Locuciones Básicas de
Ambos Idiomas y Además una Lista de 1000
Modismos y Refranes Españoles con Variantes
y Traducción al Inglés

Recopilación de
Carlos Castillo *y* Otto F. Bond

Con la ayuda de
Barbara M. García

Revisado por
D. Lincoln Canfield

The University of Chicago Press
Chicago & London

The University of Chicago

Spanish Dictionary

Third Edition, Revised and Enlarged

A New Concise Spanish-English and English-Spanish
Dictionary of Words and Phrases Basic to the Written
and Spoken Languages of Today, plus a List
of 1000 Spanish Idioms and Sayings, with Variants
and English Equivalents

Compiled by
Carlos Castillo & Otto F. Bond

With the Assistance of
Barbara M. García

Revised by
D. Lincoln Canfield

The University of Chicago Press
Chicago & London

The University of Chicago Press, Chicago 60637
The University of Chicago Press, Ltd., London

© 1948, 1972, 1977 by The University of Chicago
All rights reserved
First Edition published 1948
Third Revised Edition 1977

Printed in the United States of America

81 80 79 78 77 98765432

Library of Congress Cataloging in Publication Data

Main entry under title:

The University of Chicago Spanish dictionary.

    Added t.p. in Spanish: Diccionario inglés-
español-y español-inglés.
    Includes index.
    1. Spanish language—Dictionaries—English.
2. English language—Dictionaries—Spanish.
I. Castillo, Carlos, 1890-   II. Bond,
Otto Ferdinand, 1885-   III. García, Barbara M.
IV. Canfield, Delos Lincoln, 1903-
V. Chicago. University.
PC4640.U5 1977 463'.21 76-449

ISBN 0-226-09673-4
ISBN 0-226-09674-2 pbk.

Contents

Foreword to the Third Edition, vi

Part One Spanish-English

Parte Segunda Inglés-Español

Foreword to the Third Edition

The University of Chicago Spanish Dictionary has been compiled for the general use of the American learner of Spanish and the Spanish-speaking learner of English, with special reference to New World usages as found in the United States and in Spanish America.

With this purpose in mind, the editors and the author of the revisions and additions of this new third edition have selected the words to be defined, first according to the relative frequency of their occurrence, secondly in keeping with dialectal variants of the New World, both Anglo and Hispanic, and thirdly in accordance with the increase in technological lexicon during the past two decades.

The Spanish-English section of the Dictionary contains all the items listed in Juilland and Chang Rodriguez's *Frequency Dictionary of Spanish Words* (The Hague: Mouton & Co., 1964). The hundreds of dialectal variants which appeared in the 1972 edition as well as the entries related to developments in the fields of aviation, atomic energy, linguistics, and so forth, have been augmented. More than 1000 new entries have been added to the Spanish-English section and in the English-Spanish section some 500 new entries—in addition to the 1500 items new to the second edition—have been added. No attempt has been made to add an equal number of entries in both parts for the simple reason that in the past three decades many more new terms of universal usage have been coined in English than in Spanish. Many of these new English terms have been assimilated into Spanish.

One of the outstanding features of the third edition is the list of 1000 Spanish idioms and sayings that follows the Spanish-English section. Dialectal variants and English equivalents, also with variants, are listed for these idioms, and an English index makes locating them easy.

Also new to the third edition is syllabication of all the entries in both parts as well as a new phonetic transcription of the Spanish entries. (The English entries had been transcribed phonetically in the first edition.) In keeping with the New World application of the Dictionary, the phonetic transcriptions of the Spanish entries have been made to represent "Highland American" usage (Mexico, Guatemala, Costa Rica, Highland Colombia, Ecuador, Peru, Bolivia). Local variations have been disregarded.

Regional Spanish-American usage is still identified by abbreviations of country or area, and parenthetical identifying expressions continue to be employed to facilitate distinction among several possible definitions of a particular word.

The extensive auxiliary data of the second edition has been retained, including the list of monetary units, the adjectives of nationality, and the extensive discussion of American-Spanish and its regional dialects.

A dictionary should be an instrument for better understanding between peoples. It is the earnest wish of the editors of this one that it may serve that end.

Part One Spanish-English

List of Abbreviations

adj.	adjective	*math.*	mathematics
adv.	adverb	*neut.*	neuter
arith.	arithmetic	*num.*	numeral
conj.	conjuction	*p.p.*	past participle
contr.	contraction	*pers.*	personal
def.	definite	*pers. pron.*	personal pronoun
def. art.	definite article	*pl.*	plural
dem.	demonstrative	*poss.*	possessive
dem. adj.	demonstrative adjective	*prep.*	preposition
dem. pron.	demonstrative pronoun	*pron.*	pronoun
etc.	et cetera	*refl.*	reflexive
f.	feminine noun	*refl. pron.*	reflexive pronoun
fam.	familiar	*rel.*	relative
indef.	indefinite	*rel. adv.*	relative adverb
indef. art.	indefinite article	*rel. pron.*	relative pronoun
inf.	infinite	*sing.*	singular
interj.	interjection	*subj.*	subjunctive
interr.	interrogative	*v.*	verb
irr.	irregular	*v. irr.*	irregular verb
m.	masculine noun		

Special Words and Abbreviations Used to Indicate Regional Occurrence

Am.[1]	Spanish-American
Andalusia	
Andes	(Ecuador, Peru, Bolivia)
Arg.	Argentina
Bol.	Bolivia
Carib.	(Cuba, Puerto Rico, Dominican Republic)
C.A.	Central America (Guatemala, El Salvador, Honduras, Nicaragua, Costa Rica)
Ch.	Chile
Col.	Colombia
C.R.	Costa Rica
Cuba	
Ec.	Ecuador
Guat.	Guatemala
Hond.	Honduras
Mex.	Mexico
Nic.	Nicaragua
N.Sp.	Northern Spain
Pan.	Panama
Par.	Paraguay
Peru	
P.R.	Puerto Rico
Riopl.	Rio de la Plata region (Eastern Argentina, Uruguay)
S.A.	South America
Sal.	El Salvador
Spain	
Ur.	Uruguay
Ven.	Venezuela

Spanish Pronunciation

The Spanish of Spain (except the southwest) has 24 phonemes, or minimum units of sound-meaning distinction. The Spanish of southwest Spain and most of Spanish America has 22 phonemes. These minimum units of sound are indicated in the following charts and descriptions by slashes, /b/, /e/, /č/, and stand for

[1] This abbreviation is employed to indicate general Spanish-American usage, usually with the implication of obsolescence in Spain. It is also used to identify words that are currently little used but which may occur in literary works of bygone days.

1

Phonetic Manifestations of the Phonemes of Spanish

Voice	Bilabial		Labiodental		Interdental		Dental		Alveolar		Palatal		Velar		Glottal	
	vs	vd	vs	vd	vs	vd	vs	vd	vs	vd	vs	vd	vs	vd	vs	vd
Occlusive	p	b			t	d	t	d					k	g		
Fricative	φ	ƀ	f		θ	đ		.				y	x	ǥ	h	
Sibilant							s	z	S	Z	(š)	(ž)				
Affricate											č	ŷ				
Nasal										n		ñ		ŋ		
Lateral										l		ļ				
Vibrant										r rr						
Semiconsonant		w										j				

an abstract representation of a group or class of sounds, the individual members of which are variants or allophones. The latter are indicated by brackets: [b̥], [e], [ŷ]. Some of the phonemes of Spanish have two or three variants, depending on position within the phrase.

The two principal characteristics of Spanish pronunciation as contrasted with English are tenseness of articulation and continuity in transition from word to word within the breath group. Thus all the vowels have a clear nondiphthongal character and sound "clipped" to the English-speaking person. The consonants, especially /p/, /t/, /k/, /l/, /r/, /rr/, have much less vocalic interference than in English, and the first three have no aspiration. The glottal stop, so common in the Germanic languages, including English, is very rare in Spanish. The transition between vowels of contiguous words is smooth. **El hado, helado, el lado** sound very much alike. **Para hacerlo** is [paraasèrlo] or in rapid speech [parasèrlo]. So marked is the continuity that following sounds influence the preceding ones: **los dos niños** [lozdózniños]; **un peso** [umpèso] **en que** [èŋke].

The Consonantal Phonemes of the Spanish of Northern Spain

$$
\begin{array}{cccccc}
/p/ & /b/ & /t/ & /d/ & /k/ & /g/ \\
 & /f/ & /\theta/ & /S/ & /y/ & /x/ \\
 & & & /č/ & & \\
/m/ & & /n/ & /ñ/ & & \quad 24 \\
 & & /l/ & /ļ/ & & \\
/r/ & /rr/ & & & & \\
\end{array}
$$

The Vocalic Phonemes of Spanish

$$
\begin{array}{ccc}
i & & u \\
 e & & o \\
 & a & \\
\end{array}
$$

The Consonantal Phonemes of Andalusian and Latin American Spanish

$$
\begin{array}{cccccc}
/p/ & /b/ & /t/ & /d/ & /k/ & /g/ \\
 & /f/ & & /s/ & /y/ & /x/ \\
 & & & /č/ & & \\
/m/ & & /n/ & /ñ/ & & \quad \text{22 or 23} \\
 & & /l/ & (/ļ/) & & \text{[Bolivia, Paraguay, Peru]} \\
/r/ & /rr/ & & & & \\
\end{array}
$$

The Spanish Spelling System and the Sounds Represented

I. The Vowels

1. i as a single vowel always represents [i], similar to the second vowel of *police*. Examples: **hilo, camino, piso.** As a part of a diphthong, it represents [j], much like English /y/ in *yes, year*. Examples: **bien** [bjen], **diablo** [djablo], **ciudad, baile, reina, boina.** The first syllable of **baile** is much like *by* in English.

2. e represents [e], which has no exact equivalent in most English dialects. It is higher than the /e/ of *get* but without the diphthong of *they*. It is

much more tense in articulation than either English sound. It varies slightly according to adjacent sounds. The vowel of **perro** is more open than that of **pero**. Generally it is more open in a closed syllable. Examples: **mesa, del, hablé, en, tres.**

3. **a** represents [a], which is similar to the first vowel of *mama*, stressed on the first syllable. Examples: **caso, cano, ¡ah!, América.** Even when not stressed, it has the same clear sound. English *America* has at least two neutral or *schwa* sounds [ə].

4. **o** represents [o], which is more like the Scotch-English sound of *auld* than the British or American *old*. It has no off-glide or diphthongal character such as is heard in the latter. It varies slightly according to adjacent sounds: the first syllable of **corro** is slightly more open than the first of **coro**. **Sol** is slightly more open than **no**. Examples: **boto, modo, señor, oso, amó.**

5. **u** represents [u], which always has the value of the sound indicated by English *oo* in *boot, fool*, never that of *book*, nor that of the *u* in *union*. Examples: **cura, agudo, uno.**

    a. Note that the spelling combinations **qui, que, gui, gue** represent [ki], [ke], [gi], [ge].

    b. **u** is used to represent the semiconsonant [w] in a diphthong: **cuida, cuento, cuadro, cuota** [kwíḓa], [kwénto], [kwáḓro], [kwóta].

    c. Likewise **u** is used to represent the semivocalic element of a diphthong: **bou, deuda, causa** [bow], [déwḓa], [káwsa].

II. The Consonants

1. **p** represents [p], which never has the aspiration of English /p/ (*pill, papa*), but is like that of *spot*. Examples: **padre, capa, apuro, punto.**

2. **b** and **v** represent /b/, which has two variants, according to position in the phrase: [b], [ƀ]. These do not depend on spelling, which goes back centuries. Either letter represents [b] at the beginning of a breath group or when preceded by [m] (spelled either **m** or **n**), and is much like English /b/. Examples: **bomba, burro, en vez de, vine, invierno.** In spite of spelling, the last three examples are [embézḓe], [bíne], [imbjérno]. Either letter represents [ƀ] in all other situations. English has no equivalent. It is a /b/ with the lips slightly open. Examples: **haba, uva, Cuba, la vaca, habla, la barba.**

3. **m** represents [m], which is essentially the same as English /m/ (*much*). Examples: **madre, mano, cama.** [m] does not occur syllable final in Spanish. **Álbum** is pronounced [álƀun].

4. **f** represents [f], which is similar to the /f/ of English. In some areas and among certain strata of Hispanic society the articulation is bilabial rather than labiodental.

5. **t** represents [t], which never has the aspiration of English /t/ in prevocalic stressed position (*tea, two, ten*). It is more similar to the English /t/ of the cluster [st] (*stop, step*). Examples in Spanish: **tela, tino, tinta.** The point of articulation is dental.

6. **d** represents /d/, which has three variants according to position in the phrase: [d], [ḓ], [Ø]. At the beginning of the breath group or after /n/ and

/l/, **d** represents [d], which is similar to the English /d/ of *dame, did, darn.*
Examples: **donde, falda, conde.** In all other situations the letter represents [đ],
or even [Ø]. There is a tendency in modern Spanish to move from the
fricative [đ] (similar to the sound represented by the *th* in *mother, this, then*)
to zero articulation [Ø]. Examples: **hado, cuerda, es de, dos dados, cuadro,
padre, abad, usted, Madrid.** The last two words are usually pronounced
without final consonant, and the consonant tends to be very weak in the
ending /-ado/: **hablado, estado, mercado.**

7. **s** In Spain, except the southwest, this letter represents [S], an apicoalveolar
sibilant, similar to the /s/ of southern Scotland and that of older speakers of
the Midland dialect of the United States. Examples: **solo, casa, es.** Before
a voiced consonant within the phrase it usually represents [Z]. Examples:
desde, mismo, es verde, los labios, las manos.
In southwestern Spain and in all of Spanish America except a small area
of Colombia, this letter represents [s], a dental sibilant of high resonance
similar to the usual "feminine" sibilant of much of the United States. In
some areas it is actually lisped. Before a voiced consonant within the phrase
it usually represents [z], a voiced sibilant similar to the /z/ of English *razor,
ooze,* Examples: **desde, mismo, es verde, los labios, las manos.** In the
Caribbean and in coastal Spanish generally, there is a strong tendency to
aspirate the /s/ syllable final, and the above voicing does not occur.

8. **z,** and **c** before **e** and **i** represent in Spain, except the southwest, [θ], an
interdental fricative of tenser and more prolonged articulation than that
represented by English *th* in *thin, cloth, ether.* Examples: **zagal, zorro, luz**
[θagál], [θórro], [luθ]; or **luces, ciento, cerro** [lúθes], [θjento], [θerro].
In southwestern Spain and in Spanish America, these letters represent [s]
(see paragraph 7). Examples: **zagal, zorro, luz, luces, ciento, cerro** [sağál],
[sórro], [lus], [lúses], [sjènto], [sèrro]. Before a voiced consonant in the
phrase, the **z** represents [z] (see paragraph 7). Examples: **en vez de,
mayorazgo, la luz de.**

9. **l** always represents [l], a clear alveolar lateral that is rarely heard in
English, except in Irish and Scottish dialects. It is never velar as in English
bell, full. Examples: **lado, ala, el, al, sol.**

10. **n** represents /n/, which has variants according to the following consonants.
It stands for [n] in all cases except before /b/, /p/, /m/, where it represents
[m], and before /k/, /g/, /x/, where it represents [ŋ] (similar to the final
consonant of *sing*). Examples of [n]: **no, nada, mano, aman;** of [m]:
en vez de, en Barcelona, un peso; of [ŋ]: **anca, banco, en que, tengo,
naranja.**

11. **ll** represents [ļ] (a palatal lateral) in northern Spain and in Bolivia,
Paraguay, and most of Peru, as well as in the Bogotá area of Colombia.
This sound is similar to that heard in English *million.* In other parts of
the Spanish-speaking world, *ll* represents [y]. Examples: **calle, llano, olla.**

12. **ñ** represents [ñ] among all speakers of Spanish. It is similar to the sound
heard in English *canyon,* but is more one articulation than the English.
Examples: **cañnón, año, ñato.**

13. **ch** represents [č], which is similar to English /č/ (*church, cheek, reach*). Examples: **chato, chaleco, mucho.**

14. **y** represents [y], which varies regionally from [y] to [ž] (as in *azure*), and in most regions it represents [ŷ] (similar to *just* of English) in initial position in the phrase and after /l/ and /n/. Examples: **ayer, mayo** [ayér], [máyo]; ¡**yo**! **un yugo, el yerno** [ŷo], [unŷúǥo], [elŷérno]. In nearly all areas, Spanish /y/ has more palatal friction than English /y/.

15. a. **x** represents between vowels [ǥs] or simply [S] in Spain (see paragraph 7) and [ks] in Spanish America. Examples: **examen, próximo.**
    b. Before a consonant **x** represents [S] in Spain and [s] in Spanish America, except in affected speech, when one hears [ks]. Examples: **extranjero, experiencia.**
    c. In several Indian words of Mexico and Central America **x** represents [x] (see paragraph 20). **México** is one of these and is spelled **Méjico** in most of the Spanish-speaking world.

16. a. **c** represents [k] before **a, o, u, l,** or **r**. The [k] of Spanish does not have the aspiration of English /k/ in the unprotected prevocalic position (*can, quill, coal*) but is more like the sound in *scan*. Examples: **casa, cosa, cuna, quinto, queso, crudo, aclamar.** Note that **quinto** and **queso** are [kínto] and [kèso]. The syllable final [k] in Spanish occurs only in "learned" terms and is dealt with in various ways by the people. In Spain generally it tends to voice to [ǥ]: **técnico, acto, doctor** [téǥnico], [áǥto], doǥtór], but today in Madrid and farther north, the latter becomes [doθtór]. In Central America, Cuba, Venezuela, and Colombia [kt] often becomes [pt] and vice versa; [ps] is [ks]: **Pepsi Cola** [péksi kóla].
    b. **c** before **e** and **i** represents [θ] in Spain, except the southwest, and [s] in Spanish America (see paragraph 8).

17. **k** represents [k] in certain words of foreign origin, mainly Greek, German, and English: **kilo, kilómetro, kermesse, kiosko.**

18. **q** combined with **u** represents [k]. Examples: **queso, aquí, quien** [késo], [akí], [kjen]. **qu** occurs only before **e** and **i**.

19. a. **g** represents [g] before **a, o, u** when initial in the breath group or after /n/. Examples: **ganga, goma, guarda, tengo. gue, gui** represents [ge], [gi], **güe, güi** represent [gwe], [gwi].
    Before **a, o, u** under other circumstances, **g** represents [ǥ], a voiced velar fractive. Examples: **la guerra** [laǥérra], **lago** [láǥo], **la goma** [laǥóma], **agrado** [aǥráḍo].
    b. **g** before **e, i,** represents [x], a palatal or velar fricative, which is also represented by **j**. Examples: **gente, giro** [xénte], [xíro]. In the Caribbean and Central America, as well as in southern Spain, the /x/ is simply [h].

20. **j** always represents /x/. The usual manifestation of this phoneme is [x], but in some areas (see paragraph 19) it is [h]. Examples: **jamás, jugo, jota** [xamás], [xúǥo], [xóta].

21. **h** represents a former aspiration that is no longer present except in some rural areas of southern Spain and Spanish America. Examples: **hoja** [óxa], **humo** [úmo], **harto** [árto].

22. **r** represents [r], an alveolar single flap, similar to the sound represented by
tt in American English *kitty* in rapid speech. However, at the beginning of a
word or after **n, l, s,** it represents [rr], a multiple vibrant (trill). Examples
of [r]: **caro, farol, mero, tren, comer.** Examples of [rr] written **r: rosa, rana,
Enrique, Israel, alrededor.**
rr represents [rr] under all circumstances. Examples: **carro, correr, guerrero.**

The Noun

I. Gender[2]

A. *Masculine Gender*

1. Names of male beings are naturally masculine: **el hombre** the man; **el
muchacho** the boy; **el tío** the uncle; **el rey** the king; **el buey** the ox.

2. Nouns ending in **-o** are masculine: **el libro** the book; **el banco** the bank.
Exception: **la mano** the hand.

3. Days of the week, months, rivers, oceans, and mountains are masculine:
el martes Tuesday; **enero** January; **el Pacífico** the Pacific; **el Rin** the Rhine;
los Andes the Andes.

4. Many nouns in **-l** or **-r**, and nouns of Greek origin ending in **-ma** are
masculine: **el papel** the paper; **el azúcar** the sugar; **el favor** the favor;
el drama the drama. *Common exceptions:* **la miel** the honey; **la sal** the salt;
la catedral the cathedral; **la flor** the flower. Note that **mar** is both masculine
and feminine.

B. *Feminine Gender*

1. Names of female persons or animals are naturally feminine: **la mujer** the
woman; **la muchacha** the girl; **la tía** the aunt; **la vaca** the cow.

2. Nouns ending in **-a** are feminine: **la pluma** the pen; **la carta** the letter;
la casa the house. *Common exceptions:* **el día** the day; **el mapa** the map;
nouns of Greek origin ending in **-ma: el dogma** the dogma; **el programa**
the program.

3. Letters of the alphabet are feminine: **la** *e*, **la** *s*, **la** *t*.

4. Nouns ending in **-ión, -tad, -dad, -tud, -umbre** are feminine: **la canción** the
song; **la facultad** the faculty; **la ciudad** the city; **la virtud** the virtue;
la muchedumbre the crowd. *Exceptions:* **el gorrión** the sparrow; **el sarampión**
the measles.

C. *Formation of the Feminine*

1. Nouns ending in **-o** change **-o** to **-a: tío** uncle, **tía** aunt; **niño** boy, **niña** girl.

2. Nouns ending in **-ón, -or,** and **-án** add **-a: patrón** patron, **patrona** patroness;
pastor shepherd, **pastora** shepherdess; **holgazán** lazy man, **holgazana** lazy
woman.

[2] There is no general gender rule for the type of nouns not treated in this section.

3. Certain nouns have a special form for the feminine: **el poeta, la poetisa; el cantante, la cantatriz; el sacerdote, la sacerdotisa; el emperador, la emperatriz; el abad, la abadesa; el conde, la condesa; el duque, la duquesa.**

Note that (a) some nouns have different genders according to their meanings: **el corte** the cut or the cutting edge; **la corte** the court; **el guía** the guide; **la guía** the guidebook; **el capital** the capital (money); **la capital** the capital (city); (b) some nouns have invariable endings which are used for both the masculine and the feminine: **artista** (and all nouns ending in -**ista**), **amante, mártir, testigo, reo, demócrata, aristócrata, intérprete, consorte, comensal, homicida, suicida, indígena, cómplice, cliente.**

II. Plural of Nouns[3]

1. Nouns ending in an unaccented vowel add -**s** to form the plural: **el libro, los libros; la casa, las casas.**

2. Nouns ending in a consonant, in -**y**, or in an accented vowel add -**es**: **el papel, los papeles; la canción, las canciones: la ley, las leyes; el rubí, los rubíes.** The accepted plural, however, of **papá** is **papás**, and of **mamá** is **mamás.**

3. Nouns ending in unaccented -**es** and -**is** do not change in the plural: **el lunes** Monday, **los lunes** Mondays; **la tesis** the thesis, **las tesis** the theses.

The Adjective and the Adverb

I. The Adjective

A. *Agreement.* The adjective in Spanish agrees in gender and number with the noun it modifies: **el lápiz rojo** the red pencil; **la casa blanca** the white house; **los libros interesantes** the interesting books; **las muchachas hermosas** the beautiful girls.

B. *Formation of the plural.* Adjectives follow the same rules as nouns for the formation of the plural: **pálido, pálidos** pale; **fácil, fáciles** easy; **cortés, corteses** courteous; **capaz, capaces** capable.

C. *Formation of the feminine.*

1. Adjectives ending in -**o** change -**o** to -**a**: **blanco, blanca.**

2. Adjectives ending in other vowels are invariable: **verde** green; **fuerte** strong; **indígena** indigenous, native; **pesimista** pessimistic; **baladí** trivial.

3. Adjectives ending in a consonant are invariable: **fácil** easy; **cortés** courteous. *Exceptions:* (a) adjectives ending in -**ón, -án, -or** (except comparatives) add -**a** to form the feminine: **holgazán, holgazana** lazy; **preguntón, preguntona** inquisitive; **hablador, habladora** talkative (Note that **mayor, mejor, menor, peor, superior, inferior, exterior, interior, anterior,** and **posterior** are invariable). **Superior** adds an -**a** when it is used as a noun meaning ("mother superior"). (b) adjectives of nationality ending in a consonant add -**a** to form the feminine: **francés, francesa** French; **español, española** Spanish; **alemán, alemana** German; **inglés, inglesa** English.

Note that (a) nouns ending in -**z** change **z** to **c** before -**es**: **lápiz, lápices**; (b) nouns ending in -**ión** lose the written accent in the plural: **canción, canciones.**

[3] The plurals of certain masculine nouns may include the masculine and feminine genders: **los padres** the father(s) and mother(s), the parents; **los tíos** the uncle(s) and aunt(s); **los reyes** the king(s) and queen(s).

II. The Adverb

Many adverbs are formed by adding **-mente** to the feminine form of the adjective: **claro, claramente; lento, lentamente; fácil, fácilmente.**

III. Comparison of Adjectives and Adverbs

A. *Comparative of inequality.* The comparative of inequality is formed by placing **más** or **menos** before the positive form of the adjective or adverb: **más rico que** richer than; **menos rico que** less rich than; **más tarde** later; **menos tarde** less late. The superlative is formed by placing the definite article **el** before the comparative: **el más rico** the richest; **el menos rico** the least rich. Note the position of the article in the following examples: **la niña más linda** or **la más linda niña** the prettiest girl.

The following adjectives and adverbs have in addition irregular forms of comparison:

Positive	Comparative	Superlative
bueno	**mejor**	**el (la) mejor**
malo	**peor**	**el (la) peor**
grande	**mayor**	**el (la) mayor**
pequeño	**menor**	**el (la) menor**
alto	**superior**	**supremo**
bajo	**inferior**	**ínfimo**
mucho	**más**	
poco	**menos**	

B. *Comparative of equality.* With adjectives and adverbs the comparative of equality is formed with **tan . . . como: tan fácil como** as easy as; **tan bien como** as well as; with nouns the comparative of equality is formed with **tanto (tanta, tantos, tantas) . . . como: tanto dinero como** as much money as; **tantas personas como** as many people as.

C. *Absolute superlative of adjectives.* The absolute superlative of adjectives is formed by placing **muy** (very) before the adjective or by adding the suffix **-ísimo:**

Positive	Absolute Superlative
feliz	**muy feliz, felicísimo**
fácil	**muy fácil, facilísimo**
importante	**muy importante, importantísimo**
limpio	**muy limpio, limpísimo**
feo	**muy feo, feísimo**
rico	**muy rico, riquísimo**
largo	**muy largo, larguísimo**
notable	**muy notable, notabilísimo**

A few adjectives have, in addition, other forms derived from the Latin superlatives:

bueno	muy bueno, bonísimo[4], óptimo
malo	muy malo, malísimo, pésimo
grande	muy grande, grandísimo, máximo
pequeño	muy pequeño, pequeñísimo, mínimo

Some adjectives ending in **-ro** or **-re** revert to the corresponding Latin superlative:

acre	muy acre, acérrimo
célebre	muy célebre, celebérrimo
mísero	muy mísero, misérrimo
salubre	muy salubre, salubérrimo

D. *Absolute superlative of adverbs.* The absolute superlative of adverbs not ending in **-mente** is formed in the same manner as that of adjectives:

tarde	muy tarde, tardísimo
pronto	muy pronto, prontísimo
mucho	muchísimo
poco	poquísimo
cerca	muy cerca, cerquísima
lejos	muy lejos, lejísimos

Superlative adverbs ending in **-mente** are formed by adding the suffix **-ísima** to the corresponding feminine adjective:

claramente	muy claramente, clarísimamente
noblemente	muy noblemente, nobilísimamente

Common Spanish Suffixes

I. Diminutives

The most common diminutive endings in Spanish are:

-ito, -ita	(**-cito, -cita, -ecito, -ecita**). Examples: **librito** (from **libro**), **casita** (from **casa**), **corazoncito** (from **corazón**), **mujercita** (from **mujer**), **cochecito** (from **coche**), **florecita** (from **flor**).
-illo, -illa	(**-cillo, -cilla, -ecillo, -ecilla**). Examples: **corderillo** (from **cordero**), **dolorcillo** (from **dolor**), **viejecillo** (from **viejo**), **piedrecilla** (from **piedra**).
-ico, -ica	(**-cico, -cica, -ecico, -ecica**). Examples: **niñico** (from **niño**), **hermanica** (from **hermana**), **corazoncico** (from **corazón**), **mujercica** (from **mujer**), **pobrecico** (from **pobre**).
-uelo, -uela	(**-zuelo, -zuela, -ezuelo, -ezuela**). Examples: **arroyuelo** (from **arroyo**), **mozuela** (from **moza**), **mujerzuela** (from **mujer**), **reyezuelo** (from **rey**), **piedrezuela** (from **piedra**).
-ete, -eta	Examples: **vejete** (from **viejo**), **vejeta** (from **vieja**).
-uco, -uca	Example: **casuca** (from **casa**).
-ucho, -ucha	Examples: **serrucho** (from **sierra**), **casucha** (from **casa**).

---

[4] Also **buenísimo**.

II. Augmentatives

The most common augmentative endings in Spanish are:

-acho, -acha	Example: **ricacho** (from **rico**).
-azo, -aza	Examples: **gigantazo** (from **gigante**), **bribonazo** (from **bribón**), **manaza** (from **mano**), **bocaza** (from **boca**).
-on, -ona	Examples: **hombrón** (from **hombre**), **mujerona** (from **mujer**), **almohadón** (from **almohada**), **borrachón** (from **borracho**).
-ote, -ota	Examples: **grandote** (from **grande**), **muchachote** (from **muchacho**), muchachota (from **muchachá**).

III. Depreciatives

The most common depreciative endings in Spanish are:

-aco, -aca	Example: **pajarraco** ugly bird.
-ejo, -eja	Example: **librejo** old, worthless book.

Note that a depreciative or ironic connotation is often conveyed by many of the augmentatives and by the diminutive endings **-uelo, -ete, -uco, -ucho, -illo**.

IV. Other Suffixes

-ada

a. is sometimes equal to the English suffix *-ful:* **cucharada** spoonful; **palada** shovelful;

b. often indicates a blow: **puñada** blow with the fist; **puñalada** stab or blow with a dagger; **topetada** butt, blow with the head;

c. indicates a group or a crowd of: **peonada** a group or crowd of peons; **indiada** a group or crowd of Indians.

-al, -ar

denote a grove, field, plantation or orchard: **naranjal** orange grove; **cauchal** rubber plantation; **pinar** pine grove.

-azo

indicates a blow or explosion: **puñetazo** blow with the fist; **topetazo** butt, blow with the head; **escobazo** blow with a broom; **cañonazo** cannon shot.

-dad, -tad

are suffixes forming many abstract nouns and are usually equivalent to the English suffix *-ty:* **fraternidad** fraternity; **facultad** faculty; **cantidad** quantity; **calidad** quality.

-dizo

is an adjective-forming suffix which means sometimes *tending to,* or *in the habit of:* **resbaladizo** slippery; **olvidadizo** forgetful; **enojadizo** irritable, easily angered; **asustadizo** easily frightened, scary, timid; **movedizo** movable.

-ería

a. denotes a place where something is made or sold: **panadería** bakery; **librería** bookstore; **zapatería** shoestore; **pastelería** pastry shop;

b. indicates a profession, business or occupation: **carpintería** carpentry; **ingeniería** engineering;

c. means sometimes a collection: **pastelería** pastry, pastries;

d. is sometimes equivalent to English suffix *-ness*; it also suggests a single act or action: **tontería** foolishness; foolish act; **niñería** childishness; childish act.

-ero *a.* indicates a person who makes, sells, or is in charge of: **panadero** baker; **librero** bookseller; **zapatero** shoemaker, **carcelero** jailer; **cajaro** cashier;

b. is an adjective-forming suffix; **parlero** talkative; **guerrero** warlike.

-ez, -eza are used to make abstract nouns: **vejez** old age; **niñez** childhood; **viudez** widowhood; **grandeza** greatness.

-ía *a.* is the ending of the names of many arts and sciences: **geología** geology; **geometría** geometry; **biología** biology; *b.* see **-ería**.

-iento indicates a *resemblance*, or a *tendency to*: **ceniciento** ashlike; **soñoliento** sleepy, drowsy.

-ísimo is the ending of the absolute superlative: **hermosísimo** very beautiful.

-izo is a suffix meaning *tending to* or *somewhat*: **rojizo** reddish. See **-dizo**.

-mente is the adverbial ending attached to the feminine form of the adjective: **generosamente** generously; **claramente** clearly.

-ón *a.* is an augmentative suffix;

b. is also a suffix without an augmentative force, meaning *in the habit of*, or *full of*: **juguetón** playful; **preguntón** full of questions, inquisitive; **llorón** tearful; crybaby;

c. indicates suddenness or violence of an action: **estirón** pull, tug, jerk; **apretón** squeeze.

-or, -dor *a.* are equivalent to the English suffixes *-or*, *-er*, and indicate the agent or doer: **hablador** talker; **regulador** regulator;

b. may also be used as adjectives: **hablador** talkative; **regulador** regulating.

-oso is an adjective-forming suffix which usually means *having*, *full of*, or *characterized by*: **rocoso** rocky; **tormentoso** stormy; **fangoso** muddy; **herboso** grassy; **lluvioso** rainy; **maravilloso** marvelous; **famoso** famous.

-udo is an adjective-forming suffix meaning *having* or *characterized by*: **zancudo** long-legged; **peludo** hairy; **panzudo** big-bellied; **caprichudo** stubborn.

-ura is a suffix forming many abstract nouns: **negrura** blackness; **blancura** whiteness; **altura** height; **lisura** smoothness.

-uzco indicates *resemblance* or *a tendency to*; it is akin to the English suffix *-ish*: **blancuzco** whitish; **negruzco** blackish.

Spanish Irregular and Orthographic Changing Verbs

The superior number, or numbers, after a verb entry indicate that it is conjugated like the model verb in this section which has the corresponding number. Only the tenses which have irregular forms or spelling changes are given. The irregular forms and spelling changes are shown in bold-face type.

1. pensar (if stressed, the stem vowel **e** becomes **ie**)
    Pres. Indic. **pienso, piensas, piensa,** pensamos, pensáis, **piensan.**
    Pres. Subj. **piense, pienses, piense,** pensemos, penséis, **piensen.**
    Imper. **piensa** tú, **piense** Vd., pensemos nosotros, pensad vosotros, **piensen** Vds.

2. contar (if stressed, the stem vowel **o** becomes **ue**)
    Pres. Indic. **cuento, cuentas, cuenta,** contamos, contáis, **cuentan.**
    Pres. Subj. **cuente, cuentes, cuente,** centemos, contèis, **cuenten.**
    Imper. **cuenta** tú, **cuente** Vd. contemos nosotros, contad vosotros, **cuenten** Vds.

3.*a.* sentir (if stressed, the stem vowel **e** becomes **ie**; if unstressed, the stem vowel **e** becomes **i** when the following syllable contains stressed **a, ie,** or **ió**)
    Pres. Indic. **siento, sientes, siente,** sentimos, sentís, **sienten.**
    Pres. Subj. **sienta, sientas, sienta, sintamos, sintáis, sientan.**
    Pret. Indic. **sentí, sentiste, sintió,** sentimos, sentisteis, **sintieron.**
    Imp. Subj. **sintiera** or **sintiese, sintieras** or **sintieses, sintiera** or **sintiese, sintiéramos** or **sintiésemos, sintierais** or **sintieseis, sintieran** or **sintiesen.**
    Imper. **siente** tú, **sienta** Vd., **sintamos** nosotros, sentid vosotros, **sientan** Vds.
    Pres. Part. **sintiendo.**

    b. erguir (this verb has same vowel changes as *sentir*, but the initial **i** of the diphthong **ie** is changed to **y**. For regular spelling changes see No. 12,*a*)
    Pres. Indic. **yergo, yergues, yergue,** erguimos, erguís, **yerguen.**
    Pres. Subj. **yerga, yergas, yerga, irgamos, irgáis, yergan.**
    Pret. Indic. erguí, erguiste, **irguió,** erguimos, erguisteis, **irguieron.**
    Imp. Subj. **irguiera** or **irguiese, irguieras** or **irguieses, irguiera** or **irguieses, irguiéramos** or **irguiésemos, irguierais** or **irguieseis, irguieran** or **irguiesen.**
    Imper. **yergue** tú, **yerga** Vd., **irgamos** nosotros, erguid vosotros, **yergan** Vds.
    Pres. Part. **irguiendo.**

4. dormir (if stressed, the stem vowel **o** becomes **ue**; if unstressed, the stem vowel **o** becomes **u** when the following syllable contains stressed **a, ie,** or **ió**)
    Pres. Indic. **duermo, duermes, duerme,** dormimos, dormís, **duermen.**
    Pres. Subj. **duerma, duermas, duerma, durmamos, durmáis, duerman.**
    Pret. Indic. dormí, dormiste, **durmió,** dormimos, dormisteis, **durmieron.**

Imp. Subj.	**durmiera** or **durmiese, durmieras** or **durmieses, durmiera** or **durmiese, durmiéramos** or **durmiésemos, durmierais** or **durmieseis, durmieran** or **durmiesen.**
Imper.	**duerme** tú, **duerma** Vd., **durmanos** nosotros, dormid vosotros, **duerman** Vds.
Pres. Part.	**durmiendo.**

5. **pedir** (if stressed, the stem vowel **e** becomes **i**; if unstressed, the stem vowel **e** becomes **i** when the following syllable contains stressed **a, ie,** or **ió**)

Pres. Indic.	**pido, pides, pide,** pedimos, pedís, **piden.**
Pres. Subj.	**pida, pidas, pida, pidamos, pidáis, pidan.**
Pret. Indic.	**pedí,** pediste, **pidió,** pedimos, pedisteis, **pidieron.**
Imp. Subj.	**pidiera** or **pidiese, pidieras** or **pidieses, pidiera** or **pidiese, pidiéramos** or **pidiésemos, pidierais** or **pidieseis, pidieran** or **pidiesen.**
Imper.	**pide** tú, **pida** Vd., **pidamos** nosotros, pedid vosotros, **pidan** Vds.
Pres. Part.	**pidiendo.**

6. **buscar** (verbs ending in **car** change **c** to **qu** before **e**)

Pres. Subj.	**busque, busques, busque, busquemos, busquéis, busquen.**
Pret. Indic.	**busqué,** buscaste, buscó, buscamos, buscasteis, buscaron.
Imper.	busca tú, **busque** Vd., **busquemos** nosotros, buscad vosotros, **busquen** Vds.

7. **llegar** (verbs ending in **gar** change the **g** to **gu** before **e**)

Pres. Subj.	**llegue, llegues, llegue, lleguemos, lleguéis, lleguen.**
Pres. Indic.	**llegué,** llegaste, llegó, llegamos, llegasteis, llegaron.
Imper.	llega tú, **llegue** Vd., **lleguemos** nosotros, llegad vosotros, **lleguen** Vds.

8. **averiguar** (verbs ending in **guar** change the **gu** to **gü** before **e**)

Pres. Subj.	**averigüe, averigües, averigüe, averigüemos, averigüéis, averigüen.**
Pret. Indic.	**averigüé,** averiguaste, averiguó, averiguamos, averiguasteis, averiguaron.
Imper.	averigua tú, **averigüe** Vd., **averigüemos** nosotros, averiguad vosotros, **averigüen** Vds.

9. **abrazar** (verbs ending in **zar** change **z** to **c** before **e**)

Pres. Subj.	**abrace, abraces, abrace, abracemos, abracéis, abracen.**
Pret. Indic.	**abracé,** abrazaste, abrazó, abrazamos, abrazasteis, abrazaron.
Imper.	abraza tú, **abrace** Vd., **abracemos** nosotros, abrazad vosotros, **abracen** Vds.

10.*a.* **convencer** (verbs ending in **cer** preceded by a consonant change **c** to **z** before **a** and **o**)

Pres. Indic.	**convenzo,** convences, convence, convencemos, convencéis, convencen.
Pres. Subj.	**convenza, convenzas, convenza, convenzamos, convenzáis, convenzan.**
Imper.	convence tú, **convenza** Vd., **convenzamos** nosotros, convenced vosotros, **convenzan** Vds.

b. **esparcir** (verbs ending in **cir** preceded by a consonant change **c** to **z** before **a** and **o**)

Pres. Indic. **esparzo,** esparces, esparce, esparcimos, esparcís, esparcen.
Pres. Subj. **esparza, esparzas, esparza, esparzamos, esparzáis, esparzan.**
Imper. esparce tú, **esparza** Vd., **esparzamos** nosotros, esparcid vosotros, **esparzan** Vds.

c. mecer (some verbs ending in **cer** preceded by a vowel change **c** to **z** before **a** and **o**; see No. 13.*a*)
Pres. Indic. **mezo,** meces, mece, mecemos, mecéis, mecen.
Pres. Subj. **meza, mezas, meza, mezamos, mezáis, mezan.**
Imper. mece tú, **meza** Vd., **mezamos** nosotros, meced vosotros, **mezan** Vds.

11.*a.* dirigir (verbs ending in **gir** change **g** to **j** before **a** and **o**)
Pres. Indic. **dirijo,** diriges, dirige, dirigimos, dirigís, dirigen.
Pres. Subj. **dirija, dirijas, dirija, dirijamos, dirijáis, dirijan.**
Imper. dirige tú, **dirija** Vd., **dirijamos** nosotros, dirigid vosotros, **dirijan** Vds.

b. coger (verbs ending in **ger** change **g** to **j** before **o** and **a**)
Pres. Indic. **cojo,** coges, coge, cogemos, cogéis, cogen.
Pres. Subj. **coja, cojas, coja, cojamos, cojáis, cojan.**
Imper. coge tú, **coja** Vd., **cojamos** nosotros, coged vosotros, **cojan** Vds.

12.*a.* distinguir (verbs ending in **guir** drop the **u** before **o** and **a**)
Pres. Indic. **distingo,** distingues, distingue, distinguimos, distinguís, distinguen.
Pres. Subj. **distinga, distingas, distinga, distingamos, distingáis, distingan.**
Imper. distingue tú, **distinga** Vd., **distingamos** nosotros, distinguid vosotros, **distingan** Vds.

b. delinquir (verbs ending in **quir** change **qu** to **c** before **o** and **a**)
Pres. Indic. **delinco,** delinques, delinque, delinquimos, delinquís, delinquen.
Pres. Subj. **delinca, delincas, delinca, delincamos, delincáis, delincan.**

13.*a.* conocer (verbs ending in **cer** when preceded by a vowel insert **z** before **c** when **c** is followed by **o** or **a**; see No. 10.*c*)
Pres. Indic. **conozco,** conoces, conoce, conocemos, conocéis, conocen.
Pres. Subj. **conozca, conozcas, conozca, conozcamos, conozcáis, conozcan.**
Imper. conoce tú, **conozca** Vd., **conozcamos** nosotros, conoced vosotros, **conozcan** Vds.

b. lucir (verbs ending in **cir** when preceded by a vowel insert **z** before **c** when **c** is followed by **o** or **a**; see No. 25)
Pres. Indic. **luzco,** luces, luce, lucimos, lucís, lucen.
Pres. Subj. **luzca, luzcas, luzca, luzcamos, luzcáis, luzcan.**
Imper. luce tú, **luzca** Vd., **luzcamos** nosotros, lucid vosotros, **luzcan** Vds.

14. creer (unstressed **i** between vowels is regularly changed to **y**)
Pret. Indic. creí, creíste, **creyó,** creímos, creísteis, **creyeron.**
Imp. Subj. **creyera** or **creyese, creyeras** or **creyeses, creyera** or **creyese, creyéramos** or **creyésemos, creyerais** or **creyeseis, creyeran** or **creyesen.**
Pret. Part. **creyendo.**

15. reír (like No. 5, except that when the **i** of the stem would be followed by **ie** or **ió** the two **i**'s are reduced to one)

Pres. Indic. río, ríes, ríe, reímos, reís, **ríen.**

Pres. Subj. ría, rías, ría, riamos, riáis, rían.

Pret. Indic. reí, reíste, rió, reímos, reísteis, **rieron.**

Imp. Subj. riera or riese, rieras or rieses, riera or riese, riéramos or riésemos, rierais or rieseis, rieran or riesen.

Imper. ríe tú, ría Vd., ríamos nosotros, reíd vosotros, rían Vds.

Pres. Part. **riendo.**

16. podrir or pudrir

Pres. Indic. pudro, pudres, pudre, podrimos or pudrimos, podrís or pudrís, pudren.

Pres. Subj. pudra, pudras, pudra, pudramos pudráis, pudran.

Imp. Indic. pudría or podría, etc. (Seldom *podría* because of confusion with *poder*)

Pret. Indic. podrí or pudrí, podriste or pudriste, **pudrió,** podrimos or pudrimos, podristeis or pudristeis, **pudrieron.**

Imp. Subj. **pudriera** or **pudriese, pudrieras** or **pudrieses, pudriera** or **pudriese, pudriéramos** or **pudriésemos, pudrierais** or **pudrieseis, pudrieran** or **pudriesen.**

Fut. Indic. pudriré or podriré, etc.

Cond. pudriría or podriría, etc.

Pres. Part. **pudriendo.**

Past Part. podrido or pudrido.

17. enviar

Pres. Indic. envío, envías, envía, enviamos, enviáis, envían.

Pres. Subj. envíe, envíes, enviemos, enviéis, envíen.

Imper. envía tú, envíe Vd., enviemos nosotros, enviad vosotros, envíen Vds.

18. continuar

Pres. Indic. continúo, continúas, continúa, continuamos, continuáis, continúan.

Pres. Subj. continúe, continúes, continúe, continuemos, continuéis, continúen.

Imper. continúa tú, continúe Vd., continuemos nosotros, continuad vosotros, continúen Vds.

19. gruñir (**i** of the diphthong **ie** or **ió** is lost after **ñ**)

Pret. Indic. gruñi, gruñiste, **gruñó,** gruñisteis, **gruñeron.**

Imp. Subj. gruñera or gruñese, gruñeras or gruñeses, gruñera or gruñese, gruñéramos or gruñésemos, gruñerais or gruñeseis, gruñeran or gruñesen.

Pres. Part. gruñendo.

20. bullir (**i** of the diphthong **ie** or **ió** is lost after **ll**)

Pret. Indic. bullí, bulliste, **bulló,** bullimos, bullisteis, **bulleron.**

Imp. Subj. bullera or bullese, bulleras or bulleses, bullera or bullese, bulléramos or bullésemos, bullerais or bulleseis, bulleran or bullesen.

Pres. Part.	**bullendo.**

21. andar

Pret. Indic.	**anduve, anduviste, anduvo, anduvimos, anduvisteis, anduvieron.**
Imp. Subj.	**anduviera** or **anduviese, anduvieras** or **anduvieses, anduviera** or **anduviese, anduviéramos** or **anduviésemos, anduvierais** or **anduvieseis, anduvieran** or **anduviesen.**

22. asir

Pres. Indic.	**asgo,** ases, ase, asimos, asís, asen.
Pres. Subj.	**asga, asgas, asga, asgamos, asgáis, asgan.**
Imper.	ase tú, **asga** Vd., **asgamos** nosotros, asid vosotros, **asgan** Vds.

23. caber

Pres. Indic.	**quepo,** cabes, cabe, cabemos, cabéis, caben.
Pres. Subj.	**quepa, quepas, quepa, quepamos, quepáis, quepan.**
Pret. Indic.	**cupe, cupiste, cupo, cupimos, cupisteis, cupieron.**
Imp. Subj.	**cupiera** or **cupiese, cupieras** or **cupieses, cupiera** or **cupiese, cupiéramos** or **cupiésemos, cupierais** or **cupieseis, cupieran** or **cupiesen.**
Fut. Indic.	**cabré, cabrás, cabrá, cabremos, cabréis, cabrán.**
Cond.	**cabría, cabrías, cabría, cabríamos, cabríais, cabrían.**
Imper.	cabe tú, **quepa** Vd., **quepamos** nosotros, cabed vosotros, **quepan** Vds.

24. caer

Pres. Indic.	**caigo,** caes, cae, caemos, caéis, caen.
Pres. Subj.	**caiga, caigas, caiga, caigamos, caigáis, caigan.**
Pret. Indic.	caí, caiste, **cayó,** caímos, caísteis, **cayeron.**
Imp. Subj.	**cayera** or **cayese, cayeras** or **cayases, cayera** or **cayese, cayéramos** or **cayésemos, cayerais** or **cayeseis, cayeran** or **cayesen.**
Imper.	cae tú, **caiga** Vd., **caigamos** nosotros, caed vosotros, **caigan** Vds.
Pres. Part.	**cayendo.**

25. conducir (all verbs ending in **ducir** have the irregularities of conducir)

Pres. Indic.	**conduzco,** conduces, conduce, conducimos, conducís, conducen.
Pres. Subj.	**conduzca, conduzcas, conduzca, conduzcamos, conduzcáis, conduzcan.**
Pret. Indic.	**conduje, condujiste, condujo, condujimos, condujisteis, condujeron.**
Imp. Subj.	**condujera** or **condujese, condujeras** or **condujeses, condujera** or **condujese, condujéramos** or **condujésemos, condujerais** or **condujeseis, condujeran** or **condujesen.**
Imp.	conduce tú, **conduzca** Vd., **conduzcamos** nosotros, conducid vosotros, **conduzcan** Vds.

26. dar

Pres. Indic.	**doy,** das, da, damos, dais, dan.
Pres. Subj.	dé, des, dé, demos, deis, den.
Pret. Indic.	**dí, diste, dió, dimos, disteis, dieron.**

Imp. Subj.	diera or diese, dieras or dieses, deira or diese, diéramos or diésemos, dierais or dieseis, dieran or diesen.

27. decir

Pres. Indic.	digo, dices, dice, decimos, decís, dicen.
Pres. Subj.	diga, digas, diga, digamos, digáis, digan.
Pret. Indic.	dije, dijiste, dijo, dijimos, dijisteis, dijeron.
Imp. Subj.	dijera or dijese, dijeras or dijeses, dijera or dijese, dijéramos or dijésemos, dijerais or dijeseis, dijeran or dijesen.
Fut. Indic.	diré, dirás, dirá, diremos, deréis, dirán.
Cond.	diría, dirías, diría, diríamos, diríais, dirían.
Imper.	di tú, diga Vd., digamos nosotros, decid vosotros, **digan** Vds.
Pres. Part.	diciendo.
Past Part.	dicho.

NOTE. The compound verbs of *decir* have the same irregularities with the exception of the following:
a. The future and conditional of the compound verbs *bendecir* and *maldecir* are regular: *bendeciré, maldeciré,* etc.; *bendeciría, maldeciría,* etc.
b. The familiar imperative is regular: *bendice tu, maldice tu, contradice tu,* etc.
c. The past participles of *bendecir* and *maldecir* are regular when used with *haber*: *bendecido, maldecido;* when used as an adjective with *estar,* the forms are: *bendito, maldito.*

28. errar (like No. 1, except that the initial **ie** is spelled **ye**)

Pres. Indic.	yerro, yerras, yerra, erramos, erráis, yerran.
Pres. Subj.	yerre, yerres, yerre, erremos, erréis, yerren.
Imper.	yerra tú, yerre Vd., erremos nosotros, errad vosotros, yerren Vds.

29. estar

Pres. Indic.	estoy, estás, está, estamos, estáis, están.
Pres. Subj.	esté, estés, esté, estemos, estéis, estén.
Pret. Indic.	estuve, estuviste, estuvo, estuvimos, estuvisteis, estuvieron.
Imp. Subj.	estuviera or estuviese, estuvieras or estuvieses, estuviera or estuviese, estuviéramos or estuviésemos, estuvierais or estuvieseis, estuvieran or estuviesen.
Imper.	está tú, esté Vd., estemos nosotros, estad vosotros, estén Vds.

30. .haber

Pres. Indic.	he, has, ha, hemos, habéis, han.
Pres. Subj.	haya, hayas, haya, hayamos, hayáis, hayan.
Pret. Indic.	hube, hubiste, hubo, hubimos, hubisteis, hubieron.
Imp. Subj.	hubiera or hubiese, hubieras or hubieses, hubiera or hubiese, hubiéramos or hubiésemos, hubierais or hubieseis, hubieran or hubiesen.
Fut. Indic.	habré, habrás, habrá, habremos, habréis, habrán.
Cond.	habría, habrías, habría, habríamos, habríais, habrían.

31. hacer

Pres. Indic.	hago, haces, hace, hacemos, hacéis, hacen.
Pres. Subj.	haga, hagas, haga, hagamos, hagáis, hagan.
Pret. Indic.	hice, hiciste, hizo, hicimos, hicisteis, hicieron.
Imp. Subj.	hiciera or hiciese, hicieras or hicieses, hiciera or hiciese,

hiciéramos or hiciésemos, hicierais or hicieseis, hicieran or hiciesem.

Fut. Indic.	haré, harás, hará, haremos, haréis, harán.
Cond.	haría, harías, haría, haríamos, haríais, harían.
Imper.	haz tú, haga Vd., hagamos nosotros, haced vosotros, hagan Vds.
Past Part.	hecho.

32.a. huir

Pres. Indic.	huyo, huyes, huye, huimos, huís, huyen.
Pres. Subj.	huya, huyas, huya, huyamos, huyáis, huyan.
Pret. Indic.	huí, huiste, huyó, huimos, huisteis, huyeron.
Imp. Subj.	huyera or huyese, huyeras or huyeses, huyera or huyese, huyéramos or huyésemos, huyerais or huyeseis, huyeran or huyesen.
Imper.	huye tú, huya Vd., huyamos nosotros, huid vosotros, huyan Vds.
Pres. Part.	huyendo.

b. argüir

Pres. Indic.	arguyo, arguyes, arguye, argüimos, argüís, arguyen.
Pres. Subj.	arguya, arguyas, arguya, arguyamos, arguyáis, arguyan.
Pret. Indic.	argüí, argüiste, arguyó, argüimos, argüisteis, arguyeron.
Imp. Subj.	arguyera or arguyese, arguyeras or arguyeses, arguyera or arguyese, arguyéramos or arguyésemos, arguyerais or arguyeseis, arguyeran or arguyesen.
Imper.	arguye tú, arguya Vd., arguyamos nosotros, agrüid vosotros, arguyan Vds.
Pres. Part.	arguyendo.

33. ir

Pres. Indic.	voy, vas, va, vamos, vais, van.
Pres. Subj.	vaya, vayas, vaya, vayamos, vayáis, vayan.
Imp. Indic.	iba, ibas, iba, íbamos, ibais, iban.
Pret. Indic.	fuí, fuiste, fué, fuimos, fuisteis, fueron.
Imp. Subj.	fuera or fuese, fueras or fueses, fuera or fuese, fuéramos or fuésemos, fuerais or fueseis, fueran or fuesen.
Imper.	ve tú, vaya Vd., vayamos (vamos) nosotros, id vosotros, vayan Vds.
Pres. Part.	yendo.

34. jugar (cf. Nos. 2 and 7)

Pres. Indic.	juego, juegas, juega, jugamos, jugáis, juegan.
Pres. Subj.	juegue, juegues, juegue, juguemos, juguéis, jueguen.
Pret. Indic.	jugué, jugaste, jugó, jugamos, jugasteis, jugaron.
Imper.	juega tú, juegue Vd., jueguemos nosotros, jugad vosotros, jueguen Vds.

35. adquirir

Pres. Indic.	adquiero, adquieres, adquiere, adquirimos, adquirís, adquieren.
Pres. Subj.	adquiera, adquieras, adquiera, adquiramos, adquiráis, adquieran.
Imper.	adquiere tú, adquiera Vd., adquiramos nosotros, adquirid vosotros, adquieran Vds.

36. oír
    Pres. Indic. oigo, oyes, oye, oímos, oís, **oyen.**
    Pres. Subj. **oiga, oigas, oiga, oigamos, oigáis, oigan.**
    Pret. Indic. oí, oíste, **oyó,** oímos, oísteis, **oyeron.**
    Imp. Subj. **oyera** or **oyese, oyeras** or **oyeses, oyera** or **oyese, oyéramos** or **oyésemos, oyerais** or **oyeseis, oyeran** or **oyesen.**
    Imper. **oye** tú, **oiga** Vd., **oigamos** nosotros, oíd vosotros, **oigan** Vds.
    Pres. Part. **oyendo.**

37. oler like No. 2, except that initial **ue** is spelled **hue)**
    Pres. Indic. **huelo, hueles, huele,** olemos, oléis, **huelen.**
    Pres. Subj. **huela, huelas, huela,** olamos, oláis, **huelan.**
    Imper. **huele** tú, **huela** Vd., olamos nosotros, oled vosotros, **huelan** Vds.

38. placer
    Pres. Indic. **plazco,** places, place, placemos, placéis, placen.
    Pres. Subj. **plazca, plazcas, plazca, plazcamos, plazcáis, plazcan.** (There are also the antiquated forms, **plegue** and **plega,** used now only in the third person in poetic language.)
    Pret. Indic. In addition to the regular forms, there is the antiquated form **plugo,** used now only in poetic language.
    Imp. Subj. In addition to the regular forms, there are the antiquated forms, **pluguiera** and **pluguiese,** used now only in poetic language.

39. poder
    Pres. Indic. **puedo, puedes, puede,** podemos, podéis, **pueden.**
    Pres. Subj. **pueda, puedas, pueda,** podamos, podáis, **puedan.**
    Pret. Indic. **pude, pudiste, pudo, pudimos, pudisteis, pudieron.**
    Imp. Subj. **pudiera** or **pudiese, pudieras** or **pudieses, pudiera** or **pudiese, pudiéramos** or **pudiésemos, pudierais** or **pudieseis, pudieran** or **pudiesen.**
    Fut. Indic. **podré, podrás, podrá, podremos, podréis, podrán.**
    Cond. **podría, podrías, podría, podríamos, podríais, podrían.**
    Pres. Part. **pudiendo.**

40. poner
    Pres. Indic. **pongo,** pones, pone, ponemos, ponéis, ponen.
    Pres. Subj. **ponga, pongas, ponga, pongamos, pongáis, pongan.**
    Pret. Indic. **puse, pusiste, puso, pusimos, pusisteis, pusieron.**
    Imp. Subj. **pusiera** or **pusiese, pusieras** or **pusieses, pusiera** or **pusiese, pusiéramos** or **pusiésemos, pusierais** or **pusieseis, pusieran** or **pusiesen.**
    Fut. Indic. **pondré, pondrás, pondrá, pondremos, pondréis, pondrán.**
    Cond. **pondría, pondrías, pondría, pondríamos, pondríais, pondrían.**
    Imper. **pon** tú, **ponga** Vd., **pongamos** nosotros, poned vosotros, **pongan** Vds.
    Past Part. **puesto.**

41. querer
    Pres. Indic. **quiero, quieres, quiere,** queremos, queréis, **quieren.**
    Pres. Subj. **quiera, quieras, quiera,** queramos, queráis, **quieran.**

Pret. Indic.	quise, quisiste, quiso, quisimos, quisisteis, quisieron.
Imp. Subj.	quisiera or quisiese, quisieras or quisieses, quisiera or quisiese, quisiéramos or quisiémos, quisierais or quisieseis, quisieran or quisiesen.
Fut. Indic.	querré, querrás, querrá, querremos, querréis, querrán.
Cond.	querría, querrías, querría, querríamos, querríais, querrían.
Imper.	quiere tú, quiera Vd., queramos nosotros, quered vosotros, quieran Vds.

42. saber

Pres. Indic.	sé, sabes, sabe, sabemos, sabéis, saben.
Pres. Subj.	sepa, sepas, sepa, sepamos, sepáis, sepan.
Pret. Indic.	supe, supiste, supo, supimos, supisteis, supieron.
Imp. Subj.	supiera or supiese, supieras or supieses, supiera or supiese, supiéramos or supiésemos, supierais or supieseis, supieran or supiesen.
Fut. Indic.	sabré, sabrás, sabrá, sabremos, sabréis, sabrán.
Cond.	sabría, sabrías, sabría, sabríamos, sabríais, sabrían.
Imper.	sabe tú, sepa Vd., sepamos nosotros, sabed vosotros, sepan Vds.

43. salir

Pres. Indic.	salgo, sales, sale, salimos, salís, salen.
Pres. Subj.	salga, salgas, salga, salgamos, salgáis, salgan.
Fut. Indic.	saldré, saldrás, saldrá, saldremos, saldréis, saldrán.
Cond.	saldría, saldrías, saldría, saldríamos, saldríais, saldrían.
Imper.	sal tú, salga Vd., salgamos nosotros, salid vosotros, salgan Vds.

NOTE. The compound *sobresalir* is regular in the familiar imperative: sobresale tú.

44. ser

Pres. Indic.	soy, eres, es, somos, sois, son.
Pres. Subj.	sea, seas, sea, seamos, seáis, sean.
Imp. Indic.	era, eras, era, éramos, erais, eran.
Pret. Indic.	fuí, fuiste, fué, fuimos, fuisteis, fueron.
Imp. Subj.	fuera or fuese, fueras or fueses, fuera or fuese, fuéramos or fuésemos, fuerais or fueseis, fueran or fuesen.
Imper.	sé tú, sea Vd., seamos nosotros, sed vosotros, sean Vds.

45. tener

Pres. Indic.	tengo, tienes, tiene, tenemos, tenéis, tienen.
Pres. Subj.	tenga, tengas, tenga, tengamos, tengáis, tengan.
Pret. Indic.	tuve, tuviste, tuvo, tuvimos, tuvisteis, tuvieron.
Imp. Subj.	tuviera or tuviese, tuvieras or tuvieses, tuviera or tuviese, tuviéramos or tuviésemos, tuvierais or tuvieseis, tuvieran or tuviesen.
Fut. Indic.	tendré, tendrás, tendrá, tendremos, tendréis, tendrán.
Cond.	tendría, tendrías, tendría, tendríamos, tendríais, tendrían.
Imper.	ten tú, tenga Vd., tengamos nosotros, tened vosotros, tengan Vds.

46. traer

Pres. Indic.	traigo, traes, trae, traemos, traéis, traen.
Pres. Subj.	traiga, traigas, traiga, traigamos, traigáis, traigan.

Pret. Indic.	traje, trajiste, trajo, trajimos, trajisteis, trajeron.
Imp. Subj.	trajera or trajese, trajeras or trajeses, trajera or trajese, trajéramos or trajésemos, trajerais or trajeseis, trajeran or trajesen.
Imper.	trae tú, traiga Vd., traigamos nosotros, traed vosotros, traigan Vds.
Pres. Part.	trayendo.

47. valer

Pres. Indic.	valgo, vales, vale, valemos, valéis, valen.
Pres. Subj.	valga, valgas, valga, valgamos, valgáis, valgan.
Fut. Indic.	valdré, valdrás, valdrá, valdremos, valdréis, valdrán.
Cond.	valdría, valdrías, valdría, valdríamos, valdríais, valdrían.
Imper.	val or vale tú, valga Vd., valgamos nosotros, valed vosotros, valgan Vds.

48. venir

Pres. Indic.	vengo, vienes, viene, venimos, venís, vienen.
Pres. Subj.	venga, vengas, venga, vengamos, vengáis, vengan.
Pret. Indic.	vine, viniste, vino, vinimos, vinisteis, vinieron.
Imp. Subj.	viniera or viniese, vinieras or vinieses, viniera or viniese, viniéramos or viniésemos, vinierais or vinieseis, vinieran or viniesen.
Fut. Indic.	vendré, vendrás, vendrá, vendremos, vendréis, vendrán.
Cond.	vendría, vendrías, vendría, vendríamos, vendríais, vendrían.
Imper.	ven tú, venga Vd., vengamos nosotros, venid vosotros, vengan Vds.
Pres. Part.	viniendo.

49. ver

Pres. Indic.	veo, ves, ve, vemos, veis, ven.
Pres. Subj.	vea, veas, vea, veamos, veáis, vean.
Imp. Indic.	veía, veías, veía, veíamos, veíais, veían.
Imper.	ve tú, vea Vd., veamos, nosotros, ved vosotros, vean Vds.
Past Part.	visto.

50. yacer

Pres. Indic.	yazco or yazgo, yaces, yace, yacemos, yacéis, yacen.
Pres. Subj.	yazca or yazga, yazcas or yazgas, yazca or yazga, yazcamos or yazgamos, yazcáis or yazgáis, yazcan or yazgan.
Imper.	yace tú, yazca or yazga Vd., yazcamos or yazgamos nosotros, yaced vosotros, yazcan or yazgan Vds.

51. Defective Verbs

a. The following verbs are used only in the forms that have an i in the ending: abolir, agredir, aterirse, empedernir, transgredir.

b. atañer
This verb is used only in the third person. It is most frequently used in the present indicative: atañe, atañen.

c. concernir
This verb is used only in the third person of the following tenses:

Pres. Indic.	**concierne, conciernen.**
Pres. Subj.	**concierna, conciernan.**
Imp. Indic.	concernía, concernían.
Imp. Subj.	concerniera or concerniese, concernieran or concerniesen.
Pres. Part.	concerniendo.

d. soler

This verb is used most frequently in the present and imperfect indicative. It is less frequently used in the present subjunctive.

Pres. Indic.	**suelo, sueles, suele,** solemos, soléis, **suelen.**
Pres. Subj.	**suela, suelas, suela,** solamos, soláis, **suelan.**
Imp. Indic.	solía, solías, solía, solíamos, solíais, solían.

The preterit is seldom used. Of the compound tenses, only the present perfect is commonly used: he solido, etc. The other tenses are very rare.

e. roer

This verb has three forms in the first person of the present indicative: **roo, royo, roigo,** all of which are infrequently used. In the present subjunctive the perferable form is **roa, roas, roa,** etc., although the forms **roya** and **roiga** are found.

52. *Irregular Past Participles*

abrir—**abierto**	escribir—**escrito**
absorber—absorbido, **absorto**	freir—**frito,** freído
bendecir—bendecido, **bendito**	hacer—**hecho**
componer—**compuesto**	imprimir—**impreso**
cubrir—**cubierto**	inscribir—**inscrito, inscripto**
decir—**dicho**	maldecir—maldecido, **maldito**
deponer—**depuesto**	morir—**muerto**
descomponer—**descompuesto**	poner—**puesto**
describir—**descrito**	prescribir—**prescrito, prescripto**
descubrir—**descubierto**	proscribir—**proscrito, proscripto**
desenvolver—**desenvuelto**	proveer—proveído, **provisto**
deshacer—**deshecho**	resolver—**resuelto**
devolver—**devuelto**	revolver—**revuelto**
disolver—**disuelto**	romper—rompido, **roto**
encubrir—**encubierto**	satisfacer—**satisfecho**
entreabrir—**entreabierto**	subscribir—**subscrito**
entrever—**entrevisto**	ver—**visto**
envolver—**envuelto**	volver—**vuelto**

The Spanish Language in America

Introduction

In a sense Latin is not dead. The speech of Roman soldiers, merchants, and colonists, the Latin of another day, was taken bodily to Iberia, to Gaul, to Dacia, and to many other regions. As it developed under some influence from the languages previously spoken in these areas, it became known eventually by several other names—Spanish, Portuguese, French, Italian, Romanian, etc.

The Latin of northern Spain came to be called Castilian since its speakers were from the province of Castilla (Latin *Castella*, "castles"), and although later it was often called Spanish (**español**), to this day the people of many regions of Spanish speech refer to their language as **castellano,** and the children of Argentina and Chile, for instance, study **composición castellana.**

Castilian, among other Latin dialects, became prominent in the Iberian peninsula because of the hegemony of north central Spain in the reconquest of the peninsula from the Moors during the Middle Ages and subsequently in the discovery and settlement of America. Thus its predominance over other manifestations of Latin is not due to its own nature but rather to nonlinguistic factors: political and military power and organization, church-state relations, and finally literary ascendance.

The Spanish of Latin America, like most "colonial" speech, tends to be conservative in its structural changes compared with that of the mother country. In addition, it reflects regional traits of the southwestern part of Spain, notably Andalusia and adjacent areas, from where a large part of the sailors, conquistadores, and colonists came. In other words, the Spanish of America would seem to be Andalusian Castilian of the sixteenth and seventeenth centuries, as far as pronunciation and grammar are concerned. But in vocabulary hundreds of Indian words have entered the language, especially in Mexico, Guatemala, the Andes (Ecuador, Peru, and Bolivia), and in the Río de la Plata region. The Indian words of the Caribbean islands were taken to other parts of Latin America by the original Spanish settlers and often form a part of the general Spanish lexicon. It should be noted that these Indian languages belong to distinct, unrelated families, so that an **ahuacate** (avocado) in Mexico and Central America becomes a **palta** in the Andes. Although Spanish Americans generally have little difficulty understanding each other, the following variants represent rather extreme divergences:

	Little boy	*bus*	*blond*
Mexico	**chamaco**	**camión**	**güero**
Guatemala	**patojo**	**camioneta**	**canche**
El Salvador	**cipote**	**camioneta**	**chele**
Panamá	**chico**	**chiva**	**fulo**
Colombia	**pelado**	**autobús**	**mono**
Argentina	**pibe**	**colectivo**	**rubio**
Chile	**cabro**	**micro**	**rubio**
Cuba	**chico**	**guagua**	**rubio**

Although most of these words are actually Spanish (of Latin origin), several are from the Indian languages of the respective areas. The fact that there are differences of this sort is to be expected in a general culture that contains so many national boundaries.

Today Spanish (**castellano**) is the most extensive manifestation of the former spoken Latin. Those who think and express themselves in this language number about 200,000,000, and they live in some twenty countries, most of which have rapidly growing populations. It is estimated as of 1977 that by A.D. 2000 Spanish will be the language of nearly 500,000,000 people, most of whom will be **hispanoamericanos.** It is one of the principal languages of the world.

The Pronunciation of Latin-American Spanish

The fundamental phonological traits of American Spanish are to be found in Castilla, but only changes that have taken place in the Andalusian dialect of Castilian have become established in America. Furthermore, these changes apparently took place between the fifteenth and the eighteenth centuries, during the settlement of Latin America. Evidence indicates that inaccessible areas of Spanish America (the mountainous regions of Mexico, Guatemala, Colombia, Ecuador, Peru, Bolivia, as well as Paraguay, inland Venezuela, and northern Argentina) received only the early changes of Andalusian Castilian, while the accessible coastal areas and port cities tend to reflect both early changes and those of the late colonial period. Thus it is that Cuban and Panamanian Spanish resemble that of present-day Sevilla more than does Mexican Spanish or that of Bogotá. In the meantime Madrid Spanish (called Castilian by many North Americans) developed one or two features that never reached America.

The outstanding common feature of American-Spanish pronunciation that goes back to the early colonial period is the so-called **seseo.** About the time of Columbus the people of southwestern Spain began to confuse the two sibilant sounds of **casa** [KáSa] ("house") and **caza** [kása] ("hunt") (the capital [S] representing a "thick" alveolar sound and the [s] representing a "normal" dental sound), with the result that only the dental sound survived. Since most settlers of America were from the south, this became the general Spanish-American tendency. **Coser** and **cocer** are alike in southern Spain and in Latin America. The sibilant is a delicate dental one. In northern and central Spain a distinction between these two sounds is still maintained, and the second or dental one has become interdental [θ], similar to the voiceless *th* of English. The former [S] is still apicoalveolar, and to the foreigner approaches the sound represented by English *sh*.

In the seventeenth and eighteenth centuries other changes occurred in the pronunciation of southern Spanish. As has been indicated, these became part of the Spanish of the accessible areas of America, but most did not reach the high mountains and plateaus. The first of these was the aspiration or even the loss of /s/ syllable final. **Estos** becomes (éhtoh) or even [éto], the result of what might be termed a "relaxed" articulation. About the same time the /l̥/ (written ll) tended to be "relaxed" to the extent that it coincided with the /y/ (written y), so that **valla** and **vaya** were levelled to [báya] in Andalusia and parts of America. Today Bolivia, Paraguay, and much of Peru and Ecuador still maintain a distinction. One of the latest levelings of Andalusia was the confusion of /l/ and /r/ syllable final. This is heard today in Puerto Rico, Panama, and Venezuela, and to a certain extent in Cuba, the Dominican Republic, and central Chile. **Puerta** sounds like [pwelta], **mar** like [mal] and the infinitives seem to end in /l/. A final Andalusian trait is the velar /n/ [ŋ] as a sign of open transition. **Enamora** is [enamóra], but **en amor** is [eŋamór]. English-speakers think of *ng* when they hear **son** and **pan** pronounced [soŋ] and [paŋ].

Perhaps the only oustanding feature of American Spanish that is not traceable to Andalusia is the assibilation of /rr/ [r̃] and /r/ [r̃] final and postconsonantal. This occurs in vast areas of America: Guatemala, Costa Rica, in the eastern cordillera of Colombia, highland Ecuador, Bolivia, Chile, western and northern Argentina, and Paraguay.

Map 1

 Vos used instead of tú in informal address.

 In Chile the distinction is one of class: vos is used in the lower economic levels.

Map 2

Aspiration or loss of /s/ syllable final.

Map 3

Distinction between /ĺ/ and /y/.

Assibilation of /rr/ and /tr/.

The maps show the distribution of the distinguishing features of Spanish-American pronunciation.

Syntactic Features

The familiar form of address in Spanish, **tú**, is a direct descendant of the Latin *tu*. The Latin plural form *vos* also came down to Spanish, but by the late Middle Ages it had assumed the function of polite singular as well as familiar plural. To make the distinction, people began to say **vosotros** (you others) for the plural. In the sixteenth century there came into being a very polite form of address: **vuestra merced** (your mercy), used with the third person of the verb, as one might say, "Does his majesty wish to enter?" It has been shortened to **usted**. With this new polite form, **vos**, the former polite singular, lost prestige and became a familiar form. This was the state of affairs when the colonists came to America. As a result, vast sections of Latin America use **vos** instead of **tú** as the singular familiar form of address. All of Spanish America uses **ustedes** for the familiar plural as well as the polite plural. It will be noted in the map on page 26 that the **vos** areas are generally far from the old Viceroyalties of Mexico and Lima. Only in Chile is there a social distinction.

The verb used with **vos** is the modified plural of Old Spanish: **hablás, comés, vivís**; the imperative is **hablá, comé, viví**. The object pronoun and the possessive are from the singular, the object of the preposition, **vos: LLevate tu perro con vos**. Since the imperative of **ir** would be simply **i**, the verb **andar** is used instead: **¡andate!** Another interesting syntactic trait is the general tendency to differentiate gender of nouns of occupation and status of people and to create feminine forms where they may not have existed in so-called standard Spanish. **Presidenta, ministra, dependienta, liberala, abogada**, and **arquitecta** have been heard. Equally general are the tendencies to use adjectives as adverbs (**corre ligero, toca el piano lindo**) and to make certain adverbs "agree" with adjectives they modify (**media muerta; medias locas**) as well as to use the impersonal **haber** in the plural (**habían dos; ¿cuántos habrán?**).

The Vocabulary of Spanish America

There are three main tendencies in the development of Hispanic-American lexical elements: (1) to use words that were popular at the time of the settlement of America, especially maritime terms or rural expressions, often out of popular etymology; (2) to adopt Indian words, especially those related to the domestic scene; and (3) to borrow directly from English and to develop cases of correlative analogy due to English influence.

Of the first category are such terms as **flota** for a bus line, **amarrar** for **atar; botar** for **echar; virar** for **volverse**. In the tropical zone of America (from Guatemala south through Peru), where there are no seasons of heat and cold, since these depend on altitude, the Spaniards began to call the wet periods **invierno** (winter) and the dry, **verano** (summer). The custom continues to this day in Guatemala, El Salvador, Honduras, Nicaragua, Costa Rica, Panama, Colombia, Venezuela, Ecuador, and Peru. One may ask, ¿**qué tal el invierno?** ("How was the winter?") and receive the answer ¡**copioso!** ("copious").

Indian words entered the Spanish of America by the hundreds. In the Caribbean the Spaniards learned **tabaco, canoa, huracán, maíz, ají;** in Mexico, from Náhuatl, **chocolate, tomate, coyote, chicle, cacao;** in the Andes, from Quechua, **pampa, quinina, cóndor, puma, poncho;** and in the Río de la Plata region, from Guaraní, **ananás, ñandú, ombú, yajá, tapioca.**

During the twentieth century the influence of English has been strong in Latin America, and the direct borrowings in some areas could be counted in the hundreds: **control, lonche, lonchería, sandwich, jaibol** ("highball"), **cóctel, ponche, bar, twist, chance, fútbol, béisbol, fildear** ("to field"), **jonrón** ("home run"), **noquear** ("to knock out"), **lobista,** and even such verbs as **taipear** ("to type") and **blofear** ("to bluff"). In the realm of correlative analogy or sense loans, English has tremendous influence, and **educación** ("upbringing") takes the place of **pedagogía, instrucción,** and **enseñanza; argumento** ("plot of a story") moves into the slot of **discusión; atender** ("to wait on") into that of **asistir; audiencia** into that of **concurrencia; acta** ("minutes") takes the place of **ley; complexión** ("physical constitution") takes the place of **tez.**

Regional Features: Mexico

Among speakers of Spanish, a Mexican is recognized by his intonation and by his tendency to lengthen the articulation of his /s/ and by his general preference for the consonant over the vowel. If intonation of Spanish is represented in a pattern of four levels, Mexicans, especially males in a "man-about-town" mood, tend to strike a terminal point between standard statement and emphatic statement, giving the utterance a "minor-key" effect. The tensely-grooved /s/ of Mexican Spanish leads to the virtual elimination of unstressed vowels, especially /e/, in rapid speech: **accidentes de coches** may tend to be [aksiḍénts ḍe kočs].

Typical adjectives of Mexico are **mero** and **puro.** The first of these is so popular that it means not only "mere" but "very," "real," "just," "same," and many other things, and is even used adverbially: **ya merito** ("It won't be long now").

As has been noted, Mexico is the center of Aztec vocabulary that has entered Spanish and eventually many languages of the world; **tomate, chocolate, cacao, coyote, chicle,** and hundreds of less common terms.

Guatemala

The Spanish of Guatemala is characterized by a strong assibilated /rr/ [řř] and by [ř] for /r/ except in intervocalic position. The **jota** tends to be [h] rather than [x], and velar /n/ marks open transition. Along with those of other Central-American areas, Guatemalan speakers tend to weaken intervocalic /y/ to the extent that **silla** sounds like [sía] and **bella** like [bea]. Through a process of ultracorrection, **vea** may become [béya]. Guatemalans generally pronounce their /s/ syllable final with clarity and tension.

A fairly universal feature of the Spanish of Guatemala is the **voseo,** or use of **vos** as the subject form of familiar address in the singular. The verb used with this is the plural familiar, but the pronoun objects and possessives are always singular. **Ceando te vayas, llévate tu perro contigo,** as one might say in Spain or in Mexico, would be **Cuando te vayás, llevate tu perro con vos** in Guatemala.

Little boys are **patojos** in Guatemala, and blonds are **canches.**

El Salvador, Honduras, Nicaragua

Perhaps more than any other group of independent countries, these three form a linguistic unity in most respects. They represent in phonology a middle point between the highland conservatism (Mexico and the Andes, for instance) and the later trends of the lowlands (Cuba and Panamá, for example). The inhabitants of these countries call each other **guanacos, catrachos,** and **nicas** respectively, and are always talking of Central-American union.

The phonological phenomenon of recent discovery—although it is probably an "archaic" trait—is the occlusive pronunciation of /b/, /d/, /g/ after another consonant, a situation in which they would be fricative in "standard" Spanish.

It is in this region of Central America that one hears a lisped /s/ that approaches [θ] among many residents, and especially among the working classes. As in northern Mexico, the intervocalic /y/ (representing orthographic y and ll) tends to be a semivowel or even disappears. The jota /x/ is [h] in all speakers, and there is a strong tendency to aspirate syllable final /s/.

The Salvador-Honduras-Nicaragua region is rich in forms of combinative analogy, especially noun formation on the basis of other nouns. The suffixes **-ada** and **-ón** are of extensive application: **babosada, pendejada, lambida, atolada, paisanada, perrada, barbón, narizón, pistón, quemazón;** and the longer diminutive form **-ecito** that might be used in Spain and in Mexico is simply **-ito: llavita, lucita, crucita, piedrita.** The place where things grow or are to be found is indicated by the suffix **-al: cañal, guacal, platanal, cafetal, piñal, pinal.**

Along with Guatemala and the other Central-American countries, except Panama, this region uses the **vos** form of familiar address, and in the way described for Guatemala: **Vení y decime, ¿son vos y tu padre ladrones?**

Many indigenous words are used in everyday conversation, most of them from the Pipil, a sublanguage of the Náhuatl. A blond is a **chele,** a boy is a **cipote, pushco** is dirty, **peche** is slender, and there is the usual stock of Aztec terms that were imported after the conquest of Mexico.

Costa Rica

Like Guatemala, Costa Rica is noted for its assibilated /rr/, along with assibilated /r/ syllable final. It also shares with Guatemala a fairly conservative articulation of /s/ syllable final. As in all Central-American and Caribbean countries, the /n/ is velar when final, as a sign of open juncture: [eŋ amor] but [enamorár], and intervocalic /y/ weakens to the point of elimination through vocalization.

As a part of the syntactic structure of the dialect, **vos** and related forms operate where **tú** would prevail in Spain or Mexico today, and lexically, Costa Rica shows less Aztec influence than Guatemala, El Salvador, or Honduras.

Panama

The Spanish of Panama might be termed "trade route Spanish," in that it has the phonological character of parts of America that were in constant communication with Spain at the grass-roots level and yet were removed from the courtly influences of the viceregal centers (Mexico and Lima). It resembles strongly the Spanish of Cuba, Puerto Rico, an Venezuela and the northern coast of Colombia.

Along with other Caribbean residents, the Panamanians tend to aspirate their /s/ at the end of a syllable, or to eliminate it entirely.

Colombia

The development of the language in Colombia, which has three high mountain ranges and several important ports, might serve as an example of how American Spanish grew in disparate ways from Peninsular models. The relative inaccessibility of the high sierras and valleys makes it possible to find at least five distinct linguistic zones in the former Nueva Granada. The "dialects" therefore represent stages in the historical development of southern Peninsular Spanish, the most inaccessible regions generally representing the earliest and the most accessible in general representing the latest in Andalusian vogues, before independence.

Strange as it may seem, Colombian Spanish has two general traits in common with that of El Salvador, Honduras, and Nicaragua: the /x/ is [h] in all regions, and the /b/, /d/, /g/ are occlusive after any consonant. Thus **pardo, barba, algo, desde, las vacas,** all have occlusives where a Spaniard or a Mexican would use fricatives.

The Spanish of Bogotá has the conservative distinction of /l̯/ and /y/ and, like that of Costa Rica and Guatemala, tends to assibilate the /rr/, the /tr/, and the /r/ final.

Pastuso Spanish (of Nariño) is in many ways Ecuadorean, and like the Spanish of highland Mexico, slights the vowel in favor of the consonant, tends to pronounce the /d/ od **-ado,** and uses an apicodental /s/, strong and well defined.

Antioquia's Spanish is unique in America in one way. The /s/ is apicoalveolar [S], like that of Spain, and although no distinction is made between **casa** and **caza,** the Colombian ambassador to Spain, an **antioqueño,** gave the impression of "talking like a Spaniard." The second distinguishing feature of this region's Spanish is the /y/ of such tenseness that it even becomes affricate intervocalically [maŷo, kabaŷo].

Colombia is unusually formal in most sections as far as direct address is concerned. Many speakers use **usted** almost exclusively—even to cats and dogs. Not only is this the case within the family, but some relatives speak to each other as **su merced.** The **voseo** prevails in Antioquia and in Santander and in the **Valle,** while Bogotá and the Coast always employ the **tuteo.**

Typical of Colombia are the idiomatic expressions ¡ **siga!** and ¡ **a la orden!** The first is said to invite one to enter, and the other to ask, "What can I do for you?" Black coffee, especially the demitasse, is a **tinto,** and to invite one to partake, one says: ¿ **Le provoca un tinto?** This same sentence to a Spaniard might mean, "Does red wine make you fight?" Instead of sending regards with **saludos,** Colombians use **saludes** ("healths").

Venezuela

The speech pattern of Venezuela is for the most part that of the Caribbean, and therefore late Andalusian. One "eats" his final /s/; /l/ and /r/ are confused at syllable end; /n/ is velar as a sign of finality; and as in El Salvador, Honduras, and Nicaragua, many people pronounce the /s/ as [θ].

As far as address is concerned, most of Venezuela is **tuteo** country, but sections near the Colombian frontier are **vos** areas.

Ecuador

In a country where thousands speak Quechua (the language of the Incas) in preference to Spanish and where many are bilingual, the Spanish language of the upper inter-Andean region is very conservative in its phonological evolution. Ecuadoreans (except those of the coast) still distinguish /l̦/ and /y/ as [ž] and [y], still pronounce /s/ with deliberate tenseness and, like many Mexicans, slight the vowel in favor of the consonant. Because Quechua is so widely spoken, and because this language has a simple three-vowel system, the Spanish of the highlands tends to heighten /o/ to /u/ and /e/ to /i/. Unique in Latin America is the final /s/ as [z] before a vowel in the following word: [laz ag̦was].

Peru

About 11,000,000 **peruanos,** or as their neighbors may say, **peruleros** or **cholos,** occupy the territory of the central Inca Empire of preconquest days. Their money is counted in **soles** and their babies are **guaguas.** Along with Ecuador and Bolivia, Peru belongs to heavily populated Andean Spanish America, and besides having many Quechua-speaking inhabitants, the region boasts a clear Spanish that gives evidence of sixteenth-century origin and viceregal nurture.

Except in Lima and along the northern coast, Peruvians still distinguish the /l̦/ and /y/, and the general impression of Peruvian Spanish is similar to that of Mexico, Bolivia, and Ecuador.

Nearly all of Peru uses the **tú** form of familiar address, and as one might expect, hundreds of Quechua words have entered the Spanish of everyday life. In fact, several **quechismos** have become universal terms: **pampa, cóndor, puma, puna, quinina, llama, alpaca, gaucho, china** ("sweetheart"), **poncho,** and many others.

Chile

Linguistically, Chile can be divided into three sections, north, middle, and south. The north and the south resemble each other more than they do the middle. The heavily populated central valley partakes of many of the traits of late Andalusian, through the port of Valparaiso and the city of Santiago. Final /s/ is aspirated, /l/ and /r/ are confused in the syllable final situation, and /l̦/ and /y/ are not distinguished. Chiloé still distinguishes these latter two, and in the north there are vowel-heightening influences of Quechua. Two features that seem to characterize all Chilean Spanish are the /č/ of alveolar articulation rather than palatal and the /x/ with a palatal element of semiconsonantal nature before /e/. One seems to hear **la gente de Chile** as [la xjénte de tSíle].

Argentina, Uruguay, Paraguay

The Spanish of this vast territory is of two main types, according to the direction from which the settlers came. The western and northwestern sections were settled from Peru and Chile from about 1590. Although Buenos Aires and the humid Pampa were first settled about 1535, it was not until 1580 that a permanent settlement was established. The important factor producing the differences of today was the accessibility of Buenos Aires and surrounding country to constant influences from the ports of southern Spain in the colonial period. Thus the interior shows more conservative features: an /s/ of more tense articulation, a distinction between /l/ and /y/ in some areas, and the assibilated /rr/ of Costa Rica, Bogotá, and Guatemala.

The **porteño** of the Río de la Plata region is noted for his /y/ with strong [ž] articulation: **bayo, calle** [bážo], [káže].

Both Argentina and Uruguay are **voseo** territories, and the style has been recorded extensively in gaucho poetry. As a cattle region, the pampas have a lexicon that is rich in the terminology of the ranch and of horses. English and French are contributors to the vocabulary of the area, and one hears of **five o'clock tea a todas horas,** and the frequency of **chau** for "good-by" attests the influence of Italian, the original language of more than half of the inhabitants of Argentina. **Argentinos** are often called **che,** since they use this term to attract attention.

Paraguay, being more inaccessible, has two conservative features in its phonology: the distinction of /l/ and /y/, and the assibilation of /rr/. It is unique in that nearly all its inhabitants are bilingual. They speak the original Indian language, Guaraní, and Spanish. The occasion usually dictates which will be used, and speakers will often shift from one to the other in the same utterance.

Cuba, The Dominican Republic, and Puerto Rico

The Spanish of the Caribbean, like that of Panama, could be termed "trade route" Spanish, since it shows rather typically the American evolution of Andalusian trends of the seventeenth and eighteenth centuries, trends that do not seem to be present in the more inaccessible hinterland. Add to this the Afro-Cuban influences of slave days and the many American English loans of the twentieth century, and we have perhaps the least "conservative" Castilian.

Cubans tend to aspirate their syllable final /s/ or drop it altogether, and the tendency is as marked or more so in Puerto Rico and Santo Domingo. In all three, syllable final /l/ and /r/ are confused, most of all in Puerto Rico, where the /l/ is favored: **puerta, izquierdo** [pwélta], [ihkjéldo]. In contrast to Mexico, Ecuador, Peru, and Bolivia, where the vowel may be slighted, those of the Caribbean tend to slight the consonant in favor of the vowel. In Puerto Rico /rr/ is now velar in about half of the population. It resembles the **jota** of Spain: [x].

Cuba, Puerto Rico, and the Dominican Republic are **tuteo** countries.

This brief description of some of the features of the Castilian of America may help to show that distinctive features do not correspond to geographical or political entities to the extent that has been believed, and one might indicate as many as a hundred dialects—and yet it is all Spanish.

Numerals—Números

Cardinal Numbers	Números Cardinales	Ordinal Numbers	Números Ordinales[5]
1....... one	uno, una	first	primero
2....... two	dos	second	segundo
3....... three	tres	third	tercero
4....... four	cuatro	fourth	cuarto
5....... five	cinco	fifth	quinto
6....... six	seis	sixth	sexto
7....... seven	siete	seventh	séptimo
8....... eight	ocho	eighth	octavo
9....... nine	nueve	ninth	noveno, nono
10...... ten	diez	tenth	décimo
11...... eleven	once	eleventh	undécimo
12...... twelve	doce	twelfth	duodécimo
13...... thirteen	trece	thirteenth	décimotercio
14...... fourteen	catorce	fourteenth	décimocuarto
15...... fifteen	quince	fifteenth	décimoquinto
16...... sixteen	dieciseis, diez y seis	sixteenth	décimosexto
17...... seventeen	diecisiete, diez y siete	seventeenth	décimoséptimo
18...... eighteen	dieciocho, diez y ocho	eighteenth	décimoctavo
19...... nineteen	diecinueve, diez y nueve	nineteenth	décimonono
20...... twenty	veinte	twentieth	vigésimo
21...... twenty-one	veintiuno, veinte y uno	twenty-first	vigésimo primero
30...... thirty	treinta	thirtieth	trigésimo
40...... forty	cuarenta	fortieth	cuadragésimo
50...... fifty	cincuenta	fiftieth	quincuagésimo
60...... sixty	sesenta	sixtieth	sexagésimo
70...... seventy	setenta	seventieth	septuagésimo
80...... eighty	ochenta	eightieth	octogésimo
90...... ninety	noventa	ninetieth	nonagésimo
100..... one hundred	ciento	(one) hundredth	centésimo
101..... one hundred and one	ciento (y) uno	(one) hundred and first	centésimo primo
200..... two hundred	doscientos	two-hundredth	ducentésimo
300..... three hundred	trescientos	three-hundredth	tricentésimo

[5] The ordinals beyond the "tenth" are less used in Spanish than in English. They are often replaced by the cardinals: *Alfonso the Thirteenth* **Alfonso trece.**

Cardinal Numbers	Números Cardinales	Ordinal Numbers	Números Ordinales[5]
400...... four hundred	cuatrocientos	four-hundredth	cuadringentésimo
500...... five hundred	quinientos	five-hundredth	quingentésimo
600...... six hundred	seiscientos	six-hundredth	sexagésimo
700...... seven hundred	setecientos	seven-hundredth	septingentésimo
800...... eight hundred	ochocientos	eight-hundredth	octingentésimo
900...... nine hundred	novecientos	nine-hundredth	noningentésimo
1000..... one thousand	mil	(one thousandth	milésimo
100,000... one hundred thousand	cien mil	(one) hundred thousandth	cienmilésimo
1,000,000 one million	un millón	(one) millionth	millonésimo

Nations, Cities, and Adjectives of Nationality

Afganistán	afgano
Albania	albanés
Alto Volta	voltaico
Arabia Saudita	árabe saudita
Argelia	argelino
Argentina	argentino
Asunción	asunceño
Basutolandia	basutolandés
Bechuanalandia	bechuanalandés
Bélgica	belga
Birmania	birmano
Bogotá	bogotano
Bolivia	boliviano
Brasil	brasileño
Bruselas	bruselense
Buenos Aires	bonaerense or porteño
Bulgaria	búlgaro
Burundi	burundi
Camboya	camboyano
Camerún	camerunés
Canadá	canadiense
Caracas	caraqueño
Ceilán	ceilanés
Colombia	colombiano
Congo (both)	congoleño
Costa de Marfil	marfileño
Costa Rica	costarricense
Cuba	cubano
Chad	chadiano
Checoslovaquia	checoslovaco
Chile	chileno
China	chino
Chipre	chipriota

Dahomey	dahomeyano
Dinamarca	dinamarqués or danés
Ecuador	ecuatoriano
El Salvador	salvadoreño
España	español
Estados Unidos de América	estadounidense
Etiopía	etíope
Filipinas	filipino
Finlandia	finlandés or finés
Francia	francés
Gabón	gabonés
Gambia	gambio
Ghana	ghanés
Ginebra	ginebrino
Grecia	griego
Guatemala	guatemalteco
Guayaquil	guayaquileño
Guinea	guineo
Haití	haitiano
Honduras	hondureño
Hungría	húngaro
Ifni	ifneño
India	indio
Indonesia	indonesio
Irak	iraqués
Irán	iranio
Irlanda	irlandés
Islandia	islandés
Israel	israelí
Italia	italiano
Jamaica	jamaicano
Japón	japonés
Jordania	jordanio
Jerusalém	jerosolimitano
Kenia	kenio
Kuwait	kuwaiteño
Laos	laosiano
La Paz	paceño
Líbano	libanés
Liberia	liberiano
Liberia	
Libia	libio
Lima	limeño
Lisboa	lisboeta or lisbonense
Londres	londinense

Luxemburgo	luxemburgués
Madagascar	malache
Madrid	madrileño
Malasia	malayo
Malavi	malavio
Malí	maliense
Managua	managüense
Marruecos	marroquí
Mauritania	mauritano
México (Mejico)	mejicano (mexicano)
Mongolia	mongol
Montevideo	montevideño or montevideano
Nepal	nepalés
Nicaragua	nicaragüense
Níger	nigerino
Nigeria	nigeriano
Noruega	noruego
Nueva York	neoyorquino
Nueva Zelandia	neozelandés
Paises Bajos	holandés
Pakistán	pakistano
Panamá	panameño
Paraguay	paraguayo
París	parisiense
Perú	peruano
Polonia	polaco
Portugal	portugués
Puerto Rico	puertorriqueño or portorriqueño
Reino Unido de Gran Bretaña e Irlanda del Norte	británico
República Arabe Unida	egipcio
República Centroafricana	centroafricano
República Dominicana	dominicano
República Socialista Soviética de Bielorrusia	bieloruso
República Socialista Soviética de Ucrania	ucranio
Río de Janeiro	carioca
Río Muni	ríomuniense
Rodesia	rodesio
Rumania	rumano
Rwanda	rwandés
San José	josefino
São Paulo	paulistano

Santa Cruz	cruceño
Santiago	santiagueño or santiaguino
Senegal	senegalés
Sierra Leona	leonense
Siria	sirio
Somalia	somalí
Suazilandia	suazilandés
Sudáfrica	sudafricano
Sudán	sudanés
Suecia	sueco
Tailandia	tailandés
Tanganyica	tanganyikano
Tanzania	tanzanio
Tegucigalpa	tegucigalpense
Tenerife	tinerfeño
Tetuán	tetuaní
Togo	togolés
Trinidad y Tobago	trinitario
Túnez	tunecí
Turquía	turco
Uganda	ugandés
Unión de Repúblicas Socialistas Soviéticas	ruso
Uruguay	uruguayo
Venecia	veneciano or véneto
Venezuela	venezolano
Viena	vienés
Yemen	yemenita
Yugoslavia	yugoslavo
Washington	washingtoniano
Zambia	zambio
Zanzíbar	zanzibareño

Monetary Units and Exchange Rates

Country	Basic Unit	Standard Subdivision	Exchange Rate as of Jan. 1976*
Argentina	peso nuevo	100 centavos	$ .0255
Bolivia	peso	100 centavos	$b .0468
Brazil	cruzeiro	100 centavos	Cr$ .1200
Chile	peso	100 centésimos	$ .1400
Colombia	peso	100 centavos	$ .0330
Costa Rica	colón	100 céntimos	¢ .1160
Cuba	peso	100 centavos	$ 1.000 (official)

* U.S. dollar = 1.000

Country	Basic Unit	Standard Subdivision	Exchange Rate as of Jan. 1976*
Dominican Republic	peso	100 centavos	$ 1.000
Ecuador	sucre	100 centavos	S/ .045
El Salvador	colón	100 centavos	¢ .400
Guatemala	quetzal	100 centavos	Q 1.000
Haiti	gourde	100 centimes	G .200
Honduras	lempira	100 centavos	L .500
Mexico	peso	100 centavos	$ .0801
Nicaragua	córdoba	100 centavos	C$ .142
Panama	balboa	100 centésimos	B 1.000
Paraguay	guaraní	100 céntimos	G .0098
Peru	sol	100 centavos	S/ .0230
Spain	peseta	100 céntimos	Pts. .0172
Uruguay	peso	100 centésimos	N$ .41
Venezuela	bolívar	100 céntimos	Bs .2340

A:a **a** [a] *prep.* to; in, into; on; by.
abacería [a·ƀa·se·rí·a] *f.* grocery; grocery store; **abacero** [a·ƀa·sé·ro] *m.* grocer.
abad [a·ƀáđ] *m.* abbot; **abadía** [a·ƀa·đí·a] *f.* abbey.
abadejo [a·ƀa·đé·xo] *m. N.Sp.* codfish.
abadesa [a·ƀa·đé·sa] *f.* abbess.
abajarse [a·ƀa·xár·se] *v.* to lower oneself, humiliate oneself.
abajeño [a·ƀa·xé·ño] *adj. Mex., C.A.* lowland; *n.* lowlander.
abajo [a·ƀá·xo] *adv.* down, below; downstairs.
abalanzar⁹ [a·ƀa·lan·sár] *v.* to balance; to hurl, impel; **-se** to hurl oneself; to rush (upon), swoop down (upon); *Am.* to rear, balk.
abalear [a·ƀa·le·ár] *v.* to "shoot up"; *Am.* to winnow.
abanderado [a·ƀan·de·rá·đo] *adj.* standard-bearing; *n.* standard-bearer.
abandonamiento [a·ƀan·do·na·mjén·to] = **abandono.**
abandonar [a·ƀan·do·nár] *v.* to abandon, desert; to give up.
abandono [a·ƀan·dó·no] *m.* abandon; desertion; neglect.
abanicar⁶ [a·ƀa·ni·kár] *v.* to fan.
abanico [a·ƀa·ní·ko] *m.* fan.
abaratar [a·ƀa·ra·tár] *v.* to cheapen, lower the price of.
abarcar⁶ [a·ƀar·kár] *v.* to embrace, contain, include; *Carib., Riopl.* to buy up, monopolize.
abarrancarse⁶ [a·ƀa·rran·kár·se] *v.* to fall into an opening; to get into a difficult situation.
abarrotería [a·ƀa·rro·te·rí·a] *f. Mex., C.A., Andes* grocery, grocery store; **abarrotero** [a·ƀa·rro·té·ro] *m. Mex., C.A., Andes* grocer.
abarrotes [a·ƀa·rró·tes] *m. pl.* small packages (in hold of a ship); *Mex., C.A., Andes* groceries; **tienda de —** *Mex., C.A., Andes* grocery store.
abastecer¹³ [a·ƀas·te·sér] *v. irr.* to supply.
abastecimiento [a·ƀas·te·si·mjén·to] *m.* supply; provisions.
abasto [a·ƀás·to] *m.* supply; **no dar — a** to be unable to cope with.
abatido [a·ƀa·tí·đo] *adj.* dejected, depressed, crestfallen, humbled; fallen; lowered.
abatimiento [a·ƀa·ti·mjén·to] *m.* discouragement, dejection, depression; descent, swoop, drop.
abatir [a·ƀa·tír] *v.* to lower; to knock down; to depress; to humble; **-se** to become discouraged; to swoop down.
abdicar⁶ [aƀ·đi·kár] *v.* to abdicate.
abdomen [aƀ·đó·men] *m.* abdomen.
abecedario [a·ƀe·se·đá·rjo] *m.* alphabet; primer.
abedul [a·ƀe·đúl] *m.* birch.
abeja [a·ƀé·xa] *f.* bee; **abejera** [a·ƀe·xé·ra] *f.* beehive; **abejón** [a·ƀe·xón] *m.* drone; bumblebee; **abejorro** [a·ƀe·xó·rro] *m.* bumblebee.
aberración [a·ƀe·rra·sjón] *f.* aberration, mental or moral deviation.
abertura [a·ƀer·tú·ra] *f.* aperture, opening, hole, slit.
abeto [a·ƀé·to] *m.* fir (tree and wood).
abierto [a·ƀjér·to] *p.p. of* **abrir** opened; *adj.* open; frank; *Am.* proud, self-satisfied; *Am.* generous.
abigarrado [a·ƀi·ga·rrá·đo] *adj.* motley; multicolored; variegated.
abigeato [a·ƀi·xe·á·to] *m.* cattle stealing.
abismado [a·ƀiz·má·đo] *p.p.* absorbed, buried in thought; overwhelmed.
abismal [a·ƀiz·mál] *adj.* abysmal.

abismar [a·ƀiz·már] *v.* to overwhelm; to depress; **-se** to be plunged (into); to bury oneself (in thought, grief, etc.).
abismo [a·ƀíz·mo] *m.* abyss, precipice, chasm.
abjurar [aƀ·xu·rár] *v.* to abjure; to renounce solemnly.
ablandar [a·ƀlan·dár] *v.* to soften.
ablativo [a·ƀla·tí·ƀo] *m.* ablative.
abnegación [aƀ·ne·đa·sjón] *f.* abnegation, self-denial, self-sacrifice.
abnegado [aƀ·ne·ga·đo] *adj.* self-sacrificing.
abnegarse⁷ [aƀ·ne·gár·se] *v.* to deny oneself, sacrifice oneself.
abobado [a·ƀo·ƀá·đo] *adj.* stupid, silly.
abocar⁶ [a·ƀo·kár] *v.* to bite; to bring near; to flow into.
abocinar [a·ƀo·si·nár] *v.* to flare; to fall on one's face.
abochornar [a·ƀo·čor·nár] *v.* to overheat; to embarrass; **-se** to get overheated; to blush; to be embarrassed.
abofetear [a·ƀo·fe·te·ár] *v.* to slap.
abogacía [a·ƀo·ga·sí·a] *f.* the legal profession; a law career.
abogado [a·ƀo·gá·đo] *m.* lawyer.
abogar⁷ [a·ƀo·gár] *v.* to advocate, plead in favor of; to intercede.
abolengo [a·ƀo·lén·go] *m.* lineage, ancestry; inheritance, patrimony.
abolición [a·ƀo·li·sjón] *f.* abolition.
abolir⁵¹ [a·ƀo·lír] *v.* to abolish; to repeal.
abolsarse [a·ƀol·sár·se] *v.* to bag (said of trousers, skirts, etc.).
abollado [a·ƀo·yá·đo] *p.p. & adj.* dented; bumped; bruised.
abolladura [a·ƀo·ya·đú·ra] *f.* dent, bump.
abollar [a·ƀo·yár] *v.* to dent; to bump; to crush, crumple; to bruise.
abombar [a·ƀom·bár] *v.* to make bulge; **-se** *Riopl.* to get drunk.
abominable [a·ƀo·mi·ná·ƀle] *adj.* abominable, detestable.
abominar [a·ƀo·mi·nár] *v.* to abominate, abhor, detest.
abonado [a·ƀo·ná·đo] *m.* subscriber; *p.p. of* **abonar.**
abonar [a·ƀo·nár] *v.* to credit with; to make a payment; to endorse, back (a person); to fertilize (soil); **-se** to subscribe.
abonaré [a·ƀo·na·ré] *m.* promissory note; I.O.U.
abono [a·ƀó·no] *m.* (monetario) payment; installment; endorsement; guarantee; (del suelo) fertilizer; (suscripción) subscription.
abordar [a·ƀor·dár] *v.* to board (a ship); to dock, put into port; to approach; to undertake, take up (a matter, problem, etc.).
aborigen [a·ƀo·rí·xen] *adj.* aboriginal, indigenous, native; **aborígenes** [a·ƀo·rí·xe·nes] *m. pl.* aborigines, primitive inhabitants.
aborrascarse⁶ [a·ƀo·rras·kár·se] *v.* to become stormy.
aborrecer¹³ [a·ƀo·rre·sér] *v. irr.* to abhor, hate, detest.
aborrecible [a·ƀo·rre·si·ƀle] *adj.* abominable, hateful.
aborrecimiento [a·ƀo·rre·si·mjén·to] *m.* abhorrence; hatred.
abortar [a·ƀor·tár] *v.* to miscarry, have a miscarriage; to give birth prematurely; to fail.
aborto [a·ƀór·to] *m.* abortion, miscarriage; monster.
abotagarse⁷ [a·ƀo·ta·gár·se] *v.* to bloat; to swell.

abotonador [a·bo·to·na·dór] *m.* buttonhook.
abotonar [a·bo·to·nár] *v.* to button, button up; to bud; -se to button up.
abovedar [a·bo·be·ďár] *v.* to vault, cover with a vault; to arch.
abozalar [a·bo·sa·lár] *v.* to muzzle.
abra [á·bra] *f.* cove; mountain gap or pass; dale; *Am.* breach (*in the jungle*); *Am.* leaf (*of a door*).
abrasador [a·bra·sa·dór] *adj.* burning, very hot.
abrasar [a·bra·sár] *v.* to burn; to parch; -se to burn up, be consumed.
abrazar⁹ [a·bra·sár] *v.* to hug, embrace; to include.
abrazo [a·brá·so] *m.* hug, embrace.
abrebotellas [a·bre·bo·té·yas] *m.* bottle opener.
abrelatas [a·bre·lá·tas] *m.* can opener.
abrevadero [a·bre·ba·ďé·ro] *m.* drinking trough; watering place for cattle.
abrevar [a·bre·bár] *v.* to water (*livestock*).
abreviación [a·bre·bja·sjón] *f.* abbreviation.
abreviar [a·bre·bjár] *v.* to abbreviate, shorten, condense.
abreviatura [a·be·bja·tú·ra] *f.* abbreviation.
abrigar⁷ [a·bri·gár] *v.* to shelter, cover, protect; to wrap up; to harbor (*fear*), cherish (*hope*); -se to find shelter; to wrap oneself up.
abrigo [a·brí·go] *m.* shelter, cover, protection; wrap; overcoat.
abril [a·bríl] *m.* April.
abrillantar [a·bri·yan·tár] *v.* to polish, shine; to glaze.
abrir⁵² [a·brír] *v.* to open; to unlock.
abrochar [a·bro·čár] *v.* to button; to clasp; to fasten.
abrogación [a·bro·ga·sjón] *f.* repeal.
abrogar⁷ [a·bro·gár] *v.* to abrogate, repeal, annul.
abrojo [a·bró·xo] *m.* thistle, thorn; -s reef.
abrumador [a·bru·ma·ďór] *adj.* crushing, overwhelming; oppressive; fatiguing.
abrumar [a·bru·már] *v.* to crush, overwhelm; to trouble, annoy; -se to become foggy.
abrupto [a·brúp·to] *adj.* abrupt, steep.
absceso [ab·sé·so] *m.* abscess.
absolución [ab·so·lu·sjón] *f.* absolution; acquittal.
absoluto [ab·so·lú·to] *adj.* absolute; unconditional.
absolver²·⁵² [ab·sol·bér] *v. irr.* to absolve, free from guilt; to pardon, acquit.
absorbente [ab·sor·bén·te] *adj. & m.* absorbent.
absorber⁵² [ab·sor·bér] *v.* to absorb.
absorción [ab·sor·sjón] *f.* absorption.
absorto [ab·sór·to] *p.p. irr. of* absorber *& adj.* absorbed, engrossed; amazed.
abstenerse⁴⁵ [abs·te·nér·se] *v. irr.* to abstain, refrain.
abstinencia [abs·ti·nén·sja] *f.* abstinence; fasting.
abstracción [abs·trak·sjón] *f.* abstraction, reverie.
abstracto [abs·trák·to] *adj.* abstract.
abstraer⁴⁶ [abs·tra·ér] *v. irr.* to abstract; to withdraw, remove; -se to be lost in thought.
abstraído [abs·tra·í·ďo] *adj.* lost in thought, absent-minded; aloof.
absuelto [ab·swél·to] *p.p. of* absolver absolved, acquitted.
absurdo [ab·súr·ďo] *adj.* absurd, ridiculous, senseless; *m.* absurdity.
abuela [a·bwé·la] *f.* grandmother.
abuelo [a·bwé·lo] *m.* grandfather; -s grandparents; ancestors.
abulia [a·bú·lja] *f.* abulia, loss of will power.
abultado [a·bul·tá·ďo] *adj.* bulky, bulgy.
abultar [a·bul·tár] *v.* to bulge; to be bulky; to enlarge.

abundancia [a·bun·dá·sja] *f.* abundance, plenty.
abundante [a·bun·dán·te] *adj.* abundant, plentiful.
abundar [a·bun·dár] *v.* to abound, be plentiful.
aburrido [a·bu·rrí·ďo] *p.p. & adj.* bored; boring, tiresome; weary.
aburrimiento [a·bu·rri·mjén·to] *m.* weariness, dullness, boredom.
aburrir [a·bu·rrír] *v.* to bore, vex; -se to become bored or vexed.
abusar [a·bu·sár] *v.* to abuse, mistreat; to misuse; — de to take unfair advantage of; to impose upon.
abuso [a·bú·so] *m.* abuse; misuse.
abyecto [ab·yék·to] *adj.* abject.
acá [a·ká] *adv.* here, over here; this way, hither.
acabado [a·ka·bá·ďo] *m.* a finishing material: paint, varnish.
acabamiento [a·ka·ba·mjén·to] *m.* finish, completion, end; death; *Am.* exhaustion, physical decline.
acabar [a·ka·bár] *v.* to end, finish, complete; — de (+ *inf.*) to have just; — por (+ *inf.*) to end by; — con to put an end to, make short work of; to destroy; -se to be over, finished; to be consumed; *Am.* to wear oneself out; *Riopl., Mex., C.A.* to age or decline in health.
academia [a·ka·ďé·mja] *f.* academy; a special school; a scientific, literary, or artistic society.
académico [a·ka·ďé·mi·ko] *adj.* academic; *m.* academician, member of an academy.
acaecer¹³ [a·ka·e·sér] *v. irr.* to happen, occur.
acaecimiento [a·ka·e·si·mjén·to] *m.* event, happening.
acalorado [a·ka·lo·rá·ďo] *adj.* heated, excited, angry.
acaloramiento [a·ka·lo·ra·mjén·to] *m.* heat, ardor, excitement.
acalorar [a·ka·lo·rár] *v.* (*calentar*) to heat, warm; (*emocionar*) to excite.
acallar [a·ka·yár] *v.* to silence; to calm, quiet.
acampar [a·kam·pár] *v.* to encamp; to camp.
acanalar [a·ka·na·lár] *v.* to groove; to flute (*as a column*); to form a channel in.
acantilado [a·kan·ti·lá·ďo] *adj.* sheer, steep (*cliff*); *m.* bluff, cliff.
acantonar [a·kan·to·nár] *v.* to quarter (*troops*).
acaparar [a·ka·pa·rár] *v.* to corner (*the market*); to monopolize; to gather in (*for one's gain or profit*).
acarear [a·ka·re·ár] *v.* to bring face to face; to confront.
acariciar [a·ka·ri·sjár] *v.* to caress, pet; to cherish (*a hope or illusion*).
acarreador [a·ka·rre·a·ďór] *m.* carter; carrier.
acarrear [a·ka·rre·ár] *v.* to cart, transport; to bring about (*harm, disaster*).
acarreo [a·ka·rré·o] *m.* cartage, carriage, transport, haul.
acaso [a·ká·so] *adv.* perhaps; by chance; por si — just in case; *m.* chance, accident.
acatamiento [a·ka·ta·mjén·to] *m.* homage, reverence, respect.
acatar [a·ka·tár] *v.* to revere, respect; to pay homage to; *Mex., C.A., Ven.* to realize; *Mex., C.A., Ven.* to notice, pay attention.
acatarrar [a·ka·ta·rrár] *v.* to chill; *Mex. Ven.* to bother, annoy; -se to get chilled, catch cold; *Riopl.* to get tipsy.
acaudalado [a·kaw·da·lá·ďo] *adj.* wealthy.
acaudillar [a·kaw·ďi·yár] *v.* to lead, command.
acceder [ak·se·ďér] *v.* to accede.

accesible [ak·se·sí·ɓle] *adj.* accessible; approachable.

acceso [ak·sé·so] *m.* access; entrance, admittance; attack; fit (*of madness, anger, etc.*).

accesorio [ak·se·só·rjo] *adj. & m.* accessory.

accidentado [ak·si·ðen·tá·ðo] *adj.* seized with a fit; in a swoon; rough, uneven (*ground*).

accidental [ak·si·ðen·tál] *adj.* accidental, casual.

accidentarse [ak·si·ðen·tár·se] *v.* to have a seizure or fit; to swoon, faint.

accidente [ak·si·ðén·te] *m.* accident, mishap; chance; sudden fit, swoon.

acción [ak·sjón] *f.* (*física*) action; act; gesture; (*militar*) battle; (*de bolsa*) share of stock; — **de gracias** thanksgiving.

accionar [ak·sjo·nár] *v.* to gesticulate, make gestures; *Am.* to act, be active.

accionista [ak·sjo·nís·ta] *m. & f.*, shareholder, stockholder.

acecinar [a·se·si·nár] *v.* to dry-cure; to salt down.

acechanza [a·se·čán·sa] *f.* snare; ambush.

acechar [a·se·čár] *v.* to lurk; to spy.

acecho [a·sé·čo] *m.* ambush; spying; **al** (*or* **en**) — waiting in ambush, lying in wait.

acedo [a·sé·ðo] *adj.* rancid; acid; sour; harsh, disagreeable.

aceitar [a·sej·tár] *v.* to oil, grease.

aceite [a·séj·te] *m.* oil; — **alcanforado** camphorated oil; — **de hígado de bacalao** cod-liver oil; — **de oliva** olive oil; — **de ricino** castor oil.

aceitera [a·sej·té·ra] *f.* oil can; oil cruet (*bottle for the table*).

aceitoso [a·sej·tó·so] *adj.* oily.

aceituna [a·sej·tú·na] *f.* olive; **aceitunado** *adj.* olive green.

aceituno [a·sej·tú·no] *m.* olive tree.

aceleración [a·se·le·ra·sjón] *f.* acceleration.

acelerador [a·se·le·ra·ðór] *m.* accelerator.

acelerar [a·se·le·rár] *v.* to accelerate, speed up; to quicken, to hurry, hasten.

acémila [a·sé·mi·la] *f.* pack mule.

acendrado [a·sen·drá·ðo] *adj.* pure, without blemish; purified.

acendrar [a·sen·drár] *v.* to refine (*metals*); to purify, cleanse.

acento [a·sén·to] *m.* accent; emphasis.

acentuar[18] [a·sen·twár] *v.* to accentuate, emphasize; to accent; **-se** to become worse (*as an illness*).

acepción [a·sep·sjón] *f.* acceptation, usual meaning.

acepillar [a·se·pi·yár] *v.* to brush; to plane.

aceptación [a·sep·ta·sjón] *f.* acceptance; approval.

aceptar [a·sep·tár] *v.* to accept; to approve; to admit.

acequia [a·sé·kja] *f.* irrigation canal or ditch; *Peru, Ch.* small stream; *Ven., Mex., Andes* sewer.

acera [a·sé·ra] *f.* sidewalk.

acerado [a·se·rá·ðo] *adj.* steely, made of steel; steel-like; sharp.

acerar [a·se·rár] *v.* to steel.

acerbo [a·sér·ɓo] *adj.* bitter; harsh, cruel.

acerca de [a·sér·ka·ðe] *prep.* about, concerning.

acercamiento [a·ser·ka·mjén·to] *m.* approach; approaching; rapprochement (*coming together*).

acercar[6] [a·ser·kár] *v.* to bring near, draw up; **-se** to get near, approach.

acero [a·sé·ro] *m.* steel.

acérrimo [a·sé·rri·mo] *adj.* very sour, very tart; very harsh; very strong, stanch, stalwart, steadfast.

acertado [a·ser·tá·ðo] *adj.* accurate; right; sure.

acertar[1] [a·ser·tár] *v. irr.* to hit (*the mark*); to hit upon; find by chance; to guess right; — **a** (+ *inf.*) to happen to.

acertijo [a·ser·tí·xo] *m.* riddle.

acetileno [a·se·ti·lé·no] *m.* acetylene.

aciago [a·sjá·go] *adj.* ill-fated, unlucky.

acicalado [a·si·ka·lá·ðo] *p.p. & adj.* polished; dressed up; adorned; trim, neat.

acicalar [a·si·ka·lár] *v.* to polish; to adorn; **-se** to dress up, doll up.

acicate [a·si·ká·te] *m.* spur; incentive.

acidez [a·si·dés] *f.* acidity, sourness.

ácido [á·si·ðo] *m.* acid; *adj.* acid, sour.

acierto [a·sjér·to] *m.* right guess; lucky hit; good aim; good judgment; **con** — effectively, successfully.

aclamación [a·kla·ma·sjón] *f.* acclamation, applause.

aclamar [a·kla·már] *v.* to acclaim, cheer, hail, applaud.

aclaración [a·kla·ra·sjón] *f.* explanation.

aclarar [a·kla·rár] *v.* to clarify, explain; to clear up; to rinse; to dawn.

aclimatar [a·kli·ma·tár] *v.* to acclimatize, accustom to a climate or new environment.

acobardar [a·ko·ɓar·ðár] *v.* to frighten, intimidate.

acogedor [a·ko·xe·ðór] *adj.* friendly; hospitable.

acoger[11] [a·ko·xér] *v.* to receive; to give shelter; **-se** to take refuge.

acogida [a·ko·xí·ða] *f.* reception, welcome; refuge.

acogimiento [a·ko·xi·mjén·to] *m.* reception, welcome.

acojinar [a·ko·xi·nár] *v.* to cushion; to quilt.

acolchar [a·kol·čár] *v.* to quilt.

acólito [a·kó·li·to] *m.* acolyte, altar boy.

acometer [a·ko·me·tér] *v.* to attack; to undertake.

acometida [a·ko·me·tí·ða] *f.* **acometimiento** [a·ko·me·ti·mjén·to] *m.* attack, assault.

acomodadizo [a·ko·mo·ða·ðí·so] *adj.* obliging; accommodating.

acomodado [a·ko·mo·ðá·ðo] *adj.* well-off, wealthy; suitable, convenient; *p.p.* of **acomodar.**

acomodador [a·ko·mo·ða·ðór] *m.* usher (*in a theater*).

acomodar [a·ko·mo·ðár] *v.* (*cosa*) to arrange, adjust; (*a una persona*) to lodge; to give employment to; **-se** to make oneself comfortable; to adapt oneself.

acomodo [a·ko·mó·ðo] *m.* occupation, employment; arrangement.

acompañador [a·kom·pa·ña·ðór] *m.* companion; accompanist.

acompañamiento [a·kom·pa·ña·mjén·to] *m.* accompaniment; retinue, company.

acompañante [a·kom·pa·ñán·te] *m.* companion; escort; attendant; accompanist.

acompañar [a·kom·pa·ñár] *v.* to accompany; to escort; to be with; to enclose (*in a letter*).

acompasado [a·kom·pa·sá·ðo] *adj.* rhythmical; measured; slow, deliberate.

acondicionado [a·kon·di·sjo·ná·ðo] *adj.* conditioned; comfortable; air-conditioned; *Am.* adequate, suitable.

acondicionar [a·kon·di·sjo·nár] *v.* to condition; to prepare; to arrange; **-se** to become conditioned or prepared.

acongojar [a·koŋ·go·xár] *v.* to grieve; **-se** to grieve; to be distressed.

aconsejar [a·kon·se·xár] *v.* to advise, counsel.

acontecer[13] [a·kon·te·sér] *v. irr.* to happen, occur.

acontecimiento [a·kon·te·si·mjén·to] *m.* event, happening.

acopiar [a·ko·pjár] *v.* to gather, accumulate, store up.

acopio [a·kó·pjo] *m.* storing; accumulation; stock, store, supply.

acoplamiento [a·ko·pla·mjén·to] *m.* coupling; joint, connection.

acoplar [a·ko·plár] *v.* to couple, connect; to fit or join together; to yoke; to pair, mate.

acorazado [a·ko·ra·sá·ðo] *m.* armored ship, battleship.

acorazar[9] [a·ko·ra·sár] *v.* to armor.

acordar [a·kor·ðár] *v. irr. (estar conforme)* to arrange, to decide; *(instrumento)* to tune, put in harmony *(stringed instrument)*; *Peru, Ch., Ríopl., Mex., Cuba* to grant; *-se* to remember.

acorde [a·kór·ðe] *adj.* in harmony; in tune; *m.* chord.

acordelar [a·kor·ðe·lár] *v.* to measure with a cord; to rope off, put a cord around.

acordeón [a·kor·ðe·ón] *m.* accordion.

acordonar [a·kor·ðo·nár] *v.* to tie with a cord, string, or rope; to rope off, tie a rope around *(a place)*; to mill *(a coin).*

acornear [a·kor·ne·ár] *v.* to gore, wound with a horn; to butt.

acorralar [a·ko·rra·lár] *v.* to corral; to surround.

acortamiento [a·kor·ta·mjén·to] *m.* shortening.

acortar [a·kor·tár] *v.* to shorten, diminish; *-se* to shrink; to be shy, bashful.

acosar [a·ko·sár] *v.* to pursue, harass.

acostado [a·kos·tá·ðo] *adj.* reclining, lying down, in bed; tilted.

acostar[2] [a·kos·tár] *v. irr.* to put to bed; to lay down; *-se* to lie down, go to bed; to tilt.

acostumbrado [a·kos·tum·brá·ðo] *adj.* accustomed, used, usual, habitual.

acostumbrar [a·kos·tum·brár] *v.* to accustom, train; to be used to, be accustomed to; *-se* to get accustomed.

acotación [a·ko·ta·sjón] *f.* marginal note; stage directions *(for a play)*; boundary mark; mark on a map showing altitude.

acotar [a·ko·tár] *v.* to mark off *(with boundary marks)*; to make marginal notes or citations; to put the elevation marks on *(maps).*

acre [á·kre] *adj.* sour, tart, sharp; rude, harsh; *m.* acre.

acrecentamiento [a·kre·sen·ta·mjén·to] *m.* growth, increase.

acrecentar[1] [a·kre·sen·tár] *v. irr.* to increase; to advance, promote.

acreditar [a·kre·ði·tár] *v.* to credit; to bring fame or credit to; to accredit, authorize; *-se* to win credit or fame.

acreedor [a·kre·e·ðór] *adj.* worthy, deserving; *m.* creditor.

acribillar [a·kri·bi·yár] *v.* to riddle; to perforate; to pierce.

acriollar [a·krjo·yár] *v.* to make Spanish American; *-se* to become Spanish American like; to take on Spanish-American customs.

acróbata [a·kró·ba·ta] *m. & f.* acrobat.

acra [ák·ta] *f.* minutes *(of a meeting)*; document; **levantar —** to write the minutes.

actitud [ak·ti·túð] *f.* attitude; posture, pose.

activar [ak·ti·bár] *v.* to activate, make active; to speed up, hasten.

actividad [ak·ti·bi·ðað] *f.* activity; energy.

activista [ak·ti·bís·ta] *m. & f.* activist.

activo [ak·tí·bo] *adj.* active, lively; *m.* assets.

acto [ák·to] *m.* act; action, deed; ceremony; **— continuo** *(or* **seguido)** immediately after; **en el —** immediately.

actor [ak·tór] *m.* actor; **actriz** *f.* actress.

actuación [ak·twa·sjón] *f.* action; intervention, participation, performance; *-es* legal proceedings.

actual [ak·twál] *adj.* present *(time)*; of the present month; **-mente** *adv.* at present, nowadays.

actualidad [ak·twa·li·ðáð] *f.* present time; *-es* latest news, fashions, or events; **de —** current, up-to-date.

actuar[18] [ak·twár] *v.* to act, perform a function or act; to set in motion, cause to act.

acuarela [a·kwa·ré·la] *f.* water color.

acuario [a·kwá·rjo] *m.* aquarium.

acuartelar [a·kwar·te·lár] *v.* to quarter *(troops).*

acuático [a·kwá·ti·ko] *adj.* aquatic; **deportes -s** water sports.

acuchillar [a·ku·či·yár] *v.* to knife; to stab; to slash.

acudir [a·ku·ðír] *v.* to go or come *(to aid, or in response to a call)*; to attend, be present; to resort or turn to for help.

acueducto [a·kwe·ðúk·to] *m.* aqueduct, water channel or pipe.

acuerdo [a·kwér·ðo] *m.* agreement; decision, resolution; opinion; remembrance; **estar de —** to be in agreement; **ponerse de —** to come to an agreement; **tomar un —** to take a decision.

acullá [a·ku·yá] *adv.* yonder, over there.

acumulación [a·ku·mu·la·sjón] *f.* accumulation.

acumulador [a·ku·mu·la·ðór] *m.* storage battery.

acumular [a·ku·mu·lár] *v.* to accumulate, gather, pile up.

acuñación [a·ku·ña·sjón] *f.* coinage, minting; wedging.

acuñar [a·ku·ñár] *v.* to mint, coin, to wedge.

acuso [a·kwó·so] *adj.* watery.

acurrucarse[6] [a·ku·rru·kár·se] *v.* to cuddle, nestle; to huddle.

acusación [a·ku·sa·sjón] *f.* accusation, charge.

acusado [a·ku·sá·ðo] *p.p. & adj.* accused; *m.* defendant.

acusar [a·ku·sár] *v.* to accuse, denounce; to acknowledge *(receipt).*

acusativo [a·ku·sa·tí·bo] *adj.* accusative.

acuse [a·kú·se] *m.* acknowledgment *(of receipt).*

acústica [a·kús·ti·ka] *f.* acoustics *(science of sound).*

acústico [a·kús·ti·ko] *adj.* acoustic.

achacar[6] [a·ča·kár] *v.* to impute, attribute.

achacoso [a·ča·kó·so] *adj.* sickly.

achaparrado [a·ča·pa·rrá·ðo] *adj.* shrub, of shrub size; squat, squatty.

achaque [a·čá·ke] *m.* slight chronic illness; excuse; pretext; infirmity.

achicar[6] [a·či·kár] *v.* to shorten; to make small; to bail *(water)*; to humiliate; *Col.* to kill; *Ríopl.* to tie, fasten; *-se* to get smaller; to shrink.

achicoria [a·či·kó·rja] *f.* chicory.

adagio [a·ðá·xjo] *m.* adage, proverb, wise saying; adagio *(musical Spanish America).*

adaptar [a·ðap·tár] *v.* to adapt, fit, adjust.

adecuado [a·ðe·kwá·ðo] *adj.* adequate, fit, suitable.

adecuar [a·ðe·kwár] *v.* to fit, adapt.

adefesio [a·ðe·fé·sjo] *m.* absurdity, nonsense; ridiculous sight, dress, or person.

adelantado [a·ðe·lan·tá·ðo] *p.p. & adj.* anticipated; advanced; ahead; forward, bold; **por —** in

advance; *m.* govenor of a province (*in colonial Spanish America*).

adelantamiento [a·ḏe·lan·ta·mján·to] *m.* advancement, progress, betterment.

adelantar [a·ḏe·lan·tár] *v.* to advance; to move forward; to progress; to better; **-se** to get ahead.

adelante [a·ḏe·lán·te] *adv.* forward, ahead; **en —** from now on.

adelanto [a·ḏe·lán·to] *m.* advance; advancement, progress; betterment.

adelfa [a·ḏél·fa] *f.* oleander.

adelgazar[9] [a·ḏel·ga·sár] *v.* to thin out, taper; **-se** to get thin, slender.

ademán [a·ḏe·mán] *m.* gesture, gesticulation; attitude.

además [a·ḏe·más] *adv.* moreover, besides; **— de** *prep.* in addition to, besides.

adentro [a·ḏén·tro] *adv.* within, inside; **tierra —** inland; **mar —** out to sea; **hablar para sus -s** to talk to oneself.

aderezamiento [a·ḏe·re·sa·mján·to] *m.* dressing; adornment, decoration.

aderezar [a·ḏe·re·sár] *v.* (*embellecer*) to fix up, adorn, beautify, garnish; (*condimentar*) to season, prepare; (*almidonar*) to starch, stiffen.

aderezo [a·ḏe·ré·so] *m.* (*adorno*) adornment, garnish, trappings, finery, set of jewels; (*alimento*) seasoning; (*almidón*) starch, stiffener, filler (*used in cloth*).

adestrado [a·ḏes·trá·ḏo] *adj.* trained, skilled.

adestrar[1] [a·ḏes·trár] *v. irr.* to train; to guide.

adeudado [a·ḏew·ḏá·ḏo] *adj.* indebted; in debt; *p.p.* of **adeudar.**

adeudar [a·ḏew·ḏár] *v.* to owe; to debit, charge; **-se** to run into debt.

adeudo [a·ḏéw·ḏo] *m.* debt, indebtedness; duty (*on imports*); debit, charge.

adherencia [a·ḏe·rén·sja] *f.* adherence; attachment)

adherir[3] [a·ḏe·rír] *v. irr.* to adhere, stick.

adhesión [a·ḏe·sjón] *f.* adhesion; attachment.

adicto [a·ḏík·to] *adj.* addicted; devoted; *m.* addict; follower.

adiestrado [a·ḏjes·trá·ḏo] = **adestrado.**

adiestramiento [a·ḏjes·tra·mján·to] *m.* training; drill.

adiestrar [a·ḏjes·trár] = **adestrar.**

adinerado [a·ḏi·ne·rá·ḏo] *adj.* wealthy.

¡adiós! [a·ḏjós] *interj.* good-bye!; farewell!; hello!; *Am.* you don't say!

aditamento [a·ḏi·ta·mén·to] *m.* addition; annex.

adivinación [a·ḏi·ḇi·na·sjón] *f.* divination, prediction; guess.

adivinanza [a·ḏi·ḇi·nán·sa] *f.* conundrum, riddle.

adivinar [a·ḏi·ḇi·nár] *v.* to guess.

adivino [a·ḏi·ḇi·no] *m.* fortuneteller; soothsayer.

adjetivo [aḏ·xe·ti·ḇo] *m. & adj.* adjective.

adjudicar[6] [aḏ·xu·ḏi·kár] *v.* to adjudge, award, assign; **-se** to appropriate.

adjuntar [aḏ·xun·tár] *v.* to put with; to bring together; to enclose (*in a letter*).

adjunto [aḏ·xún·to] *adj.* adjoining; attached, enclosed.

adminículo [aḏ·mi·ní·ku·lo] *m.* accessory; gadget.

administración [aḏ·mi·nis·tra·sjón] *f.* administration, management; headquarters; *Ven., Mex., Cuba* extreme unction, last sacrament.

administrador [aḏ·mi·nis·tra·ḏór] *m.* administrator, manager.

administrar [aḏ·mi·nis·trár] *v.* to administer; to

manage; **-se** *Ven., Mex., Cuba* to receive the extreme unction or last sacrament.

administrativo [aḏ·mi·nis·tra·tí·ḇo] *adj.* administrative.

admirable [aḏ·mi·rá·ḇle] *adj.* admirable, wonderful.

admiración [aḏ·mi·ra·sjón] *f.* admiration, wonder; **punto de —** exclamation point.

admirador [aḏ·mi·ra·ḏór] *m.* admirer.

admirar [aḏ·mi·rár] *v.* to admire; **-se** to be astonished or amazed; to wonder.

admisible [aḏ·mi·sí·ḇle] *adj.* admissible, allowable.

admisión [aḏ·mi·sjón] *f.* admission; acceptance; acknowledgment.

admitir [aḏ·mi·tír] *v.* to admit; to let in; to accept; to allow, permit.

adobar [a·ḏo·ḇár] *v.* to fix, cook, prepare (*food*); to tan (*hides*); to pickle (*meats, fish*).

adobe [a·ḏó·ḇe] *m.* adobe, sun-dried mud brick.

adobo [a·ḏó·ḇo] *m.* mending; sauce for seasoning or pickling; mixture for dressing skins or cloth; rouge.

adoctrinamiento [a·ḏok·tri·na·mján·to] *m.* indoctrination, teaching, instruction.

adoctrinar [a·ḏok·tri·nár] *v.* to indoctrinate, teach, instruct.

adolecer[13] [a·ḏo·le·sér] *v. irr.* to suffer (*from an illness, defect, etc.*).

adolescencia [a·ḏo·le·sén·sja] *f.* adolescence.

adolescente [a·ḏo·le·sén·te] *adj.* adolescent.

adonde [a·ḏón·de] *rel. adv.* where; **¿adónde?** *interr. adv.* where to?; where?

adoptar [a·ḏop·tár] *v.* to adopt; to accept (*an opinion*).

adoptivo [a·ḏop·ti·ḇo] *adj.* adoptive, related by adoption; adopted.

adoración [a·ḏo·ra·sjón] *f.* adoration, worship.

adorar [a·ḏo·rár] *v.* to adore, worship.

adormecer[13] [a·ḏor·me·sér] *v. irr.* to make sleepy or drowsy; to lull; **-se** to get sleepy; to get numb; to fall asleep.

adormilado [a·ḏor·mi·lá·ḏo] *adj.* drowsy.

adornar [a·ḏor·nár] *v.* to adorn, decorate, ornament.

adorno [a·ḏór·no] *m.* adornment, ornament, decoration.

adquirir[35] [aḏ·ki·rír] *v. irr.* to acquire, gain, win, obtain.

adquisición [aḏ·ki·si·sjón] *f.* acquisition; attainment.

adrede [a·ḏré·ḏe] *adv.* on purpose, intentionally.

aduana [a·ḏwá·na] *f.* customhouse.

aduanero [a·ḏwa·né·ro] *m.* customhouse officer; *adj.* customhouse.

aduar [a·ḏwár] *m.* gypsy camp; *Riopl.* Indian camp or ranch.

aducir[25] [a·ḏu·sír] *v. irr.* to cite, allege, offer as proof.

adueñarse [a·ḏwe·ñár·se] *v.* to take possession.

adulación [a·ḏu·la·sjón] *f.* flattery.

adulador [a·ḏu·la·ḏór] *m.* flatter.

adular [a·ḏu·lár] *v.* to flatter.

adulterar [a·ḏul·te·rár] *v.* to adulterate, corrupt, make impure.

adulterio [a·ḏul·té·rjo] *m.* adultery.

adúltero [a·ḏúl·te·ro] *m.* adulterer.

adulto [a·ḏúl·to] *m. & adj.* adult.

adusto [a·ḏús·to] *adj.* stern, severe, austere.

advenedizo [aḏ·ḇe·ne·ḏi·so] *m.* newcomer, stranger; upstart; *Mex., Carib., Andes* novice, beginner; *adj.* newly arrived; upstart; *Mex., Carib., Andes* inexperienced.

advenimiento [ađ·be·ni·mién·to] *m.* advent, arrival, coming.

adverbio [ađ·bér·bjo] *m.* adverb.

adversario [ađ·ber·sá·rjo] *m.* adversary, opponent; foe.

adversidad [ađ·ber·si·đáđ] *f.* adversity; calamity.

adverso [ađ·bér·so] *adj.* adverse; contrary; unfavorable.

advertencia [ađ·ber·tén·sja] *f.* notice; warning; advice.

advertir³ [ađ·ber·tír] *v. irr.* to notice; to warn; to advise.

adyacente [ađ·ya·sén·te] *adj.* adjacent.

aéreo [a·é·re·o] *adj.* aerial; airy; correo — air mail.

aerodinámico [a·e·ro·đi·ná·mi·ko] *adj.* aerodynamic; *f.* aerodynamics.

aeródromo [a·e·ró·đro·mo] *m.* airport.

aerofluyente [a·e·ro·flu·yén·te] *adj.* streamlined.

aeronautica [a·e·ro·náw·ti·ka] *f.* aeronautics.

aeronave [a·e·ro·ná·be] *f.* airship.

aeropista [a·e·ro·pís·ta] *f.* landing strip; runway.

aeroplano [a·e·ro·plá·no] *m.* airplane.

aeropuerto [a·e·ro·pwér·to] *m.* airport.

aerosol [a·e·ro·sól] *m.* aerosol.

afabilidad [a·fa·bi·li·đáđ] *f.* friendliness, pleasantness, courtesy; afable [a·fá·ble] *adj.* affable, pleasant, courteous.

afamado [a·fa·má·đo] *adj.* famous.

afán [a·fán] *m.* eagerness, anxiety, ardor.

afanar [a·fa·nár] *v.* to urge, press; -se to hurry; to worry; to work eagerly; to toil.

afanoso [a·fa·nó·so] *adj.* laborious; hardworking.

afasia [a·fá·sja] *f.* aphasia.

afear [a·fe·ár] *v.* to make ugly; to disfigure; to blame, censure, condemn.

afección [a·fek·sjón] *f.* affection, fondness; disease.

afectado [a·fek·tá·đo] *p.p. & adj.* affected; *Am.* hurt, harmed; *Am.* estar — del corazón to have heart trouble.

afectar [a·fek·tár] *v.* (*promover*) to affect, move; (*fingir*) to pretend to have or feel; *Am.* to hurt, to harm, to injure.

afecto [a·fék·to] *m.* affection; *adj.* fond; — a fond of; given to; prone to.

afectuoso [a·fek·twó·so] *adj.* affectionate, tender.

afeitada [a·fej·tá·đa] *f. Am.* shave, shaving.

afeitar [a·fej·tár] *v.* to shave; -se to shave oneself; to put on make-up.

afeite [a·féj·te] *m.* make-up, cosmetics.

afeminado [a·fe·mi·ná·đo] *adj.* effeminate.

aferrado [a·fe·rrá·đo] *adj.* stubborn, obstinate; *p.p. of* aferrar.

aferramiento [a·fe·rra·mjén·to] *m.* grasping, seizing; attachment; stubbornness; tenacity.

aferrar [a·fe·rrár] *v.* to seize, grasp, grapple; -se to take or seize hold of; to cling; -se a una opinión to cling to an opinion.

afianzar⁹ [a·fjan·sár] *v.* to fasten, secure; to steady; to give bail or bond.

afición [a·fi·sjón] *f.* taste, inclination; fondness, affection.

aficionado [a·fi·sjo·ná·đo] *adj.* fond; *m.* amateur, fan.

aficionar [a·fi·sjo·nár] *v.* to inspire a liking or fondness; -se a to become fond of.

afiche [a·fi·če] *m. Ríopl.,* poster.

afijo [a·fí·xo] *m.* affix.

afilador [a·fi·la·đór] *m.* grinder, sharpener.

afilar [a·fi·lár] *v.* to sharpen; to grind; *Am.* to make love to, woo; *Am.* to flatter; *Am.* — con to flirt with.

afín [a·fín] *adj.* kindred, related; ideas afines related ideas.

afinador [a·fi·na·đór] *m.* piano tuner.

afinar [a·fi·nár] *v.* to refine, polish; to tune.

afinidad [a·fi·ni·đáđ] *f.* affinity; similarity; relationship.

afirmación [a·fir·ma·sjón] *f.* affirmation, assertion.

afirmar [a·fir·már] *v.* to affirm, assert; to make firm; *Am.* — un golpe to deal a blow.

afirmativa [a·fir·ma·tí·ba] *f.* affirmative.

afirmativo [a·fir·ma·tí·bo] *adj.* affirmative.

aflicción [a·flik·sjón] *f.* affliction, trouble, pain, grief.

afligir¹¹ [a·fli·xír] *v.* to afflict, trouble, grieve; *Ríopl., Ven.* to mistreat, harm, beat, strike; -se to worry, grieve.

aflojar [a·flo·xár] *v.* to slacken; to loosen, unfasten; to let go; *Mex. Ríopl., Carib.* to let go of money, spend easily; *Mex. Ríopl., Carib.* — un golpe to give a blow.

afluente [a·flwén·te] *m.* tributary; *adj.* abundant.

afluir³² [a·flwír] *v. irr.* to flow (into).

afortunado [a·for·tu·ná·đo] *adj.* fortunate; lucky.

afrenta [a·frén·ta] *f.* affront, offense, insult.

afrentar [a·fren·tár] *v.* to insult, offend, dishonor.

afrentoso [a·fren·tó·so] *adj.* outrageous, shameful, disgraceful.

africado [a·fri·ká·đo] *adj.* affricative; *f.* affricate.

africano [a·fri·ká·no] *adj. & m.* African.

afrontar [a·fron·tár] *v.* to face; to confront.

afuera [a·fwé·ra] *adv.* out, outside; -s *f. pl.* outskirts.

agachar [a·ga·čár] *v.* to lower; to bend down; -se to stoop, bend down, duck; to crouch; *Am.* to give in, yield; *Col.* -se con algo to make away with or steal something.

agalla [a·gá·ya] *f.* gill; tonsil; *Col., Ven.* greed; tener -s to have guts, have courage; *Ríopl., Ch., Carib.* to be unscrupulous and bold in business deals; *Ríopl., Ch., Carib.* to be greedy or stingy; *C.A.* to be smart, astute, cunning.

agarrar [a·ga·rrár] *v.* to seize, grasp, grab; -se to cling, hold on.

agarro [a·gá·rro] *m.* clench, clutch, grasp, grip. grab; agarrón *m.* tight clench, sudden grasp, grab; *Mex., Col., Ven., C.A.* pull, tug.

agasajar [a·ga·sa·xár] *v.* to entertain; to flatter.

agasajo [a·ga·sá·xo] *m.* entertainment, kind reception; friendliness; flattery.

agazapar [a·ga·sa·pár] *v.* to nab, seize (*a person*); -se to crouch; to squat.

agencia [a·xén·sja] *f.* agency; *Ch.* pawnshop.

agenciar [a·xen·sjár] *v.* to negotiate; to procure by negotiation; to promote.

agente [a·xén·te] *m.* agent; *Am.* officer, official.

ágil [á·xil] *adj.* agile, nimble, limber.

agilidad [a·xi·li·đáđ] *f.* agility, nimbleness.

agitación [a·xi·ta·sjón] *f.* agitation; excitement.

agitador [a·xi·ta·đór] *m.* agitator; *adj.* agitating; stirring.

agitar [a·xi·tár] *v.* to agitate, excite; to stir; to wave; to shake.

aglomeración [a·glo·me·ra·sjón] *f.* conglomeration, heap, pile, mass.

aglomerar [a·glo·me·rár] *v.* to mass together; to cluster; -se to crowd together, pile up.

aglutinante [a·glu·ti·nán·te] *adj.* agglutinative.

agobiar [a·go·bjár] *v.* to oppress, weigh down; to overwhelm.

agolparse [a·gol·pár·se] *v.* to crowd together, jam.

agonía [a·go·ní·a] *f.* agony.

AD

agonizante [a·go·ni·sán·te] *adj.* dying; *m.* dying person.

agonizar[9] [a·go·ni·sár] *v.* to be dying.

agorero [a·go·ré·ro] *adj.* ominous, of bad omen; prophetic; *m.* augur, prophet, fortune-teller.

agostar [a·gos·tár] *v.* to parch, dry up; to pasture; to plow (*in August*).

agosto [a·gós·to] *m.* August; harvest; **hacer su** — to make hay while the sun shines.

agotado [a·go·tá·ḍo] *adj. & p.p.* exhausted; out-of-print.

agotamiento [a·go·ta·mjén·to] *m.* exhaustion; draining.

agotar [a·go·tár] *v.* to exhaust, use up; to drain off; **-se** (*acabarse*) to be exhausted, used up; (*terminarse la edición*) to go out of print.

agraciado [a·gra·sjá·ḍo] *adj.* graceful; *m.* winner (*of a favor, prize, etc.*).

agraciar [a·gra·sjár] *v.* to grace; to adorn.

agradable [a·gra·ḍá·ḅle] *adj.* agreeable, pleasant.

agradar [a·gra·ḍár] *v.* to please, be agreeable (to).

agradecer[13] [a·gra·ḍe·sér] *v. irr.* to thank for; to be grateful for.

agradecido [a·gra·ḍe·si·ḍo] *adj.* thankful, grateful.

agradecimiento [a·gra·ḍe·si·mjén·to] *m.* gratitude, thankfulness.

agrado [a·gra·ḍo] *m.* agreeableness; liking, pleasure; **de su** — to his liking.

agrandar [a·gran·dár] *v.* to enlarge; to aggrandize, make greater.

agravar [a·gra·ḅár] *v.* to aggravate, make worse; to make heavier; to oppress; **-se** to get worse.

agraviar [a·gra·ḅjár] *v.* to offend, insult, affront.

agravio [a·grá·ḅjo] *m.* offense, insult, affront.

agredir[51] [a·gre·ḍír] *v.* to assail, assault, attack.

agregado [a·gre·gá·ḍo] *m.* attaché, person attached to a staff; aggregate, collection.

agregar[7] [a·gre·gár] *v.* to add; to join; to attach.

agresivo [a·gre·sí·ḅo] *adj.* aggressive, offensive.

agresor [a·gre·sór] *m.* aggressor; assailant.

agreste [a·grés·te] *adj.* rustic; wild (*fruit, flower, etc.*).

agriar[17] [a·grjár] *v.* to sour, make sour; **-se** to sour, turn sour, become sour.

agrícola [a·grí·ko·la] *adj.* agricultural.

agricultor [a·gri·kul·tór] *m.* agriculturist, farmer.

agricultura [a·gri·kul·tú·ra] *f.* agriculture.

agridulce [a·gri·ḍúl·se] *adj.* bittersweet, tart.

agrietarse [a·grje·tár·se] *v.* to crack; to chap (*said of the skin*).

agrimensura [a·gri·men·sú·ra] *f.* survey, surveying (*of land*).

agrio [á·grjo] *adj.* sour; disagreeable.

agropecuario [a·gro·pe·kwá·rjo] *adj.* farming (*crops and cattle*).

agrupación [a·gru·pa·sjón] *f.* group; bunch; grouping; gathering.

agrupar [a·gru·pár] *v.* to group, bunch up.

agrura [a·grú·ra] *f.* sourness.

agua [á·gwa] *f.* water; rain; — **abajo** downstream; — **arriba** upstream; **aguas inmundas** *f.* sewage.

aguacate [a·gwa·ká·te] *m. Am.* avocado, alligator pear; *Am.* avocado tree; *Am.* phlegmatic person.

aguacero [a·gwa·sé·ro] *m.* shower.

aguada [a·gwá·ḍa] *f.* watering place; supply of drinking water; flood in a mine; wall wash; water color.

aguadero [a·gwa·ḍé·ro] *m.* watering place.

aguado [a·gwá·ḍo] *adj.* watery; watered; *Am.* soft, unstarched; *Am.* weak, limp; *Andes* insipid,

uninteresting, dull; **sopa aguada** thin soup; *p.p. of* **aguar.**

aguaitar [a·gwaj·tár] *v. Col., Ven., Andes, Ch.* to spy; to watch; to wait for.

aguantar [a·gwan·tár] *v.* to endure, bear; to resist; **-se** to be silent, restrain oneself.

aguante [a·gwán·te] *m.* endurance, fortitude, resistance.

aguar[9] [a·gwár] *v.* to water, dilute with water; to spoil (*pleasure*); *Ríopl., Ven., C.A.* to water (*livestock*); **-se** to become diluted; to get watery; to fill up with water; **se aguó la fiesta** the party was spoiled.

aguardar [a·gwar·ḍár] *v.* to wait; to wait for.

aguardentoso [a·gwar·ḍen·tó·so] *adj.* alcoholic; hoarse, raucous.

aguardiente [a·gwar·ḍjén·te] *m.* brandy, hard liquor; — **de caña** rum.

aguarrás [a·gwa·rrás] *m.* turpentine, oil of turpentine.

aguazal [a·gwa·sál] *m.* marsh, swamp.

agudeza [a·gu·ḍé·sa] *f.* sharpness; keenness; wit; witty remark or saying.

agudo [a·gú·ḍo] *adj.* sharp; sharp-pointed; keen, witty; acute; shrill.

agüero [a·gwé·ro] *m.* augury, prediction; sign, omen; *Ríopl., Mex., Carib.* fortune-teller.

aguijar [a·gi·xár] *v.* (*picar*) to prick, goad, spur; (*animar*) to encourage, excite.

aguijón [a·gi·xón] *m.* prick; sting; spur, goad.

aguijonear [a·gi·xo·ne·ár] *v.* to goad; to prick.

águila [á·gi·la] *f.* eagle; **es un** — he is a shark.

aguileño [a·gi·lé·ño] *adj.* aquiline; eaglelike.

aguinaldo [a·gi·nál·do] *m.* Christmas or New Year's gift; bonus.

aguja [a·gú·xa] *f.* needle; crochet hook; watch hand; church spire; railroad switch.

agujerear [a·gu·xe·re·ár] *v.* to pierce, perforate; to riddle.

agujero [a·gu·xé·ro] *m.* hole; needle peddler; needle box; pincushion.

aguzar[9] [a·gu·sár] *v.* to sharpen; to goad, stimulate; — **las orejas** to prick up one's ears.

ahí [a·í] *adv.* there; **por** — over there.

ahijado [a·i·xá·ḍo] *m.* godchild.

ahijar [a·i·xár] *v.* to adopt.

ahínco [a·ín·ko] *m.* effort, eagerness, zeal.

ahogar[7] [a·o·gár] *v.* to drown; to choke, strangle; to smother; to quench, extinguish.

ahogo [a·ó·go] *m.* suffocation; breathlessness; anguish, grief.

ahondar [a·on·dár] *v.* to deepen; to dig; to penetrate, go deep into.

ahora [a·ó·ra] *adv.* now; — **mismo** right now; **por** — for the present; — **que** *Am.* as soon as; **ahorita** [a·o·rí·ta] instantly, this very minute; **ahoritica** [a·o·ri·tí·ka], **ahoritita** [a·o·ri·tí·ta] *Am.* this very second, in a jiffy.

ahorcar[6] [a·or·kár] *v.* to hang, kill by hanging.

ahorrar [a·o·rrár] *v.* to save; to spare; to avoid.

ahorro [a·ó·rro] *m.* saving, economy; **caja de -s** savings bank.

ahuecar[6] [a·we·kár] *v.* to make hollow; to hollow out; — **la voz** to speak in a hollow voice; *Am.* ¡**ahueca**! get out of here!; **-se** to become puffed up, get conceited.

ahuehuete [a·we·wé·te] *m. Am.* a Mexican cypress.

ahumado [a·u·má·ḍo] *adj.* smoked; smoky.

ahumar [a·u·már] *v.* to smoke; to fume.

ahuyentar [a·u·yen·tár] *v.* to drive away; to scare away; **-se** to go away, flee; *Ven., Carib., Mex.* to stop frequenting a place.

aindiado [ajn·djá· đo] *adj.* Indian-like.

airado [aj·ra·đo] *adj.* irate; angry.

airar [aj·rár] *v.* to annoy, irritate; **-se** to get angry.

aire [áj·re] *m.* air; wind; tune; appearance; conceit; **-cito** *m.* breeze; a little tune; a certain air or appearance.

ariear [aj·re·ár] *v.* to air, ventilate.

airoso [aj·ró·so] *adj.* windy; airy; graceful, elegant; lively, spirited.

aislador [ajz·la·đór] *m.* insulator; isolator; *adj.* insulating; isolating.

aislamiento [ajz·la·mjén·to] *m.* isolation; insulation.

aislar [ajz·lár] *v.* to isolate, place apart; to insulate.

¡aja! [a·xá] *interj.* great! fine!

ajar [a·xár] *v.* to crumple, wither.

ajedrez [a·xe·đrés] *m.* chess.

ajenjo [a·xéŋ·xo] *m.* absynthe.

ajeno [a·xé·no] *adj.* (*de otro*) another's; (*inconciente*) unaware; (*extranjero*) alien; **— a mi voluntad** beyond my control; **— de cuidados** free from cares.

ajetrearse [a·xe·tre·ár·se] *v.* to hustle and bustle; to get tired out.

ajetreo [a·xe·tré·o] *m.* bustle, hustle; hubbub; fuss; fatigue.

ají [a·xí] *m. S.A., Carib.* chili pepper, chili sauce.

ajo [a·xo] *m.* garlic; garlic clove; garlic sauce; swear word.

ajuar [a·xwár] *m.* furniture set; trousseau, bride's outfit; bride's portion or dowry.

ajustado [a·xus·tá·đo] *adj.* tight, fitting tight; agreed upon (*as a price*); **— a la ley** in accordance with the law; *p.p. of* **ajustar.**

ajustamiento [a·xus·ta·mjén·to] *m.* adjustment.

ajustar [a·xus·tár] *v.* to adjust; to fit tight; to regulate; to tighten; to settle (*accounts*); to hire (*a person*); *Col.* to stint, scrimp, save; *C.A.* — **una bofetada** to give a good slap; *C.A., Mex.* **hoy ajusta quince años** he is just fifteen years old today; **-se** to come to an agreement.

ajuste [a·xús·te] *m.* adjustment, fit; agreement; settlement (*of accounts*).

ajusticiar [a·xus·ti·sjár] *v.* to execute, put to death.

al [al] = **a** + **el** to the.

ala [á·la] *f.* wing; hat brim.

alabanza [a·la·bán·sa] *f.* praise.

alabar [a·la·bár] *v.* to praise.

alabastro [a·la·bás·tro] *m.* alabaster.

alacena [a·la·sé·na] *f.* cupboard; closet: *Am.* booth, stall, market stand.

alacrán [a·la·krán] *m.* scorpion.

alado [a·la·đo] *adj.* winged.

alambicado [a·lam·bi·ka·đo] *p.p. & adj.* distilled; over-refined, over-subtle (*applied to style*).

alambique [a·lam·bí·ke] *m.* still.

alambrada [a·lam·brá·đa] *f.* wire, entanglement.

alambrado [a·lam·brá·đo] *m.* wire fence; wire screening; wiring.

alambre [a·lám·bre] *m.* wire.

alameda [a·la·mé·đa] *f.* poplar grove; park.

álamo [á·la·mo] *m.* poplar.

alancear [a·lan·se·ár] *v.* to lance, spear.

alano [a·lá·no] *m.* mastiff.

alarde [a·lár·đe] *m.* boast, bluff, brag.

alardear [a·lar·đe·ár] *v.* to boast, brag.

alargar[7] [a·lar·gár] *v.* to lengthen; to prolong; to stretch out, extend.

alarido [a·la·rí·đo] *m.* shout, scream, howl.

alarma [a·lár·ma] *f.* alarm.

alarmar [a·lar·már] *v.* to alarm.

alazán [a·la·sán] *adj.* chestnut-colored; sorrel.

alba [ál·ba] *f.* dawn; alb (*white robe worn by priest*).

albacea [al·ba·sé·a] *m.* executor.

albañal [al·ba·ñál] *m.* sewer.

albañil [al·ba·ñíl] *m.* mason, brickmason; **albañilería** [al·ba·ñi·le·rí·a] *f.* masonry.

albaricoque [al·ba·ri·kó·ke] *m.* apricot; **albaricoquero** [al·ba·ri·ko·ke·ro] *m.* apricot tree.

abayalde [al·ba·yál·de] *m.* white lead.

albazo [al·bá·so] *m. Mex.* early morning serenade; *Mex.* bad surprise, surprise attack at dawn.

albear [al·be·ár] *v.* to show white (*in the distance*); *Am.* to rise at dawn.

albedrío [al·be·đrí·o] *m.* free will.

albéitar [al·béj·tar] *m.* veterinary.

alberca [al·bér·ka] *f.* water reservoir, tank; *Mex.* swimming pool.

albergar[7] [al·ber·gár] *v.* to house, shelter, lodge; **-se** to take shelter; to lodge.

albino [al·bí·no] *m. & f.* albino.

albo [ál·bo] *adj.* white; *Am.* white-footed (*horse*).

albóndiga [al·bón·di·ga] *f.* meat ball; fish ball.

albor [al·bór] *f.* dawn; whiteness.

alborada [al·bo·rá·đa] *f.* dawn; reveille (*morning bugle call*).

alborear [al·bo·re·ár] *v.* to dawn.

alborotador [al·bo·ro·ta·đór] *m.* agitator; troublemaker.

alborotar [al·bo·ro·tár] *v.* to disturb, upset; *Am.* to excite, arouse enthusiasm; **-se** to get upset; to mutiny, to riot; *Am.* to get excited; *Am.* to rear, balk (*said of a horse*).

alboroto [al·bo·ró·to] *m.* uproar, disturbance; riot; *Am.* excitement, enthusiasm; *Col., C.A.* popcorn, candied popcorn ball.

alborozado [al·bo·ro·sá·đo] *adj.* elated, excited.

alborozar[9] [al·bo·ro·sár] *v.* to gladden; **-se** to rejoice.

alborozo [al·bo·ró·so] *m.* joy, delight.

albricias [al·brí·sjas] *f. pl.* good news; reward (*for good news*).

alcachofa [al·ka·čó·fa] *f.* artichoke; *Ch.* sock, blow.

alachuete [al·ka·wé·te] *m.* procurer, pander; go-between; **alcahueta** *f.* bawd, procuress, go-between.

alcaide [al·káj·de] *m.* warden (*of a fortress, prison, etc.*).

alcalde [al·kál·de] *m.* mayor; justice of the peace; **— mayor** mayor.

alcance [al·kán·se] *m.* (*extensión*) reach, scope; (*capacidad*) talent, capacity; (*noticas*) last minute news, newspaper extra; **cortos -s** meagre intellect; **dar — a** to catch up with

alcancía [al·kan·sí·a] *f.* money box (*with slit for coin*); savings bank.

alcanfor [al·kan·fór] *m.* camphor.

alcantarilla [al·kan·ta·rí·ya] *f.* conduit; drain.

alcantarillado [al·kan·ta·ri·yá·đo] *m.* sewage system.

alcanzado [al·kan·sá·đo] *adj.* needy; broke, short of funds.

alcanzar[9] [al·kan·sár] *v.* to reach; to overtake; to obtain; to befall; to be enough; *Am.* to hand, pass, put within reach.

alcayata [al·ka·yá·ta] *f.* wall hook; meat hook.

alcázar [al·ká·sar] *m.* castle, fortress.

alcoba [al·kó·ḃa] *f.* alcove, bedroom.
alcohol [al·ko·ól] *m.* alcohol; **alcoholico**
  [al·ko·ó·li·ko] *adj.* alcoholic.
alcor [al·kór] *m.* hill.
alcornoque [al·kor·nó·ke] *m.* cork tree; cork wood;
  blockhead, dunce.
alcuza [al·kú·sa] *f.* oil can; cruet, oil bottle.
aldaba [al·dá·ḃa] *f.* knocker (*of a door*); crossbar,
  bolt, latch; handle (*of a door, chest, etc.*);
  tener buenas -s to have "pull", influential
  connections.
aldabón [al·da·ḃón] *m.* large iron knocker; large
  handle; **aldabonazo** [al·da·ḃo·ná·so] *m.* knock,
  knocking.
aldea [al·dé·a] *f.* village; **aldehuela** [al·de·wé·la]
  f. little village, hamlet.
aldeano [al·de·á·no] *adj.* rustic, countrified; *m.*
  villager; peasant.
aleación [a·le·a·sjón] *f.* alloy; alloying.
alear [a·le·ár] *v.* to alloy, mix (*metals*); to flutter;
  to flap (*wings, arms, etc.*).
aleccionar [a·lek·sjo·nár] *v.* to coach; to teach,
  instruct; to train; to drill.
aledaños [a·le·ḋá·ños] *m. pl.* borders, frontiers.
alegar[7] [a·le·ḡár] *v.* to allege, assert; *Am.* to argue,
  dispute.
alegato [a·le·ḡá·to] *m.* allegation; assertion.
alegrar [a·le·ḡrár] *v.* to cheer up, gladden; to
  brighten; **-se** to be glad, rejoice; to get tipsy.
alegre [a·lé·ḡre] *adj.* merry, gay, joyful, cheerful,
  bright; tipsy.
alegría [a·le·ḡrí·a] *f.* joy mirth, gaiety,
  merriment.
alejamiento [a·le·xa·mjén·to] *m.* withdrawal;
  retirement, aloofness.
alejar [a·le·xár] *v.* to remove, move away from;
  -se to move away; to withdraw, be aloof.
alelado [a·le·lá·ḋo] *adj.* stupefied, open-mouthed;
  silly.
alemán [a·le·mán] *adj. & m.* German.
alentar[1] [a·len·tár] *v. irr.* to breathe; to encourage,
  cheer, cheer up; **-se** to take heart; *Am.* to
  recover (*from illness*).
alergia [a·lér·xja] *f.* allergy.
alero [a·lé·ro] *m.* eaves; projecting edge.
alerón [a·le·rón] *m.* aileron; flap.
alerto [a·lér·to] *adj.* alert, watchful; ¡**alerta!**
  attention! look out!; **estar alerta** to be on the
  alert.
aleta [a·lé·ta] *f.* small wing; flap; fin (*of a fish*).
aletargado [a·le·tar·ḡá·ḋo] *adj.* drowsy, sluggish.
aletargarse[7] [a·le·tar·ḡár·se] *v.* to fall into a state
  of lethargy; to become drowsy.
aletazo [a·le·tá·so] *m.* flap, blow with a wing.
aletear [a·le·te·ár] *v.* to flap, flutter.
aleteo [a·le·té·o] *m.* flapping, flutter (*of wings*).
aleve [a·lé·ḃe] *adj.* treacherous.
alevosía [a·le·ḃo·sí·a] *f.* treachery.
alevoso [a·le·ḃó·so] *adj.* treacherous.
alfabeto [al·fa·ḃé·to] *m.* alphabet.
alfalfa [al·fál·fa] *f.* alfalfa; **alfalfar** [al·fa·fár] *m.*
  alfalfa field.
alfarería [al·fa·re·rí·a] *f.* pottery; **alfarero**
  [al·fa·ré·ro] *m.* potter.
alfeñicar[6] [al·fe·ñi·kár] *v.* to frost with sugar (*a
  cake, cookie, etc.*); **-se** to get frail, delicate; to act
  affectedly.
alfeñique [al·fe·ñí·ke] *m.* sugar paste; delicate
  person.
alférez [al·fé·res] *m.* ensign; second lieutenant.
alfil [al·fíl] *m.* bishop (*in chess*).

alfiler [al·fi·lér] *m.* pin; brooch; **-es** pin money;
  ponerse de veinticinco -es to doll up, dress up.
alfombra [al·fóm·bra] *f.* carpet; **alfombrilla**
  [al·fom·brí·ya] *f.* (*para el suelo*) carpet, rug;
  (*enfermedad*) measles; *Mex.* plant of the vervain
  family; *Carib.* black smallpox; *Carib.* skin
  eruption.
alforja [al·fór·xa] *f.* saddlebag; knapsack; food
  provisions for a trip; *Am.* **pasarse a la otra —**
  to take undue liberties.
alforza [al·fór·sa] *f.* tuck, fold, pleat; scar.
alga [ál·ḡa] *f.* seaweed; alga.
algarabía [al·ḡa·ra·ḃí·a] *f.* jargon; chatter; uproar.
algarrobo [al·ḡa·rró·ḃo] *m.* locust tree; carob tree.
algazara [al·ḡa·sá·ra] *f.* clamor; shouting; uproar.
álgebra [ál·xe·ḃra] *f.* algebra.
algo [ál·ḡo] *pron.* something; *adv.* somewhat.
algodón [al·ḡo·ḋón] *m.* cotton; **algodonal**
  [al·ḡo·ḋo·nál] *m.* cotton plantation.
alguacil [al·ḡwa·síl] *m.* policeman, constable.
alguien [ál·ḡjen] *pron.* somebody, someone.
algún(o) [al·ḡún(o)] *adj.* some; any; *pron.* someone.
alhaja [a·lá·xa] *f.* jewel.
alharaca [a·la·rá·ka] *f.* rumpus, clamor, racket.
aliado [a·ljá·ḋo] *adj.* allied; *m.* ally.
alianza [a·lján·sa] *f.* alliance, union; *Andes*
  wedding ring; *Am.* mixture of liquors.
aliar[17] [a·ljár] *v.* to ally; to unite; **-se** to form
  an alliance; to unite.
alicaído [a·li·ka·í·ḋo] *adj.* crestfallen, downcast,
  discouraged; drooping.
alicates [a·li·ká·tes] *m. pl.* pliers, small pincers.
aliciente [a·li·sjén·te] *m.* inducement, incentive,
  attraction.
alienista [a·lje·nís·ta] *m.* alienist (*doctor who treats
  mental diseases*).
aliento [a·ljén·to] *m.* (*de los pulmones*) breath;
  (*ánimo*) encouragement.
aligerar [a·li·xe·rár] *v.* to lighten; to hasten.
alimentación [a·li·men·ta·sjón] *f.* nourishment,
  food, nutrition; feeding.
alimentar [a·li·men·tár] *v.* to feed, nourish.
alimenticio [a·li·men·tí·sjo] *adj.* nutritious,
  nourishing.
alimento [a·li·mén·to] *m.* food.
alinear [a·li·ne·ár] *v.* to line up, put into line; to
  range; **-se** to fall in line; form into a line.
aliño [a·lí·ño] *m.* ornament, decoration; neatness;
  condiment, dressing, seasoning.
alisar [a·li·sár] *v.* to smooth; to polish; to plane.
alistamiento [a·lis·ta·mjén·to] *m.* enlistment;
  enrollment.
alistar [a·lis·tár] *v.* to enlist; to enroll; to make
  ready, **-se** to enlist; to get ready; *Am.* to dress
  up.
aliviar [a·li·ḃjár] *v.* to lighten; to alleviate, relieve,
  remedy, soothe; **-se** to get better, recover.
alivio [a·li·ḃjo] *m.* relief, remedy; aid, help;
  improvement.
aljibe [al·xi·ḃe] *m.* cistern, reservoir, tank; water
  tanker; *Ríopl.* well, artesian well, spring.
alma [ál·ma] *f.* soul, spirit; inhabitant.
almacén [al·ma·sén] *m.* warehouse; department
  store; store.
almacenaje [al·ma·se·ná·xe] *m.* storage.
almacenar [al·ma·se·nár] *v.* to store, store up; to
  put in storage.
almacenista [al·ma·se·nís·ta] *m. & f.* department
  store owner; warehouse owner or manager;
  wholesale merchant.
almanaque [al·ma·ná·ke] *m.* almanac, calendar.

AH

almeja [al·mé·xa] *f.* clam.
almendra [al·mén·dra] *f.* almond; **almendrado** [al·men·drá·ďo] *m.* almond paste; **almendro** [la·mén·dro] *m.* almond tree.
almíbar [al·mí·ƀar] *m.* syrup.
almidón [a ·mi·ďón] *m.* starch; *Col., Ven.* paste (*for gluing*).
almidonar [al·mi·ďo·nár] *v.* to starch.
alminar [al·mi·nár] *m.* turret.
almirante [al·mi·rán·te] *m.* admiral.
almirez [al·mi·rés] *m.* metal mortar.
almohada [al·mo·á·ďa] *f.* pillow; **almohadón** *m.* large cushion or pillow.
almohaza [al·mo·á·sa] *f.* currycomb (*for grooming horses*).
almoneda [al·mo·ne·ďa] *f.* auction.
almorzar[2, 9] [al·mor·sár] *v. irr.* to lunch, eat lunch.
almuerzo [al·mwér·so] *m.* lunch.
alojamientó [a·lo·xa·mjén·to] *m.* lodging.
alojar [a·lo·xár] *v.* to lodge; to house; to quarter (*troops*); **-se** to lodge, room.
alondra [a·lón·dra] *f.* lark.
alpaca [al·pá·ka] *f.* alpaca (*sheeplike animal of South America*); alpaca wool; alpaca cloth.
alpargata [al·par·gá·ta] *f.* sandal (*usually of canvas and with hemp sole*).
alpinismo [al·pi·níz·mo] *m.* mountain climbing.
alpinista [al·pi·nís·ta] *m. & f.* mountain climber.
alquería [al·ke·rí·a] *f.* farmhouse.
alquilar [al·ki·lár] *v.* to rent; to hire; **-se** to hire out.
alquiler [al·ki·lér] *m.* rent, rental; **de** — for rent, for hire.
alquitrán [al·ki·trán] *m.* tar.
alrededor [al·rre·ďe·ďór] *adv.* about, around; — **de** *prep.* around; **-es** *m. pl.* environs, outskirts.
altanería [al·ta·ne·rí·a] *f.* haughtiness.
altanero [al·ta·né·ro] *adj.* haughty, proud.
altar [al·tár] *m.* altar; — **mayor** high altar.
altavoz [al·ta·ƀós] *m.* loud-speaker.
alteración [al·te·ra·sjón] *f.* alteration, change; disturbance.
alterar [al·te·rár] *v.* to alter, change; to disturb.
altercar[6] [al·ter·kár] *v.* to argue, dispute; to quarrel.
alternador [al·ter·na·ďor] *m.* alternator.
alternar [al·ter·nár] *v.* to alternate; to take turns; — **con** to rub elbows with, be friendly with.
alternativa [al·ter·na·tí·ƀa] *f.* alternative, choice, option.
alternativo [al·ter·na·tí·ƀo] *adj.* alternating, alternative.
alterno [al·tér·no] *adj.* alternate.
alteza [al·té·sa] *f.* highness (*title*); lofty height.
altibajo [al·ti·bá·xo] *m.* downward thrust (*in fencing*); **-s** ups and downs; uneven ground.
altiplanicie [al·ti·pla·ní·sje] *f.* upland; high plateau.
altiplano [al·ti·plá·no] *m. Am.* high plateau.
altisonante [al·ti·so·nán·te] *adj.* high-sounding.
altitud [al·ti·túď] *f.* altitude.
altivez [al·ti·ƀés] *f.* haughtiness, arrogance.
altivo [al·tí·ƀo] *adj.* haughty, proud, arrogant.
alto [ál·to] *adj.* (*tamaño*) high; *m.* height; upper story (*of a building*); *Am.* heap, pile; **-s** *Am.* upper floors; *v.* hacer to halt, stop; **pasar por** — to omit, overlook; **¡—!** halt!
altoparlante [al·to·par·lán·te] *m.* loud-speaker.
altura [al·tú·ra] *f.* height, altitude.
alud [a·lúď] *m.* avalanche.
aludir [a·lu·ďír] *v.* to allude, refer indirectly.

alumbrado [a·lum·brá·ďo] *m.* lighting; *adj.* lit, lighted; tipsy.
alumbramiento [a·lum·bra·mjén·to] *m.* childbirth; lighting.
alumbrar [a·lum·brár] *v.* to light, give light; to enlighten; to give birth; **-se** to get tipsy.
aluminio [a·lu·mí·njo] *m.* aluminum.
alumnado [a·lum·ná·ďo] *m.* student body.
alumno [a·lúm·no] *m.* student.
alusión [a·lu·sjón] *f.* allusion.
alveolar [al·ƀe·o·lár] *adj.* alveolar.
alza [ál·sa] *f.* rise; lift (*for shoes*).
alzada [al·sá·ďa] *f.* height (*of a horse*).
alzamiento [al·sa·mjén·to] *m.* raising, lifting; uprising, insurrection.
alzar[9] [al·sár] *v.* to lift, raise; to cut (*cards*); **-se** to rebel, rise up in arms; *Col., Ven., C.A., Mex., Andes* to puff up with pride; **-se con algo** to run off with something, steal something.
allá [a·yá] *adv.* there, over there; **más** — farther.
allanar [a·ya·nár] *v.* to level, even off; to invade, break into (*a house*); to raid; — **una dificultad** to smooth out a difficulty.
allegado [a·ye·gá·ďo] *adj.* near; related; allied; *m.* relative; partisan, follower.
allegar[7] [a·ye·gár] *v.* to accumulate, heap up, gather.
allende [a·yén·de] *adv.* on the other side; beyond; — **el mar** across the sea, overseas.
allí [a·yi] *adv.* there; **por** — through that place, around there.
ama [á·ma] *f.* mistress, owner; — **de leche** wet nurse; — **de llaves** housekeeper.
amabilidad [a·ma·ƀi·li·ďáď] *f.* kindness, courtesy.
amable [a·má·ƀle] *adj.* kind, amiable.
amador [a·ma·ďór] *m.* lover.
amaestrar [a·ma·es·trár] *v.* to teach, coach, train.
amagar[7] [a·ma·gár] *v.* to threaten; to feint, make a threatening motion; to strike at.
amago [a·má·go] *m.* threat; indication.
amalgamar [a·mal·ga·már] *v.* to amalgamate, combine, mix, blend.
amamantar [a·ma·man·tár] *v.* to nurse, suckle.
amanecer[13] [a·ma·ne·sér] *v. irr.* to dawn; — **malo** to wake up ill; *m.* dawn, sunrise.
amanecida [a·ma·ne·sí·ďa] *f.* dawn, sunrise.
amansar [a·man·sár] *v.* to tame; to subdue; to pacify.
amante [a·mán·te] *m.* lover; — **de** fond of.
amañarse [a·ma·ñár·se] *v. Ec., Col., Ven.* to be accustomed; to acclimate oneself.
amapola [a·ma·pó·la] *f.* poppy.
amar [a·már] *v.* to love.
amargar[7] [a·mar·gár] *v.* to embitter, make bitter.
amargo [a·már·go] *adj.* bitter; *m.* bitters; *Am.* mate (*Paraguayan tea*) without sugar.
amargor [a·mar·gór] *m.* bitterness.
amargura [a·mar·gú·ra] *f.* bitterness; grief.
amarillear [a·ma·ri·ye·ár] *v.* to show or have a yellowish tinge; to turn yellow.
amarillento [a·ma·ri·yén·to] *adj.* yellowish.
amarillo [a·ma·rí·yo] *adj.* yellow.
amarra [a·má·rra] *f.* cable; rope; strap.
amarrar [a·ma·rrár] *v.* to tie, fasten, rope; to moor (*a ship*); *Am.* **amarrárselas** [a·ma·rrár·se·las] to get "tight," drunk.
amasar [a·ma·sár] *v.* to knead, mix; to mash; *Am.* to amass, accumulate (*a fortune*).
amatista [a·ma·tís·ta] *f.* amethyst.

ambages [am·bá·xes] *m. pl.* circumlocutions; **hablar sin** — to go straight to the point, speak plainly, not to beat about the bush.

ámbar [ám·bar] *m.* amber; **ambarino** [am·ba·rí·no] *adj.* amber; like amber.

ambición [am·bi·sjón] *f.* ambition; aspiration.

ambicionar [am·bi·sjo·nár] *v.* to seek, aspire after; to covet.

ambicioso [am·bi·sjó·so] *adj.* ambitious, eager; greedy, grasping.

ambiente [am·bjén·te] *m.* atmosphere, environment.

ambigüedad [am·bi·gwe·ɖáɖ] *f.* ambiguity.

ambiguo [am·bí·gwo] *adj.* ambiguous; uncertain, doubtful.

ámbito [ám·bi·to] *m.* precinct, enclosure.

ambos [ám·bos] *adj.* & *pron.* both.

ambulancia [am·bu·lán·sja] *f.* ambulance; field hospital.

ambulante [am·bu·lán·te] *adj.* walking; itinerant; moving; wandering.

amedrentar [a·me·ɖren·tár] *v.* to scare, frighten.

amenaza [a·me·ná·sa] *f.* menace, threat.

amenazador [a·me·na·sa·ɖór], **amenazante** [a·me·na·sán·te] *adj.* threatening.

amenazar⁹ [a·me·na·sár] *v.* to menace, threaten.

amenguar⁸ [a·meŋ·gwár] *v.* to lessen, diminish; to defame, dishonor.

amenidad [a·me·ni·ɖáɖ] *f.* pleasantness.

amenizar⁹ [a·me·ni·sár] *v.* to make pleasant, cheer, brighten.

ameno [a·mé·no] *adj.* pleasant, agreeable.

americana [a·me·ri·ká·na] *f.* suit coat.

americanismo [a·me·ri·ka·níz·mo] *m.* Americanism; characteristic of any part of America.

americano [a·me·ri·ká·no] *adj.* & *m.* American.

ametrallador [a·me·tra·ya·ɖór] *m.* gunner; **ametralladora** [a·me·tra·ya·ɖó·ra] *f.* machine gun.

amigable [a·mi·gá·ble] *adj.* friendly; affable, pleasant.

amígdala [a·míg·ɖa·la] *f.* tonsil; **amigdalitis** [a·mig·ɖa·li·tis] *f.* tonsilitis.

amigo [a·mí·go] *m.* friend; — **de** fond of.

aminorar [a·mi·no·rár] *v.* to lessen.

amistad [a·mis·táɖ] *f.* friendship; friendliness.

amistoso [a·mis·tó·so] *adj.* friendly.

amistía [am·nis·tí·a] *f.* amnesty.

amo [á·mo] *m.* master, owner, boss.

amodorrado [a·mo·ɖo·rrá·ɖo] *adj.* drowsy.

amodorrar [a·mo·ɖo·rrár] *v.* to make drowsy; **-se** to become drowsy.

amolador [a·mo·la·ɖór] *m.* grinder, sharpener; *adj.* grinding, sharpening.

amolar [a·mo·lár] *v. irr.* to grind, hone, sharpen; to annoy; *Col., Mex., C.A.* to ruin, harm; **-se** *Mex., C.A., Col.* to go to rack and ruin.

amoldar [a·mol·dár] *v.* to mold; to shape; to adjust; to adapt.

amonestación [a·mo·nes·ta·sjón] *f.* admonition, advice, warning; **-es** marriage bans (*or* banns).

amonestar [a·mo·nes·tár] *v.* to admonish, advise, warn.

amoníaco [a·mo·ní·a·ko] *m.* ammonia.

amontonamiento [a·mon·to·na·mjén·to] *m.* accumulation, pile, heap.

amontonar [a·mon·to·nár] *v.* to heap up, pile up, crowd up.

amor [a·mór] *m.* love; — **propio** self-esteem.

amoratado [a·mor·ta·ɖo] *adj.* livid, bluish, purplish.

amordazar⁹ [a·mor·ɖa·sár] *v.* to gag; to muzzle.

amorío [a·mo·rí·o] *m.* love affair; love-making.

amoroso [a·mo·ró·so] *adj.* loving, tender, affectionate.

amortajar [a·mor·ta·xár] *v.* to shroud.

amortiguador [a·mor·ti·gwa·ɖór] *m.* shock absorber; silencer, muffler.

amortiguar⁸ [a·mor·ti·gwár] *v.* to muffle; to deafen (*a sound*); to deaden (*a blow or sound*); to soften, tone down (*a color or sound*).

amortizar⁹ [a·mor·ti·sár] *v.* to pay on account; to liquidate, pay (*a debt*); to provide a sinking fund.

amoscarse⁶ [a·mos·kár·se] *v.* to get peeved, annoyed; *Am.* to blush, be inhibited or embarrassed.

amostazar⁹ [a·mos·ta·sár] *v.* to anger, irritate; **-se** to get angry or irritated.

amotinar [a·mo·ti·nár] *v.* to incite to rebellion; **-se** to mutiny; to riot.

amparar [am·pa·rár] *v.* to protect; to defend; *Am.* to grant mining rights; **-se** to seek protection or refuge; to protect oneself.

amparo [am·pá·ro] *m.* protection; habeas corpus (*protection against imprisonment*); *Am.* mining rights.

ampliación [am·plja·sjón] *f.* enlargement, widening.

ampliar¹⁷ [am·pljár] *v.* to enlarge, widen.

amplificador [am·pli·fi·ka·ɖór] *m.* amplifier.

amplificar⁶ [am·pli·fi·kár] *v.* to amplify, expand, extend, enlarge; to magnify.

amplio [ám·pljo] *adj.* ample; wide, large, roomy.

amplitud [am·pli·túɖ] *f.* breadth, extent, width.

ampolla [am·pó·ya] *f.* (*condición*) blister, water bubble; (*vasija*) narrow-necked bottle or vase, cruet.

ampollar [am·po·yár] *v.* to blister; **-se** to blister.

ampuloso [am·pu·ló·so] *adj.* inflated, wordy, bombastic, pompous.

amputar [am·pu·tár] *v.* to amputate, cut off.

amueblar [a·mwe·blár] *v.* to furnish (*with furniture*).

ánade [á·na·ɖe] *m.* & *f.* duck; **anadeja** [a·na·ɖé·xa] *f.* duckling.

anadear [a·na·ɖe·ár] *v.* to waddle.

anales [a·ná·les] *m. pl.* annals, historical records.

analfabeto [a·na·fa·bé·to] *adj.* & *m.* illiterate; **analfabetismo** [a·na·fa·be·tiz·mo] *m.* illiteracy.

analgésico [a·nal·xé·si·ko] *adj.* analgesic.

analisis [a·ná·li·sis] *m.* analysis.

analítico [a·na·lí·ti·ko] *adj.* analytical.

analizar⁹ [a·na·li·sár] *v.* to analyze, examine.

analogía [a·na·lo·xí·a] *f.* analogy, similarity.

análogo [a·ná·lo·go] *adj.* analogous, similar, comparable.

ananá [a·na·ná], **ananás** [a·na·nás] *f.* pineapple. *See* **pina.**

anaquel [a·na·kél] *m.* shelf; bookshelf; **anaquelería** [a·na·ke·le·rí·a] *f.* shelves, bookshelves, library stacks.

anaranjado [a·na·raŋ·xá·ɖo] *adj.* orange-colored; *m.* orange color.

anarquía [a·nar·kí·a] *f.* anarchy.

anatomía [a·na·to·mí·a] *f.* anatomy.

anatómico [a·na·tó·mi·ko] *adj.* anatomical.

anca [áŋ·ka] *f.* haunch, hind quarter, rump; *Andes* popcorn.

ancianidad [an·sja·ni·ɖáɖ] *f.* old age.

anciano [an·sjá·no] *adj.* old, aged; *m.* old man.

ancla [áŋ·kla] *f.* anchor.

anclar [aŋ·klár] *v.* to anchor.

ancho [án·čo] *adj.* wide, broad; loose; roomy; *Col.,*
Ven. self-satisfied, conceited; **a sus anchas** at
one's ease; comfortable; leisurely; *m.* width.
anchoa [an·čó·á], anchova [an·čó·ḃa] *f.* anchovy.
anchura [an·čú·ra] *f.* width, breadth; comfort, ease.
anchuroso [an·ču·ró·so] *adj.* vast, extensive;
spacious.
andada [an·dá·ḍa] *f. Mex., Ven.* walk, stroll; -s
track, footprints; **volver a las -s** to fall back
into one's old ways or habits.
andadura [an·da·ḍú·ra] *f.* gait, pace.
andaluz [an·da·lús] *adj.* Andalusian, of or
pertaining to Andalusia, Spain; *m.* Andalusian,
native or Andalusia.
andamiada [an·da·mjá·ḍa] *f.* andamiaje
[an·da·mjá·xe] *m.* scaffolding; framework.
andamio [an·dá·mjo] *m.* scaffold, scaffolding.
andanada [an·da·ná·ḍa] *f. (localidad)* grandstand;
(descarga) broadside; **soltar una** — to discharge
a broadside; to reprimand.
andante [an·dán·te] *adj.* walking; errant,
wandering; moderately slow *(music)*; **caballero**
— knight-errant.
andanzas [an·dán·sas] *f. pl.* rambles, wanderings.
andar[21] [an·dár] *v. irr.* to walk; to go, go about;
to run *(as a watch or machinery)*; — **con**
cuidado to be careful; **anda en quince años** he is
about fifteen; **a todo** — at full (walking) speed;
a más — walking briskly; **ianda!** move on!;
¿**qué andas haciendo?** what are you doing?; *Am.*
— andando to be walking around; *Am.*
iándale! hurry!
andariego [an·da·rjé·ḡo] *adj.* fond of walking;
roving; *m.* walker.
andas [án·das] *f. pl.* portable platform; litter.
andén [an·dén] *m.* railway station platform; *C.A.,*
Col., Ven., sidewalk.
andino [an·dí·no] *adj.* Andean, of or from the
Andes.
andrajo [an·drá·xo] *m.* rag.
andrajoso [an·dra·xó·so] *adj.* ragged, in rags.
anécdota [a·nék·ḍo·ta] *f.* anecdote, story.
anegar[7] [a·ne·ḡár] *v.* to drown; to flood.
anejo [a·né·xo] *adj.* annexed, attached.
anestesia [a·nes·té·sja] *f.* anesthesia.
anestésico [a·nes·té·si·ko] *m. & adj.* anesthetic.
anexar [a·nek·sár] *v.* to annex.
anexo [a·nék·so] *m.* annex; *adj.* annexed, joined.
anfibio [an·fi·ḃjo] *adj.* amphibian.
anfiteatro [an·fi·te·á·tro] *m.* amphitheater.
anfitrión [an·fi·trjón] *m.* generous host.
ángel [áŋ·xel] *m.* angel.
angélico [aŋ·xé·li·ko] *adj.* angelic.
angina [aŋ·xí·na] *f.* angina, inflammation of the
throat; *Mex., Ven.* tonsil; — **del pecho** angina
pectoris.
anglosajón [aŋ·glo·sa·xón] *adj. & m.* Anglo-Saxon.
angostar [aŋ·gos·tár] *v.* to narrow; -se to narrow,
become narrow; to contract.
angosto [aŋ·gós·to] *adj.* narrow.
angostura [aŋ·gos·tú·ra] *f.* narrowness; narrows
(narrow part of a river, valley, strait, etc.).
anguila [aŋ·gí·la] *f.* eel.
angular [aŋ·gu·lár] *adj.* angular; **piedra** —
cornerstone.
ángulo [áŋ·gu·lo] *m.* angle, corner.
anguloso [aŋ·gu·ló·so] *adj.* angular, sharp-
cornered.
angustia [aŋ·gús·tia] *f.* anguish, sorrow, grief,
worry.
angustiar [aŋ·gus·tjár] *v.* to distress, grieve, worry.

angustioso [aŋ·gus·tjó·so] *adj.* anguished, worried,
grievous; distressing.
anhelante [a·ne·lán·te] *adj.* anxious, desirous,
longing; panting.
anhelar [a·ne·lár] *v.* to long for; to breathe hard;
to pant.
anhelo [a·né·lo] *m.* longing.
anheloso [a·ne·ló·so] *adj.* anxious; eager.
anidar [a·ni·ḍár] *v.* to nest; to nestle; to dwell; to
shelter.
anillo [a·ní·yo] *m.* ring.
ánima [á·ni·ma] *f.* soul, spirit.
animación [a·ni·ma·sjón] *f.* animation, liveliness,
life.
animal [a·ni·mál] *m.* animal; *adj.* animal; stupid;
beastly; **animalejo** *m.* little animal; **animalucho**
m. insignificant animal; hideous little beast.
animar [a·ni·már] *v.* to animate, give life to; to
inspire, encourage.
ánimo [á·ni·mo] *f.* spirit, mind; courage, valor;
intention.
animosidad [a·ni·mo·si·ḍáḍ] *f.* animosity, ill will;
courage, energy.
animoso [a·ni·mó·so] *adj.* spirited; courageous.
aniñado [a·ni·ñá·ḍo] *adj.* boyish; childish; **aniñada**
girlish.
aniquilar [a·ni·ki·lár] *v.* to annihilate, wipe out,
destroy completely.
aniversario [a·ni·ḃer·sá·rjo] *m.* anniversary.
anoche [a·nó·če] *adv.* last night.
anochecer[13] [a·no·če·sér] *v. irr.* to grow dark; to
be or arrive at nightfall; *m.* nightfall.
anochecida [a·no·če·sí·ḍa] *f.* nightfall.
anonadar [a·no·na·ḍár] *v.* to annihilate; to
humiliate.
anónimo [a·nó·ni·mo] *adj.* anonymous; nameless;
m. anonymous letter or note.
anormal [a·nor·mál] *adj.* abnormal.
anotación [a·no·ta·sjón] *f.* annotation; note.
anotar [a·no·tár] *v.* to annotate, provide with
notes; to write down.
anquilosado [aŋ·ki·lo·sa·ḍo] *adj.* stiff-jointed;
gnarled.
anquilosarse [aŋ·ki·lo·sár·se] *v.* to become stiff in
the joints; to become metally stagnant.
ansia [án·sja] *f.* anxiety, anguish; longing,
eagerness; -s anguish; *Col., Ven., P.R.* nausea.
ansiar[17] [an·sjár] *v.* to long for, desire eagerly.
ansiedad [an·sje·ḍáḍ] *f.* anxiety; worry.
ansioso [an·sjó·so] *adj.* anxious, troubled; eager.
antagonismo [an·ta·go·níz·mo] *m.* antagonism.
antagonista [an·ta·go·nís·ta] *m. & f.* antagonist,
adversary, opponent.
antaño [an·tá·ño] *adv.* yesteryear, formerly; **días de**
— days of old.
ante [án·te] *prep.* before, in the presence of; —
todo above all; *m.* elk; buckskin.
anteanoche [an·te·a·nó·če] *adv.* night before last.
anteayer [an·te·a·yér] *adv.* day before yesterday.
antebrazo [an·te·ḃrá·so] *m.* forearm.
antecámara [an·te·ká·ma·ra] *f.* antechamber,
waiting room.
antecedente [an·te·se·ḍén·te] *m.* antecedent; *adj.*
antecedent, preceding.
antecesor [an·te·se·sór] *m.* ancestor; predecessor.
antedicho [an·te·ḍí·čo] *adj.* aforesaid.
antelación [an·te·la·sjón] *f.* precedence, priority *(in
time)*.
antemano [an·te·má·no] *adv.* de — beforehand.
antena [an·té·na] *f.* antenna *(of a radio or wireless)*;
lateen yard *(of a ship)*; -s antennae, feelers;

— emisora *f.* broadcasting antenna; **— receptora** *f.* receiving antenna; **— parabólica** *f.* parabolic (*TV*) antenna.

antenoche [an·te·nó·če] = **anteanoche**.

anteojera [an·te·o·xé·ra] *f.* blinder.

anteojo [an·te·ó·xo] *m.* spyglass; small telescope; eyeglass; **-s** spectacles; **-s de larga vista** field glasses.

antepasado [an·te·pa·sá·do] *adj.* passed; **año** — year before last; *m.* ancestor.

antepecho [an·te·pé·čo] *m.* sill, railing.

anteponer[40] [an·te·po·nér] *v. irr.* to place before; to prefer.

antepuesto [an·te·pwés·to] *p.p.* of **anteponer**.

anterior [an·te·rjór] *adj.* front, toward the front; earlier, previous; **el día** — the day before.

antes [án·tes] *adv.* before, formerly; **— de** *prep.* before; **— (de) que** *conj.* before.

antesala [an·te·sá·la] *f.* anteroom, waiting room.

antiaéreo [an·tja·é·re·o] *adj.* antiaircraft.

antibiótico [an·ti·bjó·ti·ko] *adj. & m.* antibiotic.

anticipación [an·ti·si·pa·sjón] *f.* anticipation, advance consideration; **con** — in advance.

anticipado [an·ti·si·pa·do] *adj.* early, ahead of time; advanced (*payment*); **por** — in advance; *p.p.* of **anticipar** anticipated.

anticipar [an·ti·si·pár] *v.* to anticipate; to advance, pay in advance; **-se** to get ahead (of).

anticipo [an·ti·sí·po] *m.* advance, advance payment.

anticlericalismo [an·ti·kle·ri·ka·líz·mo] *m.* anticlericalism (*opposition or antagonism of the clergy*).

anticoncepción [an·ti·kon·sep·sjón] *f.* contraconception; birth control.

anticuado [an·ti·kwá·do] *adj.* antiquated, out-of-date.

antídoto [an·tí·do·to] *m.* antidote.

antigualla [an·ti·gwá·ya] *f.* antique; anything old.

antigüedad [an·ti·gwe·dád] *f.* antiquity, ancient times; **-es** antique objects, antiques.

antiguo [an·tí·gwo] *adj.* ancient, old; antique.

antílope [an·tí·lo·pe] *m.* antelope.

antimonio [an·ti·mó·njo] *m.* antimony.

antiparras [an·ti·pá·rras] *f. pl.* goggles; spectacles.

antipatía [an·ti·pa·tí·a] *f.* antipathy, dislike; mutual antagonism.

antipático [an·ti·pá·ti·ko] *adj.* disagreeable; unlikeable, unpleasant.

antipoliomielítico [an·ti·po·lio·mje·lí·ti·ko] *adj.* antipolio.

antiséptico [an·ti·sép·ti·ko] *adj. & m.* antiseptic.

antisocial [an·ti·so·sjál] *adj. & m.* antisocial; criminal.

antojadizo [an·to·xa·dí·so] *adj.* fanciful, whimsical.

antojarse [an·to·xar·se] *v.*: **antojársele a uno** to take a notion or fancy to; to strike one's fancy; to want, desire.

antojo [an·tó·xo] *m.* whim, notion, fancy.

antorcha [an·tór·ča] *f.* torch.

antracita [an·tra·sí·ta] *f.* anthracite, hard coal.

antropología [an·tro·po·lo·xí·a] *f.* anthropology.

antropólogo [an·tro·pó·lo·go] *m.* anthropologist.

anual [a·nwál] *adj.* annual, yearly.

anuario [a·nwá·rjo] *m.* annual, yearbook.

anublar [a·nu·blár] *v.* to cloud; to dim, abscure; **-se** to become cloudy.

anudar [a·nu·dár] *v.* to knot; **anudársele a uno la garganta** to choke up with emotion.

anulación [a·nu·la·sjón] *f.* voiding, cancellation.

anular [a·nu·lár] *v.* to annul, void, cancel, abolish.

anunciador [a·nun·sja·dór] *m.* announcer; advertiser; *adj.* announcing; advertising.

anunciante [a·nun·sján·te] *m. & f.* announcer, advertiser.

anunciar [a·nun·sjár] *v.* to announce; to advertise.

anuncio [a·nún·sjo] *m.* announcement; advertisement.

anzuelo [an·swé·lo] *m.* fishhook; lure, attraction.

añadidura [a·ña·di·dú·ra] *f.* addition.

añadir [a·ña·dir] *v.* to add.

añejado [a·ñe·xá·do] *adj.* aged (*wine, cheese, etc.*).

añejo [a·ñé·xo] *adj.* old; of old vintage; stale.

añicos [a·ñí·kos] *m. pl.* bits, shatters, fragments; **hacer(se)** — to shatter, break into a thousand pieces.

añil [a·ñíl] *m.* indigo (*plant*); indigo blue.

año [á·ño] *m.* year; **— bisiesto** leap year; **¿cuántos -s tiene Vd?** how old are you?

añoranza [a·ño·rán·sa] *f.* nostalgia, longing.

añorar [a·ño·rár] *v.* to long for, yearn for, be homesick for; to make reminiscences.

añoso [a·ñó·so] *adj.* old, aged.

aojar [a·o·xár] *v.* to bewitch; to cast the evil eye.

apabullar [a·pa·bu·yár] *v.* to crush, crumple.

apacentar[1] [a·pa·sen·tár] *v. irr.* to graze, pasture; to feed (*the spirit, desires, passions, etc.*); **-se** to graze, pasture.

apacibilidad [a·pa·si·bi·li·dád] *f.* gentleness, mildness, pleasantness; **apacible** [a·pa·sí·ble] *adj.* pleasant, quiet, gentle.

apaciguamiento [a·pa·si·gwa·mjén·to] *m.* appeasement.

apaciguar[8] [a·pa·si·gwár] *v.* to pacify, calm, appease; **-se** to calm down.

apachurrar [a·pa·ču·rrár] *v. Mex., C.A., Carib., Andes* to crush. See **despachurrar**.

apadrinar [a·pa·dri·nár] *v.* to sponsor; to act as a godfather; to act as a second in a duel.

apagar[7] [a·pa·gár] *v.* to put out, extinguish; to deafen (*a sound*).

apagón [a·pa·gón] *m.* blackout.

apalabrar [a·pa·la·brár] *v.* to speak for, engage, reserve; **-se con** to make a verbal agreement with.

apalear [a·pa·le·ár] *v.* to beat up, thrash; to thresh.

aparador [a·pa·ra·dór] *m.* sideboard; cupboard; showcase; show window; workshop.

aparato [a·pa·rá·to] *m.* apparatus; pomp.

aparatoso [a·pa·ra·tó·so] *adj.* pompous, ostentatious.

aparcero [a·par·sé·ro] *m.* co-owner of land; *Am.* pal, comrade.

aparear [a·pa·re·ár] *v.* to mate; to match; to pair; **-se** to mate; to match; to pair.

aparecer[13] [a·pa·re·sér] *v. irr.* to appear, show up.

aparecido [a·pa·re·sí·do] *m.* ghost, specter, phantom.

aparejar [a·pa·re·xár] *v.* to prepare; to harness; to rig; to equip.

aparejo [a·pa·ré·xo] *m.* harness; packsaddle; rigging (*of a boat*); preparation; fishing tackle; **-s** equipment, tools.

aparentar [a·pa·ren·tár] *v.* to appear, seem; to pretend, feign, affect.

aparente [a·pa·rén·te] *adj.* apparent.

aparición [a·pa·ri·sjón] *f.* apparition, ghost; appearance.

apariencia [a·pa·rjén·sja] *f.* appearance.

apartado [a·par·tá·do] *m.* compartment; **— postal** post office letter box; *p.p.* of **apartar**.

apartamento [a·par·ta·mén·to] *m.* apartment.

apartamiento [a·par·ta·mjén·to] *m.* separation; retirement; aloofness; retreat, refuge; *Am.* apartment, flat.

apartar [a·par·tár] *v.* to set apart, separate; to remove; *Am.* — las reses to sort out cattle; -se to withdraw; to step aside; to go away.

aparte [a·pár·te] *adv.* apart; aside; *m.* aside (*in a play*); new paragraph; *Am.* sorting out of cattle.

apasionado [a·pa·sjo·ná·ðo] *adj.* passionate; very fond (of); impassioned, emotional.

apasionar [a·pa·sjo·nár] *v.* to arouse passion; to fill with passion; -se to become impassioned; to fall ardently in love.

apatía [a·pa·tí·a] *f.* apathy, indolence, indifference.

apático [a·pá·ti·ko] *adj.* apathetic, indifferent, indolent.

apear [a·pe·ár] *v.* (*de caballo*) dismount; (*bajar*) to lower, take down; to shackle (*a horse*); to fell (*a tree*); *Ríopl.* to fire, dismiss from a position; — el tratamiento to omit the title (*in addressing a person*); -se to get off, alight; *Am.* -se por la cola (*or* por las orejas) to go off at a tangent, make an irrelevant remark.

apechugar[7] [a·pe·ču·gár] *v.* to push with the chest; to push ahead; — con to accept reluctantly; to go through with (*something*) courageously; *P.R.* to snatch, take possession of.

apedrear [a·pe·ðre·ár] *v.* to stone, hit with stones.

apegado [a·pe·ga·ðo] *adj.* devoted, attached; *p.p.* of apegarse.

apegarse[7] [a·pe·gár·se] *v.* to become attached (to); to become fond (of).

apego [a·pé·go] *m.* attachment, fondness.

apelación [a·pe·la·sjón] *f.* appeal.

apelar [a·pe·lár] *v.* to appeal.

apelotonar [a·pe·lo·to·nár] *v.* to form or roll into a ball; to pile up, bunch together.

apellidar [a·pe·yi·ðár] *v.* to call, name; -se to be named; to have the surname of.

apellido [a·pe·yí·ðo] *m.* surname.

apenar [a·pe·nár] *v.* to grieve, afflict; -se to be grieved; *Col., Ven., C.A., Carib.* to feel embarrassed, feel ashamed.

apenas [a·pé·nas] *adv.* hardly, scarcely; *conj.* as soon as.

apéndice [a·pén·di·se] *m.* appendix.

apercibir [a·per·si·bír] *v.* to prepare beforehand; to supply; to warn, advise; to perceive; -se a la pelea to get ready to fight; *Am.* -se de to notice.

apergaminado [a·per·ga·mi·ná·ðo] *adj.* parchment-like; dried up.

aperitivo [a·pe·ri·ti·βo] *m.* aperitif, appetizer; cocktail.

aperlado [a·per·lá·ðo] *adj.* pearly, pearl-colored.

apero [a·pé·ro] *m.* farm equipment; -s tools, implements; *Ríopl., Ch., Mex., Ven., Andes* saddle and trappings.

apertura [a·per·tú·ra] *f.* opening (*act of opening or beginning*).

apestar [a·pes·tár] *v.* to infect; to corrupt; to sicken; to stink; -se to turn putrid, become corrupted; *Am.* to catch cold.

apestoso [a·pes·tó·so] *adj.* putrid, foul-smelling.

apetecer[13] [a·pe·te·sér] *v. irr.* to desire, crave.

apetecible [a·pe·te·si·βle] *adj.* desirable; appetizing.

apetencia [a·pe·tén·sja] *f.* hunger, appetite; desire.

apetito [a·pe·tí·to] *m.* appetite; hunger.

apetitoso [a·pe·ti·tó·so] *adj.* appetizing, gluttonous.

apiadarse [a·pja·ðár·se] *v.* to pity; — de to pity, take pit on.

ápice [á·pi·se] *m.* apex, top, summit.

apilar [a·pi·lár] *v.* to pile up, stack, heap.

apiñado [a·pi·ñá·ðo] *p.p. of* apiñar & *adj.* crowded, jammed; cone-shaped, shaped like a pine cone.

apiñamiento [a·pi·ña·mjén·to] *m.* crowd, jam (*of people or animals*); crowding together.

apiñar [a·pi·ñár] *v.* to cram together; to crowd; -se to pile up, crowd together.

apio [á·pjo] *m.* celery.

apisonadora [a·pi·so·na·ðó·ra] *f.* road roller.

apisonar [a·pi·so·nár] *v.* to pack down, flatten by pounding.

aplacar[6] [a·pla·kár] *v.* to appease, pacify, soothe.

aplanamiento [a·pla·na·mjén·to] *m.* flattening, leveling; dejection, depression.

aplanar [a·pla·nár] *v.* to level; to flatten; to astonish; *Am.* — las calles to tramp the streets; -se to be flattened out; to be leveled to the ground; to lose one's strength; *Col.* to give in, yield.

aplastar [a·plas·tár] *v.* to squash, crush, flatten; *Am.* to tire out, break (*a horse*); -se *Am.* to plump oneself down; *Col., Andes* to overstay a call (*remaining seated*).

aplaudir [a·plaw·ðír] *v.* to applaud, clap; to approve, praise.

aplauso [a·pláw·so] *m.* applause; praise, approval.

aplazamiento [a·pla·sa·mjén·to] *m.* postponement; adjournment.

aplazar[9] [a·pla·sár] *v.* to postpone; to adjourn.

aplicable [a·pli·ká·βle] *adj.* applicable, suitable, fitting.

aplicación [a·pli·ka·sjón] *f.* application; effort, diligence; -es appliqué (*trimming laid on a dress*).

aplicado [a·pli·ká·ðo] *adj.* industrious, diligent.

aplicar[6] [a·pli·kár] *v.* to apply; to put on, lay on; -se to apply oneself, work hard.

aplomado [a·plo·má·ðo] *adj.* gray, lead-colored; *p.p. of* aplomar.

aplomar [a·plo·már] *v.* to plumb (*a wall*); to make vertical; to make heavier; -se *Am.* to become ashamed or embarrassed; *Am.* to be slow.

aplomo [a·pló·mo] *m.* assurance, confidence, self-possession, serenity; estar — to be plumb, vertical.

apocado [a·po·ká·ðo] *adj.* cowardly; timid; *p.p. of* apocar.

apocamiento [a·po·ka·mjén·to] *m.* timidity; bashfulness; belittling.

apocar[6] [a·po·kár] *v.* to lessen; to belittle, give little importance to; -se to humble oneself.

apodar [a·po·ðár] *v.* to nickname.

apoderado [a·po·ðe·rá·ðo] *m.* attorney; proxy, substitute.

apoderar [a·po·ðe·rár] *v.* to empower, give power of attorney; -se de to take possession of, seize.

apodo [a·pó·ðo] *m.* nickname.

apogeo [a·po·xé·o] *m.* apogee (*point at which a planet, satellite, or rocket is at the greatest distance from the earth*); highest point, height (*of glory, fame, etc.*).

apolillado [a·po·li·yá·ðo] *adj.* moth-eaten; worm-eaten.

apología [a·po·lo·xí·a] *f.* praise, apologia.

apoplejía [a·po·ple·xí·a] *f.* apoplexy, stroke.

aporrear [a·po·rre·ár] *v.* to beat; to maul; *Am.* to beat (*in a game*), defeat.

aportación [a·por·ta·sjón] *f.* contribution.

aportar [a·por·tár] *v.* to bring; to contribute; to arrive in port; to reach an unexpected place (*after having gone astray*); **-se** *Am.* to appear, approach.

aporte [a·pór·te] *m.* contribution.

aposento [a·po·sén·to] *m.* room; lodging.

apostar ² [a·pos·tár] *v. irr.* to bet; to post, station.

apóstol [a·pós·tol] *m.* apostle; religious leader.

apostólico [a·pos·tó·li·ko] *adj.* apostolic (*pertaining to the apostles, or to the Pope and his authority*).

apostura [a·pos·tú·ra] *f.* elegant bearing, graceful carriage.

apoyar [a·po·yár] *v.* to lean, rest; to back, support; to aid, favor; to confirm; **-se** to lean (on).

apoyo [a·pó·yo] *m.* support; favor, protection.

apreciable [a·pre·sjá·ble] *adj.* estimable, esteemed; valuable; appraisable; noticeable.

apreciación [a·pre·sja·sjón] *f.* appreciation; valuation; estimation.

apreciar [a·pre·sjár] *v.* to appreciate, value, esteem; to price, fix the price of; to appraise.

aprecio [a·pré·sjo] *m.* esteem, high regard; appraisal, valuation, estimate; *Mex., Ven., Cuba* **hacer —** to notice, pay attention.

aprehender [a·pre·en·dér] *v.* to apprehend, seize, arrest.

aprehensión [a·pre·en·sjón], **aprensión** [a·pren·sjón] *f.* apprehension; fear, dread; seizure, arrest; *Am.* prejudice.

aprehensor [a·pre·en·sór], **aprensor** [a·pren·sór] *m.* captor.

apremiante [a·pre·mján·te] *adj.* pressing, urgent.

apremiar [a·pre·mjár] *v.* to press, urge onward, hurry.

apremio [a·pré·mjo] *m.* pressure; urgency.

aprender [a·pren·dér] *v.* to learn.

aprendiz [a·pren·dís] *m.* apprentice.

aprendizaje [a·pren·di·sá·xe] *m.* apprenticeship; learning (*act of learning*).

apresar [a·pre·sár] *v.* to seize, grab; to capture; to imprison.

aprestar [a·pres·tár] *v.* to prepare, make ready; **-se** to get ready.

apresto [a·prés·to] *m.* preparation; readiness.

apresurado [a·pre·su·rá·do] *adj.* hasty.

apresurar [a·pre·su·rár] *v.* to hurry, hasten; **-se** to hurry, hasten.

apretado [a·pre·tá·do] *adj.* tight; compact; stingy, miserly; difficult, dangerous; *p.p.* of **apretar**.

apretar ¹ [a·pre·tár] *v. irr.* to press, squeeze, tighten; to urge on; *Am.* to increase in strength or intensity (*as rain, wind, etc.*); *Am.* to redouble one's effort; **— a correr** to start to run; **-se** *Col.* to gorge, overeat.

apretón [a·pre·tón] *m.* sudden pressure; squeeze; dash, short run; **— de manos** hand-shake.

apretura [a·pre·tú·ra] *f.* jam, crush; tight squeeze, narrow place; difficulty, predicament; dire poverty.

aprieto [a·prjé·to] *m.* tight spot, difficulty.

aprisa [a·prí·sa] *adv.* quickly, fast, speedily.

aprisco [a·prís·ko] *m.* sheepfold.

aprisionar [a·pri·sjo·nár] *v.* to imprison; to tie, fasten.

aprobación [a·pro·ba·sjón] *f.* approbation, approval; consent; pass, passing grade.

aprobar ² [a·pro·bár] *v. irr.* to approve; to pass (*in an examination*).

aprontar [a·pron·tár] *v.* to make ready; to expedite; to hand over without delay; *Am.* to pay in advance.

apropiación [a·pro·pja·sjón] *f.* appropriation; confiscation.

apropiado [a·pro·pjá·do] *adj.* appropriate, proper, fitting, suitable; *p.p.* of **apropiar**.

apropiar [a·pro·pjár] *v.* to fit; to adapt; **-se** to take possession (of); to confiscate.

aprovechable [a·pro·be·čá·ble] *adj.* available; usable, fit to use.

aprovechado [a·pro·be·čá·do] *adj.* diligent, industrious; *p.p.* of **aprovechar**.

aprovechamiento [a·pro·be·ča·mjén·to] *m.* use, utilization; exploitation; profit, benefit; progress.

aprovechar [a·pro·be·čár] *v.* to profit, be profitable; to progress, get ahead; to utilize; **-se de** to take advantage of; **¡que aproveche!** may you enjoy it!

aproximado [a·prok·si·má·do] *adj.* approximate; near; nearly correct.

aproximar [a·prok·si·már] *v.* to place or bring near; to approximate; **-se** to get near, approach.

aproximativo [a·prok·si·ma·tí·bo] *adj.* approximate.

aptitud [ap·ti·túd] *f.* aptitude, capacity, ability.

apto [áp·to] *adj.* apt; competent.

apuesta [a·pwés·ta] *f.* bet, wager.

apuesto [a·pwés·to] *adj.* smart, stylish; good-looking.

apuntación [a·pun·ta·sjón] *f.* note; memorandum; musical notation, set of musical symbols or signs.

apuntalar [a·pun·ta·lár] *v.* to prop; to shore up.

apuntar [a·pun·tár] *v.* (*señalar*) to point; (*arma*) to aim; (*escribir*) to write down; (*a un actor*) to prompt; (*remendar*) to mend, to stitch; to sharpen; (*brotar*) to begin to show; **— el día** to begin to dawn; **-se** to sprout.

apunte [a·pún·te] *m.* note, memorandum.

apuñalar [a·pu·ña·lár] *v.* to stab.

apuración [a·pu·ra·sjón] *f.* worry; trouble.

apurado [a·pu·rá·do] *adj.* worried; needy; difficult; dangerous; in a hurry.

apurar [a·pu·rár] *v.* (*acabar*) to exhaust, to drain to the last drop; (*preocupar*) to worry, annoy; (*acelerar*) to hurry, press; **-se** to be or get worried; to hurry up.

apuro [a·pú·ro] *m.* need; worry; predicament; *Am.* rush, hurry.

aquejar [a·ke·xár] *v.* to grieve, afflict.

aquel [a·kél], **aquella** [a·ké·ya] *dem. adj.* that (*at a distance*); **aquellos** [a·ké·yos], **aquellas** [a·ké·yas] those; **aquél, aquélla** *m., f. dem. pron.* that one; the former; **aquello** [a·ké·yo] that, that thing; **aquéllos, aquéllas** *m., f. pl.* those; the former.

aquí [a·kí] *adv.* here; **por —** this way; through here; around here.

aquietar [a·kje·tár] *v.* to quiet, calm; to hush; **-se** to calm down, become calm.

aquilón [a·ki·lón] *m.* north wind.

ara [á·ra] *f.* altar.

árabe [á·ra·be] *adj. & m.* Arab; Arabic.

arado [a·rá·do] *m.* plow; *Am.* plowed land, piece of cultivated land.

aragonés [a·ra·go·nés] *adj.* Aragonese, of or from Aragón, Spain; *m.* Aragonese.

arancel [a·ran·sél] *m.* tariff; **— de aduanas** customs, duties; **arancelario** [a·ran·se·lá·rjo] *adj.* pertaining to tariff.

arándano [a·rán·da·no] *m.* cranberry.

araña [a·rá·ña] *f.* spider; chandelier.

arañar [a·ra·ñár] *v.* to scratch; to claw.

araño [a·rá·ño] *m.* scratch; **arañazo** [a·ra·ñá·so] *m.* big scratch.

arar [a·rár] *v.* to plow.

arbitración [ar·bi·tra·sjón] f. arbitration.
arbitrador [ar·bi·tra·đór] m. arbitrator; referee, umpire.
arbitraje [ar·bi·trá·xe] m. arbitration.
arbitrar [ar·bi·trár] v. to arbitrate; to umpire.
arbitrario [ar·bi·trá·rjo] adj. arbitrary.
arbitrio [ar·bí·trjo] m. free will; scheme, means; compromise, arbitration; sentence (of a judge); judgment.
árbitro [ár·bi·tro] m. arbitrator, sole judge, umpire.
ábol [ár·bol] m. tree; mast; arbolado [ar·bo·lá·đo] adj. wooded; m. grove of trees.
arboleda [ar·bo·le·đa] f. grove.
arbusto [ar·bús·to] m. shrub.
arca [ár·ka] f. ark; chest, coffer; arcón [ar·kón] m. large coffer or chest; bin.
arcada [ar·ka·đa] f. arcade; archway.
arcaico [ar·káj·ko] adj. archaic.
arcano [ar·ká·no] adj. hidden, secret; m. secret, mystery.
arce [ár·se] m. maple, maple tree.
arcilla [ar·sí·ya] f. clay.
arco [ár·ko] m. arc; arch; bow; violin bow; — iris rainbow.
archipiélago [ar·či·pjé·la·go] m. archipelago (group of many islands).
archisabido [ar·či·sa·bí·đo] adj. very well-known.
archivo [ar·čí·bo] m. archives; file; public records; Am. office, business office; archivero [ar·či·bé·ro] m. keeper of archives; city clerk.
arder [ar·đér] v. to burn; to be consumed (with fever or passion); Col., Carib. to smart, sting.
ardid [ar·đíd] m. trick, scheme.
ardiente [ar·đjén·te] adj. ardent, burning, fervent; passionate; fiery.
ardilla [ar·đí·ya] f. squirrel.
ardite [ar·đí·te] m. ancient coin of small value; bit, trifle; no valer un — not to be worth a penny.
ardor [ar·đór] m. ardor; heat; fervor, eagerness.
ardoroso [ar·đo·ró·so] adj. ardent, fiery.
arduo [ár·đwo] adj. arduous, hard, difficult.
área [á·re·a] f. area.
arena [a·ré·na] f. sand; arena; -s kidney stones; arenal [a·re·nál] m. sand pit.
arenga [a·rén·ga] f. address, speech.
arenisco [a·re·nís·ko] adj. sandy; gritty; piedra arenisca sandstone.
arenoso [a·re·nó·so] adj. sandy; gritty.
arenque [a·rén·ke] m. herring.
arepa [a·ré·pa] f. Col., Ven., Carib. a fried (griddle) cake made of corn meal that corresponds to the Mexican tortilla.
arete [a·ré·te] m. earring.
argamasa [ar·ga·má·sa] f. mortar.
argentar [ar·xen·tár] v. to plate (with silver); to polish.
argentino [ar·xen·tí·no] adj. silvery; Argentine; m. Argentine; Argentine gold coin worth 5 pesos.
argolla [ar·gó·ya] f. large iron ring; Am. plain finger ring, engagement ring; Am. tener — to be lucky.
argón [ar·gón] m. argon.
argucia [ar·gú·sja] f. cunning, astuteness; scheme; subtlety.
argüir³² [ar·gwír] v. irr. to argue; to deduce, infer.
argumentación [ar·gu·men·ta·sjón] f. argumentation, argument, reasoning.
argumento [ar·gu·mén·to] m. reasoning; substance, subject matter, resumé (of a play or story).
aridez [a·ri·dés] f. barrenness; dryness; drought.

árido [á·ri·đo] adj. arid, dry, barren; -s m. pl. grains and dry vegetables; medida para -s dry measure.
ariete [a·rjé·te] m. ram, battering ram; — hidráulico hydraulic ram.
arisco [a·rís·ko] adj. gruff, harsh, unsociable; Am. shy, distrustful.
arista [a·ris·ta] f. sharp edge; ridge; beard (of wheat or corn).
aristocracia [a·ris·to·krá·sja] f. aristocracy.
aristócrata [a·ris·tó·kra·ta] m. & f. aristocrat.
aristocrático [a·ris·to·krá·ti·ko] adj. aristocratic.
aritmética [a·rit·mé·ti·ka] f. arithmetic.
arma [ár·ma] f. arm, weapon; branch (of the army); -s armed forces; — arrojadiza missile weapon; — blanca sword or knife; de -s tomar ready for any emergency; ready to fight.
armada [ar·má·đa] f. armada, fleet.
armador [ar·ma·đór] m. shipbuilder; assembler.
armadura [ar·ma·đú·ra] f. armor; armature (of a generator or dynamo); framework; mounting.
armamento [ar·ma·mén·to] m. armament; equipment.
armar [ar·már] v. to arm; to set up, assemble, rig up; — una pendencia to start a quarrel; Col. — un trique to lay a snare, set a trap; Am. -se to balk, to be stubborn; Ven., Mex. -se con alguna cosa to refuse to return something.
armario [ar·má·rjo] m. wardrobe, clothes closet; cabinet.
armatoste [ar·ma·tós·te] m. unwieldy object or machine; clumsy thing; heavy, clumsy fellow.
armazón [ar·ma·són] f. framework, skeleton; m. skeleton (of an animal); Am. shelf, set of shelves.
armella [ar·mé·ya] f. staple; screw eye.
armiño [ar·mí·ño] m. ermine.
armisticio [ar·mis·tí·sjo] m. armistice.
armonía [ar·mo·ní·a] f. harmony.
armónico [ar·mó·ni·ko] adj. harmonic; harmonious.
armonioso [ar·mo·njó·so] adj. harmonious, musical.
armonizar⁹ [ar·mo·ni·sár] v. to harmonize.
arnés [ar·nés] m. harness; coat of mail; -es harness and trappings; equipment, outfit.
aro [á·ro] m. hoop; rim (of a wheel); Am. finger ring; Ch., Ríopl. earring.
aroma [a·ró·ma] f. aroma, scent, perfume.
aromático [a·ro·má·ti·ko] adj. aromatic, fragrant; spicy; sales aromáticas smelling salts.
arpa [ár·pa] f. harp.
arpía [ar·pí·a] f. shrew.
arpón [ar·pón] m. harpoon, spear.
arqueado [ar·ke·á·đo] adj. arched.
arquear [ar·ke·ár] v. to arch.
arquitecto [ar·ki·ték·to] m. architect.
arquitectónico [ar·ki·tek·tó·ni·ko] adj. architectural.
arquitectura [ar·ki·tek·tú·ra] f. architecture.
arrabal [a·rra·bál] m. outlying district; -es outskirts, suburbs.
arracada [a·rra·ká·đa] f. earring.
arraigar⁷ [a·rraj·gár] v. to root, take root; -se to become rooted, attached.
arrancado [a·rraŋ·ká·đo] adj. Mex., Carib., C.A., Andes without money, broke.
arrancar⁶ [a·rraŋ·kár] v. to uproot; to pull out; to start, start out; Ch., Mex. to flee, run away.
arranque [a·rraŋ·ke] m. start; pull; uprooting; automobile starter; — de ira fit or outburst of anger; punto de — starting point.

arras [á·rras] *f. pl.* earnest money; pledge; dowry.

arrasar [a·rra·sár] *v.* to level; to tear down, raze; to fill to the brim; **-se** to clear up (*said of the sky*); **-se de lágrimas** to fill up with tears.

arrastrado [a·rras·trá·đo] *adj.* poor, destitute; mean, vile; wretched; rascally; **llevar una vida arrastrada** to lead a dog's life.

arrastrar [a·rras·trár] *v.* to drag, haul; *Ven.* to harrow (*land*); **-se** to drag along, crawl.

arrayán [a·rra·yán] *m.* myrtle.

¡arre! [á·rre] *interj.* gee! get up there!

arrear [a·rre·ár] *v.* to drive (*mules, cattle*); *Guat.* to rustle, steal cattle; *Am.* **-le a uno una bofetada** to give a person a slap.

arrebatamiento [a·rre·ba·ta·mjén·to] *m.* snatch; ecstasy; rage.

arrebatar [a·rre·ba·tár] *v.* to snatch away; **-se de cólera** to have a fit of anger.

arrebatiña [a·rre·ba·tí·ña] *f.* grab, snatch; scramble; **arrebatón** [a·rre·ba·tón] *m.* quick or violent grab.

arrebato [a·rre·bá·to] *m.* rage; rapture, ecstasy; fit.

arrebol [a·rre·ból] *m.* red color of the sky; rouge; **-es** red clouds.

arreciar [a·rre·sjár] *v.* to increase in intensity, get stronger.

arrecife [a·rre·sí·fe] *m.* reef.

arredrar [a·rre·đrár] *v.* to frighten, intimidate; **-se** to be or get scared.

arreglar [a·rre·glár] *v.* to arrange, put in order; to regulate; to fix; to adjust, settle; *Am.* to pay (*a debt*); *Am.* to correct, punish; **-se** to doll up, fix oneself up; to settle differences, come to an agreement.

arreglo [a·rré·glo] *m.* arrangement; adjustment; settlement; conformity, agreement; **con — a** according to.

arrellanarse [a·rre·ya·nár·se] *v.* to sprawl, lounge; to be self-satisfied.

arremangado [a·rre·maŋ·gá·đo] *adj. & p.p.* turned up; **nariz arremangada** turned up nose.

arremangar[7] a·rre·maŋ·gár] *v.* to tuck up, turn up, roll up (*the sleeves, trousers, etc.*); **-se** to roll up one's sleeves; **-se los pantalones** to roll up one's trousers.

arremeter [a·rre·me·tér] *v.* to attack, assail, assault.

arremetida [a·rre·me·tí·đa] *f.* thrust, push, attack.

arremolinarse [a·rre·mo·li·nár·se] *v.* to whirl, swirl; to eddy; to mill around.

arrendamiento [a·rren·da·mjén·to] *m.* renting; lease; rental, rent.

arrendar[1] [a·rren·dár] *v. irr.* to rent, lease, let; to hire; to tie (*a horse*); to bridle; *Am.* to head for.

arrendatario [a·rren·da·tá·rjo] *m.* renter, tenant.

arreo [a·rré·o] *m.* raiment; ornament; *Am.* driving of horses or mules; *Riopl., Ch., Mex., Ven.* drove of horses or mules; **-s** trappings; equipment; finery; *adv.* uninterruptedly, without interruption.

arrepentido [a·rre·pen·tí·đo] *adj.* repentant; *p.p. of* **arrepentirse.**

arrepentimiento [a·rre·pen·ti·mjén·to] *m.* repentance, regret.

arrepentirse[3] [a·rre·pen·tír·se] *v. irr.* to repent, regret.

arrestado [a·rres·ta·đo] *adj.* daring, rash; *p.p. of* **arrestar.**

arrestar [a·rres·tár] *v.* to arrest; *Am.* to return, strike back (*a ball*); *Peru* to reprimand; **-se** to dare, venture.

arresto [a·rrés·to] *m.* arrest, imprisonment; detention; daring, rashness; rash act.

arriar[17] [a·rrjár] *v.* to haul down, lower (*the flag*); to lower (*the sails*); to slacken (*a rope*).

arriba [a·rri·ba] *adv.* above; upstairs; **de — abajo** from top to bottom; up and down; **rio —** upstream; **¡ — !** hurrah!

arribada [a·rri·bá·đa] *f.* arrival; *Am.* back talk, impudent answer.

arribar [a·rri·bár] *v.* to arrive; to put into port; *Am.* to prosper, better one's lot.

arribo [a·rri·bo] *m.* arrival.

arriendo [a·rrjén·do] = **arrendamiento.**

arriero [a·rrjé·ro] *m.* muleteer.

arriesgado [a·rrjez·gá·đo] *adj.* risky, daring.

arriesgar[7] [a·rrjez·gár] *v.* to risk; **-se** to dare, run a risk.

arrimar [a·rri·már] *v.* to bring or place near; to lay aside; to strike (*a blow*); **-se** to lean (on); to get near; to seek shelter.

arrinconar [a·rriŋ·ko·nár] *v.* to corner; to put in a corner; to lay aside; to slight, neglect; **-se** to retire; to live a secluded life.

arriscado [a·rris·ká·đo] *adj.* bold; daring; brisk; spirited (*horse*); craggy, rugged.

arriscar[6] [a·rris·kár] *v.* to risk, venture; *Mex.* to roll up, curl up, tuck up, fold back; *Col.* to have vim and vigor; *Am.* **— a** reach, amount to; **-se** to get angry; *Peru., C.A.* to dress up, doll up.

arroba [a·rró·ba] *f.* weight of 25 pounds.

arrobamiento [a·rro·ba·mjén·to] *m.* trance, rapture.

arrobarse [a·rro·bár·se] *v.* to be entranced; to be in a trance; to be enraptured.

arrodillarse [a·rro·đi·yár·se] *v.* to kneel.

arrogancia [a·rro·gán·sja] *f.* arrogance, pride.

arrogante [a·rro·gán·te] *adj.* arrogant, haughty, proud.

arrogarse[7] [a·rro·gár·se] *v.* to appropriate, usurp, assume (*power or rights*).

arrojadizo [a·rro·xa·đi·so] *adj.* missile; **arma arrojadiza** missile weapon.

arrojado [a·rro·xá·đo] *adj.* daring, rash, fearless; *p.p. of* **arrojar.**

arrojar [a·rro·xár] *v.* to throw, hurl, cast; to expel; *Am.* to throw up, vomit; **— un saldo de** to show a balance of; **-se a** to hurl oneself upon or at; to dare to.

arrojo [a·rró·xo] *m.* boldness, daring.

arrollador [a·rro·ya·đór] *adj.* sweeping, overwhelming, violent; winding (*that serves to wind or roll up*).

arrollar [a·rro·yár] *v.* to roll up; to sweep away; to trample upon; to destroy.

arropar [a·rro·pár] *v.* to wrap, cover; *Col.* to snap up, accept on the spot (*a deal*); **-se** to wrap up, cover up.

arrostrar [a·rros·trár] *v.* to face, defy; **-se** to dare, dare to fight face to face.

arroyada [a·rro·yá·đa] *f.* gully, valley of a stream; bed (*formed by a stream*); river flood.

arroyo [a·rró·yo] *m.* brook, small stream, rivulet; gutter; **arroyuelo** [a·rro·ywé·lo] *m.* rivulet.

arroz [a·rrós] *m.* rice; **arrozal** [a·rro·sál] *m.* rice field.

arruga [a·rrú·ga] *f.* wrinkle.

arrugar[7] [a·rru·gár] *v.* to wrinkle; *Carib.* to bother, annoy; **-se** to get wrinkled; *Mex., Col.* to crouch with fear, be afraid.

arruinar [a·rrwi·nár] *v.* to ruin, destroy; **-se** to become ruined; *Am.* to go "broke", lose all one's fortune.

arrullar [a·rru·yár] *v.* to lull; to coo.
arrullo [a·rrú·yo] *m.* lullaby; cooing.
arrumbar [a·rrum·bár] *v.* to lay aside (*as useless*), put away in a corner, discard; to dismiss, remove (*from office or a position of trust*); to take bearings; — **a su adversario** to corner one's opponent, overpower him.
arsenal [ar·se·nál] *m.* arsenal; navy yard.
arsénico [ar·sé·ni·ko] *m.* arsenic.
arte [ár·te] *m. & f.* art; skill, ability; cunning; craft; **por — de** by way or means of **bellas -s** fine arts.
artefacto [ar·te·fák·to] *m.* piece of workmanship, manufactured object; handiwork; contrivance.
arteria [ar·té·rja] *f.* artery.
artero [ar·té·ro] *adj.* crafty, astute.
artesa [ar·té·sa] *f.* trough.
artesano [ar·te·sá·no] *m.* artisan, craftsman; **artesanía** [ar·te·sa·ní·a] *f.* arts and crafts; workmanship, craftsmanship.
artesonado [ar·te·so·ná·ɗo] *m.* ceiling decorated with carved panels.
ártico [ár·ti·ko] *adj.* arctic.
articulación [ar·ti·ku·la·sjón] *f.* articulation; pronunciation; joint.
articular [ar·ti·ku·lár] *v.* to articulate; to join, unite.
artículo [ar·tí·ku·lo] *m.* article; — **de fondo** editorial.
artífice [ar·tí·fi·se] *m.* artisan, craftsman.
artificial [ar·ti·fi·sjál] *adj.* artificial.
artificio [ar·ti·fí·sjo] *m.* artifice, clever device; craft, skill; cunning, deceit.
artificioso [ar·ti·fi·sjó·so] *adj.* cunning, astute, deceitful; skilful.
artillería [ar·ti·ye·rí·a] *f.* artillery, gunnery; — **de plaza** (*or* **de sitio**) heavy artillery; — **de montaña** light mountain artillery.
artillero [ar·ti·yé·ro] *m.* artilleryman, gunner.
artimaña [ar·ti·má·ña] *f.* trick.
artista [ar·tís·ta] *m. & f.* artist.
artístico [ar·tís·ti·ko] *adj.* artistic.
arveja [ar·bé·xa] *f. C.A., Col., Ven.* pea. *Also referred to as* **alverja** [al·bér·xa].
arzobispo [ar·so·bís·po] *m.* archbishop.
arzón [ar·són] *m.* saddletree.
as [as] *m.* ace.
asa [á·sa] *f.* handle.
asado [a·sá·ɗo] *m.* roast; *p.p. & adj.* roasted.
asador [a·sa·ɗór] *m.* spit (*for roasting*).
asaltador [a·sal·ta·ɗór] *m.* assailant; highway robber.
asaltar [a·sal·tár] *v.* to assault, attack; **-le a uno una idea** to be struck by an idea; *Riopl., Carib.* — **la casa de un amigo** to give a surprise party.
asalto [a·sál·to] *m.* assault, attack; *Am.* surprise party.
asamblea [a·sam·blé·a] *f.* assembly, legislature; meeting.
asar [a·sár] *v.* to roast; **-se** to roast; to feel hot.
asaz [a·sás] *adv.* enough, very.
ascendencia [a·sen·dén·sja] *f.* ancestry; origin.
ascendente [a·sen·dén·te] *adj.* ascendant, ascending, upward, rising.
ascender[1] [a·sen·dér] *v. irr.* to ascend, climb; to promote; to amount (to).
ascendiente [a·sen·djén·te] *m.* ancestor; influence.
ascensión [a·sen·sjón] *f.* ascension; ascent.
ascenso [a·sén·so] *m.* ascent, rise; promotion.
ascensor [a·sen·sór] *m.* elevator.
asco [ás·ko] *m.* disgust, loathing; nausea; **me da —**

it makes me sick; it disgusts me; *Mex., Ven.* **poner a uno del —** to call a person all kinds of bad names; to soil.
ascua [ás·kwa] *f.* ember.
aseado [a·se·á·ɗo] *adj.* clean, neat; *p.p. of* **asear.**
asear [a·se·ár] *v.* to adorn; to make neat and clean; **-se** to clean oneself up.
asechanza [a·se·čán·sa] = **acechanza.**
asediar [a·se·djár] *v.* to besiege, attack.
asedio [a·sé·djo] *m.* siege.
asegurar [a·se·ǥu·rár] *v.* to assure; to secure; to affirm; to insure; **-se** to make sure; to hold on; to get insured.
asemejar [a·se·me·xár] *v.* to liken, compare; **-se a** to resemble.
asentaderas [a·sen·ta·ɗé·ras] *f. pl.* buttocks.
asentador [a·sen·ta·ɗór] *m.* razor strop.
asentar [a·sen·tár] *v.* (*poner*) to set; to put down in writing; (*afirmar*) to assert; to iron out; to establish; (*afilar*) to hone; strop; **-se** to settle.
asentimiento [a·sen·ti·mjén·to] *m.* assent, acquiescence, agreement.
asentir[3] [a·sen·tír] *v. irr.* to assent, agree.
aseo [a·sé·o] *m.* neatness, cleanliness.
asequible [a·se·ki·ble] *adj.* obtainable, available.
aserción [a·ser·sjón] *f.* assertion, affirmation.
aserradero [a·se·rra·ɗé·ro] *m.* sawmill.
aserrar[1] [a·se·rrár] *v. irr.* to saw.
aserrín [a·se·rrín] *m.* sawdust.
aserto [a·sér·to] *m.* assertion.
asesinar [a·se·si·nár] *v.* to assassinate, murder.
asesinato [a·se·si·ná·to] *m.* assassination, murder.
asesino [a·se·sí·no] *m.* assassin, murderer; *adj.* murderous.
asestar [a·ses·tár] *v.* to point, aim, direct; — **un golpe** to deal a blow; — **un tiro** to fire a shot.
aseveración [a·se·be·ra·sjón] *f.* assertion, affirmation, contention.
aseverar [a·se·be·rár] *v.* to assert, affirm.
asfalto [as·fál·to] *m.* asphalt.
asfixia [as·fik·sja] *f.* suffocation.
asfixiar [as·fik·sjár] *v.* to suffocate, smother.
así [a·sí] *adv.* so, thus, like this; therefore; — — so-so; — **que** so that; — **que** (*or* **como**) *conj.* as soon as; *Riopl., Ch., Ven., Mex., Andes* — **no más** so-so; just so.
asiático [a·sjá·ti·ko] *adj. & m.* Asiatic.
asidero [a·si·ɗé·ro] *m.* handle; hold.
asiduo [a·si·ɗwo] *adj.* assiduous, diligent, persevering.
asiento [a·sjén·to] *m.* seat; site, location; bottom; entry (*in bookkeeping*); **-s** dregs, sediment.
asignación [a·sig·na·sjón] *f.* assignment; allowance.
asignar [a·sig·nár] *v.* to assign; to allot; to attribute; to appoint.
asilado [a·si·lá·ɗo] *m.* inmate (*of an asylum*).
asilar [a·si·lár] *v.* to house, shelter; to put in an asylum.
asilo [a·si·lo] *m.* asylum, refuge, shelter.
asimilar [a·si·mi·lár] *v.* to assimilate, digest, absorb; to liken, compare.
asimismo [a·si·míz·mo] *adv.* likewise, also.
asir[22] [a·sir] *v. irr.* to seize, take hold of.
asistencia [a·sis·tén·sja] *f.* presence; attendance; assistance, help; *Mex.* sitting room; **-s** allowance; *Col., Ven., Mex.* **casa de —** boarding house.
asistente [a·sis·tén·te] *m.* assistant; helper; military orderly; *Col., Ven., P.R.* servant; **los -s** those present.

asistir [a·sis·tír] v. to attend, be present; to help; *Am.* to board, serve meals.

asno [áz·no] m. ass, donkey.

asociación [a·so·sja·sjón] f. association.

asociado [a·so·sjá·ðo] m. associate.

asociar [a·so·sjár] v. to associate; -se to join; to associate.

asolamiento [a·so·la·mjén·to] m. devastation, ravage, havoc, destruction.

asolar[2] [a·so·lár] v. *irr.* to raze; to lay waste; to parch; -se to dry up, become parched; to settle (*as liquids*).

asoleado [a·so·le·á·ðo] adj. sunny; p.p. of **asolear**.

asolear [a·so·le·ár] v. to sun; -se to bask in the sun; to get sunburnt.

asomar [a·so·már] v. to show, appear; — **la cabeza** to stick one's head out; -se to look out (*of a window*); to peep out (*or* into); *Peru* to draw near, approach.

asombrar [a·som·brár] v. (*hacer sombra*) to cast a shadow, darken; (*asustar*) to astonish, amaze, frighten; -se to be astonished, amazed.

asombro [a·sóm·bro] m. astonishment, amazement; fright.

asombroso [a·som·bró·so] adj. astonishing, amazing.

asomo [a·só·mo] m. sign, indication; conjecture, suspicion; **ni por** — by no means.

aspa [ás·pa] f. wing of a windmill; blade (*of a propeller*); reel (*for winding yarn*).

aspecto [as·pék·to] m. aspect, look, appearance.

aspereza [as·pe·ré·sa] f. roughness, ruggedness; harshness; severity.

áspero [ás·pe·ro] adj. rough, uneven, harsh; gruff.

aspiración [as·pi·ra·sjón] f. aspiration, ambition; longing; inhalation, breathing in.

aspiradora [as·pi·ra·ðó·ra] f. vacuum cleaner.

aspirante [as·pi·rán·te] m. & f. applicant; candidate.

aspirar [as·pi·rár] v. (*anhelar*) to aspire, long for, seek; (*inspirar*) to breathe in, to inhale; to aspirate (*a sound*).

asquear [as·ke·ár] v. to disgust, nauseate, sicken.

asqueroso [as·ke·ró·so] adj. loathsome, disgusting, sickening, filthy.

asta [ás·ta] f. horn; antler; mast, pole, staff, flagstaff; lance; **a media** — at half mast.

asterisco [as·te·rís·ko] m. asterisk, star (*used in printing*).

astilla [as·tí·ya] f. chip; splinter; splint.

astillar [as·ti·yár] v. to chip; to splinter; -se to splinter, break into splinters.

astillero [as·ti·yé·ro] m. dry dock; shipyard; lumber yard; rack (*for lances or spears*).

astringente [as·triŋ·xén·te] adj. & m. astringent.

astro [ás·tro] m. star; planet.

atronauta [as·tro·náw·ta] m. & f. astronaut.

astronomía [as·tro·no·mía·a] f. astronomy; **astrónomo** m. astronomer.

astucia [as·tú·sja] f. shrewdness, cunning; trick.

asturiano [as·tu·rjá·no] adj. Asturian, of or from Asturias, Spain; m. Asturian.

astuto [as·tú·to] adj. astute, shrewd, wily, crafty.

asueto [a·swé·to] m. recess, vacation; **día de** — holiday.

asumir [a·su·mír] v. to assume.

asunto [a·sún·to] m. topic, subject matter; business; affair.

asustadizo [a·sus·ta·ðí·so] adj. shy, scary, easily frightened, jumpy.

asustar [a·sus·tár] v. to frighten, scare.

atacante [a·ta·kán·te] m. attacker; adj. attacking.

atacar[6] [a·ta·kár] v. to attack; to tighten, fasten; to ram; to plug, wad (*a gun*).

atadura [a·ta·ðú·ra] f. tie, knot; fastening.

atajar [a·ta·xár] v. to intercept; to interrupt, cut off; to take a short cut; to cross out.

atajo [a·tá·xo] m. short cut; interception; *Am.* drove. *See* **hatajo**.

atalaya [a·ta·lá·ya] f. lookout, watchtower; m. lookout, watchman, guard.

atañer[19, 51] [a·ta·ñér] v. to concern.

ataque [a·tá·ke] m. attack; fit.

atar [a·tár] v. to tie, fasten; -se to get tied up; to be puzzled or perplexed.

atardecer [a·tar·ðe·sér] m. late afternoon.

atareado [a·ta·re·á·ðo] adj. busy, over-worked.

atarear [a·ta·re·ár] v. to overwork, load with work; -se to toil, work hard; to be very busy.

atascadero [a·tas·ka·ðé·ro] m. muddy place; obstruction.

atascar[6] [a·tas·kár] v. to stop up; to jam, obstruct; -se to get stuck; to stick; to jam, get obstructed; to stall.

ataúd [a·ta·úð] m. coffin.

ataviar[17] [a·ta·βjár] v. to attire, deck, adorn; -se to dress up, doll up.

atavío [a·ta·βí·o] m. attire, costume; ornaments, finery.

atemorizar[9] [a·te·mo·ri·sár] v. to frighten, scare.

atención [a·ten·sjón] f. attention, care, thought; courtesy; -es business, affairs; **en** — **a** having in mind, considering.

atender[1] [a·ten·dér] v. *irr.* to heed, pay attention; to attend to, take care of; to take into account or consideration.

atendido [a·ten·dí·ðo] adj. *Am.* attentive, courteous.

ateneo [a·te·né·o] m. literary forum.

atenerse[45] [a·te·nér·se] v. *irr.* to rely (on); to accept, abide (by).

atenido [a·te·ní·ðo] adj. Mex., Carib., C.A., Andes habitually dependent on another; p.p. of **atenerse**.

atentado [a·ten·tá·ðo] m. offense, violation; crime, violence.

atentar[1] [a·ten·tár] v. *irr.* to attempt, try; — **contra la vida de alguien** to attempt the life of someone.

atento [a·tén·to] adj. attentive; courteous, polite.

atenuar[18] [a·te·nwár] v. to attenuate, lessen; to tone down; to dim; to make thin or slender.

ateo [a·té·o] m. atheist; adj. atheistic.

aterciopelado [a·ter·sjo·pe·lá·ðo] adj. velvety.

aterido [a·te·rí·ðo] adj. stiff, numb from cold.

aterirse[3, 51] [a·te·rír·se] v. *irr.* to become numb with cold.

aterrador [a·te·rra·ðór] adj. terrifying, appalling.

aterrar [a·te·rrár] v. to terrify, frighten.

aterrizaje [a·te·rri·sá·xe] m. landing (*of a plane*); **pista de** — landing strip.

aterrizar[9] [a·te·rri·sár] v. to land (*said of a plane*).

aterronar [a·te·rro·nár] v. to make lumpy, form into lumps; -se to lump, form into lumps, become lumpy.

aterrorizar[9] [a·te·rro·ri·sár] v. to terrify, frighten, appal.

atesorar [a·te·so·rár] v. to treasure; to hoard, lay up, accumulate.

atestado [a·tes·tá·ðo] adj. crowded, jammed, stuffed; witnessed; p.p. of **atestar**.

atestar [a·tes·tár] v. (*legal*) to attest, testify, witness; (*llenar*) to fill up, cram, stuff, crowd; -se de to stuff oneself with, to get stuffed with.

atestiguar[8] [a·tes·ti·gwár] *v.* to testify, witness; to attest.

atiborrar [a·ti·ɓo·rrár] *v.* to stuff; -se to stuff oneself.

atiesar [a·tje·sár] *v.* to stiffen.

atildado [a·til·dá·ɗo] *adj.* spruce, trim; painstaking in dress or style.

atinar [a·ti·nár] *v.* to hit the mark; to guess right.

atisbar [a·tiz·ɓár] *v.* to spy, look cautiously; to watch, pry; to catch a glimpse of; to peek.

atisbo [a·tíz·ɓo] *m.* glimpse; insight; peek; spying.

atizar[9] [a·ti·sár] *v.* to poke, stir (*the fire*); to kindle, rouse; to trim (*a wick*); — **un bofetón** to give a wallop.

atlántico [aɗ·lán·ti·ko] *adj.* Atlantic; **el Atlántico** the Atlantic.

atlas [áɗ·las] *m.* atlas.

atleta [aɗ·lé·ta] *m. & f.* athlete.

atlético [aɗ·lé·ti·ko] *adj.* athletic.

atletismo [aɗ·le·tíz·mo] *m.* athletics.

atmósfera [aɗ·mós·fe·ra] *f.* atmosphere, air.

atmosférico [aɗ·mos·fé·ri·ko] *adj.* atmospheric.

atole [a·tó·le] *m. Mex.* Mexican drink made of corn meal; **atol** in C.A.

atolondrado [a·to·lon·drá·ɗo] *p.p. & adj.* confused, muddled; stunned; heedless, harebrained, thoughtless.

atolondramiento [a·to·lon·dra·mjén·to] *m.* thoughtlessness, recklessness; confusion, perplexity.

atolondrar [a·to·lon·drár] *v.* to confuse, muddle, perplex; to stun; -se to get muddled, confused; to get stunned.

atómico [a·tó·mi·ko] *adj.* atomic.

átomo [á·to·mo] *m.* atom; small particle, tiny bit.

atónito [a·tó·ni·to] *adj.* astonished, amazed.

átono [á·to·no] *adj.* unstressed.

atontado [a·ton·tá·ɗo] *adj.* stupefied, stupid, stunned.

atontar [a·ton·tár] *v.* to stupefy, stun; to confuse.

atorar [a·to·rár] *v.* to jam; to stop up, clog; *Am.* to hold up, stop; -se to get stuck (*in the mud*); to get clogged; to get jammed; to choke (*with food*).

atormentar [a·tor·men·tár] *v.* to torment; to worry, afflict; to tease, bother, vex.

atornasolado [a·tor·na·so·lá·ɗo] = **tornasolado**.

atornillar [a·tor·ni·yár] *v.* to screw; *Am.* to bother, torment.

atorrante [a·to·rrán·te] *m. & f. Col., Ch. Ríopl., Bol.* vagabond, tramp.

atrabancar[6] [a·tra·ɓaŋ·kár] *v.* to rush awkwardly; to run over; -se *Ríopl.* to get involved in difficulties; *Ríopl.* to rush into things.

atrabiliario [a·tra·ɓi·ljá·rjo] *adj.* melancholy; bad-tempered.

atracar [a·tra·kár] *v.* (*llenar*) to cram, stuff; (*amarrar*) to moor, to approach land; (*atacar*) to hold up, assault; *Am.* to seize; *Col.* to pursue, harass; *Am.* to treat severely; *Mex., C.A.* to thrash, beat; — **al muelle** to dock, moor to the wharf; -se to stuff oneself, overeat; *Ch.* to have a fist fight; *Ríopl.* to falter, stutter; -se **a** to come alongside of (*a ship*).

atracción [a·trak·sjón] *f.* attraction.

atraco [a·trá·ko] *m.* holdup, assault; *Am.* **darse un — de comida** to stuff oneself, gorge.

atracón [a·tra·kón] *m.* stuffing, gorging; *C.A.* violent quarrel; **darse un — de comida** to stuff oneself, gorge.

atractivo [a·trak·tí·ɓo] *adj.* attractive; *m.* attractiveness, charm.

atraer[46] [a·tra·ér] *v. irr.* to attract.

atragantarse [a·tra·gan·tár·se] *v.* to gobble up; to choke (*with food*).

atrancar[6] [a·traŋ·kár] *v.* to bolt, fasten with a bolt; *Am.* -le **a una cosa** to face something, stand up against something; -se to get crammed, obstructed; *Am.* to be stubborn, stick to one's opinion; *Col.* to stuff oneself, choke (*with food*).

atrapar [a·tra·pár] *v.* to trap, ensnare; to seize, grab; to overtake.

atrás [a·trás] *adv.* back; behind; backward; *Am.* **echarse** — (*or* **para** —) to back out, go back on one's word.

atrasado [a·tra·sá·ɗo] *adj.* late; behind time; backward; behind (*in one's work, payments, etc.*); slow (*said of a clock*); *p.p. of* **atrasar**.

atrasar [a·tra·sár] *v.* to delay; to be slow or behind time; -se to get behind, lose time; *Am.* to suffer a setback (*in one's health or fortune*).

atraso [a·trá·so] *m.* backwardness; delay; setback; -s arrears.

atravesar[1] [a·tra·ɓe·sár] *v. irr.* to cross; to walk across; to go through; to pierce; *Am.* to buy wholesale.

atreverse [a·tre·ɓér·se] *v.* to dare, risk; to be insolent, saucy.

atrevido [a·tre·ɓí·ɗo] *adj.* bold, daring; insolent.

atrevimiento [a·tre·ɓi·mjén·to] *m.* boldness, daring; insolence.

atribuir[32] [a·tri·ɓwír] *v. irr.* to attribute, ascribe, impute.

atribular [a·tri·ɓu·lár] *v.* to grieve, distress; -se to grieve; to be distressed.

atributo [a·tri·ɓú·to] *m.* attribute, quality.

atril [a·tríl] *m.* lectern, reading desk; book stand; music stand.

atrincherar [a·trin·če·rár] *v.* to entrench, fortify with trenches; -se to entrench oneself.

atrio [á·trjo] *m.* court, patio in front of a church; entrance hall.

atrocidad [a·tro·si·ɗáɗ] *f.* atrocity.

atronador [a·tro·na·ɗór] *adj.* thunderous, deafening.

atronar[2] [a·tro·nár] *v. irr.* to deafen; to stun.

atropellar [a·tro·pe·yár] *v.* to run over, run down, knock down; to trample upon; to insult; — **por** to knock down, overcome with violence; -se to rush.

atropello [a·tro·pé·yo] *m.* violent act; insult; outrage; trampling.

atroz [a·trós] *adj.* atrocious, awful; inhuman.

atún [a·tún] *m.* tunny fish, tuna fish.

aturdido [a·tur·ɗi·ɗo] *adj. & p.p.* stupid, awkward; stunned, bewildered.

aturdimiento [a·tur·ɗi·mjé·to] *m.* daze, bewilderment, confusion.

aturdir [a·tur·ɗír] *v.* to stun; to deafen; to bewilder.

atusar [a·tu·sár] *v.* to trim.

audacia [aw·ɗá·sja] *f.* daring, boldness.

audaz [aw·ɗás] *adj.* daring, bold.

audencia [aw·ɗjén·sja] *f.* audience, hearing; court of justice.

auditor [aw·ɗi·tór] *m.* judge advocate.

auditorio [aw·ɗi·tó·rjo] *m.* audience.

auge [áw·xe] *f.* boom (*in the market*); boost (*in prices*); topmost height (*of fortune, fame, dignity, etc.*); **estar** (*or* **ir**) **en** — to be on the increase.

augurar [aw·gu·rár] *v.* to fortell, predict.

augusto [aw·gús·to] *adj.* venerable; majestic.
aula [áw·la] *f.* schoolroom, classroom; lecture hall.
aullar [aw·yár] *v.* to howl; to shriek; to bawl.
aullido [aw·yí·đo] *m.* howl.
aumentar [aw·men·tár] *v.* to augment, increase.
aumento [aw·mén·to] *m.* increase, advance, rise.
aun [awn] (**aún**) [a·un] *adv.* even, still, yet.
aunque [áwn·ke] *conj.* though, although.
aura [áw·ra] *f.* breeze; favor, applause; *Am.* bird of prey, buzzard, vulture.
áureo [áw·re·o] *adj.* golden.
aureola [aw·re·ó·la] *f.* aureole, halo.
aureomicina [aw·re·o·mi·sí·na] *f.* Aureomycin (*trademark for chlortetracycline*).
aurora [aw·ró·ra] *f.* dawn; beginning; — **boreal** aurora borealis, northern lights.
auscultar [aws·kul·tár] *v.* to sound, examine by listening to (*the chest, lungs, heart, etc.*).
ausencia [aw·sén·sja] *f.* absence.
ausentarse [aw·sen·tár·se] *v.* to absent oneself; to be absent; to leave.
ausente [aw·sén·te] *adj.* absent.
auspicios [aws·pí·sjos] *m. pl.* auspices, patronage; omens.
austeridad [aws·te·ri·đáđ] *f.* austerity, severity, sternness, harshness.
austero [aws·té·ro] *adj.* austere, stern, strict; harsh.
austral [aws·trál] *adj.* southern.
austríaco [aws·trí·a·ko] *adj. & m.* Austrian.
austro [áws·tro] *m.* south wind.
auténtico [aw·tén·ti·ko] *adj.* authentic, true, genuine.
auto [áw·to] *m.* auto, automobile; one-act play; writ, order; — **sacramental** one-act religious play; **-s** proceedings.
autobús [aw·to·bús] *m.* bus, autobus.
autóctono [aw·tók·to·no] *adj.* indigenous, native.
autogiro [aw·to·xí·ro] *m.* autogiro.
automático [aw·to·má·ti·ko] *adj.* automatic.
automotriz [aw·to·mo·tríz] *adj.* automotive, self-moving.
automóvil [aw·to·mó·bil] *m.* automobile, auto.
automovilista [aw·to·mo·bi·lis·ta] *m. & f.* motorist.
autonomía [aw·to·no·mí·a] *f.* autonomy.
autopista [aw·to·pís·ta] *f.* expressway, superhighway, freeway, throughway, turnpike.
autor [aw·tór] *m.* author.
autoridad [aw·to·ri·đáđ] *f.* authority.
autoritario [aw·to·ri·tá·rjo] *adj.* authoritative, authoritarian, domineering; bossy.
autorización [aw·to·ri·sa·sjón] *f.* authorization, sanction.
autorizar[9] [aw·to·ri·sár] *v.* to authorize, give power (to).
autoservicio [aw·to·ser·bí·sjo] *m.* self-service.
auxiliar [awk·si·ljár] *v.* to aid, help; *adj.* auxiliary, helping, assisting; *m.* assistant.
auxilio [aek·sí·ljo] *m.* aid, help.
avaluación [a·ba·lwa·sjón] *f.* valuation, appraisal, assessment.
avaluar[18] [a·ba·lwár] *v.* to value, appraise.
avalúo [a·ba·lú·o] *m.* valuation, appraisal.
avance [a·bán·se] *m.* advance, progress, headway; advanced payment; attack.
avanzada [a·ban·sá·đa] *f.* advance guard; outpost; advanced unit, spearhead.
avanzar[9] [a·ban·sár] *v.* to advance.
avaricia [a·ba·rí·sja] *f.* avarice, greed.
avariento [a·ba·rjén·to] *adj.* avaricious, miserly; *m.* miser.
avaro [a·bá·ro] *adj.* miserly, greedy; *m.* miser.

avasallar [a·ba·sa·yár] *v.* to subject, dominate, subdue.
ave [á·be] *f.* bird; fowl; — **de corral** domestic fowl; — **de rapiña** bird of prey.
avecindarse [a·be·sin·dár·se] *v.* to settle, locate, establish oneself, take up residence (*in a community*).
avellana [a·be·yá·na] *f.* hazelnut; **avellano** [a·be·yá·no] *m.* hazel; hazelnut tree; **avellanado** [a·be·ya·ná·đo] *adj.* hazel, light brown.
avena [a·bé·na] *f.* oats.
avenencia [a·be·nén·sja] *f.* harmony, agreement; conformity.
avenida [a·be·ní·đa] *f.* avenue; flood.
avenir[48] [a·be·nír] *v. irr.* to adjust; to reconcile; **-se** a to adapt oneself to; **-se con alguien** to get along with someone.
aventador [a·ben·ta·đór] *m.* fan (*for fanning a fire*); ventilator; winnower (*machine for separating wheat from chaff*).
aventajar [a·ben·ta·xár] *v.* to excel; to be ahead (of); **-se a** to get ahead of.
aventar[1] [a·ben·tár] *v. irr.* to fan; to winnow, blow chaff from grain; to throw out, expel; *Am.* to pitch, throw; *Am.* to dry sugar (*in the open*); *Am.* to rouse (*game*), **-se** to be full of wind; to flee, run away; *Am.* to attack, hurl oneself (*on someone*).
aventura [a·ben·tú·ra] *f.* adventure; risk, danger; chance.
aventurado [a·ben·tu·rá·đo] *adj.* adventurous, risky; bold, daring.
aventurar [a·ben·tu·rár] *v.* to venture, risk; **-se a** to risk, run the risk of; to dare.
aventurero [a·ben·tu·ré·ro] *adj.* adventurous; *m.* adventurer.
avergonzar[2, 9] [a·ber·gon·sár] *v. irr.* to shame; **-se** to feel ashamed.
avería [a·be·rí·a] *f.* damage, aviary, birdhouse; *Am.* misfortune; *Mex., Cuba* mischief.
averiar[17] [a·be·rjár] *v.* to damage, spoil, hurt; **-se** to become damaged; to spoil.
averiguar[8] [a·be·ri·gwár] *v.* to find out; to investigate.
aversión [a·ber·sjón] *f.* aversion, dislike; reluctance.
avestruz [a·bes·trús] *m.* ostrich.
avezado [a·be·sá·đo] *p.p. & adj.* accustomed; trained, practiced.
aviación [a·bja·sjón] *f.* aviation.
aviador [a·bja·đór] *m.* aviator, flyer; purveyor, provider; *Am.* moneylender (*to miners or laborers*), promoter.
aviar[17] [a·bjár] *v.* to equip; to supply; to prepare, make ready; *Am.* to lend money or equipment; **estar aviado** to be surrounded by difficulties; to be in a fix.
ávido [á·bi·đo] *adj.* eager; greedy.
avinagrado [a·bi·na·grá·đo] *adj.* sour; acid; cross.
avinagrar [a·bi·na·grár] *v.* to sour, make sour or acid; **-se** to sour, become sour.
avío [a·bí·o] *m.* provision, supply; preparation; *Cuba, Mex.* loan of money or equipment; **-s** equipment; **-s de pescar** fishing tackle.
avión [a·bjón] *m.* airplane; martin (*a bird similar to a swallow*).
avisar [a·bi·sár] *v.* to inform, give notice, advise; to announce; to warn.
aviso [a·bí·so] *m.* notice, advice, announcement; warning.
avispa [a·bís·pa] *f.* wasp; **avispero** [a·bis·pé·ro] *m.* wasp's nest; **avispón** [a·bis·pón] *m.* hornet.

avispado [a·ƀis·pa·ɗo] *adj.* lively, keen, clever, wide-awake; *Am.* frightened, scared.

avispar [a·ƀis·pár] *v.* to spur, incite; **-se** to be on the alert; to be uneasy; *Am.* to become frightened, scared.

avistar [a·ƀis·tár] *v.* to glimpse, catch sight of; **-se** to see each other, meet.

avivar [a·ƀi·ƀár] *v.* to enliven, give life to; to revive; to brighten; to quicken.

avizor [a·ƀi·sór] *adj.* alert, watchful.

avizorar [a·ƀi·so·rár] *v.* to spy, watch closely.

aya [á·ya] *f.* child's nurse, governess; **ayo** [á·yo] *m.* tutor guardian.

ayer [a·yér] *adv.* yesterday.

ayuda [a·yú·ɗa] *f.* aid, help.

ayudante [a·yu·ɗán·te] *m.* assistant.

ayudar [a·yu·ɗár] *v.* to aid, help.

ayunar [a·yu·nár] *v.* to fast.

ayunas [a·yú·nas]: **en — fasting**; **en — de** totally ignorant of.

ayuno [a·yú·no] *m.* fast; **— de** wholly ignorant of.

ayuntamiento [a·yun·ta·mjén·to] *m.* municipal government; town hall.

azabache [a·sa·ƀá·če] *m.* jet; **-s** jet ornaments.

azada [a·sá·ɗa] *f.* spade; hoe; **azadón** [a·sa·ɗón] *m.* hoe.

azafata [a·sa·fá·ta] *f.* airline hostess.

azafrán [a·sa·frán] *m.* saffron.

azahar [a·sa·ár] *m.* orange or lemon blossom.

azar [a·sár] *m.* hazard; chance; accident; disaster.

azogue [a·só·ǵe] *m.* quicksilver.

azolvar [a·sol·ƀár] *v.* to clog, obstruct; **-se** to clog, get clogged.

azorar [a·so·rár] *v.* to disturb, startle; to bewilder; **-se** to be startled, astonished; to be bewildered, perplexed; to be uneasy.

azotaina [a·so·táj·na] *f.* flogging, lashing, beating.

azotar [a·so·tár] *v.* to whip, lash, beat; *Am.* to thresh (*rice*); **— las calles** to "beat the pavement", walk the streets.

azote [a·só·te] *m.* whip; lash with a whip; scourge; affliction, calamity.

azotea [a·so·té·a] *f.* flat roof.

azteca [as·té·ka] *adj., m. & f.* Aztec.

azúcar [a·sú·kar] *m.* sugar.

azucarar [a·su·ka·rár] *v.* to sugar; to sweeten; **-se** to become sweet; *Am.* to crystallize, turn to sugar.

azucarera [a·su·ka·ré·ra] *f.* sugar bowl; sugar mill.

azucarero [a·su·ka·ré·ro] *adj.* sugar (*used as adj.*); *m.* sugar manufacturer, producer or dealer; sugar bowl.

azucena [a·su·sé·na] *f.* white lily.

azufre [a·sú·fre] *m.* sulphur.

azul [a·súl] *adj.* blue; **— celeste** sky-blue; **— marino** navy blue; **— turquí** indigo; *Am.* **tiempos -es** hard times.

azulado [a·su·lá·ɗo] *adj.* bluish.

azular [a·su·lár] *v.* to dye or color blue.

azulejo [a·su·lé·xo] *m.* glazed tile; *Am.* bluebird; *adj.* bluish.

azuzar[9] [a·su·sár] *v.* to urge, egg on; to incite.

B:b

baba [bá·ƀa] *f.* drivel, slaver, saliva; slime, slimy secretion; *Am.* small alligator.

babear [ba·ƀe·ár] *v.* to drivel; to slobber.

babero [ba·ƀé·ro] *m.* baby's bib.

babor [ba·ƀór] *m.* port, port side (*of a ship*).

babosear [ba·ƀo·se·ár] *v.* to slaver, drivel; to keep one's mouth open; to act like a fool.

baboso [ba·ƀó·so] *adj.* driveling, slobbering; slimy; foolishly sentimental; *Am.* silly, idiotic, foolish; **babosa** [*f.* slug (*creature like a snail, but without a shell*).

babucha [ba·ƀú·ča] *f.* slipper; *Ríopl.* **a —** pickaback, on the back or shoulders.

bacalao [ba·ká·lá·o], **bacallao** *m.* *Andalusia, Am.* codfish.

bacía [ba·sí·a] *f.* basin.

bacilo [ba·sí·lo] *m.* bacillus.

bacín [ba·sín] *m.* pot, chamber pot; **bacinica** [ba·si·ní·ka] *f.* chamber pot.

bacteria [bak·té·rja] *f.* bacterium; **-s** bacteria.

bacteriología [bak·te·rjo·lo·xí·a] *f.* bacteriology.

bacteriológico [bak·te·rjo·ló·xi·ko] *adj.* bacteriological, pertaining to bacteriology.

báculo [bá·ku·lo] *m.* staff, cane; aid, support.

bache [bá·če] *m.* rut, hole in the road.

bachiller [ba·či·yér] *m.* bachelor (*one who holds degree*); talkative person; **bachillerato** [ba·či·ye·rá·to] *m.* bachelor's degree; studies for the bachelor's degree.

badajo [ba·ɗá·xo] *m.* clapper of a bell; foolish talker.

badana [ba·ɗá·na] *f.* sheepskin.

bagaje [ba·gá·xe] *m.* baggage; army pack mule.

bagatela [ba·ga·té·la] *f.* trifle.

bagazo [ba·gá·so] *m.* waste pulp (*of sugarcane, olives, grapes, etc.*).

bagual [ba·gwál] *adj.* *Ríopl.* wild, untamed, unruly; *Ríopl.* rude, discourteous; *Ríopl.* lanky, awkward; *m.* *Ríopl.* wild horse.

bahía [ba·í·a] *f.* bay, harbor.

bailador [baj·la·ɗór] *m.* dancer; *adj.* dancing.

bailar [baj·lár] *v.* to dance; to spin around.

bailarín [baj·la·rín] *m.* dancer; **bailarina** [baj·la·rí·na] *f.* dancer.

baile [báj·le] *m.* dance; ball; ballet.

bailotear [baj·lo·te·ár] *v.* to jig, jiggle; to dance poorly; to dance around.

baja [bá·xa] *f.* fall (*of prices*); war casualty; **dar de —** to discharge, muster out.

bajá [ba·xá] *m.* pasha.

bajada [ba·xá·ɗa] *f.* descent; slope, dip (*on a road*); **de —** on the way down; **subidas y -s** ups and downs.

bajar [ba·xár] *v.* to go down; to drop (*as price or value*); to lower; to take or carry down; to humble; **-se** to get down or off; to alight; *Am.* to stop at a hotel.

bajel [ba·xél] *m.* boat, ship.

bajeza [ba·xé·sa] *f.* vile act or remark; meanness; baseness; degradation.

bajío [ba·xí·o] *m.* shoal, sand bank; *Am.* lowland.

bajo [bñ·xo] *adj.* low; short; soft, bass (*tone or voice*); shallow (*water*); subdued (*color*); humble; base; **piso —** first floor, ground floor; *prep.* under, underneath; *m.* bass.

bala [bá·la] *f.* bullet, shot, ball; bale (*of cotton*).

balada [ba·lá·ɗa] *f.* ballad.

baladí [ba·la·ɗí] *adj.* trivial; flimsy.

balance [ba·lán·se] *m.* balance; equilibrium; balance sheet; rocking, rolling.
balancear [ba·lan·se·ár] *v.* to balance; to rock, roll; to swing, sway; to waver.
balanceo [ba·lan·séo] *m.* rocking, rolling; swinging; balancing; wavering; wobbling.
balanza [ba·lán·sa] *f.* balance, scale.
balar [ba·lár] *v.* to bleat.
balaustrada [ba·laws·trá·da] *f.* balustrade, banister, railing.
balaustre [ba·láws·tre] *m.* banister.
balazo [ba·lá·so] *m.* shot; bullet wound; *adj. Ch.* clever, cunning.
balbucear [bal·bu·se·ár] *v.* to stammer, stutter; to babble.
balbuceo [bal·bu·sé·o] *m.* babble.
balcón [bal·kón] *m.* balcony.
baldado [bal·dá·do] *m.* cripple; *adj. & p.p.* crippled.
baldar [bal·dár] *v.* to cripple; to trump (*a card*).
balde [bál·de] *m.* pail; bucket; **de** — free of charge; **en** — in vain.
baldío [bal·dí·o] *adj.* barren; fallow, uncultivated; *m.* fallow land; wasteland.
baldón [bal·dón] *m.* infamy, insult.
baldosa [bal·dó·sa] *f.* floor tile; paving stone.
balido [ba·li·do] *m.* bleat, bleating.
balneario [bal·ne·á·rjo] *m.* bathing resort; *adj.* pertaining to bathing resorts or medicinal springs.
balompié [ba·lom·pjé] *m.* football
balota [ba·ló·ta] *f.* ballot.
balotar [ba·lo·tár] *v.* to ballot, vote.
balsa [bál·sa] *f.* (*de agua*) pond, pool; (*embaracación*) raft; *Am.* marsh; *Am.* a species of ceiba (*a tropical tree*).
bálsamo [bál·sa·mo] *m.* balsam, balm.
baluarte [bal·wár·te] *m.* bulwark.
ballena [ba·yé·na] *f.* whale; whalebone.
bambolear [bam·bo·le·ár] *v.* to sway, swing, rock; **-se** to stagger; to sway.
bambú [bam·bú] *m.* bamboo.
banana [ba·ná·na] *f.* banana; **banano** [ba·ná·no] *m.* banana tree.
banasta [ba·nás·ta] *f.* large basket.
banca [bán·ka] *f.* bench; card game; banking; banking house.
bancario [baŋ·ká·rjo] *adj.* bank, pertaining to a bank.
bancarrota [baŋ·ka·rró·ta] *f.* bankruptcy; failure, collapse.
banco [bán·ko] *m.* bank; bench, stool; school (*of fish*); *Mex.* pile of grain; *Am.* small hill on a plain.
banda [bán·da] *f.* (*musical*) band; (*cinta*) ribbon, sash; (*grupo*) gang, group, party; flock; (*lindero*) side, edge, border.
bandada [ban·dá·da] *f.* flock of birds; *Am.* gang.
bandeja [ban·dé·xa] *f.* tray; *Mex., Ven., Col.* bowl.
bandera [ban·dé·ra] *f.* banner, flag; *Riopl., Cuba, Mex.* **parar uno** — to take the lead, be a gangleader.
banderilla [ban·de·ri·ya] *f.* dart with a small flag or streamers (*used in bullfights*); **clavar a uno una** — to goad or taunt someone; **tercio de** — the **banderilla** phase of the bullfight; *Am.* **pegar una** — to touch for a loan.
banderillero [ban·de·ri·yé·ro] *m.* bullfighter who sticks the **banderillas** into the bull.
banderín [ban·de·rín] *m.* small flag; signal flag; pennant; recruiting office.

banderola [ban·de·ró·la] *f.* streamer, small banner or flag; pennant.
bandidaje [ban·di·dá·xe] *m.* banditry, highway robbery; bandits.
bandido [ban·dí·do] *m.* bandit, gangster.
bando [bán·do] *m.* (*decreto*) decree, proclamation; (*partido*) party, faction.
bandolero [ban·do·lé·ro] *m.* bandit.
bandurria [ban·dú·rrja] *f.* bandore (*stringed instrument*); *Am.* a species of wading bird.
banquero [baŋ·ké·ro] *m.* banker.
banqueta [baŋ·ké·ta] *f.* bench (*without a back*); stool; footstool; *Mex.* sidewalk.
banquete [baŋ·ké·te] *m.* banquet.
banquetear [baŋ·ke·te·ár] *v.* to banquet, feast.
banquillo [baŋ·kí·yo] *m.* bench, stool.
bañada [ba·ñá·da] *f.* shower, spray; dip, bath.
bañar [ba·ñár] *v.* to bathe, wash; to dip; **-se** to take a bath.
bañera [ba·ñé·ra] *f.* bathtub.
bañista [ba·ñís·ta] *m. & f.* bather.
baño [bá·ño] *m.* (*aseo*) bath; bathtub; (*acabado*) cover, coating; — **de María** double boiler; *Am.* — **ruso** steam bath.
baqueta [ba·ké·ta] *f.* rod; whip; **-s** drumsticks; **tratar a la** — to treat scornfully, despotically.
baquiano [ba·kjá·no], **baqueano** [ba·ke·á·no] *m. Riopl., Ven., Andes* native guide (*through the wilderness, pampas, etc.*); *adj. Riopl., Andes* having an instinctive sense of direction.
bar [bar] *m.* bar, taproom, tavern.
baraja [ba·rá·xa] *f.* pack of cards.
barajar [ba·ra·xár] *v.* to shuffle; to mix, jumble together; to scuffle, wrangle; *Am.* to hinder, obstruct.
baranda [ba·rán·da] *f.* railing; **barandal** [ba·ran·dál] *m.* banister, railing.
barandilla [ba·ran·dí·ya] *f.* balustrade, rail, railing.
barata [ba·rá·ta] *f.* barter, exchange; *Am.* bargain sale; *Peru, Ch.* cockroach.
baratear [ba·ra·te·ár] *v.* to sell cheap; to cheapen; to cut the price of.
baratija [ba·ra·tí·xa] *f.* trinket, trifle.
barato [ba·rá·to] *adj.* cheap; *m.* bargain sale; money given by the winning gambler.
baratura [ba·ra·tú·ra] *f.* cheapness.
baraúnda [ba·ra·ún·da] *f.* clamor, uproar, clatter.
barba [bar·ba] *f.* chin; beard; **-s** whiskers.
barbacoa [bar·ba·kó·a] *f. Am.* barbecue; barbecued meat.
barbado [bar·bá·do] *adj.* bearded.
barbaridad [bar·ba·ri·dád] *f.* cruelty, brutality; rudeness; **una** — **de** a lot of; **¡que** —! what nonsense!; what an atrocity!
barbarie [bar·bá·rje] *f.* barbarousness; savagery; lack of culture, ignorance; cruelty, brutality.
bárbaro [bár·ba·ro] *adj.* barbarous, cruel, savage; crude, coarse; *m.* barbarian.
barbechar [bar·be·čár] *v.* to plow; to fallow.
barbecho [bar·bé·čo] *m.* first plowing; plowed land; fallow, fallow land.
barbería [bar·be·rí·a] *f.* barbershop.
barbero [bar·bé·ro] *m.* barber; flatterer.
barbilla [bar·bí·ya] *f.* point of the chin.
barbón [bar·bón], **barbudo** [bar·bú·do] *adj.* bearded.
barca [bár·ka] *f.* boat, launch, barge.
barco [bár·ko] *m.* boat, ship.
bardo [bár·do] *m.* bard, minstrel, poet.
bario [bá·rjo] *m.* barium.
barítono [ba·rí·to·no] *m.* baritone.

barlovento [bar·lo·ƀén·to] *m.* windward.
barniz [bar·nís] *m.* varnish; glaze; printer's ink.
barnizar[9] [bar·ni·sár] *v.* to varnish; to glaze.
barómetro [ba·ró·me·tro] *m.* barometer.
barquero [bar·ké·ro] *m.* boatman; bargeman.
barquillo [bar·kí·yo] *m.* rolled wafer; ice-cream cone.
barquinazo [bar·ki·ná·so] *m.* tumble, bad fall, hard bump, somersault; *Am.* lurch (*of a vehicle or boat*).
barra [bá·rra] *f.* bar; rod; railing; sand bar; claque, audience; — **de jabón** bar of soap.
barrabasada [ba·rra·ƀa·sá·ƌa] *f.* mischief, mean prank; rash, hasty act.
barraca [ba·rrá·ka] *f.* hut, cabin; *Andes* large shed, warehouse.
barranca [ba·rráŋ·ka] *f.*, **barranco** [ba·rráŋ·ko] *m.* ravine, gorge; *Am.* cliff.
barreminas [ba·rre·mí·nas] *m.* mine-sweeper.
barrena [ba·rré·na] *f.* auger, drill; gimlet (*small tool for boring holes*); spinning dive (*of a plane*).
barrenar [ba·rre·nár] *v.* to drill, bore; to scuttle (*a ship*); to blast (*a rock*).
barrendero [ba·rren·dé·ro] *m.* sweeper.
barrer [ba·rrér] *v.* to sweep; to sweep away; *Am.* to defeat; *Am.* **al** — altogether, as a whole.
barrera [ba·rré·ra] *f.* barrier; obstacle.
barreta [ba·rré·ta] *f.* small iron bar; *Mex., Cuba, Col.* pick, pickaxe.
barrica [ba·rrí·ka] *f.* cask, keg.
barrida [ba·rrí·ƌa] *f. Am.* sweep, sweeping.
barrido [ba·rrí·ƌo] *m.* sweep, sweeping; sweepings; *p.p. of* **barrer.**
barriga [ba·rrí·ga] *f.* belly; bulge.
barrigón [ba·rri·gón], **barrigudo** [ba·rri·gú·ƌo] *adj.* big-bellied.
barril [ba·rríl] *m.* barrel, keg.
barrilete [ba·rri·lé·te] *m.* clamp.
barrio [bá·rrjo] *m.* district, neighborhood, quarter; **-s bajos** slums.
barro [bá·rro] *m.* (*tierra*) mud, clay; (*granillo*) pimple; *Am.* **hacer** (*or* **cometer**) **un** — to commit a blunder.
barroso [ba·rró·so] *adj.* muddy; pimply; reddish.
barrote [ba·rró·te] *m.* short, thick bar; brace; rung (*of a ladder or chair*).
barruntar [ba·rrun·tár] *v.* to foresee; to have a presentiment; to conjecture.
barrunto [ba·rrún·to] *m.* foreboding, presentiment; guess; hint, indication, sign.
bártulos [bár·tu·los] *m. pl.* household goods; implements, tools.
barullo [ba·rú·yo] *m.* hubbub, racket, disorder.
basa [bá·sa] *f.* base, pedestal; basis, foundation.
basar [ba·sár] *v.* to base; to put on a base.
basca [bás·ka] *f.* nausea, sickness to one's stomach; **tener -s** to be nauseated, sick to one's stomach.
báscula [bás·ku·la] *f.* scale (*for weighing*), platform scale.
base [bá·se] *f.* base, basis, foundation.
básico [bá·si·ko] *adj.* basic.
basquear [bas·ke·ár] *v.* to heave, try to vomit; to be nauseated, sick to one's stomach.
basquetbol [bas·ke·ƀól] *m.* basketball.
bastante [bas·tán·te] *adj.* enough, sufficient; *adv.* enough.
bastar [bas·tár] *v.* to be enough; to suffice.
bastardilla [bas·tar·ƌí·ya] *f.* italic type, italics.
bastardo [bas·tár·ƌo] *adj.* bastard.
bastidor [bas·ti·ƌór] *m.* wing (*of a stage*); frame; embroidery frame; window sash; easel (*support*

for a picture, blackboard, etc.); **entre -es** behind the scenes, off stage.
bastilla [bas·tí·ya] *f.* hem.
bastimento [bas·ti·mén·to] *m.* supply, provisions; vessel, ship.
basto [bás·to] *adj.* coarse; *m.* club (*in cards*); *Am.* saddle pad.
bastón [bas·tón] *m.* cane, walking stick.
basura [ba·sú·ra] *f.* rubbish, scraps; garbage; refuse.
basurero [ba·su·ré·ro] *m.* garbage or rubbish dump; manure pile; garbage man, rubbish man; street cleaner.
bata [bá·ta] *f.* lounging robe; housecoat, wrapper, dressing gown; smock; **batín** [ba·tín] *m.* smock.
batahola [ba·ta·ó·la] *f.* hubbub, racket, uproar.
batalla [ba·tá·ya] *f.* battle; struggle.
batallar [ba·ta·yár] *v.* to battle, fight, struggle.
batallón [ba·ta·yón] *m.* battalion.
batata [ba·tá·ta] *f. Caribe, Sp.* sweet potato.
bate [bá·te] *m.* baseball bat.
batea [ba·té·a] *f.* tray; trough; bowl; barge; *Am.* washtub.
bateador [ba·te·a·ƌór] *m.* batter (*in baseball*).
batear [ba·te·ár] *v.* to bat.
batería [ba·te·rí·a] *f.* battery (*military, naval, or electric*); — **de cocina** set of kitchen utensils; — **de jazz** a jazz combo; *Mex.* **dar** — to raise a rumpus; to plod, work hard.
batidor [ba·ti·ƌór] *m.* beater; scout.
batintín [ba·tin·tín] *m.* gong.
batir [ba·tír] *v.* (*combatir*) to beat, whip, defeat; (*reconocer*) reconnoiter, explore; (*mover*) to flap; *Ch.* to rinse (*clothes*); *Ríopl.* to denounce; **-se** to fight; — **palmas** to clap, applaud.
batisfera [ba·tis·fé·ra] *f.* bathysphere.
baturrillo [ba·tu·rrí·yo] *m.* medley, mixture; hodgepodge.
batuta [ba·tú·ta] *f.* orchestra conductor's baton or wand; **llevar la** — to lead; to be the leader.
baúl [ba·úl] *m.* trunk, chest; — **mundo** large trunk.
bautismo [baw·tíz·mo] *m.* baptism, christening; **nombre de** — Christian name.
bautista [baw·tís·ta] *m. & f.* Baptist; baptizer.
bautizar[9] [baw·ti·sár] *v.* to baptize, christen.
bautizo [baw·tí·so] *m.* christening, baptism.
baya [bá·ya] *f.* berry.
bayeta [ba·yé·ta] *f.* flannel, flannelette; **bayetón** *m.* thick wool cloth; *Col.* long poncho lined with flannel.
bayo [bá·yo] *adj.* bay, reddish-brown.
baza [bá·sa] *f.* trick (*cards played in one round*); **meter** — to meddle; to butt into a conversation; **no dejar meter** — not to let a person put a word in edgewise.
bazar [ba·sár] *m.* bazaar; department store.
bazo [bá·so] *m.* spleen.
bazofia [ba·só·fja] *f.* scraps, refuse, garbage; dregs.
beatitud [be·a·ti·túd] *f.* bliss, blessedness.
beato [be·á·to] *adj.* blessed; beatified; devout; overpious; hypocritical.
bebé [be·ƀé] *m.* baby.
bebedero [be·ƀe·ƌé·ro] *m.* drinking trough; watering place; spout.
bebedor [be·ƀe·ƌór] *m.* drinker; drunkard.
beber [be·ƀér] *v.* to drink; to drink in, absorb.
bebida [be·ƀí·ƌa] *f.* drink, beverage; **dado a la** — given to drink.
beca [bé·ka] *f.* scholarship, fellowship; sash worn over the academic gown.

becario [be·ká·rjo] *m.* scholar, fellow, holder of a scholarship.

becerro [be·sé·rro] *m.* young bull (*less than a year old*); calf; calfskin.

becuadro [be·kwá·ḍro] *m.* natural sign (*in music*).

bedel [be·ḍél] *m.* beadle.

befa [bé·fa] *f.* scoff, jeer.

befar [be·fár] *v.* to scoff, jeer at, mock.

bejuco [be·xú·ko] *m.* reed; **silla de** — cane chair.

beldad [bel·dáḍ] *f.* beauty.

belga [bél·ga] *adj., m. & f.* Belgian.

bélico [bé·li·ko] *adj.* warlike.

beligerante [be·li·xe·rán·te] *adj., m. & f.* belligerent.

bellaco [be·yá·ko] *adj.* sly, deceitful; *m.* villain; rascal.

bellaquear [be·ya·ke·ár] *v.* to cheat; to play tricks; *Am.* to rear, stand up on the hind legs; *Am.* to balk; *Am.* to be touchy, oversensitive.

bellaquería [be·ya·ke·rí·a] *f.* cunning, trickery; sly act or remark.

belleza [be·yé·sa] *f.* beauty.

bello [bé·yo] *adj.* beautiful.

bellota [be·yó·ta] *f.* acorn.

bemol [be·mól] *adj.* flat (*in music*); **tener -es** to have difficulties.

bendecir[27, 52] [ben·de·sír] *v. irr.* to bless.

bendición [ben·di·sjón] *f.* benediction, blessing; *Mex., C.A., Col., Ven.* **echarle la — a una cosa** to give something up for lost.

bendito [ben·di·to] *adj.* blessed; saintly; **es un —** he is a saint, he is a simple soul; *p.p. of* **bendecir.**

benefactor [be·ne·fak·tór] *m.* benefactor; patron.

beneficencia [be·ne·fi·sén·sja] *f.* beneficence, kindness, charity; — **pública** welfare.

beneficiar [be·ne·fi·sjár] *v.* to benefit, do good; to cultivate (*land*); to exploit (*a mine*); to treat (*metals*); *Col., Ven.* to slaughter (*cattle*) for marketing.

beneficio [be·ne·fí·sjo] *m.* (*provecho*) benefit, profit; exploitation of a mine; (*cultivo*) cultivation of land; *Am.* fertilizer; *Am.* slaughtering (*of cattle*).

benéfico [be·né·fi·ko] *adj.* beneficent, good, kind.

benemérito [be·ne·mé·ri·to] *m.* worthy, notable; *adj.* worthy.

benevolencia [be·ne·ḅo·len·sja] *f.* benevolence, kindness.

benévolo [be·né·ḅo·lo] *adj.* benevolent, good, kindly.

benigno [be·nig·no] *adj.* benign, gentle, mild, kind.

beodo [be·ó·ḍo] *adj.* drunk; *m.* drunkard.

berbiquí [ber·ḅi·kí] *m.* carpenter's brace.

berenjena [be·reṇ·xí·na] *f.* eggplant; *Mex., C.A.* kind of squash; **berenjenal** *m.* egg-plant patch; **meterse uno en un —** to get into a mess.

bergantín [ber·gan·tín] *m.* brigantine, brig (*square-rigged ship with two masts*).

beriberi [be·ri·ḅé·ri] *m.* beriberi.

berilio [be·ri·ljo] *m.* beryllium.

bermejo [ber·mé·xo] *adj.* crimson, bright red.

bermellón [ber·me·yón] *adj.* vermilion (*bright red*).

berrear [be·rre·ár] *v.* to bellow; to scream; to sing off key.

berrido [be·rrí·ḍo] *m.* bellow, bellowing; scream.

berrinche [be·rrín·če] *m.* fit of anger; tantrum.

berro [bé·rro] *m.* water cress.

berza [bér·sa] *f.* cabbage.

besar [be·sár] *v.* to kiss.

beso [bé·so] *m.* kiss.

bestia [bés·tja] *f.* beast.

bestialidad [bes·tja·li·ḍáḍ] *f.* bestiality, brutality.

besugo [be·sú·go] *m.* sea bream (*a fish*).

besuquear [be·su·ke·ár] *v.* to kiss repeatedly.

betabel [be·ta·ḅél] *f. Mex.* beet.

betún [be·tún] *m.* bitumen (*combustible mineral*); black pitch; shoeblacking.

Biblia [bí·ḅlja] *f.* Bible.

bíblico [bí·ḅli·ko] *adj.* Biblical.

biblioteca [bi·ḅljo·té·ka] *f.* library; set of volumes; bookcase.

bibliotecario [bi·ḅljo·te·ká·rjo] *m.* librarian.

bicarbonato [bi·kar·ḅo·ná·to] *m.* bicarbonate.

bicicleta [bi·si·klé·ta] *f.* bicycle; **biciclista** [bi·si·klís·ta], **bicicletista** [bi·si·kle·tís·ta] *m. & f.* bicyclist, bicycle rider.

bicho [bí·čo] *m.* insect, bug; any small animal; an insignificant person.

biela [bjé·la] *f.* connecting rod (*of an engine*).

bien [bjen] *adv.* well; — **que** although; **ahora —** now then; **más —** rather; **si —** although; *m.* good, benefit; **-es** property; **-es inmuebles** real estate; **-es raíces** real estate.

bienaventurado [bje·na·ḅen·tu·rá·ḍo] *adj.* blessed, happy.

bienaventuranza [bje·na·ḅen·tu·ran·sa] *f.* blessedness; beatitude; bliss.

bienestar [bje·nes·tár] *m.* well-being, comfort, welfare.

bienhechor [bje·ne·čór] *m.* benefactor.

bienvenida [bjem·be·ní·ḍa] *f.* welcome.

bienvenido [bjem·be·ní·ḍo] *adj.* welcome.

biftec [bif·ték], **bistec** [bis·ték], **bisté** [bis·té] *m.* beefsteak.

bifurcación [bi·fur·ka·sjón] *f.* fork, forking, branching out; railway junction; branch railroad.

bifurcarse[6] [bi·fur·kár·se] *v.* to fork, branch off, divide into two branches.

bigamía [bi·ga·mí·a] *f.* bigamy.

bigote [bi·gó·te] *m.* mustache.

bikini [bi·ki·ni] *m.* bikini bathing suit.

bilabial [bi·la·ḅjál] *adj.* bilabial.

bilingüe [bi·liṇ·gwe] *adj.* bilingual.

bilingüismo [bi·liṇ·gwíz·mo] *m.* bilingualism.

bilis [bí·lis] *f.* bile.

billar [bi·yár] *m.* billiards; billiard room.

billete [bi·yé·te] *m.* ticket; note; bill, banknote.

billón [bi·yón] *m.* billion.

bimestre [bi·més·tre] *m.* two-month period; bi-monthly salary, rent, etc.; *adj.* bi-monthly; **bimestral** [bi·mes·trál] *adj.* bimonthly.

biografía [bjo·gra·fí·a] *f.* biography.

biología [bjo·lo·xí·a] *f.* biology.

biombo [bjom·bo] *m.* folding screen.

birlar [bir·lár] *v.* to snatch away; to steal; to kill or knock down with one blow.

birrete [bi·rré·te] *m.* academic cap; mortarboard.

bisabuelo [bi·sa·ḅwé·lo] *m.* great-grandfather; **bisabuela** *f.* great-grandmother.

bisagra [bi·sá·gra] *f.* hinge.

bisel [bi·sél] *m.* bevel.

bisiesto [bi·sjés·to] *adj.* leap (*year*).

bismuto [biz·mú·to] *m.* bismuth.

bisojo [bi·só·xo] *adj.* squint-eyed.

bisonte [bi·són·te] *m.* bison; the American buffalo.

bisturí [bis·tu·rí] *m.* bistoury, surgical knife.

bitoque [bi·tó·ke] *m.* barrel plug, stopper; *Am.* faucet; *Col., Cuba, Mex.* injection point (*of a syringe*).

bizarría [bi·sa·rrí·a] *f.* gallantry, bravery; generosity.

bizarro [bi·sá·rro] *adj.* gallant, brave; generous.

bizco [bís·ko] *adj.* cross-eyed.
bizcocho [bis·kó·čo] *m.* hardtack, hard biscuit; cake; cookie; — **borracho** cake dipped in wine.
biznieto [biz·njé·to] *m.* great-grandson; **biznieta** *f.* great-granddaughter.
blanco [bláŋ·ko] *adj. (color)* white; *m.* white man; *(nada escrito)* blank, blank sheet; *(objeto de tiro)* target, goal.
blancura [blaŋ·kú·ra] *f.* whiteness.
blancuzco [blaŋ·kús·ko], **blanquecino** [blaŋ·ke·sí·no], **blanquizco** [blaŋ·kís·ko] *adj.* whitish.
blandir [blan·dír] *v.* to brandish, flourish, swing.
blando [blán·do] *adj.* bland, smooth; soft; **blanducho** *adj.* flabby; soft.
blandura [blan·dú·ra] *f.* softness; mildness, gentleness.
blanquear [blaŋ·ke·ár] *v.* to whiten, bleach; to whitewash; to show white; to begin to turn white.
blanqueo [blaŋ·ké·o] *m.* whitening, bleach, bleaching.
blanquillo [blaŋ·kí·yo] *adj.* whitish; white *(flour)*; *m. Mex., C.A.* egg; *Peru, Ch., Andes* white peach.
blasfemar [blas·fe·már] *v.* to blaspheme, curse, swear.
blasfemia [blas·fé·mja] *f.* blasphemy.
blasón [bla·són] *m.* coat of arms; honor, glory.
blasonar [bla·so·nár] *v.* to boast.
blindaje [blin·dá·xe] *m.* armor, armor plating.
blindar [blin·dár] *v.* to armor.
bloc [blok] *m. Am.* tablet, pad of paper.
blocaje [blo·ká·xe] *m.* action of blocking.
blondo [blón·do] *adj.* blond.
bloque [bló·ke] *m.* block *(of stone, wood, etc.)*; *Am.* tablet, pad of paper; *Cuba, Mex., Ríopl.* political bloc.
bloquear [blo·ke·ár] *v.* to blockade.
bloqueo [blo·ké·o] *m.* blockade.
blusa [blú·sa] *f.* blouse.
boato [bo·á·to] *m.* pomp, ostentation.
bobada [bo·bá·da] *f.* foolishness, folly.
bobalicón [bo·ba·li·kón] *adj.* foolish, silly; *m.* simpleton, blockhead, dunce.
bobear [bo·be·ár] *v.* to act like a fool; to fool around; to gawk, stare foolishly.
bobería [bo·be·rí·a] *f.* foolishness, folly; nonsense; foolish remark.
bobina [bo·bí·na] *f.* bobbin, reel; electric coil; — **distribuidora** feeding reel; — **receptora** rewind reel *(on a tape recorder)*.
bobo [bo·bo] *adj.* simple, foolish, stupid; *m.* booby, fool, dunce.
boca [bó·ka] *f.* mouth; opening; — **abajo** face downward; — **arriba** face upward; **a — de jarro** at close range; **bocaza** *f.* large mouth.
bocacalle [bo·ka·ká·ye] *f.* street intersection.
bocado [bo·ká·do] *m.* mouthful, morsel, bite; bit *(of a bridle)*; **bocadillo** [bo·ka·dí·yo], **bocadito** [bo·ka̧·dí·to] *m.* snack; sandwich; tidbit; *Am.* piece of candy.
bocanada [bo·ka·ná·da] *f.* mouthful; puff *(of smoke)*.
boceto [bo·sé·to] *m.* sketch; outline; skit.
bocina [bo·sí·na] *f.* horn; trumpet; automobile horn; speaking tube; megaphone.
bochorno [ba·čór·no] *m.* sultry weather; suffocating heat; blush, flush; embarrassment.
bochornoso [bo·čor·nó·so] *adj.* sultry; embarrassing.
boda [bó·da] *f.* marriage, wedding; — **de negros**

a noisy party; **-s de Camacho** lavish feast, banquet.
bodega [bo·dé·ga] *f.* cellar; wine cellar; storeroom; warehouse; *Cuba, Ven., Col.* grocery store; **bodeguero** *m.* keeper of a wine cellar; liquor dealer; *Cuba, Ven., Col.* grocer.
bodoque [bo·dó·ke] *m.* wad; lump; dunce; *Am.* bump, swelling.
bofe [bó·fe] *m.* lung; *P.R.* snap, easy job; **echar uno los -s** to throw oneself into a job; to work hard; *Am.* **ser un —** to be a bore; to be repulsive.
bofetada [bo·fe·tá·da] *f.* slap; **bofetón** *m.* big slap, blow, hard sock, wallop.
boga [bó·ga] *f.* vogue, fashion; rowing; *m.* rower.
bogar[7] [bo·gár] *v.* to row.
bohemio [bo·é·mjo] *adj. & m.* Bohemian.
bohío [bo·í·o] *m. Carib., Ven.* cabin, shack, hut.
boina *f.* cap.
bola [bó·la] *f. (esfera)* ball, bowling; *(mentira)* fib, lie; *(betún)* shoe polish; *Am.* disturbance, riot, false rumor; **no dar pie con —** not to do things right; not to hit the mark; to make mistakes; *Am.* **darle a la —** to hit the mark.
boleada [bo·le·áda] *f. Ríopl.* lassoing with **boleadoras**; *Ríopl.* hunting expedition *(with* **boleadoras***)*; *Mex.* shoeshine; *Col.* affront, insult.
boleadoras [bo·le·a·dó·ras] *f. pl. Ríopl.* throwing weapon made of three united thongs with balls at the ends.
bolear [bo·le·ár] *v.* to play billiards; to bowl; to lie, fib; *Am.* to lasso with **boleadoras**; *Am.* to entangle; *Am.* to polish *(shoes)*; *Am.* to dismiss; *Am.* to blackball, vote against; *Am.* to flunk; **-se** *Am.* to rear, balk *(said of a horse)*; *Am.* to blush, be ashamed.
boleta [bo·lé·ta] *f.* certificate; pass; pay order; *Mex., C.A.* ballot; *Ch.* first draft of a deed.
boletín [bo·le·tín] *m.* bulletin.
boleto [bo·lé·to] *m. Am.* ticket; **boletería** *f. Am.* ticket office.
boliche [bo·lí·če] *m.* bowl *(wooden ball for bowling)*; bowling alley; *Ríopl.* cheap tavern; *Ch.* gambling joint; *Ríopl.* cheap store or shop, notions store, variety store.
bolígrafo [bo·lí·gra·fo] *m.* ball point pen.
bolillo *m. Mex., C.A.* hard roll.
bolita [bo·lí·ta] *f.* small ball; *Am.* ballot *(small ball used in voting)*; *Col., Ven.* marble; *Am.* armadillo.
bolo [bó·lo] *m.* one of the ninepins *(used in bowling)*; dunce, stupid fellow; **-s** bowls, bowling; **jugar a los -s** to bowl.
bolsa [ból·sa] *f.* bag, purse; stock exchange; *Ríopl.* pocket.
bolsillo [bol·sí·yo] *m.* pocket; pocketbook.
bolsista [bol·sís·ta] *m.* stockbroker, market operator.
bollo [bó·yo] *m.* bun, muffin; bump, lump; puff *(in a dress)*; tuft *(on upholstery)*; *Andes* loaf of bread; *Am.* a kind of tamale; **-s** *Am.* difficulties, troubles.
bomba [bóm·ba] *f.* pump; lamp globe; bomb; — **atómica** atomic bomb; — **de hidrógeno** hydrogen bomb; *Carib.* false news; *Am.* stanza improvised by a dancer; *Ríopl.* firecracker, skyrocket; *Mex., Col.* satirical remark; *Am.* large drum; — **para incendios** fire engine; *Am.* **estar con una —** to be drunk; **bombita** *f.* soap bubble; *Col.* shame, embarrassment.

bombachas [bom·bá·čas] *f. pl. Ríopl.* loose-fitting breeches.
bombacho [bom·bá·čo] *adj.* loose-fitting *(trousers or breeches).*
bombardear [bom·bar·ḍe·ár] *v.* to bomb.
bombardeo [bom·bar·ḍé·o] *m.* bombardment, bombing; **avión de** — bomber, bombing plane.
bombardero [bom·bar·ḍé·ro] *m.* bombardier; bomber.
bombear [bom·be·ár] *v.* *(echar bombas)* to bomb; *(alabar)* to praise, extol; *Am.* to pump; *Col.* to fire, dismiss; *Am.* to puff hard on a cigar or cigarette.
bombero [bom·bé·ro] *m.* fireman; pumper.
bombilla [bom·bí·ya] *f.* electric-light bulb; *Am.* kerosene lamp tube; *Am.* small tube for drinking mate.
bombo [bóm·bo] *m.* large drum; bass drum; player on a bass drum; *Mex., Col., Ch.* pomp, ostentation; *Ríopl.* buttocks, rump; **dar** — to praise, extol *(in the press or newspapers)*; *Col., Ríopl.* **darse** — to put on airs; *Am.* **irse uno al** — to fail; *adj.* stunned; *Am.* lukewarm; *Am.* slightly rotten; *Am.* stupid, silly, simple; *Cuba* **fruta bomba** papaya *(tropical fruit).*
bombón [bom·bón] *m.* bonbon, candy; — **de altea** marshmallow.
bonachón [bon·na·čón] *adj.* good-natured; naïve, simple.
bonanza [bo·nán·sa] *f.* fair weather; prosperity; rich vein of ore.
bondad [bon·dáḍ] *f.* goodness.
bondadoso [bon·da·ḍó·so] *adj.* good, kind.
boniato [bo·njá·to] *m. Am.* sweet potato.
bonito [bo·ní·to] *adj.* pretty; *m.* striped tunny *(a fish).*
bono [bó·no] *m.* certificate; bond.
boñiga [bo·ñí·ga] *f.* dung, manure.
boqueada [bo·ke·á·ḍa] *f.* gape, gasp.
boquear [bo·ke·ár] *v.* to open one's mouth; to gape, gasp; to be dying.
boquete [bo·ké·te] *m.* breach, gap, hole, opening.
boquiabierto [bo·kja·bjér·to] *adj.* openmouthed.
boquilla [bo·ki·ya] *f.* *(abertura)* little mouth; small opening; *(de cigarro)* holder; tip; *(de instrumento)* mouthpiece.
borbollón [bor·bo·yón], **borbotón** [bor·bo·tón] *m.* spurt; spurting; big bubble; bubbling up; **a -es** in spurts.
borbotar [bor·bo·tár] *v.* to bubble up; to spurt, gush forth; to boil over.
bordado [bor·dá·ḍo] *m.* embroidery.
bordadura [bor·da·ḍú·ra] *f.* embroidery.
bordar [bor·dár] *v.* to embroider.
borde [bór·ḍe] *m.* border, edge.
bordear [bor·ḍe·ár] *v.* to skirt, go along the edge of; *Am.* to trim with a border; *Am.* to make a **bordo** *(small, temporary dam)*; **-se** *Ch., Mex., Ven.* to approach, get near.
bordo [bór·ḍo] *m.* board, side of a ship; tack *(of a ship)*; *Mex., Ven.* ridge *(of a furrow)*; *Mex.* small dam; **a** — on board.
borla [bór·la] *f.* *(indumentaria)* tassel; doctor's cap; *(título)* doctor's degree; *(cosmético)* powder puff; tuft; **tomar uno la** — to get a doctor's degree.
borlarse [bor·lár·se] *v. Am.* to get a doctor's degree.
boro [bó·ro] *m.* boron.
borrachera [bo·rra·čé·ra] *f.* drunkenness; drunken spree.
borrachín [bo·rra·čín] *m.* toper.

borracho [bo·rrá·čo] *adj.* drunk; *m.* drunkard; **borrachón** [bo·rra·čón] *m.* drunkard, heavy drinker.
borrador [bo·rra·ḍór] *m.* rough draft; *Am.* rubber eraser.
borrar [bo·rrár] *v.* to blot out; to erase.
borrasca [bo·rrás·ka] *f.* storm, tempest.
borrascoso [bo·rras·kó·so] *adj.* stormy.
borrego [bo·rré·go] *m.* lamb; fool, simpleton; *Mex.,* *C.A.* false news.
borrico [bo·rrí·ko] *m.* donkey, ass; fool; sawhorse.
borrón [bo·rrón] *m.* blotch *(of ink)*, blot.
borronear [bo·rro·ne·ár] *v.* to blot, blotch; to scribble; to blur; to make a rough sketch.
boruca [bo·rú·ka] *f.* racket, noise.
boscaje [bos·ká·xe] *m.* grove, thicket, woods; landscape *(picture of natural scenery).*
bosque [bós·ke] *m.* forest, woods; **bosquecillo** *m.* small forest, grove.
bosquejar [bos·ke·xár] *v.* to sketch; to outline.
bosquejo [bos·ké·xo] *m.* sketch, plan, outline, rough draft.
bostezar[9] [bos·te·sár] *v.* to yawn.
bostezo [bos·té·so] *m.* yawn.
bota [bó·ta] *f.* *(calzado)* boot; *(bolsa)* leather wine bag; *adj. Am.* stupid, clumsy; *Mex.* drunk.
botar [bo·tár] *v.* *(echar)* to launch; to fling; to throw away; *(rebotar)* to bounce; *Ven.* to waste, squander; *Am.* to fire, dismiss; **-se** *Am.* to lie down.
botarate [bo·ta·rá·te] *m.* fool; braggart; *Mex.,* *Carib.* spendthrift.
bote [bó·te] *m.* *(jarro)* small jar; *(embarcación)* boat; *(rebote)* bounce; *(golpe)* blow; jump; *Ríopl.* liquor bottle; *Mex., C.A.* jail; **estar de** — **en** — to be crowded, completely filled up.
botella [bo·té·ya] *f.* bottle.
botica [bo·tí·ka] *f.* drugstore.
boticario [bo·ti·ká·rjo] *m.* druggist.
botija [bo·tí·xa] *f.* earthen jug; fat person; *Am.* buried treasure; *Am.* belly; *Col.* **poner a uno como** — **verde** to dress down, scold, insult a person.
botijo [bo·tí·xo] *m.* earthen jar with spout and handle.
botín [bo·tín] *m.* booty, plunder; high shoe; *Am.* sock.
botiquín [bo·ti·kín] *m.* medicine cabinet; medicine kit; *Am.* liquor store, wine shop.
botón [bo·tón] *m.* bud; button; knob; handle; **-es** bellboy.
bóveda [bó·be·ḍa] *f.* arched roof; vault, underground cellar; burial place.
boxeador [bok·se·a·ḍór] *m.* boxer.
boxear [bok·se·ár] *v.* to box, fight with the fists.
boxeo [bok·sé·o] *m.* boxing.
boya [bó·ya] *f.* buoy; float net; *Am.* crease, dent; *Am.* rich mineral vein; *Am.* **estar en la buena** — to be in good humor.
bozal [bo·sál] *m.* *(de animal)* nuzzle; *(cascabel)* bells on a harness; *(novicio)* novice; *(negro)* Negro native of Africa; *Am.* headstall *(of a halter)*; *Spain* person *(especially a Negro)* who speaks broken Spanish; *Am.* coarse, crude individual; *adj.* green, inexperienced; wild, untamed; stupid.
bozo [bó·so] *m.* down *(on the upper lip)*; mustache; outside part of the mouth; headstall *(of a halter).*
bracear [bra·se·ár] *v.* to swing one's arms; to struggle; to crawl, swim with a crawl.

bracero [bra·sé·ro] *m.* laborer; **de** — arm in arm; **servir de** — **a una señora** to serve as an escort, give a lady one's arm.

bracete [bra·sé·te]: **de** — arm in arm.

bramante [bra·mán·te] *m.* hemp cord, hemp string; Brabant linen; *adj.* roaring, bellowing.

bramar [bra·már] *v.* to bellow, roar, howl; to rage.

bramido [bra·mí·đo] *m.* roar; howl; bellow.

brasa [brá·sa] *f.* red-hot coal.

brasero [bra·sé·ro] *m.* brazier *(pan for burning coal)*, grate; hearth; *Ríopl.* brick cooking stove.

bravata [bra·bá·ta] *f.* bravado, boastfulness, defiance.

bravear [bra·be·ár] *v.* to bluster; to bully.

bravío [bra·bí·o] *adj.* savage, wild; rustic.

bravo [brá·bo] *adj. (agresivo)* wild, ferocious, harsh; ill-tempered; *(valiente)* brave; *Carib., C.A., Andes* angry; *Am.* hot, highly seasoned.

bravura [bra·bú·ra] *f.* fierceness; courage; bravado, show of boldness.

braza [brá·sa] *f.* fathom; stroke.

brazada [bra·sá·đa] *f.* armful; movement of the arms *(swimming stroke)*; **a una** — at arm's length.

brazalete [bra·sa·lé·te] *m.* bracelet.

brazo [brá·so] *m.* arm; branch; **-s** day laborers; *Ríopl., Cuba* **de** — arm in arm; **luchar a** — **partido** to wrestle; to fight hand to hand.

brea [bré·a] *f.* pitch; tar; canvas.

brecha [bré·ča] *f.* breach, gap.

brega [bré·ga] *f.* fight, scrap.

bregar [bre·gár] *v.* to struggle; to fight.

breña [bré·ña] *f.* rough, craggy ground covered with brambles; bramble; **breñal** *m.* brambles; bush country.

breve [bré·be] *adj.* brief, short; **en** — shortly.

brevedad [bre·be·đáđ] *f.* brevity, shortness.

bribón [bri·bón] *adj.* idle, indolent; *m.* rascal, rogue; **bribonazo** *m.* scoundrel, cheat.

brida [brí·đa] *f.* bridle; rein.

brigada [bri·gá·đa] *f.* brigade.

brillante [bri·yán·te] *adj.* brilliant, bright; *m.* diamond.

brillantez [bri·yan·tés] *f.* brilliance, dazzle.

brillar [bri·yár] *v.* to shine.

brillo [brí·yo] *m.* luster, sparkle, shine.

brincar [briŋ·kár] *v.* to hop, skip, jump, bounce.

brinco [bríŋ·ko] *m.* hop, skip, bounce, leap.

brindar [brin·dár] *v.* to toast, drink to the health of; to offer.

brindis [brín·dis] *m.* toast *(to a person's health)*.

brío [brí·o] *m.* vigor, liveliness; valor, courage.

brioso [brjó·so] *adj.* lively; brave.

brisa [brí·sa] *f.* breeze.

británico [bri·tá·ni·ko] *adj.* British.

brizna [bríz·na] *f.* particle, chip, fragment; blade of grass.

brocal [bro·kál] *m.* curb, curbstone *(of a well)*.

brocha [bró·ča] *f.* painter's brush; loaded dice; **cuadro de** — **gorda** badly done painting; **pintor de** — **gorda** house painter **brochada** *f.* stroke of the brush, brush stroke; **brochazo** *m.* blow with a brush; brush stroke.

broche [bró·če] *m.* brooch; clasp, clip, fastener; hook and eye.

broma [bró·ma] *f.* jest, joke; fun, merriment; *Am.* disappointment, irritation; **de** — in jest; **fuera de** — all joking aside.

bromear [bro·me·ár] *v.* to joke, jest.

bronca [bróŋ·ka] *f.* quarrel, dispute, wrangle;

armar una — to cause a disturbance, raise a rumpus.

bronce [brón·se] *m.* bronze.

bronceado [bron·se·áđo] *adj.* bronzed; bronze-colored; *m.* bronze finish.

bronco [bróŋ·ko] *adj.* hoarse; raspy, harsh; coarse, rough; uncouth; wild, untamed *(horse)*.

bronquio [bróŋ·kjo] *m.* bronchus, bronchial tube.

broquel [bro·kél] *m.* buckler, shield *(worn on the arm)*.

brotar [bro·tár] *v.* to shoot forth; to bud; to break out *(on the skin)*; to gush, flow; to spring forth.

broza [bró·sa] *f.* brushwood, underbush; rubbish, refuse, trash; coarse, hard brush.

bruces [brú·ses]: **de** — face downward.

bruja [brú·xa] *f.* witch; hag; owl; *adj. Mex.* broke, poor; **brujo** *m.* sorcerer, magician, wizard.

brújula [brú·xu·la] *f. (compás)* compass; magnetic needle; *(mira)* peephole; gunsight.

bruma [brú·ma] *f.* mist, fog; **brumoso** *adj.* foggy, misty, hazy.

bruñir[19] [bru·ñír] *v. irr.* to burnish, polish; to put on make-up.

brusco [brús·ko] *adj.* blunt, rude, abrupt.

brutal [bru·tál] *adj.* brutal, beastly, savage.

brutalidad [bru·ta·li·đáđ] *f.* brutality.

bruto [brú·to] *adj. (tonto)* stupid, brutal; *(burdo)* coarse, rough; **peso** — gross weight; **diamante en** — diamond in the rough, unpolished diamond; *m.* brute, beast.

bucal [bu·kál] *adj.* oral, pertaining to the mouth.

bucear [bu·se·ár] *v.* to dive; to dive into, plunge into; to explore thoroughly a subject.

bucle [bú·kle] *m.* curl, ringlet.

buche [bú·če] *m.* crop *(of a bird)*; mouthful *(of water)*; wrinkle, bag *(in clothes)*; *Ríopl. Mex., Ven.* goiter.

budín *m.* pudding.

buen(o) [bwé·n(o)] *adj.* good; kind; useful; well, in good health; **de buenas a primeras** all of a sudden, unexpectedly, on the spur of the moment; **por la(s) buena(s) o por la(s) mala(s)** willingly or unwillingly, by hook or crook.

buey [bwej] *m.* ox.

búfalo [bú·fa·lo] *m.* buffalo.

bufanda [bu·fán·da] *f.* muffler, scarf.

bufar [bu·fár] *v.* to snort; to puff with anger; **-se** *Mex.* to swell, bulge *(as a wall)*.

bufete [bu·fé·te] *m.* desk, writing table; lawyer's office.

bufido [bu·fí·đo] *m.* snort.

bufón [bu·fón] *m.* buffoon, jester, clown; *adj.* comical, funny; **bufonada** [bu·fo·ná·đa] *f.* wisecrack; jest.

bufonear [bu·fo·ne·ár] *v.* to clown; to jest.

buhardilla [bu·ar·đí·ya], [bwar·đí·ya] *f.* garret, attic; skylight.

buho [bú·o] *m.* owl.

buhonero [bu·o·né·ro] *m.* peddler.

buitre [bwí·tre] *m.* vulture.

buje [bú·xe] *m.* bushing; axle box.

bujía [bu·xí·a] *f.* candle; candle power; candlestick; spark plug.

bula [bú·la] *f.* bull *(papal document)*; papal seal.

buldózer [bul·dó·ser] *m.* bulldozer.

bulevar [bu·le·bár] *m.* boulevard.

bulto [búl·to] *m. (cuerpo)* body, bundle, shadow, lump, swelling; *(tamaño)* bulk, volume; **a** — haphazardly, by guess; **escurrir el** — to dodge; **imagen de** — statue, sculpture; **una verdad de** — an evident truth.

bulla [bú·ya] *f.* shouting, uproar; noisy crowd.
bullicio [bu·yí·sjo] *m.* noise, uproar.
bullicioso [bu·yi·sjó·so] *adj.* boisterous, noisy; gay, lively; turbulent, stormy.
bullir[20] [bu·yír] *v. irr.* to boil; to buzz about; to bustle; to stir, move; *Am.* to deride.
buñuelo [bu·ñwé·lo] *m.* fritter; botch, poor piece of work.
buque [bú·ke] *m.* ship, boat.
burbuja [bur·bú·xa] *f.* bubble.
burdo [búr·ḍo] *adj.* coarse.
burgués [bur·gés] *adj.* bourgeois, middle-class.
burla [búr·la] *f.* jest, mockery; **de —** in jest.
burlador [bur·la·ḍór] *m.* practical joker; jester; scoffer; seducer.
burlar [bur·lár] *v.* to mock, ridicule, deceive; **-se de** to scoff at; to make fun of
burlón [bur·lón] *m.* jester, teaser.
burocracia [bu·ro·krá·sja] *f.* bureaucracy.
burócrata [bu·ró·kra·ta] *m.* bureaucrat.
burro [bú·rro] *m.* ass, donkey; *Mex., Cuba, Riopl.* stepladder; *adj.* stupid; **burrito** *m.* small donkey; *Am.* saddle rack.
busca [bús·ka] *f.* search; hunting party; *Am.* **-s** profit on the side; graft.
buscar[6] [bus·kár] *v.* to seek, search, look for; *Andes* to provoke.
búsqueda [bús·ke·ḍa] *f.* search.
busto [bús·to] *m.* bust (*upper part of body*).
butaca [bu·tá·ka] *f.* armchair; orchestra seat; **butacón** [bu·ta·kón] *m.* large armchair.
buzo [bú·so] *m.* diver; deep-sea or "skin" diver.
buzón [bu·són] *m.* mailbox; letter drop.

C:c **cabal** [ka·bál] *adj.* complete, entire; exact; **estar uno en sus -es** to be in one's right mind.
cabalgar[7] [ka·bal·gár] *v.* to ride, mount (*a horse*); to ride horseback.
caballa [ka·bá·ya] *f.* horse mackerel.
caballada [ka·ba·yá·ḍa] *f.* herd of horses; *Am.* nonsense, stupidity, blunder.
caballejo [ka·ba·yè·xo] *m.* nag; poor horse.
caballeresco [ka·ba·ye·rés·ko] *adj.* gentlemanly; knightly; chivalrous, gallant.
caballería [ka·ba·ye·rí·a] *f.* cavalry; horsemanship; mount, horse; knighthood; chivalry.
caballeriza [ka·ba·ye·rí·sa] *f.* stable; horses of a stable.
caballerizo [ka·ba·ye·rí·so] *m.* groom, stableman.
caballero [ka·ba·yé·ro] *m.* gentleman; knight, horseman; *adj.* gentlemanly.
caballerosidad [ka·ba·ye·ro·si·ḍáḍ] *f.* chivalry, gentlemanly conduct.
caballeroso [ka·ba·ye·ró·so] *adj.* chivalrous, gentlemanly.
caballete [ka·ba·yé·te] *m.* (*de casa*) ridge of a roof; (*madero*) sawhorse; (*de la cara*) bridge of the nose.
caballo [ka·bá·yo] *m.* horse; knight (*in chess*); *Am.* stupid or brutal person; **a —** on horseback; **caballuco** [ka·ba·yú·ko] *m.* nag.
cabaña [ka·bá·ña] *f.* hut, cabin; *Am.* cattle ranch.
cabecear [ka·be·se·ár] *v.* to nod; to shake the head; to pitch (*as a boat*); *Am.* to begin to rise or fall (*said of a river*).
cabeceo [ka·be·sé·o] *m.* nodding; pitching (*of a boat*).

cabecera [ka·be·sé·ra] *f.* head (*of bed or table*); seat, chief city (*of a district*).
cabecilla [ka·be·sí·ya] *f.* small head; *m.* ringleader.
cabellera [ka·be·yé·ra] *f.* head of hair, long hair; wig; tail of a comet.
cabello [ka·bé·yo] *m.* hair; **traer algo por los -s** to bring in a far-fetched fact or quotation; **-s de ángel** cotton candy.
cabelludo [ka·be·yú·ḍo] *adj.* hairy; **cuero —** scalp.
caber[23] [ka·bér] *v. irr.* to fit into, go into; to have enough room for; to befall; **no cabe duda** there is no doubt; **no cabe más** there is no room for more; **no — uno en sí** to be puffed up with pride; **no cabe en lo posible** it is absolutely impossible.
cabestro [ka·bés·tro] *m.* halter; leading ox; *Carib., Mex.* rope, cord; *Am.* advance payment; **cabestrillo** [ka·bes·trí·yo] *m.* sling (*for an arm*).
cabeza [ka·bé·sa] *f.* (*parte superior*) head; upper part; (*director*) chief, leader; capital (*of a district*); *Carib.* source (*of a river*); **— de playa** beachhead; **— de puente** bridgehead; **— sonora** recording head.
cabezada [ka·be·sá·ḍa] *f.* butt (*with the head*); bump on the head; nod; shake of the head; pitching (*of a ship*); headgear (*of a harness*).
cabezazo [ka·be·sá·so] *m.* butt (with the head); bump on the head.
cabezudo [ka·be·sú·ḍo] *adj.* big-headed; hard-headed, pig-headed, stubborn, headstrong.
cabezón [ka·be·són] *adj.* big-headed; pig-headed, stubborn; *Ch.* strong (*liquor*); *m.* large head; cavesson (*iron noseband used in breaking a horse*); *Col.* rapids or whirlpool in a river.
cabida [ka·bí·ḍa] *f.* space, room, capacity; **tener — con alguien** to have influence with someone.
cabildo [ka·bíl·do] *m.* cathedral chapter; municipal council; council room; town hall.
cabina [ka·bí·na] *f.* cabin (*of an airplane*).
cabizbajo [ka·biz·bá·xo] *adj.* crestfallen, downcast; pensive.
cable [ká·ble] *m.* cable.
cablegrafiar[17] [ka·ble·gra·fjár] *v.* to cable.
cablegrama [ka·ble·grá·ma] *m.* cablegram.
cabo [ká·bo] *m.* (*cosa*) end, tip, handle; piece of rope; (*geográfico*) cape, headland; (*persona*) foreman, corporal; *al* — finally; **al fin y al —** anyway, in the long run; **de — a rabo** from beginning to end; **estar al — de** to be well informed about; **llevar a —** to carry out, finish.
cabotaje [ka·bo·tá·xe] *m.* coastal trade or traffic.
cabra [ká·bra] *f.* goat; *Col.* fraud, trick; *Am.* loaded dice; *Am.* light two-wheeled carriage; **cabrillas** [ka·brí·yas] *f. pl.* whitecaps (*small waves with white crests*); Pleiades (*constellation*); game of skipping stones on the water.
cabrero [ka·bré·ro] *m.* goatherd.
cabrío [ka·brí·o] *adj.* goatish; **macho —** he-goat; *m.* herd of goats.
cabriola [ka·brjó·la] *f.* caper, leap, hop, skip; somersault; **hacer -s** to cut capers; to prance.
cabriolar [ka·brjo·lár] *v.* to prance; to caper; to romp, frolic, frisk.
cabrito [ka·brí·to] *m.* kid; **cabritilla** [ka·bri·tí·ya] *f.* kid, kidskin.
cabrón [ka·brón] *m.* he-goat; cuckold (*man whose wife is unfaithful*).
caca [ká·ka] *f.* excrement (popular children's expression).

cacahuate [ka·ka·wá·te] *m. Mex., C.A.* peanut; *Spain* cacahuete [ka·ka·wé·te], cacahuey ka·ka·wéj].

cacao [ka·ká·o] *m.* cocoa.

cacarear [ka·ka·re·ár] *v.* to cackle; to boast; *Am.* to run away from a fight.

cacareo [ka·ka·ré·o] *m.* cackle.

cacería [ka·se·rí·a] *f.* hunt, hunting.

cacerola [ka·se·ró·la] *f.* saucepan.

cacique [ka·sí·ke] *m.* chief; political boss; *Mex.* tyrant; *Ch., Ven.* one who leads an easy life.

caciquismo [ka·si·kíz·mo] *m.* political bossism (*rule by political bosses*).

cacofonía [ka·ko·fo·ní·a] *f.* cacophony.

cacto [kák·to] *m.* cactus.

cacumen [ka·kú·men] *m.* acumen, keen insight.

cacha [ká·ča] *f.* handle (*of a knife or pistol*); *Am.* the horns of a bull; *C.A.* hacer la — to complete a task, to get.

cacharro [ka·čá·rro] *m.* earthen pot or vase; broken piece of a pot; crude utensil; *Am.* cheap trinket.

cachaza [ka·čá·sa] *f.* slowness; calm; rum.

cachazudo [ka·ča·sú· đo] *adj.* slow, easy going.

cachetada [ka·če·tá·đa] *f. Am.* slap on the face.

cachete [ka·čé·te] *m.* cheek; slap on the cheek.

cachimbo [ka·čím·bo] *m. Am.* pipe (*for smoking*); *Cuba* small sugar mill; also cachimba [ka·čím·ba].

cachivache [ka·či·bá·če] *m.* piece of junk; worthless fellow; *Mex., Carib., Ven.* trinket.

cacho [ká·čo] *m. Am.* horn (of an animal); *adj.* bent, crooked.

cachorro [ka·čó·rro] *m.* cub; small pistol; *Am.* rude, ill-bred person.

cachucha [ka·čú·ča] *f.* cap; rowboat; popular Andalusian dance, song and music; *Am.* slap.

cada [ká·đa] *adj.* each, every; — uno each one; — y cuando que whenever; *Am.* a — nada every second.

cadalso [ka·đál·so] *m.* gallows; scaffold, platform.

cadáver [ka·đá·ber] *m.* corpse; cadavérico [ka·đa·bé·ri·ko] *adj.* deadly, ghastly, pale, like a corpse.

cadena [ka·đé·na] *f.* chain.

cadencia [ka·đen·sja] *f.* cadence.

cadencioso [ka·đen·sjó·so] *adj.* rhythmical.

cadera [ka·đé·ra] *f.* hip.

cadete [ka·đé·te] *m.* cadet.

cadmio [kađ·mjo] *m.* cadmium.

caducar⁶ [ka·đu·kár] *v.* to dote, be in one's dotage; to lapse, expire; to become extinct, fall into disuse.

caduco [ka·đú·ko] *adj.* decrepit, very old, feeble; perishable.

caer²⁴ [ka·ér] *v. irr.* to fall; to fall down; to fall off; -se to fall down, tumble; — a to face, overlook; — bien to fit, be becoming; — en cama to fall ill; — en la cuenta to catch on, get the point; — en gracia to please; al — de la noche at nightfall; dejar — to drop.

café [ka·fé] *m.* coffee, café; *Am.* annoyance, bad time.

cafeína [ka·fe·í·na] *f.* caffein.

cafetal [ka·fe·tál] *m.* coffee plantation.

cafetera [ka·fe·té·ra] *f.* coffeepot; woman café owner, coffee vendor or merchant; coffee-bean picker.

cafetería [ka·fe·te·rí·a] *f.* café, bar, lunchroom.

cafetero [ka·fe·té·ro] *adj.* pertaining to coffee; *m.*

coffee grower; coffee merchant; owner of a café or coffee-house; *Am.* coffee drinker.

cafeto [ka·fé·to] *m.* coffee bush.

cagar⁷ [ka·gár] *v. irr.* to defecate (*popular term*).

caída [ka·í·đa] *f.* fall, drop; descent; a la — del sol (*or* de la tarde) at sunset.

caimán [kaj·mán] *m.* cayman, alligator.

caja [ká·xa] *f.* case, box; — de ahorros savings bank; — de cambios transmission (*automobile*); — de píldora pillbox; — fuerte safe; echar a uno con -s destempladas to give someone the gate.

cajero [ka·xé·ro] *m.* cashier; box maker.

cajetilla [ka·xe·tí·ya] *f.* small box; package of cigarettes.

cajón [ka·xón] *m.* large box, chest; drawer; vendor's booth or stand; *Ch., Mex.* narrow conyon; — de muerto coffin; *Mex.* — de ropa dry-goods and clothing store.

cal [kal] *f.* lime (*mineral*).

calabaza [ka·la·ba·sa] *f.* pumpkin, squash; gourd; an ignorant person; dar -s to jilt, turn down (*a suitor*); to flunk; fail.

calabozo [ka·la·bó·so] *m.* dungeon; prison cell.

calado [ka·lá·đo] *m.* drawn work; openwork (*in wood, metal linen, etc.*), fretwork; draft (*of a ship*).

calamar [ka·la·már] *m.* squid, cuttlefish.

calambre [ka·lám·bre] *m.* cramp.

calamidad [ka·la·mi·đáđ] *f.* calamity, misfortune.

calandria [ka·lan·drja] *f.* lark, skylark.

calar [ka·lár] *v.* (*penetrar*) to pierce, penetrate; to soak through; to make openwork (*in cloth, metal*); (*probar*) to probe, search into; -se el sombrero to put on one's hat; to pull down one's hat.

calavera [ka·la·bé·ra] *f.* skull; *m.* madcap, rounder, reckless fellow; *Mex.* taillight.

calcar⁶ [kal·kár] *v.* to trace; to copy, imitate.

calceta [kal·sé·ta] *f.* hose, stocking; hacer — to knit; calcetería [kal·se·te·rí·a] *f.* hosiery shop; hosiery (*business of making hose*).

calcetín [kal·se·tín] *m.* sock.

calcinar [kal·si·nár] *v.* to burn, char, heat.

calcio [kál·sjo] *m.* calcium.

calco [kál·ko] *m.* tracing, traced copy; exact copy; imitation.

calculadora [kal·ku·la·đó·ra] *f.* calculator (*machine for performing mathematical operations*); — electrónica computer.

calcular [kal·ku·lár] *v.* to calculate, figure, estimate.

cálculo [kál·ku·lo] *m.* calculation, estimate; calculus; gravel (*in the gall bladder, kidney, etc.*).

caldear [kal·de·ár] *v.* to heat; to weld; -se *Am.* to become overheated, excited; *Am.* to get "lit up", get drunk.

caldera [kal·dé·ra] *f.* boiler; caldron, kettle; calderilla [kal·de·rí·ya] *f.* copper coin.

caldo [kál·do] *m.* broth; gravy.

calefacción [ka·le·fak·sjón] *f.* heat, heating.

calendario [ka·len·dá·rjo] *m.* calendar; almanac.

caléndula [ka·lén·du·la] *f.* marigold.

calentador [ka·len·ta·đór] *m.* heater.

calentar¹ [ka·len·tár] *v. irr.* to warm, heat; to spank; *Am.* to annoy, bother; -se to warm oneself; to become heated, excited; to be in heat; *Am.* to become angry.

calentura [ka·len·tú·ra] *f.* fever; *Col.* fit of temper; — de pollo feigned illness; calenturón [ka·len·tu·rón] *m.* high fever.

calenturiento [ka·len·tu·rjén·to] *adj.* feverish; *Ch.* tubercular.

caletre [ka·lé·tre] *m.* judgment, acumen, keen insight.

calibrar [ka·li·ɓrár] *v.* to gauge, measure; to measure the caliber of.

calibre [ka·lí·ɓre] *m.* caliber; bore, gauge (*of a gun*); diameter (*of a pipe, tube, wire*).

calicanto [ka·li·kán·to] *m.* stone masonry.

calicó [ka·li·kó] *m.* calico, cotton cloth.

calidad [ka·li·ɗáɗ] *f.* quality.

cálido [ká·li·ɗo] *adj.* warm, hot.

caliente [ka·ljén·te] *adj.* warm, hot; heated; fiery; *Am.* angry; *Col.* bold brave; *m. Am.* brandy in hot water; **calientito** *adj.* nice and warm.

calificación [ka·li·fi·sjón] *f.* qualification; grade, mark (*in a course or examination*); judgment.

calificar[6] [ka·li·fi·kár] *v.* to qualify; to rate, consider, judge; to grade; *Am.* to compute (*election returns*); **-se** *Ch.* to qualify or register (*as a voter*).

caligrafia [ka·li·gra·fí·a] *f.* penmanship.

calina [ka·li·na] *f.* haze, mist.

cáliz [ká·lis] *m.* chalice, communion cup; cup, goblet; calyx (*of a flower*).

calma [kál·ma] *f.* calm, quiet.

calmante [kal·mán·te] *adj.* soothing; *m.* sedative.

calmar [kal·már] *v.* to calm, quiet, soothe.

calmo [kál·mo] *adj.* calm, quiet.

calmoso [kal·mó·so] *adj.* calm; soothing; phlegmatic, slow.

caló [ka·ló] *m.* underworld slang.

calor [ka·lór] *m.* heat, warmth; ardor.

caloría [ka·lo·rí·a] *f.* calorie.

calorifero [ka·lo·rí·fe·ro] *m.* heater, radiator; furnace.

calosfrío [ka·los·frí·o], **calofrío** [ka·lo·frí·o] *m.* chill.

calumnia [ka·lúm·nja] *f.* slander.

calumniar [ka·lum·njár] *v.* to slander.

caluroso [ka·lu·ró·so] *adj.* (*literal*) hot, warm; (*figurado*) heated, excited; cordial, enthusiastic.

calva [kál·ɓa] *f.* bald head; bald spot; barren spot.

calvario [kal·ɓá·rjo] *m.* Calvary, place of the Cross; suffering, tribulation.

calvo [kál·ɓo] *adj.* bald; barren.

calza [kál·sa] *f.* wedge; shoehorn; *Col., Ven.* gold inlay, tooth filling; **-s** breeches.

calzada [kal·sá·ɗa] *f.* paved road; highway; *Mex., Carib.* wide avenue.

calzado [kal·sá·ɗo] *m.* footwear.

calzador [kal·sa·ɗór] *m.* shoehorn.

calzar[9] [kal·sár] *v.* to put on (*shoes, gloves, spurs*); to put a wedge under a wheel; *Am.* to fill (*a tooth*).

calzón [kal·són] *m.* (*or* **calzones** [kal·só·nes]) breeches, short trousers; *Mex., Ven.* drawers; *Mex.* white cotton trousers; **calzoncillos** [kal·son·sí·yos] *m. pl.* drawers, men's shorts; **calzoneras** [kal·so·né·ras] *f. pl. Mex.* trousers open down the sides.

callado [ka·yá·ɗo] *adj.* silent, quiet.

callar [ka·yár] *v.* to be silent; to hush; **-se** to be or keep silent.

calle [ká·ye] *f.* street.

calleja [ka·yé·xa] *f.* small street, alley, lane; **callejuela** [ka·ye·xwé·la] *f.* small, narrow street; lane.

callejear [ka·ye·xe·ár] *v.* to walk the streets, ramble.

callejero [ka·ye·xé·ro] *m.* street-rambler, street-stroller; street-loiterer; *adj.* fond of walking the streets; rambling.

callejón [ka·ye·xón] *m.* alley; lane; narrow pass; **— sin salida** blind alley.

callo [ká·yo] *m.* callus, corn; *Spain* **-s** tripe (*food*).

calloso [ka·yó·so] *adj.* callous, hard.

cama [ká·ma] *f.* bed, couch, cot; litter **caer en —** to fall ill; **guardar —** to be confined to bed; *Am.* **tenderle uno la — a otro** to help one in his love affairs; to set a trap for someone; **camastro** [ka·más·tro] *m.* poor, uncomfortable bed.

camada [ka·má·ɗa] *f.* litter; brood.

camaleón [ka·ma·le·ón] *m.* chameleon.

cámara [ká·ma·ra] *f.* chamber, hall, parlor; house (*of a legislative body*); cabin, stateroom; chamber (*of a gun*); **— de aire** inner tube; **— fotográfica** camera.

camarada [ka·ma·rá·ɗa] *m.* comrade; **camaradería** [ka·ma·ra·ɗe·rí·a] *f.* comradeship, companionship.

camarera [ka·ma·ré·ra] *f.* waitress; chambermaid; stewardess.

camarero [ka·ma·ré·ro] *m.* waiter; chamberlain; steward; valet.

camarilla [ka·ma·rí·ya] *f.* political lobby; small group of politicians, "kitchen cabinet", group of unofficial advisers; small room.

camarón [ka·ma·rón] *m.* shrimp.

camarote [ka·ma·ró·te] *m.* cabin, stateroom.

cambalache [kam·ba·lá·če] *m.* swap, barter, exchange.

cambalachear [kam·ba·la·če·ár] *v.* to swap, barter, exchange.

cambiador [kam·bja·ɗór] *m.* barterer; money changer; *Am.* switchman.

cambiante [kam·bján·te] *adj.* changing; exchanging; **-s** *m. pl.* iridescent colors.

cambiar [kam·bjár] *v.* to change; to exchange; to shift; **— de marcha** to shift gears.

cambiavía [kam·bja·ɓí·a] *m. Carib., Mex., Andes* railway switchman. *See* **guardagujas** *and* **cambiador**.

cambio [kám·bjo] *m.* change; exchange; railway switch; **libre —** free trade; **en —** on the other hand; in exchange.

cambista [kam·bís·ta] *m.* exchange broker, banker; *Am.* railway switchman.

camello [ka·mé·yo] *m.* camel.

camilla [ka·mí·ya] *f.* stretcher; cot; **camillero** [ka·mi·yé·ro] *m.* stretcher bearer.

caminante [ka·mi·nán·te] *m. & f.* walker, traveler.

caminar [ka·mi·nár] *v.* to travel; to walk; *Am.* to progress, prosper.

caminata [ka·mi·ná·ta] *f.* long walk; hike; jaunt.

camino [ka·mí·no] *m.* road; course; *Riopl.* table runner; *Am.* hall runner; **— de hierro** railroad; **— real** highway; **de —** on the way.

camión [ka·mjón] *m.* truck; wagon; *Mex.* bus; **camionero** [ka·mjo·né·ro] *m.* truck driver; **camioneta** [ka·mjo·né·ta] *f.* small truck; station wagon; *C.A.* bus.

camisa [ka·mí·sa] *f.* shirt; **— de fuerza** straitjacket; **meterse en — de once varas** to attempt more than one can manage, bite off more than one can chew; **camiseta** [ka·mi·sé·ta] *f.* undershirt.

camisón [ka·mi·són] *m.* long shirt; *Am.* nightgown; *Am.* gown, dress.

camote [ka·mó·te] *m. Am.* a kind of sweet potato.

campamento [kam·pa·mén·to] *m.* encampment; camp.

campana [kam·pá·na] *f.* bell; *Riopl., Andes* spy, lookout (*for thieves*); **campanada**

[kam·pa·ná·ɗa] *f.* stroke of a bell; *Am.* **por — de vacante** once in a blue moon, very seldom.
campanario [kam·pa·ná·rjo] *m.* bell tower.
campanilla [kam·pa·ní·ya] *f.* small bell; bubble; uvula; tassel; bell-flower.
campanillazo [kam·pa·ni·yá·so] *m.* loud ring of a bell.
campanilleo [kam·pa·ni·yé·o] *m.* ringing; tinkling.
campaña [kam·pá·ña] *f.* level, open country; campaign; period of active service.
campear [kam·pe·ár] *v.* to pasture; to grow green (*said of the fields*); to excel; to be prominent, stand out; to be in the field; *Ríopl.* to search the plains for lost cattle; *Col., Ven.* to act the bully.
campechano [kam·pe·čá·no] *adj.* frank, open.
campéon [kam·pe·ón] *m.* champion; defender.
campeonato [kam·pe·o·ná·to] *m.* championship.
campero [kam·pé·ro] *adj.* out in the open; related to the country.
campesino [kam·pe·sí·no] *adj.* rural, rustic; *m.* peasant, countryman; farmer.
campestre [kam·pés·tre] *adj.* rural, rustic.
campiña [kam·pí·ña] *f.* large field; open country.
campo [kám·po] *m.* country; field; camp; **a — raso** in the open; **a — traviesa** (*or* **travieso**) cross-country.
camposanto [kam·po·sán·to] *m.* churchyard, cemetery.
camuesa [ka·mwé·sa] *f.* pippin (*a variety of apple*).
camuflaje [ka·mu·flá·xe] *m.* camouflage.
can [kan] *m.* dog; trigger (*of a gun*).
cana [ká·na] *f.* white hair, grey hair; *Carib.* a kind of palm; **echar una — al aire** to go out for a good time; to go out on a fling.
canadiense [ka·na·ɗjén·se] *adj., m. & f.* Canadian.
canal [ka·nál] *m.* canal, channel; *f.* eaves trough.
canalla [ka·ná·ya] *f.* rabble, mob; *m.* mean fellow.
canana [ka·ná·na] *f.* cartridge belt; **-s** *Col., Ven.* handcuffs.
canapé [ka·na·pé] *m.* couch, lounge, sofa; settee.
canario [ka·ná·rjo] *m.* canary; native of the Canary Islands; *interj.* great Scott!
canasta [ka·nás·ta] *f.* basket; crate.
cancelación [kan·se·la·sjón] *f.* cancellation.
cancelar [kan·se·lár] *v.* to cancel.
canciller [kan·si·yór] *m.* chancellor.
canción [kan·sjón] *f.* song; a kind of lyric poem; **volver a la misma —** to repeat, harp on the same thing.
cancha [kán·ča] *f.* court (*for tennis, etc.*); sports ground or field; cockpit, enclosure for cockfights; *Perú* roasted corn or beans; *Am.* **¡abran —!** gangway!; make room!
candado [kan·dá·ɗo] *m.* padlock; *Col.* goatee.
candela [kan·dé·la] *f.* candle; fire, forest fire; light.
candelabro [kan·de·lá·βro] *m.* candelabrum.
candelero [kan·de·lé·ro] *m.* candlestick.
candente [kan·dén·te] *adj.* incandescent, white-hot, red-hot.
candidato [kan·di·ɗá·to] *m.* candidate.
candidatura [kan·di·ɗa·tú·ra] *f.* candidacy.
candidez [kan·di·ɗés] *f.* candor, simplicity.
cándido [kán·di·ɗo] *adj.* candid, simple, innocent; white.
candil [kan·díl] *m.* lamp; *Ríopl., Mex.* chandelier;
candileja [kan·di·lé·xa] *f.* small oil lamp; oil receptacle (*of a lamp*); **-s** footlights (*of a stage*).
candor [kan·dór] *m.* candor, simplicity, innocence; frankness, sincerity.
canela [ka·né·la] *f.* cinnamon; an exquisite thing.

caney [ka·nej] *m. Caribe* hut; crude structure (*often without walls*).
cangrejo [kan·gré·xo] *m.* crab.
canguro [kan·gú·ro] *m.* kangaroo.
caníbal [ka·ní·βal] *m.* cannibal.
canica [ka·ní·ka] *f.* marble (*small glass or marble ball*).
canilla [ka·ní·ya] *f.* long bone (*of the arm or leg*); cock (*of a barrel*), faucet; spool (*for a sewing machine*); *C.A.* slender leg; *Ch., Col., Ríopl.* calf (*of the leg*); *Mex., Ven.* **tener —** to have physical strength; **canillita** [ka·ni·yí·ta] *m. Ríopl., Ch., C.A., Andes* newspaper boy.
canino [ka·ní·no] *adj.* canine; **tener un hambre canina** to be ravenous; to be hungry as a dog.
canje [kán·xe] *m.* interchange, exchange.
canjear [kaŋ·xe·ár] *v.* to exchange, interchange.
cano [ká·no] *adj.* grey-headed, grey-haired.
canoa [ka·nó·a] *f.* canoe.
canon [ká·non] *m.* canon; precept, rule, principle.
canónigo [ka·nó·ni·ɠo] *m.* canon (*churchman*).
canonizar[9] [ka·no·ni·sár] *v.* to canonize, saint.
canoso [ka·nó·so] *adj.* grey, grey-haired.
cansado [kan·sá·ɗo] *adj.* tired; tiresome, boring.
cansancio [kan·sán·sjo] *m.* fatigue, weariness.
cansar [kan·sár] *v.* to tire, fatigue; **-se** to get tired.
cantar [kan·tár] *v.* to sing; to squeal, confess; *Am.* **— alto** to ask a high price; **— claro** (*or* **-las claras**) to speak with brutal frankness; *m.* song, epic poem.
cántaro [kán·ta·ro] *m.* pitcher, jug.
cantatriz [kan·ta·trís] *f.* singer.
cantera [kan·té·ra] *f.* quarry; *Ríopl., Mex., Carib.* stone block.
cántico [kán·ti·ko] *m.* canticle, religious song.
cantidad [kan·ti·ɗáɗ] *f.* quantity.
cantilena [kan·ti·lé·na] *f.* song, ballad; monotonous repetition.
cantimplora [kan·tim·pló·ra] *f.* canteen; metal vessel for cooling water; *Col.* flask for carrying gunpowder.
cantina [kan·tí·na] *f.* mess hall; wine cellar; wine shop; canteen; *Carib., Mex., Ríopl.* barroom, tavern; *Col.* saddlebag.
cantinela [kan·ti·né·la] *f.* = **cantilena**.
cantinero [kan·ti·né·ro] *m.* bartender; tavern keeper.
canto [kán·to] *m.* song; singing; canto (*division of a long poem*); stone; edge; *Col.* lap; *Am.* piece.
cantón [kan·tón] *m.* canton, region; corner; *Am.* cotton cloth.
cantor [kan·tór] *m.* singer; song bird.
canturrear [kan·tu·rre·ár], **canturriar** [kan·tu·rrjár] *v.* to hum, sing softly.
canturreo [kan·tu·rré·o] *m.* hum, humming.
caña [ká·ña] *f.* cane, reed; tall, thin glass; stem; *Ríopl., Col., Ven.* sugar-cane brandy; *Am.* a kind of dance; *Am.* bluff, boast.
cañada [ka·ñá·ɗa] *f.* narrow canyon, dale, dell, gully, ravine; *Am.* brook.
cáñamo [ká·ña·mo] *m.* hemp; hemp cloth; *Am.* hemp cord, rope; **cañamazo** [ka·ña·má·so] *m.* canvas.
cañaveral [ka·ña·βe·rál] *m.* cane field; reed patch; sugar-cane plantation.
cañería [ka·ñe·rí·a] *f.* conduit, pipe line; tubing, piping; gas or water main.
caño [ká·ño] *m.* pipe, tube; spout; sewer; narrow channel; *Ven.* branch of a river, stream.
cañón [ka·ñón] *m.* (*arma*) cannon, gun; barrel (*of a gun*); (*topográfico*) ravine, gorge, canyon;

(*tubo*) pipe, tube; (*figurado*) beard stubble; pinfeather; quill (*of a feather*); chimney shaft; **cañonazo** [ka·ño·ná·so] *m.* cannon shot.

cañonear [ka·ño·ne·ár] *v.* to cannonade, bombard.

cañoneo [ka·ño·né·o] *m.* cannonade; bombardment.

cañonero [ka·ño·né·ro] *m.* gunboat; gunner; **lancha cañonera** gunboat.

caoba [ka·ó·ba] *f.* mahogany.

caos [ká·os] *m.* chaos, confusion.

capa [ká·pa] *f.* (*ropa*) cape, cloak; (*cubierta*) covering, coating; layer; scum; **so — de** under the guise of, under pretense of.

capacidad [ka·pa·si·dád] *f.* capacity; ability.

capacitar [ka·pa·si·tár] *v.* to enable, prepare, fit, qualify; *Col.* to empower, authorize.

capataz [ka·pa·tás] *m.* boss, foreman, overseer.

capaz [ka·pás] *adj.* capable, able, competent; spacious, roomy.

capellán [ka·pe·yán] *m.* chaplain, priest, clergyman.

caperuza [ka·pe·rú·sa] *f.* pointed hood.

capicúa [ka·pi·kú·a] *f.* a number which reads the same from right to left as from left to right.

capilla [ka·pí·ya] *f.* chapel; hood.

capirote [ka·pi·ró·te] *m.* hood; **tonto de —** dunce, plain fool.

capital [ka·pi·tál] *m.* capital, funds; *f.* capital, capital city; *adj.* capital; **capitalismo** [ka·pi·ta·líz·mo] *m.* capitalism; **capitalista** [ka·pi·ta·lís·ta] *m.* & *f.* capitalist; *adj.* capitalistic.

capitalino [ka·pi·ta·lí·no] *adj.* relative to the capital city; *m.* a resident of the capital.

capitalizar[9] [ka·pi·ta·li·sár] *v.* to capitalize.

capitán [ka·pi·tán] *m.* captain.

capitanear [ka·pi·ta·ne·ár] *v.* to command, lead.

capitolio [ka·pi·tó·ljo] *m.* capitol.

capitular [ka·pi·tu·lár] *v.* to surrender; to come to an agreement.

capítulo [ka·pí·tu·lo] *m.* chapter.

caporal [ka·po·rál] *m.* boss, leader; *Am.* foreman in a cattle ranch.

capote [ka·pó·te] *m.* cloak (*with sleeves*); bullfighter's cloak; *Ch.* thrashing, beating; **decir para su —** to say to oneself; *Am.* **de —** in an underhanded way; *Ven., Carib.* **dar —** to get ahead; to deceive.

capricho [ka·prí·čo] *m.* caprice, whim, notion.

caprichoso [ka·pri·čó·so] *adj.* capricious, whimsical; changeable, fickle.

caprichudo [ka·pri·čú·do] *adj.* whimsical; stubborn, willful.

cápsula [káp·su·la] *f.* capsule; percussion cap, cartridge shell; metal cap (*on bottles*).

captar [kap·tár] *v.* to win, attract; to capitivate; *Am.* to get, tune in on (*a radio station*).

captura [kap·tú·ra] *f.* capture.

capturar [kap·tu·rár] *v.* to capture, arrest.

capucha [ka·pú·ča] *f.* hood.

capullo [ka·pú·yo] *m.* cocoon; bud; acorn cup.

cara [ká·ra] *f.* face; expression, countenance; front; **de —** opposite; **echar** (*or* **dar**) **en —** to reproach, blame; **sacar la — por alguien** to take someone's part, defend him.

carabina [ka·ra·bí·na] *f.* carbine, rifle.

caracol [ka·ra·kól] *m.* snail; winding stairs; *Am.* embroidered blouse; *Am.* curl.

caracolear [ka·ra·ko·le·ár] *v.* to caper, prance around (*said of horses*); *Col., Ven.* to muddle, entangle; *Am.* to sidestep an obligation.

caracoleo [ka·ra·ko·lé·o] *m.* prancing around; winding, turn.

carácter [ka·rák·ter] *m.* character; temper.

característico [ka·rak·te·rís·ti·ko] *adj.* characteristic; **característica** [ka·rak·te·rís·ti·ka] *f.* characteristic, trait.

caracterizar[9] [ka·rak·te·ri·sár] *v.* to characterize.

¡caramba! [ka·rám·ba] *interj.* great guns! great Scott!

carámbano [ka·rám·ba·no] *m.* icicle.

caramelo [ka·ra·mé·lo] *m.* caramel.

caramillo [ka·ra·mí·yo] *m.* reed pipe, small flute; **armar un —** to raise a rumpus, create a disturbance.

carancho [ka·rán·čo] *m.* *Ríopl.* hawk, buzzard.

carátula [ka·rá·tu·la] *f.* mask; *Col., Ven., Ríopl., Carib., Andes* title page of a book; *C.A., Mex., Andes* dial, face of a watch.

caravana [ka·ra·bá·na] *f.* caravan.

caray [ka·ráj] *m.* tortoise shell; *interj.* gosh!

carbólico [kar·bó·li·ko] *adj.* carbolic.

carbón [kar·bón] *m.* carbon; coal; **— de leña** charcoal; **carbono** [kar·bó·no] *m.* carbon.

carbonera [kar·bo·né·ra] *f.* coal bin; coal cellar; woman coal or charcoal vendor; *Am.* coal mine; **carbonero** [kar·bo·né·ro] *m.* coal dealer; charcoal vendor; *adj.* coal, relating to coal or charcoal.

carburador [kar·bu·ra·dór] *m.* carburetor.

carajada [kar·ka·xá·da] *f.* loud laughter, peal of laughter.

cárcel [kár·sel] *f.* jail, prison.

carcelero [kar·se·lé·ro] *m.* jailer; *adj.* relating to a jail.

carcomido [kar·ko·mí·do] *adj.* worm-eaten; decayed.

cardán [kar·dán] *m.* universal joint.

cardar [kar·dár] *v.* to card, comb (*wool*).

cardenal [kar·de·nál] *m.* cardinal; cardinal bird; bruise.

cárdeno [kár·de·no] *adj.* dark-purple.

cardo [kár·do] *m.* thistle; a kind of cactus.

carear [ka·re·ár] *v.* to confront, bring face to face; to compare; **-se** to meet face to face.

carecer[13] [ka·re·sér] *v. irr.* to lack, be in need of.

carencia [ka·rén·sja] *f.* lack, want.

carente [ka·rén·te] *adj.* lacking.

carero [ka·ré·ro] *adj.* overcharging; profiteering; *m.* profiteer.

carestía [ka·res·tí·a] *f.* dearth, scarcity; high price.

careta [ka·ré·ta] *f.* mask.

carga [kár·ga] *f.* load, burden; freight; cargo; charge or gunpowder; **volver a la —** to insist again and again.

cargado [kar·gá·do] *p.p. & adj.* loaded; strong (*as tea or coffee*); cloudy, sultry; **— de espaldas** round-shouldered, stoop-shouldered.

cargador [kar·ga·dór] *m.* loader; stevedore; *Am.* carrier, errand boy, mover.

cargamento [kar·ga·mén·to] *m.* cargo.

cargar[6] [kar·gár] *v.* (*poner carga*) to load; to charge; (*atacar*) to charge; (*molestar*) to bother, annoy; *Am.* to carry, lug; *Am.* to punish; **— con** to carry away; to assume (*responsibility*); **— con el muerto** to get the blame (*unjustly*).

cargo [kár·go] *m.* charge, position, duty, burden; loading; accusation; **hacerse — de** to take charge of; to realize.

carguero [kar·gé·ro] *adj.* load-carrying; freight-carrying; *m. Am.* beast of burden; *Am.* skilled loader of pack animals; *Am.* patient, long-suffering person.

caribe [ka·rí·ƀe] *adj.* Caribbean; *m.* Carib, Caribbean Indian; cannibal; savage.

caricatura [ka·ri·ka·tú·ra] *f.* caricature; cartoon.

caricia [ka·rí·sja] *f.* caress.

caridad [ka·ri·ðáð] *f.* charity; alms.

caries [ká·rjes] *f.* decay (*of a bone*); tooth cavity.

cariño [ka·rí·ño] *m.* affection, love; *Am.* gift.

cariñoso [ka·ri·ñó·so] *adj.* affectionate, loving.

caritativo [ka·ri·ta·tí·ƀo] *adj.* charitable.

cariz [ka·rís] *m.* aspect, appearance.

carmesí [kar·me·sí] *adj.* & *m.* crimson.

carmín [kar·mín] *m.* crimson.

carnal [kar·nál] *adj.* carnal, sensual.

carnaval [kar·na·ƀál] *m.* carnival.

carne [kár·ne] *f.* meat; flesh; — **de gallina** "goose flesh", "goose pimples"; **echar -s** to put on weight, get fat; *Am.* — **de res** beef.

carneada [kar·ne·á·ða] *f. Ríopl.* butchering, slaughtering.

carnear [kar·ne·ár] *v. Ríopl.* to butcher; *Ríopl.* to kill.

carnero [kar·né·ro] *m.* (*animal*) ram, male sheep; (*carne*) mutton; *Am.* a weak-willed person; *Am.* waste basket; *Am.* — **de la tierra** llama (*or any fleece-bearing animal*); *Am.* **cantar uno el** — to die.

carnet [kar·né] *m.* identification card; notebook.

carnicería [kar·ni·se·rí·a] *f.* (*tienda*) meat market; (*matanza*) butchery, slaughter; *C.A., Ec.* slaughterhouse.

carnicero [kar·ni·sé·ro] *m.* butcher; *adj.* carnivorous, flesh-eating; cruel.

carnívoro [kar·ní·ƀo·ro] *adj.* carnivorous.

carnosidad [kar·no·si·ðáð] *f.* fleshiness, fatness; abnormal growth (*on animal or plant tissues*).

carnoso [kar·nó·so] *adj.* fleshy; meaty; pulpy.

caro [ká·ro] *adj.* expensive; dear; *adv.* at a high price.

carona [ka·ró·na] *f.* saddle pad.

carozo [ka·ró·so] *m.* cob, corncob.

carpa [kár·pa] *f.* carp (*fresh-water fish*); *Am.* canvas tent, circus tent; — **dorada** goldfish.

carpeta [kar·pé·ta] *f.* (*cubierta*) table cover; desk pad; (*cartera*) portfolio, letter case or file; *Andes* office desk; *Am.* bookkeeping department; **carpetazo** [kar·pe·tá·so]: **dar** — to table (*a motion*); to set aside, pigeonhole or dismiss.

carpintería [kar·pin·te·rí·a] *f.* carpentry; carpenter's workshop.

carpintero [kar·pin·té·ro] *m.* carpenter; **pájaro** — woodpecker.

carraspear [ka·rras·pe·ár] *v.* to cough up; to clear one's throat; to be hoarse.

carraspera [ka·rras·pé·ra] *f.* hoarseness.

carrera [ka·rré·ra] *f.* career; race, run; course; stocking run.

carreta [ka·rré·ta] *f.* long narrow wagon; cart; *Col., Ven.* wheelbarrow.

carretaje [ka·rre·tá·xe] *m.* cartage (*transporting by cart, truck, etc.*); price paid for cartage.

carrete [ka·rré·te] *m.* spool; reel — **distribuidor** feeding reel; — **receptor** take-up reel (*tape recorder*).

carretel [ka·rre·tél] *m.* reel, spool, bobbin; fishing reel; log reel (*of a boat*).

carretera [ka·rre·té·ra] *f.* highway.

carretero [ka·rre·té·ro] *m.* carter, teamster; cart maker; **camino** — highway.

carretilla [ka·rre·tí·ya] *f.* wheelbarrow; small cart;

baggage truck; *Ríopl.* wagon; *Am.* jaw; *Col.* string, series (*of lies, blunders, etc.*); *Am.* firecracker; **repetir de** — to rattle off, repeat mechanically.

carretón [ka·rre·tón] *m.* truck; wagon, cart.

carril [ka·rríl] *m.* rail; rut; furrow.

carrillo [ka·rrí·yo] *m.* (*de la cara*) cheek; (*mecánico*) pulley; cart.

carrizo [ka·rrí·so] *m.* reed; reed grass.

carro [ká·rro] *m.* cart; cartload; *Am.* car, auto, streetcar, coach; *Am.* **pararle a uno el** — to restrain someone; *Am.* **pasarle a uno el** — to suffer an injury or misfortune; **carroza** [ka·rró·sa] *f.* large and luxurious carriage; chariot; *Am.* hearse.

carrocería [ka·rro·se·rí·a] *f.* chassis; frame for a parade float.

carroña [ka·rró·ña] *f.* dead and decaying flesh; putrid, decaying carcass.

carruaje [ka·rrwá·xe] *m.* carriage, vehicle.

carta [kár·ta] *f.* (*misiva*) letter; (*naipe*) card; (*documento*) charter; map; — **blanca** full authority, freedom to act; — **de naturaleza** naturalization papers; — **de venta** bill of sale; *Ch.* **retirar** — to repent, back down; *Am.* **ser la última** — **de la baraja** to be the worst or most insignificant person or thing.

cartearse [kar·te·ár·se] *v.* to correspond, write to each other.

cartel [kar·tél] *m.* poster, handbill; cartel, written agreement; **cartela** [kar·té·la] *f.* tag, slip of paper, small card, piece of cardboard; **cartelera** [kar·te·lé·ra] *f.* billboard; **cartelón** [kar·te·lón] *m.* large poster.

cartera [kar·té·ra] *f.* (*objeto*) wallet; briefcase; desk pad; (*puesto*) portfolio, cabinet post; **carterista** [kar·te·rís·ta] *m.* & *f.* pickpocket.

cartero [kar·té·ro] *m.* mailman, letter carrier, postman.

cartilla [kar·tí·ya] *f.* primer; note, short letter; **leerle a uno la** — to scold, lecture someone concerning his duties.

cartografiar[17] [kar·to·gra·fjár] *v.* to chart; to make charts.

cartón [kar·tón] *m.* cardboard; pasteboard; **cartulina** [kar·tu·lí·na] *f.* fine cardboard.

cartuchera [kar·tu·čé·ra] *f.* cartridge belt.

cartucho [kar·tú·čo] *m.* cartridge; roll of coins; paper cone or bag.

casa [ká·sa] *f.* (*doméstica*) house, home; household; (*negocio*) business firm; square (*of a chessboard*); *Am.* bet, wager; — **de empeños** pawnshop; — **de huéspedes** boardinghouse; **echar la** — **por la ventana** to spend recklessly, squander everything; **poner** — to set up housekeeping.

casabe [ka·sá·ƀe], **cazabe** *m. Am.* cassava; *Am.* cassava bread.

casaca [ka·sá·ka] *f.* long military coat; **volver** — to be a turncoat, change sides or parties.

casamiento [ka·sa·mjén·to] *m.* wedding; marriage.

casar [ka·sár] *v.* to marry; to match; *Am.* to graft (*trees*); **-se** to get married.

cascabel [kas·ka·ƀél] *m.* jingle bell, tinkle bell; snake's rattle; *Am.* rattlesnake; **cascabela** [kas·ka·ƀé·la] *f. C.R.* rattlesnake.

cascada [kas·ká·ða] *f.* cascade, waterfall.

cascajo [kas·ká·xo] *m.* coarse gravel; crushed stone; pebble; fragment; rubbish.

cascanueces [kas·ka·nwé·ses] *m.* nutcracker.

cascar[6] [kas·kár] *v.* to crack, break; **-se** to crack or break open.

cáscara [kás·ka·ra] *f.* shell, husk, hull, rind; bark of a tree; *Ríopl.* **dar a uno — de novillo** to give someone a whipping; **cascarudo** [kas·ka·rú·ḍo] *adj.* having a thick husk; having a thick rind.

cascarrabias [kas·ka·rrá·ḅjas] *m. & f.* crab, grouch, ill-tempered person; *adj.* grouchy, cranky, irritable.

casco [kás·ko] *m.* helmet; hoof; skull; broken piece of earthenware; cask; empty bottle; hull of a ship; *Mex., Ríopl.* compound, main buildings of a farm; **caliente de -s** hot-headed; **ligero de -s** light-headed, frivolous; **romperse los -s** to rack one's brain.

caserío [ka·se·rí·o] *m.* hamlet, small settlement.

casero [ka·sé·ro] *adj.* domestic; homemade; *m.* landlord; janitor, caretaker; *Ch.* customer; *Col., Peru, Ven.* delivery boy; **casera** [ka·sé·ra] *f.* landlady; housekeeper.

caseta [ka·sé·ta] *f.* small house, cottage; booth, stall.

casi [ká·si] *adv.* almost.

casilla [ka·sí·ya] *f.* (*puesto*) stall, booth; (*apartado*) post office box; pigeonhole; **sacarle a uno de sus -s** to change someone's way of life or habits; to irritate, annoy, try someone's patience; **salirse de sus -s** to lose one's temper; to do something out of the way.

casino [ka·sí·no] *m.* club, society; clubhouse; recreation hall.

caso [ká·so] *m.* case; point; matter; event — **que** (*or* **en — de que**) in case that; **dado —** supposing; **hacer — de** to pay attention to; **hacer — omiso de** to omit; **no viene al —** that is not to the point.

casorio [ka·só·rjo] *m.* wedding, marriage.

caspa [kás·pa] *f.* dandruff.

casta [kás·ta] *f.* race, breed; caste, distinct class; quality, kind.

castaña [kas·tá·ña] *f.* chestnut; jug; knot or roll of hair; *Am.* small barrel; *Mex.* trunk, large suitcase.

castañetear [kas·ta·ñe·te·ár] *v.* to rattle the castanets; to chatter (*said of the teeth*); to crackle (*said of the knees or joints*); — **con los dedos** to snap one's fingers.

castañeteo [kas·ta·ñe·té·o] *m.* rattle or sound of castanets; chatter, chattering (*of the teeth*).

castaño [kas·tá·ño] *m.* chestnut (*tree and wood*); *adj.* chestnut-colored.

castañuela [kas·ta·ñwé·la] *f.* castanet.

castellano [kas·te·yá·no] *adj. & m.* Castilian, Spanish.

castidad [kas·ti·ḍáḍ] *f.* chastity.

castigar[7] [kas·ti·gár] *v.* to chastise, punish.

castigo [kas·tí·go] *m.* punishment; correction.

castillo [kas·tí·yo] *m.* castle.

castizo [kas·tí·so] *adj.* pure, correct (*language*); pure-blooded.

casto [kás·to] *adj.* chaste, pure.

castor [kas·tór] *m.* beaver; beaver cloth.

casual [ka·swál] *adj.* casual, accidental.

casualidad [ka·swa·li·ḍáḍ] *f.* chance, accident.

casuca [ka·sú·ka] *f.* little house; hut, shanty.

casucha [ka·sú·ča] *f.* hut, hovel, shack.

catadura [ka·ta·ḍú·ra] *f.* aspect, appearance.

catalán [ka·ta·lán] *adj.* Catalan, Catalonian, of or from Catalonia, Spain; *m.* Catalan.

catalejo [ka·ta·lé·xo] *m.* telescope.

catalogar[7] [ka·ta·lo·gár] *v.* to catalogue.

catálogo [ka·tá·lo·go] *m.* catalogue.

catar [ka·tár] *v.* to look at, examine; to taste, sample.

catarata [ka·ta·rá·ta] *f.* cataract; waterfall.

catarro [ka·tá·rro] *m.* catarrh, cold.

catástrofe [ka·tás·tro·fe] *f.* catastrophe, mishap.

catear [ka·te·ár] *v.* to explore, look around; *Ch., C.A., Mex.* to search or raid (*a home*); *Am.* to explore for ore; *Col., Ríopl.* to test, try.

catecismo [ka·te·síz·mo] *m.* catechism.

cátedra [ká·te·ḍra] *f.* class; subject; chair, professorship.

catedral [ka·te·ḍrál] *f.* cathedral.

catedrático [ka·te·ḍrá·ti·ko] *m.* professor.

categoría [ka·te·go·rí·a] *f.* category, rank; kind, class.

categórico [ka·te·gó·ri·ko] *adj.* categorical, positive.

catequizar[9] [ka·te·ki·sár] *v.* to catechize, give religious instruction (to); to induce, persuade.

católico [ka·tó·li·ko] *adj.* Catholic; universal; *m.* Catholic; **catolicismo** [ka·to·li·síz·mo] *m.* Catholicism.

catre [ká·tre] *m.* cot, small bed; *Am.* raft, float; *C.A.*, camp stool, folding stool; — **de tijera** folding cot.

catrín [ka·trín] *m. Am.* dandy; *adj. Mex., C.A.* over-elegant, dressy.

cauce [káw·se] *m.* river bed.

caución [kaw·sjón] *f.* precaution; security, guarantee; bail.

cauchero [kaw·cé·ro] *m. Am.* rubber gatherer; *Am.* rubber producer; *adj. Am.* rubber, pertaining to rubber.

caucho [káw·čo] *m.* rubber; — **sintético** [synthetic rubber; *Am.* rubber tree; *Col.* rubber raincoat or cloak; **cauchal** [kaw·čál] *m.* rubber grove or plantation.

caudal [kaw·ḍál] *m.* (*monetario*) wealth; (*torrente*) river current; volume of water.

caudaloso [kaw·ḍa·ló·so] *adj.* wealthy; abundant.

caudillaje [kaw·ḍi·yá·xe] *m.* military leadership; *Am.* political bossism; *Am.* tyranny.

caudillo [kaw·ḍí·yo] *m.* leader, chief; *Am.* political boss.

causa [káw·sa] *f.* cause; case, lawsuit; *Am.* light lunch, snack; **a causa de** on account of.

causar [kaw·sár] *v.* to cause.

cautela [kaw·té·la] *f.* caution; cunning, craftiness; trick, deception.

cauteloso [kaw·te·ló·so] *adj.* cautious; crafty.

cautivar [kaw·ti·ḅár] *v.* to capture; to charm, fascinate.

cautiverio [kaw·ti·ḅé·rjo] *m.* captivity.

cautivo [kaw·tí·ḅo] *m.* captive, war prisoner.

cauto [káw·to] *adj.* cautious.

cavar [ka·ḅár] *v.* to dig, spade; to excavate.

caverna [ka·ḅér·na] *f.* cavern, cave.

cavernoso [ka·ḅer·nó·so] *adj.* cavernous, like a cavern; hollow; **voz cavernosa** deep, hollow voice.

cavidad [ka·ḅi·ḍáḍ] *f.* cavity.

cayado [ka·yá·ḍo] *m.* shepherd's crook, staff.

cayo [ká·yo] *m.* key, island reef.

caza [ká·sa] *f.* hunt, hunting; wild game; *m.* attack plane; **dar —** to pursue, track down.

cazador [ka·sa·ḍór] *adj.* hunting; *m.* hunter.

cazar[9] [ka·sár] *v.* to chase, hunt; to track down.

cazatorpedero [ka·sa·tor·pe·ḍé·ro] *m.* destroyer, torpedo-boat.

cazo [ká·so] *m.* dipper; pot, pan.

cazuela [ka·swé·la] *f.* stewing pan; earthenware cooking pan; topmost theatre gallery; *Ven.*

stewed hen; *P.R.* candied sweet potatoes with spices.

cebada [se·bá·da] *f.* barley; *Am.* brewing of **mate**; **cebadal** [se·ba·dál] *m.* barley field.

cebar [se·bár] *v.* to feed, fatten (*animals*); to encourage, nourish (*a passion*); to prime (*a gun*, *pump*, *etc.*); to bait (*a fishhook*); *Ríopl.* to brew and serve **mate** or tea; **-se** to vent one's fury.

cebo [sé·bo] *m.* feed (*for animals*); bait; incentive.

cebolla [se·bó·ya] *f.* onion.

cebollar [se·bo·yár] *m.* onion patch.

cecear [se·se·ár] *v.* to lisp.

ceceo [se·sé·o] *m.* lisp, lisping.

cecina [se·sí·na] *f.* dried beef, jerked beef.

cedazo [se·dá·so] *m.* sieve.

ceder [se·dér] *v.* to cede, transfer; to yield, surrender, submit; to diminish, abate.

cedilla [se·dí·ya] *f.* cedilla.

cedro [sé·dro] *m.* cedar.

cédula [sé·du·la] *f.* slip of paper; certificate; — **de vecindad** (*or* — **personal**) official identification card.

céfiro [sé·fi·ro] *m.* zephyr, soft breeze; *Am.* fine muslin.

cegar[1, 7] [se·gár] *v. irr.* to blind; to become blind; to confuse; to fill up, stop up (*a hole*).

ceguedad [se·ge·dád], **ceguera** [se·gé·ra] *f.* blindness.

ceiba [séj·ba] *f. Am.* ceiba, silk-cotton tree.

ceja [sé·xa] *f.* eyebrow; brow of a hill.

cejar [se·xár] *v.* to go backward; to back; to back down, give in, yield; to slacken.

cejijunto [se·xi·xún·to] *adj.* frowning; with knitted eyebrows.

celada [se·lá·da] *f.* ambush, snare, trap.

celaje [se·lá·xe] *m.* colored clouds; skylight; presage, portent; *P.R.* shadow, ghost; *Am.* **como un** — like lightning.

celar [se·lár] *v.* to guard, watch; to watch over jealously; to conceal.

celda [sél·da] *f.* cell.

celebración [se·le·bra·sjón] *f.* celebration.

celebrar [se·le·brár] *v.* to celebrate; to praise, honor; to be glad.

célebre [sé·le·bre] *adj.* famous; funny, witty; *Col.* graceful, pretty (*woman*).

celebridad [se·le·bri·dád] *f.* fame, renown; celebrity, famous person; celebration.

celeridad [se·le·ri·dád] *f.* swiftness, speed.

celeste [se·lés·te] *adj.* celestial, heavenly.

celestial [se·les·tjál] *adj.* celestial, heavenly, divine.

celibe [sé·li·be] *adj.* unmarried; *m.* & *f.* unmarried person.

celo [sé·lo] *m.* (*humano*) zeal, ardor; envy; (*animal*) heat (*sexual excitement in animals*); **-s** jealousy, suspicion; **tener -s** to be jealous.

celosía [se·lo·sí·a] *f.* window lattice; Venetian blind.

celoso [se·ló·so] *adj.* jealous; zealous, eager; suspicious.

célula [sé·lu·la] *f.* cell.

celuloide [se·lu·lój·de] *m.* celluloid.

cellisca [se·yís·ka] *f.* sleet; rain and snow.

cementar [se·men·tár] *v.* to cement.

cementerio [se·men·té·rjo] *m.* cemetery.

cemento [se·mén·to] *m.* cement; — **armado** reinforced concrete.

cena [sé·na] *f.* supper.

cenagal [se·ne·gál] *m.* quagmire, muddy ground, swamp.

cenagoso [se·na·gó·so] *adj.* muddy, miry.

cenar [se·nár] *v.* to eat supper.

cencerrada [sen·se·rrá·da] *f.* racket, noise (*with cowbells, tin cans, etc.*); tin pan serenade.

cencerrear [sen·se·rre·ár] *v.* to make a racket (*with cowbells, tin cans, etc.*).

cencerro [sen·sé·rro] *m.* cowbell.

cendal [sen·dál] *m.* gauze; thin veil.

cenicero [se·ni·sé·ro] *m.* ash tray; ash pit; ash pan.

cenicienta [se·ni·sjén·ta] *f.* a Cinderella.

ceniciento [se·ni·sjén·to] *adj.* ashen, ash-colored.

cenit [sé·nit] *m.* zenith.

ceniza [se·ní·sa] *f.* ashes, cinders.

cenizo [se·ní·so] *adj.* ash-colored.

censo [sén·so] *m.* census.

censor [sen·sór] *m.* censor.

censura [sen·sú·ra] *f.* censure, criticism, disapproval; censorship.

censurador [sen·su·ra·dór] *m.* censor, critic; critical person; *adj.* critical.

censurar [sen·su·rár] *v.* to censure, criticize, reprove; to censor.

centavo [sen·tá·bo] *m.* cent.

centella [sen·té·ya] *f.* lightning, flash; spark.

centelleante [sen·te·ye·án·te] *adj.* sparkling, flashing.

centellear [sen·te·ye·ár] *v.* to twinkle; to sparkle, glitter; to flash.

centelleo [sen·te·yé·o] *m.* glitter, sparkle.

centenar [sen·te·nár] *m.* one hundred; field of rye.

centenario [sen·te·ná·rjo] *m.* centennial, one hundredth anniversary; *adj.* centennial; old, ancient.

centeno [sen·té·no] *m.* rye.

centésimo [sen·té·si·mo] *adj.* & *m.* hundredth.

centímetro [sen·tí·me·tro] *m.* centimeter (*one hundredth part of a meter*).

céntimo [sén·ti·mo] *m.* one hundredth part of a peseta.

centinela [sen·ti·né·la] *m.* sentry, sentinel.

central [sen·trál] *adj.* central; *f.* main office; headquarters; *Am.* main sugar mill or refinery.

centrar [sen·trár] *v.* to center.

céntrico [sén·tri·ko] *adj.* central.

centrífugo [sen·trí·fu·go] *adj.* centrifugal.

centrípeto [sen·trí·pe·to] *adj.* centripetal.

centro [sén·tro] *m.* center, middle.

ceñidor [se·ñi·dór] *m.* girdle, belt, sash.

ceñir[5, 19] [se·ñír] *v. irr.* (*redear*) to gird, girdle; to tighten; to encircle; (*abreviar*) to diminish; to limit; **-se a** to limit oneself to.

ceño [sé·ño] *m.* frown; scowl; **fruncir el** — to frown; to scowl.

cepa [sé·pa] *f.* stump, stub (*of a tree or plant*); vinestock; origin, stock (*of a family*); *Am.* mass of plants growing from a common root; *Am.* excavation (*for a building*), hole, pit (*for planting trees*); **de buena** — of good stock.

cepillo [se·pí·yo] *m.* brush; alms box; carpenter's plane; *Am.* flatterer; — **de dientes** toothbrush.

cepo [sé·po] *m.* branch, stock.

cera [sé·ra] *f.* wax.

cerámica [se·rá·mi·ka] *f.* ceramics, pottery.

cerca [sér·ka] *adv.* near, near by; — **de** *prep.* near, nearly; *f.* fence, low wall.

cercado [ser·ká·do] *m.* enclosure; fenced-in garden; fence; *Am.* Peruvian political division; *p.p. of* **cercar.**

cercanía [ser·ka·ní·a] *f.* proximity; **-s** surroundings, vicinity.

cercano [ser·ká·no] *adj.* near; neighboring.

cercar⁶ [ser·kár] *v.* to fence, enclose; to surround; to besiege.

cercenar [ser·se·nár] *v.* to clip off; to curtail, diminish, reduce.

cerciorar [ser·sjo·rár] *v.* to assure, affirm; **-se** to ascertain, find out.

cerco [sér·ko] *m.* fence enclosure; siege; circle; *Ch.* small farm or orchard.

cerda [sér·da] *f.* bristle; *Am.* **ir en -s** to go halves or share in a deal.

cerdo [sér·do] *m.* hog; pig; pork.

cerdoso [ser·dó·so] *adj.* bristly.

cereal [se·re·ál] *m.* cereal, grain.

cerebro [se·ré·bro] *m.* brain.

ceremonia [se·re·mó·nja] *f.* ceremony.

ceremonial [se·re·mo·njál] *adj. & m.* ceremonial.

ceremonioso [se·re·mo·njó·so] *adj.* ceremonious.

cereza [se·ré·sa] *f.* cherry; **cerezo** [se·ré·so] *m.* cherry tree; cherry wood.

cerilla [se·rí·ya] *f.* wax taper; wax match; earwax.

cerillo [se·rí·yo] *m. Mex., C.A., Ven., Andes* match.

cerner¹ [ser·nér] *v. irr.* to sift; to drizzle; *Am.* to strain through a sieve; **-se** to hover (*as a bird or plane*).

cero [sé·ro] *m.* zero; nothing.

cerquita [ser·kí·ta] *adv.* quite near, nice and near.

cerrado [se·rrá·do] *adj.* closed; cloudy; thick (*beard*); reserved (*person*); dull; *Am.* stubborn.

cerradura [se·rrá·dú·ra] *f.* locking, closing; lock; **— de golpe** spring lock.

cerrajería [se·rra·xe·rí·a] *f.* locksmith's shop; locksmith's trade.

cerrajero [se·rra·xé·ro] *m.* locksmith.

cerrar¹ [se·rrár] *v. irr.* to close, shut, lock; **-se** to close; **-se el cielo** to become overcast or cloudy.

cerrazón [se·rra·són] *f.* cloudiness, darkness.

cerro [sé·rro] *m.* hill.

cerrojo [se·rró·xo] *m.* latch, bolt.

certamen [ser·tá·men] *m.* contest, literary contest; debate; competition.

certero [ser·té·ro] *adj.* accurate, exact; well-aimed; **tirador —** good shot.

certeza [ser·té·sa] *f.* certainty.

certidumbre [ser·ti·dúm·bre] *f.* certainty.

certificado [ser·ti·fi·ká·do] *adj.* certified, registered; *m.* certificate.

certificar⁶ [ser·ti·fi·kár] *v.* to certify; to register (*a letter*).

cervato [ser·bá·to] *m.* fawn, young deer.

cerveza [ser·bé·sa] *f.* beer; **cervecería** [ser·be·se·rí·a] *f.* beer tavern; brewery.

cerviz [ser·bís] *f.* cervix.

cesante [se·sán·te] *adj.* unemployed.

cesar [se·sár] *v.* to cease, stop; to quit.

cesio [sé·sjo] *m.* cesium.

cesta [sés·ta] *f.* basket; a kind of racket for playing jai alai (*Basque ball game*).

cesto [sés·to] *m.* large basket, hamper.

cetrino [se·trí·no] *adj.* greenish-yellow, lemon-colored; citronlike; melancholy, gloomy.

cetro [sé·tro] *m.* scepter, staff.

cibernética [si·ber·né·ti·ka] *f.* cybernetics, computer science.

cicatero [si·ka·té·ro] *adj.* miserly, stingy.

cicatriz [si·ka·trís] *f.* scar.

cicatrizar⁹ [si·ka·tri·sár] *v.* to heal, close (*a wound*).

ciclo [sí·klo] *m.* cycle; period of time; school term.

ciclón [si·klón] *m.* cyclone.

ciclotrón [si·klo·trón] *m.* cyclotron.

ciego [sjé·go] *adj.* blind; **a ciegas** blindly; *m.* blindman.

cielo [sjé·lo] *m.* sky; heaven; **— de la boca** palate; **poner en el —** to praise, extol; **poner el grito en el —** to "hit the ceiling"; **cielito** *m. Am.* gaucho group dance and tune.

ciempiés [sjem·pjés], **cientopiés** [sjen·to·pjés] *m.* centipede.

ciénaga [sjé·na·ga] *f.* swamp, bog, quagmire, marsh.

ciencia [sjén·sja] *f.* science; learning; skill; **a** (*or* **de**) **— cierta** with certainty.

cieno [sjé·no] *m.* mud, mire.

científico [sjen·tí·fi·ko] *adj.* scientific; *m.* scientist.

cierre [sjé·rre] *m.* clasp, fastener; zipper; closing, fastening, locking; method of closing.

cierto [sjér·to] *adj.* certain, true, sure; **por —** certainly; *Col., C.A.* **ciertas hierbas** so-and-so (*person not named*).

ciervo [sjér·bo] *m.* deer; **cierva** [sjér·ba] *f.* doe, hind, female deer.

cierzo [sjér·so] *m.* north wind.

cifra [sí·fra] *f.* cipher, number; figure; abridgment, summary; code; monogram; emblem.

cifrar [si·frár] *v.* to write in code; to summarize; **— la esperanza en** to place one's hope in.

cigarra [si·gá·rra] *f.* cicada, locust.

cigarrera [si·ga·rré·ra] *f.* cigar or cigarette case; woman cigar maker or vendor.

cigarrillo [si·ga·rrí·yo] *m.* cigarette.

cigarro [si·gá·rro] *m.* cigar, cigarette.

cigüeña [si·gwé·ña] *f.* stork; crank, handle (*for turning*).

cigüeñal [si·gwe·ñál] *m.* crankshaft.

cilíndrico [si·lín·dri·ko] *adj.* cylindrical.

cilindro [si·lín·dro] *m.* cylinder; *Mex.* hand organ.

cima [sí·ma] *f.* peak, summit, top; **dar —** to complete, carry out.

cimarrón [si·ma·rrón] *adj. Ríopl., Mex., Carib., Ven., Andes* wild, untamed; *Ríopl.* **mate —** black, bitter **mate.**

cimarronear [si·ma·rro·ne·ár] *v. Ríopl.* to drink **mate** without sugar.

cimbrar [sim·brár], **cimbrear** [sim·bre·ár] *v.* to brandish, flourish, swing; to shake; to bend; *Am.* to swing around, change suddenly one's direction, **— a uno de un golpe** to knock a person down with a blow; **-se** to swing, sway; to vibrate, shake.

cimiento [si·mjén·to] *m.* foundation, base; source, root; **abrir los -s** to break ground for a building.

cinc [siŋk] *m.* zinc.

cincel [sin·sél] *m.* chisel.

cincelar [sin·se·lár] *v.* to chisel; to engrave.

cincha [sín·ča] *f.* cinch, girth; *Am.* blows with the flat of a sword; *Col., Ríopl.* **a revienta -s** unwillingly; hurriedly; at breakneck speed.

cinchar [sin·čár] *v.* to cinch, tighten the saddle girth; *Am.* to hit with the flat of a sword.

cine [sí·ne], **cinema** [si·né·ma] *m.* cinema, motion picture, movie; **cinematógrafo** [si·ne·ma·tó·gra·fo] *m.* motion picture.

cinematografía [si·ne·ma·to·gra·fí·a] *f.* cinematography, the science of motion picture photography.

cíngulo [síŋ·gu·lo] *m.* girdle, cord, belt.

cínico [sí·ni·ko] *adj.* cynical, sarcastic, sneering; *m.* cynic.

cinta [sín·ta] *f.* ribbon, band; tape; strip; movie film; coarse fishing net; *Am.* tin can.

cintarada [sin·ta·rá·da] *f.* beating, flogging; **cintarazo** *m.* blow with the flat of a sword.

cintilar [sin·ti·lár] v. to sparkle, twinkle; to glimmer.
cinto [sín·to] m. belt; girdle.
cintura [sin·tú·ra] f. waist; meter en — to subdue, subject.
cinturón [sin·tu·rón] m. belt; — de seguridad safety belt.
ciprés [si·prés] m. cypress.
circo [sír·ko] m. circus.
circonio [sir·kó·njo] m. zirconium.
circuito [sir·kwí·to] m. circuit.
circulación [sir·ku·la·sjón] f. circulation; traffic.
circular [sir·ku·lár] v. to circulate; to circle; adj. circular; f. circular letter, notice.
círculo [sír·ku·lo] m. circle; group; club; clubhouse.
circundante [sir·kun·dán·te] adj. surrounding.
circundar [sir·kun·dár] v. to surround.
circunferencia [sir·kun·fe·rén·sja] f. circumference.
circunlocución [sir·kun·lo·ku·sjón] f. circumlocution, roundabout expression.
circunspección [sir·kun·spek·sjón] f. circumspection, decorum, prudence, restraint.
circunspecto [sir·kuns·pék·to] adj. circumspect, prudent.
circunstancia [sir·kuns·tán·sja] f. circumstance.
circunstante [sir·kuns·tán·te] adj. surrounding; present; -s m. pl. bystanders, onlookers, audience.
circunvecino [sir·kum·be·sí·no] adj. neighboring, surrounding.
cirio [sí·rjo] m. wax candle; saguaro cactus.
ciruela [si·rwé·la] f. plum; prune; — pasa prune, dried prune; ciruelo m. plum tree.
cirugía [si·ru·xí·a] f. surgery.
cirujano [si·ru·xá·no] m. surgeon.
cisne [síz·ne] m. swan; Riopl. powder puff.
cisterna [sis·tér·na] f. cistern.
cita [sí·ta] f. date, appointment; citation; summons; quotation.
citación [si·ta·sjón] f. citation, quotation; summons.
citar [si·tár] v. (convocar) to make a date or appointment with; (referir) to cite, quote; (incitar) incite, provoke; to summon.
cítrico [sí·tri·ko] adj. citric.
ciudad [sju·dád] f. city.
ciudadano [sju·da·dá·no] m. citizen; resident of a city; adj. of or pertaining to a city; ciudadanía [sju·da·da·ní·a] f. citizenship.
ciudadela [sju·da·dé·la] f. citadel.
cívico [sí·bi·ko] adj. civic.
civil [si·bíl] adj. civil; polite, courteous.
civilidad [si·bi·li·dád] f. civility, courtesy.
civilización [si·bi·li·sa·sjón] f. civilization.
civilizador [si·bi·li·sa·dór] adj. civilizing; m. civilizer.
civilizar⁹ [si·bi·li·sár] v. to civilize.
cizaña [si·sá·ña] f. weed; vice; discord; sembrar — to sow discord.
clamar [kla·már] v. to clamor, shout; to whine.
clamor [kla·mór] m. clamor, shout; whine; knell.
clamoreo [kla·mo·ré·o] m. clamoring; shouting.
clamorear [kla·mo·re·ár] v. to clamor, shout; to toll, knell.
clandestino [klan·des·tí·no] adj. clandestine, underhanded, secret.
clara [klá·ra] f. white of egg; bald spot; thin spot (in a fabric); a las -s clearly, openly, frankly.
claraboya [kla·ra·bó·ya] f. skylight.
clarear [kla·re·ár] v. (poner claro), to clarify, make

clear; (haber más luz) to grow light, begin to dawn; to clear up; Am. to pierce through and through; -se to become transparent; to reveal oneself.
claridad [kla·ri·dád] f. clarity, clearness; blunt remark, slam; fame.
claridoso [kla·ri·dó·so] adj. Mex., Ven., C.A. blunt, outspoken, plainspoken.
clarificar⁶ [kla·ri·fi·kár] v. to clarify, make clear.
clarín [kla·rín] m. bugle; bugler; organ stop; Am. song bird.
clarinete [kla·ri·né·te] m. clarinet; clarinet player.
clarito [kla·rí·to] adj. & adv. quite clear, nice and clear.
clarividencia [kla·ri·bi·dén·sja] f. clairvoyance; keen insight.
claro [klá·ro] adj. clear; light (color); illustrious; adv. clearly; m. skylight; space, gap; clearing (in a forest); pasar la noche de — en — not to sleep a wink; Mex., Carib. en — without eating or sleeping; Am. poner en — to copy (a rough draft).
clase [klá·se] f. class; classroom; kind, sort.
clásico [klá·si·ko] adj. classic, classical.
clasificación [kla·si·fi·ka·sjón] f. classification.
clasificar⁶ [kla·si·fi·kár] v. to classify.
claustro [kláws·tro] m. cloister; meeting of a university faculty; — de profesores university faculty.
cláusula [kláw·su·la] f. clause.
clausura [klaw·sú·ra] f. closing; seclusion, monastic life.
clavado [kla·bá·do] m. Mex. a dive.
clavar [kla·bár] v. to nail; to fix; to deceive, cheat; -se to be deceived; Mex. to fall into a trap; Mex. to dive.
clave [klá·be] f. key, code; keystone; clef.
clavel [kla·bél] m. carnation, pink.
clavetear [kla·be·te·ár] v. to nail; to stud with nails.
clavícula [kla·bí·ku·la] f. collarbone.
clavija [kla·bí·xa] f. peg; electric plug; peg (of a stringed instrument).
clavijero [kla·bi·xé·ro] m. hat or clothes rack.
clavo [klá·bo] m. nail; clove (spice); sharp pain or grief; sick headache; Mex. rich mineral vein; Am. bother, worry; Col. surprise, disappointment; Riopl. drug on the market (unsaleable article); dar en el — to hit the nail on the head; Am. meter a uno en un — to put a person in a predicament; Am. ser un — to be punctual, exact.
clemencia [kle·mén·sja] f. mercy; clemente [kle·mén·te] adj. merciful.
clerical [kle·ri·kál] adj. clerical, of a clergyman or the clergy.
clérigo [klé·ri·go] m. clergyman.
clero [klé·ro] m. clergy.
cliché [kli·čé] m. photographic plate; also clisé.
cliente [kljén·te] m. & f. client; customer;
clientela [kljen·té·la] f. clientele, clients; customers.
clima [klí·ma] m. climate.
clímax [klí·maks] m. climax.
clínica [klí·ni·ka] f. clinic.
clíper [klí·per] m. clipper.
cloaca [klo·á·ka] f. sewer.
cloquear [klo·ke·ár] v. to cluck.
cloqueo [klo·ké·o] m. cluck, clucking.
cloro [kló·ro] m. chlorine.
clorofila [klo·ro·fí·la] f. chlorophyll.

cloruro [klo·rú·ro] *m.* chloride.
club [kluḃ] *m.* club, society.
clueca [klwé·ka] *f.* brooding hen.
coacción [ko·ak·sjón] *f.* compulsion, force; enforcement.
coagular [ko·a·ġu·lár] *v.* to coagulate, thicken, clot; to curd, curdle; **-se** to coagulate, clot; to curd, curdle.
coágulo [ko·á·ġu·lo] *m.* coagulation, clot.
coartar [ko·ar·tár] *v.* to restrain, limit.
coba [kó·ḃa] *f.* flattery; fib; **dar** — to flatter; to tease.
cobalto [ko·ḃál·to] *m.* cobalt.
cobarde [ko·ḃár·ḋe] *adj.* cowardly; timid; weak; *m.* coward.
cobardía [ko·ḃar·ḋí·a] *f.* cowardice.
cobertizo [ko·ḃer·tí·so] *m.* shed; shanty.
cobertor [ko·ḃer·tór] *m.* bedcover, quilt.
cobertura [ko·ḃer·tú·ra] *f.* cover, covering.
cobija [ko·ḃí·xa] *f.* cover; shelter; roof; *Am.* blanket; *Am.* shawl, serape, poncho; **-s** *Am.* bedclothes.
cobijar [ko·ḃi·xár] *v.* to cover; to shelter.
cobrador [ko·ḃra·ḋór] *m.* collector; ticket collector.
cobranza [ko·ḃrán·sa] *f.* collection (*of a sum of money*); cashing.
cobrar [ko·ḃrár] *v.* to collect (*bills, debts*); to charge; to cash (*a draft, check, etc.*); to recover, regain; to gain, acquire; *Am.* to demand payment; — **cariño a** to take a liking to.
cobre [kó·ḃre] *m.* copper; copper kitchen utensils; *Am.* copper coin; **-s** brass musical instruments; **batir el** — to hustle, work with energy; *Am.* **mostrar el** — to show one's worse side.
cobrizo [ko·ḃrí·so] *adj.* coppery, copper-colored.
cobro [kó·ḃro] *m.* collection (*of bills*); **poner en** — to put in a safe place; **ponerse en** — to take refuge, get to a safe place.
coca [kó·ka] *f.* *Am.* coca (*South American shrub and its leaves*); *Am.* cocaine; *Am.* coca tea; *Am.* eggshell; *Am.* fruit skin or rind; *Am.* **de** — free of charge; in vain.
cocaína [ko·ka·í·na] *f.* cocaine.
cocear [ko·se·ár] *v.* to kick.
cocer[2, 10] [ko·sér] *v. irr.* to cook; to boil; to bake.
cocido [ko·sí·ḋo] *m.* Spanish stew; *p.p. of* **cocer.**
cociente [ko·sjén·te] *m.* quotient.
cocimiento [ko·si·mjén·to] *m.* cooking; baking; liquid concoction (*generally made of medicinal herbs*).
cocina [ko·sí·na] *f.* kitchen; cuisine, cooking; — **económica** stove, range.
cocinar [ko·si·nár] *v.* to cook.
cocinero [ko·si·né·ro] *m.* cook.
coco [kó·ko] *m.* coconut; coconut palm; bogeyman, goblin; *Am.* derby hat; *Mex., Carib., Riopl.* head; *Am.* blow on the head; **hacer -s a** to make eyes at, flirt with; *Col., Ven., Andes* **pelar a** — to crop the hair; **cocotal** [ko·ko·tál] *m.* grove of coconut palms; coconut plantation; **cocotero** [ko·ko·té·ro] *m.* coconut palm.
cocodrilo [ko·ko·ḋrí·lo] *m.* crocodile.
coche [kó·če] *m.* coach; car; taxi.
cochero [ko·čé·ro] *m.* coachman; cabman; taxi driver.
cochinada [ko·či·ná·ḋa] *f.* filth, filthiness; filthy act or remark; dirty trick; herd of swine.
cochinilla [ko·či·ní·ya] *f.* cochineal (*insect*).
cochino [ko·čí·no] *m.* hog, pig; dirty person; *Ch.* stingy person; *Am.* — **de monte** wild boar; *adj.* filthy, dirty; *Ch.* miserly, stingy.

codazo [ko·ḋá·so] *m.* nudge; poke (*with the elbow*).
codear [ko·ḋe·ár] *v.* to elbow; to nudge; **-se con alguien** to rub elbows with someone.
códice [kó·ḋi·se] *m.* codex.
codicia [ko·ḋi·sja] *f.* greed; greediness.
codiciar [ko·ḋi·sjár] *v.* to covet.
codicioso [ko·ḋi·sjó·so] *adj.* covetous, greedy.
código [kó·ḋi·ġo] *m.* code of laws.
codo [kó·ḋo] *m.* elbow; bend; **alzar** (*or* **empinar**) **el** — to drink too much; **hablar por los -s** to talk too much; **meterse** (*or* **estar metido**) **hasta los -s** to be up to the elbows, be very busy.
codorniz [ko·ḋor·nís] *f.* partridge.
coetáneo [ko·e·tá·ne·o] *adj.* contemporary.
cofrade [ko·frá·ḋe] *m.* & *f.* fellow member (*of a brotherhood, club, society, etc.*).
cofradía [ko·fra·ḋí·a] *f.* brotherhood; sisterhood; guild; trade union.
cofre [kó·fre] *m.* coffer, jewel box; chest, trunk.
coger[1] [ko·xér] *v.* to seize; to catch; to grasp; to gather; *Am.* **-se una cosa** to steal something.
cogollo [ko·ġó·yo] *m.* heart (of lettuce), head (of cabbage).
cogote [ko·ġó·te] *m.* nape, back of the neck.
cohechar [ko·e·čár] *v.* to bribe.
coheredero [ko·e·re·ḋé·ro] *m.* joint heir.
coherente [ko·e·rén·te] *adj.* coherent; connected.
cohete [ko·é·te] *m.* skyrocket; rocket; *Riopl.* **al** — in vain, uselessly.
cohetería [ko·e·te·rí·a] *f.* rocketry; rocket weaponry; shop for making fireworks.
cohibición [koj·ḃi·sjón] *f.* repression, inhibition, restraint.
cohibido [koj·ḃí·ḋo] *p.p.* & *adj.* inhibited; embarrassed, uneasy.
cohibir [koj·ḃír] *v.* to restrain, repress; to inhibit.
coincidencia [kojn·si·ḋén·sja] *f.* coincidence.
coincidir [kojn·si·ḋír] *v.* to coincide.
cojear [ko·xe·ár] *v.* to limp; **cojeamos del mismo pie** we both have the same weakness.
cojera [ko·xé·ra] *f.* limp, lameness.
cojín [ko·xín] *m.* cushion; pad; **cojincillo** *m.* pad.
cojinete [ko·xi·né·te] *m.* small pillow or cushion, pad; bearing, ball bearing.
cojo [kó·xo] *adj.* lame, crippled; one-legged.
col [kol] *f.* cabbage; — **de Bruselas** Brussels sprouts.
cola [kó·la] *f.* (*rabo*) tail; train of a dress; (*hilera de gente*) line of people; **piano de** — grand piano; **piano de media** — baby grand; **hacer** — to stand in line; *Am.* **comer** — to be the last one in a contest.
colaboración [ko·la·ḃo·ra·sjón] *f.* collaboration, mutual help.
colaborar [ko·la·ḃo·rár] *v.* to collaborate, work together.
coladera [ko·la·ḋé·ra] *f.* colander, strainer, sieve; *Mex., Ven.* drain.
colar[2] [ko·lár] *v. irr.* to strain, filter; to bleach with lye; **-se** to slip in or out, sneak in.
colcha [kól·ča] *f.* quilt; bedspread; **-s** *Riopl.* saddle and trappings; *Riopl.* gaucho clothing.
colchón [kol·čón] *m.* mattress.
colear [ko·le·ár] *v.* to wag the tail; to grab a bull by the tail and throw him over; *Am.* to flunk (*a student*); *Am.* to trail, tag behind (*a person*); *Col.* to bother, nag, harass; *Am.* to smoke one cigarette after another.
colección [ko·lek·sjón] *f.* collection; set; gathering.
coleccionar [ko·lek·sjo·nár] *v.* to collect, make a collection.

coleccionista [ko·lek·sjo·nís·ta] *m. & f.* collector (*of stamps, curios, etc.*).

colecta [ko·lék·ta] *f.* collection of voluntary gifts; assessment; collect (*a short prayer of the mass*).

colectivo [ko·lek·tí·ƀo] *adj.* collective; *m.* small bus.

colector [ko·lek·tór] *m.* collector; water pipe, drain.

colega [ko·lé·ga] *m. & f.* colleague, fellow worker.

colegiatura [ko·le·xja·tú·ra] *f.* college fellowship or scholarship; *C.A.* tuition in a college.

colegio [ko·lé·xjo] *m.* boarding school; school, academy; college, body of professional men.

colegir[5, 11] [ko·le·xír] *v.* to gather; to conclude, infer.

cólera [kó·le·ra] *f.* anger, rage; *m.* cholera (*disease*).

colérico [ko·lé·ri·ko] *adj.* irritable; angry.

coleto [ko·lé·to] *m.* leather jacket; one's inner self; *Am.* impudence, shamelessness; **decir para su —** to say to oneself; **echarse al —** to drink down; to devour.

colgadero [kol·ga·ɖé·ro] *m.* hanger; hook, peg; hat or clothes rack.

colgadura [kol·ga·ɖú·ra] *f.* drape, hanging; drapery; tapestry.

colgante [kol·gán·te] *adj.* hanging; dangling; **puente —** suspension bridge.

colgar[2, 7] [kol·gár] *v. irr.* (*suspender*) to hang, suspend; to dangle; to drape (*walls*); (*achacar*) to impute, attribute; *Cuba* to flunk, fail (*a student*); *Col.* **-se** to fall behind.

colibrí [ko·li·ƀrí] *m.* hummingbird.

coliflor [ko·li·flór] *f.* cauliflower.

coligarse[7] [ko·li·gár·se] *v.* to league together, band together.

colilla [ko·lí·ya] *f.* small tail; butt (*of a cigarette*), stub (*of a cigar*).

colina [ko·lí·na] *f.* hill.

colindante [ko·lin·dán·te] *adj.* contiguous, neighboring, adjacent.

colindar [ko·lin·dár] *v.* to border (on); to be adjoining.

colisión [ko·li·sjón] *f.* collision, clash.

colmar [kol·már] *v.* to fill to the brim; **— de** to fill with; to shower with (*gifts, favors, etc.*); **-le a uno el plato** to exhaust one's patience.

colmena [kol·mé·na] *f.* beehive; *Mex.* bee.

colmillo [kol·mí·yo] *m.* eyetooth, canine tooth; tusk; fang.

colmo [kól·mo] *m.* overfullness; limit; **— de la locura** height of folly; **¡eso es el —!** that's the limit! *adj.* overfull, filled to the brim.

colocación [ko·lo·ka·sjón] *f.* placing, arrangement; position, job.

colocar[6] [ko·lo·kár] *v.* to place; to put in place, arrange; to give employment to.

colocho [ko·ló·čo] *m. C.A.* curly hair; wood shavings.

colombiano [ko·lom·bjá·no] *adj.* Colombian, of or pertaining to Colombia, South America.

colon [kó·lon] *m.* colon (*of the large intestine*).

colonia [ko·ló·nja] *f.* colony; silk ribbon; *Mex., Carib.* city district; *Am.* sugar plantation.

coloniaje [ko·lo·njá·xe] *m. Am.* colonial period.

colonial [ko·lo·njál] *adj.* colonial.

colonización [ko·lo·ni·sa·sjón] *f.* colonization.

colonizador [ko·lo·ni·sa·ɖór] *m.* colonizer, colonist; *adj.* colonizing.

colonizar[9] [ko·lo·ni·sár] *v.* to colonize.

colono [ko·ló·no] *m.* colonist, settler; tenant farmer; *Carib.* owner of a sugar plantation; *Am.* bootlicker, flatterer.

coloquio [ko·ló·kjo] *m.* conversation, talk; literary dialogue; *Col.* street comedy farce.

color [ko·lór] *m.* color; coloring; paint; rouge; **so — de** under the pretext of.

coloración [ko·lo·ra·sjón] *f.* coloring.

colorado [ko·lo·ra·ɖo] *adj.* red, reddish; colored; **ponerse —** to blush.

colorante [ko·lo·rán·te] *adj. & m.* coloring.

colorar [ko·lo·rár] *v.* to color; to stain; to dye.

colorear [ko·lo·re·ár] *v.* to color; to redden; to give color to.

colorete [ko·lo·ré·te] *m.* rouge.

colorido [ko·lo·rí·ɖo] *m.* coloring; color; *adj.* colored; colorful.

colosal [ko·lo·sál] *adj.* colossal, huge.

columbrar [ko·lum·brár] *v.* to see faintly; to glimpse.

columna [ko·lúm·na] *f.* column.

columpiar [ko·lum·pjár] *v.* to swing; **-se** to swing; to sway.

columpio [ko·lúm·pjo] *m.* swing.

collado [ko·yá·ɖo] *m.* hillock, knoll.

collar [ko·yár] *m.* necklace; dog collar; *Am.* collar (*of a draft horse*); **collera** [ko·yé·ra] *f.* collar (*for draft animals*).

coma [kó·ma] *f.* comma; *m.* coma, stupor, prolonged unconsciousness.

comadre [ko·má·ɖre] *f.* (*amiga*) woman friend; (*chismosa*) gossip; (*partera*) midwife; (*alcahueta*) go-between; *name used to express kinship between mother and godmother*; **comadrona** [ko·ma·ɖró·na] *f.* midwife.

comadreja [ko·ma·ɖré·xa] *f.* weasel.

comandancia [ko·man·dán·sja] *f.* command; position and headquarters of a commander.

comandante [ko·man·dán·te] *m.* major; commander.

comandar [ko·man·dár] *v.* to command (*troops*).

comandita [ko·man·dí·ta] *f.* silent partnership; **sociedad en —** limited company.

comando [ko·mán·do] *m.* military command.

comarca [ko·már·ka] *f.* district, region.

comba [kóm·ba] *f.* bulge, warp.

combar [kom·bár] *v.* to warp, bend, twist; **-se** to warp; to sag; to bulge.

combate [kom·bá·te] *m.* combat, battle, fight.

combatiente [kom·ba·tjén·te] *m.* combatant, fighter.

combatir [kom·ba·tír] *v.* to combat; to fight.

combinación [kom·bi·na·sjón] *f.* combination.

combinar [kom·bi·nár] *v.* to combine, unite.

comburente [kom·bu·rén·te] *m.* the chemical agent that causes combustion, e.g., oxygen; *adj.* causing combustion.

combustible [kom·bus·tí·ƀle] *adj.* combustible; *m.* fuel.

combustión [kom·bus·tjón] *f.* combustion.

comedero [ko·me·ɖé·ro] *m.* trough (*for feeding animals*); *adj.* edible, eatable.

comedia [ko·mé·ɖja] *f.* comedy; farce.

comediante [ko·me·ɖján·te] *m.* actor, comedian.

comedido [ko·me·ɖí·ɖo] *adj.* courteous, polite; obliging; *p.p.* of **comedirse**.

comedirse[5] [ko·me·ɖír·se] *v. irr.* to be civil, polite, obliging; *Ec.* to meddle; *Am.* **— a hacer algo** to volunteer to do something.

comedor [ko·me·ɖór] *m.* dining room; great eater.

comején [ko·me·xén] *m.* termite.

comelón [ko·me·lón] *m. Am.* big eater. See **comilón**.

comendador [ko·men·da·ɖór] *m.* commander (*of certain military orders*).

comensal [ko·men·sál] *m. & f.* table companion; dinner guest.
comentador [ko·men·ta·dór] *m.* commentator.
comentar [ko·men·tár] *v.* to comment.
comentario [ko·men·tá·rjo] *m.* commentary, explanation.
comentarista [ko·men·ta·rís·ta] *m. & f.* commentator.
comenzar[1,9] [ko·men·sár] *v. irr.* to begin.
comer [ko·mér] *v.* to eat; to dine; to take (*in chess or checkers*); **dar de** — to feed; **ganar de** — to earn a living; **-se** to eat; to eat up; to skip (*a letter, syllable, word, etc.*); *Ríopl., Col.* **-se uno a otro** to deceive each other.
comercial [ko·mer·sjál] *adj.* commercial.
comerciante [ko·mer·sján·te] *m.* merchant; storekeeper.
comerciar [ko·mer·sjár] *v.* to trade; to have dealings (with).
comercio [ko·mér·sjo] *m.* commerce, trade.
comestible [ko·mes·tí·ble] *adj.* edible, eatable; **-s** *m. pl.* food, groceries.
cometa [ko·mé·ta] *m.* comet; *C.A.* person seldom seen; *f.* kite.
cometer [ko·me·tér] *v.* to commit; to entrust; to use (*a figure of speech*).
cometido [ko·me·tí·do] *m.* commission, assignment, charge; task, duty.
comezón [ko·me·són] *f.* itch.
comicios [ko·mí·sjos] *m. pl.* primaries, elections.
cómico [kó·mi·ko] *adj.* comic, of comedy; comical, funny, amusing; *m.* comedian, actor.
comida [ko·mí·da] *f.* meal; dinner; good; **comidilla** *f.* small meal; gossip; **la comidilla de la vecindad** the talk of the town.
comienzo [ko·mjén·so] *m.* beginning; origin.
comilitona [ko·mi·li·tó·na] *f.* spread, big feast.
comilón [ko·mi·lón] *m.* big eater.
comillas [ko·mí·yas] *f. pl.* quotation marks.
comino [ko·mí·no] *m.* cuminseed.
comisario [ko·mi·sá·rjo] *m.* commissary, deputy, delegate; manager; *Am.* police inspector.
comisión [ko·mi·sjón] *f.* commission; committee.
comisionado [ko·mi·sjo·ná·do] *adj.* commissioned, charged, delegated; *m.* commissioner; *Am.* constable.
comisionar [ko·mi·sjo·nár] *v.* to commission.
comistrajo [ko·mis·trá·xo] *m.* mess, strange food concoction, mixture.
comité [ko·mi·té] *m.* committee, commission.
comitiva [ko·mi·tí·ba] *f.* retinue, group of attendants or followers.
como [kó·mo] *adv. & conj.* as, like, such as; if, provided that, since, when; *Mex., Ven.* about, approximately; **¿cómo?** [kó·mo] *interr. adv.* how?; what (did you say)?; *Am.* **¡cómo no!** yes, of course!
cómoda [kó·mo·da] *f.* bureau, chest of drawers.
comodidad [ko·mo·di·dád] *f.* comfort; convenience.
comodín [ko·mo·dín] *m.* joker, wild card.
cómodo [kó·mo·do] *adj.* comfortable; convenient; *m. Am.* bedpan.
compacto [kom·pák·to] *adj.* compact.
compadecer[13] [kom·pa·de·sér] *v. irr.* to pity, sympathize with; **-se con** to be in harmony with; **-se de** to take pity on.
compadrazgo [kom·pa·dráz·go] *m.* compaternity (*spiritual affinity between the godfather and the parents of a child*); friendship; relationship; clique, group of friends.
compadre [kom·pá·dre] *m.* (*amigo*) pal, crony,

comrade; (*padrino*) cosponsor; *name used to express kinship between father and godfather.*
compañero [kom·pa·ñé·ro] *m.* companion; partner; mate; **compañerismo** [kom·pa·ñe·ríz·mo] *m.* companionship.
compañía [kom·pa·ñí·a] *f.* company; *Am.* — **del ahorcado** silent companion, poor company.
comparación [kom·pa·ra·sjón] *f.* comparison.
comparar [kom·pa·rár] *v.* to compare.
comparativo [kom·pa·ra·tí·bo] *adj.* comparative.
comparecer[13] [kom·pa·re·sér] *v. irr.* to appear (*before a judge or tribunal*).
compartimiento [kom·par·ti·mjén·to] *m.* compartment.
compartir [kom·par·tír] *v.* to share; to divide into shares.
compás [kom·pás] *m.* compass; measure; beat; **llevar el** — to beat time.
compasión [kom·pa·sjón] *f.* compassion, pity.
compasivo [kom·pa·sí·bo] *adj.* compassionate, sympathetic.
compatible [kom·pa·tí·ble] *adj.* compatible, in harmony.
compatriota [kom·pa·trjó·ta] *m. & f.* compatriot, fellow countryman.
compeler [kom·pe·lér] *v.* to compel, force.
compendiar [kom·pen·djár] *v.* to abstract, summarize, condense.
compendio [kom·pén·djo] *m.* summary, condensation.
compensación [kom·pen·sa·sjón] *f.* compensation; recompense.
compensar [kom·pen·sár] *v.* to balance; to make equal; to compensate, recompense.
competencia [kom·pe·tén·sja] *f.* competition, rivalry; competence, ability.
competente [kom·pe·tén·te] *adj.* competent; capable; adequate.
competidor [kom·pe·ti·dór] *m.* competitor; rival; *adj.* competing.
competir[5] [kom·pe·tír] *v. irr.* to compete, vie.
compilar [kom·pi·lár] *v.* to compile.
compinche [kom·pín·če] *m.* chum, pal, comrade.
complacencia [kom·pla·sén·sja] *f.* complacency, satisfaction, contentment.
complacer[38] [kom·pla·sér] *v. irr.* to please, humor; to comply; **-se** to take pleasure or satisfaction (in).
coplaciente [kom·pla·sjén·te] *adj.* obliging, agreeable, willing to please.
complejidad [kom·ple·xi·dád] *f.* complexity.
complejo [kom·ple·xo] *adj. & m.* complex.
complemento [kom·ple·mén·to] *m.* complement; object (*of a verb*).
completamiento [kom·ple·ta·mjén·to] *m.* completion.
completar [kom·ple·tár] *v.* to complete; to finish.
completo [kom·plé·to] *adj.* complete, full, perfect.
complexión [kom·plek·sjón] *f.* constitution, make-up.
complicar[6] [kom·pli·kár] *v.* to complicate.
cómplice [kóm·pli·se] *m. & f.* accomplice, companion in crime.
complot [kom·plót] *m.* plot, conspiracy; intrigue.
componenda [kom·po·nén·da] *f.* adjustment; compromise.
componente [kom·po·nén·te] *adj.* component, constituent; *m.* component, essential part.
componer[40] [kom·po·nér] *v. irr.* to fix, repair; to

fix up; to adorn, trim; to compose; to set up (*type*); to settle (*a dispute*); *Col.* to set (*bones*).

comportamiento [kom·por·ta·mjén·to] *m.* conduct, behavior.

composición [kom·po·si·sjón] *f.* composition; settlement.

compositor [kom·po·si·tór] *m.* composer.

compostura [kom·pos·tú·ra] *f.* (*arreglo*) repair; settlement, adjustment; (*aseo*) neatness, composition; (*dignidad*) composure, dignity.

compota [kom·pó·ta] *f.* fruit preserves; — **de manzana** applesauce.

compra [kóm·pra] *f.* purchase; buying; **ir de -s** to go shopping.

comprador [kom·pra·dór] *m.* buyer, purchaser.

comprar [kom·prár] *v.* to buy, purchase.

comprender [kom·pren·dér] *v.* to understand, grasp, comprehend; to comprise, embrace.

comprensible [kom·pren·sí·ble] *adj.* comprehensible, understandable.

comprensión [kom·pren·sjón] *f.* understanding; comprehension; keenness.

comprensivo [kom·pren·si·bo] *adj.* comprehensive; understanding.

compresión [kom·pre·sjón] *f.* compression.

compresor [kom·pre·sór] *m.* compressor.

comprimido [kom·pri·mí·do] *adj.* compressed; *m.* medicinal tablet.

comprimir [kom·pri·mír] *v.* to compress; to repress.

comprobación [kom·pro·ba·sjón] *f.* confirmation, check, proof, test.

comprobante [kom·pro·bán·te] *adj.* proving, verifying; *m.* proof; evidence; certificate; voucher; warrant.

comprobar[2] [kom·pro·bár] *v. irr.* to verify; to check; to prove.

comprometer [kom·pro·me·tér] *v.* (*exponer*) to compromise; to endanger; to bind; to force; (*concordar*) to come to an agreement; **-se** to promise, bind oneself; to become engaged; to compromise oneself.

compromiso [kom·pro·mí·so] *m.* (*convenio*) compromise; (*obligación*) engagement; appointment; (*dificultad*) predicament, trouble.

compuerta [kom·pwér·ta] *f.* sluice (*gate to control the flow of water*), floodgate.

compuesto [kom·pwés·to] *p.p. of* **componer** & *adj.* repaired; fixed, adorned; composed; composite; compound; *m.* composite; compound.

compungirse[11] [kom·pun·xír·se] *v.* to feel regret or remorse.

computadora electrónica [kom·pu·ta·dó·ra e·lek·tró·ni·ka] *f.* electronic computer.

computar [kom·pu·tár] *v.* to compute, calculate.

cómputo [kóm·pu·to] *m.* computation, calculation.

comulgar[7] [ko·mul·gár] *v.* to commune, take communion.

común [ko·mún] *adj.* common; **por lo —** generally; *m.* toilet; **el — de las gentes** the majority of the people; the average person.

comunero [ko·mu·né·ro] *adj.* common, popular; *Am.* pertaining to a community; *m.* commoner (*one of the common people*); *Col., Ven., Andes* member of an Indian community.

comunicación [ko·mu·ni·ka·sjón] *f.* communication.

comunicar[6] [ko·mu·ni·kár] *v.* to communicate; to notify; **-se** to communicate; to correspond; to be in touch (with); to connect.

comunicativo [ko·mu·ni·ka·tí·bo] *adj.* communicative, talkative.

comunidad [ko·mu·ni·dád] *f.* community; commonwealth; the common people; commonness; guild.

comunión [ko·mu·njón] *f.* communion; political party.

comunismo [ko·mu·níz·mo] *m.* communism; **comunista** [ko·mu·nís·ta] *m.* & *f.* communist; *adj.* communistic, communist.

con [kon] *prep.* with; — **ser** in spite of being; — **tal que** provided that; — **todo** however.

conato [ko·ná·to] *m.* attempt, effort; assault (*law*).

concavidad [kon·ka·bi·dád] *f.* hollow, cavity; hollowness.

cóncavo [kón·ka·bo] *adj.* concave, hollow.

concebible [kon·se·bí·ble] *adj.* conceivable.

concebir[5] [kon·se·bír] *v. irr.* to conceive; to imagine; to understand, grasp.

conceder [kon·se·dér] *v.* to concede, grant; to admit.

concejal [kon·se·xál] *m.* councilman, alderman.

concejo [kon·sé·xo] *m.* town council.

concentración [kon·sen·tra·sjón] *f.* concentration.

concentrar [kon·sen·trár] *v.* to concentrate.

concepción [kon·sep·sjón] *f.* conception.

concepto [kon·sép·to] *m.* concept, idea, thought.

concernir[51] [kon·ser·nir] *v. irr.* to concern.

concertar[1] [kon·ser·tár] *v. irr.* (*arreglar*) to arrange, plan, settle; to conclude (*a treaty or business deal*); (*concordar*) to harmonize; to agree.

concesión [kon·se·sjón] *f.* concession, grant; granting; acknowledgment.

conciencia [kon·sjén·sja] *f.* conscience.

concienzudo [kon·sjen·sú·do] *adj.* conscientious.

concierto [kon·sjér·to] *m.* concert; harmony; agreement; **de —** by common agreement.

conciliar [kon·si·ljár] *v.* to conciliate, win over; to reconcile, bring into harmony; **— el sueño** to get to sleep.

concilio [kon·sí·ljo] *m.* council.

concision [kon·si·sjón] *f.* conciseness, brevity.

conciso [kon·sí·so] *adj.* concise, brief.

conciudadano [kon·sju·da·dá·no] *m.* fellow citizen, fellow countryman.

concluir[32] [kon·klwír] *v. irr.* to conclude, finish; to infer.

conclusión [kon·klu·sjón] *f.* conclusion.

concordancia [kon·kor·dán·sja] *f.* concord, agreement, harmony.

concordar[2] [kon·kor·dár] *v. irr.* to agree; to be in harmony; to put in harmony.

concordia [kon·kór·dja] *f.* concord, harmony, agreement.

concretar [kon·kre·tár] *v.* to summarize, condense; to limit; **-se a** to limit oneself to.

concreto [kon·kré·to] *adj.* concrete, real, specific; **en —** concretely; to sum up; *m. Am.* concrete.

concupiscente [kon·ku·pi·sen·te] *adj.* sensual.

concurrencia [kon·ku·rrén·sja] *f.* gathering, audience; concurrence, simultaneous meeting or happening; competition.

concurrido [kon·ku·rrí·do] *adj.* well-patronized, well-attended, much frequented.

concurrir [kon·ku·rrír] *v.* to concur, meet together; to happen at the same time or place; to attend; to agree.

concurso [kon·kúr·so] *m.* gathering; contest; competitive examination; assistance.

concha [kón·ča] *f.* shell; shellfish; prompter's box; *Mex.* **tener — to** be indifferent, unruffled, tough.

conchabar [kon·ča·ɓár] v. to unite, join; *Mex., S.A.*
to hire (*labor*); -se to join, gang together; to
conspire; *Ríopl.* to hire oneself out, get a job.
conchabo [kon·čá·ɓo] m. *Am.* hiring of a laborer
or servant; *Ríopl.* job, menial job.
conde [kón·de] m. count; condesa *f.* countess.
condecoración [kon·de·ko·ra·sjón] *f.* decoration;
badge, medal.
condecorar [kon·de·ko·rár] v. to decorate (*with a
badge or medal*).
condena [kon·dé·na] *f.* term in prison, sentence,
penalty.
condenación [kon·de·na·sjón] *f.* condemnation;
conviction (*of a prisoner or criminal*);
damnation.
condenar [kon·de·nár] v. to condemn; to sentence;
Am. to annoy, irritate; -se to be damned, go to
hell.
condensar [kon·den·sár] v. to condense.
condescendencia [kon·de·sen·dén·sja] *f.*
condescension, patronizing attitude.
condescender[1] [kon·de·sen·dér] v. *irr.* to
condescend; to comply, yield.
condición [kon·di·sjón] *f.* condition.
condimentar [kon·di·men·tár] v. to season.
condimento [kon·di·mén·to] m. condiment,
seasoning.
condiscípulo [kon·di·sí·pu·lo] m. schoolmate,
classmate.
condolerse[2] [kon·do·lér·se] v. *irr.* to condole (with),
sympathize (with), be sorry (for).
cóndor [kón·dor] m. *Am.* condor, vulture; *Am.* gold
coin of Ecuador, Chile and Colombia.
conducir[25] [kon·du·sír] v. *irr.* to conduct, lead;
to drive (*an auto*); -se to behave, act.
conducta [kon·dúk·ta] *f.* conduct; behavior;
convoy, escort; management.
conducto [kon·dúk·to] m. conduit, pipe, channel;
por — de through.
conductor [kon·duk·tór] adj. conducting; m. leader;
chauffeur; guide; conductor (*electrical*); *Am.*
conductor, ticket collector (*on trains, buses,
streetcars*); *Am.* teamster, driver.
conectar [ko·nek·tár] v. to connect.
conejera [ko·ne·xé·ra] *f.* burrow; rabbit warren
(*piece of land for breeding rabbits*); den, joint,
dive (*of ill repute*).
conejo [ko·né·xo] m. rabbit; *Am.* guinea pig;
conejillo de Indias [ko·ne·xí·yo de ín·djas]
guinea pig.
conexión [ko·nek·sjón] *f.* connection.
conexo [ko·nék·so] adj. connected; coherent.
confección [kon·fek·sjón] *f.* making; confection;
manufactured article; workmanship;
concoction, compound.
confeccionar [kon·fek·sjo·nár] v. to make; to
manufacture; to mix, put up (*a prescription*).
confederación [kon·fe·ɗe·ra·sjón] *f.* confederation,
alliance, league.
confederar [kon·fe·ɗe·rár] v. to confederate; -se to
confederate, form into a confederacy.
conferencia [kon·fe·rén·sja] *f.* lecture; conference,
meeting.
conferenciante [kon·fe·ren·sján·te] m. & *f.* lecturer.
conferencista [kon·fe·ren·sís·ta] m. & *f.* lecturer.
conferir[3] [kon·fe·rír] v. *irr.* to confer; to give,
bestow.
confesar[1] [kon·fe·sár] v. *irr.* to confess.
confesión [kon·fe·sjón] *f.* confession.
confesionario [kon·fe·sjo·ná·rjo] m. confessional,
confessional box.

confesor [kon·fe·sór] m. confessor.
confiado [kon·fjá·ɗo] adj. confident, trusting,
credulous; presumptuous, self-confident.
confianza [kon·fján·sa] *f.* confidence, trust;
familiarity; informality; **reunión de** — informal
gathering or party.
confianzudo [kon·fjan·sú·ɗo] adj. over-friendly,
over-familiar; *Am.* meddlesome.
confiar[17] [kon·fjár] v. to confide, entrust; to trust,
hope firmly.
confidencia [kon·fi·ɗén·sja] *f.* confidence, trust;
secret, confidential remark; **confidencial**
[kon·fi·ɗen·sjál] adj. confidential.
confidente [kon·fi·ɗén·te] m. confidant; spy, secret
agent; settee or sofa for two people, love seat;
adj. faithful, trustworthy.
confín [kon·fín] m. limit, border, boundary; adj.
bordering, limiting.
confinar [kon·fi·nár] v. to border (upon); to
confine, exile to a specific place.
confirmación [kon·fir·ma·sjón] *f.* confirmation.
confirmar [kon·fir·már] v. to confirm.
confiscar[6] [kon·fis·kár] v. to confiscate.
confitar [kon·fi·tár] v. to candy (*with sugar syrup*);
to make into candy or preserves; to sweeten.
confite [kon·fí·te] m. candy, bonbon; **confitería**
[kon·fi·te·rí·a] *f.* confectionery; candy shop;
confitura [kon·fi·tú·ra] *f.* confection.
conflicto [kon·flík·to] m. conflict.
confluencia [kon·flwén·sja] *f.* junction (*of two
rivers*).
conformar [kon·for·már] v. to adapt, adjust; -se to
conform, comply; to agree; to be resigned (to);
to be satisfied.
conforme [kon·fór·me] adj. in agreement; resigned,
satisfied; alike, similar; — **a** in accordance with.
conformidad [kon·for·mi·ɗáɗ] *f.* conformity;
agreement, harmony; compliance; — **con la
voluntad de Dios** resignation to the will of God;
en — **con** in compliance with; **estar de** — **con**
to be in accordance or agreement with.
confortar [kon·for·tár] v. to comfort, console.
confraternidad [kon·fra·ter·ni·ɗáɗ] *f.* brotherhood.
confrontar [kon·fron·tár] v. to confront; to face; to
compare, check.
confundir [kon·fun·dír] v. to confound, confuse,
mix up; to bewilder; to shame.
confusión [kon·fu·sjón] *f.* confusion.
confuso [kon·fú·so] adj. confused, bewildered;
blurred; vague.
congelado [koŋ·xe·lá·ɗo] p.p. & adj. frozen; icy.
congelar [koŋ·xe·lár] v. to congeal, freeze.
congenial [koŋ·xe·njál] adj. congenial.
congeniar [koŋ·xe·njár] v. to be congenial (with);
to harmonize, be in harmony (with).
congoja [koŋ·gó·xa] *f.* anguish, grief, anxiety.
congratular [koŋ·gra·tu·lár] v. to congratulate.
congregación [koŋ·gre·ɡa·sjón] *f.* congregation,
assembly; religious fraternity.
congregar[7] [koŋ·gre·ɡár] v. to congregate, call
together; to assemble; -se to congregate,
assemble.
congresista [koŋ·gre·sís·ta] m. congressman;
conventionite; *f.* congresswoman.
congreso [koŋ·gré·so] m. congress, assembly;
convention; — **de los Diputados** House of
Representatives.
conjetura [koŋ·xe·tú·ra] *f.* conjecture, guess,
surmise.
conjeturar [koŋ·xe·tu·rár] v. to conjecture, guess,
surmise.

CO

conjugación [koŋ·xu·ga·sjón] *f.* conjugation; coupling, joining together.
conjugar[7] [koŋ·xu·gár] *v.* to conjugate.
conjunción [koŋ·xun·sjón] *f.* conjunction; union, combination.
conjunto [koŋ·xún·to] *m.* total, whole, entirety; **en** — as a whole; *adj.* joined; related, allied.
conjuración [koŋ·xu·ra·sjón] *f.* conspiracy, plot.
conjurado [koŋ·xu·rá·ðo] *m.* conspirator.
conjurar [koŋ·xu·rár] *v.* to conspire, plot; to join a conspiracy; to entreat; to conjure; to ward off.
conjuro [kon·xu·ro] *m.* conspiracy; exorcism.
conmemorar [kom·me·mo·rár] *v.* to commemorate.
conmemorativo [kom·me·mo·ra·tí·ßo] *adj.* memorial, serving to commemorate.
conmigo [kom·mí· go] with me.
conminación [kom·mi·na·sjón] *f.* threat.
conminatorio [kom·mi·na·tó·rjo] *adj.* threatening.
conmoción [kom·mo·sjón] *f.* commotion.
conmovedor [kom·mo·ße·ðór] *adj.* moving, touching; stirring.
conmover[2] [kom·mo·ßér] *v. irr.* to move, touch, affect (*with emotion*); to stir (*emotions*).
conmutador [kom·mu·ta·ðór] *m.* electric switch; **cuadro** — switchboard.
connatural [kon·na·tu·rál] *adj.* inborn.
cono [kó·no] *m.* cone; pine cone.
conocedor [ko·no·se·ðór] *adj.* knowing, aware, expert; *m.* connoisseur, judge, expert; **ser** — **de** to be judge of.
conocer[13] [ko·no·sér] *v. irr.* (*tener idea de*) to know, be acquainted with; to recognize; (*llegar a conocer*) to meet; **se conoce que** it is clear or evident that.
conocido [ko·no·si·ðo] *p.p.* & *adj.* known; well-known; *m.* acquaintance.
conocimiento [ko·no·si·mjén·to] *m.* (*inteligencia*) knowledge, understanding; acquaintance; (*documento*) bill of lading; **-s** knowledge, learning; **poner en** — to inform.
conque [kóŋ·ke] *conj.* so then, well then, and so.
conquista [koŋ·kís·ta] *f.* conquest.
conquistador [koŋ·kis·ta·ðór] *m.* conqueror; *adj.* conquering, victorious.
conquistar [koŋ·kis·tár] *v.* to conquer, defeat; to win.
consabido [kon·sa·ßí·ðo] *adj.* aforementioned, aforesaid.
consagración [kon·sa·gra·sjón] *f.* consecration.
consagrar [kon·sa·grár] *v.* to consecrate.
consciencia [kons·sjén·sja] *f.* consciousness.
consciente [kons·sjén·te] *adj.* conscious.
consecución [kon·se·ku·sjón] *f.* attainment.
consecuencia [kon·se·kwén·sja] *f.* consequence; result; **a** — **de** as a result of; **por** (*or* **en**) — therefore; consequently.
consecuente [kon·se·kwén·te] *adj.* consequent, logical; consistent; *m.* consequence, result.
consecutivo [kon·se·ku·tí·ßo] *adj.* consecutive, successive.
conseguir[5, 12] [kon·se·gír] *v. irr.* to get, obtain; to reach, attain.
conseja [kon·sé·xa] *f.* old wives' tale, fable.
consejero [kon·se·xé·ro] *m.* adviser counselor.
consejo [kon·sé·xo] *m.* counsel, advice; council; council hall.
consentimiento [kon·sen·ti·mjén·to] *m.* consent.
consentir[3] [kon·sen·tír] *v. irr.* to consent, permit; to pamper, spoil.
conserje [kon·sér·xe] *m.* janitor, caretaker.

conserva [kon·sér·ßa] *f.* preserve; pickled fruit or vegetables; *Ch.* filling (*for tarts or candy*).
conservación [kon·ser·ßa·sjón] *f.* conservation.
conservador [kon·ser·ßa·ðór] *m.* conservative; preserver; guardian; *adj.* conservative.
conservar [kon·ser·ßár] *v.* to conserve, keep; to preserve.
considerable [kon·si·ðe·rá·ßle] *adj.* considerable.
consideración [kon·si·ðe·ra·sjón] *f.* consideration.
considerado [kon·si·ðe·rá·ðo] *adj.* considerate, thoughtful; respected; prudent.
considerar [kon·si·ðe·rár] *v.* to consider; to treat with consideration.
consigna [kon·síg·na] *f.* watchword, password; *Am.* checkroom.
consignar [kon·sig·nár] *v.* to consign; to deliver; to deposit; to assign; to check (*baggage*).
consigo [kon·sí·go] with oneself; with himself (herself, themselves).
consiguiente [kon·si·gjén·te] *adj.* consequent; *m.* consequence; **por** — consequently.
consistente [kon·sis·tén·te] *adj.* firm, substantial.
consistir [kon·sis·tír] *v.* to consist; to be based on; **¿en qué consiste?** why?; what is the explanation for it?
consocio [kon·só·sjo] *m.* associate, partner.
consolación [kon·so·la·sjón[*f.* consolation.
consolar[2] [kon·so·lár] *v. irr.* to console, cheer.
consolidar [kon·so·li·ðár] *v.* to consolidate, make solid; to unite, combine.
consonante [kon·so·nán·te] *m.* perfect rhyme; *f.* consonant; *adj.* in harmony.
consorte [kon·sór·te] *m.* & *f.* consort; mate; companion.
conspicuo [kons·pí·kwo] *adj.* conspicuous.
conspiración [kons·pi·ra·sjón] *f.* conspiracy, plot.
conspirador [kons·pi·ra·ðór] *m.* conspirator, plotter.
conspirar [kons·pi·rár] *v.* to conspire, plot.
constancia [kons·tán·sja] *f.* (*firmeza*) constancy; perseverance; (*certeza*) evidence, certainty; *Am.* documentary proof, record.
constante [kons·tán·te] *adj.* constant; continual; firm, faithful. ·
constar [kons·tár] *v.* to be evident, clear; to consist (of); be composed (of); to be on record.
constatación [kons·ta·ta·sjón] *f. Am.* proof, check, evidence.
constelación [kons·te·la·sjón] *f.* constellation.
constipado [kons·ti·pá·ðo] *adj.* suffering from a cold; *m.* cold in the head.
constipar [kons·ti·pár] *v.* to stop up (*the nasal passages*); to cause a cold; **-se** to catch cold.
constitución [kons·ti·tu·sjón] *f.* constitution.
constitucional [kons·ti·tu·sjo·nál] *adj.* constitutional.
constituir[32] [kons·ti·twír] *v. irr.* to constitute, form; to set up, establish; **-se en** to set oneself up as.
constitutivo [kons·ti·tu·tí·ßo] = **constituyente**.
constituyente [kons·ti·tu·yén·te] *adj.* constituent.
constreñir[5, 19] [kons·tre·ñír] *v. irr.* to constrain; to compel, oblige.
construcción [kons·truk·sjón] *f.* construction; structure; building.
construir[32] [kons·trwír] *v. irr.* to construct, build.
consuelo [kon·swé·lo] *m.* consolation, comfort; relief; cheer.
consuetudinario [kon·swe·tu·ði·ná·rjo] *adj.* habitual, customary; **derecho** — common law.
cónsul [kón·sul] *m.* consul.
consulado [kon·su·lá·ðo] *m.* consulate.

consulta [kon·súl·ta] *f.* consultation; opinion.
consultar [kon·sul·tár] *v.* to consult.
consultorio [kon·sul·tó·rjo] *m.* office for consultation; doctor's office or clinic.
consumado [kon·su·má·ɗo] *p.p.* of **consumar**; *adj.* consummate, perfect, complete; accomplished.
consumar [kon·su·már] *v.* to consummate, complete.
consumidor [kon·su·mi·ɗór] *m.* consumer; *adj.* consuming.
consumir [kon·su·mír] *v.* to consume; to waste; **-se** to be consumed; to burn out; to be exhausted; to waste away.
consumo [kon·sú·mo] *m.* consumption (*of food, provisions, etc.*).
consunción [kon·sun·sjón] *f.* consumption (*illness*).
contabilidad [kon·ta·ƀi·li·ɗáɗ] *f.* accounting; bookkeeping.
contacto [kon·ták·to] *m.* contact.
contado [kon·tá·ɗo]: **al** — in cash; **de** — immediately; **por de** — of course; **contados** *adj.* few, scarce, rare.
contador [kon·ta·ɗór] *m.* accountant; purser, cashier; counter; meter (*for water, gas, or electricity*); — **geiger** Geiger counter; Geiger-Müller counter.
contaduría [kon·ta·ɗu·rí·a] *f.* accountant's or auditor's office; box office; cashier's office; accounting.
contagiar [kon·ta·xjár] *v.* to infect; to corrupt; to contaminate.
contagio [kon·tá·xjo] *m.* contagion; infection.
contagioso [kon·ta·xjó·so] *adj.* contagious; infectious.
contaminar [kon·ta·mi·nár] *v.* to contaminate, defile; to corrupt.
contar[2] [kon·tár] *v. irr.* to count; to tell, relate; — **con** to count on, rely on; **a** — **desde** starting from, beginning with.
contemplación [kon·tem·pla·sjón] *f.* contemplation; gazing; meditation.
contemplar [kon·tem·plár] *v.* to contemplate, gaze at; to examine; to meditate.
contemporáneo [kon·tem·po·rá·ne·o] *adj.* contemporary.
contender[1] [kon·ten·dér] *v. irr.* to contend, fight; to compete.
contener[45] [kon·te·nér] *v. irr.* to contain; to restrain, check; **-se** to refrain; to restrain oneself.
contenido [kon·te·ni·ɗo] *m.* contents; *adj.* restrained, moderate.
contentamiento [kon·ten·ta·mjén·to] *m.* contentment, joy.
contentar [kon·ten·tár] *v.* to give pleasure, make happy; **-se** to be satisfied, pleased; *Am.* to make up, renew friendship.
contento [kon·tén·to] *adj.* content, contented, satisfied, glad; *m.* gladness, contentment.
contera [kon·té·ra] *f.* metal tip (*of a cane, umbrella, etc.*); tip, end; refrain of a song; **por** — as a finishing touch.
contertulio [kon·ter·tú·ljo] *m.* fellow-member.
contestación [kon·tes·ta·sjón] *f.* answer, reply; argument.
contestar [kon·tes·tár] *v.* to answer, reply.
contextura [kon·tes·tú·ra] *f.* texture, composition; structure (*of animal or vegetable tissues*).
contienda [kon·tjén·da] *f.* fight; dispute; contest.
contigo [kon·tí·ɡo] with you (with thee).
contiguo [kon·tí·gwo] *adj.* contiguous, next, neighboring.

continental [kon·ti·nen·tál] *adj.* continental.
continente [kon·ti·nén·te] *m.* continent; countenance; *adj.* continent, moderate, sober.
contingencia [kon·tiŋ·xén·sja] *f.* contingency, possibility; risk.
contigente [kon·tiŋ·xén·te] *adj.* contingent, accidental; *m.* quota; military contingent.
continuación [kon·ti·nwa·sjón] *f.* continuation; continuance; **a** — below, as follows.
continuar[18] [kon·ti·nwár] *v.* to continue; to last.
continuidad [kon·ti·nwi·ɗáɗ] *f.* continuity.
continuo [kon·tí·nwo] *adj.* continuous, connected; continual; steady, constant.
contonearse [kon·to·ne·ár·se] *v.* to strut, swagger; to waddle.
contoneo [kon·to·né·o] *m.* strut; waddle.
contorno [kon·tór·no] *m.* (*circuito*) environs, surrounding country (*usually used in plural*); (*línea*) contour, outline.
contra [kón·tra] *prep.* against; **el pro y el** — the pro and con; *f.* opposition; *Am.* antidote, remedy; **-s** *Am.* play-off, final game (*to determine the winner*); **llevar a uno la** — to contradict a person, take the opposite view.
contraalmirante [kon·tra·al·mi·rán·te] *m.* rear admiral.
contrabajo [kon·tra·ƀá·xo] *m.* bass fiddle, string bass.
contrabandear [kon·tra·ƀan·de·ár] *v.* to smuggle.
contrabandista [kon·tra·ƀan·dís·ta] *m.* smuggler.
contrabando [kon·tra·ƀán·do] *m.* contraband; smuggled goods; smuggling.
contracción [kon·trak·sjón] *f.* contraction; *Ch., Peru* diligence, application, devotion.
contradecir[27] [kon·tra·ɗe·sír] *v. irr.* to contradict.
contradicción [kon·tra·ɗik·sjón] *f.* contradiction.
contradictorio [kon·tra·ɗik·tó·rjo] *adj.* contradictory, contrary, opposing.
contradicho [kon·tra·ɗí·čo] *p.p.* of **contradecir**.
contraer[46] [kon·tra·ér] *v. irr.* to contract; — **matrimonio** to get married; **-se** to shrink; to contract.
contrafuerte [kon·tra·fwér·te] *m.* buttress; spur (*of a mountain*); **-s** secondary chain of mountains.
contrahacer[31] [kon·tra·a·sér] *v. irr.* to counterfeit; to forge; to copy, imitate; to mimic.
contrahecho [kon·tra·é·čo] *p.p.* of **contrahacer** & *adj.* counterfeit; forged; deformed.
contralor [kon·tra·lór] *m. Am.* controller or comptroller (*of accounts or expenditures*). See **controlador**.
contraorden [kon·tra·ór·ɗen] *f.* countermand; cancellation of an order.
contrapelo [kon·tra·pé·lo]: **a** — against the grain.
contrapesar [kon·tra·pe·sár] *v.* to counterbalance, balance; to offset.
contrapeso [kon·tra·pé·so] *m.* counterpoise, counterweight, counterbalance; *Am.* fear, uneasiness.
contrariar[17] [kon·tra·rjár] *v.* to oppose; to contradict; to irritate, vex.
contrariedad [kon·tra·rje·ɗáɗ] *f.* opposition; contradiction; bother, irritation; disappointment.
contrario [kon·trá·rjo] *adj.* contrary; opposite; *m.* opponent.
contrarrestar [kon·tra·rres·tár] *v.* to counteract; to resist, oppose; to strike back (*a ball*).
contrarrevolución [kon·tra·rre·ƀo·lu·sjón] *f.* counterrevolution.
contraseña [kon·tra·sé·ña] *f.* password, watchword

mark; check (*for baggage*); — **de salida** theatre check (*to re-enter during the performance*).
contrastar [kon·tras·tár] *v*. (*contrapesar*) to contrast; to test (*scales, weights, measures, etc.*); to assay (*metals*); (*resistir*) to resist, oppose.
contraste [kon·trás·te] *m*. contrast; assay, test; assayer, tester; assayer's office.
contrata [kon·trá·ta] *f*. contract, bargain, agreement.
contratar [kon·tra·tár] *v*. to contract for; to trade; to engage, hire (*men*); -**se** to come to, or make, an agreement.
contratiempo [kon·tra·tjém·po] *m*. accident, mishap.
contratista [kon·tra·tís·ta] *m*. & *f*. contractor.
contrato [kon·trá·to] *m*. contract.
contraventana [kon·tra·ƀen·tá·na] *f*. shutter.
contribución [kon·tri·ƀu·sjón] *f*. contribution; tax.
contribuir[32] [kon·tri·ƀwír] *v*. *irr*. to contribute.
contribuyente [kon·tri·ƀu·yén·te] *m*. contributor; tax-payer; *adj*. contributing.
control [kon·tról] *m*. *Am*. control.
controlador [kon·tro·la·ɖór] *m*. *Am*. controller.
controlar [kon·tro·lár] *v*. *Am*. to control.
controversia [kon·tro·ƀér·sja] *f*. controversy.
contumacia [kon·tu·má·sja] *f*. stubbornness, obstinacy; contempt of court, failure to appear in court; rebelliousness.
contumaz [kon·tu·más] *adj*. stubborn; rebellious.
contusión [kon·tu·sjón] *f*. bruise.
convalecer[13] [kom·ba·le·sér] *v*. *irr*. to convalesce, recover from an illness.
convecino [kom·be·sí·no] *adj*. near, neighboring; *m*. neighbor.
convencedor [kom·ben·se·ɖór] *adj*. convincing.
convencer[10] [kom·ben·sér] *v*. to convince.
convencimiento [kom·ben·si·mjén·to] *m*. conviction; belief; convincing.
convención [kom·ben·sjón] *f*. convention, assembly; pact, agreement; *Ríopl., Col., Ven., Mex., Carib*. political convention; **convencional** [kom·ben·sjo·nál] *adj*. conventional.
convenido [kom·be·ní·ɖo] *adj*. agreed; O.K., all right; *p.p. of* **convenir**.
conveniencia [kom·be·njén·sja] *f*. convenience; comfort; utility, profit.
conveniente [kom·be·njén·te] *adj*. convenient, useful, profitable; fit, proper, suitable; opportune.
convenio [kom·bé·njo] *m*. pact, agreement.
convenir[48] [kom·be·nír] *v*. *irr*. to agree; to convene, assemble; to be suitable, proper, advisable; to suit, fit; -**se** to agree.
conventillo [kom·ben·tí·yo] *m*. *Ríopl., Ch*. tenement house.
convento [kom·bén·to] *m*. convent.
convergente [kom·ber·xén·te] *adj*. convergent, coming together.
converger[11] [kom·ber·xér], **convergir**[11] [kom·ber·xír] *v*. to converge.
conversación [kom·ber·sa·sjón] *f*. conversation.
conversar [kom·ber·sár] *v*. to converse.
conversión [kom·ber·sjón] *f*. conversion.
convertir[3] [kom·ber·tír] *v*. *irr*. to convert.
convicción [kom·bik·sjón] *f*. conviction.
convicto [kom·bík·to] *p.p. irr. of* **convencer**; convicted, guilty.
convidado [kom·bi·ɖá·ɖo] *m*. guest; *Am*. — **y con ollita** guest who abuses hospitality.
convidar [kom·bi·ɖár] *v*. to invite; -**se** to volunteer one's services; to invite oneself.

convincente [kom·bin·sén·te] *adj*. convincing.
convite [kom·bí·te] *m*. invitation; banquet.
convocación [kom·bo·ka·sjón] *f*. convocation.
convocar[6] [kom·bo·kár] *v*. to convoke, call together.
convoyar [kom·bo·yár] *v*. to convoy, escort.
convulsión [kom·bul·sjón] *f*. convulsion.
convulsivo [kom·bul·si·ƀo] *adj*. convulsive; **tos convulsiva** whooping cough.
conyugal [kon·ŷu·ǵál] *adj*. conjugal, pertaining to marriage or a married couple; **vida** — married life.
cónyuge [kón·yu·xe] *m*. husband; *f*. wife.
cooperación [ko·o·pe·ra·sjón] *f*. cooperation.
cooperador [ko·o·pe·ra·ɖór] *adj*. cooperating, cooperative; *m*. cooperator, co-worker.
cooperar [ko·o·pe·rár] *v*. to cooperate.
cooperativo [ko·o·pe·ra·tí·ƀo] *adj*. cooperative; **cooperativa** *f*. cooperative, cooperative society.
coordinación [ko·or·ɖi·na·sjón] *f*. coordination.
coordinar [ko·or·ɖi·nár] *v*. to coordinate.
copa [kó·pa] *f*. (*vaso*) goblet; (*de árbol*) treetop; (*de sombrero*) crown; (*palo de la baraja*) card in the suit of **copas** (*Spanish deck of cards*); *Am*. **empinar la** — to drink, get drunk.
copartícipe [ko·par·tí·si·pe] *adj*. participant; *m*. & *f*. joint partner.
copete [ko·pé·te] *m*. tuft; crest; top, summit; ornamental top on furniture; **de** — of high rank, important; proud; **estar uno hasta el** — to be stuffed; to be fed up; **tener mucho** — to be arrogant, haughty.
copia [kó·pja] *f*. copy; imitation; abundance.
copiar [ko·pjár] *v*. to copy.
copioso [ko·pjó·so] *adj*. copious, abundant.
copita [ko·pí·ta] *f*. little glass; little drink.
copla [kó·pla] *f*. couplet; stanza (*of variable length and meter*); popular song.
copo [kó·po] *m*. (*de nieve*) snowflake; (*mechón*) wad, tuft (*of wool or cotton*).
copularse [ko·pu·lár·se] *v*. to have sexual relations.
coqueta [ko·ké·ta] *f*. coquette, flirt.
coquetear [ko·ke·te·ár] *v*. to flirt.
coquetería [ko·ke·te·rí·a] *f*. coquetry, flirting.
coraje [ko·rá·xe] *m*. courage, valor; anger.
coral [ko·rál] *m*. coral; *Am*. red poisonous snake; -**es** coral beads; *adj*. choral, pertaining to a choir; **coralino** [ko·ra·lí·no] *adj*. coral, like coral.
coraza [ko·rá·sa] *f*. cuirass, armor; armor plate or plating; shell (*of a turtle*).
corazón [ko·ra·són] *m*. heart; core, center; **corazonada** [ko·ra·so·ná·ɖa] *f*. presentiment, foreboding; hunch.
corbata [kor·bá·ta] *f*. necktie; cravat; *Am*. colorful kerchief, scarf.
corcel [kor·sél] *m*. charger, steed.
corcova [kor·kó·ba] *f*. hump, hunch; **corcovado** [kor·ko·bá·ɖo] *adj*. hunchbacked; *m*. hunchback.
corcovear [kor·ko·be·ár] *v*. to prance about, leap; *Am*. to kick, protest against.
corchete [kor·čé·te] *m*. hook and eye.
corcho [kór·čo] *m*. cork; beehive; *adj*. *Am*. cork-like, spongy.
cordel [kor·dél] *m*. cord, rope.
cordero [kor·ɖé·ro] *m*. lamb; lambskin.
cordial [kor·ɖjál] *adj*. cordial, friendly; **dedo** — middle finger.
cordialidad [kor·ɖja·li·ɖáɖ] *f*. cordiality, friendliness, warmth.
cordillera [kor·ɖi·yé·ra] *f*. mountain range.
cordobés [kor·ɖo·ƀés] *adj*. Cordovan, of or

pertaining to Cordova; *m.* native of Cordova.

cordón [kor·dón] *m.* cord; braid; cordon, line of soldiers; *Riopl.* — **de la acera** curb, curbstone of the sidewalk; **cordonería** [kor·do·ne·rí·a] *f.* lace or cord maker's shop; collection of cords and laces; cordmaker's work; braiding.

cordoncillo [kor·don·sí·yo] *m.* small cord, drawstring, lace, lacing; braid; mill (*ridged edge of a coin*); ridge, rib (*of certain fabrics*).

cordura [kor·dú·ra] *f.* good judgment, wisdom; sanity.

cornada [kor·ná·da] *f.* goring; butt with the horns; **dar -s** to gore, horn, butt with the horns.

corneta [kor·né·ta] *f.* cornet; bugle; horn; *m.* bugler.

cornisa [kor·ní·sa] *f.* cornice.

coro [kó·ro] *m.* choir; chorus.

corona [ko·ró·na] *f.* crown; wreath.

coronar [ko·ro·nár] *v.* to crown; to top.

coronel [ko·ro·nél] *m.* colonel.

coronilla [ko·ro·ní·ya] *f.* small crown; crown of the head; **estar uno hasta la** — to be fed up, be satiated.

corpanchón [kor·pan·čón] *m.* large body; carcass.

corpiño [kor·pí·ño] *m.* bodice.

corporación [kor·po·ra·sjón] *f.* corporation.

corporal [kor·po·rál] *adj.* corporal, of the body; *m.* corporal (*small piece of linen used at Mass*).

corpóreo [kor·pó·re·o] *adj.* corporeal, bodily; tangible, material.

corpulento [kor·pu·lén·to] *adj.* corpulent, fat, stout.

corral [ko·rrál] *m.* yard; corral, cattle yard; **corralón** [ko·rra·lón] *m.* large corral; *Am.* lumber warehouse.

correa [ko·rré·a] *f.* leather strap; resistance; *Ch.* **-s** leather blanket carrier; *Am.* **tener muchas -s** to be phlegmatic, calm.

corrección [ko·rrek·sjón] *f.* correction; correctness.

correcto [ko·rrék·to] *adj.* correct, proper.

corredizo [ko·rre·dí·so] *adj.* sliding, slipping; **nudo** — slip knot.

corredor [ko·rre·dór] *m.* (*que corre*) runner, racer; (*pasillo*) corridor; gallery around a patio; (*revendedor*) broker; *Carib., Andes* covered porch; *Am.* beater of wild game; *adj.* running; speedy.

corregidor [ko·rre·xi·dór] *m.* corrector; Spanish magistrate.

corregir[5, 11] [ko·rre·xír] *v. irr.* to correct; to reprove; to punish; **-se** to mend one's ways.

correligionario [ko·rre·li·xjo·ná·rjo] *adj.* of the same religion; of the same political party or sympathies; *m.* coreligionist.

correntada [ko·rren·tá·da] *f. Ch., Riopl., C.A., Carib.* strong river current.

correo [ko·rré·o] *m.* mail; mail service; postman; post office; — **aéreo** air mail.

correón [ko·rre·ón] *m.* large strap.

correoso [ko·rre·ó·so] *adj.* flexible; leathery; tough; **correosidad** [ko·rre·o·si·dád] *f.* toughness, flexibility.

correr [ko·rrér] *v.* (*caminar*) to run; to blow (*said of the wind*); (*encarrera*) to race; to chase; (*pasar*) to pass, elapse (*time*); to draw (*a curtain*); *Am.* to dismiss, throw out; **-se** to slip through; to slide; to be embarrassed.

correría [ko·rre·rí·a] *f.* foray, raid for plunder; excursion, short trip; **-s** wanderings, travels; raids.

correspondencia [ko·rres·pon·dén·sja] *f.* correspondence; letters, mail; agreement;

interchange.

corresponder [ko·rres·pon·dér] *v.* to reciprocate, return (*love, favors*); to belong; to concern; to correspond (*one thing with another*).

correspondiente [ko·rres·pon·djén·te] *adj.* corresponding, agreeing; respective; *m.* correspondent.

corresponsal [ko·rres·pon·sál] *m.* correspondent; agent; newspaper reporter.

corretear [ko·rre·te·ár] *v.* to run around; to roam, rove; *Am.* to pursue, chase.

corrida [ko·rrí·da] *f.* race; *Ch.* row, file; *P.R.* night spree; *Am.* beating up of game; — **del tiempo** swiftness of time; — **de toros** bullfight; **de** — without stopping.

corrido [ko·rrí·do] *adj.* embarrassed, ashamed; worldly-wise; flowing, fluent; **de** — without stopping; *m. Mex., Col., Ven., Riopl., Andes* popular ballad.

corriente [ko·rrjén·te] *adj.* (*que corre*) running; flowing, fluent; (*común*) usual, common, ordinary; *Am.* frank, open; **¡** — **!** all right! O.K.!; **el ocho del** — the eighth of the current month; **estar al** — to be up-to-date; to be well-informed (*about current news*); **poner a uno al** — to keep someone posted or well informed; *f.* current; flow; course; *Am.* **hay que llevarle la** — one must humor him.

corrillo [ko·rrí·yo] *m.* circle or group of gossipers.

corro [kó·rro] *m.* group of talkers or spectators.

corroer[51] [ko·rro·ér] *v. irr.* to corrode.

corromper [ko·rrom·pér] *v.* to corrupt; to seduce; to bribe; **-se** to rot; to become corrupted.

corrompido [ko·rrom·pí·do] *adj.* corrupt; rotten, spoiled; degenerate; *p.p. of* **corromper**.

corrupción [ko·rrup·sjón] *f.* corruption.

corrupto [ko·rrúp·to] *adj.* corrupt, rotten.

corsé [kor·sé] *m.* corset.

cortada [kor·tá·da] *f. Col., Ven., Carib.* cut, slash.

cortador [kor·ta·dór] *m.* cutter.

cortadura [kor·ta·dú·ra] *m.* cut; gash; slash.

cortante [kor·tán·te] *adj.* cutting; sharp.

cortaplumas [kor·ta·plú·mas] *m.* penknife.

cortar [kor·tár] *v.* to cut; to cut off; to cut out; to cut down; to interrupt; *Ven.* to harvest, pick (*fruit*); to gossip, speak ill of someone; **-se** to be embarrassed, ashamed; to sour, curdle (*said of milk*); *Am.* to become separated, cut off; *Mex., Cuba* to leave in a hurry; *Am.* to die.

corte [kór·te] *m.* cut; cutting; cutting edge; fit, style; *Carib., Mex., Riopl.* cut (*in cards*); *Am.* harvest; *Am.* weeding; *Am.* gracefulness in dancing; *f.* royal court; retinue; *P.R., Ven.* court of justice; **-s** Spanish parliament; **hacer la** — to court, woo; *Am.* **darse uno** — to put on airs.

cortedad [kor·te·dád] *f.* smallness; timidity; bashfulness, shyness.

cortejar [kor·te·xár] *v.* to court, woo.

cortejo [kor·té·xo] *m.* cortege, procession; retinue; courtship; suitor.

cortés [kor·tés] *adj.* courteous, polite.

cortesana [kor·te·sá·na] *f.* courtesan, prostitute.

cortesano [kor·te·sá·no] *m.* courtier; *adj.* courtlike; courteous.

cortesía [kor·te·sí·a] *f.* courtesy, politeness.

corteza [kor·té·sa] *f.* bark; crust; peel.

cortijo [kor·tí·xo] *m.* farmhouse.

cortina [kor·tí·na] *m.* curtain.

corto [kór·to] *adj.* short; scanty; bashful.

corveta [kor·bé·ta] *f.* buck, leap, bound (*of a horse*); **hacer -s** to prance.

CO

corvo [kór·ƀo] *adj. see* **curvo.**

cosa [kó·sa] *f.* thing; — **de** approximately, about; **no es** — it is not worth anything; **otra** — something else; **como si tal** — serene, as if nothing had happened; *Am.* **ni por una de estas nueve -s** absolutely not, not for anything in the world.

cosecha [ko·sé·ča] *f.* crop; harvest.

cosechar [ko·se·čár] *v.* to reap; to harvest.

coser [ko·sér] *v.* to sew; to stitch.

cosmético [koz·mé·ti·ko] *m. & adj.* cosmetic.

cosquillas [kos·kí·yas] *f. pl.* ticklishness; tickling; **hacer** — to tickle; to excite (*one's desire or curiosity*); **tener** — to be ticklish.

cosquillear [kos·ki·ye·ár] *v.* to tickle; to excite (*one's curiosity or desire*).

cosquilleo [kos·ki·yé·o] *m.* tickle, tickling sensation.

cosquilloso [kos·ki·yó·so] *adj.* ticklish; touchy.

costa [kós·ta] *f.* coast; cost, expense, price; **a toda** — at all costs, by all means.

costado [kos·tá·đo] *m.* side; flank.

costal [kos·tál] *m.* sack; **estar hecho un — de huesos** to be nothing but skin and bones; to be very thin.

costanero [kos·ta·né·ro] *adj.* coastal, relating to a coast; sloping.

costar[2] [kos·tár] *v. irr.* to cost; — **trabajo** to be difficult.

costarricense [kos·ta·rri·sén·se] *adj., m. & f.* Costa Rican.

coste [kós·te], **costo** [kós·to] *m.* cost; expense.

costear [kos·te·ár] *v.* (*pagar*) to defray or pay costs; to pay, be profitable; (*pasar junto a*) to navigate along the coast; to go along the edge of; **no costea** it does not pay.

costero [kos·té·ro] *adj.* coastal; **navegación costera** coastal navigation.

costilla [kos·tí·ya] *f.* rib; chop, cutlet.

costoso [kos·tó·so] *adj.* costly, expensive.

costra [kós·tra] *f.* crust; scab.

costroso [kos·tró·so] *adj.* crusty, scabby.

costumbre [kos·túm·bre] *f.* custom, habit.

costura [kos·tú·ra] *f.* sewing; stitching; seam.

costurera [kos·tu·ré·ra] *f.* seamstress.

costurero [kos·tu·ré·ro] *m.* sewing table or cabinet; sewing box; sewing room.

costurón [kos·tu·rón] *m.* coarse stitching; large seam; patch, mend; big scar.

cotejar [ko·te·xár] *v.* to confront, compare.

cotejo [ko·té·xo] *m.* comparison.

contense [ko·tén·se] *m. Ch., Mex.* burlap.

cotidiano [ko·ti·đjá·no] *adj.* daily.

cotizable [ko·ti·sá·ƀle] *adj.* quotable (*price*).

cotización [ko·ti·sa·sjón] *f.* quotation of prices; current price.

cotizar[9] [ko·ti·sár] *v.* to quote (*prices*); *Ch.* to contribute one's share or quota; *Am.* to prorate, distribute proportionally.

coto [kó·to] *m.* enclosure; landmark; limitation; limit, boundary; **poner** — **a** to set a limit to; to put an end to.

cotón [ko·tón] *m. Mex., C.A.* shirt of cheap fabric.

cotorra [ko·tó·rra] *f.* small parrot; magpie; talkative person, chatterbox.

cotorrear [ko·to·rre·ár] *v.* to chatter; to gossip.

covacha [ko·ƀá·ča] *f.* small cave; grotto; *Mex., Cuba, Andes* hut, shanty; *Col.* cubbyhole, small dark room.

coyote [ko·yó·te] *m. Am.* coyote, prairie wolf; *Mex.* shyster, tricky, lawyer; *C.A.* agent, broker (*often illegal*).

coyuntura [ko·yun·tú·ra] *f.* joint; articulation; occasion; precise moment.

coz [kos] *f.* kick; recoil of a gun; butt of a firearm; **dar** (*or* **tirar**) **coces** to kick.

cráneo [krá·ne·o] *m.* cranium, skull.

craso [krá·so] *adj.* fat; thick, coarse, gross; **ignorancia crasa** gross ignorance.

cráter [krá·ter] *m.* crater of a volcano.

creación [kre·a·sjón] *f.* creation.

creador [kre·a·đór] *m.* creator; *adj.* creating, creative.

crear [kre·ár] *v.* to create.

crecer[13] [kre·sér] *v. irr.* to grow; to increase; **-se** to swell (*as a river*); to become or feel important.

crecida [kre·sí·đa] *f.* river flood.

crecido [kre·sí·đo] *adj.* grown, increased; large; swollen.

creciente [kre·sjén·te] *adj.* growing, increasing; crescent (*moon*); *f.* river flood; *m.* crescent.

crecimiento [kre·si·mjén·to] *m.* growth, increase.

credenciales [kre·đen·sjá·les] *f. pl.* credentials.

crédito [kré·đi·to] *m.* credit; credence, belief; fame, reputation; letter of credit; **dar a** — to loan on credit.

credo [kré·đo] *m.* creed; **en un** — in a jiffy, in a minute.

crédulo [kré·đu·lo] *adj.* credulous, too ready to believe.

creencia [kre·én·sja] *f.* belief, faith.

creer[14] [kre·ér] *v.* to believe; to think, suppose; **¡ya lo creo!** I should say so!; yes, of course!

creíble [kre·í·ƀle] *adj.* credible, believable.

crema [kré·ma] *f.* cream; custard; cold cream.

cremallera [kre·ma·yé·ra] *f.* rack (*rack and pinion*).

crepitar [kre·pi·tár] *v.* to crackle, snap; to creak; to rattle.

crepuscular [kre·pús·ku·lár] *adj.* twilight.

crepúsculo [kre·pús·ku·lo] *m.* twilight.

crespo [krés·po] *adj.* curly; artificial (*style*); angry; crisp.

crespón [kres·pón] *m.* crepe.

cresta [krés·ta] *f.* crest; top, summit; tuft, comb (*of a bird*).

cretona [kre·tó·na] *f.* cretonne.

creyente [kre·yén·te] *m. & f.* believer; *adj.* believing.

creyón [kre·yón] *m. Am.* crayon.

cría [krí·a] *f.* brood; suckling; breeding.

criadero [krja·đé·ro] *m.* tree nursery; breeding place; hotbed; rich mine.

criado [krjá·đo] *m.* servant; *adj.* bred; **mal** — ill-bred; **criada** *f.* maid, servant.

criador [krja·đór] *m.* breeder, raiser, rearer; creator; *adj.* creating, creative; breeding; nourishing.

crianza [krján·sa] *f.* breeding; nursing; manners.

criar[17] [krjar] *v.* to breed; to bring up, rear, educate; to nurse.

criatura [krja·tú·ra] *f.* creature; baby, child.

criba [krí·ƀa] *f.* sieve.

cribar [kri·ƀár] *v.* to sift.

crimen [krí·men] *m.* crime.

criminal [kri·mi·nál] *adj., m. & f.* criminal.

crin [krin] *f.* mane.

crinudo [kri·nú·đo] *adj. Am.* with a long or thick mane.

criollo [krjó·yo] *m. Am.* Creole; native of America (*especially Spanish America*); *adj. Am.* national, domestic (*not foreign to Spanish America*).

criptón [krip·tón] *m.* krypton.

crisantema [kri·san·té·ma] *f.*, **crisantemo**
[kri·san·té·mo] *m.* chrysanthemum.
crisis [krí·sis] *f.* crisis.
crisol [kri·sól] *m.* crucible, melting pot; hearth of
a blast furnace.
crispar [kris·pár] *v.* to contract (*muscles*); to clench
(*fists*); to put (*nerves*) on edge.
cristal [kris·tál] *m.* crystal; glass; mirror; lens.
cristalería [kris·ta·le·rí·a] *f.* glassware shop or
factory; glassware.
cristalino [kris·ta·li·no] *adj.* crystalline, transparent,
clear; *m.* lens of the eye.
cristalizar[9] [kris·ta·li·sár] *v.* to crystallize.
cristiandad [kris·tjan·dád] *f.* Christianity;
Christendom.
cristianismo [kris·tja·níz·mo] *m.* Christianity.
cristiano [kris·tjá·no] *m.* Christian; person; **hablar
en** — to speak clearly; *adj.* Christian.
criterio [kri·té·rjo] *m.* criterion, rule, standard;
judgment.
crítica [krí·ti·ka] *f.* criticism; censure; gossip.
criticador [kri·ti·ka·dór] *adj.* critical; *m.* critic,
faultfinder.
criticar[6] [kri·ti·kár] *v.* to criticize; to censure; to
find fault with.
crítico [krí·ti·ko] *adj.* critical; *m.* critic, judge;
Am. faultfinder, slanderer; **criticón** [kri·ti·kón]
m. critic, knocker, faultfinder; *adj.* critical,
over-critical, faultfinding.
croar [kro·ár] *v.* to croak.
cromo [kró·mo] *m.* chromium.
cromosoma [kro·mo·só·ma] *m.* chromosome.
crónica [kró·ni·ka] *f.* chronicle, history; **cronista**
[kro·nís·ta] *m. & f.* chronicler.
crónico [kró·ni·ko] *adj.* chronic.
cronómetro [kro·nó·me·tro] *m.* chronometer,
timepiece.
croquis [kró·kis] *m.* rough sketch.
cruce [krú·se] *m.* crossing; crossroads;
crossbreeding.
crucero [kru·sé·ro] *m.* (*cruciforme*) crossing;
crossbearer; crossroads; transept (*of a church*);
crossbeam; cross (*a constellation*); (*buque*)
cruiser.
cruceta [kru·sé·ta] *f.* crosspiece; crosstree;
universal joint (*automobile*).
crucificar[6] [kru·si·fi·kár] *v.* to crucify.
crucifijo [kru·si·fí·xo] *m.* crucifix.
crucigrama [kru·si·grá·ma] *m.* crossword puzzle.
crudo [krú·do] *adj.* raw; uncooked; unripe; harsh;
agua cruda hard water; **petróleo** — crude oil;
Mex. **estar** — to have a hang-over; **cruda** *f.*
Mex. hang-over.
cruel [krwel] *adj.* cruel.
crueldad [krwel·dád] *f.* cruelty.
crujido [kru·xi·do] *m.* creak, crack, creaking; rustle.
crujir [kru·xir] *v.* to creak, crackle; to grate (*one's
teeth*); to rustle; to crunch.
cruz [krus] *f.* cross.
cruzada [kru·sá·da] *f.* crusade; holy war;
campaign.
cruzado [kru·sá·do] *m.* crusader; *adj.* crossed; cross,
crosswise, transverse.
cruzamiento [kru·sa·mjén·to] *m.* crossing;
crossroads.
cruzar[9] [kru·sár] *v.* to cross; *Am.* to fight,
dispute; **-se con** to meet.
cuaco [kwá·ko] *m. Mex.* horse; *Am.* cassava flour.
cuaderno [kwa·dér·no] *m.* notebook; memorandum
book; booklet; *Mex., Ven.* pamphlet.
cuadra [kwá·dra] *f.* hall, large room; stable;

hospital or prison ward; *Am.* city block; *Am.*
reception room.
cuadrado [kwa·drá·do] *adj.* square; *m.* square;
square ruler; die, metal block or plate.
cuadrante [kwa·drán·te] *m.* dial, face of a clock or
watch; sundial; quadrant (*fourth part of circle*;
instrument used in astronomy).
cuadrar [kwa·drár] *v.* (*cuadriforme*) to square; to
form into a square; (*agradar*) to please; to
conform; to harmonize; to set well; *Am.* to be
becoming (*said of clothes*); *Am.* to be ready;
Am. to contribute a large sum; *Am.* to come
out well, succeed; **-se** to stand at attention.
cuadricular [kwa·dri·ku·lár] *v.* to square off, divide
into squares.
cuadrilla [kwa·drí·ya] *f.* group, troupe, gang;
armed band; quadrille, square dance.
cuadro [kwá·dro] *m.* square; picture; scene; frame;
flower bed; *Am.* blackboard; *Ch.* slaughterhouse.
cuajada [kwa·xá·da] *f.* curd.
cuajado [kwa·xá·do] *p.p. & adj.* coagulated,
curdled; filled, covered; — **de** full or covered
with (*flowers, dew, etc.*).
cuajar [kwa·xár] *v.* to coagulate, thicken, curd,
curdle; to turn out well; to jell; to please; *Am.*
to chatter, prattle; **-se** to coagulate, curd; to
become crowded, be filled; **la cosa no cuajó** the
thing did not work, did not jell.
cuajarón [kwa·xa·rón] *m.* clot.
cual [kwal] *rel. pron.* which; **cada** — each one;
— **más** — **menos** some people more, others less;
el —, **la** —, **los -es**, **las -es** which; who; **lo** —
which; *adv.* as, like; **¿cuál?** *interr. pron.* which
one? what?
cualidad [kwa·li·dád] *f.* quality; trait.
cualquier(a) [kwal·kjér(a)] *indef. adj. & pron.* any,
anyone; whichever; **un hombre cualquiera** any
man whatever.
cuando [kwán·do] *rel. adv. & conj.* when; **aun** —
even though; **¿cuándo?** *interr. adv.* when?
cuantía [kwan·tí·a] *f.* quantity; rank, importance.
cuantioso [kwan·tjó·so] *adj.* plentiful, abundant;
numerous.
cuanto [kwán·to] *rel. adj. & pron.* as much as, as
many as; all that; — **antes** as soon as possible,
immediately; **en** — *conj.* as soon as; — **a**
as for, with regard to; **unos -s** a few; **¿cuánto?**
interr. adj. & pron. how much?; **¿cuántos?** how
many?
cuaquerismo [kwa·ke·ríz·mo] *m.* the Quaker sect,
or doctrine.
cuáquero [kwá·ke·ro] *m.* Quaker.
cuarentena [kwa·ren·té·na] *f.* quarantine; forty
units of anything; period of forty days, months,
or years.
cuarentón [kwa·ren·tón] *m.* man in his forties;
cuarentona [kwa·ren·tó·na] *f.* woman in her
forties.
cuaresma [kwa·réz·ma] *f.* Lent.
cuarta [kwár·ta] *f.* fourth, fourth part; span of a
hand; *Am.* horse whip; *P.R.* **echar** — to beat,
flog.
cuartear [kwar·te·ár] *v.* to quarter, divide into
quarters; *P.R.* to whip; **-se** to crack, split (*said
of walls or ceilings*); *Mex.* to back down, go
back on one's word.
cuartel [kwar·tél] *m.* quarter, one fourth; quarters,
barracks; district; quarter, mercy; **no dar** — to
give no quarter.
cuartelada [kwar·te·lá·da] *f.* military coup d'état,
uprising, insurrection.

CO

cuartelazo [kwar·te·lá·so] *m. Am.* military coup d'état, insurrection.

cuarterón [kwar·te·rón] *m.* quarter, fourth part; fourth of a pound; panel (*of a door or window*); *adj. & m.* quarter-breed (*one fourth Indian and three fourths Spanish*); quadroon (*person of quarter negro blood*).

cuarteto [kwar·té·to] *m.* quartet; quatrain (*stanza of four lines*).

cuartilla [kwar·tí·ya] *f.* (*hoja*) sheet of paper; (*medida*) about 4 quarts; about 1½ pecks; fourth of an **arroba** (about 6 pounds); *Am.* three cents' worth; *Am.* **no valer uno** — not to be worth a penny.

cuartillo [kwar·tí·yo] *m.* fourth of a peck; about a pint; fourth of a **real.**

cuarto [kwár·to] *m.* room; quarter, one fourth; **tener -s** to have money; *adj.* fourth.

cuarzo [kwár·so] *m.* quartz.

cuate [kwá·te] *adj., m. & f. Mex.* twin; pal, buddy.

cuatrero [kwa·tré·ro] *m.* horse thief, cattle thief; *Am.* Indian who speaks "broken" Spanish.

cuba [kú·ba] *f.* cask, barrel; tub, vat; big-bellied person; drunkard.

cubano [ku·bá·no] *adj. & m.* Cuban.

cubeta [ku·bé·ta] *f.* small barrel or keg; bucket, pail.

cúbico [kú·bi·ko] *adj.* cubic.

cubierta [ku·bjér·ta] *f.* cover; covering; envelope; deck (*of a ship*); *Am.* sheath.

cubierto [ku·bjér·to] *p.p. of* **cubrir**; *m.* cover; place setting for one person at a table.

cubismo [ku·bíz·mo] *m.* cubism.

cubo [kú·bo] *m.* cube; bucket, pail; hub of a wheel; mill pond; *Am.* finger bowl.

cubremesa [ku·bre·mé·sa] *f.* table cover.

cubrir[52] [ku·brír] *v.* to cover; to hide; to coat; to settle, pay (*a bill*); **-se** to cover oneself; to put on one's hat.

cucaracha [ku·ka·rá·ča] *f.* cockroach.

cuclillas [ku·klí·yas] **en** — in a squatting position; **sentarse en** — to squat.

cuclillo [ku·klí·yo] *m.* cuckoo.

cuco [kú·ko] *adj.* dainty, cute; sly, shrewd; *m.* cuckoo; a kind of caterpillar; card game; *Ríopl.* peach, peach tree; *Am.* **hacer** — **a** to make fun of; to fool.

cucurucho [ku·ku·rú·čo] *m.* paper cone; *Am.* peak, summit; *Peru, C.A., Mex.* cowl, cloak with a hood (*worn by penitents in Holy Week processions*).

cuchara [ku·čá·ra] *f.* spoon; scoop; *Am.* mason's trowel; **media** — mediocre person; *Am.* mason's helper; *Am.* **hacer** — to pout; *Am.* **meter uno su** — to butt into a conversation; to meddle;

cucharada [ku·ča·rá·da] *f.* spoonful; scoop;

cucharón [ku·ča·rón] *m.* large spoon; ladle; dipper; scoop.

cuchichear [ku·či·če·ár] *v.* to whisper.

cuchicheo [ku·či·čé·o] *m.* whispering, whisper.

cuchillo [ku·čí·yo] *m.* knife; gore (*in a garment*); — **de monte** hunting knife; **cuchillería** *Mex., P.R.* mountain ridge; *Am.* gore (*in a garment*); *Am.* narrow tract of land.

cuchillada [ku·či·yá·da] *f.* thrust with a knife, stab, slash; cut, gash.

cuchillo [ku·čí·yo] *m.* knife; gore (*in a garment*); — **de monte** hunting knife; **cuchillería** [ku·či·ye·rí·a] *f.* cutlery; cutlery shop.

cueca [kwé·ka] *f. Am.* a Chilean dance.

cuello [kwé·yo] *m.* neck; collar.

cuenca [kwéŋ·ka] *f.* river basin; narrow valley; wooden bowl; socket of the eye.

cuenco [kwéŋ·ko] *m.* earthen bowl.

cuenta [kwén·ta] *f.* (*cálculo*) count, calculation; bill; account; (*bolita*) bead (*of a rosary or necklace*); **a fin de -s** in the final analysis; **caer en la** — to see, get the point; **darse** — to realize; *Col.* **de toda** — anyway; **eso corre de mi** — that is my responsibility; I'll take charge of that; **eso no me tiene** — that does not pay me; it is of no profit to me; **en resumidas -s** in short; *P.R.* **hacerle** — **una cosa a uno** to be useful or profitable for one; **tomar en** — to take into account; **tomar una cosa por su** — to take charge of something, take the responsibility for it; **vamos a -s** let's understand or settle this.

cuentagotas [kwen·ta·gó·tas] *m.* dropper (*for counting drops*).

cuento [kwén·to] *m.* story, tale; — **de nunca acabar** never-ending tale; **déjese de -s** come to the point; **no viene a** — it is not opportune or to the point.

cuerda [kwér·da] *f.* cord, string, rope; chord; watch spring; **dar** — **a** to wind (*a watch*).

cuerdo [kwér·do] *adj.* sane; wise.

cuereada [kwe·re·á·da] *f. Mex., C.A., Col., Ven.* flogging, whipping; *Am.* skinning of an animal.

cuerear [kwe·re·ár] *v. Am.* to flog, whip; *Am.* to harm, dishonor; *Am.* to beat (*in a game*); *Am.* to skin (*an animal*).

cuerno [kwér·no] *m.* horn; antenna, feeler; **poner -s a** to be unfaithful to, deceive (*a husband*); *Am.* **mandar al** — to send to the devil.

cuero [kwé·ro] *m.* hide, skin; leather; wineskin; *Col., Ven.* whip; **en -s** naked.

cuerpeada [kwer·pe·á·da] *f. Ríopl.* dodge; evasion.

cuerpo [kwér·po] *m.* body; bulk; corps; **en** — without hat or coat; **luchar** — **a** to fight in single combat; *Am.* **sacar el** — to dodge; to escape, avoid doing something.

cuervo [kwér·bo] *m.* crow; raven; *Ven.* buzzard; *Am.* dishonest priest; *Ríopl., Ch.* **hacer uno la del** — to leave abruptly and not return.

cuesta [kwés·ta] *f.* hill, slope; **a -s** on one's shoulders or back; in one's care; — **abajo** downhill; — **arriba** uphill.

cuestión [kwes·tjón] *f.* question; controversy, dispute; problem, matter.

cuestionario [kwes·tjo·ná·rjo] *m.* questionnaire, list of questions.

cueva [kwé·ba] *f.* cave, cavern; cellar.

cuico [kwí·ko] *m. Mex.* cop, policeman; *Am.* gossiper, tattletale, "squealer"; *Ch., Bol., Peru* half-breed; *Ríopl.* short, chubby person.

cuidado [kwi·dá·do] *m.* care, attention; worry, misgiving; **al** — de in care of; **tener** — to be careful; ¡ — ! look out!; be careful! **¡cuidadito!** be very careful!

cuidadoso [kwi·da·dó·so] *adj.* careful; attentive; anxious.

cuidar [kwi·dár] *v.* to take care of, look after, keep; to make or do carefully.

cuita [kwí·ta] *f.* grief, care, anxiety; misfortune; *C.A.* bird dung.

cuitado [kwi·tá·do] *adj.* unfortunate; timid, shy.

culata [ku·lá·ta] *f.* haunch, buttock; rear; butt (*of a firearm*).

culatazo [ku·la·tá·so] *f.* blow with the butt of a rifle; recoil, kick of a firearm.

culebra [ku·le·bra] *f.* snake; coil; *Mex.* money belt.

culebrear [ku·le·bre·ár] *v.* to zigzag; to twist,

wriggle.

culminación [kul·mi·na·sjón] *f.* culmination, climax.

culminar [kul·mi·nár] *v.* to culminate; to come to a climax.

culo [kú·lo] *m.* anus, behind.

culpa [kúl·pa] *f.* fault; guilt; blame; **echar la — a** to blame; **tener la —** to be to blame.

culpabilidad [kul·pa·ƀi·li·ɗáɗ] *f.* guilt; **culpable** [kul·pá·ƀle] *adj.* guilty.

culpar [kul·pár] *v.* to blame; to declare guilty.

cultivación [kul·ti·ƀa·sjón] *f.* cultivation.

cultivador [kul·ti·ƀa·ɗór] *m.* cultivator; **máquina cultivadora** cultivator.

cultivar [kul·ti·ƀár] *v.* to cultivate.

cultivo [kul·ti·ƀo] *m.* cultivation, culture.

culto [kúl·to] *adj.* cultured; *m.* cult, worship; religious sect; **rendir — a** to pay homage to; to worship.

cultura [kul·tú·ra] *f.* culture; cultivation.

cumbre [kúm·bre] *f.* summit; top.

cumpleaños [kum·ple·á·ños] *m.* birthday.

cumplido [kum·plí·ɗo] *adj.* (*completo*) complete, full; perfect; (*cortés*) courteous; *p.p.* fulfilled; due, fallen due; **tiene tres años -s** he is just over three years old; *m.* courtesy, attention; compliment.

cumplimentar [kum·pli·men·tár] *v.* to compliment; to congratulate; to pay a courtesy visit.

cumplimiento [kum·pli·mjén·to] *m.* fulfilment; courtesy; completion; compliment; **de —** formal, ceremonious.

cumplir [kum·plír] *v.* to fulfill; to comply; to carry out; to fall due; **— año,** to have a birthday; to be (*so many*) years old.

cúmulo [kú·mu·lo] *m.* pile, heap; accumulation; cumulus (*mass of clouds*).

cuna [kú·na] *f.* cradle; origin; *Am.* coffin for the poor; *Am.* dive, den (*for gambling and dancing*).

cundir [kun·dír] *v.* to spread (*as news, disease, liquids*); to propagate, extend, multiply.

cuña [kú·ña] *f.* wedge; splinter; *Ch., Ríopl.* influential person.

cuñado [ku·ñá·ɗo] *m.* brother-in-law; **cuñada** [ku·ñá·ɗa] *f.* sister-in-law.

cuota [kwó·ta] *f.* quota; dues, fee; **— de entrada** admission fee.

cuotidiano [kwo·ti·ɗjá·no] *adj.* everyday, daily.

cupé [ku·pé] *m.* coupé.

cupo [kú·po] *m.* quota; *Col.* place, seat (*on a plane or train*).

cupón [ku·pón] *m.* coupon.

cúpula [kú·pu·la] *f.* dome.

cura [kú·ra] *f.* cure; *m.* curate, priest.

curación [ku·ra·sjón] *f.* cure.

curandero [ku·ran·dé·ro] *m.* healer (*not a doctor*); quack; medicine man (*among Indians*).

curar [ku·rár] *v.* to cure, heal; to treat; to cure (*meats, tobacco*); to tan (*skins*); *Am.* to load (*dice*), fix (*cards*); **— de** to take care of; **-se** to cure oneself; to get well; *Ríopl.* to get drunk.

curiosear [ku·rjo·se·ár] *v.* to snoop, peek, peer, pry; to observe with curiosity.

curiosidad [ku·rjo·si·ɗáɗ] *f.* curiosity; neatness, daintiness.

curioso [ku·rjó·so] *adj.* curious; neat, dainty; **libros raros y -s** rare books.

curro [kú·rro] *adj.* showy, gaudy, flashy; *m.* dandy.

currutaco [ku·rru·tá·ko] *adj.* fop, dandy; *adj.* affected (*in one's dress*).

cursi [kúr·si] *adj.* common, in bad taste; cheap,

ridiculous; **cursilería** [kur·si·le·rí·a] *f.* bad taste, cheapness, false elegance; group of cheap, ridiculous people.

curso [kúr·so] *m.* course, direction; scholastic year; course of study.

curtidor [kur·ti·ɗór] *m.* tanner.

curtiduría [kur·ti·ɗu·rí·a] *f.* tannery.

curtir [kur·tír] *v.* to tan; to harden, accustom to hardships; *Col., Ven.* to dirty, soil; **-se** to get tanned or sunburned; to become accustomed to hardships.

curva [kúr·ƀa] *f.* curve.

curvo [kúr·ƀo] *adj.* curved; bent, crooked; arched.

cúspide [kús·pi·ɗe] *f.* summit, peak, top; spire, steeple.

custodia [kus·tó·ɗja] *f.* custody; guard, guardian; monstrance (*vessel in which the consecrated Host is exposed*).

custodiar [kus·to·ɗjár] *v.* to guard, watch; to keep in custody.

custodio [kus·tó·ɗjo] *m.* guardian, keeper.

cutícula [ku·ti·ku·la] *f.* cuticle.

cutis [kú·tis] *m.* skin; complexion.

cuyo [kú·yo] *rel. poss. adj.* whose, of whom, of which.

cuz! [kus] *interj.* come here! here! (*to a dog*).

CH : ch

chabacano [ča·ƀa·ká·no] *adj.* crude, unpolished; inartistic; cheap, in bad taste; *m. Mex.* a variety of apricot.

chacota [ča·kó·ta] *f.* fun; jest; **echar a —** to take as a joke; **hacer — de** to make fun of.

chacotear [ča·ko·te·ár] *v.* to frolic, joke, make merry; to be boisterous; to show off.

chacra [čá·kra] *f. Ec., Peru, Ch.* small farm; *Col., Ec.* cultivated field.

chagra [čá·ɡra] *f. Col., Ec.* farm, piece of farm land; *m. & f. Ec.* peasant; *adj.* uncivilized, unrefined.

chal [čal] *m.* shawl.

chalán [ča·lán] *m.* horse trader; *Am.* broncobuster, horse breaker.

chaleco [ča·lé·ko] *m.* waistcoat, vest.

chalupa [ča·lú·pa] *f.* sloop, sailboat; launch; *Mex., Col., Ven., Ríopl.* canoe; *P.R.* raft; *Mex.* Mexican tortilla with sauce.

chamaco [ča·má·ko] *m. Mex., C.A.* boy; **chamaquito** *m. Mex., C.A.* little boy.

chamarra [ča·má·rra] *f.* coarse wool jacket or sweater; *Mex.* sheepskin jacket, leather jacket; *Am.* heavy wool blanket.

chamarreta [ča·ma·rré·ta] *f.* short loose jacket; *Am.* square poncho.

chambergo [čam·bér·ɡo] *m.* gaucho sombrero.

chambón [čam·bón] *adj.* clumsy, awkward, unskillful; *m.* bungler, clumsy performer, awkward workman; clumsy player.

champaña [čam·pá·ña] *f.* champagne.

champú [čam·pú] *m.* shampoo.

champurrado [čam·pu·rrá·ɗo] *m. Mex.* a mixed drink of chocolate and **atole**; *Col.* a mixed alcoholic beverage.

champurrar [čam·pu·rrár], *Am.* **champurrear** [čam·pu·rre·ár] *v.* to mix (*drinks*).

chamuscada [ča·mus·ká·ɗa], **chamuscadura** [ča·mus·ka·ɗú·ra] *f. Am.* singe, scorch.

chamuscar[6] [ča·mus·kár] *v.* to scorch; to singe; to sear; *Am.* to sell at a low cost; **-se** to get scorched, singed, or seared; *Am.* to get peeved, offended.

chamusquina [ča·mus·kí·na] *f.* singe, scorch.

chancear [čan·se·ár] *v.* to fool, joke, jest.

chancero [čan·sé·ro] *m.* jester, joker; *adj.* jolly.

chancla [čáṇ·kla] *f.* slipper; old shoe; **chancleta** *f.* slipper; *m. Am.* good-for-nothing.

chanclo [čáṇ·klo] *m.* galosh, overshoe; clog; rubber overshoe; **-s** rubbers.

chancho [čán·čo] *m. S.A.* pig, pork.

changador [čaṇ·ga·ḏór] *m. Ríopl.* carrier, porter; *Am.* handy man, person who does odd jobs.

chango [čáṇ·go] *m. Mex.* monkey; **ponerse** — to be alert, wary.

chantaje [čan·tá·xe] *m.* blackmail, blackmailing.

chanza [čán·sa] *f.* joke, jest.

chapa [čá·pa] *f.* metal plate; veneer (*thin leaf of wood*); rosy spot on the cheeks; *Mex., C.A., Andes* lock; *Am.* Indian spy; **-s** game of tossing coins; **hombre de** — serious, reliable man.

chapado [ča·pá·ḏo] *adj.* veneered (*covered with a thin layer of wood or other material*); **— a la antigua** old-fashioned.

chapalear [ča·pa·le·ár] = **chapotear.**

chapapote [ča·pa·pó·te] *m.* tar; asphalt.

chaparro [ča·pá·rro] *m.* scrub oak; short, chubby person; *Am.* a kind of tropical shrub with rough leaves; *Am.* short whip; *adj. Mex., C.A.* short, squatty.

chaparrón [ča·pa·rrón] *m.* downpour, heavy shower.

chapetón [ča·pe·tón] *m.* red spot on the cheek; *Col.* nickname for a Spaniard.

chapitel [ča·pi·tél] *m.* spire, steeple; capital (*of a column*).

chapotear [ča·po·te·ár] *v.* to splash, paddle in the water.

chapoteo [ča·po·té·o] *m.* splash.

chapucear [ča·pu·se·ár] *v.* to fumble; to botch, bungle, do or make clumsily; *Am.* to deceive, trick.

chapulín [ča·pu·lín] *m. Mex., C.A.* grasshopper.

chapurrar [ča·pu·rrár] *v.* to speak (*a language*) brokenly; to mix (*drinks*).

chapuz [ča·pús] *m.* dive, duck, ducking.

chapuza [ča·pú·sa] *f.* botch, clumsy piece of work; *Am.* foul trick, fraud.

chapuzar[9] [ča·pu·sár] *v.* to duck; to dive.

chaqueta [ča·ké·ta] *f.* jacket; **chaquetón** [ča·ke·tón] *m.* long jacket, coat.

charamusca [ča·ra·mús·ka] *f. Mex.* twisted candy stick or cane; *Col., Ven.* brushwood, firewood; *C.A.* hubbub, uproar.

charamusquero [ča·ra·mus·ké·ro] *m. Am.* candystick maker or vendor.

charca [čár·ka] *f.* pond.

charco [čár·ko] *m.* puddle, pool; **pasar el** — to cross the pond, cross the ocean.

charla [čár·la] *f.* chat, chatter, prattle.

charladuría [čar·la·ḏu·rí·a] *f.* chatter, gossip.

charlar [čar·lár] *v.* to chat, chatter, prate.

charlatán [čar·la·tán] *m.* chatterer, prater; gossiper; charlatan, quack.

charol [ča·ról] *m.* varnish; patent leather; *Col.* tray; **charola** *f. Mex.* tray.

charolar [ča·ro·lár] *v.* to varnish, polish.

charqui [čar·ki] *m.* jerky, jerked beef.

charro [čá·rro] *m. Spain* a villager of Salamanca province; *Mex.* Mexican horseman of special costume and cultural status.

charrúa [ča·rrú·a] *m. & f. Am.* Charruan Indian (*Indian of Uruguay*).

chascarrillo [čas·ka·rrí·yo] *m.* joke, funny story.

chasco [čás·ko] *m.* joke, prank; surprise; disillusionment, disappointment; **llevar-se** — to be disappointed, surprised or fooled; *adj. Am.* thick, curly (*hair*); *Am.* ruffled (*plumage*).

chasquear [čas·ke·ár] *v.* to play a trick on; to disappoint; to crack (*a whip*); to smack (*the lips*); to click (*the tongue*); to crack, snap; *Col., Ven.* to chatter (*said of the teeth*); *Am.* to munch (*food*); **-s** to be disappointed or disillusioned; to be tricked or fooled.

chasqui [čás·ki] *m. Andes, Ríopl.* courier, messenger.

chasquido [čas·kí·ḏo] *m.* crack of a whip; crackle; smack (*of the lips*); click (*of the tongue*).

chata [čá·ta] *f.* bedpan; scow, barge, flat-bottomed boat; *Am.* platform wagon, platform car, flatcar; **chatita** [ča·tí·ta] *f. Mex.* "honey", "cutie", "funny face".

chato [čá·to] *adj.* snub-nosed, flat-nosed; flat; flattened; squatty; *Mex.* **quedarse uno** — to be left flat or in the lurch; to be disappointed.

chaval [ča·bál] *m.* lad; young man.

chayote [ča·yó·te] *m. Am.* vegetable pear (*a tropical fruit growing on a vine*); *Am.* dunce, silly fool.

che [če] *interj. Ríopl.* word used to attract attention among intimates; say! listen! hey!; nickname for citizens of Argentina.

cheque [čé·ke] *m.* check, bank check.

chica [čí·ka] *f.* little girl; girl, maid, servant.

chicle [čí·kle] *m. Am.* chicle; *Am.* chewing gum.

chico [čí·ko] *adj.* small, little; *m.* child, boy; *Col.* each game of billiards; *Am.* = **chicozapote** [čí·ko·sa·pó·te] (*tropical fruit and tree from which chicle is extracted*).

chicote [čí·kó·te] *m.* cigar; piece of rope; *Am.* whip; *Col., Ven.* cigar butt.

chicotear [čí·ko·te·ár] *v. Ríopl., Col., Peru* to lash, whip, flog; *Am.* to fight, quarrel; *Am.* to kill.

chicoteo [čí·ko·té·o] *m. Ríopl.* whipping; *Am.* shooting, killing; *Am.* crackling, rattling (*as of machine guns*); *Am.* quarreling.

chicha [čí·ča] *f. Peru, Col., Ch., Ríopl., C.A.* chicha (*a popular alcoholic beverage*); *Peru* thick-soled shoe; **no ser ni — ni limonada** to be worth nothing, be neither fish nor fowl.

chícharo [čí·ča·rro] *m.* pea; *Col.* bad cigar; *Am.* apprentice.

chicharra [čí·čá·rra] *f.* cicada, locust; talkative person; *Mex.* person with a shrill voice; *Am.* rickety, squeaky car; *Ch.* harsh-sounding musical instrument or bell; *C.A., Mex., Cuba* piece of fried pork skin.

chicharrón [čí·ča·rrón] *m.* crackling, crisp piece of fried pork skin; burned piece of meat; sunburnt person; *Am.* dried-up, wrinkled person; *Am.* bootlicker, flatterer.

chiche [čí·če] *m. Mex., C.A.* breast, teat; wet nurse.

chichón [čí·čón] *m.* bump, lump; *Am.* joker, jester; **chichona** [čí·čó·na] *adj. Mex., C.A.* large-breasted.

chiflado [čí·flá·ḏo] *adj.* "cracked", "touched", crazy; *p.p. of* **chiflar.**

chifladura [čí·fla·ḏú·ra] *f.* craziness, mania; mockery, jest.

chiflar [čí·flár] *v.* to whistle; to hiss; *Am.* to sing (*said of birds*); **-se** to lose one's head; to become unbalanced, crazy.

chiflido [či·flí·ḍo] *m.* whistle; hiss; *Am.* **en un —** in a jiffy, in a second.

chile [čí·le] *m.* chili, red pepper.

chileno [či·lé·no] *adj. & m.* Chilean.

chillante [či·yán·te] *adj.* flashy, bright, showy, loud; shrieking.

chillar [či·yár] *v.* to shriek, scream; to hiss; *Am.* to shout, protest, moan; *Am.* to "squeal", turn informer; *Ríopl., Ven., C.A., P.R.* **no —** not to say a word; *Mex.* **-se** to be piqued, offended.

chillido [či·yí·ḍo] *m.* shriek, scream.

chillón [či·yón] *adj.* shrieking, screaming; shrill; loud, gaudy; *Col., Andes* whining, discontented; *Ríopl.* touchy.

chimenea [či·me·né·a] *f.* chimney; fireplace, hearth.

china [čí·na] *f. (de la China)* Chinese woman; China silk or cotton; porcelain; *(piedra)* pebble; marble; *Andes, Ch., Ríopl., Col.* girl, young woman *(usually half-breed or Indian)*; *Am.* servant girl; *P.R.* sweet orange; *Col.* spinning top; **chinita** [či·ní·ta] *f. Am.* little Indian girl; darling.

chinche [čín·če] *f.* bedbug; thumbtack; tiresome person, bore; *Col., Ven., Ríopl.* touchy or irritable person; *Am.* plump, squatty person.

chinchilla [čin·čí·ya] *f.* chinchilla.

chinchorro [čin·čó·rro] *m. Ven., Col.* hammock.

chino [čí·no] *adj.* Chinese; *Mex.* curly; *m. Ríopl.* Chinese; Chinaman; *Am.* pig; *Am.* half-breed *(Negro and Indian, white and Indian)*; *Am.* Indian; *Col.* house servant; *Am.* coarse, rough, ugly person; *Col.* straight, coarse hair.

chiquero [či·ké·ro] *m.* pigsty, pigpen; pen for bulls; goat shelter.

chiquilín [či·ki·lín] *m. Am.* tot, little boy; **chiquilina** [či·ki·lí·na] *f. Am.* little girl.

chiquito [či·kí·to] *adj.* tiny, very small; *m.* tiny tot, tiny child; **chiquitico** [či·ki·tí·ko] *adj.* tiny.

chiripa [či·rí·pa] *f.* stroke of good luck.

chiripá [či·ri·pá] *m. Ríopl.* loose riding trousers *(square of cloth draped from the waist and between the legs)*.

chirola [ği·ró·la] *f. Mex., Ven., Ríopl.* "jug", jail; *Am.* coin of low value.

chirona [či·ró·na] *f.* "jug", jail.

chirriado [či·rrjá·ḍo] *adj. Col.* attractive; lively.

chirriar[17] [či·rrjár] *v.* to squeak, creak; to sizzle; to chirp; to sing out of tune; *Col.* to go on a spree.

chirrido [či·rrí·ḍo] *m.* creak, squeak; chirp; squeaking, creaking; chirping.

chisguete [čiz·ǵé·te] *m.* squirt.

chisme [čiz·me] *m.* gossip, piece of gossip; trifle, trinket, knickknack, gadget.

chismear [čiz·me·ár] *v.* to gossip; to tattle.

chismería [čiz·me·rí·a] *f.* gossiping, talebearing.

chismero [čiz·mé·ro] *adj.* gossiping; *m.* gossip.

chismoso [čiz·mó·so] *adj.* gossiping; *m.* gossip, talebearer, tattletale.

chispa [čís·pa] *f.* spark; small diamond; wit; *Col.* false rumor, lie; *Am.* two-wheeled cart; *Mex.* brazen, shameless woman; *Am.* **da —** it clicks, works, functions; *Am.* **ponerse —** to get drunk.

chispeante [čis·pe·án·te] *adj.* sparkling.

chispear [čis·pe·ár] *v.* to spark; to sparkle; to twinkle; to drizzle.

chisporrotear [čis·po·rro·te·ár] *v.* to sputter, throw off sparks.

chiste [čís·te] *m.* joke, jest; **dar en el —** to guess right, hit the nail on the head.

chistera [čis·té·ra] *f.* top hat; fish basket.

chistoso [čis·tó·so] *adj.* funny, amusing, humorous.

¡chito! [čí·to] **¡chitón!** [čí·tón] *interj.* hush!

chiva [čí·ḅa] *f.* female goat; *Am.* goatee; *Pan., Col.* flivver, small bus; **chivo** *m.* he-goat; *Am.* fit of anger; *Am.* insulting remark; *Am.* **estar hecho un —** to be very angry; *Am.* angry; **chivato** [či·ḅá·to] *m. Cuba* informer, squealer.

chocante [čo·kán·te] *adj.* striking, surprising; shocking; disgusting; *Col., Andes* tiresome, annoying, impertinent.

chocar[6] [čo·kár] *v.* to bump, collide, clash; to fight; to shock, surprise, disgust; **me choca ese hombre** I loathe that man.

chocarrear [čo·ka·rre·ár] *v.* to tell coarse jokes; to clown.

chocarrería [čo·ka·rre·rí·a] *f.* coarse joke; **chocarrero** [čo·ka·rré·ro] *adj.* coarse, vulgar; clownish.

choclo [čó·klo] *m.* overshoe; clog; *Mex.* low shoe or slipper; *Andes, Col., Ch., Ríopl.* ear of corn; *Am.* corn stew; *Am.* spike, ear of wheat.

chocolate [čo·ko·lá·te] *m.* chocolate.

chochear [čo·če·ár] *v.* yo be in one's dotage, act senile.

chochera [čo·čé·ra], **chochez** [čo·čés] *f.* senility, dotage; **chocheras** [čo·čé·ras], **chocheces** [čo·čé·ses] senile actions or habits.

chocho [čó·čo] *adj.* doting; *m.* childish old man.

chófer [čó·fer], [čo·fér] *m.* chauffeur.

cholo [čó·lo] *m. Andes, Ríopl., Ch.* half-breed; *Am.* half-civilized Indian; *Am.* coarse, rude; *C.R.* dark-skinned; *Ch.* black *(dog)*.

chopo [čó·po] *m.* black poplar; *adj. Am.* stupid.

choque [čó·ke] *m.* collision, bump; shock; clash, conflict; dispute.

chorizo [čo·rí·so] *m.* sausage; *Am.* string of things; *Am.* fool.

chorrada [čo·rrá·so] *m.* spurt, large stream or jet.

chorrear [čo·rre·ár] *v.* to drip; to spout.

chorro [čó·rro] *m.* spurt, jet; stream, flow; *Am.* strand of a whip; *Am.* river rapids.

choteador [čo·te·a·ḍór] *m. Am.* joker, jester.

chotear [čo·te·ár] *v. Cuba* to make fun of, jeer, jest, mock, kid; *Mex., C.A.* to idle, fool around; *Am.* to pamper.

choteo [čo·té·o] *m. Cuba* joking, jeering, kidding.

choza [čó·sa] *f.* hut, cabin.

chubasco [ču·bás·ko] *m.* squall, sudden shower; **aguantar el —** to weather the storm.

chuchería [ču·če·rí·a] *f.* trifle, trinket; knick-knack; tidbit.

chueco [čwé·ko] *adj. Am.* crooked, bent; *Col.* crook-legged, bow-legged, knock-kneed; *Am.* worn-out, dejected; *Mex.* disgusted, annoyed; *Am.* **commerciar en —** to trade in stolen goods.

chuleta [ču·lé·ta] *f.* cutlet, chop; blow, slap.

chulo [ču·lo] *m.* dandy; effeminate man; clownish fellow; bullfighter's assistant; *Col.* buzzard; *Am.* coarse, thick brush; *adj. C.A., Col., Mex.* goodlooking pretty.

chumpipe [čum·pí·pe] *m. C.A.* turkey; also **chompipe.**

chupada [ču·pá·ḍa] *f.* sucking; suction; suck, sip; *Mex., C.A., Ven., Andes* puff from a cigarette; *Ríopl.* big swallow of liquor.

chupador [ču·pa·ḍór] *m.* sucker; teething ring; *Am.* toper, heavy drinker; *Am.* smoker.

chupaflor [ču·pa·flór], **chuparrosa** [ču·pa·rró·sa] *m. Am.* hummingbird.

chupar [ču·pár] *v.* to suck; to sip; to absorb,

take in; *Am.* to smoke; *C.A., Ríopl., Andes* to drink, get drunk; -se to shrivel up.
churrasco [ču·rrás·ko] *m. Ríopl., Andes* roasted meat; *Ríopl., Andes* barbecued meat; *Ríopl., Andes* large piece of meat for barbecuing.
churrasquear [ču·rras·ke·ár] *v. Ríopl., Andes* to barbecue, roast over coals; *Ríopl., Andes* to prepare (*meat*) for barbecuing; *Ríopl., Andes* to eat barbecued meat.
churrasquito [ču·rras·kí·to] *m.* small piece of roast.
churrigueresco [ču·rri·ge·rés·ko] *adj.* baroque, ornate (*architecture*).
churro [čú·rro] *adj.* coarse; *m. Spain* doughnut-like fritter.
chuscada [čus·ká·ḏa] *f.* jest, joke.
chusco [čús·ko] *adj.* funny, witty; ridiculous; *Peru* **perro** — mongrel dog.
chusma [čúz·ma] *f.* rabble, mob.
chuzo [čú·so] *m.* pike or cane carried by the watchman (*sereno*).

D:d **dable** [dá·ḇle] *adj.* feasible, possible.
daca [dá·ka] = **da acá**.
dávida [dá·ḏi·ḇa] *f.* gift.
dadivoso [da·ḏi·ḇó·so] *adj.* liberal, generous.
dado [dá·ḏo] *m.* die; -s dice.
dador [da·ḏór] *m.* giver.
daga [dá·ga] *f.* dagger.
dama [dá·ma] *f.* lady; **jugar a las -s** to play checkers.
damajuana [da·ma·xwá·na] *f.* demijohn.
damasquinado [da·mas·ki·ná·ḏo] *m.* damascene (*incrustation of gold in steel*).
damisela [da·mi·sé·la] *f.* damsel, girl.
danza [dán·sa] *f.* dance.
danzante [dan·sán·te] *m.* & *f.* dancer.
danzar[9] [dan·sár] *v.* to dance.
danzarina [dan·sa·rí·na] *f.* dancer.
dañar [da·ñár] *v.* to harm, hurt, damage; -se to spoil, rot; to get hurt; to get damaged.
dañino [da·ñí·no] *adj.* harmful; destructive.
daño [dá·ño] *m.* damage, harm, loss.
dañoso [da·ñó·so] *adj.* harmful.
dar[26] [dar] *v. irr.* (*hacer don*) to give, confer; (*golpear*) to strike, hit; (*emitir*) give off, emit; — **a luz** to give birth to; to publish; — **con** to encounter, find; — **de comer** to feed; — **de sí** to give, stretch; — **en** to hit upon; to persist in; — **largas a un asunto** to prolong or postpone a matter; *C.A., Ven., Col.* — **cuero** (**guasca, puños**) to beat, thrash, lash; **lo misma da** it makes no difference; -se to give up; **dárselas de** to boast of.
dardo [dár·ḏo] *m.* dart, arrow.
dares y tomares [dá·res·i·to·má·res] *m. pl.* give-and-take, disputes; dealings.
dársena [dár·se·na] *f.* dock, wharf.
datar [da·tár] *v.* to date; — **de** to date from.
dátil [dá·til] *m.* date (*fruit of the date palm*).
dato [dá·to] *m.* datum, fact; -s data.
de [de] *prep.* of, from; about, concerning; in (*after a superlative*); if (*before inf.*); — **no llegar** if he does not arrive; **el — la gorra azul** the one with the blue cap; **el mejor — América** the best in America; **más — lo que dice** more than he says.
debajo [de·ḇá·xo] *adv.* under, underneath; — **de** *prep.* under.

debate [de·ḇá·te] *m.* debate; dispute, quarrel.
debatir [de·ḇa·tír] *v.* to debate, argue, discuss; to fight; -se to struggle.
debe [de·ḇe] *m.* debit.
debelar [de·ḇe·lár] *v.* to subdue, defeat.
deber [de·ḇér] *v.* to owe; to have to (must, should, ought); **debe de ser** it must be, probably is; **íme la debes!** I have an account to settle with you!
deber [de·ḇér] *m.* duty, obligation; debt; debit, debit side (*in bookkeeping*).
debido [de·ḇí·ḏo] *adj.* due, owing; just, appropriate.
débil [dé·ḇil] *adj.* weak, feeble.
debilidad [de·ḇi·li·ḏáḏ] *f.* debility, weakness.
debilitación [de·ḇi·li·ta·sjón] *f.*, **debilitamiento** [de·ḇi·li·ta·mjén·to] *m.* weakening; weakness.
debilitar [de·ḇi·li·tár] *v.* to weaken.
débito [dé·ḇi·to] *m.* debt; debit.
debutar [de·ḇu·tár] *v.* to make a debut, make a first public appearance.
década [dé·ka·ḏa] *f.* decade, ten years; series of ten.
decadencia [de·ka·ḏén·sja] *f.* decadence, decline, falling off.
decaer[24] [de·ka·ér] *v. irr.* to decay, decline, wither, fade; to fall to leeward.
decaimiento [de·kaj·mjén·to] *m.* decline, decay; dejection; weakness.
decano [de·ká·no] *m.* dean; senior member of a group.
decantado [de·kan·tá·ḏo] *p.p.* & *adj.* much talked about; overrated.
decapitar [de·ka·pi·tár] *v.* to behead.
decencia [de·sén·sja] *f.* decency; **decente** [de·sén·te] *adj.* decent; respectable; fair.
decenio [de·sé·njo] *m.* decade.
decepción [de·sep·sjón] *f.* disillusion, disappointment.
decepcionante [de·sep·sjo·nán·te] *adj.* disappointing.
decepcionar [de·sep·sjo·nár] *v.* to disillusion, disappoint.
decibel [de·si·ḇél] *m.* decibel (*unit for the measurement of the intensity of sound*).
decidir [de·si·ḏír] *v.* to decide, resolve; -se a to make up one's mind to; to decide to.
décima [dé·si·ma] *f.* tenth; tithe; stanza of ten octosyllabic lines.
décimo [dé·si·mo] *adj.* tenth.
decir[27] [de·sír] *v. irr.* to say; to tell; to speak; **es** — that is; **querer** — to mean, signify.
decisión [de·si·sjón] *f.* decision.
decisivo [de·si·sí·ḇo] *adj.* decisive, final.
declamar [de·kla·már] *v.* to declaim, recite.
declaración [de·kla·ra·sjón] *f.* declaration; statement; deposition; testimony.
declarar [de·kla·rár] *v.* to declare, state, affirm; to testify; -se to propose, declare one's love; to give one's views or opinion.
declinar [de·kli·nár] *v.* to decline; to go down; to lose vigor, decay; to bend down.
declive [de·klí·ḇe] *m.* declivity, slope.
decoración [de·ko·ra·sjón] *f.* decoration, ornament; stage setting.
decorar [de·ko·rár] *v.* to decorate, adorn.
decorativo [de·ko·ra·tí·ḇo] *adj.* decorative, ornamental.
decoro [de·kó·ro] *m.* decorum, propriety, dignity; honor.
decoroso [de·ko·ró·so] *adj.* decorous, becoming, proper, decent.
decrépito [de·kré·pi·to] *adj.* decrepit, old, feeble.

decretar [de·kre·tár] *v.* to decree.
decreto [de·kré·to] *m.* decree; decision, order.
dechado [de·čá·do] *m.* model, pattern, example.
dedal [de·dál] *m.* thimble.
dedicar[6] [de·di·kár] *v.* to dedicate; to devote; **-se** to apply oneself.
dedicatoria [de·di·ka·tó·rja] *f.* dedication, inscription.
dedo [dé·do] *m.* (*de la mano*) finger; (*del pie*) toe; — **del corazón** middle finger; — **meñique** little finger; — **pulgar** thumb; **no mamarse el** — not to be easily fooled; **dedillo** *m.* small finger; **saber al dedillo** to know perfectly, know by heart.
deducción [de·duk·sjón] *f.* deduction; inference.
deducir[25] [de·du·sír] *v. irr.* to deduce, conclude; to deduct.
defecar[6] [de·fe·kár] *v. irr.* to defecate.
defecto [de·fék·to] *m.* defect, fault.
defectuoso [de·fek·twó·so] *adj.* defective, faulty.
defender[1] [de·fen·dér] *v. irr.* to defend.
defensa [de·fén·sa] *f.* defense; *Am.* automobile bumper.
defensivo [de·fen·sí·bo] *adj.* defensive; *m.* defense, safeguard; **defensiva** [de·fen·si·ba] *f.* defensive.
defensor [de·fen·sór] *m.* defender.
deficiencia [de·fi·sjén·sja] *f.* deficiency; **deficiente** [de·fi·sjén·te] *adj.* deficient.
déficit [dé·fi·sit] *m.* deficit, shortage.
definición [de·fi·ni·sjón] *f.* definition.
definido [de·fi·ni·do] *adj.* definite; *p.p. of* **definir**.
definir [de·fi·nír] *v.* to define, explain; to determine.
definitivo [de·fi·ni·tí·bo] *adj.* definitive, conclusive, final; **en definitiva** in short, in conclusion; definitely.
deformación [de·for·ma·sjón] *f.* deformation, deformity.
deformar [de·for·már] *v.* to deform; **-se** to become deformed; to lose its shape or form.
deforme [de·for·me] *adj.* deformed; ugly.
deformidad [de·for·mi·dad] *f.* deformity.
defraudar [de·fraw·dár] *v.* to defraud, cheat, rob of.
defunción [de·fun·sjón] *f.* death, decease.
degenerado [de·xe·ne·rá·do] *adj. & m.* degenerate.
degenerar [de·xe·ne·rár] *v.* to degenerate.
deglución [de·glu·sjón] *f.* swallowing.
deglutir [de·glu·tír] *v.* to swallow.
degollar[2] [de·go·yár] *v. irr.* to behead; to slash the throat; to cut (*a dress*) low in the neck.
degradar [de·gra·dár] *v.* to degrade; to debase.
degüello [de·gwé·yo] *m.* beheading; throat-slashing.
dehesa [de·é·sa] *f.* pasture, grazing ground.
deidad [dej·dad] *f.* deity.
dejadez [de·xa·dés] *f.* lassitude, languor, listlessness; self-neglect, slovenliness.
dejado [de·xá·do] *adj.* indolent, listless; solvenly.
dejar [de·xár] *v.* (*abandonar*) to leave; to quit; to abandon; to omit; (*permitir*) to permit, let; (*soltar*) to let go; — **de** to stop, cease; — **caer** to drop; *Am.* **no -se** not to be an easy mark, not to let others pick on one.
dejo [dé·xo] *m.* (*sabor*) aftertaste; slight taste; (*acento*) slight accent, peculiar inflection.
del [del] = **de** + **el** of the.
delantal [de·lan·tál] *m.* apron.
delante [de·lán·te] *adv.* before, in front; — **de** *prep.* in front of.
delantera [de·lan·té·ra] *f.* lead, forepart, front.
delantero [de·lan·té·ro] *adj.* front, foremost, first.
delatar [de·la·tár] *v.* to denounce, accuse, inform against.

delator [de·la·tór] *m.* accuser, informer.
delegación [de·le·ga·sjón] *f.* delegation.
delegado [de·le·gá·do] *m.* delegate.
delegar[7] [de·le·gár] *v.* to delegate.
deleitable [de·lej·tá·ble] *adj.* delightful, enjoyable.
deleitar [de·lej·tár] *v.* to delight, please.
deleite [de·léj·te] *m.* delight, joy, pleasure.
deleitoso [de·lej·tó·so] *adj.* delightful.
deletrear [de·le·tre·ár] *v.* to spell.
deleznable [de·lez·ná·ble] *adj.* perishable; brittle.
delfín [del·fín] *m.* dolphin; dauphin.
delgadez [del·ga·dés] *f.* thinness; slimness; fineness.
delgado [del·gá·do] *adj.* thin, slender, slim.
deliberado [de·li·be·rá·do] *adj.* deliberate; *p.p. of* **deliberar**.
deliberar [de·li·be·rár] *v.* to deliberate, consider, ponder.
delicadeza [de·li·ka·dé·sa] *f.* fineness; delicacy; softness, exquisiteness.
delicado [de·li·ká·do] *adj.* delicate; weak, frail; exquisite, dainty; tender.
delicia [de·lí·sja] *f.* delight.
delicioso [de·li·sjó·so] *adj.* delicious, delightful.
delincuente [de·liŋ·kwén·te] *adj.*, *m. & f.* deliquent.
delineación [de·li·ne·a·sjón] *f.*, **delineamiento** [de·li·ne·a·mjén·to] *m.* delineation, design, outline, drawing; portrayal.
delinear [de·li·ne·ár] *v.* to delineate, sketch, outline.
delirante [de·li·rán·te] *adj.* delirious, raving.
delirar [de·li·rár] *v.* to be delirious; to rave, talk wildly or foolishly.
delirio [de·lí·rjo] *m.* delirium, temporary madness; wild excitement; foolishness.
delito [de·lí·to] *m.* crime; misdemeanor.
demacrado [de·ma·krá·do] *adj.* scrawny, emaciated, thin.
demanda [de·mán·da] *f.* demand; petition; question; claim; complaint; lawsuit.
demandado [de·man·dá·do] *m.* defendant; *p.p. of* **demandar**.
demandante [de·man·dán·te] *m. & f.* plaintiff.
demandar [de·man·dár] *v.* to demand; to petition; to sue, file a suit; to indict.
demás [de·más] *indef. adj. & pron.*: **los** — the rest; the others; **las** — **personas** the other people; **lo** — the rest; **por** — useless; uselessly; **por lo** — as to the rest; moreover.
demasía [de·ma·sí·a] *f.* excess; boldness, insolence; offense, outrage; **en** — excessively.
demasiado [de·ma·sjá·do] *adv.* too much, excessively; too; *adj.* too much, excessive.
demente [de·mén·te] *adj.* demented, insane, crazy.
democracia [de·mo·krá·sja] *f.* democracy;
demócrata [de·mó·kra·ta] *m. & f.* democrat;
democrático [de·mo·krá·ti·ko] *adj.* democratic.
demoler[2] [de·mo·lér] *v. irr.* to demolish, tear down.
demonio [de·mó·njo] *m.* demon, devil; evil spirit.
demontre [de·món·tre] *m.* devil; ¡ — ! the deuce!
demora [de·mó·ra] *f.* delay.
demorar [de·mo·rár] *v.* to delay; to retard; **-se** to linger; to be delayed.
demostración [de·mos·tra·sjón] *f.* demonstration; proof, explanation.
demostrar[2] [de·mos·trár] *v. irr.* to demonstrate, show, prove, explain.
demostrativo [de·mos·tra·tí·bo] *adj.* demonstrative.
demovilizar[9] [de·mo·bi·li·sár] *v.* to demobilize.
demudar [de·mu·dár] *v.* to change, alter; to disguise; **-se** to change color or one's facial expression; to turn pale.
dengoso [deŋ·gó·so], **denguero** [deŋ·gé·ro] *adj.*

affected; finicky.
dengue [déŋ·ge] *m.* primness; coyness, affectation; dengue, breakbone fever; *Am.* marigold; *Col.* zigzag; *Am.* swagger **hacer -s** to act coy, make grimaces.
denigrar [de·ni·grár] *v.* to blacken, defame, revile, insult.
denodado [de·no·dá·do] *adj.* dauntless, daring.
denominación [de·no·mi·na·sjón] *f.* denomination; name, title, designation.
denominar [de·no·mi·nár] *v.* to name, call, entitle.
denostar[2] *v. irr.* to insult, outrage, revile.
denotar [de·no·tár] *v.* to denote, indicate, mean.
densidad [den·si·dád] *f.* density.
denso [dén·so] *adj.* dense, compact; thick.
dentado [den·tá·do] *adj.* toothed, notched.
dentadura [den·ta·dú·ra] *f.* set of teeth.
dentar[1] [den·tár] *v. irr.* to tooth, furnish (*a saw*) with teeth; to indent; to cut teeth, grow teeth (*referring to a child*).
dentellada [den·te·yá·da] *f.* bite; tooth mark; **a -s** with big bites.
dentición [den·ti·sjón] *f.* teething.
dentífrico [den·tí·fri·ko] *m.* dentrifice, tooth cleanser; **pasta dentífrica** toothpaste; **polvos dentífricos** toothpowder.
dentista [den·tís·ta] *m.* dentist.
dentro [dén·tro] *adv.* inside, within; **— de** *prep.* inside of; **por — on** the inside.
denuedo [de·nwé·do] *m.* spirit, courage, daring.
denuesto [de·nwés·to] *m.* affront, insult.
denuncia [de·nún·sja] *f.* denunciation; condemnation, accusation; miner's claim.
denunciar [de·nun·sjár] *v.* to denounce, accuse; to proclaim, advise, give notice; to claim (*a mine*).
deparar [de·pa·rár] *v.* to furnish, offer, supply.
departamento [de·par·ta·mén·to] *m.* department; compartment; apartment.
departir [de·par·tír] *v.* to talk, converse.
dependencia [de·pen·dén·sja] *f.* dependence; dependency; branch office.
depender [de·pen·dér] *v.* to depend, rely (on).
dependiente de·pen·djén·te] *m.* clerk; dependent, subordinate; *adj.* dependent.
depilar [de·pi·lár] *v.* to depilate.
depilatorio [de·pi·la·tó·rjo] *adj.* & *m.* depilatory.
deplorar [de·plo·rár] *v.* to deplore, lament, regret.
deponer[40] [de·po·nér] *v. irr.* to set aside; to depose, remove (*an official*); to testify, declare; to have a bowel movement; *Am.* to vomit.
deportar [de·por·tár] *v.* to deport, banish.
deporte [de·pór·te] *m.* sport; pastime, recreation.
deportista [de·por·tís·ta] *m.* sportsman; *f.* sportswoman.
deportivo [de·por·ti·bo] *adj.* sport, sports (*used as an adj.*); **copa deportiva** loving cup.
deposición [de·po·si·sjón] *f.* declaration, assertion; testimony; dismissal, removal (*from office or power*); bowel movement.
depositar [de·po·si·tár] *v.* to deposit; to deliver, intrust.
depositario [de·po·si·tá·rjo] *m.* receiver, trustee.
depósito [de·pó·si·to] *m.* deposit; storage; warehouse; **— de agua** reservoir.
depravado [de·pra·bá·do] *adj.* depraved, corrupt, degenerate.
depravar [de·pra·bár] *v.* to corrupt, pervert, contaminate.
depreciar [de·pre·sjár] *v.* to depreciate, lessen the value of.
depresión [de·pre·sjón] *f.* depression; dip, sag.

deprimente [de·pri·mén·te] *adj.* depressing.
deprimir [de·pri·mír] *v.* to depress; to press down; to humiliate, belittle.
depuesto [de·pwés·to] *p.p. of* **deponer.**
depurar [de·pu·rár] *v.* to purify.
derecha [de·ré·ča] *f.* right hand; right side; right wing (*in politics*); **a la — to** the right; **derechazo** [de·re·čá·so] *m.* a blow with the right hand, a right (*boxing*).
derechista [de·re·čís·ta] *adj.* & *m. f.* rightist.
derecho [de·ré·čo] *adj.* right; straight; *m.* law; duty, tax; fee.
derechura [de·re·čú·ra] *f.* straightness.
deriva [de·rí·ba] *f.* drift (*of a boat or plane*); **irse** (*or* **andar**) **a la —** to drift, be drifting.
derivar [de·ri·bár] *v.* to derive; to come (from).
derogar[7] [de·ro·gár] *v.* to revoke, repeal, abolish.
derramamiento [de·rra·ma·mjén·to] *m.* spill, spilling, shedding; overflow; scattering; **— de sangre** bloodshed.
derramar [de·rra·már] *v.* to spill; to spread, scatter; to shed.
derrame [de·rrá·me] *m.* spill, spilling, shedding; overflow; discharge (*of secretion, blood, etc.*); slope.
derredor [de·rre·dór] *m.* circuit; contour; **al —** around; **en — around.**
derrengado [de·rreŋ·ga·do] *p.p.* & *adj.* lame, crippled; dislocated (*said of hip or spine*).
derrengar[1,7] [de·rreŋ·gár] *v. irr.* to dislocate or sprain (*hip or spine*); to cripple; to bend.
derretimiento [de·rre·ti·mjén·to] *m.* thaw, thawing, melting.
derretir[5] [de·rre·tír] *v. irr.* to melt, dissolve; **-se** to be consumed; to melt.
derribar [de·rri·bár] *v.* to demolish, knock down, fell; to overthrow; **-se** to lie down, throw oneself down.
derrocamiento [de·rro·ka·mjén·to] *m.* overthrow.
derrocar[6] [de·rro·kár] *v.* to fling down; to fell; to overthrow.
derrochador [de·rro·ča·dór] *m.* squanderer, spendthrift; *adj.* wasteful, extravagant.
derrochar [de·rro·čár] *v.* to waste; to squander.
derroche [de·rró·če] *m.* waste; dissipation, lavish spending.
derrota [de·rró·ta] *f.* rout, defeat; ship's route or course.
derrotar [de·rro·tár] *v.* to defeat; to squander; to destroy, ruin; to lose or shift its course (*said of a ship*).
derrotero [de·rro·té·ro] *m.* course, direction; ship's course; book of marine charts.
derrumbadero [de·rrum·ba·dé·ro] *m.* precipice.
derrumbamiento [de·rrum·ba·mjén·to] *m.* landslide; collapse.
derrumbar [de·rrum·bár] *v.* to fling down; *Am.* to knock down; *Am.* to go down in a hurry; **-se** to crumble away; to topple over; *Col., Ven.* to dwindle (*as a business*).
derrumbe [de·rrúm·be] *m.* landslide; collapse.
desabotonar [de·sa·bo·to·nár] *v.* to unbutton.
desabrido [de·sa·brí·do] *adj.* tasteless, insipid; harsh; sour.
desabrigar[7] [de·sa·bri·gár] *v.* to uncover; **-se** to uncover oneself.
desabrimiento [de·sa·bri·mjén·to] *m.* tastelessness; harshness; sourness.
desabrochar [de·sa·bro·čár] *v.* to unfasten, unbutton, unclasp; **-se** to unbutton oneself, unfasten one's clothes.

desacato [de·sa·ká·to] *m.* irreverence, disrespect; profanation.

desacierto [de·sa·sjér·to] *m.* mistake, error.

desacoplar [de·sa·ko·plár] *v.* to uncouple, disconnect.

desacostumbrado [de·sa·kos·tum·brá·ďo] *adj.* unaccustomed; unusual; *p.p. of* **desacostumbrar.**

desacostumbrar [de·sa·kos·tum·brár] *v.* to disaccustom, rid of a habit; **-se** to become unaccustomed; to lose a custom.

desacreditar [de·sa·kre·ďi·tár] *v.* to discredit; to disgrace.

desacuerdo [de·sa·kwér·ďo] *m.* disagreement; discord; blunder; forgetfulness.

desafiar[17] [de·sa·fjár] *v.* to challenge; to compete; to defy.

desafinado [de·sa·fi·ná·ďo] *adj.* out of tune.

desafinar [de·sa·fi·nár] *v.* to be discordant; to be out of tune; **-se** to get out of tune.

desafío [de·sa·fí·o] *m.* challenge, defiance; duel; contest.

desafortunado [de·sa·for·tu·ná·ďo] *adj.* unfortunate, unlucky.

desafuero [de·sa·fwé·ro] *m.* violation; outrage, abuse.

desagradable [de·sa·gra·ďá·ble] *adj.* disagreeable, unpleasant.

desagradar [de·sa·gra·ďár] *v.* to displease.

desagradecido [de·sa·gra·ďe·si·ďo] *adj.* ungrateful.

desagrado [de·sa·grá·ďo] *m.* displeasure; discontent.

desagraviar [de·sa·gra·ƀjár] *v.* to make amends; to compensate for a damage or injury; to right a wrong; to apologize; to vindicate.

desagravio [de·sa·grá·ƀjo] *m.* reparation; compensation for a wrong or injury; vindication; apology.

desaguadero [de·sa·ǥwa·ďé·ro] *m.* drain, drain, pipe, water outlet.

desaguar[8] [de·sa·ǥwár] *v.* to drain, draw off; to flow (into); *Ch.* to wash (*something*) two or more times; *Am.* to extract the juice from; *Col., Ven., Mex.* to urinate; **-se** to drain.

desagüe [de·sá·ǥwe] *m.* drainage; drain.

desaguisado [de·sa·ǥi·sá·ďo] *m.* outrage, violence, wrong.

desahogado [de·sa·o·gá·ďo] *p.p. & adj.* (*aliviado*) relieved; (*espacioso*) roomy, spacious; **estar — to** be in easy or comfortable circumstances; to be well-off.

desahogar[7] [de·sa·o·gár] *v.* to relieve from pain or trouble; **-se** to find relief or release; to unbosom oneself, disclose one's feelings.

desahogo [de·sa·ó·ǥo] *m.* relief from pain or trouble; release; ease, comfort, relaxation; freedom, unrestraint.

desairar [de·saj·rár] *v.* to slight, snub, disdain; to rebuff; to disappoint; to neglect.

desaire [de·sáj·re] *m.* rebuff, snub, slight, disdain.

desajustar [de·sa·xus·tár] *v.* to put out of order.

desalentar[1] [de·sa·len·tár] *v. irr.* to put out of breath; to discourage; **-se** to get discouraged.

desaliento [de·sa·ljén·to] *m.* discouragement, dejection.

desaliñado [de·sa·li·ñá·ďo] *adj.* disheveled, slovenly, unkempt, untidy; disorderly.

desaliño [de·sa·lí·ño] *m.* slovenliness, untidiness; neglect, carelessness; disorder.

desalmado [de·sal·má·ďo] *adj.* soulless, cruel, inhuman.

desalojar [de·sa·lo·xár] *v.* to dislodge; to evict,

expel from a lodging; to vacate.

desamarrar [de·sa·ma·rrár] *v.* to untie, unfasten; to unmoor (*a ship*).

desamparar [de·sam·pa·rár] *v.* to abandon, forsake.

desamparo [de·sam·pá·ro] *m.* desertion, abandonment.

desamueblado [de·sa·mwe·ƀlá·ďo] *adj.* unfurnished.

desangrar [de·saŋ·grár] *v.* to bleed, draw blood from; to drain; **-se** to bleed, lose blood.

desanimado [de·sa·ni·má·ďo] *adj.* discouraged; lifeless; dull (*said of a party, meeting, etc.*).

desanimar [de·sa·ni·már] *v.* to dishearten, discourage.

desaparecer[13] [de·sa·pa·re·sér] *v. irr.* to disappear; to hide; **-se** to disappear, vanish.

desaparición [de·sa·pa·ri·sjón] *f.* disappearance.

desapasionado [de·sa·pa·sjo·ná·ďo] *adj.* dispassionate; free from passion; calm; impartial.

desapego [de·sa·pe·ǥo] *m.* aloofness, indifference, detachment.

desapercibido [de·sa·per·si·ƀí·ďo] *adj.* unprepared; unprovided; unnoticed.

desaprobación [de·sa·pro·ƀa·sjón] *f.* disapproval.

desaprobar[2] [de·sa·pro·ƀár] *v. irr.* to disapprove.

desarmar [de·sar·már] *v.* to disarm; to dismount, take apart.

desarme [de·sár·me] *m.* disarmament.

desarraigar[7] [de·sa·rraj·gár] *v.* to root out, uproot.

desarreglado [de·sa·rre·glá·ďo] *p.p. & adj.* disordered; disorderly; slovenly.

desarreglar [de·sa·rre·glár] *v.* to disarrange, disorder, disturb, upset.

desarreglo [de·sa·rré·glo] *m.* disorder, confusion.

desarrollar [de·sa·rro·yár] *v.* to unroll, unfold; to develop, explain; **-se** to develop; to unfold.

desarrollo [de·sa·rró·yo] *m.* development.

desaseado [de·sa·se·á·ďo] *adj.* unkempt, untidy.

desaseo [de·sa·sé·o] *m.* slovenliness, untidiness.

desasir[22] [de·sa·sir] *v. irr.* to loosen, unfasten; **-se** to get loose (from); to let go (of).

desasosiego [de·sa·so·sjé·ǥo] *m.* unrest, uneasiness, restlessness.

desastrado [de·sas·trá·ďo] *adj.* unfortunate, unhappy; ragged, dirty, untidy.

desastre [de·sás·tre] *m.* disaster.

desastroso [de·sas·tró·so] *adj.* disastrous, unfortunate.

desatar [de·sa·tár] *v.* to untie, loosen; to dissolve; to unravel, clear up; **-se** to let loose, let go; to break loose; **-se en improperios** to let out a string of insults.

desatascar[6] [de·sa·tas·kár] *v. irr.* to extricate, dislodge; to pull out of the mud.

desatención [de·sa·ten·sjón] *f.* inattention, lack of attention; discourtesy.

desatender[1] [de·sa·ten·dér] *v. irr.* to disregard, pay no attention (to); to slight, neglect.

desatento [de·sa·tén·to] *adj.* inattentive; discourteous.

desatinado [de·sa·ti·ná·ďo] *adj.* senseless; reckless.

desatinar [de·sa·ti·nár] *v.* to act foolishly; to talk nonsense; to blunder; to rave; to lose one's bearings.

desatino [de·sa·tí·no] *m.* blunder, error; folly; nonsense.

desatracar[6] [de·sa·tra·kár] *v.* to push off (*from shore or from another ship*); to cast off, unmoor.

desavenencia [de·sa·ƀe·nén·sja] *f.* disagreement, discord; dispute, misunderstanding.

desayunar [de·sa·yu·nár·se] *v.* to eat breakfast;

—con la noticia to hear a piece of news for the first time.
desayuno [de·sa·yú·no] *m.* breakfast.
desazón [de·sa·són] *f.* uneasiness, anxiety; insipidity, flatness, tastelessness; displeasure.
desbandarse [dez·ƀan·dár·se] *v.* to disband, scatter, disperse; to desert the army or a party.
desbaratar [dez·ƀa·ra·tár] *v.* to destroy, ruin; to upset, disturb; to disperse, put to flight; to talk nonsense; **-se** to be upset, be in disorder; to fall to pieces.
desbocado [dez·ƀo·ká·ɖo] *adj.* runaway (*horse*), dashing headlong; foul-mouthed, abusive; broken-mouthed (*jar, pitcher, etc.*).
desbordamiento [dez·ƀor·ɖa·mjén·to] *m.* overflow, flood.
desbordante [dez·ƀor·ɖán·te] *adj.* overflowing; *Am.* frantic.
desbordar [dez·ƀor·ɖár] *v.* to overflow, flood; **-se** to spill over; to get overexcited.
desbravar [dez·ƀra·ƀár] *v.* to tame; **-se** to calm down.
descabalar [des·ka·ƀa·lár] *v.* to break (*a given amount, making it thereby incomplete*).
descabello [des·ka·ƀé·yo] *m.* the act of killing the bull by piercing the brain with the sword.
descabezado [des·ka·ƀe·sá·ɖo] *p.p.* beheaded; *adj.* headless; harebrained, thoughtless.
descabezar⁹ [des·ka·ƀe·sár] *v.* to behead; to chop off the head or tip of; **—el sueño** to take a nap; **-se** to break one's head; to rack one's brain.
descaecido [des·ka·e·sí·ɖo] *adj.* feeble, weak; **—de ánimo** depressed, dejected, despondent.
descaecimiento [des·ka·e·si·mjén·to] *m.* languor, weakness; depression, dejection.
descalabradura [des·ka·la·ƀra·ɖú·ra] *f.* blow or wound on the head; scar on the head.
descalabrar [des·ka·la·ƀrár] *v.* to wound on the head; to hurt, injure; to damage; **-se** to suffer a head wound or skull fracture.
descalabro [des·ka·lá·ƀro] *m.* loss, misfortune.
descalzar⁹ [des·kal·sár] *v.* to take off (*someone's*) shoes or (and) stockings; **-se** to take off one's shoes or (and) stockings; to lose a shoe (*said of horses*).
descalzo [des·kál·so] *adj.* barefoot; shoeless.
descaminar [des·ka·mi·nár] *v.* to mislead, lead astray; **-se** to go astray.
descamisado [des·ka·mi·sá·ɖo] *adj.* shirtless; in rags; *m.* ragamuffin, ragged fellow.
descansar [des·kan·sár] *v.* to rest.
descanso [des·kán·so] *m.* rest; staircase landing.
descarado [des·ka·rá·ɖo] *adj.* shameless, impudent, brazen.
descarga [des·kár·ga] *f.* discharge; unloading.
descargar⁷ [des·kar·gár] *v.* to discharge; to unload.
descargo [des·kár·go] *m.* discharge (*of a duty or obligation*); unloading; relief.
descargue [des·kár·ge] *m.* unloading; discharge.
descarnado [des·kar·ná·ɖo] *adj.* fleshless, scrawny.
descarnar [des·kar·nár] *v.* to pull the flesh from the bone; to corrode, eat away; **-se** to become thin, emaciated.
descaro [des·ká·ro] *m.* effrontery, shamelessness, impudence, audacity.
descarriar¹⁷ [des·ka·rrjár] *v.* to mislead, lead astray; to separate (*cattle*) from the herd; **-se** to stray; to go astray.
descarrilar [des·ka·rri·lár] *v.* to derail (*cause a train to run off the track*); to wreck (*a train*);

-se to get or run off the track; to go astray.
descartar [des·kar·tár] *v.* to discard; to put aside.
descascarado [des·kas·ka·rá·ɖo] *p.p. & adj.* peeled off; chipped off.
descascarar [des·kas·ka·rár] *v.* to shell, hull, husk; to peel; to chip off (*plaster*); *Am.* to defame, discredit; *Col.* to flay; **-se** to chip off, peel off.
descendencia [de·sen·dén·sja] *f.* descent, lineage; descendants, offspring.
descendente [de·sen·dén·te] *adj.* descending, downward.
descender¹ [de·sen·dér] *v. irr.* to descend, go down; to get down; to come (from), originate.
descendiente [de·sen·djén·te] *m. & f.* descendant; *adj.* descending.
descendimiento [de·sen·di·mjén·to] *m.* descent.
descenso [de·sén·so] *m.* descent; fall.
descifrar [de·si·frár] *v.* to decipher, puzzle out, figure out.
descolgar²‚ ⁷ [des·kol·gár] *v. irr.* to unhang, take down; to let down; **-se** to climb down (*a rope, tree, etc.*); to drop in, appear unexpectedly.
descolorar [des·ko·lo·rár] *v.* to discolor; to fade; **-se** to fade, lose its color; to discolor.
descolorido [des·ko·lo·rí·ɖo] *adj.* pale.
descollar² [des·ko·yár] *v. irr.* to excel; to stand out; tower (above).
descomedido [des·ko·me·ɖí·ɖo] *adj.* rude, discourteous, impolite; unobliging.
descompletar [des·kom·ple·tár] *v.* to make incomplete, break (*a unit, sum, set, etc.*)
descomponer⁴⁰ [des·kom·po·nér] *v. irr.* (*estorbar*) to upset, disturb; (*echar a perder*) to put out of order; to decompose; **-se** to decompose, rot; to become upset, ill; to get out of order; *Col., Ven., C.A., Carib., Mex.* **se me descompuso el brazo** I dislocated my arm, my arm got out of joint.
descomposición [des·kom·po·si·sjón] *f.* decomposition; decay, corruption; disorder, confusion.
descompuesto [des·kom·pwés·to] *p.p. of* **descomponer**; *adj.* out of order; insolent; brazen; immodest.
descomunal [des·ko·mu·nál] *adj.* colossal, enormous, monstrous.
desconcertante [des·kon·ser·tán·te] *adj.* disconcerting, disturbing, confusing, baffling, embarrassing.
desconcertar¹ [des·kon·ser·tár] *v. irr.* to disconcert, bewilder, confuse; to disturb; **-se** to be confused, perplexed.
desconcierto [des·kon·sjér·to] *m.* disorder; confusion; disagreement; feeling of discomfort.
desconchadura [des·kon·ča·ɖú·ra] *f.* chip (*chipped off place*); chipping off, peeling off (*of plaster, varnish, etc.*).
desconchar [des·kon·čár] *v.* to scrape off (*plaster or stucco*); **-se** to peel off, chip off (*as plaster*).
desconectar [des·ko·nek·tár] *v.* to disconnect.
desconfiado [des·kon·fjá·ɖo] *adj.* distrustful, suspicious.
desconfianza [des·kon·fján·sa] *f.* mistrust, distrust.
desconfiar¹⁷ [des·kon·fjár] *v.* to distrust; to lose confidence.
desconocer¹³ [des·ko·no·sér] *v. irr.* to fail to recognize or remember; to disown; to disregard, slight; not to know.
desconocido [des·ko·no·sí·ɖo] *adj.* unknown; unrecognizable; *m.* stranger.
desconocimiento [des·ko·no·si·mjén·to] *m.*

disregard; ignorance.
desconsolado [des·kon·so·lá·ḍo] *p.p & adj.*
disconsolate, forlorn; disheartened, grieved.
desconsolador [des·kon·so·la·ḍór] *adj.*
disheartening, saddening.
desconsolar² [des·kon·so·lár] *v. irr.* to sadden,
grieve; to discourage; **-se** to become
disheartened, grieved.
desconsuelo [des·kon·swé·lo] *m.* dejection, sadness,
distress.
descontar² [des·kon·tár] *v. irr.* to discount, deduct;
to allow for.
descontentadizo [des·kon·ten·ta·ḍí·so] *adj.*
discontented, fretful, hard to please.
descontentar [des·kon·ten·tár] *v.* to displease.
descontento [des·kon·tén·to] *adj.* discontent,
displeased; *m.* discontent, displeasure.
descorazonado [des·ko·ra·so·ná·ḍo] *adj.*
disheartened, discouraged, depressed.
descorchar [des·kor·čár] *v.* to uncork; to remove
the bark from (*a cork tree*); to force or break
open.
descortés [des·kor·tés] *adj.* discourteous, rude,
impolite.
descortesía [des·kor·te·sí·a] *f.* discourtesy, rudeness,
impoliteness.
descortezar⁹ [des·kor·te·sár] *v.* to bark, strip the
bark from (*trees*); to remove the crust or shell
from; to peel; to civilize, remove the rough
manners from.
descoser [des·ko·sér] *v.* to rip, unsew, unstitch;
-se to rip, come unstitched; to talk too much
or indiscreetly.
descosido [des·ko·sí·ḍo] *m.* rip; *adj.* too talkative,
indiscreet; disorderly; *p.p. of* **descoser**.
descostrar [des·kos·trár] *v.* to flake; to scale off;
to remove the crust from; **-se** to flake, scale off.
descoyuntado [des·ko·yun·tá·ḍo] *p.p. & adj.*
dislocated, out of joint.
descoyuntar [des·ko·yun·tár] *v.* to dislocate, put
out of joint; **-se** to get out of joint.
descrédito [des·kré·ḍi·to] *m.* discredit.
descreído [des·kre·í·ḍo] *adj.* incredulous,
unbelieving; *m.* unbeliever.
descreimiento [des·krej·mjén·to] *m.* unbelief, lack
of faith.
describir⁵² [des·kri·ḅír] *v.* to describe.
descripción [des·krip·sjón] *f.* description.
descriptivo [des·krip·ti·ḅo] *adj.* descriptive.
descrito [des·krí·to] *p.p. irr. of* **describir**.
descuartizar⁹ [des·kwar·ti·sár] *v.* to quarter (*an
animal*; to tear or cut into parts.
descubierto [des·ku·ḅjér·to] *p.p. of* **descubrir** & *adj.*
(*sin cubierta*) uncovered; hatless, bareheaded;
(*hallado*) discovered; *m.* deficit, shortage; **al—**
openly, in the open; **en—** uncovered, unpaid.
descubridor [des·ku·ḅri·ḍór] *m.* discoverer.
descubrimiento [des·ku·ḅri·mjén·to] *m.* discovery;
find; invention.
descubrir⁵² [des·ku·ḅrír] *v.* to discover; to uncover;
-se to uncover; to take off one's hat.
descuento [des·kwén·to] *m.* discount; deduction.
descuidado [des·kwi·ḍá·ḍo] *adj.* careless, negligent;
untidy, slovenly; unaware; thoughtless.
descuidar [des·kwi·ḍár] *v.* to neglect; to overlook;
to be careless or negligent; **-se** to be careless
or negligent.
descuido [des·kwí·ḍo] *m.* carelessness; neglect;
oversight; disregard; inattention; slip, error.
desde [déz·ḍe] *prep.* from; since; **—luego** of
course; **—que** *conj.* since, ever since.

desdecir²⁷ [dez·ḍe·sir] *v. irr.* to be out of harmony
(with); to detract (from); **-se** to retract; to
contradict oneself.
desdén [dez·ḍén] *m.* disdain, scorn.
desdentado [dez·ḍen·tá·ḍo] *adj.* toothless.
desdeñar [dez·ḍe·ñár] *v.* to disdain, scorn.
desdeñoso [dez·ḍe·ñó·so] *adj.* disdainful, scornful.
desdicha [dez·ḍí·ča] *f.* misfortune; misery; poverty.
desdichado [dez·ḍi·čá·ḍo] *adj.* unfortunate;
unhappy, wretched; miserable; *m.* wretch.
desdoblamiento [dez·ḍo·ḅla·mjén·to] *m.* unfolding.
desdoblar [dez·ḍo·ḅlár] *v.* to unfold; to spread out.
desdorar [dez·ḍo·rár] *v.* to remove the gilt from;
to tarnish; to dishonor.
desdoro [dez·ḍó·ro] *m.* tarnish, blemish; dishonor.
deseable [de·se·á·ḅle] *adj.* desirable.
desear [de·se·ár] *v.* to desire, want.
desecación [de·se·ka·sjón] *f.*, **desecamiento**
[de·se·ka·mjén·to] *m.* drying; drainage.
desecar⁶ [de·se·kár] *v.* to dry; to dry up; to drain
(*land*).
desechar [de·se·čár] *v.* to discard; to reject; to
refuse, decline; *Col.* to cut across, take a short
cut.
desecho [de·sé·čo] *m.* remainder, residue; waste
material; piece of junk; discard; **-s** refuse, scraps,
junk; **hierro de—**scrap iron; **papel de—**
wastepaper, scraps of paper.
desembalar [de·sem·ba·lár] *v.* to unpack.
desembarazar⁹ [de·sem·ba·ra·sár] *v.* to rid, free,
clear; *Ch.* to give birth; **-se** to get rid of.
desembarazo [de·sem·ba·rá·so] *m.* freedom, ease,
naturalness; *Ch.* childbirth.
desembarcadero [de·sem·bar·ka·ḍé·ro] *m.* dock,
wharf, pier.
desembarcar⁶ [de·sem·bar·kár] *v.* to disembark,
land; to unload; to go ashore.
desembarco [de·sem·bár·ko], **desembarque**
[de·sem·bár·ke] *m.* landing; unloading.
desembocadura [de·sem·bo·ka·ḍú·ra] *f.* mouth (*of a
river, canal, etc.*); outlet.
desembocar⁶ [de·sem·bo·kár] *v.* to flow (into); to
lead (to).
desembolsar [de·sem·bol·sár] *v.* to disburse, pay
out.
desembolso [de·sem·ból·so] *m.* disbursement,
outlay, expenditure.
desembragar⁷ [de·sem·bra·ǵár] *v.* to throw out the
clutch; to disconnect.
desemejante [de·se·me·xán·te] *adj.* unlike.
desempacar⁶ [de·sem·pa·kár] *v.* to unpack.
desempañar [de·sem·pa·ñár] *v.* to wipe clean; to
remove steam or smudge (*from glass*).
desempeñar [de·sem·pe·ñár] *v.* to recover, redeem,
take out of pawn; **—un cargo** to perform the
duties of a position; **—un papel** to play a part;
-se to get out of debt.
desempeño [de·sem·pé·ño] *m.* fulfillment, carrying
out, discharge; performance (*of a duty*); acting
(*of a role*); redeeming (*of a thing pawned*).
desempleado [de·sem·ple·á·ḍo] *adj.* unemployed.
desempleo [de·sem·plé·o] *m.* unemployment.
desempolvar [de·sem·pol·ḅár] *v.* to dust, remove
the dust from.
desencadenar [de·sen·ka·ḍe·nár] *v.* to unchain, free
from chains; to loosen, set free; **-se** to free
oneself; to break loose.
desencajado [de·seŋ·ka·xá·ḍo] *p.p. & adj.* disjointed;
disfigured; sunken (*eyes*); emaciated.
desencajar [de·seŋ·ka·xár] *v.* to dislocate; **-se** to
become dislocated.

DE

desencantar [de·sen̦·kan·tár] v. to disillusion. disappoint.

desencanto [de·sen̦·kán·to] m. disillusion, disappointment.

desenfadar [de·sen·fa·ḍár] v. to free of anger; -se to calm down.

desenfado [de·sen·fá·ḍo] m. ease, freedom; calmness.

desenfrenado [de·sen·fre·ná·ḍo] p.p. & adj. unbridled; wanton, reckless; loose, immoral.

desenganchar [de·seŋ·gan·čár] v. to unhitch; to unhook; to unfasten.

desengañador [de·seŋ·ga·ña·ḍór] adj. disappointing, disillusioning.

desengañar [de·seŋ·ga·ñár] v. to undeceive, disillusion, disappoint.

desengaño [de·seŋ·gá·ño] m. disillusion, disappointment, blighted hope.

desengranar [de·seŋ·gra·nár] v. to throw out of gear.

desenmarañar [de·sem·ma·ra·ñár] v. to untangle; to unravel.

desenmascarar [de·sem·mas·ka·rár] v. to unmask.

desenredar [de·sen·rre·ḍár] v. to disentangle, unravel.

desenrollar [de·sen·rro·yár] v. to unroll.

desensartar [de·sen·sar·tár] v. to unstring; to unthread; to unfasten from a ring.

desensillar [de·sen·si·yár] v. to unsaddle.

desentenderse[1] [de·sen·ten·dér·se] v. irr. to neglect, ignore, pay no attention to; to pretend not to see, hear or understand.

desentendido [de·sen·ten·dí·ḍo] adj. unmindful, heedless; p.p. of **desentenderse; hacerse el**—to pretend not to notice.

desenterrar[1] [de·sen·te·rrár] v. irr. to unearth, dig up.

desentonado [de·sen·to·ná·ḍo] adj. inharmonious, out of tune.

desentonar [de·sen·to·nár] v. to be out of tune; to be out of harmony; to sing off key, play out of tune.

desenvoltura [de·sem·bol·tú·ra] f. freedom, ease, abandon; boldness, impudence.

desenvolver[2, 52] [de·sem·bol·ḅér] v. irr. to unroll, unfold; to unwrap; to develop.

desenvolvimiento [de·sem·bol·ḅi·mjén·to] m. development, unfolding.

desenvuelto [de·sem·bwél·to] adj. free, easy; forward, bold; shameless, brazen; p.p. of **desenvolver**.

deseo [de·sé·o] m. desire, wish.

deseoso [de·se·ó·so] adj. desirous, eager.

desequilibrado [de·se·ki·li·ḅrá·ḍo] adj. unbalanced; p.p. of **desequilibrar**.

desequilibrar [de·se·ki·li·ḅrár] v. to unbalance; to derange.

desequilibrio [de·se·ki·li·ḅrjo] m. lack of balance; derangement, mental disorder.

deserción [de·ser·sjón] f. desertion.

desertar [de·ser·tár] v. to desert; to abandon; **-se de** to desert.

desertor [de·ser·tór] m. deserter; quitter.

desesperación [de·ses·pe·ra·sjón] f. despair; desperation; fury.

desesperado [de·ses·pe·rá·ḍo] adj. desperate; despairing; hopeless; p.p. of **desesperar**.

desesperanzado [de·ses·pe·ran·sá·ḍo] p.p. & adj. discouraged; hopeless; desperate, in despair.

desesperanzar[9] [de·ses·pe·ran·sár] v. to discourage, deprive of hope; **-se** to be discouraged; to

despair, lose one's hope.

desesperar [de·ses·pe·rár] v. to despair, lose hope; to make (someone) despair; **-se** to despair, be desperate; to be furious.

desfachatez [des·fa·ča·tés] f. shamelessness, effrontery, impudence.

desfalcar[6] [des·fal·kár] v. to embezzle; to remove a part of.

desfalco [des·fál·ko] m. embezzlement; diminution, decrease.

desfallecer[13] [des·fa·ye·sér] v. irr. to grow weak; to faint.

desfallecimiento [des·fa·ye·si·mjén·to] m. faintness; weakness; languor; swoon, faint.

desfavorable [des·fa·ḅo·rá·ḅle] adj. unfavorable.

desfigurar [des·fi·ġu·rár] v. to disfigure; to deface; to distort.

desfiladero [des·fi·la·ḍé·ro] m. narrow passage, narrow gorge; road on the edge of a precipice.

desfilar [des·fi·lár] v. to march, parade, pass by.

desfile [des·fí·le] m. parade.

desgana [dez·ġá·na] f. lack of appetite; reluctance.

desgarrado [dez·ġa·rrá·ḍo] p.p. torn; adj. shameless; impudent.

desgarradura [dez·ġa·rra·ḍú·ra] f. tear.

desgarrar [dez·ġa·rrár] v. to tear, rend; to expectorate, cough up; **-se** to tear; to separate oneself (from).

desgastar [dez·ġas·tár] v. to waste, consume, wear away; **-se** to waste away, lose one's strength or vigor; to wear off.

desgaste [dez·ġás·te] m. waste; wear and tear.

desgracia [dez·ġrá·sja] f. misfortune, mishap; disgrace.

desgraciado [dez·ġra·sjá·ḍo] adj. unfortunate, wretched.

desgranar [dez·ġra·nár] v. to thrash, thresh (grain); to remove the grain from; to shell (peas, beans, etc.).

desgreñado [dez·ġre·ñá·ḍo] adj. disheveled.

desgreñar [dez·ġre·ñár] v. to dishevel; **-se** to muss up one's own hair.

deshabitado [des·a·ḅi·li·tá·ḍo] adj. uninhabited, deserted; empty, vacant.

deshacer[31] [des·a·sér] v. irr. to undo; to dissolve; to destroy; to untie; **-se** to dissolve; to melt; to waste away; **-se de** to get rid of.

desharrapado, desarrapado [de·sa·rra·pá·ḍo] adj. ragged, shabby, tattered.

deshecha [de·sé·ča] f. simulation, pretense; **hacer la**—to feign, pretend.

deshecho [de·sé·čo] p.p. of **deshacer** & adj. undone; ruined, destroyed, in pieces; violent (said of rainstorms); worn-out, fatigued; Am. disorderly, untidy.

deshelar[1] [de·se·lár] v. irr. to melt; to thaw; **-se** to melt; to thaw.

desherbar[1] [de·ser·ḅár] v. irr. to weed.

deshielo [dez·yé·lo] m. thaw.

deshierbe [dez·yér·ḅe] m. weeding.

deshilachar [de·si·la·čár] v. to ravel, fray.

deshilar [de·si·lár] v. to unravel; **-se** to unravel; to fray.

deshojar [de·so·xár] v. to strip off the leaves, petals, or pages; **-se** to lose its leaves (said of a plant or book); to lose petals.

deshollejar [de·so·ye·xár] v. to husk, hull; to peel, pare, skin; to shell (beans).

deshonesto [de·so·nés·to] adj. immodest; unchaste, lewd.

deshonra [de·són·rra] f. dishonor; disgrace.

deshonrar [de·son·rrár] *v.* to dishonor, disgrace; to insult, offend; to seduce.

deshonroso [de·son·rró·so] *adj.* dishonorable; shameful.

deshora [de·só·ra] *f.* inopportune time; **a** — (*or* **a -s**) unexpectedly; **comer a** — to piece, eat between meals.

deshuesar [dez·we·sár] *v.* to stone, remove the pits or stones from (*fruits*); to bone, remove the bones from (*an animal*).

deshumanizar[9] [de·su·ma·ni·sár] *v. irr.* to dehumanize.

desidia [de·sí·dja] *f.* indolence, laziness.

desidioso [de·si·djó·so] *adj.* indolent, negligent, lazy; listless.

desierto [de·sjér·to] *adj.* deserted, uninhabited; alone; lonely; *m.* desert, wilderness.

designación [de·sig̣·na·sjón] *f.* designation; appointment.

designar [de·sig̣·nár] *v.* to designate, appoint, select; to design, plan, intend.

designio [de·sig̣·njo] *m.* design, plan, purpose.

desigual [de·si·g̣wál] *adj.* unequal; uneven; variable, changeable.

desigualdad [de·si·g̣wa·li·dád] *f.* inequality; unevenness; roughness (*of the ground*).

desilusión [de·si·lu·sjón] *f.* disillusion, disappointment.

desilusionar [de·si·lu·sjo·nár] *v.* to disillusion, disappoint; **-se** to become disillusioned; to lose one's illusions.

desinencia [de·si·nén·sja] *f.* termination, ending (*of a word*).

desinfectante [de·sin·fek·tán·te] *adj.* disinfecting; *m.* disinfectant.

desinfectar [de·sin·fek·tár] *v.* to disinfect.

desinflado [de·sin·flá·do] *adj.* deflated, not inflated, flat.

desinflar [de·sin·flár] *v.* to deflate.

desinterés [de·sin·te·rés] *m.* disinterestedness, unselfishness, impartiality.

desinteresado [de·sin·te·re·sá·do] *adj.* disinterested, unselfish, fair, impartial.

desistir [de·sis·tír] *v.* to desist, stop, cease.

deslavado [dez·la·ba·do] *p.p. & adj.* half-washed; weakened; faded; pale; saucy.

deslavar [dez·la·bár] *v.* to wash away; to fade; to wash superficially.

desleal [dez·le·ál] *adj.* disloyal, faithless.

desleír[15] [dez·le·ír] *v. irr.* to dissolve; to dilute, make thin or weak; **-se** to become diluted.

deslindar [dez·lin·dár] *v.* to mark off, mark the boundaries of.

desliz [dez·lís] *m.* slip, slide; error.

deslizador [dez·li·sa·dór] *m.* glider.

deslizamiento [dez·li·sa·mjén·to] *m.* slip, slipping; glide; sliding, skidding.

deslizar[9] [dez·li·sár] *v.* to slip, slide; **-se** to slip; to skid; to glide; to slip out.

deslucido [dez·lu·sí·do] *p.p. & adj.* tarnished; dull; discredited; dingy, shabby; awkward, ungraceful; inelegant.

deslucir[13] [dez·lu·sír] *v. irr.* to tarnish, dull the luster of; to discredit.

deslumbrador [dez·lum·bra·dór] *adj.* dazzling, glaring.

deslumbramiento [dez·lum·bra·mjén·to] *m.* dazzle, glare; daze, confusion.

deslumbrar [dez·lum·brár] *v.* to dazzle.

deslustrado [dez·lus·trá·do] *adj. & p.p.* tarnished; dim, dull; opaque.

deslustrar [dez·lus·trár] *v.* to tarnish; to soil, stain (*one's honor or reputation*).

deslustre [dez·lús·tre] *m.* tarnish; disgrace.

desmadejado [dez·ma·de·xá·do] *p.p. & adj.* enervated, exhausted; depressed.

desmadejar [dez·ma·de·xár] *v.* to enervate, weaken.

desmán [dez·mán] *m.* misconduct, abuse, insult; calamity, disaster.

desmantelar [dez·man·te·lár] *v.* to dismantle, strip of furniture, equipment, etc.

desmañado [dez·ma·ñá·do] *adj.* unskillful, awkward, clumsy.

desmayar [dez·ma·yár] *v.* to dismay; to lose strength, courage; **-se** to faint.

desmayo [dez·má·yo] *m.* faint, swoon; dismay, discouragement.

desmazalado [dez·ma·sa·lá·do] *adj.* dejected, depressed.

desmedido [dez·me·dí·do] *adj.* limitless; excessive.

desmejorar [dez·me·xo·rár] *v.* to impair; to make worse; **-se** to grow worse; to waste away, lose one's health.

desmentir[3] [dez·men·tír] *v. irr.* to contradict; to give the lie; **-se** to contradict oneself; to retract, take back one's word.

desmenuzar[9] [dez·me·nu·sár] *v.* to crumble, break into bits; to mince; to shred; **-se** to crumble, fall to pieces.

desmerecer[13] [dez·me·re·sér] *v. irr.* to become unworthy of; to deteriorate, lose merit or value; to be inferior to.

desmigajar [dez·mi·g̣a·xár] *v.* to crumb (*bread*); to crumble; **-se** to crumble.

desmochar [dez·mo·čár] *v.* to cut off, chop off (*the top or tip*).

desmolado [dez·mo·lá·do] *adj.* toothless, without molars.

desmontar [dez·mon·tár] *v.* to dismount; to cut down (*a forest*); to clear or level off (*ground*); to dismantle, take apart; to tear down; **-se** to dismount, alight, get off.

desmoronar [dez·mo·ro·nár] *v.* to crumble; **-se** to crumble down, fall gradually to pieces.

desnatar [dez·na·tár] *v.* to skim, take the cream from (*milk*).

desnaturalizado [dez·na·tu·ra·li·sá·do] *adj.* unnatural, cruel; **alcohol** — denatured alcohol (*made unfit for drinking*); **madre desnaturalizada** unnatural mother (*one without motherly instincts*).

desnudar [dez·nu·dár] *v.* to undress, uncover; **-se** to undress.

desnudez [dez·nu·dés] *f.* nudity, nakedness.

desnudo [dez·nú·do] *adj.* nude, naked, bare.

desobedecer[13] [de·so·be·de·sér] *v. irr.* to disobey.

desobediencia [de·so·be·djén·sja] *f.* disobedience; **desobediente** [de·so·be·djén·te] *adj.* disobedient.

desocupación [de·so·ku·pa·sjón] *f.* unemployment; idleness; vacationing.

desocupado [de·so·ku·pá·do] *adj.* unoccupied; unemployed, idle; empty, vacant.

desocupar [de·so·ku·pár] *v.* to empty, vacate; **-se de un negocio** to get rid of, or not pay attention to, a business.

desoír[36] [de·so·ír] *v. irr.* to turn a deaf ear to, not to heed; to refuse (*a petition*).

desolación [de·so·la·sjón] *f.* desolation; ruin; loneliness; anguish, affliction, grief.

desolado [de·so·lá·do] *adj.* desolate; *p.p. of* **desolar.**

desolar[2] [de·so·lár] *v. irr.* to lay waste, ruin; **-se** to

DE

be in anguish; to grieve.

desollar[2] [de·so·yár] *v. irr.* to skin, flay; to fleece, extort money from.

desorbitado [de·sor·ƀi·tá·ɖo] *adj.* out of its orbit; out of place or proportion; decentered; *Ch. Andes* popeyed, with bulging eyes; *Am.* crazy, eccentric.

desorden [de·sór·ɖen] *m.* disorder, confusion.

desordenado [de·sor·ɖe·ná·ɖo] *adj.* disorderly; lawless; unsettled; *p.p. of* **desordenar.**

desordenar [de·sor·ɖe·nár] *v.* to disturb, confuse, upset.

desorientar [de·so·rjen·tár] *v.* to throw off one's bearings; to lead astray; to misdirect, mislead; to confuse; **-se** to lose one's bearings; to go astray, get lost.

desoxidar [de·sok·si·ɖár] *v.* to deoxidize.

despabilado [des·pa·ƀi·lá·ɖo] *adj.* wakeful; wide-awake; bright, lively.

despabilar [des·pa·ƀi·lár] *v.* to snuff, trim the wick of (*a candle*); to enliven, awaken (*the mind*), sharpen (*the wits*); **-se** to wake up, rouse oneself, shake off drowsiness.

despacio [des·pá·sjo] *adv.* slowly.

despacioso [des·pa·sjó·so] *adj.* slow.

despachar [des·pa·čár] *v.* to dispatch; to send; to facilitate; to ship.

despacho [des·pá·čo] *m.* (*oficina*) office, bureau; salesroom; (*communicación*) dispatch; (*envío*) sending; shipment; (*sin demora*) promptness; *Ch.* country store, farm store.

despachurrar [des·pa·ču·rrár] *v.* to crush, squash.

desparejo [des·pa·ré·xo] *adj.* unequal, uneven.

desparpajar [des·par·pa·xár] *v.* to upset, disarrange; to rant, talk too much; *Mex.* to disperse, scatter.

desparpajo [des·par·pá·xo] *m.* ease, freedom of manner; freshness, pertness; *Col.* dispersion, scattering; *Am.* disorder, jumble.

desparramar [des·pa·rra·már] *v.* to scatter, spread; to spill; to squander; **-se** to "spread" oneself, spend lavishly; to scatter; to spill.

desparramo [des·pa·rrá·mo] *m. Ch., C.A.* scattering, spreading, spilling; *Riopl., Carib.* disorder, commotion.

despatarrarse [des·pa·ta·rrár·se] *v.* to sprawl; to fall sprawling to the ground.

despecho [des·pé·čo] *m.* spite; grudge; despair; weaning; **a — de** in spite of.

despedazar[9] [des·pe·ɖa·sár] *v.* to break, cut, tear into pieces.

despedida [des·pe·ɖí·ɖa] *f.* farewell; departure; dismissal.

despedir[5] [des·pe·ɖír] *v. irr.* (*cesar*) to discharge, dismiss; (*emitir*) emit, throw off, give off; to see (*a person*) off (*at a station, airport, etc.*); **-se** to take leave, say good-bye.

despegar[7] [des·pe·ǥár] *v.* to detach; to unfasten; to take off (*said of a plane*); *Am.* to unhitch; **no — los labios** not to say a word, not to open one's mouth; **-se** to grow apart; to come loose or become detached.

despego [des·pé·ǥo] = **desapego.**

despegue [des·pé·ǥe] *m.* takeoff (*of an airplane*).

despejado [des·pe·xá·ɖo] *adj.* clear, cloudless; smart, bright; *p.p. of* **despejar.**

despejar [des·pe·xár] *v.* to clear; to remove obstacles from; **-se** to clear up (*as the sky*); to clear one's mind.

despellejar [des·pe·ye·xár] *v.* to skin, flay.

despensa [des·pén·sa] *f.* pantry; storeroom (*for food*); food provisions.

despensero [des·pen·sé·ro] *m.* butler; steward.

despeñadero [des·pe·ña·ɖé·ro] *m.* steep cliff, precipice.

despeñar [des·pe·ñár] *v.* to fling down a precipice; **-se** to fall down a precipice; to throw oneself down a cliff.

despepitar [des·pe·pi·tár] *v.* to seed, remove seeds from; **-se** to talk or shout vehemently; to rave, talk wildly; **-se por una cosa** to long for something; to be crazy about something.

desperdiciado [des·per·ɖi·sjá·ɖo] *adj.* wasteful; *p.p. of* **desperdiciar.**

desperdiciar [des·per·ɖi·sjár] *v.* to squander; to waste.

desperdicio [des·per·ɖí·sjo] *m.* waste; extravagance; **-s** leftovers, garbage; residue.

desperdigar[7] [des·per·ɖi·ǥár] *v.* to disperse; to scatter; to strew.

desperezarse[9] [des·pe·re·sár·se] *v.* to stretch oneself.

desperfecto [des·per·fék·to] *m.* damage; flaw, defect.

despertador [des·per·ta·ɖór] *m.* alarm clock.

despertar[1] [des·per·tár] *v. irr.* to awaken; to wake up; **-se** to wake up.

despiadado [des·pja·ɖá·ɖo] *adj.* pitiless, heartless, cruel.

despierto [des·pjér·to] *adj.* awake; wide-awake.

despilfarrado [des·pil·fa·rrá·ɖo] *adj.* wasteful, extravagant; ragged; *p.p. of* **despilfarrar.**

despilfarrar [des·pil·fa·rrár] *v.* to squander; to waste.

despilfarro [des·pil·fá·rro] *m.* extravagance, squandering; waste.

despistar [des·pis·tár] *v.* to throw off the track.

desplantador [des·plan·ta·ɖór] *m.* garden trowel.

desplante [des·plán·te] *m.* arrogance; impudent remark or act.

desplazar[9] [des·pla·sár] *v.* to displace.

desplegar[1, 7] [des·ple·ǥár] *v. irr.* to unfold; to unfurl; to show, manifest.

desplomar [des·plo·már] *v.* to cause (*a wall*) to lean; **-se** to slump; to topple over, tumble down, collapse.

desplome [des·pló·me] *m.* collapse; toppling over; landslide.

desplumar [des·plu·már] *v.* to pick, pluck (*a fowl*); to fleece, skin, rob, strip; **-se** to molt, shed the feathers.

despoblado [des·po·ƀlá·ɖo] *adj.* uninhabited, desolate; **— de árboles** treeless; *m.* open country; uninhabited place; wilderness.

despojar [des·po·xár] *v.* to despoil, rob; to strip (of), deprive (of); **-se** to undress; to deprive oneself.

despojo [des·pó·xo] *m.* plundering, robbery; spoil, booty; leftover, scrap; **-s** remains.

desportilladura [des·por·ti·ya·ɖú·ra] *f.* chip; nick.

desportillar [des·por·ti·yár] *v.* to chip; to nick.

desposar [des·po·sár] *v.* to marry; **-se** to become formally engaged; to get married.

déspota [dés·po·ta] *m & f.* despot, tyrant.

despótico [des·pó·ti·ko] *adj.* despotic, tyrannical.

despotismo [des·po·tíz·mo] *m.* despotism, tyranny.

despreciable [des·pre·sjá·ƀle] *adj.* contemptible; worthless; insignificant, negligible.

despreciar [des·pre·sjár] *v.* to despise, scorn.

desprecio [des·pré·sjo] *m.* scorn, contempt.

desprender [des·pren·dér] *v.* to unfasten, loosen; to detach; **-se** to get loose, come unfastened; to climb down; to get rid (of); to be inferred, be deduced.

desprendimiento [des·pren·di·mjén·to] *m.*
detachment; generosity; unfastening; landslide.
despreocupado [des·pre·o·ku·pá·ḍo] *p.p. & adj.*
unbiased; liberal, broadminded; unconventional,
carefree; *Am.* careless, slovenly; *Am.* indifferent
to criticism.
desprestigiar [des·pres·ti·xjár] *v.* to discredit, harm
the reputation of; **-se** to lose one's prestige.
desprestigio [des·pres·tí·xjo] *m.* discredit, loss of
prestige.
desprevenido [des·pre·ḅe·ní·ḍo] *adj.* unprepared;
unaware.
despropósito [des·pro·pó·si·to] *m.* absurdity,
nonsense.
desprovisto [des·pro·ḅís·to] *adj.* destitute; lacking;
devoid.
después [des·pwés] *adv.* after, afterward; then,
later; **— de** *prep,* after; **— (de) que** *conj.* after.
despuntado [des·pun·tá·ḍo] *adj.* blunt, dull; *p.p. of*
despuntar.
despuntar [des·pun·tár] *v.* (*quitar la punta*) to
blunt; to cut off (*a point*); nip; (*brotar*) to bud
or sprout; (*sobresalir*) to excel; to be clever,
witty; **— el alba** to begin to dawn.
desquiciar [des·ki·sjár] *v.* to unhinge; to perturb.
desquitar [des·ki·tár] *v.* to retrieve, restore (*a loss*);
-se to get even, take revenge; to win back one's
money; to make up (for).
desquite [des·ki·te] *m.* retaliation, revenge; getting
even; recovery of a loss; return game or match.
desrazonable [des·rra·so·ná·ḅle] *adj.* unreasonable.
destacado [des·ta·ká·ḍo] *adj.* outstanding; *p.p. of*
destacar.
destacamento [des·ta·ka·mjén·to] *m.* military
detachment.
destacar[6] [des·ta·kár] *v.* to detach (*troops*); to
make stand out; to stand out; **hacer —** to
emphasize; to make stand out; **-se** to stand out.
destapar [des·ta·pár] *v.* to uncover; to uncork;
Am. to start running; **-se** to uncover, get
uncovered; to get uncorked; *Am.* to burst out
talking.
destartalado [des·tar·ta·la·ḍo] *adj.* in disorder; in
rack and ruin; dismantled, stripped of
furniture.
destechado [des·te·čá·ḍo] *adj.* roofless.
destellar [des·te·yár] *v.* to flash; to sparkle,
twinkle; to gleam.
destello [des·té·yo] *m.* flash, sparkle, gleam.
destemplado [des·tem·plá·ḍo] *adj.* out of tune, out
of harmony; immoderate; **sentirse —** not to feel
well; to feel feverish.
desteñir[5, 19] [des·te·ñír] *v. irr.* to discolor; to fade;
to bleach; **-se** to become discolored; to fade.
desternillarse [des·ter·ni·yár·se] *v.* **— de risa** to
split one's sides with laughter.
desterrado [des·te·rrá·ḍo] *m.* exile; outcast; *p.p. &*
adj. exiled, banished.
desterrar[1] [des·te·rrár] *v. irr.* to exile, banish; to
remove earth (from).
destetar [des·te·tár] *v.* to wean.
destierro [des·tjé·rro] *m.* exile.
destilación [des·ti·la·sjón] *f.* distillation,
destiladera [des·ti·la·ḍé·ra] *f.* still; *Am.* filter.
destilar [des·ti·lár] *v.* to distill; to drip, trickle; to
filter.
destilería [des·ti·le·rí·a] *f.* distillery.
destinación [des·ti·na·sjón] *f.* destination.
destinar [des·ti·nár] *v.* to destine; to employ.
destinatario [des·ti·na·tá·rjo] *m.* addressee.
destino [des·tí·no] *m.* destiny, fate; destination;

employment, job.
destituido [des·ti·twí·ḍo] *adj.* destitute; *p.p. of*
destituir.
destituir[32] [des·ti·twír] *v. irr.* to deprive.
destorcer[10] [des·tor·sér] *v. irr.* to untwist.
destornillador [des·tor·ni·ya·ḍór] *m.* screwdriver.
destornillar [des·tor·ni·yár] *v.* to unscrew.
destrabar [des·tra·ḅár] *v.* to unlock, unfasten; to
untie; to separate; to unfetter.
destreza [des·tré·sa] *f.* dexterity, skill, ability.
destronar [des·tro·nár] *v.* to dethrone, depose,
overthrow.
destrozar[9] [des·tro·sár] *v.* to shatter, cut to pieces;
to destroy; to squander.
destrozo [des·tró·so] *m.* destruction; ruin.
destrucción [des·truk·sjón] *f.* destruction.
destructivo [des·truk·tí·ḅo] *adj.* destructive.
destructor [des·truk·tór] *adj.* destructive; *m.*
destroyer.
destruir[32] [des·trwír] *v. irr.* to destroy; to ruin.
desunir [de·su·nír] *v.* to divide, separate.
desusado [de·su·sá·ḍo] *adj.* unusual,
unaccustomed; obsolete, out of use.
desuso [de·sú·so] *m.* disuse; obsoleteness.
desvaído [dez·ḅa·í·ḍo] *adj.* lanky, tall and
awkward; gaunt; dull, faded.
desvainar [dez·ḅaj·nár] *v.* to shell (*peas, beans, etc.*).
desvalido [dez·ḅa·lí·ḍo] *adj.* abandoned; destitute;
helpless.
desvalijar [dez·ḅa·li·xár] *v.* to ransack the contents
of a valise; to rob.
desván [dez·ḅán] *m.* garret, attic.
desvanecer[13] [dez·ḅa·ne·sér] *v. irr.* to fade,
dissolve; to make vain; to make dizzy; **-se** to
evaporate; to vanish; to fade out, disappear; to
get dizzy.
desvanecido [dez·ḅa·ne·sí·ḍo] *adj.* (*desmayado*)
dizzy, faint; (*orgulloso*) proud, haughty; *p.p. of*
desvanecer.
desvanecimiento [dez·ḅa·ne·si·mjén·to] *m.* dizziness,
faintness; vanity.
desvariar[17] [dez·ḅa·rjár] *v.* to rave, be delirious;
to rant, talk excitedly; to talk nonsense.
desvarío [dez·ḅa·rí·o] *m.* raving; delirium;
madness; inconstancy.
desvelado [dez·ḅe·lá·ḍo] *adj.* sleepless, awake;
watchful; *p.p. of* **desvelar.**
desvelar [dez·ḅe·lár] *v.* to keep (*another*) awake;
-se to keep awake; to have insomnia, lose sleep;
to be worried, anxious.
desvelo [dez·ḅé·lo] *m.* lack of sleep; restlessness;
vigilance, watchfulness; worry, anxiety.
desvencijado [dez·ḅen·si·xá·ḍo] *adj.* tottering,
rickety, shaky, falling apart.
desventaja [dez·ḅen·tá·xa] *f.* disadvantage.
desventura [dez·ḅen·tú·ra] *f.* misfortune,
unhappiness.
desventurado [dez·ḅen·tu·rá·ḍo] *adj.* unfortunate,
unhappy, miserable, wretched.
desvergonzado [dez·ḅer·ɡon·sá·ḍo] *adj.* shameless,
brazen.
desvergüenza [dez·ḅer·ɡwén·sa] *f.* shamelessness;
disgrace; shame; insolence; impudent word.
desvestir[5] [dez·ḅes·tír] *v. irr.* to undress; **-se** to
undress.
desviación [dez·ḅja·sjón] *f.* deviation, turning aside,
shift; detour.
desviar[17] [dez·ḅjár] *v.* to deviate, turn aside; to
swerve; **-se** to shift direction; to branch off, turn
off the main road; to swerve.
desvío [dez·ḅí·o] *m.* deviation, turning aside;

indifference, coldness; side track, railroad siding; detour.

desvirtuar[18] [dez·þir·twár] *v.* to impair, diminish the value or quality of.

desvivirse [dez·þi·þír·se] *v.* — **por** to long for; to be excessively fond of, be crazy about, make a fuss over; to do one's best for; **ella se desvive por complacerme** she does her utmost to please me.

desyerbar [dez·yer·þár] = **desherbar.**

detallar [de·ta·yár] *v.* to detail, report in detail; to retail.

detalle [de·tá·ye] *m.* detail; retail; ¡**ahí está el —** ! that's the point.

detallista [de·ta·yís·ta] *m. & f.* retailer; detailer, person fond of detail.

detective [de·tek·tí·þe], **detectivo** [de·tek·ti·þo] *m.* detective.

detención [de·ten·sjón] *f.* detention, arrest; stop, halt; delay.

detener[45] [de·te·nér] *v. irr.* to detain, stop; to arrest; **-se** to halt; to delay oneself, stay.

detenimiento [de·te·ni·mjén·to] *m.* detention; delay; care, deliberation.

deteriorar [de·te·rjo·rár] *v.* to deteriorate, damage; **-se** to deteriorate, become impaired or damaged; to wear out.

deterioro [de·te·rjó·ro] *m.* deterioration, impairment.

determinación [de·ter·mi·na·sjón] *f.* determination; firmness.

determinar [de·ter·mi·nár] *v.* to determine; to decide; **-se** to resolve, decide.

detestable [de·tes·tá·þle] *adj.* detestable; hateful.

detestar [de·tes·tár] *v.* to detest.

detonación [de·to·na·sjón] *f.* detonation, report (*of a gun*), loud explosion; pop.

detonar [de·to·nár] *v.* to detonate, explode with a loud noise; to pop.

detrás [de·trás] *adv.* behind; **— de** *prep.* behind; **por —** from the rear, by the rear, from behind.

deuda [déw·da] *f.* debt; indebtedness.

deudo [déw·do] *m.* relative, kinsman.

deudor [dew·dór] *m.* debtor; *adj.* indebted, obligated.

devanar [de·þa·nár] *v.* to spool, wind on a spool; **-se los sesos** to rack one's brain.

devaneo [de·þa·né·o] *m.* frenzy; dissipation; wandering; idle pursuit; giddiness.

devastar [de·þas·tár] *v.* to devastate, lay waste, destroy.

devenir[48] [de·þe·nír] *v. irr.* to befall; to become, be transformed into.

devoción [de·þo·sjón] *f.* devotion; piety; attachment.

devocionario [de·þo·sjo·ná·rjo] *m.* prayer book.

devolución [de·þo·lu·sjón] *f.* return, giving back; replacement.

devolver[2, 52] [de·þol·þér] *v. irr.* to return, give back, pay back.

devorador [de·þo·ra·dór] *adj.* devouring; absorbing; ravenous; *m.* devourer.

devorar [de·þo·rár] *v.* to devour, gobble up.

devoto [de·þó·to] *adj.* devout, religious, pious; very fond (of).

devuelto [de·þwél·to] *p.p. of* **devolver.**

día [dí·a] *m.* day; **al otro —** on the next day; **hoy —** nowadays; **un — sí y otro no** every other day.

diablo [djá·þlo] *m.* devil, demon.

diablura [dja·þlú·ra] *f.* deviltry, mischief, devilish prank.

diabólico [dja·þó·li·ko] *adj.* diabolic, devilish, fiendish.

diácono [djá·ko·no] *m.* deacon.

diadema [dja·dé·ma] *f.* diadem, crown.

diáfano [djá·fa·no] *adj.* transparent, clear; sheer.

diagnosticar[6] [djag·nos·ti·kár] *v.* to diagnose.

diagrama [dja·grá·ma] *m.* diagram; graph.

dialecto [dja·lék·to] *m.* dialect.

dialectología [dja·lek·to·lo·xí·a] *f.* dialectology.

dialogar[7] [dja·lo·gár] *v.* to dialogue.

diálogo [djá·lo·go] *m.* dialogue.

diamante [dja·mán·te] *m.* diamond.

diámetro [djá·me·tro] *m.* diameter.

diantre [dján·tre] *m.* devil.

diapasón [dja·pa·són] *m.* pitch (*of a sound*); tuning fork.

diapositiva [dja·po·si·tí·þa] *f. Spain* slide, lantern slide.

diario [djá·rjo] *adj.* daily; *m.* newspaper; daily expense; journal, diary.

diarrea [dja·rré·a] *f.* diarrhea.

dibujante [di·þu·xán·te] *m. & f.* draftsman; designer.

dibujar [di·þu·xár] *v.* (*diseñar*) to draw, make a drawing of; (*describir*) depict, portray; describe; **-se** to appear, show.

dibujo [di·þú·xo] *m.* drawing; delineation, portrayal, picture; **— natural** drawing of the human figure, drawing from life.

dicción [dik·sjón] *f.* diction; word; choice of words, style.

diciembre [di·sjém·bre] *m.* December.

dictado [dik·tá·do] *m.* dictation; title; dictate; **escribir al —** to take dictation.

dictador [dik·ta·dór] *m.* dictator.

dictadura [dik·ta·dú·ra] *f.* dictatorship.

dictamen [dik·tá·men] *m.* opinion, judgment.

dictaminar [dik·ta·mi·nár] *v.* to give an opinion or judgment.

dictar [dik·tár] *v.* to dictate.

dicha [dí·ča] *f.* happiness; good luck.

dicharachero [di·ča·ra·čé·ro] *adj.* fond of making wisecracks; witty.

dicharacho [di·ča·rá·čo] *m.* wisecrack, smart remark; malicious remark.

dicho [dí·čo] *p.p. of* **decir** said; **— y hecho** no sooner said than done; *m.* saying, popular proverb.

dichoso [di·čó·so] *adj.* happy, lucky.

diente [djén·te] *m.* tooth; tusk; **— de león** dandelion; **de -s afuera** insincerely; *Am.* **pelar el —** to smile affectedly.

diéresis [djé·re·sis] *f.* diaeresis (*as in* **vergüenza**).

diesel [di·sel] *m.* diesel; diesel motor.

diestra [djés·tra] *f.* right hand.

diestro [djés·ro] *adj.* skillful; right; *m.* matador; skillful swordsman; halter.

dieta [djé·ta] *f.* diet; assembly; salary, fee.

diezmo [djéz·mo] *m.* tithe.

difamación [di·fa·ma·sjón] *f.* libel, slander.

difamador [di·fa·ma·dór] *m.* slanderer.

difamar [di·fa·már] *v.* to defame, libel, malign, slander.

difamatorio [di·fa·ma·tó·rjo] *adj.* scandalous, slandering.

diferencia [di·fe·rén·sja] *f.* difference.

diferencial [di·fe·ren·sjál] *m.* differential.

diferenciar [di·fe·ren·sjár] *v.* to differentiate, distinguish; to differ, disagree; **-se** to distinguish oneself; to become different.

diferente [di·fe·rén·te] *adj.* different.

diferir[3] [di·fe·rír] *v. irr.* to defer, put off, delay;

to differ, disagree; to be different.

difícil [di·fí·sil] *adj.* difficult.

dificultad [di·fi·kul·tád] *f.* difficulty.

dificultar [di·fi·kul·tár] *v.* to make difficult; — **el paso** to impede or obstruct the passage; **-se** to become difficult.

dificultoso [di·fi·kul·tó·so] *adj.* difficult, hard.

difteria [dif·té·rja] *f.* diphtheria.

difundir [di·fun·dír] *v.* to diffuse, spread out, scatter; to broadcast by radio.

difunto [di·fún·to] *adj.* deceased, dead; *m.* corpse.

difusión [di·fu·sjón] *f.* diffusion, spreading, scattering; wordiness; broadcasting.

difuso [di·fú·so] *adj.* diffuse; diffused, widespread.

digerible [di·xe·rí·ble] *adj.* digestible.

digerir[3] [di·xe·rír] *v. irr.* to digest.

dignarse [dig·nár·se] *v.* to deign, condescend.

dignatario [dig·na·tá·rjo] *m.* dignitary (*person in a high office*).

dignidad [dig·ni·dád] *f.* dignity.

digno [díg·no] *adj.* worthy; dignified.

digresión [di·gre·sjón] *f.* digression.

dije [dí·xe] *m.* trinket, small piece of jewelry; locket; woman of fine qualities, a "jewel"; *Am.* locket or charm.

dilación [di·la·sjón] *f.* delay.

dilatado [di·la·tá·do] *adj.* vast, spacious; extensive; *p.p. of* **dilatar**.

dilatar [di·la·tár] *v.* to dilate, widen, enlarge; to expand; to lengthen, extend; to spread out; to defer, put off, retard; **-se** to expand; to be diffuse, wordy; *Am.* to delay oneself, take long.

diligencia [di·li·xén·sja] *f.* diligence, care, industry; speed; stagecoach; business, errand.

diligente [di·li·xén·te] *adj.* diligent; quick, speedy.

diluir[3,2] [di·lwír] *v. irr.* to dilute.

diluvio [di·lú·bjo] *m.* flood.

dimensión [di·men·sjón] *f.* dimension.

dimes: — **y diretes** [dí·mes·i·di·ré·tes] quibbling, arguing; **andar en** — **y diretes** to quibble, argue.

diminución [di·mi·nu·sjón] *f.* diminution, decrease.

diminutivo [di·mi·nu·tí·bo] *adj.* diminutive, tiny; diminishing; *m.* diminutive.

diminuto [di·mi·nú·to] *adj.* tiny, little.

dimisión [di·mi·sjón] *f.* resignation (*from an office*).

dimitir [di·mi·tír] *v.* to resign, give up (*a position, office, etc.*).

dinámica [di·ná·mi·ka] *f.* dynamics; **dinámico** *adj.* dynamic.

dinamismo [di·na·míz·mo] *m.* vigor, forcefulness; dynamic force or energy.

dinamita [di·na·mí·ta] *f.* dynamite.

dínamo [dí·na·mo] *m.* dynamo.

dinastía [di·nas·tí·a] *f.* dynasty.

dineral [di·ne·rál] *m.* a lot of money.

dinero [di·né·ro] *m.* money; currency; *Peru* Peruvian silver coin equivalent to about ten cents; — **contante y sonante** ready cash, hard cash.

dios [djos] *m.* god: **Dios** God; **a la buena de** — without malice; without plan, haphazard, at random.

diosa [djó·sa] *f.* goddess.

diplomacia [di·plo·má·sja] *f.* diplomacy; tact.

diplomático [di·plo·má·ti·ko] *adj.* diplomatic; tactful; *m.* diplomat.

diputación [di·pu·ta·sjón] *f.* deputation; committee.

diputado [di·pu·tá·do] *m.* deputy, representative.

diputar [di·pu·tár] *v.* to depute, delegate,

commission.

dique [dí·ke] *m.* dike; barrier; — **de carena** dry dock.

dirección [di·rek·sjón] *f.* direction, course; advice, guidance; management; board of directors; office of the board of directors; address.

directivo [di·rek·tí·bo] *adj.* directive, directing, guiding; **mesa directiva** board of directors.

directo [di·rék·to] *adj.* direct, straight.

director [di·rek·tór] *m.* director, manager; *adj.* directing.

directorio [di·rek·tó·rjo] *adj.* directory, directive, directing; *m.* directory, book of instructions; directorate, board of directors.

dirigente [di·ri·xén·te] *adj.* directing, leading; *m.* leader, director.

dirigible [di·ri·xí·ble] *adj. & m.* dirigible.

dirigir[11] [di·ri·xír] *v.* to direct, manage, govern; to guide; to address (*letters, packages*); to dedicate; **-se a** to address (*a person*); to go to or toward.

discernimiento [di·ser·ni·mjén·to] *m.* discernment, keen judgment, insight, discrimination.

discernir[3] [di·ser·nír] *v. irr.* to discern; to distinguish; to discriminate.

disciplina [di·si·plí·na] *f.* discipline, training; rule of conduct; order; any art or science; scourge, whip.

disciplinar [di·si·pli·nár] *v.* to discipline; train; to drill; **-se** to discipline oneself; to scourge oneself.

discípulo [di·sí·pu·lo] *m.* pupil; disciple.

disco [dís·ko] *m.* disk; discus; phonograph record.

díscolo [dís·ko·lo] *adj.* unruly, disobedient; unfriendly.

discordancia [dis·kor·dán·sja] *f.* discord, disagreement.

discordia [dis·kór·dja] *f.* discord.

discreción [dis·kre·sjón] *f.* discretion; keenness; wit; **darse** (*or* **rendirse**) **a** — to surrender unconditionally; **discrecional** [dis·kre·sjo·nál] *adj.* optional.

discrepancia [dis·kre·pán·sja] *f.* discrepancy.

discreto [dis·kré·to] *adj.* discreet, prudent; clever.

disculpa [dis·kúl·pa] *f.* excuse; apology.

disculpable [dis·kul·pá·ble] *adj.* excusable.

disculpar [dis·kul·pár] *v.* to excuse, free from blame; **-se** to excuse oneself, apologize.

discurrir [dis·ku·rrír] *v.* (*charlar*) to discuss; (*recorrer*) to ramble about; (*imaginar*) to invent, think out.

discursear [dis·kur·se·ár] *v.* to make speeches.

discurso [dis·kúr·so] *m.* discourse; speech; reasoning; lapse of time.

discusión [dis·ku·sjón] *f.* discussion.

discutible [dis·ku·tí·ble] *adj.* debatable, questionable.

discutir [dis·ku·tír] *v.* to discuss.

disecar[6] [di·se·kár] *v.* to dissect; to stuff and mount (*the skins of animals*).

diseminación [di·se·mi·na·sjón] *f.* dissemination, spread, scattering.

diseminar [di·se·mi·nár] *v.* to disseminate, scatter, spread.

disensión [di·sen·sjón] *f.* dissension, dissent, disagreement.

disentería [di·sen·te·rí·a] *f.* dysentery.

disentir[3] [di·sen·tír] *v. irr.* to dissent, differ, disagree.

diseñador [di·se·ña·dór] *m.* designer.

diseñar [di·se·ñár] *v.* to design; to sketch, outline.

diseño [di·sé·ño] *m.* design; sketch, outline.

DE

disertar [di·ser·tár] *v.* to discourse, discuss.
disforme [dis·fór·me] *adj.* deformed; ugly, hideous; out of proportion.
disfraz [dis·frás] *m.* disguise, mask; masquerade costume.
disfrazar[9] [dis·fra·sár] *v.* to disguise, conceal; -se to disguise oneself; to masquerade.
disfrutar [dis·fru·tár] *v.* to enjoy; to reap benefit or advantage; to make use of.
disfrute [dis·frú·te] *m.* enjoyment, benefit, use.
disgustar [diz·gus·tár] *v.* to disgust, displease; -se to get angry; to get bored.
disgusto [diz·gús·to] *m.* displeasure; unpleasantness; annoyance; quarrel; grief; disgust.
disidente [di·si·ðén·te] *m.* & *f.* dissident; protester.
disimulado [di·si·mu·lá·ðo] *adj.* underhanded, sly, cunning; *p.p. of* **disimular.**
disimular [di·si·mu·lár] *v.* to feign, hide, mask; to overlook, excuse.
disimulo [di·si·mú·lo] *m.* dissimulation, feigning, pretense; slyness; reserve.
disipación [di·si·pa·sjón] *f.* dissipation; waste, extravagance.
disipar [di·si·pár] *v.* to dissipate, scatter; to squander; -se to vanish.
dislocar[6] [diz·lo·kár] *v.* to dislocate, put out of joint; -se to become dislocated, get out of joint.
disminución [diz·mi·nu·sjón] = **diminución.**
disminuir[32] [diz·mi·nwír] *v. irr.* to diminish, decrease, lessen.
disociación [di·so·sja·sjón] *f.* dissociation, separation.
disociar [di·so·sjár] *v.* to dissociate, separate.
disolución [di·so·lu·sjón] *f.* dissolution, breaking up; dissoluteness, lewdness.
disoluto [di·so·lú·to] *adj.* dissolute, loose, immoral, dissipated.
disolver[2, 52] [di·sol·ßér] *v. irr.* to dissolve; to melt.
disonancia [di·so·nán·sja] *f.* discord.
disparada [dis·pa·rá·ða] *f. C.A., Mex., Carib., Ríopl.* rush, run.
disparar [dis·pa·rár] *v.* to shoot, fire, discharge; to throw; -se to run away, dart out.
disparatado [dis·pa·ra·tá·ðo] *adj.* absurd, foolish, senseless.
disparatar [dis·pa·ra·tár] *v.* to talk nonsense; to blunder; to act foolishly.
disparate [dis·pa·rá·te] *m.* nonsense, blunder.
disparidad [dis·pa·ri·ðáð] *f.* inequality.
disparo [dis·pá·ro] *m.* shooting, discharge, explosion; shot; sudden dash, run.
dispensa [dis·pén·sa] *f.* dispensation; exemption.
dispensar [dis·pen·sár] *v.* to excuse, absolve, pardon; to grant, give.
dispensario [dis·pen·sá·rjo] *m.* dispensary; pharmaceutical laboratory; pharmacopoeia (*book containing list and description of drugs*).
dispersar [dis·per·sár] *v.* to disperse, scatter.
dispersión [dis·per·sjón] *f.* dispersion, dispersal.
displicencia [dis·pli·sén·sja] *f.* displeasure, discontent, dislike.
displicente [dis·pli·sén·te] *adj.* unpleasant, disagreeable, cross.
disponer[40] [dis·po·nér] *v. irr.* (*arreglar*) to dispose; to arrange, put in order; to prepare; (*mandar*) to order, command; -se to get ready; to make one's will and testament.
disponible [dis·po·ní·ßle] *adj.* spare, available; on hand.
disposición [dis·po·si·sjón] *f.* disposition;

arrangement; order, command; aptitude; disposal.
dispuesto [dis·pwés·to] *p.p. of* **disponer** & *adj.* disposed; ready; fit; smart, clever.
disputa [dis·pú·ta] *f.* dispute.
disputar [dis·pu·tár] *v.* to dispute.
distancia [dis·tán·sja] *f.* distance.
distante [dis·tán·te] *adj.* distant.
distar [dis·tár] *v.* to be distant, far (from).
distender[1] [dis·ten·dér] *v. irr.* to distend, stretch; to inflate; -se to distend, expand.
distinción [dis·tin·sjón] *f.* distinction.
distinguido [dis·tiŋ·gí·ðo] *adj.* & *p.p.* distinguished.
distinguir[12] [dis·tiŋ·gír] *v.* to distinguish; -se to distinguish oneself, excel; to differ, be different.
distintivo [dis·tin·tí·ßo] *adj.* distinctive, distinguishing; *m.* distinguishing characteristic; mark, sign; badge.
distinto [dis·tín·to] *adj.* distinct, plain, clear; different.
distracción [dis·trak·sjón] *f.* distraction; diversion, amusement; lack of attention.
distraer[46] [dis·tra·ér] *v. irr.* to distract; to divert, amuse; to lead astray; to divert (*funds*); -se to have a good time; to be absentminded; to be inattentive.
distraído [dis·tra·í·ðo] *adj.* distracted; inattentive; absentminded; *Am.* slovenly, untidy.
distribución [dis·tri·ßu·sjón] *f.* distribution, apportionment.
distribuidor [dis·tri·ßwi·ðór] *m.* distributor; *adj.* distributing.
distribuir[32] [dis·tri·ßwír] *v. irr.* to distribute; to sort; classify.
distrito [dis·trí·to] *m.* district; region.
disturbio [dis·túr·ßjo] *m.* disturbance.
disuadir [di·swa·ðír] *v.* to dissuade.
disuelto [di·swél·to] *p.p. of* **disolver.**
diurno [djúr·no] *adj.* day, of the day.
divagación [di·ßa·ga·sjón] *f.* rambling, digression.
divagar[7] [di·ßa·gár] *v.* to ramble; to digress.
diván [di·ßán] *m.* divan, sofa.
divergencia [di·ßer·xén·sja] *f.* divergence; difference (*of opinion*).
divergir[11] [di·ßer·xír] *v.* to diverge; to differ.
diversidad [di·ßer·si·ðáð] *f.* diversity; variety.
diversión [di·ßer·sjón] *f.* amusement.
diverso [di·ßér·so] *adj.* diverse; different; -s several, various.
divertido [di·ßer·tí·ðo] *adj.* amusing, funny.
divertir[3] [di·ßer·tír] *v. irr.* to amuse, entertain; to divert, turn aside; -se to have a good time, amuse oneself.
dividendo [di·ßi·ðén·do] *m.* dividend.
dividir [di·ßi·ðir] *v.* to divide, split.
divinidad [di·ßi·ni·ðáð] *f.* divinity, deity; ¡qué—! what a beauty!
divino [di·ßi·no] *adj.* divine.
divisa [di·ßi·sa] *f.* device, emblem; foreign exchange.
divisar [di·ßi·sár] *v.* to sight; to make out, distinguish.
división [di·ßi·sjón] *f.* division.
divisorio [di·ßi·só·rjo] *adj.* dividing.
divorcid [di·ßor·sjár] *v.* to divorce; to separate.
divorcio [di·ßor·sjo] *m.* divorce.
divulgar[7] [di·ßul·gár] *v.* to divulge, spread, make public, give out.
diz [dis] = **dice; dizque** [dís·ke] they say that . . .
do [do] *m.* the first note of the diatonic scale in solfeggio.

dobladillar [do·βla·đi·yár] v. to hem.
dobladillo [do·βla·đí·yo] m. hem; — **de ojo** hemstitch.
doblar [do·βlár] v. to bend, fold; to double; to toll, knell; *Ríopl.* to knock down; — **la esquina** to turn the corner; **-se** to stoop; to bend down; to give in.
doble [dó·βle] adj. double, twofold; double-faced, hypocritical; *Am.* broke, poor; m. fold; toll, tolling of bells, knell.
doblegar[7] [do·βle·gár] v. to bend; to fold; **-se** to bend over; to stoop; to submit, yield.
doblete [do·βlé·te] m. doublet; a two-base hit.
doblez [do·βlés] m. fold, crease; duplicity, hypocrisy.
docena [do·sé·na] f. dozen.
docente [do·sén·te] adj. teaching; educational; **cuerpo** — faculty (*of a school*).
dócil [dó·sil] adj. docile, obedient, manageable, meek; flexible; **docilidad** [do·si·li·đáđ] f. obedience, meekness, gentleness; flexibility.
docto [dók·to] adj. learned; expert.
doctor [dok·tór] m. doctor.
doctorar [dok·to·rár] v. to grant a doctor's degree to; **-se** to get a doctor's degree.
doctrina [dok·trí·na] f. doctrine.
documentar [do·ku·men·tár] v. to document.
documento [do·ku·mén·to] m. document.
dogal [do·gál] m. halter; noose.
dogma [dóg·ma] m. dogma; **dogmático** [dog·má·ti·ko] adj. dogmatic, pertaining to dogma; positive.
dolencia [do·lén·sja] f. ailment; ache, aching.
doler[2] [do·lér] v. irr. to ache, hurt, cause pain; to cause grief; **-se de** to feel pity for, feel sorry for; to repent from.
doliente [do·ljén·te] adj. sorrowful; suffering; aching; m. sick person, patient; mourner.
dolor [do·lór] m. pain, ache; sorrow, grief.
dolorido [do·lo·rí·đo] adj. aching, sore; afflicted; repentant; doleful.
doloroso [do·lo·ró·so] adj. painful; sorrowful.
doma [dó·ma] f. breaking of horses.
domador [do·ma·đór] m. horsebreaker, broncobuster.
domar [do·már] v. to tame, subdue.
domeñar [do·me·ñár] v. to tame; to subdue; to dominate.
domesticar[6] [do·mes·ti·kár] v. to domesticate, tame.
doméstico [do·més·ti·ko] adj. domestic; m. house servant.
domiciliar [do·mi·si·ljár] v. to house, lodge; *Ríopl.* to address (*a letter*); **-se** to take up residence; to settle down; to dwell, reside.
domicilio [do·mi·sí·ljo] m. home, dwelling.
dominación [do·mi·na·sjón] f. domination, rule, authority.
dominador [do·mi·na·đór] adj. dominant, dominating; domineering, bossy; m. ruler, boss.
dominante [do·mi·nán·te] adj. dominant; domineering; tyrannical; prevailing; predominant.
dominar [do·mi·nár] v. to dominate, rule, lead; to stand out, tower above; to master.
dómine [dó·mi·ne] m. teacher; pedagogue; pedant.
domingo [do·mín·go] m. Sunday; — **de ramos** Palm Sunday.
dominio [do·mi·njo] m. domain; dominion; authority; mastery (*of a science, art, language, etc.*).

dominó [do·mi·nó] m. domino.
don [don] m. gift; ability, knack; Don (*title used only before Christian names of men*).
donación [do·na·sjón] f. donation; grant.
donador [do·na·đór] m. donor, giver.
donaire [do·náj·re] m. grace, elegance; wit; humor; witty remark.
donairoso [do·naj·ró·so] adj. elegant, graceful; witty.
donar [do·nár] v. to donate.
doncella [don·sé·ya] f. virgin, maiden; maidservant; *Col.* felon (*sore or inflammation near a finger or toenail*).
donde [dón·de] rel. adv. where, in which; **a** — (**adonde**) where, to which; *C.A., Ríopl.* to the house of; **de** — from where, from which; **en** — where, in which; **por** — where, through which; wherefore; — **no** otherwise; if not; **¿donde?** interr. adv. where?; **¿por** —? which way?
dondequiera [don·de·kjé·ra] adv. wherever; anywhere.
donjuanismo [don·xwa·níz·mo] m. Don Juanism, conduct reminiscent of Don Juan Tenorio.
donoso [do·nó·so] adj. witty, gay; graceful.
doña [dó·ña] f. Doña (*title used only before Christian names of women*).
dorada [do·rá·đa] f. gilthead (fish).
dorado [do·rá·đo] p.p. & adj. gilded, gilt; golden; m. gilding; *Am.* a kind of hummingbird; **doradillo** [do·ra·đí·yo] adj. *Am.* honey-colored, golden (*applied to horses*).
dorar [do·rár] v. to gild.
dormir[4] [dor·mír] v. irr. to sleep; **-se** to go to sleep, fall asleep; to become numb.
dormitar [dor·mi·tár] v. to doze.
dormitorio [dor·mi·tó·rjo] m. dormitory; bedroom.
dorso [dór·so] m. back, reverse.
dosel [do·sél] m. canopy.
dosis [dó·sis] f. dose.
dotación [do·ta·sjón] f. endowment, endowing; donation, foundation; dowry; complement (*personnel of a warship*); office force.
dotar [do·tár] v. to endow; to provide with a dowry.
dote [dó·te] m. & f. dowry; f. natural gift, talent, or quality.
draga [drá·ga] f. dredge, dredging machine.
dragado [dra·gá·đo] m. dredging.
dragaminas [dra·ga·mí·nas] m. mine sweeper.
dragar[7] [dra·gár] v. to dredge.
dragón [dra·gón] m. dragon.
drama [drá·ma] m. drama.
dramático [dra·má·ti·ko] adj. dramatic; m. dramatic actor; playwright, dramatist.
dramatizar[9] [dra·ma·ti·sár] v. to dramatize.
dramaturgo [dra·ma·túr·go] m. playwright, dramatist.
drenaje [dre·ná·xe] m. *Am.* drainage.
drenar [dre·nár] v. *Am.* to drain.
dril [dril] m. drill (*strong cotton or linen cloth*).
droga [dró·ga] f. (*medicina*) drug, medicine; (*mentira*) lie, fib; trick; (*molestia*) bother, nuisance; *Peru, Carib.* bad debt; *Ríopl.* drug on the market unsalable article.
droguería [dro·ge·rí·a] f. drugstore; drug business.
droguero [dro·gé·ro] m. druggist; *Am.* cheat, debt evader.
droguista [dro·gís·ta] m. & f. druggist; cheat, crook.
dúctil [dúk·til] adj. ductile.
ducha [dú·ča] f. shower bath; douche.

DI

ducho [dú·čo] *adj.* expert, skillful.
duda [dú·ḍa] *f.* doubt.
dudable [du·ḍá·ḅle] *adj.* doubtful.
dudar [du·ḍár] *v.* to doubt; to hesitate.
dudoso [du·ḍó·so] *adj.* doubtful; uncertain.
duela [dwé·la] *f.* stave (*of a barrel*); *Mex., Andes* long, narrow floor board.
duelo [dwé·lo] *m.* (*luto*) grief, sorrow; mourning; mourners; (*pleito*) duel; **estar de** — to be in mourning; to mourn.
duende [dwén·de] *m.* goblin.
dueña [dwé·ña] *f.* owner, landlady; duenna, chaperon or governess.
dueño [dwé·ño] *m.* owner; master.
dueto [dwé·to], **dúo** [dú·o] *m.* duet.
dulce [dúl·se] *adj.* sweet; pleasant, agreeable; fresh (*water*); soft (*metal*); *m.* sweetmeat; candy; preserves; *Am.* sugar, honey; **dulcería** [dul·se·rí·a] *f.* candy shop.
dulcificar[6] [dul·si·fi·kár] *v.* to sweeten; to soften.
dulzón [dul·són] *adj.* over-sweet, sickeningly sweet.
dulzura [dul·sú·ra] *f.* sweetness; meekness.
duna [dú·na] *f.* dune, sand dune.
duplicado [du·pli·ká·ḍo] *adj.* & *m.* duplicate; **por** — in duplicate; *p.p. of* **duplicar**.
duplicar[6] [du·pli·kár] *v.* to duplicate, double; to repeat.
duplicidad [du·pli·si·ḍáḍ] *f.* duplicity, deceit, deceitfulness, treachery.
duque [dú·ke] *m.* duke.
duquesa [du·ké·sa] *f.* duchess.
durabilidad [du·ra·ḅi·li·ḍáḍ] *f.* durability, durable quality, wear.
durable [du·rá·ḅle] *adj.* durable.
duración [du·ra·sjón] *f.* duration.
duradero [du·ra·ḍé·ro] *adj.* durable, lasting.
durante [du·rán·te] *prep.* during, for.
durar [du·rár] *v.* to last, endure; to wear well.
durazno [du·ráz·no] *m.* peach; peach tree; **duraznero** [du·raz·né·ro] *m.* peach tree.
dureza [du·ré·sa] *f.* hardness; harshness.
durmiente [dur·mjén·te] *adj.* sleeping; *m.* sleeper; crossbeam; *Col., Ven., Mex., Ch.* railroad tie.
duro [dú·ro] *adj.* (*sólido*) hard; firm, solid; untiring; (*cruel*) cruel; harsh; rigid; (*tacaño*) stubborn; stingy; **a duras penas** with difficulty; *Am.* — **y parejo** eagerly, tenaciously; *Am.* **hacer** — to resist stubbornly; *m.* **duro** (*Spanish dollar*).

E:e **e** [e] *conj.* and (*before words beginning with* **i** *or* **hi**).
ebanista [e·ḅa·nís·ta] *m.* cabinetmaker.
ébano [é·ḅa·no] *m.* ebony.
ebrio [é·brjo] *adj.* drunk.
ebullición [e·ḅu·yi·sjón] *f.* boiling, bubbling up.
eclesiástico [e·kle·sjás·ti·ko] *adj.* ecclesiastic, belonging to the church; *m.* clergyman.
eclipsar [e·klip·sár] *v.* to eclipse; to outshine, surpass.
eclipse [e·klíp·se] *m.* eclipse.
écloga [é·klo·ḡa] *f.* eclogue, pastoral poem, idyll.
eco [é·ko] *m.* echo.
economía [e·ko·no·mí·a] *f.* economy; — **política** economics, political economy.
económico [e·ko·nó·mi·ko] *adj.* economic;

economical, saving; **economista** [e·ko·no·mís·ta] *m.* economist.
economizar[9] [e·ko·no·mi·sár] *v.* to economize, save.
ecuación [e·kwa·sjón] *f.* equation.
ecuador [e·kwa·ḍór] *m.* equator.
echar [e·čár] *v.* (*tirar*) to throw, cast; to expel; to throw out; (*emitir*) to give off; to sprout; — **a correr** to run away; -(**se**) **a perder** to spoil; — **a pique** to sink; -(**se**) **a reir** to burst out laughing; — **carnes** to get fat; — **de menos** to miss; — **de ver** to notice; to make out; — **mano** to seize; — **papas** to fib; — **raíces** to take root; — **suertes** to draw lots; -**se** to lie down; *Am.* **echársela** [e·čár·se·la] to boast.
edad [e·ḍáḍ] *f.* age.
edecán [e·ḍe·kán] *m.* aide-de-camp.
edén [e·ḍén] *m.* Eden; paradise.
edición [e·ḍi·sjón] *f.* edition; publication.
edificación [e·ḍi·fi·ka·sjón] *f.* edification (*moral or spiritual uplift*); construction.
edificar[6] [e·ḍi·fi·kár] *v.* to construct, build; to edify, uplift.
edificio [e·ḍi·fí·sjo] *m.* edifice, building.
editar [e·ḍi·tár] *v.* to publish.
editor [e·ḍi·tór] *m.* publisher; *adj.* publishing.
editorial [e·ḍi·to·rjál] *adj.* publishing, editorial; *m.* editorial; *f.* publishing house.
edredón [e·ḍre·ḍón] *m.* down quilt, comforter, quilted blanket.
educación [e·ḍu·ka·sjón] *f.* education, training; breeding, manners.
educador [e·ḍu·ka·ḍór] *m.* educator; *adj.* educating.
educando [e·ḍu·kán·do] *m.* pupil; inmate (*of an orphanage, boarding school, etc.*).
educar[6] [e·ḍu·kár] *v.* to educate, teach, train, raise, bring up.
educativo [e·ḍu·ka·tí·ḅo] *adj*— educational.
efectivo [e·fek·tí·ḅo] *adj.* effective; real; in operation, active; *m.* cash.
efecto [e·fék·to] *m.* (*resultado*) effect, result; (*fin*) end, purpose, -**s** goods, personal property; **en** — in fact, actually; **llevar a** — to carry out; **surtir** — to come out as expected; to give good results.
efectuar[18] [e·fek·twár] *v.* to effect, bring about.
eficacia [e·fi·ká·sja] *f.* efficacy; efficiency; effectiveness.
eficaz [e·fi·kás] *adj.* effective; active; efficient.
eficiencia [e·fi·sjén·sja] *f.* efficiency; **eficiente** [e·fi·sjén·te] *adj.* efficient.
efímero [e·fí·me·ro] *adj.* ephemeral, short-lived, brief.
efluvio [e·flú·ḅjo] *m.* emanation, exhalation, vapors.
efusión [e·fu·sjón] *f.* effusion, unrestrained expression of feeling, gushy manner; — **de sangre** bloodshed.
efusivo [e·fu·sí·ḅo] *adj.* effusive, too demonstrative, over-emotional.
egipcio [e·xip·sjo] *adj.* & *m.* Egyptian.
egocéntrico [e·go·sén·tri·ko] *adj.* egocentric, self-centered.
egoísmo [e·go·íz·mo] *m.* selfishness.
egoísta [e·go·ís·ta] *adj.* selfish; *m.* & *f.* selfish person.
egolatría [e·go·la·trí·a] *f.* self-worship.
eje [é·xe] *m.* axis; axle.
ejecución [e·xe·ku·sjón] *f.* execution; carrying out.
ejecutar [e·xe·ku·tár] *v.* to execute; to carry out; to perform, do.

ejecutivo [e·xe·ku·tí·ɓo] *adj.* executive; active; *m.* executive.

ejecutor [e·xe·ku·tór] *m.* executor; — **de la justicia** executioner.

ejemplar [e·xem·plár] *adj.* exemplary, model; *m.* copy; specimen.

ejemplo [e·xém·plo] *m.* example; model, pattern.

ejercer[10] [e·xer·sér] *v.* to practice (*a profession*); to exert.

ejercicio [e·xer·sí·sjo] *m.* exercise; practice; military drill; exercise (*of authority*); **hacer** — to take exercise.

ejercitar [e·xer·si·tár] *v.* to practice, exercise; to drill, train; **-se** to train oneself; to practice.

ejército [e·xér·si·to] *m.* army.

ejido [e·xí·đo] *m.* public land, common.

ejote [e·jó·te] *m. Mex., Guat.* string bean.

el [el] *def. art. m.* the; — **de** the one with, that one with; — **que** *rel. pron.* he who, the one that; **él** *pers. pron.* he; him, it (*after a prep.*).

elaboración [e·la·ɓo·ra·sjón] *f.* manufacture, making; development.

elaborar [e·la·ɓo·rár] *v.* to elaborate.

elasticidad [e·las·ti·si·đáđ] *f.* elasticity.

elástico [e·lás·ti·ko] *adj.* elastic; flexible; *m.* elastic; elastic tape; wire spring; **-s** *Am.* suspenders.

elección [e·lek·sjón] *f.* election; choice.

electo [e·lék·to] *adj.* elect, chosen; *m.* elect, person chosen.

elector [e·lek·tór] *m.* elector, voter; *adj.* electoral, electing.

electoral [e·lek·to·rál] *adj.* electoral.

electricidad [e·lek·tri·si·đáđ] *f.* electricity.

electricista [e·lek·tri·sís·ta] *m.* electrician; electrical engineer.

eléctrico [e·lék·tri·ko] *adj.* electric, electrical.

electrizar[9] [e·lek·tri·sá] *v.* to electrify; to thrill, excite; *Am.* to anger, irritate.

electrocardiógrafo [e·lek·tro·kar·đjó·gra·fo] *m.* electrocardiograph.

electroimán [e·lek·troj·mán] *m.* electromagnet.

electrólisis [e·lek·tró·li·sis] *f.* electrolysis.

electromagnético [e·lek·tro·mag·né·ti·ko] *adj.* electromagnetic.

electrón [e·lek·trón] *m.* electron.

electrónico [e·lek·tró·ni·ko] *adj.* electronic; **electrónica** [e·lek·tro·ni·ka] *f.* electronics.

elefante [e·le·fán·te] *m.* elephant.

elegancia [e·le·gán·sja] *f.* elegance, grace, distinguished manner.

elegante [e·le·gán·te] *adj.* elegant, graceful, polished; stylish.

elegir[5, 11] [e·le·xír] *v. irr.* to elect, choose.

elemental [e·le·men·tál] *adj.* elementary; elemental, fundamental.

elemento [e·le·mén·to] *m.* element; **-s** elements, fundamentals; personnel; — **químicos** chemical elements, simple substances; *Am.* **ser** (*or* **estar**) **hecho un** — to be an idiot, a fool.

elevación [e·le·ɓa·sjón] *f.* elevation; height; rise; rapture.

elevador [e·le·ɓa·đór] *m. Am.* elevator, hoist.

elevar [e·le·ɓár] *v.* to elevate, raise, lift; **-se** to go up; to soar.

eliminación [e·li·mi·na·sjón] *f.* elimination, removal.

eliminar [e·li·mi·nár] *v.* to eliminate.

elocuencia [e·lo·kwén·sja] *f.* eloquence.

elocuente [e·lo·kwén·te] *adj.* eloquent.

elogiar [e·lo·xjár] *v.* to praise.

elogio [e·ló·xjo] *m.* praise.

elote [e·ló·te] *m. Mex., C.A.* ear of corn, corn on the cob.

elucidación [e·lu·si·đa·sjón] *f.* elucidation, explanation.

elucidar [e·lu·si·đár] *v.* to elucidate, illustrate, explain.

eludir [e·lu·đír] *v.* to elude, avoid, dodge.

ella [é·ya] *pers. pron.* she; her, it (*after a prep*).

ello [é·yo] *pron.* it; — **es que** the fact is that.

emanación [e·ma·na·sjón] *f.* emanation, flow; fumes, vapor, odor; manifestation.

emanar [e·ma·nár] *v.* to emanate, spring, issue.

emancipación [e·man·si·pa·sjón] *f.* emancipation.

emancipar [e·man·si·pár] *v.* to emancipate, set free; **-se** to become free.

embajada [em·ba·xá·đa] *f.* embassy; errand, mission.

embajador [em·ba·xá·đor] *m.* ambassador.

embalador [em·ba·la·đór] *m.* packer.

embalaje [em·ba·lá·xe] *m.* packing.

embalar [em·ba·lár] *v.* to pack; to bale, crate.

embaldosar [em·bal·do·sár] *v.* to pave with flagstones or tiles.

embalsamar [em·bal·sa·már] *v.* to embalm; to scent, perfume.

embarazar[9] [em·ba·ra·sár] *v.* (*impedir*) to hinder, to obstruct; (*preñar*) to make pregnant; **-se** to become pregnant; to become embarrassed.

embarazo [em·ba·rá·so] *m.* (*obstáculo*) impediment, obstacle; (*preñez*) pregnancy; (*timidez*) bashfulness, awkwardness.

embarazoso [em·ba·ra·só·so] *adj.* embarrassing; cumbersome, unwieldly.

embarcación [em·bar·ka·sjón] *f.* ship, boat; embarkation.

embarcadero [em·bar·ka·đé·ro] *m.* wharf, pier.

embarcador [em·bar·ka·đór] *m.* shipper.

embarcar[6] [em·bar·kár] *v.* to embark; to ship; *Am.* to ship by train or any vehicle; **-se** to embark, sail; to engage (in); *Am.* to board, get on a train.

embarco [em·bár·ko] *m.* embarkation.

embargar[7] [em·bar·gár] *v.* to impede; to restrain; to attach, confiscate; to lay an embargo on; **estar embargado de emoción** to be overcome with emotion.

embargo [em·bár·go] *m.* embargo, restriction on commerce; attachment, confiscation; **sin** — nevertheless.

embarque [em·bár·ke] *m.* shipment.

embarrado [em·ba·rrá·đo] *p.p. & adj.* smeared: plastered; muddy.

embarrar [em·ba·rrár] *v.* to smear, daub.

embaucador [em·baw·ka·đór] *m.* cheat, impostor.

embaucar[6] [em·baw·kár] *v.* to fool, trick, swindle, deceive.

embebecido [em·be·ɓe·sí·đo] *p.p. & adj.* absorbed; amazed.

embebecimiento [em·be·ɓe·si·mjén·to] *m.* absorption; rapture.

embeber [em·be·ɓér] *v.* to imbibe, absorb; to soak; to shrink, **-se** to be fascinated; to be absorbed.

embelesar [em·be·le·sár] *v.* to enrapture, delight, charm.

embeleso [em·be·lé·so] *m.* delight, ectasy.

embellecer[13] [em·be·ye·sér] *v. irr.* to embellish, beautify, adorn.

embestida [em·bes·tí·đa] *f.* sudden attack, onset, assault.

embestir[5] [em·bes·tír] *v. irr.* to attack, assail.

embetunar [em·be·tu·nár] *v.* to cover with pitch; to black.

emblanquecer[13] [em·blaŋ·ke·sér] *v. irr.* to whiten; to bleach; to become white; **-se** to whiten, become white.

emblema [em·blé·ma] *m.* emblem.

embobar [em·bo·bár] *v.* to fool; to amuse; to fascinate; to amaze; **-se** to be amazed; to be fascinated.

embobinado [em·bo·bi·ná·do] *m.* reel assembly (*of a tape recorder or computer*).

embocadura [em·bo·ka·dú·ra] *f.* mouth (*of a river*); entrance (*through a narrow passage*); mouthpiece (*of a wind instrument*); bit (*of a bridle*); taste, flavor (said of *wines*).

embolado [em·bo·lá·do] *m.* bull whose horns have been tipped with balls; impotent, ineffectual person; *p.p. of* **embolar**.

embolar [em·bo·lár] *v.* (*al toro*) to tip a bull's horns with balls; (*dar lustre*) to polish, to black; **-se** *C.A.* to get drunk.

émbolo [ém·bo·lo] *m.* piston; plunger (*of a pump*); embolus (*clot in a blood vessel*).

embolsar [em·bol·sár] *v.* to put into a pocket or purse; **-se** to pocket, put into one's pocket.

emborrachar [em·bo·rra·čár] *v.* to intoxicate; **-se** to get drunk.

emborronar [em·bo·rro·nár] *v.* to blot; to scribble.

emboscada [em·bos·ká·da] *f.* ambush.

emboscar[6] [em·bos·kár] *v.* to ambush; **-se** to lie in ambush; to go into a forest.

embotado [em·bo·tá·do] *adj.* dull, blunt; *p.p. of* **embotar**.

embotamiento [em·bo·ta·mjén·to] *m.* dullness, bluntness; dulling, blunting.

embotar [em·bo·tár] *v.* to dull, blunt; to enervate, weaken.

embotellador [em·bo·te·ya·dór] *m.* bottling machine; **embotelladora** [em·bo·te·ya·dó·ra] bottling works.

embotellar [em·bo·te·yár] *v.* to bottle; to bottle up; *Am.* to jail.

embozado [em·bo·sá·do] *adj.* cloaked; muffled, covered up to the face.

embozar[7] [em·bo·sár] *v.* to muffle; to cloak, conceal, disguise; to muzzle; **-se** to muffle oneself, wrap oneself.

embragar[7] [em·bra·gár] *v.* to engage or throw in the clutch.

embrague [em·brá·ge] *m.* clutch (*of a machine*); coupling.

embriagar[7] [em·brja·gár] *v.* to intoxicate; **-se** to get drunk, intoxicated.

embriaguez [em·brja·gés] *f.* intoxication; drunkenness.

embrión [em·brjón] *m.* embryo.

embrollar [em·bro·yár] *v.* to involve, ensnare, entangle; to confuse.

embrollo [em·bró·yo] *m.* confusion, tangle; trickery, lie, deception.

embromar [em·bro·már] *v.* to chaff, make fun of "kid"; *Am.* to bother, molest; *Am.* to delay unnecessarily; *Col., Ven.* to ruin, harm; **-se** *Am.* to be bothered, disgusted; *Mex.* to get delayed.

embrujar [em·bru·xár] *v.* to bewitch, enchant.

embrujo [em·brú·xo] *m.* charm, enchantment; glamour.

embrutecer[13] [em·bru·te·sér] *v. irr.* to stupefy, render brutish; to dull the mind, make insensible.

embudo [em·bú·do] *m.* funnel; trick.

embuste [em·bús·te] *m.* lie, fraud; trinket.

embustero [em·bus·té·ro] *m.* liar; *adj.* deceitful, tricky.

embutido [em·bu·tí·do] *m.* sausage; inlaid work; *Am.* insertion of embroidery or lace; *p.p. of* **embutir.**

embutir [em·bu·tír] *v.* to insert, inlay; to stuff.

emerger[11] [e·mer·xér] *v.* to emerge, come out.

emigración [e·mi·gra·sjón] *f.* emigration.

emigrante [e·mi·grán·te] *m. & f.* emigrant.

emigrar [e·mi·grár] *v.* to emigrate; to migrate.

eminencia [e·mi·nén·sja] *f.* eminence; height.

eminente [e·mi·nén·te] *adj.* eminent, high, lofty.

emisión [e·mi·sjón] *f.* issue (*of bonds, money, etc.*); radio broadcast.

emisor [e·mi·sór] *adj.* emitting; broadcasting; *m.* radio transmitter; **emisora** [e·mi·só·ra] *f.* broadcasting station.

emitir [e·mi·tír] *v.* to emit, give off; to utter; to send forth; to issue; to broadcast.

emoción [e·mo·sjón] *f.* emotion.

emocional [e·mo·sjo·nál] *adj.* emotional.

emocionante [e·mo·sjo·nán·te] *adj.* moving, touching, thrilling.

emocionar [e·mo·sjo·nár] *v.* to cause emotion, touch, move; **-se** to be touched, moved, stirred.

emotivo [e·mo·tí·bo] *adj.* emotional.

empacador [em·pa·ka·dór] *m.* packer.

empacar[6] [em·pa·kár] *v.* to pack up, wrap up, bale, crate; *Ríopl.* to goad, irritate (*an animal*); **-se** to be stubborn; to get angry; *Ríopl.* to balk; *Ríopl.* to put on airs.

empachado [em·pa·čá·do] *p.p. & adj.* (*relleno*) clogged; stuffed; upset from indigestion; (*tímido*) embarrassed; bashful.

empachar [em·pa·čár] *v.* to stuff, cram; to cause indigestion; **-se** to get upset; to get clogged; to be stuffed; to suffer indigestion; to get embarrassed.

empacho [em·pá·čo] *m.* indigestion; bashfulness; **no tener — en** to have no objection to; to feel free to.

empalagar[7] [em·pa·la·gár] *v.* to cloy; to pall on, become distasteful; to disgust.

empalagoso [em·pa·la·gó·so] *adj.* cloying; sickeningly sweet; boring, wearisome.

empalizada [em·pa·li·sá·da] *f.* stockade, palisade.

empalmar [em·pal·már] *v.* to splice; to join; **— con** to join (*as railroads or highways*).

empalme [em·pál·me] *m.* junction; joint, connection; splice.

empanada [em·pa·ná·da] *f.* pie, meat pie; swindle, fraud.

empanizar[9] [em·pa·ni·sár] *v. Carib., C.A., Mex.* to bread.

empañado [em·pa·ñá·do] *adj. & p.p.* tarnished; dim, blurred.

empañar [em·pa·ñár] *v.* to blur, dim, tarnish.

empapada [em·pa·pá·da] *f. Am.* drenching, soaking.

empapar [em·pa·pár] *v.* to soak, drench, saturate.

empapelador [em·pa·pe·la·dór] *m.* paper hanger.

empapelar [em·pa·pe·lár] *v.* to paper; to wrap in paper.

empaque [em·pá·ke] *m.* (*bulto*) packing; (*parecer*) looks, appearance, air; airs, importance; *Am., Peru* impudence.

empaquetar [em·pa·ke·tár] *v.* to pack; to pack in; to make a package; **-se** to dress up, doll up.

emparedado [em·pa·re·dá·do] *adj.* shut up, confined between walls; *m.* sandwich; prisoner confined in a narrow cell.

emparejar [em·pa·re·xár] v. to even up, level off; to match; to pair off; to overtake, catch up with.

emparentado [em·pa·ren·tá·do] adj. & p.p. related by marriage.

emparentar [em·pa·ren·tár] v. to become related by marriage.

emparrado [em·pa·rrá·do] m. vine arbor.

empastar [em·pas·tár] v. to paste; to fill (a tooth); to bind (books); -se Ch. to get lost in the pasture; Mex. to become overgrown with grass.

empaste [em·pás·te] m. tooth filling; binding (of a book).

empatar [em·pa·tár] v. (igualar) to tie (in a game), have an equal score; to have an equal number of votes; (impedir) to hinder, obstruct; Col., Ven., Carib. to tie, join.

empate [em·pá·te] m. tie, draw, equal score, equal number of votes; hindrance, obstruction; Am. joint, junction.

empecinado [em·pe·si·ná·do] adj. Am. stubborn.

empedernido [em·pe·der·ni·do] adj. hardened, hardhearted.

empedernir[51] [em·pe·der·nír] v. to harden, toughen; -se to become hardened.

empedrado [em·pe·drá·do] m. cobblestone pavement; p.p. & adj. paved with stones.

empedrar[1] [em·pe·drár] v. irr. to pave with stones.

empeine [em·péj·ne] m. instep; groin (hollow between lower part of abdomen and thigh).

empellón [em·pe·yón] m. push, shove; a -es by pushing.

empeñar [em·pe·ñár] v. (dar en prenda) to pawn; (obligar) to oblige, compel; -se to persist, insist; to apply oneself; to go into debt; -se por to plead for, intercede for; se empeñaron en una lucha they engaged in a fight.

empeño [em·pé·ño] m. (fianza) pledge, pawn; (deseo) persistence, insistence; eagerness; perseverance; Am. pawnshop; tener — en to be eager to.

empeorar [em·pe·o·rár] v. to impair; to make worse; to grow worse; -se to grow worse.

empequeñecer[13] [em·pe·ke·ñe·sér] v. irr. to diminish, make smaller; to belittle.

emperador [em·pe·ra·dór] m. emperor; emperatriz [em·pe·ra·trís] f. empress.

emperifollar [em·pe·ri·fo·yár] v. to decorate, adorn; -se to dress up, deck out, doll up.

empero [em·pé·ro] conj. however, nevertheless.

empezar[1, 9] [em·pe·sár] v. irr. to begin.

empiezo [em·pjé·so] m. Carib., Mex., C.A. beginning.

empinado [em·pi·ná·do] adj. steep; lofty.

empinar [em·pi·nár] v. to raise, lift; to incline, bend; — el codo to drink; -se to stand on tiptoes; to rear (said of horses); to rise high; Am. to overeat.

empiojado [em·pjo·xá·do] adj. lousy, full of lice.

emplasto [em·plás·to] m. plaster, poultice.

empleado [em·ple·á·do] m. employee; p.p. of emplear.

emplear [em·ple·ár] v. to employ; to invest, spend; -se en to be employed in.

empleo [em·plé·o] m. employment, position, job; employ; occupation; aim; investment.

emplumar [em·plu·már] v. to feather; to adorn with feathers; to tar and feather; C.A. to deceive; Ec. to send away to a house of correction or prison; Am. — con algo to run away with something, steal it; Ch., Col., Ven. -las (or emplumárselas [em·plu·már·se·las]) to

take to one's heels, flee, escape.

empobrecer[13] [em·po·bre·sér] v. irr. to impoverish; -se to become poor.

empobrecimiento [em·po·bre·si·mjén·to] m. impoverishment.

empolvado [em·pol·bá·do] adj. dusty, covered with dust or powder.

empolvar [em·pol·bár] v. to sprinkle powder; to cover with dust; -se to get dusty; to powder one's face.

empollar [em·po·yár] v. to hatch, brood.

emponzoñar [em·pon·so·ñár] v. to poison.

emprendedor [em·pren·de·dór] adj. enterprising.

emprender [em·pren·dér] v. to undertake.

empreñar [em·pre·ñár] v. to impregnate, make pregnant.

empresa [em·pré·sa] f. enterprise, undertaking; symbol; company, management.

empresario [em·pre·sá·rjo] m. manager; impresario, promoter.

empréstito [em·prés·ti·to] m. loan.

empujar [em·pu·xár] v. to push, shove.

empuje [em·pú·xe] m. push; shove; impulse; energy.

empujón [em·pu·xón] m. shove, push.

empuñar [em·pu·ñár] v. to grasp, grab, clutch, seize.

émulo [é·mu·lo] m. rival, competitor.

en [en] prep. in, on, upon.

enaguas [e·ná·gwas] f. pl. underskirt, petticoat; short skirt.

enajenamiento [e·na·xe·na·mjén·to] m. trance; abstraction, absence of mind; transfer (of property); — mental mental disorder; — de los sentidos loss of consciousness.

enajenar [e·na·xe·nár] v. (distraer) to enrapture, charm; to deprive (of one's sense); (trasladar) to transfer property; to dispossess; — el afecto de to alienate the affection of; -se to be enraptured, be in a trance.

enaltecer[13] [e·nal·te·sér] v. to extol, exalt.

enamorado [e·na·mo·rá·do] adj. in love; m. lover.

enamorar [e·na·mo·rár] v. to make love, woo, court; to enamor; -se to fall in love.

enano [e·ná·no] m. dwarf; adj. dwarfish, tiny, little.

enarbolar [e·nar·bo·lár] v. to hoist, lift, raise on high; to brandish (a sword, cane, etc.); -se to rear, balk.

enarcado [e·nar·ká·do] p.p. arched.

enarcar[6] [e·nar·kár] v. to arch; to hoop (barrels, kegs, etc.); — las cejas to arch one's eyebrows.

enardecer[13] [e·nar·de·sér] v. irr. to excite, kindle, fire with passion; -se to become excited; to get angry.

enardecimiento [e·nar·de·si·mjén·to] m. ardor, passion, unbridled enthusiasm; inflaming.

encabezado [eŋ·ka·be·sá·do] m. headline; heading.

encabezamiento [eŋ·ka·be·sa·mjén·to] m. heading; headline; list or roll of taxpayers; registration of taxpayers.

encabezar[9] [eŋ·ka·be·sár] v. to give a heading or title to; to head; to lead; to make up (a list or tax roll); to strengthen (wine).

encabritarse [eŋ·ka·bri·tár·se] v. to rear, rise up on the hind legs.

encadenar [eŋ·ka·de·nár] v. to chain; to link together.

encajar [eŋ·ka·xár] v. to thrust in, fit into, insert; -se to squeeze into; to intrude, meddle.

encaje [eŋ·ká·xe] m. lace; adjustment; fitting

EM

together; socket, groove, hole; inlaid work.

encajonar [eŋ·ka·xo·nár] v. to box (put or pack in a box).

encallar [eŋ·ka·yár] v. to strand, run aground; to get stuck.

encamado [eŋ·ka·má·ḍo] p.p. confined in bed.

encaminar [eŋ·ka·mi·nár] v. to direct, guide; -se to betake oneself, go (toward); to start out on a road.

encanecer¹³ [eŋ·ka·ne·sér] v. irr. to get grey, get grey-haired.

encanijado [eŋ·ka·ni·xá·ḍo] adj. emaciated, thin, sickly.

encanijarse [eŋ·ka·ni·xár·se] v. to get thin, emaciated.

encantado [eŋ·kan·tá·ḍo] p.p. & adj. delighted, charmed; enchanted.

encantador [eŋ·kan·ta·ḍór] adj. charming; m. charmer, enchanter.

encantamiento [eŋ·kan·ta·mjén·to] m. enchantment.

encantar [eŋ·kan·tár] v. to charm, enchant.

encanto [eŋ·kán·to] m. charm, enchantment, delight.

encapillar [eŋ·ka·pi·yár] v. P.R. to confine in the death cell.

encapotado [eŋ·ka·po·tá·ḍo] p.p. & adj. cloaked; overcast, cloudy; in a bad humor.

encapotarse [eŋ·ka·po·tár·se] v. to become overcast, cloudy; to cover up, put on a cloak or raincoat; to frown.

encapricharse [eŋ·ka·pri·čár·se] v. to persist in one's whims; to get stubborn.

encaramar [eŋ·ka·ra·már] v. to raise; to elevate; to extol; -se to climb; to climb upon, get upon, perch upon; Ch. to be ashamed; Carib. to go to one's head (said of liquor).

encarar [eŋ·ka·rár] v. to face; to aim; -se con to face; to confront.

encarcelación [eŋ·kar·se·la·sjón] f. imprisonment.

encarcelamiento [eŋ·kar·se·la·mjén·to] = **encarcelación.**

encarcelar [eŋ·kar·se·lár] v. to imprison, jail.

encarecer¹³ [eŋ·ka·re·sér] v. irr. (alzar precio) to go up in value; to make dear, raise the price of; (ponderar) to exaggerate; to extol; to recommend highly, to enhance.

encarecidamente [eŋ·ka·re·si·ḍa·mén·te] adv. earnestly.

encargar⁷ [eŋ·kar·ǥár] v. (dar cargo) to put in charge; to entrust; to commission; (aconsejar) to recommend, advise; (pedir), to order; to beg; -se de to take charge of.

encargo [eŋ·kár·ǥo] m. recommendation, advice; charge; order; commission; errand.

encariñado [eŋ·ka·ri·ñá·ḍo] adj. & p.p. attached, fond, enamored.

encariñamiento [eŋ·ka·ri·ña·mjén·to] m. affection, fondness, attachment.

encariñar [eŋ·ka·ri·ñár] v. to awaken love or affection; -se to become fond (of), attached (to).

encarnado [eŋ·kar·ná·ḍo] adj. flesh-colored; red; p.p. of **encarnar.**

encarnar [eŋ·kar·nár] v. to incarnate, embody; to bait (a fishhook).

encarnizado [eŋ·kar·ni·sá·ḍo] adj. bloody; hard-fought, fierce.

encarnizar⁹ [eŋ·kar·ni·sár] v. to infuriate, enrage; -se to get furious, enraged; to fight with fury.

encasillar [eŋ·ka·si·yár] v. to pigeonhole, put in a pigeonhole or compartment; to put in a stall; to classify, sort out.

encender¹ [en·sen·dér] v. irr. to light, kindle; to set on fire; -se to take fire, be on fire; to get red.

encendido [en·sen·di·ḍo] adj. red; p.p. of **encender;** m. ignition (of a motor).

encerado [en·se·rá·ḍo] m. blackboard; oilcloth; wax coating; p.p. & adj. waxed; wax-colored; papel — wax paper.

encerar [en·se·rár] v. to wax; to thicken (lime).

encerramiento [en·se·rra·mjén·to] m. enclosure, confinement; locking up; retreat; prison.

encerrar¹ [en·se·rrár] v. irr. to enclose; to lock up; to contain; -se to lock oneself up, go into seclusion.

encía [en·sí·a] f. gum (of the teeth).

enciclopedia [en·si·klo·pé·ḍja] f. encyclopedia.

encierro [en·sjé·rro] m. confinement; retreat; prison.

encima [en·sí·ma] adv. above, overhead, over, on top; besides, in addition; — de on top of; por — de over; Am. de — besides, in addition; Col., C.A., Riopl., Carib. echárselo todo — to spend everything on clothes.

encina [en·sí·na] f. live oak.

encinta [en·sín·ta] adj. pregnant.

encintado [en·sin·tá·ḍo] m. curb (of a sidewalk).

enclaustrar [en·klaws·trár] v. to cloister.

enclavar [eŋ·kla·ḅár] v. to nail, fix, fasten.

enclenque [eŋ·klén·ke] adj. sickly, wan; weak, feeble.

enclítico [eŋ·klí·ti·ko] adj. enclitic.

encobar [eŋ·ko·ḅár] v. to brood.

encoger¹¹ [eŋ·ko·xér] v. to shrink, shrivel, shorten, contract; -se to shrink; to shrivel; -se de hombros to shrug one's shoulders.

encogido [eŋ·ko·xi·ḍo] p.p. & adj. shrunk, shrivelled; timid, shy.

encogimiento [eŋ·ko·xi·mjén·to] m. shrinking; timidity; — de hombros shrug.

encolerizar⁹ [eŋ·ko·le·ri·sár] v. to anger; -se to get angry.

encomendar¹ [eŋ·ko·men·dár] v. irr. (encargar) to charge, advise; to entrust; (recomendar) to recommend, commend; -se to put oneself in the hands (of); to send regards; to pray (to).

encomiar [eŋ·ko·mjár] v. to extol, praise.

encomienda [eŋ·ko·mjén·da] f. charge, commission; recommendation; royal land grant (including Indian inhabitants); Am. warehouse (for agricultural products); Am. parcel-post package.

encomio [eŋ·kó·mjo] m. encomium, high praise.

enconado [eŋ·ko·ná·ḍo] p.p. & adj. inflamed; infected; sore; angry.

enconar [eŋ·ko·nár] v. to inflame; to infect; to irritate; -se to become inflamed, infected; to get irritated.

encono [eŋ·kó·no] m. rancor, animosity, ill will; Cuba, Mex. inflammation, swelling.

encontrado [eŋ·kon·trá·ḍo] adj. opposite; opposing; contrary; p.p. of **encontrar.**

encontrar² [eŋ·kon·trár] v. irr. to encounter, meet; to find; -se to meet; to coincide; to be; to be found, be situated; to collide; to conflict; -se con to come across, meet up with.

encontrón [eŋ·kon·trón], **encontronazo** [eŋ·kon·tro·ná·so] m. bump, collision; **darse un** — to collide (with) bump (into); to bump into each other.

encordelar [eŋ·kor·ḍe·lár] v. to string; to tie with strings.

encorvar [eŋ·kor·ḅár] v. to curve, bend; -se to bend down; to stoop.

encrespar [eŋ·kres·pár] *v.* (*rizar*) to curl; to ruffle; (*agitar*) to irritate; **-se** to curl; to get ruffled; to become involved or entangled (*a matter or affair*); to become rough (*said of the sea*).

encrucijada [eŋ·kru·si·xá·da] *f.* crossroads, street intersection; ambush.

encuadernación [eŋ·kwa·der·na·sjón] *f.* binding (*of books*).

encuadernar [eŋ·kwa·der·nár] *v.* to bind (*books*).

encuadrar [eŋ·kwa·drár] *v.* to enclose in a frame; to encompass; to fit (into); *Am.* to suit; *Ven.* to summarize briefly, give a synthesis of.

encubierto [eŋ·ku·bjér·to] *p.p. of* **encubrir.**

encubrir[52] [eŋ·ku·brír] *v.* to cover, hide.

encuentro [eŋ·kwén·tro] *m.* (*hallazgo*) encounter, meeting; find, finding; (*conflicto*) conflict, clash; collision; **salir al — de** to go out to meet; to make a stand against, oppose; *Am.* **llevarse de —** to run over, knock down; to drag along.

encuerado [eŋ·kwe·rá·do] *adj. Am.* naked.

encuerar [eŋ·kwe·rár] *v. Am.* to strip of clothes; *Am.* to skin, fleece, strip of money; **-se** *Am.* to strip, get undressed.

encuesta [eŋ·kwés·ta] *f.* search, inquiry, investigation; survey.

encumbrado [eŋ·kum·brá·do] *p.p. & adj.* elevated; exalted; high, lofty.

encumbramiento [eŋ·kum·bra·mjén·to] *m.* elevation; exaltation; height; eminence.

encumbrar [eŋ·kum·brár] *v.* to elevate; to exalt, extol; **-se** to climb to the top; to rise up; to hold oneself high; to soar.

encurtido [eŋ·kur·tí·do] *m.* pickle; *p.p. of* **encurtir.**

encurtir [eŋ·kur·tír] *v.* to pickle.

enchilada [en·či·lá·da] *f. Mex. C.A.* rolled **tortilla** served with chili.

enchuecar[6] [en·čwe·kár] *v.* to bend, twist; **-se** *Col., Ven., Mex., Ríopl.* to get bent or twisted.

enchufar [en·ču·fár] *v.* to plug in; to telescope; to fit (*a tube or pipe*) into another.

enchufe [en·čú·fe] *m.* socket; plug; electric outlet; *Spain* influence; position obtained through influence.

ende [én·de]: **por — hence, therefore.**

endeble [en·dé·ble] *adj.* weak, feeble; flimsy.

endemoniado [en·de·mo·njá·do] *adj.* possessed by the devil; devilish, fiendish; mischievous.

endentar[1] [en·den·tár] *v. irr.* to indent, form notches in; to furnish (*a saw, wheel, etc.*) with teeth; to mesh.

enderezar[9] [en·de·re·sár] *v.* to straighten; to set upright; to right, correct; to direct; to address; **-se** to go straight (to); to straighten up.

endeudado [en·dew·dá·do] *p.p. & adj.* indebted; in debt.

endeudarse [en·dew·dár·se] *v.* to get into debt, become indebted.

endiablado [en·dja·blá·do] *adj.* devilish; possessed by the devil; ugly; mean, wicked; *Col., Ven., Mex., Ríopl.* dangerous, risky.

endomingado [en·do·miŋ·gá·do] *p.p. & adj.* dressed up in one's Sunday, or best, clothes.

endosante [en·do·sán·te] *m.* endorser.

endosar [en·do·sár] *v.* to endorse (*a check, draft, etc.*).

endose [en·dó·se], **endoso** [en·dó·so] *m.* endorsement.

endulzar[9] [en·dul·sár] *v.* to sweeten; to soften.

endurecer[13] [en·du·re·sér] *v. irr.* to harden; **-se** to get hardened; to get cruel.

enebro [e·né·bro] *m.* juniper.

enemigo [e·ne·mí·go] *m.* enemy; devil; *adj.* hostile; unfriendly; **ser — de una cosa** to dislike a thing.

enemistad [e·ne·mis·tád] *f.* enmity, hatred.

enemistar [e·ne·mis·tár] *v.* to cause enmity between; **-se con** to become an enemy of.

energía [e·ner·xí·a] *f.* energy; **— nuclear** nuclear energy.

enérgico [e·nér·xi·ko] *adj.* energetic.

enero [e·né·ro] *m.* January.

enervar [e·ner·bár] *v.* to enervate, weaken.

enfadar [en·fa·dár] *v.* to anger; **-se** to get angry.

enfado [en·fá·do] *m.* anger, disgust.

enfadoso [en·fa·dó·so] *adj.* annoying.

enfardar [en·far·dár] *v.* to bale, pack.

énfasis [én·fa·sis] *m.* emphasis; **enfático** [en·fá·ti·ko] *adj.* emphatic.

enfermar [en·fer·már] *v.* to become ill; to make ill; to weaken; **-se** to become ill.

enfermedad [en·fer·me·dád] *f.* sickness, illness.

enfermería [en·fer·me·rí·a] *f.* infirmary.

enfermero [en·fer·mé·ro] *m.* male nurse; **enfermera** [en·fer·mé·ra] *f.* nurse (*for the sick*).

enfermizo [en·fer·mí·so] *adj.* sickly; unhealthy.

enfermo [en·fer·mo] *adj.* sick, ill; feeble; *m.* patient.

enflaquecer[13] [en·fla·ke·sér] *v. irr.* to become thin; to make thin; to weaken.

enfocar[6] [en·fo·kár] *v.* to focus.

enfrenar [en·fre·nár] *v.* to bridle; to brake, put the brake on; to check, curb.

enfrentar [en·fren·tár] *v.* to put face to face; **-se con** to confront, face, meet face to face.

enfrente [en·frén·te] *adv.* in front, opposite; **— de** in front of, opposite.

enfriamiento [en·frja·mjén·to] *m.* cooling; chill; refrigeration.

enfriar[17] [en·frjár] *v.* to cool, chill; *Carib.* to kill; **-se** to cool, cool off; to get chilled.

enfurecer[13] [en·fu·re·sér] *v. irr.* to infuriate, enrage; **-se** to rage; to get furious; to get rough, stormy (*said of the sea*).

enfurruñarse [en·fu·rru·ñár·se] *v.* to get angry; to grumble.

engalanar [eŋ·ga·la·nár] *v.* to adorn, decorate; **-se** to dress up, primp.

enganchamiento [eŋ·gan·ča·mjén·to] = **enganche.**

enganchar [eŋ·gan·čár] *v.* to hitch; to hook; to ensnare; to draft; to attract into the army; *Col., Ven., Mex., Ríopl.* to hire (*labor with false promises*); **-se** to engage, interlock; to get hooked; to enlist in the army.

enganche [eŋ·gán·če] *m.* hooking; coupling; draft (*into the army*); *Col., Ven., Mex., Ríopl.* enrolling of laborers (*for a rubber plantation or other risky business under false promises*); *Mex.* down payment.

engañador [eŋ·ga·ña·dór] *adj.* deceitful, deceiving; *m.* deceiver.

engañar [eŋ·ga·ñár] *v.* to deceive; to while away (*time*); to ward off (*hunger or sleep*); **-se** to deceive oneself; to be mistaken.

engaño [eŋ·gá·ño] *m.* deceit, trick, fraud; mistake, misunderstanding; *Ch., C.A.* bribe.

engañoso [eŋ·ga·ñó·so] *adj.* deceitful; tricky; misleading.

engastar [eŋ·gas·tár] *v.* to mount, set (*jewels*).

engaste [eŋ·gás·te] *m.* setting (*for a gem or stone*).

engatusar [eŋ·ga·tu·sár] *v.* to coax, entice; to.fool.

engendrar [eŋ·xen·drár] *v.* to engender, beget. produce; to cause.

engolfarse [eŋ·gol·fár·se] *v.* to get deep (into); to go deeply (into); to become absorbed, lost in thought.

engomar [eŋ·go·már] *v.* to gum; to glue.

engordar [eŋ·gor·ḍár] *v.* to fatten; to get fat; to get rich.

engorroso [eŋ·go·rró·so] *adj.* cumbersome; bothersome.

engranaje [eŋ·gra·ná·xe] *m.* gear, gears, gearing.

engranar [eŋ·gra·nár] *v.* to gear, throw in gear; to mesh gears.

engrandecer[13] [eŋ·gran·de·sér] *v. irr.* to aggrandize, make greater; to magnify; to exalt.

engrane [eŋ·grá·ne] *m.* engagement (*of gears*); gear.

engrasar [eŋ·gra·sár] *v.* to lubricate, grease; to stain with grease; to fertilize, manure; to dress (*cloth*).

engrase [eŋ·grá·se] *m.* grease job.

engreído [eŋ·gre·í·ḍo] *adj. & p.p.* conceited, vain; *Col.* attached, fond.

engreír[15] [eŋ·gre·ír] *v. irr.* to make vain, conceited; -se to puff up, get conceited; *Col.* to become fond (of), become attached (to).

engrosar[2] [eŋ·gro·sár] *v. irr.* to enlarge; to thicken; to fatten; to get fat.

engrudo [eŋ·grú·ḍo] *m.* paste (*for gluing*).

engullir[20] [eŋ·gu·yír] *v.* to gobble, devour; to gorge.

enhebrar [en·e·ḅrár] *v.* to thread (*a needle*); to string (*beads*).

enhiesto [en·jés·to] *adj.* straight, upright, erect.

enhorabuena [en·o·ra·ḅwé·na] *f.* congratulation; *adv.* safely; well and good; all right; with much pleasure.

enigma [e·níǵ·ma] *m.* enigma, riddle, puzzle.

enjabonar [en·xa·ḅo·nár] *v.* to soap; to soft-soap, flatter.

enjaezar[9] [eŋ·xa·e·sár] *v.* to harness.

enjalbegar[7] [eŋ·xal·ḅe·ǵar] *v.* to whitewash; -se to paint (*one's face*).

enjambre [eŋ·xám·bre] *m.* swarm of bees; crowd.

enjaular [eŋ·xaw·lár] *v.* to cage; to confine; to jail.

enjuagar[7] [eŋ·xwa·ǵár] *v.* to rinse, rinse out.

enjuague [eŋ·xwá·ǵe] *m.* mouth wash; rinse; rinsing; scheme, plot.

enjugar[7] [eŋ·xu·ǵár] *v.* to dry; to wipe; -se to dry oneself.

enjuiciar [eŋ·xwi·sjár] *v.* to indict; to prosecute, bring suit against; to try (*a case*); to judge.

enjundia [eŋ·xún·dja] *f.* substance, essence; fat; force, strength.

enjuto [en·xú·to] *adj.* dried; thin, skinny; -s *m. pl.* dry kindling.

enlace [en·lá·se] *m.* link; tie, bond; marriage.

enladrillado [en·la·ḍri·yá·ḍo] *m.* brick pavement or floor.

enladrillar [en·la·ḍri·yár] *v.* to pave with bricks.

enlatar [en·la·tár] *v.* to can; *Col.* to roof with tin.

enlazar[9] [en·la·sár] *v.* to join, bind, tie; to rope; *Ven., Mex.* to lasso; -se to join; to marry; to become related through marriage.

enlodar [en·lo·ḍár] *v.* to cover with mud; to smear, sully, soil, dirty; -se to get in the mud; to get muddy.

enloquecer[13] [en·lo·ke·sér] *v. irr.* to make crazy; to drive mad; to lose one's mind; -se to go crazy.

enlosado [en·lo·sá·ḍo] *m.* flagstone pavement; *p.p. of* enlosar.

enlosar [en·lo·sár] *v.* to pave with flagstones.

enmantecado [em·man·te·ká·ḍo] *m. Am.* ice cream. *See* mantecado.

enmantecar[6] [em·man·te·kár] *v.* to butter; to grease (*with lard or butter*).

enmarañar [emma·ra·ñár] *v.* to entagle; to snarl; to confuse, mix up.

enmascarar [em·mas·ka·rár] *v.* to mask; -se to put on a mask; to masquerade.

enmendar[1] [em·men·dár] *v. irr.* to amend, correct; to indemnify, compensate; -se to reform, mend one's ways.

enmienda [em·mjén·da] *f.* correction; amendment; reform; indemnity, compensation.

enmohecer[13] [em·mo·e·sér] *v.* to rust; to mold; -se to rust, become rusty; to mold.

enmudecer[13] [em·mu·ḍe·sér] *v. irr.* to silence; to remain silent; to lose one's voice; to become dumb.

ennegrecer[13] [en·ne·ǵre·sér] *v. irr.* to blacken; to darken; -se to become dark; to get cloudy.

ennoblecer[13] [en·no·ḅle·sér] *v. irr.* to ennoble, dignify.

enojadizo [e·no·xa·ḍí·so] *adj.* irritable, ill-tempered.

enojado [e·no·xá·ḍo] *adj.* angry.

enojar [e·no·xár] *v.* to make angry, vex, annoy; -se to get angry.

enojo [e·nó·xo] *m.* anger; annoyance.

enojoso [e·no·xó·so] *adj.* annoying, bothersome.

enorgullecer[13] [e·nor·ǵu·ye·sér] *v. irr.* to fill with pride; -se to swell up with pride; to be proud.

enorme [e·nór·me] *adj.* enormous.

enramada [en·rra·má·ḍa] *f.* arbor, bower; shady grove.

enrarecer[13] [en·rra·re·sér] *v. irr.* to rarefy, thin, make less dense (*as air*); -se to become rarefied; to become scarce.

enrarecimiento [en·rra·re·si·mjén·to] *m.* rarity, thinness (*of the air*); rarefaction (*act of making thin, rare or less dense*).

enredadera [en·rre·da·dé·ra] *f.* climbing vine.

enredar [en·rre·ḍár] *v.* (*enmarañar*) to entangle, snare; to snarl; to mix up; to wind (*on a spool*); (*enemistar*) to raise a rumpus; to get tangled up, mixed up; to get trapped; -se con to have an affair with.

enredista [en·rre·ḍís·ta] *m. Am.* liar; *Am.* talebearer.

enredo [en·rré·ḍo] *m.* tangle; confusion; lie; plot.

enredoso [en·rre·ḍó·so] *adj.* tangled up; *Am.* tattler.

enrejado [en·rre·xá·ḍo] *m.* trellis; grating.

enrevesado [en·rre·ḅe·sá·ḍo] *adj.* turned around; intricate, complicated; unruly.

enriquecer[13] [en·rri·ke·sér] *v. irr.* to enrich; to become rich; -se to become rich.

enrojecer[13] [en·rro·xe·sér] *v. irr.* to redden; -se to get red, blush.

enrollar [en·rro·yár] *v.* to roll, roll up; to coil.

enronquecer[13] [en·rroŋ·ke·sér] *v. irr.* to make hoarse; to become hoarse; -se to become hoarse.

enroscar[6] [en·rros·kár] *v.* to coil; to twist, twine; -se to coil; to curl up.

ensacar[6] [en·sa·kár] *v.* to sack, bag, put in a bag or sack.

ensalada [en·sa·lá·ḍa] *f.* salad; hodgepodge, mixture.

ensalmo [en·sál·mo] *m.* incantation.

ensalzar[9] [en·sal·sár] *v.* to exalt, praise.

ensanchar [en·san·čár] *v.* to widen, enlarge; -se to expand; to puff up.

ensanche [en·sán·če] *m.* widening, expansion, extension.

ensangrentado [en·saŋ·gren·tá·ḍo] *adj.* gory, bloody; *p.p. of* ensangrentar.

ensangrentar [en·saŋ·gren·tár] *v.* to stain with blood; -se to be covered with blood; to get red with anger.

ensartar [en·sar·tár] v. to string; to thread; to link; to rattle off (*tales, stories, etc.*); *Ch.* to tie to a ring; *Am.* to swindle, trick; **-se** *Andes* to fall into a trap.

ensayar [en·sa·yár] v. to try; to attempt; to test; to rehearse; **-se** to practice, train oneself.

ensayo [en·sá·yo] m. trial, attempt; rehearsal; test; experiment; essay.

ensenada [en·se·ná·ḍa] f. small bay, cove.

enseñanza [en·se·ñán·sa] f. teaching; education, training.

enseñar [en·se·ñár] v. to show; to teach; to train; to point out.

enseres [en·sé·res] m. pl. household goods; utensils; implements; equipment.

ensillar [en·si·yár] v. to saddle; *Ch.* to abuse, mistreat, domineer; *Riopl.* — **el picazo** to get angry.

ensimismarse [en·si·miz·már·se] v. to become absorbed in thought; *Col., Ven., Ch.* to become conceited or vain.

ensoberbecer[13] [en·so·ḅer·ḅe·sér] v. irr. to make proud or haughty; **-se** to puff up with pride; to become haughty; to get rough, choppy (*said of the sea*).

ensordecer[13] [en·sor·ḍe·sér] v. irr. to deafen; to become deaf.

ensortijar [en·sor·ti·xár] v. to curl; to ring the nose of (*an animal*); **-se** to curl.

ensuciar [en·su·sjár] v. to dirty, soil; to stain; **-se** to get dirty; to soil oneself.

ensueño [en·swé·ño] m. illusion, dream.

entablar [en·ta·ḅlár] v. to board up; to plank; to splint; — **una conversación** to start a conversation; — **un pleito** to bring a lawsuit.

entablillar [en·ta·ḅi·yár] v. to splint; *Mex.* to cut (*chocolate*) into tablets or squares.

entallar [en·ta·yár] v. to fit closely (*a dress*); to carve.

entapizar[9] [en·ta·pi·sár] v. to cover with tapestry; to drape with tapestries; to upholster.

entarimar [en·ta·ri·már] v. to floor (*with boards*).

ente [én·te] m. entity, being; queer fellow.

enteco [en·té·ko] adj. sickly, skinny.

entender[1] [en·ten·dér] v. irr. to understand; — **de** to know, to be an expert in; — **en** to take care of; to deal with; **-se con** to have dealings or relations with; to have an understanding with.

entendido [en·ten·dí·ḍo] p.p. understood; adj. wise, prudent; well-informed; able, skilful; **no darse por** — to pretend not to hear or understand; not to take the hint.

entendimiento [en·ten·di·mjén·to] m. understanding; intellect; mind.

enterado [en·te·rá·ḍo] p.p. & adj. informed; aware.

enterar [en·te·rár] v. to inform, acquaint; **-se** to know, learn, find out; to understand, get the idea.

entereza [en·te·ré·sa] f. entirety; integrity; fortitude; serenity; firmness; perfection.

enternecedor [en·ter·ne·se·ḍór] adj. touching, moving, pitiful.

enternecer[13] [en·ter·ne·sér] v. irr. to soften, touch, stir, move; **-se** to become tender; to be touched, stirred.

entero [en·té·ro] adj. (*completo*) entire, whole; (*justo*) just, right; firm; m. integer, whole number; *Col.* payment, reimbursement; *Ch.* balance of an account; **caballo** — stallion.

enterramiento [en·te·rra·mjén·to] m. burial.

enterrar[1] [en·te·rrár] v. irr. to bury; *Am.* to sink,

stick into.

entibiar [en·ti·ḅjár] v. to make lukewarm; **-se** to become lukewarm.

entidad [en·ti·ḍáḍ] f. entity; unit, group, organization; **de** — of value or importance.

entierro [en·tjé·rro] m. burial; funeral; grave; *Am.* hidden treasure.

entintar [en·tin·tár] v. to ink; to stain with ink; to dye.

entoldar [en·tol·dár] v. to cover with an awning; **-se** to puff up with pride; to become overcast, cloudy.

entonación [en·to·na·sjón] f. intonation.

entonar [en·to·nár] v. to sing in tune; to start a song (*for others to follow*); to be in tune; to harmonize; **-se** to put on airs.

entonces [en·tón·ses] adv. then, at that time; **pues** — well then.

entornado [en·tor·ná·ḍo] adj. half-open; half-closed, ajar.

entornar [en·tor·nár] v. to half-open.

entorpecer[13] [en·tor·pe·sér] v. irr. to stupefy; to be numb, make numb; to delay, obstruct; to thwart, frustrate.

entorpecimiento [en·tor·pe·si·mjén·to] m. numbness; dullness; delay, obstruction.

entrada [en·trá·ḍa] f. (*apertura*) entrance; entry; gate; opening; (*acción o privilegio*) entering, admission; entrée (*dish or dinner course*); *Am.* attack, assault, goring; *Mex.* beating; **-s** cash receipts.

entrambos [en·trám·bos] adj. & pron. both.

entrampar [en·tram·pár] v. to trap, ensnare; to trick; to burden with debts; **-se** to get trapped or entangled; to run into debt.

entrante [en·trán·te] adj. entering; incoming; **el año** — next year.

entraña [en·trá·ña] f. entrail; innermost recess; heart; disposition, temper; **-s** entrails, "innards", insides; **hijo de mis -s** child of my heart; **no tener -s** to be cruel.

entrar [en·trár] v. to enter, go in, come in; to attack; **me entró miedo** I became afraid; **-se** to slip in, get in, sneak in; to enter.

entre [én·tre] prep. between; among; **dijo** — **sí** he said to himself; — **tanto** meanwhile; *Am.* — **más habla menos dice** the more he talks the less he says.

entreabierto [en·tre·a·ḅjér·to] p.p. of **entreabrir**; adj. ajar, half-open, partly open.

entreabrir[52] [en·tre·a·ḅrir] v. to half-open.

entreacto [en·tre·ák·to] m. intermission; intermezzo (*entertainment between the acts*); small cigar.

entrecano [en·tre·ká·no] adj. greyish.

entrecejo [en·tre·sé·xo] m. space between the eyebrows; **fruncir el** — to wrinkle one's brow.

entrecortado [en·tre·kor·tá·ḍo] adj. hesitating, faltering (*speech*); breathless, choking; p.p. interrupted.

entrecortar [en·tre·kor·tár] v. to cut halfway through or in between; to interrupt at intervals.

entrecruzar[9] [en·tre·kru·sár] v. to intercross, cross; to interlace; **-se** to cross.

entredicho [en·tre·ḍi·čo] m. prohibition, injunction.

entrega [en·tré·ḡa] f. (*acto de ceder*) delivery; surrender; (*parte suelta*) installment (*of a book*); **novela por -s** serial novel.

entregar[7] [en·tre·ḡár] v. to deliver, hand over; **-se** to surrender, submit, give up; to devote oneself (to); to abandon oneself (to).

entrelazar[9] [en·tre·la·sár] v. to interlace; to weave

together.
entremés [en·tre·més] *m.* relish, side dish (*of olives, pickles, etc.*); one-act farce (*formerly presented between the acts of a play.*)
entremeter [en·tre·me·tér] *v.* to insert; to place between; **-se** to meddle; to intrude.
entremetido [en·tre·me·tí·ḍo] *adj.* meddlesome; *m.* meddler; intruder.
entremetimiento [en·tre·me·ti·mjén·to] *m.* intrusion, meddling.
entremezclar [en·tre·mes·klár] *v.* to intermix, intermingle.
entrenador [en·tre·na·ḍór] *m. Am.* trainer.
entrenamiento [en·tre·na·mjén·to] *m. Am.* training, drill.
entrenar [en·tre·nár] *v. Am.* to train, drill; **-se** *Am.* to train.
entresacar[6] [en·tre·sa·kár] *v.* to pick out, select.
entresuelo [en·tre·swé·lo] *m.* mezzanine; second floor.
entretanto [en·tre·tán·to] *adv.* meanwhile.
entretejer [en·tre·te·xér] *v.* to weave together; to intertwine.
entretener[45] [en·tre·te·nér] *v. irr.* to delay, detain; to amuse, entertain; **-se** to amuse oneself; to delay oneself; **— el tiempo** to while away the time.
entretenido [en·tre·te·ní·ḍo] *adj.* entertaining, amusing; *p.p. of* **entretener.**
entretenimiento [en·tre·te·ni·mjén·to] *m.* entertainment; pastime; delay.
entrever[49] [entre·ḅér] *v.* to glimpse, catch a glimpse of; to half-see, see vaguely.
entreverar [en·tre·ḅe·rár] *v.* to intermingle, intermix.
entrevista [en·tre·ḅís·ta] *f.* interview; date, appointment.
entrevistar [en·tre·ḅis·tár] *v.* to interview; **-se con** to have an interview with.
entrevisto [en·tre·ḅís·to] *p.p. of* **entrever.**
entristecer[13] [en·tris·te·sér] *v. irr.* to sadden, make sad; **-se** to become sad.
entrometer [en·tro·me·tér] = **entremeter.**
entrometido [en·tro·me·tí·ḍo] = **entremetido.**
entumecer[13] [en·tu·me·sér] *v. irr.* to make numb; **-se** to get numb; to surge; to swell.
entumido [en·tu·mí·ḍo] *adj.* numb, stiff; *Am.* timid, shy, awkward.
entumirse [en·tu·mír·se] *v.* to get numb.
enturbiar [en·tur·ḅjár] *v.* to make muddy; to muddle; to disturb; to obscure; **-se** to get muddy; to get muddled.
entusiasmar [en·tu·sjaz·már] *v.* to excite, fill with enthusiasm; **-se** to get enthusiastic, excited.
entusiasmo [en·tu·sjáz·mo] *m.* enthusiasm.
entusiasta [en·tu·sjás·ta] *m. & f.* enthusiast; **entusiástico** *adj.* enthusiastic.
enumeración [e·nu·me·ra·sjón] *f.* enumeration, counting.
enumerar [e·nu·me·rár] *v.* to enumerate.
enunciar [e·nun·sjár] *v.* to express, state, declare.
envainar [em·baj·nár] *v.* to sheathe.
envalentonar [em·ba·len·to·nár] *v.* to make bold or haughty; **-se** to get bold; to brag, swagger.
envanecer[13] [em·ba·ne·sér] *v. irr.* to make vain; **-se** to become vain.
envasar [em·ba·sár] *v.* to pack, put up in any container; to bottle; to can.
envase [em·bá·se] *m.* packing; container, jar, bottle, can (*for packing*).
envejecer[13] [em·be·xe·sér] *v. irr.* to make old; to

grow old, get old; **-se** to grow old, get old.
envenenamiento [em·be·ne·na·mjén·to] *m.* poisoning.
envenenar [em·be·ne·nár] *v.* to poison; to infect.
envergadura [em·ber·ga·ḍú·ra] *f.* span (*of an airplane*); spread (*of a bird's wings*); breadth (*of sails*).
envés [em·bés] *m.* back or wrong side.
enviado [em·bjá·ḍo] *m.* envoy.
enviar[17] [em·bjár] *v.* to send; **— a uno a paseo** to give someone his walking papers.
enviciar [em·bi·sjár] *v.* to vitiate, corrupt; **-se** to become addicted (to), overly fond (of).
envidar [em·bi·ḍár] *v.* to bid (*in cards*); to bet.
envidia [em·bi·ḍja] *f.* envy.
envidiable [em·bi·ḍjá·ḅle] *adj.* enviable, desirable.
envidiar [em·bi·ḍjár] *v.* to envy.
envidioso [em·bi·ḍjó·so] *adj.* envious.
envilecer[13] [em·bi·le·sér] *v. irr.* to revile, malign, degrade; **-se** to degrade or lower oneself.
envilecimiento [em·bi·le·si·mjén·to] *m.* degradation, humiliation, shame.
envío [em·bí·o] *m.* remittance, sending; shipment.
envite [em·bí·te] *m.* bid; stake (*in cards*); offer; push.
envoltorio [em·bol·tó·rjo] *m.* bundle, package.
envoltura [em·bol·tú·ra] *f.* wrapping, cover; wrapper.
envolver[2, 52] [em·bol·ḅér] *v. irr.* to involve, entangle; to wrap; to wind (*a thread, rope, etc.*); to surround; **-se** to become involved, entangled; to cover up, wrap up.
envuelto [em·bwél·to] *p.p. of* **envolver.**
enyesar [en·ỹe·sár] *v.* to plaster; to chalk.
enzolvar [en·sol·ḅár] *v. Am.* to clog, obstruct; *Am.* **-se** to clog, get clogged. *See* **azolvar.**
¡epa! [é·pa] *interj. Riopl., Ven., Col., Mex.* hey! listen! stop! look out!
épico [é·pi·ko] *adj.* epic.
epidemia [e·pi·ḍe·mja] *f.* epidemic.
episodio [e·pi·só·ḍjo] *m.* episode.
epístola [e·pís·to·la] *f.* epistle; letter.
epitafio [e·pi·tá·fjo] *m.* epitaph.
época [é·po·ka] *f.* epoch.
epopeya [e·po·pé·ya] *f.* epic poem.
equidad [e·ki·ḍáḍ] *f.* equity, justice, fairness.
equidistante [e·ki·ḍis·tán·te] *adj.* equidistant, equally distant, halfway, midway.
equilibrar [e·ki·li·ḅrár] *v.* to balance, poise.
equilibrio [e·ki·lí·ḅrjo] *m.* equilibrium, balance; poise.
equilibrista [e·ki·li·ḅrís·ta] *m. & f.* acrobat.
equipaje [e·ki·pá·xe] *m.* baggage, luggage; equipment, outfit; crew.
equipar [e·ki·pár] *v.* to equip, fit out; to man, equip and provision (*a ship*).
equipo [e·kí·po] *m.* (*materiales*) equipment, equipping; outfit; (*grupo*) work crew; sport team; **— de novia** trousseau.
equitación [e·ki·ta·sjón] *f.* horsemanship; horseback riding.
equitativo [e·ki·ta·tí·ḅo] *adj.* fair, just.
equivalente [e·ki·ḅa·lén·te] *adj.* equivalent.
equivaler[47] [e·ki·ḅa·lér] *v. irr.* to be equivalent.
equivocación [e·ki·ḅo·ka·sjón] *f.* error, mistake.
equivocado [e·ki·ḅo·ká·ḍo] *p.p. & adj.* mistaken.
equivocar[6] [e·ki·ḅo·kár] *v.* to mistake; **-se** to be mistaken; to make a mistake.
equívoco [e·kí·ḅo·ko] *adj.* equivocal, ambiguous, vague; *Am.* mistaken; *m.* pun, play on words; *Am.* mistake, error.

era [é·ra] *f.* era, age; threshing floor.
erario [e·rá·rjo] *m.* public treasury.
erguido [er·ǵi·ḍo] *adj.* erect; *p.p. of* **erguir.**
erguir[3] [er·ǵir] *v. irr.* to erect, set upright; to lift *(the head);* **-se** to sit up or stand erect; to become proud and haughty.
erial [e·rjál] *m.* uncultivated land; *adj.* unplowed, untilled.
erigir[11] [e·ri·xír] *v.* to erect, build; to found.
erizado [e·ri·sá·ḍo] *adj.* bristly, prickly; — **de** bristling with.
erizar[9] [e·ri·sár] *v.* to set on end, make bristle; **-se** to bristle; to stand on end *(hair).*
erizo [e·rí·so] *m.* hedgehog, porcupine; thistle; — **de mar** sea urchin; **ser un** — to be irritable, harsh.
ermitaño [er·mi·tá·ño] *m.* hermit.
erosion [e·ro·sjón] *f.* erosion.
errabundo [e·rra·ƀún·do] *adj.* wandering.
errado [e·rrá·ḍo] *adj.* mistaken, wrong, in error; *p.p. of* **errar.**
errante [e·rrán·te] *adj.* errant, roving, wandering.
errar[28] [e·rrár] *v. irr.* to err, make mistakes; to miss *(target, road);* to rove, wander.
errata [e·rrá·ta] *f.* misprint, printer's error.
erróneo [e·rró·ne·o] *adj.* erroneous, mistaken, wrong, incorrect.
error [e·rrór] *m.* error, fault, mistake.
eructar [e·ruk·tár] *v.* to belch.
eructo [e·rúk·to] *m.* belch.
erudición [e·ru·ḍi·sjón] *f.* erudition, learning.
erudito [e·ru·ḍí·to] *adj.* erudite, scholarly, learned; *m.* scholar.
erupción [e·rup·sjón] *f.* eruption; outburst; rash.
esbelto [ez·ƀel·to] *adj.* slender.
esbozar[9] [ez·ƀo·sár] *v.* to sketch, outline.
esbozo [ez·ƀó·so] *m.* sketch, outline.
escabechar [es·ka·ƀe·čár] *v.* to pickle.
escabeche [es·ka·ƀé·če] *m.* pickled fish; pickle *(solution for pickling).*
escabel [es·ka·ƀél] *m.* stool; footstool.
escabrosidad [es·ka·ƀro·si·ḍáḍ] *f.* roughness, unevenness; harshness; improper word or phrase.
escabroso [es·ka·ƀró·so] *adj.* rough; rugged; scabrous, rather indecent.
escabullirse[20] [es·ka·ƀu·yír·se] *v. irr.* to slip away; to slip through; to scoot, scamper, scurry.
escala [es·ká·la] *f.* ladder; scale; port of call; stopover; **hacer** — **en** to stop over at; **escalafón** [es·ka·la·fón] *m.* army register.
escalar [es·ka·lár] *v.* to scale; to climb.
escaldar [es·kal·dár] *v.* to scald; to make red-hot; **-se** to get scalded.
escalera [es·ka·lé·ra] *f.* stairs, staircase; ladder; — **mecánica** escalator.
escalfar [es·kal·fár] *v.* to poach *(eggs).*
escalinata [es·ka·li·ná·ta] *f.* flight of stairs *(usually on the outside).*
escalofriarse[17] [es·ka·lo·frjár·se] *v.* to become chilled.
escalofrío [es·ka·lo·frí·o] *m.* chill; **-s** chills and fever.
escalón [es·ka·lón] *m.* step *(of a ladder or staircase);* stepping stone; *Am.* **-es** tribe of quichua Indians.
escalonar [es·ka·lo·nár] *v.* to echelon *(arrange in step-like formation);* to terrace; **-se** to rise in terraces.
escama [es·ká·ma] *f.* scale, fish scale; flake.
escamoso [es·ka·mó·so] *adj.* scaly.

escamotear [es·ka·mo·te·ár] *v.* to whisk out of sight; to steal or snatch away with cunning; to conceal by a trick of sleight of hand.
escampar [es·kam·pár] *v.* to clear *(weather).*
escandalizar[9] [es·kan·da·li·sár] *v.* scandalize, shock; **-se** to be shocked.
escándalo [es·kán·da·lo] *m.* scandal; bad example.
escandaloso [es·kan·da·ló·so] *adj.* scandalous, shocking; *Mex., C.A., Col., Andes* showy, loud *(color).*
escandio [es·kán·djo] *m.* scandium.
escapada [es·ka·pá·ḍa] *f.* escape, flight.
escapar [es·ka·pár] *v.* to escape, flee, avoid; **-se** to run away, escape.
escaparate [es·ka·pa·rá·te] *m.* show window; glass case, glass cabinet or cupboard.
escapatoria [es·ka·pa·tó·rja] *f.* escape, loophole, excuse.
escape [es·ká·pe] *m.* escape; vent, outlet; exhaust; **a** — rapidly, at full speed.
escarabajo [es·ka·ra·ƀá·xo] *m.* black beetle.
escaramuza [es·ka·ra·mú·sa] *f.* skirmish; quarrel.
escarbar [es·kar·ƀár] *v.* to scrape, scratch; to dig out; to pry into, investigate.
escarcear [es·kar·se·ár] *v. Ch., Ríopl.* to prance.
escarcha [es·kár·ča] *f.* frost; frosting.
escarchar [es·kar·čár] *v.* to frost; to freeze.
escardar [es·kar·ḍár] *v.* to weed; to weed out.
escarlata [es·kar·lá·ta] *f.* scarlet; scarlet fever; scarlet cloth; **escarlatina** [es·kar·la·tí·na] *f.* scarlet fever.
escarmentar[1] [es·kar·men·tár] *v. irr.* to punish *(as an example or warning);* to profit by one's misfortunes, punishment, etc.; — **en cabeza ajena** to profit by another's mistake or misfortune.
escarmiento [es·kar·mjén·to] *m.* lesson, example, warning; punishment.
escarnecer[13] [es·kar·ne·sér] *v. irr.* to jeer, insult, mock.
escarnio [es·kár·njo] *m.* scoff, jeer.
escarpa [es·kár·pa] *f.* steep slope, bluff, cliff; scarp *(of a fortification).*
escarpado [es·kar·pá·ḍo] *adj.* steep; rugged.
escarpia [es·kár·pja] *f.* hook *(for hanging something).*
escasear [es·ka·se·ár] *v.* to be scarce; to grow less, become scarce; to stint.
escasez [es·ka·sés] *f.* scarcity, lack, scantiness.
escaso [es·ká·so] *adj.* scarce, limited; scant; scanty; stingy.
escatimar [es·ka·ti·már] *v.* to stint, skimp; to curtail.
escena [e·sé·na] *f.* scene; scenery, theatre, stage.
escenario [e·se·ná·rjo] *m.* stage.
escenificación [e·se·ni·fi·ka·sjón] *f.* dramatization, stage adaptation.
escepticismo [e·sep·ti·síz·mo] *m.* scepticism; doubt, unbelief.
escéptico [e·sép·ti·ko] *m. & adj.* sceptic.
esclarecer[13] [es·kla·re·sér] *v. irr.* to lighten, illuminate; to elucidate, make clear, explain.
esclarecimiento [es·kla·re·si·mjén·to] *m.* clarification, illumination, illustration; worth, nobility.
esclavitud [es·kla·ƀi·túḍ] *f.* slavery.
esclavizar[9] [es·kla·ƀi·sár] *v.* to enslave.
esclavo [es·klá·ƀo] *m.* slave.
esclusa [es·klú·sa] *f.* lock *(of a canal);* sluice, floodgate.
escoba [es·kó·ƀa] *f.* broom.
escobazo [es·ko·ƀá·so] *m.* blow with a broom.

escobilla [es·ko·ƀí·ya] *f.* whisk broom; small broom.

escobillón [es·ko·ƀi·yón] *m.* swab; push broom.

escocer[2,10] [es·ko·sér] *v. irr.* to sting, smart.

escocés [es·ko·sés] *adj.* Scottish; Scotch; *m.* Scot; Scotchman.

escoger[11] [es·ko·xér] *v.* to choose, select, pick out.

escolar [es·ko·lár] *adj.* scholastic, academic; *m.* scholar, student.

escolástico [es·ko·lás·ti·ko] *adj. & m.* scholastic.

escolta [es·kól·ta] *f.* escort; convoy.

escoltar [es·kol·tár] *v.* to escort; to convoy.

escollo [es·kó·yo] *m.* reef; danger; obstacle.

escombro [es·kóm·bro] *m.* debris, rubbish; mackerel.

esconder [es·kon·dér] *v.* to hide, conceal; **-se** to hide, go into hiding.

escondidas [es·kon·dí·ɖas]: **a — on the sly, under cover**; *Am.* **jugar a las — to play hide-and-seek.**

escondite [es·kon·dí·te] *m.* hiding place; *Spain* **jugar al — to play hide-and-seek.**

escondrijo [es·kon·dri·xo] *m.* hiding place.

escopeta [es·ko·pé·ta] *f.* shotgun.

escopetazo [es·ko·pe·tá·so] *m.* gunshot; gunshot wound; sudden bad news; *Am.* offensive or ironic remark.

escoplo [es·kó·plo] *m.* chisel.

escoria [es·kó·rja] *f.* slag; scum; **escorial** [es·ko·rjál] *m.* dump, dumping place; pile of slag.

escorpión [es·kor·pjón] *m.* scorpion.

escote [es·kó·te] *m.* low neck; **convite a — Dutch treat** *(where everyone pays his share).*

escotilla [es·ko·tí·ya] *f.* hatchway; **escotillón** *m.* hatch, hatchway; trap door.

escozor [es·ko·zór] *m.* smarting sensation, sting.

escribano [es·kri·ƀá·no] *m.* court clerk; lawyer's clerk; notary.

escribiente [es·kri·ƀjén·te] *m.* clerk, office clerk.

escribir[52] [es·kri·ƀír] *v.* to write.

escritc [es·krí·to] *p.p. of* **escribir** written; *m*— writing; manuscript.

escritor [es·kri·tór] *m.* writer.

escritorio [es·kri·tó·rjo] *m.* desk; office.

escritura [es·kri·tú·ra] *f.* writing, handwriting; deed, document; **Sagrada Escritura Holy Scripture.**

escrúpulo [es·krú·pu·lo] *m.* scruple, doubt.

escrupuloso [es·kru·pu·ló·so] *adj.* scrupulous; particular, exact.

escrutador [es·kru·ta·ɖór] *adj.* scrutinizing, examining; peering; penetrating; *m.* scrutinizer, examiner; inspector of election returns.

escrutar [es·kru·tár] *v.* to scrutinize.

escrutinio [es·kru·tí·njo] *m.* scrutiny, careful inspection.

escuadra [es·kwá·ɖra] *f.* squadron; fleet; square *(instrument for drawing or testing right angles).*

escuadrón [es·kwa·ɖrón] *m.* squadron.

escualidez [es·kwa·li·ɖés] *f.* squalor.

escuálido [es·kwá·li·ɖo] *adj.* squalid, filthy; thin, emaciated.

escuchar [es·ku·čár] *v.* to listen; to heed.

escudar [es·ku·ɖár] *v.* to shield.

escudero [es·ku·ɖé·ro] *m.* squire.

escudo [es·kú·ɖo] *m.* shield; escutcheon, coat of arms; gold crown *(ancient coin)*; *Am.* Chilean gold coin.

escudriñar [es·ku·ɖri·ñár] *v.* to scrutinize, search, pry into.

escuela [es·kwé·la] *f.* school.

escuelante [es·kwe·lán·te] *m. & f. Col.* schoolboy; schoolgirl.

escueto [es·kwé·to] *adj.* plain, unadorned, bare.

esculcar[6] [es·kul·kár] *v. Am.* to search; *Carib., Col., Ven.* to frisk *(a person's pockets).*

esculpir [es·kul·pír] *v.* to sculpture; to engrave.

escultor [es·kul·tór] *m.* sculptor.

escultura [es·kul·tú·ra] *f.* sculpture.

escupidera [es·ku·pi·ɖé·ra] *f.* cuspidor.

escupir [es·ku·pír] *v.* to spit.

escurridero [es·ku·rri·ɖé·ro] *m.* drain pipe; drainboard.

escurrir [es·ku·rrír] *v.* to drip; to drain; to trickle; **-se** to ooze out, trickle; to slip out, sneak out.

ese [é·se], **esa** [é·sa] *dem. adj.* that; **esos** [é·sos], **esas** [é·sas] those; **ése, ésa** *m., f. dem. pron.* that one; **ésos, ésas** *m., f. pl.* those.

esencia [e·sén·sja] *f.* essence.

esencial [e·sen·sjál] *adj.* essential.

esfera [es·fé·ra] *f.* sphere; clock dial.

esférico [es·fé·ri·ko] *adj.* spherical.

esforzado[2,9] [es·for·sá·ɖo] *adj.* strong; valiant; courageous.

esforzar[2,9] [es·for·sár] *v. irr.* to give or inspire strength; to encourage; **-se** to make an effort; to strive, try hard.

esfuerzo [es·fwér·so] *m.* effort; spirit, courage, vigor; stress.

esfumar [es·fu·már] *v.* to shade, tone down; **-se** to vanish, disappear.

esgrima [ez·ɡrí·ma] *f.* fencing.

esgrimir [ez·ɡri·mír] *v.* to fence; to brandish; to wield *(the sword or pen).*

eslabón [ez·la·ƀón] *m.* link of a chain; steel knife sharpener; black scorpion.

eslabonar [ez·la·ƀo·nár] *v.* to link; to join; to connect.

esmaltar [ez·mal·tár] *v.* to enamel; to beautify; adorn.

esmalte [ez·mál·te] *m.* enamel; enamel work; smalt *(a blue pigment).*

esmerado [ez·me·rá·ɖo] *adj.* painstaking, careful, conscientious; *p.p. of* **esmerar.**

esmeralda [ez·me·rál·da] *f.* emerald; *Am.* an eel-like fish; *Col.* hummingbird; *Mex.* variety of pineapple.

esmerar [ez·me·rár] *v.* to polish, clean; **-se** to strive, take special pains, use great care.

esmero [ez·mé·ro] *m.* care, precision.

esmoquin [ez·mó·kin] *m.* tuxedo, dinner coat.

eso [é·so] *dem. pron.* that, that thing, that fact; **— es that is it**; **a — de at about** *(referring to time)*; *Am.* **¡eso! that's right!**

espaciar[17] [es·pa·sjár] *v.* to space; to spread; to expand; **-se** to enlarge *(upon a subject)*: to relax, amuse oneself.

espacio [es·pá·sjo] *m.* space; interval; slowness, delay; *adv. Mex.* slowly.

espacioso [es·pa·sjó·so] *adj.* spacious; slow.

espada [es·pá·ɖa] *f.* sword; skilled swordsman; matador *(bull-fighter who kills the bull)*; **-s swords** *(Spanish card suit).*

espalda [es·pál·da] *f.* back, shoulders; **-s back, back part**; **a -s behind one's back**; **de -s on one's back**; **dar la — a to turn one's back on**; **espaldilla** [es·pal·dí·ya] *f.* shoulder blade.

espaldar [es·pal·dár] *m.* back *(of a chair)*; trellis *(for plants)*; backplate of a cuirass *(armor).*

espantadizo [es·pan·ta·ɖí·so] *adj.* scary, shy, timid.

espantajo [es·pan·tá·xo] *m.* scarecrow.

espantapájaros [es·pan·ta·pá·xa·ros] *m.* scarecrow.

espantar [es·pan·tár] v. to frighten, scare; to scare away; *Col.* to haunt; **-se** to be scared; to be astonished; *Mex.* **espantárselas** [es·pan·tár·se·las] to be wide-awake, catch on quickly.

espanto [es·pán·to] m. fright, terror; astonishment; *Col., Ven., Mex.* ghost.

espantoso [es·pan·tó·so] adj. frightful, terrifying; wonderful.

español [es·pa·ñól] adj. Spanish; m. Spaniard; Spanish language.

esparadrapo [es·pa·ra·drá·po] m. court plaster, adhesive tape. *See* **tela adhesiva.**

esparcir[10] [es·par·sír] v. to scatter, spread; **-se** to relax, amuse oneself.

espárrago [es·pá·rra·go] m. asparagus.

esparto [es·pár·to] m. esparto grass (used for making ropes, mats, etc.).

espasmo [es·páz·mo] m. spasm; horror.

espátula [es·pá·tu·la] f. spatula.

especia [es·pé·sja] f. spice.

especial [es·pe·sjál] adj. special; **en** — in particular. specially.

especialidad [es·pe·sja·li·dád] f. specialty.

especialista [es·pe·sja·lís·ta] m. & f. specialist.

especializar[9] [es·pe·sja·li·sár] v. to specialize; **-se en** to specialize in.

especie [es·pé·sje] f. species; kind, sort; pretext; idea.

especificar[6] [es·pe·si·fi·kár] v. to specify; to name.

específico [es·pe·si·fi·ko] adj. specific; m. specific (medicine).

espécimen [es·pé·si·men] m. specimen, sample.

espectacular [es·pek·ta·ku·lár] adj. spectacular.

espectáculo [es·pek·tá·ku·lo] m. spectacle.

espectador [es·pek·ta·dór] m. spectator.

espectro [es·pék·tro] m. spectre, ghost; spectrum.

espectrógrafo [es·pek·tró·gra·fo] m. spectrograph.

especulación [es·pe·ku·la·sjón] f. speculation.

especulador [es·pe·ku·la·dór] m. speculator.

especular [es·pe·ku·lár] v. to speculate.

especulativo [es·pe·ku·la·tí·bo] adj. speculative.

espejismo [es·pe·xíz·mo] m. mirage; illusion.

espejo [es·pé·xo] m. mirror; model; — **de cuerpo entero** full-length mirror.

espeluznante [es·pe·luz·nán·te] adj. hair-raising, terrifying.

espeluznarse [es·pe·luz·nár·se] v. to be terrified; to bristle with fear.

espera [es·pé·ra] f. wait; stay (granted by judge), delay; extension of time (for payment); **sala de** — waiting room; **estar en** — **de** to be waiting for; to be expecting.

esperanza [es·pe·rán·sa] f. hope; expectation.

esperanzado [es·pe·ran·sá·do] adj. hopeful.

esperanzar[9] [es·pe·ran·sár] to give hope to.

esperar [es·pe·rár] v. (tener esperanza) to hope; to expect; to trust; (permanecer) to wait, wait for; — **en alguien** to place hope or confidence in someone.

esperezarse [es·pe·re·sár·se] = **desperezarse.**

esperma [es·pér·ma] f. sperm.

esperpento [es·per·pén·to] m. ugly thing; nonsense.

espesar [es·pe·sár] v. to thicken; to make dense; **-se** to thicken; to become thick or dense.

espeso [es·pé·so] adj. thick, dense; compact; slovenly; *Ríopl.* bothersome, boring.

espesor [es·pe·sór] m. thickness.

espesura [es·pe·sú·ra] f. density, thickness; thicket; thickest part (of a forest).

espetar [es·pe·tár] v. to spring (a joke, story, etc.)

on (a person), surprise with (a joke, speech, story, etc.); to pop (a question); to run a spit through (meat, fish, etc. for roasting); to pierce; **-se** to be stiff, pompous.

espía [es·pí·a] m. & f. spy.

espiar[17] [es·pjár] v. to spy; *Col., Mex.* **-se** to bruise the hoofs, get lame (said of horses).

espiga [es·pí·ga] f. ear of wheat; peg; spike.

espigar[7] [es·pi·gár] v. to glean; to grow spikes (said of corn or grain); **-se** to grow tall and slender.

espina [es·pí·na] f. thorn; sharp splinter; fish bone; spine; fear, suspicion; **darle a uno mala** — to arouse one's suspicion.

espinaca [es·pi·ná·ka] f. spinach.

espinazo [es·pi·ná·so] m. spine, backbone.

espinilla [es·pi·ní·ya] f. shin (front part of leg); blackhead (on the skin).

espino [es·pí·no] m. hawthorn; thorny shrub; thorny branch.

espinoso [es·pi·nó·so] adj. thorny; difficult, dangerous.

espionaje [es·pjo·ná·xe] m. espionage, spying.

espiral [es·pi·rál] adj. & f. spiral.

espirar [es·pi·rár] v. to exhale; to emit, give off; to die. *See* **expirar.**

espíritu [es·pí·ri·tu] m. spirit; soul; courage; vigor; essence; ghost.

espiritual [es·pi·ri·tuál] adj. spiritual.

espita [es·pí·ta] f. spigot, faucet, tap; toper, drunkard.

esplendidez [es·plen·di·dés] f. splendor.

espléndido [es·plén·di·do] adj. splendid.

esplendor [es·plen·dór] m. splendor.

esplendoroso [es·plen·do·ró·so] adj. resplendent, shining.

espliego [es·pljé·go] m. lavender (plant).

espolear [es·po·le·ár] v. to spur; to incite.

espoleta [es·po·lé·ta] f. bomb fuse.

espolón [es·po·lón] m. spur (on a cock's leg); ram (of a boat); spur; buttress.

espolvorear [es·pol·bo·re·ár] v. to powder, sprinkle with powder.

esponja [es·pón·xa] f. sponge; sponger, parasite; *Col., Peru, Ch., Ríopl.* souse, habitual drunkard.

esponjado [es·poŋ·xá·do] adj. fluffy; spongy; puffed up; p.p. of **esponjar.**

esponjar [es·poŋ·xár] v. to fluff; to make spongy or porous; **-se** to fluff up; to become spongy or porous; to swell, puff up; to puff up with pride.

esponjoso [es·poŋ·xó·so] adj. spongy.

esponsales [es·pon·sá·les] m. pl. betrothal.

espontaneidad [es·pon·ta·nej·dád] f. spontaneity, ease, naturalness.

espontáneo [es·pon·tá·ne·o] adj. spontaneous.

esposa [es·pó·sa] f. wife; **-s** handcuffs.

esposo [es·pó·so] m. husband.

espuela [es·pwé·la] f. spur.

espulgar[7] [es·pul·gár] v. to delouse, remove lice or fleas from; to scrutinize.

espuma [es·pú·ma] f. foam, froth; scum; — **de jabón** suds.

espumar [es·pu·már] v. to skim; to froth, foam.

espumarajo [es·pu·ma·rá·xo] m. froth, foam (from the mouth); **echar -s** to froth at the mouth; to be very angry.

espumoso [es·pu·mó·so] adj. foamy.

esputo [es·pú·to] m. sputum, spit, saliva.

esquela [es·ké·la] f. note, letter; announcement.

esqueleto [es·ke·lé·to] m. skeleton; carcass; framework; *Mex., C.A., Col., Ven.* blank (to fill

ES

out); *Am.* outline.
esquema [es·ké·ma] *f.* scheme, outline.
esquí [es·kí] *m.* ski, skiing; — **náutico,** — **acuático** water ski.
esquiar[17] [es·kjár] *v.* to ski.
esquila [es·kí·la] *f.* small bell; cow bell; sheep-shearing.
esquilar [es·ki·lár] *v.* to shear; to clip; to crop.
esquina [es·kí·na] *f.* corner, angle; **esquinazo** [es·ki·ná·so] *m.* corner; *Am.* serenade; **dar esquinazo** to avoid meeting someone; to "ditch" someone.
esquivar [es·ki·ƀár] *v.* to avoid, dodge; to shun; **-se** to withdraw, shy away.
esquivez [es·ki·ƀés] *f.* shyness; aloofness; disdain.
esquivo [es·kí·ƀo] *adv.* reserved, unsociable; shy; disdainful, aloof.
estabilidad [es·ta·ƀi·li·ḍáḍ] *f.* stability.
estable [es·tá·ƀle] *adj.* stable, firm, steady.
establecer[13] [es·ta·ƀle·sér] *v. irr.* to establish; to found; to decree, ordain.
establecimiento [es·ta·ƀle·si·mjén·to] *m.* establishment; foundation; statute, law.
establo [es·tá·ƀlo] *m.* stable; **establero** [es·ta·ƀlé·ro] *m.* groom.
estaca [es·tá·ka] *f.* stake, club; stick; picket.
estacada [es·ta·ká·ḍa] *f.* stockade; picket fence; *Am.* predicament.
estacar[6] [es·ta·kár] *v.* to stake; to tie on a stake; to stake off, mark with stakes; *Am.* to fasten down with stakes; **-se** to remain stiff or rigid.
estación [es·ta·sjón] *f.* station; season; railway station.
estacionar [es·ta·sjo·nár] *v.* to station; to place; to park (*a car*); **-se** to remain stationary; to park.
estacionario [es·ta·sjo·ná·rjo] *adj.* stationary; motionless.
estada [es·tá·ḍa] *f.* sojourn, stay.
estadía [es·ta·ḍí·a] *f.* detention, stay; stay in port (*beyond time allowed for loading and unloading*); *C.A., Carib.* sojourn, stay (*in any sense*).
estadio [es·tá·ḍjo] *m.* stadium.
estadista [es·ta·ḍis·ta] *m.* statesman.
estadística [es·ta·ḍís·ti·ka] *f.* statistics.
estado [es·tá·ḍo] *m.* state, condition; station, rank; estate; — **mayor** army staff; **hombre de** — statesman; *Am.* **en** — **interesante** pregnant.
estadounidense [es·ta·ḍow·ni·ḍén·se] *adj.* from the United States, American.
estafa [es·tá·fa] *f.* swindle, fraud, trick.
estafador [es·ta·fa·ḍór] *m.* swindler, crook.
estafar [es·ta·fár] *v.* to swindle, defraud, cheat.
estalactita [es·ta·lak·tí·ta] *f.* stalactite.
estalagmita [es·ta·laǥ·mí·ta] *f.* stalagmite.
estallar [es·ta·yár] *v.* to explode, burst; to creak, crackle.
estallido [es·ta·yí·ḍo] *m.* explosion, outburst; crash; creaking; crack (*of a gun*), report (*of a gun or cannon*).
estambre [es·tám·bre] *m.* woolen yarn; stamen (*of a flower*).
estampa [es·tám·pa] *f.* image; print; stamp; cut, picture; footprint; figure, appearance.
estampado [es·tam·pá·ḍo] *m.* print, printed fabric; printing.
estampar [es·tam·pár] *v.* to stamp, print.
estampida [es·tam·pí·ḍa] *f.* crack, sharp sound; *Col., Ven., C.A.* stampede (*sudden scattering of a herd of cattle or horses*).
estampido [es·tam·pí·ḍo] *m.* crack, sharp sound; report of a gun.

estampilla [es·tam·pí·ya] *f.* stamp, seal; *Mex., C.A., Andes* postage stamp.
estancar[6] [es·taŋ·kár] *v.* to stem; to stanch; to stop the flow of; to corner (*a market*); **-se** to stagnate, become stagnant.
estancia [es·tán·sja] *f.* (*permanencia*) stay; (*lugar*) hall, room; mansion; *Riopl.* farm, cattle ranch; *Carib.* main building of a farm or ranch.
estanciero [es·tan·sjé·ro] *m. Riopl.* rancher, ranch-owner, cattle raiser; *adj.* pertaining to an **estancia.**
estanco [es·táŋ·ko] *m.* monopoly; government store (*for sale of monopolized goods such as tobacco, stamps and matches*); tank, reservoir; *Ec., C.A.* liquor store.
estándar [es·tán·dar] *m. Am.* standard, norm.
estandardizar [es·tan·dar·ḍi·sár], **estandarizar**[9] [es·tan·da·ri·sár] *v. Am.* to standardize.
estandarte [es·tan·dár·te] *m.* standard, flag, banner.
estanque [es·táŋ·ke] *m.* pond, pool, reservoir.
estanquillo [es·táŋ·kí·yo] *m.* tobacco store; *Am.* small store; *C.A., Mex.* small liquor store, tavern.
estante [es·tán·te] *m.* shelf; bookshelf; *Am.* prop, support; **estantería** [es·tan·te·rí·a] *f.* shelves; bookcases.
estaño [es·tá·ño] *m.* tin.
estaquilla [es·ta·kí·ya] *f.* peg; spike.
estar[29] [es·tár] *v. irr.* to be; **-le bien a uno** to be becoming to one; — **de prisa** to be in a hurry; *¿a* **cuántos estamos?** what day of the month is it today?; **-se** to keep, remain.
estático [es·tá·ti·ko] *adj.* static; **estática** [es·tá·ti·ka] *f.* statics; radio static.
estatua [es·tá·twa] *f.* statue.
estatura [es·ta·tú·ra] *f.* stature, height.
estatuto [es·ta·tú·to] *m.* statute.
este [és·te], **esta** [és·ta] *dem. adj.* this; **estos** [és·tos], **estas** [és·tas] these; **éste, ésta** *m., f. dem. pron.* this one, this thing; the latter; **esto** [és·to] this, this thing; **éstos, éstas** *m., f. pl.* these; the latter.
este [és·te] *m.* east; east wind.
estela [es·té·la] *f.* wake of a ship.
estenógrafo [es·te·nó·ǥra·fo] *m.* stenographer.
estentóreo [es·ten·tó·re·o] *adj.* loud, thundering (*voice*).
estepa [es·té·pa] *f.* steppe, treeless plain.
estera [es·té·ra] *f.* matting; mat.
estercolar [es·ter·ko·lár] *v.* to manure, fertilize with manure.
estercolero [es·ter·ko·lé·ro] *m.* manure pile, manure dump; manure collector.
estereoscopio [es·te·re·os·kó·pjo] *m.* stereoscope.
estereotipo [es·te·re·o·tí·po] *m.* stereotype.
estéril [es·té·ril] *adj.* sterile, barren.
esterilidad [es·te·ri·li·ḍáḍ] *f.* sterility, barrenness.
esterilizar[9] [es·te·ri·li·sár] *v.* to sterilize.
esterlina [es·ter·lí·na] *adj.* sterling; **libra** — pound sterling.
estero [es·té·ro] *m.* estuary.
estertor [es·ter·tór] *m.* death-rattle; snort.
estético [es·té·ti·ko] *adj.* aesthetic; **estética** [es·té·ti·ka] *f.* aesthetics.
estetoscopio [es·te·tos·kó·pjo] *m.* stethoscope.
estibador [es·ti·ƀa·ḍór] *m.* stevedore, longshoreman.
estibar [es·ti·ƀár] *v.* to stow (*in a boat*); to pack down, compress.
estiércol [es·tjér·kol] *m.* manure; fertilizer.
estigma [es·tíǥ·ma] *m.* stigma; brand, mark of disgrace; birthmark.

estilar [es·ti·lár] v. to use, be accustomed to using; -**se** to be in style (said of clothes).
estilete [es·ti·lé·te] m. stiletto, narrow-bladed dagger; stylet (instrument for probing wounds); long, narrow sword.
estilo [es·tí·lo] m. style; fashion.
estima [es·tí·ma] f. esteem.
estimación [es·ti·ma·sjón] f. esteem, regard; valuation.
estimar [es·ti·már] v. to esteem, regard highly; to estimate, appraise; to judge, think.
estimulante [es·ti·mu·lán·te] adj. stimulant, stimulating; m. stimulant.
estimular [es·ti·mu·lár] v. to stimulate, excite, goad.
estímulo [es·tí·mu·lo] m. stimulation, incitement; stimulus.
estío [es·tí·o] m. summer.
estipulación [es·ti·pu·la·sjón] f. stipulation, specification, provision, proviso.
estipular [es·ti·pu·lár] v. to stipulate, specify.
estirado [es·ti·rá·ḍo] p.p. & adj. stretched; extended, drawn out; stuck-up, conceited.
estirar [es·ti·rár] v. to stretch, extend; — **la pata** to die; -**se** to stretch out; Am. to die.
estirón [es·ti·rón] m. hard pull, tug; stretch; **dar un** — to grow suddenly (said of a child).
estirpe [es·tír·pe] f. lineage, family, race.
estival [es·ti·ḅál] adj. summer, relating to the summer.
estocada [es·to·ká·ḍa] f. thrust, stab; stab wound.
estofa [es·tó·fa] f. stuff, cloth; class, quality; **gente de baja** — low class people, rabble.
estofado [es·to·fá·ḍo] m. stew, stewed meat; p.p. of **estofar.**
estofar [es·to·fár] v. to quilt; to stew.
estoico [es·tój·ko] adj. & m. stoic.
estola [es·tó·la] f. stole; — **de visón** mink wrap.
estómago [es·tó·ma·/go] m. stomach.
estopa [es·tó·pa] f. burlap; oakum (loose fiber of old ropes).
estoque [es·tó·ke] m. long, narrow sword.
estorbar [es·tor·ḅár] v. to hinder; to obstruct.
estorbo [es·tór·ḅo] m. hindrance; nuisance, bother.
estornudar [es·tor·nu·ḍár] v. to sneeze.
estornudo [es·tor·nú·ḍo] m. sneeze.
estrado [es·trá·ḍo] m. dais (platform for a throne, seats of honor, etc.); main part of a parlor or drawing room.
estragado [es·tra·ǵá·ḍo] p.p. & adj. corrupted; spoiled; ruined; tired, worn out.
estragar[7] [es·tra·ǵár] v. to corrupt, contaminate; to spoil; to ruin.
estrago [es·trá·ǵo] m. havoc, ruin; massacre.
estrangulador [es·traŋ·gu·la·ḍór] m. strangler, choke (of an automobile); adj. strangling.
estrangular [es·traŋ·gu·lár] v. to strangle; to choke, throttle.
estratagema [es·tra·ta·xé·ma] f. stratagem, scheme.
estrategia [es·tra·té·xja] f. strategy.
estratégico [es·tra·té·xi·ko] adj. strategic; m. strategist, person trained or skilled in strategy.
estrato [es·trá·to] m. stratum, layer (of mineral).
estratorreactor [es·tra·to·rre·ak·tór] m. supersonic jet plane.
estratosfera [es·tra·tos·fé·ra] f. stratosphere.
estrechar [es·tre·čár] v. to tighten; to narrow down; to embrace, hug; — **la mano** to squeeze, grasp another's hand; to shake hands.
estrechez [es·tre·čés], **estrechura** [es·tre·čú·ra] f. narrowness; tightness; austerity; dire straits;

poverty; closeness.
estrecho [es·tré·čo] adj. narrow; tight; m. strait, narrow passage.
estrella [es·tré·ya] f. star; — **de mar** starfish.
estrellado [es·tre·yá·ḍo] adj. starry; spangled with stars; **huevos -s** fried eggs.
estrellar [es·tre·yár] v. to shatter; to dash to pieces; to star, spangle with stars; -**se** to shatter, break into pieces; to fail.
estremecer[13] [es·tre·me·sér] v. irr. to shake; -**se** to shiver, shudder; to vibrate.
estremecimiento [es·tre·me·si·mjén·to] m. shiver, shudder; vibration; shaking.
estrenar [es·tre·nár] v. to wear for the first time; to perform (a play) for the first time; to inaugurate; to begin.
estreno [es·tré·no] m. début, first appearance or performance.
estreñimiento [es·tre·ñi·mjén·to] m. constipation.
estreñir[5, 19] [es·tre·ñír] v. irr. to constipate; -**se** to become constipated.
estrépito [es·tré·pi·to] m. racket, noise, crash.
estrepitoso [es·tre·pi·tó·so] adj. noisy; boisterous.
estriado [es·trjá·ḍo] p.p. & adj. fluted, grooved; streaked.
estriar[17] [es·trjár] v. to groove; to flute (as a column).
estribación [es·tri·ḅa·sjón] f. spur (of a mountain or mountain range).
estribar [es·tri·ḅár] v. to rest (upon); **eso estriba en que** . . . the basis or reason for it is that . . .
estribillo [es·tri·ḅí·yo] m. refrain.
estribo [es·trí·ḅo] m. (de caballo o vehículo) stirrup; footboard, running board; (apoyo) support; brace; spur (of a mountain); **perder los -s** to lose one's balance; to lose control of oneself.
estribor [es·tri·ḅór] m. starboard.
estricto [es·trík·to] adj. strict.
estrofa [es·tró·fa] f. strophe, stanza.
estroncio [es·trón·sjo] m. strontium.
estropajo [es·tro·pá·xo] m. fibrous mass (for scrubbing); **tratar a uno como un** — to treat someone scornfully.
estropear [es·tro·pe·ár] v. to spoil, ruin, damage; to cripple.
estructura [es·truk·tú·ra] f. structure.
estructural [es·truk·tu·rál] adj. structural.
estruendo [es·trwén·do] m. clatter; clamor, din, racket.
estruendoso [es·trwen·dó·so] adj. thunderous, uproarious, deafening.
estrujamiento [es·tru·xa·mjén·to] m. crushing, squeezing.
estrujar [es·tru·xár] v. to squeeze, press, crush.
estrujón [es·tru·xón] m. squeeze, crush; smashing.
estuario [es·twá·rjo] m. estuary.
estuco [es·tú·ko] m. stucco.
estuche [es·tú·če] m. jewel box; instrument case, kit; small casket; sheath.
estudiantado [es·tu·ḍjan·ta·ḍo] m. the student body (of a school or college).
estudiante [es·tu·ḍján·te] m. & f. student.
estudiantil [es·tu·ḍjan·tíl] adj. pertaining to students.
estudiar [es·tu·ḍjár] v. to study.
estudio [es·tú·ḍjo] m. study; studio.
estudioso [es·tu·ḍjó·so] adj. studious; m. learner.
estufa [es·tú·fa] f. heater; stove; hothouse; steam room; steam cabinet.
estupefacto [es·tu·pe·fák·to] adj. stunned; speechless.

ES

estupendo [es·tu·pén·do] *adj.* stupendous, marvelous.

estupidez [es·tu·pi·déṣ] *f.* stupidity.

estúpido [es·tú·pi·đo] *adj.* stupid.

esturión [es·tu·rjón] *m.* sturgeon.

etapa [e·tá·pa] *f.* stage, lap (*of a journey or race*); army food rations; epoch, period.

éter [é·ter] *m.* ether.

etéreo [e·té·re·o] *adj.* ethereal; heavenly.

eternidad [e·ter·ni·đáđ] *f.* eternity.

eternizar[9] [e·ter·ni·sár] *v.* to prolong excessively; to perpetuate, make eternal.

eterno [e·tér·no] *adj.* eternal, everlasting.

ética [é·ti·ka] *f.* ethics; **ético** *adj.* ethical, moral.

etimología [e·ti·mo·lo·xí·a] *f.* etymology.

etiqueta [e·ti·ké·ta] *f.* etiquette; formality; tag; **de — formal** (*dress, function, etc.*).

étnico [ét·ni·ko] *adj.* ethnic.

eucalipto [ew·ka·líp·to] *m.* eucalyptus.

Eucaristía [ew·ka·ris·tí·a] *f.* Eucharist.

euforia [ew·fó·rja] *f.* euphoria.

europeo [ew·ro·pé·o] *adj.* & *m.* European.

evacuación [e·ƀa·kwa·sjón] *f.* evacuation; bowel movement.

evacuar[18] [e·ƀa·kwár] *v.* to evacuate, empty; to vacate.

evadir [e·ƀa·đír] *v.* to evade, elude; **-se** to slip away, escape.

evaluar[18] [e·ƀa·lwar] *v.* to evaluate, appraise.

evangelio [e·ƀaŋ·xé·ljo] *m.* gospel.

evaporar [e·ƀa·po·rár] *v.* to evaporate; **-se** to evaporate; to vanish, disappear.

evasión [e·ƀa·sjón] *f.* evasion, dodge, escape.

evasiva [e·ƀa·sí·ƀa] *f.* evasion, dodge, escape.

evasivo [e·ƀa·sí·ƀo] *adj.* evasive.

evasor [e·ƀa·sór] *m.* evader, dodger.

evento [e·ƀén·to] *m.* event.

evidencia [e·ƀi·đén·sja] *f.* evidence.

evidenciar [e·ƀi·đen·sjár] *v.* to prove, show, make evident.

evidente [e·ƀi·đén·te] *adj.* evident.

evitable [e·ƀi·tá·ƀle] *adj.* avoidable.

evitar [e·ƀi·tár] *v.* to avoid, shun.

evocar[6] [e·ƀo·kár] *v.* to evoke, call forth.

evolución [e·ƀo·lu·sjón] *f.* evolution.

evolucionar [e·ƀo·lu·sjo·nár] *v.* to evolve; to perform maneuvers; to go through changes.

exacerbar [ek·sa·ser·ƀár] *v.* to exasperate, irritate; to aggravate, make worse.

exactitud [ek·sak·ti·túđ] *f.* exactness, precision; punctuality.

exacto [ek·sák·to] *adj.* exact, precise; punctual.

exagerar [ek·sa·xe·rár] *v.* to exaggerate.

exaltación [ek·sal·ta·sjón] *f.* exaltation; excitement.

exaltado [ek·sal·tá·đo] *adj.* elated; excited; hotheaded.

exaltar [ek·sal·tár] *v.* to exalt, elevate, glorify; to praise; **-se** to get excited; to become upset emotionally.

examen [ek·sá·men] *m.* examination; inspection.

examinar [ek·sa·mi·nár] *v.* to examine; to inspect.

exangüe [ek·sáŋ·gwe] *adj.* lacking blood; anemic; exhausted.

exánime [ek·sá·ni·me] *adj.* lifeless, motionless; weak, faint.

exasperar [ek·sas·pe·rár] *v.* to exasperate, irritate, annoy.

excavar [es·ka·ƀár] *v.* to excavate, dig, dig out.

excedente [ek·se·đén·te] *m.* surplus; *adj.* exceeding, extra.

exceder [ek·se·đér] *v.* to exceed, surpass; to

overdo; **-se** to go beyond the proper limit; to misbehave.

excelencia [ek·se·lén·sja] *f.* excellence, superiority; excellency (*title*).

excelente [ek·se·lén·te] *adj.* excellent.

excelso [ek·sél·so] *adj.* lofty, elevated; sublime; **El Excelso** the Most High.

excéntrico [ek·sén·tri·ko] *adj.* eccentric; queer, odd.

excepción [ek·sep·sjón] *f.* exception.

excepcional [ek·sep·sjo·nál] *adj.* exceptional, unusual.

excepto [ek·sép·to] *adv.* except, with the exception of.

exceptuar[18] [ek·sep·twár] *v.* to except.

excesivo [ek·se·sí·ƀø] *adj.* excessive.

exceso [ek·sé·so] *m.* excess; crime; **— de equipaje** excess baggage; **en —** in excess, excessively.

excitación [ek·si·ta·sjón] *f.* excitement.

excitante [ek·si·tán·te] *adj.* exciting; stimulating.

excitar [ek·si·tár] *v.* to excite, stir; **-se** to get excited.

exclamación [es·kla·ma·sjón] *f.* exclamation.

exclamar [es·kla·már] *v.* to exclaim.

excluir[32] [es·klwír] *v. irr.* to exclude.

exclusivo [es·klu·sí·ƀo] *adj.* exclusive.

excomunicar[6] [es·ko·mu·ni·kár] *v.* to excommunicate.

excomunión [es·ko·mu·njón] *f.* excommunication.

excrecencia [es·kre·sén·sja], **excrescencia** [es·kre·sén·sja] *f.* excrescence (*abnormal growth or tumor*).

excremento [es·kre·mén·to] *m.* excrement.

excursión [es·kur·sjón] *f.* excursion, tour, outing.

excusa [es·kú·sa] *f.* excuse.

excusado [es·ku·sá·đo] *p.p.* & *adj.* excused; exempt; superfluous; unnecessary; reserved, private; *m.* toilet.

excusar [es·ku·sár] *v.* (*disculpar*) to excuse; to exempt; (*evitar*) to avoid, shun; **-se** to excuse oneself, apologize; to decline.

exención [ek·sen·sjón] *f.* exemption.

exentar [ek·sen·tár] *v.* to exempt. *See* **eximir.**

exento [ek·sén·to] *adj.* exempt, freed; free, unobstructed.

exequias [ek·sé·kjas] *f. pl.* obsequies, funeral rites.

exhalar [ek·sa·lár] *v.* to exhale; to emit, give off; to breathe forth; **-se** to evaporate; to run away.

exhibición [ek·si·ƀi·sjón] *f.* exhibition; exposition; *Mex.* payment of an installment.

exhibir [ek·si·ƀír] *v.* to exhibit; *Mex.* to pay for in installments (*stocks, policies, etc.*); **-se** to exhibit oneself, show off.

exhortar [ek·sor·tár] *v.* to exhort, admonish.

exigencia [ek·si·xén·sja] *f.* demand; urgent want; emergency.

exigente [ek·si·xén·te] *adj.* demanding, exacting; urgent.

exigir[11] [ek·si·xír] *v.* to require; to demand; to exact.

exiguo [ek·sí·ǥwo] *adj.* scanty, meager.

eximio [ek·sí·mjo] *adj.* very distinguished.

eximir [ek·si·mír] *v.* to exempt, except, excuse; **-se de** to avoid, shun.

existencia [ek·sis·tén·sja] *f.* existence; **-s** stock on hand, goods; **en —** in stock, on hand.

existente [ek·sis·tén·te] *adj.* existent, existing; in stock.

existir [ek·sis·tír] *v.* to exist.

éxito [ék·si·to] *m.* outcome, result; success; **tener buen (mal) —** to be successful (unsuccessful).

éxodo [ék·so·đo] *m.* exodus, emigration.

exonerar [ek·so·ne·rár] *v.* to exonerate, free from blame; to relieve of a burden or position; to dismiss.

exorbitante [ek·sor·ƀi·tán·te] *adj.* exorbitant, excessive, extravagant.

exótico [ek·só·ti·ko] *adj.* exotic, foreign, strange; quaint.

expansión [es·pan·sjón] *f.* expansion; relaxation; recreation.

expansivo [es·pan·sí·ƀo] *adj.* expansive; demonstrative, effusive.

expatriar [es·pa·trjár] *v.* to expatriate, exile; -se to expatriate oneself, renounce one's citizenship; to emigrate.

expectación [es·pek·ta·sjón] *f.* expectation.

expectativa [es·pek·ta·tí·ƀa] *f.* expectation; hope, prospect; **estar en — de algo** to be expecting, or on the lookout for, something.

expectorar [es·pek·to·rár] *v.* to expectorate, cough up.

expedición [es·pe·ɖi·sjón] *f.* expedition; dispatch, promptness; papal dispatch or bull.

expedicionario [es·pe·ɖi·sjo·ná·rjo] *adj.* expeditionary; *m.* member of an expedition; explorer.

expediente [es·pe·ɖjén·te] *m.* certificate; papers pertaining to a business matter; expedient, means; dispatch, promptness.

expedir[5] [es·pe·ɖír] *v. irr.* to dispatch; to issue officially; to remit, send.

expeler [es·pe·lér] *v.* to expel, eject.

experiencia [es·pe·rjén·sja] *f.* experience; experiment.

experimentado [es·pe·ri·men·tá·ɖo] *adj. & p.p.* experienced.

experimental [es·pe·ri·men·tál] *adj.* experimental.

experimentar [es·pe·ri·men·tár] *v.* to experiment, try, test; to experience, feel.

experimento [es·pe·ri·mén·to] *m.* experiment, trial.

experto [es·pér·to] *adj.* expert, skillful; *m.* expert.

expiación [es·pja·sjón] *f.* expiation, atonement.

expiar[17] [es·pjár] *v.* to atone for; to make amends for; to purify.

expirar [es·pi·rár] *v.* to die; to expire, come to an end.

explayar [es·pla·yár] *v.* to extend; -se to become extended; to relax in the open air; to enlarge upon a subject; -se con un amigo to unbosom oneself, speak with utmost frankness with a friend.

explicable [es·pli·ká·ƀle] *adj.* explainable.

explicación [es·pli·ka·sjón] *f.* explanation.

explicar[6] [es·pli·kár] *v.* to explain; — una cátedra to teach a course; -se to explain oneself; to account for one's conduct.

explicativo [es·pli·ka·tí·ƀo] *adj.* explanatory, explaining.

explícito [es·plí·si·to] *adj.* explicit, express, clear, definite.

exploración [es·plo·ra·sjón] *f.* exploration.

explorador [es·plo·ra·ɖór] *m.* explorer, scout; *adj.* exploring.

explorar [es·plo·rár] *v.* to explore.

explosión [es·plo·sjón] *f.* explosion.

explosivo [es·plo·sí·ƀo] *adj. & m.* explosive.

explotación [es·plo·ta·sjón] *f.* exploitation; operation of a mine; development of a business; plant.

explotar [es·plo·tár] *v.* to exploit, operate, develop; to utilize, profit by; to make unfair use of; *Am.* to explode.

exponer[40] [es·po·nér] *v. irr.* (*dejar ver*) to expose, reveal; to show, exhibit; to display; (*sin protección*) to leave unprotected, to expose (*film*); (*explicar*) to expound; to explain; -se a to expose oneself to; to run the risk of.

exportación [es·por·ta·sjón] *f.* exportation; export.

exportar [es·por·tár] *v.* to export.

exposición [es·po·si·sjón] *f.* exposition; exhibition; explanation; exposure.

exprés [es·prés] *m. Am.* express; *Am.* express company.

expresar [es·pre·sár] *v.* to express; -se to express oneself, speak.

expresión [es·pre·sjón] *f.* expression; utterance; -es regards.

expresivo [es·pre·sí·ƀo] *adj.* expressive; affectionate.

expreso [es·pré·so] *adj.* expressed; express, clear, exact; fast; *m.* express train.

exprimir [es·pri·mír] *v.* to squeeze, extract (*juice*); to wring out; to express, utter.

expuesto [es·pwés·to] *p.p. of* exponer & *adj.* exposed; expressed; displayed; risky, dangerous; **lo — what has been said.**

expulsar [es·pul·sár] *v.* to expel, eject.

expulsión [es·pul·sjón] *f.* expulsion, expelling.

exquisitez [es·ki·si·tés] *f.* exquisiteness.

exquisito [es·ki·sí·to] *adj.* exquisite.

extasiado [es·ta·sjá·ɖo] *adj.* rapt, in ecstasy; *p.p. of* extasiar.

extasiar[17] [es·ta·sjár] *v.* to delight; -se to be in ecstasy; to be entranced.

éxtasis [és·ta·sis] *m.* ecstasy.

extender[1] [es·ten·dér] *v. irr.* to extend; to spread; to unfold; to draw up (*a document*); -se to extend, spread; to expatiate, be too wordy.

extensión [es·ten·sjón] *f.* extension; extent; expanse; expansion.

extensivo [es·ten·sí·ƀo] *adj.* extensive.

extenso [es·tén·so] *p.p. of* extender & *adj.* extensive, vast, spacious; **por — extensively, in detail.**

extenuado [es·te·nwá·ɖo] *adj.* wasted, weak, emaciated.

exterior [es·te·rjór] *adj.* exterior, outer; *m.* exterior; outside; outward appearance.

exterminar [es·ter·mi·nár] *v.* to exterminate.

exterminio [es·ter·mí·njo] *m.* extermination, destruction.

externo [es·tér·no] *adj.* external, outward.

extinguir[12] [es·tiŋ·gír] *v.* to extinguish, put out; to destroy.

extinto [es·tín·to] *adj.* extinct.

extintor [es·tin·tór] *m.* extinguisher; — de espuma fire extinguisher.

extirpar [es·tir·pár] *v.* to eradicate, pull out by the roots, root out, remove completely; to destroy completely.

extorsión [es·tor·sjón] *f.* extortion.

extorsionar [es·tor·sjo·nár] *v. Am.* to extort, extract money, blackmail.

extorsionista [es·tor·sjo·nís·ta] *m. Am.* extortioner, profiteer, racketeer.

extracto [es·trák·to] *m.* extract; abstract, summary.

extraer[46] [es·tra·ér] *v. irr.* to extract.

extranjero [es·traŋ·xé·ro] *adj.* foreign; *m.* foreigner.

extrañamiento [es·tra·ña·mjén·to] *m.* wonder, surprise, amazement.

extrañar [es·tra·ñár] *v.* to wonder at; to banish; *Am.* to miss (*a person or thing*); -se to marvel, be astonished.

extrañeza [es·tra·ñé·sa] *f.* strangeness; surprise,

astonishment; oddity, odd thing.
extraño [es·trá·ño] *adj.* strange; rare; odd; *m.* stranger.
extraordinario [es·tra·or·ḍi·ná·rjo] *adj.* extraordinary.
extravagancia [es·tra·ḅa·ǥán·sja] *f.* extravagance; folly.
extravagante [es·tra·ḅa·ǥán·te] *adj.* extravagant, fantastic; queer, odd.
extraviar[17] [es·tra·ḅjár] *v.* to lead astray; to strand; to misplace; **-se** to lose one's way; to get stranded; to get lost; to miss the road.
extravío [es·tra·ḅí·o] *m.* deviation, straying; error; misconduct; damage.
extremado [es·tre·má·ḍo] *adj.* extreme; extremely good or extremely bad; *p.p. of* **extremar**.
extremar [es·tre·már] *v.* to carry to an extreme; **-se** to take great pains, exert great effort.
extremidad [es·tre·mi·ḍáḍ] *f.* extremity; extreme degree; remotest part; **-es** extremities, hands and feet.
extremo [es·tré·mo] *adj.* extreme, last; farthest; excessive; utmost; *m.* extreme, highest degree or point; end, extremity; extreme care; **con (en** or **por) —** very much, extremely.
exuberante [ek·su·ḅe·rán·te] *adj.* exuberant; luxuriant.

F·f fa [fa] *m.* fourth note of the musical scale (*solfa syllables*).
fabada [fa·ḅá·ḍa] *f.* a bean and bacon soup popular in Spain.
fábrica [fá·ḅri·ka] *f.* manufacture; factory, mill; structure.
fabricación [fa·ḅri·ka·sjón] *f.* manufacture.
fabricante [fa·ḅri·kán·te] *m.* manufacturer, maker.
fabricar[6] [fa·ḅri·kár] *v.* to manufacture, make; to construct, build; to fabricate, make up, invent.
fabril [fa·ḅríl] *adj.* manufacturing.
fábula [fá·ḅu·la] *f.* fable, tale; falsehood.
fabuloso [fa·ḅu·ló·so] *adj.* fabulous; false, imaginary.
facción [fak·sjón] *f.* faction, band, party; battle; **-es** features; **estar de —** to be on duty.
faceta [fa·se·ta] *f.* facet.
faceto [fa·sé·to] *adj. Am.* cute, funny; *Am.* affected.
fácil [fá·sil] *adj.* easy; docile, yielding, manageable; likely; probable.
facilidad [fa·si·li·ḍáḍ] *f.* facility, ease; opportunity.
facilitar [fa·si·li·tár] *v.* to facilitate, make easy; to furnish; give; **— todos los datos** to furnish all the data.
facón [fa·kón] *m. Riopl., Bol.* dagger, large knife; **faconazo** [fa·ko·ná·so] *m. Riopl., Bol.* stab.
factible [fak·tí·ḅle] *adj.* feasible.
factor [fak·tór] *m.* factor; element, joint cause; commercial agent; baggage man.
factoría [fak·to·rí·a] *f.* trading post; *Am.* factory.
factura [fak·tú·ra] *f.* (*cuenta*) invoice, itemized bill; (*hechura*) workmanship, form; *Am.* roll, biscuit, muffin; **— simulada** temporary invoice, memorandum.
facturar [fak·tu·rár] *v.* to invoice, bill; to check (*baggage*).
facultad [fa·kul·táḍ] *f.* faculty; ability, aptitude; power, right; permission; branch of learning; school or college of a university.
facultativo [fa·kul·ta·tí·ḅo] *m.* doctor, physician.

facundia [fa·kún·dja] *f.* eloquence, fluency, facility in speaking, gift of expression.
facha [fá·ča] *f.* appearance, figure, aspect, looks.
fachada [fa·čá·ḍa] *f.* façade, front (*of a building*); title page.
fachenda [fa·čén·da] *f.* ostentation, vanity.
fachendoso [fa·čen·dó·so] *adj.* vain, boastful, ostentatious.
faena [fa·é·na] *f.* task, job, duty; *Carib., Mex., C.A.* extra job; *Ch.* work crew, labor gang.
faja [fá·xa] *f.* sash; girdle; band; *Am.* belt, waist band.
fajar [fa·xár] *v.* to girdle; to bind, wrap, or bandage with a strip of cloth; *Am.* to beat, strike, thrash; *Am.* **— un latigazo a uno** to whip, thrash someone; **-se** to put on a sash or belt; to tighten one's sash or belt; *Am.* **-se con** to have a fight with, come to blows with.
fajo [fá·xo] *m.* bundle; sheaf.
falaz [fa·lás] *adj.* illusive, illustory; deceitful, deceiving.
falda [fál·da] *f.* skirt; lap; hat brim; foothill, slope; **faldón** [fal·dón] *m.* coattail; shirttail.
faldear [fal·de·ár] *v.* to skirt (*a hill*).
falsario [fal·sá·rjo] *m.* crook, forger; liar.
falsear [fal·se·ár] *v.* to falsify, misrepresent; to counterfeit; to forge; to pick (*a lock*); to flag, grow weak; to hit a wrong note.
falsedad [fal·se·ḍáḍ] *f.* falsehood, lie; deceit.
falsificación [fal·si·fi·ka·sjón] *f.* falsification, forgery; counterfeit.
falsificar[6] [fal·si·fi·kár] *v.* to falsify, make false; to counterfeit; to forge.
falso [fál·so] *adj.* false; untrue, unreal; deceitful; counterfeit; sham; *C.A.* cowardly; *m.* inside facing of a dress; lining; *Mex.* false testimony, slander; **en —** upon a false foundation; without proper security; *Am.* **coger a uno en —** to catch one lying.
falta [fál·ta] *f.* (*defecto*) lack, want; fault, mistake; defect; absence; (*infracción*) misdemeanor, offense; **a — de** for want of; **hacer —** to be necessary; to be missing; **me hace —** I need it; **sin —** without fail.
faltar [fal·tár] *v.* to be lacking, wanting; to be absent or missing; to fail, be of no use or help; to fail to fulfill (*a promise or duty*); to die; *Mex., C.A.* to insult; **— poco para las cinco** to be almost five o'clock; **¡no fáltaba más!** that's the last straw!; why, the very idea!
falto [fál·to] *adj.* lacking; deficient, short; *Am.* foolish, stupid.
faltriquera [fal·tri·ké·ra] *f.* pocket.
falla [fá·ya] *f.* fault, defect; failure; fault (*fracture in the earth's crust*); *Riopl.* baby's bonnet; **-s** popular *fiestas* of Valencia, Spain.
fallar [fa·yár] *v.* (*juzgar*) to render a verdict; (*fracasar*) to fail, be deficient; to default; to miss; to fail to hit; to give way, break; to trump.
fallecer[13] [fa·ye·sér] *v. irr.* to die.
fallecimiento [fa·ye·si·mjén·to] *m.* decease, death.
fallido [fa·yí·ḍo] *adj.* frustrated; bankrupt.
fallo [fá·yo] *m.* verdict, judgment; decision; *adj.* lacking (*a card, or suit, in card games*); *Ch.* silly, foolish.
fama [fá·ma] *f.* fame, reputation; rumor, report; *Ch.* bull's-eye, center of a target.
famélico [fa·mé·li·ko] *adj.* ravenous, hungry, starved.
familia [fa·mí·lja] *f.* family.
familiar [fa·mi·ljár] *adj.* domestic, homelike;

familiar, well-known; friendly, informal; colloquial (*phrase or expression*); *m.* intimate friend; member of a household; domestic servant; familiar spirit, demon; *Am.* relative.
familiaridad [fa·mi·lja·ri·ḏáḏ] *f.* familiarity, informality.
familiarizar[9] [fa·mi·lja·ri·sar] *v.* to familiarize, acquaint; **-se** to acquaint oneself, become familiar (with).
famoso [fa·mó·so] *adj.* famous; excellent.
fanal [fa·nál] *m.* beacon, lighthouse; lantern; headlight; bell jar, glass cover.
fanático [fa·ná·ti·ko] *adj.* & *m.* fanatic.
fanatismo [fa·na·tíz·mo] *m.* fanaticism.
fanega [fa·né·ga] *f.* Spanish bushel; **— de tierra** land measure (*variable according to region*).
fanfarrón [fan·fa·rrón] *m.* braggart, boaster; bluffer.
fanfarronada [fan·fa·rro·ná·ḏa] *f.* boast, brag, swagger, bluff.
fanfarronear [fan·fa·rro·ne·ár] *v.* to bluff, brag; to swagger.
fango [fáŋ·go] *m.* mud, mire.
fangoso [faŋ·gó·so] *adj.* muddy, miry.
fantasear [fan·ta·se·ár] *v.* to fancy; to imagine.
fantasía [fan·ta·sí·a] *f.* fantasy, imagination, fancy, whim; **-s** string of pearls; *Ven.* **tocar por —** to play by ear.
fantasma [fan·táz·ma] *m.* phantom, image; vision, ghost; *f.* scarecrow.
fantasmagórico [fan·taz·ma·ǵó·ri·ko] *adj.* fantastic, unreal, illusory.
fantástico [fan·tás·ti·ko] *adj.* fantastic.
fardel [far·ḏél] *m.* knapsack, bag; bundle.
fardo [fár·ḏo] *m.* bundle; bale, *Ríopl., Andes* **pasar el —** to "pass the buck", shift the responsibility to someone else.
faringe [fa·ríŋ·xe] *f.* pharynx.
faríngeo [fa·ríŋ·xe·o] *adj.* pharyngeal.
farmacéutico [far·ma·séw·ti·ko] *m.* pharmacist, druggist; *adj.* pharmaceutical (*pertaining to a pharmacy or pharmacists*).
farmacia [far·má·sja] *f.* pharmacy; drugstore.
faro [fá·ro] *m.* lighthouse; beacon; *Am.* headlight.
farol [fa·ról] *m.* (*linterna*) lantern; street lamp; (*fachendoso*) conceit, self-importance; *Ríopl.* balcony; *Am.* presumptuous man; *Am.* bluff; **darse —** to show off; to put on airs.
farola [fa·ró·la] *f.* street light; lamppost.
farolero [fa·ro·lé·ro] *adj.* vain, ostentatious; *m.* lamp maker or vendor; lamplighter (*person*).
farra [fá·rra] *f.* *Ríopl., Ch., Col., Ven., Andes* spree, revelry, wild party, noisy merrymaking; *Ríopl., Ch., Col., Ven., Andes* **ir de —** to go on a spree.
farsa [fár·sa] *f.* farce; company of actors; sham, fraud.
farsante [far·sán·te] *m.* charlatan, bluffer; quack; comedian; wag.
fascinación [fa·si·na·sjón] *f.* fascination; glamour.
fascinador [fa·si·na·ḏór] *adj.* fascinating, glamorous; charming.
fascinar [fa·si·nár] *v.* to fascinate, bewitch, charm; to allure.
fascismo [fa·síz·mo] *m.* fascism.
fascista [fa·sís·ta] *m.* & *f.* fascist.
fase [fá·se] *f.* phase, aspect.
fastidiar [fas·ti·ḏjár] *v.* to annoy, bother; to bore; *Col., P.R.* to hurt, harm, ruin.
fastidio [fas·ti·ḏjo] *m.* boredom; disgust; nuisance, annoyance.
fastidioso [fas·ti·ḏjó·so] *adj.* annoying, bothersome; boring, tiresome.

fatal [fa·tál] *adj.* fatal; mortal, deadly; unfortunate.
fatalidad [fa·ta·li·ḏáḏ] *f.* fatality, destiny; calamity, misfortune.
fatalismo [fa·ta·líz·mo] *m.* fatalism.
fatiga [fa·tí·ga] *f.* fatigue, weariness; toil; **-s** hardships.
fatigar[7] [fa·ti·gár] *v.* to fatigue, weary; to bother.
fatigoso [fa·ti·ǵó·so] *adj.* fatiguing, tiring.
fatuo [fá·two] *adj.* foolish, stupid; vain; **fuego —** will-o'-the-wisp.
favor [fa·ḇór] *m.* favor; kindness; help, aid; protection; *Am.* ribbon bow; **a — de** in favor of; **hágame el —** please.
favorable [fa·ḇó·rá·ḇle] *adj.* favorable.
favorecer[13] [fa·ḇo·re·sér] *v. irr.* to favor, help, protect.
favoritismo [fa·ḇo·ri·tíz·mo] *m.* favoritism.
favorito [fa·ḇo·rí·to] *adj.* & *m.* favorite.
faz [fas] *f.* face.
fe [fe] *f.* faith; **— de bautismo** baptismal certificate.
fealdad [fe·al·dáḏ] *f.* ugliness, homeliness; foulness, foul or immoral action.
febrero [fe·ḇré·ro] *m.* February.
febril [fe·ḇríl] *adj.* feverish.
fécula [fé·ku·la] *f.* starch.
fecundar [fe·kun·dár] *v.* to fertilize.
fecundo [fe·kún·do] *adj.* fruitful, fertile, productive.
fecha [fé·ča] *f.* date.
fechar [fe·čár] *v.* to date.
fechoría [fe·čo·rí·a] *f.* misdeed, misdemeanor.
federación [fe·ḏe·ra·sjón] *f.* federation, union.
federal [fe·ḏe·rál] *adj.* federal.
felicidad [fe·li·si·ḏáḏ] *f.* happiness; **¡-es!** congratulations.
felicitación [fe·li·si·ta·sjón] *f.* congratulation.
felicitar [fe·li·si·tár] *v.* to congratulate.
feligrés [fe·li·grés] *m.* parishioner.
feliz [fe·lís] *adj.* happy; lucky.
felpa [fél·pa] *f.* plush.
felpudo [fel·pú·ḏo] *adj.* plushy, like plush; *m.* small plushlike mat; door mat.
femenil [fe·me·níl] *adj.* womanly, feminine.
femenino [fe·me·ní·no] *adj.* feminine.
fementido [fe·men·tí·ḏo] *adj.* false; treacherous.
fenecer[13] [fe·ne·sér] *v. irr.* to die; to finish, end.
fénico [fé·ni·ko] *adj.* carbolic; **acido —** carbolic acid.
fénix [fé·nis] *m.* phoenix (*mythical bird*).
fenómeno [fe·nó·me·no] *m.* phenomenon.
feo [fe·o] *adj.* ugly, homely; *Am.* bad (*referring to taste or odor*); **feote** [fe·ó·te] *adj.* hideous, very ugly.
féretro [fé·re·tro] *m.* bier; coffin.
feria [fé·rja] *f.* fair; market; *Mex.* change (*money*); *Am.* tip; **-s** *Am.* present given to servants or the poor during holidays.
feriante [fe·rján·te] *m.* & *f.* trader at fairs; trader; peddler.
feriar [fe·rjár] *v.* to trade.
fermentar [fer·men·tár] *v.* to ferment.
fermento [fer·mén·to] *m.* ferment; yeast, leaven.
ferocidad [fe·ro·si·ḏáḏ] *f.* ferocity, fierceness.
feroz [fe·rós] *adj.* ferocious, wild, fierce.
férreo [fé·rre·o] *adj.* ferrous (*pertaining to or derived from iron*); ironlike; harsh; **vía férrea** railroad.
ferretería [fe·rre·te·rí·a] *f.* hardware shop; hardware.
ferrocarril [fe·rro·ka·rríl] *m.* railroad.
ferroviario [fe·rro·ḇjá·rjo] *adj.* railway, railroad (*used as adj.*); *m.* railroad man; railroad

EX

employee.
fértil [fér·til] *adj.* fertile, productive; **fertilidad** [fer·ti·li·ḍaḍ] *f.* fertility.
fertilizar[9] [fer·ti·li·sár] *v.* to fertilize.
ferviente [fer·ḅjén·te] *adj.* fervent, ardent.
fervor [fer·ḅór] *m.* fervor, zeal, devotion.
fervoroso [fer·ḅo·ró·so] *adj.* fervent, ardent; pious, devout; zealous.
festejar [fes·te·xár] *v.* to feast, entertain; to celebrate; to woo; *Mex.* to thrash, beat.
festejo [fes·té·xo] *m.* entertainment, festival, celebration; courtship; *Am.* revelry.
festín [fes·tín] *m.* feast; banquet.
festividad [fes·ti·ḅi·ḍaḍ] *f.* festival; holiday; holy day; festivity, gaiety, rejoicing.
festivo [fes·tí·ḅo] *adj.* festive, gay; **día** — holiday.
fétido [fé·ti·ḍo] *adj.* foul, foul-smelling.
fiado [fjá·ḍo] *p.p.* of **fiar**; **al** — on credit.
fiador [fja·ḍór] *m.* guarantor, backer, bondsman; *Ec., Ch.* chin strap, hat guard.
fiambre [fjám·bre] *m.* cold meat; cold or late news; *Riopl., Mex., Col., Ven.* cold meat salad; *Am.* flop, failure (*referring to a party*).
fianza [fján·sa] *f.* bond, security, surety, guarantee; bail.
fiar[17] [fjar] to trust; to guarantee, back; *Am.* to borrow on credit; **-se de** to place confidence in.
fibra [fí·ḅra] *f.* fiber; **fibroso** *adj.* fibrous.
ficción [fik·sjón] *f.* fiction.
ficticio [fik·tí·sjo] *adj.* fictitious.
ficha [fí·ča] *f.* (*pieza*) chip; token; domino; (*tarjeta*) file card; *Am.* check (*used in barbershops and stores*); *Am.* rascal, scamp;
fichero [fi·čé·ro] *m.* file, card index, filing cabinet.
fidedigno [fi·ḍe·ḍíg·no] *adj.* trustworthy, reliable.
fidelidad [fi·ḍe·li·ḍaḍ] *f.* fidelity, faithfulness.
fideo [fi·ḍé·o] *m.* vermicelli, thin noodle; thin person.
fiebre [fjé·ḅre] *f.* fever; excitement, agitation; *Ch.* astute person.
fiel [fjel] *adj.* faithful; true, accurate; *m.* public inspector; pointer of a balance or scale; pin of the scissors; **los -es** the worshipers, the congregation.
fieltro [fjél·tro] *m.* felt; felt hat; felt rug.
fiera [fjé·ra] *f.* wild beast; *Am.* go-getter, hustler; **ser una** — **para el trabajo** to be a demon for work.
fiereza [fje·ré·sa] *f.* ferocity, fierceness; cruelty; ugliness.
fiero [fjé·ro] *adj.* fierce, ferocious, wild; cruel; ugly, horrible; huge; *m.* threat; **echar** (*or* **hacer**) **-s** to threaten; to boast.
fierro [fjé·rro] *m. Am.* iron; *Am.* iron bar; *Am.* cattle brand; **-s** *Am.* tools, implements. See **hierro.**
fiesta [fjés·ta] *f.* festivity, celebration, entertainment; holiday; **estar de** — to be in a holiday mood; **hacer -s a uno** to fawn on a person.
fiestero [fjes·té·ro] *adj.* fond of parties, fond of entertaining; gay, festive; playful; *m.* merrymaker.
figón [fi·gón] *m.* cheap eating house, "joint."
figura [fi·gú·ra] *f.* figure; shape, form; countenance; face card.
figurado [fi·gu·rá·ḍo] *adj.* figurative.
figurar [fi·gu·rár] *v.* to figure; to form; to represent, symbolize; **-se** to imagine; **se me figura** I think, guess, or imagine.
figurín [fi·gu·rín] *m.* fashion plate; dandy.

fijar [fi·xár] *v.* to fix, fasten; to establish; **-se** to settle; **-se en** to notice, pay attention to.
fijeza [fi·xé·sa] *f.* firmness, solidity, steadiness.
fijo [fí·xo] *adj.* fixed; firm; secure.
fila [fí·la] *f.* row, tier; rank.
filamento [fi·la·mén·to] *m.* filament.
filatelia [fi·la·té·lja] *f.* philately.
filete [fi·lé·te] *m.* (*moldura*) edge, rim; (*carne*) fillet, tenderloin; (*freno*) snaffle bit (*for horses*); hem; screw thread.
filial [fi·ljál] *adj.* filial.
filigrana [fi·li·grá·na] *f.* filigree.
filmar [fil·már] *v.* to film, screen (*a play or novel*).
filo [fí·lo] *m.* cutting edge; *Andes* hunger; **por** — exactly; *Am.* **de** — resolutely.
filología [fi·lo·lo·xí·a] *f.* philology.
filólogo [fi·ló·lo·go] *m.* philologist.
filón [fi·lón] *m.* seam, layer (*of metallic ore*).
filoso [fi·ló·so] *adj. Am.* sharp, sharp-edged.
filosofía [fi·lo·so·fí·a] *f.* philosophy.
filosófico [fi·lo·só·fi·ko] *adj.* philosophic, philosophical.
filósofo [fi·ló·so·fo] *m.* philosopher.
filtrar [fil·trár] *v.* to filter; **-se** to leak through, leak out; to filter.
filtro [fíl·tro] *m.* filter.
filudo [fi·lú·ḍo] *adj. Am.* sharp, sharp-edged.
fin [fin] *m.* end, ending; purpose; **al** — at last; **al — y al cabo** at last; anyway; in the end; **a — de que** so that; **a -es del mes** toward the end of the month; **en** — in conclusion; well; in short.
finado [fi·ná·ḍo] *m.* the deceased.
final [fi·nál] *adj.* final.
finalizar[9] [fi·na·li·sár] *v.* to finish; to end.
financiamiento [fi·nan·sja·mjén·to] *m. Am.* financing.
financiar [fi·nan·sjár] *v. Am.* to finance.
financiero [fi·nan·sjé·ro] *adj.* financial; *m.* financier.
financista [fi·nan·sís·ta] *m. Am.* financier.
finanza [fi·nán·sa] *f. Am.* finance; **-s** *Am.* public treasury, government funds.
finca [fíŋ·ka] *f.* real estate; property; country house; *Am.* ranch, farm.
fincar [fiŋ·kár] *v.* to buy real estate; *Am.* to rest (on), be based (on); *Am.* to build a farmhouse or country house.
fineza [fi·né·sa] *f.* fineness; nicety; courtesy; favor, kindness; present.
fingimiento [fiŋ·xi·mjén·to] *m.* pretense, sham.
fingir[11] [fiŋ·xír] *v.* to feign, pretend, fake; to imagine.
finiquito [fi·ni·kí·to] *m.* settlement (*of an account*); quittance, final receipt; **dar** — to finish up.
fino [fí·no] *adj.* fine; nice; delicate; sharp; subtle; refined.
finura [fi·nú·ra] *f.* fineness; nicety; subtlety; courtesy, good manners.
fiordo [fjór·ḍo] *m.* fjord.
firma [fír·ma] *f.* signature; firm, firm name.
firmamento [fir·ma·mén·to] *m.* firmament, sky.
firmante [fir·mán·te] *m. & f.* signer.
firmar [fir·már] *v.* to sign.
firme [fír·me] *adj.* firm; solid, hard; **de** — without stopping, hard, steadily.
firmeza [fir·mé·sa] *f.* firmness.
fiscal [fis·kál] *m.* public prosecutor, district attorney; *adj.* fiscal.
fisgar[7] [fiz·gár] *v.* to pry; to snoop; to spy on.
fisgón [fiz·gón] *m.* snoop, snooper; *adj.* snooping; curious.

fisgonear [fiz·go·ne·ár] *v.* to pry about; to snoop.
física [fí·si·ka] *f.* physics.
físico [fí·si·ko] *adj.* physical; *Am.* vain, prudish, affected; *Am.* real; *m.* physicist.
fisiología [fi·sjo·lo·xía] *f.* physiology.
fisiológico [fi·sjo·ló·xi·ko] *adj.* physiological.
fisionomía [fi·sjo·no·mí·a] *f.* face, features.
flaco [flá·ko] *adj.* lean, skinny; frail, weak; **su lado** — his weak side, his weakness.
flacura [fla·kú·ra] *f.* thinness.
flama [flá·ma] *f.* flame.
flamante [fla·mán·te] *adj.* bright, shiny; brand-new.
flameante [fla·me·án·te] *adj.* flaming, flashing.
flamear [fla·me·ár] *v.* to flame; to flap, flutter (*in the wind*).
flamenco [fla·méŋ·ko] *adj.* Flemish; *C.A., P.R.* skinny; *m.* Flemish, Flemish language; flamingo; Andalusian dance.
flan [flan] *m.* custard.
flanco [fláŋ·ko] *m.* flank, side.
flanquear [flaŋ·ke·ár] *v.* to flank.
flaps [fla(p)s] *m. pl.* flaps (*of an airplane*).
flaquear [fla·ke·ár] *v.* to weaken, flag.
flaqueza [fla·ké·sa] *f.* thinness, leanness; weakness, frailty.
flauta [fláw·ta] *f.* flute; **flautista** [flaw·tís·ta] *m. & f.* flute player.
fleco [flé·ko] *m.* fringe; bangs, fringe of hair.
flecha [flé·ča] *f.* arrow, dart.
flechar [fle·čár] *v.* to dart, shoot (*an arrow*); to strike, wound or kill with an arrow; to cast an amorous or ardent glance; *Ven.* to prick, sting; *Am.* to burn (*said of the sun*).
flechazo [fle·čá·so] *m.* arrow shot; wound from an arrow.
flema [flé·ma] *f.* phlegm.
fletamento [fle·ta·mén·to] *m.* charter, charter party (*of a ship*).
fletar [fle·tár] *v.* to charter (*a ship*); to freight; *Ch.* to hire (*pack animals*); *Peru* to let loose (*strong words*); *Am.* to scatter (*false rumors*); **-se** *Col., Mex., Carib., Ch.* to run away, slip away; *Am.* to slip in uninvited; *Am.* **salir fletado** to leave on the run.
flete [flé·te] *m.* freight, freightage; cargo; load; *Am.* fine horse, race horse; *Am.* bother, nuisance; *Col., Ven.* **salir sin -s** to leave in a hurry.
flexibilidad [flek·si·βi·li·đáđ] *f.* flexibility; **flexible** [flek·sí·βle] *adj.* flexible.
flexión [flek·sjón] *f.* bending, bend; sag.
flojear [flo·xe·ár] *v.* to slacken; to weaken; to idle, to be lazy.
flojedad [flo·xe·đáđ] *f.* laxity, looseness; slackness; laziness; slack.
flojera [flo·xé·ra] = **flojedad.**
flojo [fló·xo] *adj.* (*mal atado*) lax; loose, slack; (*sin fuerza*) lazy; weak.
flor [flor] *f.* flower, blossom; compliment; — **de la edad** prime; — **de lis** iris (*flower*); — **y nata** the best, the cream, the chosen few; **a** — **de** flush with; **echar -es** to throw a bouquet; to compliment, flatter.
floreado [flo·re·á·đo] *p.p. & adj.* flowered; made of the finest wheat.
florear [flo·re·ár] *v.* to decorate with flowers; to brandish, flourish; to make a flourish on the guitar; to flatter, compliment; to bolt, sift out (*the finest flour*); *Am.* to flower, bloom; *Am.* to choose the best; **-se** *C.A.* to shine, excel; *Am.* to burst open like a flower.

florecer[13] [flo·re·sér] *v. irr.* to flower, bloom; to flourish, thrive.
floreciente [flo·re·sjén·te] *adj.* flourishing, thriving; prosperous.
florecimiento [flo·re·si·mjén·to] *m.* flourishing, flowering, bloom.
floreo [flo·ré·o] *m.* flourish; idle talk; flattery, compliment.
florería [flo·re·rí·a] *f.* florist's shop.
florero [flo·ré·ro] *m.* florist; flower vase; flatterer; *adj.* flattering.
floresta [flo·rés·ta] *f.* wooded place, grove; arbor.
florete [flo·ré·te] *m.* fencing foil.
florido [flo·rí·đo] *adj.* flowery.
flota [fló·ta] *f.* fleet; *Col.,* **echar -s** to brag, boast.
flotador [flo·ta·đór] *m.* floater; float; pontoon (*of a hydroplane*); *adj.* floating.
flotante [flo·tán·te] *adj.* floating; *m. Col., Ven.* bluffer, braggart.
flotar [flo·tár] *v.* to float.
flote [fló·te]: **a** — afloat.
fluctuación [fluk·twa·sjón] *f.* fluctuation; wavering, hesitation.
fluctuar[18] [fluk·twár] *v.* to fluctuate; to waver; to hesitate.
fluente [flwén·te] *adj.* fluent, flowing.
fluidez [flwi·đés] *f.* fluidity, easy flow, fluency.
fluido [flú·i·đo] *adj.* fluid, flowing, fluent; *m.* fluid.
fluir[32] [flwir] *v. irr.* to flow.
flujo [flú·xo] *m.* flux; flow; flood tide.
flúor [flú·or] *m.* fluorin.
fluorescente [flwo·re·sén·te] *adj.* fluorescent.
flux [flus] *f.* flush (*in cards*); *P.R., Col., Ven.* suit of clothes; **hacer** — to use up one's funds, lose everything; *Am.* **tener uno** — to be lucky.
foca [fó·ka] *f.* seal, sea lion.
foco [fó·ko] *m.* focus, center; *Am.* electric-light bulb.
fofo [fó·fo] *adj.* spongy, porous; light (*in weight*); soft.
fogata [fo·gá·ta] *f.* fire, blaze, bonfire.
fogón [fo·gón] *m.* hearth, fireplace; grill (*for cooking*); vent of a gun; *C.A., Mex.* fire, bonfire; **fogonazo** [fo·go·ná·so] *m.* flash (*of gunpowder*).
fogoso [fo·gó·so] *adj.* fiery, ardent; lively, spirited.
follaje [fo·yá·xe] *m.* foliage.
folletín [fo·ye·tín] *m.* small pamphlet; serial story.
folleto [fo·yé·to] *m.* pamphlet.
fomentar [fo·men·tár] *v.* to foment, encourage, promote, foster.
fomento [fo·mén·to] *m.* promotion, encouragement; development; aid.
fonda [fón·da] *f.* inn; restaurant.
fondear [fon·de·ár] *v.* to cast anchor; to sound, make soundings; to search (*a ship*); to sound out; **-se** *Cuba* to save up for the future.
fondero [fon·dé·ro] *m. Am.* innkeeper.
fondillos [fon·di·yos] *m. pl.* seat of trousers.
fondista [fon·dís·ta] *m. & f.* innkeeper.
fondo [fón·do] *m.* (*hondura*) bottom; depth; background; back, rear end; (*esencia*) mature, heart, inner self; fund; *Cuba, Ven.* underskirt; **-s funds;** **a** — thoroughly; **echar a** — to sink.
fonducho [fon·dú·čo] *m.* cheap eating place.
fonema [fo·né·ma] *m.* phoneme.
fonética [fo·né·ti·ka] *f.* phonetics, study of pronunciation.
fonógrafo [fo·nó·gra·fo] *m.* phonograph.
fonología [fo·no·lo·xí·a] *f.* phonology.
forajido [fo·ra·xí·đo] *m.* outlaw, fugitive; highwayman, bandit.

foráneo [fo·rá·ne·o] *adj.* foreign; *m.* outsider, stranger.

forastero [fo·ras·té·ro] *m.* stranger; foreigner; outsider; *adj.* foreign.

forcejear [for·se·xe·ár], **forcejar** [for·se·xar] *v.* to struggle; to strive; to oppose, resist.

forja [fór·xa] *f.* forge; forging; blacksmith's shop.

forjador [for·xa·dór] *m.* forger (*of metals*); smith, blacksmith; inventor (*of lies, stories, tricks, etc.*).

forjar [for·xár] *v.* to forge; to form, shape; to invent, feign, fake.

forma [fór·ma] *f.* form, shape, figure; manner; format (*size and shape of a book*); host (*unleavened bread for communion*).

formación [for·ma·sjón] *f.* formation.

formal [for·mál] *adj.* formal; serious, trustworthy, punctual; reliable.

formalidad [for·ma·li·dád] *f.* formality; seriousness, reliability; gravity, dignity; punctuality; red tape.

formalismo [for·ma·líz·mo] *m.* formality, red tape (*excess of formalities*); **formalista** [for·ma·lís·ta] *adj.* fond of excessive formalities, fond of red tape.

formalizar[9] [for·ma·li·sár] *v.* to give proper form to; to legalize; to make official; **-se** to settle down, become serious.

formar [for·már] *v.* to form; to shape, mold; **-se** to get into line; to be molded, educated; to take form.

fórmico [fór·mi·ko] *adj.* formic.

formidable [for·mi·dá·ble] *adj.* formidable; fearful.

formón [for·món] *m.* wide chisel.

fórmula [fór·mu·la] *f.* formula.

formular [for·mu·lár] *v.* to formulate, word.

fornido [for·ní·do] *adj.* stout, strong, sturdy.

foro [fó·ro] *m.* stage; back, rear (*of a stage*); forum, court; bar (*profession of law*).

forraje [fo·rrá·xe] *m.* forage, green grass, fodder, feed.

forrajear [fo·rra·xe·ár] *v.* to forage, gather forage.

forrar [fo·rrár] *v.* to line; to cover, put a sheath, case, or covering on; **-se** *Riopl., C.A.* to eat well; *Am.* to supply oneself with provisions; *Riopl., Mex., Cuba* to save money.

forro [fó·rro] *m.* lining; sheathing, casing; covering; book cover.

fortalecer[13] [for·ta·le·sér] *v. irr.* to fortify; to strengthen.

fortaleza [for·ta·lé·sa] *f.* fortress; fortitude; strength, vigor; *Ch.* stench, stink.

fortificación [for·ti·fi·ka·sjón] *f.* fortification; fort.

fortificar[6] [for·ti·fi·kár] *v.* to fortify.

fortuito [for·twí·to] *adj.* fortuitous, accidental, unexpected.

fortuna [for·tú·na] *f.* fortune; fate, chance; wealth; **por —** fortunately.

forzar[9] [for·sár] *v. irr.* to force; to compel; to take (*a fort*); to rape; **— la entrada en** to break into.

forzoso [for·só·so] *adj.* compulsory; necessary.

fosa [fó·sa] *f.* grave; cavity.

fosco [fós·ko] *adj.* dark; cross, irritable, frowning; *see* **hosco.**

fosfato [fos·fá·to] *m.* phosphate.

fosforecer[13] [fos·fo·re·sér], **fosforescer** [fos·fo·re·sér] *v.* to glow.

fósforo [fós·fo·ro] *m.* phosphorus; match.

fósil [fó·sil] *adj. & m.* fossil.

foso [fó·so] *m.* hole, pit; stage pit; ditch.

foto [fó·to] *f.* snapshot.

fotoeléctrico [fo·to·e·lék·tri·ko] *adj.* photoelectric.

fotograbado [fo·to·gra·bá·do] *m.* photoengraving.

fotografía [fo·to·gra·fí·a] *f.* photograph; photography.

fotografiar[17] [fo·to·gra·fjár] *v.* to photograph.

fotógrafo [fo·tó·gra·fo] *m.* photographer.

fotosíntesis [fo·to·sín·te·sis] *f.* photosynthesis.

fracasado [fra·ka·sá·do] *adj.* failed; *m.* failure.

fracasar [fra·ka·sár] *v.* to fail; to come to ruin; to crumble to pieces.

fracaso [fra·ká·so] *m.* failure, ruin; calamity; crash.

fracción [frak·sjón] *f.* fraction.

fractura [frak·tú·ra] *f.* fracture; break, crack.

fracturar [frak·tu·rár] *v.* to fracture, break.

fragancia [fra·gán·sja] *f.* fragrance, scent, perfume.

fragante [fra·gán·te] *adj.* fragrant; **en —** in the act.

fragata [fra·gá·ta] *f.* frigate.

frágil [frá·xil] *adj.* fragile, breakable; frail, weak.

fragmento [frag·mén·to] *m.* fragment.

fragor [fra·gór] *m.* clang, din; crash.

fragoroso [fra·go·ró·so] *adj.* deafening, thunderous.

fragoso [fra·gó·so] *adj.* rugged, craggy, rough, uneven; noisy.

fragua [frá·gwa] *f.* forge; blacksmith's shop.

fraguar [fra·gwár] *v.* to forge; to scheme, hatch (*a plot*).

fraile [fráj·le] *m.* friar; priest; **frailuco** [fraj·lú·ko] *m.* little old friar.

frambuesa [fram·bwé·sa] *f.* raspberry; **frambueso** [fram·bwé·so] *m.* raspberry bush.

francés [fran·sés] *adj.* French; *m.* Frenchman; French language.

franco [fráŋ·ko] *adj.* (*sincero*) frank, open, candid, sincere; (*exento*) free; *m.* franc; **francote** [fraŋ·kó·te] *adj.* very frank, blunt, outspoken.

franela [fra·né·la] *f.* flannel.

franja [fráŋ·xa] *f.* fringe, border; stripe; braid.

franquear [fraŋ·ke·ár] *v.* to exempt; to free; to frank (*a letter*); to dispatch, send; to make grants; **— el paso** to permit the passage (of); **-se** to unbosom oneself, disclose one's innermost thoughts and feelings.

franqueo [fraŋ·ké·o] *m.* postage; franking (*of a letter*); freeing (*of slaves or prisoners*).

franqueza [fraŋ·ké·sa] *f.* frankness; freedom.

franquicia [fraŋ·kí·sja] *f.* franchise, grant, privilege; freedom or exemption (*from fees*).

frasco [frás·ko] *m.* flask, vial, small bottle.

frase [frá·se] *f.* phrase; sentence.

fraternal [fra·ter·nál] *adj.* fraternal, brotherly.

fraternidad [fra·ter·ni·dád] *f.* fraternity; brotherhood.

fraude [fráw·de] *m.* fraud.

fraudulento [fraw·du·lén·to] *adj.* fraudulent, tricky, deceitful, dishonest.

fray [fraj] *m.* (*contr. of* **fraile** [fráj·le], *used before Christian name*) friar.

frazada [fra·sá·da] *f.* blanket.

frecuencia [fre·kwén·sja] *f.* frequency; **con —** frequently.

frecuentar [fre·kwen·tár] *v.* to frequent.

frecuente [fre·kwén·te] *adj.* frequent.

fregadero [fre·ga·dé·ro] *m.* sink.

fregado [fre·gá·do] *m.* scrub, scrubbing; *p.p. of* **fregar;** *adj. Ch., Andes* bothersome, annoying; *Col.* stubborn; *Mex., C.A.* brazen.

fregar[7] [fre·gár] *v. irr.* to scour; to scrub; to rub; to wash (*dishes*); *Am.* to molest, annoy.

fregona [fre·gó·na] *f.* scrub woman; dishwasher, kitchen maid.

freír[15] [fre·ír] *v. irr.* to fry; to tease, bother.

frenar [fre·nár] *v.* to apply the brakes; to restrain.

frenesí [fre·ne·sí] *m.* frenzy, madness.
frenético [fre·né·ti·ko] *adj.* frantic; furious; in a frenzy.
freno [fré·no] *m.* bridle; brake; control; bit (*for horses*).
frente [frén·te] *f.* forehead; countenance; *m.* front; **en — de** in front of; **— a** in front of, facing; **hacer —** to face.
fresa [fré·sa] *f.* strawberry.
fresca [frés·ka] *f.* fresh air; fresh remark.
fresco [frés·ko] *adj.* (*bastante frío*) fresh; cool, (*sereno*) calm, serene; (*descarado*) forward, bold; *m.* coolness; cool air; fresco (*painting*); *C.A., Col.* refreshment; **al —** in the open air; **pintura al —** painting in fresco.
frescor [fres·kór] *m.* freshness, coolness.
frescura [fres·kú·ra] *f.* (*temperatura baja*) freshness; coolness; (*serenidad*) calm; freedom; ease; (*insolencia*) boldness, impudence; impudent remark.
fresno [fréz·no] *m.* ash, ash tree.
fresquecillo [fres·ke·sí·yo] *adj.* nice and cool; *m.* cool air, fresh breeze; **fresquecito** [fres·ke·sí·to], **fresquito** [fres·kí·to] *adj.* nice and cool.
frialdad [frjal·dád] *f.* coldness; coolness, indifference.
fricativo [fri·ka·tí·ƀo] *adj.* fricative.
fricción [frik·sjón] *f.* friction, rub, rubbing.
friccionar [frik·sjo·nár] *v.* to rub; to massage.
friega [frjé·ǥa] *f.* rub, rubbing; *Am.* bother, nuisance, irritation; *Am.* flogging, beating.
frigorífico [fri·ǥo·rí·fi·ko] *adj.* freezing; *m. Spain* refrigerator, icebox; *Ríopl.* meatpacking house.
frijol [fri·xól] *m.* bean; kidney bean, navy bean.
frío [frí·o] *adj.* cold; frigid; cool, indifferent; *m.* cold; **-s** *Mex.* chills and fever; *Col., C.A., Ven.* malaria.
friolento [frjo·lén·to] *adj.* cold-blooded, sensitive to cold; chilly.
friolera [frjo·lé·ra] *f.* trifle.
fritada [fri·tá·ḏa] *f.* dish of fried food.
frito [fri·to] *p.p. irr. of* **freír** fried; *m.* fry, dish of fried food.
fritura [fri·tú·ra] *f.* fry, dish of fried food; fritter.
frivolidad [fri·ƀo·li·ḏáḏ] *f.* frivolity; **frívolo** [fri·ƀo·lo] *adj.* frivolous.
fronda [frón·da] *f.* leaf; fern leaf; foliage.
frondoso [fron·dó·so] *adj.* leafy.
frontera [fron·té·ra] *f.* frontier, border; **fronterizo** [fron·te·rí·so] *adj.* frontier (*used as an adj.*); opposite, facing.
frontero [fron·té·ro] *adj.* facing, opposite.
frontis [frón·tis] *m.* façade, front (*of a building*).
frontispicio [fron·tis·pí·sjo] *m.* front, façade (*front of a building*); title page.
frontón [fron·tón] *m.* main wall of a handball court; handball court; jai alai court; game of *pelota*.
frotación [fro·ta·sjón] *f.* friction, rubbing.
frotar [fro·tár] *v.* to rub; to scour.
frote [fró·te] *m.* rubbing; friction.
fructificar[6] [fruk·ti·fi·kár] *v.* to fruit, bear or produce fruit; to yield profit.
fructuoso [fruk·twó·so] *adj.* fruitful.
frugal [fru·ǥál] *adj.* frugal, economical, saving, thrifty; **frugalidad** [fru·ǥa·li·ḏáḏ] *f.* frugality, thrift.
fruncir[10] [frun·sír] *v.* to wrinkle; to gather in pleats; to contract, shrivel; **— las cejas** to frown; to knit the eyebrows; **— los labios** to purse or curl the lips.

fruslería [fruz·le·rí·a] *f.* trifle, trinket.
frustración [frus·tra·sjón] *f.* frustration; failure.
frustrar [frus·trár] *v.* to frustrate, thwart, foil; **-se** to fail, be thwarted.
fruta [frú·ta] *f.* fruit (*not a vegetable*); **frutería** [fru·te·rí·a] *f.* fruit store.
frutero [fru·té·ro] *m.* fruit vendor; fruit dish; *adj.* fruit (*used as adj.*); **buque —** fruit boat; **plato —** fruit dish.
fruto [frú·to] *m.* fruit (*any organic product of the earth*); result; benefit, profit.
¡fuche! [fú·če] *interj. Mex.* phew! ugh! pew! phooey!
fuego [fwé·ǥo] *m.* (*incendio*) fire; (*pasión*) passion; (*erupción*) skin eruption; *Am.* cold sore; **-s artificiales** fireworks; **hacer —** to fire, shoot; **estar hecho un —** to be very angry; **romper —** to begin to fire, start shooting.
fuelle [fwé·ye] *m.* (*instrumento*) bellows; (*arruga*) pucker, wrinkle, fold; (*hablador*) tattletale, windbag, gossiper.
fuente [fwén·te] *f.* fountain; source, origin; spring; platter, serving dish.
fuera [fwé·ra] *adv.* outside, out; **— de** *prep.* outside of; in addition to.
fuereño [fwe·ré·ño] *m. Mex., Ven., Andes* outsider, stranger.
fuero [fwé·ro] *m.* law, statute; power, jurisdiction; code of laws; exemption, privilege.
fuerte [fwér·te] *adj.* (*robusto*) strong; loud; secure, fortified; (*grave*) grave, serious; (*áspero*) excessive; *Ch.* stinking; *m.* fort; forte, strong point; forte (*music*); *Mex.* alcohol, liquor; *adv.* strongly; excessively; loud; hard.
fuerza [fwér·sa] *f.* force; power, strength; violence, compulsion; **a —** de by dint of; **a la —** (**por —**, **por la —**, **de por —**, *Am.* **de —**) by force, forcibly; necessarily; **ser —** to be necessary.
fuete [fwé·te] *m. Col., Cuba, Ríopl., Mex., Ven., Andes* whip; **fuetazo** [fwe·tá·so] *m. Am.* lash.
fuga [fú·ǥa] *f.* flight, escape; leak, leakage; fugue (*musical composition*).
fugarse[7] [fu·ǥár·se] *v.* to flee, escape.
fugaz [fu·ǥás] *adj.* fleeing; fleeting, brief, passing.
fugitivo [fu·xi·tí·ƀo] *adj.* fugitive; fleeting, passing; perishable; *m.* fugitive.
fulano [fu·lá·no] *m.* so-and-so (*referring to person*).
fulgor [ful·ǥór] *m.* radiance, brilliance.
fulgurar [ful·ǥu·rár] *v.* to gleam, flash, shine.
fulminar [ful·mi·nár] *v.* to thunder, thunder forth; to utter (*threats*).
fulo [fú·lo] *m. Pan.* blond.
fullero [fu·yé·ro] *m.* cardsharp; crooked gambler; cheat.
fumada [fu·má·ḏa] *f.* puff, whiff (*of smoke*).
fumadero [fu·ma·ḏé·ro] *m.* smoking room.
fumador [fu·ma·ḏór] *m.* smoker, habitual smoker.
fumar [fu·már] *v.* to smoke (*tobacco*); *Am.* **-se a uno** to swindle or cheat someone.
fumigar[7] [fu·mi·ǥár] *v.* to fumigate.
función [fun·sjón] *f.* (*actividad*) function; functioning; (*empleo*) office; occupation; (*espectáculo*) show, performance; religious festival.
funcionamiento [fun·sjo·na·mjén·to] *m.* functioning, action, working, operation.
funcionar [fun·sjo·nár] *v.* to function; to work, run (*said of machines*).
funcionario [fun·sjo·ná·rjo] *m.* public employee, officer or official.
funda [fún·da] *f.* cover, case; *Col.* skirt; **— de**

FO

almohada pillowcase.
fundación [fun·da·sjón] *f.* foundation.
fundador [fun·da·dór] *m.* founder.
fundamental [fun·da·men·tál] *adj.* fundamental.
fundamento [fun·da·mén·to] *m.* foundation, groundwork; basis; *Col.* skirt.
fundar [fun·dár] *v.* to found, establish; to erect; to base, ground.
fundición [fun·di·sjón] *f.* foundry; smelting.
fundir [fun·dír] *v.* to smelt, fuse, melt; to cast, mold; *Am.* to ruin; **-se** to fuse, melt together; to unite; *Ríopl., Mex.* to be ruined.
fundo [fún·do] *m.* farm, country estate; property, land.
fúnebre [fú·ne·bre] *adj.* funeral; funereal, gloomy, dismal.
funeral [fu·ne·rál] *adj. & m.* funeral.
funeraria [fu·ne·rá·rja] *f.* undertaking establishment, funeral parlor.
funesto [fu·nés·to] *adj.* ill-fated, unlucky; sad, unfortunate.
fungosidad [fun·go·si·dád] *f.* fungus, fungous growth.
funicular [fu·ni·ku·lár] *adj. & m.* funicular.
furgón [fur·gón] *m.* freight car, boxcar; baggage car; **furgonada** [fur·go·ná·da] *f.* carload.
furia [fú·rja] *f.* fury, rage; speed.
furibundo [fu·ri·bún·do] *adj.* furious.
furioso [fu·rjó·so] *adj.* furious.
furor [fu·rór] *m.* fury, rage, anger; frenzy.
furtivo [fur·tí·bo] *adj.* furtive, sly, secret.
fuselaje [fu·se·lá·xe] *m.* fuselage (*of an airplane*).
fusible [fu·sí·ble] *adj.* fusible; *m.* electric fuse.
fusil [fu·síl] *m.* gun, rifle.
fusilar [fu·si·lár] *v.* to shoot, execute.
fusión [fu·sjón] *f.* fusion; melting; **— nuclear** nuclear fusion.
fustigar[7] [fus·ti·gár] *v.* to lash, whip; to censure severely, scold sharply.
fútbol [fú·bol] *m.* soccer.
fútil [fú·til] *adj.* futile, useless; trivial; **futilidad** [fu·ti·li·dád] *f.* futility, uselessness.
futuro [fu·tú·ro] *adj.* future; *m.* fiancé, future husband; future.

G:g

gabacho [ga·bá·čo] *adj.* from or of the Pyrenees; Frenchlike; *Am.* **me salió —** it turned out wrong; *m.* Frenchman (*used depreciatively*).
gabán [ga·bán] *m.* overcoat.
gabeta [ga·bé·ta] = **gaveta.**
gabinete [ga·bi·né·te] *m.* cabinet (*of a government*); studio; study, library room; dressing room; sitting room; private room; dentist's office; laboratory; *Am.* glassed-in **mirador.**
gaceta [ga·sé·ta] *f.* gazette, official newspaper; professional periodical; *Am.* any newspaper.
gacetilla [ga·se·tí·ya] *f.* short newspaper article; column of short news items; gossip column; *m. & f.* newsmonger, tattletale; **gacetillero** [ga·se·ti·yé·ro] *m.* newspaper reporter; newsmonger.
gacha [ga·ča] *f.* watery mass or mush; *Col.* china or earthenware bowl; **-s** porridge, mush; caresses; **-s de avena** oatmeal.
gacho [gá·čo] *adj.* drooping; bent downward; turned down; stooping; slouching; with horns

curved downward; **sombrero —** slouch hat; **a gachas** on all fours; **con las orejas gachas** with drooping ears; crestfallen, discouraged.
gafas [gá·fas] *f. pl.* spectacles; grappling hooks.
gaita [gáj·ta] *f.* flageolet, a kind of flute; *Am.* good-for-nothing, lazy bum; **— gallega** bagpipe; **sacar la —** to stick out one's neck; **gaitero** [gaj·té·ro] *m.* piper, bagpipe player.
gaje [gá·xe] *m.* fee; **-s** wages, salary; fees.
gajo [gá·xo] *m.* broken branch; bunch.
gala [gá·la] *f.* elegance; full dress or uniform; ostentation; *Am.* award, prize, tip; **-s** finery, regalia, best clothes; **-s de novia** trousseau; **hacer — de** to boast of.
galán [ga·lán] *m.* gallant, lover; leading man (*in a play*).
galante [ga·lán·te] *adj.* gallant, attentive to ladies; polite.
galanteador [ga·lan·te·a·dór] *m.* gallant, lady's man; flatterer.
galantear [ga·lan·te·ár] *v.* to court, woo; to make love.
galanteo [ga·lan·té·o] *m.* wooing, courtship.
galantería [ga·lan·te·rí·a] *f.* gallantry, compliment, attention to ladies; courtesy; gracefulness; generosity.
galardón [ga·lar·dón] *m.* recompense, reward.
galeote [ga·le·ó·te] *m.* galley slave.
galera [ga·lé·ra] *f.* galley; large wagon; women's jail; printer's galley; *Mex.* jail; *Ch., Ríopl.* tall hat.
galerada [ga·le·rá·da] *f.* galley, galley proof; wagon load, van load.
galería [ga·le·rí·a] *f.* gallery; corridor.
galgo [gál·go] *m.* greyhound; *adj. Col.* gluttonous, always hungry.
galicismo [ga·li·síz·mo] *m.* gallicism.
galillo [ga·lí·yo] *m.* uvula.
galio [gá·ljo] *m.* gallium.
galón [ga·lón] *m.* galloon, braid, trimming; gallon.
galoneado [ga·lo·ne·á·do] *adj.* gallooned, trimmed with braid.
galopada [ga·lo·pá·da] *f.* gallop; **pegar una —** to break into a gallop.
galopar [ga·lo·pár] *v.* to gallop.
galope [ga·ló·pe] *m.* gallop; **a (al or de) —** at a gallop; speedily.
galopear [ga·lo·pe·ár] = **galopar.**
galpón [gal·pón] *m. Ríopl., Andes* large open shed.
galvanómetro [gal·ba·nó·me·tro] *m.* galvanometer.
gallardete [ga·yar·dé·te] *m.* streamer.
gallardía [ga·yar·dí·a] *f.* elegance; gracefulness; bravery.
gallardo [ga·yár·do] *adj.* elegant, graceful; brave.
gallego [ga·yé·go] *adj.* Galician, from or of Galicia, Spain; *m.* Galician; *Carib., Ríopl.* Spaniard (*used as a nickname*).
galleta [ga·yé·ta] *f.* cracker; hardtack, hard biscuit; hard cookie; blow, slap; small pot; *Ríopl.* bread of coarse meal or bran; *Ch.* reproof; *Am.* **colgarle la — a uno** to fire, dismiss someone; *Am.* **tener —** to have strength, muscle.
gallina [ga·yí·na] *f.* hen; *m. & f.* chickenhearted person.
gallinero [ga·yi·né·ro] *m.* chicken coop, house, or yard; flock of chickens; basket for carrying chickens; poultryman; noisy gathering; top gallery of a theater.
gallo [gá·yo] *m.* cock, rooster; aggressive, bossy person; cork float; false note (*in singing*); frog (*in one's throat*); *Am.* secondhand clothing; *Am.*

fire wagon; *Mex., Riopl.* serenade.
gamba [gám·ba] *f. Spain* large shrimp.
gamo [gá·mo] *m.* buck, male deer.
gamonal [ga·mo·nál] *m. Am.* boss; overseer.
gamuza [ga·mú·sa] *f.* chamois, chamois skin (*soft leather made from the skin of sheep, goats, deer, etc.*).
gana [gá·na] *f.* desire, appetite; **de buena (mala)** — willingly (unwillingly); **tener** — (*or* **-s**) to feel like, want to; **no me da la** — I don't want to.
ganadero [ga·na·dé·ro] *m.* cattleman; cattle dealer; *adj.* cattle, pertaining to cattle.
ganado [ga·ná·do] *m.* cattle; herd; livestock; — **mayor** cattle; horses; mules; — **menor** sheep; — **de cerda** swine.
ganador [ga·na·dór] *m.* winner; *adj.* winning.
ganancia [ga·nán·sja] *f.* profit, gain; *Am.* something to boot, something extra.
gananancioso [ga·nan·sjó·so] *adj.* winning; profitable; *m.* winner.
ganar [ga·nár] *v.* to win; to profit, gain; to earn; to get ahead of.
gancho [gán·čo] *m.* hook; hooked staff; *Mex., Cuba, Riopl., Col., C.A.* hairpin; *Am.* bait, lure, trick; **aguja de** — crochet hook; **echar a uno el** — to hook someone; **tener** — to be attractive, alluring.
gandul [gan·dúl] *m.* bum, loafer.
ganga [gáŋ·ga] *f.* bargain; snap, easy job; kind of prairie hen.
gangoso [gáŋ·gó·so] *adj.* twangy, nasal (*voice*).
gangrena [gaŋ·gré·na] *f.* gangrene.
gangrenar [gaŋ·gre·nár] *v.* to gangrene, cause gangrene; **-se** to gangrene.
ganguear [gan·ge·ár] *v.* to talk "through the nose."
ganoso [ga·no·so] *adj.* desirous; *Am.* lively, spirited (*horse*).
ganso [gán·so] *m.* goose, gander; lazy, slovenly person; dunce.
ganzúa [gan·sú·a] *f.* hook; picklock (*tool for picking locks*); *m. & f.* burglar.
garabato [ga·ra·bá·to] *m.* hook; scrawl, scribble; **hacer -s** to scribble, write poorly.
garaje [ga·rá·xe] *m.* garage.
garantía [ga·ran·tí·a] *f.* to guaranty; security; bail, bond.
garantizar[9] [ga·ran·ti·sár] *v.* to guarantee, vouch for.
garañón [ga·ra·ñón] *m.* jackass, male ass; male camel (*for breeding*); *Riopl., Mex., C.A.* stallion.
garapiñar [ga·ra·pi·ñár] *v.* to candy (*almonds, fruits, etc.*).
garbanzo [gar·bán·so] *m.* chickpea.
garbo [gár·bo] *m.* elegance, graceful air, good carriage.
garboso [gar·bó·so] *adj.* graceful; elegant; sprightly.
garduña [gar·dú·ña] *f.* marten.
garfio [gár·fjo] *m.* hook.
garganta [gar·gán·ta] *f.* throat, neck; gorge, ravine; **gargantilla** [gar·gan·tí·ya] *f.* necklace.
gárgara [gár·ga·ra] *f.* gargling; **-s** *Am.* gargle, gargling solution; **hacer -s** to gargle.
gargarear [gar·ga·re·ár] *v. Am.* to gargle.
gargarismo [gar·ga·riz·mo] *m.* gargling; gargle, gargling solution.
gargarizar[9] [gar·ga·ri·sár] *v.* to gargle.
garita [ga·rí·ta] *f.* sentry box; watchman's booth; *Col.* vendor's booth.
garito [ga·rí·to] *m.* gambling house, gambling joint; gambler's winnings.
garra [gá·rra] *f.* claw, paw; hook; *Am.* strength;

Col. leather or cloth remnant; *Am.* skinny person or animal; *Am.* margin of profit in a business deal; **echar la** — to arrest; to grab; *Mex., C.A., Ven., Andes* **hacer -s** to tear to pieces.
garrafa [ga·rrá·fa] *f.* decanter; **garrafón** [ga·rra·fón] *m.* large decanter; demijohn.
garrapata [ga·rra·pá·ta] *f.* tick (*an insect*).
garrapatear [ga·rra·pa·te·ár] *v.* to scribble, scrawl, write poorly.
garrocha [ga·rró·ča] *f.* pole; iron-pointed staff; **salto de** — pole vault; *Am.* goad (*for goading oxen*).
garrote [ga·rró·te] *m.* club, cudgel, heavy stick; *Mex., Ur.* brake; **dar** — to strangle; *Am.* to brake, set the brakes; **garrotazo** [ga·rro·tá·so] *m.* blow with a club; huge stick.
garrotero [ga·rro·té·ro] *m. Mex., Ven.* brakeman; *Am.* beater (*one who beats with a club*); *adj. Am.* stingy.
garrucha [ga·rrú·ča] *f.* pulley.
garúa [ga·rú·a] *f. C.A., Riopl., Ven., Andes* drizzle.
garza [gar·sa] *f.* heron; egret.
garzo [gár·so] *adj.* blue, bluish; blue-eyed.
gas [gas] *m.* gas, vapor; *Col., Riopl., Ven.* gasoline; — **lacrimógeno** tear gas.
gasa [gá·sa] *f.* gauze.
gaseosa [ga·se·ó·sa] *f.* soda water; soda pop.
gaseoso [ga·se·ó·so] *adj.* gaseous.
gasolina [ga·so·lí·na] *f.* gasoline.
gastador [gas·ta·dór] *adj.* lavish, extravagant, wasteful; *m.* spendthrift, lavish spender.
gastar [gas·tár] *v.* to spend; to wear; to use; to waste; **-se** to wear out; to get old.
gasto [gás·to] *m.* expense, expenditure; wear.
gatas [gá·tas] **a** — on all fours; **andar a** — to creep, crawl; **salir a** — to crawl out of a difficulty.
gateado [ga·te·á·do] *adj.* catlike; veined, streaked; *m. Am.* light-colored horse with black streaks.
gatear [ga·te·ár] *v.* to creep, crawl; to walk on all fours; to claw, scratch; to steal.
gatillo [ga·tí·yo] *m.* kitten; trigger; forceps (*for extracting teeth*); petty thief.
gato [gá·to] *m.* cat; moneybag; jack (*for lifting weights*); sneak thief; sly fellow; *Am.* trigger; *Am.* outdoor market; *Am.* hot-water bottle; *Am.* a gaucho song and tap dance (*by extension*, the dancer); *Am.* blunder.
gatuperio [ga·tu·pé·rjo] *m.* fraud, intrigue.
gauchada [gaw·čá·da] *f. Riopl.* gaucho deed or exploit.
gauchaje [gaw·čá·xe] *m. Riopl.* band of Gauchos, Gaucho folk.
gauchesco [gaw·čés·ko] *adj. Am.* relating to Gauchos.
gaucho [gáw·čo] *m. Am.* Gaucho, Argentine and Uruguayan cowboy; *Riopl., Ven.* good horseman; *adj. Am.* relating to Gauchos, Gaucho-like; *Am.* sly, crafty.
gaveta [ga·bé·ta] *f.* drawer.
gavilla [ga·bí·ya] *f.* sheaf; gang, band (*of rogues, thieves, etc.*).
gaviota [ga·bjó·ta] *f.* sea gull.
gaza [gá·sa] *f.* loop; *Carib.* noose of a lasso.
gazmoñería [gaz·mo·ñe·rí·a] *f.* prudery, affected modesty; **gazmoño** [gaz·mó·ño] *adj.* prudish, affected, coy.
gaznate [gaz·ná·te] *m.* windpipe; a kind of fritter; *Andes* a sweetmeat made a pineapple or coconut.
gazpacho [gas·pá·čo] *m. Spain* cold vegetable soup.

FU

gelatina [xe·la·tí·na] *f.* gelatin; jelly.
gema [xé·ma] *f.* gem, jewel; bud.
gemelo [xe·mé·lo] *m.* twin; **-s** twins; binoculars, opera glasses, field glasses; cuff links.
gemido [xe·mí·do] *m.* moan; wail, cry.
gemir [xe·mír] *v. irr.* to moan; to wail, cry.
gendarme [xen·dár·me] *m. Mex., Ven., Riopl., C.A.* policeman.
genealogía [xe·ne·a·lo·xí·a] *f.* genealogy.
generación [xe·ne·ra·sjón] *f.* generation.
generador [xe·ne·ra·dór] *m.* generator; — **molecular** atom smasher.
general [xe·ne·rál] *adj. & m.* general; **por lo** — generally.
generalidad [xe·ne·ra·li·dád] *f.* generality; majority.
generalizar[9] [xe·ne·ra·li·sár] *v.* to generalize; **-se** to spread, become general.
genérico [xe·né·ri·ko] *adj.* generic.
género [xé·ne·ro] *m. (clase)* kind, sort, class; gender; *(tela)* goods, material, cloth; — **humano** human race.
generosidad [xe·ne·ro·si·dád] *f.* generosity.
generoso [xe·ne·ró·so] *adj.* generous; best *(wine).*
genial [xe·njál] *adj.* genial, jovial, pleasant.
genio [xé·njo] *m.* genius; temperament, disposition; spirit.
gente [xén·te] *f. (personas)* people; crowd; *(pueblo)* race, nation; clan; *Am.* — **bien** upper-class or important person; *Am.* **ser** — to be a somebody; to be cultured; to be socially important.
gentil [xen·tíl] *adj.* graceful; genteel; courteous; gentile; *m.* pagan; gentile.
gentileza [xen·ti·lé·sa] *f.* grace, courtesy; nobility; gavor.
gentilicio [xen·ti·lí·sjo] *adj.* national; *m.* name used to identify national or local origin.
gentío [xen·tí·o] *m.* crowd, throng.
gentuza [xen·tú·sa] *f.* rabble.
genuino [xe·nwí·no] *adj.* genuine.
geofísica [xe·o·fí·si·ka] *f.* geophysics.
geografía [xe·o·gra·fí·a] *f.* geography; **geográfico** [xe·o·grá·fi·ko] *adj.* geographical.
geología [xe·o·lo·xí·a] *f.* geology; **geológico** [xe·o·ló·xi·ko] *adj.* geological.
geometría [xe·o·me·trí·a] *f.* geometry; **geométrico** [xe·o·mé·tri·ko] *adj.* geometric.
geranio [xe·rá·njo] *m.* geranium.
gerencia [xe·rén·sja] *f.* management, administration.
gerente [xe·rén·te] *m.* manager.
germen [xér·men] *m.* germ; origin, source.
germinar [xer·mi·nár] *v.* to germinate.
gerundio [xe·rún·djo] *m.* gerund; present participle.
gesticular [xes·ti·ku·lár] *v.* to gesticulate.
gestión [xes·tjón] *f.* action, step, maneuver; intervention; **-es** negotiations.
gestionar [xes·tjo·nár] *v.* to manage; to take steps; to negotiate or carry out *(a deal, transaction, etc.).*
gesto [xés·to] *m.* face, expression; grimace; gesture; **estar de buen** *(or* **mal)** — to be in a good *(or* bad) humor; **hacer -s a** to make faces at.
giba [xí·ba] *f.* hump, hunch.
gigante [xi·gán·te] *adj.* gigantic; *m.* giant.
gigantesco [xi·gan·tés·ko] *adj.* gigantic.
gimnasia [xim·ná·sja] *f.* gymnastics; **gimnasio** [xim·ná·sjo] *m.* gymnasium; German institute *(for secondary instruction).*
gimotear [xi·mo·te·ár] *v.* to whimper, whine.
gimoteo [xi·mo·té·o] *m.* whimper, whining.
ginebra [xi·né·bra] *f.* gin *(liquor).*
ginecología [xi·ne·ko·lo·xí·a] *f.* gynecology.

gira [xí·ra] *f.* excursion, tour; outing, picnic.
girador [xi·ra·dór] *m.* drawer *(of a check or draft).*
girar [xi·rár] *v.* to revolve, rotate, whirl; to send, issue, or draw *(checks, drafts, etc.);* to manage *(a business).*
girasol [xi·ra·sól] *m.* sunflower.
giratorio [xi·ra·tó·rjo] *adj.* rotary, revolving.
giro [xí·ro] *m. (movimiento circular)* rotation; bend, turn; *(dirección)* direction, trend; *(estructura)* turn of phrase; *(monetario)* draft; — **postal** money order; *adj.* yellowish *(rooster); Am.* black and white *(rooster); Am.* cocky.
gitano [xi·tá·no] *adj.* gypsy; gypsylike; sly, clever; *m.* gypsy.
gitomate [xi·to·má·te] *Am.* = **jitomate.**
glacial [gla·sjál] *adj.* glacial, icy, very cold.
glaciar [gla·sjár] *m.* glacier.
glándula [glán·du·la] *f.* gland.
glasear [gla·se·ár] *v.* to glaze *(paper, fruits, etc.),* make glossy.
glaucoma [glaw·kó·ma] *m.* glaucoma.
globo [gló·bo] *m.* globe, sphere; world; balloon.
glóbulo [gló·bu·lo] *m.* globule; corpuscle.
gloria [gló·rja] *f.* glory; gloria *(song of praise to God).*
gloriarse[17] [glo·rjár·se] *v.* to glory (in), delight (in), be proud (of); to boast (of).
glorieta [glo·rjé·ta] *f.* arbor, bower; secluded nook in a park *(with benches).*
glorificar[6] [glo·ri·fi·kár] *v.* to glorify; **-se** to glory (in), take great pride (in).
glorioso [glo·rjó·so] *adj.* glorious.
glosa [gló·sa] *f.* gloss.
glosar [glo·sár] *v.* to gloss, comment upon, explain *(a text).*
glosario [glo·sá·rjo] *m.* glossary.
glotal [glo·tál] *adj.* glottal.
glotis [gló·tis] *f.* glottis.
glotón [glo·tón] *adj.* gluttonous; *m.* glutton.
glotonería [glo·to·ne·rí·a] *f.* gluttony.
gobernador [go·ber·na·dór] *adj.* governing; *m.* governor, ruler.
gobernante [go·ber·nán·te] *adj.* governing, ruling; *m.* governor, ruler.
gobernar[1] [go·ber·nár] *v. irr.* to govern, rule; to lead, direct; to steer *(a boat).*
gobierno [go·bjér·no] *m.* government; management; control; helm, rudder.
goce [gó·se] *m.* enjoyment; joy.
goleta [go·lé·ta] *f.* schooner, sailing vessel.
golfo [gól·fo] *m.* gulf; open sea; faro *(gambling game);* vagabond, bum, ragamuffin.
golondrina [go·lon·drí·na] *f.* swallow; swallow fish.
golosina [go·lo·sí·na] *f.* sweet, dainty, tidbit; trifle; appetite, desire.
goloso [go·ló·so] *adj.* sweet-toothed, fond of sweets; gluttonous.
golpazo [gol·pá·so] *m.* bang, whack, heavy blow, hard knock.
golpe [gól·pe] *m.* blow, hit, stroke; knock; beat; *Col.* facing *(of a garment); Am.* sledge hammer; — **de fortuna** stroke of good luck; — **de gente** crowd, throng; — **de gracia** death blow; finishing stroke; **de** — suddenly; **de un** — all at once; **pestillo de** — spring latch; *Am.* **al** — instantly, at once; *Am.* **al** — **de vista** at one glance.
golpear [gol·pe·ár] *v.* to strike, hit; to knock; to beat; *Am.* to knock at a door.
golpetear [gol·pe·te·ár] *v.* to tap, knock or pound continuously; to flap; to rattle.
golpeteo [gol·pe·té·o] *m.* tapping, pounding,

knocking; flapping; rattling.

gollería [go·ye·rí·a] *f.* dainty, delicacy; superfluous thing.

goma [gó·ma] *f.* gum; rubber; elastic; eraser; tire; — **de repuesto** spare tire; *Am.* **estar de** — to have a hang-over (*after excessive drinking*).

gomero [go·mé·ro] *adj.* rubber, pertaining to rubber; *m. Riopl.* gum or rubber tree; *Am.* rubber producer; *Am.* rubber-plantation worker; *Ven.* glue container or bottle.

gomífero [go·mí·fe·ro] *adj.* rubber-bearing, rubber-producing.

gomoso [go·mó·so] *adj.* gummy, sticky; *m.* dandy.

gordiflón [gor·di·flón] *adj.* fat; chubby.

gordo [gór·do] *adj.* fat; plump; *m.* suet, fat; **gorda** [gór·da] *f. Mex.* thick tortilla or cornmeal cake; **se armó la gorda** all hell broke loose; there was a big rumpus.

gordura [gor·dú·ra] *f.* fatness; stoutness; fat.

gorgojo [gor·gó·xo] *m.* weevil; puny person; *Am.* wood borer, wood louse; **gorgojoso** *adj.* infested with weevils.

gorila [go·rí·la] *m.* gorilla.

gorjeador [gor·xe·a·dór] *m.* warbler; *adj.* warbling; **pájaro** — warbler.

gorjear [gor·xe·ár] *v.* to warble; to chirp.

gorjeo [gor·xé·o] *m.* warble; warbling.

gorra [gó·rra] *f.* cap; bonnet; **de** — at another's expense; **vivir de** — to sponge, live at another's expense.

gorrino [go·rrí·no] *m.* sucking pig.

gorrión [go·rrjón] *m.* sparrow.

gorro [gó·rro] *m.* cap; bonnet.

gorrón [go·rrón] *m.* sponge, parasite; bum; rake (*dissolute fellow*).

gota [gó·ta] *f.* (*líquido*) drop; (*enfermedad*) gout; **sudar la** — **gorda** to sweat profusely, toil, work hard.

gotear [go·te·ár] *v.* to drip; to leak; to dribble, **gotear** [go·te·ár] *v.* to drip; to leak; to dribble, trickle; to sprinkle, begin to rain; **-se** to leak.

goteo [go·té·o] *m.* trickle, drip.

gotera [go·té·ra] *f.* leak, hole (*in the roof*); eaves, trough; **-s** *Mex.* surroundings, outskirts.

gotero [go·té·ro] *m. Carib., Mex.* dropper (*for counting drops*).   •

gótico [gó·ti·ko] *adj.* Gothic; *m.* Goth; Gothic language.

gozar[9] [go·sár] *v.* to enjoy; to possess, have; **-se** to rejoice.

gozne [góz·ne] *m.* hinge.

gozo [go·so] *m.* pleasure, joy.

gozoso [go·só·so] *adj.* joyful, glad, merry.

gozque [gós·ke] **gozquejo,** [gos·ké·xo] **gozquecillo** [gos·ke·sí·yo] *m.* a small dog.

grabación [gra·ba·sjón] *f.* recording (*tape*).

grabado [gra·bá·do] *adj.* engraved; recorded; *m.* engraving; woodcut, print; — **al agua fuerte** etching.

grabadora [gra·ba·dó·ra] *f.* tape recorder; *Spain* **grabadora magnetofónica.**

grabar [gra·bár] *v.* to engrave; to carve; to fix, impress; to record on tape; — **al agua fuerte** to etch.

gracejada [gra·se·xá·da] *f. C.A.* clownish act or expression.

gracejo [gra·sé·xo] *m.* grace; cuteness; humor, wit.

gracia [grá·sja] *f.* (*humorismo*) witty remark; joke; humor; (*garbo*) grace; gracious act; (*favor*) favor; pardon; **caer en** — to please; **hacer** — to amuse, make (*someone*) laugh; **¡-s!** thanks!; **dar -s to**

thank.

gracioso [gra·sjó·so] *adj.* (*chistoso*) amusing; funny; witty; (*con garbo*) graceful, attractive; *m.* comedian, clown.

grada [grá·da] *f.* step of a staircase; harrow; **-s** steps; seats of an amphitheater; bleachers.

gradación [gra·da·sjón] *f.* gradation.

gradería [gra·de·rí·a] *f.* series of steps; rows of seats (*in an amphitheater or stadium*); — **cubierta** grandstand; **-s** bleachers.

grado [grá·do] *m.* (*medida*) degree; step; (*título*) degree; **de** (**buen**) — willingly, with pleasure; **de mal** — unwillingly; **de** — **en** — by degrees, gradually.

graduación [gra·dwa·sjón] *f.* graduation; military rank.

gradual [gra·dwál] *adj.* gradual; *m.* response sung at mass.

graduar[18] [gra·dwár] *v.* to graduate, give a diploma, rank or degree to; to gauge; to classify, grade; **-se** to graduate, take a degree.

gráfico [grá·fi·ko] *adj.* graphic; vivid, lifelike; **gráfica** *f.* graph, diagram, chart.

grafito [gra·fi·to] *m.* graphite.

grajo [grá·xo] *m.* rook; crow.

grama [grá·ma] *f.* grama grass.

gramática [gra·má·ti·ka] *f.* grammar; **gramatical** [gra·ma·ti·kál] *adj.* grammatical; **gramático** [gra·má·ti·ko] *adj.* grammatical; *m.* grammarian.

gramo [grá·mo] *m.* gram.

gran [gran] *contr. of* **grande.**

grana [grá·na] *f.* cochineal, kermes (*insects used for producing a red dye*); scarlet color; scarlet cloth; any small seed.

granada [gra·ná·da] *f.* pomegranate; grenade, shell, small bomb; — **de mano** hand grenade.

granado [gra·ná·do] *m.* pomegranate tree; *adj.* notable; illustrious; select.

grande [grán·de] *adj.* large, big; great, grand; *Mex., C.A., Ven.,* Andes **mamá** (**papá**) — grandmother (grandfather); *m.* grandee (*Spanish or Portuguese nobleman*); **en** — on a large scale.

grandeza [gran·dé·sa] *f.* greatness; grandeur, splendor; bigness; size; grandeeship; body of grandees.

grandiosidad [gran·djo·si·dád] *f.* grandeur, grandness; greatness; **grandioso** [gran·djó·so] *adj.* grandiose, great, grand, magnificent.

granero [gra·né·ro] *m.* granary; grain bin; country or region rich in grain.

granito [gra·ní·to] *m.* granite; small grain; small pimple.

granizada [gra·ni·sá·da] *f.* hailstorm; shower, volley.

granizar[9] [gra·ni·sár] *v.* to hail.

granizo [gra·ní·so] *m.* hail; hailstorm; web or film in the eye; *adj. Mex.* spotted (*horse*).

granja [gráŋ·xa] *f.* grange, farm; country house.

granjear [graŋ·xe·ár] *v.* to earn, gain; to acquire, obtain; *Ch., C.A.* to steal; **-se** to win for oneself (*favor, goodwill, esteem, etc.*).

granjería [graŋ·xe·rí·a] *f.* farming; business profit.

granjero [graŋ·xé·ro] *m.* farmer.

grano [grá·no] *m.* (*cereal*) grain; seed; grain (*unit of measure*); **ir al** — to come to the point.

granuja [gra·nú·xa] *f.* ragamuffin, urchin; scamp.

granular [gra·nu·lár] *v.* to granulate; **-se** to become granulated; to break out with pimples.

grapa [grá·pa] *f.* clamp; staple; (*carbunclo*) pimple.

grasa [grá·sa] *f.* grease; fat; tallow; *Mex., Riopl., Ven.* shoe polish; *Am.* **dar** — to polish (*shoes*).

GE

grasiento [gra·sjén·to] *adj.* greasy, oily.
grasoso [gra·só·so] *adj.* greasy, oily.
gratificación [gra·ti·fi·ka·sjón] *f.* gratuity, bonus, tip; recompense, reward.
gratis [grá·tis] *adv.* gratis, for nothing, free of charge.
gratitud [gra·ti·túḍ] *f.* gratitude.
grato [grá·to] *adj.* pleasing, pleasant; gratuitous; **su grata** your favor, your letter.
gratuito [gra·twí·to] *adj.* gratuitous, free, free of charge.
grava [grá·ḅa] *f.* gravel.
gravamen [gra·ḅá·men] *m.* burden; mortgage.
grave [grá·ḅe] *adj.* grave; serious; weighty, heavy; grievous; deep, low (*in pitch*).
gravedad [gra·ḅe·dáḍ] *f.* (*fuerza*) gravity; (*seriedad*) seriousness, gravity; (*tono*) depth (*of a sound*).
gravoso [gra·ḅó·so] *adj.* burdensome; **serle a uno —** to be burdensome; to weigh on one's conscience.
graznar [graz·nár] *v.* to caw, croak, squawk, cackle, quack.
graznido [graz·ní·ḍo] *m.* caw, croak, squawk, cackle, quack.
greca [gré·ka] *f.* fret; ornamental design.
greda [gré·ḍa] *f.* clay, chalk; chalk cleaner.
gremial [gre·mjál] *adj.* pertaining to a labor union; *m.* member of a union.
gremio [gré·mjo] *m.* guild, society, brotherhood, trade union; fold (*referring to the Church*).
greña [gré·ña] *f.* shock of hair, tangled mop of hair (*usually* **greñas**); **greñudo** [gre·ñú·ḍo] *adj.* shaggy, with long, unkempt hair.
grey [grej] *f.* flock; congregation (*of a church*).
griego [grjé·ǥo] *adj.* Greek, Grecian; *m.* Greek.
grieta [grjé· ta] *f.* crevice; crack; fissure.
grifo [grí·fo] *m.* faucet; *Andes* cheap tavern (*where* **chicha** *is sold*); *Peru* gas station; *Am.* colored person; *Col.* drug addict; *Am.* drunkard; *adj.* curly, kinky, woolly (*hair*); *Col.* vain, conceited; **letra grifa** script; **ponerse —** to bristle, stand on end (*said of hair*).
grillo [grí·yo] *m.* cricket; sprout, shoot; **-s** fetters; obstacle, hindrance.
grima [grí·ma] *f.* uneasiness; displeasure, disgust; *Riopl., Carib.* sadness, compassion, pity; *Am.* bit, small particle; **dar —** to disgust; to make uneasy; *Am.* to make sad, inspire pity.
gringo [griŋ·go] *adj. Ch. Riopl.* (*Italian*) foreign (*not Spanish*); *m. Ch., Riopl.* (*Italian*) foreigner (*not Spanish*); *Mex., C.A., Andes, Col., Ven.* Yankee or English-speaking person.
gripe [grí·pe] *f.* grippe, flu, influenza.
gris [gris] *adj.* grey; **grisáceo** *adj.* greyish.
grita [grí·ta] *f.* shouting, hooting; clamor, uproar.
gritar [gri·tár] *v.* to shout, cry.
gritería [gri·te·rí·a] *f.* shouting, clamor, uproar.
grito [grí·to] *m.* shout, cry; **poner el — en el cielo** to complain loudly, "hit the ceiling".
grosella [gro·sé·ya] *f.* currant; **— blanca** gooseberry; **grosellero** [gro·se·yé·ro] *m.* currant bush.
grosería [gro·se·rí·a] *f.* rudeness; coarseness; crudeness; insult.
grosero [gro·sé·ro] *adj.* rough, coarse; rude, impolite.
grosor [gro·sór] *m.* thickness.
grotesco [gro·tés·ko] *adj.* grotesque, fantastic; absurd.
grúa [grú·a] *f.* crane, derrick.
gruesa [grwé·sa] *f.* gross, twelve dozen.
grueso [grwé·so] *adj.* (*voluminoso*) fat, stout; thick; bulky, big, heavy; (*burdo*) dense; coarse; *m.* thickness; bulk; density; main part; **en —** in gross, in bulk, by wholesale.
grulla [grú·ya] *f.* crane (*bird*).
gruñido [gru·ñí·ḍo] *m.* growl, grumble; grunt.
gruñir [gru·ñír] *v. irr.* to grunt; to growl; to snarl; to grumble.
gruñón [gru·ñón] *adj.* growling; grunting; grumbly; *m.* growler; grumbler.
grupa [grú·pa] *f.* rump; **volver -s** to turn around (*usually on horseback*).
grupo [grú·po] *m.* group; set.
gruta [grú·ta] *f.* grotto, cavern.
guacal [gwa·kál] *m. Col., Mex., C.A.* crate (*for transporting fruit, vegetables, etc., carried on the back*). *Also* **huacal.**
guacamayo [gwa·ka·má·yo] *m. Am.* macaw (*large parrot*); *Am.* flashily dressed person.
guacamole [gwa·ka·mó·le] *m. Mex., C.A., Cuba* avocado salad; also **guacamol.**
guacho [gwá·čo] *m.* birdling, chick; young animal; *Andes, Riopl.* orphan; *Andes, Riopl.* foundling, abandoned child; *adj. Am.* odd, not paired; *Andes, Riopl.* forlorn, alone, abandoned.
guadal [gwa·dál] *m. Am.* small dune, sand hill; *Ven.* quagmire, bog, swamp; *Am.* growth of bamboo grass.
guadaña [gwa·dá·ña] *f.* scythe.
guagua [gwá·ǥwa] *f. Carib., Ven.* bus; trifle, insignificant thing; *m. & f. Andes, Ch., Riopl.* baby; **de —** for nothing, gratis, free.
guaje [gwá·xe] *m. Am.* a species of gourd; *Am.* vessel or bowl made of a gourd; *Am.* simpleton, fool; *Am.* trifle, trinket, piece of junk; *adj. Am.* foolish; *Am.* **hacerse uno —** to play the fool; *Am.* **hacer a uno —** to fool, deceive someone.
guajiro [gwa·xí·ro] *m.* Indian of the Guajira peninsula (*in Venezuela and Colombia*); *Cuba* rustic, peasant.
guajolote [gwa·xo·ló·te] *m. Mex.* turkey; *Mex.* fool.
guanaco [gwa·ná·ko] *m. Andes, Ch., Riopl.* guanaco (*a kind of llama*); *Am.* tall, lanky, gawky person; *Am.* fool, simpleton; nickname for Salvadoreans.
guanajo [gwa·ná·xo] *m. Am.* turkey; *Am.* fool, dunce.
guano [gwá·no] *m. Carib.* palm tree; *Carib.* palm leaves (*used for thatching*); *Am.* guano, bird dung, fertilizer.
guantada [gwan·tá·ḍa] *f.* wallop, blow, slap.
guante [gwán·te] *m.* glove; *Andes* whip, scourge; **echar el — a uno** to seize or grab a person; **guantelete** [gwan·te·lé·te] *m.* gauntlet.
guapo [gwá·po] *adj.* handsome, good-looking; ostentatious, showy; daring, brave; *Ch., Andes* harsh, severe; *Carib., Mex.* angry; *m.* brawler, quarreler, bully.
guarache [gwa·rá·če] *m. Mex.* Mexican leather sandal; *Mex.* tire patch. *Also* **huarache** [wa·rá·če].
guaraní [gwa·ra·ní] *adj.* pertaining to the Guarani Indians of Paraguay; *m. & f.* Guarani Indian.
guarapo [gwa·rá·po] *m. Col., C.A., Andes* juice of the sugar cane; *Col., C.A., Andes* sugar-cane liquor; *Col., C.A., Andes* low-grade brandy.
guarda [gwár·ḍa] *m. & f.* guard; keeper; *Riopl.* ticket collector on a streetcar; *f.* custody, care, keeping; observance of a law; **-s** outside ribs of a fan; flyleaves.
guardabarros [gwar·ḍa·ḅa·rros], **guardafango** [gwar·ḍa·fáŋ·go] *m.* fender.
guardabosques [gwar·ḍa·ḅós·kes] *m.* forest ranger,

forester, forest keeper.
guardabrisa [gwar·ḍa·ḅrí·sa] *f.* windshield.
guardacostas [gwar·ḍa·kós·tas] *m.* coast guard.
guardafrenos [gwar·ḍa·fré·nos] *m.* brakeman.
guardagujas [gwar·ḍa·ǵú·xas] *m.* switchman.
guardamonte [gwar·ḍa·món·te] *m.* trigger guard;
forest keeper.
guardapapeles [gwar·ḍa·pa·pé·les] *m.* file, filing
cabinet or box.
guardapelo [gwar·ḍa·pé·lo] *m.* locket.
guardar [gwar·ḍár] *v.* to guard, watch over; to
keep; to store; to observe (*laws, customs*); **-se de**
to guard against, keep from, avoid.
guardarropa [gwar·ḍa·rró·pa] *m.* wardrobe;
cloakroom; keeper of a cloakroom.
guardia [gwár·/ja] *f.* guard, body of guards;
defense, protection; *m.* guard, guardsman.
guardiamarina [gwar·ḍja·ma·rí·na] *f.* midshipman.
guardián *m.* guardian, keeper; superior of a
Franciscan monastery.
guarecer[13] [gwa·re·sér] *v. irr.* to protect, shelter;
-se to take shelter.
guarida [gwa·rí·da] *f.* den, cave, lair.
guarismo [gwa·ríz·mo] *m.* number.
guarnecer[13] [gwar·ne·sér] *v. irr.* to garnish,
decorate; to adorn; to trim; to harness; to
garrison; to set (*jewels*).
guarnición [gwar·ni·sjón] *f.* adornment; trimming;
setting of a jewel; guard of a sword; garrison;
-es trappings, harness.
guaro [gwá·ro] *m. C.A.* rum.
guasa [gwá·sa] *f.* joking; foolishness.
guasca [gwás·ka] *f. Andes, Ch., Riopl.* leather
thong; *Andes, Ch., Riopl.* rope, cord; *Andes, Ch.*
whip; *Andes, Ch., Riopl.* **dar** — to whip, beat,
thrash.
guaso [gwá·so] *m. Am.* stag, male deer; *Ch., Andes,
Ríopl.* peasant; *Cuba* half-breed; *Am.* lasso; *adj.*
rustic, peasant-like.
guasón [gwa·són] *adj.* funny, comical; *m.* joker,
jester.
guata [gwá·ta] *f. Am.* padding; *Ven.* fib; *Col.* a
species of potato; *Ch., Andes* paunch, belly; *Am.*
echar — to get fat.
guatemalteco [gwa·te·mal·té·ko] *m. & adj.*
Guatemalan.
guayaba [gwa·yá·ḅa] *f.* guava (*pear-shaped tropical
fruit*); **guayabo** *m.* guava tree; *Am.* lie, fraud, trick.
guayabera [gwa·ya·ḅé·ra] *f.* tropical pleated jacket.
gubernativo [gu·ḅer·na·tí·ḅo] *adj.* governmental,
administrative.
guedeja [ge·ḍé·xa] *f.* forelock; lock of hair; lion's
mane.
güero [gwé·ro] *adj. Mex.* blond; *m. Ven.* cassava
liquor. *See* **huero.**
guerra [gé·rra] *f.* war; — **a muerte** war to the
finish; **dar** — to bother, trouble.
guerrear [ge·rre·ár] *v.* to war; *Am.* to do mischief
or to bother (*said of children*).
guerrero [ge·rré·ro] *adj.* warlike, martial; *m.* warrior,
soldier.
guerrilla [ge·rrí·ya] *f.* small war; skirmish; body of
soldiers; band of fighters.
guerrillero [ge·rri·yé·ro] *m.* guerrilla fighter.
guía [gí·a] *m. & f.* guide, leader; *f.* guidebook,
directory; signpost; shoot, sprout; *Ríopl.* garland
of flowers.
guiar[17] [gjar] *v.* to guide; to drive (*a car*).
guija [gi·xa] *f.* pebble; **guijarro** [gi·xá·rro] *m.*
cobblestone.
guijo [gí·xo] *m.* gravel.

guinda [gín·da] *f.* sour cherry.
guindilla [gin·dí·ya] *f. Spain* small hot pepper.
guineo [gi·né·o] *m. C.A.* banana.
guiñada [gi·ñá·ḍa] *f.* wink.
guiñapo [gi·ñá·po] *m.* tag, tatter, rag; ragamuffin,
ragged person.
guiñar [gi·ñár] *v.* to wink.
guiño [gí·ño] *m.* wink.
guión [gjón] *m.* hyphen; repeat sign (*in music*); cross
(*carried before a prelate in a procession*); guide,
leader (*among birds and animals*); leader in a
dance.
guirnalda [gir·nál·da] *f.* garland, wreath.
guisa [gí·sa] *f.* way, manner; **a — de** like, in the
manner of.
guisado [gi·sá·ḍo] *m.* stew.
guisante [gi·sán·te] *m.* pea; — **de olor** sweet pea.
guisar [gi·sár] *v.* to cook; to prepare, arrange.
guiso [gí·so] *m.* dish, dish of food.
güisquil [gwis·kil] *m. C.A.* chayote (*a pear-shaped
fruit*).
guitarra [gi·tá·rra] *f.* guitar.
gula [gú·la] *f.* gluttony.
gusano [gu·sá·no] *m.* worm; caterpillar; — **de la
conciencia** remorse; — **de luz** glowworm; *Col.,
Mex.* **matar el** — to satisfy a need or desire
(*particularly hunger or thirst*).
gustar [gus·tár] *v.* (*agradar*) to please, be pleasing;
(*saborear*) to taste; to experience; **-le a uno una
cosa** to like something; — **de** to have a liking
for, be fond of.
gusto [gús·to] *m.* (*agrado*) pleasure; whim, fancy;
(*sabor*) taste; flavor; **dar** — to please; **estar a** —
to be comfortable, contented; **tener** — **en** to be
glad to; **tomar el** — **a una cosa** to become fond
of something.
gustoso [gus·tó·so] *adj.* (*con agrado*) glad; pleasant;
willing; merry; (*sabroso*) tasty; *adv.* willingly.

H:h

haba [á·ḅa] *f.* large bean; Lima
bean.
habano [a·ḅá·no] *m.* Havana
cigar.

haber[30] [a·ḅér] *v. irr.* to have (*auxiliary verb*);
habérselas con to have it out with; **ha de llegar
mañana** he is to arrive tomorrow; **ha de ser
verdad** it must be true; **hay** (**había, hubo,** *etc.*)
there is, there are (there was, there were, *etc.*);
hay que (+ *inf.*) it is necessary; **no hay de qué**
you are welcome? **¿qué hay?** what's the matter?
haber [a·ḅér] *m.* credit, credit side (*in book-keeping*);
-es property, goods, cash, assets.
habichuela [a·ḅi·čwé·la] *f.* bean; — **verde** string
bean.
hábil [á·ḅil] *adj.* skilful, capable, able.
habilidad [a·ḅi·li·ḍáḍ] *f.* ability, skill.
habilitar [a·ḅi·li·tár] *v.* to enable; to equip; to
qualify.
habitación [a·ḅi·ta·sjón] *f.* apartment; room;
lodging.
habitante [a·ḅi·tán·te] *m.* inhabitant; resident.
habitar [a·ḅi·tár] *v.* to inhabit; to live, reside.
hábito [á·ḅi·to] *m.* habit; custom.
habitual [a·ḅi·twál] *adj.* habitual, customary.
habituar[18] [a·ḅi·twár] *v.* to accustom; **-se** to get
used, accustomed.
habla [á·ḅla] *f.* speech; language, dialect; **al** —
within speaking distance; in communication

GR

(with).

hablador [a·β̣la·ḍór] *m.* talker; gossip; *adj.* talkative.

habladuría [a·β̣la·ḍu·rí·a] *f.* gossip, rumor; empty talk; impertinent remark.

hablar [a·β̣lár] *v.* to speak; to talk; — **alto** (*or* **en voz alta**) to speak loudly; — **bajo** (**quedo** *or* **en voz baja**) to speak softly; — **por los codos** to chatter constantly.

hablilla [a·β̣li·ya] *f.* gossip, rumor, malicious tale.

hacedero [a·se·ḍé·ro] *adj.* feasible.

hacedor [a·se·ḍór] *m.* maker; **el Supremo Hacedor** the Maker.

hacendado [a·sen·dá·ḍo] *m.* landholder; *Ríopl., Ch., Ven.* owner of a farm, plantation, or ranch.

hacendoso [a·sen·ḍó·so] *adj.* industrious, diligent.

hacer[31] [a·sér] *v. irr.* (*crear*) to do; to make; (*formar*) to form; to accustom; (*causar*) to cause, order (*followed by inf.*); — **caso** to mind, pay attention; — **frío** (**calor**) to be cold (warm); — **la maleta** to pack one's suitcase; — **un papel** to play a part; *Am.* — **aprecio** to pay attention; *Ríopl., Mex.* — **caras** (*or* **caritas**) to flirt; **no le hace** it makes no difference; **-se** to become, grow, get to be; **-se a** to get used to; **-se de rogar** to want to be coaxed.

hacia [á·sja] *prep.* toward; about; — **adelante** forward; — **atrás** backward.

hacienda [a·sjén·da] *f.* estate; property; finance; large farm; *Ríopl.* cattle, livestock.

hacina [á·si·na] *f.* shock (*of grain*), stack, pile.

hacinar [a·si·nár] *v.* to shock (*grain*); to stack, pile up; to accumulate.

hacha [á·ča] *f.* ax; hatchet; torch.

hachero [a·čé·ro] *m.* axman, woodcutter.

hada [á·ḍa] *f.* fairy.

hado [á·ḍo] *m.* fate, fortune, destiny.

halagar[7] [a·la·g̣ár] *v.* to coax; to flatter; to allure, attract.

halago [a·lá·g̣o] *m.* flattery; caress; allurement.

halagüeño [a·la·g̣wé·ño] *adj.* alluring, attractive; flattering; promising.

halar [a·lár] = **jalar**.

halcón [al·kón] *m.* falcon.

hálito [á·li·to] *m.* breath; vapor.

hallar [a·yár] *v.* to find; to discover, find out; **-se** to be; to fare, get along.

hallazgo [a·yáz·g̣o] *m.* find; discovery; reward (*for finding something*).

hamaca [a·má·ka] *f.* hammock.

hambre [ám·bre] *f.* hunger; famine; appetite; **tener** — to be hungry; **hambruna** [am·brú·na] *f. Am.* great hunger, starvation.

hambrear [am·bre·ár] *v.* to starve; to be hungry.

hambriento [am·brjén·to] *adj.* hungry; greedy; *C.A., Mex., Andes* stingy.

hampa [ám·pa] *f. Spain* underworld.

hangar [aŋ·g̣ár] *m.* hangar.

haragán [a·ra·g̣án] *adj.* lazy, indolent; *m.* loafer, idler.

haraganear [a·ra·g̣a·ne·ár] *v.* to lounge, loaf, be lazy.

haraganería [a·ra·g̣a·ne·rí·a] *f.* laziness.

harapiento [a·ra·pjén·to] *adj.* tattered, ragged.

harapo [a·rá·po] *m.* rag, tatter; **andar hecho un** — to be in tatters.

haraposo [a·rá·pó·so] *adj.* tattered, ragged.

harina [a·rí·na] *f.* flour; **eso es — de otro costal** that is something entirely different; **harinoso** [a·ri·nó·so] *adj.* floury; flourlike.

harmonía [ar·mo·ní·a] *f.* harmony.

hartar [ar·tár] *v.* to fill up, gorge; to sate, satiate;

-se to have one's fill; to overeat, eat too much.

harto [ár·to] *adj.* full; sated, satiated; fed up; too much; *adv.* too much; *Mex., C.A., Col., Ven., Ríopl., Andes* much, very much.

hasta [ás·ta] *prep.* till, until; up to; — **luego** good-bye, see you later; *conj.* even; — **que** until.

hastiar[17] [as·tjár] *v.* to surfeit; to cloy; to disgust.

hastío [as·tí·o] *m.* surfeit, excess; boredom; loathing, disgust.

hato [á·to] *m.* herd; flock; sheepfold; shepherd's hut; gang, crowd; pile; *Col., Ven.* cattle ranch.

haya [á·ya] *f.* beech; **hayuco** *m.* beechnut.

haz [as] *f.* face; surface; *m.* fagot, bundle, bunch.

hazaña [a·sá·ña] *f.* deed, exploit, feat.

hazmerreír [az·me·rre·ír] *m.* laughing stock.

he [e] (*used with* **aquí** *or* **allí**) behold, here is, here you have; **heme aquí** here I am; **helo aquí** here it is.

hebilla [e·β̣i·ya] *f.* buckle.

hebra [é·β̣ra] *f.* thread; fiber; fine string; *Am.* **de una** — all at once, at one stroke, *Am.* **ni** — absolutely nothing; **hebroso** *adj.* fibrous, stringy.

hecatombe [e·ka·tóm·be] *m.* massacre, great slaughter; hecatomb (*sacrifice of 100 oxen*).

hectárea [ek·tá·re·a] *m.* hectare.

hechicera [e·či·sé·ra] *f.* witch, enchantress; hag.

hechicería [e·či·se·rí·a] *f.* witchcraft; magic; charm; enchantment.

hechicero [e·či·sé·ro] *adj.* bewitching, charming; *m.* magician; charmer; sorcerer.

hechizar[9] [e·či·sár] *v.* to bewitch; to charm.

hechizo [e·čí·so] *m.* charm; enchantment.

hecho [é·čo] *m.* fact; act, deed; **de** — in fact; *p.p. of* **hacer** done, made.

hechura [e·čú·ra] *f.* make; shape, cut; workmanship.

heder[1] [e·ḍér] *v. irr.* to stink; to reek.

hediondez [e·ḍjon·dés] *f.* stink, stench.

hediondo [e·ḍjón·do] *adj.* foul-smelling, stinking; filthy; *m. Ríopl.* skunk.

hedor [e·ḍór] *m.* stink, stench.

helada [e·lá·ḍa] *f.* frost.

helado [e·lá·ḍo] *adj.* frozen; freezing; frosty; icy; *m.* ice cream; ice, sherbet; **heladería** [e·la·ḍe·rí·a] *f. Am.* ice-cream parlor.

heladora [e·la·ḍó·ra] *f.* freezer.

helar[1] [e·lár] *v. irr.* to freeze.

helecho [e·lé·čo] *m.* fern.

hélice [é·li·se] *f.* screw propeller; helix, spiral.

helicóptero [e·li·kóp·te·ro] *m.* helicopter.

helio [e·ljo] *m.* helium.

helipuerto [e·li·pwér·to] *m.* heliport.

hembra [ém·bra] *f.* female; staple; nut (*of a screw*); **macho y** — hook and eye.

hemisferio [e·mis·fé·rjo] *m.* hemisphere.

hemofilia [e·mo·fí·lja] *f.* hemophilia.

hemoglobina [e·mo·g̣lo·β̣i·na] *f.* hemoglobin.

hemorragia [e·mo·rrá·xja] *f.* hemorrhage.

henchir[5] [en·čír] *v. irr.* to swell, stuff, fill.

hendedura [en·de·ḍú·ra], **hendidura** [en·di·ḍú·ra] *f.* crack, crevice, fissure.

hender[1] [en·dér] *v. irr.* to split, crack, cleave.

henequén [e·ne·kén] *m. Mex., Ven., C.A., Col.* sisal, sisal hemp.

heno [é·no] *m.* hay.

henil [e·níl] *m.* hayloft.

hepatitis [e·pa·tí·tis] *f.* hepatitis.

heráldico [e·rál·di·ko] *adj.* heraldic; **heráldica** heraldry.

heraldo [e·rál·do] *m.* herald.

herbazal [er·β̣a·sál] *m.* field of grass.

herboso [er·b̶ó·so] *adj.* grassy; weedy.
heredad [e·re·d̶á̶d̶] *f.* parcel of land; rural property; estate.
heredar [e·re·d̶ár] *v.* to inherit; to bequeath, leave in a will.
heredero [e·re·d̶é·ro] *m.* heir; successor; **heredera** [e·re·d̶é·ra] *f.* heiress.
hereditario [e·re·d̶i·tá·rjo] *adj.* hereditary.
hereje [e·ré·xe] *m.* heretic; **cara de —** hideous face.
herejía [e·re·xí·a] *f.* heresy; offensive remark.
herencia [e·ren·sja] *f.* inheritance; heritage; heredity.
herida [e·rí·d̶a] *f.* wound; injury.
herido [e·rí·d̶o] *adj.* wounded; *m.* wounded man; *Am.* small drainage channel.
herir[3] [e·rír] *v. irr.* to wound; to hurt; to strike; to offend.
hermana [er·má·na] *f.* sister.
hermanastro [er·ma·nás·tro] *m.* stepbrother, half brother; **hermanastra** [er·ma·nás·tra] *f.* stepsister, half sister.
hermandad [er·man·dá̶d̶] *f.* brotherhood, fraternity.
hermano [er·má·no] *m.* brother.
hermético [er·mé·ti·ko] *adj.* hermetic; airtight; tight-lipped; close-mouthed; **hermetismo** [er·me·tiz·mo] *m.* complete silence.
hermosear [er·mo·se·ár] *v.* to beautify, adorn.
hermoso [er·mó·so] *adj.* beautiful, handsome.
hermosura [er·mo·sú·ra] *f.* beauty.
hernia [ér·nja] *f.* hernia.
héroe [é·ro·é] *m.* hero; **heroína** [e·ro·í·na] *f.* heroine; heroin (*drug*).
heroico [e·rój·ko] *adj.* heroic.
heroísmo [e·ro·íz·mo] *m.* heroism.
herradura [e·rra·d̶ú·ra] *f.* horseshoe.
herraje [e·rrá·xe] *m.* ironwork; iron trimmings; horseshoes and nails; *Am.* silver saddle trimmings; *Am.* horseshoe.
herramienta [e·rra·mjén·ta] *f.* tool; *pl.* set of tools.
herrar[1] [e·rrár] *v. irr.* to shoe (*a horse*); to brand; to trim with iron.
herrería [e·rre·rí·a] *f.* blacksmith's shop or trade; forge; ironworks.
herrero [e·rré·ro] *m.* blacksmith.
herrete [e·rré·te] *m.* metal tip (*for a shoelace, for instance*); *Am.* branding iron.
herrumbre [e·rrúm·bre] *f.* rust; plant rot.
hervidero [er·b̶i·d̶é·ro] *m.* bubbling sound (*of boiling water*); bubbling spring; swarm, crowd; **un — de gente** a swarm of people.
hervir[3] [er·b̶ír] *v. irr.* to boil; **— de gente** to swarm with people.
hervor [er·b̶ór] *m.* boiling; boiling point; **soltar el —** to come to a boil.
heterodoxia [e·te·ro·d̶ók·sja] *f.* heterodoxy.
heterogéneo [e·te·ro·xé·ne·o] *adj.* heterogeneous.
hez [es] *f.* scum; **la — del pueblo** the scum of society; **heces** [é·ses] dregs, sediment.
hiato [já·to] *m.* hiatus.
híbrido [í·b̶ri·d̶o] *adj. & m.* hybrid.
hidalgo [i·d̶al·g̶o] *m.* hidalgo (*Spanish nobleman*); *adj.* noble, courteous.
hidalguía [i·d̶al·g̶í·a] *f.* nobility; generosity; courtesy.
hidrato [i·d̶rá·to] *m.* hydrate.
hidráulico [i·d̶ráw·li·ko] *adj.* hydraulic; **fuerza hidráulica** water power; **ingeniero —** hydraulic engineer.
hidroavión [i·d̶ro·a·b̶jón] *m.* hydroplane, seaplane.
hidroeléctrico [i·d̶ro·e·lék·tri·ko] *adj.* hydroelectric.
hidrógeno [i·d̶ró·xe·no] *m.* hydrogen.

hidropesía [i·d̶ro·pe·sí·a] *f.* dropsy.
hidroplano [i·d̶ro·plá·no] *m.* hydroplane.
hiedra [jé·d̶ra] *f.* ivy.
hiel [jel] *f.* gall, bile; bitterness.
hielo [jé·lo] *m.* ice; frost.
hierba [jér·b̶a] *f.* grass; herb; weed; *Ríopl., Andes* mate (*Paraguayan tea*); *Mex., Ven., Cuba* marihuana (*a narcotic*); *C.A.* **ciertas -s** so-and-so (*person not named*).
hierbabuena [jer·b̶a·b̶wé·na] *f.* mint. *Also* **yerbabuena** [ỳer·b̶a·b̶wé·na].
hierro [jé·rro] *m.* iron; brand; iron tool, instrument, or weapon; **-s** irons, chains, handcuffs.
hígado [í·g̶a·d̶o] *m.* (*órgano*) liver; (*valentía*) courage; valor; **malos -s** ill will.
higiene [i·xjé·ne] *f.* hygiene; **higiénico** [i·xjé·ni·ko] *adj.* hygienic, sanitary.
higo [í·g̶o] *m.* fig; **higuera** [i·g̶é·ra] *f.* fig tree; **higuerilla** [i·g̶e·rí·ya] *f. Am.* castor-oil plant.
hija [í·xa] *f.* daughter; native daughter.
hijo [í·xo] *m.* son; native son; offspring; fruit, result.
hilachas [i·lá·čas] *f. pl.* lint; **mostrar uno la hilacha** to show one's worst side or nature; **hilachos** [i·lá·čos] *m. pl. Am.* rags, tatters.
hilado [i·lá·d̶o] *m.* yarn; *p.p. of* **hilar.**
hilandera [i·lan·dé·ra] *f.* spinner.
hilandería [i·lan·de·rí·a] *f.* spinning mill; art of spinning; spinning.
hilandero [i·lan·dé·ro] *m.* spinner; spinning room.
hilar [i·lár] *v.* to spin, make into thread; **— muy delgado** to be very subtle.
hilas [í·las] *f. pl.* lint, fine ravelings (*for dressing wounds*).
hilaza [i·lá·sa] *f.* coarse thread; yarn.
hilera [i·lé·ra] *f.* file, row, line; **— de perlas** strand or string of pearls. ·
hilo [í·lo] *m.* (*hebra*) thread; fine yarn; string; (*alambre*) filament; thin wire; (*tela*) linen; **a —** without interruption; **al —** along the thread; *Am.* very well, all right; **de —** straight, without stopping; *Am.* **de un —** constantly, without stopping; **tener el alma en un —** to be frightened to death; to be in great anxiety or suspense.
hilván [il·b̶án] *m.* basting stitch; basting; *Am.* hem.
hilvanar [il·b̶a·nár] *v.* to baste; to put together, connect; to do hastily; *Am.* to hem.
himno [ím·no] *m.* hymn.
hincapié [iŋ·ka·pjé] **: hacer —** to emphasize, stress; to insist (upon).
hincar[6] [iŋ·kár] *v.* to drive, thrust (into); **-se** (*or* **-se de rodillas**) to kneel down.
hinchado [in·čá·d̶o] *adj. & p.p.* swollen; inflated; presumptuous.
hinchar [in·čár] *v.* to swell; **-se** to swell; to swell up, puff up.
hinchazón [in·ča·són] *f.* swelling; inflation; conceit; bombast, inflated style.
hinojos [i·nó·xos] **: de —** on one's knees.
hipérbole [i·pér·b̶o·le] *f.* hyperbole.
hiperbólico [i·per·b̶ó·li·ko] *adj.* hyperbolic.
hipo [í·po] *m.* hiccough; sob; longing; grudge, ill will.
hipocresía [i·po·kre·sía] *f.* hypocrisy.
hipócrita [i·pó·kri·ta] *adj.* hypocritical, insincere; *m. & f.* hypocrite.
hipódromo [i·pó·d̶ro·mo] *m.* race track.
hipoteca [i·po·té·ka] *f.* mortgage.
hipotecar[6] [i·po·te·kár] *v.* to mortgage.
hipótesis [i·pó·te·sis] *f.* hypothesis, theory.

HA

hipotético [i·po·té·ti·ko] *adj.* hypothetic(al).
hirviente [ir·bjén·te] *adj.* boiling.
hispanidad [is·pa·ni·ḍáḍ] *f.* Hispanic solidarity.
hispanista [is·pa·nís·ta] *m. & f.* Hispanist; one who is interested in Hispanic studies.
hispano [is·pá·no] *adj.* Hispanic, Spanish; *m.* Spanish-speaking person.
hispanoamericano [is·pa:no·a·me·ri·ká·no] *adj.* Spanish-American.
histamina [is·ta·mí·na] *f.* histamine.
histérico [is·té·ri·ko] *adj.* hysterical.
historia [is·tó·rja] *f.* history; story; tale, fable; **dejarse de -s** to stop fooling and come to the point; **historieta** [is·to·rjé·ta] *f.* story, anecdote.
historiador [is·to·rja·ḍór] *m.* historian.
historial [is·to·rjal] *m.* record, data (*concerning a person or firm*); *adj.* historic.
histórico [is·tó·ri·ko] *adj.* historic, historical.
hito [í·to] *adj.* firm, fixed; **de hito en hito** fixedly.
hocico [o·sí·ko] *m.* snout; **caer de -s** to fall on one's face; **meter el — en todo** to meddle, stick one's nose in everything.
hogaño [o·gá·ño] *adv.* nowadays.
hogar [o·gár] *m.* hearth, fireplace; home.
hogareño [o·ga·ré·ño] *adj.* home-loving, domestic; homelike.
hoguera [o·gé·ra] *f.* bonfire.
hoja [ó·xa] *f.* leaf; petal; sheet of paper or metal; blade; **— de lata** tin plate.
hojalata [o·xa·lá·ta] *f.* tin plate.
hojaldre [o·xál·dre] *m. & f.* puff pastry.
hojarasca [o·xa·rás·ka] *f.* fallen leaves; dry foliage; superfluous ornament; trash; useless words.
hojear [o·xe·ár] *v.* to leaf, turn the pages of; to browse.
hojuela [o·xwé·la] *f.* leaflet, small leaf; thin leaf (*of metal*); flake; thin pancake; **— de estaño** tin foil.
¡hola! [ó·la] *interj.* hello!; ho!; ah!
holandés [o·lan·dés] *adj.* Dutch; *m.* Dutchman; Dutch language.
holgado [ol·gá·ḍo] *adj.* (*libre*) free, at leisure; comfortable; (*ancho*) wide, loose; roomy, spacious; *p.p. of* **holgar.**
holganza [ol·gán·sa] *f.* idleness.
holgar [ol·gár] *v. irr.* to rest; to loaf; **-se** to be glad; to relax, have a good time; **huelga decir** needless to say.
holgazán [ol·ga·sán] *m.* idler, loafer; *adj.* lazy, idle.
holgazanear [ol·ga·sa·ne·ár] *v.* to loiter, lounge, idle, bum around.
holgazanería [ol·ga·sa·ne·rí·a] *f.* idleness, laziness.
holgorio [ol·gó·rjo] *m.* spree.
holgura [ol·gú·ra] *f.* (*descanso*) ease; rest, comfort; (*lugar*) roominess, plenty of room.
holocausto [o·lo·káws·to] *m.* holocaust, burnt offering, sacrifice.
hollar [o·yár] *v.* to tread, trample upon.
hollejo [o·yé·xo] *m.* skin, peel; husk.
hollín [o·yín] *m.* soot.
hombrada [om·brá·ḍa] *f.* manly act; show of bravery.
hombre [óm·bre] *m.* man; **hombría** [om·brí·a] *f.* manliness, manly strength; **— de bien** honesty.
hombro [óm·bro] *m.* shoulder; **arrimar** (*or* **meter**) **el —** to help.
hombruno [om·brú·no] *adj.* mannish, masculine.
homenaje [o·me·ná·xe] *m.* homage, honor.
homeópata [o·me·ó·pa·ta] *adj.* homeopathic.
homicida [o·mi·sí·ḍa] *m.* murderer; *f.* murderess; *adj.* homicidal, murderous.
homicidio [o·mi·sí·ḍjo] *m.* homicide, murder.

homófono [o·mó·fo·no] *adj.* homophonous.
homogeneidad [o·mo·xe·nej·ḍáḍ] *f.* homogeneity.
homogéneo [o·mo·xé·ne·o] *adj.* homogeneous, of the same kind or nature.
honda [ón·da] *f.* sling, slingshot.
hondo [ón·do] *adj.* deep; low; *m.* bottom, depth.
hondonada [on·do·ná·ḍa] *f.* hollow, dip, gully, ravine.
hondura [on·dú·ra] *f.* depth; **meterse en -s** to go beyond one's depth; to get into trouble.
honestidad [o·nes·ti·ḍáḍ] *f.* chastity, modesty, decency; decorum, propriety.
honesto [o·nés·to] *adj.* chaste, modest, decent; just; honest.
hongo [óŋ·go] *m.* mushroom; fungus; derby hat.
honor [o·nór] *m.* honor; glory; dignity.
honorario [o·no·rá·rjo] *m.* fee (*for professional services*); *adj.* honorary.
honorífico [o·no·rí·fi·ko] *adj.* honorary; **mención honorífica** honorable mention.
honra [ón·rra] *f.* honor; reputation; **-s** obsequies, funeral rites.
honradez [on·rra·ḍés] *f.* honesty, honor, integrity.
honrado [on·rrá·ḍo] *adj.* honest, honorable; honored.
honrar [on·rrár] *v.* to honor; **-se** to be honored; to consider it an honor.
honroso [on·rró·so] *adj.* honorable; honoring.
hora [ó·ra] *f.* hour; time; **-s** canonical hours, office (*required daily prayers for priests and nuns*); **es — de** it is time to; **no ver la — de** (+ *inf.*) to be anxious to; **¿qué — es?** what time is it?
horadar [o·ra·ḍár] *v.* to pierce, bore, perforate.
horario [o·rá·rjo] *m.* schedule, timetable; hour hand.
horca [ór·ka] *f.* (*cadalso*) gallows; (*horcón*) pitchfork; *P.R.* birthday present; **— de ajos** string of garlic.
horcajadas [or·ka·xá·ḍas]: **a —** astride (*with one leg on each side*); **ponerse a —** to straddle.
horcón [or·kón] *m.* forked pole, forked prop; *Mex., Cuba, Ven.* post, roof support; *Am.* roof.
horda [ór·ḍa] *f.* horde.
horizontal [o·ri·son·tál] *adj.* horizontal.
horizonte [o·ri·són·te] *m.* horizon.
horma [ór·ma] *f.* form, mold; block (*for shaping a hat*); shoe last; shoe tree.
hormiga [or·mí·ga] *f.* ant.
hormigón [or·mi·gón] *m.* concrete.
hormigonera [or·mi·go·né·ra] *f.* concrete mixer.
hormiguear [or·mi·ge·ár] *v.* to swarm; to be crawling with ants; **me hormiguea el cuerpo** I itch all over.
hormigueo [or·mi·ge·o] *m.* itching, creeping sensation; tingle, tingling sensation.
hormiguero [or·mi·gé·ro] *m.* ant hill; ant nest; swarm; **oso —** anteater.
hormona [or·mó·na] *f.* hormone.
hornada [or·ná·ḍa] *f.* batch of bread, baking.
hornear [or·ne·ár] *v.* to bake (*in an oven*).
hornilla [or·ní·ya] *f.* burner; grate (*of a stove*).
hornillo [or·ní·yo] *m.* kitchen stove; hot plate.
horno [or·no] *m.* furnace; oven; kiln (*for baking bricks*); **alto —** blast furnace.
horquilla [or·ki·ya] *f.* hairpin; forked pole; small pitchfork.
horrendo [o·rrén·do] *adj.* horrible, hideous.
horrible [o·rri·ble] *adj.* horrible.
horripilante [o·rri·pi·lán·te] *adj.* horrifying.
horror [o·rrór] *m.* horror; atrocity; **dar —** to cause fright; to horrify; **tenerle — a uno** to feel a

strong dislike for one.

horrorizar[9] [o·rro·ri·sár] *v.* to horrify, shock, terrify.

horroroso [o·rro·ró·so] *adj.* horrid; frightful, hideous.

hortaliza [or·ta·li·sa] *f.* vegetables; vegatable garden.

hortelano [or·te·lá·no] *m.* gardener.

hosco [ós·ko] *adj.* sullen; frowning; dark.

hospedaje [os·pe·ḍá·xe] *m.* board and lodging; lodging.

hospedar [os·pe·ḍár] *v.* to lodge, give lodging; -se to take lodging; to room, to stop (*at a hotel*).

hospedero [os·pe·ḍé·ro] *m.* innkeeper.

hospicio [os·pí·sjo] *m.* asylum; orphanage, orphan asylum; poorhouse; **hospiciano** [os·pi·sjá·no] *m.* inmate of a poorhouse or asylum.

hospital [os·pi·tál] *m.* hospital; — **de primera sangre** first-aid station.

hospitalidad [os·pi·ta·li·ḍáḍ] *f.* hospitality.

hostería [os·te·rí·a] *f.* hostelry, inn.

hostia [ós·tja] *f.* host (*consecrated wafer*).

hostigar[7] [os·ti·gár] *v.* to harass, vex; to beat, lash; *C.A., Col.* to cloy.

hostil [os·tíl] *adj.* hostile; **hostilidad** [os·ti·li·ḍáḍ] *f.* hostility.

hotel [o·tél] *m.* hotel; villa; **hotelero** [o·te·lé·ro] *m.* hotel-keeper; *adj.* pertaining to hotels.

hoy [oj] *adv.* today; — **día** nowadays; **de — en adelante** from now on; — **por** — at present; **de — más** henceforth.

hoya [ó·ya] *f.* pit, hole; grave; valley; *Am.* river basin.

hoyo [ó·yo] *m.* hole; pit; grave; *Ríopl., Carib.* dimple.

hoyuelo [o·ywé·lo] *m.* dimple; tiny hole.

hoz [os] *f.* sickle; narrow ravine.

hozar[9] [o·sár] *v.* to root, turn up the earth with the snout (*as hogs*).

huacal [wa·kál] = **guacal.**

huarache [wa·rá·če] = **guarache.**

huaso [wá·so] = **guaso.**

hueco [wé·ko] *adj.* (*vacío*) hollow, empty; (*vano*) vain, affected; puffed up; high-sounding; *m.* gap, space, hole.

huelga [wél·ga] *f.* labor strike; rest; leisure; **declararse en** — to strike.

huelguista [wel·gís·ta] *m.* striker.

huella [wé·ya] *f.* trace; footprint.

huérfano [wér·fa·no] *adj.* & *m.* orphan.

huero [wé·ro] *adj.* empty; rotten, spoiled (*egg*). *See* **güero.**

huerta [wér·ta] *f.* orchard and vegetable garden; irrigated land.

huerto [wér·to] *m.* small orchard and vegetable garden; garden patch.

hueso [wé·so] *m.* bone; stone, pit; big seed; **la sin** — the tongue; **soltar la sin** — to talk too much; **no dejarle un — sano** to pick him to pieces.

huésped [wés·peḍ] *m.* (*convidado*) guest; (*anfitrión*) host; **ser — en su casa** to be seldom at home.

hueste [wés·te] *f.* host, army, multitude.

huesudo [we·sú·ḍo] *adj.* bony.

huevo [wé·ḅo] *m.* egg; — **duro** hard-boiled egg; — **estrellado** fried egg; — **pasado por agua** soft-boiled egg; -s **revueltos** scrambled eggs; *Mex., C.A., Col., Ven.* -s **tibios** soft-boiled eggs; *Col., Ven.* -s **pericos** scrambled eggs; *Ven., Andes* **costar un** — to be very expensive.

huída [wi·ḍa] *f.* flight; escape.

huir[32] [wir] *v. irr.* to flee, escape; to avoid, shun.

huizache [wi·sá·ce] *m. Mex., C.A.* huisache (*a species of acacia*).

hule [ú·le] *m.* rubber; oilcloth; *Col., Ven.* rubber tree.

hulla [ú·ya] *f.* soft coal.

humanidad [u·ma·ni·ḍáḍ] *f.* humanity, mankind; humaneness; -es humanities, letters.

humanitario [u·ma·ni·tá·rjo] *adj.* humanitarian, humane, kind, charitable.

humano [u·má·no] *adj.* human; humane; *m.* man, human being.

humareda [u·ma·ré·ḍa] *f.* cloud of smoke.

humeante [u·me·án·te] *adj.* smoking, smoky; steaming.

humear [u·me·ár] *v.* to smoke, give off smoke; to steam; *Am.* to fumigate.

humedad [u·me·ḍáḍ] *f.* humidity, moisture, dampness.

humedecer[13] [u·me·ḍe·sér] *v. irr.* to moisten, wet, dampen.

húmedo [ú·me·ḍo] *adj.* humid, moist, wet, damp.

humildad [u·mil·dáḍ] *f.* humility; humbleness; meekness.

humilde [u·míl·de] *adj.* humble, lowly, meek.

humillación [u·mi·ya·sjón] *f.* humiliation; submission.

humillar [u·mi·yár] *v.* to humiliate, humble, lower, crush; -se to humiliate oneself; to bow humbly.

humillos [u·mí·yos] *m. pl.* airs, conceit, vanity.

humo [ú·mo] *m.* smoke, fume, vapor; -s conceit, vanity.

humor [u·mór] *m.* substance; mood, disposition.

humorada [u·mo·rá·ḍa] *f.* pleasantry, witty remark; caprice, notion.

humorismo [u·mo·ríz·mo] *m.* humor, humorous style.

humorístico [u·mo·rís·ti·ko] *adj.* humorous.

humoso [u·mó·so] *adj.* smoky.

hundimiento [un·di·mjén·to] *m.* sinking, collapse, cave-in.

hundir [un·dír] *v.* (*sumir*) to sink, submerge; (*batir*) to crush, oppress; to destroy; -se to sink; to collapse, cave in.

huracán [u·ra·kán] *m.* hurricane.

huraño [u·rá·ño] *adj.* diffident, shy, bashful; unsociable.

¡hurra! [ú·rra] *interj.* hurrah!

hurtadillas [ur·ta·ḍí·yas]: **a** — on the sly, secretly, stealthily.

hurtar [ur·tár] *v.* to steal, rob; -se to withdraw, slip away; to hide; — **el cuerpo** to dodge; to flee.

hurto [úr·to] *m.* robbery, theft; stolen article; **a** — stealthily, on the sly.

husmear [uz·me·ár] *v.* to scent, smell, follow the track of; to nose, pry (into).

husmeo [uz·mé·o] *m.* sniff, sniffing, smelling; prying.

huso [ú·so] *m.* spindle.

I:i **ibérico** [i·ḅé·ri·ko], **ibero** [i·ḅé·ro] *adj.* Iberian; **iberoamericano** [i·ḅe·ro·a·mé·ri·ká·no] *adj.* Ibero-American (*Spanish or Portuguese American*).

iconoclasta [i·ko·no·klás·ta] *m.* & *f.* iconoclast.

ida [í·ḍa] *f.* departure; sally; **billete de — y vuelta** round-trip ticket; -s **y venidas** goings and comings.

idea [i·dé·a] *f.* idea; notion.
ideal [i·de·ál] *m.* & *adj.* ideal.
idealismo [i·de·a·líz·mo] *m.* idealism.
idealista [i·de·a·lís·ta] *adj.* idealistic; *m.* & *f.* idealist; dreamer.
idear [i·de·ár] *v.* to form an idea of; to devise, think out, plan.
idem [í·den] idem (*abbreviation:* id.), ditto, the same.
idéntico [i·dén·ti·ko] *adj.* identical.
identidad [i·den·ti·dád] *f.* identity.
identificar[6] [i·den·ti·fi·kár] *v.* to identify
idilio [i·dí·ljo] *m.* idyl.
idioma [i·dí·ljo] *m.* language, tongue.
idiosincrasia [i·djo·siŋ·krá·sja] *f.* idiosyncrasy.
idiota [i·djó·ta] *m.* & *f.* idiot; *adj.* idiotic, foolish.
idiotez [i·djo·tés] *f.* idiocy.
idiotismo [i·djo·tíz·mo] *m.* idiom; idiocy.
idolatrar [i·do·la·trár] *v.* to idolize, worship.
ídolo [í·do·lo] *m.* idol.
idóneo [i·dó·ne·o] *adj.* fit, suitable; qualified.
iglesia [i·glé·sja] *f.* church.
ignición [ig·ni·sjón] *f.* ignition.
ignominia [ig·no·mi·nja] *f.* infamy, shame, disgrace.
ignominioso [ig·no·mi·njó·so] *adj.* ignominious; infamous, shameful, disgraceful.
ignorancia [ig·no·rán·sja] *f.* ignorance.
ignorante [ig·no·rán·te] *adj.* ignorant.
ignorar [ig·no·rár] *v.* to be ignorant of, not to know.
ignoto [ig·nó·to] *adj.* unknown, undiscovered.
igual [i·gwál] *adj.* (*semejante*) equal; (*liso*) even, smooth; uniform; (*siempre*) constant; **serle — a uno** to be all the same to one, make no difference to one; *m.* equal; **al — equally.**
igualar [i·gwa·lár] *v.* to equal; to equalize; to match; to level, smooth; to adjust; to be equal.
igualdad [i·gwal·dád] *f.* equality.
igualitario [i·gwa·li·tá·rjo] *adj.* equalitarian (*promoting the doctrine of equality*).
iguana [i·gwá·na] *f.* iguana.
ijada [i·xá·da] *f.* loin; flank (*of an animal*); pain in the side; **ijar** *m.* flank (*of an animal*).
ilegal [i·le·gál] *adj.* illegal, unlawful.
ilegítimo [i·le·xí·ti·mo] *adj.* illegitimate; illegal.
ileso [i·lé·so] *adj.* unharmed, uninjured, unhurt, safe and sound.
ilícito [i·lí·si·to] *adj.* illicit, unlawful.
ilimitado [i·li·mi·tá·do] *adj.* unlimited.
iluminación [i·lu·mi·na·sjón] *f.* illumination.
iluminar [i·lu·mi·nár] *v.* to illuminate; to light; to enlighten.
ilusión [i·lu·sjón] *f.* illusion.
ilusivo [i·lu·sí·bo] *adj.* illusive.
iluso [i·lú·so] *adj.* deluded; *m.* visionary, dreamer.
ilusorio [i·lu·só·rjo] *adj.* illusive; deceptive; worthless.
ilustración [i·lus·tra·sjón] *f.* illustration; elucidation, explanation.
ilustrado [i·lus·trá·do] *adj.* learned; enlightened.
ilustrador [i·lus·tra·dór] *m.* illustrator.
ilustrar [i·lus·trár] *v.* to illustrate.
ilustre [i·lús·tre] *adj.* illustrious, distinguished.
imagen [i·má·xen] *f.* image.
imaginable [i·ma·xi·ná·ble] *adj.* imaginable, conceivable.
imaginación [i·ma·xi·na·sjón] *f.* imagination.
imaginar [i·ma·xi·nár] *v.* to imagine.
imaginario [i·ma·xi·ná·rjo] *adj.* imaginary.
imaginativo [i·ma·xi·na·tí·bo] *adj.* imaginative; **imaginativa** [i·ma·xi·na·tí·ba] *f.* imagination.

imán [i·mán] *m.* magnet; attraction.
imantar [i·man·tár] *v.* to magnetize.
imbécil [im·bé·sil] *adj.* imbecile, stupid.
imborrable [im·bo·rrá·ble] *adj.* indelible, not erasable; unforgettable.
imbuir[32] [im·bwír] *v. irr.* to imbue; to instill, infuse, inspire (with).
imitación [i·mi·ta·sjón] *f.* imitation.
imitador [i·mi·ta·dor] *m.* imitator; follower; *adj.* imitative, imitating.
imitar [i·mi·tár] *v.* to imitate.
impaciencia [im·pa·sjén·sja] *f.* impatience.
impaciente [im·pa·sjén·te] *adj.* impatient.
impar [im·pár] *adj.* odd; **número — odd number.**
imparcial [im·par·sjál] *adj.* impartial; **imparcialidad** [im·par·sja·li·dád] *f.* impartiality, fairness, justice.
impasible [im·pa·sí·ble] *adj.* impassive, insensitive, insensible, unfeeling, unmoved.
impávido [im·pá·bi·do] *adj.* fearless; calm; *Am.* impudent, brazen.
impedimento [im·pe·di·mén·to] *m.* impediment, hindrance, obstacle.
impedir[5] [im·pe·dír] *v. irr.* to impede, prevent, hinder.
impeler [im·pe·lér] *v.* to impel, push; to incite, spur.
impenetrable [im·pe·ne·trá·ble] *adj.* impenetrable; impervious; incomprehensible.
impensado [im·pen·sá·do] *adj.* unforeseen, unexpected; offhand, done without thinking; **impensadamente** [im·pen·sa·da·mén·te] *adv.* offhand, without thinking; unexpectedly.
imperar [im·pe·rár] *v.* to rule, command, dominate.
imperativo [im·pe·ra·tí·bo] *adj.* imperative; urgent, compelling; *m.* imperative mood.
imperceptible [im·per·sep·tí·ble] *adj.* imperceptible.
imperdible [im·per·dí·ble] *m.* safety pin; *adj.* safe, that cannot be lost.
imperecedero [im·pe·re·se·dé·ro] *adj.* imperishable, enduring, everlasting.
imperfecto [im·per·fék·to] *adj.* imperfect; *m.* imperfect tense.
imperial [im·pe·rjál] *adj.* imperial; *f.* coach top; top seats on a coach or bus.
impericia [im·pe·rí·sja] *f.* inexperience.
imperio [im·pé·rjo] *m.* empire; command, rule; sway, influence.
imperioso [im·pe·rjó·so] *adj.* imperious, arrogant, domineering; urgent.
impermeable [im·per·me·á·ble] *adj.* waterproof, impervious, rainproof; *m.* raincoat.
impersonal [im·per·so·nál] *adj.* impersonal.
impertinencia [im·per·ti·nén·sja] *f.* impertinence; impudence; insolent remark or act; **decir -s to** talk nonsense; to make insolent remarks.
impertinente [im·per·ti·nén·te] *adj.* impertinent, impudent; meddlesome; irrelevant, not to the point; **-s** *m. pl.* lorgnette (*eyeglasses mounted on a handle*).
ímpetu [ím·pe·tu] *m.* impetus; violent force; impulse; *C.A., Ríopl.* vehement desire; **— de ira** fit of anger.
impetuoso [im·pe·twó·so] *adj.* impetuous, violent.
impío [im·pí·o] *adj.* impious, irreligious; profane.
implacable [im·pla·ká·ble] *adj.* implacable, relentless.
implantación [im·plan·ta·sjón] *f.* implantation; establishment, introduction (*of a system*).
implantar [im·plan·tár] *v.* to implant, establish, introduce.

implicar⁶ [im·pli·kár] v. to imply; to implicate, involve.

implorar [im·plo·rár] v. to implore, entreat, beg.

imponente [im·po·nén·te] adj. imposing.

imponer⁴⁰ [im·po·nér] v. irr. to impose; to invest (money); — miedo to inspire fear; — respeto to inspire or command respect; -se to inspire fear or respect; to dominate; Am. -se a to get accustomed ur used to.

importancia [im·por·tán·sja] f. importance.

importante [im·por·tán·te] adj. important.

importar [im·por·tár] v. to be important; to matter; to amount to; to be necessary; to concern; to import.

importe [im·pór·te] m. amount, price, value.

importunar [im·por·tu·nár] v. to importune, nag, tease, pester.

importuno [im·por·tú·no] adj. annoying, persistent.

imposibilidad [im·po·si·ƀi·li·ḍáḍ] f. impossibility.

imposibilitado [im·po·si·ƀi·li·tá·ḍo] p.p. & adj. disabled, unfit; helpless.

imposibilitar [im·po·si·ƀi·li·tár] v. to make impossible; to disable.

imposible [im·po·sí·ƀle] adj. impossible; intolerable, unbearable; Col., Ven. disabled (because of illness); Am. slovenly, untidy.

imposición [im·po·si·sjón] f. imposition; burden; tax.

impostor [im·pos·tór] m. impostor, cheat;

impostura [im·pos·tú·ra] f. imposture, fraud, deceit.

impotencia [im·po·ten·sja] f. impotence.

impotente [im·po·tén·te] adj. impotent, powerless.

impreciso [im·pre·sí·so] adj. vague, indefinite; inaccurate.

impregnar [im·preǵ·nár] v. to impregnate, saturate.

imprenta [im·prén·ta] f. press; printing shop; printing.

imprescindible [im·pre·sin·di·ƀle] adj. essential, indispensable.

impresión [im·pre·sjón] f. impression; printing; mark; footprint.

impresionante [im·pre·sjo·nán·te] adj. impressive.

impresionar [im·pre·sjo·nár] v. to impress; to move, affect, stir; -se to be stirred, moved.

impreso [im·pré·so] p.p. irr. of imprimir printed; impressed, imprinted; m. printed matter.

impresor [im·pre·sór] m. printer.

imprevisión [im·pre·ƀi·sjón] f. carelessness, lack of foresight.

imprevisto [im·pre·ƀís·to] adj. unforeseen, unexpected.

imprimir [im·pri·mír] v. to print; to imprint, impress.

improbable [im·pro·ƀá·ƀle] adj. improbable, unlikely.

improperio [im·pro·pé·rjo] m. affront, insult.

impropio [im·pró·pjo] adj. improper; unsuitable.

improvisar [im·pro·ƀi·sár] v. to improvise.

improviso [im·pro·ƀí·so] adj. unforeseen; de — suddenly; Col., Ven., Mex. en un — in a moment, in the twinkling of an eye.

imprudencia [im·pru·ḍén·sja] f. imprudence, indiscretion, rash act.

imprudente [im·pru·ḍén·te] adj. imprudent; unwise; indiscreet.

impuesto [im·pwés·to] p.p. of imponer imposed; informed; Am. estar — a to be used or accustomed to; m. tax, duty.

impulsar [im·pul·sár] v. to impel, push, move; to force.

impulso [im·púl·so] m. impulse; push.

impureza [im·pu·ré·sa] f. impurity.

impuro [im·pú·ro] adj. impure.

imputar [im·pu·tár] v. to impute, attribute.

inacabable [i·na·ka·ƀá·ƀle] adj. unending, endless.

inacabado [i·na·ka·ƀá·ḍo] adj. unfinished.

inaccesible [i·nak·se·sí·ƀle] adj. inaccessible, unobtainable.

inacción [i·nak·sjón] f. inaction, inactivity, idleness.

inaceptable [i·na·sep·tá·ƀle] adj. unacceptable, unsatisfactory.

inactividad [i·nak·ti·ƀi·ḍáḍ] f. inactivity.

inactivo [i·nak·tí·ƀo] adj. inactive.

inadecuado [i·na·ḍe·kwá·ḍo] adj. inadequate.

inadvertencia [i·naḍ·ƀer·tén·sja] f. oversight; inattention, heedlessness.

inadvertido [i·naḍ·ƀer·tí·ḍo] adj. careless, heedless; unnoticed.

inafectado [i·na·fek·tá·ḍo] adj. unaffected.

inagotable [i·na·ǵo·ta·ƀle] adj. inexhaustible.

inaguantable [i·na·ǵwan·tá·ƀle] adj. insufferable, unbearable.

inalámbrico [i·na·lám·bri·ko] adj. wireless.

inalterable [i·nal·te·rá·ƀle] adj. unalterable, unchangeable.

inalterado [i·nal·te·rá·ḍo] adj. unchanged.

inamovible [i·na·mo·ƀi·ƀle] = inmovible.

inanición [i·na·ni·sjón] f. starvation.

inanimado [i·na·ni·má·ḍo] adj. inanimate, lifeless.

inapelable [i·na·pe·lá·ƀle] adj. unappealable; unavoidable.

inapetencia [i·na·pe·tén·sja] f. lack of appetite.

inaplicable [i·na·pli·ká·ƀle] adj. inapplicable, unsuitable; — al caso irrelevant.

inapreciable [i·na·pre·sjá·ƀle] adj. invaluable; inappreciable, too small to be perceived, very slight.

inasequible [i·na·se·ki·ƀle] adj. inaccessible, not obtainable; hard to attain or obtain.

inaudito [i·naw·ḍí·to] adj. unheard-of; unprecedented.

inauguración [i·naw·ǵu·ra·sjón] f. inauguration.

inaugurar [i·naw·ǵu·rár] v. to inaugurate, begin, open.

incaico [iŋ·káj·ko], incásico [iŋ·ká·si·ko] adj. Incan (of or pertaining to the Incas).

incalculable [iŋ·kal·ku·lá·ƀle] adj. incalculable; innumerable, untold.

incandescente [iŋ·kan·de·sén·te] adj. incandescent.

incansable [iŋ·kan·sá·ƀle] adj. untiring, tireless.

incapacidad [iŋ·ka·pa·si·ḍáḍ] f. incompetence, inability, unfitness.

incapacitar [iŋ·ka·pa·si·tár] v. to cripple, disable, handicap, unfit, make unfit.

incapaz [iŋ·ka·pás] adj. incapable, unable.

incauto [iŋ·káw·to] adj. unwary, heedless, reckless.

incendiar [in·sen·djár] v. to set fire to; -se to catch fire.

incendio [in·sén·djo] m. conflagration, fire.

incentivo [in·sén·ti·ƀo] m. incentive, inducement.

incertidumbre [in·ser·ti·ḍúm·bre] f. uncertainty, doubt.

incesante [in·se·sán·te] adj. incessant.

incidental [in·si·den·tál] adj. incidental.

incidente [in·si·ḍén·te] adj. incidental; m. incident.

incienso [in·sjén·so] m. incense.

incierto [in·sjér·to] adj. uncertain, doubtful; unstable; unknown; untrue.

incisión [in·si·sjón] f. incision, cut, slit, gash.

incisivo [in·si·sí·ƀo] adj. incisive; m. incisor.

incitamiento [in·si·ta·mjén·to] m. incitement,

inducement, incentive.
incitar [in·si·tár] *v.* to incite, rouse, stir up.
incivil [in·si·ƀíl] *adj.* uncivil, rude, impolite.
inclemencia [in·kle·mén·sja] *f.* inclemency, severity, harshness; **inclemente** [in·kle·mén·te] *adj.* unmerciful, merciless.
inclinación [in·kli·na·sjón] *f.* inclination, affection; tendency, bent; bow; incline, slope.
inclinar [in·kli·nár] *v.* (*bajar*) to incline; (*persuadir*) to persuade; **-se** to bow; to stoop; to incline, slope, slant; to lean, bend.
incluir[32] [in·klwír] *v. irr.* to include; to inclose.
inclusive [in·klu·sí·ƀe] *adv.* inclusive, including; even; **inclusivo** [in·klu·sí·ƀo] *adj.* inclusive; comprehensive.
incluso [in·klú·so] *adj.* inclosed; included; including; even.
incógnito [in·kóǥ·ni·to] *adj.* unknown; **de —** incognito (*with one's name or rank unknown*); **incógnita** *f.* unknown quantity (*in mathematics*).
incoherente [in·ko·e·rén·te] *adj.* incoherent, disconnected, rambling.
incoloro [in·ko·ló·ro] *adj.* colorless.
incombustible [in·kom·bus·ti·ƀle] *adj.* incombustible; fireproof.
incomestible [in·ko·mes·ti·ƀle] *adj.* inedible.
incomodar [in·ko·mo·ɖár] *v.* to inconvenience, disturb, trouble, annoy.
incomodidad [in·ko·mo·ɖi·ɖáɖ] *f.* inconvenience, discomfort; bother, annoyance.
incómodo [in·kó·mo·ɖo] *adj.* inconvenient, bothersome: uncomfortable.
incomparable [in·kom·pa·ra·ƀle] *adj.* incomparable.
incompasivo [in·kom·pa·sí·ƀo] *adj.* merciless, pitiless.
incompatible [in·kom·pa·ti·ƀle] *adj.* incompatible; unsuitable, uncongenial.
incompetencia [in·kom·pe·tén·sja] *f.* incompetence, inability, unfitness; **incompentente** [in·kom·pe·tén·te] *adj.* incompetent, unfit.
incompleto [in·kom·plé·to] *adj.* incomplete.
incomprensible [in·kom·pren·sí·ƀle] *adj.* incomprehensible.
inconcebible [in·kon·se·ƀi·ƀle] *adj.* inconceivable.
inconcluso [in·kon·klú·so] *adj.* unfinished.
incondicional [in·kon·di·sjo·nál] *adj.* unconditional.
inconexo [in·ko·nék·so] *adj.* unconnected; incoherent, disconnected.
inconfundible [in·kon·fun·di·ƀle] *adj.* unmistakable.
incongruente [in·kon·grwén·te] *adj.* unsuitable, not appropriate; not harmonious.
inconquistable [in·kon·kis·tá·ƀle] *adj.* unconquerable.
inconsciencia [in·kon·sjén·sja] *f.* unconsciousness; unawareness.
inconsciente [in·kon·sjén·te] *adj.* unconscious; unaware.
inconsecuente [in·kon·se·kwén·te] *adj.* inconsistent; illogical.
inconsiderado [in·kon·si·ɖe·rá·ɖo] *adj.* inconsiderate, thoughtless.
inconstancia [in·kons·tán·sja] *f.* inconstancy, changeableness, fickleness.
inconstante [in·kons·tán·te] *adj.* inconstant, fickle, changeable, variable.
incontable [in·kon·tá·ƀle] *adj.* countless, innumerable.
inconveniencia [in·kom·be·njén·sja] *f.* inconvenience; trouble.
inconveniente [in·kom·be·njén·te] *adj.* inconvenient; improper; *m.* obstacle; objection.

incorporar [in·kor·po·rár] *v.* to incorporate, unite; to embody; to include; **-se** to sit up; **-se a** to join.
incorrecto [in·ko·rrék·to] *adj.* incorrect.
incredulidad [in·kre·ɖu·li·ɖáɖ] *f.* incredulity, unbelief.
incrédulo [in·kré·ɖu·lo] *adj.* incredulous, unbelieving; *m.* unbeliever.
increíble [in·kre·í·ƀle] *adj.* incredible, unbelievable.
incremento [in·kre·mén·to] *m.* increment, increase.
incrustar [in·krus·tár] *v.* to inlay; to encrust (*cover with a crust or hard coating*); **-se en** to penetrate impress itself deeply into.
incubadora [in·ku·ƀa·ɖó·ra] *f.* incubator.
inculcar[6] [in·kul·kár] *v.* to inculcate, instill, impress.
inculto [in·kúl·to] *adj.* uncultured; uncultivated; unrefined.
incumbencia [in·kum·bén·sja] *f.* concern, duty, obligation; **no es de mi —** it does not concern me, it is not within my province.
incurable [in·ku·rá·ƀle] *adj.* incurable.
incurrir [in·ku·rrír] *v.* to incur, fall (into); **— en un error** to fall into or commit an error; **— en el odio de** to incur the hatred of.
incursión [in·kur·sjón] *f.* raid, invasion.
indagación [in·da·ǥa·sjón] *f.* investigation, inquiry.
indagador [in·da·ǥa·ɖór] *m.* investigator; inquirer; *adj.* investigating; inquiring.
indagar[7] [in·da·ǥár] *v.* to find out, investigate; to inquire.
indebido [in·de·ƀí·ɖo] *adj.* undue, improper; illegal; **indebidamente** [in·de·ƀi·ɖa·mén·te] *adv.* unduly; illegally.
indecencia [in·de·sén·sja] *f.* indecency, obscenity, indecent act or remark.
indecente [in·de·sén·te] *adj.* indecent, improper.
indecible [in·de·sí·ƀle] *adj.* inexpressible, untold.
indeciso [in·de·sí·so] *adj.* undecided; doubtful, uncertain.
indefectible [in·de·fek·tí·ƀle] *adj.* unfailing; **-mente** unfailingly.
indefenso [in·de·fén·so] *adj.* defenseless, unprotected.
indefinible [in·de·fi·ní·ƀle] *adj.* indefinable.
indefinido [in·de·fi·ni·ɖo] *adj.* indefinite.
indeleble [in·de·le·ƀle] *adj.* indelible.
indemnización [in·dem·ni·sa·sjón] *f.* indemnity, compensation.
indemnizar[9] [in·dem·ni·sár] *v.* to indemnify, compensate.
independencia [in·de·pen·dén·sja] *f.* independence.
independiente [in·de·pen·djén·te] *adj.* independent.
indescriptible [in·des·krip·tí·ƀle] *adj.* indescribable.
indeseable [in·de·se·á·ƀle] *adj.* undesirable, unwelcome.
indiada [in·djá·ɖa] *f. Ríopl., C.A., Col.* community, group, or crowd of Indians; *Col., Ven., Carib., Andes* an Indian-like remark or act; *Am.* an uncontrollable fit of anger.
indianista [in·dja·nís·ta] *m. & f.* student of Indian culture; *adj.* pertaining to Indian culture.
indiano [in·djá·no] *adj.* of or pertaining to the West or East Indies; *m.* Spaniard who goes back to settle in his country after having lived for some time in Spanish America.
indicación [in·di·ka·sjón] *f.* indication.
indicar[6] [in·di·kár] *v.* to indicate, show, point out.
indicativo [in·di·ka·tí·ƀo] *adj.* indicative; *m.* indicative, indicative mood.
índice [ín·di·se] *m.* index; catalogue; sign; pointer;

forefinger.
indicio [in·dí·sjo] *m.* indication, sign.
indiferencia [in·di·fe·rén·sja] *f.* indifference.
indiferente [in·di·fe·rén·te] *adj.* indifferent.
indígena [in·dí·xe·na] *adj.* indigenous, native; *m.* &
f. native inhabitant; *Am.* Indian.
indigestión [in·di·xes·tjón] *f.* indigestion.
indignación [in·dig·na·sjón] *f.* indignation.
indignado [in·dig·ná·do] *p.p.* & *adj.* indignant,
irritated, angry.
indignar [in·dig·nár] *v.* to irritate, anger; **-se** to
become indignant, angry.
indignidad [in·dig·ni·dád] *f.* indignity, affront,
insult; unworthy or disgraceful act.
indigno [in·dig·no] *adj.* unworthy; low,
contemptible.
indio [ín·djo] *adj.* & *m.* Indian; Hindu; indium
(*element*).
indirecta [in·di·rék·ta] *f.* hint, indirect remark,
innuendo, insinuation.
indirecto [in·di·rék·to] *adj.* indirect.
indisciplinado [in·di·si·pli·ná·do] *adj.* undisciplined,
untrained.
indiscreto [in·dis·kré·to] *adj.* indiscreet, imprudent,
unwise, rash.
indiscutible [in·dis·ku·tí·ƀle] *adj.* indisputable,
unquestionable.
indispensable [in·dis·pen·sá·ƀle] *adj.* indispensable.
indisponer⁴⁰ [in·dis·po·nér] *v. irr.* to indispose; to
make ill; **— a uno con otro** to prejudice someone
against another; **-se** to become ill; **-se con** to fall
out with, quarrel with.
indisposición [in·dis·po·si·sjón] *f.* indisposition,
upset, slight illness; reluctance, unwillingness.
indispuesto [in·dis·pwés·to] *p.p. of* **indisponer** & *adj.*
indisposed, unwilling; ill.
indisputable [in·dis·pu·tá·ƀle] *adj.* unquestionable.
indistinto [in·dis·tín·to] *adj.* indistinct, dim, vague,
not clear.
individual [in·di·ƀi·dwál] *adj.* individual.
individualidad [in·di·ƀi·dwa·li·dád] *f.* individuality.
individualismo [in·di·ƀi·dwa·líz·mo] *m.*
individualism.
individuo [in·di·ƀí·dwo] *adj.* individual; indivisible;
m. individual; person; member.
indócil [in·dó·sil] *adj.* unruly, disobedient,
headstrong.
indocto [in·dók·to] *adj.* uneducated, ignorant.
índole [ín·do·le] *f.* disposition, temper; kind, class.
indolencia [in·do·lén·sja] *f.* indolence, laziness;
insensitiveness, indifference.
indolente [in·do·lén·te] *adj.* indolent, lazy;
insensitive, indifferent.
indomable [in·do·má·ƀle] *adj.* indomitable,
unconquerable; unmanageable; untamable.
indómito [in·dó·mi·to] *adj.* untamed;
uncontrollable, unruly.
inducir²⁵ [in·du·sír] *v. irr.* to induce; to persuade.
indudable [in·du·dá·ƀle] *adj.* unquestionable,
certain.
indulgencia [in·dul·xén·sja] *f.* indulgence, tolerance,
forgiveness; remission of sins.
indulgente [in·dul·xén·te] *adj.* indulgent, lenient.
indultar [in·dul·tár] *v.* to pardon, set free; to
exempt.
indulto [in·dúl·to] *m.* pardon, forgiveness;
exemption; privilege.
indumentaria [in·du·men·tá·rja] *f.* costume, dress;
manner of dressing.
industria [in·dús·trja] *f.* industry; cleverness, skill;
de — intentionally, on purpose.

industrial [in·dus·trjál] *adj.* industrial; *m.*
industrialist; manufacturer.
industrioso [in·dus·trjó·so] *adj.* industrious.
inédito [i·né·di·to] *adj.* unpublished.
inefable [i·ne·fá·ƀle] *adj.* ineffable, inexpressible.
ineficaz [i·ne·fi·kás] *adj.* ineffective; inefficient.
inepto [i·nép·to] *adj.* incompetent; unsuitable.
inequívoco [i·ne·kí·ƀo·ko] *adj.* unmistakable.
inercia [i·nér·sja] *f.* inertia, lifelessness; inactivity.
inerme [i·nér·me] *adj.* unarmed, defenseless.
inerte [i·nér·te] *adj.* inert; inactive, sluggish, slow.
inesperado [i·nes·pe·rá·do] *adj.* unexpected.
inestable [i·nes·tá·ƀle] *adj.* unstable; unsettled;
unsteady.
inestimable [i·nes·ti·má·ƀle] *adj.* inestimable,
invaluable.
inevitable [i·ne·ƀi·tá·ƀle] *adj.* inevitable,
unavoidable.
inexacto [i·nek·sák·to] *adj.* inexact, inaccurate.
inexorable [i·nek·so·rá·ƀle] *adj.* inexorable.
inexperiencia [i·nes·pe·rjén·n·sja] *f.* inexperience.
inexperto [i·nes·pér·to] *adj.* unskilful, unskilled,
inexperienced.
inexplicable [i·nes·pli·ká·ƀle] *adj.* inexplicable.
inextinguible [i·nes·tiŋ·gí·ƀle] *adj.* inextinguishable,
unquenchable.
infalible [in·fa·lí·ƀle] *adj.* infallible.
infame [in·fá·me] *adj.* infamous; *m.* scoundrel.
infamia [in·fá·mja] *f.* infamy, dishonor; wickedness.
infancia [in·fán·sja] *f.* infancy.
infante [in·fán·te] *m.* infant; infante (*royal prince of
Spain, except the heir to the throne*); infantryman.
infantería [in·fan·te·rí·a] *f.* infantry.
infantil [in·fan·tíl] *adj.* infantile, childlike, childish.
infatigable [in·fa·ti·gá·ƀle] *adj.* tireless, untiring.
infausto [in·fáws·to] *adj.* unfortunate; unhappy.
infección [in·fek·sjón] *f.* infection; **infeccioso** *adj.*
infectious.
infectar [in·fek·tár] *v.* to infect; to corrupt; **-se** to
become infected.
infeliz [in·fe·lís] *adj.* unhappy, unfortunate; *m.* poor
wretch.
inferior [in·fe·rjór] *adj.* inferior; lower; *m.* inferior.
inferioridad [in·fe·rjo·ri·dád] *f.* inferiority.
inferir³ [in·fe·rír] *v. irr.* (*concluir*) to infer; to
imply; (*causar*) to inflict.
infernal [in·fer·nál] *adj.* infernal.
infestar [in·fes·tár] *v.* to infest, invade, overrun,
plague; to corrupt, infect.
inficionar [in·fi·sjo·nár] *v.* to infect; to contaminate.
infiel [in·fjél] *adj.* unfaithful, faithless; infidel;
inaccurate.
infiernillo [in·fjer·ni·yo] *m.* chafing dish.
infierno [in·fjér·no] *m.* hell; **en el quinto —** very
far away.
infiltrar [in·fil·trár] *v.* to filter through; **-se** to leak
(into), filter (through), infiltrate.
infinidad [in·fi·ni·dád] *f.* infinity; **una — de** a large
number of.
infinito [in·fi·ní·to] *adj.* infinite; *adv.* infinitely; *m.*
infinity.
inflamación [in·fla·ma·sjón] *f.* inflammation.
inflamado [in·fla·má·do] *p.p.* & *adj.* inflamed; sore.
inflamar [in·fla·már] *v.* to inflame, excite; to kindle,
set on fire; **-se** to become inflamed.
inflar [in·flár] *v.* to inflate; to exaggerate; **-se** to
become inflated; to swell up with pride.
inflexible [in·flek·sí·ƀle] *adj.* inflexible, stiff, rigid;
unbending.
inflexión [in·flek·sjón] *f.* inflection.
infligir¹¹ [in·fli·xír] *v.* to inflict.

IN

influencia [in·flwén·sja] *f.* influence.
influenza [in·flwén·sa] *f.* influenza, grippe, flu.
influir [in·flwír] *v. irr.* to influence.
influjo [in·flú·xo] *m.* influence; influx, inward flow.
influyente [in·flu·yén·te] *adj.* influential.
información [in·for·ma·sjón] *f.* information.
informal [in·for·mál] *adj.* informal; unconventional; unreliable, not dependable, not punctual.
informar [in·for·már] *v.* to inform; to give form to; to give a report; to present a case; **-se** to find out.
informe [in·fór·me] *m.* report, account; information; brief; *adj.* formless, shapeless.
infortunio [in·for·tú·njo] *m.* misfortune, mishap; misery.
infracción [in·frak·sjón] *f.* infraction, breach, violation (*of a law, treaty, etc.*).
infractor [in·frak·tór] *m.* transgressor, lawbreaker, violator (*of a law*).
infrascrito [in·fras·krí·to] *m.* undersigned, subscriber, signer (*of a letter, document, etc.*); **el** — **secretario** the secretary whose signature appears below.
infringir[11] [in·friŋ·xír] *v.* to infringe, break, violate.
infructuoso [in·fruk·twó·so] *adj.* fruitless.
ínfulas [ín·fu·las] *f. pl.* airs, false importance; **darse** — to put on airs.
infundado [in·fun·dá·ḍo] *adj.* groundless, without foundation.
infundir [in·fun·dír] *v.* to infuse, inspire; to instill.
infusión [in·fu·sjón] *f.* infusion (*liquid extract obtained by steeping*); infusion, inspiration; **poner en** — to steep (*as tea leaves*).
ingeniería [iŋ·xe·nje·rí·a] *f.* engineering.
ingeniero [iŋ·xe·njé·ro] *m.* engineer.
ingenio [iŋ·xé·njo] *m.* genius; talent; ingenuity; mentality, mental power, mind; wit; — **de azúcar** sugar refinery; sugar plantation.
ingeniosidad [iŋ·xe·njo·si·ḍáḍ] *f.* ingenuity, cleverness.
ingenioso [iŋ·xe·njó·so] *adj.* ingenious, clever.
ingenuidad [iŋ·xe·nwi·ḍáḍ] *f.* candor, frankness; unaffected simplicity.
ingenuo [iŋ·xé·nwo] *adj.* frank, sincere; simple, unaffected; naive.
ingerir [iŋ·xe·rír] = **injerir.**
ingestión [iŋ·xes·tjón] *f.* ingestion.
ingle [íŋ·gle] *f.* groin.
inglés [iŋ·glés] *adj.* English; **a la inglesa** in the English fashion; *Am.* **ir a la inglesa** to go Dutch treat; *m.* Englishman; the English language.
ingobernable [iŋ·go·ḇer·ná·ḇle] *adj.* ungovernable, unruly, uncontrollable.
ingratitud [iŋ·gra·ti·túḍ] *f.* ingratitude.
ingrato [iŋ·grá·to] *adj.* ungrateful, thankless; harsh; cruel; disdainful.
ingrediente [iŋ·gre·ḍjén·te] *m.* ingredient.
ingresar [iŋ·gre·sár] *v.* to enter; — **en** to join (*a society, club, etc.*).
ingreso [iŋ·gré·so] *m.* entrance; entry; **-s** receipts, profits; revenue.
inhábil [i·ná·ḇil] *adj.* unskilled; unskilful; unfit.
inhabilidad [i·na·ḇi·li·ḍáḍ] *f.* inability; unfitness.
inhabilitar [i·na·ḇi·li·tár] *v.* to disqualify; to unfit, disable.
inherente [i·ne·rén·te] *adj.* inherent.
inhibir [i·ni·ḇír] *v.* to inhibit.
inhospitalario [i·nos·pi·ta·lá·rjo] *adj.* inhospitable.
inhumano [i·nu·má·no] *adj.* inhuman, cruel.
iniciador [i·ni·sja·ḍór] *m.* initiator; pioneer; *adj.* initiating.

inicial [i·ni·sjál] *adj. & f.* initial.
iniciar [i·ni·sjár] *v.* to initiate; to begin.
iniciativa [i·ni·sja·ti·ḇa] *f.* initiative.
inicuo [i·ni·kwo] *adj.* wicked.
iniquidad [i·ni·ki·ḍáḍ] *f.* iniquity, wickedness; sin.
injerir[3] [iŋ·xe·rír] *v. irr.* to inject, insert; **-se** to interfere, meddle.
injertar [iŋ·xer·tár] *v.* to graft.
injerto [iŋ·xér·to] *m.* graft.
injuria [iŋ·xú·rja] *f.* affront, insult; harm, damage.
injuriar [iŋ·xu·rjár] *v.* to insult, offend; to harm, damage.
injurioso [iŋ·xu·rjó·so] *adj.* insulting, offensive; harmful.
injusticia [iŋ·xus·tí·sja] *f.* injustice.
injustificado [iŋ·xus·ti·fi·ká·ḍo] *adj.* unjustified; unjustifiable.
injusto [iŋ·xús·to] *adj.* unjust, unfair.
inmaculado [im·ma·ku·lá·ḍo] *adj.* immaculate, clean; pure.
inmediación [im·me·ḍja·sjón] *f.* vicinity; nearness; **-es** environs, outskirts.
inmediato [im·me·ḍjá·to] *adj.* near, close; *Am.* **de** — immediately; suddenly; **inmediatamente** *adv.* immediately, at once.
inmejorable [im·me·xo·rá·ḇle] *adj.* unsurpassable.
inmensidad [im·men·si·ḍáḍ] *f.* immensity, vastness; vast number.
inmenso [im·mén·so] *adj.* immense, vast, huge; boundless.
inmersión [im·mer·sjón] *f.* immersion, dip.
inmigración [im·mi·ḡra·sjón] *f.* immigration.
inmigrante [im·mi·ḡrán·te] *adj.,. m. & f.* immigrant.
inmigrar [im·mi·ḡrár] *v.* to immigrate.
inminente [im·mi·nén·te] *adj.* imminent.
inmiscuir[32] [im·mis·kwír] *v. irr.* to mix; **-se** to meddle, interfere.
inmoble [im·mó·ḇle] *adj.* motionless; unshaken.
inmoral [im·mo·rál] *adj.* immoral; **inmoralidad** [im·mo·ra·li·ḍáḍ] *f.* immorality.
inmortal [im·mor·tál] *adj.* immortal; **inmortalidad** *f.* immortality.
inmovible [im·mo·ḇí·ḇle] *adj.* immovable, fixed; steadfast.
inmóvil [im·mó·ḇil] *adj.* motionless, still; immovable.
inmuebles [im·mwé·ḇles] *m. pl.* real estate.
inmundicia [im·mun·di·sja] *f.* filth, dirt; nastiness.
inmundo [im·mún·do] *adj.* filthy, dirty; impure; nasty.
inmune [im·mú·ne] *adj.* immune; exempt.
inmunidad [im·mu·ni·ḍáḍ] *f.* immunity.
inmutable [im·mu·tá·ḇle] *adj.* unchangeable, invariable.
inmutar [im·mu·tár] *v.* to alter, change; **-se** to show emotion (*either by turning pale or blushing*).
innato [in·ná·to] *adj.* innate, natural, inborn.
innecesario [in·ne·se·sá·rjo] *adj.* unnecessary.
innegable [in·ne·ḡá·ḇle] *adj.* undeniable, not to be denied.
innocuo [in·nó·kwo] *adj.* innocuous, harmless.
innocuidad *f.* harmlessness.
innovación [in·no·ḇa·sjón] *f.* innovation; novelty.
innumerable [in·nu·me·rá·ḇle] *adj.* innumerable.
inobservancia [i·noḇ·ser·ḇán·sja] *f.* nonobservance, violation (*of a law*), lack of observance (*of a law, rule, or custom*).
inocencia [i·no·sén·sja] *f.* innocence.
inocente [i·no·sén·te] *adj.* innocent; *m.* innocent person; **inocentón** *adj.* quite foolish or simple; easily fooled; *m.* dupe, unsuspecting victim.

inocular [i·no·ku·lár] *v.* to inoculate.
inodoro [i·no·dó·ro] *adj.* odorless; *m.* C.A., Ven., Col. toilet, water closet.
inofensivo [i·no·fen·sí·ƀo] *adj.* inoffensive; harmless.
inolvidable [i·nol·ƀi·ɗá·ƀle] *adj.* unforgettable.
inopinado [i·no·pi·ná·ɗo] *adj.* unexpected.
inoportuno [i·no·por·tú·no] *adj.* inopportune, untimely, unsuitable.
inoxidable [i·nok·si·ɗá·ƀle] *adj.* rust proof.
inquietar [iŋ·kje·tár] *v.* to worry, disturb, make uneasy; **-se** to become disturbed, uneasy.
inquieto [iŋ·kjé·to] *adj.* restless; uneasy, anxious.
inquietud [iŋ·kje·túɗ] *f.* restlessness; anxiety, uneasiness; fear.
inquilino [iŋ·ki·lí·no] *m.* tenant, renter; lodger.
inquina [iŋ·kí·na] *f.* aversion, grudge, dislike.
inquirir[35] [iŋ·ki·rír] *v. irr.* to inquire, investigate; to find out.
inquisición [iŋ·ki·si·sjón] *f.* inquisition; inquiry, investigation.
insaciable [in·sa·sjá·ƀle] *adj.* insatiable, never satisfied, greedy.
insalubre [in·sa·lu·ƀre] *adj.* unhealthy, unhealthful, unwholesome.
insano [in·sá·no] *adj.* insane, crazy; unhealthy.
inscribir[52] [ins·kri·ƀír] *v.* to inscribe; to register, enroll; to record; **-se** to register.
inscripción [ins·krip·sjón] *f.* inscription; registration.
inscripto [ins·kríp·to], **inscrito** [ins·krí·to] *p.p. of* inscribir.
insecto [in·sék·to] *m.* insect.
inseguro [in·se·ǥú·ro] *adj.* insecure; unsafe; doubtful, uncertain.
insensato [in·sen·sá·to] *adj.* senseless; foolish.
insensibilidad [in·sen·si·ƀi·li·ɗáɗ] *f.* insensibility, unconsciousness; lack of feeling.
insensible [in·sen·si·ƀle] *adj.* insensible; unfeeling; imperceptible.
inseparable [in·se·pa·rá·ƀle] *adj.* inseparable.
inserción [in·ser·sjón] *f.* insertion; insert.
insertar [in·ser·tár] *v.* to insert.
inserto *adj.* inserted.
inservible [in·ser·ƀí·ƀle] *adj.* useless.
insidioso [in·si·ɗjó·so] *adj.* insidious; sly, crafty.
insigne [in·siǥ·ne] *adj.* famous.
insignia [in·siǥ·nja] *f.* badge, medal, decoration; flag, pennant; **-s** insignia.
insignificante [in·siǥ·ni·fi·kán·te] *adj.* insignificant.
insinuación [in·si·nwa·sjón] *f.* insinuation; intimation, hint.
insinuar[18] [in·si·nwár] *v.* to insinuate, hint; **-se** to insinuate oneself (*into another's friendship*); to creep (into) gradually.
insipidez [in·si·pi·ɗés] *f.* flatness, tastelessness, dullness; **insípido** *adj.*, insipid; tasteless.
insistencia [in·sis·tén·sja] *f.* insistence, persistence, obstinacy; **insistente** [in·sis·tén·te] *adj.* insistent, persistent.
insistir [in·sis·tír] *v.* to insist; to persist.
insociable [in·so·sjá·ƀle] *adj.* unsociable.
insolación [in·so·la·sjón] *f.* sunstroke.
insolencia [in·so·lén·sja] *f.* insolence.
insolentarse [in·so·len·tár·se] *v.* to sauce, become insolent, act with insolence.
insolente [in·so·lén·te] *adj.* insolent.
insólito [in·só·li·to] *adj.* unusual; uncommon.
insolvente [in·sol·ƀén·te] *adj.* insolvent, bankrupt.
insomne [in·sóm·ne] *adj.* sleepless.
insondable [in·son·dá·ƀle] *adj.* fathomless, deep; impenetrable.

insoportable [in·so·por·tá·ƀle] *adj.* unbearable.
insospechado [in·sos·pe·čá·ɗo] *adj.* unsuspected.
inspección [ins·pek·sjón] *f.* inspection.
inspeccionar [ins·pek·sjo·nár] *v.* to inspect.
inspector [ins·pek·tór] *m.* inspector; overseer.
inspiración [ins·pi·ra·sjón] *f.* inspiration; inhalation, breathing in.
inspirar [ins·pi·rár] *v.* to inspire; to inhale.
instalación [ins·ta·la·sjón] *f.* installation.
instalar [ins·ta·lar] *v.* to install.
instancia [ins·tán·sja] *f.* instance, urgent request; petition; **a -s de** at the request of.
instantánea [ins·tan·tá·ne·a] *f.* snapshot.
instantáneo [ins·tan·tá·ne·o] *adj.* instantaneous; sudden.
instante [ins·tán·te] *m.* instant, moment; **al** — at once, immediately; **por -s** continually; from one moment to another; *adj.* instant, urgent.
instar [ins·tár] *v.* to urge, press; to be urgent.
instigar[7] [ins·ti·ǥár] *f.* instance, urge on, incite.
instintivo [ins·tin·tí·ƀo] *adj.* instinctive.
instinto [ins·tín·to] *m.* instinct.
institución [ins·ti·tu·sjón] *f.* institution; establishment, foundation; **-es** institutes, collection of precepts and principles.
instituir[32] [ins·ti·twír] *v. irr.* to institute; — **por heredero** to appoint as heir.
instituto [ins·ti·tú·to] *m.* institute; — established principle, law, or custom; — **de segunda enseñanza** high school.
institutriz [ins·ti·tu·trís] *f.* governess.
instrucción [ins·truk·sjón] *f.* instruction; education.
instructivo [ins·truk·tí·ƀo] *adj.* instructive.
instruir[32] [ins·trwír] *v. irr.* to instruct, teach; to inform.
instrumento [ins·tru·mén·to] *m.* instrument.
insuficiencia [in·su·fi·sjén·sja] *f.* insufficiency, deficiency; incompetence; dearth, scarcity, lack.
insuficiente [in·su·fi·sjén·te] *adj.* insufficient.
insufrible [in·su·frí·ƀle] *adj.* insufferable, unbearable.
insula [in·su·la] *f.* island.
insulina [in·su·lí·na] *f.* insulin.
insultante [in·sul·tán·te] *adj.* insulting, abusive.
insultar [in·sul·tár] *v.* to insult; **-se** to be seized with a fit.
insulto [in·súl·to] *m.* insult; sudden fit or attack.
insuperable [in·su·pe·rá·ƀle] *adj.* insuperable; insurmountable.
insurgente [in·sur·xén·te] *adj., m. & f.* insurgent.
insurrección [in·su·rrek·sjón] *f.* insurrection, uprising, revolt.
insurrecto [in·su·rrék·to] *m.* insurgent, rebel; *adj.* rebellious.
intacto [in·ták·to] *adj.* intact.
intachable [in·ta·čá·ƀle] *adj.* faultless, irreproachable.
integral [in·te·ǥrál] *adj.* integral; *f.* integral (*math*).
integrante [in·te·ǥrán·te] *adj.* integral; integrating.
integrar [in·te·ǥrár] *v.* to form; to integrate.
integridad [in·te·ǥri·ɗáɗ] *f.* integrity; wholeness; honesty; purity.
íntegro [in·te·ǥro] *adj.* whole, complete; honest, upright.
intelecto [in·te·lék·to] *m.* intellect.
intelectual [in·te·lek·twál] *adj.* intellectual.
inteligencia [in·te·li·xén·sja] *f.* intelligence.
inteligente [in·te·li·xén·te] *adj.* intelligent.
intemperancia [in·tem·pe·rán·sja] *f.* intemperance, excess.
intemperie [in·tem·pé·rje] *f.* open air; bad weather;

IN

a la — unsheltered, outdoors, in the open air; exposed to the weather.

intención [in·ten·sjón] *f.* intention; **intencional** [in·ten·sjo·nál] *adj.* intentional.

intendente [in·ten·dén·te] *m.* manager, superintendent, supervisor; *Riopl.* governor of a province; *Am.* police commissioner.

intensidad [in·ten·si·dáḍ] *f.* intensity; stress.

intenso [in·tén·so] *adj.* intense; intensive; ardent, vehement.

intentar [in·ten·tár] *v.* to attempt, try; to intend.

intento [in·tén·to] *m.* intent, purpose, intention; **de** — on purpose.

intercalar [in·ter·ka·lár] *v.* to insert, place between.

intercambio [in·ter·kám·bjo] *m.* interchange; exchange.

interceder [in·ter·se·ḍér] *v.* to intercede.

interceptar [in·ter·sep·tár] *v.* to intercept.

intercesión [in·ter·se·sjón] *f.* intercession, mediation.

interdental [in·ter·ḍen·tál] *adj.* interdental.

interdicción [in·ter·ḍik·sjón] *f.* interdiction; prevention.

interés [in·te·rés] *m.* interest.

interesante [in·te·re·sán·te] *adj.* interesting.

interesar [in·te·re·sár] *v.* to interest; to give an interest or share; **-se** to be or become interested.

interferencia [in·ter·fe·rén·sja] *f.* interference.

interin [ín·te·rin] *m.* interim, meantime; **en al** — in the meantime.

interino [in·te·rí·no] *adj.* acting, temporary.

interior [in·te·rjór] *adj.* interior; inner; internal; *m.* interior, inside.

interjección [in·ter·xek·sjón] *f.* interjection, exclamation.

interlineal [in·ter·li·ne·ál] *adj.* interlinear.

interlocutor [in·ter·lo·ku·tór] *m.* participant in a dialogue.

intermedio [in·ter·me·ḍjo] *adj.* intermediate; intervening; *m.* intermission; interval; **por** — **de** by means of, through the intervention of.

interminable [in·ter·mi·ná·ḅle] *adj.* interminable, unending, endless.

intermisión [in·ter·mi·sjón] *f.* intermission, interruption, pause, interval.

intermitente [in·ter·mi·tén·te] *adj.* intermittent, occurring at intervals; **calentura** (*or* **fiebre**) — intermittent fever.

internacional [in·ter·na·sjo·nál] *adj.* international.

internado [in·ter·ná·ḍo] *m.* a boarding student.

internar [in·ter·nár] *v.* to intern, confine; **-se** to penetrate, go into the interior.

interno [in·tér·no] *adj.* internal; interior; *m.* boarding-school student.

interoceánico [in·te·ro·se·á·ni·ko] *adj.* interoceanic; transcontinental.

interpelar [in·ter·pe·lár] *v.* to interrogate, question, demand explanations; to ask the aid of.

interponer[40] [in·ter·po·nér] *v. irr.* to interpose, put between, insert; to place as a mediator; **-se** to intervene, mediate.

interpretación [in·ter·pre·ta·sjón] *f.* interpretation.

interpretar [in·ter·pre·tár] *v.* to interpret.

intérprete [in·tér·pre·te] *m. & f.* interpreter.

interpuesto [in·ter·pwés·to] *p.p. of* **interponer.**

interrogación [in·te·rro·ɡa·sjón] *f.* interrogation, question; **signo de** — question mark.

interrogador [in·te·rro·ɡa·ḍór] *m.* questioner; *adj.* questioning.

interrogar[7] [in·te·rro·ɡár] *v.* to interrogate, question.

interrogativo [in·te·rro·ɡa·tí·ḅo] *adj.* interrogative.

interrogatorio [in·te·rro·ɡa·tó·rjo] *m.* interrogation, questioning.

interrumpir [in·te·rrum·pír] *v.* to interrupt.

interrupción [in·te·rrup·sjón] *f.* interruption.

interruptor [in·te·rrup·tór] *m.* interrupter; electric switch.

intersección [in·ter·sek·sjón] *f.* intersection.

intersticio [in·ters·tí·sjo] *m.* interval.

intervalo [in·ter·ḅá·lo] *m.* interval.

intervención [in·ter·ḅen·sjón] *f.* intervention; mediation; participation; auditing of accounts.

intervenir[48] [in·ter·ḅe·nír] *v. irr.* to intervene; to mediate; to audit (*accounts*).

interventor [in·ter·ḅen·tór] *m.* inspector; controller, comptroller; auditor.

intestino [in·tes·tí·no] *m.* intestine; *adj.* intestine, internal.

intimación [in·ti·ma·sjón] *f.* intimation; hint, insinuation, suggestion.

intimar [in·ti·már] *v.* to announce, notify; to intimate, hint; to become intimate, become friendly.

intimidad [in·ti·mi·ḍáḍ] *f.* intimacy.

intimidar [in·ti·mi·ḍár] *v.* to intimidate.

íntimo [ín·ti·mo] *adj.* intimate.

intitular [in·ti·tu·lár] *v.* to entitle; to give a title to (*a person or a thing*); **-se** to be entitled, be called; to call oneself (*by a certain name*).

intolerable [in·to·le·rá·ḅle] *adj.* intolerable.

intolerancia [in·to·le·rán·sja] *f.* intolerance; **intolerante** [in·to·le·rán·te] *adj.* intolerant, narrow-minded.

intoxicante [in·tok·si·kán·te] *m.* poison.

intoxicar[6] [in·tok·si·kár] *v.* to poison.

intranquilo [in·traŋ·kí·lo] *adj.* disturbed, uneasy.

intranquilidad [in·traŋ·ki·li·ḍáḍ] *f.* uneasiness, restlessness.

intransigencia [in·tran·si·xén·sja] *f.* uncompromising act or attitude; intolerance.

intransigente [in·tran·si·xén·te] *adj.* uncompromising, unwilling to compromise or yield; intolerant.

intratable [in·tra·tá·ḅle] *adj.* unsociable; rude; unruly.

intravenoso [in·tra·ḅe·nó·so] *adj.* intravenous (*within a vein or the veins; into a vein*).

intrepidez [in·tre·pi·ḍés] *f.* fearlessness, courage.

intrépido [in·tré·pi·ḍo] *adj.* intrepid, fearless.

intriga [in·trí·ɡa] *f.* intrigue; scheme; plot.

intrigante [in·tri·ɡán·te] *m. & f.* intriguer, plotter; *adj.* intriguing.

intrigar[7] [in·tri·ɡár] *v.* to intrigue.

intrincado [in·triŋ·ká·ḍo] *adj.* intricate, complicated, entangled.

introducción [in·tro·ḍuk·sjón] *f.* introduction.

introducir[25] [in·tro·ḍu·sír] *v. irr.* to introduce; **-se** to introduce oneself; to get in; to penetrate.

intromisión [in·tro·mi·sjón] *f.* meddling; insertion.

introvertido [in·tro·ḅer·tí·ḍo] *m. & f.* introvert.

intruso [in·trú·so] *adj.* intrusive, intruding; *m.* intruder.

intuición [in·twi·sjón] *f.* intuition.

intuir[32] [in·twír] *v. irr.* to sense, feel by intuition.

inundación [i·nun·da·sjón] *f.* inundation, flood.

inundar [i·nun·dár] *v.* to inundate, flood.

inusitado [i·nu·si·tá·ḍo] *adj.* unusual, rare.

inútil [i·nú·til] *adj.* useless.

inutilidad [i·nu·ti·li·ḍáḍ] *f.* uselessness.

inutilizar[9] [i·nu·ti·li·sár] *v.* to make useless, put out of commission; to disable; to ruin, spoil.

invadir [im·ba·ḍír] *v.* to invade.

invalidar [im·ba·li·dár] *v.* to render invalid; to void, annul.

inválido [im·bá·li·ɖo] *adj.* invalid; void, null; sickly, weak; *m.* invalid.

invariable [im·ba·rjá·ƀle] *adj.* invariable.

invasión [im·ba·sjón] *f.* invasion.

invasor [im·ba·sór] *m.* invader; *adj.* invading; **ejército —** invading army.

invencible [im·ben·sí·ƀle] *adj.* invincible, unconquerable.

invención [im·ben·sjón] *f.* invention.

invendible [im·ben·di·ƀle] *adj.* unsaleable.

inventar [im·ben·tár] *v.* to invent.

inventariar[17] [im·ben·ta·rjár] *v.* to inventory, take an inventory of.

inventario [im·ben·tá·rjo] *m.* inventory.

inventiva [im·ben·tí·ƀa] *f.* inventiveness, power of inventing, ingenuity.

inventivo [im·ben·tí·ƀo] *adj.* inventive.

invento [im·bén·to] *m.* invention.

inventor [im·ben·tór] *m.* inventor; storyteller, fibber.

invernáculo [im·ber·ná·ku·lo] *m.* greenhouse, hothouse.

invernada [im·ber·ná·ɖa] *f.* wintering; *Am.* pasturing.

invernadero [im·ber·na·ɖé·ro] *m.* winter quarters; winter resort; winter pasture; greenhouse, hothouse.

invernal [im·ber·nál] *adj.* wintry, winter.

invernar[1] [im·ber·nár] *v. irr.* to winter, spend the winter.

inverosímil [im·be·ro·sí·mil] **inverisímil** [im·be·ri·sí·mil] *adj.* unlikely, improbable.

inversión [im·bér·sjón] *f.* inversion; investment.

inverso [im·bér·so] *adj.* inverse, inverted; reverse; **a** (*or* **por**) **la inversa** on the contrary.

invertir[3] [im·ber·tír] *v. irr.* to invert; to reverse; to invest; to employ, spend (*time*).

investigación [im·bes·ti·ga·sjón] *f.* investigation.

investigador [im·bes·ti·ga·ɖór] *m.* investigator; *adj.* investigating.

investigar[7] [im·bes·ti·gár] *v.* to investigate.

invicto [im·bík·to] *adj.* unconquered; always victorious.

invierno [im·bjér·no] *m.* winter; *C.A., Col., Ven., Ec., Peru* the rainy season.

invisible [im·bi·si·ƀle] *adj.* invisible.

invitación [im·bi·ta·sjón] *f.* invitation.

invitar [im·bi·tár] *v.* to invite.

invocación [im·bo·ka·sjón] *f.* invocation.

invocar[6] [im·bo·kár] *v.* to invoke.

involuntario [im·bo·lun·tá·rjo] *adj.* involuntary.

inyección [in·ŷek·sjón] *f.* injection.

inyectado [in·ŷek·tá·ɖo] *p.p.* injected; *adj.* bloodshot, inflamed.

inyectar [in·ŷek·tár] *v.* to inject.

ion [jon] *m.* ion.

ionizar[9] [jo·ni·sár] *v. irr.* to ionize.

ir[33] [ir] *v. irr.* to go; to walk; **— corriendo** to be running; **— entendiendo** to understand gradually; to begin to understand; **— a caballo** to ride horseback; **— a pie** to walk; **— en automóvil** to drive, ride in an automobile; **no irle ni venirle a uno** to make no difference to one; **¿cómo le va?** how are you? **no me va nada en eso** that doesn't concern me; **¡vamos!** let's go! come on! **¡vaya!** **¡vaya un hómbre!** what a man!; **-se** to go, go away; to escape; **-se abajo** to fall down, topple over; to collapse; **-se a pique** yo founder, sink.

ira [í·ra] *f.* ire, anger.

iracundo [i·ra·kún·do] *adj.* irritable; angry.

iridio [i·ri·ɖjo] *m.* iridium.

iris [í·ris] *m.* iris (*of the eye*); **arco —** rainbow.

irisado [i·ri·sá·ɖo] *adj.* iridescent, rainbow-hued.

ironía [i·ro·ní·a] *f.* irony.

irónico [i·ró·ni·ko] *adj.* ironic, ironical.

irracional [i·rra·sjo·nál] *adj.* irrational, unreasonable.

irradiar [i·rra·ɖjár] *v.* to radiate.

irreal [i·rre·ál] *adj.* unreal.

irreflexión [i·rre·flek·sjón] *f.* thoughtlessness.

irreflexivo [i·rre·flek·sí·ƀo] *adj.* thoughtless.

irrefrenable [i·rre·fre·ná·ƀle] *adj.* uncontrollable.

irrefutable [i·rre·fu·tá·ƀle] *adj.* irrefutable.

irregular [i·rre·gu·lár] *adj.* irregular.

irreligioso [i·rre·li·xjó·so] *adj.* irreligious.

irremediable [i·rre·me·ɖjá·ƀle] *adj.* irremediable; hopeless, incurable.

irreprochable [i·rre·pro·čá·ƀle] *adj.* irreproachable, flawless.

irresistible [i·rre·sis·tí·ƀle] *adj.* irresistible.

irresoluto [i·rre·so·lú·to] *adj.* irresolute, undecided, hesitating.

irrespetuoso [i·rres·pe·twó·so] *adj.* disrespectful.

irreverencia [i·rre·ƀe·rén·sja] *f.* irreverence.

irreverente [i·rre·ƀe·rén·te] *adj.* irreverent.

irrigación [i·rre·ga·sjón] *f.* irrigation.

irrigar[7] [i·rri·gár] *v.* to irrigate.

irrisión [i·rri·sjón] *f.* mockery, ridicule, derision.

irritación [i·rri·ta·sjón] *f.* irritation.

irritante [i·rri·tán·te] *adj.* irritating.

irritar [i·rri·tár] *v.* to irritate.

irrumpir [i·rrum·pír] *v.* to enter violently; to invade.

irrupción [i·rrup·sjón] *f.* sudden attack, raid, invasion.

isla [íz·la] *f.* island.

islamismo [iz·la·míz·mo] *m.* islamism.

islandés [iz·lan·dés] *adj.* Icelandic.

isleno [iz·lé·ño] *m.* islander.

isobara [i·so·ƀá·ra] *f.* isobar.

islote [iz·ló·te] *m.* islet, small rocky island.

istmo [íz·mo] *m.* isthmus.

italiano [i·ta·ljá·no] *adj. & m.* Italian.

itinerario [i·ti·ne·rá·rjo] *m.* itinerary; timetable, schedule; railroad guide.

itrio [í·trjo] *m.* yttrium.

izar[9] [i·sár] *v.* to hoist; to heave.

izquierda [is·kjér·ɖa] *f.* left hand; left side; left wing (*in politics*); **a la —** to the left; **izquierdista** [is·kjer·ɖís·ta] *m. & f.* leftist, radical.

izquierdo [is·kjér·ɖo] *adj.* left; left-handed.

J:j

jabalí [xa·ƀa·lí] *m.* wild boar.

jabalina [xa·ƀa·lí·na] *f.* javelin; wild sow.

jabón [xa·ƀón] *m.* soap; *Ríopl.* fright, fear; **dar —** to soft-soap, flatter; **dar un —** to give a good scolding; to beat, thrash.

jabonadura [xa·ƀo·na·ɖú·ra] *f.* washing, soaping; **-s** suds, lather; **dar a uno una —** to reprimand or scold someone.

jabonar [xa·ƀo·nár] *v.* (*lavar*) to lather, soap; (*reprender*) to scold; reprimand.

jabonera [xa·ƀo·né·ra] *f.* soap dish; woman soap vendor or maker.

jaca [xá·ka] *f.* pony, small horse; **jaco** [xa·ko] *m.* small nag; poor horse.

jacal [xa·kál] *m. Mex.* shack, adobe hut; **jacalucho** [xa·ka·lú·čo] *m. Am.* poor, ugly shack.

jacinto [xa·sín·to] *m.* hyacinth.
jactancia [xak·tán·sja] *f.* boast, brag; boasting.
jactancioso [xak·tan·sjó·so] *adj.* braggart, boastful.
jactarse [xak·tár·se] *v.* to brag, boast.
jaculatoria [xa·ku·la·tó·rja] *f.* short, fervent prayer.
jadeante [xa·de·án·te] *adj.* breathless, panting, out of breath.
jadear [xa·de·ár] *v.* to pant.
jadeo [xa·dé·o] *m.* pant, panting.
jaez [xa·és] *m.* harness; kind, sort; **jaeces** [xa·é·ses] trappings.
jaguar [xa·gwár] *m.* jaguar.
jagüey [xa·gwéj] *m.* puddle, pool.
jai alai [xaj·a·láj] *m.* Basque game played with basket and *pelota*.
jalar [xa·lár] *v.* to pull; to haul; to jerk; *C.A.* to court, make love; *Ven., Andes* to flunk (*a student*); *Mex.* **ijala!** [xá·la] (*or* **ijálale!** [xá·la·le]) get going! get a move on there!; **-se** *Am.* to get drunk; *Mex.* to go away, move away.
jalea [xa·lé·a] *f.* jelly.
jalear [xa·le·ár] *v.* to shout (*to hunting dogs*); to rouse, beat up (*game*); to shout and clap (*to encourage dancers*)
jaleo [xa·lé·o] *m.* shouting and clapping (*to encourage dancers*); an Andalusian dance; revelry, merrymaking; jesting; gracefulness.
jaletina [xa·le·tí·na] *f.* gelatin.
jalón [xa·lón] *m.* marker (*for boundaries*); *Am.* pull, jerk, tug; *Mex., C.A.* swallow of liquor; *Bol., C.A.* stretch, distance.
jalonear [xa·lo·ne·ár] *v. C.A., Mex.* to pull, jerk.
jamás [xa·más] *adv.* never.
jamón [xa·món] *m.* ham; *P.R.* fix, difficulty.
jamona [xa·mó·na] *f.* popular term for a fat middle-aged woman.
japonés [xa·po·nés] *adj. & m.* Japanese.
jaque [xá·ke] *m.* check (*in chess*); braggart, bully; **— mate** checkmate (*in chess*); **tener a uno en —** to hold someone under a threat.
jaqueca [xa·ké·ka] *f.* headache; sick headache.
jara [xá·ra] *f.* rockrose (*shrub*); *Ven., Col.* reed; **jaral** [xa·rál] *m.* bramble of rockroses; *Am.* reeds, clump of reeds.
jarabe [xa·rá·be] *m.* syrup; sweet beverage; *Mex., C.A.* a kind of tap dance; *Mex.* song and musical accompaniment of the **jarabe**.
jarana [xa·rá·na] *f.* merrymaking, revelry; trick; fib; jest; *Col., Ec., Carib.* a dance; *Mex.* small guitar; **ir de —** to go on a spree.
jarcia [xár·sja] *f.* rigging (*ropes, chains, etc. for the masts, yards and sails of a ship*); fishing tackle; pile, heap; jumble of things.
jardín [xar·dín] *m.* flower garden.
jardinero [xar·di·né·ro] *m.* gardener.
jarra [xá·rra] *f.* jar, vase, pitcher; **de** (*or* **en**) **-s** akimbo (*with hands on the hips*).
jarro [xá·rro] *m.* jar, jug, pitcher.
jarrón *m.* large vase or jar.
jaspe [xás·pe] *m.* jasper; veined marble; **jaspeado** *adj.* veined, streaked, mottled.
jaula [xáw·la] *f.* cage; cagelike cell or prison; *Am.* roofless cattle car or freight car.
jauría [xaw·rí·a] *f.* pack of hounds.
jazmín [xaz·mín] *m.* jasmine.
jefatura [xe·fa·tú·ra] *f.* position of chief; headquarters of a chief.
jefe [xé·fe] *m.* chief, leader, head.
jengibre [xeŋ·xí·bre] *m.* ginger.
jerez [xe·rés] *m.* sherry wine.
jerga [xér·ga] *f.* (*tela*) thick coarse cloth; straw

mattress; (*dialecto*) jargon; slang; *Am.* saddle pad; *Col.* poncho made of coarse cloth.
jergón [xer·gón] *m.* (*material*) straw mattress; ill-fitting suit or dress; (*persona*) big clumsy fellow; *Ríopl., Mex., Ven.* cheap coarse rug.
jerigonza [xe·ri·gón·sa] *f.* jargon; slang.
jeringa [xe·riŋ·ga] *f.* syringe; **jeringazo** [xe·riŋ·gá·so] *m.* injection; squirt.
jeringar[7] [xe·riŋ·gár] *v.* to inject; to squirt; to bother, molest, vex, annoy.
jeroglífico [xe·ro·glí·fi·ko] *m.* hieroglyphic.
jesuita [xe·swi·ta] *m.* Jesuit.
jeta [xé·ta] *f.* snout; thick lips.
jiba [xí·ba] = **giba.**
jíbaro [xí·ba·ro] *adj. P.R.* rustic, rural, rude, uncultured; *m. P.R.* bumpkin, peasant.
jibia [xi·bja] *f.* cuttlefish.
jícara [xí·ka·ra] *f.* chocolate cup; *Am.* small bowl made out of a gourd; *Am.* any small bowl; *Am.* bald head.
jilguero [xil·gé·ro] *m.* linnet.
jinete [xi·né·te] *m.* horseman, rider.
jineteada [xi·ne·te·á·da] *f. Ríopl., C.A.* roughriding, horse-breaking.
jinetear [xi·ne·te·ár] *v.* to ride horseback; to perform on horseback; *Am.* to break in (*a horse*); *Am.* to ride a bronco or bull.
jira [xí·ra] *f.* excursion, tour; outing, picnic; strip of cloth.
jirafa [xi·rá·fa] *f.* giraffe; boom mike (*broadcasting*).
jitomate [xi·to·má·te] *m. Mex.* tomato. *Also* **gitomate.**
jocoso [xo·kó·so] *adj.* jocular.
jofaina [xo·fáj·na] *f.* basin, washbowl.
jolgorio [xol·gó·rjo] = **holgorio.**
jornada [xor·ná·da] *f.* day's journey; military expedition; working day; act (*of a Spanish play*).
jornal [xor·nál] *m.* day's wages; bookkeeping journal; **a —** by the day.
jornalero [xor·na·lé·ro] *m.* day laborer.
joroba [xo·ró·ba] *f.* hump; nuisance, annoyance.
jorobado [xo·ro·bá·do] *adj.* hunchbacked; annoyed, bothered, in a bad fix; *m.* hunchback.
jorobar [xo·ro·bár] *v.* to bother, pester, annoy.
jorongo [xo·róŋ·go] *m. Mex.* Mexican poncho.
jota [xó·ta] *f.* name of the letter *j*; iota (*anything insignificant*); Aragonese and Valencian dance and music; *Am.* (= **ojota**) leather sandal; **no saber una —** not to know anything.
joven [xó·ben] *adj.* young; *m. & f.* youth; young man; young woman.
jovial [xo·bjál] *adj.* jovial, jolly, merry; **jovialidad** [xo·bja·li·dád] *f.* gaiety, merriment, fun.
joya [xó·ya] *f.* jewel; piece of jewelry; **-s** jewels; trousseau.
joyería [xo·ye·rí·a] *f.* jeweler's shop.
joyero [xo·yé·ro] *m.* jeweler; jewel box.
juanete [xwa·né·te] *m.* bunion.
jubilación [xu·bi·la·sjón] *f.* retirement (*from a position or office*); pension.
jubilar [xu·bi·lár] *v.* to pension; to retire; **-se** to be pensioned or retired; to rejoice; *Col.* to decline, fall into decline; *Ven., Guat.* to play hooky or truant.
jubileo [xu·bi·lé·o] *m.* jubilee; time of rejoicing; concession by the Pope of plenary (*complete*) indulgence.
júbilo [xú·bi·lo] *m.* joy, glee.
jubiloso [xu·bi·ló·so] *adj.* jubilant, joyful.
jubón [xu·bón] *m.* jacket; bodice.

judía [xu·ḍí·a] *f. Spain* bean; string bean; Jewess; -s tiernas (*or* verdes) string beans.

judicial [xu·ḍi·sjál] *adj.* judicial; -mente *adv.* judicially.

judío [xu·ḍí·o] *adj.* Jewish; *m.* Jew.

judo [xú·ḍo] *m.* judo.

juego [xwé·ġo] *m.* game; play; sport; gambling; pack of cards; set; — de palabras pun, play on words; — de te tea set; hacer — to match; poner en — to coordinate; to set in motion.

juerga [xwér·ġa] *f.* spree, revelry, wild festivity; irse de — to go out on a spree; juerguista *m. & f.* merrymaker.

jueves [xwé·ḅes] *m.* Thursday.

juez [xwes] *m.* judge; juror, member of a jury; — arbitrador (*or* árbitro) arbitrator, umpire.

jugada [xu·ġá·ḍa] *f.* play, move; stroke; trick.

jugador [xu·ġa·ḍór] *m.* player; gambler; — de manos juggler.

jugar³⁴ [xu·ġár] *v. irr.* to play; to gamble; to toy; — a la pelota to play ball; *Am.* — a dos cartas to be double-faced.

jugarreta [xu·ġa·rré·ta] *f.* bad play, wrong play; mean trick; tricky deal; *Am.* noisy game.

jugo [xú·ġo] *m.* juice; sap.

jugosidad [xu·ġo·si·ḍáḍ] *f.* juiciness; jugoso *adj.* juicy.

juguete [xu·ġé·te] *m.* plaything, toy; jest, joke; — cómico skit; por (*or* de) — jokingly.

juguetear [xu·ġe·te·ár] *v.* to play around, romp, frolic; to toy; to tamper (with), fool (with).

juguetón [xu·ġe·tón] *adj.* playful.

juicio [xwi·sjo] *m.* judgment; sense, wisdom; opinion; trial; perder el — to lose one's mind, go crazy.

juicioso [xwi·sjó·so] *adj.* judicious, wise; sensible.

julio [xú·ljo] *m.* July.

jumento [xu·mén·to] *m.* ass, donkey.

juncal [xun·kál] *m.* growth of rushes.

junco [xúŋ·ko] *m.* rush, reed; junk (*Chinese sailboat*).

jungla [xúŋ·gla] *f. Am.* jungle.

junio [xú·njo] *m.* June.

junquillo [xuŋ·kí·yo] *m.* reed; jonquil (*yellow flower similar to the daffodil*), species of narcissus.

junta [xún·ta] *f.* (*reunión*) meeting, conference; (*funcionarios*) board, council.

juntar [xun·tár] *v.* to join, unite; to connect; to assemble; to collect; -se to assemble, gather; to be closely united; to associate (with).

junto [xún·to] *adj.* joined, united;-s together; *adv.* near; — a near to, close to; en — all together, in all; por — all together, in a lump; wholesale.

juntura [xun·tú·ra] *f.* juncture; junction; joint, seam.

jurado [xu·rá·ḍo] *m.* jury; juror, juryman; *adj. & p.p.* sworn.

juramentar [xu·ra·men·tár] *v.* to swear in; -se to take an oath, be sworn in.

juramento [xu·ra·mén·to] *m.* oath; vow; curse.

jurar [xu·rár] *v.* to swear, vow; to take oath; to curse.

jurisconsulto [xu·ris·kon·súl·to] *m.* jurist, expert in law; lawyer.

jurisdicción [xu·riz·ḍik·sjón] *f.* jurisdiction.

jurisprudencia [xu·ris·pru·ḍén·sja] *f.* jurisprudence, law.

juro: de — [xú·ro] *adv.* certainly, of course.

justa [xús·ta] *f.* joust, tournament, combat (*between horsemen with lances*); contest.

justicia [xus·tí·sja] *f.* justice; court of justice; judge; police.

justiciero [xus·ti·sjé·ro] *adj.* strictly just, austere (*in matters of justice*).

justificación [xus·ti·fi·ka·sjón] *f.* justification.

justificante [xus·ti·fi·kán·te] *adj.* justifying; *m.* voucher; written excuse; proof.

justificar⁶ [xus·ti·fi·kár] *v.* to justify; to vindicate, clear of blame.

justo [xús·to] *adj.* just; pious; exact, correct; tight; *adv.* duly; exactly; tightly; *m.* just man; los -s the just.

juvenil [xu·ḅe·níl] *adj.* juvenile, young, youthful.

juventud [xu·ḅen·túḍ] *f.* youth; young people.

juzgado [xuz·ġá·ḍo] *m.* court, tribunal.

juzgar⁷ [xuz·ġár] *v.* to judge.

K:k

kermesse [ker·mé·se] *f.* country fair; bazaar for charity.

keroseno [ke·ro·sé·no] *f.* kerosene, coal oil.

kilo [kí·lo] *m.* kilo, kilogram.

kilociclo [ki·lo·sí·klo] *m.* kilocycle.

kilogramo [ki·lo·ġrá·mo] *m.* kilogram.

kilometraje [ki·lo·me·trá·xe] *m.* number of kilometers.

kilómetro [ki·ló·me·tro] *m.* kilometer.

kilovatio [ki·lo·ḅá·tjo] *m.* kilowatt.

L:l

la [la] *def. art. f.* the; — de the one with, that one with; *obj. pron.* her; it; — que rel. pron. she who, the one that; which.

la [la] *m.* sixth note on the musical scale.

laberinto [la·ḅe·rín·to] *m.* labyrinth, maze; labyrinth, internal ear.

labia [la·ḅja] *f.* fluency, talkativeness, gift of gab; tener mucha — to be a good talker.

labial [la·ḅjál] *adj.* labial.

labio [lá·ḅjo] *m.* lip.

labiodental [la·ḅjo·ḍen·tál] *adj.* labiodental.

labor [la·ḅór] *f.* (*trabajo*) labor, work; (*cosido*) embroidery; needlework; (*agrícola*) tillage; — de punto knitting; laborable [la·ḅo·rá·ḅle] *adj.* workable; tillable; día laborable work day; laboral [la·ḅo·rál] *adj.* pertaining to labor.

laboratorio [la·ḅo·ra·tó·rjo] *m.* laboratory.

laboriosidad [la·ḅo·rjo·si·ḍáḍ] *f.* laboriousness, industry.

laborioso [la·ḅo·rjó·so] *adj.* laborious; industrious.

laborista [la·ḅo·rís·ta] *m. & f.* laborite.

labrado [la·ḅrá·ḍo] *p.p. & adj.* (*agrícola*) tilled, cultivated; (*hecho*) wrought; manufactured; carved; *m.* carving; — en madera woodwork, carving; -s cultivated lands.

labrador [la·ḅra·ḍór] *m.* farmer; peasant.

labranza [la·ḅrán·sa] *f.* farming, tillage, plowing; cultivated land, farm.

labrar [la·ḅrár] *v.* (*la tierra*) to till, cultivate, farm; to plow; (*crear*) to carve; to embroider; to work (*metals*); to build (*a monument*).

labriego [la·ḅrjé·ġo] *m.* peasant.

laca [lá·ka] *f.* lacquer; shellac.

lacayo [la·ká·yo] *m.* lackey, footman, flunky.

lacio [lá·sjo] *adj.* withered; languid; limp; straight

(hair).
lacra [lá·kra] *f.* trace of an illness; blemish, defect; *Am.* sore, ulcer, scab, scar.
lacre [lá·kre] *m.* red sealing wax; *adj. Am.* red.
lacrimógeno [la·kri·mó·xe·no] *adj.* tear-producing.
lactar [lak·tár] *v.* to nurse, suckle; to feed with milk.
lácteo [lák·te·o] *adj.* milky; **fiebre láctea** milk fever; **régimen** — milk diet; **Vía láctea** milk Way.
ladear [la·de·ár] *v.* to tilt, tip; to go along the slope or side of; to turn aside (*from a way or course*); **-se** to tilt; to sway; to incline or lean (towards); to move to one side; *Am.* to fall in love.
ladeo [la·dé·o] *m.* inclination, tilt.
ladera [la·dé·ra] *f.* slope.
ladino [la·dí·no] *adj.* crafty, sly, shrewd; conversant with two or three languages; *m.* Sephardic Jew (*Spanish-speaking*); Romansch (*a Romance language of Switzerland*); *Guat.* Spanish-speaking person (*as opposed to one who speaks an Indian language*); *Am.* mestizo, half-breed; *Mex., Ven.* talker, talkative person.
lado [lá·do] *m.* side; **al** — near, at hand, at one's side; **de** — tilted, obliquely; sideways; — **a** — side by side; **¡a un** —! gangway! **hacerse a un** — to move over, step aside, move to one side; *Mex., Ven.* **echársela de** — to boast.
ladrar [la·drár] *v.* to bark.
ladrido [la·drí·do] *m.* bark, barking.
ladrillo [la·drí·yo] *m.* brick.
ladrón [la·drón] *m.* thief, robber; **ladronzuelo** [la·dron·swé·lo] *m.* petty thief.
lagartija [la·gar·tí·xa] *f.* small lizard.
lagarto [la·gár·to] *m.* lizard; rascal, sly fellow.
lago [lá·go] *m.* lake.
lágrima [lá·gri·ma] *f.* tear; **llorar a** — **viva** to weep abundantly.
lagrimear [la·gri·me·ár] *v.* to weep, shed tears.
laguna [la·gú·na] *f.* lagoon; gap, blank space.
laico [láj·ko] *adj.* lay; *m.* layman.
laísta [la·ís·ta] *m. & f.* one who uses *la* for indirect object.
laja [lá·xa] *f.* slab; flat stone.
lamedero [la·me·dé·ro] *m.* salt lick (*for cattle*).
lamentable [la·men·tá·ble] *adj.* lamentable, pitiful.
lamentación [la·men·ta·sjón] *f.* lamentation.
lamentar [la·men·tár] *v.* to lament, deplore; **-se** to moan, complain, wail.
lamento [la·mén·to] *m.* lament, moan, cry.
lamer [la·mér] *v.* to lick; to lap.
lamida [la·mí·da] *f. Mex., C.A.* lick; also **lambida**.
lámina [lá·mi·na] *f.* metal plate; sheet of metal; engraving; book illustration.
laminar [la·mi·nár] *v.* to laminate.
lámpara [lá·pa·ra] *f.* lamp.
lampiño [lam·pi·ño] *adj.* hairless; beardless.
lana [lá·na] *f.* wool; *Am.* tramp, vagabond.
lanar [la·nar] *adj.* wool-bearing; of wool.
lance [lán·se] *m.* occurrence, event; cast, throw, move, turn; accident; quarrel; predicament.
lancear [lan·se·ár] *v.* to lance, spear.
lancha [lán·ča] *f.* launch; boat; slab; **lanchón** [lan·čón] *m.* barge.
langosta [laŋ·gós·ta] *f.* lobster; locust.
languidecer[13] [laŋ·gi·de·sér] *v. irr.* to languish.
languidez [laŋ·gi·dés] *f.* languor, faintness, weakness.
lánguido [láŋ·gi·do] *adj.* languid.
lanilla [la·ní·ya] *f.* nap (*of cloth*).

lanudo [la·nú·do] *adj.* woolly; *Ven.* coarse, crude, ill-bred; *Am.* dull, slow, weak-willed; *Ch., C.A., Col.* wealthy.
lanza [lán·sa] *f.* lance, spear; *Col.* swindler, cheat; *m.* **lanzabombas** [lan·sa·bóm·bas] bomb launcher; *m.* **lanzacohetes** [lan·sa·ko·é·tes] rocket launcher; *m.* **lanzallamas** [lan·sa·yá·mas] flame thrower.
lanzada [lan·sá·da] *f.* thrust (*with a spear*).
lanzadera [lan·sa·dé·ra] *f.* shuttle.
lanzamiento [lan·sa·mjén·to] *m.* launching (*boat or rocket*).
lanzar[9] [lan·sár] *v.* to fling, throw; to eject; to launch; **-se** to rush, fling oneself; to dart out.
lanzazo [lan·sá·so] *m.* thrust with a lance.
lapicero [la·pi·sé·ro] *m.* pencil (*a mechanical pencil, one with an adjustable lead*).
lápida [lá·pi·da] *f.* slab, tombstone; stone tablet.
lapidar [la·pi·dár] *v.* to stone; *Col., Ch.* to cut precious stones.
lapidario [la·pi·dá·rjo] *m.* lapidary.
lápiz [lá·pis] *f.* pencil; crayon; — **para los labios** lipstick.
lapso [láp·so] *m.* lapse.
lardo [lár·do] *m.* lard.
lares [lá·res] *m. pl.* home.
largar[7] [lar·gár] *v.* to loosen; to let go; to set free; to unfold (*a flag or sails*); *Am.* to hurl, throw; *Col.* to strike (*a blow*); *Ríopl.* to give, hand over; **-se** to go away, slip away; to leave.
largo [lár·go] *adj.* long; generous; *m.* length; largo (*music*); **a la larga** in the long run; slowly; **a lo** — along; lengthwise; **¡— de aquí!** get out of here!
largor [lar·gór] *m.* length.
largucho [lar·gú·čo] *adj.* lanky.
largueza [lar·ge·sa] *f.* generosity, liberality; length.
larguísimo [lar·gí·si·mo] *adj.* very long.
largura [lar·gú·ra] *f.* length.
laringe [la·ríŋ·xe] *f.* larynx.
laríngeo [la·ríŋ·xe·o] *adj.* laryngeal.
laringitis [la·riŋ·xí·tis] *f.* laryngitis.
larva [lár·ba] *f.* larva.
las [las] *def. art. f. pl.* the; *obj. pron.* them; — **que** *rel. pron.* those which; which.
lascivia [la·sí·bja] *f.* lewdness.
lascivo [la·sí·bo] *adj.* lascivious, lewd.
lástima [lás·ti·ma] *f.* pity; compassion, grief.
lastimadura [las·ti·ma·dú·ra] *f.* sore, hurt.
lastimar [las·ti·már] *v.* to hurt; to offend; **-se** to get hurt; **-se de** to feel pity for.
lastimero [las·ti·mé·ro] *adj.* pitiful; mournful.
lastimoso [las·ti·mó·so] *adj.* pitiful.
lastre [lás·tre] *m.* ballast, weight.
lata [lá·ta] *f.* (*metal*) tin plate; tin can, can; (*madero*) small log; thin board; (*pesadez*) annoyance; embarrassment; boring speech; *Am.* gaucho saber; *Am.* prop.
latente [la·tén·te] *adj.* latent.
lateral [la·te·rál] *adj.* lateral, side; [1] (*phonetically*).
latido [la·tí·do] *m.* palpitation, throb, beat; bark, howl.
latifundio [la·ti·fún·djo] *m.* large landed estate.
latigazo [la·ti·gá·so] *m.* lash, stroke with a whip; crack of a whip; harsh reprimand; unexpected blow or offense.
látigo [lá·ti·go] *m.* whip; *Am.* whipping, beating; *Ch.* end or goal of a horse race.
latín [la·tín] *m.* Latin language.
latinismo [la·ti·níz·mo] *m.* Latinism; imitating

Latin.

latino [la·tí·no] *adj.* Latin; *m.* Latinist, Latin scholar; Latin.

latir [la·tír] *v.* to throb, beat, palpitate; to bark.

latitud [la·ti·túd] *f.* latitude; extent, breadth.

latón [la·tón] *m.* brass.

latrocinio [la·tro·sí·njo] *m.* larceny, theft, robbery.

laúd [la·úd] *m.* lute; catboat (*long, narrow boat with a lateen sail*).

laudable [law·dá·ƀle] *adj.* laudable, praiseworthy.

laurel [law·rél] *m.* laurel; laurel wreath.

lauro [láw·ro] *m.* laurel; glory, fame.

lava [lá·ƀa] *f.* lava; washing of minerals.

lavable [la·ƀá·ƀle] *adj.* washable.

lavabo [la·ƀá·ƀo] *m.* lavatory, washroom; washstand; washbowl.

lavadero [la·ƀa·dé·ro] *m.* washing place.

lavado [la·ƀá·do] *m.* wash, washing; laundry, laundry work; — **de cerebro** brain washing.

lavador [la·ƀa·dór] *m.* washer; cleaner; *adj.* washing; cleaning; **lavadora** [la·ƀa·dó·ra] *f.* washer, washing machine.

lavadura [la·ƀa·dú·ra] *f.* washing; slops, dirty water.

lavamanos [la·ƀa·má·nos] *m.* lavatory, washbowl, washstand.

lavandera [la·ƀan·dé·ra] *f.* laundress, washerwoman.

lavandería [la·ƀan·de·rí·a] *f.* laundry.

lavar [la·ƀár] *v.* to wash; to launder; to whitewash.

lavativa [la·ƀa·tí·ƀa] *f.* enema; syringe; bother, nuisance.

lavatorio [la·ƀa·tó·rjo] *m.* washing (*act of washing*); wash (*liquid or solution for washing*); lavatory (*ceremonial act of washing*); washbowl, washstand; *Am.* washroom.

lavazas [la·ƀá·sas] *f. pl.* slops, dirty water.

laxante [lak·sán·te] *m.* laxative.

lazada [la·sá·da] *f.* bow, bowknot; *Am.* throwing of the lasso, lassoing.

lazar[9] [la·sár] *v.* to rope, lasso; to noose.

lazarillo [la·sa·rí·yo] *m.* blindman's guide.

lazo [lá·so] *m.* (*nudo*) bow, knot; slipknot; lasso, lariat; (*vínculo*) tie, bond; (*trampa*) snare, trap; trick.

le [le] *obj. pron.* him; you (*formal*); to him; to her; to you (*formal*).

leal [le·ál] *adj.* loyal.

lealtad [le·al·tád] *f.* loyalty.

lebrel [le·ƀrél] *m.* greyhound.

lebrillo [le·ƀrí·yo] *m.* earthenware basin or tub.

lección [lek·sjón] *f.* lesson; reading; **dar la** — to recite the lesson; **dar** — to teach; **tomarle a uno la** — to have someone recite his lesson.

lector [lek·tór] *m.* reader; lecturer.

lectura [lek·tú·ra] *f.* reading; **libro de** — reader.

lechada [le·čá·da] *f.* whitewash; *Am.* milking.

leche [lé·če] *f.* milk; *Col., Ven., C.A., Andes, Ríopl.* luck (*in games*).

lechería [le·če·rí·a] *f.* dairy, creamery; **lechero** [le·čé·ro] *adj.* milk; milch, giving milk (*applied to animals*); *Am.* lucky (*in games of chance*); *m.* milkman; **lechera** [le·čé·ra] *f.* milkmaid; milk can; milk pitcher.

lecho [lé·čo] *m.* bed; river bed.

lechón [le·čón] *m.* suckling pig; pig.

lechoso [le·čó·so] *adj.* milky; *m.* papaya tree; **lechosa** [le·čó·sa] *f. P.R.* papaya (*tropical fruit*).

lechuga [le·čú·ga] *f.* lettuce.

lechuza [le·čú·sa] *f.* screech owl, barn owl.

leer[14] [le·ér] *v.* to read.

legación [le·ga·sjón] *f.* legation.

legado [le·gá·do] *m.* (*donación*) legacy; legato; (*representante*) representative, ambassador.

legajo [le·gá·xo] *m.* bundle of papers; dossier.

legal [le·gál] *adj.* legal, lawful; truthful; reliable; *Col., Ven., Andes* excellent, best; *Am.* just, honest.

legalizar[9] [le·ga·li·sár] *v.* to legalize.

legar[7] [le·gár] *v.* to will, bequeath; to send as a delegate.

legendario [le·xen·dá·rjo] *adj.* legendary.

legión [le·xjón] *f.* legion.

legislación [le·xiz·la·sjón] *f.* legislation.

legislador [le·xiz·la·dór] *m.* legislator; *adj.* legislating, legislative.

legislar [le·xiz·lár] *v.* to legislate.

legislativo [le·xiz·la·tí·ƀo] *adj.* legislative.

legislatura [le·xiz·la·tú·ra] *f.* legislature, legislative assembly.

legítimo [le·xí·ti·mo] *adj.* legitimate; real, genuine.

lego [lé·go] *adj.* lay; ignorant; *m.* layman.

legua [lé·gwa] *f.* league (*about 3 miles*).

leguleyo [le·gu·lé·yo] *m.* shyster.

legumbre [le·gúm·bre] *f.* vegetable.

leída [le·í·da] *f. Am.* reading. See **lectura**.

leísta [le·ís·ta] *m. & f.* one who uses the pronoun **le** for masculine direct object (*le conozco*).

lejanía [le·xa·ní·a] *f.* distance; distant place.

lejano [le·xá·no] *adj.* distant; remote.

lejía [le·xí·a] *f.* lye; harsh reprimand.

lejos [lé·xos] *adv.* far, far away; **a lo** — in the distance; *Am.* **a un** — in the distance; **de** (or **desde**) — from afar; *m.* view, perspective; background.

lelo [lé·lo] *adj.* silly, stupid, foolish.

lema [lé·ma] *m.* motto; theme; slogan.

lencería [len·se·rí·a] *f.* dry goods; dry-goods store; linen room or closet.

lengua [léŋ·gwa] *f.* tongue; language; interpreter; — **de tierra** point, neck of land.

lenguado [leŋ·gwá·do] *m.* flounder, sole (*a fish*).

lenguaje [leŋ·gwá·xe] *m.* language (*manner of expression*).

lenguaraz [leŋ·gwa·rás] *adj.* talkative, loose-tongued.

lengüeta [leŋ·gwé·ta] *f.* small tongue; **lengüetada** [leŋ·gwe·ta·da] *f.* lick.

leninismo [le·ni·níz·mo] *m.* Leninism.

lente [lén·te] *m. & f.* lens; -**s** *m. pl.* eyeglasses.

lenteja [len·té·xa] *f.* lentil; lentil seed; **lentejuela** [len·te·xwé·la] *f.* spangle.

lentitud [len·ti·túd] *f.* slowness.

lento [lén·to] *adj.* slow; dull.

leña [lé·ña] *f.* firewood; kindling; beating; **leñera** [le·ñé·ra] *f.* woodshed; woodbox.

leñador [le·ña·dór] *m.* woodcutter; woodman.

leño [lé·ño] *m.* log; timber; piece of firewood.

león [le·ón] *m.* lion; **leona** [le·ó·na] *f.* lioness.

leonera [le·o·né·ra] *f.* lion's den or cage; dive, gambling joint; disorderly room.

leontina [le·on·tí·na] *f. Mex., Carib., Col.* watch chain.

leopardo [le·o·pár·do] *m.* leopard.

leopoldina [le·o·pol·dí·na] *f. Mex., Ven.* watch chain.

lerdo [lér·do] *adj.* dull, heavy, stupid, slow.

les [les] *obj. pron.* to them; to you (*formal*).

lesión [le·sjón] *f.* wound, injury.

lesionar [le·sjo·nár] *v.* to injure; to wound; to hurt; to damage.

lesna [léz·na] = **lezna.**

LA

letargo [le·tár·go] *m.* lethargy, stupor, drowsiness.
letra [lé·tra] *f.* letter (*of the alphabet*); printing type; hand; handwriting; letter (*exact wording or meaning*); words of a song; — **abierta** letter of credit; — **de cambio** draft, bill of exchange; — **mayúscula** capital letter; — **minúscula** small letter; **al pie de la** — literally; **-s** letters, learning.
letrado [le·trá·do] *adj.* learned; *m.* lawyer.
letrero [le·tré·ro] *m.* notice, poster, sign; legend (*under an illustration*).
leva [lé·ƀa] *f.* levy, draft; weighing anchor, setting sail; **echar** — to draft, conscript; *Col.* **echar -s** to boast.
levadizo [le·ƀa·dí·so] *adj.* lift (*bridge*).
levadura [le·ƀa·dú·ra] *f.* leaven, yeast.
levantamiento [le·ƀan·ta·mjén·to] *m.* (*revuelta*) uprising, revolt, insurrection; (*altura*) elevation; lifting, raising; adjournment (*of a meeting*); — **de un plano** surveying.
levantar [le·ƀan·tár] *v.* to raise, lift; to set up; to erect; to rouse, stir up; to recruit; *Ch.* to break land, plow; — **el campo** to break camp; — **la mesa** to clear the table; — **la sesión** to adjourn the meeting; — **un plano** to survey, map out; — **falso testimonio** to bear false witness; **-se** to stand up, get up, rise; to rebel.
levante [le·ƀán·te] *m.* east; east wind.
levantisco [le·ƀan·tís·ko] *adj.* turbulent; rebellious.
levar [le·ƀár] *v.* to weigh (*anchor*); — **el ancla** to weigh anchor; **-se** to weigh anchor, set sail.
leve [lé·ƀe] *adj.* light; slight; unimportant.
levita [le·ƀí·ta] *f.* frock coat; *m.* Levite, member of the tribe of Levi.
léxico [lék·si·ko] *m.* lexicon, dictionary; vocabulary; glossary.
lexicografía [lek·si·ko·gra·fí·a] *f.* lexicography.
lexicología [lek·si·ko·lo·xí·a] *f.* lexicology.
ley [lej] *f.* law; rule; loyalty; standard quality; **de buena** — of good quality; **plata de** — sterling silver; **-es** jurisprudence, law; system of laws.
leyenda [le·yén·da] *f.* legend; reading; inscription.
lezna [léz·na] *f.* awl.
liar[17] [ljar] *v.* to tie, bind; to roll up; to deceive; **-se** to bind oneself; to get tangled up.
libelo [li·ƀé·lo] *m.* libel.
libélula [li·ƀé·lu·la] *f.* dragon fly.
liberación [li·ƀe·ra·sjón] *f.* liberation; deliverance.
liberal [li·ƀe·rál] *adj.* liberal; generous; **liberalidad** [li·ƀe·ra·li·dád] *f.* liberality; generosity.
liberalismo [li·ƀe·ra·líz·mo] *m.* liberalism.
libertad [li·ƀer·tád] *f.* liberty.
libertador [li·ƀer·ta·dór] *m.* liberator, deliverer.
libertar [li·ƀer·tár] *v.* to liberate, free, set free; **-se** to get free; to escape.
libertinaje [li·ƀer·ti·ná·xe] *m.* license, licentiousness, lack of moral restraint.
libertino [li·ƀer·tí·no] *m.* libertine (*person without moral restraint*).
libido [li·ƀí·do] *m.* libido.
libra [lí·ƀra] *f.* pound; Libra (*sign of the Zodiac*).
librador [li·ƀra·dór] *m.* drawer (*of a bill, draft, etc.*); deliverer, liberator; measuring scoop.
libranza [li·ƀrán·sa] *f.* bill of exchange, draft.
librar [li·ƀrár] *v.* to free, set free; to issue; to draw (*a draft*); — **guerra** to wage war; **-se** to save oneself; to escape; **-se de** to get rid of, escape from.
libre [lí·ƀre] *adj.* free; unmarried; loose; vacant.
librea [li·ƀré·a] *f.* livery (*uniform*).
librería [li·ƀre·rí·a] *f.* bookstore.
librero [li·ƀré·ro] *m.* bookseller; *Am.* bookcase,

bookshelves.
libreta [li·ƀré·ta] *f.* notebook, memorandum book,
libreto [li·ƀré·to] *m.* libretto.
libro [lí·ƀro] *m.* book; — **de caja** cashbook; — **mayor** ledger.
licencia [li·sén·sja] *f.* license; permission; furlough, leave; looseness; license to practice.
licenciado [li·sen·sjá·do] *m.* licenciate (*person having a degree approximately equivalent to a master's degree*); *Riopl., Mex., C.A.* lawyer.
licenciar [li·sen·sjár] *v.* to license; to give a license or permit; to dismiss, discharge (*from the army*); to confer the degree of **licenciado**; **-se** to get the degree of **licenciado**.
licenciatura [li·sen·sja·tú·ra] *f.* degree of **licenciado**.
licencioso [li·sen·sjó·so] *adj.* licentious, lewd.
liceo [li·sé·o] *m.* lyceum; high school; *Col.* primary school or high school.
lícito [lí·si·to] *adj.* lawful; permissible, allowable.
licor [li·kór] *m.* liquid; liquor.
lid [lid] *f.* fight; contest.
líder [lí·der] *m. Am.* leader.
lidiar [li·djár] *v.* to fight; to combat; to contend.
liebre [ljé·ƀre] *f.* hare; coward.
lienzo [ljén·so] *m.* cotton or linen cloth; canvas; painting.
liga [lí·ga] *f.* (*alianza*) league; alliance; (*cinta*) garter; alloy; birdlime.
ligadura [li·ga·dú·ra] *f.* binding; tie, bond.
ligar[7] [li·gár] *v.* to bind, tie, unite; to alloy (*combine metals*); **-se** to unite, combine, form an alliance.
ligereza [li·xe·ré·sa] *f.* lightness; swiftness; flippancy; frivolity.
ligero [li·xé·ro] *adj.* (*leve*) light; (*rápido*) swift; nimble; flippant; *adv. Am.* quickly; **a la ligera** quickly, superficially.
lija [lí·xa] *f.* sandpaper.
lijar [li·xár] *v.* to sandpaper.
lila [lí·la] *f.* lilac; pinkish-purple.
lima [lí·ma] *f.* file; lime (*fruit*); finishing, polishing.
limar [li·már] *v.* to file; to file down; to smooth, polish.
limeño [li·mé·ño] *adj.* of or from Lima, Peru.
limero [li·mé·ro] *m.* lime tree.
limitación [li·mi·ta·sjón] *f.* limitation; district.
limitar [li·mi·tár] *v.* to limit; to restrict; to bound.
límite [lí·mi·te] *m.* limit; boundary.
limítrofe [li·mí·tro·fe] *adj.* limiting; bordering.
limo [lí·mo] *m.* slime.
limón [li·món] *m.* lemon; lemon tree; **limonada** *f.* lemonade; **limonero** *m.* lemon tree lemon dealer or vendor.
limosna [li·móz·na] *f.* alms, charity.
limosnero [li·moz·né·ro] *m.* beggar.
limpiabotas [lim·pja·ƀó·tas] *m.* bootblack; *Ch.* bootlicker, flatterer.
limpiadientes [lim·pja·djén·tes] *m.* toothpick.
limpiaparabrisas [lim·pja·pa·ra·ƀrí·sas] *m.* windshield wiper.
limpiar [lim·pjár] *v.* to clean; to wipe; to cleanse, purify; *Am.* to beat up, whip, lash.
límpido [lím·pi·do] *adj.* limpid, clear.
limpieza [lim·pjé·sa] *f.* cleanliness, neatness; purity; honesty.
limpio [lím·pjo] *adj.* clean; neat; pure; **poner en** — to make a clean copy; *Am.* — **y soplado** absolutely broke, wiped out.
linaje [li·ná·xe] *m.* lineage, family, race.
linajudo [li·na·xú·do] *adj.* highborn.
linaza [li·ná·sa] *f.* linseed.

lince [lín·se] *m.* lynx; sharp-sighted person.
linchar [lin·čár] *v.* to lynch.
lindar [lin·dár] *v.* to border, adjoin.
linde [lín·de] *m. & f.* limit, border, boundary; landmark.
lindero [lin·dé·ro] *adj.* bordering upon; *m. Carib., C.A.* landmark; boundary.
lindeza [lin·dé·sa] *f.* prettiness; exquisiteness; neatness; witty act or remark.
lindo [lín·do] *adj.* pretty; **de lo** — wonderfully; very much; to the utmost.
línea [lí·ne·a] *f.* line; limit.
lineal [li·ne·ál] *adj.* lineal, linear.
lingüista [liŋ·gwís·ta] *m. & f.* linguist.
lingüística [liŋ·gwís·ti·ka] *f.* linguistics.
lingüístico [liŋ·gwís·ti·ko] *adj.* linguistic.
lino [lí·no] *m.* linen; flax; **linón** *m.* lawn, thin linen or cotton.
linotipia [li·no·tí·pja] *f.* linotype.
linterna [lin·tér·na] *f.* lantern.
lío [lí·o] *m. (bulto)* bundle; *(enredo)* fib; mess, confusion; **armar un** — to raise a rumpus; to cause confusion; **hacerse un** — to be confused, get tangled up; **meterse en un** — to get oneself into a mess.
liquidación [li·ki·da·sjón] *f.* liquidation; settlement *(of an account).*
liquidar [li·ki·dár] *v.* to liquidate; to settle *(an account).*
líquido [lí·ki·do] *m.* liquid.
lira [lí·ra] *f.* lyre, small harp; a type of metrical composition; lira *(Italian coin).*
lírico [lí·ri·ko] *adj.* lyric, lyrical; *Am.* fantastic; *m. Ríopl.* visionary, dreamer.
lirio [lí·rjo] *m.* lily.
lirismo [li·ríz·mo] *m.* lyricism *(lyric quality); Am.* idle dream, fantasy.
lisiado [li·sjá·do] *adj.* lame, hurt, injured.
liso [lí·so] *adj.* smooth, even; flat; evident, clear; *Am.* crafty, sly; *Col., Ven., C.A., Andes* fresh, impudent.
lisonja [li·sóŋ·xa] *f.* flattery.
lisonjear [li·soŋ·xe·ár] *v.* to flatter; to fawn on; to please.
lisonjero [li·soŋ·xé·ro] *adj.* flattering, pleasing; *m.* flatterer.
lista [lís·ta] *f.* list; strip; stripe; **pasar** — to call the roll; — **de correos** general delivery.
listado [lis·tá·do] *adj.* striped.
listar [lis·tár] *v.* to register, enter in a list; *Ríopl., Mex., Ven.* to stripe, streak.
listo [lís·to] *adj.* ready, prompt; clever; *Ríopl., Ch.* mischievous.
listón [lis·tón] *m.* ribbon, tape; strip.
lisura [li·sú·ra] *f.* smoothness; sincerity, frankness; *Am.* freshness, impudence; *Andes* insulting or filthy remark.
litera [li·té·ra] *f.* berth *(on a boat or train);* litter *(for carrying a person).*
literario [li·te·rá·rjo] *adj.* literary.
literato [li·te·rá·to] *adj.* literary, learned; *m.* literary man, writer.
literatura [li·te·ra·tú·ra] *f.* literature.
litigio [li·tí·xjo] *m.* litigation, lawsuit.
litio [lí·tjo] *m.* lithium.
litoral [li·to·rál] *adj.* seaboard, coastal; *m.* coast, shore.
litro [lí·tro] *m.* liter *(about 1.05 quarts).*
liviandad [li·bja·ni·dád] *f.* lightness; frivolity; lewdness.
liviano [li·bjá·no] *adj. (leve)* light; slight,

unimportant; *(lascivo)* frivolous, fickle; lewd; unchaste.
lívido [lí·bi·do] *adj.* livid, having a dull-bluish color; pale.
lo [lo] *obj. pron.* him; you *(formal);* it; so; *dem. pron.* — **de** that of, that affair of, that matter of; — **bueno** the good, what is good; **sé** — **bueno** que **Vd. es** I know how good you are; — **que** that which, what.
loable [lo·á·ble] *adj.* laudable, worthy of praise.
loar [lo·ár] *v.* to praise.
lobanillo [lo·ba·ní·yo] *m.* growth, tumor.
lobo [ló·bo] *m.* wolf.
lóbrego [ló·bre·go] *adj.* dark, gloomy.
lobreguez [lo·bre·gés] *f.* darkness, gloominess.
lóbulo [ló·bu·lo] *m.* lobe.
lobuno [lo·bú·no] *adj.* related to the wolf.
local [lo·kál] *adj.* local; *m.* place, quarters; site; premises.
localidad [lo·ka·li·dád] *f.* location; locality, town; place; seat *(in a theater).*
localización [lo·ka·li·sa·sjón] *f.* localization, localizing.
localizar[9] [lo·ka·li·sár] *v.* to localize.
loco [ló·ko] *adj.* insane, mad, crazy; — **de remate** stark mad; *m.* lunatic, insane person.
locomotor [lo·ko·mo·tór] *adj.* locomotive.
locomotora [lo·ko·mo·tó·ra] *f.* locomotive; — **diesel** diesel locomotive.
locuaz [lo·kwás] *adj.* loquacious, talkative.
locución [lo·ku·sjón] *f.* phrase; diction.
locura [lo·kú·ra] *f.* madness, insanity.
locutor [lo·ku·tór] *m.* radio announcer.
lodazal [lo·da·sál] *m.* muddy place; mire.
lodo [ló·do] *m.* mud; **lodoso** [lo·dó·so] *adj.* muddy, miry.
logaritmo [lo·ga·rím·mo] *m.* logarithm.
logia [ló·xja] *f.* lodge *(secret society).*
lógica [ló·xi·ka] *f.* logic; reasoning.
lógico [ló·xi·ko] *adj.* logical.
lograr [lo·grár] *v.* to gain, obtain, accomplish; — (+ *inf.*) to succeed in; **-se** to succeed; to turn out well.
logrero [lo·gré·ro] *m.* usurer; profiteer.
logro [ló·gro] *m.* profit, gain; usury; attainment; realization.
loísta [lo·ís·ta] *m. & f.* one who uses the pronoun *lo* for the masculine direct object *(lo conozco).*
loma [ló·ma] *f.* small hill; **lomerío** [lo·me·rí·o] *m. Am.* group of hills.
lombriz [lom·brís] *f.* earthworm.
lomillo [lo·mí·yo] *m.* cross-stitch.
lomo [ló·mo] *m.* back *(of an animal, book, knife, etc.);* loin; ridge between two furrows; *Mex., Ven.* **hacer** — to bear with patience, resign oneself.
lona [ló·na] *f.* canvas.
lonche [lón·če] *m. Col., Ven., Mex.* lunch; **lonchería** [lon·če·rí·a] *f. Col., Ven., Mex.* lunchroom.
londinense [lon·di·nén·se] *m. & f.* of or from London.
longaniza [loŋ·ga·ní·sa] *f.* pork sausage.
longevidad [loŋ·xe·bi·dád] *f.* longevity, long life; span of life, length of life.
longitud [loŋ·xi·túd] *f.* longitude; length.
longitudinal [loŋ·xi·tu·di·nál] *adj.* longitudinal, lengthwise; **-mente** *adv.* longitudinally, lengthwise.
lonja [lóŋ·xa] *f. (mercado)* exchange; market; *(carne)* slice of meat; *(correa)* leather strap; *Ríopl.* raw hide.

LE

lontananza [lon·ta·nán·sa] *f.* background; **en** — in the distance, in the background.
loro [ló·ro] *m.* parrot.
los [los] *def. art. m. pl.* the; *obj. pron.* them; — **que** *rel. pron.* those which; which.
losa [ló·sa] *f.* flagstone; slab; gravestone.
lote [ló·te] *m.* lot, share, part; *Am.* remnant lot; *Col.* swallow of liquor; *Am.* blockhead, dunce.
lotear [lo·te·ár] *v. Am.* to subdivide into lots; *Am.* to divide into portions.
lotería [lo·te·rí·a] *f.* lottery; raffle.
loza [ló·sa] *f.* fine earthenware; crockery; — **fina** chinaware.
lozanía [lo·sa·ní·a] *f.* luxuriance (*rich foliage or growth*); vigor.
lozano [lo·sá·no] *adj.* luxuriant; exuberant, vigorous, lusty.
lubricar[6] [lu·bri·kár] *v.* to lubricate, or grease.
lucero [lu·sé·ro] *m.* morning star; any bright star; star on the forehead of certain animals; splendor, brightness.
lúcido [lú·si·do] *adj.* lucid, clear; shining, bright.
luciente [lu·sjén·te] *adj.* shining, bright.
luciérnaga [lu·sjér·na·ga] *f.* firefly; glowworm.
lucimiento [lu·si·mjén·to] *m.* splendor; brilliance; success.
lucir[13] [lu·sír] *v. irr.* (*brillar*) to shine; to illuminate; to brighten; (*superar*) to excel; (*alardear*) to show off; **-se** to shine, be brilliant; show off; to be successful.
lucrativo [lu·kra·tí·bo] *adj.* lucrative, profitable.
lucro [lú·kro] *m.* profit, gain.
luctuoso [luk·twó·so] *adj.* sad, mournful, dismal.
lucha [lú·ča] *f.* fight, struggle; dispute; wrestling match.
luchador [lu·ča·dór] *m.* fighter; wrestler.
luchar [lu·čár] *v.* to fight; to wrestle; to struggle; to dispute.
luego [lwé·go] *adv.* soon, presently; afterwards, then, next; **desde** — immediately, at once; naturally; — **de** after; — **que** as soon as; **hasta** — good-bye, so long; — — right away.
luengo [lwén·go] *adj.* long; **-s años** many years.
lugar [lu·gár] *m.* (*sitio*) place; site; town; space; (*empleo*) position, employment; (*ocasión*) time, occasion, opportunity; **dar** — **a** to give cause or occasion for; **hacer** (*or* **dar**) — to make room; **en** — **de** instead of.
lugareño [lu·ga·ré·ño] *m.* villager.
lúgubre [lú·gu·bre] *adj.* mournful, gloomy.
lujo [lú·xo] *m.* luxury, extravagance.
lujoso [lu·xó·so] *adj.* luxurious; elegant; showy.
lujuria [lu·xú·rja] *f.* lust, lewdness, sensuality.
lujurioso [lu·xu·rjó·so] *adj.* lustful, lewd, sensual.
lumbre [lúm·bre] *f.* fire; brightness.
luminoso [lu·mi·nó·so] *adj.* luminous, bright, shining.
luna [lú·na] *f.* moon; mirror, glass for mirrors.
lunar [lu·nár] *adj.* lunar; *m.* mole; blemish, spot.
lunático [lu·ná·ti·ko] *adj. & m.* lunatic.
lunes [lú·nes] *m.* Monday; *Ch.* **hacer San Lunes** to lay off on Monday.
lunfardo [lun·fár·do] *m.* social dialect of the Buenos Aires underworld.
lustre [lús·tre] *m.* luster, shine; glory.
lustroso [lus·tró·so] *adj.* lustrous, glossy, shining.
luto [lú·to] *m.* mourning; sorrow, grief.
luz [lus] *f.* light; clarity; hint, guidance; **dar a** — to give birth; to publish; **entre dos luces** at twilight.

LL:ll

llaga [yá·ga] *f.* wound; ulcer, sore.
llama [yá·ma] *f.* flame; llama (*a South American beast of burden*).
llamada [ya·má·da] *f.* call; beckon, sign; knock; reference mark (*as an asterisk*).
llamador [ya·ma·dór] *m.* knocker (*of a door*); caller.
llamamiento [ya·ma·mjén·to] *m.* call, calling; calling together; appeal.
llamar [ya·már] *v.* to call; to summon; to name; to invoke; — **a la puerta** to knock at the door; **-se** to be called, named; *Am.* to break one's word or promise.
llamarada [ya·ma·rá·da] *f.* flash; sudden flame or blaze; sudden flush, blush.
llamativo [ya·ma·tí·bo] *adj.* showy, loud, gaudy, flashy; thirst-exciting.
llameante [ya·me·án·te] *adj.* flaming.
llana [yá·na] *f.* mason's trowel.
llanero [ya·né·ro] *m. Ven., Col.* plainsman.
llaneza [ya·né·sa] *f.* simplicity; frankness; sincerity; plainness.
llano [yá·no] *adj.* plain, simple; even, smooth, level; frank; *m.* plain, flat ground.
llanta [yán·ta] *f. Spain* rim of a wheel; *Am.* tire; tire casing; *Peru* large sunshade (*used in Peruvian markets*).
llanto [yán·to] *m.* crying, weeping; tears.
llanura [ya·nú·ra] *f.* extensive plain; prairie; evenness, flatness.
llapa [yá·pa] *f. Andes, Ríopl.* a small gift from the vendor to the purchaser; also **yapa, ñapa.**
llave [yá·be] *f.* key; faucet; clef; — **de tuercas** wrench; — **inglesa** monkey wrench; — **maestra** master key.
llavera [ya·bé·ra] *f. Am.* housekeeper.
llavero [ya·bé·ro] *m.* key ring; key maker; keeper of the keys.
llavín [ya·bín] *m.* small key.
llegada [ye·gá·da] *f.* arrival.
llegar[7] [ye·gár] *v.* to arrive; to reach; to amount; — **a ser** to get or come to be; — **a las manos** to come to blows; **-se** to approach, get near.
llenar [ye·nár] *v.* to fill; to stuff; **-se** to fill up; to overeat; **-se de** to get filled with; to get covered with, spattered with.
lleno [yé·no] *adj.* full; *m.* fullness, completeness; **de** — totally, completely; **un** — **completo** a full house (*said of a theater*).
llenura [ye·nú·ra] *f.* fullness; abundance.
llevadero [ye·ba·dé·ro] *adj.* bearable, tolerable.
llevar [ye·bár] *v.* (*transportar*) to carry; to bear; to transport; to wear; (*conducir*) to take; to lead; (*cobrar*) to charge; to ask a certain price; to keep (*accounts*); — **ventaja** to be ahead, have the advantage; — **un año a** to be one year older than; — **un mes aquí** to have been here one month; — **un castigo** to suffer punishment; **-se** to carry away; **-se bien con** to get along with.
llorar [yo·rár] *v.* to cry, weep.
lloriquear [yo·ri·ke·ár] *v.* to whimper, whine, weep.
lloriqueo [yo·ri·ké·o] *m.* whimper, whining.
lloro [yó·ro] *m.* weeping.
llorón [yo·rón] *adj.* weeping; **sauce** — a weeping willow; *m.* weeper, crybaby, whiner.
llorona [yo·ró·na] *f.* weeping woman; **-s** *Am.* large spurs.
lloroso [yo·ró·so] *adj.* tearful; weeping.
llovedizo [yo·be·dí·so] *adj.* rain (*used as adj.*); **agua llovediza** rain water.

llover[2] [ỹo·ḃér] *v. irr.* to rain, shower.
llovizna [ỹo·ḃíz·na] *f.* drizzle.
lloviznar [ỹo·ḃiz·nár] *v.* to drizzle, sprinkle.
lluvia [ỹu·ḃja] *f.* rain; shower.
lluvioso [ỹu·ḃjó·so] *adj.* rainy.

M:m

macana [ma·ká·na] *f. Am.* club, cudgel, stick; *Am.* lie, absurdity, nonsense.
macanudo [ma·ka·nú·ḍo] *adj. Ríopl.* tremendous! great!
macarrón [ma·ka·rrón] *m.* macaroon; **-es** macaroni.
maceta [ma·sé·ta] *f. (tiesto)* flowerpot; *(martillo)* small mallet; stonecutter's hammer; handle of tools; *Am.* head; *adj. Am.* slow.
macilento [ma·si·lén·to] *adj.* thin, emaciated; pale.
macizo [ma·sí·so] *adj.* solid, firm; massive; *m.* massiveness; firmness; thicket; clump.
machacar[6] [ma·ča·kár] *v.* to pound, crush; to insist, harp on.
machacón [ma·ča·kón] *adj.* persistent; tenacious.
machete [ma·čé·te] *m.* machete, large heavy knife; **machetazo** *m.* large machete; blow with a machete.
machismo [ma·číz·mo] *m.* the quality of being a male; proven daring.
macho [má·čo] *m.* male; he-mule; hook *(of a hook and eye)*; abutment; pillar; stupid fellow; sledgehammer; *C.R.* a blond; North American; *Am.* **pararle a uno el** — to halt or repress a person; *adj.* masculine, male; strong.
machucar[6] [ma·ču·kár] *v.* to pound, beat, bruise; *Am.* to crush; *Am.* to break *(a horse)*.
machucón [ma·ču·kón] *m.* smash; bruise.
madeja [ma·ḍé·xa] *f.* skein; mass of hair; limp, listless person.
madera [ma·ḍé·ra] *f.* wood; timber; lumber; **maderero** *m.* lumberman, lumber dealer.
maderaje [ma·ḍe·rá·xe] *m.* timber, lumber; timber work; woodwork.
maderamen [ma·ḍe·rá·men] *m.* timber; timber work; woodwork.
madero [ma·ḍé·ro] *m.* beam; plank; timber, piece of lumber; blockhead, dunce.
madrastra [ma·ḍrás·tra] *f.* stepmother.
madre [má·ḍre] *f.* mother; womb; root, origin; river bed; **salirse de** — to overflow *(said of rivers)*.
madrepeña [ma·ḍre·pé·ña] *f. Am.* moss.
madreperla [ma·ḍre·pér·la] *f.* mother-of-pearl.
madreselva [ma·ḍre·sél·ḃa] *f.* honeysuckle.
madriguera [ma·ḍri·ǵé·ra] *f.* burrow; den, lair.
madrileño [ma·ḍri·lé·ño] *adj.* Madrilenian, from or pertaining to Madrid; *m.* Madrilenian.
madrina [ma·ḍrí·na] *f. (patrocinadora)* godmother; bridesmaid; sponsor; *(correa)* strap for yoking two horses; *(ganado)* leading mare; prop; *Am.* small herd of tame cattle *(used for leading wild cattle)*.
madrugada [ma·ḍru·ǵá·ḍa] *f.* dawn; early morning; **de** — at daybreak.
madrugador [ma·ḍru·ǵa·ḍór] *m.* early riser.
madrugar[7] [ma·ḍru·ǵár] *v.* to rise early; to be ahead of others; to "get the jump" on someone.
madurar [ma·ḍu·rár] *v.* to mature; to ripen.
madurez [ma·ḍu·rés] *f.* maturity; ripeness.
maduro [ma·ḍú·ro] *adj.* ripe; mature; prudent,

wise; *Am.* bruised, sore.
maestría [ma·es·trí·a] *f.* mastery; great skill; advanced teaching degree.
maestro [ma·és·tro] *m.* master, teacher; chief craftsman; *adj.* master; masterly, skillful; **llave maestra** master key; **obra maestra** masterpiece.
magia [má·xja] *f.* magic; charm.
mágico [má·xi·ko] *adj.* magic; *m.* magician.
magín [ma·xín] *m.* imagination, fancy.
magisterio [ma·xis·té·rjo] *m.* teaching profession.
magistrado [ma·xis·trá·ḍo] *m.* magistrate, judge.
magistral [ma·xis·trál] *adj.* masterly; masterful; authoritative.
magnánimo [maǵ·ná·ni·mo] *adj.* magnanimous, noble, generous.
magnesia [maǵ·né·sja] *f.* magnesia.
magnesio [maǵ·né·sjo] *m.* magnesium.
magnético [maǵ·né·ti·ko] *adj.* magnetic; attractive.
magnetofónico [maǵ·ne·to·fó·ni·ko] *adj.* recording *(tape or wire)*.
magnetófono [maǵ·ne·tó·fo·no] *m.* tape recorder.
magnificencia [maǵ·ni·fi·sén·sja] *f.* magnificence, splendor.
magnífico [maǵ·ní·fi·ko] *adj.* magnificent, splendid.
magnitud [maǵ·ni·túḍ] *f.* magnitude, greatness.
magno [máǵ·no] *adj.* great.
magnolia [maǵ·nó·lja] *f.* magnolia.
mago [má·ǵo] *m.* magician, wizard; **los tres Reyes Magos** the Three Wise Men.
magra [máǵ·ra] *f.* slice of ham.
magro [máǵ·ro] *adj.* lean.
maguey [ma·ǵéj] *m.* maguey, century plant.
magullar [ma·ǵu·yár] *v.* to bruise; to maul; to mangle; *Ríopl., Ch., Col., Andes, P.R.* to crumple.
magullón [ma·ǵu·yón] *m.* a bruise.
mahometano [ma·o·me·tá·no] *adj. & m.* Mohammedan.
maicillo [maj·sí·yo] *m. Am.* gravel.
maíz [ma·ís] *m.* corn; **maizal** [maj·sál] *m.* cornfield.
majada [ma·xá·ḍa] *f.* sheepfold; dung, manure; *Ríopl., Ch.* flock of sheep or goats.
majadería [ma·xa·ḍe·rí·a] *f.* foolishness, nonsense.
majadero [ma·xa·ḍé·ro] *adj.* foolish; bothersome.
majar [ma·xár] *v.* to pound; to crush; to bruise; to crumple; to mash; to annoy, bother.
majestad [ma·xes·táḍ] *f.* majesty; dignity.
majestuoso [ma·xes·twó·so] *adj.* majestic, stately.
majo [má·xo] *adj.* gaudy, showy; gaily attired; pretty; *m.* dandy; **maja** [má·xa] *f.* belle.
mal [mal] *m.* evil; illness; harm; wrong. *See* **malo**.
malabarista [ma·la·ḃrís·ta] *m. & f.* juggler; *Ch.* sly thief.
malacate [ma·la·ká·te] *m.* hoist, hoisting machine; winch; *Am.* spindle *(for cotton)*; *Am.* **parecer uno un** — to be constantly on the go, be in constant motion.
malagueña [ma·la·ǵé·ña] *adj.* song and dance of Málaga.
malandanza [ma·lan·dán·sa] *f.* misfortune.
malaquita [ma·la·kí·ta] *f.* malachite.
malaventura [ma·la·ḃen·tú·ra] *f.* misfortune, disaster.
malazo [ma·lá·so] *adj.* perverse, evil, wicked; vicious.
malbaratar [mal·ḃa·ra·tár] *v.* to undersell, sell at a loss; to squander.
malcontento [mal·kon·tén·to] *adj.* discontented; *m.* malcontent, troublemaker.
malcriado [mal·krjá·ḍo] *adj.* ill-bred, rude.
maldad [mal·dáḍ] *f.* badness, evil, wickedness.

LO

maldecir[27,52] [mal·de·sír] *v. irr.* to curse; to damn.
maldiciente [mal·di·sjén·te] *adj.* cursing.
maldición [mal·di·sjón] *f.* curse.
maldispuesto [mal·dis·pwés·to] *adj.* unwilling, not inclined.
maldito [mal·dí·to] *p.p. of* **maldecir** & *adj.* cursed; wicked; damned; *Am.* tricky; *Am.* bold, boastful.
maleable [ma·le·á·ƀle] *adj.* malleable; easily spoiled.
maleante [ma·le·án·te] *m.* crook, rogue, rascal, villain.
malecón [ma·le·kón] *m.* mole; dike.
maledicencia [ma·le·ɖi·sén·sja] *f.* slander.
maleficio [ma·le·fi·sjo] *m.* spell, charm, witchery.
maléfico [ma·lé·fi·ko] *adj.* evil, harmful.
malestar [ma·les·tár] *m.* indisposition; slight illness; discomfort.
maleta [ma·lé·ta] *f.* travelling bag; suitcase; *Col., Ven., C.A.* bundle of clothes; *Col.* hump (*on the back*); *Am.* saddlebag; *C.A.* rogue, rascal; *Am.* lazy fellow.
maletín [ma·le·tín] *m.* small valise, satchel.
malevo [ma·lé·ƀo] *adj. Bol., Ríopl.* bad, wicked.
malévolo [ma·lé·ƀo·lo] *adj.* bad, evil, wicked.
maleza [ma·lé·sa] *f.* underbrush; thicket; weeds.
malgastar [mal·ǥas·tár] *v.* to squander, waste.
¡malhaya! [ma·lá·ya] *interj.* cursed; *Ríopl.* were it so!
malhechor [ma·le·čór] *m.* malefactor, evildoer, criminal.
malhora [ma·ló·ra] *f. Ríopl., C.A., Ven.* trouble, misfortune.
malhumorado [ma·lu·mo·rá·ɖo] *adj.* ill-humored.
malicia [ma·lí·sja] *f.* malice; wickedness; shrewdness; suspicion; *Ch.* bit of brandy or cognac added to another drink.
maliciar [ma·li·sjár] *v.* to suspect.
malicioso [ma·li·sjó·so] *adj.* malicious; wicked; shrewd; suspicious.
maligno [ma·liǥ·no] *adj.* malign, malignant; pernicious, harmful.
malmandado [mal·man·dá·ɖo] *adj.* disobedient; stubborn.
mal(o) [mál(o)] *adj.* bad, evil; wicked; ill; difficult; *Am.* **a la mála** treacherously; *Ríopl.* **de malas** by force; **estar de malas** to be out of luck; **por la mala** unwillingly, by force; **venir de malas** to come with evil intentions; **mal** *adv.* badly; poorly; wrongly.
malograr [ma·lo·ǥrár] *v.* to waste, lose; **-se** to turn out badly; to fail.
malón [ma·lón] *m.* mean trick; *Ríopl.* surprise Indian raid; *Ven.* tin-pan serenade, boisterous surprise party.
malpagar[7] [mal·pa·ǥár] *v.* to underpay, pay poorly.
malparto [mal·pár·to] *m.* miscarriage, abortion.
malquerencia [mal·ke·rén·sja] *f.* aversion, dislike, ill will.
malsano [mal·sá·no] *adj.* unhealthy; sickly.
malta [mál·ta] *f.* malt.
maltratar [mal·tra·tár] *v.* to treat badly; to misuse, abuse.
maltrato [mal·trá·to] *m.* mistreatment, abuse.
maltrecho [mal·tré·čo] *adj.* battered, bruised, injured.
malvado [mal·ƀá·ɖo] *adj.* wicked; malicious.
malversación [mal·ƀer·sa·sjón] *f.* graft, corruption, misuse of public funds.
malversar [mal·ƀer·sár] *v.* to misuse (*funds in one's trust*); to embezzle.
malla [má·ya] *f.* mesh; coat of mail; *Ch.* species of

potato; **hacer** — to knit.
mamá [ma·má] *f.* mamma.
mamada [ma·má·ɖa] *f.* suck, sucking.
mamado [ma·má·ɖo] *adj. Am.* drunk.
mamar [ma·már] *v.* to suckle; to suck; to gorge; **-se** *Ríopl., C.A.* to get drunk; *Col.* to go back on one's promise; *Am.* to fold up, crack up; **-se a uno** to get the best of someone, decieve someone; *Col., C.A.* to kill someone.
mamarracho [ma·ma·rrá·čo] *m.* a mess; a worthless guy.
mamífero [ma·mí·fe·ro] *m.* mammal; *adj.* mammalian, of mammals.
mamón [ma·món] *adj.* suckling; *m.* suckling (*very young animal or child*); shoot, sucker (*of a tree*); *Ríopl.* cherimoya (*tree and fruit*); *Am.* papaya (*tree and fruit*); *Mex.* a kind of cake; *C.A.* public employee.
mampara [mam·pá·ra] *f.* screen.
mampostería [mam·pos·te·rí·a] *f.* masonry, stone masonry.
manada [ma·ná·ɖa] *f.* herd; drove; pack; flock.
manantial [ma·nan·tjál] *m.* spring; source, origin.
manar [ma·nár] *v.* to spring, flow (from); to abound.
manaza [ma·ná·sa] *f.* large hand.
manazo [ma·ná·so] *m. Ríopl.* slap. *See* **manotazo.**
mancarrón [maŋ·ka·rrón] *m.* one-armed or one-handed man; cripple; old nag; *Ríopl., Andes* crude, clumsy fellow; *Am.* disabled workman; *Am.* dike, small dam.
mancebo [man·sé·ƀo] *m.* youth, young man; bachelor.
mancera [man·sé·ra] *f.* handle of a plough.
mancilla [man·sí·ya] *f.* stain, spot; dishonor.
manco [máŋ·ko] *adj.* one-armed; one-handed; maimed; lame (*referring to an arm* or *the front leg of an animal*); faulty, defective; *m. Ch.* nag.
mancuerna [maŋ·kwér·na] *f.* pair of animals tied together; *Mex., C.A. f. pl.* cuff links.
mancha [mán·ča] *f.* spot, stain, blemish; *Am.* cloud, swarm; *Ven., Cuba, Col.* roving herd of cattle.
manchar [man·čár] *v.* to stain, soil, spot; to tarnish.
manchego [man·čé·ǥo] *adj.* of or belonging to La Mancha (*region of Spain*); *m.* inhabitant of La Mancha.
manchón [man·čón] *m.* large stain; large patch.
mandadero [man·da·ɖé·ro] *m.* messenger, errand boy.
mandado [man·dá·ɖo] *m.* (*orden*) command, order; (*recado*) errand; *p.p. of* **mandar; bien** — well-behaved; **mal** — ill-behaved.
mandamiento [man·da·mjén·to] *m.* command, order; writ; commandment.
mandar [man·dár] *v.* (*pedir*) to command, order; rule; (*enviar*) to send; to bequeath; will; *Col., Ven.* to throw, hurl; — **hacer** to have made, order; *Col., Ven., Mex., Carib., Andes* — **una bofetada** to give a slap; *Col., Ven., Mex., Carib., Andes* — **una pedrada** to throw a stone; **-se** *Am.* to be impudent; **-se mudar** *Ríopl., Carib.* to go away.
mandatario [man·da·tá·rjo] *m.* attorney, representative; *Am.* magistrate, chief.
mandato [man·dá·to] *m.* mandate; order, command; term of office.
mandíbula [man·di·ƀu·la] *f.* jaw, jawbone.
mandioca [man·djó·ka] *f.* manioc.
mando [mán·do] *m.* command, authority, power.
mandolina [man·do·lí·na] *f.* mandolin.

mandón [man·dón] *adj.* bossy, domineering; *m.* bossy person; *Am.* boss or foreman of a mine; *Am.* race starter.

maneador [ma·ne·a·dór] *m. Ríopl., Ven., Col.* hobble, leather lasso (*for the legs of an animal*); *Am.* whip; *Ven., Andes* halter.

manear [ma·ne·ár] *v.* to hobble, lasso, tie the legs of (*an animal*); -se *Col., Ven.* to get tangled up.

manecilla [ma·ne·sí·ya] *f.* small hand; hand of a watch or clock.

manejable [ma·ne·xá·ƀle] *adj.* manageable.

manejar [ma·ne·xár] *v.* to manage, handle; to drive (*a car*); -se to move about, get around (*after an illness or accident*); *Carib., Ven.* to behave oneself.

manejo [ma·né·xo] *m.* handling; management; trick, intrigue.

manera [ma·né·ra] *f.* manner, way, mode; side opening in a shirt; front opening in breeches; -s customs; manners, behavior; **a — de** (*or* **a la — de**) like, in the style of; **de — que** so that; **sobre —** exceedingly; extremely.

manga [máŋ·ga] *f.* sleeve; bag; hose (*for watering*); body of troops; *Am.* multitude, herd, swarm; *Am.* cattle chute (*narrow passageway*); *Am.* corral; **— de agua** waterspout, whirlwind over the ocean; *Am.* **— de hule** raincape; **por angas o por -s** by hook or crook, in one way or another.

mangana [maŋ·gá·na] *f.* lariat, lasso.

manganeso [maŋ·ga·né·so] *m.* manganese.

mangle [máŋ·gle] *m.* mangrove.

mango [máŋ·go] *m.* handle; *Am.* mango (*tropical tree and its fruit*).

manguera [maŋ·gé·ra] *f.* hose (*for water*); waterspout; *Ríopl.* large corral (*for livestock*).

manguito [maŋ·gi·to] *m.* muff; knitted half-sleeve (*worn on the forearm*); oversleeve.

maní [ma·ní] *m. Carib., C.A., Ch., Andes, Ven., Col.* peanut; **manicero** [ma·ni·sé·ro] *m. Carib., C.A., Ch., Andes, Ven., Col.* peanut vendor.

manía [ma·ní·a] *f.* mania, frenzy; craze, whim.

maniatar [ma·nja·tár] *v.* to tie the hands; to handcuff; to hobble (*an animal*).

maniático [ma·njá·ti·ko] *m.* crank, queer fellow; *adj.* cranky, queer, odd.

manicomio [ma·ni·kó·mjo] *m.* insane asylum.

manicura [ma·ni·kú·ra] *f.* manicure; manicurist.

manicurar [ma·ni·ku·rár] *v.* to manicure.

manido [ma·ní·ɖo] *adj.* rotting; *Ríopl., Carib., Col., Andes* trite, commonplace.

manifestación [ma·ni·fes·ta·sjón] *f.* manifestation; demonstration.

manifestar[1] [ma·ni·fes·tár] *v. irr.* to manifest; to show.

manifiesto [ma·ni·fjés·to] *adj.* manifest, clear, plain; *m.* manifesto, public declaration; customhouse manifest.

manigua [ma·ní·ǥwa] *f. Col., Ríopl., Cuba, P.R.* Cuban jungle or thicket; *Carib.* **coger —** to get feverish; *Ríopl., Carib.* **irse a la —** to rise up in rebellion.

manija [ma·ní·xa] *f.* handle; crank; fetter.

manilla [ma·ní·ya] *f.* small hand; bracelet; -s **de hierro** handcuffs.

maniobra [ma·njó·ƀra] *f.* maneuver; operation.

maniobrar [ma·njo·ƀrár] *v.* to maneuver.

manipulación [ma·ni·pu·la·sjón] *f.* manipulation.

manipular [ma·ni·pu·lár] *v.* to manipulate, handle.

maniquí [ma·ni·kí] *m.* manikin, model, dummy, figure of a person; puppet.

manivela [ma·ni·ƀé·la] *f.* crank.

manjar [maŋ·xár] *m.* dish, food; choice bit of food.

mano [má·no] *f.* (*del cuerpo*) hand; forefoot; (*reloj*) clock hand; (*acabado*) coat of paint or varnish; quire (*25 sheets*) of paper; *Am.* adventure, mishap; *Am.* handful; **— de obra** workmanship; labor; **a —** at hand; by hand; *Am.* **estamos a —** we are even, we are quits; *Am.* **doblar las -s** to give up; **ser —** to be first (*in a game*); to lead (*in a game*); **venir a las -s** to come to blows.

manojo [ma·nó·xo] *m.* handful; bunch.

manopla [ma·nó·pla] *f.* gauntlet; heavy glove; huge hand.

manosear [ma·no·se·ár] *v.* to handle, touch, feel with the hand; *Am.* to fondle, pet, caress.

manotada [ma·no·tá·ɖa] *f.* slap, blow; sweep of the hand; *Col.* handful, fistful; **manotazo** [ma·no·tá·so] *m.* slap.

manotear [ma·no·te·ár] *v.* to gesticulate; to strike with the hands; *Ríopl.* to embezzle, steal; *Am.* to snatch away (*what is given*).

mansalva [man·sál·ƀa]: **a —** without danger or risk; treacherously; **matar a —** to kill without warning or without giving a person a chance to defend himself.

mansedumbre [man·se·ɖúm·bre] *f.* meekness; gentleness.

mansión [man·sjón] *f.* sojourn, stay; abode, dwelling.

manso [mán·so] *adj.* meek; mild, gentle; tame; *Ríopl., Ch.* cultivated (*plant*), civilized (*Indian*); *m.* leading sheep, goat, or ox.

manta [mán·ta] *f.* blanket; large shawl; tossing in a blanket; *Mex., C.A., Ven., Ríopl.* coarse cotton cloth; *Am.* poncho; *Am.* **— mojada** dull person, dunce; **darle a uno una —** to toss someone in a blanket.

mantear [man·te·ár] *v.* to toss (*someone*) in a blanket.

manteca [man·té·ka] *f.* fat; lard; butter; *Am.* **— de cacao** cocoa butter; *Am.* **— de coco** coconut oil; **mantequera** [man·te·ké·ra] *f.* churn; butter dish; woman who makes or sells butter.

mantecado [man·te·ká·ɖo] *m.* ice cream.

mantel [man·tél] *m.* tablecloth; altar cloth; *C.A., Mex.* **estar de -es largos** to dine in style.

mantener[45] [man·te·nér] *v. irr.* to maintain; to support; to sustain; to defend; -se to continue, remain, to support oneself; -se **firme** to remain firm; -se **quieto** to stay or keep quiet.

mantenimiento [man·te·ni·mjén·to] *m.* maintenance, support; sustenance; livelihood.

mantequilla [man·te·ki·ya] *f.* butter; **mantequillería** [man·te·ki·ye·rí·a] *f. Am.* creamery, dairy (*for making butter*).

mantilla [man·tí·ya] *f.* mantilla (*Spanish veil or scarf for the head*); saddlecloth.

manto [mán·to] *m.* mantle, cloak; cape: large mantilla; mantel, mantelpiece.

mantón [man·tón] *m.* large shawl; **— de Manila** embroidered silk shawl.

manuable [ma·nwá·ƀle] *adj.* handy, easy to handle.

manual [ma·nwál] *adj.* manual; handy; *m.* manual, handbook.

manubrio [ma·nú·ƀrjo] *m.* crank; handle.

manufacturar [ma·nu·fak·tu·rár] *v.* to manufacture.

manufacturero [ma·nu·fak·tu·ré·ro] *adj.* manufacturing; *m.* manufacturer.

manuscrito [ma·nus·krí·to] *adj.* written by hand; *m.* manuscript.

manutención [ma·nu·ten·sjón] *f.* maintenance; support; conservation.

MA

manzana [man·sá·na] *f.* apple; block of houses; *Ríopl., Ch., Col., Ven., C.A.* Adam's apple; **manzano** [man·sá·no] *m.* apple tree.

manzanar [man·sa·nár] *m.* apple orchard.

maña [má·ña] *f.* skill, knack; cunning; **malas -s** bad tricks or habits.

mañana [ma·ñá·na] *f.* morning; *Ríopl.* **media** — mid-morning snack; *adv.* tomorrow, in the near future; **pasado** — day after tomorrow; **muy de** — very early in the morning; *m.* morrow; **mañanitas** [ma·ña·ní·tas] *f. pl. Mex., C.A.* popular song sung early in the morning to celebrate a birthday, saint's day, etc.

mañanero [ma·ña·né·ro] *m.* early riser; *adj.* early rising; **mañanista** [ma·ña·nís·ta] *m. & f. Am.* procrastinator, one who puts things off until tomorrow.

mañero [ma·ñe·ro] *adj.* astute, artful, clever; *Am.* tricky; *Ch.* shy (*animal*); *Ríopl.* indolent, lazy (*child*).

mañoso [ma·ñó·so] *adj.* skillful; clever; sly; tricky; deceitful; *Am.* slow, lazy; *Am.* greedy, gluttonous (*child*).

mapa [má·pa] *m.* map, chart.

mapache [ma·pá·če] *m. Ch.* raccoon.

mapurite [ma·pu·rí·te], **mapurito** [ma·pu·rí·to] *m. Col., Ven.* skunk. *See* zorrino, zorrillo.

máquina [má·ki·na] *f.* machine; engine; — **de coser** sewing machine; — **de escribir** typewriter.

maquinación [ma·ki·na·sjón] *f.* machination, scheming, plotting; plot, scheme.

maquinador [ma·ki·na·ɖór] *m.* schemer, plotter.

maquinal [ma·ki·nál] *adj.* mechanical, automatic; **-mente** *adv.* mechanically, automatically, in a mechanical manner.

maquinar [ma·ki·nár] *v.* to plot, scheme.

maquinaria [ma·ki·ná·rja] *f.* machinery; mechanism; mechanics.

maquinista [ma·ki·nís·ta] *m.* engineer, locomotive engineer; machinist; mechanic.

mar [mar] *m. & f.* sea; — **alta** rough sea; — **llena** high tide (*see* pleamar); — **de fondo** swell; **a -es** abundantly; **baja** — low tide; **en alta** — on the high seas; **la** — **de cosas** a lot of things.

maraca [ma·rá·ka] *f. Carib., Col., Ven.* maraca (*rhythm instrument made of a dried gourd filled with seeds or pebbles*).

maraña [ma·rá·ña] *f.* tangle; snarl; thicket; maze; plot, intrigue.

marañón [ma·ra·ñón] *m.* cashew.

maravedí [ma·ra·þe·ɖí] *m.* maravedi (*an old Spanish coin*).

maravilla [ma·ra·þí·ya] *f.* wonder, marvel; marigold; **a las mil -s** wonderfully, perfectly.

maravillar [ma·ra·þi·yár] *v.* to astonish, dazzle; **-se** to wonder, marvel.

maravilloso [ma·ra·þi·yó·so] *adj.* marvellous, wonderful.

marbete [mar·þé·te] *m.* label, stamp; baggage tag or check.

marca [már·ka] *f.* mark, stamp; sign; brand, make; gauge, rule; march, frontier province; — **de fábrica** trademark; **de** — of excellent quality.

marcar[6] [mar·kár] *v.* to mark, stamp, brand; to note, observe.

marcial [mar·sjál] *adj.* martial, warlike; frank, abrupt.

marco [már·ko] *m.* frame; mark (*German coin*); mark (*unit of weight, equal to 8 ounces*).

marcha [már·ča] *f.* march; course, progress; speed; gait; running, functioning; movement of a watch.

marchamo [mar·čá·mo] *m.* customhouse mark; *Am.* tax on each slaughtered animal.

marchante [mar·čán·te] *m.* (*vendedor*) merchant, dealer; (*cliente*) customer, regular client.

marchar [mar·čár] *v.* to march, mark step; to walk; to parade; to run (*said of machinery*); **-se** to go away.

marchitar [mar·či·tár] *v.* to wither; **-se** to wither; to fade; to shrivel up.

marchito [mar·čí·to] *adj.* withered; faded; shriveled up.

marea [ma·ré·a] *f.* tide; *Ríopl., Ch.* sea fog.

mareado [ma·re·á·ɖo] *adj.* seasick; dizzy.

marear [ma·re·ár] *v.* (*navegar*) to navigate, sail; (*fastidiar*) to annoy, upset (*a person*); to make dizzy; **-se** to get seasick, nauseated; dizzy.

mareo [ma·ré·o] *m.* seasickness; nausea; vexation, annoyance.

marfil [mar·fil] *m.* ivory; *Ven.* fine-toothed comb.

margarita [mar·ga·rí·ta] *f.* marguerite, daisy; pearl.

margen [már·xen] *m. & f.* margin, border; river bank; **dar** — **a** to give an occasion to.

mariachi [ma·rjá·či] *m. Mex.* band and music typical of Guadalajara; *pl.* members of the band.

maricón [ma·ri·kón] *adj.* sissy, effeminate; *m.* sissy.

marido [ma·rí·ɖo] *m.* husband.

marimacho [ma·ri·má·čo] *m.* mannish woman.

marimba [ma·rím·ba] *f.* marimba.

marina [ma·rí·na] *f.* (*costa*) seacoast, shore; (*fuerza naval*) fleet; navy; (*arte u oficio*) seascape; seamanship; — **de guerra** navy; — **mercante** merchant marine.

marinero [ma·ri·né·ro] *m.* mariner, seaman, sailor.

marino [ma·rí·no] *adj.* marine; *m.* mariner, seaman, sailor.

mariposa [ma·ri·pó·sa] *f.* butterfly; moth; *Am.* blindman's buff (*a game*).

mariquita [ma·ri·kí·ta] *f.* sissy; (*cap.*) Molly.

mariscal [ma·ris·kál] *m.* marshal; blacksmith; — **de campo** field marshal.

marisco [ma·rís·ko] *m.* shellfish.

marítimo [ma·rí·ti·mo] *adj.* maritime, marine.

marmita [mar·mí·ta] *f.* kettle, boiler, teakettle.

mármol [már·mol] *m.* marble.

marmóreo [mar·mó·re·o] *adj.* marble, of marble, like marble.

maroma [ma·ró·ma] *f.* rope; *Am.* somersault; *Am.* acrobatic performance; *Col.* sudden change of political views; **andar en la** — to walk the tightrope; **maromero** [ma·ro·mé·ro] *m. Carib.* acrobat.

marqués [mar·kés] *m.* marquis.

marquesa [mar·ké·sa] *f.* marquise; *Ch.* couch.

marrano [ma·rrá·no] *m.* pig, hog; filthy person.

marrazo [ma·rrá·so] *m. Am.* bayonet, dagger.

marrón [ma·rrón] *adj.* maroon.

marroquí [ma·rro·kí] *adj.* from Morocco; *pl.* **marroquíes** [ma·rro·kí·es].

marrullero [ma·rru·yé·ro] *adj.* sly, wily.

martes [már·tes] *m.* Tuesday; — **de carnestolendas** Shrove Tuesday (*Tuesday before Lent*).

martillar [mar·ti·yár] *v.* to hammer, pound.

martillo [mar·tí·yo] *m.* hammer.

martinete [mar·ti·ne·te] *m.* pile driver; drop hammer; hammer of a piano.

mártir [már·tir] *m. & f.* martyr.

martirio [mar·tí·rjo] *m.* martyrdom; torture, torment.

martirizar[9] [mar·ti·ri·sár] *v.* to martyr; to torture, torment.

marxismo [mark·síz·mo] *m.* Marxism.
marzo [már·so] *m.* March.
mas [mas] *conj.* but.
más [mas] *adj.* more; most; *adv.* more; most; plus; — **bien** rather; — **de** more than, over; — **que** more than; **no** ... — **que** only; **a** — **de** in addition to; **a lo** — at the most; **está de** — it is superfluous, unnecessary; *Am.* **no** — only; *Am.* **no quiero** — **nada** (*instead of* **no quiero nada** —) I don't want anything more.
masa [má·sa] *f.* (*volumen*) mass; volume; (*pueblo*) crowd, the masses; (*pasta*) dough, paste; mortar; — **coral** glee club, choral society; **agarrarle a uno con las manos en la** — to catch someone in the act; **masilla** *f.* putty.
masaje [ma·sá·xe] *m.* massage.
mascada [mas·ká·ḍa] *f.* chewing; *Am.* mouthful; *Ríopl.* chew or quid of tobacco; *Am.* reprimand, scolding; *Mex.* silk handkerchief, scarf.
mascar[6] [mas·kár] *v.* to chew.
máscara [más·ka·ra] *f.* mask; **-s** masquerade; *m.* & *f.* masquerader; **mascarada** [mas·ka·rá·ḍa] *f.* masquerade.
masculino [mas·ku·lí·no] *adj.* masculine.
mascullar [mas·ku·yár] *v.* to mumble; to munch.
masón [ma·són] *m.* mason, freemason; **masonería** [ma·so·ne·rí·a] *f.* masonry, freemasonry.
masticar[6] [mas·ti·kár] *v.* to chew.
mástil [más·til] *m.* mast; post.
mastín [mas·tín] *m.* mastiff.
mastuerzo [mas·twér·so] *m.* (*flor*) nasturtium; (*tonto*) simpleton, fool.
mata [má·ta] *f.* shrub, plant, bush; grove; clump of trees; *Ven., Col.* thicket, jungle; — **de pelo** head of hair.
matadero [ma·ta·ḍé·ro] *m.* slaughterhouse; hard work.
matador [ma·ta·ḍór] *m.* killer, murderer; bullfighter who kills the bull.
matamoros [ma·ta·mó·ros] *m.* bully; boastful person.
matamoscas [ma·ta·mós·kas] *m.* fly swatter.
matanza [ma·tán·sa] *f.* massacre, butchery; slaughter of livestock; *Mex.* slaughterhouse.
matar [ma·tár] *v.* to kill; to murder; **-se** to commit suicide; to overwork; **-se con alguien** to fight with somebody.
matasanos [ma·ta·sá·nos] *m.* quack, quack doctor.
matasellos [ma·ta·sé·yos] *m.* canceller (*of stamps*).
mate [má·te] *m.* checkmate (*winning move in chess*); *Ríopl., Ch.* Paraguayan tea (*used also in Argentina and Uruguay*); *Andes, Col.* teapot (*for* mate), any small pot; *Am.* bald head; *adj.* unpolished, dull (*surface*).
matear [ma·te·ár] *v.* to plant seeds or shoots; to hunt among the bushes; *Ríopl., Ch.* to drink mate; *Am.* to checkmate (*make the winning move in chess*).
matemática [ma·te·má·ti·ka] *f. pl.* mathematics.
matemático [ma·te·má·ti·ko] *adj.* mathematical; *m.* mathematician.
materia [ma·té·rja] *f.* matter; material; school subject; pus; — **prima** (*or* **primera** —) raw material.
material [ma·te·rjál] *adj.* material; rude, coarse; *m.* ingredient; material; equipment; *Ven.* **de** — made of adobe.
maternal [ma·ter·nál] *adj.* maternal.
maternidad [ma·ter·ni·ḍáḍ] *f.* maternity, motherhood.
materno [ma·tér·no] *adj.* maternal.

matinal [ma·ti·nál] *adj.* morning, of the morning.
matiné [ma·ti·né] *m. Am.* matinée.
matiz [ma·tís] *m.* tint, shade, color, hue; shading.
matizar[9] [ma·ti·sár] *v.* to blend (*colors*); to tint; to shade, tone down.
matón [ma·tón] *m.* bully.
matorral [ma·to·rrál] *m.* thicket.
matoso [ma·tó·so] *adj.* bushy; weedy, full of weeds.
matrero [ma·tré·ro] *adj.* astute, shrewd; cunning, sly; *m. Col.* trickster, swindler; *Ríopl.* bandit, outlaw, cattle thief.
matrícula [ma·tri·ku·la] *f.* register, list; matriculation, registration; certificate of registration.
matricular [ma·tri·ku·lár] *v.* to matriculate, enroll, register.
matrimonio [ma·tri·mó·njo] *m.* matrimony, marriage; married couple.
matriz [ma·trís] *f.* matrix, mold, form; womb; screw nut; *adj.* main, principal, first; **casa** — main office (*of a company*).
matungo [ma·tún·go] *m. Ríopl.* nag, old worn-out horse.
matutino [ma·tu·tí·no] *adj.* morning, of the morning.
maula [máw·la] *m.* a good-for-nothing.
maullar [maw·yár] *v.* to mew.
maullido, [maw·yi·ḍo] **maúllo** [ma·ú·yo] *m.* mew.
máxima [mák·si·ma] *f.* maxim, rule; proverb.
máxime [mák·si·me] *adj.* principally, especially.
máximo [mák·si·mo] *adj. & m.* maximum.
maya [má·ya] *f.* daisy; May queen; *m. & f.* Maya, Mayan Indian; *m.* Mayan language.
mayo [má·yo] *m.* May; Maypole; *Am.* Mayo Indian (*from Sonora, Mexico*); *Am.* language of the Mayo Indian.
mayonesa [ma·yo·né·sa] *f.* mayonnaise; dish served with mayonnaise.
mayor [ma·yór] *adj.* greater; larger; older; greatest; largest; oldest; main; major; high (*altar, mass*); *m.* major; chief; **-es** elders; ancestors; — **de edad** of age; **por** — (*or* **al por** —) wholesale; *f.* major premise (*of a syllogism*).
mayoral [ma·yo·rál] *m.* head shepherd; stagecoach driver; foreman; overseer, boss.
mayorazgo [ma·yo·ráz·g̣o] *m.* primogeniture (*right of inheritance by the first-born*); first-born son and heir; family estate left to the eldest son.
mayordomo [ma·yor·ḍó·mo] *m.* majordomo, steward, butler; manager of an estate.
mayorear [ma·yo·re·ár] *v. Am.* to wholesale, sell at wholesale.
mayoreo [ma·yo·ré·o] *m. Am.* wholesale.
mayoría [ma·yo·rí·a] *f.* majority.
mayorista [ma·yo·rís·ta] *m. Am.* wholesale dealer.
maza [má·sa] *f.* mace (*weapon, staff*); — **química** chemical mace.
mazmorra [maz·mó·rra] *f.* dungeon.
mazo [má·so] *m.* mallet; sledgehammer; bunch, handful.
mazorca [ma·sór·ka] *f.* ear of corn; *Ríopl.* tyrannical government; *Am.* cruel torture (*imposed by tyrants*).
me [me] *obj. pron.* me; to me; for me; myself.
mear [me·ár] *v.* to urinate.
mecánico [me·ká·ni·ko] *adj.* mechanical; *m.* mechanic, machinist, repairman; driver, chauffeur.
mecanismo [me·ka·níz·mo] *m.* mechanism.
mecanografía [me·ka·no·g̣ra·fí·a] *f.* stenography, typewriting.

MA

mecanógrafo [me·ka·nó·ǵra·fo] *m.* stenographer, typist.
mecate [me·ká·te] *m. Mex., C.A., Col., Ven.* rope, cord.
mecedor [me·se·ḍór] *m.* swing; *adj.* swinging, rocking.
mecedora [me·se·ḍó·ra] *f.* rocking chair.
mecer[10] [me·sér] *v.* to swing, rock, sway; to shake.
mecha [mé·ča] *f.* wick; lock of hair; fuse; strip of salt pork or bacon (*for larding meat*); *Ven.* tip of a whip; *Am.* scare, fright; *Andes, Col.* fib; *Andes, Col.* jest, joke; *Col.* trifle, worthless thing.
mechar [me·čár] *v.* to lard (*meat or fowl*).
mechero [me·čé·ro] *m.* (*canutillo*) lamp burner; gas jet; candlestick socket; (*encendedor*) pocket lighter; large wick; *Col.* disheveled hair; *Am.* joker, jester.
mechón [me·čón] *m.* large wick; large lock of hair.
medalla [me·ḍa·ya] *f.* medal.
médano [mé·ḍa·no] *m.* dune, sand hill,.sand bank; *Ríopl., Carib.* sandy marshland.
media [mé·ḍja] *f.* stocking; *Col., Ríopl., Ven.* — **corta** (*or* —) sock.
mediación [me·ḍja·sjón] *f.* mediation.
mediador [me·ḍja·ḍór] *m.* mediator.
mediados: [me·ḍjá·ḍos] **a — de** about the middle of.
medianero [me·ḍja·né·ro] *m.* mediator; go-between; *adj.* mediating; intermediate; **pared medianera** partition wall.
medianía [me·ḍja·ní·a] *f.* mediocrity; average; middle ground; moderate circumstances; moderation; *Col.* partition wall.
mediano [me·ḍjá·no] *adj.* medium; moderate; middle-sized; average; mediocre.
medianoche [me·ḍja·nó·če] *f.* midnight.
mediante [me·ḍján·te] *adj.* intervening; **Dios —** God willing; *prep.* by means of, through, with the help of.
mediar [me·ḍjár] *v.* to mediate, intervene; to intercede; to arrive at, or be in, the middle.
medible [me·ḍí·ƀle] *adj.* measurable.
medicamento [me·ḍi·ka·mén·to] *m.* medicament, medicine.
medicastro [me·ḍi·kás·tro] *m.* quack, quack doctor.
medicina [me·ḍi·si·na] *f.* medicine.
medicinar [me·ḍi·si·nár] *v.* to doctor, treat, prescribe medicine for; **-se** to take medicine.
medición [me·ḍi·sjón] *f.* measurement; measuring.
médico [mé·ḍi·ko] *m.* doctor, physician; *adj.* medical.
medida [me·ḍí·ḍa] *f.* measure; measurement; gauge, rule; — **para áridos** dry measure; **a — del deseo** according to one's desire; **a — que** as, in proportion as; at the same time as.
medidor [me·ḍi·ḍór] *m. Am.* meter, gauge.
medio [mé·ḍjo] *adj.* half; middle; intermediate; medium, average; **media noche** midnight; **hacer una cosa a medias** to do something halfway; **ir a medias** to go halves; *adv.* half, not completely; *m.* middle; means, way; medium; environment; **-s** means, resources; **meterse de por —** to intervene, meddle in a dispute.
mediocre [me·ḍjó·kre] *adj.* mediocre; **mediocridad** [me·ḍjo·kri·ḍáḍ] *f.* mediocrity.
mediodía [me·ḍjo·ḍí·a] *m.* midday, noon; south.
medioeval [me·ḍjo·e·ƀál], **medieval** [me·ḍje·ƀál] *adj.* medieval.
medir[5] [me·ḍír] *v. irr.* to measure; to scan (*verses*); *Col., Ven., Mex.* — **las calles** to walk the streets, be out of a job; **-se** to measure one's words or

actions; *Mex., C.A., Ven., Col., Ríopl.* **-se con otro** to try one's strength or ability against another; to fight with another.
meditación [me·ḍi·ta·sjón] *f.* meditation.
meditar [me·ḍi·tár] *v.* to meditate; to muse.
medrar [me·ḍrár] *v.* to flourish, thrive; to prosper.
medroso [me·ḍró·so] *adj.* timid, faint-hearted; fearful, dreadful.
médula [mé·ḍu·la] *f.* marrow; pith; — **oblongada** medulla ablongata (*the posterior part of the brain tapering off into the spinal cord*).
megáfono [me·ǵá·fo·no] *m.* megaphone.
megatón [me·ǵa·ton] *m.* megaton.
mejicano [me·xi·ká·no] *adj.* Mexican; *m.* Mexican; the Aztec language; inhabitant of Mexico City. *Also* **mexicano.**
mejilla [me·xi·ya] *f.* cheek.
mejor [me·xór] *adj.* better; **el —** the best; *adv.* better; **a lo —** suddenly, unexpectedly; **tanto —** so much the better.
mejora [me·xó·ra] *f.* betterment; improvement.
mejoramiento [me·xo·ra·mjén·to] *m.* improvement.
mejorar [me·xo·rár] *v.* to better, improve; to get better, recover; **-se** to get better, recover.
mejoría [me·xo·rí·a] *f.* betterment, improvement; superiority.
melado [me·lá·ḍo] *adj.* honey-colored; *m.* sugar-cane syrup; honey cake.
melancolía [me·laŋ·ko·lí·a] *f.* melancholy, gloom.
melancólico [me·laŋ·kó·li·ko] *adj.* melancholy, gloomy.
melaza [me·lá·sa] *f.* molasses.
melena [me·lé·na] *f.* mane.
melindre [me·lín·dre] *m.* (*acto*) affectation; affected act or gesture; whim; (*comestible*) fritter, marzipan (*sweetmeat made of almond paste*).
melindroso [me·lin·dró·so] *adj.* affected; too particular, finicky, fussy.
melocotón [me·lo·ko·tón] *m.* peach; **melocotonero** [me·lo·ko·to·ne·ro] *m.* peach tree.
melodía [me·lo·dí·a] *f.* melody; **melodioso** [me·lo·djó·so] *adj.* melodious.
melón [me·lón] *m.* melon; cantaloupe; musk-melon; melon vine.
melosidad [me·lo·si·ḍáḍ] *f.* sweetness; softness, gentleness.
meloso [me·ló·so] *adj.* honeyed; soft, sweet; *m. Am.* honey-voiced person; *Am.* over-affectionate person.
mella [mé·ya] *f.* nick; dent; **hacer —** to make a dent or impression; to cause pain, worry, or suffering.
mellar [me·yár] *v.* to notch; to nick; to dent; to impair, damage.
mellizo [me·yí·so] *adj. & m.* twin.
membrete [mem·ƀré·te] *m.* heading; letterhead; memorandum.
membrillo [mem·brí·yo] *m.* quince (*tree and its fruit*).
membrudo [mem·brú·ḍo] *adj.* sinewy, robust, strong, muscular.
memorable [me·mo·rá·ƀle] *adj.* memorable, notable.
memorándum [me·mo·rán·dun] *m.* memorandum, note; memorandum book, notebook.
memoria [me·mór·ja] *f.* memory; remembrance; reminiscence; memoir, note, account; memorandum; **de —** by heart; **hacer —** to remember, recollect; — **de gallo** poor memory; **-s** regards; memoirs.
memorial [me·mo·rjál] *m.* memorandum book;

memorial, brief, petition.
mención [men·sjón] *f.* mention.
mencionar [men·sjo·nár] *v.* to mention.
mendigar[7] [men·di·gár] *v.* to beg; to ask alms.
mendigo [men·di·go] *m.* beggar.
mendrugo [men·drú·go] *m.* crumb of bread.
menear [me·ne·ár] *v.* to move, shake, stir; to wiggle; to wag; **-se** to hustle about; to wag; to wiggle.
meneo [me·né·o] *m.* shaking; swaying; wagging; wiggle; wiggling.
menester [me·nes·tér] *m.* need; job, occupation; **-es** bodily needs; implements, tools; tasks, chores; **ser — to** be necessary.
menesteroso [me·nes·te·ró·so] *adj.* needy, in want.
mengua [mén·gwa] *f.* diminution, decrease; waning; poverty, want; discredit.
menguante [men·gwán·te] *adj.* waning, diminishing, declining.
menguar[8] [men·gwár] *v.* to diminish, decrease; to wane.
menjurje [men·xúr·xe] *m.* stuff, mixture.
menor [me·nór] *adj.* smaller, lesser, younger; smallest, least, youngest; minor; *m. & f.* **— de edad** minor; *m.* minor (*music*); Minorite, Franciscan; *f.* minor premise (*of a syllogism*); **por — (al por —)** at retail; in small quantities.
menoría [me·no·rí·a] **= minoría.**
menos [mé·nos] *adv.* less; least; except; *adj. & pron.* less, least; *m.* minus; **— de** (*or* **— que**) less than; **a lo — (al —,** *or* **por lo —)** at least; **a — que** unless; **echar de —** to miss, feel or notice the absence of ; **no puede — de hacerlo** he cannot help doing it; **venir a —** to decline; to become weak or poor.
menoscabar [me·nos·ka·bár] *v.* to diminish, lessen; to impair, damage; **— la honra de** to undermine the reputation of.
menoscabo [me·nos·ká·bo] *m.* impairment; damage; diminution, lessening.
menospreciar [me·nos·pre·sjár] *v.* to despise, scorn; to underestimate.
menosprecio [me·nos·pré·sjo] *m.* scorn, contempt; underestimation.
mensaje [men·sa·xe] *m.* message.
mensajero [men·sa·xé·ro] *m.* messenger.
menstruo [méns·trwo] *m.* menstruation.
mensual [men·swál] *adj.* monthly.
mensualidad [men·swa·li·dáḍ] *f.* monthly allowance; monthly payment.
mensurable [men·su·rá·ble] *adj.* measurable.
menta [mén·ta] *f.* mint; peppermint; *Ríopl.* rumor, hearsay; *Ríopl, Andes* **por -s** by hearsay; *Ríopl.* **persona de — famous** person.
mentado [men·tá·do] *adj.* famous; *p.p.* mentioned.
mental [men·tál] *adj.* mental.
mentalidad [men·ta·li·dáḍ] *f.* mentality.
mentar[1] [men·tár] *v. irr.* to mention; to call, name.
mente [mén·te] *f.* mind; intellect.
mentecato [men·te·ká·to] *adj.* foolish, simple; *m.* fool.
mentir[3] [men·tír] *v. irr.* to lie, tell lies.
mentira [men·tí·ra] *f.* lie, falsehood, fib; white spot on the fingernails.
mentiroso [men·ti·ró·so] *adj.* lying; deceptive, false; *m.* liar, fibber; **mentirosillo** *m.* little fibber.
mentís [men·tís]: **dar un —** to give the lie (to).
mentón [men·tón] *m.* chin.
menú [me·nú] *m.* menu.
menudear [me·nu·de·ár] *v.* to occur frequently; to repeat over and over; to fall incessantly (*as rain,*

stones, projectiles, *etc.*); to tell in detail; *Am.* to retail, sell at retail; *Am.* to meet together often.
menudeo [me·nu·dé·o] *m.* retail; **vender al — to** retail, sell at retail.
menudo [me·nú·do] *adj.* minute, small; insignificant; exact, detailed; **dinero — change; a — often; por —** in detail; retail; *m.* entrails, "innards"; change, small coins.
meñique [me·ñí·ke] *adj.* tiny, wee; **dedo — little** finger.
meollo [me·ó·yo] *m.* marrow; pith; kernel; substance; brain; brains.
meple [mé·ple] *m. Ríopl.* maple.
merca [mér·ka] *f.* purchase.
mercachifle [mer·ka·čí·fle] *m.* peddler, vendor; cheap merchant; cheap fellow.
mercader [mer·ka·dér] *m.* trader, merchant.
mercadería [mer·ka·de·rí·a] *f.* merchandise; trade.
mercado [mer·ká·do] *m.* market; mart.
mercancía [mer·kan·sí·a] *f.* merchandise; goods.
mercantil [mer·kan·tíl] *adj.* mercantile, commercial.
mercar[6] [mer·kár] *v.* to purchase, buy.
merced [mer·séḍ] *f.* favor; present, gift; mercy; **Vuestra Merced** Your Honor; **a — de** at the mercy of; at the expense of.
mercería [mer·se·rí·a] *f.* notions (*pins, buttons, etc.*); notions store; *Ríopl., P.R.* drygoods store.
mercurio [mer·kú·rjo] *m.* mercury; quicksilver.
merecedor [me·re·se·dór] *adj.* worthy, deserving.
merecer[13] [me·re·sér] *v. irr.* to deserve.
merecido [me·re·sí·do] *adj. & p.p.* deserved; *m.* deserved punishment.
merecimiento [me·re·si·mjén·to] *m.* merit.
merendar[1] [me·ren·dár] *v. irr.* to have an afternoon snack or refreshment; *Carib., Ven.* **-se uno a alguien** to fleece or skin someone (*in a game or business deal*); to kill someone.
merendero [me·ren·dé·ro] *m.* lunchroom.
meridiano [me·ri·djá·no] *adj. & m.* meridian.
meridional [me·ri·djo·nál] *adj.* southern; *m.* southerner.
merienda [me·rjén·da] *f.* light afternoon meal; afternoon refreshments.
mérito [mé·ri·to] *m.* merit; **de —** notable.
merito [me·rí·to] *dim. of* **mero.**
meritorio [me·ri·tó·rjo] *adj.* meritorious, worthy, deserving; *m.* employee without salary (*learning trade or profession*).
merluza [mer·lú·sa] *f.* hake (*species of codfish*); drunken state.
merma [mér·ma] *f.* reduction, decrease.
mermar [mer·már] *v.* to dwindle; to decrease, reduce.
mermelada [mer·me·lá·da] *f.* marmalade.
mero [mé·ro] *adj.* mere, pure; *Mex., C.A.* exact, real; **la mera verdad** the real truth; *adv. Mex., C.A.* very, very same, exactly; *Mex., C.A.* soon; *Col.* only; *Mex., C.A.* **una mera de las tres** only one of the three; *Mex., C.A.* **ya —** (*or* **merito**) very soon; *Mex., C.A.* **allí —** (*or* **merito**) right there; *m.* species of perch; *Ch.* species of thrush.
merodear [me·ro·de·ár] *v.* to rove in search of plunder.
mes [mes] *m.* month.
mesa [mé·sa] *f.* table; executive board; staircase landing; mesa, plateau; **levantar la —** to clear the table; **poner la —** to set the table; *Col., Carib., C.A., Mex.* **quitar la —** to clear the table.
mesada [me·sá·da] *f.* monthly salary or allowance.
mesarse [me·sár·se] *v.* to tear (*one's hair or beard*).
mesero [me·sé·ro] *m. Mex., C.A., Ven., Col.* waiter.

ME

meseta [me·sé·ta] *f.* plateau; staircase landing.
mesón [me·són] *m.* inn (*usually a large one-story shelter for men and pack animals*).
mesonero [me·so·né·ro] *m.* innkeeper.
mestizo [mes·tí·so] *adj.* half-breed; hybrid; **perro — mongrel dog**; *m.* mestizo, half-breed.
mesura [me·sú·ra] *f.* moderation; composure; dignity; politeness.
mesurado [me·su·rá·đo] *adj.* moderate, temperate; dignified.
meta [mé·ta] *f.* goal; objective.
metabolismo [me·ta·ƀo·líz·mo] *m.* metabolism.
metafísica [me·ta·fí·si·ka] *f.* metaphysics.
metáfora [me·tá·fo·ra] *f.* metaphor.
metafórico [me·ta·fó·ri·ko] *adj.* metaphorical.
metal [me·tál] *m.* metal.
metálico [me·tá·li·ko] *adj.* metallic, metal; *m.* specie, coined money; cash in coin.
metalurgia [me·ta·lúr·xja] *f.* metallurgy.
metamorfosis [me·ta·mor·fó·sis] *f.* metamorphosis.
metate [me·tá·te] *m. Mex.* flat stone (*used for grinding corn, etc.*).
metátesis [me·tá·te·sis] *f.* metathesis.
meteorito [me·te·o·rí·to] *m.* meteorite.
meteoro [me·te·ó·ro] *m.* meteor.
meteorología [me·te·o·ro·lo·xí·a] *f.* meteorology; **meteorológico** [me·te·o·ro·ló·xi·ko] *adj.* meteorological; **oficina meteorológica** weather bureau.
meter [me·tér] *v.* to put (in); to get (in); to insert; to smuggle; to make (*noise, trouble, etc.*); to cause (*fear*); *Carib.* to strike (*a blow*); *Riopl., Carib.* **-le** to hurry up; **-se** to meddle, interfere; to plunge (into); **-se monja** (*Am.* **-se de monja**) to become a nun; also **-se a monja**; **-se con** to pick a quarrel with.
metódico [me·tó·đi·ko] *adj.* methodical.
método [mé·to·đo] *m.* method.
metralleta [me·tra·yé·ta] *f.* hand machine gun.
metrico [mé·tri·ko] *adj.* metric.
metro [mé·tro] *m.* meter; subway.
metrópoli [me·tró·po·li] *f.* metropolis.
metropolitano [me·tro·po·li·tá·no] *adj.* metropolitan; *m.* archbishop.
mexicano [me·xi·ká·no] = **mejicano** (*pronounced identically*).
mezcal [mes·kál] *m. Mex.* mescal (*a species of* **maguey** *and an alcoholic beverage made from it*).
mezcla [més·kla] *f.* mixture; mortar; mixed cloth; **mezclilla** [mes·klí·ya] *f.* mixed cloth (*generally black and white*); tweed.
mezclar [mes·klár] *v.* to mix, blend; **-se** to mix, mingle; to meddle.
mezcolanza [mes·ko·lán·sa] *f.* jumble, mess, mixture.
mezquindad [mes·ki·ni·đáđ] *f.* meanness; stinginess; dire poverty.
mezquino [mes·kí·no] *adj.* poor, needy; mean, stingy; meager; small, tiny; *m. Col., Mex.* wart (*usually on a finger*).
mezquita [mes·kí·ta] *f.* mosque.
mi [mi] *adj.* my.
mí [mi] *pers. pron.* (*used after prep.*) me, myself.
miaja [mjá·xa] = **migaja**.
miau [mjáw] *m.* mew.
mico [mí·ko] *m.* long-tailed monkey; *C.A.* jack (*for lifting heavy objects*).
microbio [mi·kró·ƀjo] *m.* microbe.
microbús [mi·kro·ƀús] *m.* microbus.
microfilm [mi·kro·fíln] *m.* microfilm.
micrófono [mi·kró·fo·no] *m.* microphone.

microscopio [mi·kros·kó·pjo] *m.* microscope; — **electrónico** electron microscope; **microscópico** [mi·kro·skó·pi·ko] *adj.* microscopic.
miedo [mjé·đo] *m.* fear; dread; **tener — to be afraid**.
miedoso [mje·đó·so] *adj.* afraid, fearful, timid.
miel [mjel] *m.* honey; molasses.
mielga [mjél·ga] *f.* plot of ground for planting.
miembro [mjém·bro] *m.* member; limb.
mientes [mjén·tes] *f. pl.* thought, mind; **parar — en** to consider, reflect on; **traer a las — to recall**; **venírsele a uno a las — to occur to one, come to one's mind**.
mientras [mjén·tras] *conj.* while; — **que** while; — **tanto** in the meantime, meanwhile; — **más ... — menos ...** the more ... the less ...
miércoles [mjér·ko·les] *m.* Wednesday.
mies [mjes] *f.* ripe grain; harvest; **-es** fields of grain.
miga [mí·ga] *f.* crumb; soft part of bread; substance; **-s** crumbs; fried crumbs of bread; **hacer buenas -s** (*or* **malas -s**) **con** to get along well (*or* badly) with.
migaja [mi·gá·xa] *f.* crumb; bit, fragment, small particle.
migración [mi·gra·sjón] *f.* migration.
milagro [mi·lá·gro] *m.* miracle; wonder.
milagroso [mi·la·gró·so] *adj.* miraculous.
milicia [mi·lí·sja] *f.* militia; military science; military profession.
miligramo [mi·li·grá·mo] *m.* milligram.
milimetro [mi·li·mé·tro] *m.* millimeter.
militar [mi·li·tár] *adj.* military; *m.* soldier, military man; *v.* to serve in the army; to militate, fight (against).
milpa [mil·pa] *f. Mex., C.A.* cornfield.
milla [mí·ya] *f.* mile.
millar [mi·yár] *m.* thousand; **-es** thousands, a great number.
millón [mi·yón] *m.* million; **millonario.** [mi·yo·ná·rjo] *adj. & m.* millionaire; **millonésimo** [mi·yo·né·si·mo] *adj. & m.* millionth.
mimar [mi·már] *v.* to pamper, spoil, humor; to pet.
mimbre [mím·bre] *m.* wicker; **mimbrera** [mim·bré·ra] *f.* willow.
mímico [mí·mi·ko] *adj.* mimic.
mimo [mí·mo] *m.* pampering, caress; coaxing.
mimoso [mi·mó·so] *adj.* tender, sensitive; delicate; finicky, fussy.
mina [mí·na] *f.* mine; source; fortune.
minar [mi·nár] *v.* to mine; to undermine; to sow with explosive mines.
mineral [mi·ne·rál] *m.* mineral; mine; ore; wealth, fortune; *adj.* mineral.
minería [mi·ne·rí·a] *f.* mining; miners.
minero [mi·né·ro] *m.* miner; wealth, fortune; source; *adj.* mining; **compañía minera** mining company.
miniatura [mi·nja·tú·ra] *f.* miniature.
minifalda [mi·ni·fál·da] *f.* miniskirt.
minifundio [mi·ni·fún·djo] *m.* small farm (*privately owned*).
mínimo [mí·ni·mo] *adj.* least, smallest; *m.* minimum.
minino [mi·ní·no] *m.* kitten, kitty, pussy.
ministerio [mi·nis·té·rjo] *m.* ministry; administration, ministering; portfolio (*office of a cabinet member*); minister's office.
ministrar [mi·nis·trár] *v.* to minister; to give (*money, aid, etc.*).
ministro [mi·nís·tro] *m.* minister; cabinet member;

office of justice.
minoría [mi·no·rí·a] *f.* minority.
minoridad [mi·no·ri·ðáð] *f.* minority (*in age*).
minucioso [mi·nu·sjó·so] *adj.* minute, detailed; scrupulous.
minúsculo [mi·nús·ku·lo] *adj.* small; **letra minúscula** small letter.
minuta [mi·nú·ta] *f.* minutes; memorandum; first draft (*of a contract, deed, etc.*); memorandum list; lawyer's bill; *Am.* **a la —** breaded and fried (*said of meat or fish*).
minuto [mi·nú·to] *m.* minute; **minutero** [mi·nu·té·ro] *m.* minute hand.
mío [mí·o] *poss. adj.* my, of mine; *poss. pron.* mine; *Riopl., Ch.* **detrás —** behind me.
miope [mjó·pe] *adj.* shortsighted, nearsighted; *m. & f.* nearsighted person.
miopía [mjo·pí·a] *f.* near-sightedness.
mira [mí·ra] *f.* (*de puntería*) gun sight; guiding point; (*intención*) intention, design; outlook; **estar a la — de** to be on the lookout for; to be on the alert for; **poner la — en** to fix one's eyes on; to aim at.
mirada [mi·rá·ða] *f.* glance, gaze, look.
mirador [mi·ra·ðór] *m.* mirador, enclosed balcony (*commanding an extensive view*); watchtower; lookout site; onlooker, spectator; *Riopl.* penthouse (*small house built on a roof for recreation*).
miramiento [mi·ra·mjén·to] *m.* consideration, respect, regard; reverence; circumspection, prudence.
mirar [mi·rár] *v.* to look; to glance; to behold; to see; **— por alguien** to take care of someone; **imira (tú)!** look!
miríada [mi·rjá·ða] *f.* myriad, multitude, great number.
miriñaque [mi·ri·ñá·ke] *m.* crinoline.
mirlo [mír·lo] *m.* blackbird.
mirón [mi·rón] *m.* bystander, onlooker, spectator; *adj.* curious.
mirra [mí·rra] *f.* myrrh.
mirto [mír·to] *m.* myrtle.
misa [mí·sa] *f.* mass; **— del gallo** midnight mass.
misántropo [mi·sán·tro·po] *m.* misanthrope.
misceláneo [mis·se·lá·ne·o] *adj.* miscellaneous.
miserable [mi·se·rá·ḅle] *adj.* miserable, unhappy; forlorn; miserly, stingy; mean.
miseria [mi·sé·rja] *f.* misery; poverty; stinginess; bit, trifle.
misericordia [mi·se·ri·kor·ðja] *f.* mercy, compassion, pity.
misericordioso [mi·se·ri·kor·ðjó·so] *adj.* merciful, compassionate.
mísero [mí·se·ro] *adj.* miserable, unhappy; forlorn; stingy.
misi [mí·si] *interj.* word used to call cats.
misión [mi·sjón] *f.* mission.
misionero [mi·sjo·né·ro] *m.* missionary.
mismo [míz·mo] *adj.* same; self, very; **ahora —** right away.
misterio [mis·té·rjo] *m.* mystery; secret.
misterioso [mis·te·rjó·so] *adj.* mysterious.
místico [mís·ti·ko] *adj.* mystical, mystic; *m.* mystic.
mitad [mi·táð] *f.* half; middle.
mitigar [mi·ti·gár] *v.* to mitigate, soften, soothe.
mitin [mí·tin] *m.* meeting.
mito [mí·to] *m.* myth; **mitología** [mi·to·lo·xí·a] *f.* mythology.
mitra [mí·tra] *f.* bishop's miter.
mixto [mís·to] *adj.* mixed; half-breed; *m.*

composite; match; explosive compound.
mobiliario [mo·ḅi·ljá·rjo] *m.* furniture.
moblaje [mo·ḅlá·xe] = **mueblaje.**
mocasín [mo·ka·sín] *m.* moccasin.
mocedad [mo·se·ðáð] *f.* youth; youthfulness; youthful prank.
mocetón [mo·se·tón] *m.* tall, robust lad.
moción [mo·sjón] *f.* motion.
moco [mó·ko] *m.* mucus; snot.
mocoso [mo·kó·so] *adj.* sniffling; *m.* brat, scamp; sniffling boy.
mochar [mo·čár] *v. Am.* to cut off, chop off, cut, trim (*see* **desmochar**); *Am.* to snitch, pilfer; *Col.* to depose, dismiss, put out of a job.
mochila [mo·čí·la] *f.* knapsack; soldier's kit.
mocho [mó·čo] *adj.* cut off; cropped, shorn; *Am.* maimed, mutilated; *Mex.* reactionary, conservative; *m.* butt of a firearm; *Col., Ven.* nag; *Carib.* cigar butt.
moda [mó·ða] *f.* mode, custom, style, fashion; **de —** fashionable.
modelar [mo·ðe·lár] *v.* to model.
modelo [mo·ðé·lo] *m.* model, copy, pattern; *m. & f.* life model.
moderación [mo·ðe·ra·sjón] *f.* moderation.
moderado [mo·ðe·rá·ðo] *adj.* moderate; conservative.
moderar [mo·ðe·rár] *v.* to moderate, temper; to regulate; to restrain.
moderno [mo·ðér·no] *adj.* modern.
modestia [mo·ðés·tja] *f.* modesty.
modesto [mo·ðés·to] *adj.* modest.
módico [mó·ði·ko] *adj.* moderate, reasonable (*price*).
modificación [mo·ði·fi·ka·sjón] *f.* modification.
modificar[6] [mo·ði·fi·kár] *v.* to modify.
modismo [mo·ðíz·mo] *m.* idiom.
modista [mo·ðís·ta] *f.* dressmaker; milliner.
modo [mó·ðo] *m.* mode, manner, way; mood (*grammar*); **a** (*or* **al**) **— de** like, in the manner of; **de — que** so that; and so; **de todos -s** at any rate, anyway.
modorra [mo·ðo·rra] *f.* drowsiness; gid (*a disease of sheep*).
modular [mo·ðu·lár] *v.* to modulate, tone down.
mofa [mó·fa] *f.* scoff, jeer, taunt; mockery.
mofar [mo·fár] *v.* to mock, scoff, jeer; **-se de** to make fun of, scoff at.
moflete [mo·flé·te] *m.* fat cheek; **mofletudo** [mo·fle·tú·ðo] *adj.* fat-cheeked.
mohín [mo·ín] *m.* grimace; wry face.
mohíno [mo·í·no] *adj.* moody, discontented, sad, melancholy; black (*referring to a horse, cow, or bull*).
moho [mó·o] *m.* rust; mold.
mohoso [mo·ó·so] *adj.* musty, moldy; rusty.
mojada [mo·xá·ða] *f.* drench, drenching, wetting.
mojado [mo·xá·ðo] *adj.* wet, damp, moist; *p.p. of* **mojar.**
mojadura [mo·xa·ðú·ra] *f.* wetting, dampening, drenching.
mojar [mo·xár] *v.* to dampen, wet, moisten; *Riopl.* to accompany (*a song*); *Am.* to bribe; *Riopl., Carib., Mex.* to celebrate by drinking; *Am.* **mojársele a uno los papeles** to get things mixed up.
mojicón [mo·xi·kón] *m.* punch, blow; muffin, bun.
mojigatería [mo·xi·ga·te·rí·a] *f.* prudery; false humility; affected piety.
mojigato [mo·xi·gá·to] *adj.* prudish; affectedly pious, overzealous (*in matters of religion*);

hypocritical; *m.* prude; hypocrite.
mojón [mo·xón] *m.* landmark; milestone; heap, pile.
molde [mól·de] *m.* mold, cast; form; pattern, model; **venir de** — to come pat, be to the point; **letras de** — printed letters; print.
moldear [mol·de·ár] *v.* to mold; to cast; to decorate with moldings.
moldura [mol·dú·ra] *f.* molding.
mole [mó·le] *f.* mass, bulk; *adj.* soft, mild; *m. Mex.* — **de guajolote** a Mexican dish of turkey served with a chili gravy.
molécula [mo·lé·ku·la] *f.* molecule.
moler[2] [mo·lér] *v. irr.* to mill; to grind; to tire, fatigue; to wear out, destroy; to bother; — **a palos** to give a thorough beating.
molestar [mo·les·tár] *v.* to molest, disturb; to bother, annoy.
molestia [mo·lés·tja] *f.* bother, annoyance; discomfort.
molesto [mo·lés·to] *adj.* bothersome, annoying; uncomfortable.
molibdeno [mo·lib·dé·no] *m.* molybdenum.
molicie [mo·lí·sje] *f.* softness; fondness for luxury.
molienda [mo·ljén·da] *f.* grind, grinding, milling; portion to be, or that has been, ground; grinding season (*for sugar cane or olives*); fatigue, weariness; bother.
molinero [mo·li·né·ro] *m.* miller.
molinete [mo·li·né·te] *m.* small mill; ventilating fan; pin wheel; twirl, whirl, flourish.
molinillo [mo·li·ní·yo] *m.* small mill or grinder; chocolate beater; restless person.
molino [mo·lí·no] *m.* mill; restless person; — **de viento** windmill.
molusco [mo·lús·ko] *m.* mollusk.
mollera [mo·yé·ra] *f.* crown of the head; judgment, good sense; **ser duro de** — to be stubborn; **no tener sal en la** — to be dull, stupid.
momentáneo [mo·men·tá·ne·o] *adj.* momentary; sudden, quick.
momento [mo·mén·to] *m.* moment; importance; momentum; **al** — immediately, without delay; **a cada** — continually; frequently.
mona [mó·na] *f.* female monkey; mimic; drunkenness; **dormir la** — to sleep it off; **pillar una** — to get drunk.
monada [mo·ná·da] *f.* (*típico de mono*) monkeyshine; monkey face; (*cosa graciosa*) cute little thing; cute gesture; nonsense; flattery.
monarca [mo·nár·ka] *m.* monarch.
monarquía [mo·nar·kí·a] *f.* monarchy.
monasterio [mo·nas·té·rjo] *m.* monastery.
mondadientes [mon·da·djén·tes] *m.* toothpick.
mondadura [mon·da·dú·ra] *f.* trimming; peeling.
mondar [mon·dár] *v.* to pare; to peel; to prune; to clean out; *Am.* to beat, thrash; *Am.* to beat, defeat; **-se los dientes** to pick one's teeth.
moneda [mo·né·da] *f.* coin; money; — **corriente** currency; — **menuda** (*or* **suelta**) change, small coins; **casa de** — mint.
monería [mo·ne·rí·a] *f.* monkeyshine, antic; trifle, trinket; cute little thing.
monetario [mo·ne·tá·rjo] *adj.* monetary; pertaining to money; financial.
monigote [mo·ni·gó·te] *m.* puppet, ridiculous figure; dunce.
monitorear [mo·ni·to·re·ár] *v.* to monitor (*a radio or TV program*).
monja [món·xa] *f.* nun.
monje [món·xe] *m.* monk.

mono [mó·no] *m.* monkey; silly fool; mimic; coveralls; *Ch.* pile of fruit or vegetables (*in a market*); **-s** *Ch.* worthless household utensils and furniture; *Am.* **meterle a uno los -s en el cuerpo** to frighten, terrify someone; *adj.* pretty, neat, cute; *Am.* sorrel, reddish-brown; *Col.* blond.
monóculo [mo·nó·ku·lo] *m.* monocle.
monologar[7] [mo·no·lo·gár] *v.* to soliloquize, talk to oneself; to recite monologues; to monopolize the conversation.
monólogo [mo·nó·lo·go] *m.* monologue.
monopolio [mo·no·pó·ljo] *m.* monopoly.
monopolizar[9] [mo·no·po·li·sar] *v.* to monopolize; to corner (*a market*).
monosílabo [mo·no·sí·la·ḅo] *adj.* monosyllabic, of one syllable; *m.* monosyllable.
monotonía [mo·no·to·ní·a] *f.* monotony; **monótono** [mo·nó·to·no] *adj.* monotonous.
monserga [mon·sér·ga] *f.* gabble.
monstruo [móns·trwo] *m.* monster.
monstruosidad [mons·trwo·si·dáḍ] *f.* monstrosity; monster, freak.
monstruoso [mons·trwó·so] *adj.* monstrous.
monta [món·ta] *f.* amount, sum; value, importance; **de poca** — of little value or importance.
montaje [mon·tá·xe] *m.* assembly, assembling (*of machinery*); mount, support for a cannon.
montante [mon·tán·te] *m.* broadsword; transom; upright; post; *Carib., Ven.* sum, amount, cost; *f.* high tide.
montaña [mon·tá·ña] *f.* mountain; — **rusa** roller coaster.
montañés [mon·ta·ñés] *adj.* mountain (*used as adj.*) of, from or pertaining to the mountains; *m.* mountaineer; native of the province of Santander, Spain.
montañismo [mon·ta·níz·mo] *m.* mountaineering.
montañoso [mon·ta·ñó·so] *adj.* mountainous.
montar [mon·tár] *v.* to mount; to ride horseback; to amount (to); to set (*jewels*); to cock (*a gun*); to assemble, set up (*machinery*); *Carib., C.A.* to organize, establish.
montaraz [mon·ta·rás] *adj.* wild, primitive, uncivilized; *m.* forester.
monte [món·te] *m.* mount, mountain; forest; thicket; monte (*a card game*); *C.A., Mex.* grass, pasture; *Am.* country, outskirts; **montecillo** [mon·te·sí·yo] *m.* mound, small hill; **montepío** [mon·te·pí·o] *m.* pawnshop.
montera [mon·té·ra] *f.* cap; *Andes* Bolivian cone-shaped hat (*worn by Indians*).
montés [mon·tés] *adj.* wild, mountain (*used as adj.*); **cabra** — mountain goat; **gato** — wildcat.
montículo [mon·tí·ku·lo] *m.* mound.
montón [mon·tón] *m.* pile, heap; mass, great number; **a -es** in abundance, in heaps, by heaps.
montonera [mon·to·né·ra] *f. Col., Ven., Riopl.* band of mounted rebels or guerrilla fighters (*Col.* pile of wheat, hay, straw, etc.; *Am.* pile, heap (*of anything*).
montuoso [mon·twó·so] *adj.* hilly; mountainous.
montura [mon·tú·ra] *f.* mount, horse; saddle and trappings.
monumento [mo·nu·mén·to] *m.* monument; **monumental** [mo·nu·men·tál] *adj.* monumental.
moña [mó·ña] *f.* doll; hair ribbon.
moño [mó·ño] *m.* knot or roll of hair; bow of ribbon; crest; tuft of feathers; *Mex.* forelock (*lock of hair on the fore part of the head*); *Am.* crest, peak (*of anything*); *Col.* whim; *Am.* a

Colombian popular dance; **-s** frippery, gaudy ornaments; *Col.* **estar con el — torcido** to be in an ugly humor.

mora [mó·ra] *f.* blackberry; mulberry; brambleberry; *Ch.* blood pudding, sausage.

morada [mo·rá·ḍa] *f.* dwelling, residence; stay.

morado [mo·rá·ḍo] *adj.* purple.

morador [mo·ra·ḍór] *m.* dweller, resident.

moral [mo·rál] *adj.* moral; *f.* ethics, moral philosophy; morale; *m.* mulberry tree; blackberry bush.

moraleja [mo·ra·lé·xa] *f.* moral, lesson, maxim.

moralidad [mo·ra·li·ḍáḍ] *f.* morality.

moralista [mo·ra·lís·ta] *m. & f.* moralist.

morar [mo·rár] *v.* to live, dwell, reside.

morbidez [mor·ƀi·ḍés] *f.* softness; mellowness.

mórbido [mór·ƀi·ḍo] *adj.* morbid; soft.

morboso [mor·ƀó·so] *adj.* morbid, unhealthy, diseased.

morcilla [mor·sí·ya] *f.* blood pudding, blood sausage; gag (*an amusing remark by a comedian*).

mordacidad [mor·ḍa·si·ḍáḍ] *f.* sharpness (*of tongue*).

mordaz [mor·ḍás] *adj.* biting, cutting, sarcastic.

mordaza [mor·ḍá·sa] *f.* gag (*for the mouth*).

mordedor [mor·ḍe·ḍór] *adj.* biting; snappy; *m.* biter; slanderer.

mordedura [mor·ḍe·ḍú·ra] *f.* bite; sting.

mordelón [mor·ḍe·lón] *adj. Col., Ven.* biting, snappy; *m. Am.* biter; *Mex.* public official who accepts a bribe.

morder[2] [mor·ḍér] *v. irr.* to bite; to nip; to gnaw; to corrode; to backbite, slander; *Ven.* to swindle; *Mex., C.A.* to "shake down", exact a bribe.

mordida [mor·ḍi·ḍa] *f. Am.* bite; *Mex., C.A., Carib., Ven.* graft, money obtained by graft.

mordiscar[6] [mor·ḍis·kár], **mordisquear** [mor·ḍis·ke·ár] *v.* to nibble; to gnaw.

mordisco [mor·ḍis·ko] *m.* bite; nibble.

moreno [mo·ré·no] *adj.* brown; dark, brunette; *m. Ríopl., Carib., Mex., Ven., Andes* colored person.

moretón [mo·re·tón] *m.* bruise, black-and-blue mark.

morfema [mor·fé·ma] *m.* morpheme.

morfina [mor·fí·na] *f.* morphine; **morfinómano** [mor·fi·nó·ma·no] *m.* morphine addict, drug fiend.

morfología [mor·fo·lo·xi·a] *f.* morphology.

moribundo [mo·ri·ƀún·do] *adj.* dying.

morir[4, 52] [mo·rír] *v. irr.* to die; **-se** to die; to die out, be extinguished.

morisco [mo·rís·ko] *adj.* Moorish; Moresque, in the Moorish style; *m.* Morisco (*Christianized Moor*); language of the Moriscos.

mormonismo [mor·mo·níz·mo] *m.* Mormonism.

moro [mó·ro] *adj.* Moorish; *Mex., Ven., Ríopl., Cuba* dappled, spotted (*horse*); *Col., Ch., Andes* unbaptized; *m.* Moor; *Am.* frosted cookie.

morocho [mo·ró·čo] *adj. Am.* robust, strong; *Ríopl.* of dark complexion; *Ch.* rough, tough; *Andes* of low social condition.

morral [mo·rrál] *m.* nose bag; knapsack; hunter's bag.

morrillo [mo·rrí·yo] *m.* fat of the neck (*especially the bull*).

morriña [mo·rrí·ña] *f.* melancholy, blues, sadness.

morro [mó·rro] *m.* knoll.

morsa [mór·sa] *f.* walrus.

mortaja [mor·tá·xa] *f.* shroud; *Am.* cigarette paper.

mortal [mor·tál] *adj.* mortal; fatal; deadly; *m.* mortal; **mortalidad** [mor·ta·li·ḍáḍ] *f.* mortality;

death rate.

mortandad [mor·tan·dáḍ] *f.* mortality, death rate; massacre, slaughter.

mortecino [mor·te·sí·no] *adj.* deathly pale; dying; **hacer la mortecina** to pretend to be dead.

morterete [mor·te·ré·te] *m.* small mortar, small canon.

mortero [mor·té·ro] *m.* mortar (*for grinding*).

mortífero [mor·tí·fe·ro] *adj.* deadly, fatal.

mortificar[6] [mor·ti·fi·kár] *v.* to mortify; to torment; to vex, annoy; **-se** to do penance; to be grieved; *Mex., C.A., Ven.* to be embarrassed.

mortuorio [mor·twó·rjo] *adj.* funeral; funereal, mournful; *m.* funeral, burial.

mosaico [mo·sáj·ko] *adj. & m.* mosaic.

mosca [mós·ka] *f.* fly; bore; bother; *Am.* sponger, parasite; *Mex., C.A., Ven.* bull's-eye, center of a target; **moscón** *m.* large fly; *Am.* **ir de moscón** to go along as a chaperone.

mosquear [mos·ke·ár] *v.* to brush off or drive away flies; to whip, beat; *Ríopl.* to rage, be furious; **-se** to show pique or resentment; *Ch.* to go away.

mosquito [mos·kí·to] *m.* mosquito; gnat; *Am.* Mosquito Indian of Nicaragua; **mosquitero** *m.* mosquito net.

mostacho [mos·tá·čo] *m.* mustache.

mostaza [mos·tá·sa] *f.* mustard; mustard seed; bird shot.

mostrador [mos·tra·ḍór] *m.* demonstrator; store counter; clock dial.

mostrar[2] [mos·trár] *v. irr.* to show; to demonstrate; to exhibit.

mostrenco [mos·tréŋ·ko] *adj.* (*sin dueño*) ownerless; homeless; stray (*animal*); (*torpe*) slow, dull; fat, heavy; *m.* dunce; *C.A.* worthless animal.

mota [mó·ta] *f.* mote, speck; knot in cloth; slight defect; mound, knoll; *Col., Ven., Carib.* powder puff; *Am.* tuft.

mote [mó·te] *m.* motto; slogan; nickname; *Andes, Ch., Col.* stewed corn; *Andes* grammatical error (*made by illiterate people and children*); *Am.* — **pelado** hominy.

motear [mo·te·ár] *v.* to speck, speckle; to spot; *Am.* to mispronounce, enunciate badly.

motejar [mo·te·xár] *v.* to jeer at; to call bad names; to insult; to censure; — **de** to brand as.

motín [mo·tín] *m.* mutiny; riot.

motivar [mo·ti·ƀár] *v.* to cause; to give a cause for.

motivo [mo·tí·ƀo] *m.* motive, reason; motif, theme; *m.* **con — de** because of; on the occasion of; *adj.* motive.

motocicleta [mo·to·si·klé·ta] *f.* motorcycle; **motociclista** [mo·to·si·kle·tís·ta] *m. & f.* motorcyclist, motorcycle rider.

motociclismo [mo·to·si·klíz·mo] *m.* motorcycling.

motor [mo·tór] *m.* motor; — **de reacción** jet engine; *adj.* motor, causing motion.

motorista [mo·to·rís·ta] *m. & f.* motorist; motorman, motorwoman.

motorreactor [mo·to·rre·ak·tór] *m.* jet engine.

motriz [mo·trís] *adj.* motive, impelling, driving; **fuerza** — power, driving force.

movedizo [mo·ƀe·ḍi·so] *adj.* movable; shaky; shifting; **arena movediza** quicksand.

mover[2] [mo·ƀér] *v. irr.* (*físicamente*) to move; (*persuadir*) to persuade; to stir, excite; to touch, affect; **-se** to move.

movible [mo·ƀi·ƀle] *adj.* movable; mobile; fickle.

móvil [mó·ƀil] *m.* motive, inducement, incentive; *adj.* mobile, movable; unstable.

MO

movilización [mo·bi·li·sa·sjón] *f.* mobilization.
mobilizar[9] [mo·bi·li·sár] *v.* to mobilize.
movimiento [mo·bi·mjén·to] *m.* movement; motion; commotion, disturbance.
moza [mó·sa] *f.* maid; girl; last hand of a game; *Ch.* last song or dance of a fiesta.
mozalbete [mo·sal·bé·te] *m.* youth, lad.
mozárabe [mo·sá·ra·be] *adj.* Mozarabic (*Christian in Moslem Spain*).
mozo [mó·so] *adj.* young; unmarried; *m.* youth; manservant; waiter; porter; errand boy; **buen —** handsome man.
mozuela [mo·swé·la] *f.* lass, young girl.
mozuelo [mo·swé·lo] *m.* lad, young boy.
mucama [mu·ká·ma] *f. Andes, Ríopl.* servant girl; **mucamo** [mu·ká·mo] *m. Andes, Ríopl.* servant.
mucoso [mu·kó·so] *adj.* mucous; slimy; **membrana mucosa** mucous membrane.
muchacha [mu·čá·ča] *f.* child; girl; servant, maid.
muchacho [mu·čá·čo] *m.* child; boy, lad.
muchedumbre [mu·če·đúm·bre] *f.* multitude; crowd.
mucho [mú·čo] *adj.* much, a lot of; long (*referring to time*); **-s** many; *adv.* much; a great deal; **ni con —** not by far, not by a long shot; **ni — menos** not by any means, nor anything like it; **por — que** no matter how much; **no es — que** it is no wonder that.
muda [mú·đa] *f.* change; change of clothes; molt (*act or time of shedding feathers*); *Ríopl.* relay of draft animals.
mudable [mu·đá·ble] *adj.* changeable; fickle.
mudanza [mu·đán·sa] *f.* change; removal; inconstancy.
mudar [mu·đár] *v.* to change; to remove; to molt; **— de casa** to move; **— de traje** to change one's suit or costume; **-se** to change one's clothes; to change one's habits; to move, change one's abode.
mudez [mu·đés] *f.* muteness, dumbness.
mudo [mú·đo] *adj.* mute, dumb; silent; *m.* dumb person.
mueblaje [mwe·blá·xe] *m.* furniture.
mueble [mwé·ble] *m.* piece of furniture; **-s** furniture, household goods; *adj.* movable; **bienes -s** chattels, movable possessions.
mueblería [mwe·ble·rí·a] *f.* furniture store.
mueca [mwé·ka] *f.* grimace; wry face.
muela [mwé·la] *f.* (*diente*) molar tooth; (*piedra*) millstone; grindstone; **— cordal** (*or* **— del juicio**) wisdom tooth.
muelle [mwé·ye] *adj.* soft; voluptuous; *m.* spring; wharf; loading platform; **— real** main spring of a watch.
muerte [mwér·te] *f.* death.
muerto [mwér·to] *p.p. of* **morir** & *adj.* dead; withered; faded; **naturaleza muerta** still life; *m.* corpse.
muesca [mwés·ka] *f.* notch; groove.
muestra [mwés·tra] *f.* sample; pattern, model; shop sign; sign, indication; presence, bearing; face, dial (*of a clock or watch*); **muestrario** [mwes·trá·rjo] *m.* book or collection of samples.
mugido [mu·xí·đo] *m.* moo; mooing, lowing of cattle.
mugir[11] [mu·xír] *v.* to moo, low.
mugre [mú·gre] *f.* dirt, grime.
mugriento [mu·grjén·to] *adj.* grimy, dirty.
mujer [mu·xér] *f.* woman; wife.
mujeriego [mu·xe·rjé·go] *adj.* fond of women; womanly.
mujeril [mu·xe·ríl] *adj.* womanly, feminine;

womanish, like a woman.
mula [mú·la] *f.* mule; *Am.* cushion for carrying loads; *Am.* worthless merchandise; *Ríopl.* cruel, treacherous person; *Am.* **echar a uno la —** to give someone the dickens, scold someone.
muladar [mu·la·đár] *m.* rubbish pile or dump; dunghill, pile of manure.
mulato [mu·lá·to] *adj.* & *m.* mulatto.
muleta [mu·lé·ta] *f.* crutch; red cloth draped over a rod (*used by bullfighters*).
muletilla [mu·le·ti·ya] *f.* cane with a crutchlike handle; red cloth draped over a rod (*used by bullfighters*); cliché (*hackneyed or trite phrase*); refrain; repetitious word or phrase; braid frog (*fastener for a coat*).
mulo [mú·lo] *m.* mule.
multa [múl·ta] *f.* fine.
multicolor [mul·ti·ko·lór] *adj.* many-colored, motley.
múltiple [múl·ti·ple] *adj.* multiple.
multiplicación [mul·ti·pli·ka·sjón] *f.* multiplication.
multiplicar[6] [mul·ti·pli·kár] *v.* to multiply.
multiplicidad [mul·ti·pli·si·đáđ] *f.* multiplicity, manifold variety.
múltiplo [múl·ti·plo] *m.* multiple number.
multitud [mul·ti·túđ] *f.* multitude; crowd.
mullido [mu·yí·đo] *adj.* soft; fluffy; *m.* stuffing for mattresses or pillows; soft cushion or mattress.
mullir[20] [mu·yír] *v.* to fluff; to soften.
mundanal [mun·da·nál] *adj.* worldly.
mundano [mun·dá·no] *adj.* mundane, worldly.
mundial [mun·djál] *adj.* universal; **la guerra —** the World War.
mundo [mún·do] *m.* world; trunk; **todo el —** everybody.
munición [mu·ni·sjón] *f.* ammunition; buckshot; **es de guerra** war supplies.
municipal [mu·ni·si·pál] *adj.* municipal; **municipalidad** [mu·ni·si·pa·li·đáđ] *f.* municipality; town hall; city government.
municipio [mu·ni·sí·pjo] *m.* municipality.
muñeca [mu·ñé·ka] *f.* doll; wrist; manikin (*figure for displaying clothes*); **muñeco** *m.* boy doll; dummy, puppet.
muñón [mu·ñón] *m.* stump (*of an arm or leg*).
muralla [mu·rá·ya] *f.* surrounding wall; rampart.
murciano [mur·sjá·no] *adj.* of or from Murcia, Spain; *m.* native of Murcia.
murciélago [mur·sjé·la·go] *m.* bat.
murga [múr·ga] *f.* brass band.
murmullo [mur·mú·yo] *m.* murmur, rumor; whisper; muttering.
murmuración [mur·mu·ra·sjón] *f.* slander, gossip; grumbling.
murmurar [mur·mu·rár] *v.* to murmur; to slander, gossip; to whisper; to grumble.
muro [mú·ro] *m.* wall.
murria [mú·rrja] *f.* sulkiness, sullenness, melancholy, blues; **tener —** to be sulky; to have the blues.
musa [mú·sa] *f.* Muse; muse, poetic inspiration; poetry; **-s** fine arts.
muscular [mus·ku·lár] *adj.* muscular.
musculatura [mus·ku·la·tú·ra] *f.* muscles; muscular system.
músculo [mús·ku·lo] *m.* muscle.
musculoso [mus·ku·ló·so] *adj.* muscular; sinewy.
muselina [mu·se·lí·na] *f.* muslin.
museo [mu·sé·o] *m.* museum.
musgo [múz·go] *m.* moss.
musgoso [muz·gó·so] *adj.* mossy.

música [mú·si·ka] *f.* music.
musical [mu·si·kál] *adj.* musical.
músico [mú·si·ko] *adj.* musical; *m.* musician.
musitar [mu·si·tár] *v.* to mutter, mumble; to whisper.
muslo [múz·lo] *m.* thigh.
mustio [mús·tjo] *adj.* sad; withered; humble.
mutación [mu·ta·sjón] *f.* mutation; unsettled weather.
mutilar [mu·ti·lár] *v.* to mutilate; to butcher; to mar.
mutismo [mu·tíz·mo] *m.* muteness, silence.
mutuo [mú·two] *adj.* mutual; reciprocal.
muy [mwi(múj)] *adv.* very; greatly; most.

N:n
nabo [ná·ƀo] *m.* turnip.
nácar [ná·kar] *m.* mother-of-pearl; pearl color.
nacarado [na·ka·rá·ɖo] *adj.* pearly.
nacer[13] [na·sér] *v. irr.* (*salir del vientre*) to be born; (*brotar*) to spring, originate; to bud; to sprout, grow (*said of plants*); — **de pie** (*or* — **de pies**) to be born lucky.
naciente [na·sjén·te] *adj.* rising (*sun*); *m.* orient, east.
nacimiento [na·si·mjén·to] *m.* birth; origin; beginning; descent; source; crèche (*representation of the Nativity*).
nación [na·sjón] *f.* nation.
nacional [na·sjo·nál] *adj.* national; *m.* national, citizen.
nacionalidad [na·sjo·na·li·ɖáɖ] *f.* nationality.
nada [ná·ɖa] *f.* nothingness; *indef. pron.* nothing, not ... anything; *adv.* not at all; **de** — you are welcome, don't mention it (*as a reply to* «gracias»); *Am.* **a cada** — constantly; **una nadita** [na·ɖí·ta] a trifle, just a little.
nadada [na·ɖá·ɖa] *f.* swim.
nadador [na·ɖa·ɖór] *m.* swimmer; *Ven.* fish-net float.
nadar [na·ɖár] *v.* to swim; to float.
nadería [na·ɖe·rí·a] *f.* a mere nothing, trifle, worthless thing.
nadie [ná·ɖje] *indef. pron.* nobody, no one, not ... anyone.
nafta [náf·ta] *f.* naphtha.
naguas [ná·ǵwas] = **enaguas.**
náhuatl [ná·watl] *adj.* the language of the Aztec Indians.
naipe [nái·pe] *m.* playing card.
nalgas [nál·ǵas] *f. pl.* buttocks; rump; **nalgada** [nal·ǵá·ɖa] *f.* spank; **-s** spanking.
nana [ná·na] *f.* grandma; lullaby; *Mex., Riopl., Ven.* child's nurse; *Spain* nice old lady.
naranja [na·ráŋ·xa] *f.* orange; — **tangerina** [taŋ·xe·rí·na] tangerine; **naranjada** [na·raŋ·xá·ɖa] *f.* orangeade; orange juice; orange marmalade; **naranjal** [na·raŋ·xál] *m.* orange grove; **naranjo** [na·ráŋ·xo] *m.* orange tree.
narciso [nar·sí·so] *m.* narcissus; daffodil; fop, dandy.
narcótico [nar·kó·ti·ko] *adj. & m.* narcotic.
narcotizar[9] [nar·ko·ti·sár] *v.* to dope, drug with narcotics.
nariz [na·rís] *f.* nose; nostril; **narices** [na·rí·ses] nostrils.
narración [na·rra·sjón] *f.* narration, account, story.

narrar [na·rrár] *v.* to narrate, tell, relate.
narrativo [na·rra·tí·ƀo] *adj.* narrative; **narrativa** [na·rra·tí·ƀa] *f.* narrative.
nata [ná·ta] *f.* cream; best part; scum; **-s** whipped cream with sugar; custard; **natoso** [na·tó·so] *adj.* creamy.
natación [na·ta·sjón] *f.* swimming.
natal [na·tál] *adj.* natal; native; **natalicio** [na·ta·lí·sjo] *m.* birthday; **natalidad** [na·ta·li·ɖáɖ] *f.* birth rate.
natillas [na·tí·yas] *f. pl.* custard.
nativo [na·tí·ƀo] *adj.* native.
natural [na·tu·rál] *adj.* natural; native; simple, unaffected; *m. & f.* native; *m.* nature, disposition; **al** — without affectation; **del** — from nature, from life.
naturaleza [na·tu·ra·lé·sa] *f.* nature; disposition; nationality; naturalization; — **muerta** still life.
naturalidad [na·tu·ra·li·ɖáɖ] *f.* naturalness; simplicity; birthright.
naturalista [na·tu·ra·lís·ta] *adj.* naturalistic; *m. & f.* naturalist.
naturalización [na·tu·ra·li·sa·sjón] *f.* naturalization.
naturalizar[9] [na·tu·ra·li·sár] *v.* to naturalize; to acclimatize, accustom to a new climate; **-se** to become naturalized.
naufragar[7] [naw·fra·ǵár] *v.* to be shipwrecked; to fail.
naufragio [naw·frá·xjo] *m.* shipwreck; failure, ruin.
náufrago [náw·fra·ǵo] *m.* shipwrecked person.
náusea [náw·se·a] *f.* nausea; **dar -s** to nauseate, sicken; to disgust; **tener -s** to be nauseated, be sick to one's stomach.
nauseabundo [naw·se·a·ƀún·do] *adj.* nauseating, sickening.
nauseado [naw·se·á·ɖo] *adj.* nauseated, sick to one's stomach.
náutica [náw·ti·ka] *f.* navigation (*science of navigation*).
navaja [na·ƀá·xa] *f.* jackknife, pocketknife; penknife; razor.
navajazo [na·ƀa·xá·so] *m.* stab with a jackknife or razor; stab wound.
naval [na·ƀál] *adj.* naval.
navarro [na·ƀá·rro] *adj.* Navarrese, of or pertaining to Navarre, Spain; *m.* Navarrese.
nave [ná·ƀe] *f.* ship, boat; nave; — **cósmica** spaceship; — **cósmica pilotada** manned space vehicle.
navegable [na·ƀe·ǵá·ƀle] *adj.* navigable.
navegación [na·ƀe·ǵa·sjón] *f.* navigation; sea voyage; — **aérea** aviation.
navegador [na·ƀe·ǵa·ɖór] **navegante** [na·ƀe·ǵán·te] *m.* navigator; *adj.* navigating.
navegar[7] [na·ƀe·ǵár] *v.* to navigate; to sail.
navidad [na·ƀi·ɖáɖ] *f.* Nativity; Christmas; **-es** Christmas season.
navideño [na·ƀi·ɖé·ño] *adj.* pertaining to Christmas.
navío [na·ƀí·o] *m.* vessel, ship — **de guerra** warship.
neblina [ne·ƀlí·na] *f.* fog, mist.
nebulosidad [ne·ƀu·lo·si·ɖáɖ] *f.* cloudiness; nebulousness.
necedad [ne·se·ɖáɖ] *f.* foolishness, nonsense.
necesario [ne·se·sá·rjo] *adj.* necessary.
neceser [ne·se·sér] *m.* toilet case; sewing kit.
necesidad [ne·se·si·ɖáɖ] *f.* necessity, need, want.
necesitado [ne·se·si·tá·ɖo] *adj.* needy; in need, destitute, poor; *p.p.* of **necesitar**; *m.* needy person.
necesitar [ne·se·si·tár] *v.* to need; to necessitate.
necio [né·sjo] *adj.* stupid, ignorant; foolish.

stubborn; *Col.* touchy.
necrología [ne·kro·lo·xí·a] *f.* necrology.
nefando [ne·fán·do] *adj.* abominable; wicked.
nefasto [ne·fás·to] *adj.* ominous; tragic.
nefritis [ne·frí·tis] *f.* nephritis.
negación [ne·ga·sjón] *f.* negation, denial; negative (*negative particle*).
negar [1, 7] [ne·gár] *v. irr.* to deny; to refuse; to prohibit; to disown; **-se** to refuse, decline.
negativa [ne·ga·tí·ba] *f.* negative; denial, refusal.
negativo [ne·ga·tí·bo] *adj.* negative.
negligencia [ne·gli·xén·sja] *f.* negligence, neglect, carelessness.
negligente [ne·gli·xén·te] *adj.* negligent, neglectful, careless.
negociación [ne·go·sja·sjón] *f.* negotiation; business; business house; management; transaction, deal.
negociante [ne·go·sján·te] *m.* merchant, trader, dealer; businessman; *adj.* negotiating.
negociar [ne·go·sjár] *v.* to negotiate; to trade; to transact.
negocio [ne·gó·sjo] *m.* business; business deal; negotiation, transaction; *Ríopl., Carib., C.A., Ven., Andes* store; **hombre de -s** businessman.
negrear [ne·gre·ár] *v.* to become black; to appear black, look black (*in the distance*).
negrero [ne·gré·ro] *m.* slave trader.
negro [né·gro] *adj.* black; dark; sad, gloomy; unfortunate; *m.* black color; negro; *Ríopl., C.A., Ven., Col.* dear, darling; **negra** [né·gra] *f.* negress; *Ríopl., C.A., Ven., Col.* dear, darling.
negrura [ne·grú·ra] *f.* blackness.
negruzco [ne·grús·ko] *adj.* blackish.
nena [né·na] *f.* baby girl; **nene** [né·ne] *m.* baby boy.
neón [ne·ón] *m.* neon.
neófito [ne·ó·fi·to] *m.* & *f.* neophyte.
neologismo [ne·o·lo·xíz·mo] *m.* neologism.
neoplasma [ne·o·pláz·ma] *m.* neoplasm.
nepotismo [ne·po·tíz·mo] *m.* nepotism.
nervio [ner·bjo] *m.* nerve.
nervioso [ner·bjó·so], **nervoso** [ner·bó·so] *adj.* nervous, sinewy, strong.
nerviosidad [ner·bjo·si·dáđ], **nervosidad** [ner·bo·si·dáđ] *f.* nervousness; flexibility; vigor.
nervudo [ner·bú·đo] *adj.* sinewy, tough, powerful.
neto [né·to] *adj.* clear, pure; net (*profit, price, etc.*); **netamente** [ne·ta·mén·te] *adv.* clearly, distinctly.
neumático [new·má·ti·ko] *m.* tire; *adj.* pneumatic.
neuralgia [new·rál·xja] *f.* neuralgia.
neurastenia [new·ras·té·nja] *f.* neurasthenia.
neutralidad [new·tra·li·đáđ] *f.* neutrality.
neutralizar [9] [new·tra·li·sár] *v.* to neutralize, counteract.
neutro [néw·tro] *adj.* neutral; neuter; sexless.
neutrón [new·trón] *m.* neutron.
nevada [ne·bá·đa] *f.* snowfall.
nevado [ne·bá·đo] *adj.* snowy, white as snow; covered with snow.
nevar [1] [ne·bár] *v. irr.* to snow.
nevasca [ne·bás·ka] *f.* snowstorm.
nevera [ne·be·ra] *f.* icebox; refrigerator; ice storehouse; ice or ice-cream vendor (*woman*).
nevería [ne·be·rí·a] *f.* ice cream parlor.
ni [ni] *conj.* & *adv.* not; not even; neither; — **siquiera** not even.
nicotina [ni·ko·tí·na] *f.* nicotine.
nicho [ní·čo] *m.* niche; recess, hollow in a wall.
nidada [ni·đá·đa] *f.* nestful of eggs; brood of chicks; hatch, brood.
nido [ní·đo] *m.* nest; abode; *Am.* **patearle el — a**

alguien to "upset the applecart", upset someone's plans.
niebla [njé·bla] *f.* fog, mist; confusion.
nieto [njé·to] *m.* grandson, grandchild; **nieta** [njé·ta] *f.* granddaughter.
nieve [njé·be] *f.* snow; *Mex., Ríopl., Ven.* sherbet, ice cream; **tiempo de -s** snowy season.
nigua [ní·gwa] *f.* chigger, chigoe, "sand flea," "red bug."
nihilismo [ni·i·líz·mo] *m.* nihilism.
nimio [ní·mjo] *adj.* miserly, stingy; *Am.* very small, insignificant.
ninfa [nín·fa] *f.* nymph.
ningun(o) [niŋ·gún(o)] *indef. adj.* & *pron.* no one, none, not ... any; nobody.
niña [ní·ña] *f.* girl; baby girl; *Andes, Ríopl., Mex., Carib.* lady, mistress (*title of respect and endearment given to adults*); — **del ojo** pupil of the eye.
niñada [ni·ña·đa] *f.* childishness, childish act or remark.
niñera [ni·ñé·ra] *f.* child's nurse.
niñería [ni·ñé·rí·a] *f.* childish act; child's play; trifle; foolishness.
niñez [ni·ñés] *f.* infancy; childhood.
niño [ní·ño] *m.* child, boy; infant; *Am.* master (*title of respect given to a young man by his servants*); *adj.* childlike, childish; very young, immature.
níquel [ní·kel] *m.* nickel.
niquelado [ni·ke·lá·đo] *adj.* nickel-plated; *m.* nickel plating; nickel plate.
níspero [nís·pe·ro] *m.* loquat; medlar tree.
nitidez [ni·ti·đés] *f.* clarity, clearness.
nítido [ní·ti·đo] *adj.* clear.
nitrato [ni·trá·to] *m.* nitrate; saltpeter.
nítrico [ní·tri·ko] *adj.*
nitro [ní·tro] *m.* niter, saltpeter.
nitrógeno [ni·tró·xe·no] *m.* nitrogen.
nitroglicerina [ni·tro·gli·se·rí·na] *f.* nitroglycerine.
nivel [ni·bél] *m.* level.
nivelar [ni·be·lár] *v.* to level; to grade; to equalize.
no [no] *adv.* no; not; nay; — **bien** as soon as; **un — sé qué** something indefinable; **por sí o por** — just in case, anyway.
noble [nó·ble] *adj.* noble; *m.* nobleman.
nobleza [no·blé·sa] *f.* nobility; nobleness.
noción [no·sjón] *f.* notion, idea.
nocivo [no·sí·bo] *adj.* noxious, harmful, injurious.
nocturno [nok·túr·no] *adj.* nocturnal, night, nightly; *m.* nocturne (*musical or lyrical composition*).
noche [nó·če] *f.* night; darkness; **a la** — tonight; **de** — by (at) night; **por (en) la** — at night, in the evening; **dejar a uno a buenas -s** to leave a person in the lurch.
Nochebuena [no·če·bwé·na] *f.* Christmas Eve.
nocherniego [no·čer·njé·go] *m.* night owl (*person*).
nodriza [no·drí·sa] *f.* child's nurse; wet nurse.
nogal [no·gál] *m.* walnut (*tree and wood*).
nomás [no·más] *Am* = **no más** just; only.
nombradía [nom·bra·đí·a] *f.* renown, fame.
nombramiento [nom·bra·mjén·to] *m.* nomination; appointment; naming.
nombrar [nom·brár] *v.* to name; to name; to appoint.
nombre [nóm·bre] *m.* name; fame; noun; watchword; — **de pila** (*or* — **de bautismo**) Christian name.
nomenclatura [no·meŋ·kla·tú·ra] *f.* nomenclature.
nomeolvides [no·me·ol·bí·des] *f.* forget-me-not.
nómina [nó·mi·na] *f.* list (*of names*); pay roll.
nominación [no·mi·na·sjón] *f.* nomination;

appointment.
nominal [no·mi·nál] *adj.* nominal; **valor** — small, insignificant value.
nominar [no·mi·nár] *v.* to nominate.
non [non] *adj.* odd, uneven; *m.* odd number, uneven number; **estar** (*or* **quedar**) **de** — to be left alone, be left without a partner or companion.
nonada [no·ná·da] *f.* trifle, mere nothing.
nopal [no·pál] *m.* nopal, prickly pear tree (*species of cactus*).
nordeste [nor·dés·te] *adj. & m.* northeast.
nórdico [nór·di·ko] *adj.* Nordic.
noria [nó·rja] *f.* draw well; chain pump.
norma [nór·ma] *f.* norm, standard, model.
normal [nor·mál] *adj.* normal; standard; *f.* perpendicular line.
normalizar[9] [nor·ma·li·sár] *v.* to normalize, make normal; to standardize.
noroeste [nor·o·és·te] *adj. & m.* northwest.
nortada [nor·tá·da] *f.* strong north wind.
nortazo [nor·tá·so] *m. Mex., Ven.* sudden gust of wind, strong north wind.
norte [nór·te] *m.* north; north wind; guide; North Star; direction.
norteamericano [nor·te·a·me·ri·ká·no] *adj.* North American; American (*from or of the United States*).
nortear [nor·te·ár] *v.* to blow from the north; *Sal.* to blow from any direction.
norteño [nor·té·ño] *adj.* northern; *m.* northener.
noruego [no·rwé·go] *adj. & m.* Norwegian.
nostalgia [nos·tál·xja] *f.* nostalgia, longing, homesickness.
nostálgico [nos·tál·xi·ko] *adj.* homesick; lonesome; longing.
nota [nó·ta] *f.* note; mark; fame.
notable [no·tá·ble] *adj.* notable; noticeable.
notar [no·tár] *v.* to note, observe; to mark; to write down.
notario [no·tá·rjo] *m.* notary.
noticia [no·tí·sja] *f.* notice, information; news; **recibir -s** to receive word, hear (from).
noticiario [no·ti·sjá·rjo] *m.* news sheet, news column, news bulletin or film; **noticiero** [no·ti·sjé·ro] *m.* = **noticiario**; *adj.* news (*used as adj.*); newsy, full of news.
noticioso [no·ti·sjó·so] *adj.* newsy, full of news; well-informed.
notificación [no·ti·fi·ka·sjón] *f.* notification, notifying; notice; summons.
notificar[6] [no·ti·fi·kár] *v.* to notify.
notorio [no·tó·rjo] *adj.* well-known; obvious, evident.
novato [no·bá·to] *m.* novice, beginner.
novedad [no·be·dád] *f.* novelty; latest news, event, or fashion; change; newness; **hacerle a uno** — to seem strange or new to one; to excite one's curiosity or interest; **sin** — as usual; well.
novel [no·bél] *adj.* new, inexperienced.
novela [no·bé·la] *f.* novel; fiction.
novelesco [no·be·lés·ko] *adj.* novelistic, fictional; fantastic.
novelista [no·be·lís·ta] *m. & f.* novelist.
novena [no·bé·na] *f.* novena of the Church.
novia [nó·bja] *f.* fiancée; sweetheart; bride.
noviazgo [no·bjáz·go] *m.* betrothal, engagement; courtship.
novicio [no·bí·sjo] *m.* novice; beginner; apprentice; *adj.* inexperienced.
noviembre [no·bjém·bre] *m.* November.
novilla [no·bí·ya] *f.* heifer, young cow.

novillada [no·bi·yá·da] *f.* herd of young bulls; bullfight (*using young bulls*).
novillero [no·bi·yé·ro] *m.* a novice bullfighter; a fighter of 3-year-old bulls.
novillo [no·bí·yo] *m.* young bull; steer; **-s** bullfight (*using young bulls*); **hacer -s** to play hooky, cut classes; to play truant.
novio [nó·bjo] *m.* fiancé; sweetheart; bridegroom.
nubarrón [nu·ba·rrón] *m.* large storm cloud.
nube [nú·be] *f.* cloud; film on the eyeball; **poner por las -s** to praise to the skies.
nublado [nu·blá·do] *m.* storm cloud; imminent danger; *adj.* cloudy.
nublar [nu·blar] *v.* to cloud; to darken, obscure; **-se** to grow cloudy.
nubloso [nu·bló·so] *adj.* cloudy; gloomy.
nuboso [nu·bó·so] *adj. Spain* cloudy.
nuca [nú·ka] *f.* nape.
nuclear [nu·kle·ár] *adj.* nuclear.
núcleo [nú·kle·o] *m.* nucleus; kernel.
nudillo [nu·dí·yo] *m.* small knot; knuckle; loop, knitted stitch.
nudo [nú·do] *m.* (*vínculo*) knot; joint; union, bond, tie (*crisis*) crisis, turning point (*of a play*); knot, nautical mile; — **ciego** hard knot.
nudoso [nu·dó·so] *adj.* knotty, gnarled, knotted.
nuera [nwé·ra] *f.* daughter-in-law.
nueva [nwé·ba] *f.* news.
nuevecito [nwe·be·sí·to] *adj.* nice and new, brandnew.
nuevo [nwé·bo] *adj.* new; newly arrived; **de** — again; ¿**qué hay de** —? what's new? what's the news?
nuez [nwes] *f.* walnut; nut; — (*or* — **de Adán**) Adam's apple; — **moscada** (*or* — **de especia**) nutmeg.
nulidad [nu·li·dád] *f.* nullity (*state or quality of being null*); incompetence; nonentity, a nobody.
nulo [nú·lo] *adj.* null, void; useless.
numeral [nu·me·rál] *adj. & m.* numeral.
numerar [nu·me·rár] *v.* to number; to calculate; to enumerate.
numérico [nu·mé·ri·ko] *adj.* numerical.
número [nú·me·ro] *m.* number; numeral.
numeroso [nu·me·ró·so] *adj.* numerous.
numismática [nu·miz·má·ti·ka] *f.* numismatics.
nunca [nún·ka] *adv.* never; **no ...** — not ... ever; **más que** — more than ever.
nuncio [nún·sjo] *m.* herald, messenger; nuncio, Papal envoy.
nupcial [nup·sjál] *adj.* nuptial, relating to marriage or weddings.
nupcias [núp·sjas] *f. pl.* nuptials, wedding.
nutria [nú·trja] *f.* otter.
nutrición [nu·tri·sjón] *f.* nutrition; nourishment.
nutrido [nu·trí·do] *adj.* full, abundant; substantial; *p.p. of* **nutrir**.
nutrimento [nu·tri·mén·to], **nutrimiento** [nu·tri·mjén·to] *m.* nutrition; nourishment, food.
nutrir [nu·trír] *v.* to nourish, feed.
nutritivo [nu·tri·tí·bo] *adj.* nutritious, nourishing.
nylon [náj·lon] *m.* nylon.

NE

Ñ:ñ

ñandú [ñan·dú] *m.* nandu; American ostrich.
ñapa [ñá·pa] *f. Andes, Ríopl., Cuba, Ven., Col.* additional amount, something extra; *Am.* **de** — to boot, in addition, besides.
ñato [ñá·to] *adj. C.A., Col., Ven., Andes* flat-nosed, pug-nosed, snub-nosed; *Am.* ugly, deformed; *Am.* insignificant.
ñoñería [ño·ñe·rí·a] *f.* silly remark or action; *Am.* dotage.
ñoño [ñó·ño] *adj.* feeble-minded; silly; *Am.* old, decrepit, feeble; *Col., Ec.* old-fashioned, out of style.
ñu [ñu] *m.* gnu.

O:o

o [o] *conj.* or, either.
oasis [o·á·sis] *m.* oasis.
obedecer[13] [o·be·de·sér] *v. irr.* to obey; — **a cierta causa** to arise from, be due to, a certain cause; **esto obedece a que** ... this is due to the fact that ...
obediencia [o·be·djén·sja] *f.* obedience.
obediente [o·be·djén·te] *adj.* obedient.
obelisco [o·be·lís·ko] *m.* obelisk.
obertura [o·ber·tú·ra] *f.* musical overture.
obispado [o·bis·pá·do] *m.* bishopric.
obispo [o·bís·po] *m.* bishop; *Cubp, Andes* **a cada muerte de** (*or* **por la muerte de un**) — once in a blue moon.
objeción [ob·xe·sjón] *f.* objection.
objetar [ob·xe·tár] *v.* to object.
objetivo [ob·xe·tí·bo] *adj.* objective; *m.* objective (*lens of any optical instrument*); objective.
objeto [ob·xé·to] *m.* object, purpose, aim; thing.
oblea [o·blé·a] *f.* water.
oblicuo [o·blí·kwo] *adj.* oblique, slanting, bias.
obligación [o·bli·ga·sjón] *f.* obligation; duty; bond, security; engagement.
obligar[7] [o·bli·gár] *v.* to oblige; to obligate, bind, compel, put under obligation; **-se** to bind oneself, obligate oneself.
obligatorio [o·bli·ga·tó·rjo] *adj.* obligatory; compulsory; binding.
oboe [o·bó·e] *m.* oboe.
óbolo [ó·bo·lo] *m.* mite, small contribution.
obra [ó·bra] *f.* (*resultado de acción*) work; act; labor, toil; (*creación artística*) book; building (*under construction*); masterpiece of art; repair; — **de** approximately; **por** — **de** through, by virtue of power of; **hacer mala** — to interfere, hinder; **poner por** — to undertake, begin; to put into practice.
obrar [o·brár] *v.* to work; to act; to operate; to function; to perform; to make; to do; **obra en nuestro poder** we are in receipt of; **la carta que obra en su poder** the letter that is in his possession.
obrero [o·bré·ro] *m.* workman, laborer.
obscenidad [ob·se·ni·dád] *f.* obscenity.
obsceno [ob·sé·no] *adj.* obscene.
obscurecer[13] [obs·ku·re·sèr] *v. irr.* to obscure. darken; to tarnish; to grow dark; **-se** to get dark or cloudy.
obscuridad [obs·ku·ri·dád] *f.* obscurity; darkness; dimness.
obscuro [obs·kú·ro] *adj.* obscure; dark; dim; **a obscuras** (=**a oscuras**) in the dark; *m.* shade (*in painting*).

obsequiar [ob·se·kjár] *v.* to regale, entertain; to court; *Am.* to give, make a present of.
obsequio [ob·sé·kjo] *m.* attention, courtesy; gift; **en** — **de** for the sake of, in honor of.
obsequioso [ob·se·kjó·so] *adj.* attentive, courteous, obliging; obsequious, servile.
observación [ob·ser·ba·sjón] *f.* observation; remark.
observador [ob·ser·ba·dór] *m.* observer; *adj.* observing.
observancia [ob·ser·bán·sja] *f.* observance (*of a law, rule, custom, etc.*).
observante [ob·ser·bán·te] *adj.* observant (*of a law, custom, or rule*).
observar [ob·ser·bár] *v.* to observe; to watch; to remark.
observatorio [ob·ser·ba·tó·rjo] *m.* observatory.
obsesión [ob·se·sjón] *f.* obsession.
obsesionar [ob·se·sjo·nár] *v.* to obsess.
obstáculo [obs·tá·ku·lo] *m.* obstacle.
obstante: obstante [obs·tán·te] **no** — notwithstanding; nevertheless.
obstar [obs·tár] *v.* to hinder, impede, obstruct.
obstétrica [obs·té·tri·ka] *f.* obstetrics.
obstinación [obs·ti·na·sjón] *f.* obstinacy. stubbornness.
obstinado [obs·ti·ná·do] *adj.* obstinate, stubborn.
obstinarse [obs·ti·nár·se] *v.* to persist (in); to be obstinate, stubborn (about).
obstrucción [obs·truk·sjón] *f.* obstruction.
obstruir[32] [obs·trwír] *v. irr.* to obstruct, block.
obtener[45] [ob·te·nér] *v. irr.* to obtain, get; to attain.
obtenible [ob·te·ní·ble] *adj.* obtainable, available.
obturador [ob·tu·ra·dór] *m.* choke (*of an automobile*); throttle; plug, stopper; shutter (*of a camera*).
obviar [ob·bjár] *v.* to obviate, clear away, remove.
obvio [ób·bjo] *adj.* obvious.
ocasión [o·ka·sjón] *f.* occasion, opportunity; cause; danger, risk; **de** — reduced, bargain; **avisos de** — want "ads" (*advertisements*); *Am.* **esta** — this time.
ocasional [o·ka·sjo·nál] *adj.* occasional.
ocasionar [o·ka·sjo·nár] *v.* to occasion, cause.
ocaso [o·ká·so] *m.* sunset; setting (*of any star or planet*); west; decadence, decline, end.
occidental [ok·si·den·tál] *adj.* occidental, western.
occidente [ok·si·dén·te] *m.* occident, west.
océano [o·sé·a·no] *m.* ocean.
oceanografía [o·se·a·no·gra·fi·a] *f.* oceanography.
ocelote [o·se·ló·te] *m.* ocelot.
ocio [ó·sjo] *m.* leisure, idleness; recreation, pastime.
ociosidad [o·sjo·si·dád] *f.* idleness, leisure.
ocioso [o·sjó·so] *adj.* idle; useless.
ocre [ó·kre] *m.* ocher.
octava [ok·tá·ba] *f.* octave.
octubre [ok·tú·bre] *m.* October.
ocular [o·ku·lár] *adj.* ocular; **testigo** — eye witness; *m.* eyepiece, lens (*for the eye in a microscope or telescope*).
oculista [o·ku·lís·ta] *m. & f.* oculist; *Am.* flatterer.
ocultar [o·kul·tár] *v.* to hide, conceal.
oculto [o·kúl·to] *adj.* hidden, concealed; *m. Am.* species of mole (*small animal*).
ocupación [o·ku·pa·sjón] *f.* occupation; employment.
ocupante [o·ku·pán·te] *m. & f.* occupant.
ocupar [o·ku·pár] *v.* to occupy; to employ; **-se en**

(*Am.* **-se de**) to be engaged in; to pay attention to, be interested in.
ocurrencia [o·ku·rrén·sja] *f.* occurrence, event; witticism, joke; bright or funny idea.
ocurrente [o·ku·rrén·te] *adj.* witty, funny, humorous; occurring.
ocurrir [o·ku·rrír] *v.* to occur.
ocurso [o·kúr·so] *m. Ríopl.* petition, application.
ochavo [o·čá·βo] *m.* an ancient coin; **no tener —** not to have a red cent.
ochentón [o·čen·tón] *m.* octogenarian.
oda [ó·ða] *f.* ode.
odiar [o·djár] *v.* to hate.
odio [ó·djo] *m.* hatred.
odioso [o·djó·so] *adj.* odious, hateful.
odontología [o·ðon·to·lo·xí·a] *f.* odontology.
odre [ó·ðre] *m.* wine bag; drunk.
oeste [o·és·te] *m.* west; west wind.
ofender [o·fen·dér] *v.* to offend; to displease; **-se** to get offended; to become angry, take offense.
ofensa [o·fén·sa] *f.* offense.
ofensivo [o·fen·sí·βo] *adj.* offensive; obnoxious; attacking; **ofensiva** [o·fen·sí·βa] *f.* offensive.
ofensor [o·fen·sór] *m.* offender; *adj.* offending.
oferta [o·fér·ta] *f.* offer; promise.
oficial [o·fi·sjál] *m.* official, officer, skilled workman; *adj.* official.
oficiar [o·fi·sjár] *v.* to officiate, serve, minister, perform the duties of a priest or minister; to communicate officially; **— de** to serve as, act as.
oficina [o·fi·sí·na] *f.* office; shop; **oficinesco** *adj.* clerical, pertaining to an office.
oficio [o·fi·sjo] *m.* trade; function; official communication; religious office (*prayers*).
oficioso [o·fi·sjó·so] *adj.* officious, meddlesome.
ofrecer[13] [o·fre·sér] *v. irr.* to offer; to promise; **-se** to offer, occur, present itself; to offer oneself, volunteer; **¿qué se le ofrece a Vd.?** what do you wish?
ofrecimiento [o·fre·si·mjén·to] *m.* offer; offering.
ofrenda [o·frén·da] *f.* offering, gift.
ofuscamiento [o·fus·ka·mjén·to] *m.* clouded vision, blindness; cloudiness of the mind, bewilderment, mental confusion.
ofuscar[6] [o·fus·kár] *v.* to darken, cast a shadow on; to blind; to cloud; to bewilder, confuse.
ogro [ó·ɡro] *m.* ogre.
oído [o·í·ðo] *m.* hearing; ear; **al —** confidentially; **de** (*or* **al**) **—** by ear; **de -s** (*or* **de oidas**) by hearsay or rumor.
oidor [oj·ðór] *m.* hearer, listener; judge.
oír[36] [o·ír] *v. irr.* to hear; to listen; to understand; **— misa** to attend mass; **— decir que** to hear that; **— hablar de** to hear about.
ojal [o·xál] *m.* buttonhole; hole.
¡ojalá! [o·xa·lá] *interj.* God grant!; I hope so!; **— que** would that. I hope that.
ojazo [o·xá·so] *m.* large eye.
ojeada [o·xe·á·ða] *f.* glimpse, quick glance.
ojear [o·xe·ár] *v.* to eye, stare; to bewitch; to beat up, rouse (*wild game*).
ojera [o·xé·ra] *f.* dark circle under the eye; eyecup.
ojeriza [o·xe·rí·sa] *f.* grudge, spite.
ojeroso [o·xe·ró·so] *adj.* with dark circles under the eyes.
ojete [o·xé·te] *m.* eyelet.
ojiva [o·xí·βa] *f.* pointed arch; **ojival** [o·xi·βál] *adj.* pointed (*arch*); **ventana ojival** window with a pointed arch.
ojo [ó·xo] *m.* (*órgano*) eye; (*agujero*) keyhole; hole; **¡—!** careful! look out!; **a —** by sight, by guess;

a -s vistas visibly, clearly; **— de agua** spring (*of water*); **— de buey** porthole; **mal** (*or* **mal de**) **—** evil eye; *Am.* **hacer —** to cast the evil eye; *Am.* **pelar el —** to be alert, keep one's eye peeled; *Mex., Ven.* **poner a uno los -s verdes** to deceive someone; **tener entre -s a** to have ill will toward, have a grudge against.
ojoso [o·xó·so] *adj.* full of holes.
ojota [o·xó·ta] *f. Andes, Ch., Ríopl.* leather sandal.
ola [ó·la] *f.* wave.
¡ole! [ó·le] *interj.* bravo! good!
oleada [o·le·á·ða] *f.* big wave; swell; surge; abundant yield of oil.
oleaje [o·le·á·xe], **olaje** [o·lá·xe] *m.* swell, surge, succession of waves.
oleo [ó·le·o] *m.* oil, holy oil; **pintura al —** oil painting.
oleoducto [o·le·o·dúk·to] *m.* pipe line.
oleoso [o·le·ó·so] *adj.* oily.
oler[37] [o·lér] *v. irr.* to smell; to scent; **— a** to smack of; to smell like; *Am.* **olérselas** to suspect it, "smell a rat".
olfatear [ol·fa·te·ár] *v.* to scent, sniff, smell.
olfateo [ol·fa·té·o] *m.* sniff, sniffing.
olfato [ol·fá·to] *m.* sense of smell.
olfatorio [ol·fa·tó·rjo] *adj.* olfactory.
oligarquía [o·li·ɡar·kí·a] *f.* oligarchy.
olimpiada [o·lim·pjá·ða] *f.* Olympiad; Olympic games.
olímpico [o·lím·pi·ko] *adj.* Olympian.
oliva [o·lí·βa] *f.* olive; olive tree; **olivar** *m.* olive grove; **olivo** *m.* olive tree.
olmo [ól·mo] *m.* elm.
olor [o·lór] *m.* (*en el olfato*) smell, odor, fragrance; (*fama*) smack, trace, suspicion; *Am.* spice; **olorcillo** [o·lor·sí·yo] *m.* faint odor.
oloroso [o·lo·ró·so] *adj.* fragrant.
olote [o·ló·te] *m. Mex., C.A.* cob, corncob.
olvidadizo [ol·βi·ða·dí·so] *adj.* forgetful.
olvidar [ol·βi·ðár] *v.* to forget; to neglect; **-se de** to forget; **olvidársele a uno algo** to forget something.
olvido [ol·βí·ðo] *m.* forgetfulness; oblivion; neglect; **echar al —** to cast into oblibion; to forget on purpose.
olla [ó·ya] *f.* pot, kettle; olla (*vegetable and meat stew*); **— podrida** Spanish stew of mixed vegetables and meat.
ombligo [om·bli·ɡo] *m.* navel; middle center.
ombú [om·bú] *m.* umbra tree.
omisión [o·mi·sjón] *f.* omission; oversight, neglect.
omiso [o·mí·so] *adj.* careless, neglectful; *N. Arg.* guilty; **hacer caso —** to omit.
omitir [o·mi·tír] *v.* to omit; to overlook.
ómnibus [óm·ni·βus] *m.* omnibus, bus.
omnipotente [om·ni·po·tén·te] *adj.* omnipotent, almighty.
onda [ón·da] *f.* wave; ripple; sound wave; scallop.
ondear [on·de·ár] *v.* to wave; to waver; to ripple; to sway, swing.
ondulación [on·du·la·sjón] *f.* undulation, waving motion; wave; **— permanente** permanent wave.
ondulado [on·du·lá·ðo] *p.p. & adj.* wavy; scalloped (*edge*); **— permanente** permanent wave.
ondulante [on·du·lán·te] *adj.* wavy, waving.
ondular [on·du·lár] *v.* to undulate; to wave.
oneroso [o·ne·ró·so] *adj.* onerous.
onomástico [o·no·más·ti·ko] *adj.* onomastic; saint's day.
onomatopeya [o·no·ma·to·pé·ya] *f.* onomatopoeia.
ontología [on·to·lo·xí·a] *f.* ontology.

onza [ón·sa] *f*. ounce; ounce, wildcat; *Ríopl., Bol.* small tiger.

opacidad [o·pa·si·dád] *f*. opacity; sadness.

opaco [o·pá·ko] *adj*. opaque, dim, dull.

ópalo [ó·pa·lo] *m*. opal.

ópera [ó·pe·ra] *f*. opera.

operación [o·pe·ra·sjón] *f*. operation; business transaction.

operador [o·pe·ra·dór] *m*. operator, surgeon.

operante [o·pe·rán·te] *adj*. operant (*behavior*).

operar [o·pe·rár] *v*. to operate; to take effect, work; to speculate (*in business*); to manipulate, handle.

operario [o·pe·rá·rjo] *m*. operator, workman, worker.

opereta [o·pe·ré·ta] *f*. operetta.

opinar [o·pi·nár] *v*. to express an opinion; to think; to judge; to argue.

opinión [o·pi·njón] *f*. opinion; reputation.

opio [ó·pjo] *m*. opium.

oponer[40] [o·po·nér] *v*. *irr*. to oppose; **-se** to disapprove; **-se a** to oppose, be against.

oporto [o·pór·to] *m*. port wine.

oportunidad [o·por·tu·ni·dád] *f*. opportunity.

oportuno [o·por·tú·no] *adj*. opportune; convenient, timely.

oposición [o·po·si·sjón] *f*. opposition; competition; **-es** competitive examinations.

opositor [o·po·si·tór] *m*. opponent; competitor.

opresión [o·pre·sjón] *f*. oppression.

opresivo [o·pre·sí·ƀo] *adj*. oppressive.

opresor [o·pre·sór] *m*. oppressor.

oprimir [o·pri·mír] *v*. to oppress; to crush; to press down.

oprobio [o·pró·ƀjo] *m*. infamy; insult; shame; dishonor.

optar [op·tár] *v*. to choose, select; — **por** to decide upon; to choose.

óptica [óp·ti·ka] *f*. optics.

óptico [óp·ti·ko] *adj*. optical, optic; *m*. optician.

optimismo [op·ti·míz·mo] *m*. optimism; **optimista** *m*. & *f*. optimist; *adj*. optimistic.

óptimo [óp·ti·mo] *adj*. very good, very best.

opuesto [o·pwés·to] *p.p*. of **oponer** opposed; *adj*. opposite; contrary.

opulencia [o·pu·lén·sja] *f*. opulence, abundance, wealth.

opulento [o·pu·lén·to] *adj*. opulant, wealthy.

oquedad [o·ke·dád] *f*. cavity, hollow; chasm.

ora [ó·ra] *conj*. now, then; whether; either.

oración [o·ra·sjón] *f*. oration; prayer; sentence.

oráculo [o·rá·ku·lo] *m*. oracle.

orador [o·ra·dór] *m*. orator, speaker.

oral [o·rál] *adj*. oral.

orar [o·rár] *v*. to pray.

oratoria [o·ra·tó·rjo] *f*. oratory, eloquence.

oratorio [o·ra·tó·rjo] *m*. oratory, private chapel; oratorio (*a religious musical composition*); *adj*. oratorical, pertaining to oratory.

orbe [ór·ƀe] *m*. orb, sphere, globe; the earth; world, universe.

órbita [ór·ƀi·ta] *f*. orbit; eye socket.

orden [ór·den] *m*. (*colocación*) order; succession, series; class, group; relation; proportion; *f*. (*mando*) order, command; (*sociedad*) honorary or religious order; *m*. & *f*. sacrament of ordination; **a sus órdenes** at your service.

ordenado [or·de·ná·do] *p.p*. & *adj*. ordered; ordained; orderly; neat.

ordenanza [or·de·nán·sa] *f*. ordinance, decree, law; command, order; *m*. orderly (*military*).

ordenar [or·de·nár] *v*. to arrange, put in order; to order, command; to ordain; **-se** to become ordained.

ordeño [or·dé·ña] *m*. milking.

ordeñar [or·de·ñár] *v*. to milk.

ordinariez [or·di·na·rjés] *f*. commonness, lack of manners.

ordinario [or·di·ná·rjo] *adj*. ordinary; usual; common, coarse; *m*. ordinary (*a bishop or judge*); ordinary mail; daily household expense; **de** — usually, ordinarily.

orear [o·re·ár] *v*. to air; **-se** to be exposed to the air; to dry in the air.

orégano [o·ré·ga·no] *m*. wild marjoram, oregano.

oreja [o·ré·xa] *f*. ear; hearing; loop; small flap; *Am*. handle (*shaped like an ear*); **orejano** [o·re·xá·no] *adj*. unbranded (*cattle*); *Ven., Col.* cautious; *Am*. Cuba aloof, unsociable person; **orejera** [o·re·xé·ra] *f*. ear muff, ear flap; **orejón** [o·re·xón] *m*. pull by the ear; *Col.* rancher or inhabitant of the *sabana*; *adj. Col.* long-eared, long-horned; *Col.* unbranded (*cattle*); *Col.* coarse, crude, uncouth.

orfandad [or·fan·dád] *f*. orphanage (*state of being an orphan*).

orfanato [or·fa·ná·to] *m*. orphanage, orphan asylum.

orfanatorio [or·fa·na·tó·rjo] *Am*. = **orfanato**.

orfebre [or·fé·ƀre] *m*. goldsmith; silversmith.

orfebrería [or·fe·ƀre·rí·a] *f*. silver or gold work.

orfeón [or·fe·ón] *m*. glee club, choir.

orgánico [or·gá·ni·ko] *adj*. organic.

organillo [or·ga·ní·yo] *m*. hand organ, hurdy-gurdy.

organismo [or·ga·níz·mo] *m*. organism.

organización [or·ga·ni·sa·sjón] *f*. organization.

organizador [or·ga·ni·sa·dór] *m*. organizer.

organizer[9] [or·ga·ni·sár] *v*. to organize; to arrange.

órgano [ór·ga·no] *m*. organ; **organillo** [or·ga·ní·yo] *m*. hand organ.

orgía [or·xí·a] *f*. orgy, wild revel.

orgullo [or·gú·yo] *m*. pride; haughtiness, arrogance.

orgulloso [or·gu·yó·so] *adj*. proud; haughty, arrogant.

oriental [o·rjen·tál] *adj*. oriental, eastern.

orientar [or·rjen·tár] *v*. to orientate, orient; **-se** to orient oneself, find one's bearings.

oriente [o·rjén·te] *m*. orient, east; east wind; source, origin.

orificación [o·ri·fi·ka·sjón] *f*. gold filling.

orificio [o·ri·fi·sjo] *m*. orifice, small hole, aperture, outlet.

origen [o·rí·xen] *m*. origin; source.

original [o·ri·xi·nál] *adj*. original; strange, quaint; *m*. original; manuscript, copy; queer person; **originalidad** [o·ri·xi·na·li·dád] *f*. originality.

originar [o·ri·xi·nár] *v*. to originate, cause to be; **-se** originate, arise.

orilla [o·rí·ya] *f*. shore, bank; beach; edge, border; **-s** *Am*. outskirts, environs.

orillar [o·ri·yár] *v*. to border, trim the edge of; to skirt, go along the edge of; to reach the edge or shore.

orín [o·rín] *m*. rust; **orines** *m*. pl. urine.

orina [o·rí·na] *f*. urine.

orinar [o·ri·nár] *v*. to urinate.

oriol [o·rjól] *m*. oriole.

oriundo [o·rjún·do] *adj*. native; **ser** — **de** to hail from, come from.

orla [ór·la] *f*. border; trimming, fringe.

orlar [or·lár] *v*. to border, edge, trim with a border or fringe.

orlón [or·lón] *m.* orlon.
ornado [or·ná·ḍo] *adj.* ornate; *p.p.* adorned, ornamented.
ornamentar [or·na·men·tár] *v.* to ornament, adorn.
ornamento [or·na·mén·to] *m.* ornament; decoration; **-s** sacred vestments.
ornar [or·nár] *v.* to adorn.
oro [ó·ro] *m.* gold; gold ornament; **-s** "gold coins" (*Spanish card suit*).
orondo [o·rón·do] *adj.* self-satisfied, puffed up, vain; *Am.* serene, calm.
oropel [o·ro·pél] *m.* tinsel.
orquesta [or·kés·ta] *f.* orchestra.
orquestar [or·kés·tár] *v.* to orchestrate.
orquídea [or·kí·de·a] *f.* orchid.
ortiga [or·tí·ga] *f.* nettle.
ortodoxo [or·to·dók·so] *adj.* orthodox.
ortografía [or·to·gra·fí·a] *f.* orthography, spelling.
ortográfico [or·to·grá·fi·ko] *adj.* orthographic (*pertaining to orthography or spelling*).
oruga [o·rú·ga] *f.* caterpillar.
orzuelo [or·swé·lo] *m.* sty (*on the eyelid*).
osadía [o·sa·ḍí·a] *f.* boldness, daring.
osado [o·sá·ḍo] *adj.* bold, daring.
osamenta [o·sa·mén·ta] *f.* bones; skeleton.
osar [o·sár] *v.* to dare, venture.
oscilación [o·si·la·sjón] *f.* oscillation, sway; fluctuation, wavering.
oscilar [o·si·lár] *v.* to oscillate, swing, sway; to waver.
oscilatorio [o·si·la·tó·rjo] *adj.* oscillatory.
oscurecer [os·ku·re·sér] = **obscurecer**.
oscuridad [os·ku·ri·ḍáḍ] = **obscuridad**.
oscuro [os·kú·ro] = **obscuro**.
oso [ó·so] *m.* bear; — **blanco** polar bear; — **hormiguero** anteater; — **marino** seal.
ostentación [os·ten·ta·sjón] *f.* ostentation, show. display.
ostentar [os·ten·tár] *v.* to display, show; to show off; to boast.
ostentoso [os·ten·tó·so] *adj.* ostentatious, showy.
ostión [os·tjón] *m.* large oyster.
ostra [ós·tra] *f.* oyster.
otate [o·tá·te] *m. Mex., C.A.* species of bamboo; *Mex., C.A.* bamboo stick or cane.
otero [o·té·ro] *m.* hillock, small hill, knoll.
otoñal [o·to·ñál] *adj.* autumnal, of autumn.
otoño [o·tó·ño] *m.* autumn, fall.
otorgar[7] [o·tor·gár] *v.* to grant; to promise; to consent to.
otro [ó·tro] *adj.* another; **otra vez** again; *Am.* **como dijo el** — as someone said.
otrora [o·tró·ra] *adv.* formerly, in other times.
ovación [o·ba·sjón] *f.* ovation, enthusiastic applause.
oval [o·bál], **ovalado** [o·ba·lá·ḍo] *adj.* oval; **óvalo** [ó·ba·lo] *m.* oval.
oveja [o·bé·xa] *f.* sheep.
ovejero [o·be·xé·ro] *m.* shepherd; sheep dog.
ovejuno [o·be·xú·no] *adj.* sheep, pertaining or relating to sheep.
overo [o·bé·ro] *adj.* peach-colored (*applied to horses and cattle*); *Ríopl.* mottled, spotted; *Ríopl.* multicolored; *Ríopl.* **ponerle a uno** — to insult someone.
overol [o·be·ról], **overoles** [o·be·ró·les] *m. Ch., Col.* overalls.
ovillar [o·bi·yár] *v.* to ball, wind or form into a ball; **-se** to curl up into a ball.
ovillo [o·bí·yo] *m.* ball of yarn or thread; tangle; **hacerse uno un** — to curl up into a ball; to

become entangled, confused.
oxidado [ok·si·ḍá·ḍo] *p.p.* rusted; *adj.* rusty.
oxidar [ok·si·ḍár] *v.* to oxidize; to rust; **-se** to become oxidized; to rust.
óxido [ók·si·ḍo] *m.* oxide.
oxígeno [ok·sí·xeno] *m.* oxygen.
oyente [o·yén·te] *m. & f.* listener, auditor, hearer; *adj.* listening.
ozono [o·só·no] *m.* ozone.

P:p

pabellón [pa·be·yón] *m.* pavilion; canopy; banner, flag; shelter, covering; external ear.
pabilo [pa·bí·lo] *m.* wick; snuff (*of a candle*).
pacer[13] [pa·sér] *v. irr.* to pasture; to graze.
paciencia [pa·sjén·sja] *f.* patience.
paciente [pa·sjén·te] *adj.* patient; *m. & f.* patient.
pacienzudo [pa·sjen·sú·ḍo] *adj.* patient, long-suffering.
pacificar[6] [pa·si·fi·kár] *v.* to pacify; to appease.
pacífico [pa·sí·fi·ko] *adj.* pacific, peaceful, calm.
pacifismo [pa·si·fíz·mo] *m.* pacifism.
pacto [pák·to] *m.* pact, agreement.
padecer[13] [pa·de·sér] *v. irr.* to suffer.
padecimiento [pa·de·si·mjén·to] *m.* suffering.
padrastro [pa·drás·tro] *m.* stepfather; hangnail.
padre [pá·ḍre] *m.* father; **-s** parents; ancestors; *adj. Am.* very great, stupendous.
padrenuestro [pa·ḍre·nwés·tro] *m.* paternoster, the Lord's Prayer.
padrino [pa·ḍrí·no] *m.* godfather; sponsor, patron; second in a duel; best man (*at a wedding*).
paella [pa·é·ya] *f.* a popular rice dish with chicken, vegetables, etc.
paga [pá·ga] *f.* payment; pay, salary.
pagadero [pa·ga·dé·ro] *adj.* payable.
pagado [pa·gá·ḍo] *p.p. & adj.* paid; self-satisfied, conceited; — **de sí mismo** pleased with oneself.
pagador [pa·ga·ḍór] *m.* payer; paymaster; paying teller (*in a bank*).
paganismo [pa·ga·níz·mo] *m.* paganism, heathenism.
pagano [pa·gá·no] *adj.* pagan; *m.* pagan; payer; dupe, sucker.
pagar[7] [pa·gár] *v.* to pay; to pay for; to requite, return (*love*); **-se de** to be proud of; to boast of; to be pleased with; *Ríopl.* **-se de palabras** to let oneself be tricked; *Am.* — **a nueve** to pay in excess.
pagaré [pa·ga·ré] *m.* promissory note; I.O.U.
página [pá·xi·na] *f.* page.
paginar [pa·xi·nár] *v.* to page.
pago [pá·go] *m.* (*premio*) payment; prize, reward; (*distrito*) country district; *Ríopl.* one's native farm land or district; *adj.* paid; *Am.* **estar -s** to be quits.
paila [pái·la] *f.* large pan; *C.A.* saucer.
país [pa·ís] *m.* nation, country; region.
paisaje [paj·sá·xe] *m.* landscape.
paisanaje [paj·sa·ná·xe] *m.* peasantry, country people; civilians; *Andes* gang of farm laborers.
paisano [paj·sá·no] *m.* countryman; peasant; fellow countryman; civilian.
paja [pá·xa] *f.* straw; chaff; rubbish; *Andes* grass for pasture; **echar -s** to draw lots; **por quítame allá esas -s** for an insignificant reason or pretext; **en un quítame allá esas -s** in a jiffy, in a second; **a**

humo de -s thoughtlessly; lightly; **no lo hizo a humo de -s** he did not do it without a special reason or intention.

pajar [pa·xár] *m.* straw loft, barn.

pájaro [pá·xa·ro] *m.* bird; shrewd, cautious person; *Ch.* absent-minded person; *Ch., Riopl.* person of suspicious conduct; — **carpintero** woodpecker; — **mosca** humming bird.

paje [pá·xe] *m.* page, valet, attendant.

pajizo [pa·xí·so] *adj.* made of straw; covered with straw; straw colored.

pajonal [pa·xo·nál] *m.* plain or field of tall coarse grass.

pala [pá·la] *f.* shovel; trowel; scoop; paddle; blade of an oar; racket; upper (*of a shoe*); cunning, craftiness; **meter la** — to deceive with cunning; *Am.* **hacer la** — to deceive with cunning; to stall, pretend to work; to flatter; **palada** [pa·lá·da] *f.* scoop, shovelful; stroke of an oar.

palabra [pa·lá·ḇra] *f.* word; promise; **de** — by word of mouth; **cuatro -s** a few words; **empeñar la** — to promise, pledge; **tener la** — to have the floor; *Am.* **i—!** I mean it, it is true!

palabrero [pa·la·ḇré·ro] *adj.* wordy, talkative.

palabrita [pa·la·ḇrí·ta] *f.* a little word, a few words; a word of advice.

palacio [pa·lá·sjo] *m.* palace; **palaciego** [pa·la·sjé·ǥo] *m.* courtier; *adj.* relating to a palace or court; court (*used as an adj.*).

paladar [pa·la·ḍár] *m.* palate; taste, relish.

paladear [pa·la·ḍe·ár] *v.* to relish, taste with relish.

paladín [pa·la·ḍín] *m.* knight; champion, defender.

paladio [pa·lá·djo] *m.* palladium.

palanca [pa·láŋ·ka] *f.* lever; crowbar; bar used for carrying a load; influence, a "pipe line".

palangana [pa·laŋ·gá·na] *f.* washbowl, basin; *S.A.* platter; *Ch.* large wooden bowl; *m. Andes* bluffer, charlatan.

palatal [pa·la·tál] *adj.* palatal.

palco [pál·ko] *m.* theater box; — **escénico** stage.

palenque [pa·léŋ·ke] *m.* palisade, fence; enclosure; *Riopl.* hitching post or plank.

paleta [pa·lé·ta] *f.* small flat shovel; mason's trowel; shoulder blade; blade (*of a rudder, of a ventilating fan*); paddle (*of a paddle wheel*); painter's palette; *Am.* candy, sweetmeat or ice cream attached to a stick; *Am.* a wooden paddle to stir with, or for beating clothes; **en dos -s** in a jiffy, in a second; **paletilla** [pa·le·tí·ya] *f.* shoulder blade.

- **palidecer**[13] [pa·li·ḍe·sér] *v. irr.* to turn pale.

palidez [pa·li·ḍés] *f.* pallor, paleness.

pálido [pá·li·ḍo] *adj.* pallid, pale.

palillo [pa·lí·yo] *m.* small stick; toothpick; **tocar todos los -s** (*Ch.* **menear uno los -s**) to try every possible means.

paliza [pa·lí·sa] *f.* beating (*with a stick*), thrashing.

palizada [pa·li·sá·ḍa] *f.* palisade; stockade.

palma [pál·ma] *f.* palm tree; palm leaf; palm of the hand; **batir -s** to clap, applaud; **llevarse la** — to triumph, win, carry off the honors; to be the best.

palmada [pal·má·ḍa] *f.* slap; clap.

palmario [pal·má·rjo] *adj.* clear, evident.

palmatoria [pal·ma·tó·rja] *f.* small candlestick with handle.

palmear [pal·me·ár] *v.* to clap, applaud; *Am.* to pat, clap on the back; *Riopl.* to flatter.

palmera [pal·mé·ra] *f.* palm tree.

palmo [pál·mo] *m.* span (*about 9 inches*); — **a** — slowly, foot by foot.

palmotear [pal·mo·te·ár] *v.* to clap, applaud.

palo [pá·lo] *m.* stick; pole; log; mast; wood; blow with a stick; suit (*in a deck of cards*); *Am.* tree; *Riopl.* reprimand, reproof; *P.R., Ven.* large swallow of liquor; — **del Brasil** Brazil wood; *Ven.* — **a pique** rail fence, barbed wire fence; *Mex., C.A.* **a medio** — half-done; half-drunk; *Am.* **a** — **entero** drunk.

paloma [pa·ló·ma] *f.* dove, pigeon; pleasant, mild person; **-s** whitecaps.

palomar [pa·lo·már] *m.* dovecot (*shelter for doves or pigeons*).

palomilla [pa·lo·mí·ya] *f.* little dove; moth; small butterfly; **-s** small whitecaps.

palomita [pa·lo·mí·ta] *f.* little dove; **-s** *Am.* popcorn.

palpable [pal·pá·ḇle] *adj.* palpable (*that can be felt or touched*); clear, obvious, evident.

palpar [pal·pár] *v.* to feel; to touch; to grope.

palpitación [pal·pi·ta·sjón] *f.* palpitation; beat, throb.

palpitante [pal·pi·tán·te] *adj.* palpitating. throbbing, trembling; exciting; **la cuestión** — the burning question.

palpitar [pal·pi·tár] *v.* to palpitate; to throb, beat.

palta [pál·ta] *f. Col., Ven., Andes, Riopl., Ch.* avocado, alligator pear; **palto** [pál·to] *m. Col., Ven., Andes, Riopl., Ch.* avocado tree. *See* **aguacate.**

palúdico [pa·lú·ḍi·ko] *adj.* marshy; **fiebre palúdica** malarial, or marsh fever; malaria; **paludismo** *m.* malaria.

pampa [pám·pa] *f. Am.* (*vast treeless plain of South America*); *Am.* prairie; *Ch.* drill field (*military*); *m. & f.* pampa Indian of Argentina; *m. Am.* language of the pampa Indian; *adj. Am.* pertaining to the pampa Indian *Riopl.* **caballo** — horse with head and body of different colors; *Riopl.* **trato** — dubious or dishonest deal; *Am.* **estar a la** — to be in the open; *Riopl.* **tener todo a la** — to be ragged or to be indecently exposed; *Ch.* **quedar en** — to be left without clothes; to be left in the lurch.

pampeano [pam·pe·á·no] *adj. Riopl.* of, or pertaining to, the pampa.

pampero [pam·pé·ro] *adj. Riopl.* of, or pertaining to, the pampas; *Riopl.* inhabitant of the pampas; *Riopl.* violent wind of the pampa.

pan [pan] *m.* bread; loaf of bread; wheat; **-es** fields of grain; breadstuffs; *Am.* **echar -es** to brag, boast.

pana [pá·na] *f.* corduroy.

panadería [pa·na·ḍe·rí·a] *f.* bakery.

panadero [pa·na·ḍé·ro] *m.* baker; *Ch.* flatterer.

panal [pa·nál] *m.* honeycomb; sweetmeat (*made of sugar, egg white, and lemon*).

panamericano [pa·na·me·ri·ká·no] *adj.* Pan-American.

pandearse [pan·de·ár·se] *v.* to bulge, warp; to sag.

pandeo [pan·dé·o] *m.* sag; bulge.

pandilla [pan·dí·ya] *f.* gang, band.

panela [pa·né·la] *f. Col., C.A.* unrefined sugar.

panfleto [pan·flé·to] *m. Am.* pamphlet.

pánico [pá·ni·ko] *m.* panic; *adj.* panic, panicky.

panne [pán·ne] *f.* accident, car trouble.

panocha [pa·no·ča] *f.* ear of corn; *Mex.* Mexican raw sugar; *Col., C.R.* a kind of tamale.

panqué [paŋ·ké] *m. Col., C.A., Mex.* small cake, cup cake; *Am.* pancake.

pantalón [pan·ta·lón] *m.* trousers; pants; **un par de -es** a pair of trousers.

pantalla [pan·tá·ya] *f.* light shade; screen; fireplace screen; motion-picture screen; *C.R.* fan, palm leaf fan; *P.R.* earring.

pantano [pan·tá·no] *m.* swamp; dam; difficulty.

pantanoso [pan·ta·nó·so] *adj.* swampy, marshy; muddy.

panteón [pan·te·ón] *m.* cemetery.

pantera [pan·té·ra] *f.* panther.

pantorrilla [pan·to·rrí·ya] *f.* calf (*of the leg*).

pantufla [pan·tú·fla] *f.* bedrom slipper.

panza [pán·sa] *f.* paunch, belly.

panzón [pan·són], **panzudo** [pan·sú·ḍo] *adj.* big-bellied.

pañal [pa·ñál] *m.* diaper; **estar en -es** to be in one's infancy; to have little or no knowledge of a thing.

paño [pá·ño] *m.* cloth (*any cloth, especially woolen*); blotch or spot on the skin; film on the eyeball; *Mex., Cuba* parcel of tillable land; *Mex.* kerchief; shawl; — **de manos** towel; — **de mesa** tablecloth; **al** — off-stage; **-s** clothes, garments; **-s menores** underwear; **pañero** *m.* clothier.

pañolón [pa·ño·lón] *m.* scarf, large kerchief; shawl.

pañuelo [pa·ñwé·lo] *m.* handkerchief.

papa [pá·pa] *m.* Pope; *f.* potato; fib, lie; *Am.* snap, easy job; **-s** pap (*soft food for babies*); soup; *Riopl., Ch.* **cosa** — something good to eat; **echar -s** to fib, lie; *Am.* **importarle a uno una** — not to matter to one a bit; *Am.* **no saber ni** — not to a know a thing; to be completely ignorant.

papá [pa·pá] *m.* papa; *Mex., C.A., Andes* — **grande** grandfather.

papagayo [pa·pa·ǵá·yo] *m.* parrot; talker, chatterer.

papal [pa·pál] *adj.* papal.

papalote [pa·pa·ló·te], **papelote** [pa·pe·ló·te] *m.* *Carib., Mex.* kite.

papamoscas [pa·pa·mós·kos] *m.* flycatcher (*a bird*); simpleton, half-wit, dunce.

papanatas [pa·pa·ná·tas] *m.* simpleton, fool, dunce.

paparrucha [pa·pa·rrú·ča] *f.* fib, lie; **paparruchero** [pa·pa·rru·čé·ro] *m.* fibber.

papaya [pa·pá·ya] *f.* papaya.

papel [pa·pél] *m.* (*hoja*) paper; sheet of paper; document; (*parte dramática*) role; — **de estraza** brown wrapping paper; — **de lija** sandpaper; — **de seda** tissue paper; — **moneda** paper money; — **secante** blotting paper; **hacer el** — **de** to play the role of; **hacer buen** (*or* **mal**) — to cut a good (*or* bad) figure.

papelera [pa·pe·lé·ra] *f.* folder, file, case or device for keeping papers; *Am.* wastepaper basket; **papelero** [pa·pe·lé·ro] *m.* paper manufacturer; *adj.* pertaining to paper; vain, ostentatious.

papelería [pa·pe·le·rí·a] *f.* stationery store; stationery; lot of papers.

papeleta [pa·pe·lé·ta] *f.* card, file card, slip of paper.

papelucho [pa·pe·lú·čo] *m.* worthless piece of paper.

papera [pa·pé·ra] *f.* goiter; **-s** mumps.

paquete [pa·ké·te] *m.* package; bundle; dandy; packet boat (*mail boat*); *adj. Am.* dolled up, dressed up; *Riopl., Col.* important, pompous; *Riopl., Col.* insincere.

par [pár] *adj.* even; *m.* pair, couple; peer; **a la** — at par; jointly; at the same time; **al** — **de** on a par with; **bajo** — below par; **sin** — peerless, without an equal, having no equal; **sobre** — above par; **de** — **en** — wide-open.

para [pá·ra] *prep.* for; to; toward; in order to; ¿— **qué?** what for; — **que** so that; — **siempre** forever; — **mis adentros** to myself; **sin qué ni** — **qué** without rhyme or reason; *m. Riopl.* Paraguayan tobacco; *Riopl.* Paraguayan (*used as nickname*).

parabién [pa·ra·ḃjén] *m.* congratulations; **dar el** — to congratulate.

parabrisas [pa·ra·ḃrí·sas] *m.* windshield.

paracaídas [pa·ra·ka·í·ḍas] *m.* parachute; **paracaidista** [pa·ra·kaj·ḍís·ta] *m. & f.* parachutist.

parachoques [pa·ra·čó·kes] *m.* bumper.

parada [pa·rá·ḍa] *f.* stop; stopping place; bet, stake; military review; *P.R.* parade; *Riopl.* boastfulness; *Riopl.* **tener mucha** — to dress very well.

paradero [pa·ra·ḍé·ro] *m.* stopping place; whereabouts; end.

parado [pa·rá·ḍo] *p.p. & adj.* stopped; unoccupied, unemployed; fixed, motionless; *Am.* standing, erect, straight up; *Ch., P.R.* stiff, proud; *Riopl.* cold, unenthusiastic; *P.R., Ch., Andes* **caer uno** — to land on one's feet; to be lucky; *Am.* **estar bien** — to be well-fixed, well-established; to be lucky; *m. Am.* air, appearance.

paradoja [pa·ra·ḍó·xa] *f.* paradox.

paradójico [pa·ra·ḍó·xi·ko] *adj.* paradoxical.

parafina [pa·ra·fí·na] *f.* paraffin.

paráfrasis [pa·rá·fra·sis] *f.* paraphrase.

paraguas [pa·rá·ǵwas] *m.* umbrella; **paragüero** [pa·ra·ǵwé·ro] *m.* umbrella stand; umbrella maker or seller.

paraguayo [pa·ra·ǵwá·yo] *adj. & m.* Paraguayan.

paraíso [pa·ra·í·so] *m.* paradise, heaven; upper gallery (*in a theater*).

paraje [pa·rá·xe] *m.* place; spot; situation.

paralelo [pa·ra·lé·lo] *adj.* parallel; similar; **paralela** [pa·ra·lé·la] *f.* parallel line; **paralelismo** [pa·ra·le·líz·mo] *m.* parallelism.

parálisis [pa·rá·li·sis] *f.* paralysis.

paralítico [pa·ra·lí·ti·ko] *adj.* paralytic.

paralizar[9] [pa·ra·li·sár] *v.* to paralyze; to stop.

parámetro [pa·rá·me·tro] *m.* parameter.

páramo [pá·ra·mo] *m.* high, bleak plain; cold region; *Andes* blizzard or a cold drizzle.

parangón [pa·raŋ·gón] *m.* comparison.

parangonar [pa·raŋ·go·nár] *v.* to compare.

paraninfo [pa·ra·nín·fo] *m.* assembly hall, lecture hall, auditorium.

parapeto [pa·ra·pé·to] *m.* parapet.

parar [pa·rár] *v.* to stop; to end, end up, come to an end; to parry (*in fencing*); to set up (*type*); *Am.* to stand, place in upright position; — **atención** to notice; — **mientes en** to observe; notice; *Riopl.* **las orejas** to prick up one's ears; to pay close attention; **-se** to stop; *Am.* to stand up, get up.

pararrayos [pa·ra·rrá·yos] *m.* lightning rod.

parásito [pa·rá·si·to] *m.* parasite; *adj.* parasitic.

parasol [pa·ra·sól] *m.* parasol.

parcela [par·sé·la] *f.* parcel of land; particle, small piece.

parcial [par·sjál] *adj.* partial; *m.* follower, partisan; **parcialidad** [par·sja·li·ḍáḍ] *f.* partiality; faction, party.

parche [pár·če] *m.* mending patch; sticking plaster; medicated plaster; drum.

pardal [par·ḍál] *m.* sparrow; linnet; sly fellow.

PA

pardear [par·de·ár] *v.* to grow dusky; to appear brownish-grey.

pardo [pár·do] *adj.* dark-grey; brown; dark; cloudy; *m.* leopard; *Carib.*, *Riopl.* mulatto;

pardusco [par·dús·ko] *adj.* greyish; brownish.

parear [pa·re·ár] *v.* to pair, couple, match, mate.

parecer[13] [pa·re·sér] *v. irr.* to seem; to appear, show up; **-se** to resemble each other, look alike; *m.* opinion; appearance, looks; **al** — apparently, seemingly.

parecido [pa·re·sí·do] *adj.* alike, similar; **bien** — good-looking; *p.p. of* **parecer**; *m.* similarity, likeness, resemblance.

pared [pa·réd] *f.* wall; — **maestra** main wall; — **medianera** partition wall.

paredón [pa·re·dón] *m.* execution wall; thick wall.

pareja [pa·ré·xa] *f.* pair; couple; match; partner; *Am.* team of two horses; *Riopl.* horse race.

parejero [pa·re·xé·ro] *m. Riopl.* race horse; *Riopl.* over-familar person, backslapper, hail-fellow-well-met.

parejo [pa·ré·xo] *adj.* even; smooth; equal; *adv. Riopl.* hard.

parentela [pa·en·té·la] *f.* relatives, kin.

parentesco [pa·ren·tés·ko] *m.* kinship, relationship.

paréntesis [pa·rén·te·sis] *m.* parenthesis; digression; **entre** — by the way.

pargo [pár·go] *m.* red snapper.

paria [pá·rja] *m. & f.* outcast.

paridad [pa·ri·dád] *f.* par, equality.

pariente [pa·rjén·te] *m. & f.* relative, relation.

parir [pa·rír] *v.* to give birth; to bear (*children*).

parlamentar [par·la·men·tár] *v.* to converse; to parley, discuss terms with an enemy.

parlamentario [par·la·men·tá·rjo] *adj.* parliamentary; *m.* member of parliament; envoy to a parley.

parlamento [par·la·mén·to] *m.* speech (*of a character in a play*); parley; parliament, legislative assembly.

parlanchín [par·lan·čín] *adj.* talkative; *m.* talker, chatterer.

parlero [par·lé·ro] *adj.* talkative; gossipy; chattering, chirping.

parlotear [par·lo·te·ár] *v.* to prate, prattle, chatter, chat.

parloteo [par·lo·té·o] *m.* chatter, prattle, idle talk.

paro [pá·ro] *m.* work, stoppage; lockout; *Am.* throw (*in the game of dice*); *Am.* — **y pinta** game of dice.

parodia [pa·ró·dja] *f.* parody, take-off, humorous imitation.

parodiar [pa·ro·djár] *v.* to parody, take off, imitate.

parótidas [pa·ró·ti·das] *f. pl.* mumps.

parpadear [par·pa·de·ár] *v.* to wink; to blink; to flutter the eyelids; to twinkle.

parpadeo [par·pa·dé·o] *m.* winking; blinking; fluttering of the eyelids; twinkling.

párpado [pár·pa·do] *m.* eyelid.

parque [pár·ke] *m.* park; *Am.* ammunition.

parra [pá·rra] *f.* grapevine; earthenware jug.

parrafada [pa·rra·fá·da] *f.* chat.

párrafo [pá·rra·fo] *m.* paragraph; **echar un** — **con** to have a chat with.

parral [pa·rrál] *m.* grape arbor.

parranda [pa·rrán·da] *f.* revel, orgy, spree; *Col.* gang, band; **andar** (*or* **ir**) **de** — to go on a spree.

parrandear [pa·rran·de·ár] *v.* to revel, make merry, go on a spree.

parrilla [pa·rrí·ya] *f.* grill, gridiron, broiler; grate.

párroco [pá·rro·ko] *m.* parish priest.

parroquia [pa·rró·kja] *f.* parish; parish church; clientele, customers.

parroquiano [pa·rro·kjá·no] *m.* client, customer; parishioner; *adj.* parochial, of a parish.

parsimonia [par·si·mó·nja] *f.* thrift, economy; moderation; prudence.

parsimonioso [par·si·mo·njó·so] *adj.* thrifty; stingy; cautious; slow.

parte [pár·te] *f.* part; share; place; party (*legal term*); **-s** qualities; **parte** *m.* notice, announcement; *Am.* unnecessary excuses or explanations; **de algún tiempo a ésta** — for some time past; **de** — **de** on behalf of; in favor of; **de** — **a** — through, from one side to the other; **dar** — to inform; **echar a mala** — to take amiss; **en** — partly; **por todas -s** everywhere; *m.* telegram; message.

partera [par·té·ra] *f.* midwife.

partición [par·ti·sjón] *f.* partition, division.

participación [par·ti·si·pa·sjón] *f.* participation, share; notice.

participante [par·ti·si·pán·te] *m. & f.* participant; *adj.* participating, sharing.

participar [par·ti·si·pár] *v.* to participate, share; to inform, notify.

partícipe [par·tí·si·pe] *m. & f.* participant; *adj.* participating.

participio [par·ti·sí·pjo] *m.* participle.

partícula [par·tí·ku·la] *f.* particle.

particular [par·ti·ku·lár] *adj.* particular, special; peculiar; private; personal; odd, strange; **en** — specially; **lecciones -es** private lessons; *m.* private citizen; individual; point, detail; matter.

partida [par·tí·da] *f.* (*salida*) departure, leave; (*entidad*) item, entry; record; band, group; squad; shipment; game; set (*in tennis*); *Am.* part in the hair; — **de bautismo** (**de matrimonio** *or* **de defunción**) birth (marriage, *or* death) certificate; — **de campo** picnic; — **de caza** hunting party; — **doble** double-entry bookkeeping; *Mex.*, *Riopl.* **confesar la** — to tell the truth, speak plainly; **jugar una mala** — to play a mean trick.

partidario [par·ti·dá·rjo] *m.* partisan, follower, supporter.

partido [par·tí·do] *m.* party, faction, group; contest, game; profit; district; *Bol.* **a** (*or* **al**) — in equal shares; *Am.* **dar** — to give a handicap or advantage (*in certain games*); **darse a** — to yield, give up; **sacar** — **de** to derive advantage from, make the best of; **tomar un** — to decide, make a decision.

partir [par·tír] *v.* (*dividir*) to split, divide; to crack, break; (*salir*) to depart, leave; **a** — **de hoy** starting today; from this day on; *Am.* **a** (*or* **al**) — in equal parts; *Am.* — **a uno por el eje** to ruin someone.

partitura [par·ti·tú·ra] *f.* musical score.

parto [pár·to] *m.* childbirth, delivery; product, offspring; **estar de** — to be in labor.

parvada [par·bá·da] *f.* pile of unthreshed grain; brood; *Andes* flock (*of birds or children*).

parvedad [par·be·dád] *f.* smallness; trifle; snack, bit of food.

párvulo [pár·bu·lo] *m.* child; *adj.* small; innocent.

pasa [pá·sa] *f.* raisin; woolly hair of negros.

pasada [pa·sá·da] *f.* passing, passage; *Am.* stay; *Am.* embarrassment; shame; **una mala** — a mean trick; **de** — on the way; incidentally, by the way; **dar una** — **por** to pass by, walk by.

pasadizo [pa·sa·dí·so] *m.* aisle; narrow hall;

narrow passageway.

pasado [pa·sá·d̦o] *m.* past; *p.p.* past, gone; *adj.* overripe, spoiled; *Mex.* dried (*fruits*). *Col.* thin, bony (*animal*); — **mañana** day after tomorrow; **el año** — last year; **en días -s** in days gone by.

pasaje [pa·sá·xe] *m.* passage; fare, ticket; total number of passengers; *Carib., Mex., Col.* private alley; *Col., Ven.* anecdote.

pasajero [pa·sa·xé·ro] *adj.* passing, temporary, fleeting, transitory; *m.* passenger; guest (*of a hotel*).

pasamano [pa·sa·má·no] *m.* railing, hand rail; gangplank; gangway (*of a ship*).

pasaporte [pa·sa·pór·te] *m.* passport.

pasar [pa·sár] *v.* to pass; to cross; to surpass, exceed; to pierce; to go forward; to go over (in, by, to); to enter; to carry over, take across; to happen; to get along; to swallow; to overlook; to tolerate; to suffer; — **las de Caín** to have a hard time; — **por alto** to omit, overlook; — **por las armas** to execute; **-se** to transfer, change over; to get overripe, spoiled; to exceed, go beyond; **se me pasó decirte** I forgot to tell you; *Ch.* **pasársela a uno** to deceive someone, break someone's confidence; **un buen** — enough to live on.

pasarela [pa·sa·ré·la] *f.* gangplank.

pasatiempo [pa·sa·tjém·po] *m.* pastime; *Am.* cookie.

pascua [pás·kwa] *f.* Easter; Jewish Passover; — **florida** (*or* **de resurrección**) Easter Sunday; — **de Navidad** Christmas.

pase [pá·se] *m.* pass, permit; thrust (*in fencing*); pass (*with the cape in bullfighting*).

pasear [pa·se·ár] *v.* to walk; to take a walk; to ride; **-se** to take a walk; to parade; **-se en automóvil** to take an automobile ride; **-se a caballo** to go horseback riding.

paseo [pa·sé·o] *m.* walk, ride; parade; public park; boulevard; — **en automóvil** automobile ride; **dar un** — to take a walk.

pasillo [pa·sí·yo] *m.* aisle; hallway, corridor; short step; short skit; *Col., Ec.* a type of dance music; *Mex.* runner, hall carpet.

pasión [pa·sjón] *f.* passion; suffering.

pasivo [pa·sí·b̦o] *adj.* passive; inactive; *m.* liabilities, debts; debit, debit side (*in bookkeeping*).

pasmar [paz·már] *v.* to astound, stun; **-se** to be amazed, stunned; to marvel; to get a sudden chill; to get frostbitten; *P.R.* to become dried up, shriveled up; *P.R., Mex.* to get bruised by the saddle or pack (*said of horses and mules*).

pasmo [páz·mo] *m.* amazement, astonishment; wonder, awe.

pasmoso [paz·mó·so] *adj.* astonishing, astounding; marvellous.

paso [pá·so] *m.* pass; step; pace; gait; passage; passing; skit; incident; *P.R., Ch., Andes* ford; *Mex.* ferry, ferryboat wharf; *adv.* slowly; **de** — by the way, in passing; **al** — **que** while; **salir del** — to get out of a difficulty; *Am.* **marcar el** — to mark step, obey humbly; *adj.* dried (*figs, grapes, prunes, etc.*); **paso a nivel** grade crossing.

pasta [pás·ta] *f.* paste; dough; noodles; book cover, binding; *Am.* cookie, cracker; **de buena** — of good temper or disposition.

pastal [pas·tál] *m. Am.* range, grazing land, large pasture.

pastar [pas·tár] *v.* to pasture, graze.

pastear [pas·te·ár] *v. Mex., Riopl.* to graze, pasture.

pastel [pas·tél] *m.* pie; pastry roll; filled pastry;

trick, fraud; secret pact, plot; pastel crayon; **pintura al** — pastel painting.

pastelería [pas·te·le·rí·a] *f.* pastry shop, bakery; pastry.

pastelero [pas·te·lé·ro] *m.* pastry cook; *Cuba* turncoat (*person who changes easily from one political party to another*); *Riopl.* political intriguer.

pasterizar[9] [pas·te·ri·sár], **pasteurizar**[9] [pas·tew·ri·sár] *v.* to pasteurize.

pastilla [pas·tí·ya] *f.* tablet (*of medicine, candy, etc.*); bar (*of chocolate*); cake (*of soap*).

pastizal [pas·ti·sál] *m.* pasture, grassland.

pasto [pás·to] *m.* pasture; grassland; grazing; nourishment; *Am.* grass; **a todo** — without restraint.

pastor [pas·tór] *m.* shepherd; pastor.

pastoral [pas·to·rál] *adj.* pastoral; *f.* pastoral play; idyll; pastoral letter; **pastorela** [pas·to·ré·la] *f.* pastoral, pastoral play; **pastoril** [pas·tó·ril] *adj.* pastoral.

pastoso [pas·tó·so] *adj.* pasty, soft; mellow (*said of the voice*); *Am.* grassy.

pastura [pas·tú·ra] *f.* pasture; fodder, feed.

pata [pá·ta] *f.* foot, leg (*of an animal, table, chair, etc.*); female duck; — **de gallo** crow's-foot (*wrinkle at the corner of the eye*); *Ch., Andes* — **de perro** wanderer; *Riopl.* **hacer** — **ancha** to stand firm, face a danger; **meter la** — to put one's foot in it, make an embarrassing blunder; **-s arriba** upside down, head over heels.

patacón [pa·ta·kón] *m. Riopl.* silver coin worth about one peso.

patada [pa·tá·d̦a] *f.* kick; stamp (*with the foot*); footprint; "kick," intoxicating effect; **a -s** with kicks; in great abundance; *Andes* **en dos -s** in a jiffy, in a second.

patalear [pa·ta·le·ár] *v.* to kick around; to stamp.

pataleo [pa·ta·lé·o] *m.* kicking; stamping.

pataleta [pa·ta·lé·ta] *f.* convulsion; fainting fit.

patán [pa·tán] *m.* boor, ill-mannered person; rustic; *adj.* rude, boorish, ill-mannered.

patata [pa·tá·ta] *f.* potato.

patear [pa·te·ár] *v.* to kick; to stamp the foot; to tramp about; to trample on; to humiliate; *Am.* to kick, spring back (*as a gun*); *Ch.* to have a kick or intoxicating effect.

patentar [pa·ten·tár] *v.* to patent.

patente [pa·tén·te] *adj.* patent, evident, clear; *f.* patent; grant; privilege; *Carib.* **de** — excellent, of best quality.

patentizar[9] [pa·ten·ti·sár] *v.* to evidence, reveal, show.

paternal [pa·ter·nál] *adj.* paternal; fatherly.

paternidad [pa·ter·ni·d̦ád̦] *f.* paternity, fatherhood; authorship.

paterno [pa·tér·no] *adj.* paternal, fatherly.

patético [pa·té·ti·ko] *adj.* pathetic.

patibulario [pa·ti·b̦u·lá·rjo] *adj.* harrowing, frightful, hair-raising; criminal.

patíbulo [pa·tí·b̦u·lo] *m.* scaffold, gallows.

patilla [pa·tí·ya] *f.* small foot or paw; *Col., Ven.* watermelon; *Riopl.* stone or brick bench (*near a wall*); *Riopl.* railing of a balcony; *Ch.* slip from a plant; **-s** side whiskers; **Patillas** [pa·tí·yas] the Devil.

patín [pa·tín] *m.* skate; a small patio; goosander (*a kind of duck*); — **de ruedas** roller skate.

patinadero [pa·ti·na·d̦é·ro] *m.* skating rink.

patinar [pa·ti·nár] *v.* to skate; to skid.

patio [pá·tjo] *m.* patio, open court, courtyard;

PA

Am. railway switchyard; *Am.* **pasarse uno al —** to take undue liberties.

patitieso [pa·ti·tjé·so] *adj.* dumbfounded.

patituerto [pa·ti·twér·to] *adj.* crook-legged; knock-kneed; bow-legged.

patizambo [pa·ti·sám·bo] *adj.* knock-kneed.

pato [pá·to] *m.* duck; **pagar el —** to be the goat; to get the blame; *Ríopl.* **andar —** to be flat broke, penniless; *Am.* **hacerse —** to play the fool; *Mex., Ríopl.* **pasarse de — a ganso** to take undue liberties; *Am.* **ser el — de la boda** to be the life of the party; **patito** *m.* duckling.

patochada [pa·to·čá·da] *f.* stupidity, blunder, nonsense.

patojo [pa·tó·xo] *adj.* crooked-legged; bowlegged; *m. & f. Guat.* child; young person.

patología [pa·to·lo·xí·a] *f.* pathology.

patológico [pa·to·ló·xi·ko] *adj.* pathological.

patraña [pa·trá·ña] *f.* fabulous tale; lie, falsehood.

patria [pá·trja] *f.* fatherland, native country.

patriarca [pa·trjár·ka] *m.* patriarch; **patriarcal** [pa·trjar·kál] *adj.* patriarchal.

patrimonio [pa·tri·mó·njo] *m.* patrimony; inheritance.

patrio [pá·trjo] *adj.* native, of one's native country; paternal, belonging to the father.

patriota [pa·trjó·ta] *m. & f.* patriot.

patriótico [pa·trjó·ti·ko] *adj.* patriotic.

patriotismo [pa·trjo·tíz·mo] *m.* patriotism.

patrocinar [pa·tro·si·nár] *v.* to patronize, favor, sponsor.

patrocinio [pa·tro·sí·njo] *m.* patronage, protection.

patrón [pa·trón] *m.* (*protector*) patron; patron saint; sponsor; (*amo*) master, boss; proprietor, landlord; host; skipper; (*dechado*) pattern, standard, model; **patrona** [pa·tró·na] *f.* landlady; patroness; hostess.

patronato [pa·tro·ná·to] *m.* board of trustees; foundation (*for educational, cultural, or charitable purposes*).

patrono [pa·tró·no] *m.* patron, protector; trustee; patron saint.

patrulla [pa·trú·ya] *f.* patrol; squad, gang.

patrullar [pa·tru·yár] *v.* to patrol.

pausa [páw·sa] *f.* pause, stop, rest.

pausar [paw·sár] *v.* to pause.

pauta [páw·ta] *f.* norm, rule, standard; guide lines (*for writing*).

pava [pá·ḅa] *f.* turkey hen; *Ríopl.* kettle, teapot, teakettle; *Andes, Ch.* jest, coarse joke; **pelar la —** to talk by night at the window (*said of lovers*).

pavear [pa·ḅe·ár] *v.* to talk nonsense.

pavesa [pa·ḅé·sa] *f.* cinder; small firebrand; burnt wick or snuff of a candle; **-s** cinders.

pavimentar [pa·ḅi·men·tár] *v.* to pave.

pavimento [pa·ḅi·mén·to] *m.* pavement.

pavo [pá·ḅo] *m.* turkey; *Ch.* sponger, parasite; **— real** peacock; **comer —** to be a wallflower at a dance; *adj.* silly, foolish; vain.

pavón [pa·ḅón] *m.* peacock.

pavonearse [pa·ḅo·ne·ár·se] *v.* to strut, swagger.

pavoneo [pa·ḅo·né·o] *m.* strut, swagger.

pavor [pa·ḅór] *m.* awe, dread, terror.

pavoroso [pa·ḅo·ró·so] *adj.* frightful, dreadful.

payador [pa·ya·dór] *m. Ríopl.* one who sings an improvised song accompanied on the guitar.

payasada [pa·ya·sá·da] *f.* clownish act or remark.

payasear [pa·ya·se·ár] *v.* to clown, play the fool.

payaso [pa·yá·so] *m.* clown.

paz [pas] *f.* peace.

pazguato [paz·ǵwá·to] *adj.* simple, dumb, stupid;

m. simpleton.

peaje [pe·á·xe] *m.* toll (*for crossing a bridge or ferry*).

peal [pe·ál] = **pial.**

pealar [pe·a·lár] = **pialar.**

peatón [pe·a·tón] *m.* pedestrian.

peca [pé·ka] *f.* freckle.

pecado [pe·ká·do] *m.* sin.

pecador [pe·ka·dór] *m.* sinner; *adj.* sinful.

pecaminoso [pe·ka·mi·nó·so] *adj.* sinful.

pecar[6] [pe·kár] *v.* to sin; **— de bueno** to be too good; **— de oscuro** to be exceedingly unclear, too complicated.

pecera [pe·sé·ra] *f.* fish bowl.

pécora [pé·ko·ra] *f.* head of sheep.

pecoso [pe·kó·so] *adj.* freckly, freckled.

peculado [pe·ku·lá·do] *m.* embezzlement.

peculiar [pe·ku·ljár] *adj.* peculiar; **peculiaridad** [pe·ku·lja·ri·dád] *f.* peculiarity.

pechada [pe·čá·da] *f. Ríopl.* bump, push, shove with the chest; *Am.* bumping contest between two riders; *Ríopl., Ch.* overthrowing an animal (*by bumping it with the chest of a horse*).

pechar [pe·čár] *v. Ríopl., Ch.*; *Bol.* to bump, push, shove with the chest; *Ríopl., Ch., Bol.* to drive one's horse against; *Ch., Ríopl.* to borrow, strike (*someone*) for a loan.

pechera [pe·čé·ra] *f.* shirtfront; chest protector; bib (*of an apron*).

pecho [pé·čo] *m.* chest; breast; bosom; heart; courage; **dar el —** to nurse; **tomar a -s** to take to heart; *P.R., Col.* **a todo —** shouting; *Am.* **en -s de camisa** in shirt sleeves.

pechuga [pe·čú·ǵa] *f.* breast, breast meat of a fowl; bosom; *C.A., Col., Ch., Andes* courage, nerve, audacity, impudence.

pedagogía [pe·da·ǵo·xí·a] *f.* pedagogy, science of education.

pedagógico [pe·da·ǵó·xi·ko] *adj.* pedagogic, relating to education or teaching.

pedagogo [pe·da·ǵó·ǵo] *m.* pedagogue, teacher, educator.

pedal [pe·dál] *m.* pedal.

pedalear [pe·da·le·ár] *v.* to pedal.

pedante [pe·dán·te] *adj.* pedantic, affected, vain; superficial; *m.* pedant; **pedantesco** [pe·dan·tés·ko] *adj.* pedantic.

pedazo [pe·dá·so] *m.* piece, portion, bit; **hacer -s** to tear or break into pieces; **caerse a -s** fall into pieces.

pedernal [pe·der·nál] *m.* flint.

pedestal [pe·des·tál] *m.* pedestal, base.

pedestre [pe·dés·tre] *adj.* pedestrian, walking, going on foot; commonplace, vulgar, low.

pedido [pe·dí·do] *m.* commercial order; request, petition; *p.p. of* **pedir.**

pedigüeño [pe·di·ǵwé·ño] *adj.* begging, demanding.

pedir[5] [pe·dír] *v. irr.* to ask, beg, petition; to ask for; to demand; to require; to order (*merchandise*); **a — de boca** exactly as desired.

pedo [pé·do] *m.* wind, flatulence; *Mex.* **andar —** to be drunk.

pedrada [pe·drá·da] *f.* hit or blow with a stone; throw with a stone; mark or bruise made by a stone (*thrown*); **a -s** by stoning; with stones; **dar una —** to hit with a stone; **echar a alguien a -s** to stone someone out; **matar a -s** to stone to death.

pedregal [pe·dre·ǵál] *m.* rocky ground, ground strewn with rocks.

pedregoso [pe·dre·ǵó·so] *adj.* rocky, stony, pebbly.

pedrería [pe·dre·rí·a] *f.* precious stones; precious stone ornament; jewelry.

pedrusco [pe·drús·ko] *m.* boulder.

pedúnculo [pe·dúŋ·ku·lo] *m.* stem (*of a leaf, flower or fruit*), stalk.

pegajoso [pe·ga·xó·so] *adj.* sticky; contagious.

pegar[7] [pe·gár] *v.* (*golpear*) to hit, strike, slap, beat; (*adherir*) to stick, paste, glue; to sew on (*a button*); to infect; to be becoming; to be fitting, opportune, to the point; *Am.* to tie, fasten; *Am.* to yoke; — **fuego** to set on fire; — **un chasco** to play a trick; to surprise; disappoint; — **un susto** to give a scare; — **un salto** (**una carrera**) to take a jump (a run); **-se** to stick, cling; **pegársela a uno** to fool somebody.

pegote [pe·gó·te] *m.* sticky thing; sticking plaster; clumsy patch; sponger; thick, sticky concoction; clumsy addition or insertion (*in a literary or artistic work*).

peinado [pej·ná·do] *m.* coiffure, hairdo; hairdressing; *p.p.* combed; groomed; *adj.* effeminate; **bien** — spruce, trim.

peinador [pej·na·dór] *m.* hairdresser; short wrapper or dressing gown; **peinadora** [pej·na·dó·ra] *f.* woman hairdresser.

peinar [pej·nár] *v.* to comb; *Ríopl.* to flatter.

peine [péj·ne] *m.* comb.

peineta [pej·né·ta] *f.* large ornamental comb.

peje [pé·xe] *m. C.A.* fish.

peladilla [pe·la·dí·ya] *f.* small pebble.

pelado [pe·lá·do] *p.p. & adj.* peeled; plucked; skinned; hairless; featherless; barren, treeless, bare; penniless, broke; *m. Mex.* ragged fellow (*generally a peon*); *Mex.* ill-bred person; *Col.* child.

pelafustán [pe·la·fus·tán] *m.* tramp, vagabond.

pelagatos [pe·la·gá·tos] *m.* ragged fellow, tramp.

pelaje [pe·lá·xe] *m.* animal's coat, fur; external appearance.

pelar [pe·lár] *v.* to cut the hair of; to pluck the feathers or hair from; to peel, shell, skin, husk; to fleece, rob; *Am.* to beat, thrash; *Am.* to slander; *C.R.* — **los dientes** to show one's teeth; to smile affectedly; *C.A., Mex., Carib., Col., Andes* — **los ojos** to keep one's eyes peeled; to open one's eyes wide; **-se** to peel off; to lose one's hair; *Col., Ven.* to be confused; *Col., Ven.* to be careless, unaware; *Col., Ven.* to slip away; *Col., Ven.* to die; **pelárselas por algo** to be dying for something, want something very much.

peldaño [pel·dá·ño] *m.* step (*of a staircase*).

pelea [pe·lé·a] *f.* fight, quarrel.

pelear [pe·le·ár] *v.* to fight; to quarrel.

peletería [pe·le·te·rí·a] *f.* fur store; fur trade; furs; *Am.* leather goods, leather shop; *Cuba* shoe store.

pelicano [pe·li·ká·no] *adj.* gray-haired.

pelícano [pe·lí·ka·no] *m.* pelican.

película [pe·lí·ku·la] *f.* thin skin; membrane; film; motion-picture film.

peligrar [pe·li·grár] *v.* to be in danger.

peligro [pe·li·gro] *m.* danger.

peligroso [pe·li·gró·so] *adj.* dangerous.

pelillo [pe·lí·yo] *m.* short, fine hair; **-s** trouble, nuisance; **echar -s a la mar** to "bury the hatchet", become reconciled; **no pararse en -s** not to stop at small details, not to bother about trifles; **no tener -s en la lengua** to speak frankly.

pelirrojo [pe·li·rró·xo] *adj.* redheaded, red-haired.

pelo [pé·lo] *m.* (*cabello*) hair; (*haz*) nap (*of cloth*); (*fibra*) grain (*in wood*); **al** — perfectly; agreed;

apropos, to the point; along the grain; **eso me viene al** — that suits me perfectly; **con todos sus -s y señales** with every possible detail; *Am.* **por** (*or* **en**) **un** — on the point of, almost, by a hair's breadth; **montar en** — to ride bareback; **tomar el** — **a** to kid, make fun of; *Ríopl., Carib., Mex., Andes* **no aflojar un** — not to yield an inch.

pelón [pe·lón] *adj.* bald.

pelota [pe·ló·ta] *f.* ball; ball game; *Am.* boat made of cowhide; **en** — (*or* **en -s**) naked; *Am.* **darle a la** — to hit upon by chance; **pelotilla** [pe·lo·tí·ya] *f.* pellet, little ball.

pelotari [pe·lo·tá·ri] *m.* pelota (*jai-alai*) player.

pelotera [pe·lo·té·ra] *f.* brawl, row, riot; *C.A., Ven.* crowd.

pelotón [pe·lo·tón] *m.* large ball; crowd, gang; heap, pile; platoon of soliders; firing squad.

peluca [pe·lú·ka] *f.* wig.

pelucón [pe·lu·kón] *adj.* wig-wearing; *Ch.* conservative.

peludo [pe·lú·do] *adj.* hairy; shaggy; *m.* plush carpet with shaggy pile; *Am.* a species of armadillo; *Ríopl.* **agarrar un** — to get drunk.

peluquería [pe·lu·ke·rí·a] *f.* barbershop, hairdresser's shop.

peluquero [pe·lu·ké·ro] *m.* hairdresser, barber.

pelusa [pe·lú·sa] *f.* down; fuzz; nap (*of cloth*).

pellejo [pe·yé·xo] *m.* hide; skin; peel; **salvar el** — to save one's skin, escape punishment; *Am.* **jugarse el** — to gamble one's life.

pellizcar[6] [pe·yis·kár] *v.* to pinch, nip.

pellizco [pe·yís·ko] *m.* pinching, nipping; pinch, nip.

pena [pé·na] *f.* penalty; grief, worry; hardship; toil; *Mex., Carib., C.A., Col., Ven.* embarrassment; **a duras -s** with great difficulty; hardly; **me da** — it grieves me; *C.A., Ven., Col., Carib.* it embarrasses me; **valer la** — to be worthwhile; **tener** (*or* **estar con**) **mucha** — to be terribly sorry; *Am.* to be greatly embarrassed.

penacho [pe·ná·čo] *m.* tuft, crest; plume.

penado [pe·ná·do] *adj.* afflicted.

penal [pe·nál] *adj.* penal; **código** — penal code.

penalidad [pe·na·li·dád] *f.* hardship; trouble; penalty.

penar [pe·nár] *v.* to suffer; to worry, fret; to impose a penalty; — **por** to long for; to suffer because of.

penca [pén·ka] *f.* leaf of a cactus plant; *Am.* sweetheart; *Ven.* **coger una** — to get drunk.

penco [pén·ko] *m.* nag, horse; *Am.* boor.

pendencia [pen·dén·sja] *f.* quarrel; scuffle, fight.

pendenciero [pen·den·sjé·ro] *adj.* quarrelsome.

pender [pen·dér] *v.* to hang; to dangle; to depend.

pendiente [pen·djén·te] *f.* slope; *m.* earring; pendant; *Am.* watch chain; *adj.* hanging, dangling; pending.

pendón [pen·dón] *m.* banner.

péndulo [pén·du·lo] *m.* pendulum.

pene [pé·ne] *m.* penis.

penetración [pe·ne·tra·sjón] *f.* penetration; acuteness; keen judgment.

penetrante [pe·ne·trán·te] *adj.* penetrating; acute; keen.

penetrar [pe·ne·trár] *v.* to penetrate; to pierce; to fathom, comprehend.

penicilina [pe·ni·si·lí·na] *f.* penicillin.

península [pe·nín·su·la] *f.* peninsula.

peninsular [pe·nin·su·lár] *adj.* peninsular.

penitencia [pe·ni·tén·sja] *f.* penance.

PA

penitenciaría [pe·ni·ten·sja·rí·a] *f.* penitentiary.
penitente [pe·ni·tén·te] *adj.* repentant, penitent; *m.* & *f.* penitent.
penoso [pe·nó·so] *adj.* painful; hard, difficult; embarrassing; fatiguing; *Mex., Carib., C.A., Ven., Col.* timid, shy.
pensador [pen·sa·ðór] *m.* thinker; *adj.* thinking.
pensamiento [pen·sa·mjén·to] *m.* thought; mind; pansy.
pensar[1] [pen·sár] *v. irr.* to think; to think over; to intend.
pensativo [pen·sa·tí·ƀo] *adj.* pensive.
pensión [pen·sjón] *f.* pension; board; scholarship for study; boardinghouse; *Col.* apprehension, anxiety; — **completa** room and board.
pensionado [pen·sjo·ná·ðo] *m.* pensioner (*person receiving a pension*); *adj.* & *p.p.* pensioned.
pensionar [pen·sjo·nár] *v.* to pension.
pensionista [pen·sjo·nís·ta] *m.* & *f.* boarder; pensioner (*person receiving a pension*).
pentagrama [pen·ta·ǥrá·ma] *m.* musical staff.
penúltimo [pe·núl·ti·mo] *adj.* next to the last.
penumbra [pe·núm·bra] *f.* partial shadow, dimness.
penumbroso [pe·num·bró·so] *adj.* dim.
peña [pé·ña] *f.* rock, large stone.
peñasco [pe·ñás·ko] *m.* large rock; crag.
peñascoso [pe·ñas·ko·so] *adj.* rocky.
peón [pe·ón] *m.* unskilled laborer; foot soldier; spinning top; pawn (*in chess*); *Ch., Riopl., C.A., Carib., Mex.* farm hand; *Am.* apprentice; *Mex.* — **de albañil** mason's helper.
peonada [pe·o·ná·ða] *f.* gang of laborers or peons.
peonaje [pe·o·ná·xe] *m.* gang of laborers.
peonza [pe·on·sa] *f.* top (*toy*).
peor [pe·ór] *adj.* & *adv.* worse; worst; — **que** worse than; — **que** — that is even worse; **tanto** — so much the worse.
pepa [pé·pa] *f. Andes, Col., Ven., Ch., Mex., Riopl.* seed (*of an apple, melon, etc.*); *Mex.* marble (*to play with*); **Pepa** nickname for **Josefa.**
pepenar [pe·pe·nár] *v. Mex.* to pick up; *Am.* to seize, grab.
pepino [pe·pí·no] *m.* cucumber.
pepita [pe·pí·ta] *f.* seed (*of an apple, melon, etc.*); pip (*a disease of birds*); nugget (*lump of gold or other minerals*); *Am.* fruit stone, pit; **Pepita** = **Josefita** dim. of **Josefa.**
pequeñez [pe·ke·ñés] *f.* smallness; childhood; trifle; meanness.
pequeño [pe·ké·ño] *adj.* small, little; young; low, humble; *m.* child.
pera [pé·ra] *f.* pear; goatee; sinecure, easy job; *Am.* Peruvian alligator pear (*see* **aguacate**); *Am.* **hacerle a uno la** — to play a trick on someone; **peral** *m.* pear tree; pear orchard.
percal [per·kál] *m.* percale (*fine cotton cloth*).
percance [per·kán·se] *m.* misfortune, accident; occurrence.
percepción [per·sep·sjón] *f.* perception; idea.
perceptible [per·sep·ti·ƀle] *adj.* perceptible, noticeable.
percibir [per·si·ƀír] *v.* to perceive; to collect, receive.
percudido [per·ku·ðí·ðo] *adj.* dirty, grimy.
percudir [per·ku·ðír] *v.* to soil, make dirty or grimy; -**se** to get grimy.
percusión [per·ku·sjón] *f.* percussion.
percusor [per·ku·sór] *m.* firing pin.
percha [pér·ča] *f.* clothes or hat rack; pole; perch, roost; perch (*a fish*); **perchero** [per·čé·ro] *m.* clothes or hat rack.

perder[1] [per·ðér] *v. irr.* to lose; to squander; to ruin, harm; to miss (*a train*); — **de vista** to lose sight of; -**se** to lose one's way; to get lost; to go astray; to get spoiled; to become ruined.
perdición [per·ði·sjón] *f.* perdition, damnation, hell, ruin.
pérdida [pér·ði·ða] *f.* loss; damage.
perdidamente [per·ði·da·mén·te] *adv.* excessively.
perdido [per·ði·ðo] *p.p.* & *adj.* lost; strayed; mislaid; ruined; **estar** — **por alguien** to be crazy about, or very fond of, someone; *m.* rake, dissolute fellow; bum, vagabond.
perdigón [per·ði·ǥón] *m.* young partridge; bird shot, buckshot; losing gambler.
perdiz [per·ðís] *f.* partridge.
perdón [per·ðón] *m.* pardon; forgiveness; remission.
perdonar [per·ðo·nár] *v.* to pardon; to forgive.
perdulario [per·ðu·lá·rjo] *m.* rake, dissolute person; reckless fellow; good-for-nothing; tramp.
perdurable [per·ðu·rá·ƀle] *adj.* lasting, everlasting.
perdurar [per·ðu·rár] *v.* to last, endure.
perecedero [pe·re·se·ðé·ro] *adj.* perishable.
perecer[13] [pe·re·sér] *v. irr.* to perish; to die; -**se** to long (*for*), pine (*for*).
peregrinación [pe·re·ǥri·na·sjón] *f.* pilgrimage; long journey.
peregrinar [pe·re·ǥri·nár] *v.* to journey; to go through life.
peregrino [pe·re·ǥrí·no] *m.* pilgrim; *adj.* foreign, strange; rare; beautiful, perfect; travelling, wandering; **ave peregrina** migratory bird, bird of passage.
perejil [pe·re·xíl] *m.* parsley; -**es** frippery, showy clothes or ornaments.
perenne [pe·rén·ne] *adj.* perennial, enduring, perpetual.
pereza [pe·ré·sa] *f.* laziness; idleness.
perezoso [pe·re·só·so] *adj.* lazy; *m. Am.* sloth (*an animal*); *Am.* safety pin; *Am.* bed cushion.
perfección [per·fek·sjón] *f.* perfection; **a la** — to perfection, perfectly.
perfeccionamiento [per·fek·sjo·na·mjén·to] *m.* perfecting, perfection; completion.
perfeccionar [per·fek·sjo·nár] *v.* to perfect, finish, complete.
perfecto [per·fék·to] *adj.* perfect.
perfidia [per·fí·ðja] *f.* perfidy, treachery.
pérfido [pér·fi·ðo] *adj.* perfidious, treacherous, faithless.
perfil [per·fíl] *m.* profile; outline; *Am.* pen or pen point.
perfilar [per·fi·lár] *v.* to silhouette; to outline; -**se** to show one's profile; to be silhouetted.
perforación [per·fo·ra·sjón] *f.* perforation, hole; puncture; perforating, boring, drilling.
perforar [per·fo·rár] *v.* to perforate, pierce; to drill, bore.
perfumar [per·fu·már] *v.* to perfume, scent.
perfume [per·fú·me] *m.* perfume; fragrance.
perfumería [per·fu·me·rí·a] *f.* perfumery; perfume shop.
pergamino [per·ǥa·mí·no] *m.* parchment.
pericia [pe·rí·sja] *f.* expertness, skill.
perico [pe·rí·ko] *m.* parakeet, small parrot; *Col.* **huevos -s** scrambled eggs.
perifollos [pe·ri·fó·yos] *m. pl.* frippery, finery, showy ornaments.
perifrasear [pe·ri·fra·se·ár] *v.* to paraphrase.
perifrasis [pe·rí·fra·sis] *f.* paraphrase.
perigeo [pe·ri·xé·o] *m.* perigee.

perilla [pe·rí·ya] *f.* small pear; pear-shaped ornament; knob; pommel of a saddle; goatee; de — apropos, to the point.

perímetro [pe·rí·me·tro] *m.* perimeter.

periódico [pe·rjó·di·ko] *m.* newspaper; periodical; *adj.* periodic, periodical.

periodismo [pe·rjo·díz·mo] *m.* journalism; periodista [pe·rjo·dís·ta] *m. & f.* journalist; newspaper editor or publisher; periodístico [pe·rjo·dís·ti·ko] *adj.* journalistic.

período [pe·rí·o·do] [pe·rjó·do] *m.* period; cycle; sentence.

peripecia [pe·ri·pé·sja] *f.* vicissitude, change in fortune; unforeseen incident.

peripuesto [pe·ri·pwés·to] *adj.* dressed up, dolled up, decked out.

perito [pe·rí·to] *adj.* learned; experienced; skillful; skilled; *m.* expert.

peritoneo [pe·ri·to·né·o] *m.* peritoneum.

peritonitis [pe·ri·to·ní·tis] *f.* peritonitis.

perjudicar[6] [per·xu·di·kár] *v.* to damage, impair, harm.

perjudicial [per·xu·di·sjál] *adj.* harmful, injurious.

perjuicio [per·xwí·sjo] *m.* damage, ruin, mischief; harm.

perjurar [per·xu·rár] *v.* to perjure oneself; to commit perjury; to curse, swear.

perjurio [per·xú·rjo] *m.* perjury.

perla [pér·la] *f.* pearl; de -s perfectly, just right, to the point.

perlino [per·lí·no] *adj.* pearly, pearl-colored.

permanecer[13] [per·ma·ne·sér] *v. irr.* to remain, stay.

permanencia [per·ma·nén·sja] *f.* permanence, duration; stability; stay, sojourn.

permanente [per·ma·nén·te] *adj.* permanent.

permiso [per·mí·so] *m.* permission; permit.

permitir [per·mi·tír] *v.* to permit, let; to grant.

permuta [per·mú·ta] *f.* exchange, barter.

permutar [per·mu·tár] *v.* to exchange; to barter; to change around.

pernetas [per·né·tas] : en — barelegged, with bare legs.

pernicioso [per·ni·sjó·so] *adj.* pernicious, harmful.

perno [pér·no] *m.* bolt; spike; -s *Am.* tricks, frauds.

pero [pé·ro] *conj.* but, except, yet; *m.* objection, exception; defect; a variety of apple tree; a variety of apple; perón [pe·rón] *m. Am.* a variety of apple.

perogrullada [pe·ro·gru·yá·da] *f.* platitude, trite or commonplace remark.

peroración [pe·ro·ra·sjón] *f.* peroration, speech, harangue.

perorar [pe·ro·rár] *v.* to make an impassioned speech; to declaim, harangue; to plea, make a plea.

perorata [pe·ro·rá·ta] *f.* harangue, speech.

peróxido [pe·rók·si·do] *m.* peroxide.

perpendicular [per·pen·di·ku·lár] *adj., m. & f.* perpendicular.

perpetuar[18] [per·pe·twár] *v.* to perpetuate.

perpetuo [per·pé·two] *adj.* perpetual; perpetua [per·pé·twa] *f.* everlasting (*plant*).

perplejidad [per·ple·xi·dád] *f.* perplexity.

perplejo [per·plé·xo] *adj.* perplexed, bewildered.

perra [pé·rra] *f.* bitch, female dog; drunkenness; — chica five-centime copper coin; — grande (*or* gorda) ten-centime copper coin.

perrada [pe·rrá·da] *f.* pack of dogs; hacer una — to play a mean trick.

perrera [pe·rré·ra] *f.* kennel; toil, hard work, hard

job; tantrum; *Carib., Mex., Ven.* brawl, dispute.

perrilla [pe·rrí·ya] *f. Am.* sty (*on the eyelid*). See orzuelo.

perro [pé·rro] *m.* dog; — de busca hunting dog; — dogo bulldog; — de lanas poodle; *adj.* dogged, tenacious; *Mex., C.A.* hard, selfish, mean, stingy; *Ven.,* vagabond.

perruno [pe·rrú·no] *adj.* canine, doglike.

persecución [per·se·ku·sjón] *f.* persecution; pursuit.

perseguidor [per·se·gi·dór] *m.* pursuer; persecutor.

perseguimiento [per·se·gi·mjén·to] *m.* pursuit; persecution.

perseguir[5, 12] [per·se·gír] *v. irr.* to pursue; to persecute; to harass, annoy.

perseverancia [per·se·be·rán·sja] *f.* perseverance.

perseverar [per·se·be·rár] *v.* to persevere.

persiana [per·sjá·na] *f.* Venetian blind; window shade.

persistencia [per·sis·tén·sja] *f.* persistence; persistente [per·sis·tén·te] *adj.* persistent.

persistir [per·sis·tír] *v.* to persist.

persona [per·só·na] *f.* person; personage.

personaje [per·so·ná·xe] *m.* personage; character (*in a book or play*).

personal [per·so·nál] *adj.* personal; *m.* personnel.

personalidad [per·so·na·li·dád] *f.* personality; individuality; person, personage.

personalismo [per·so·na·liz·mo] *m.* personalism; individualism.

perspectiva [per·spek·ti·ba] *f.* perspective; view; appearance; outlook; prospect.

perspicacia [pers·pi·ká·sja] *f.* keenness of mind, penetration, keen insight.

perspicaz [pers·pi·kás] *adj.* keen, shrewd.

persuadir [per·swa·dír] *v.* to persuade.

persuasión [per·swa·sjón] *f.* persuasion.

persuasivo [per·swa·sí·bo] *adj.* persuasive.

pertenecer[13] [per·te·ne·sér] *v. irr.* to belong; to pertain; to concern.

perteneciente [per·te·ne·sjén·te] *adj.* pertaining, belonging, concerning.

pértiga [per·ti·ga] *f.* pole, bar, rod; salto con — pole vault.

pertinente [per·ti·nén·te] *adj.* pertinent, to the point, apt, fitting.

pertrechos [per·tré·čos] *m. pl.* military supplies; tools, implements.

perturbación [per·tur·ba·sjón] *f.* uneasiness, agitation, disturbance.

perturbar [per·tur·bár] *v.* to perturb, disturb.

perunano [pe·rwá·no] *adj. & m.* Peruvian.

perulero [pe·ru·lé·ro] *adj. m. & f.* Peruvian (*slang expression*).

perversidad [per·ber·si·dád] *f.* perversity, wickedness.

perverso [per·bér·so] *adj.* perverse, wicked; *m.* pervert.

pervertir[3] [per·ber·tír] *v. irr.* to pervert; to; corrupt to distort; -se to become perverted; to go wrong.

pesa [pé·sa] *f.* weight (*for scales*); — de reloj clock weight; -s y medidas weights and measures.

pesadez [pe·sa·dés] *f.* heaviness; dullness, drowsiness; slowness; bother; stubbornness.

pesadilla [pe·sa·dí·ya] *f.* nightmare.

pesado [pe·sá·do] *adj.* heavy; sound (*sleep*); tiresome, boring, annoying; slow; dull.

pesadumbre [pe·sa·dúm·bre] *f.* grief, sorrow; weight, heaviness.

pésame [pé·sa·me] *m.* condolence, expression of sympathy.

PE

pesantez [pe·san·tés] *f.* gravity; heaviness.
pesar [pe·sár] *v.* (*penar*) to cause grief, sorrow, or regret; (*tener gravedad*) to weigh; to consider, to have weight, value, or importance; *m.* grief, sorrow; **a — de** in spite of.
pesaroso [pe·sa·ró·so] *adj.* grieved, sad; repentant.
pesca [pés·ka] *f.* fishing; catch, fish caught.
pescadería [pes·ka·de·rí·a] *f.* fish market; **pescadero** [pes·ka·dé·ro] *m.* fishmonger, dealer in fish.
pescado [pes·ká·do] *m.* fish (*especially after being caught*); salted codfish.
pescador [pes·ka·dór] *m.* fisherman.
pescar[6] [pes·kár] *v.* to fish; to catch; to catch unaware, catch in the act.
pescozón [pes·ko·són] *m.* blow on the back of the head or neck.
pescuezo [pes·kwé·so] *m.* neck.
pesebre [pe·sé·bre] *m.* manger.
peseta [pe·sé·ta] *f.* peseta (*monetary unit of Spain*).
pesimismo [pe·si·míz·mo] *m.* pessimism; **pesimista** [pe·si·mis·ta] *m. & f.* pessimist; *adj.* pessimistic.
pésimo [pé·si·mo] *adj.* very bad.
peso [pé·so] *m.* weight; weighing; burden; importance; *Am.* peso (*monetary unit of several Spanish American countries*).
pesquera [pes·ké·ra] *f.* fishery (*place for catching fish*); **pesquería** [pes·ke·rí·a] *f.* fishery; fishing.
pesquero [pes·ké·ro] *adj.* fishing; **buque —** fishing boat; **industria pesquera** fishing industry.
pesquisa [pes·ki·sa] *f.* investigation, inquiry; *m. Am.* police investigator.
pestaña [pes·tá·ña] *f.* eyelash; edging, fringe; **quemarse las -s** to burn the midnight oil, study hard at night.
pestañear [pes·ta·ñe·ár] *v.* to blink; to wink; to flicker.
peste [pés·te] *f.* pest, pestilence, plague; epidemic; strench, stink, foul odor; overabundance. excess; *Am.* smallpox; *Col.* head cold; **echar -s** to utter insults.
pestillo [pes·tí·yo] *m.* bolt; latch; lock.
pesuña [pe·sú·ña] *f.* hoof (*cloven*).
pesuño [pe·sú·ño] *m.* half of the cloven hoof.
petaca [pe·tá·ka] *f.* tobacco pouch; cigar case; leather covered hamper (*used as a pack*); *Mex.,* *adj.* Andes heavy, clumsy.
pétalo [pé·ta·lo] *m.* petal.
petate [pe·tá·te] *m.* bundle; impostor; *Mex., C.A., Ven., Col.* mat (*of straw or palm leaves*); *Am.* dunce; *Andes* coward; **liar el —** to pack up and go; *Mex.* to die; *Col., Ven.* **dejar a uno en un —** to ruin a person, leave him penniless.
petición [pe·ti·sjón] *f.* petition, request.
petirrojo [pe·ti·rró·xo] *m.* robin, robin redbreast.
petiso [pe·tí·so] *adj. Riopl., Ch., Andes* small, short, dwarfish; *m. Am.* small horse, pony.
pétreo [pé·tre·o] *adj.* stone, stony.
petróleo [pe·tró·le·o] *m.* petroleum.
petrolero [pe·tro·lé·ro] *m.* oil man; dealer in petroleum; **compañía petrolera** oil company.
petulancia [pe·tu·lán·sja] *f.* flippancy; insolence; **petulante** [pe·tu·lán·te] *adj.* impertinent, flippant.
petunia [pe·tú·nja] *f.* petunia.
pez [pes] *m.* fish; *f.* pitch, tar.
pezón [pe·són] *m.* nipple; stem, stalk (*of a fruit, leaf or flower*); small point of land.
pezuña [pe·sú·ña] *f.* hoof.
piadoso [pja·dó·so] *adj.* pious; kind, merciful.
pial [pjal] *m. Mex.* lasso, lariat (*thrown in order to trip an animal*); *Riopl.* snare, trap.
pialar [pja·lár] *v.* to lasso by tripping with a **pial.**

piano [pjá·no] *m.* piano; — **de cola** grand piano; — **vertical** upright piano.
piar[17] [pjar] *v.* to peep, chirp; to cry, whine.
pibe [pi·be] *m. Riopl.* urchin, boy.
pica [pí·ka] *f.* pike, spear; picador's goad or lance; stonecutter's hammer; *Ven.* tapping of rubber trees; *Col.* trail; *Col., Ch.* pique, resentment; *Am.* cockfight.
picada [pi·ká·da] *f.* prick; bite (*as of an insect or fish*); puncture; sharp pain; dive (*of a plane*); *Cuba, Riopl.* path, trail (*cut through a forest*); *Am.* narrow ford; *Col., Ven., Mex.* peck.
picadillo [pi·ka·dí·yo] *m.* meat and vegetable hash; minced meat, mincement.
picador [pi·ka·dór] *m.* picador (*mounted bullfighter armed with a goad*); horse-breaker; chopping block; *Ven.* tree tapper.
picadura [pi·ka·dú·ra] *f.* biting; pricking; bite; prick; sting; puncture; cut tobacco.
picante [pi·kán·te] *adj.* (*acerbo*) pricking, biting, stinging; (*con chile o ají*) spicy; highly seasoned; *m.* strong seasoning; *Am.* highly seasoned sauce (*usually containing chili pepper*).
picapleitos [pi·ka·pléj·tos] *m.* quarrelsome person (*one who likes to pick a fight*); shyster.
picaporte [pi·ka·pór·te] *m.* latch; latchkey; door knocker.
picar[6] [pi·kár] *v.* to prick; to pierce; to bite (*said of fish or insects*); to sting; to peck; to nibble; to mince, chop up; to goad; to stick, poke; to hew, chisel; to pique, vex; to itch, smart, burn; *Am.* to chop (*wood*); *Am.* to open a trail; *Am.* to tap (*a tree*); *Am.* to slaughter (*cattle*); — **muy alto** to aim very high; — **en** to border on, be somewhat of; *Mex., Ven.* **¡pícale!** [pí·ka·le] hurry! **-se** to be piqued, angry; to be motheaten; to begin to sour; to begin to rot; *C.A., Ven.* to get tipsy; **-se de** to boast of.
picardía [pi·kar·dí·a] *f.* roguishness; offensive act or remark; roguish trick; mischief.
picaresco [pi·ka·rés·ko] *adj.* picaresque, roguish.
pícaro [pí·ka·ro] *m.* rogue, rascal; *adj.* roguish; mischievous; crafty, sly; low, vile; **picarón** [pa·ka·rón] *m.* big rascal.
picazón [pi·ka·són] *f.* itch, itching.
pico [pí·ko] *m.* beak, bill; sharp point; peak; pickaxe, pick, spout; mouth; additional amount, a little over; *C.A., Carib., Riopl., Ven.* a small balance; *Mex.* a goodly sum; **tener el — de oro** to be very eloquent; **tener mucho —** to be very talkative.
picotada [pi·ko·tá·da] *f.,* **picotazo** [pi·ko·tá·so] *m.* peck.
picotear [pi·ko·te·ár] *v.* to peck; to chatter; *Am.* to mince, cut into small pieces.
pichel [pi·čél] *m.* pitcher; mug.
pichón [pi·čón] *m.* young pigeon; *C.A.* any male bird (*except a rooster*); *Am.* dupe, easy mark; *Am.* novice, inexperienced person, apprentice; *adj. Am.* timid, shy.
pie [pje] *m.* foot; leg; stand; stem; base; *Am.* down payment; *Mex.* strophe, stanza; *Am.* — **de amigo** prop; — **de banco** silly remark; **a — juntillas** steadfastly, firmly; **al — de la letra** to the letter, literally, exactly; **de —** (*or* **en —**) standing; **a cuatro -s** on all fours; **dar —** to give an opportunity or occasion; *Am.* **estar a — en** to be ignorant of; **ir a —** to walk.
piececito [pje·se·sí·to], **piecito** [pje·sí·to] *m.* little foot.
piedad [pje·dád] *f.* piety; pity; mercy; **monte de —**

pawnshop.

piedra [pjé·ḏra] *f.* stone; gravel; hailstone; *Ven.* piece of a domino set; — **angular** (*or* **fundamental**) cornerstone; — **caliza** limestone; — **pómez** pumice, pumice stone; **a** — **y lodo** shut tight; **ser** — **de escándalo** to be an object; of scandal.

piel [pjel] *f.* skin; hide; leather; fur.

piélago [pjé·la·ǥo] *m.* high sea; sea; great abundance, great plenty.

pienso [pjén·so] *m.* feed; thought; **ni por** — not even in thought.

pierna [pjér·na] *f.* leg; **dormir a** — **suelta** to sleep like a log, sleep soundly; *Am.* **ser una buena** — to be a good fellow, be always in a good mood.

pieza [pjé·sa] *f.* (*pedazo*) piece; part; (*cuarto*) room; (*comedia*) play; **de una** — solid, in one piece; *Am.* **ser de una** — to be an honest, upright man.

pifia [pí·fja] *f.* a miss, miscue.

pigmento [piǥ·men·to] *m.* pigment.

pijama [pi·yá·ma] [pi·xá·ma] *m.* pajamas.

pila [pí·la] *f.* (*pieza cóncava*) basin; baptismal font; trough; (*cúmulo*) pile; heap; electric battery; — **atómica** atomic pile; *Am.* fountain; *Andes* hairless dog; *Am.* bald head; **nombre de** — Christian name; *Andes* **andar** — to go naked; *Mex.* **tener las -s** (*or* **tener por -s**) to have a lot, have heaps.

pilar [pi·lár] *m.* pillar, column; basin of a fountain.

pilcha [píl·ča] *f. Ríopl.* any article of clothing; *Am.* mistress; **-s** *Ríopl.* belongings.

píldora [píl·do·ra] *f.* pill.

pilmama [pil·má·ma] *f. Mex.* child's nurse, wet nurse.

pilón [pi·lón] *m.* basin (*of a fountain*); watering trough; sugar loaf; large wooden or metal mortar (*for grinding grain*); counterpoise; *Mex.* an additional amount, premium (*given to a buyer*); *Mex.* **de** — to boot, in addition, besides;

piloncillo [pi·lon·sí·yo] *m. Am.* unrefined sugar loaf.

pilotar [pi·lo·tár], **pilotear** [pi·lo·te·ár] *v.* to pilot.

pilote [pi·ló·te] *m.* pile (*for building*).

piloto [pi·ló·to] *m.* pilot; *Mex.* generous entertainer or host.

pillaje [pi·yá·xe] *m.* pillage, plunder.

pillar [pi·yár] *v.* to pillage, plunder; to pilfer; to seize, snatch, grasp; to catch; *Am.* to surprise, catch in the act.

pillo [pí·yo] *adj.* roguish; sly, crafty; *m.* rogue, rascal; *Am.* a species of heron; *Am.* long-legged person; **pilluelo** [pi·ywé·lo] *m.* little rascal, scamp.

pimentero [pi·men·té·ro] *m.* pepper plant; pepperbox, pepper shaker.

pimentón [pi·men·tón] *m.* large pepper; cayenne, red pepper; paprika.

pimienta [pi·mjén·ta] *f.* black pepper.

pimiento [pi·mjén·to] *m.* green pepper; red pepper.

pimpollo [pim·pó·yo] *m.* rosebud; bud; shoot, sprout; attractive youth.

pináculo [pi·ná·ku·lo] *m.* pinnacle, top, summit.

pinar [pi·nár] *m.* pine grove.

pincel [pin·sél] *m.* artist's brush; **pincelada** [pin·se·lá·ḏa] *f.* stroke of the brush.

pinchar [pin·čár] *v.* to prick; to puncture.

pinchazo [pin·čá·so] *m.* prick; puncture; stab.

pingajo [piŋ·gá·xo] *m.* tag, tatter, rag.

pingo [píŋ·go] *m. Ríopl., Andes* saddle horse; *Mex.* devil.

pingüe [píŋ·gwe] *adj.* abundant, copious; fat, greasy.

pingüino [piŋ·gwí·no] *m.* penguin.

pino [pí·no] *m.* pine; *Am.* filling for a meat pie; **hacer -s** (*or* **hacer pinitos**) to begin to walk (*said of a baby*); to begin to do things (*said of a novice*).

pinta [pín·ta] *f.* spot, mark; outward sign, aspect; pint; *Mex.* **hacer** — to play hooky, cut class.

pintar [pin·tár] *v.* to paint; to describe, depict; to feign; to begin to turn red, begin to ripen (*said of fruit*); to fancy, imagine; *Mex.* to play hooky, play truant; *Am.* to fawn, flatter; **no** — **nada** to be worth nothing, count for nothing; **las cosas no pintaban bien** things did not look well; *Mex.* — **venados** to play hooky; **-se** to put on make-up; *Am.* to excel (in); to praise oneself; *Ven.* to go away.

pintarrajear [pin·ta·rra·xe·ár] *v.* to daub; to smear with paint or rouge.

pinto [pín·to] *adj. Am.* spotted, speckled.

pintor [pin·tór] *m.* painter, artist; — **de brocha gorda** house painter; poor artist; *adj. Am.* boastful, conceited.

pintoresco [pin·to·rés·ko] *adj.* picturesque.

pintura [pin·tú·ra] *f.* painting; picture; paint, color; description.

pinzas [pín·sas] *f. pl.* pincers; tweezers; claws (*of lobsters, crabs, etc.*); *Ríopl., Mex., Carib.* pliers, tongs.

piña [pí·ña] pineapple; pine cone; piña cloth; cluster; *Cuba* pool (*a billiard game*).

piñata [pi·ñá·ta] *f.* pot; hanging pot or other container (*filled with candies, fruit, etc.*).

piñón [pi·ñón] *m.* pine nut; nut pine; pinion.

pio [pí·o] *adj.* pious, devout; kind; merciful; dappled, spotted (*horse*); **obras pías** pious works, charitable deeds.

piocha [pjó·ča] *adj. Mex.* great! excellent.

piojo [pjó·xo] *m.* louse.

piojoso [pjo·xó·so] *adj.* lousy; mean, stingy.

pionero [pjo·né·ro] *m.* pioneer; boy scout.

pipa [pí·pa] *f.* tobacco pipe; keg, barrel; reed pipe (*musical instrument*); fruit seed (*of a lemon, orange, melon*); *Col.* green coconut; *Am.* potato; *Ven.* **estar** — to be drunk; *m. Am.* species of green frog.

pipiar [1][7] [pi·pjár] *v.* to peep, chirp.

pipiolo [pi·pjó·lo] *m.* novice, beginner; *Am.* child, youngster.

pique [pí·ke] *m.* pique, resentment; chigger (*insect*); flea; *Am.* small chili pepper; *Am.* trail; **a** — **de** in danger of, on the point of; **echar a** — to sink (*a ship*); to destroy; **irse a** — to capsize; to sink.

piquete [pi·ké·te] *m.* prick; bite, sting (*of insects*); small hole; picket, stake; picket (*military*); *Am.* small band of musicians; *Am.* small corral; *Am.* cutting edge of scissors.

piragua [pi·rá·ǥwa] *f. Ríopl., Carib., Ven., Col., Andes* Indian canoe; dugout.

pirámide [pi·rá·mi·ḏe] *f.* pyramid.

pirata [pi·rá·ta] *m.* pirate.

piratear [pi·ra·te·ár] *v.* to pirate.

piropo [pi·ró·po] *m.* flattery, compliment; a variety of garnet (*a semiprecious stone*); **echar un** — to "throw a bouquet"; to compliment.

pirotecnia [pi·ro·ték·nja] *f.* pyrotechnics; fireworks.

pirueta [pi·rwé·ta] *f.* whirl; somersault; caper; **hacer -s** to cut capers; to turn somersaults; to do stunts.

pisada [pi·sá·ḏa] *f.* footstep; footprint; **dar una** — to step on, stamp on; **seguir las -s de** to follow in the footsteps of; to imitate.

pisapapeles [pi·sa·pa·pé·les] *m.* paperweight.

pisar [pi·sár] *v.* to step on, tread upon; to trample under foot; to pound; to cover (*said of a male bird*).

piscina [pi·sí·na] *f.* swimming pool, swimming tank; fish pond.

pisco [pís·ko] *m. Peru, Col.* a rum-based mixed drink.

pise [pí·se] *m. Ven.* rut; *Am.* tread (*of a wheel*). See **rodadura**.

piso [pí·so] *m.* floor; story; pavement; apartment, flat; tread; *Riopl., Mex., Carib., Ven.* fee for pasturage rights; *Am.* table scarf; *Am.* stool, footstool; *Am.* small rug.

pisón [pi·són] *m.* heavy mallet (*for pounding, flattening, crushing*).

pisotear [pi·so·te·ár] *v.* to tramp, tramp on, trample; to tread.

pisotón [pi·so·tón] *m.* hard step, stamp (*of the foot*); **dar un —** to step hard, stamp (upon).

pista [pís·ta] *f.* track, trace, trail; clew; race track; **— de aterrizaje** landing field.

pistola [pis·tó·la] *f.* pistol; **pistolera** [pis·to·lé·ra] *f.* holster.

pistolero [pis·to·lé·ro] *m.* gangster; body guard.

pistón [pis·tón] *m.* piston; *Col.* cornet.

pita [pí·ta] *f. Am.* agave or century plant; *Am.* fiber, or thread made from the fiber, of the agave or maguey.

pitar [pi·tár] *v.* to toot; to whistle; *Riopl., Andes* to smoke; *Ven.* to hiss; *Carib., Mex.* to slip away, escape; *Am.* **-se una cosa** to steal something; *Ch., Col., Ven., C.A.* (*pitado*) **salir pitando** to leave on the run.

pitazo [pi·tá·so] *m.* toot, whistle, blast.

pitillo [pi·tí·yo] *m. Spain* cigarette; **pitillera** [pi·ti·yé·ra] *f.* cigarette case.

pito [pí·to] *m.* whistle; cigarette; *Am.* tick (*an insect*); **no vale un —** it is not worth a straw; *Am.* **no saber ni — de una cosa** not to know anything about a subject.

pitón [pi·tón] *m.* lump; horn of an animal.

pizarra [pi·sá·rra] *f.* slate; blackboard; **pizarrín** [pi·sa·rrín] *m.* slate pencil; **pizarrón** [pi·sa·rrón] *m.* blackboard.

pizca [pís·ka] *f.* pinch, small bit; *Mex.* harvest.

placa [plá·ka] *f.* badge, insignia; plaque, tablet; metal plate; photographic plate; license plate; *Ven.* scab or skin blemish.

placentero [pla·sen·té·ro] *adj.* pleasant, agreeable.

placer[38] [pla·sér] *v. irr.* to please, content; *m.* pleasure; sand bank, shoal; placer (*place where gold is obtained by washing*); *Am.* pearl fishing.

placero [pla·sé·ro] *m.*, **placera** *f.* market vendor.

plácido [plá·si·do] *adj.* placid, calm.

plaga [plá·ga] *f.* plague; calamity.

plagar[7] [pla·gár] *v.* to plague, infest; **-se de** to become plagued or infested with.

plagiar [pla·xjár] *v.* to plagiarize, steal and use as one's own (*the writings, ideas, etc. of another*); to kidnap, abduct.

plan [plan] *m.* plan; design; project; drawing; mine floor; *Am.* clearing; *Am.* building grounds of a ranch.

plana [plá·na] *f.* page (*of a newspaper*); plain, flat country; mason's trowel; tally sheet; **enmendar la — a uno** to correct a person's mistakes.

plancton [pláŋk·ton] *m.* plankton.

plancha [plán·ča] *f.* flatiron; metal plate; gangplank; blunder; *Cuba* railway flatcar; *Ven.,*

Col. dental plate; **— de blindaje** armor plate; **hacer una —** to make a ridiculous blunder; **tirarse una —** to place oneself in a ridiculous situation.

planchado [plan·čá·do] *m.* ironing; clothes ironed or to be ironed; *adj. Am.* smart, clever; *Am.* brave; *Ven.* dolled up, dressed up; *Am.* broke, penniless.

planchar [plan·čár] *v.* to iron; to smooth out; *Mex.* to leave (*someone*) waiting; *Am.* to strike with the flat of a blade; *Am.* to flatter; *Mex., Ven.* — **el asiento** to be a wallflower at a dance.

planeador [pla·ne·a·dór] *m.* glider airplane.

planear [pla·ne·ár] *v.* to plan; to glide (*said of an airplane or bird*).

planeo [pla·né·o] *m.* planning; glide, gliding (*of an airplane*).

planeta [pla·né·ta] *m.* planet.

planetario [pla·ne·tá·rjo] *m.* planetary.

plano [plá·no] *adj.* plane, flat, level; *m.* plane; plan; map; **de —** flatly, clearly, openly; **dar de —** to hit with the flat of anything.

planta [plán·ta] *f.* (*ser orgánico*) plant; plantation; (*proyecto*) plan; ground plan, ground floor; (*del pie*) sole of the foot; — **baja** ground floor; **buena —** good looks; **echar -s** to brag.

plantación [plan·ta·sjón] *f.* plantation; planting.

plantar [plan·tár] *v.* plant; to strike (*a blow*); **-se** to stand firm; to balk; *Am.* to doll up, dress up; **dejar a uno plantado** to "stand someone up", keep someone waiting indefinitely.

plantear [plan·te·ár] *v.* to plan; to establish; to carry out; to state, present (*a problem*); to try.

plantel [plan·tél] *m.* establishment; firm; plant; nursery.

plantío [plan·tí·o] *m.* planting; plantation; recently planted garden; tree nursery.

plañidero [pla·ñi·dé·ro] *m.* professional mourner.

plasma [pláz·ma] *m.* plasma.

plástico [plás·ti·ko] *adj.* plastic.

plata [plá·ta] *f.* silver; silver money; **hablar en —** to speak in plain language; *Carib., C.A., Ven., Col.* money.

plataforma [pla·ta·fór·ma] *f.* platform; — **de lanzamiento** launching pad.

platanal [pla·ta·nál], **platanar** [pla·ta·nár] *m.* grove of banana trees; banana plantation.

plátano [plá·ta·no] *m.* banana; banana tree; plane tree.

platea [pla·té·a] *f.* main floor of a theatre; a lower box seat.

plateado [pla·te·á·do] *adj.* silver-plated; silvery.

platear [pla·te·ár] *v.* to silver, plate, cover with silver.

platel [pla·tél] *m.* platter; tray.

platero [pla·té·ro] *m.* silversmith; jeweler.

plática [plá·ti·ka] *f.* conversation, talk, chat; informal lecture.

platicador[6] [pla·ti·ka·dór] *m.* talker; *adj.* talkative.

platicar[6] [pla·ti·kár] *v.* to converse, talk, chat.

platillo [pla·tí·yo] *m.* saucer; pan (*of a pair of scales*); cymbal; stew.

platino [pla·tí·no] *m.* platinum.

plato [plá·to] *m.* plate; dish; dinner course; **— de tocadiscos** turntable.

platón [pla·tón] *m.* large plate; platter.

platudo [pla·tú·do] *adj. Am.* wealthy, rich.

playa [plá·ya] *f.* beach, shore; *Ven.* wide, open space in front of a ranch house; *Riopl., Andes* — **de estacionamiento** parking lot.

plaza [plá·sa] *f.* (*pública*) plaza, public square;

public market; (*empleo*) job; employment; *Ríopl.*,
Ch., Cuba, Ven. park, promenade; — **de armas**
parade ground; public square; fortress; — **fuerte**
fortress; — **de gallos** cockpit (*for cockfights*); —
de toros bull ring; **sacar a** — to bring out into
the open, make public; **sentar** — to enlist;
plazoleta [pla·so·lé·ta], **plazuela** [pla·swé·la] *f.*
small square, court.
plazo [plá·so] *m.* term, time; **a** — on credit; in
installments.
pleamar [ple·a·már] *m.* flood tide, high tide.
plebe [plé·be] *f.* rabble; masses.
plebeyo [ple·bé·yo] *adj.* plebeian.
plebiscito [ple·bi·sí·to] *m.* plebiscite, direct vote.
plegadizo [ple·ga·dí·so] *adj.* folding; pliable, easily
bent.
plegar[1,7] [ple·gár] *v.* to fold; to pleat; to crease;
-se to bend, yield, submit.
plegaria [ple·gá·rja] *f.* supplication, prayer; prayer
hour.
pleito [pléj·to] *m.* litigation, lawsuit; dispute;
debate; duel; — **de acreedores** bankruptcy
proceedings; **pleitista** *m. & f.* quarrelsome
person.
plenario [ple·ná·rjo] *adj.* plenary (*session*).
plenipotenciario [ple·ni·po·ten·sjá·rjo] *m.*
plenipotentiary (*diplomatic agent having full
power or authority*); *adj.* plenipotentiary, having
full power.
plenitud [ple·ni·túd] *f.* plenitude, fullness,
completeness; abundance.
pleno [plé·no] *adj.* full, complete; **sesión plena** joint
session; **en** — **día** in broad daylight, openly; **en**
— **rostro** (*or* **en plena cara**) right on the face; *m.*
joint session (*of a legislative body*).
pleuresía [plew·re·sí·a] *f.* pleurisy.
pliego [pljé·go] *m.* sheet of paper; sealed letter or
document.
pliegue [pljé·ge] *m.* fold, crease, pleat.
plomada [plo·má·da] *f.* plumb, lead weight, plumb
bob.
plomazo [plo·má·so] *m. Col., Ven., Mex.* shot,
bullet.
plomería [plo·me·rí·a] *f.* plumbing; plumber's
shop; lead roof.
plomero [plo·mé·ro] *m.* plumber.
plomizo [plo·mí·so] *adj.* leaden, lead-colored.
plomo [pló·mo] *m.* lead; plumb, lead weight;
bullet; boring person; **a** — vertical; vertically;
adj. Carib., Mex. lead-colored.
pluma [plú·ma] *f.* (*de ave*) feather; plume;
(*instrumento*) pen; quill; — **estilográfica** (*or* —
fuente) fountain pen; **plumada** [plu·má·da] *f.*
dash, stroke of the pen, flourish; **plumaje**
[plu·má·xe] *m.* plumage; plume, **plumero**
[plu·mé·ro] *m.* feather duster; box for feathers;
feather ornament (*on hats, helmets, etc.*); **plumón**
[plu·món] *m.* down; feather mattress; **plumoso**
[plu·mó·so] *adj.* downy, feathery.
plural [plu·rál] *adj.* plural.
plutonio [plu·tó·njo] *m.* plutonium.
pluralidad [plu·ra·li·dád] *f.* plurality.
pluvial [plu·bjál] *adj.* rain (*used as adj.*); **capa** —
cope (*long cape used by priests during certain
religious ceremonies*).
pluviómetro [plu·bjó·me·tro] *m.* rain gauge.
población [po·bla·sjón] *f.* (*acto*) populating;
settlement; (*número*) population; (*lugar*) town,
city.
poblado [po·blá·do] *m.* inhabited place; village; *p.p.*
populated; covered with growth.

poblador [po·bla·dór] *m.* settler (*of a colony*).
poblar[2] [po·blár] *v. irr.* to populate, people; to
colonize, settle; to stock (*a farm*); to breed; -se
to become covered (*with leaves or buds*).
pobre [pó·bre] *adj.* poor; *m.* poor man; beggar;
pobrete [po·bré·te] *m.* poor devil, poor wretch;
pobretón [po·bre·tón] *m.* poor old fellow, poor
wretch.
pobreza [po·bré·sa] *f.* poverty; need; lack, scarcity;
barrenness.
pocilga [po·síl·ga] *f.* pigsty, pigpen.
pocillo [po·sí·yo] *m.* cup.
poco [pó·ko] *adj.* little, scanty; small; short (*time*);
-s few, some; *m.* a little, a bit; *adv.* little; **a** —
presently, after a short time; **a** — **rato** (*or* **al** —
rato) after a short while; — **a** — slowly, little by
little; **a los -s meses** after a few months; **por** —
me caigo I almost fell; **tener en** — to hold in
low esteem.
podadera [po·da·dé·ra] *f.* pruning hook or knife.
podar [po·dár] *v.* to prune, trim, cut off.
podenco [po·dén·ko] *m.* hound.
poder[39] [po·dér] *v. irr.* to be able; can; may; **él**
puede mucho (*or* **poco**) he has much (*or* little)
power; **puede que** it is possible that, it may be
that, perhaps; **hasta más no** — to the utmost, to
the limit; **no** — **más** not to be able to do more;
to be exhausted; **no puede menos de hacerlo** he
cannot help doing it; **no** — **con la carga** not to
be equal to the burden, not to be able to lift the
load; *Col., Ven.* **-le a uno algo** to be worried or
affected by something, *m.* power, authority.
poderío [po·de·rí·o] *m.* power, dominion; might;
wealth.
poderoso [po·de·ró·so] *adj.* powerful; wealthy.
podre [pó·dre] *f.* pus; decayed matter; **podredumbre**
[po·dre·dúm·bre] *f.* corruption, decay; pus;
rotten matter.
podrido [po·drí·do] *adj.* rotten; *p.p. of* podrir.
podrir[16] [po·drír] = pudrir[16].
poema [po·é·ma] *m.* poem.
poesía [po·e·sí·a] *f.* poetry; poem.
poeta [po·é·ta] *m.* poet; **poetastro** [po·e·tás·tro] *m.*
bad poet.
poético [po·é·ti·ko] *adj.* poetic; **poética** [po·é·ti·ka]
f. poetics.
poetisa [po·e·tí·sa] *f.* poetess.
polaco [po·lá·ko] *adj.* Polish; *m.* Polish, Polish
language; Pole.
polaina [po·láj·na] *f.* legging.
polar [po·lár] *adj.* polar.
polea [po·lé·a] *f.* pulley.
polémica [po·lé·mi·ka] *f.* controversy; polemics.
polen [pó·len] *m.* pollen.
policía [po·li·sí·a] *f.* police; *m.* policeman.
policial [po·li·sjál] *m. Col., Ven.* policeman.
policiaco [po·li·sjá·ko] [po·li·sí·a·ko] *adj.* police,
detective (*story*).
poligamia [po·li·gá·mja] *f.* polygamy.
polígota [po·lí·glo·ta] *m. & f.* polyglot; one who
speaks several languages.
polilla [po·lí·ya] *f.* moth; larva of the moth.
poliomielitis [po·ljo·mje·li·tis] *f.* poliomyelitis,
polio.
política [po·lí·ti·ka] *f.* politics; policy; *Am.* — **de**
campanario politics of a clique.
politicastro [po·lí·ti·kás·tro] *m.* bad or incapable
politician.
político [po·lí·ti·ko] *adj.* political; politic; polite;
madre política mother-in-law; *m.* politician.
póliza [pó·li·sa] *f.* policy, written contract; draft;

customhouse certificate; — **de seguros** insurance policy.
polizonte [po·li·són·te] *m.* policeman.
polo [pó·lo] *m.* pole (*of a* magnet *or of an axis*); polo (*a game*); — **acuático** water polo.
polonio [po·ló·njo] *m.* polonium.
poltrón [pol·trón] *adj.* lazy, idle; **silla poltrona** easy chair.
polvareda [pol·ba·ré·da] *f.* cloud of dust; **armar** (*or* **levantar**) **una** — to kick up the dust; to raise a rumpus.
polvera [pol·bé·ra] *f.* powder box; compact; powder puff.
polvo [pól·bo] *m.* dust; powder; pinch of snuff or powder; — **férrico** iron oxide filings (*coating for recording tape*); **-s** toilet powder; **-s para dientes** tooth powder; **limpio de** — **y paja** entirely free; net; *Am.* cleaned out, without a penny; *Am.* innocent, ignorant, unaware; *Mex., Col., Ven.* **tomar el** — to escape, "beat it".
pólvora [pól·bo·ra] *f.* gunpowder; fireworks.
polvorear [pol·bo·re·ár] *v.* to powder, sprinkle with powder.
polvoriento [pol·bo·rjén·to] *adj.* dusty.
polvorín [pol·bo·rín] *m.* powder magazine; priming powder; powder flask; *Am.* tick (*parasitic insect*); *Ríopl.* spitfire, quick-tempered person.
polla [pó·ya] *f.* pullet (*young hen*); young lass; pool (*in cards*).
pollada [po·yá·da] *f.* hatch, brood; flock of chicks.
pollera [po·yé·ra] *f.* woman who raises and sells chickens; chicken coop; a bell-shaped basket for chickens; petticoat; *Ríopl., Ch., Col., Andes* skirt.
pollino [po·yí·no] *m.* young donkey, ass.
pollo [pó·yo] *m.* young chicken ; nestling, young bird; *Spain* young man; **polluelo** [po·ywé·lo] *m.* chick.
pomelo [po·mé·lo] *m. Spain* grapefruit.
pómez [pó·mes] *m.* pumice.
pompa [póm·pa] *f.* pomp; pageant, procession; bubble; pump.
pomposo [pom·pó·so] *adj.* pompous.
pómulo [pó·mu·lo] *m.* cheek bone.
ponche [pón·če] *m.* punch (*a beverage*); **ponchera** [pon·čé·ra] *f.* punch bowl.
poncho [pón·čo] *m. Andes, Ch., Ríopl.* poncho; cape.
ponderación [pon·de·ra·sjón] *f.* pondering, careful consideration, weighing; exaggeration.
ponderar [pon·de·rár] *v.* (*pensar*) to ponder, consider, weigh; (*exagerar*) to exaggerate; to extol.
ponderativo [pon·de·ra·ti·bo] *adj.* exaggerating.
ponderoso [pon·de·ró·so] *adj.* ponderous, heavy.
poner[40] [po·nér] *v. irr.* to put; to place; to set; to lay; to suppose; — **como nuevo a alguien** to cover someone with insults; — **en claro** to clarify; — **en limpio** to recopy, make a clean copy; — **todo de su parte** to do one's best; **pongamos que** . . . let us suppose that . . .; **-se** to place oneself; to become; **-se a** to begin to; **-se al corriente** to become informed; **-se de pie** to stand up; *Carib., Mex., Ch., Andes* **-se bien con alguien** to ingratiate oneself with someone, get on his good side; *Am.* **ponérsela** to get drunk.
poniente [po·njén·te] *m.* west; west wind; **el sol** — the setting sun.
pontón [pon·tón] *m.* pontoon; scow, flat-bottomed boat; log bridge; pontoon bridge.
ponzoña [pon·só·ña] *f.* venom, poison.

ponzoñoso [pon·so·ñó·so] *adj.* venomous, poisonous.
popa [pó·pa] *f.* poop, stern; **viento en** — speedily; going well.
popote [po·pó·te] *m. Mex.* straw for brooms; *Mex.* drinking straw or tube.
populacho [po·pu·lá·čo] *m.* populace, rabble.
popular [po·pu·lár] *adj.* popular.
popularidad [po·pu·la·ri·dád] *f.* popularity.
populoso [po·pu·ló·so] *adj.* populous, densely populated.
popurrí [po·pu·rrí] *m.* potpourri.
poquito [po·kí·to] *adj.* very little; *Cuba, Ven., Col.* timid, shy; *m.* a small bit; **a -s** in small quantities.
por [por] *prep.* by; for; for the sake of, on account of, on behalf of; because of; through; along; on exchange for; in the place of; during; about, around; to, with the idea of; — **ciento** percent; — **consiguiente** consequently; — **entre** among, between; — **escrito** in writing; — **poco se muere** he almost died; **está** — **hacer** it is yet to be done; **él está** — **hacerlo** he is in favor of doing it; **recibir** — **esposa** to receive as a wife; **tener** — to consider, think of as; ¿ — **que?** *interr. adv.* why? for what reason?
porcelana [por·se·lá·na] *f.* porcelain, china; enamel.
porcentaje [por·sen·tá·xe] *m.* percentage.
porcino [por·sí·no] *adj.* porcine; related to the pig.
porción [por·sjón] *f.* portion; part, share; **una** — **de** **gente** a lot of people.
porche [pór·če] *m.* porch.
pordiosear [por·djo·se·ár] *v.* to beg.
pordiosero [por·djo·sé·ro] *m.* beggar.
porfía [por·fí·a] *f.* stubbornness, obstinacy; persistence, insistence; **a** — in competition; with great insistence.
porfiado[por·fjá·do] *adj.* stubborn, obstinate, persistent.
porfiar[17] [por·fjár] *v.* to persist; to insist; to dispute obstinately; to argue.
pormenor [por·me·nór] *m.* detail.
pormenorizar[9] [por·me·no·ri·sár] *v.* to detail, tell in detail; to itemize.
pornografía [por·no·gra·fi·a] *f.* pornography.
pornográfico [por·no·grá·fi·ko] *adj.* pornographic.
poro [pó·ro] *m.* pore.
poroso [po·ró·so] *adj.* porous.
poroto [po·ró·to] *m. Ch., Ríopl., Andes* bean; *Ch., Ríopl., Andes* runt; urchin.
porque [pór·ke] *conj.* because; so that.
porqué [por·ké] *m.* cause, reason, motive.
porquería [por·ke·rí·a] *f.* filth; filthy act or word; nasty piece of food; trifle, worthless object.
porra [pó·rra] *f.* club, stick; *Am.* **mandar a uno a la** — to send someone to the devil; **porrazo** *m.* blow; knock; bump; **porrón** *m.* wine vessel with long snout.
porta [pór·ta] *f.* porthole; cover for a porthole; goal (*in football*).
portaaviones [por·ta·a·bjó·nes] *m.* airplane carrier.
portada [por·tá·da] *f.* façade, front (*of a building*); title page.
portador [por·ta·dór] *m.* carrier; bearer; tray.
portal [por·tál] *m.* portal; entrance, vestibule; portico, porch; *Am.* Christmas crèche; **-es** arcades, galleries; **portalón** [por·ta·lón] *m.* large portal; gangway (*of a ship*).
portamonedas [por·ta·mo·ne·das] *m.* pocketbook, coin purse.

portapapeles [por·ta·pa·pé·les] *m.* briefcase.
portaplumas [por·ta·plú·mas] *m.* penholder.
portar [por·tár] *v. Am.* to carry; **-se** to behave.
portátil [por·tár] *adj.* portable.
portaviones [por·ta·ƀjo·nes] *m.* aircraft carrier; also **portaaviones.**
portavoz [por·ta·ƀos] *m.* megaphone; mouthpiece; spokesman.
portazgo [por·táz·ɡo] *m.* toll.
portazo [por·tá·so] *m.* bang or slam of a door; **dar un —** to bang or slam the door.
porte [pór·te] *m.* portage, cost of carriage; freight; postage; manner, bearing; size, capacity; *Am.* birthday present; *C.A.* size.
portear [por·te·ár] *v.* to carry on one's back; *Am.* to get out in a hurry.
portento [por·tén·to] *m.* portent; wonder, marvel.
portentoso [por·ten·tó·so] *adj.* marvelous, extraordinary, amazing, terrifying.
porteño [por·té·ño] *adj.* from a port; *Ríopl.* from Buenos Aires.
portería [por·te·ría] *f.* porter's quarters; main door of a building.
portero [por·té·ro] *m.* doorkeeper, doorman; janitor.
pórtico [pór·ti·ko] *m.* portico, porch.
portilla [por·tí·ya] *f.* porthole; small gate or passageway.
portón *m.* gate.
portugués [por·tu·ɡés] *adj.* Portuguese; *m.* Portuguese; Portuguese language.
porvenir [por·ƀe·nír] *m.* future.
pos [pos]: **en — de** after; in pursuit of.
posada [po·sá·ða] *f.* lodging; inn; boardinghouse; dwelling, home; *Mex.* **las -s** a Christmas festivity lasting nine days; **posadero** [po·sa·ðé·ro] *m.* innkeeper.
posaderas [po·sa·ðé·ras] *f. pl.* posterior, buttocks, rump.
posar [po·sár] *v.* to lodge; to rest; to sit down; to pose (*as a model*); to perch (*said of birds*); **-se** to settle (*said of sediment*); to perch (*said of birds*).
posdata [poz·ðá·ta] *f.* postscript.
poseedor [po·se·e·ðór] *m.* possessor, owner.
poseer[14] [po·se·ér] *v.* to possess, own; to master, know well; **-se** to have control of oneself.
posesión [po·se·sjón] *f.* possession.
posesivo [po·se·sí·ƀo] *adj. & m.* possessive.
posesor [po·se·sór] *m.* possessor, owner.
posibilidad [po·si·ƀi·li·ðáð] *f.* possibility.
posible [po·sí·ƀle] *adj.* possible; **hacer lo —** to do one's best; **-s** *m. pl.* goods, property, means.
posición [po·si·sjón] *f.* position; posture; status, rank, standing; placing.
positivo [po·si·tí·ƀo] *adj.* positive; effective; true; practical.
posponer[40] [pos·po·nér] *v. irr.* to postpone, put off; to put after; to subordinate.
pospuesto [pos·pwés·to] *p.p. of* **posponer.**
posta [pós·ta] *f.* (*bala*) small bullet; (*apuesta*) bet, wager; (*relevo*) relay (*of post horses*); post station; **-s** buckshot; **por la —** posthaste; fast, speedily; *m.* postboy, courier, messenger.
postal [pos·tál] *adj.* postal; **tarjeta —** postcard.
postdata [poz·ðá·ta] = **posdata.**
poste [pós·te] *m.* post, pillar.
postergar[7] [pos·ter·ɡár] *v.* to delay; to postpone; to disregard someone's right.
posteridad [pos·te·ri·ðáð] *f.* posterity.
posterior [pos·te·rjór] *adj.* posterior, back, rear; later.

postigo [pos·tí·ɡo] *m.* wicket, small door or gate; shutter; peep window.
postizo [pos·tí·so] *adj.* false, artificial; *m.* switch, false hair.
postración [pos·tra·sjón] *f.* prostration, collapse, exhaustion; dejection, lowness of spirits.
postrar [pos·trár] *v.* to prostrate; to humiliate; to throw down; to weaken, exhaust; **-se** to kneel to the ground; to be weakened, exhausted; to · collapse.
postre [pós·tre] *m.* dessert; **a la —** at last.
postrer(o) [pos·tré·r(o)] *adj.* last; hindmost, nearest the rear.
postulante [pos·tu·lán·te] *m. & f.* petitioner; applicant, candidate.
póstumo [pós·tu·mo] *adj.* posthumous, after one's death.
postura [pos·tú·ra] *f.* posture, position; bid; wager; pact, agreement; egg-laying.
potable [po·tá·ƀle] *adj.* drinkable; **agua —** drinking water.
potaje [po·tá·xe] *m.* pottage, thick soup; porridge; mixed drink.
potasio [po·tá·sjo] *m.* potassium.
pote [pó·te] *m.* pot; jar; jug; *Carib., Ven., Mex., Ríopl.* flask; *Am.* buzzard.
potencia [po·tén·sja] *f.* potency; power; faculty, ability; powerful nation.
potentado [po·ten·tá·ðo] *m.* potentate.
potente [po·tén·te] *adj.* potent, powerful, strong.
potestad [po·tes·táð] *f.* power; dominion, authority.
potranca [po·trán·ka] *f.* filly, young mare.
potrero [po·tré·ro] *m.* herdsman of colts; fenced-in pasture land; *Carib., Mex., C.A., Ven., Col., Ch.* cattle ranch, stock farm.
potro [pó·tro] *m.* colt; rack, torture; *Col., Ven., Mex., Ch., Ríopl.* wild horse.
poyo [pó·yo] *m.* stone or brick bench (*usually built against a wall*).
pozo [pó·so] *m.* well; hole, pit; mine shaft; hold of a ship; *Am.* pool, puddle; *Ríopl., Ch., Ven., Col., Mex.* spring, fountain.
pozole [po·só·le] *m. Mex.* stew made of hominy and pig's head.
práctica [prák·ti·ka] *f.* practice; exercise; custom, habit; method.
practicante [prak·ti·kán·te] *m. & f.* doctor's assistant; hospital intern.
practicar[6] [prak·ti·kár] *v.* to practice; to put into practice.
práctico [prák·ti·ko] *adj.* practical; experienced, skilful; *m.* **— de puerto** harbor pilot.
pradera [pra·ðé·ra] *f.* prairie; meadow.
prado [prá·ðo] *m.* meadow, field; lawn.
preámbulo [pre·ám·bu·lo] *m.* preamble, introduction, prologue.
precario [pre·ká·rjo] *adj.* precarious.
precaución [pre·kaw·sjón] *f.* precaution.
precaver [pre·ka·ƀér] *v.* to guard (against), keep (from); to warn, caution; **-se** to guard oneself (against); to take precautions.
precavido [pre·ka·ƀí·ðo] *adj.* cautious, on guard.
precedencia [pre·se·dén·sja] *f.* precedence; priority.
precedente [pre·se·dén·te] *adj.* preceding; *m.* precedent.
preceder [pre·se·dér] *v.* to precede; to have precedence.
precepto [pre·sép·to] *m.* precept; rule; order.
preceptor [pre·sep·tór] *m.* teacher, tutor.
preciado [pre·sjá·ðo] *adj.* prized, esteemed; precious, valuable.

PO

preciar [pre·sjár] v. to appraise; to value; **-se de** to boast of, be proud of.
precio [pré·sjo] m. price; value, worth; esteem.
precioso [pre·sjó·so] adj. precious, valuable; fine, exquisite; beautiful.
precipicio [pre·si·pí·sjo] m. precipice; ruin.
precipitación [pre·si·pi·ta·sjón] f. precipitation; rush, haste, hurry.
precipitado [pre·si·pi·tá·ḍo] adj. precipitate, hasty, rash; m. precipitate (chemical term).
precipitar [pre·si·pi·tár] v. to precipitate; to hasten, rush; to hurl, throw headlong; **-se** to throw oneself headlong; to rush (into).
precipitoso [pre·si·pi·tó·so] adj. precipitous, steep; rash.
precisar [pre·si·sár] v. to determine precisely; to force, compel, make necessary; Riopl., Col., Ven., Mex., Andes; to be necessary or urgent; Am. to need.
precisión [pre·si·sjón] f. precision, exactness; accuracy; compulsion, force, necessity; Am. haste.
preciso [pre·si·so] adj. necessary; precise, exact; clear; m. Am. small travelling bag.
precoz [pre·kós] adj. precocious.
precursor [pre·kur·sór] m. precursor, forerunner.
predecir²⁷ [pre·ḍe·sír] v. irr. to predict, prophesy, forecast, foretell.
predestinar [pre·ḍes·ti·nár] v. to predestine.
predicación [pre·ḍi·ka·sjón] f. preaching.
predicado [pre·ḍi·ká·ḍo] adj. & m. predicate; p.p. of predicar.
predicador [pre·ḍi·ka·ḍór] m. preacher.
predicar⁶ [pre·ḍi·kár] v. to preach.
predicción [pre·ḍik·sjón] f. prediction.
predilección [pre·ḍi·lek·sjón] f. predilection, preference, liking.
predilecto [pre·ḍi·lek·to] adj. favorite, preferred.
predisponer⁴⁰ [pre·ḍis·po·nér] v. irr. to predispose, bias, prejudice.
predispuesto [pre·ḍis·pwés·to] p.p. of predisponer & adj. predisposed, prejudiced, biased.
predominante [pre·ḍo·mi·nán·te] adj. predominant; prevailing, ruling.
predominar [pre·ḍo·mi·nár] v. to predominate, prevail.
predominio [pre·ḍo·mí·njo] m. predominance; sway, influence.
prefacio [pre·fa·sjo] m. preface.
prefecto [pre·fék·to] m. prefect (military or civil chief; sometimes a mayor, sometimes governor of a province, as in Peru).
preferencia [pre·fe·rén·sja] f. preference; **de —** with preference; preferably.
preferente [pre·fe·rén·te] adj. preferable; preferred; preferential; **acciones -s** preferred shares.
preferible [pre·fe·rí·ḃle] adj. preferable.
preferir³ [pre·fe·rír] v. irr. to prefer.
prefijar [pre·fi·xár] v. to prefix; to set beforehand (as a date).
prefijo [pre·fí·xo] m. prefix.
pregonar [pre·ġo·nár] v. to proclaim, cry out; to make known.
pregunta [pre·ġún·ta] f. question; **hacer una —** to ask a question.
preguntar [pre·ġun·tár] v. to ask, inquire.
preguntón [pre·ġun·tón] adj. inquisitive.
prejuicio [pre·xwí·sjo] m. prejudice.
prejuzgar⁷ [pre·xuz·ġár] v. irr. to prejudge.
prelado [pre·lá·ḍo] m. prelate.
preliminar [pre·li·mi·nár] adj. & m. preliminary.

preludiar [pre·lu·ḍjár] v. to be the prelude or beginning of; to initiate, introduce; to try out (a musical instrument).
preludio [pre·lú·ḍjo] m. prelude; introduction.
prematuro [pre·ma·tú·ro] adj. premature, untimely.
premeditado [pre·me·ḍi·tá·ḍo] adj. premeditated, deliberate.
premiar [pre·mjár] v. to reward.
premio [pré·mjo] m. prize; reward; recompense; premium; **a —** with interest, at interest.
premisa [pre·mí·sa] f. premise (either of the first two propositions of a syllogism).
premura [pre·mú·ra] f. pressure, urgency, haste.
prenda [prén·da] f. (fianza) pawn, pledge, security; token; (partes del vestido) article of clothing; anything valuable; loved person; jewel; **-s** good qualities, gifts, talents; **— de vestir** garment; **juego de -s** game of forfeits; **en — de** as a proof of, as a pledge of.
prendar [pren·dár] v. to pawn, pledge; to charm, please; **-se de** to get attached to; to fall in love with.
prendedor [pren·de·ḍór] m. clasp; stickpin; tie pin; brooch; Am. light.
prender [pren·dér] v. (asir) to seize, catch, grab; to bite (said of an insect); to fasten, clasp; to arrest, imprison; (empezar) to take root; to begin to burn; catch fire; Riopl., Carib., C.A., Mex. to light (a lamp); Am. to start, begin, undertake; **— el fuego** to start the fire; Col. **-las** to take to one's heels; **-se** to dress up.
prendero [pren·dé·ro] m. pawnbroker; second-hand dealer.
prensa [prén·sa] f. press; printing press.
prensar [pren·sár] v. to press.
prensil [pren·síl] adj. prehensile.
preñado [pre·ñá·ḍo] adj. pregnant; full.
preñez [pre·ñés] f. pregnancy.
preocupación [pre·o·ku·pa·sjón] f. preoccupation; worry; bias, prejudice.
preocupar [pre·o·ku·pár] v. to preoccupy; to worry; to prejudice; **-se** to be preoccupied; to worry; to be prejudiced.
preparación [pre·pa·ra·sjón] f. preparation.
preparar [pre·pa·rár] v. to prepare; **-se** to get ready; to be prepared.
preparativo [pre·pa·ra·tí·ḃo] adj. preparatory; m. preparation.
preparatorio [pre·pa·ra·tó·rjo] adj. preparatory.
preponderancia [pre·pon·de·rán·sja] f. preponderance.
preposición [pre·po·si·sjón] f. preposition.
prerrogativa [pre·rro·ġa·tí·ḃa] f. prerogative, right, privilege.
presa [pré·sa] f. prey; dam; fang, tusk; claw; **hacer —** to seize.
presagiar [pre·sa·xjár] v. to foretell.
presagio [pre·sá·xjo] m. presage, omen, sign.
presbítero [prez·ḃí·te·ro] m. priest.
prescindir [pre·sin·dír] v. to disregard, set aside, leave aside; to omit; to dispense (with).
prescribir⁵² [pres·kri·ḃír] v. to prescribe.
prescrito [pres·krí·to] p.p. of prescribir.
presencia [pre·sén·sja] f. presence; figure, bearing; **— de ánimo** presence of mind, serenity.
presenciar [pre·sen·sjár] v. to see, witness; to be present at.
presentación [pre·sen·ta·sjón] f. presentation; personal introduction; Ven. petition.
presentar [pre·sen·tár] v. to present; to introduce; **-se** to appear, present oneself; to introduce

oneself; to offer one's services; *Am.* to have recourse to justice, file suit.

presente [pre·sén·te] *adj.* present; *m.* present, gift; **al** — now, at the present time; **por el (la,** *or* **lo)** — for the present; **mejorando lo** — present company excepted; **tener** — to bear in mind.

presentimiento [pre·sen·ti·mjén·to] *m.* presentiment, foreboding.

presentir³ [pre·sen·tír] *v. irr.* to have a presentiment, foreboding or hunch.

preservación [pre·ser·ba·sjón] *f.* preservation.

preservar [pre·ser·bár] *v.* to preserve, guard, protect, keep.

presidencia [pre·si·dén·sja] *f.* presidency; office of president; presidential term; chairmanship.

presidencial [pre·si·den·sjál] *adj.* presidential.

presidente [pre·si·dén·te] *m.* president; chairman; presiding judge.

presidiario [pre·si·djá·rjo] *m.* prisoner, convict.

presidio [pre·sí·djo] *m.* garrison; fortress; penitentiary, prison; **diez años de** — ten years at hard labor (*in a prison*).

presidir [pre·si·dír] *v.* to preside; to direct.

presilla [pre·sí·ya] *f.* loop, fastener; clip.

presión [pre·sjón] *f.* pressure.

preso [pré·so] *m.* prisoner; *p.p. irr.* of **prender** imprisoned.

prestado [pres·tá·do] *adj.* & *p.p.* loaned, lent; **dar** — to lend; **pedir** — to borrow.

prestamista [pres·ta·mís·ta] *m.* & *f.* moneylender.

préstamo [prés·ta·mo] *m.* loan.

prestar [pres·tár] *v.* to loan, lend; *Col., Ven., C.A., Andes* to borrow; — **ayuda** to give help; — **atención** to pay attention; *Andes* **presta acá** give it here, give it to me; **-se** to lend oneself or itself.

presteza [pres·té·sa] *f.* promptness, speed.

prestidigitación [pres·ti·di·xi·ta·sjón] *f.* juggling, sleight of hand.

prestidigitador [pres·ti·di·xi·ta·dór] *m.* juggler.

prestigio [pres·tí·xjo] *m.* prestige; influence, authority; good reputation.

presto [prés·to] *adj.* quick; nimble; prompt; ready; *adv.* soon, at once; **de** — quickly, promptly.

presumido [pre·su·mi·do] *adj.* conceited, presumptuous; *p.p. of* **presumir.**

presumir [pre·su·mír] *v.* to presume; to boast; to show off; *Am.* to court, woo; — **de valiente** to boast of one's valor.

presunción [pre·sun·sjón] *f.* presumption, assumption; conceit, arrogance.

presunto [pre·sún·to] *adj.* presumed; supposed; prospective; **heredero** — heir apparent.

presuntuoso [pre·sun·twó·so] *adj.* presumptuous, conceited.

presuponer⁴⁰ [pre·su·po·nér] *v. irr.* to presuppose, take for granted, imply; to estimate.

presupuesto [pre·su·pwés·to] *p.p. of* **presuponer** presupposed; estimated; *m.* budget, estimate.

presuroso [pre·su·ró·so] *adj.* quick, prompt; hasty.

pretencioso [pre·ten·sjó·so] *adj.* presumptuous; conceited.

pretender [pre·ten·dér] *v.* to pretend; to solicit; seek; to claim; to try; to court.

pretendiente [pre·ten·djén·te] *m.* pretender, claimant; suitor; office seeker.

pretensión [pre·ten·sjón] *f.* pretension; claim; presumption; pretense.

pretérito [pre·té·ri·to] *adj.* preterite, past; *m.* preterite, the past tense.

pretexto [pre·tés·to] *m.* pretext, pretense, excuse.

pretil [pre·tíl] *m.* stone or brick railing; *Am.* ledge; *Mex., Ven.* stone or brick bench (*built against a wall*).

pretina [pre·tí·na] *f.* belt, girdle; waistband.

prevalecer¹³ [pre·ba·le·sér] *v. irr.* to prevail.

prevaleciente [pre·ba·le·sjén·te] *adj.* prevalent, current.

prevención [pre·ben·sjón] *f.* prevention; foresight, preparedness; bias, prejudice; provision, supply; admonition, warning; police station; guardhouse.

prevenido [pre·be·ni·do] *adj.* & *p.p.* prepared, ready; forewarned; cautious; supplied.

prevenir⁴⁸ [pre·be·nír] *v. irr.* to prevent, avoid; to prepare beforehand; to foresee; to warn; to predispose; **-se** to get prepared, get ready.

prever⁴⁹ [pre·bér] *v. irr.* to foresee.

previo [pré·bjo] *adj.* previous; *m. Am.* preliminary examination.

previsión [pre·bi·sjón] *f.* foresight.

previsto [pre·bís·to] *p.p. of* **prever.**

prieto [prjé·to] *adj.* dark, black; tight; compact; *Ríopl., Ven., Col., Mex., C.A., Andes* dark-complexioned, swarthy.

prima [prí·ma] *f.* female cousin; premium; prime (*first of the canonical hours*).

primacía [pri·má·sja] *f.* priority, precedence; superiority.

primario [pri·má·rjo] *adj.* primary, principal.

primavera [pri·ma·bé·ra] *f.* spring; primrose; print, flowered silk cloth.

primaveral [pri·ma·be·rál] *adj.* spring, pertaining to spring.

primer(o) [pri·mér(o)] *adj.* first; former; leading, principal; **primera enseñanza** primary education; **primera materia** raw material; **de buenas a primeras** all of a sudden, unexpectedly; **a primera luz** at dawn; *adv.* first; rather.

primicia [pri·mi·sja] *f.* first fruit; first profit; **-s** first fruits.

primitivo [pri·mi·tí·bo] *adj.* primitive; primary; original.

primo [prí·mo] *m.* cousin; simpleton, sucker, dupe; — **hermano** (*or* **carnal**) first cousin; *Carib.* **coger a uno de** — to deceive someone easily; *adj.* first; **número** — prime number.

primogénito [pri·mo·xé·ni·to] *adj.* & *m.* first-born; **primogenitura** [pri·mo·xe·ni·tú·ra] *f.* birthright; rights of the first-born.

primor [pri·mór] *m.* beauty; excellence; exquisiteness; skill, ability.

primordial [pri·mor·djál] *adj.* primordial.

primoroso [pri·mo·ró·so] *adj.* excellent, fine, exquisite; skillful.

prímula [prí·mu·la] *f.* primrose.

princesa [prin·sé·sa] *f.* princess.

principal [prin·si·pál] *adj.* principal; renowned, famous; **piso** — main floor (*usually, the second floor*); *m.* principal, capital sum; chief, head.

príncipe [prín·si·pe] *m.* prince; *adj.* princeps, first (*edition*).

principiante [prin·si·pján·te] *m.* beginner.

principiar [prin·si·pjár] *v.* to begin.

principio [prin·sí·pjo] *m.* principle; beginning; origin, source; entrée (*main dinner course*); **a -s de** towards the beginning of.

pringar⁷ [prin·gár] *v. irr.* to dip (*in grease*).

pringoso [prin·gó·so] *adj.* greasy.

pringue [prin·ge] *m.* & *f.* grease drippings (*from bacon, ham, etc.*).

prioridad [prjó·ri·dád] *f.* priority; precedence.

PR

prisa [prí·sa] *f.* speed, haste; **de** (*or* **a**) — quickly, speedily; **a toda** — with the greatest speed; **eso corre** — that is urgent; **dar** — **a** to hurry; **darse** — to hurry; **tener** (*or* **estar de**) — to be in a hurry.
prisión [pri·sjón] *f.* prison; imprisonment; seizure; shackle; **-es** shackles, fetters, chains.
prisionero [pri·sjo·né·ro] *m.* prisoner.
prisma [príz·ma] *f.* prism.
pristino [pris·tí·no] *adj.* first, early, former, primitive.
privación [pri·βa·sjón] *f.* privation; want, lack; loss.
privado [pri·βá·do] *adj.* private; personal; unconscious; *p.p.* deprived; *m.* favorite.
privar [pri·βár] *v.* (*destituir*) to deprive; to prohibit; (*tener aceptación*) to enjoy the favor of someone; to be in vogue; **-le a uno del sentido** to stun, daze; **ya no privan esas costumbres** those customs are no longer in vogue or in existence; **-se** to lose consciousness; **-se de** to deprive oneself of.
privativo [pri·βa·tí·βo] *adj.* exclusive; particular, distinctive.
privilegiado [pri·βi·le·xjá·do] *adj.* privileged.
privilegiar [pri·βi·le·xjár] *v.* to favor; to give a privilege to.
privilegio [pri·βi·lé·xjo] *m.* privilege; exemption; patent; copyright; — **de invención** patent on an invention.
pro [pro] *m. & f.* profit, advantage; **en — de** on behalf of; **en — y en contra** pro and con, for and against; **hombre de** — man of worth.
proa [pró·a] *f.* prow.
probabilidad [pro·βa·βi·li·dád] *f.* probability.
probable [pro·βá·ble] *adj.* probable.
probar[2] [pro·βár] *v. irr.* (*examinar*) to test; to taste; to prove; to try; to try on; (*gustar*) to suit, agree with; **no me prueba el clima** the climate does not agree with me.
probeta [pro·βé·ta] *f.* test tube; pressure gauge.
probidad [pro·βi·dád] *f.* integrity, uprightness, honesty.
problema [pro·βlé·ma] *m.* problem.
problemático [pro·βle·má·ti·ko] *adj.* problematic.
procedente [pro·se·dén·te] *adj.* proceeding (from), originating; according to law.
proceder [pro·se·dér] *v.* to proceed; to originate; to behave; to take action (against); *m.* behavior, conduct.
procedimiento [pro·se·di·mjén·to] *m.* procedure; method; process; conduct.
prócer [pró·ser] *m.* distinguished person; hero; great statesman.
procesado [pro·se·sá·do] *p.p. & adj.* relating to, or included in, a lawsuit; accused, prosecuted; *m.* defendant.
procesar [pro·se·sár] *v.* to prosecute; to accuse; to indict; to sue.
procesión [pro·se·sjón] *f.* procession; parade.
proceso [pro·sé·so] *m.* process; lawsuit, legal proceedings; lapse of time; — **verbal** minutes, record.
proclama [pro·klá·ma] *f.* proclamation, ban; marriage banns.
proclamación [pro·kla·ma·sjón] *f.* proclamation.
proclamar [pro·kla·már] *v.* to proclaim.
proclítico [pro·klí·ti·ko] *adj.* proclitic.
procurador [pro·ku·ra·dór] *m.* attorney.
procurar [pro·ku·rár] *v.* (*pretender*) to try, endeavor; (*obtener*) to procure, obtain, get.
prodigar[7] [pro·di·gár] *v.* to lavish; to bestow

upon; to squander, waste.
prodigio [pro·dí·xjo] *m.* prodigy, wonder, marvel; miracle.
prodigioso [pro·di·xjóso] *adj.* prodigious, marvelous; fine, exquisite.
pródigo [pró·di·go] *adj.* prodigal, wasteful; lavish; generous; *m.* spendthrift.
producción [pro·duk·sjón] *f.* production; produce.
producir[25] [pro·du·sír] *v. irr.* to produce; to bring about; to yield; **-se** to express oneself, explain oneself; *Col., Ven.* to occur, happen.
productivo [pro·duk·tí·βo] *adj.* productive; fruitful; profitable.
producto [pro·dúk·to] *m.* product; yield; result.
productor [pro·duk·tór] *m.* producer; *adj.* producing, productive.
proeza [pro·é·sa] *f.* prowess; *Col.* boast, exaggeration.
profanación [pro·fa·na·sjón] *f.* profanation.
profanar [pro·fa·nár] *v.* to profane; to defile.
profano [pro·fá·no] *adj.* profane, not sacred; irreverent; lay, uninformed (*about a branch of learning*).
profecía [pro·fe·sí·a] *f.* prophecy; prediction.
proferir[3] [pro·fe·rír] *v. irr.* to utter, express, speak.
profesar [pro·fe·sár] *v.* to profess; to avow, confess.
profesión [pro·fe·sjón] *f.* profession; avowal, declaration.
profesional [pro·fe·sjo·nál] *adj., m. & f.* professional.
profesionista [pro·fe·sjo·nís·ta] *m. & f. Am.* professional.
profesor [pro·fe·sór] *m.* professor, teacher; **profesorado** [pro·fe·so·rá·do] *m.* faculty; body of teachers; teaching profession; professorship.
profeta [pro·fé·ta] *m.* prophet.
profético [pro·fé·ti·ko] *adj.* prophetic.
profetizar[9] [pro·fe·ti·sár] *v.* to prophesy.
proficiente [pro·fi·sjén·te] *adj.* proficient, skilled.
profilaxis [pro·fi·lák·sis] *f.* prophylaxis (*disease prevention*).
prófugo [pró·fu·go] *adj. & m.* fugitive.
profundidad [pro·fun·di·dád] *f.* profundity, depth.
profundizar[9] [pro·fun·di·sár] *v.* to deepen; to go deep into.
profundo [pro·fún·do] *adj.* profound; deep; low.
profuso [pro·fú·so] *adj.* profuse; lavish.
progenitor [pro·xe·ni·tór] *m.* progenitor.
programa [pro·grá·ma] *m.* program; plan.
programar [pro·gra·már] *v.* to plan; to program.
progresar [pro·gre·sár] *v.* to progress.
progresista [pro·gre·sís·ta] *m., & f. & adj.* progressive.
progresivo [pro·gre·sí·βo] *adj.* progressive.
progreso [pro·gré·so] *m.* progress.
prohibición [proj·βi·sjón] *f.* prohibition; ban.
prohibir [proj·βír] *v.* to prohibit, forbid.
prohijar [pro·i·xár] *v.* to adopt.
prójimo [pró·xi·mo] *m.* neighbor, fellow being; *Ríopl., Carib., C.A.* **ese** — that fellow.
prole [pró·le] *f.* progeny, offspring.
proletariado [pro·le·ta·rjá·do] *m.* proletariat, working class.
proletario [pro·le·tá·rjo] *adj.* proletarian, belonging to the working class; plebeian; *m.* proletarian.
prolijo [pro·lí·xo] *adj.* prolix, too long, drawn out, too detailed; boring, tedious.
prologar[7] [pro·lo·gár] *v.* to preface, write a preface for.
prólogo [pró·lo·go] *m.* prologue.
prolongación [pro·loŋ·ga·sjón] *f.* prolongation,

extension; lengthening.
prolongar[7] [pro·lon·gár] *v.* to prolong, lengthen, extend.
promediar [pro·me·djár] *v.* to average; to divide or distribute into two equal parts; to mediate; **antes de — el mes** before the middle of the month.
promedio [pro·mé·djo] *m.* middle; average.
promesa [pro·mé·sa] *f.* promise.
prometedor [pro·me·te·dór] *adj.* promising, hopeful.
prometer [pro·me·tér] *v.* to promise; to show promise; *Ríopl., C.A.* to affirm, assure; **-se** to become engaged, betrothed.
prometido [pro·me·tí·do] *adj. & p.p.* betrothed; *m.* fiancé, betrothed; promise.
prominente [pro·mi·nén·te] *adj.* prominent.
promiscuo [pro·mís·kwo] *adj.* promiscuous.
promisorio [pro·mi·só·rjo] *adj.* promissory.
promoción [pro·mo·sjón] *f.* promotion, advancement.
promontorio [pro·mon·tó·rjo] *m.* promontory, headland, cape; anything bulky; bulge.
promotor [pro·mo·tór] *m.* promoter.
promovedor [pro·mo·be·dór] *m.* promoter.
promover[2] [pro·mo·bér] *v. irr.* to promote; to advance.
promulgación [pro·mul·ga·sjón] *f.* promulgation, publication, proclamation (*of a law*).
promulgar[7] [pro·mul·gár] *v.* to promulgate, proclaim, announce publicly.
pronombre [pro·nóm·bre] *m.* pronoun.
pronominal [pro·no·mi·nál] *adj.* pronominal.
pronosticar[6] [pro·nos·ti·kár] *v.* to prophesy, predict.
pronóstico [pro·nós·ti·ko] *m.* forecast; prediction; omen.
prontitud [pron·ti·túd] *f.* promptness; quickness.
pronto [prón·to] *adj.* quick, speedy; ready; prompt; *adv.* soon; quickly; **de —** suddenly; **al —** at first; **por de** (*or* **por lo**) — for the present; *m.* sudden impulse.
pronunciación [pro·nun·sja·sjón] *f.* pronunciation.
pronunciar [pro·nun·sjár] *v.* to pronounce; to utter; **-se** to rise up in rebellion.
propagación [pro·pa·ga·sjón] *f.* propagation, spread, spreading.
propaganda [pro·pa·gán·da] *f.* propaganda; advertising.
propagar[7] [pro·pa·gár] *v.* to propagate, reproduce; to spread.
propalar [pro·pa·lár] *v.* to spread (*news*).
propasarse [pro·pa·sár·se] *v.* to overstep one's bounds; to exceed one's authority, go too far.
propensión [pro·pen·sjón] *f.* tendency, inclination; bent, natural tendency or ability.
propenso [pro·pén·so] *adj.* prone, susceptible, inclined.
propiciar [pro·pi·sjár] *v.* to calm one's anger; *Am.* to propose.
propicio [pro·pí·sjo] *adj.* propitious, favorable.
propiedad [pro·pje·dád] *f.* property; ownership; attribute, quality; propriety, appropriateness.
propietario [pro·pje·tá·rjo] *m.* proprietor, owner.
propina [pro·pí·na] *f.* tip (*voluntary gift of money for service*).
propinar [pro·pi·nár] *v.* to give (*something to drink*); to give (*a beating, kick, slap*); *Am.* to tip, give a tip to; **— una paliza** to give a beating.
propio [pró·pjo] *adj.* proper; suitable; own; same; **amor —** vanity, pride, self-esteem; *m.* messenger.
proponer[40] [pro·po·nér] *v. irr.* to propose; to

resolve; to present; **-se** to resolve, make a resolution.
proporción [pro·por·sjón] *f.* proportion; dimension; ratio; opportunity, chance.
proporcionar [pro·por·sjo·nár] *v.* to proportion; to adapt, adjust; to furnish, supply; give.
proposición [pro·po·si·sjón] *f.* proposition; proposal; assertion.
propósito [pro·pó·si·to] *m.* purpose, aim, design; **a —** apropos, suitable, fitting; by the way; **de —** on purpose; **fuera de —** irrelevant, beside the point.
propuesto [pro·pwés·to] *f.* proposal, offer; proposition.
propuesto [pro·pwés·to] *p.p. of* **proponer**.
propulsar [pro·pul·sár] *v.* to propel.
propulsión [pro·pul·sjón] *f.* propulsion; **— a chorro** (*por reacción*) jet propulsion; **— a cohete** rocket propulsion.
propulsor [pro·pul·sór] *m.* propeller; *adj.* propelling; *m.* propelling force.
prorratear [pro·rra·te·ár] *v.* to prorate, distribute or assess proportionally; to average.
prorrateo [pro·rra·té·o] *m.* apportionment, proportional distribution.
prórroga [pró·rro·ga] *f.* renewal, extension of time.
prorrogar[7] [pro·rro·gár] *v.* to put off, postpone; to adjourn; to extend (*time limit*).
prorrumpir [pro·rrum·pír] *v.* to break forth; **— en llanto** to burst into tears; **— en una carcajada** to let out a big laugh.
prosa [pró·sa] *f.* prose.
prosaico [pro·sáj·ko] *adj.* prosaic; dull; tedious.
proscribir[52] [pros·kri·bír] *v.* to proscribe, banish; to outlaw.
proscripción [pros·krip·sjón] *f.* banishment.
proscripto [pros·krip·to], **proscrito** [pros·krí·to] *p.p. of* **proscribir**; *m.* exile, outlaw.
proseguir[5, 12] [pro·se·gír] *v. irr.* to continue; to follow.
prosélito [pro·sé·li·to] *m.* proselyte.
prosódico [pro·só·di·ko] *adj.* prosodic.
prosperar [pros·pe·rár] *v.* to prosper.
prosperidad [pros·pe·ri·dád] *f.* prosperity; success.
próspero [prós·pe·ro] *adj.* prosperous; successful.
próstata [prós·ta·ta] *f.* prostate.
prostituir[32] [pros·ti·twír] *v.* to prostitute, corrupt.
prostituta [pros·ti·tú·ta] *f.* prostitute.
protagonista [pro·ta·go·nis·ta] *m. & f.* protagonist (*main character or actor*).
protección [pro·tek·sjón] *f.* protection; support.
proteccionista [pro·tek·sjo·nis·ta] *adj.* protective; **tarifa —** protective tariff; *m. & f.* protectionist (*follower of the economic principles of protection*).
protector [pro·tek·tór] *m.* protector, guardian; *adj.* protecting, protective.
protectorado [pro·tek·to·rá·do] *m.* protectorate.
proteger[11] [pro·te·xér] *v.* to protect; to shelter; to defend.
protegido [pro·te·xi·do] *m.* protege.
proteína [pro·te·í·na] *f.* protein.
proteínico [pro·te·í·ni·ko] *adj.* related to the proteins.
protesta [pro·tés·ta] *f.* protest; protestation.
protestación [pro·tes·ta·sjón] *f.* protestation, solemn declaration; protest.
protestante [pro·tes·tán·te] *m.* Protestant; one who protests.
protestar [pro·tes·tár] *v.* (*confesar*) to assert, assure; to avow publicly; (*negar*) to protest;

PR

— **una letra** to protest a draft.
protocolo [pro·to·kó·lo] *m.* protocol.
protón [pro·tón] *m.* proton.
protoplasma [pro·to·pláz·ma] *m.* protoplasm.
protuberancia [pro·tu·ƀe·rán·sja] *f.* protuberance, bulge.
protuberante [pro·tu·ƀe·rán·te] *adj.* protuberant, prominent, bulging.
provecho [pro·ƀé·čo] *m.* profit; benefit; utility; advantage; **hombre de** — worthy, useful man.
provechoso [pro·ƀe·čó·so] *adj.* profitable; useful; beneficial; advantageous.
proveedor [pro·ƀe·e·ɖór] *m.* provisioner, provider; supply man.
proveer[14, 52] [pro·ƀe·ér] *v. irr.* to provide; to supply; to confer, bestow; to decide; **-se de** to supply oneself with.
provenir[48] [pro·ƀe·nír] *v. irr.* to originate, arise, come (from).
proverbio [pro·ƀer·ƀjo] *m.* proverb.
providencia [pro·ƀi·ɖén·sja] *f.* providence; foresight; Providence, God; legal decision, sentence; provision, measure; **tomar una** — to take a step or measure.
providencial [pro·ƀi·ɖen·sjál] *adj.* providential.
provincia [pro·ƀín·sja] *f.* province.
provincial [pro·ƀin·sjál] *adj.* provincial.
provinciano [pro·ƀin·sjá·no] *adj.* & *m.* provincial.
provisión [pro·ƀi·sjón] *f.* provision; supply, stock.
provisional [pro·ƀi·sjo·nál] *adj.* temporary; provisional.
provisorio [pro·ƀi·só·rjo] *adj.* provisional, temporary.
provisto [pro·ƀís·to] *p.p. of* **proveer**.
provocación [pro·ƀo·ka·sjón] *f.* provocation; dare, defiance.
provocador [pro·ƀo·ka·ɖór] *adj.* provoking; — provoker.
provocar[6] [pro·ƀo·kár] *v.* to provoke; to excite, rouse; to stimulate.
provocativo [pro·ƀo·ka·tí·ƀo] *adj.* provocative.
proximidad [prok·si·mi·ɖáɖ] *f.* proximity, nearness.
próximo [prók·si·mo] *adj.* next; neighboring; near; **del** — **pasado** of last month.
proyección [pro·yek·sjón] *f.* projection; jut.
proyectar [pro·yek·tár] *v.* to project; to plan; to throw; to cast; **-se** to be cast (*as a shadow*).
proyectil [pro·yek·tíl] *m.* projectile.
proyectista [pro·yek·tís·ta] *m.* & *f.* designer; schemer, planner.
proyecto [pro·yék·to] *m.* project; plan; — **de ley** bill (*in a legislature*).
prudencia [pru·ɖén·sja] *f.* prudence, practical wisdom, discretion.
prudente [pru·ɖén·te] *adj.* prudent, wise, discreet.
prueba [prwé·ƀa] *f.* proof; trial; test; fitting; sample; evidence; *Andes, Ríopl., Col., C.A.* acrobatic performance, stunt, trick, sleight of hand; **a** — **de incendio** fireproof.
prurito [pru·rí·to] *m.* itch; keen desire.
psicología [si·ko·lo·xí·a] *f. see* **sicología**.
psicosis [si·kó·sis] *f. see* **sicosis**.
psiquiatría [si·kja·trí·a] *f. see* **siquiatría**.
psitacosis [si·ta·kó·sis] *f. see* **sitacosis**.
ptomaína [toma·í·na] *f.* ptomaine.
púa [pú·a] *f.* prick; barb; prong; thorn; quill (*of a porcupine, etc.*); sharp, cunning person; *Ríopl.* cock's spur; **alambre de -s** barbed wire.
publicación [pu·ƀli·ka·sjón] *f.* publication.
publicar[6] [pu·ƀli·kár] *v.* to publish; to reveal; to announce.

publicidad [pu·ƀli·si·ɖáɖ] *f.* publicity.
público [pú·ƀli·ko] *adj.* & *m.* public.
puchero [pu·čé·ro] *m.* pot, kettle; meat and vegetable stew; pout; **hacer -s** to pout.
pucho [pú·čo] *m.* cigar or cigarette butt; *C.A.* something of little value.
pudiente [pu·ɖjén·te] *adj.* powerful; rich, wealthy; *m.* man of means.
pudín [pu·ɖín] *m.* pudding.
pudor [pu·ɖór] *m.* modesty; shyness.
pudrir[16] [pu·ɖrír] *v.* to rot; to vex, annoy; **-se** to rot.
pueblero [pwe·ƀlé·ro] *m. Ríopl.* townsman (*as opposed to countryman*).
pueblo [pwé·ƀlo] *m.* town, village; people, race, nation; populace; common people.
puente [pwén·te] *m.* bridge; *Carib., Mex., Ríopl.* dental bridge; *Am.* knife and fork rest; — **colgante** suspension bridge; — **levadizo** drawbridge.
puerca [pwér·ka] *f.* sow.
puerco [pwér·ko] *m.* pig, hog; — **espín** porcupine; — **jabalí** wild boar; *adj.* filthy, dirty; coarse, ill-bred.
pueril [pwe·ríl] *adj.* puerile, childish.
puerro [pwé·rro] *m.* scallion.
puerta [pwér·ta] *f.* door; gate; entrance; — **accessoria** (**excusada,** *or* **falsa**) side door; — **de golpe** spring door; trap door; — **franca** open door; free entrance or entry; — **trasera** back door; **a** — **cerrada** secretly, behind closed doors; *Am.* **en** — in view, in sight, very near.
puerto [pwér·to] *m.* port; harbor; refuge; mountain pass; — **franco** free port.
puertorriqueño [pwer·to·rri·ké·ño] *adj.* & *m.* Puerto Rican.
pues [pwes] *conj.* since, because, for, inasmuch as; then; *adv.* then; well; — **bien** well then, well; — **que** since.
puesta [pwés·ta] *f.* set, setting (*of a star or planet*); stake at cards; — **de sol** sunset.
puestero [pwes·té·ro] *m. Carib., Mex., Ríopl.* vendor, seller (*at a stand or stall*); *Ríopl.* man in charge of livestock on Argentine ranches.
puesto [pwés·to] *p.p. of* **poner** placed, put, set; **mal** (*or* **bien**) — badly (*or* well) dressed; *m.* place; vendor's booth or stand; post, position, office; military post; *Andes, Ríopl.* station for watching and taking care of cattle on a ranch; — **de socorros** first-aid station; — **que** *conj.* since.
pugilato [pu·xi·lá·to] *m.* boxing.
pugilista [pu·xi·lís·ta] *m.* boxer, prize fighter.
pugna [púg·na] *f.* struggle; conflict; **estar en** — **con** to be in conflict with; to be opposed to.
pugnar [pug·nár] *v.* to fight; to struggle; to strive; to persist.
pujanza [pu·xán·sa] *f.* push, force, power.
pujar [pu·xár] *v.* to make a strenuous effort; to grope for words; to falter; to outbid (*offer a higher bid than*); *C.A.* to grunt; *Am.* to reject; *Ven.* to dismiss; *Am.* — **para adentro** to forbear, keep silent; *Am.* **andar pujado** to go around crestfallen; to be in disgrace.
pujido [pu·xí·ɖo] *m. Am.* grunt (*due to strenuous effort*).
pulcritud [pul·kri·túɖ] *f.* neatness, trimness; excellence, perfection.
pulcro [púl·kro] *adj.* neat, trim; beautiful.
pulga [púl·ga] *f.* flea; *Ríopl.* small and insignificant person; **tener malas -s** to be illtempered; *Col.,*

Andes **ser de pocas -s** to be touchy, oversensitive; **pulgón** *m.* blight, plant louse.
pulgada [pul·gá·ḍa] *f.* inch.
pulgar [pul·gár] *m.* thumb.
pulguero [pul·gé·ro] *m.* jail (*slang*).
pulido [pu·li·ḍo] *adj.* polished, refined; polite; neat; exquisite.
pulidor [pu·li·ḍór] *adj.* polishing; *m.* polisher.
pulimentar [pu·li·men·tár] *v.* to polish.
pulimento [pu·li·mén·to] *m.* polish; gloss.
pulir [pu·lír] *v.* to polish.
pulmón [pul·món] *m.* lung.
pulmonar [pul·mo·nár] *adj.* pulmonary, pertaining to the lungs.
pulmonía [pul·mo·ní·a] *f.* pneumonia.
pulpa [púl·pa] *f.* pulp; boneless meat.
pulpería [pul·pe·rí·a] *f. Riopl., C.A., Ch., Ven., Andes* country general store; *Am.* tavern.
pulpero [pul·pé·ro] *m. Riopl., C.A., Ch., Ven., Andes* owner of a country store or tavern.
púlpito [púl·pi·to] *m.* pulpit.
pulpo [púl·po] *m.* octopus.
pulque [púl·ke] *m. Mex.* pulque (*fermented juice of the maguey*).
pulquería [pul·ke·rí·a] *f. Mex.* pulque bar or *cantina.*
pulsación [pul·sa·sjón] *f.* pulsation, beat, throb; pulse, beating.
pulsar [pul·sár] *v.* to pulsate, throb, beat; to feel the pulse of; to sound out; examine; to play (*the harp*); *Mex., C.A.* to judge or try the weight of (*by lifting*).
pulsera [pul·sé·ra] *f.* bracelet; wrist bandage; **reloj de —** wrist watch.
pulso [púl·so] *m.* pulse; steadiness; tract; *Riopl., Carib., Col.* bracelet, wrist watch; **un hombre de —** a prudent, steady man; *Cuba, Mex.* **beber a —** to drink straight down, gulp down; **levantar a —** to lift with the strength of the wrist or hand; **sacar a — un negocio** to carry out a deal by sheer perseverance.
pulsorreactor [pul·so·rre·ak·tór] *m.* jet engine of movable intake valves.
pulular [pu·lu·lár] *v.* to swarm; to multiply rapidly; to sprout, bud.
pulverizar[9] [pul·ḅe·ri·sár] *v.* to pulverize.
pulla [pú·ya] *f.* taunt; mean dig, quip, cutting remark; filthy word or remark.
puma [pú·ma] *f.* puma, mountain lion.
puna [pú·na] *f. Andes* cold, arid tableland of the Andes; *Riopl.* desert; *Andes* sickness caused by high altitude.
pundonor [pun·do·nór] *m.* point of honor.
púnico [pú·ni·ko] *adj.* Punic.
punta [pún·ta] *f.* point, tip; bull's horn; cigar or cigarette butt; *Ven.,* gang, band, herd, a lot (*of things, people, etc.*); *Am.* small leaf of fine tobacco; *Am.* jeer, cutting remark; **-s** point lace; scallops; **de — on end; de -s** (*or* **de puntillas**) on tiptoe; *Am.* **a — de** by dint of, by means of; **estar de — con** to be on bad terms with; **sacar — a un lápiz** to sharpen a pencil; **tener sus -s de poeta** to be something of a poet.
puntada [pun·ta·ḍa] *f.* stitch; hint; *Andes* prick, pricking, sting, sharp pain; **no he dado — en este asunto** I have left this matter completely untouched.
puntal [pun·tál] *m.* prop; support, basis; bull's horn; *Col.* snack (*between meals*).
puntapié [pun·ta·pjé] *m.* kick (*with the toe of the shoe.*)

puntazo [pun·tá·so] *m. Col., Ven., Mex., Cuba* stab, jab.
puntear [pun·te·ár] *v.* to pluck (*the strings of a guitar*); to play (*a guitar*); to make dots; to engrave, draw or paint by means of dots; to stitch; to tack (*said of a boat*).
puntería [pun·te·rí·a] *f.* aim.
puntero [pun·té·ro] *m.* pointer; chisel; blacksmith's punch; *C.A., Col., Ch.* clock or watch hand; *Am.* leader of a parade; *Cuba, Mex., Ven., Col.* leading ox (*or other animal*); *Am.* guide.
pentiagudo [pun·tja·ǵu·ḍo] *adj.* sharp, sharp-pointed.
puntilla [pun·tí·ya] *f.* small point; tip; small dagger; tracing point; point lace; *Ven.* penknife; *Am.* toe rubber; *Am.* ridge (*of a hill*); **de -s** on tiptoe; **puntillazo** *m.* stab (*with a dagger*).
punto [pún·to] *m.* (*parada*) period; stop; point; dot; (*puntada*) stitch; mesh; (*sitio*) place; moment; (*mira*) gun sight; **— de admiración** exclamation mark; **— de interrogación** question mark; **— y coma** semicolon; **dos -s** colon; **al — at once, immediately; a — de** on the point of; **de —** knitted, porous knit, stockinet or jersey weave; **en —** exactly, on the dot; **a — fijo** with certainty; **subir de —** to increase or get worse.
puntuación [pun·twa·sjón] *f.* punctuation.
puntual [pun·twál] *adj.* punctual, prompt; exact.
puntualidad [pun·twa·li·ḍáḍ] *f.* punctuality, promptness; certainty.
puntuar[18] [pun·twár] *v.* to punctuate.
punzada [pun·sá·ḍa] *f.* puncture; prick; sharp pain.
punzante [pun·sán·te] *adj.* sharp; pricking; piercing, penetrating.
punzar[9] [pun·sár] *v.* to puncture; to sting; to prick; to punch, perforate.
punzón [pun·són] *m.* punch, puncher; pick; awl.
puñada [pu·ñá·ḍa] *f.* punch, box, blow with the fist.
puñado [pu·ñá·ḍo] *m.* fistful, handful; **a -s** abundantly; by handfuls.
puñal [pu·ñál] *m.* dagger.
puñalada [pu·ña·la·ḍa] *f.* stab; sharp pain; **coser a -s** to stab to death.
puñetazo [pu·ñe·tá·so] *m.* punch, blow with the fist.
puño [pú·ño] *m.* fist; fistful, handful; cuff; hilt, handle; *Ven., Col.* blow with the fist; **a — cerrado** firmly; **ser como un —** to be stingy; **tener -s** to be strong, courageous.
pupila [pu·pi·la] *f.* pupil (*of the eye*).
pupilo [pu·pi·lo] *m.* ward; boarding-school pupil; boarder.
pupitre [pu·pí·tre] *m.* desk, school desk.
puré [pu·ré] *m.* purée, thick soup.
pureza [pu·ré·sa] *f.* purity; chastity.
purga [púr·ga] *f.* purge, laxative, physic.
purgante [pur·gán·te] *adj.* purgative, laxative; *m.* purgative, physic, laxative.
purgar[7] [pur·gár] *v.* to purge; to purify; to atone for; **-se** to purge oneself; to take a laxative.
purgatorio [pur·ga·tó·rjo] *m.* purgatory.
purificar[6] [pu·ri·fi·kár] *v.* to purify.
purista [pu·rís·ta] *m. & f.* purist.
puro [pú·ro] *adj.* (*limpio*) pure; clean; chaste; (*sólo*) mere, only, sheer; **a pura fuerza** by sheer force; **a puros gritos** by just shouting; *m.* cigar.
púrpura [púr·pu·ra] *f.* purple; purple cloth.
purpúreo [pur·pú·re·o] *adj.* purple.
pus [pus] *m.* pus.
pusilánime [pu·si·lá·ni·me] *adj.* pusillanimous.
puta [pú·ta] *f.* whore, prostitute.
putativo [pu·ta·tí·ḅo] *adj.* reputed, supposed; **padre**

— foster father.

putrefacción [pu·tre·fak·sjón] *f.* putrefaction, decay, rotting.

putrefacto [pu·tre·fák·to] *adj.* putrid, rotten, decayed.

puya [pú·ya] *f.* goad; lance head.

Q:q

que [ke] *rel. pron.* that; which; who; whom; **el** — who; which; the one who; the one which; *conj.* that; for, because; **más (menos)** — more (less) than; **el mismo** — the same as; — (= *subj.*) let, may you, I hope that; **por mucho** no matter how much; **quieras** — no whether you wish or not.

qué [ke] *interr. adj. & pron.* what?; what a!; *interr. adv.* how; **¡**— **bonito!** how beautiful!; **¿a** —? what for?; **¿para** —? what for?; **¿por** —? why?; **¿** — **tal?** how?; hello!; **¡**— **más da!** what's the difference!; **¡a mí** —! so what! and what's that to me!

quebracho [ke·ƀrá·čo] *m.* quebracho, breakax wood.

quebrada [ke·ƀrá·ɖa] *f.* ravine; gorge; failure, bankruptcy; *Ríopl., Col., Ven., C.A., Mex.* brook.

quebradizo [ke·ƀra·ɖi·so] *adj.* breakable; brittle; fragile; delicate.

quebrado [ke·ƀrá·ɖo] *adj.* broken; weakened; ruptured; bankrupt; rough or rugged (*ground*); *m.* common fraction; *Ven.* navigable waters between reefs.

quebrantar [ke·ƀran·tár] *v.* to break; to break open; to pound, crush; to violate (*a law*); to weaken; to vex; *Mex., Col.* to tame, break in (*a colt*); — **el agua** to take the chill off the water.

quebranto [ke·ƀrán·to] *m.* breaking; grief, affliction; discouragement; damage, loss.

quebrar[1] [ke·ƀrár] *v. irr.* to break; to crush; to interrupt; to wither (*said of the complexion*); to become bankrupt; **-se** to break; to get broken; to be ruptured; **-se uno la cabeza** to rack one's brain.

quebrazón [ke·ƀra·són] *m. Ven., Col.* breakage, breaking.

quechua [ké·čwa] *adj. Am.* Quichuan; *m. & f.* Quichua, Quichuan Indian; *m.* Quichuan language.

quedar [ke·ɖár] *v.* to stay; to remain; to be left over; to be left (*in a state or condition*); — **en** to agree to; *Am.* — **de** to agree to; — **bien** to acquit oneself well; to come out well; *Am.* to suit, become (*said of a dress, hat, etc.*); *Am.* — **bien con alguien** to please someone; **-se** to remain; **-se con una cosa** to keep something; to take something (*buy it*); *Am.* **-se como si tal cosa** to act as if nothing had happened.

quedo [ké·ɖo] *adj.* quiet, still; gentle; *adv.* softly; in a low voice; **quedito** [ke·ɖi·to] *adj.* nice and quiet; *adv.* very softly.

quehacer [ke·a·sér] *m.* work, occupation; task, duty, chore.

queja [ké·xa] *f.* complaint; groan, moan; grudge.

quejarse [ke·xár·se] *v.* to complain; to grumble; to moan; to lament.

quejido [ke·xí·ɖo] *m.* moan; groan.

quejoso [ke·xó·so] *adj.* complaining, whining.

quejumbre [ke·xúm·bre] *f.* whine, moan; murmur,

complaint; **-s** *m. Cuba, Ven.* grumbler, whiner; **quejumbroso** [ke·xum·bró·so] *adj.* whining, complaining.

quemada [ke·má·ɖa] *f.* burned forest; *Am.* burn.

quemado [ke·má·ɖo] *m.* burned portion of a forest; *Col.* burned field; *Am.* hot alcoholic drink; *adj.* dark, tan; *Am.* peeved, piqued; *Col., Ven., Cuba, Mex.* ruined; *p.p. of* **quemar.**

quemadura [ke·ma·ɖú·ra] *f.* burn; scald; smut (*plant disease*).

quemar [ke·már] *v.* to burn; to scald; to scorch; to sell at a loss; to annoy; *Am.* to deceive, swindle; **-se** to burn; to be hot.

quemazón [ke·ma·són] *f.* (*calor*) burn, burning; great heat; fire, conflagration; (*desazón*) pique, anger; bargain sale; *Am.* mirage on the pampas.

quena [ké·na] *f. Andes* flute of the Quechua Indians.

querella [ke·ré·ya] *f.* quarrel; complaint; controversy.

querellarse [ke·re·yár·se] *v.* to complain.

querencia [ke·rén·sja] *f.* affection; longing; favorite spot; haunt; stable.

querer[41] [ke·rér] *v. irr.* to want, wish, desire; to will; to be willing; to love; — **decir** to mean; **sin** — unwillingly; **no quiso hacerlo** he refused to do it; **quiere llover** it is trying to rain, it is about to rain; **como quiera** in any way; **como quiera que** since; no matter how; **cuando quiera** whenever; **donde quiera** wherever; anywhere; **-se** to love each other; *Ríopl., Ven., Col.* to be on the point of, be about to; **se quiere caer esa pared** that wall is about to fall.

querido [ke·rí·ɖo] *p.p.* wanted, desired; *adj.* beloved, dear; *m.* lover; **querida** *f.* darling; mistress.

queroseno [ke·ro·sé·no] *m. variant of* **keroseno.**

querubín [ke·ru·ƀín] *m.* cherub.

quesería [ke·se·rí·a] *f.* dairy, creamery, cheese factory; **quesera** [ke·sé·ra] *f.* dairy, cheese factory; cheese dish; dairymaid, woman cheese vendor or cheesemaker; **quesero** [ke·sé·ro] *adj.* pertaining to cheese; *m.* cheesemaker.

queso [ké·so] *m.* cheese; *Ven.* — **de higos** fig paste.

quetzal [ket·sál] *m.* bird of paradise; quetzal (*monetary unit of Guatemala*).

quicio [kí·sjo] *m.* hinge of a door; **sacar a uno de** — to exasperate someone.

quichua [kí·čwa] = **quechua.**

quiebra [kjé·ƀra] *f.* (*rotura*) break; crack; fissure; fracture; (*pérdida*) loss, damage; bankruptcy.

quien [kjen] *rel. pron.* who, whom; he who, she who; **quién** *interr. pron.* who? whom?

quienquiera [kjen·kjé·ra] *pron.* whoever, whosoever, whomsoever.

quieto [kjé·to] *adj.* quiet, still; calm.

quietud [kje·túɖ] *f.* quiet, stillness, calmness.

quijada [ki·xá·ɖa] *f.* jaw; jawbone.

quijotada [ki·xo·tá·ɖa] *f.* quixotic deed.

quilate [ki·lá·te] *m.* carat (*twenty-fourth part in weight and value of gold*); unit of weight for precious stones and pearls; **-s** qualities; degree of perfection or purity.

quilla [kí·ya] *f.* keel.

quimera [ki·mé·ra] *f.* absurd idea, wild fancy.

química [kí·mi·ka] *f.* chemistry.

químico [kí·mi·ko] *adj.* chemical; *m.* chemist.

quina [kí·na], **quinina** [ki·ní·na] *f.* quinine.

quincalla [kin·ká·ya] *f.* hardware.

quincallería [kin·ka·ye·rí·a] *f.* hardware; hardware store; hardware trade.

quincena [kin·sé·na] *f.* fortnight; semimonthly pay.
quinqué [kin·ké] *m.* oil lamp.
quinta [kín·ta] *f.* (*casa*) villa, country house; (*militar*) draft, military conscription; (*cartas*) sequence of five cards.
quintaesencia [kin·ta·e·sén·sja] *f.* quintessence, pure essence, purest form.
quiosco [kjós·ko] *m.* kiosk, small pavilion.
quirúrgico [ki·rúr·xi·ko] *adj.* surgical.
quisquilloso [kis·ki·yó·so] *adj.* touchy, oversensitive.
quisto [kís·to]: **bien —** well-liked, well received, welcome; **mal —** disliked; unwelcome.
quitamanchas [ki·ta·mán·čas] *m.* cleaner, stain remover.
quitar [ki·tár] *v.* to remove; to take away (off, *or* from); to rob of; to deprive of; to subtract; to parry (*in fencing*); **-se** to take off (*clothing*); to remove oneself, withdraw; **-se de una cosa** to give up something, get rid of something; **-se a alguien de encima** to get rid of someone; **¡quita allá!** don't tell me that!; **¡quítese de aquí!** get out of here!
quitasol [ki·ta·sól] *m.* large sunshade, parasol.
quite [kí·te] *m.* parry (*in fencing*); revenge; dodge, dodging; *Ven., Col., Mex.* **andar a los -s** to be on the defensive; to take offense easily; to be afraid of one's own shadow; **eso no tiene —** that can't be helped.
quizá [ki·sá], **quizás** [ki·sás] *adv.* perhaps, maybe.

R·r

rabadilla [rra·ba·dí·ya] *f.* end of the spinal column; tail of a fowl; rump.
rábano [rrá·ba·no] *m.* radish; **tomar el — por las hojas** to take one thing for another; to misinterpret something.
rabia [rrá·bja] *f.* rabies; rage; **tener — a alguien** to hate someone; *Ríopl., Carib., Mex.* **volarse de —** to get furious, angry.
rabiar [rra·bjár] *v.* to have rabies; to rage; to rave; to suffer a severe pain; **— por** to be dying to or for, be very eager to; **quema que rabia** it burns terribly.
rabieta [rra·bjé·ta] *f.* tantrum, fit of temper.
rabino [rra·bí·no] *m.* rabbi.
rabioso [rra·bjó·so] *adj.* rabid (*having rabies*), mad; furious, angry, violent.
rabo [rrá·bo] *m.* tail; **de cabo a —** from beginning to end; **mirar con el — del ojo** to look out of the corner of one's eye.
rabón [rra·bón] *m.* bobtail.
racimo [rra·si·mo] *m.* bunch; cluster.
raciocinio [rra·sjo·sí·njo] *m.* reasoning.
ración [rra·sjón] *f.* ration; allowance; supply.
racional [rra·sjo·nál] *adj.* rational; reasonable.
racionamiento [rra·sjo·na·mjén·to] *m.* rationing.
racionar [rra·sjo·nár] *v.* to ration.
racismo [rra·siz·mo] *m.* racism.
racista [rra·sís·ta] *m. & f.* racist.
radar [rra·dár] *m.* radar.
radaroscopio [rra·da·ros·kó·pjo] *m.* radarscope.
radiación [rra·dja·sjón] *f.* radiation; **— cósmica** cosmic radiation.
radiatividad [rra·djak·ti·bi·dáḍ] *f.* radioactivity.
radiactivo [rra·djak·ti·bo] *adj.* radioactive.
radiador [rra·dja·dór] *m.* radiator.
radiante [rra·dján·te] *adj.* radiant; shining;

beaming.
radiar [rra·djár] *v.* to radiate; to radio; to broadcast.
radical [rra·di·kál] *adj.* (*básico*) fundamental, basic; radical; (*extremista*) extreme; *m.* radical; root of a word.
radicalismo [rra·di·ka·líz·mo] *m.* radicalism.
radicar[6] [rra·di·kár] *v.* to take root; to be, be found (*in a certain place*); **-se** to take root; to locate, settle.
radio [rrá·djo] *m.* radius; radium; *m. & f.* radio.
radiodifundir [rra·djo·di·fun·dír] *v.* to broadcast by radio. See **difundir**.
radiodifusión [rra·djo·di·fu·sjón] *f.* broadcasting. See **difusión**.
radiodifusora [rra·djo·di·fu·só·ra], **radioemisora** [rra·djo·e·mi·só·ra] *f.* broadcasting station.
radioeléctrico [rra·djo·e·lék·tri·ko] *adj.* radioelectric.
radioescucha [rra·djo·es·kú·ča] *m. & f.* radio listener.
radiofónico [rra·djo·fó·ni·ko] *adj.* radio (*used as adj.*); **estación radiofónica** radio station.
radiografía [rra·djo·gra·fí·a] *f.* radiography, X-ray photography; X-ray picture.
radiografiar[17] [rra·djo·gra·fjár] *v.* to take X-ray pictures.
radiolocutor [rra·djo·lo·ku·tór] *m.* radio announcer. See **locutor**.
radiotelefonía [rra·djo·te·le·fo·ní·a] *f.* radiotelephony, radio, wireless.
radiotelegrafía [rra·djo·te·le·gra·fí·a] *f.* radiotelegraphy, radio, wireless telegraphy.
radiotransmisor [rra·djo·trans·mi·sór] *m.* radio transmitter.
radon [rra·don] *m.* radon.
radioyente [rra·djo·yén·te] = **radioescucha.**
raer[24] [rra·ér] *v. irr.* to scrape off; to rub off; to scratch off; to fray; to erase.
ráfaga [rrá·fa·ga] *f.* gust of wind; flash of light.
raído [rra·í·do] *p.p. & adj.* scraped off; rubbed off; frayed; worn, threadbare.
raigón [rraj·gón] *m.* large root; root of a tooth.
raíz [rra·ís] *f.* root; origin; foundation; **— cuadrada** square root; **a —** de close to, right after; **de —** by the roots, completely; **echar raíces** to take root, become firmly fixed.
raja [rrá·xa] *f.* slice; splinter; crack; split, crevice; **hacer -s** to slice; to tear into strips; to cut into splinters; **hacerse uno -s** to wear oneself out (*by dancing, jumping or any violent exercise*).
rajá [rra·xá] *m.* rajah.
rajadura [rra·xa·dú·ra] *f.* crack, crevice.
rajar [rra·xár] *v.* to split; to crack; to cleave; to slice; to chatter; to brag; *Col., Cuba, Mex., Andes* to defame, insult; *Col.* to flunk, fail (*a student*); **-se** to split open; to crack; *Mex.* to get afraid, back down.
rajatablas [rra·xa·tá·blas] *m. Col.* reprimand, scolding; **a —** in great haste.
ralea [rra·lé·a] *f.* breed, race, stock; species, kind.
ralear [rra·le·ár] *v.* to thin out, make less dense; to become less dense.
ralo [rrá·lo] *adj.* sparse, thin, thinly scattered.
rallador [rra·ya·dór] *m.* grater.
rallar [rra·yár] *v.* to grate; to grate on, annoy; *Am.* to goad, spur.
rama [rrá·ma] *f.* branch, limb; **en —** crude, raw; **andarse por las -s** to beat about the bush, not to stick to the point.
ramada [rra·má·da] *f.* branches, foliage; arbor;

Am. shed, tent.
ramaje [rra·má·xe] *m.* foliage; branches.
ramal [rra·mál] *m.* strand (*of a rope, etc.*); branch; branch railway line; halter.
rambla [rrám·bla] *f.* avenue (*especially in Barcelona*).
ramera [rra·mé·ra] *f.* harlot, prostitute.
ramificarse[6] [rra·mi·fi·kár·se] *v.* to branch off, divide into branches.
ramillete [rra·mi·yé·te] *m.* bouquet; flower cluster.
ramo [rrá·mo] *m.* bunch (*of flowers*), bouquet; line, branch (*of art, science, industry, etc.*); branch, bough; **domingo de -s** Palm Sunday.
ramonear [rra·mo·ne·ár] *v.* to cut off twigs or tips of branches; to nibble grass, twigs, or leaves; *Am.* to eat scraps or leftovers.
rampa [rrám·pa] *f.* ramp; apron (*airport*); — **de cohetes,** — **de lanzamiento** launching ramp.
ramplón [rram·plón] *adj.* coarse; crude, uncouth; slovenly.
ramplonería [rram·plo·ne·rí·a] *f.* coarse act or remark; crudeness, coarseness; slovenliness.
rana [rrá·na] *f.* frog.
rancio [rrán·sjo] *adj.* rancid, stale; old (*wine*); **linaje** — old, noble lineage.
ranchero [rran·čé·ro] *m. Mex.* rancher, farmer; **ranchería** [rran·če·rí·a] *f.* group of huts; *Col.* inn (*for* **arrieros**).
rancho [rrán·čo] *m.* camp; hamlet; mess (*meal for a group and the group itself*); *Carib., Ven., Col., Andes, Ríopl.* hut; *Carib., Ven., Col., Andes, Ríopl.* country house; *Mex.* ranch, small farm (*usually for cattle raising*).
rango [rraŋ·go] *m.* rank, position.
ranura [rra·nú·ra] *f.* groove; slot.
rapar [rra·pár] *v.* to shave off; to crop (*hair*); to strip bare, rob of everything.
rapaz [rra·pás] *adj.* rapacious, grasping, greedy; *m.* lad; **rapaza** *f.* lass, young girl.
rape [rrá·pe] *m.* quick or close haircut.
rapé [rra·pé] *m.* snuff (*pulverized tobacco*).
rapidez [rra·pi·dés] *f.* rapidity, speed.
rápido [rrá·pi·do] *adj.* rapid, swift; *m.* rapids.
rapiña [rra·pí·ña] *f.* plunder; **ave de** — bird of prey.
rapiñar [rra·pi·ñár] *v.* to plunder; to steal.
raposa [rra·pó·sa] *f.* fox.
raptar [rrap·tár] *v.* to kidnap, abduct.
rapto [rráp·to] *m.* (*delito*) abduction, kidnapping; (*sentimiento*) ecstasy, rapture; outburst.
raqueta [rra·ké·ta] *f.* racket (*used in games*); tennis.
raquítico [rra·kí·ti·ko] *adj.* rickety, feeble, weak, skinny, sickly.
rareza [rra·ré·sa] *f.* rarity; oddity; strangeness; freak; curiosity; queer act or remark; peculiarity; **por** — seldom.
raro [rrá·ro] *adj.* rare; thin, not dense; scarce; strange, odd; ridiculous; **rara vez** (*or* **raras veces**) rarely, seldom.
ras [rras] : **a** — **de** flush with, even with; **al** — **con** flush with; **estar** — **con** — to be flush, perfectly even.
rascacielos [rras·ka·sjé·los] *m.* skyscraper.
rascar[6] [rras·kár] *v.* to scratch; to scrape; *Andes* to dig up potatoes; *Am.* — **uno para adentro** to seek one's own advantage, look out for oneself.
rasete [rra·sé·te] *m.* sateen.
rasgado [rraz·gá·do] *adj.* torn; open; *Col.* generous; *Am.* outspoken; **ojos -s** large, wideopen eyes.

rasgadura [rraz·ga·dú·ra] *f.* tear, rip, rent.
rasgar[7] [rraz·gár] *v.* to tear; to rip.
rasgo [rráz·go] *m.* (*propiedad*) trait, characteristic; (*rúbrica*) stroke of the pen, flourish; (*hazaña*) feat; *Am.* irrigation ditch; *Ven.* **un** — **de terreno** a parcel of land; **-s** features; traits.
rasgón [rraz·gón] *m.* large tear, rent, rip.
rasguñar [rraz·gu·ñár] *v.* to scratch; to claw.
rasguño [rraz·gú·ño] *m.* scratch.
raso [rrá·so] *adj.* (*llano*) plain; flat, smooth; (*despejado*) clear, cloudless; *Ríopl., Mex.* even, level (*when measuring wheat, corn, etc.*); *Am.* scarce, scanty; **soldado** — private; **al** — in the open air; *m.* satin.
raspadura [rras·pa·dú·ra] *f.* scrape; scraping; erasure; shaving (*of wood or metal*).
raspar [rras·pár] *v.* to scrape, scrape off; to steal; *Andes* to scold, upbraid; *Col.* to leave.
rastra [rrás·tra] *f.* drag; sled; large rake; harrow; **a -s** dragging; unwillingly.
rastreador [rras·tre·a·dór] *m.* trailer, tracker, tracer.
rastrear [rras·tre·ár] *v.* to trail, track, trace; to rake, harrow; to drag (*a dragnet*); to skim, scrape the ground.
rastrero [rras·tré·ro] *adj.* low, vile.
rastrillar [rras·tri·yár] *v.* to rake; to comb (*flax or hemp*); *Ven.* to scrape; *Am.* to shoot; *Am.* to barter, exchange; *Am.* to pilfer, steal (*in stores*).
rastrillo [rras·trí·yo] *m.* rake; *Am.* barter, exchange; *Am.* business deal.
rastro [rrás·tro] *m.* track, trail, scent; trace, sign; rake, harrow; slaughterhouse.
rastrojo [rras·tró·xo] *m.* stubble.
rasura [rra·sú·ra] *f.* shave, shaving.
rasurar [rra·su·rár] *v.* to shave.
rata [rrá·ta] *f.* rat; *m.* pickpocket.
ratear [rra·te·ár] *v.* to pilfer; to pick pockets; to creep, crawl.
ratería [rra·te·rí·a] *f.* petty larceny; meanness.
ratero [rra·té·ro] *m.* pickpocket; *adj.* contemptible, mean.
ratificar[6] [rra·ti·fi·kár] *v.* to ratify.
rato [rrá·to] *m.* short time, little while; **buen** — pleasant time; long time; **-s perdidos** leisure hours; **a -s** at intervals, from time to time; **pasar el** — to while away the time, kill time; *Am.* ¡**hasta cada** —! so long!; see you later!
ratón [rra·tón] *m.* mouse; *Am.* **tener un** — to have a hangover; **ratonera** [rra·to·né·ra] *f.* mousetrap.
raudal [rraw·dál] *m.* torrent, downpour, flood; *Ríopl., Ch., Col., Ven., Andes* rapids.
raudo [rraw·do] *adj.* rapid swift.
raya [rrá·ya] *f.* line; dash; stripe; boundary line; part in the hair; *Mex.* pay, wage; *Mex.* **día de** — payday; **tener a** — to keep within bounds; to hold in check; **pasar de la** — to overstep one's bounds, take undue liberties; *m.* sting ray (*a species of fish*).
rayador [rra·ya·dór] *m. Mex.* paymaster; *Am.* umpire in a game.
rayar [rra·yár] *v.* to line, make lines on; to streak; to scratch, mark; to cross out; *Mex.* to pay or collect wages; *Am.* to stop a horse all of a sudden; *Am.* to spur a horse to run at top speed; — **el alba** to dawn; — **en** to border on; *Am.* **-se uno** to help oneself; to get rich.
rayo [rrá·yo] *m.* ray, beam; lightning, thunderbolt; spoke; **-s X** X-rays; **-s infrarrojos** infrared rays.
rayón [rra·yón] *m.* rayon.
raza [rrá·sa] *f.* race; clan; breed; fissure, crevice; **caballo de** — thoroughbred horse.

razón [rra·són] *f.* (*facultad*) reason; (*justicia*) right, justice; (*cuenta*) ratio; account, information, word, message; — **social** firm, firm name; **a** — **de** at the rate of; **icon** —! no wonder!; **dar** — to inform; **dar la** — **a una persona** to admit that a person is right; **perder la** — to lose one's mind; **poner en** — to pacify; **tener** — to be right.

razonable [rra·so·ná·ƀle] *adj.* reasonable.

razonamiento [rra·so·na·mjén·to] *m.* reasoning.

razonar [rra·so·nár] *v.* to reason; to discourse, talk; to argue.

re [rre] *m.* second note of the musical scale (*solfeggio*).

reabierto [rre·a·ƀjér·to] *p.p. of* **reabrir**.

reabrir[52] [rre·a·ƀrír] *v.* to reopen.

reacción [rre·ak·sjón] *f.* reaction; — **nuclear** nuclear reaction; — **en cadena** chain reaction.

reaccionar [rre·ak·sjo·nár] *v.* to react.

reaccionario [rre·ak·sjo·ná·rjo] *adj. & m.* reactionary.

reacio [rre·á·sjo] *adj.* stubborn, obstinate.

reactor [rre·ak·tór] *m.* reactor; — **atómico** atomic reactor; — **nuclear** nuclear reactor.

reajustar [rre·a·xus·tár] *v.* to readjust.

reajuste [rre·a·xús·te] *m.* readjustment.

real [rre·ál] *adj.* real; royal; *m.* army camp; fairground; real (*Spanish coin worth one fourth of a peseta*); **-es** *Andes* money (*in general*); **levantar el** — (*or* **los -es**) to break camp.

realce [rre·ál·se] *m.* (*adorno*) embossment, raised work, relief; (*lustre*) prestige; lustre, splendor; **dar** — to enhance; to emphasize.

realeza [rre·a·lé·sa] *f.* royalty (*royal dignity*).

realidad [rre·a·li·dád] *f.* reality; truth; fact; **en** — really, truly, in fact.

realismo [rre·a·líz·mo] *m.* realism; royalism.

realista [rre·a·lis·ta] *adj.* realistic; royalist; *m.* realist; royalist.

realización [rre·a·li·sa·sjón] *f.* realization, fulfillment; conversion into money, sale.

realizar[9] [rre·a·li·sár] *v.* to realize, fulfill, make real; to convert into money; to sell out.

realzar[9] [rre·al·sár] *v.* to emboss; to raise; to enhance; to make stand out; to emphasize.

reanimar [rre·a·ni·már] *v.* to revive; to comfort; to cheer; to encourage.

reanudación [rre·a·nu·da·sjón] *f.* renewal.

reanudar [rre·a·nu·dár] *v.* to renew, resume, begin again.

reaparecer[13] [rre·a·pa·re·sér] *v. irr.* to reappear.

reasumir [rre·a·su·mír] *v.* to resume.

reata [rre·á·ta] *f.* lariat, rope, lasso.

reavivar [rre·a·ƀi·ƀár] *v.* to revive.

rebaja [rre·ƀá·xa] *f.* deduction; reduction; discount.

rebajar [rre·ƀa·xár] *v.* to diminish; to lower, reduce; to tone down (*a painting*); to humiliate; **-se** to lower or humble oneself.

rebanada [rre·ƀa·ná·da] *f.* slice.

rebanar [rre·ƀa·nár] *v.* to slice.

rebaño [rre·ƀá·ño] *m.* flock; herd.

rebatir [rre·ƀa·tír] *v.* to beat over and over; to repel, resist; to refute; to rebut (*come back with an argument*); to argue; to parry (*in fencing*).

rebato [rre·ƀá·to] *m.* alarm, call to arms; surprise attack.

rebelarse [rre·ƀe·lár·se] *v.* to rebel.

rebelde [rre·ƀél·de] *adj.* rebellious; *m.* rebel; defaulter (*one who fails to appear in court*).

rebeldía [rre·ƀel·dí·a] *f.* rebelliousness; defiance; default, failure to appear in court; **en** — in revolt.

rebelión [rre·ƀe·ljón] *f.* rebellion, revolt.

rebencazo [rre·ƀeŋ·ká·so] *m. Ríopl., Ch., Andes* crack of a whip; *Am.* lash, stroke with a whip.

rebenque [rre·ƀéŋ·ke] *m.* rawhide whip.

reborde [rre·ƀór·de] *m.* edge, border.

rebosante [rre·ƀo·sán·te] *adj.* brimming, overflowing.

rebosar [rre·ƀo·sár] *v.* to overflow, brim over; to abound.

rebotar [rre·ƀo·tár] *v.* to rebound, bounce back or again; to make rebound; to repel, reject; to annoy, vex; **-se** to become vexed, upset; *Col., Mex.* to become cloudy or muddy (*said of water*); *Am.* **rebotársele a uno la bilis** to get angry, become upset.

rebote [rre·ƀó·te] *m.* rebound, bounce; **de** — on the rebound; indirectly.

rebozar[9] [rre·ƀo·sár] *v.* to muffle up; **-se** to muffle oneself up; to wrap oneself up.

rebozo [rre·ƀó·so] *m.* shawl; **sin** — frankly, openly.

rebullir[20] [rre·ƀu·yír] *v. irr.* to stir, move; to boil up.

rebusca [rre·ƀús·ka] *f.* research; search; searching; gleaning; residue.

rebuscar[6] [rre·ƀus·kár] *v.* to search thoroughly; to pry into; to glean.

rebuznar [rre·ƀuz·nár] *v.* to bray.

rebuzno [rre·ƀúz·no] *m.* bray.

recabar [rre·ka·ƀár] *v.* to obtain, gain by entreaty.

recado [rre·ká·do] *m.* message; errand; gift; daily food supply, daily marketing; precaution; equipment; *Ríopl., Andes* saddle and trappings; — **de escribir** writing materials; **-s a** regards to.

recaer[24] [rre·ka·ér] *v. irr.* to fall (upon); to fall again; to relapse; to have a relapse.

recaída [rre·ka·í·da] *f.* relapse; falling again.

recalar [rre·ka·lár] *v.* to saturate, soak through; to reach port; to come within sight of land; to land, end up, stop at; *Am.* — **con alguien** to "land" on somebody, take it out on somebody.

recalcar[6] [rre·kal·kár] *v.* to emphasize; to harp on; to press down.

recalcitrante [rre·kal·si·trán·te] *adj.* obstinate, disobedient, stubborn.

recalentar[1] [rre·ka·len·tár] *v. irr.* to reheat, warm over; to overheat, heat too much.

recamar [rre·ka·már] *v.* to embroider (*usually with gold or silver*).

recámara [rre·ká·ma·ra] *f.* dressing room; *Mex., C.A., Col.* bedroom; *Ríopl., Col.* chamber for an explosive charge.

recapitular [rre·ka·pi·tu·lár] *v.* to recapitulate, sum up, tell briefly.

recargar[7] [rre·kar·gár] *v.* to overload; to emphasize.

recargo [rre·kár·go] *m.* overload; extra load; extra charge; increase (*of fever*); new charge, new accusation.

recatado [rre·ka·tá·do] *adj.* cautious, prudent; modest; *p.p.* concealed.

recatar [rre·ka·tár] *v.* to cover, conceal; **-se** to show timidity; to be cautious; to hide (from), shun.

recato [rre·ká·to] *m.* caution, prudence; reserve, restraint, secrecy; modesty.

recaudación [rre·kaw·da·sjón] *f.* collection, collecting; office of tax collector.

recaudador [rre·kaw·da·dór] *m.* tax collector.

recaudar [rre·kaw·dár] *v.* to collect (*money, taxes, rents, etc.*).

RA

recaudo [rre·kaw·ḏo] *m.* collection, collecting; precaution; bond, security; *Mex.* spices, seasonings; *Am.* daily supply of vegetables; **estar a buen** — to be safe; **poner a buen** — to place in safety.

recelar [rre·se·lár] *v.* to suspect, fear; **-se de** to be suspicious or afraid of.

recelo [rre·sé·lo] *m.* suspicion, fear.

receloso [rre·se·ló·so] *adj.* suspicious, distrustful, fearful.

recepción [rre·sep·sjón] *f.* reception; admission.

receptáculo [rre·sep·tá·ku·lo] *m.* receptacle.

receptivo [rre·sep·ti·ḇo] *adj.* receptive, capable of receiving, quick to receive.

receptor [rre·sep·tór] *m.* receiver; *adj.* receiving.

receta [rre·sé·ta] *f.* recipe; prescription.

recetar [rre·se·tár] *v.* to prescribe (*a medicine*).

recibidor [rre·si·ḇi·ḏór] *m.* receiver; reception room.

recibimiento [rre·si·ḇi·mjén·to] *m.* reception; welcome; reception room; parlor.

recibir [rre·si·ḇír] *v.* to receive; to admit, accept; to go out to meet; — **noticias de** to hear from; **-se de** to receive a title or degree of.

recibo [rre·sí·ḇo] *m.* (*monetario*) receipt; (*acción*) reception; (*sala*) reception room; parlor; **sala de** — reception room; **estar de** — to be at home for receiving callers; **ser de** — to be acceptable, be fit for use.

reciedumbre [rre·sje·ḏúm·bre] *f.* strength, force, vigor.

recién [rre·sjén] *adv.* recently, lately, newly (*used before a past participle*); *Ríopl., Ch., Andes* just now; *Ríopl., Ch., Andes* a short time ago; *Ríopl., Ch., Andes* — **entonces** just then.

reciente [rre·sjén·te] *adj.* recent, new.

recinto [rre·sín·to] *m.* enclosure; precinct.

recio [rré·sjo] *adj.* strong, robust; harsh; hard, severe; fast; *adv.* strongly; harshly; rapidly; hard; loud.

recipiente [rre·si·pjén·te] *m.* receptable, container; recipient, receiver (*he who receives*).

recíproco [rre·sí·pro·ko] *adj.* reciprocal, mutual.

recitación [rre·si·ta·sjón] *f.* recitation, recital.

recital [rre·si·tál] *m.* musical recital.

recitar [rre·si·tár] *v.* to recite.

reclamación [rre·kla·ma·sjón] *f.* protest, complaint; claim, demand.

reclamador [rre·kla·ma·ḏór] *m.* claimant; complainer.

reclamante [rre·kla·mán·te] *m. & f.* claimant; complainer; *adj.* complaining; claiming.

reclamar [rre·kla·már] *v.* (*protestar*) to complain, protest (*against*); (*exigir*) to claim, demand; to lure, call back (*a bird*).

reclamo [rre·klá·mo] *m.* (*protesta*) protest; claim; advertisement; (*llamada*) call; bird call; decoy bird; lure.

reclinar [rre·kli·nár] *v.* to recline, lean; **-se** to recline, lean back.

recluir[32] [rre·klwír] *v. irr.* to seclude, shut up; **-se** to isolate oneself.

recluso [rre·klú·so] *m.* recluse, hermit; *adj.* shut in, shut up.

recluta [rre·klú·ta] *f.* recruiting; *Am.* roundup of cattle; *m.* recruit.

reclutamiento [rre·klu·ta·mjén·to] *m.* recruiting; levy, draft.

reclutar [rre·klu·tár] *v.* to recruit, enlist; *Am.* to round up (*cattle*).

recobrar [rre·ko·ḇrár] *v.* to recover, regain; **-se** to recover; to recuperate.

recobro [rre·kó·ḇro] *m.* recovery.

recodo [rre·kó·ḏo] *m.* bend, turn; elbow (*of a road*).

recoger[11] [rre·ko·xér] *v.* (*juntar*) to gather; to collect; to pick up; (*ceñir*) to take in, tighten; (*abrigar*) to shelter; **-se** to retire, go home; to withdraw; to seclude oneself; to take shelter.

recogida [rre·ko·xí·ḏa] *f.* harvest.

recogimiento [rre·ko·xi·mjén·to] *m.* seclusion; concentration of thought, composure; retreat; collecting, gathering.

recolección [rre·ko·lek·sjón] *f.* collecting, gathering; harvest, crop; summary.

recolectar [rre·ko·lek·tár] *v.* to harvest; to gather.

recomendable [rre·ko·men·dá·ḇle] *adj.* praiseworthy, laudable; advisable.

recomendación [rre·ko·men·da·sjón] *f.* recommendation; request.

recomendar[1] [rre·ko·men·dár] *v. irr.* to recommend; to commend, praise; to enjoin, urge; to advise.

recompensa [rre·kom·pén·sa] *f.* recompense; compensation.

recompensar [rre·kom·pen·sár] *v.* to recompense, reward; to compensate.

reconcentrar [rre·kon·sen·trár] *v.* to concentrate, bring together; to hide in the depth of one's heart; **-se** to concentrate, become absorbed in thought, collect one's thoughts.

reconciliación [rre·kon·si·lja·sjón] *f.* reconciliation.

reconciliar [rre·kon·si·ljár] *v.* to reconcile; **-se** to become reconciled.

recóndito [rre·kón·di·to] *adj.* hidden, concealed; profound.

reconocer[13] [rre·ko·no·sér] *v. irr.* to recognize; to admit, acknowledge; to examine carefully; to reconnoiter, scout, explore.

reconocimiento [rre·ko·no·si·mjén·to] *m.* recognition; acknowledgment; gratitude; examination; scouting, exploring.

reconstruir[32] [rre·kons·trwír] *v. irr.* to reconstruct, rebuild.

recontar[2] [rre·kon·tár] *v. irr.* to recount; to tell, relate.

recopilar [rre·ko·pi·lár] *v.* to compile; to digest, make a digest of.

récord [rré·kor] *m.* record.

recordación [rre·kor·ḏa·sjón] *f.* recollection; remembrance.

recordar[2] [rre·kor·ḏár] *v. irr.* to remember; to recall; to remind; *Am.* to rouse, awaken; **-se** to remember; to wake up.

recordativo [rre·kor·ḏa·ti·ḇo] *adj.* reminding.

recordatorio [rre·kor·ḏa·tó·rjo] *m.* reminder.

recorrer [rre·ko·rrér] *v.* to go over; to travel over; to read over; to look over; to overhaul.

recorrido [rre·ko·rri·ḏo] *m.* trip, run; mileage, distance traveled.

recortar [rre·kor·tár] *v.* to trim, clip; to shorten; to cut out (*figures*); to pare off; **-se** to project itself (*as a shadow*); to outline itself.

recorte [rre·kór·te] *m.* clipping; cutting; outline; *Mex.* gossip, slander.

recostar [rre·kos·tár] *v.* to recline, lean; **-se** to recline, lean back.

recoveco [rre·ko·ḇé·ko] *m.* turn, bend, nook; sly or underhanded manner.

recreación [rre·kre·a·sjón] *f.* recreation.

recrear [rre·kre·ár] *v.* to entertain, amuse; to gratify, please; **-se** to amuse oneself; to take delight (in).

recreo [rre·kré·o] *m.* recreation, entertainment; place of amusement.

recrudecer[13] [rre·kru·de·sér] *v.* to recur, break out again, flare up, become worse (*said of an illness or evil*).

rectángulo [rrek·táŋ·gu·lo] *m.* rectangle; *adj.* rectangular, right-angled.

rectificar[6] [rrek·ti·fi·kár] *v.* to rectify, correct, amend; to refine (*liquors*).

rectitud [rrek·ti·túḍ] *f.* rectitude, uprightness, righteousness; straightness; accuracy.

recto [rrék·to] *adj.* straight; right; just, honest; **ángulo** — right angle; *m.* rectum; *adv.* *C.A.* straight ahead.

rector [rrek·tór] *m.* college or university president; principal; rector, curate, priest.

recua [rré·kwa] *f.* drove of pack animals; drove, crowd.

recuento [rre·kwén·to] *m.* recount.

recuerdo [rre·kwér·ḍo] *m.* remembrance; recollection; souvenir, keepsake; memory; **-s** regards; *adj. Ríopl., Col., Ven.* awake.

reculada [rre·ku·lá·ḍa] *f.* recoil.

recular [rre·ku·lár] *v.* to recoil, spring back; to fall back, go back, retreat; to yield, back down.

recuperación [rre·ku·pe·ra·sjón] *f.* recovery.

recuperar [rre·ku·pe·rár] *v.* to recuperate, recover, regain; **-se** to recuperate, recover one's health.

recurrir [rre·ku·rrír] *v.* to resort (to); to have recourse (to).

recurso [rre·kúr·so] *m.* recourse, resort; petition, appeal; **-s** means, resources; **sin** — without remedy; without appeal.

recusar [rre·ku·sár] *v.* to reject, decline.

rechazar[9] [rre·ča·sár] *v.* to reject; to repel, drive back; to rebuff.

rechifla [rre·čí·fla] *f.* hooting; hissing; ridicule.

rechiflar [rre·či·flár] *v.* to hoot; to hiss; to ridicule.

rechinamiento [rre·či·na·mjén·to] *m.* creak; squeak; squeaking; gnashing.

rechinar [rre·či·nár] *v.* to squeak; to creak; *Am.* to be furious, angry; *Am.* to grumble, growl; — **los dientes** to gnash one's teeth.

rechino [rre·čí·no] = **rechinamiento.**

rechoncho [rre·čon·čo] *adj.* plump; chubby; squat.

rechuparse [rre·ču·pár·se] *v.* to smack one's lips.

red [rreḍ] *f.* net; netting; network; snare; **redecilla** [rre·de·sí·ya] *f.* small net; mesh; hair net.

redacción [rre·ḍak·sjón] *f.* (*acto*) wording; editing; (*lugar*) newspaper offices; editorial department; (*cuerpo*) editorial staff.

redactar [rre·ḍak·tár] *v.* to word, compose; to edit.

redactor [rre·ḍak·tór] *m.* editor.

redada [rre·ḍá·ḍa] *f.* catch; haul (*of criminals*).

redarguir[32] [rre·ḍar·ǥwír] *v.* *irr.* to retort, answer back; to contradict, call in question; to reargue.

rededor [rre·ḍe·ḍór] *m.* surroundings; **al** (*or* **en**) — around, about.

redención [rre·ḍen·sjón] *f.* redemption.

redentor [rre·ḍen·tór] *m.* redeemer, savior; **el Redentor** the Savior.

redil [rre·ḍíl] *m.* sheepfold.

redimir [rre·ḍi·mír] *v.* to redeem; to ransom; to set free.

rédito [rré·ḍi·to] *m.* interest, revenue, yield.

redituar[18] [rre·ḍi·twár] *v.* to produce, yield (*interest*).

redoblar [rre·ḍo·ƀlár] *v.* to double; to clinch (*a nail*); to reiterate, repeat; to roll (*a drum*).

redoble [rre·ḍó·ƀle] *m.* roll (*of a drum*).

redoma [rre·ḍó·ma] *f.* flask, vial.

redomón [rre·ḍo·món] *m. Ríopl.* half-tame horse or bull; *adj. Ríopl.* half-civilized, rustic.

redonda [rre·ḍón·da] *f.* surrounding district, neighborhood; whole note (*music*); **a la** — all around, round-about.

redondear [rre·ḍon·de·ár] *v.* to round, make round; to round off; to round out.

redondel [rre·ḍon·dél] *m.* arena, bull ring; circle.

redondez [rre·ḍon·dés] *f.* roundness.

redondo [rre·ḍón·do] *adj.* round; whole, entire; clear, evident; *Andes* stupid; *Mex.* honest; **en** — all around.

redopelo [rre·ḍo·pé·lo]: **a** — against the grain.

redor [rre·ḍór] *m.* round mat; **en** — around.

reducción [rre·ḍuk·sjón] *f.* reduction; cut, discount; decrease.

reducido [rre·ḍu·sí·ḍo] *p.p.* & *adj.* reduced; compact, small.

reducir[25] [rre·ḍu·sír] *v.* *irr.* to reduce; to diminish; to convert (into); to reset (*a bone*); **-se** to adapt oneself, adjust oneself; to be constrained, forced.

redundante [rre·ḍun·dán·te] *adj.* redundant.

reedificar[6] [rre·e·ḍi·fi·kár] *v.* to rebuild, reconstruct.

reelección [rre·e·lek·sjón] *f.* re-election.

reelegir[11] [rre·e·le·xír] *v.* to re-elect.

reembolsar [rre·em·bol·sár] *v.* to reimburse, refund, repay, pay back.

reembolso [rre·em·ból·so] *m.* reimbursement, refund.

reemitir [rre·mi·tír] *v.* to emit again; to issue again; to rebroadcast; to relay (*a broadcast*).

reemplazable [rre·em·pla·sá·ƀle] *adj.* replaceable.

reemplazar[9] [rre·em·pla·sár] *v.* to replace; to substitute.

reemplazo [rre·em·plá·so] *m.* replacement; substitute, substitution.

reexpedir[5] [rre·es·pe·ḍír] *v.* *irr.* to forward (*mail*).

refacción [rre·fak·sjón] *f.* (*alimento*) light lunch, refreshment; (*compostura*) repair, reparation; *Mex., Col.* spare part; *Carib.* help, aid, loan.

refajo [rre·fá·xo] *m.* underskirt; short skirt.

referencia [rre·fe·rén·sja] *f.* reference; narration, account.

referente [rre·fe·rén·te] *adj.* referring.

referir[3] [rre·fe·rír] *v.* *irr.* to refer; to narrate; to relate; **-se** to refer (to), relate (to).

refinamiento [rre·fi·na·mjén·to] *m.* refinement.

refinar [rre·fi·nár] *v.* to refine; to purify.

refinería [rre·fi·ne·rí·a] *f.* refinery.

reflector [rre·flek·tór] *m.* reflector; floodlight.

reflejar [rre·fle·xár] *v.* to reflect; to think over; **-se** to be reflected.

reflejo [rre·flé·xo] *m.* reflection, image, reflex; *adj.* reflected; reflex.

reflexión [rre·flek·sjón] *f.* reflection, meditation, consideration.

reflexionar [rre·flek·sjo·nár] *v.* to reflect, meditate, think over.

reflexivo [rre·flek·sí·ƀo] *adj.* reflexive; reflective, thoughtful.

reflujo [rre·flú·xo] *m.* ebb; ebb tide.

refocilar [rre·fo·si·lár] *v.* to cheer.

reforma [rre·fór·ma] *f.* reform; reformation; improvement.

reformador [rre·for·ma·ḍór] *m.* reformer.

reformar [rre·for·már] *v.* to reform; to correct, amend; to improve, **-se** to reform.

reformista [rre·for·mís·ta] *m.* & *f.* reformer.

reforzar[2, 9] [rre·for·sár] *v.* *irr.* to reinforce; to

RE

strengthen.
refracción [rre·frak·sjón] *f.* refraction.
refractario [rre·frak·tó·rjo] *adj.* refractory;
impervious; rebellious, unruly; stubborn.
refrán [rre·frán] *m.* popular proverb or saying.
refrenar [rre·fre·nár] *v.* to restrain, keep in check;
to curb; to rein.
refrendar [rre·fren·dár] *v.* to legalize by signing; to
countersign (*confirm by another signature*); —
un pasaporte to visé a passport.
refrescante [rre·fres·kán·te] *adj.* refreshing.
refrescar[6] [rre·fres·kár] *v.* to refresh, renew; to
cool; to get cool (*said of the weather*); **-se** to
cool off; to take the fresh air; to take a cooling
drink or refreshment; *Cuba, C.A.* to take an
afternoon refreshment.
refresco [rre·frés·ko] *m.* refreshment.
refresquería [rre·fres·ke·rí·a] *f. Mex., C.A., Ven.*
refreshment shop, outdoor refreshment stand.
refriega [rre·frjé·ga] *f.* strife, fray, scuffle.
refrigeración [rre·fri·xe·ra·sjón] *f.* refrigeration;
light meal or refreshment.
refrigerador [rre·fri·xe·ra·dór] *m. Am.* refrigerator,
freezer; *adj.* refrigerating, freezing; refreshing.
refrigerar [rre·fri·xe·rár] *v.* to cool.
refrigerio [rre·fri·xé·rjo] *m.* refreshment; relief,
comfort; coolness.
refrito [rre·frí·to] *adj.* refried; frijoles refritos
(*Mexican fried beans*).
refuerzo [rre·fwér·so] *m.* reinforcement.
refugiado [rre·fu·xjá·do] *m.* refugee; *p.p. of* **refugiar.**
refugiar [rre·fu·xjár] *v.* to shelter; **-se** to take
shelter or refuge.
refugio [rre·fú·xjo] *m.* refuge, shelter.
refulgente [rre·ful·xén·te] *adj.* refulgent, radiant,
shining.
refundir [rre·fun·dír] *v.* to remelt, refound, recast
(*metals*); to recast, rewrite, reconstruct.
refunfuñar [rre·fun·fu·ñár] *v.* to grumble, mumble,
growl, mutter.
refunfuño [rre·fun·fú·ño] *m.* grumble, growl;
refunfuñón [rre·fun·fu·ñón] *adj.* grouchy;
grumbly, grumbling.
refutar [rre·fu·tár] *v.* to refute.
regadera [rre·ga·dé·ra] *f.* sprinkler; *Mex.* shower
bath.
regadío [rre·ga·dí·o] *adj.* irrigable, that can be
irrigated; irrigated; *m.* irrigated land; **tierras de**
— irrigable lands.
regalar [rre·ga·lár] *v.* (*dar*) to give, present as a
gift; to regale; (*recrear*) to entertain; to delight,
please; **-se** to treat oneself well, live a life of
ease.
regalo [rre·gá·lo] *m.* present, gift; pleasure,
delight; dainty, delicacy; luxury, comfort.
regañadientes [rre·ga·ña·djén·tes]: **a** — much
against one's wishes; unwillingly.
regañar [rre·ga·ñár] *v.* to growl; to grumble; to
quarrel; to scold.
regaño [rre·gá·ño] *m.* scolding, reprimand.
regañón [rre·ga·ñón] *adj.* grumbling; scolding;
quarrelsome; *m.* growler, grumbler, scolder.
regar[1, 7] [rre·gár] *v. irr.* to irrigate; to water; to
sprinkle, scatter; *Col.* to spill, throw off (*said of
a horse*); **-se** *Am.* to scatter, disperse (*said of a
group, herd, etc.*).
regatear [rre·ga·te·ár] *v.* to haggle, bargain; to
dispute; to sell at retail; to race (*in a regatta or
boat race*).
regateo [rre·ga·té·o] *m.* bargaining.
regazo [rre·gá·so] *m.* lap.

regencia [rre·xén·sja] *f.* regency.
regentar [rre·xen·tár] *v.* to direct, conduct,
manage; — **una cátedra** to teach a course (*at
a university*).
regente [rre·xén·te] *m.* regent; manager; *adj.* ruling.
regidor [rre·xi·dór] *m.* councilman, alderman; *adj.*
governing, ruling.
régimen [rré·xi·men] *m.* regime; government, rule,
management; — **lácteo** milk diet.
regimiento [rre·xi·mjén·to] *m.* regiment;
(*administrativo*) administration; municipal
council; position of alderman.
regio [rré·xjo] *adj.* regal, royal; splendid,
magnificent.
región [rre·xjón] *f.* region.
regir[5, 11] [rre·xír] *v. irr.* to rule, govern; to direct,
manage; to be in force (*said of a law*); to move
(*said of the bowels*).
registrador [rre·xis·tra·dór] *m.* registrar, recorder;
city clerk, official in charge of records; inspector
(*in a customhouse*); searcher; *adj.* registering;
caja registradora cash register.
registrar [rre·xis·trár] *v.* to examine, inspect,
scrutinize; to register, record; **-se** to register,
enroll.
registro [rre·xís·tro] *m.* search, inspection;
registration; census; registration office; register;
record; registration certificate; watch regulator;
bookmark; organ stop; *Ven.* wholesale textile
store.
regla [rré·gla] *f.* (*precepto*) rule; ruler; order;
precept, principle; (*medida*) measure,
moderation; menstruation; **en** — in order, in
due form; **por** — **general** as a general rule;
usually.
reglamento [rre·gla·mén·to] *m.* regulations, rules;
rule, bylaw.
regocijado [rre·go·si·xá·do] *adj.* joyful, merry, gay;
p.p. of **regocijar.**
regocijar [rre·go·si·xár] *v.* to gladden, delight; **-se**
to be glad; to rejoice.
regocijo [rre·go·sí·xo] *m.* joy; rejoicing.
regordete [rre·gor·dé·te] *adj.* plump.
regresar [rre·gre·sár] *v.* to return.
regreso [rre·gré·so] *m.* return; **estar de** — to be
back.
reguero [rre·gé·ro] *m.* stream, rivulet; trickle;
irrigation ditch.
regulación [rre·gu·la·sjón] *f.* regulation;
adjustment.
regulador [rre·gu·la·dór] *m.* regulator; controller,
governor (*of a machine*); *adj.* regulating.
regular [rre·gu·lár] *v.* to regulate; to adjust; *adj.*
regular; ordinary; moderate; fair, medium; **por**
lo — as a rule, usually; *adv.* fairly well.
regularidad [rre·gu·la·ri·dád] *f.* regularity.
regularizar[9] [rre·gu·la·ri·sár] *v.* to regulate, make
regular.
rehacer[31] [rre·a·sér] *v. irr.* to remake; to make over;
to repair; **-se** to recover one's strength; to rally.
rehén [rre·én] *m.* hostage; **en rehenes** as a hostage.
rehuir[32] [rre·wír] *v. irr.* to shun, avoid; to shrink
(from).
rehusar [rre·u·sár] *v.* to refuse; **-se a** to refuse to.
reina [réj·na] *f.* queen.
reinado [rrej·ná·do] *m.* reign.
reinante [rrej·nán·te] *adj.* reigning; prevailing.
reinar [rrej·nár] *v.* to reign; to rule; to prevail.
reincidir [rrej·si·dír] *v.* to relapse, slide back (into).
reino [rré·no] *m.* kingdom.
reintegro [rrejn·te·gro] *m.* reimbursement, refund.

reir[15] [rre·ír] *v. irr.* to laugh; **-se de** to laugh at; *Ríopl., Andes, Col., Ven., Carib.* — **de dientes para afuera** to laugh outwardly, laugh hypocritically.

reiterar [rrej·te·rár] *v.* to reiterate, repeat.

reivindicación [rrej·ḇin·di·ka·sjón] *f.* recovery.

reja [rré·xa] *f.* grate, grating; plowshare *(blade of the plow)*; plowing; *Carib., C.A.* jail.

rejilla [rre·xí·ya] *f.* small grating, lattice; small latticed window; fireplace grate; cane upholstery; *Ch.* wire dish-cover.

rejo [rré·xo] *m.* point; plow share.

rejonear [rre·xo·ne·ár] *v.* to fight a bull from horseback *(Portuguese style)*.

rejuvenecer[13] [rre·xu·ḇe·ne·sér] *v. irr.* to rejuvenate, make young; **-se** to become rejuvenated.

relación [rre·la·sjón] *f.* relation; story, account; long speech in a play; *Ríopl.* verse recited alternately by a couple in a folk dance; **-es** personal relations, connections; acquaintances.

relacionar [rre·la·sjo·nár] *v.* to relate, connect; **-se** to be related, connected; to become acquainted; establish friendly connections.

relajación [rre·la·xa·sjón] *f.*, **relajamiento** [rre·la·xa·mjén·to] *m.* relaxation; laxity; slackening; hernia.

relajar [rre·la·xár] *v.* to relax; to slacken; to release from a vow or oath; **-se** to get a hernia or rupture; to become weakened; to become lax *(said of laws, customs, etc.)*.

relajo [rre·lá·xo] *m. Carib., Mex.* disorderly conduct; lewdness; scandal.

relamerse [rre·la·mér·se] *v.* to lick one's lips; to gloat; to boast; to slick oneself up.

relámpago [rre·lám·pa·ǵo] *m.* lightning; flash.

relampaguear [rre·lam·pa·ǵe·ár] *v.* to lighten; to flash; to sparkle.

relampagueo [rre·lam·pa·ǵé·o] *m.* flashing; sheet lightning.

relatar [rre·la·tár] *v.* to relate, narrate.

relativo [rre·la·tí·ḇo] *adj.* relative; — **a** relative to, regarding.

relato [rre·lá·to] *m.* narration, account, story.

relé [rre·lé] *m.* relay; — **de televisión** television relay system.

relegar[7] [rre·le·ǵár] *v.* to relegate, banish; to postpone; to set aside, put away.

relente [rre·lén·te] *m.* night dampness; *Am.* fresh night breeze.

relevar [rre·le·ḇár] *v.* to relieve; to release; to absolve; to replace, substitute; to emboss; to make stand out in relief.

relevo [rre·lé·ḇo] *m.* relief *(from a post or military duty; person who relieves another from the performance of a duty)*.

relicario [rre·li·ká·rjo] *m.* reliquary *(small box or casket for keeping relics); Col., Ven., Cuba, Mex., Andes* locket.

relieve [rre·ljé·ḇe] *m.* relief, embossment, raised work; **-s** scraps, leftovers; **de** — in relief; prominent, outstanding; **poner de** — to make stand out; to emphasize.

religión [rre·li·xjón] *f.* religion.

religiosidad [rre·li·xjo·si·ḍáḍ] *f.* religiousness, piety; faithfulness.

religioso [rre·li·xjó·so] *adj.* religious; faithful; punctual; *m.* friar, monk.

relinchar [rre·lin·čár] *v.* to neigh.

relincho [rre·lín·čo] *m.* neigh.

reliquia [rre·li·kja] *f.* relic; vestige; **-s** relics, remains.

reloj [rre·ló] *m.* clock; watch; — **de pulsera** wristwatch; — **de sol** *(or* — **solar)** sundial; — **despertador** alarm clock.

relojería [rre·lo·xe·rí·a] *f.* watch shop; jewelry store.

reluciente [rre·lu·sjén·te] *adj.* shining; sparkling.

relucir[13] [rre·lu·sír] *v. irr.* to glitter, sparkle; to shine.

relumbrante [rre·lum·brán·te] *adj.* brilliant, flashing, resplendent.

relumbrar [rre·lum·brár] *v.* to glare; to glitter.

relumbre [rre·lúm·bre] *m.* glare, glitter.

rellenar [rre·ye·nár] *v.* to refill; to fill up; to pad; to stuff.

relleno [rre·yé·no] *adj.* stuffed; *m.* meat stuffing; filling.

remachar [rre·ma·čár] *v.* to clinch; to hammer down; to flatten; to rivet; to fix firmly; **-se** *Am.* to be tight-lipped, stubbornly silent.

remache [rre·má·če] *m.* clinching; fastening; securing; riveting; rivet.

remanente [rre·ma·nén·te] *m.* remainder, balance; remnant; residue.

remar [rre·már] *v.* to row; to struggle.

rematado [rre·ma·tá·ḍo] *adj. & p.p. (acabado)* finished; *(vendido en subasta)* sold at auction; **loco** — completely crazy.

rematar [rre·ma·tár] *v. (acabar)* to finish; to end; to give the final or finishing stroke; *(vender)* to auction; *(afianzar)* to fasten *(a stitch)*; *Am.* to stop *(a horse)* suddenly; *Am.* to buy or sell at auction; **-se** to be finished, be completely destroyed or ruined.

remate [rre·má·te] *m. (fin)* finish, end; *(postura)* highest bid at an auction; sale at auction; *(punta)* pinnacle, spire; *Am.* selvage, edge of a fabric; **de** — absolutely, without remedy; **loco de** — completely crazy, stark mad.

remedar [rre·me·ḍár] *v.* to imitate; to mimic.

remediar [rre·me·ḍjár] *v.* to remedy; to help; to avoid.

remedio [rre·mé·ḍjo] *m.* remedy; help; amendment; recourse, resort; **sin** — without help, unavoidable; **no tiene** — it can't be helped.

remedo [rre·mé·ḍo] *m.* imitation; mockery.

remembranza [rre·mem·brán·sa] *f.* remembrance, memory.

rememorar [rre·me·mo·rár] *v.* to remember, call to mind.

remendar[1] [rre·men·dár] *v. irr.* to mend, patch; to darn; to repair.

remendón [rre·men·dón] *m.* cobbler, shoe repairman; mender, patcher.

remero [rre·mé·ro] *m.* rower.

remesa [rre·mé·sa] *f.* shipment; remittance, payment.

remesar [rre·me·sár] *v.* to remit; to ship.

remiendo [rre·mjén·do] *m.* mend; mending; patch; darn; repair; **a -s** piecemeal, piece by piece.

remilgado [rre·mil·gá·ḍo] *adj.* prudish, prim, affected.

remilgo [rre·míl·ǵo] *m.* prudery, primness, affection.

reminiscencia [rre·mi·nis·sén·sja] *f.* reminiscence.

remisión [rre·mi·sjón] *f. (disculpa)* remission; forgiveness; *(remesa)* remittance, remitting; *(diminución)* abatement, slackening; *Mex., Ven.* anything shipped or sent.

remitente [rre·mi·tén·te] *m. & f.* sender; shipper.

remitir [rre·mi·tír] *v. (enviar)* to remit; to send; *(diferir)* to defer; to pardon; to refer; to abate; **-se** to defer, yield *(to another's judgment)*.

RE

remo [rré·mo] *m.* oar; hard and long work; leg of a horse; **al —** at the oar; at hard labor.
remojar [rre·mo·xár] *v.* to soak; to steep; *Am.* to tip, bribe.
remojo [rre·mó·xo] *m.* soaking; steeping; *Am.* tip, bribe.
remolacha [rre·mo·lá·ča] *f.* beet.
remolcador [rre·mol·ka·ḍór] *m.* towboat, tug, tugboat; **lancha remolcadora** tugboat.
remolcar[6] [rre·mol·kár] *v.* to tow, tug; to take (*a person*) in tow.
remolino [ree·mo·lí·no] *m.* swirl, whirl; whirlwind; whirlpool; commotion; *Ríopl.* pin wheel; *Am.* ventilating wheel (*fan*); **— de gente** throng, crowd.
remolón [rre·mo·lón] *adj.* indolent, lazy.
remolque [rre·mól·ke] *m.* tow; towrope; **llevar a —** to tow; to take in tow.
remontar [rre·mon·tár] *v.* (*alzar*) to elevate, raise; (*reparar*) to repair, patch up; to resole; to revamp; *Am.* to go up; *Ríopl., Carib., C.A., Ven., Col.* to go upstream; **-se** to rise; to soar, fly upward; to date (from), go back (to); *Ríopl.* to take to the woods or hills.
rémora [rré·mo·ra] *f.* impediment, obstacle, hindrance.
remorder[4] [rre·mor·ḍér] *v. irr.* to sting.
remordimiento [rre·mor·ḍi·mjén·to] *m.* remorse.
remoto [rre·mó·to] *adj.* remote, distant; improbable.
remover[2] [rre·mo·ḅér] *v. irr.* to remove; to dismiss; to stir.
rempujar [rrem·pu·xár] *v.* to jostle, push.
rempujón [rrem·pu·xón] *m.* jostle, push.
remuda [rre·mú·ḍa] *f.* change; substitution; replacement; change of clothes; spare tire; relay of horses; *Am.* spare horse, spare pack animal.
remudar [rre·mu·ḍár] *v.* to change; to replace.
remuneración [rre·mu·ne·ra·sjón] *f.* remuneration, compensation, pay, reward.
remunerar [rre·mu·ne·rár] *v.* to remunerate, compensate, pay, reward (*for services*).
renacer[13] [rre·na·sér] *v. irr.* to be reborn; to spring up, grow up again.
renacimiento [rre·na·si·mjén·to] *m.* renascence, renaissance; revival; rebirth.
rencilla [rren·sí·ya] *f.* quarrel.
renco [rréŋ·ko] *adj.* lame.
rencor [rreŋ·kór] *m.* rancor, resentment, hatred, grudge.
rencoroso [rreŋ·ko·ró·so] *adj.* resentful, spiteful.
rendición [rren·di·sjón] *f.* surrender; submission; yield, profit.
rendido [rren·dí·ḍo] *p.p. & adj.* tired out, fatigued; devoted; obsequious, servile.
rendija [rren·dí·xa] *f.* crack, crevice.
rendimiento [rren·di·mjén·to] *m.* yield, output, profit; surrender, submission; fatigue.
rendir[5] [rren·dír] *v. irr.* to subdue; to surrender, hand over; to yield, produce; to fatigue; to render, do (*homage*); *Cuba, Ven.* **— la jornada** to end or suspend the day's work; **-se** to surrender, give up; to become fatigued, worn out.
renegado [rre·ne·ǵá·ḍo] *m.* renegade, traitor; *adj.* renegade, disloyal; wicked.
renegar[1, 7] [rre·ne·ǵárd] *v. irr.* to deny insistently; to detest; to blaspheme, curse; **— de** to deny, renounce (*one's faith*); *Am.* to hate, protest against.
renglón [rreŋ·glón] *m.* line (*written or printed*);

item; *Ríopl., Col., Ven., Mex., Carib., Andes* line of business, specialty.
renio [rré·njo] *m.* rhenium.
reno [rré·no] *m.* reindeer.
renombrado [rre·nom·brá·ḍo] *adj.* renowned, famous.
renombre [rre·nóm·bre] *m.* renown, fame.
renovación [rre·no·ḅa·sjón] *f.* renovation, restoration; renewal.
renovar[2] [rre·no·ḅár] *v. irr.* to renovate; to renew; to replace.
renquear [rreŋ·ke·ár] *v.* to limp.
renta [rrén·ta] *f.* rent, rental; income; revenue.
renuencia [rre·nwén·sja] *f.* reluctance, unwillingness.
renuente [rre·nwén·te] *adj.* reluctant, unwilling.
renuevo [rre·nwé·ḅo] *m.* (*vástago*) sprout, shoot; (*acto*) renovation, restoration.
renunciar [rre·nun·sjár] *v.* to renounce; to resign; to refuse; to renege (*fail to follow suit in cards*).
reñidor[5, 19] [rre·ñi·ḍór] *adj.* quarrelsome.
reñir[5, 19] [rre·ñír] *v. irr.* to quarrel; to fight; to scold.
reo [rré·o] *adj.* guilty; *m.* culprit, criminal; defendant.
reojo : [rre·ó·xo] **mirar de —** to look out of the corner of one's eye; to look scornfully.
repantigarse[7] [rre·pan·ti·ǵár·se] *v.* to lounge, stretch out (*in a chair*).
reparación [rre·pa·ra·sjón] *f.* reparation; repair; indemnity.
reparar [rre·pa·rár] *v.* (*renovar*) to repair; to regain; to recover; (*corregir*) to make amends for, atone for; to remedy; to ward off (*a blow*); *Am.* to rear, buck (*said of horses*); **— en** to observe, notice.
reparo [rre·pá·ro] *m.* (*arreglo*) repair; restoration; (*observación*) notice; observation; (*duda*) doubt, objection; (*abrigo*) shelter; parry (*fencing*); *Mex.* sudden bound or leap of a horse.
repartimiento [rre·par·ti·mjén·to] *m.* distribution, division; assessment.
repartir [rre·par·tír] *v.* to distribute; to allot.
reparto [rre·pár·to] *m.* distribution; mail delivery; cast of characters.
repasar [rre·pa·sár] *v.* to review, look over, go over again; to mend (*clothes*); to pass by again.
repaso [rre·pá·so] *m.* review; revision.
repelente [rre·pe·lén·te] *adj.* repellent, repulsive, repugnant.
repeler [rre·pe·lér] *v.* to repel; to reject.
repelón [rre·pe·lón] *m.* pull; kink.
repente [rre·pén·te] *m.* sudden movement; *Am.* attack, fit; **de —** suddenly.
repentino [rre·pen·tí·no] *adj.* sudden.
repercutir [rre·per·ku·tír] *v.* to resound, echo back; to rebound; to reflect back (*as light*).
repetición [rre·pe·ti·sjón] *f.* repetition.
repetido [rre·pe·tí·ḍo] *p.p.* repeated; **repetidas veces** repeatedly, often.
repetir[5] [rre·pe·tír] *v. irr.* to repeat; to belch.
repicar[6] [rre·pi·kár] *v.* (*tañer*) to chime, ring; (*hacer menudo*) to mince, chop fine; *Carib., Ven.* to drum, tap (*with the fingers or heels*); **-se** to boast; to be conceited.
repique [rre·pí·ke] *m.* (*tañido*) chime, ringing, peal; (*acción de picar*) mincing, chopping.
repiquetear [rre·pi·ke·te·ár] *v.* to chime, ring; to jingle; *Am.* to tap (*with fingers or heels*).
repiqueteo [rre·pi·ke·té·o] *m.* chiming, ringing; jingling, tinkling; *Ríopl., Carib., Ven.* clicking

sound of heels.

repisa [rre·pí·sa] *f*. shelf, ledge; sill; wall bracket; — **de ventana** window sill.

replegar[1, 7] [rre·ple·gár] *v. irr.* to fold, pleat; **-se** to retreat, fall back.

réplica [rré·pli·ka] *f*. reply, answer, retort; replica, copy; *Am. m.* examiner.

replicar[6] [rre·pli·kár] *v*. to reply, answer back; to retort.

repliegue [rre·pljé·ge] *m*. fold, crease; retreat (*of troops*).

repollo [rre·pó·yo] *m*. cabbage.

reponer[20] [rre·po·nér] *v. irr.* (*devolver*) to replace, put back; to restore; (*contestar*) to reply, retort; **-se** to recover one's health or fortune; to collect oneself, become calm.

reportaje [rre·por·tá·xe] *m*. newspaper report; reporting.

reportar [rre·por·tár] *v*. to check, control, restrain; to attain, obtain; to bring; to carry; *Am.* to report; **-se** to control oneself.

reporte [rre·pór·te] *m*. report, news.

repórter [rre·pór·ter], **reportero** *m*. reporter.

reposado [rre·po·sá·do] *p.p. & adj.* reposed; quiet, calm; restful.

reposar [rre·po·sár] *v*. to repose; to rest; to lie buried; **-se** to settle (*said of sediment*).

reposición [rre·po·si·sjón] *f*. replacement; recovery (*of one's health*).

reposo [rre·pó·so] *m*. repose, rest; calm.

repostada [rre·pos·tá·da] *f*. sharp answer, back talk.

repostería [rre·pos·te·rí·a] *f*. pastry shop.

reprender [rre·pren·dér] *v*. to reprimand, scold.

reprensible [rre·pren·si·ble] *adj.* reprehensible, deserving reproof.

reprensión [rre·pren·sjón] *f*. reproof, rebuke.

represa [rre·pré·sa] *f*. dam; damming, stopping; *Col., Ven.* reservoir.

represalia [rre·pre·sá·lja] *f*. reprisal.

represar [rre·pre·sár] *v*. to bank, dam; to recapture (*a ship*) from the enemy; to repress, check.

representación [rre·pre·sen·ta·sjón] *f*. representation; play, performance; authority, dignity; petition, plea.

representante [rre·pre·sen·tán·te] *adj.* representing; *m. & f*. representative; actor.

representar [rre·pre·sen·tár] *v*. (*declarar*) to represent; to declare, state; to express, show; (*actuar*) to act, play, perform; **-se** to imagine, picture to oneself.

representativo [rre·pre·sen·ta·ti·bo] *adj.* representative.

represión [rre·pre·sjón] *f*. repression, control, restraint.

reprimenda [rre·pri·mén·da] *f*. reprimand, rebuke.

reprimir [rre·pri·mir] *v*. to repress, check, curb; **-se** to repress oneself; to refrain.

reprobar[2] [rre·pro·bár] *v. irr.* to reprove, blame; to condemn; to flunk, fail.

reprochar [rre·pro·čár] *v*. to reproach.

reproche [rre·pró·če] *m*. reproach.

reproducción [rre·pro·duk·sjón] *f*. reproduction.

reproducir[25] [rre·pro·du·sir] *v. irr.* to reproduce.

reptil [rrep·til] *m*. reptile.

república [rre·pú·bli·ka] *f*. republic.

republicano [rre·pu·bi·ká·no] *adj. & m.* republican.

repudiar [rre·pu·djár] *v*. to repudiate; to disown.

repuesto [rre·pwés·to] *m*. stock, supply, provisions; sideboard; **de** — spare, extra; *p.p. of* **reponer** *& adj.* recovered (*from an illness, loss, fright, etc.*);

replaced; restored.

repugnancia [rre·pug·nán·sja] *f*. repugnance, disgust; aversion; dislike, reluctance.

repugnante [rre·pug·nán·te] *adj.* repugnant, disgusting, loathsome.

repugnar [rre·pug·nár] *v*. to be repugnant; to disgust; to oppose, contradict.

repulido [rre·pu·lí·do] *adj.* polished up, slick; shiny; spruce.

repulsa [rre·púl·sa] *f*. repulse; rebuff; rebuke.

repulsar [rre·pil·sár] *v*. to repulse, repel, reject.

repulsivo [rre·pul·si·bo] *adj.* repulsive, repugnant.

repuntar [rre·pun·tár] *v. Am.* to round up (*cattle*).

reputación [rre·pu·ta·sjón] *f*. reputation.

reputar [rre·pu·tár] *v*. to repute.

requebrar[1] [rre·ke·brár] *v. irr.* to compliment; to flatter; to flirt with; to court, woo; to break again.

requemado [rre·ke·má·do] *p.p. & adj.* burned; parched; tanned, sunburned.

requemar [rre·ke·már] *v*. to parch, dry up; to burn; to overcook; **-se** to become overheated; to burn inwardly; to get tanned, sunburned.

requerimiento [rre·ke·ri·mjén·to] *m*. requisition; requirement; summons; **-s** amorous advances, insinuations.

requerir[3] [rre·ke·rir] *v. irr.* (*exigir*) to require; to need; to summon; (*indagar*) to examine, investigate; (*avisar*) to notify; — **de amores** to court, woo.

requesón [rre·ke·són] *m*. cottage cheese.

requiebro [rre·kjé·bro] *m*. flattery; compliment.

requisito [rre·ki·si·to] *m*. requirement, requisite; — **previo** prerequisite.

res [rres] *f*. head of cattle; any large animal.

resabio [rre·sa·bjo] *m*. disagreeable aftertaste; bad habit.

resaca [rre·sá·ka] *f*. undertow; surge; surf; redraft (*of a bill of exchange*); *Am.* beating, thrashing; *Mex., Riopl.* mud and slime (*left by a flood*).

resaltar [rre·sal·tár] *v*. to stand out; to project, jut out; to rebound, bounce or spring back; to be evident, obvious.

resarcir[10] [rre·sar·sir] *v*. to indemnify, compensate, repay; to make amends for; **-se de** to make up for.

resbaladero [rrez·ba·la·dé·ro] *m*. slide, slippery place.

resbaladizo [rrez·ba·la·di·so] *adj.* slippery.

resbalar [rrez·ba·lár] *v*. to slide; **-se** to slip; to slide; to skid; **resbalársele a uno una cosa** to let a thing slide off one's back, be impervious to a thing.

resbalón [rrez·ba·lón] *m*. sudden or violent slip; slide; error; **darse un** — to slip.

resbaloso [rrez·ba·ló·so] *adj.* slippery.

rescatar [rres·ka·tár] *v*. to ransom; to redeem; to barter, exchange, trade; *Am.* to resell.

rescate [rres·ká·te] *m*. ransom; redemption; barter, exchange.

rescoldo [rres·kól·do] *m*. embers, hot cinders, hot ashes; doubt, scruple.

resecar[6] [rre·se·kár] *v*. to dry up; to parch.

reseco [rre·sé·ko] *adj.* very dry; dried up, parched; thin, skinny.

resentimiento [rre·sen·ti·mjén·to] *m*. resentment; impairment, damage (*to one's health*).

resentirse[3] [rre·sen·tir·se] *v. irr* (*tener pesar*) to show resentment, hurt, or grief; to resent; (*empeorar*) to weaken; to become worse.

reseña [rre·sé·ña] *f*. military review; book review;

RE

brief account; sign, signal.
reseñar [rre·se·ñár] *v.* to review (*a book*); to review (*troops*); to outline briefly, give a short account of.
resero [rre·sé·ro] *m. Riopl.* cowboy, herdsman; *Am.* dealer in livestock.
reserva [rre·ser·ḅa] *f.* reserve; reservation; exception; caution; **a — de** reserving the right to, intending to; **sin —** without reserve, frankly.
reservación [rre·ser·ḅa·sjón] *f.* reservation.
reservar [rre·ser·ḅár] *v.* to reserve; to put aside; to postpone; to exempt; to keep secret; **-se** to conserve one's strength, spare oneself (*for another time*).
resfriado [rres·frjá·ḍo] *m.* cold (*illness*); *p.p. of* **resfriar**; *adj. Riopl.* indiscreet.
resfriar[17] [rres·frjár] *v.* to cool; to chill; **-se** to catch cold; to cool.
resfrío [rres·frí·o] *m.* chill; cold.
resguardar [rrez·ǵwar·ḍár] *v.* to guard, defend; to shield; **-se de** to guard oneself against; to seek shelter from.
resguardo [rrez·ǵwár·ḍo] *m.* defense; security; guarantee; guard.
residencia [rre·si·ḍén·sja] *f.* residence; office or post of a resident foreign minister; *Am.* luxurious dwelling.
residente [rre·si·ḍén·te] *adj.* resident, residing; *m.* & *f.* resident, dweller; resident foreign minister; *Col., C.A., Riopl.* alien resident.
residir [rre·si·ḍír] *v.* to reside; to live, dwell; to be inherent, belong (to).
residuo [rre·sí·ḍwo] *m.* residue; remainder.
resignación [rre·sig̈·na·sjón] *f.* resignation.
resignar [rre·sig̈·nár] *v.* to resign; to hand over; **-se** to resign oneself.
resina [rre·si·na] *f.* resin.
resistencia [rre·sis·tén·sja] *f.* resistance.
resistente [rre·sis·tén·te] *adj.* resistant; resisting.
resistir [rre·sis·tír] *v.* to resist; to tolerate, endure; **-se** to resist, struggle.
resolución [rre·so·lu·sjón] *f.* (*ánimo*) resolution; courage, determination; (*resultado*) solution; **en — in brief.**
resolver[2, 52] [rre·sol·ḅér] *v. irr.* to resolve, decide; to solve; to dissolve; **-se** to resolve, decide; to be reduced (to), dissolve (into).
resollar[2] [rre·so·yár] *v. irr.* to breathe hard; to pant.
resonar[2] [rre·so·nár] *v. irr.* to resound.
resoplar [rre·so·plár] *v.* to puff, breathe hard; to snort.
resoplido [rre·so·plí·ḍo] *m.* puff, pant; snort.
resorte [rre·sór·te] *m.* spring; elasticity; means (*to attain an object*); *Col.* elastic, rubber band; *Ven.* **no es de mi —** it doesn't concern me.
respaldar [rres·pal·dár] *v.* to endorse; to guarantee; *Am.* to back, support; **-se** to lean back; *Ch.* to protect one's rear.
respaldo [rres·pál·ḍo] *m.* back (*of a chair or sheet of paper*); protecting wall; endorsement; *Am.* protection, security, guarantee.
respectivo [rres·pek·tí·ḅo] *adj.* respective.
respecto [rres·pék·to] *m.* respect, relation, reference; point, matter; (**con**) **— a** (*or* **— de**) with respect to, with regard to.
respetable [rres·pe·tá·ḅle] *adj.* respectable.
respetar [rres·pe·tár] *v.* to respect.
respeto [rres·pé·to] *m.* respect; reverence, regard; consideration.
respetuoso [rres·pe·twó·so] *adj.* respectful;

respectable.
respingar[7] [rres·piŋ·gár] *v.* to buck; to balk (*said of a horse*); to grumble; to curl up (*said of the edge of a garment*).
respingo [rres·píŋ·go] *m.* buck, balking; muttering, grumbling.
respiración [rres·pi·ra·sjón] *f.* respiration, breathing.
respirar [rres·pi·rár] *v.* to breathe.
respiro [rres·pí·ro] *m.* breathing; breath; respite, pause, moment of rest; extension of time (*for payment*).
resplandecer[13] [rres·plan·de·sér] *v. irr.* to shine; to glitter.
resplandeciente [rres·plan·de·sjén·te] *adj.* resplendent, shining.
resplandor [rres·plan·dór] *m.* splendor, brilliance, brightness; *Am.* sun's glare.
responder [rres·pon·dér] *v.* to respond; to answer; to correspond, harmonize; to answer (for), be responsible (for).
respondón [rres·pon·dón] *adj.* saucy, pert, insolent (*in answering*).
responsabilidad [rres·pon·sa·ḅi·li·ḍáḍ] *f.* responsibility.
responsable [rres·pon·sá·ḅle] *adj.* responsible.
respuesta [rres·pwés·ta] *f.* response; answer, reply.
resquebradura [rres·ke·ḅra·dú·ra], **resquebrajadura** [rres·ke·ḅra·xa·dú·ra] *f.* fissure, crevice, crack.
resquebrajar [rres·ke·ḅrá·xár] = **resquebrar.**
resquebrar[1] [rres·ke·ḅrár] *v. irr.* to crack; to split.
resquicio [rres·kí·sjo] *m.* crack, slit, crevice; opening; *Col., Ven., Mex.* vestige, sign, trace.
resta [rrés·ta] *f.* subtraction (*as an arithmetical operation*); remainder.
restablecer[13] [rres·ta·ḅle·sér] *v. irr.* to re-establish; to restore; **-se** to recover.
restante [rres·tán·te] *adj.* remaining; *m.* residue, remainder.
restañar [rres·ta·ñár] *v.* to staunch (*a wound*); to check the flow of.
restar [rres·tár] *v.* to deduct; to subtract; to remain, be left over; to strike back (*a ball*).
restauración [rres·taw·ra·sjón] *f.* restoration.
restaurante [rres·taw·rán·te] *m.* restaurant.
restaurar [rres·taw·rár] *v.* to restore; to recover; to re-establish; to repair.
restitución [rres·ti·tu·sjón] *f.* restitution, restoration, return.
restituir[32] [rres·ti·twír] *v. irr.* to return, give back; to restore.
resto [rrés·to] *m.* rest, remainder; stakes at cards; return (*of a tennis ball*); player who returns the ball; **-s** remains.
restorán [rres·to·rán] *m. Am.* restaurant.
restregar[1, 7] [rres·tre·gár] *v. irr.* to rub hard; to scrub.
restricción [rres·trik·sjón] *f.* restriction; restraint; curb; limitation.
restringir[11] [rres·triŋ·xír] *v.* to restrict; to restrain; to limit.
resucitar [rre·su·si·tár] *v.* to resuscitate, bring to life; to come to life; to revive.
resuelto [rre·swél·to] *p.p. of* **resolver** resolved, determined; *adj.* resolute, bold; quick.
resuello [rre·swé·yo] *m.* breath; breathing, panting.
resulta [rre·súl·ta] *f.* result; effect, consequence; **de -s** as a result, in consequence.
resultado [rre·sul·tá·ḍo] *m.* result, effect, consequence.
resultante [rre·sul·tán·te] *adj.* resulting; *f.* resultant

(*force*).

resultar [rre·sul·tár] *v.* to result; to spring, arise as a consequence; to turn out to be; **resulta que** it turns out that.

resumen [rre·sú·men] *m.* résumé, summary; **en —** summing up, in brief.

resumidero [rre·su·mi·ḍé·ro] *m. Am.* = **sumidero.**

resumir [rre·su·mír] *v.* to summarize, sum up; **-se** to be reduced or condensed.

resurgir[11] [rre·sur·xír] *v.* to arise again; to reappear.

retablo [rre·tá·ƀlo] *m.* altarpiece; religious picture hung as a votive offering; series of pictures that tell a story.

retaguardia [rre·ta·ǵwár·ḍja] *f.* rear guard.

retal [rre·tál] *m.* remnant.

retar [rre·tár] *v.* to challenge, defy; to reprimand, scold; *Ch., Andes* to insult.

retardar [rre·tar·ḍár] *v.* to retard, delay.

retazo [rre·tá·so] *m.* remnant; piece; fragment.

retener[45] [rre·te·nér] *v. irr.* to retain; to keep; to withhold; to detain.

retintín [rre·tin·tín] *m.* jingle, tinkle; sarcastic tone of ring.

retirada [rre·ti·rá·ḍa] *f.* retreat; withdrawal.

retirado [rre·ti·rá·ḍo] *p.p. & adj.* retired; distant, remote; isolated; pensioned.

retirar [rre·ti·rár] *v.* to withdraw; to take away; **-se** to retire, withdraw; to retreat.

retiro [rre·tí·ro] *m.* retreat; retirement; place of refuge; pension of a retired officer.

reto [rré·to] *m.* challenge; defiance; *Ríopl.* scolding; *Andes* insult.

retobado [rre·to·ƀá·ḍo] *adj. Col., Ríopl.* saucy; *Andes* stubborn, unruly; *Andes* peevish; *Am.* sly, astute.

retobar [rre·to·ƀár] *v. Col., Andes* to cover with leather; *Am.* to wrap with leather, oilcloth, or burlap; *Am.* to tan (*leather*); **-se** *Ríopl.* to revel, talk back, act saucy; *Andes, Col.* to become disagreeable and aloof.

retocar[6] [rre·to·kár] *v.* to retouch, touch up; to finish, perfect.

retoñar [rre·to·ñár] *v.* to sprout; to bud; to sprout again; to reappear.

retoño [rre·tó·ño] *m.* sprout, shoot; bud.

retoque [rre·tó·ke] *m.* retouching; finishing touch.

retorcer[2, 10] [rre·tor·sér] *v. irr.* to twist; to retort; to distort; **-se** to wriggle; to squirm.

retorcimiento [rre·tor·si·mjén·to] *m.* twisting; squirming.

retórica [rre·tó·ri·ka] *f.* rhetoric.

retornar [rre·tor·nár] *v.* to return; to give back.

retorno [rre·tór·no] *m.* return; repayment; barter.

retozar[9] [rre·to·sár] *v.* to gambol, frisk about, frolic, romp; to stir within (*said of passions*).

retozo [rre·tó·so] *m.* frolic; **retozón** [rre·to·són] *adj.* frisky, playful.

retractarse [rre·trak·tár·se] *v.* to retract, take back one's word.

retraer[46] [rre·tra·ér] *v. irr.* to withdraw, draw back, take back; **-se de** to withdraw from; to keep aloof or away from; to shun.

retraído [rre·tra·i·ḍo] *adj.* shy, reserved.

retraimiento [rre·traj·mjén·to] *m.* retirement; reserve, aloofness, shyness.

retranca [rre·tráŋ·ka] *f. Cuba* brake; **retranquero** [rre·traŋ·ké·ro] *m. Am.* brakeman.

retrancar[6] [rre·traŋ·kár] *v. Cuba* to brake, put the brake on; *Cuba* **se ha retrancado el asunto** the

affair has come to a standstill.

retrasado [rre·tra·sá·ḍo] *p.p. & adj.* behind, behind time; backward; postponed, delayed.

retrasar [rre·tra·sár] *v.* to delay, retard; to set back; to go backward; **-se** to fall behind; to be late, behind time.

retraso [rre·trá·so] *m.* delay.

retratar [rre·tra·tár] *v.* to portray; to photograph; to copy, imitate; **-se** to be portrayed; to be photographed; to be reflected.

retrato [rre·trá·to] *m.* portrait; photograph; copy, imitation; reflection.

retrete [rre·tré·te] *m.* toilet, water closet; place of retreat.

retroactivo [rre·tro·ak·ti·ƀo] *adj.* retroactive.

retroceder [rre·tro·se·ḍér] *v.* to turn back; to fall back, draw back; to recede.

retroceso [rre·tro·sé·so] *m.* retrogression, backward step; retreat; setback, relapse.

retrocohete [rre·tro·ko·é·te] *m.* retro-rocket.

retropropulsión [rre·tro·pro·pul·sjon] *f.* retropropulsion.

retruécano [rre·trwé·ka·no] *m.* pun.

retumbar [rre·tum·bár] *v.* to resound; to rumble.

retumbo [rre·túm·bo] *m.* loud echo or sound; rumble (*of thunder, cannon, etc.*).

reuma [rréw·ma] *m. & f.,* **reumatismo** [rrew·ma·tíz·mo] *m.* rheumatism.

reunión [rrew·njón] *f.* reunion; meeting.

reunir [rrew·nír] *v.* to reunite; to unite; to group; to gather; to assemble; to collect; **-se** to meet, assemble; to reunite.

revancha [rre·ƀán·ča] *f.* revenge; return game or match.

revelación [rre·ƀe·la·sjón] *f.* revelation.

revelador [rre·ƀe·la·ḍór] *adj.* revealing; *m.* developer (*in photography*).

revelar [rre·ƀe·lár] *v.* to reveal; to develop (*a film*).

revendedor [rre·ƀen·de·ḍór] *m.* retailer; reseller; ticket scalper.

reventa [rre·ƀén·ta] *f.* resale.

reventar[1] [ree·ƀen·tár] *v. irr.* (*estallar*) to burst; to burst forth; to explode; to smash; (*fatigar*) to fatigue, exhaust; to bother; **-se** to burst; to blow out, explode.

reventón [rre·ƀen·tón] *m.* burst, bursting; blowout; steep hill; hard work, toil; *adj.* bursting.

reverdecer[13] [rre·ƀer·ḍe·sér] *v. irr.* to grow fresh and green again; to gain new strength and vigor.

reverencia [rre·ƀe·rén·sja] *f.* reverence; bow.

reverenciar [rre·ƀe·ren·sjár] *v.* to revere, venerate.

reverendo [rre·ƀe·rén·do] *adj.* reverend; *Cuba, Ríopl., Mex., Andes* large, big (*ironically*).

reverente [rre·ƀe·rén·te] *adj.* reverent.

reverso [rre·ƀér·so] *m.* reverse; back side.

revertir[3] [rre·ƀer·tír] *v. irr.* to revert.

revés [rre·ƀés] *m.* reverse; back, wrong side; black stroke or slap; backhanded thrust (*in fencing*); misfortune; **al —** backwards; wrong side out; in the opposite way; from left to right.

revestir[5] [rre·ƀes·tír] *v. irr.* to dress, clothe; to coat, cover with a coating; **-se** to dress, put on an outer garment or vestment; to be invested (*with power, authority, etc.*); **-se de paciencia** to arm oneself with patience.

revisar [rre·ƀi·sár] *v.* to revise; to review; to examine, inspect.

revisión [rre·ƀi·sjón] *m.* revision; review (*of a case*), new trial; inspection (*of baggage*).

revisor [rre·ƀi·sór] *m.* corrector; inspector,

RE

overseer.

revista [rre·βís·ta] *f.* (*inspección*) review; inspection; (*publicación*) magazine, journal; (*proceso*) second trial or hearing; **pasar** — to pass in review; to examine carefully; to review (*troops*).

revistar [rre·βis·tár] *v.* to review, inspect (*troops*).

revivir [rre·βi·βír] *v.* to revive.

revocación [rre·βo·ka·sjón] *f.* repeal, cancellation.

revocar⁶ [rre·βo·kár] *v.* to revoke, repeal.

revolcar⁶ [rre·βol·kár] *v.* (*derribar*) to knock down; to turn over and over; to floor, defeat; (*suspender*) to fail, flunk; **-se** to wallow; to roll over and over; to flounder.

revolotear [rre·βo·lo·te·ár] *v.* to fly about, flutter around; to hover; to circle around.

revoltijo [rre·βol·tí·xo], **revoltillo** [rre·βol·tí·yo] *m.* jumble, mixture, mess; tangle, muddle; **revoltillo de huevos** scrambled eggs.

revoltoso [rre·βol·tó·so] *adj.* turbulent, unruly, rebellious; mischievous; intricate; *m.* agitator, troublemaker; rebel.

revolución [rre·βo·lu·sjón] *f.* revolution.

revolucionario [rre·βo·lu·sjo·ná·rjo] *adj.* revolutionary; *m.* revolutionist, revolutionary.

revolver² [rre·βol·βér] *v. irr.* to revolve; to turn over; to stir up; to mix up; to turn around swiftly (*a horse*); **-se** to move back and forth; to roll over and over; to change (*said of the weather*).

revólver [rre·βól·βer] *m.* revolver, pistol.

revuelo [rre·βwé·lo] *m.* whirl; stir, commotion; flying around.

revuelta [rre·βwél·ta] *f.* revolt, revolution; second turn; turn, bend; quarrel, fight; *Am.* sudden turning of a horse.

revuelto [rre·βwél·to] *p.p. of* **revolver** & *adj.* confused; mixed up; intricate, complicated; choppy (*sea*); changeable (*weather*); **huevos -s** scrambled eggs.

rey [rrej] *m.* king.

reyerta [rre·yér·ta] *f.* quarrel, dispute.

rezagado [rre·sa·gá·ðo] *adj.* back, behind; *m.* straggler, slowpoke, latecomer.

rezagar⁷ [rre·sa·gár] *v.* to leave behind; to separate (*the weak cattle*) from the herd; *Am.* to reserve, set aside; **-se** to lag behind.

rezar⁹ [rre·sár] *v.* to pray; to say or recite (*a prayer*); to mutter, grumble; **así lo reza el libro** so the book says; **eso no reza conmigo** that has nothing to do with me.

rezo [rré·so] *m.* prayer.

rezongar⁷ [rre·son·gár] *v.* to grumble, growl, mutter.

rezongón⁷ [rre·son·gón] *adj.* growling, grumbling; *m.* grumbler, growler; scolder.

rezumar [rre·su·már] *v.* to ooze; to leak; **se rezuma** it oozes, it seeps through.

ria [rrí·a] *f.* mouth of a river, estuary.

riachuelo [rrja·čwé·lo] *m.* rivulet, brook.

ribazo [rri·βá·so] *m.* bank, ridge.

ribera [rri·βé·ra] *f.* shore, bank, beach.

ribereño [rri·βe·ré·ño] *adj.* of, pertaining to, or living on, a river bank.

ribete [rri·βé·te] *m.* trimming, border, edge, binding; addition; **tiene sus -s de poeta** he is something of a poet.

ribetear [rri·βe·te·ár] *v.* to bind, put a binding on; to border, trim the edge or border of.

ricacho [rri·ká·čo] *adj.* quite rich (*often said sarcastically*); **ricachón** [rri·ka·čón] *adj.* extremely rich, disgustingly rich.

rico [rrí·ko] *adj.* rich, wealthy; delicious; exquisite; **ricote** [rri·kó·te] = **ricacho.**

ridiculizar ⁹ [rri·ði·ku·li·sár] *v.* to ridicule, deride.

ridículo [rri·ði·ku·lo] *adj.* ridiculous; queer, strange; *m.* ridicule; ridiculous situation; **hacer el** — to be ridiculous; to act the fool.

riego [rrjé·go] *m.* irrigation; watering.

riel [rrjel] *m.* rail; **-es** track, railroad track.

rienda [rrjén·da] *f.* rein, bridle; moderation, restraint; **a** — **suelta** with free rein, without restraint; violently, swiftly; **soltar la** — to let loose, act without restraint; **tirar las -s** to draw rein, tighten the reins; to restrain.

riente [rrjén·te] *adj.* laughing, smiling.

riesgo [rrjez·go] *m.* risk.

rifa [rrí·fa] *f.* raffle; scuffle, quarrel.

rifar [rrí·fár] *v.* to raffle; to scuffle, quarrel.

rifeño [rri·fé·ño] *m.* riff.

rifle [rrí·fle] *m.* rifle.

rigidez [rri·xi·ðés] *f.* rigidity, stiffness; severity, strictness.

rígido [rrí·xi·ðo] *adj.* rigid, stiff; severe, strict.

rigor [rri·gór] *m.* rigor; severity; harshness; rigidity, stiffness; **en** — in reality; strictly; **ser de** — to be absolutely indispensable, be required by custom.

rigoroso [rri·go·ró·so], **riguroso** [rri·gu·ró·so] *adj.* rigorous; harsh; severe; strict.

rima [rrí·ma] *f.* rhyme; **-s** poems.

rimar [rri·már] *v.* to rhyme.

rimbombante [rrim·bom·bán·te] *adj.* high-sounding; resounding.

rimero [rri·mé·ro] *m.* pile, heap.

rincón [rriŋ·kón] *m.* corner; nook; *Am.* narrow valley.

rinconada [rriŋ·ko·ná·ða] *f.* corner; nook.

rinconera [rriŋ·ko·né·ra] *f.* corner cupboard, corner table, corner bracket.

ringlera [rriŋ·glé·ra] *f.* tier, row, line.

rinoceronte [rri·no·se·rón·te] *m.* rhinoceros.

riña [rrí·ña] *f.* quarrel, dispute, fight.

riñón [rri·ñón] *m.* kidney; center, interior.

río [rrí·o] *m.* river.

ripio [rrí·pjo] *m.* rubble, stone or brick fragments; padding (*in a verse, speech, etc.*), useless word.

riqueza [rri·ké·sa] *f.* riches; wealth.

risa [rrí·sa] *f.* laugh; laughter; **reventar de** — to burst with laughter; **tomar a** — to take lightly; to laugh off.

risada [rri·sá·ða] *f.* gale of laughter, loud laugh.

risco [rrís·ko] *m.* rocky cliff, crag; honey fritter.

risible [rri·sí·βle] *adj.* laughable, ridiculous.

risotada [rri·so·tá·ða] *f.* guffaw, big laugh.

ristra [rrís·tra] *f.* string (*of onions, garlic, etc.*); series, row.

risueño [rri·swé·ño] *adj.* smiling; pleasant; delightful.

rítmico [rríd·mi·ko] *adj.* rhythmical.

ritmo [rríd·mo] *m.* rhythm.

rito [rrí·to] *m.* rite, ceremony.

rival [rri·βál] *m. & f.* rival, competitor; enemy.

rivalidad [rri·βa·li·ðáð] *f.* rivalry, competition; enmity.

rivalizar⁹ [rri·βa·li·sár] *v.* to rival, compete.

rizado [rri·sá·ðo] *p.p.* curled; *adj.* wavy, curly; *m.* curling; curls.

rizar⁹ [rri·sár] *v.* to curl; to ripple; to ruffle, gather into ruffles; **-se** to curl one's hair; to curl.

rizo [rrí·so] *m.* curl; *adj.* curly; **rizoso** [rri·só·so] *adj.* curly.

roano [rro·á·no] *adj.* roan (*red, bay, or chestnut-colored, mixed with white; applied to a horse*).

robalo [rro·ḇá·lo] *m.* bass.
robar [rro·ḇár] *v.* to rob, steal; to abduct, kidnap.
roble [rró·ḇle] *m.* oak tree; oak wood; **robledal**
[rro·ḇle·dál], **robledo** [rro·ḇlé·do] *m.* oak grove.
robo [rró·ḇo] *m.* robbery, theft; loot, plunder.
robusto [rró·ḇús·to] *adj.* robust, vigorous.
roca [rró·ka] *f.* rock, boulder; rocky cliff, crag.
rocalloso [rro·ka·yó·so] *adj.* rocky.
roce [rró·se] *m.* graze; friction; contact; **no tener**
— **con** to have no contact with (*a person*).
rociada [rro·sjá·ḏa] *f.* sprinkling; spray; dew;
sprinkle, shower; volley of harsh words.
rociar[17] [rro·sjár] *v.* to sprinkle; to spray; to fall
(*said of dew*).
rocín [rro·sín] *m.* nag, hack; draft horse; coarse,
ill-bred man; *Riopl., Mex., Andes* riding horse.
rocío [rro·sí·o] *m.* dew; sprinkle; shower; spray; *adj.*
Am. reddish, roan (*horse*).
rocoso [rro·kó·so] *adj.* rocky.
rodada [rro·ḏá·ḏa] *f.* rut, wheel track; *Riopl.*
tumble, fall.
rodado [rro·ḏáḏ·ḏo] *adj.* dapple (*horse*); *p.p. of*
rodar.
rodadura [rro·ḏa·ḏú·ra] *f.* rolling; rut; — **del**
neumático tire tread.
rodaja [rro·ḏá·xa] *f.* disk; small wheel; round slice.
rodaje [rro·ḏá·xe] *m.* works (*of a watch*); — **de**
película the filming of a movie.
rodar[2] [rro·ḏár] *v. irr.* to roll; to revolve; to roam,
wander about; to fall down (*rolling*); *Am.* — **a**
patadas to kick down.
rodear [rro·ḏe·ár] *v.* to go around; to go by a
roundabout way; to surround, encircle; *Riopl.,*
Cuba, Ven. to round up (*cattle*).
rodela [rro·ḏé·la] *f.* round shield; *Mex.* padded
ring for carrying loads on the head; *Am.* round
slice; *Am.* kettle lid; *Am.* hoop; *Am.* game of
rolling a hoop.
rodeo [rro·ḏé·o] *m.* detour, roundabout way;
circumlocution, roundabout expression; dodge,
evasion; corral, stockyard; rodeo, roundup.
rodilla [rro·ḏi·ya] *f.* knee; **de** -**s** on one's knees;
hincarse de -**s** to kneel down.
rodillo [rro·ḏí·yo] *m.* roller; rolling pin; road
roller.
rodio [rró·ḏjo] *m.* rhodium.
rododendro [rro·ḏo·ḏén·dro] *m.* rhododendron.
roedor [rro·e·ḏór] *m.* rodent.
roer[51] [rro·ér] *v. irr.* to gnaw; to corrode, eat
away; to torment, harass.
rogar[2, 7] [rro·gár] *v. irr.* to pray, beg, beseech;
hacerse de — to let oneself be coaxed.
rojez [rro·xés] *f.* redness.
rojizo [rro·xí·so] *adj.* reddish.
rojo [rró·xo] *adj.* red; red, radical.
rojura [rro·xú·ra] *f.* redness.
rollizo [rro·yí·so] *adj.* plump; *m.* log.
rollo [rró·yo] *m.* roll; bundle; rolling pin; log.
romadizo [rro·ma·ḏí·so] *m.* nasal catarrh, head
cold.
romance [rro·mán·se] *adj.* Romance, Romanic
(*language*); *m.* Romance language; Spanish
language; romance, chivalric novel; ballad;
eight-syllable meter with even verses rhyming in
assonance; **en buen** — in plain language.
románico [rro·má·ni·ko] *adj.* Romanesque
(*architecture*); Romance (*language*).
romano [rro·má·no] *adj. & m.* Roman.
romanticismo [rro·man·ti·siz·mo] *m.* romanticism.
romántico [rro·mán·ti·ko] *adj.* romantic;
sentimental; *m.* romantic; sentimentalist.

rombo [rróm·bo] *m.* rhombus.
romería [rro·me·rí·a] *f.* pilgrimage.
romero [rro·mé·ro] *m.* pilgrim; rosemary (*shrub*).
romo [rró·mo] *adj.* blunt; snub-nosed.
rompe [rróm·pe]: **de** — **y rasga** resolute, bold;
al — *Am.* suddenly.
rompecabezas [rrom·pe·ka·ḇé·sas] *m.* puzzle,
riddle.
rompenueces [rrom·pe·nwé·ses] *m.* nutcracker.
rompeolas [rrom·pe·ó·las] *m.* breakwater, mole.
romper[52] [rrom·pér] *v.* to break; to shatter; to
tear; to wear through; *Ven.* to leave suddenly or
on the run; — **el alba** to dawn; — **a** to start to;
-**se** to break.
rompiente [rrom·pjén·te] *m.* shoal, sand bank, reef;
-**s** breakers, surf.
rompimiento [rrom·pi·mjén·to] *m.* rupture, break;
crack; breach; quarrel.
rompopo [rrom·pó·po] *m.* eggnog.
ron [rron] *m.* rum.
roncar[6] [rroŋ·kár] *v.* to snore; to roar; to brag.
ronco [rróŋ·ko] *adj.* hoarse; harsh-sounding.
roncha [rrón·ča] *f.* hive; welt.
ronda [rrón·da] *f.* patrol; night serenaders; round
(*of a game, of drinks, etc.*); *Riopl., C.A., Andes*
ring-around-a-rosy (*a children's game*); **hacer la**
— **a** to court; *Am.* to surround, trap (*an*
animal).
rondar [rron·dár] *v.* to go around, hover around;
to patrol; to make the rounds; to serenade.
ronquera [rron·ké·ra] *f.* hoarseness.
ronquido [rron·ki·ḏo] *m.* snore; snort.
ronronear [rron·rro·ne·ár] *v.* to purr.
ronroneo [rron·rro·né·o] *m.* purr.
ronzal [rron·sál] *m.* halter.
roña [rró·ña] *f.* scab, mange; filth; infection;
stinginess; trickery; *Riopl., Col., Ven., Cuba* ill
will, grudge; *Am.* **hacer** — to fake an illness.
roñoso [rro·ñó·so] *adj.* scabby, mangy; dirty;
stingy; *Carib., Mex.* spiteful; *Am.* fainthearted,
cowardly.
ropa [rró·pa] *f.* clothing, clothes; — **blanca** linen;
— **vieja** old colthes; stew made from leftover
meat; **a quema** — at close range (*when*
shooting); suddenly, without warning.
ropaje [rro·pá·xe] *m.* clothes, clothing, apparel;
robe.
ropería [rro·pe·rí·a] *f.* clothing store.
ropero [rro·pé·ro] *m.* clothier; wardrobe,
clothespress; wardrobe keeper; *Am.* clothes rack.
roqueño [rro·ké·ño] *adj.* rocky; hard, like rock.
rorro [rró·rro] *m.* popular term for a baby.
rosa [rró·sa] *f.* rose; red spot on the skin; rose
color; *Ch., Mex.* rosebush; — **de los vientos** (*or*
— **náutica**) mariner's compass.
rosado [rro·sá·ḏo] *adj.* rosy, rose-colored; frosted
(*drink*); *Am.* roan, reddish-brown (*horse*).
rosal [rro·sál] *m.* rosebush.
rosario [rro·sá·rjo] *m.* rosary; — **de desdichas** chain
of misfortunes.
rosbif [rroz·ḇíf] *m.* roast beef.
rosca [rrós·ka] *f.* screw and nut; screw thread;
spiral, twist; ring-shaped roll; *Mex., Ven., Col.*
ring-shaped cushion (*for carrying loads on the*
head); *Am.* circle of card players.
roseta [rro·sé·ta] *f.* rosette; small rose; -**s** popcorn.
rosetón [rro·se·tón] *m.* large rosette; rose
window.
rosillo [rro·sí·yo] *adj.* light red; roan (*horse*).
rostro [rrós·tro] *m.* face; **hacer** — to face.
rota [rró·ta] *f.* rout, defeat; ship's course; Rota

(*ecclesiastical court*); rattan palm tree.
rotación [rro·ta·sjón] *f.* rotation.
rotario [rro·tá·rjo] *m.* member of the Rotary Club.
rotativo [rro·ta·tí·βo] *adj.* rotary; *f.* printing press.
rotatorio [rro·ta·tó·rjo] *adj.* rotary.
roto [rró·to] *p.p. irr.* of **romper** & *adj.* broken; shattered; torn; worn out, ragged; *m. Ch.* person of the poorer class.
rotular [rro·tu·lár] *v.* to label; to letter.
rótulo [rró·tu·lo] *m.* title, inscription; label.
rotundo [rro·tún·do] *adj.* round; sonorous; **una negativa rotunda** a flat denial.
rotura [rro·tú·ra] *f.* breach, opening; break; tear, rip; rupture; fracture.
roturar [rro·tu·rár] *v.* to break ground; to plow (*new ground*).
rozadura [rro·sa·dú·ra] *f.* friction; chafe; chafing.
rozamiento [rro·sa·mjén·to] *m.* friction; rubbing.
rozar[9] [rro·sár] *v.* to graze; to scrape; to chafe; to clear of underbush; **-se con alguien** to have connections, contact, or dealings with someone.
rozón [rro·són] *m.* graze, sudden or violent scrape; short, broad scythe.
ruana [rrwá·na] *f. Col., Ven.* a woolen poncho.
ruano [rrwá·no] = **roano**.
rubí [rru·βí] *m.* ruby.
rubicundo [rru·βi·kún·do] *adj.* reddish; ruddy, healthy red; reddish-blond.
rubidio [rru·βí·djo] *m.* rubidium.
rubio [rrú·βjo] *adj.* blond, blonde.
rubor [rru·βór] *m.* blush; bashfulness, shyness.
ruborizarse[9] [rru·βo·ri·sar·se] *v.* to blush; to feel ashamed.
rúbrica [rrú·βri·ka] *f.* scroll, flourish (*added to a signature*); title, heading; **de** — according to ritual, rule, or custom.
rucio [rrú·sjo] *adj.* grey (*horse or donkey*); — **rodado** dapple-grey.
rudeza [rru·dé·sa] *f.* rudeness; coarseness; roughness.
rudo [rrú·do] *adj.* rude; coarse; rough; stupid.
rueca [rrwé·ka] *f.* distaff (*used for spinning*).
rueda [rrwé·da] *f.* (*maquina*) wheel; circle; spread of a peacock's tail; round object; (*grupo*) circle; group; **en** — in turn; in a circle; **hacer la** — **a** to court; to flatter.
ruedo [rrwé·do] *m.* circuit, tour; border, rim; circumference.
ruego [rrwé·go] *m.* prayer, supplication, request.
rufián [rru·fján] *m.* ruffian; bully.
rugido [rru·xi·do] *m.* roar; rumbling.
rugir[11] [rru·xír] *v.* to roar; to bellow.
rugoso [rru·gó·so] *adj.* wrinkled; furrowed.
ruibarbo [rrwi·βár·βo] *m.* rhubarb.
ruidazo [rrwi·dá·so] *m.* big noise.
ruido [rrwi·do] *m.* noise; din; dispute; talk, rumor; **hacer** (*or* **meter**) — to make a noise; to create a sensation; to cause a disturbance.
ruidoso [rrwi·dó·so] *adj.* noisy; loud; sensational.
ruin [rrwin] *adj.* (*vicioso*) vile, base, mean; vicious (*animal*); (*mezquino*) small; petty; puny; stingy.
ruina [rrwi·na] *f.* ruin; destruction; downfall.
ruindad [rrwin·dád] *f.* baseness; meanness; stinginess; mean or vile act.
ruinoso [rrwi·nó·so] *adj.* ruinous; in a state of ruin or decay.
ruiseñor [rrwi·se·ñór] *m.* nightingale.
rumba [rrúm·ba] *f. Ven., Col., Carib., Mex., Riopl.* rumba (*dance and music*); *Carib., Ven., Andes* spree; *Carib., Ven., Andes* **irse de** — to go on a spree.

rumbear [rrum·be·ár] *v. Riopl., Andes* to head (towards), take a certain direction; *Am.* to cut a path through a forest; *Am.* to go on a spree.
rumbo [rrúm·bo] *m.* (*ruta*) direction, course; route; (*pompa*) pomp; ostentation; *Am.* cut on the head; *Am.* revel, noisy spree; **hacer** — **a** to head or sail towards; *Am.* **ir al** — to be going in the right direction, be on the right track.
rumboso [rrum·bó·so] *adj.* pompous, ostentatious; generous.
rumiante [rru·mján·te] *m.* ruminant.
rumiar [rru·mjár] *v.* to ruminate; to chew the cud; to ponder, meditate.
rumor [rru·mór] *m.* rumor, report; murmur; rumble.
runfla [rrún·fla] *f.* series (*of things of the same kind*); sequence (*in cards*).
runrún [rrun·rrún] *m.* rumor; murmur.
ruptura [rrup·tú·ra] *f.* rupture; break; fracture.
rural [rru·rál] *adj.* rural.
ruso [rrú·so] *adj.* Russian; *m.* Russian; Russian language.
rústico [rrús·ti·ko] *adj.* rustic, rural; crude, coarse; *m.* peasant; **en** (*or* **a la**) **rústica** unbound, paper-bound.
ruta [rrú·ta] *f.* route, course, way.
rutenio [rru·té·njo] *m.* ruthenium.
rutina [rru·tí·na] *f.* routine.

S:s **sábado** [sá·βa·do] *m.* Saturday.
sábalo [sá·βa·lo] *m.* shad; *Am.* tarpon.
sábana [sá·βa·na] *f.* bed sheet; altar cloth.
sabana [sa·βá·na] *f. Col.* savanna, treeless plain; *Col.* **ponerse en la** — to become suddenly rich.
sabandija [sa·βan·dí·xa] *f.* small reptile; small lizard.
sabañón [sa·βa·ñón] *m.* chilblain.
sabedor [sa·βe·dór] *adj.* knowing; aware, informed.
saber[42] [sa·βér] *v. irr.* to know; to know how to, be able to; to learn, find out; *Riopl., Ven., Col.* to be in the habit of; — **a** to taste of, taste like; **sabe bien** it tastes good; **a** — namely; that is; *Am.* **¿a** — **si venga!** who knows whether he will come!; **un no sé qué** an indefinable something; **¿sabe Vd. a la plaza?** do you know the way to the square?; *m.* knowledge, learning.
sabiduría [sa·βi·du·rí·a] *f.* wisdom; knowledge.
sabiendas [sa·βjén·das] : **a** — consciously, knowingly.
sabino [sa·βí·no] *adj.* roan.
sabio [sá·βjo] *adj.* wise; judicious; learned; *m.* savant, scholar; sage, wise man.
sable [sá·βle] *m.* saber; **sablazo** [sa·βlá·so] *m.* blow with a saber; saber wound; **dar un sablazo** to strike for a loan.
sabor [sa·βór] *m.* savor, taste, flavor.
saborear [sa·βo·re·ár] *v.* to savor, flavor, season; to relish, taste with pleasure; to enjoy; **-se** to eat or drink with relish; to smack one's lips.
sabotaje [sa·βo·tá·xe] *m.* sabotage.
sabotear [sa·βo·te·ár] *v.* to sabotage.
sabroso [sa·βró·so] *adj.* savory, tasty; delicious; delightful.
sabueso [sa·βwé·so] *m.* hound.
sacabocados [sa·ka·βo·ká·dos] *m.* punch (*tool*).
sacacorchos [sa·ka·cór·čos] *m.* corkscrew.

sacamuelas [sa·ka·mwé·las] *m.* & *f.* tooth puller; quack dentist.

sacar[6] [sa·kár] *v.* to draw, draw out, pull out, get out, or take out; to get, obtain; to infer; to make (*a copy*); to take (*a snapshot or picture*); to stick out (*one's tongue*); to serve (*a ball*); — **a bailar** to ask to dance, lead on to the dance floor; — **a luz** to publish; — **el cuerpo** to dodge; — **en claro** (*or* — **en limpio**) to deduce, conclude; *Am.* — **el sombrero** to take off one's hat; *Am.* ¡**sáquese de allí**! get out of there!

sacarina [sa·ka·rí·na] *f.* saccharine.

sacerdocio [sa·ser·ḍó·sjo] *m.* priesthood.

sacerdote [sa·ser·ḍó·te] *m.* priest.

saciar [sa·sjár] *v.* to satiate, satisfy; **-se** to be satiated, satisfied completely.

saco [sá·ko] *m.* sack, bag; sackful, bagful; loose-fitting coat; sack, plundering; *Am.* suit coat; — **de noche** overnight bag, satchel.

sacramento [sa·kra·mén·to] *m.* sacrament.

sacrificar[6] [sa·kri·fi·kár] *v.* to sacrifice.

sacrificio [sa·kri·fí·sjo] *m.* sacrifice.

sacrilegio [sa·kri·lé·xjo] *m.* sacrilege.

sacrílego [sa·krí·le·ḡo] *adj.* sacrilegious.

sacristán [sa·kris·tán] *m.* sacristan, sexton; *Am.* busybody, meddler.

sacro [sá·kro] *adj.* sacred.

sacrosanto [sa·kro·sán·to] *adj.* sacrosanct, holy and sacred.

sacudida [sa·ku·ḍí·ḍa] *f.* shake, jolt, jerk.

sacudimiento [sa·ku·ḍi·mjén·to] *m.* shaking; shake, jerk; shock, jolt.

sacudir [sa·ku·ḍír] *v.* to shake; to jerk; to beat; to beat the dust from; to shake off; **-se** to shake oneself; to brush oneself off; **-se de alguien** to shake someone off, get rid of someone.

sádico [sá·ḍi·ko] *adj.* sadistic, cruel.

sadismo [sa·ḍíz·mo] *m.* sadism.

saeta [sa·é·ta] *f.* arrow, dart.

sagacidad [sa·ḡa·si·ḍáḍ] *f.* sagacity.

sagaz [sa·ḡás] *adj.* sagacious, shrewd.

sagrado [sa·ḡrá·ḍo] *adj.* sacred; consecrated; *m.* asylum, refuge.

sahumar [sa·u·már] *v.* to perfume with incense; to fumigate.

sahumerio [sa·u·mé·rjo] *m.* vapor, fume; incense; burning of incense; fumigation.

sainete [sáj·né·te] *m.* one-act comedy or farce; delicacy, tasty tidbit; flavor, relish; sauce.

sajón [sa·xón] *adj.* & *m.* Saxon.

sal [sal] *f.* salt; wit, humor; grace; *Mex., Cuba, C.A., Col., Andes* misfortune, bad luck.

sala [sá·la] *f.* parlor; hall, large room; — **de justicia** courtroom.

salado [sa·lá·ḍo] *adj.* salty; salted; witty; charming; *Am.* costly; *Mex., Cuba, C.A., Col., Andes* **estar** — to be unlucky; *m. Am.* salt pit, salt mine.

salar [sa·lár] *v.* to salt; to cure or preserve with salt; *Mex., Cuba, C.A., Col., Andes* to bring bad luck (to); *Am.* to dishonor; *Am.* to ruin, spoil; *Am.* to bribe; *Am.* to feed salt to cattle; *m. Am.* salt pit.

salario [sa·lá·rjo] *m.* salary, wages.

salchicha [sal·čí·ča] *f.* sausage; **salchichón** [sal·či·čón] *m.* large sausage.

saldar [sal·dár] *v.* to balance, settle (*an account*).

saldo [sál·do] *m.* balance, settlement (*of an account*); bargain sale.

saledizo [sa·le·ḍí·so] = **salidizo**.

salero [sa·lé·ro] *m.* (*vaso*) saltcellar, saltshaker;

place for storing salts; salt lick; (*gracia*) wit, grace, charm; *Am.* salt dealer.

saleroso [sa·le·ró·so] *adj.* charming; witty; attractive (*more common in feminine*).

salida [sa·lí·ḍa] *f.* departure; exit; sally; outlet; way out; loophole; outskirts; outcome; jut, projection; outlay, expenditure; witty remark; — **de pie de banco** silly remark, nonsense; — **del sol** sunrise; *Cuba* — **de teatro** evening wrap.

salidizo [sa·li·ḍí·so] *m.* jut, ledge, projection; *adj.* salient, jutting, projecting.

saliente [sa·ljén·te] *adj.* salient, standing out; projecting; *m.* salient, salient angle; jut, projection.

salina [sa·lí·na] *f.* salt mine or pit; salt works.

salir[43] [sa·lír] *v. irr.* (*partir*) to go out; to leave; depart; to get out (*of*); to come out; to sprout; to come (*from*); (*resultar*) to turn out to be; — **bien** to turn out well; to come out well; — **a su padre** to turn out to be or look like his father; *Am.* — **a mano** to come out even; **-se** to get out, slip out; to leak out; **-se con la suya** to get one's own way.

salitral [sa·li·trál] *m.* saltpeter bed or mine.

salitre [sa·lí·tre] *m.* saltpeter; **salitrera** [sa·li·tré·ra] *f.* saltpeter mine or bed; **salitroso** [sa·li·tró·so] *adj.* nitrous, abounding in saltpeter.

saliva [sa·lí·ḅa] *f.* saliva.

salmo [sál·mo] *m.* psalm.

salmodiar [sal·mo·ḍjár] *v.* to chant; to talk in a monotone or singsong.

salmón [sal·món] *m.* salmon.

salmuera [sal·mwé·ra] *f.* brine.

salobre [sa·ló·ḅre] *adj.* briny, salty.

salón [sa·lón] *m.* salon, hall, large room; salted meat or fish.

salpicadero [sal·pi·ka·ḍé·ro] *m.* dashboard.

salpicadura [sal·pi·ka·ḍú·ra] *f.* spatter, splash.

salpicar[6] [sal·pi·kár] *v.* to sprinkle, spray, spatter.

salpicón [sal·pi·kón] *m.* hash; hodgepodge; *Ec.* fruit drink.

salpimentar[1] [sal·pi·men·tár] *v. irr.* to salt and pepper.

salpimienta [sal·pi·mjén·ta] *f.* salt and pepper.

salpullido [sal·pu·yí·ḍo] *m.* rash, skin eruption.

salsa [sál·sa] *f.* sauce; gravy; *Am.* sound whipping or beating; **salsera** [sal·sé·ra] *f.* sauce dish.

saltamontes [sal·ta·món·tes] *m.* grasshopper.

saltar [sal·tár] *v.* (*brincar*) to jump; to jump over; to leap; to bounce; to skip; (*estallar*) to burst, break into pieces; to come off; — **a la vista** to be obvious, evident; — **a tierra** to disembark, land; *Mex.* — **las trancas** to lose one's patience; to lose one's head.

salteador [sal·te·a·ḍór] *m.* bandit, highway robber.

saltear [sal·te·ár] *v.* to assault, attack; to hold up, rob; to take by surprise; to jump or skip around.

salto [sál·to] *m.* jump; leap; precipice; gap; — **de agua** waterfall; **a -s** by jumps; **en un** (*or* **de un**) — in a jiffy; quickly; **dar un** — to jump, leap.

saltón [sal·tón] *adj.* jumping, skipping, hopping; jumpy; protruding; *Col.* half-cooked; **ojos -es** popeyes, bulging eyes; *m.* grasshopper.

salubre [sa·lú·ḅre] *adj.* healthy, healthful.

salubridad [sa·lu·ḅri·ḍáḍ] *f.* healthfulness, health; sanitation.

salud [sa·lúḍ] *f.* health; welfare; salvation; ¡—! greetings!; your health!

saludable [sa·lu·ḍá·ḅle] *adj.* wholesome, healthful beneficial.

saludador [sa·lu·ḏa·ḏór] *m.* greeter; healer, quack.
saludar [sa·lu·ḏár] *v.* to salute, greet; to fire a salute.
saludo [sa·lú·ḏo] *m.* salute, nod, greeting.
salutación [sa·lu·ta·sjón] *f.* salutation; greeting.
salva [sál·ḅa] *f.* salvo, salute with guns; greeting; welcome.
salvación [sal·ḅa·sjón] *f.* salvation.
salvado [sal·ḅá·ḏo] *m.* bran.
salvador [sal·ḅa·ḏór] *m.* savior, rescuer; Savior (Saviour); *adj.* saving.
salvaguardar [sal·ḅa·ǥwar·ḏár] *v.* to safeguard, defend, protect.
salvaguardia [sal·ḅa·ǥwár·ḏja] *m.* safeguard, protection; guard; *f.* safe-conduct paper, passport; password.
salvajada [sal·ḅa·xá·ḏa] *f.* savage act or remark.
salvaje [sal·ḅá·xe] *adj.* savage, wild; *m.* savage.
salvajez [sal·ḅa·xés] *f.* wildness, savagery.
salvajismo [sal·ḅa·xíz·mo] *m.* savagery; *Am.* savage act or remark. *See* **salvajada.**
salvamento [sal·ḅa·mén·to] *m.* salvation, rescue; place of safety; salvage (*rescue of property*); **bote de —** lifeboat.
salvar [sal·ḅár] *v.* (*librar*) to save; to except; to exclude; (*vencer*) to clear, jump over; **-se** to be saved; to save oneself, escape.
salvavidas [sal·ḅa·ḅí·ḏas] *m.* life preserver; **lancha —** lifeboat.
¡salve! [sál·ḅe] *interj.* hail!; **Salve** [sál·ḅe] *f.* Salve Regina, prayer to the Virgin Mary.
salvia [sál·ḅja] *f.* sage (*a plant*).
salvo [sál·ḅo] *adj.* saved; safe; *prep.* save, except but; **a —** safe, without injury; **en —** in safety; out of danger.
salvoconducto [sal·ḅo·kon·dúk·to] *m.* safe-conduct, pass.
san [san] *adj.* (*contr. of* **santo**) saint.
sánalotodo [sá·na·lo·tó·ḏo] *m.* cure-all.
sanar [sa·nár] *v.* to heal, cure; to recover, get well.
sanatorio [sa·na·tó·rjo] *m.* sanitarium.
sanción [san·sjón] *f.* sanction.
sancionar [san·sjo·nár] *v.* to sanction; to authorize, ratify.
sancocho [saŋ·kó·čo] *m.* parboiled meat.
sandalia [san·dá·lja] *f.* sandal.
sandez [san·dés] *f.* stupidity; folly; foolish remark.
sandía [san·dí·a] *f.* watermelon.
sandio [san·dí·o] *adj.* silly, foolish.
saneamiento [sa·ne·a·mjén·to] *m.* sanitation; drainage of land.
sanear [sa·ne·ár] *v.* to make sanitary (*land, property, etc.*); to drain, dry up (*land*).
sangrar [saŋ·gár] *v.* to bleed; to drain; to tap (*a tree*); to pilfer; to exploit (*someone*); to indent (*a line*).
sangre [sáŋ·gre] *f.* blood; **— fría** calmness, coolness of mind; **a — fría** in cold blood.
sangría [saŋ·grí·a] *f.* a refreshing Spanish drink made of red wine, fruit juice, and sugar.
sangriento [saŋ·grjén·to] *adj.* bleeding; bloody; bloodstained; bloodthirsty, cruel.
sanguijuela [saŋ·gi·xwé·la] *f.* leech.
sanguinario [saŋ·gi·ná·rjo] *adj.* bloody, cruel; bloodthirsty, murderous.
sanidad [sa·ni·ḏáḏ] *f.* health; soundness; healthfulness; sanitation; **— publica** health department.
sanitario [sa·ni·tá·rjo] *adj.* sanitary.
sano [sá·no] *adj.* (*de salud*) sound, healthy; healthful; sane, sensible; (*integro*) whole;

unbroken; undamaged; **— y salvo** safe and sound.
sanseacabó [san·se·a·ka·ḅó] that's all; that's the end.
santiamén [san·tja·mén]: **en un —** in a jiffy.
santidad [san·ti·ḏáḏ] *f.* sanctity, holiness, saintliness; **su Santidad** his Holiness.
santificar[6] [san·ti·fi·kár] *v.* to sanctify; to consecrate.
santiguar[8] [san·ti·ǥwár] *v.* to bless; to make the sign of the cross; to beat, hit, punish; **-se** to cross oneself; to show astonishment (*by crossing oneself*).
santísimo [san·tí·si·mo] *adj.* most holy; *m.* the Holy Sacrament.
santo [sán·to] *adj.* saintly, holy; sacred; **esperar todo el — día** to wait the whole blessed day; **— y bueno** well and good; *Ríopl., Col., Ven., Mex., Carib., Andes* **¡santa palabra!** that's my final and last word! *m.* saint; saint's day; *Mex., Ven.* **tener el — de espaldas** to have a streak of bad luck; **santurrón** *m.* religious hypocrite, affectedly pious person.
santuario [san·twá·rjo] *m.* sanctuary; *Col.* buried treasure; *Am.* Indian idol.
saña [sá·ña] *f.* fury, rage.
sañudo [sa·ñú·ḏo] *adj.* furious, enraged.
sapo [sá·po] *m.* toad; *Col.* despicable little man; *Col.* chubby person; *Am.* sly person; **echar -s y culebras** to swear, curse.
saque [sá·ke] *m.* serve, service (*in tennis*); server.
saquear [sa·ke·ár] *v.* to sack, plunder, pillage, loot.
saqueo [sa·ké·o] *m.* sacking, pillaging, plunder; loot, booty.
saquillo [sa·kí·yo] *m.* small bag, handbag, satchel.
sarampión [sa·ram·pjón] *m.* measles.
sarao [sa·rá·o] *m.* soirée, evening party.
sarape [sa·rá·pe] *m. Mex.* serape, blanket.
sarcasmo [sar·káz·mo] *m.* sarcasm.
sarcástico [sar·kás·ti·ko] *adj.* sarcastic.
sarcófago [sar·kó·fa·ǥo] *m.* sarcophagus.
sardina [sar·ḏi·na] *f.* sardine.
sardo [sár·ḏo] *adj.* Sardinian.
sargento [sar·xén·to] *m.* sergeant.
sarmentoso [sar·men·tó·so] *adj.* vinelike; full of vine shoots; gnarled, knotty.
sarmiento [sar·mjén·to] *m.* shoot or branch of a vine.
sarna [sár·na] *f.* itch; mange.
sarnoso [sar·nó·so] *adj.* itchy, scabby, mangy.
sarpullido [sar·pu·yí·ḏo] = **salpullido.**
sarro [sá·rro] *m.* tartar (*on teeth*); crust, sediment (*in utensils*).
sarta [sár·ta] *f.* string (*of beads*); series.
sartén [sar·tén] *f.* frying pan.
sastre [sás·tre] *m.* tailor.
sastrería [sas·tre·rí·a] *f.* tailor shop.
satánico [sa·tá·ni·ko] *adj.* satanic, devilish.
satélite [sa·té·li·te] *m.* satellite; suburban development; **— artificial** artificial satellite.
satén [sa·tén] *m.* sateen.
sátira [sá·ti·ra] *f.* satire.
satírico [sa·tí·ri·ko] *adj.* satirical.
satirizar[9] [sa·ti·ri·sár] *v.* to satirize.
satisfacción [sa·tis·fak·sjón] *f.* satisfaction; apology, excuse; **tomar —** to vindicate oneself; to take revenge; **dar una —** to offer an apology; to apologize.
satisfacer[31] [sa·tis·fa·sér] *v. irr.* to satisfy; to pay (*a debt*); **— una letra** to honor a draft; **-se** to be satisfied; to take satisfaction.

satisfactorio [sa·tis·fak·tó·rjo] *adj.* satisfactory.
satisfecho [sa·tis·fé·čo] *p.p. of* **satisfacer** satisfied, gratified; *adj.* content, contented.
saturar [sa·tu·rár] *v.* to saturate; to satiate.
sauce [sáw·se] *m.* willow.
savia [sá·bja] *f.* sap.
saxófono [sak·só·fo·no] *m.* saxophone; also **saxofón** [sak·so·fón], **sazón** [sa·són] *f.* (*época*) season, opportune time; (*sabor*) taste, flavor; ripeness; **a la** — then, at that time; **en** — in season; ripe; opportunely; *adj. Ríopl., Mex., Cuba* ripe.
sazonado [sa·so·ná·ḍo] *adj. & p.p.* seasoned; mellow, ripe; expressive (*said of a phrase*).
sazonar [sa·so·nár] *v.* to season; to flavor; **-se** to become seasoned; to ripen, mature.
se [se] *obj. pron.* (*before* **le, la, lo, las,** *and* **los**) to him, to her; to you (*formal*); to them; *refl. pron.* himself, herself, yourself (*formal*), yourselves (*formal*) themselves; *reciprocal pron.* each other, one another.
sebo [sé·ḅo] *m.* tallow, fat.
seboso [se·ḅó·so] *adj.* fatty; tallowy.
secador [se·ka·ḍór] *m. Am.* dryer (*clothes, hair*).
secante [se·kán·te] *adj.* drying, blotting; **papel** — blotter; *f.* secant (*math.*).
secar[6] [se·kár] *v.* to dry; to wipe dry; **-se** to dry or wipe oneself; to dry up; to wither; to get thin.
sección [sek·sjón] *f.* section; division; cutting.
seccionar [sek·sjo·nár] *v.* to section.
seco [sé·ko] *adj.* (*sin humedad*) dry; dried; withered; (*áspero*) harsh; abrupt; plain, unadorned; **en** — on dry land, out of the water; **parar en** — to stop short, stop suddenly; **a secas** plain; alone, without anything else; *Mex., Carib., Ríopl., Andes* simply, straight to the point; **comer pan a secas** to eat just bread; *Mex., Ven.* **bailar a secas** to dance without musical accompaniment.
secreción [se·kre·sjón] *f.* secretion.
secretar [se·kre·tár] *v.* to secrete.
secretaría [se·kre·ta·rí·a] *f.* secretary's office; position of secretary.
secretariado [se·kre·ta·rjá·ḍo] *m.* secretariat.
secretario [se·kre·tá·rjo] *m.* secretary; confidant; **secretaria** [se·kre·ta·rja] *f.* woman secretary; secretary's wife.
secretear [se·kre·te·ár] *v.* to whisper; **-se** to whisper to each other.
secreto [se·kré·to] *adj.* secret, hidden; secretive; *m.* secret; secrecy; secret place; — **a voces** open secret; **en** — secretly; **hablar en** — to whisper.
secta [sék·ta] *f.* sect.
secuaz [se·kwás] *m.* partisan, follower.
secuela [se·kwé·la] *f.* sequel, outcome, consequence.
secuencia [se·kwén·sja] *f.* sequence.
secuestrador [se·kwes·tra·ḍór] *m.* kidnapper; confiscator.
secuestrar [se·kwes·trár] *v.* to seize; to kidnap; to confiscate.
secuestro [se·kwés·tro] *m.* kidnapping; seizure.
secular [se·ku·lár] *adj.* secular; lay, worldly; centennial; *m.* secular, secular priest.
secundar [se·kun·dár] *v.* to second, favor, back up.
secundario [se·kun·dá·rjo] *adj.* secondary.
sed [seḍ] *f.* thirst; craving, desire; **tener** — to be thirsty.
seda [sé·da] *f.* silk; **como una** — soft as silk; sweet-tempered; smoothly, easily.
sedal [se·ḍál] *m.* fishing line.

sedán [se·ḍán] *m.* sedan.
sedativo [se·ḍa·tí·ḅo] *adj. & m.* sedative.
sede [sé·ḍe] *f.* seat, see; **Santa Sede** Holy See.
sedentario [se·ḍen·tá·rjo] *adj.* sedentary.
sedeño [se·ḍé·ño] *adj.* silky, silken.
sedería [se·ḍe·rí·a] *f.* silk goods; silk shop.
sedero [se·ḍé·ro] *m.* silk dealer or weaver; *adj.* silk, pertaining to silk; **industria sedera** silk industry.
sedición [se·ḍi·sjón] *f.* sedition.
sedicioso [se·ḍi·sjó·so] *adj.* seditious, turbulent.
sediento [se·ḍjén·to] *adj.* thirsty; dry, parched; anxious, desirous.
sedimento [se·ḍi·mén·to] *m.* sediment; dregs, grounds.
sedoso [se·ḍó·so] *adj.* silken, silky.
seducción [se·ḍuk·sjón] *f.* seduction.
seducir[25] [se·ḍu·sír] *v. irr.* to seduce; to entice; to charm.
seductivo [se·ḍuk·tí·ḅo] *adj.* seductive, alluring; inviting, enticing.
seductor [se·ḍuk·tór] *adj.* tempting, fascinating; *m.* seducer; tempter; charming person.
sefardí [se·far·ḍí] *adj.* Sephardic; *m.* Spanish-speaking Jew.
segador [se·ḡa·ḍór] *m.* harvester, reaper; **segadora** [se·ḡa·ḍó·ra] *f.* harvester, mowing machine; woman reaper.
segar[1, 7] [se·ḡár] *v. irr.* to mow, reap; to cut off.
seglar [se·ḡlár] *adj.* secular, lay; *m.* layman.
segmento [seḡ·mén·to] *m.* segment.
segregar[7] [se·ḡre·ḡár] *v. irr.* to segregate.
seguida [se·ḡí·ḍa] *f.* succession; series, continuation; **de** — without interruption, continuously; **en** — at once, immediately.
seguido [se·ḡí·ḍo] *p.p.* followed; continued; *adj.* continuous; straight, direct; *adv.* without interruption; *Am.* often; *Col., Ven.* **de** — at once, immediately.
seguidor [se·ḡi·ḍór] *m.* follower.
seguimiento [se·ḡi·mjén·to] *m.* pursuit.
seguir[5, 12] [se·ḡír] *v. irr.* to follow; to continue; to pursue; **-se** to follow as a consequence.
según [se·ḡún] *prep.* according to; *conj.* as; according to; — **y conforme** (*or* — **y como**) exactly as, just as; that depends.
segundar [se·ḡun·dár] *v.* to repeat a second time; to second.
segundero [se·ḡun·dé·ro] *m.* second hand (*of a watch or clock*).
segundo [se·ḡún·do] *adj. & m.* second.
segundón [se·ḡun·dón] *m.* second child.
seguridad [se·ḡu·ri·ḍáḍ] *f.* security; safety; certainty; **alfiler de** — safety pin.
seguro [se·ḡú·ro] *adj.* secure; sure, certain; safe; *Ríopl., Mex., Carib., Andes* honest, trustworthy; *m.* assurance; insurance; safety device; **a buen** — (**al** —, *or* **de** —) truly, certainly; **en** — in safety; **sobre** — without risk; without taking a chance; *Am.* **irse uno del** — to lose one's temper; *Ch., Mex., Cuba, Andes* **a la segura** without risk.
seibó [sej·ḅó] *m. Cuba, Ven.* sideboard, hutch.
selección [se·lek·sjón] *f.* selection choice.
seleccionar [se·lek·sjo·nár] *v.* to select, choose.
selecto [se·lék·to] *adj.* select, choice.
selenio [se·lé·njo] *m.* selenium.
selectivo [se·lek·tí·ḅo] *adj.* selective.
selva [sél·ḅa] *f.* forest; jungle.
sellar [se·yár] *v.* (*imprimir*) to stamp; to seal; (*cerrar*) to close tightly, seal; (*concluir*) to

conclude.

sello [sé·yo] *m.* seal; stamp; *Am.* official stamped paper.

semáforo [se·má·fo·ro] *m.* traffic light.

semana [se·má·na] *f.* week; week's wages; **días de** — week days; **entre** — during the week.

semanal [se·ma·nál] *adj.* weekly; **-mente** *adv.* weekly, every week.

semanario [se·ma·ná·rjo] *m.* weekly publication; *adj.* weekly.

semblante [sem·blán·te] *m.* countenance; facial expression; appearance.

semblanza [sem·blán·sa] *f.* portrait, literary sketch.

sembrado [sem·brá·ḍo] *m.* sown ground; cultivated field.

sembradora [sem·bra·ḍó·ra] *f.* seeder, sowing machine.

sembrar[1] [sem·brár] *v. irr.* to sow; to scatter.

semejante [se·me·xán·te] *adj.* similar, like; such a; *m.* fellow man; **nuestros -s** our fellow men.

semejanza [se·me·xán·sa] *f.* resemblance, similarity; simile; **a — de** in the manner of.

semejar [se·me·xár] *v.* to resemble; **-se** to resemble.

semental [se·men·tál] *adj.* sowing (*crops*); breeding (*animals*); used as stud.

semestre [se·més·tre] *m.* semester.

semiconsonante [se·mi·kon·so·nán·te] *f.* semiconsonant.

semilla [se·mí·ya] *f.* seed.

semillero [se·mi·yé·ro] *m.* seed bed; plant nursery; **— de vicios** hotbed of vice.

seminario [se·mi·ná·rjo] *m.* seminary; plant nursery, seed plot.

semítico [se·mí·ti·ko] *adj.* Semitic.

semivocal [se·mi·ḅo·kál] *f.* semivowel.

sempiterno [sem·pi·tér·no] *adj.* everlasting; evergreen.

senado [se·ná·ḍo] *m.* senate.

senador [se·na·ḍór] *m.* senator.

sencillez [sen·si·yés] *f.* simplicity; plainness.

sencillo [sen·si·yo] *adj.* simple; easy; plain; unadorned; unaffected; *m.* loose change, small coins.

senda [sén·da] *f.* path; way, course.

sendero [sen·dé·ro] *m.* path.

sendos [sén·dos] *adj. pl.* one for each of two or more persons or things.

senectud [se·nek·túḍ] *f.* senility, old age.

senil [se·nil] *adj.* senile.

seno [sé·no] *m.* (*pecho*) breast, bosom; (*hueco*) cavity, hollow; womb; lap; cove, bay; innermost recess; sinus (*cavity in a bone*); sine (*math.*); *C.A.* armpit.

sensación [sen·sa·sjón] *f.* sensation.

sensacional [sen·sa·sjo·nál] *adj.* sensational.

sensatez [sen·sa·tés] *f.* prudence, common sense.

sensato [sen·sá·to] *adj.* sensible, wise, prudent.

sensibilidad [sen·si·ḅi·li·ḍáḍ] *f.* sensibility; sensitiveness.

sensible [sen·si·ḅle] *adj.* sensitive; perceptible; regrettable.

sensitivo [sen·si·ti·ḅo] *adj.* sensitive.

sensual [sen·swál] *adj.* sensual; sensuous.

sensualidad [sen·swa·li·ḍáḍ] *f.* sensuality; lewdness.

sentada [sen·tá·ḍa] *f.* sitting; **de una — at** one sitting.

sentado [sen·tá·ḍo] *adj.* seated, sitting; **dar por —** to take for granted.

sentar[1] [sen·tár] *v. irr.* to seat; to set; to establish; to become, suit, fit; to agree with one (*as food or climate*); **-se** to sit down; to settle down; *Col.* **-se**

en la palabra to do all the talking, monopolize the conversation.

sentencia [sen·tén·sja] *f.* sentence; verdict; judgment, maxim, proverb; statement.

sentenciar [sen·ten·sjár] *v.* to sentence; to pass judgment on; to decide.

sentido [sen·ti·ḍo] *p.p.* felt; experienced; *adj.* heartfelt, filled with feeling; sensitive; touchy; **darse por —** to take offense; to have one's feelings hurt; **estar — con alguien** to be offended or peeved at someone; *m.* sense; meaning; judgment; **aguzar el —** to prick up one's ears; **perder el —** to faint.

sentimental [sen·ti·men·tál] *adj.* sentimental.

sentimentalismo [sen·ti·men·ta·líz·mo] *m.* sentimentalism, sentimentality.

sentimiento [sen·ti·mjén·to] *m.* sentiment; sensation, feeling; grief, regret.

sentir[3] [sen·tír] *v. irr.* to feel; to sense; to hear; to regret; **-se** to feel (*well, strong, sad, etc.*); to feel oneself, consider oneself; to feel resentment; to feel a pain; **sin —** without being realized or felt; inadvertently; unnoticed; *m.* feeling; judgment, opinion.

seña [sé·ña] *familiar contraction of* **señora.**

seña [sé·ña] *f.* sign, mark; signal; password; **-s** address (*name and place of residence*); **por mas -s** as an additional proof.

señal [se·ñál] *f.* (*marca*) sign, mark; signal; trace, vestige; scar; (*indicio*) reminder; indication; token, pledge; *Riopl., Andes* earmark, brand (*on the ear of livestock*); **en — de** in proof of, in token of.

señalar [se·ña·lár] *v.* to mark; to point out; to indicate; to determine, fix; to appoint; to signal; to assign; *Am.* to earmark, brand (*cattle*); **-se** to distinguish oneself.

señero [se·ñé·ro] *adj.* unique.

señor [se·ñór] *m.* mister; sir; owner; master, lord; gentleman; **el Señor** the Lord.

señora [se·ñó·ra] *f.* lady; madam; mistress; Mrs.

señorear [se·ño·re·ár] *v.* to lord it over, domineer; to dominate; to master, control.

señoría [se·ño·rí·a] *f.* lordship.

señoril [se·ño·ríl] *adj.* lordly.

señorío [se·ño·rí·o] *m.* dominion, rule; domain of a lord; lordship; dignity; mastery, control; body of noblemen.

señorita [se·ño·rí·ta] *f.* miss; young lady.

señorito [se·ño·rí·to] *m.* master, young gentleman.

señuelo [se·ñwé·lo] *m.* decoy; lure, bait; *Ven.* leading or guiding oxen.

separación [se·pa·ra·sjón] *f.* separation.

separado [se·pa·rá·ḍo] *p.p. & adj.* separate; separated; **por —** separately.

separar [se·pa·rár] *v.* to separate; to set aside; to remove (from); to dismiss (from); **-se** to separate; to retire, resign; to withdraw, leave.

separata [se·pa·rá·ta] *f.* reprint (*of an article*).

septentrional [sep·ten·trjo·nál] *adj.* northern.

septiembre [sep·tjém·bre] *m.* September.

sepulcral [se·pul·král] *adj.* sepulchral (*pertaining to sepulchers or tombs*); **lápida —** tombstone.

sepulcro [se·púl·kro] *m.* sepulcher, tomb, grave.

sepultar [se·pul·tár] *v.* to bury; to hide.

sepultura [se·pul·tú·ra] *f.* burial; grave; **dar —** to bury.

sepulturero [se·pul·tu·ré·ro] *m.* gravedigger.

sequedad [se·ke·ḍáḍ] *f.* dryness; gruffness.

sequía [se·ki·a] *f.* drought.

séquito [sé·ki·to] *m.* retinue, following.

ser⁴⁴ [ser] *v. irr.* to be; to exist; to happen, occur; — **de** (*or* **para**) **ver** to be worth seeing; *m.* being; essence, nature; existence; *Am.* **estar en un** — to be always in the same condition.

serafín [se·ra·fín] *m.* seraph.

serenar [se·re·nár] *v.* to pacify; to calm down; *Col.* to drizzle, rain gently; **-se** to become serene, calm down; to clear up (*said of the weather*).

serenata [se·re·ná·ta] *f.* serenade.

serenidad [se·re·ni·dád] *f.* serenity, calm.

sereno [se·ré·no] *adj.* serene, calm; clear, cloudless; *m.* night humidity, dew; night watchman; **al** — in the night air.

serie [sé·rje] *f.* series.

seriedad [se·rje·dád] *f.* seriousness; gravity; earnestness; dignity.

serio [sé·rjo] *adj.* serious; grave; earnest; dignified; formal; **en** — seriously.

sermón [ser·món] *m.* sermon; reproof.

sermonear [ser·mo·ne·ár] *v.* to preach; to admonish, reprimand.

serpentear [ser·pen·te·ár] *v.* to wind, twist, turn, zigzag.

serpentino [ser·pen·tí·no] *adj.* serpentine.

serpiente [ser·pjén·te] *f.* serpent, snake.

serrado [se·rrá·do] *adj.* toothed, notched (*like a saw*); jagged.

serrana [se·rrá·na] *f.* mountain girl; **serranilla** [se·rra·ní·ya] *f.* lyric poem with a rustic theme.

serranía [se·rra·ní·a] *f.* mountainous region; chain of mountains.

serrano [se·rrá·no] *m.* mountaineer; *adj.* of, pertaining to, or from the mountains.

serrar [se·rrár] = **aserrar**.

serrín [se·rrín] *m.* sawdust.

serrucho [se·rrú·čo] *m.* handsaw.

servible [ser·ßí·ßle] *adj.* serviceable, useful.

servicial [ser·ßi·sjál] *adj.* helpful, obliging.

servicio [ser·ßí·sjo] *m.* service; table service; tea or coffee set; chamber pot; *Am.* toilet, water closet.

servidor [ser·ßi·dór] *m.* servant; waiter; — **de Vd.** at your service; **su seguro** — yours truly.

servidumbre [ser·ßi·dúm·bre] *f.* domestic help, servants; servitude, slavery; service.

servil [ser·ßíl] *adj.* servile; **servilón** [ser·ßi·lón] *adj.* very servile; *m.* bootlicker, great flatterer.

servilismo [ser·ßi·líz·mo] *m.* servility, servile behavior or attitude; servile submission.

servilleta [ser·ßi·yé·ta] *f.* napkin.

servir⁵ [ser·ßír] *v. irr.* to serve; to be of use; — **de** to serve as, act as; to be used as; — **para** to be good for; to be used for; **-se** to serve or help oneself; to be pleased to; **-se de** to make use of; **sírvase Vd. hacerlo** please do it.

seseo [se·sé·o] *m.* pronunciation of all sibilantsas /s/.

sesgado [sez·gá·do] *adj.* slanting, oblique, bias.

sesgar⁷ [sez·gár] *v.* to slant; to cut on the bias; to follow an oblique line.

sesgo [séz·go] *m.* bias; slant; diagonal cut; turn; **al** — on the bias; diagonally, obliquely.

sesión [se·sjón] *f.* session; meeting, conference.

seso [sé·so] *m.* brain; wisdom, intelligence; **devanarse los -s** to rack one's brain.

sestear [ses·te·ár] *v.* to snooze, take a nap.

sesudo [se·sú·do] *adj.* sensible, wise, prudent; *Mex., C.A.* stubborn.

seta [sé·ta] *f.* mushroom.

setiembre [se·tjém·bre] *m. Spain* preferred form for **septiembre.**

sétimo [sé·ti·mo] *adj. Spain* preferred form for **séptimo.**

seto [sé·to] *m.* fence; hedge.

seudónimo [sew·dó·ni·mo] *m.* pseudonym, pen name.

severidad [se·ße·ri·dád] *f.* severity; strictness; seriousness.

severo [se·ßé·ro] *adj.* severe; strict; stern.

sevillano [se·ßi·yá·no] *adj.* of, from, or pertaining to Seville, Spain.

sexo [sék·so] *m.* sex.

sexual [sek·swál] *adj.* sexual.

si [si] *conj.* if; whether; **i— ya te lo dije!** but I already told you!; — **bien** although; **por —** **acaso** just in case.

sí [si] *adv.* yes; — **que** certainly, really; **un — es no es** a trifle, somewhat; *m.* assent, consent; *refl. pron.* (*used after a prep.*) himself, herself, yourself (*formal*), themselves; **de por —** separately, by itself; **estar sobre —** to be on the alert.

sibilante [si·ßi·lán·te] *adj.* sibilant, whistling.

sicología [si·ko·lo·xí·a] *f.* psychology.

sicológico [si·ko·ló·xi·ko] *adj.* psychological.

sicólogo [si·kó·lo·go] *m.* psychologist.

sicosis [si·kó·sis] *f.* psychosis.

siderurgia [si·de·rúr·xja] *f.* iron and steel industry.

sidra [sí·dra] *f.* cider.

siega [sjé·ga] *f.* reaping, mowing; harvesting; harvest, harvest season.

siembra [sjém·bra] *f.* sowing; seedtime, sowing time; sown field.

siempre [sjém·pre] *adv.* always; *Mex., C.A., Col., Andes* in any case, anyway; **para** (*or* **por**) — forever, for always; **por — jamás** forever and ever; — **que** whenever; provided that; *Am.* — **si me voy** I've decided to go anyway.

siemprepreviva [sjem·pre·ßi·ßa] *f.* evergreen; everlasting.

sien [sjen] *f.* temple (*of the forehead*).

sierpe [sjér·pe] *f.* serpent, snake.

sierra [sjé·rra] *f.* saw; rocky mountain range.

siervo [sjér·ßo] *m.* serf; slave; servant.

siesta [sjés·ta] *f.* siesta, afternoon nap; early afternoon; **dormir la** — to take an afternoon nap.

sifón [si·fón] *m.* siphon; siphon bottle; trap (*in plumbing fixtures*).

sigilo [si·xi·lo] *m.* secret; secrecy.

sigla [sí·gla] *f.* initial abbreviation.

siglo [sí·glo] *m.* century; period, epoch; the world, worldly matters.

significación [sig·ni·fi·ka·sjón] *f.* meaning; significance.

significado [sig·ni·fi·ká·do] *m.* significance, meaning.

significar⁶ [sig·ni·fi·kár] *v.* to signify; to mean; to make known, show; to matter, have importance.

significativo [sig·ni·fi·ka·tí·ßo] *adj.* significant.

signo [síg·no] *m.* sign; mark; symbol.

siguiente [si·gjén·te] *adj.* following.

sílaba [sí·la·ßa] *f.* syllable.

silabario [si·la·ßá·rjo] *m.* speller, spelling book.

silabear [si·la·ße·ár] *v.* to syllabicate.

silbar [sil·ßár] *v.* to whistle; to hiss.

silbato [sil·ßá·to] *m.* whistle.

silbido [sil·ßí·do] *m.* whistle; hiss.

silenciador [si·len·sja·dór] *m.* silencer; muffler (*of an automobile*).

silencio [si·lén·sjo] *m.* silence; pause; *adj. Am.* silent, quiet, motionless.

silencioso [si·len·sjó·so] *adj.* silent, quiet.

SE

silicio [si·li·sjo] *m.* silicon.
silo [sí·lo] *m.* silo; cave.
silogismo [si·lo·xíz·mo] *m.* syllogism.
silueta [si·lwé·ta] *f.* silhouette.
silvestre [sil·βés·tre] *adj.* wild, uncultivated.
silvicultor [sil·βi·kul·tór] *m.* forester; **silvicultura** [sil·βi·kul·tú·ra] *f.* forestry.
silla [sí·ya] *f.* chair; saddle; — **de montar** saddle; *Ven.* — **de balanza** rocking chair. *See* **mecedora.**
sillón [si·yón] *m.* large chair; easy chair; *Am.* — **de hamaca** rocking chair.
sima [sí·ma] *f.* chasm, abyss.
simbólico [sim·bó·li·ko] *adj.* symbolic.
simbolismo [sim·bo·líz·mo] *m.* symbolism.
símbolo [sím·bo·lo] *m.* symbol; — **de la fe** (*or* **de los Apóstoles**) the Apostle's creed.
simetría [si·me·trí·a] *f.* symmetry.
simétrico [si·mé·tri·ko] *adj.* symmetrical.
simiente [si·mjén·te] *f.* seed.
símil [sí·mil] *m.* simile; similarity; *adj.* similar.
similar [si·mi·lár] *adj.* similar.
simpatía [sim·pa·tí·a] *f.* attraction, attractiveness; accord, harmony; liking.
simpático [sim·pá·ti·ko] *adj.* sympathetic, congenial; pleasant, agreeable, nice.
simpatizar[9] [sim·pa·ti·sár] *v.* to be attractive to; to get on well with; to be congenial; **no me simpatiza** I don't like him.
simple [sim·ple] *adj.* simple; mere; plain; pure, unmixed; naïve, innocent; silly, foolish; *m.* simpleton.
simpleza [sim·plé·sa] *f.* simplicity; simpleness, stupidity, foolishness.
simplicidad [sim·pli·si·ðáð] *f.* simplicity; candor.
simplificar[6] [sim·pli·fi·kár] *v.* to simplify.
simplista [sim·plís·ta] *adj.* simplistic; *m. & f.* a person who is inclined to oversimplify.
simplón [sim·plón] *m.* simpleton.
simposio [sim·pó·sjo] *m.* symposium.
simulacro [si·mu·lá·kro] *m.* mimic battle, sham or mock battle; image, vision.
simular [si·mu·lár] *v.* to simulate, feign.
simultáneo [si·mul·tá·ne·o] *adj.* simultaneous.
sin [sin] *prep.* without; besides, not counting; — **que** *conj.* without; — **embargo** nevertheless, still, yet; — **qué ni para qué** without rhyme or reason.
sinagoga [si·na·ǥó·ǥa] *f.* synagogue.
sinapismo [si·na·píz·mo] *m.* mustard plaster; irritating person, nuisance, pest, bore.
sincerar [sin·se·rár] *v.* to square, justify, excuse; **-se** to square oneself (with), justify oneself (with).
sinceridad [sin·se·ri·ðáð] *f.* sincerity.
sincero [sin·sé·ro] *adj.* sincere.
síncopa [sín·ko·pa] *f.* syncopation; syncope.
sincronizar[9] [sin·kro·ni·sár] *v. irr.* to synchronize.
sindicar[6] [sin·di·kár] *v.* to syndicate; **-se** to syndicate, form a syndicate.
sindicato [sin·di·ká·to] *m.* syndicate; labor union.
síndico [sín·di·ko] *m.* receiver (*person appointed to take charge of property under litigation or to liquidate a bankrupt business*); trustee.
sinecura [si·ne·kú·ra] *f.* sinecure (*easy and well paid position*).
sinfonía [sin·fo·ní·a] *f.* symphony.
singular [sin·gu·lár] *adj.* singular; unique; striking; odd, strange.
singularizar[9] [sin·gu·la·ri·sár] *v.* to single out, choose; to distinguish; **-se** to distinguish oneself; to be singled out.
siniestro [si·njés·tro] *adj.* sinister; left (*side*); *m.* unforeseen loss, damage; **siniestra** [si·njés·tra] *f.*

left hand; left-hand side.
sinnúmero [sin·nú·me·ro] *m.* great number, endless number.
sino [sí·no] *conj.* but; *prep.* except; **no hace** — **lo que le mandan** he only does what he is told; — **que** *conj.* but; *m.* fate, destiny.
sinónimo [si·nó·ni·mo] *m.* synonym; *adj.* synonymous.
sinrazón [sin·rra·són] *f.* injustice, wrong.
sinsabor [sin·sa·βór] *m.* displeasure; trouble, grief, distress.
sintaxis [sin·ták·sis] *f.* syntax.
síntesis [sin·te·sis] *f.* synthesis; summary.
sintético [sin·té·ti·ko] *adj.* synthetic.
sintetizar[9] [sin·te·ti·sár] *v.* to synthesize.
síntoma [sín·to·ma] *m.* symptom; indication, sign.
sintonizar[9] [sin·to·ni·sár] *v.* to tune in (on).
sinuoso [si·nwó·so] *adj.* sinuous, winding; wavy.
sinvergüenza [sim·ber·ǥwén·sa] *m. & f.* shameless person; scoundrel.
siquiatra [si·kjá·tra] *m. & f.* psychiatrist, alienist.
siquiatría [si·kja·trí·a] *f.* psychiatry.
siquiera [si·kjé·ra] *adv.* at least; even; **ni** — not even; *conj.* even though.
sirena [si·ré·na] *f.* siren; whistle, foghorn.
sirviente [sir·βjén·te] *m.* servant; waiter; **sirvienta** [sir·βjén·ta] *f.* housemaid; waitress.
sisa [sí·sa] *f.* petty theft; dart (*made in a garment*).
sisal [si·sál] *m. Am.* sisal or sisal hemp (*fiber used in ropemaking*).
sisar [si·sár] *v.* to take in (*a garment*); to pilfer; to cheat out of, defraud.
sisear [si·se·ár] *v.* to hiss.
siseo [si·sé·o] *m.* hiss, hissing.
sistema [sis·té·ma] *m.* system.
sistemático [sis·te·má·ti·ko] *adj.* systematic.
sitial [si·tjál] *m.* chair of a presiding officer; place of honor.
sitiar [si·tjál] *v.* to besiege; to surround.
sitio [sí·tjo] *m.* site, location; place, spot, space; siege; *Am.* cattle ranch; *Mex.* taxicab station; **poner** — **a** to lay siege to.
sito [sí·to] *adj.* situated, located.
situación [si·twa·sjón] *f.* situation; position; location; state, condition; *Mex., Carib., Ven., Col.* **hombre de la** — man of the hour, man of influence.
situado [si·twá·ðo] *p.p.* situated; placed.
situar[18] [si·twár] *v.* to locate; to place; **-se** to station oneself, place oneself; to be located, placed, situated.
snobismo [ez·no·βíz·mo] *m.* snobism (*in the European sense*); the tendency to try to do whatever seems to be in style.
so [so]: — **capa de** under the guise of; — **pena de** under penalty of; — **pretexto de** under the pretext of.
sobaco [so·βá·ko] *m.* armpit.
sobar [so·βár] *v.* (*ablandar*) to rub; to knead; to massage; to touch, handle; to fondle, pet; (*fastidiar*) to bother; to beat, slap; *Col., Ven., Mex.* to set bones; *Col.* to flay, skin; *Am.* to win (*in a fight*); *Am.* to tire out (*a horse*).
soberanía [so·βe·ra·ní·a] *f.* sovereignty.
soberano [so·βe·rá·no] *adj. & m.* sovereign.
soberbia [so·βer·βja] *f.* pride, arrogance; ostentation, pomp.
soberbio [so·βer·βjo] *adj.* proud, haughty, arrogant; pompous; superb, magnificent; spirited (*horse*).
sobornar [so·βor·nár] *v.* to bribe.

soborno [so·βór·no] *m.* bribery; bribe; *Andes* overload (*on a pack animal*), extra load.

sobra [só·βra] *f.* surplus, excess; **-s** leftovers, leavings; **de —** more than enough; superfluous, unnecessary.

sobrado [so·βrá·ḍo] *m.* attic; loft; *Am.* pantry shelf; **-s** *Col., Ven.* leftovers, leavings; *adj.* leftover; excessive; superfluous; forward, brazen; **sobradas veces** many times, repeatedly.

sobrante [so·βrán·te] *adj.* leftover, surplus, excess, spare; *m.* surplus, excess, remainder.

sobrar [so·βrár] *v.* to exceed; to remain, be left over; to be more than enough.

sobre [só·βre] *prep.* (*encima de*) over; above; on, upon; (*acerca de*) about; approximately; besides; **— manera** excessively; **estar — sí** to be cautious, on the alert; **— que** besides, in addition to the fact that; *m.* envelope; address (*on an envelope*).

sobrecama [so·βre·ká·ma] *f.* bedspread.

sobrecarga [so·βre·kár·ɣa] *f.* overload; overburden.

sobrecargar[7] [so·βre·kar·ɣár] *v.* to overload; to overburden.

sobrecargo [so·βre·kár·ɣo] *m.* purser (*on a ship*); *f.* airline hostess.

sobrecoger[11] [so·βre·ko·xér] *v.* to surprise, catch unaware; to startle; **-se** to be startled; **-se de miedo** to be seized with fear.

sobreexcitación [so·βre·ek·si·ta·sjón] *f.* overexcitement; thrill.

sobreexcitar [so·βre·ek·si·tár] *v.* to overexcite.

sobrehumano [so·βre·u·má·no] *adj.* superhuman.

sobrellevar [so·βre·ye·βár] *v.* to endure, bear; to tolerate; to lighten (*another's burden*).

sobremesa [so·βre·mé·sa] *f.* table runner; after dinner conversation at the table; **de —** during the after dinner conversation.

sobrenadar [so·βre·na·ḍár] *v.* to float.

sobrenatural [so·βre·na·tu·rál] *adj.* supernatural.

sobrenombre [so·βre·nóm·bre] *m.* surname; nickname.

sobrentender[1] [so·βren·ten·dér] *v. irr.* to assume, understand; **-se** to be assumed, be obvious, be understood.

sobrepasar [soβ·re·pa·sár] *v.* to exceed; to excel; **-se** to overstep, go too far.

sobreponer[40] [so·βre·po·nér] *v. irr.* to lay on top; **-se** to dominate oneself; **-se a** to overcome; to dominate.

sobrepuesto [so·βre·pwés·to] *p.p. of* **sobreponer**; *m.* appliqué (*trimming laid on a dress*); *C.A.* mend, patch.

sobrepujar [so·βre·pu·xár] *v.* to exceed, excel, surpass; to outweigh.

sobresaliente [so·βre·sa·ljén·te] *adj.* outstanding; projecting; excellent; *m. & f.* substitute (*a person*); understudy (*substitute actor*).

sobresalir[43] [so·βre·sa·lír] *v. irr.* to stand out; to project, jut out; to excel.

sobresaltar [so·βre·sal·tár] *v.* to startle, frighten; to assail; to stand out clearly **-se** to be startled, frightened.

sobresalto [so·βre·sál·to] *m.* start, scare, fright, shock; **de —** suddenly.

sobrescrito [so·βres·krí·to] *m.* address (*on an envelope*).

sobresdrújulo [so·βrez·drú·xu·lo] *adj.* accented on syllable before antepenult.

sobrestante [so·βres·tán·te] *m.* overseer; boss, foreman.

sobresueldo [so·βre·swél·do] *m.* overtime pay, extra

pay or wages.

sobretodo [so·βre·tó·ḍo] *m.* overcoat.

sobrevenir[48] [so·βre·βe·nír] *v. irr.* to happen, occur, come unexpectedly; to follow, happen after.

sobreviviente [so·βre·βi·βjén·te] *m. & f.* survivor; *adj.* surviving.

sobrevivir [so·βre·βi·βír] *v.* to survive.

sobriedad [so·brje·ḍáḍ] *f.* sobriety, soberness, temperance, moderation.

sobrina [so·βrí·na] *f.* niece.

sobrino [so·βrí·no] *m.* nephew.

sobrio [só·βrjo] *adj.* sober, temperate, moderate.

socarrón [so·ka·rrón] *adj.* cunning, sly, crafty.

socarronería [so·ka·rro·ne·rí·a] *f.* craftiness, slyness, cunning.

socavar [so·ka·βár] *v.* to dig under; to undermine.

socavón [so·ka·βón] *m.* tunnel; cave, cavern; underground passageway.

social [so·sjál] *adj.* social; sociable, friendly.

socialismo [so·sja·líz·mo] *m.* socialism.

socialista [so·sja·lís·ta] *adj.* socialist, socialistic; *m. & f.* socialist.

sociedad [so·sje·ḍáḍ] *f.* society; partnership; company, firm, corporation; **— anónima** (*or* **— por acciones**) stock company.

socio [só·sjo] *m.* associate, partner; member.

sociología [so·sjo·lo·xí·a] *f.* sociology.

socorrer [so·ko·rrér] *v.* to help, aid, assist.

socorro [so·kó·rro] *m.* help, aid, assistance, relief; *Am.* partial advance payment on a workman's wages.

sodio [só·djo] *m.* sodium.

sodomía [so·ḍo·mí·a] *f.* sodomy.

soez [so·és] *adj.* low, vile, vulgar; coarse, ill-mannered.

sofá [so·fá] *m.* sofa, davenport.

sofocante [so·fo·kán·te] *adj.* suffocating, stifling.

sofocar[6] [so·fo·kár] *v.* to suffocate, choke; to smother; to bother; to embarrass.

sofoco [so·fó·ko] *m.* suffocation, choking; upset, annoyance; embarrassment.

sofrenar [so·fre·nár] *v.* to check; to control; to reprimand.

sofrito [so·frí·to] *m.* a preparation of lightly fried ingredients.

soga [só·ɣa] *f.* rope; *Ven., Col., Andes, Ch.* leather lasso or rope.

sojuzgamiento [so·xuz·ɣa·mjén·to] *m.* subjugation, subjection.

sojuzgar[7] [so·xuz·ɣár] *v.* to subjugate, subdue, subject.

sol [sol] *m.* sun; sunshine; sol (*fifth note of the scale*); *Am.* sol (*monetary unit of Peru*); **de — a —** from sunrise to sunset; **hace —** it is sunny; **tomar el —** to bask in the sun; to enjoy the sunshine.

solana [so·lá·na] *f.* sunny place; sunroom; sun porch; intense sunlight; **solanera** [so·la·né·ra] *f.* sunburn; sunny place.

solapa [so·lá·pa] *f.* lapel.

solapado [so·la·pá·ḍo] *adj.* sly, crafty, cunning, deceitful, underhanded.

solar [so·lár] *m.* lot, plot of ground; ancestral mansion; manor; *Carib., Mex.* tenement house; *Mex., Ven.* back yard; *Col.* town lot, field (*for growing alfalfa, corn, etc.*); *adj.* solar, of the sun.

solar[2] [so·lár] *v. irr.* to sole (*shoes*); to pave, floor.

solariego [so·la·rjé·ɣo] *adj.* manorial, pertaining to a manor; **casa solariega** ancestral manor or mansion.

solaz [so·lás] *m.* solace, comfort; relaxation,

recreation.
solazar[9] [so·la·sár] *v.* to console, cheer, comfort;
-se to seek relaxation or pleasure; to enjoy
oneself.
soldado [sol·dá·đo] *m.* soldier; — **raso** private; —
de línea regular soldier.
soldadura [sol·da·đú·ra] *f.* soldering; welding;
solder.
soldar[2] [sol·dár] *v. irr.* to solder; to weld.
soleado [so·le·á·đo] *adj.* sunny; *p.p.* sunned.
solear [so·le·ár] = **asolear.**
soledad [so·le·đáđ] *f.* solitude; loneliness;
homesickness; lonely retreat.
solemne [so·lém·ne] *adj.* solemn; imposing; —
disparate downright foolishness, huge blunder.
solemnidad [so·lem·ni·đáđ] *f.* solemnity; solemn
ceremony.
soler[2,51] [so·lér] *v. irr.* to have the custom of, be in
the habit of.
solfeo [sol·fé·o] *m.* sol-faing, solfeggio style.
solferino [sol·fe·ri·no] *adj.* reddish-purple.
solicitante [so·li·si·tán·te] *m. & f.* solicitor;
applicant.
solicitar [so·li·si·tár] *v.* to solicit; to apply for; to
beg, ask for; to court, woo.
solícito [so·lí·si·to] *adj.* solicitous, careful; anxious,
concerned, diligent.
solicitud [so·li·si·túđ] *f.* solicitude; care, concern,
anxiety.
solidaridad [so·li·đa·ri·đáđ] *f.* solidarity; union;
bond, community of interests.
solidez [so·li·đés] *f.* solidity; compactness.
solidificar[6] [so·li·đi·fi·kár] *v.* to solidify.
sólido [so·li·đo] *adj.* solid; firm; strong; *m.*
solid.
soliloquio [so·li·ló·kjo] *m.* soliloquy, monologue.
solista [so·lís·ta] *m. & f.* soloist.
solitaria [so·li·tá·rja] *f.* tapeworm.
solitario [so·li·tá·rjo] *adj.* solitary; lonely; *m.*
recluse, hermit; solitaire (*card game*); solitaire
(*gem set by itself*).
sólito [só·li·to] *adj.* customary.
solo [só·lo] *adj.* sole, only; single; alone; lonely **a
solas** alone; *m.* solo; **sólo** [só·lo] *adv.* only.
solomillo [so·lo·mí·yo], **solomo** [so·ló·mo] *m.*
sirloin; loin; loin of pork.
solsticio [sols·tí·sjo] *m.* solstice.
soltar[2] [sol·tár] *v. irr.* to loosen, untie, unfasten; to
let loose; to set free; to let go; to let out; to
utter; -se to set oneself free; to come loose; to
lose restraint; to loosen up; -se a to begin to,
start to.
soltero [sol·té·ro] *adj.* single, unmarried; *m.*
bachelor; **soltera** [sol·té·ra] *f.* spinster; **solterón**
[sol·te·rón] *m.* old bachelor; **solterona**
[sol·te·ró·na] *f.* old maid.
soltura [sol·tú·ra] *f.* looseness; freedom; facility,
ease; agility, nimbleness; release (*of a prisoner*).
solución [so·lu·sjón] *f.* solution; loosening, untying.
solucionar [so·lu·sjo·nár] *v.* to solve, to resolve.
solventar [sol·ƀen·tár] *v.* to pay (*a bill*), settle (*an
account*); to solve (*a problem or difficulty*).
sollozar[9] [so·yo·sár] *v.* to sob.
sollozo [so·yó·so] *m.* sob.
sombra [sóm·bra] *f.* (*oscuridad*) shadow; shade;
darkness; (*abrigo*) shelter, protection; (*imagen*)
image, reflection (*in the water*); *Am.* guide lines
(*under writing paper*); *Ven.* awning, sunshade;
hacer — to shade; to cast a shadow (on).
sombreado [som·bre·á·đo] *adj.* shady; shaded.
sombrear [som·bre·ár] *v.* to shade; -se *Mex., Ven.,*

Col. to seek the shade, stand in the shade.
sombrería [som·bre·re·rí·a] *f.* hat shop.
sombrero [som·bré·ro] *m.* hat; — **de copa** top hat,
high hat; — **hongo** derby; — **de jipijapa** Panama
hat; *C.A., Col., Ven.* — **de pelo** top hat.
sombrilla [som·brí·ya] *f.* parasol, sunshade.
sombrío [som·brí·o] *adj.* somber, gloomy; shady.
somero [so·mé·ro] *adj.* superficial, shallow;
summary, concise.
someter [so·me·tér] *v.* to submit; to subject; -se to
submit.
sometimiento [so·me·ti·mjén·to] *m.* submission;
subjection.
somnolencia [som·no·lén·sja] *f.* drowsiness,
sleepiness; **con** — sleepily.
son [son] *m.* sound; tune; rumor; **en** — **de guerra**
in a warlike manner; **sin ton ni** — without
rhyme or reason.
sonaja [so·ná·xa] *f.* jingles, tambourine (*to
accompany certain dances*); rattle; **sonajero**
[so·na·xé·ro] *m.* child's rattle.
sonámbulo [so·nám·bu·lo] *m.* sleepwalker.
sonante [so·nán·te] *adj.* sounding; ringing;
sonorous; **en dinero** — **y contante** in hard cash.
sonar[2] [so·nár] *v. irr.* to sound; to ring; to sound
familiar; — **a** to sound like; seem like; -se to
blow one's nose; **se suena que** it is rumored that.
sonda [són·da] *f.* plumb, string with lead weight
(*for sounding the depth of water*); sounding;
surgeon's probe.
sondar [son·dár] = **sondear.**
sondear [son·de·ár] *v.* to sound, fathom; to sound
out; to probe; to examine into.
sondeo [son·dé·o] *m.* sounding, fathoming.
soneto [so·né·to] *m.* sonnet.
sonido [so·ní·đo] *m.* sound.
sonoro [so·nó·ro] *adj.* sonorous; **consonante sonora**
voiced consonant.
sonreír[15] [son·rre·ír] *v. irr.* to smile; -se to smile.
sonriente [son·rrjén·te] *adj.* smiling, beaming,
radiant.
sonrisa [son·rrí·sa] *f.* smile.
sonrojarse [son·rro·xár·se] *v.* to blush.
sonrojo [son·rró·xo] *m.* blush.
sonrosado [son·rro·sá·đo] *adj.* rosy.
sonsacar[6] [son·sa·kár] *v.* to lure away; to draw
(*someone*) out; to extract (*a secret*); to take on
the sly.
sonsonete [son·so·né·te] *m.* singsong; rhythmical
tapping sound.
soñador [so·ña·đór] *m.* dreamer.
soñar[2] [so·ñár] *v. irr.* to dream; — **con** (*or* — **en**)
to dream of; — **despierto** to daydream.
soñoliento [so·ño·ljén·to] *adj.* sleepy, drowsy.
sopa [só·pa] *f.* soup; sop; **estar hecho una** — to be
sopping wet; *Am.* **es un -s** he is a fool.
sopapo [so·pá·po] *m.* chuck, tap, pat (*under the
chin*); slap.
sopera [so·pé·ra] *f.* soup tureen.
sopero [so·pé·ro] *m.* soup dish.
sopetón [so·pe·tón] *m.* box, slap; **de** — all of a
sudden, unexpectedly.
soplar [so·plár] *v.* (*despedir aire*) to blow; to blow
away; to blow up, inflate; (*robar*) to swipe, steal;
(*informar*) to prompt; to "squeal" on, inform
against; *Col., Ven., Mex., Cuba, Andes* — **una
bofetada** to strike a blow; -se to swell up, puff up;
to eat up, gobble up; to gulp down; **se sopló el
pastel** he gobbled up the pie; *Am.* -se a uno to
deceive someone, get the best of someone.
soplete [so·plé·te] *m.* blow torch; blowpipe.

soplo [só·plo] *m.* (*de aire*) blowing; puff, gust of wind; breath; (*aviso*) whispered warning or advice; "squealing", informing; **en un —** in a jiffy, in a second.

soplón [so·plón] *m.* informer, "squealer" (*one who tells on someone*), tattletale.

sopor [so·pór] *m.* stupor; lethargy.

soportal [so·por·tál] *m.* arcade.

soportar [so·por·tár] *v.* to support, hold up, bear; to stand, endure, tolerate.

soporte [so·pór·te] *m.* support.

sorber [sor·ḅér] *v.* to sip; to suck; to swallow; to absorb; to snuff up one's nose.

sorbete [sor·ḅé·te] *m.* sherbet; fruit ice; *C.A., Mex., Ven.* cone, ice-cream cone; *Am.* silk top hat.

sorbo [sór·ḅo] *m.* sip, swallow, gulp; sniff.

sordera [sor·ḍé·ra], **sordez** [sor·ḍés] *f.* deafness.

sórdido [sór·ḍi·ḍo] *adj.* sordid.

sordina [sor·ḍi·na] *f.* mute (*of a musical instrument*).

sordo [sór·ḍo] *adj.* deaf; silent, noiseless; dull; muffled; **consonante sorda** voiceless consonant; *m.* deaf person; **hacerse el —** to pretend not to hear; to turn a deaf ear.

sordomudo [sor·ḍo·mú·ḍo] *adj.* deaf and dumb; *m.* deaf-mute.

sorna [sór·na] *f.* slyness, cunning; sneer.

soroche [so·ró·če] *m. Andes* shortness of breath, sickness caused by high altitude; *Am.* blush, flush.

sorprendente [sor·pren·dén·te] *adj.* surprising.

sorprender [sor·pren·dér] *v.* to surprise; **-se** to be surprised.

sorpresa [sor·pré·sa] *f.* surprise.

sortear [sor·te·ár] *v.* to draw lots; to raffle; to dodge; to shun; to fight (*bulls*) skillfully.

sorteo [sor·té·o] *m.* drawing or casting of lots; raffle.

sortija [sor·ti·xa] *f.* ring; finger ring; ringlet, curl.

sosa [só·sa] *f.* soda.

sosegado [so·se·ǵá·ḍo] *adj.* calm, quiet, peaceful.

sosegar[1,7] [so·se·ǵár] *v.* to calm, quiet; to be quiet; **-se** to quiet down.

sosiego [so·sjé·ǵo] *m.* calm, peace, quiet.

soslayo [soz·lá·yo]: **al —** obliquely; slanting; on the bias; **de —** oblique, slanting; at a slant; sideways; **mirada de —** side glance; **pegar de —** to glance, hit at a slant.

soso [só·so] *adj.* flat, tasteless, insipid; dull, silly; awkward.

sospecha [sos·pé·ča] *f.* suspicion; mistrust.

sospechar [sos·pe·čár] *v.* to suspect; to mistrust.

sospechoso [sos·pe·čó·so] *adj.* suspicious; *m.* suspect.

sostén [sos·tén] *m.* support; prop; supporter; brassière.

sostener[4,5] [sos·te·nér] *v. irr.* to sustain; to hold; to support, maintain; to defend, uphold; to endure.

sostenido [sos·te·ní·ḍo] *p.p. & adj.* sustained; supported, held up; *m.* sharp (*in music*).

sota [só·ta] *f.* jack (*at cards*); *m. Am.* foreman, boss, overseer.

sotana [so·tá·na] *f.* cassock (*black outer robe of a priest*).

sótano [só·ta·no] *m.* cellar, basement.

soterrar [so·te·rrár] *v.* to bury.

soto [só·to] *m.* grove; thicket.

sotreta [so·tré·ta] *m. Andes, Riopl.* nag, old horse.

soviet [so·ḅjét] *m.* soviet; **soviético** [so·ḅjé·ti·ko] *adj.* soviet, of, or pertaining to, soviets.

sténcil [es·tén·sil] *m.* stencil.

suave [swá·ḅe] *adj.* soft; smooth; mild; bland; gentle.

suavidad [swa·ḅi·ḍáḍ] *f.* softness; smoothness; mildness; gentleness.

suavizar[9] [swa·ḅi·sár] *v.* to smooth; to soften.

subalterno [su·ḅal·tér·no] *adj. & m.* subordinate.

subasta [su·ḅás·ta] *f.* public auction.

subastar [su·ḅás·tar] *v.* to sell at auction.

subconsciente [suḅ·kon·sjén·te] *adj.* subconscious.

subdesarrollado [suḅ·ḍe·sa·rro·yá·ḍo] *adj.* underdeveloped.

súbdito [súḅ·ḍi·to] *m.* subject.

subida [su·ḅí·ḍa] *f.* rise; ascent; carrying up; **de —** on the way up; **muchas -s y bajadas** many ups and downs; much going up and down.

subir [su·ḅír] *v.* to ascend, go up, climb; to raise, lift; to carry up; to mount; **— al tren** to board the train, get on the train.

súbito [sú·ḅi·to] *adj.* sudden; **de —** suddenly.

sublevación [su·ḅle·ḅa·sjón] *f.* revolt, uprising, insurrection.

sublevar [suḅ·le·ḅár] *v.* to excite to rebellion; **-se** to revolt.

sublimado [suḅ·li·má·ḍo] *adj.* sublimated.

sublime [su·ḅlí·me] *adj.* sublime.

submarino [suḅ·ma·rí·no] *m. & adj.* submarine; *m.* **— atómico** atomic submarine.

subordinado [su·ḅor·ḍi·ná·ḍo] *adj. & m.* subordinate.

subordinar [su·ḅor·ḍi·nár] *v.* to subordinate; to subdue.

subrayar [suḅ·rra·yár] *v.* to underline; to emphasize.

subsanar [suḅ·sa·nár] *v.* to mend, remedy, repair (*a damage, error, defect, etc.*); to make up for (*an error, fault, etc.*); to excuse (*a fault or error*).

subscribir [suḅs·kri·ḅír] = **suscribir.**

subscripción [suḅs·krip·sjón] = **suscripción.**

subscriptor [suḅs·krip·tór] = **suscritor.**

subsecretario [suḅ·se·kre·tá·rjo] *m.* undersecretary.

subsecuente [suḅ·se·kwén·te] *adj.* subsequent.

subsiguiente [suḅ·si·ǵjén·te] *adj.* subsequent.

subsistencia [suḅ·sis·tén·sja] *f.* living, livelihood; sustenance; permanence.

subsistir [suḅ·sis·tír] *v.* to subsist; to exist; to last.

substancia [suḅs·tán·sja] = **sustancia.**

substancial [suḅs·tan·sjál] = **sustancial.**

substancioso [suḅs·tan·sjó·so] = **sustancioso.**

substituible [suḅs·ti·twí·ḅle] = **sustituible.**

substantivo [suḅs·tan·ti·ḅo] = **sustantivo.**

substitución [suḅs·ti·tu·sjón] = **sustitución.**

substituir [suḅs·ti·twír] = **sustituir.**

substituto [suḅs·ti·tú·to] = **sustituto.**

substracción [suḅs·trak·sjón] = **sustracción.**

substraer [suḅs·tra·ér] = **sustraer.**

subsuelo [suḅ·swé·lo] *m.* subsoil.

subteniente [suḅ·te·njén·te] *m.* second lieutenant.

subterfugio [suḅ·ter·fú·xjo] *m.* subterfuge.

subterráneo [suḅ·te·rrá·ne·o] *adj.* subterranean, underground; *m.* underground; cave, tunnel, vault.

suburbano [su·ḅur·ḅá·no] *adj.* suburban; *m.* suburban resident.

suburbio [su·ḅur·ḅjo] *m.* suburb.

subvención [suḅ·ḅen·sjón] *f.* subsidy.

subvencionar [suḅ·ḅen·sjo·nár] *v.* to subsidize.

subyugar [suḅ·yu·ǵár] *v.* to subdue.

succión [suk·sjón] *f.* suction.

suceder [su·se·ḍér] *v.* to happen, occur; to succeed, follow.

sucesión [su·se·sjón] *f.* succession; heirs, offspring.

sucesivo [su·se·sí·ḅo] *adj.* successive; **en lo —**

hereafter, in the future.

suceso [su·sé·so] *m.* event; outcome, result.

sucesor [su·se·sór] *m.* successor.

suciedad [su·sje·ḍáḍ] *f.* dirt, filth; filthiness; filthy act or remark.

sucinto [su·sín·to] *adj.* compact, concise, brief.

sucio [sú·sjo] *adj.* dirty; foul, filthy.

suculento [su·ku·lén·to] *adj.* juicy.

sucumbir [su·kum·bír] *v.* to succumb; to yield.

sucursal [su·kur·sál] *f.* branch, branch office (*of a post office, bank, etc.*); *adj.* branch (*used as an adj.*).

suche [sú·če] *adj. Ven.* sour, unripe; *m. Andes* pimple; *Ch.* office boy, insignificant employee; *Andes* suche (*a tree*).

sud [suḍ] *m.* south; south wind; **sudeste** [su·ḍés·te] *m. & adj.* southeast; **sudoeste** [su·ḍo·és·te] *m. & adj.* southwest.

sudamericano [su·ḍa·me·ri·ká·no] *adj. & m.* South American.

sudar [su·ḍár] *v.* to sweat, perspire; to ooze; to toil.

sudario [su·ḍá·rjo] *m.* shroud.

sudor [su·ḍór] *m.* sweat, perspiration; toil.

sudoroso [su·ḍo·ró·so] *adj.* sweaty, sweating, perspiring.

sueco [swé·ko] *adj.* Swedish; *m.* Swede; Swedish language; **hacerse el —** to pretend not to see or understand.

suegra [swé·ǥra] *f.* mother-in-law.

suegro [swé·ǥro] *m.* father-in-law.

suela [swé·la] *f.* sole of a shoe; shoe leather.

sueldo [swél·do] *m.* salary.

suelo [swé·lo] *m.* soil, ground; floor; pavement; bottom.

suelto [swél·to] *adj.* (*no atado*) loose; free, easy; (*ágil*) agile, nimble; blank (*verse*); *m.* small change; short newspaper article, news item.

sueño [swé·ño] *m.* sleep; dream; sleepiness, drowsiness; **en -s** in one's sleep; **conciliar el —** to get to sleep; **tener —** to be sleepy.

suero [swé·ro] *m.* serum.

suerte [swér·te] *f.* (*fortuna*) fate; fortune; chance; luck; (*clase*) sort, kind; way, manner; (*truco*) trick; **de — que** so that, in such a way that; and so; **echar -s** to cast lots; **tener —** to be lucky; **tocarle a uno la —** to fall to one's lot; to be lucky.

suéter [swé·ter] *m. Am.* sweater.

suficiente [su·fi·sjén·te] *adj.* sufficient; competent, able.

sufijo [su·fí·xo] *m.* suffix; *adj.* suffixed.

sufragar[7] [su·fra·ǥár] *v.* to defray, pay; to help, aid; *Am.* **— por** to vote for.

sufragio [su·frá·xjo] *m.* suffrage; vote; help, aid.

sufrido [su·fri·ḍo] *adj.* suffering, long-suffering, patient; **mal —** impatient.

sufridor [su·fri·ḍór] *m.* sufferer; *adj.* suffering.

sufrimiento [su·fri·mjén·to] *m.* suffering; patience; endurance.

sufrir [su·frír] *v.* to suffer; to endure; to allow, permit; to sustain; to undergo; **— un examen** to take an examination.

sugerencia [su·xe·rén·sja] *f. Am.* suggestion, hint.

sugerir[3] [su·xe·rír] *v. irr.* to suggest; to hint.

sugestión [su·xes·tjón] *f.* suggestion; hint.

sugestivo [su·xes·tí·βo] *adj.* suggestive.

suicida [swi·sí·ḍa] *m. & f.* suicide (*person who commits suicide*). ·

suicidarse [swi·si·ḍár·se] *v.* to commit suicide.

suicidio [swi·sí·ḍjo] *m.* suicide (*act of suicide*).

suizo [swí·so] *adj. & m.* Swiss.

sujeción [su·xe·sjón] *f.* subjection; control; submission.

sujetapapeles [su·xe·ta·pa·pé·les] *m.* paper clip.

sujetar [su·xe·tár] *v.* to subject; to control; to subdue; to fasten; to grasp, hold; **-se** to subject oneself; to submit; to adhere (to).

sujeto [su·xé·to] *adj.* subject; liable; fastened; under control; *m.* subject matter; subject; fellow, individual.

sulfamida [sul·fa·mí·ḍa] *f.* common name for the sulfa drugs.

sulfato [sul·fá·to] *m.* sulphate.

sulfurarse [sul·fu·rár·se] *v.* to get angry.

sulfúrico [sul·fú·ri·ko] *adj.* sulphuric.

sulfuro [sul·fú·ro] *m.* sulphide.

sultán [sul·tán] *m.* sultan.

suma [sú·ma] *f.* sum; addition; substance; summary; **en —** in short.

sumador [su·ma·ḍór] *adj.* adding; **máquina sumadora** adding machine.

sumar [su·már] *v.* to add; to add up (to), amount (to); to sum up; **-se a** to join.

sumario [su·má·rjo] *m.* summary; indictment; *adj.* summary, brief, concise; swift (*punishment*).

sumergible [su·mer·xí·βle] *adj.* submergible; *m.* submarine.

sumergir[11] [su·mer·xír] *v.* to submerge, plunge, sink; to immerse; **-se** to submerge; to sink.

sumidero [su·mi·ḍé·ro] *m.* sink; sewer, drain.

suministrar [su·mi·nis·trár] *v.* to give, supply with, provide with.

sumir [su·mír] *v.* to sink; to submerge; to immerse; *Riopl., Mex., Carib.* to dent; **-se** to sink; *Andes* to shrink, shrivel; *Andes* to cower, crouch in fear; *Am.* **-se el sombrero hasta las cejas** to pull one's hat over one's eyes.

sumisión [su·mi·sjón] *f.* submission; obedience.

sumiso [su·mí·so] *adj.* submissive; obedient; meek.

sumo [sú·mo] *adj.* supreme, highest, high; greatest; **— pontífice** Sovereign Pontiff (*the Pope*); **a lo —** at the most.

suntuoso [sun·twó·so] *adj.* sumptuous, magnificent, luxurious.

superable [su·pe·rá·βle] *adj.* superable.

superabundancia [su·pe·ra·βun·dán·sja] *f.* superabundance, great abundance, overflow.

superar [su·pe·rár] *v.* to surpass; to exceed; to overcome.

superávit [su·pe·rá·βit] *m.* surplus.

superficial [su·per·fi·sjál] *adj.* superficial; shallow; frivolous; **superficialidad** [su·per·fi·sja·li·ḍáḍ] *f.* superficiality, shallowness, frivolity.

superficie [su·per·fí·sje] *f.* surface; area.

superfluo [su·pér·flwo] *adj.* superfluous.

superintendente [su·pe·rin·ten·dén·te] *m.* superintendent; supervisor; overseer.

superior [su·pe·rjór] *adj.* superior; higher; better; upper; *m.* superior; father superior; **superiora** [su·pe·rjó·ra] *f.* superior, mother superior.

superioridad [su·pe·rjo·ri·ḍáḍ] *f.* superiority; excellence.

superlativo [su·per·la·tí·βo] *adj. & m.* superlative.

supersónico [su·per·só·ni·ko] *adj.* supersonic.

superstición [su·pers·ti·sjón] *f.* superstition.

supersticioso [su·pers·ti·sjó·so] *adj.* superstitious.

supervivencia [su·per·βi·βén·sja] *f.* survival.

superviviente [su·per·βi·βjén·te] = **sobreviviente**.

suplantar [su·plan·tár] *v.* to supplant; to forge (*a document or check*).

suplementar [su·ple·men·tár] *v.* supplement.

suplementario [su·ple·men·tá·rjo] *adj.*
supplementary, extra.
suplemento [su·ple·mén·to] *m.* supplement; supply,
supplying.
suplente [su·plén·te] *adj., m. & f.* substitute.
súplica [sú·pli·ka] *f.* entreaty; request; petition;
prayer.
suplicante [su·pli·kán·te] *adj.* suppliant, beseeching;
m. & f. suppliant; petitioner.
suplicar[6] [su·pli·kár] *v.* to beg, entreat, implore; to
pray humbly; to appeal, petition.
suplicio [su·plí·sjo] *m.* torture; torment; anguish;
execution; instrument of torture; scaffold,
gallows.
suplir [su·plír] *v.* to supply; to make up for; to
substitute, take the place of (*temporarily*).
suponer[40] [su·po·nér] *v. irr.* to suppose; to assume;
to be important.
suposición [su·po·si·sjón] *f.* supposition;
assumption.
supremacía [su·pre·má·sía] *f.* supremacy.
supremo [su·pré·mo] *adj.* supreme; final, last.
supresión [su·pre·sjón] *f.* suppression; omission;
elimination.
suprimir [su·pri·mír] *v.* to suppress; to abolish; to
omit.
supuesto [su·pwés·to] *p.p. of* **suponer** supposed,
assumed; — **que** supposing that; since; **por** —
of course; naturally; *m.* supposition;
assumption.
supuración [su·pu·ra·sjón] *f.* formation or
discharge of pus.
supurar [su·pu·rár] *v.* to fester, form or discharge
pus.
sur [sur] *m.* south; south wind; **sureste** [su·rés·te]
m. southeast; **suroeste** [su·ro·és·te] *m.* southwest.
suramericano [su·ra·me·ri·ká·no] = **sudamericano.**
surcar[6] [sur·kár] *v.* to furrow; to plow; to plow
through; to cut through.
surco [súr·ko] *m.* furrow; rut; groove; wrinkle.
sureño [su·ré·ño] *adj.* southern, from the south;
m. a southerner.
surgir[11] [sur·xír] *v.* to surge, rise; to spurt; spout;
to appear.
surrealismo [su·rre·a·líz·mo] *m.* surrealism.
surtido [sur·tí·do] *m.* stock, supply, assortment;
adj. assorted.
surtidor [sur·ti·dór] *m.* supplier; spout, jet.·
surtir [sur·tír] *v.* to provide, supply, stock (with);
to spout, spurt; — **efecto** to produce the desired
result; — **un pedido** to fill an order.
susceptible [sus·sep·tí·ble] *adj.* susceptible; sensitive;
touchy.
suscitar [su·si·tár] *v.* to raise, stir up, provoke.
suscribir[52] [sus·kri·bír] *v.* to subscribe; to endorse;
to agree (to); **-se** to subscribe.
suscripción [sus·krip·sjón] *f.* subscription.
suscrito [sus·kri·to] *p.p. of* **suscribir.**
suscritor [sus·kri·tór] *m.* subscriber.
susodicho [su·so·dí·čo] *adj.* aforesaid,
above-mentioned.
suspender [sus·pen·dér] *v.* (*colgar*) to suspend; to
hang; (*detener*) to stop; to defer; (*no aprobar*)
to fail, flunk; to dismiss temporarily; to
astonish.
suspensión [sus·pen·sjón] *f.* suspension;
postponement, delay; uncertainty; cessation; a
system of supporting devices (*automobile*).
suspenso [sus·pén·so] *adj.* suspended; hanging;
pending; perplexed, astonished; **en** — in
suspense; *m.* failure (*in an examination*).

suspicaz [sus·pi·kás] *adj.* suspicious.
suspirar [sus·pi·rár] *v.* to sigh; to sigh (for), long
(for).
suspiro [sus·pí·ro] *m.* sight; brief pause (*in music*).
sustancia [sus·tán·sja] *f.* substance; essence; *Andes*
broth.
sustancial [sus·tan·sjál] *adj.* substantial; nourishing.
sustancioso [sus·tan·sjó·so] *adj.* substantial;
nourishing.
sustantivo [sus·tan·tí·bo] *m.* noun; *adj.* substantive;
real; independent.
sustentar [sus·ten·tár] *v.* to sustain; to support; to
feed, nourish; to maintain; uphold.
sustento [sus·tén·to] *m.* sustenance; food; support.
sustitución [sus·ti·tu·sjón] *f.* substitution.
sustituible [sus·ti·twi·ble] *adj.* replaceable.
sustituir[32] [sus·ti·twír] *v. irr.* to substitute.
sustituto [sus·ti·tú·to] *m.* substitute.
susto [sús·to] *m.* scare, fright.
sustracción [sus·trak·sjón] *f.* subtraction.
sustraer[46] [sus·tra·ér] *v. irr.* to subtract; to remove,
withdraw; **-se** a to evade, avoid, slip away from.
susurrar [su·su·rrár] *v.* to whisper; to murmur;
to rustle; **-se** to be whispered or rumored about.
susurro [su·sú·rro] *m.* whisper; murmur; rustle.
sutil [su·til] *adj.* subtle; keen; clever; crafty; thin,
fine, delicate.
sutileza [su·ti·lé·sa], **sutilidad** [su·ti·li·dád] *f.*
subtlety; keenness, cleverness; cunning; thinness,
fineness.
suyo [sú·yo] *adj.* his, of his; her, of hers; your, of
yours (*formal*); their, of theirs; *pron.* his, hers,
yours (*formal*), theirs; **de** — naturally, by
nature; **salirse con la suya** to get one's own way;
hacer de las suyas to be up to one's tricks;
los -s his (hers, theirs); his (her, their) own
people.

T:t tabaco [ta·bá·ko] *m.* tobacco; *Carib.,
Ven., Col.* cigar; snuff; *Col.* blow
with the fist; **tabaquería**
[ta·ba·ke·rí·a] *f.* tobacco store,
cigar store.
tábano [tá·ba·no] *m.* horsefly, gadfly.
taberna [ta·bér·na] *f.* tavern, bar, liquor store.
tabernáculo [ta·ber·ná·ku·lo] *m.* tabernacle.
tabique [ta·bí·ke] *m.* partition, partition wall.
tabla [tá·bla] *f.* board, plank; plate of metal; slab;
table, list; strip of ground; *Col.* chocolate tablet;
-s draw, tie (*in games*); stage boards, the stage;
a raja — cost what it may; *Am.* in great haste;
hacer — **rasa de algo** to disregard, omit, or
ignore something; *Am.* to clear away all
obstacles in the way of something.
tablado [ta·blá·do] *m.* platform, stage; scaffold;
floor boards.
tablero [ta·blé·ro] *m.* board; panel; timber, piece
of lumber; chessboard, checkerboard; store
counter; large work table; gambling table; *Col.,
Ven., Mex.* blackboard; **poner al** — to risk,
endanger; — **de mando** control panel.
tableta [ta·blé·ta] *f.* tablet; small thin board;
memorandum pad.
tabletear [ta·ble·te·ár] *v.* to rattle; to make a
continuous rattling or tapping sound.
tableteo [ta·ble·té·o] *m.* rattling sound; tapping.
tablilla [ta·blí·ya] *f.* tablet; slat, small thin board;
splint; small bulletin board; **-s** wooden clappers.
tablón [ta·blón] *m.* plank; large, thick board.

SU

taburete [ta·ḃu·ré·te] *m.* stool; footstool; *Sal.* chair.

tacañería [ta·ka·ñe·rí·a] *f.* stinginess, tightness, miserliness.

tacaño [ta·ka·ño] *adj.* stingy, tight, miserly; sly.

tácito [tá·si·to] *adj.* tacit, implied; silent.

taciturno [ta·si·túr·no] *adj.* taciturn, silent, sullen; sad.

taco [tá·ko] *m.* wad; roll; plug, stopper; billiard cue; bite, snack; swear word; *Mex., C.A.* Mexican folded tortilla sandwich; *Am.* leather legging; *Ch., Andes* short, fat person; *Mex.* heel of a shoe; *Am.* pile, heap; **echar -s** to curse, swear; *Mex.* **darse uno** — to strut, put on airs.

tacón [ta·kón] *m.* heel of a shoe.

taconear [ta·ko·ne·ár] *v.* to click the heels, walk hard on one's heels.

taconeo [ta·ko·né·o] *m.* click, clicking (*of the heels*).

táctica [ták·ti·ka] *f.* tactics.

tacto [ták·to] *m.* tact; touch, sense of touch.

tacha [tá·ča] *f.* flaw, defect, blemish.

tachar [ta·čár] *v.* (*borrar*) to cross out; to scratch out; to blot out; (*culpar*) to blame; to find fault with; to censure.

tachón [ta·čón] *m.* stud; trimming, braid; blot.

tachonar [ta·čo·nár] *v.* to stud, ornament with studs; to adorn with trimming.

tachuela [ta·čwé·la] *f.* tack, small nail; *Am.* metal dipper; *Am.* runt, "shorty".

tafetán [ta·fe·tán] *m.* taffeta; — **inglés** court plaster; — **adhesivo** "Band-Aid".

tahur [ta·úr] *m.* gambler; cardsharp.

taimado [taj·má·ḍo] *adj.* sly, crafty; *Am.* sullen, gloomy, gruff.

taita [táj·ta] = **tatita**. *See* **tata**.

tajada [ta·xá·ḍa] *f.* slice; cut.

tajalápiz [ta·xa·lá·pis] *m.* pencil sharpener.

tajante [ta·xán·te] *adj.* cutting, sharp.

tajar [ta·xár] *v.* to slice; to cut; to sharpen (*a pencil*).

tajo [tá·xo] *m.* cut; gash; cutting edge; sheer cliff; chopping block.

tal [tal] *adj.* such; such a; — **cual** such as; so-so, fair; — **vez** perhaps; **el** — **Pedro** that fellow Peter; **un** — **García** a certain García; — **para cual** two of a kind; **un** — **por cual** a nobody; *adv.* just as, in such a way; **estaba** — **como le dejé** he was just as I left him; **con** — **(de) que** provided that; **¿qué** —? how are you?; hello!

talabarte [ta·la·ḃár·te] *m.* sword belt.

taladrar [ta·la·ḍrár] *v.* to bore, drill; to pierce; to penetrate.

taladro [ta·lá·ḍro] *m.* auger, drill; bore, drill hole; *Am.* mine tunnel.

tálamo [tá·la·mo] *m.* bridal bed or chamber.

talante [ta·lán·te] *m.* disposition; mood; appearance, manner.

talar [ta·lár] *v.* to cut down; *Am.* to prune.

talco [tál·ko] *m.* talc (*a soft mineral*); — **en polvo** talcum powder.

talega [ta·lé·ḡa] *f.* money bag, sack.

talento [ta·lén·to] *m.* talent; ability, natural gift.

talentoso [ta·len·tó·so] *adj.* talented, gifted.

talio [tá·ljo] *m.* thallium.

talismán [ta·liz·mán] *m.* talisman, charm.

talón [ta·lón] *m.* heel; stub, check, coupon.

talonario [ta·lo·ná·rjo] *m.* stub book; **libro** — stub book.

talonear [ta·lo·ne·ár] *v.* to tap with one's heel; to walk briskly.

taloneo [ta·lo·né·o] *m.* tapping with the heel; loud footsteps.

talla [tá·ya] *f.* (*altura*) stature, height; size; (*labrado*) carving; (*lance entero*) round of a card game; (*rescate*) ransom; *Am.* chat; *Am.* thrashing, beating.

tallar [ta·yár] *v.* to carve; to cut (*stone*); to appraise; to deal (*cards*); *Am.* to court, make love; *Andes, Col.* to bother, disturb.

tallarín [ta·ya·rín] *m.* noodle.

talle [tá·ye] *m.* figure, form; waist; fit (*of a dress*); looks, appearance; *Ven.* bodice.

taller [ta·yér] *m.* workshop; laboratory; studio; factory.

tallo [tá·yo] *m.* stalk; stem; shoot, sprout.

tamal [ta·mál] *m. Mex., C.A.* tamale; *Am.* vile trick, intrigue; *Am.* clumsy bundle.

tamaño [ta·má·ño] *m.* size; *adj.* such a; of the size of; — **disparate** such a (big) mistake; — **como un elefante** big as an elephant; **tamañito** [ta·ma·ñí·to] *adj.* very small; **tamañito así** about this little; **se quedó tamañito** he was (left) astonished, amazed.

tamarindo [ta·ma·rín·do] *m.* tamarind; *Mex.* traffic cop (*because of color of uniform*).

tambalearse [tam·ba·le·ár·se] *v.* to totter, stagger, sway, reel.

también [tam·bjén] *adv.* also, too; likewise.

tambor [tam·bór] *m.* drum; drum-like object; drummer; pair of embroidery hoops; *Mex.* bedspring, spring mattress; — **de freno** brake drum; **tambora** [tam·bó·ra] *f.* bass drum; **tamboril** [tam·bo·ríl] *m.* small drum; **tamborilero** [tam·bo·ri·lé·ro] *m.* drummer.

tamborilear [tam·bo·ri·le·ár] *v.* to drum; to extol.

tamiz [ta·mís] *m.* fine sieve.

tamizar [ta·mi·sár] *v.* to sift; to blend.

tampoco [tam·pó·ko] *conj.* either (*after a negative*); **no lo hizo** — he did not do it either; **ni yo** — nor I either.

tan [tan] *adv.* (*contr. of* **tanto**) so, as; such a.

tanda [tán·da] *f.* turn; round, bout; task; gang, group; shift, relay; *Col., Ven., Mex., Carib.* section of a theatrical performance.

tangente [taŋ·xén·te] *adj. & f.* tangent; **salirse por la** — to go off at a tangent; to avoid the issue.

tangible [taŋ·xí·ḃle] *adj.* tangible.

tango [táŋ·go] *m.* tango.

tanque [táŋ·ke] *m.* tank; reservoir; *Col., Ven.* pond; *Mex.* swimming pool.

tantán [tan·tán] *m.* clang; knock! knock!; sound of a bell, drum, etc.

tantear [tan·te·ár] *v.* to probe, test; to sound out, feel out; to estimate, calculate approximately; *Cuba, Ven., Riopl.* to grope, feel one's way; *Am.* to lie in wait; *Mex.* to fool, make a fool of; *Ven., Mex., C.A.* **¡tantee Vd.!** just imagine!

tanteo [tan·té·o] *m.* trial, test; calculation, estimate; score; **al** — by guess; hit or miss.

tanto [tán·to] *adj., pron. & adv.* so much, as much; so; **-s** so many, as many; *m.* certain amount; counter, chip (*to keep score*); **cuarenta y -s** forty odd; **el** — **por ciento** percentage, rate; **un** — (*or* **algún** —) somewhat; — **como** as well as; as much as; — **... como** both ... and; — **en la ciudad como en el campo** both in the city and in the country; **entre** (*or* **mientras**) — meanwhile; **por lo** — therefore.

tañer [ta·ñér] *v.* to play (*an instrument*); to ring.

tañido [ta·ñí·ḍo] *m.* sound, tune; ring; twang (*of a guitar*).

tapa [tá·pa] *f.* cover; lid; book cover; heel lift.

tapacubos [ta·pa·kú·ƀos] *m.* hubcap.
tapadera [ta·pa·ɗé·ra] *f.* cover, lid; one who shields another.
tapar [ta·pár] *v.* to cover; to plug, stop up; to veil; to hide; *Am.* to fill (*a tooth*); *Am.* to crush, crumple; *Am.* to cover with insults; **-se** to cover up; to wrap oneself up.
taparrabo [ta·pa·rrá·ƀo] *m.* loincloth; trunks.
tapera [ta·pé·ra] *f. Am.* ruins; *Ríopl., Andes* abandoned room or house.
tapete [ta·pé·te] *m.* rug; table scarf.
tapia [tá·pja] *f.* abode wall; wall fence.
tapiar [ta·pjár] *v.* to wall up; to block up (*a door or window*).
tapicería [ta·pi·se·rí·a] *f.* tapestry; upholstery; tapestry shop; tapestry making.
tapioca [ta·pjó·ka] *f.* tapioca.
tapiz [ta·pís] *m.* tapestry.
tapizar[9] [ta·pi·sár] *v. irr.* to carpet; to cover.
tapón [ta·pón] *m.* plug, stopper, cork; bottle cap.
taquigrafía [ta·ki·ǥra·fí·a] *f.* shorthand.
taquígrafo [ta·kí·ǥra·fo] *m.* stenographer.
taquilla [ta·kí·ya] *f.* ticket office; box office; file (*for letters, papers, etc.*); *Am.* tavern, liquor store.
tarántula [ta·rán·tu·la] *f.* tarantula.
tararear [ta·ra·re·ár] *v.* to hum.
tarareo [ta·ra·ré·o] *m.* hum, humming.
tarascada [ta·ras·ká·ɗa] *f.* snap, bite; snappy or harsh answer.
tardanza [tar·ɗán·sa] *f.* delay; slowness.
tardar [tar·ɗár] *v.* to delay; to be late; to be long (in); to take long (in); **-se** to delay oneself; to be delayed; **a más** — at the very latest.
tarde [tár·de] *f.* afternoon; *adv.* late; **de — en —** from time to time, now and then.
tardío [tar·ɗí·o] *adj.* late; slow.
tardo [tár·ɗo] *adj.* slow, lazy; tardy, late; stupid, dull; **tardón** [tar·ɗón] *adj.* very slow; *m.* slowpoke, slow person.
tarea [ta·ré·a] *f.* task, job; anxiety, care.
tarifa [ta·rí·fa] *f.* tariff; list of duties, taxes, or prices; fare.
tarima [ta·rí·ma] *f.* wooden platform; low bench.
tarjeta [tar·xé·ta] *f.* card; **— postal** postcard.
tarro [tá·rro] *m.* earthen jar; glass jar; *Mex.* horn (*of an animal*); *Ch., Cuba, Andes* can; *Andes* top hat.
tarta [tár·ta] *f.* tart.
tartamudear [tar·ta·mu·ɗe·ár] *v.* to stutter, stammer.
tartamudeo [tat·ta·mu·ɗé·o] *m.* stammer, stammering.
tartamudo [tar·ta·mú·ɗo] *m.* stutterer, stammerer; *adj.* stuttering, stammering.
tártaro [tár·ta·ro] *m.* tartar.
tartera [tar·té·ra] *f.* griddle; baking pan.
tarugo [tar·ú·ǥo] *m.* wooden block; wooden peg; blockhead, dunce; *adj. Andes* mischievous, devilish.
tasa [tá·sa] *f.* measure; standard; rate; appraisal; valuation.
tasación [ta·sa·sjón] *f.* assessment, valuation, appraisal.
tasajo [ta·sá·xo] *m.* piece of jerked beef.
tasar [ta·sár] *v.* to measure; to appraise; to rate.
tata [tá·ta] *f.* daddy, dad; *Mex., Andes* chief (*said by Indians to a superior*); **tatita** [ta·tí·ta] *m.* daddy; *Mex., Andes* dear chief or daddy (*said by Indians*).
tataranieto [ta·ta·ra·njé·to] *m.* great-great-grandson.
tatuar[18] [ta·twár] *v.* to tattoo.
taurino [taw·rí·no] *adj.* related to bullfighting.
tauromaquia [taw·ro·má·kja] *f.* bullfighting.
taxear [tak·se·ár] *v.* to taxi (*said of a plane*).
taxi [ták·si], **taxímetro** [tak·sí·me·tro] *m.* taxi, taxicab.
taxista [tak·sís·ta] *m. & f.* taxi driver.
taxonomía [tak·so·no·mí·a] *f.* taxonomy.
taza [tá·sa] *f.* cup; bowl; basin of a fountain.
tazón [ta·són] *m.* large cup; bowl; basin of a fountain.
té [te] *m.* tea; *f.* T-square, T-shaped ruler.
te [te] *obj. pron.* you (*fam. sing.*); to you; for you; yourself.
teatral [te·a·trál] *adj.* theatrical.
teatro [te·á·tro] *m.* theater; stage; scene, setting; **hacer** — to put on airs, show off.
tecla [té·kla] *f.* key (*of a piano, typewriter, etc.*); **dar uno en la** — to hit the nail on the head, find the right way to do something.
teclado [te·klá·ɗo] *m.* keyboard.
teclear [te·kle·ár] *v.* to finger the keys; to play the piano; to type.
tecleo [te·klé·o] *m.* fingering; movement of the keys (*typewriter, piano*).
técnica [ték·ni·ka] *f.* technique.
técnico [ték·ni·ko] *adj.* technical; *m.* technical expert, technician.
tecnología [tek·no·lo·xí·a] *f.* technology.
tecolote [te·ko·ló·te] *m. Mex.* owl.
techado [te·čá·ɗo] *m.* roof; shed; *p.p. of* **techar**.
techar [te·čár] *v.* to roof.
techo [té·čo] *m.* roof; ceiling.
techumbre [te·čúm·bre] *f.* roof; ceiling.
tedio [te·ɗjo] *m.* tediousness; boredom; bother.
tedioso [te·ɗjó·so] *adj.* tedious, boring, tiresome.
teja [té·xa] *f.* tile; linden tree; *Am.* rear part of a saddle; **de -s abajo** here below, in this world.
tejado [te·xá·ɗo] *m.* roof; shed.
tejamanil [te·xa·ma·níl] *m.* shingle; small thin board.
tejar [te·xár] *m.* tile factory; *v.* to cover with tiles.
tejedor [te·xe·ɗór] *m.* weaver.
tejer [te·xér] *v.* to weave; to interlace; to braid; to knit.
tejido [te·xí·ɗo] *m.* textile, fabric; texture; weave; weaving; tissue.
tejo [té·xo] *m.* disk; quoit; weight.
tejón [te·xón] *m.* badger; bar of gold.
tela [té·la] *f.* cloth; membrane; web; film (*on the surface of liquids*); **— adhesiva** adhesive tape; **— de cebolla** onion skin; flimsy fabric; *Am.* **— emplástica** court plaster; **— metálica** wire screen; **poner en — de juicio** to call in question.
telar [te·lár] *m.* loom.
telaraña [te·la·rá·ña] *f.* cobweb, spider's web.
teleférico [te·le·fé·ri·ko] *m.* telpher; car suspended on aerial cables.
telefonear [te·le·fo·ne·ár] *v.* to telephone.
telefónico [te·le·fó·ni·ko] *adj.* telephonic, telephone (*used as adj.*); **receptor** — telephone receiver.
teléfono [te·lé·fo·no] *m.* telephone; **telefonista** [te·le·fo·nísta] *m. & f.* telephone operator.
telegrafía [te·le·ǥra·fí·a] *f.* telegraphy.
telegrafiar[17] [te·le·ǥra·fjár] *v.* to telegraph.
telegráfico [te·le·ǥrá·fi·ko] *adj.* telegraphic.
telégrafo [te·lé·gra·fo] *m.* telegraph; **— sin hilos** (*or* **— inalámbrico**) wireless telegraph; **telegrafista** [te·le·ǥra·fís·ta] *m. & f.* telegraph operator.

TA

telegrama [te·le·ǵra·ma] *m.* telegram.
telémetro [te·lé·me·tro] *m.* telemeter; range finder.
telepatía [te·le·pa·tí·a] *f.* telepathy.
telescopio [te·les·kó·pjo] *m.* telescope.
telesquí [te·les·kí] *m.* ski lift.
teletipo [te·le·tí·po] *m.* teletype.
televidente [te·le·ƀi·dén·te] *m. & f.* televiewer; one who watches television.
televisión [te·le·ƀi·sjón] *f.* television.
telón [te·lón] *m.* theater curtain; — **de boca** drop curtain; — **de foro** drop scene.
telurio [te·lú·rjo] *m.* tellurium.
tema [té·ma] *m.* theme; subject; *f.* fixed idea, mania.
temático [te·má·ti·ko] *adj.* thematic; persistent.
temblar[1] [tem·blár] *v. irr.* to tremble; to shake; to quiver.
temblón [tem·blón] *adj.* tremulous, trembling, shaking, quivering.
temblor [tem·blór] *m.* tremor, trembling; shiver; quake; — **de tierra** earthquake.
tembloroso [tem·blo·ró·so] *adj.* trembling, shaking.
temer [te·mér] *v.* to fear; to dread; to suspect.
temerario [te·me·rá·rjo] *adj.* rash, reckless.
temeridad [te·me·ri· đáđ] *f.* temerity, recklessness; folly.
temeroso [te·me·ró·so] *adj.* fearful; suspicious; timid.
temible [te·mí·ƀle] *adj.* terrible, dreadful.
temor [te·mór] *m.* fear; dread, suspicion.
témpano [tém·pa·no] *m.* thick slice or chunk (*of anything*); kettledrum; drumhead (*parchment stretched over the end of a drum*); — **de hielo** block of ice; iceberg.
temperamento [tem·pe·ra·mén·to] *m.* temperament; climate.
temperatura [tem·pe·ra·tú·ra] *f.* temperature.
tempestad [tem·pes·táđ] *f.* tempest, storm.
tempestuoso [tem·pes·twó·so] *adj.* tempestuous, stormy.
templado [tem·plá·đo] *p.p. & adj.* (*moderado*) tempered; tuned; moderate; temperate; lukewarm; (*valiente*) brave; *Andes* in love; *Am.* half-drunk; *Am.* hard, severe; **estar mal** — to be in a bad humor.
templanza [tem·plán·sa] *f.* temperance; moderation; mildness.
templar [tem·plár] *v.* to temper; to moderate; to calm; to soften; to tune; **-se** to be tempered, moderate; to control oneself; *Andes* to fall in love; *Col.* to take to one's heels; *Am.* to stuff oneself.
temple [tém·ple] *m.* temper; temperament; valor, courage; harmony (*of musical instruments*); *Am.* sweetheart; **de mal** — in a bad humor.
templo [tém·plo] *m.* temple; church.
temporada [tem·po·rá·đa] *f.* period of time, season; — **de ópera** opera season.
temporal [tem·po·rál] *adj.* temporal; secular, worldly; temporary; *m.* weather; storm; spell of rainy weather.
tempranero [tem·pra·né·ro] *adj.* habitually early or ahead of time; **ser** — to be an early riser.
temprano [tem·prá·no] *adj.* early; premature; *adv.* early.
tenacidad [te·na·si·đáđ] *f.* tenacity; tenaciousness; perseverance.
tenacillas [te·na·sí·yas] *f. pl.* small tongs; pincers, tweezers; sugar tongs; curling iron.
tenaz [te·nás] *adj.* tenacious; firm; strong, resistant; stubborn.

tenazas [te·ná·sas] *f. pl.* pincers; pliers; tongs; forceps (*for pulling teeth*); **tenazuelas** [te·na·swé·las] *f. pl.* tweezers, small pincers.
tendedero [ten·de·đé·ro] *m.* place to hang or spread clothes; clothesline.
tendencia [ten·dén·sja] *f.* tendency, inclination.
tender[1] [ten·dér] *v. irr.* (*extender*) to spread out; to hang to dry; to stretch out; to lay out; (*propender*) to tend, have a tendency, move (*toward*); *Carib., Mex., C.A., Riopl., Andes* to make (*a bed*); **-se** to stretch oneself out; to lay all one's cards on the table; to run at full gallop.
ténder [tén·der] *m.* tender (*of a train*).
tendero [ten·dé·ro] *m.* storekeeper; tentmaker.
tendido [ten·dí·đo] *m.* laying; a wash hung up to dry.
tendón [ten·dón] *m.* tendon, sinew.
tenducho [ten·dú·čo] *m.* wretched little shop.
tenebroso [te·ne·ƀró·so] *adj.* dark, shadowy; gloomy.
tenedor [te·ne·đór] *m.* table fork; holder, possessor, keeper; — **de libros** bookkeeper.
teneduría [te·ne·đu·rí·a] *f.* office and position of bookkeeper; — **de libros** bookkeeping.
tener[45] [te·nér] *v. irr.* to have; to possess; to hold; — **en mucho** to esteem highly; — **por** to consider, judge; — **que** (+ *inf.*) to have to; — **gana** (*or* — **ganas**) **de** to desire, feel like; — **miedo** (**sueño, frío, hambre**, *etc.*) to be afraid (sleepy, cold, hungry, *etc.*); — **... años** to be ... years old; **-se** to stand firm; to hold on.
tenería [te·ne·rí·a] *f.* tannery.
tenia [té·nja] *f.* tapeworm.
teniente [te·njén·te] *m.* first lieutenant; substitute, deputy.
tenis [té·nis] *m.* tennis.
tenista [te·nís·ta] *m. & f.* tennis player.
tenor [te·nór] *m.* tenor; text, literal meaning; kind, sort, nature.
tensión [ten·sjón] *f.* tension; strain.
tenso [tén·so] *adj.* tense; tight, taut.
tentación [ten·ta·sjón] *f.* temptation.
tentáculo [ten·tá·ku·lo] *m.* tentacle, feeler.
tentador [ten·ta·đór] *adj.* tempting; *m.* tempter; the devil.
tentalear [ten·ta·le·ár] *v.* to grope, feel around; to finger, touch; to fumble (*for something*).
tentar[1] [ten·tár] *v. irr.* to tempt; to touch, feel with the fingers; to grope; to attempt, try; to test; to probe, examine with a probe.
tentativa [ten·ta·tí·ƀa] *f.* attempt, trial.
tentativo [ten·ta·tí·ƀo] *adj.* tentative.
tenue [té·nwe] *adj.* delicate, thin; flimsy; worthless.
teñir[5,19] [te·ñir] *v. irr.* to dye; to tinge; to darken (*the color of a painting*).
teologal [te·o·lo·ǵál], **teológico** *adj.* theological.
teología [te·o·lo·xi·a] *f.* theology.
teólogo [te·ó·lo·ǵo] *m.* theologian.
teoría [te·o·rí·a] *f.* theory.
teórico [te·ó·ri·ko] *adj.* theoretical.
tequila [te·kí·la] *m. Mex.* tequila (*liquor made from the maguey plant*).
terapéutico [te·ra·péw·ti·ko] *adj.* therapeutic.
tercero [ter·sé·ro] *adj.* third; *m.* third person; mediator; go-between; tertiary (*member of the third order of St. Francis*).
terciar [ter·sjár] *v.* (*atravesar*) to sling across one's shoulders; (*dividir*) to divide into three parts; (*intervenir*) to intervene, mediate; to meddle, join (*in*); (*equilibrar*) to balance the load on a pack animal; *Mex., Col.* to load or carry on the

back; *Am.* to adulterate, add water to; *Am.* to mix.

tercio [tér·sjo] *adj.* third; *m.* one third; half of a mule load; military regiment or division; *Col., Carib., Mex.* bale, bundle; **hacer uno mal** — to hinder, interfere; — **de varas** the banderilla part of the bullfight.

terciopelo [ter·sjo·pé·lo] *m.* velvet.

terco [tér·ko] *adj.* obstinate, stubborn; hard; *Am.* harsh, severe.

tergiversar [ter·xi·ßer·sár] *v.* to distort, twist.

terminación [ter·mi·na·sjón] *f.* termination, end; ending.

terminal [ter·mi·nál] *adj.* terminal, final.

terminante [ter·mi·nán·te] *adj.* closing, ending; decisive, final.

terminar [ter·mi·nár] *v.* to terminate, end; to finish; **-se** to end.

término [tér·mi·no] *m.* end; completion; goal, object; boundary, limit; terminal; term; word, phrase; **en otros -s** in other words; **por** — **medio** on an average; as a rule; **primer** — foreground.

termo [tér·mo] *m.* thermos bottle.

termómetro [ter·mó·me·tro] *m.* thermometer.

termonuclear [ter·mo·nu·kle·ár] *adj.* thermonuclear.

Termos [tér·mos] *f.* Thermos bottle (*trademark*).

termóstato [ter·mós·ta·to] *m.* thermostat.

ternera [ter·né·ra] *f.* calf; veal.

terneza [ter·né·sa] *f.* tenderness; softness; affection; affectionate word; caress.

terno [tér·no] *m.* group or combination of three; suit of clothes; *Carib., Mex.* set of jewels (*earrings, necklace, and brooch*); *Am.* cup and saucer; **echar** (*or* **soltar**) **un** — to utter a bad word; to curse, swear.

ternura [ter·nú·ra] *f.* tenderness.

terquedad [ter·ke·ðáð] *f.* obstinacy, stubbornness.

terrado [te·rrá·ðo] *m.* terrace; flat roof.

terramicina [te·rra·mi·sí·na] *f.* Terramycin.

terraplén [te·rra·plén] *m.* railroad embankment.

terrateniente [te·rra·te·njén·te] *m. & f.* landholder.

terraza [te·rrá·sa] *f.* terrace, veranda; flat roof.

terremoto [te·rre·mó·to] *m.* earthquake.

terrenal [te·rre·nál] *adj.* earthly, worldly.

terreno [te·rré·no] *m.* land; ground; field; *adj.* earthly, worldly.

terrestre [te·rrés·tre] *adj.* terrestrial; earthly.

terrible [te·rrí·ßle] *adj.* terrible.

terrífico [te·rrí·fi·ko] *adj.* terrific.

territorial [te·rri·to·rjál] *adj.* territorial.

territorio [te·rri·tó·rjo] *m.* territory.

terrón [te·rrón] *m.* clod; lump (*of sugar*).

terror [te·rrór] *m.* terror.

terrorista [te·rro·rís·ta] *m. & f.* terrorist.

terruño [te·rrú·ño] *m.* native soil.

terso [tér·so] *adj.* polished, smooth.

tertulia [ter·tú·lja] *f.* evening party; social gathering; club; conversation; *Riopl., Cuba, Ven.* theater gallery.

tertuliano [ter·tu·ljá·no], **tertulio** [ter·tú·ljo] *m.* member of a **tertulia**.

tesis [té·sis] *f.* thesis.

tesón [te·són] *m.* grit, endurance, pluck, persistence.

tesonero [te·so·né·ro] *adj. Mex., Cuba, Andes* tenacious, stubborn, persevering, persistent.

tesorería [te·so·re·rí·a] *f.* treasury; **tesorero** [te·so·ré·ro] *m.* treasurer.

tesoro [te·só·ro] *m.* treasure; treasury.

testa [tés·ta] *f.* head; crown of the head; front.

testamento [tes·ta·mén·to] *m.* testament; will.

testarudez [tes·ta·ru·ðés] *f.* stubbornness, obstinacy.

testarudo [tes·ta·rú·ðo] *adj.* stubborn.

testigo [tes·tí·ɣo] *m. & f.* witness; *m.* testimony, proof, evidence; — **de cargo** witness for the prosecution; — **de vista** eyewitness.

testimoniar [tes·ti·mo·njár] *v.* to give testimony of; to serve as a witness.

testimonio [tes·ti·mó·njo] *m.* testimony; proof, evidence; **levantar falso** — to bear false witness.

testuz [tes·tús] *m.* nape; crown of the head (*of certain animals*).

teta [té·ta] *f.* teat, nipple; breast; udder.

tétano [té·ta·no] *m.* tetanus.

tetera [te·té·ra] *f.* teapot; teakettle; *Mex., Cuba, Col.* **tetero** [te·té·ro] nursing bottle.

tétrico [té·tri·ko] *adj.* sad, melancholy, gloomy.

teutónico [tew·tó·ni·ko] *adj.* teutonic.

textil [tes·til] *adj.* textile.

texto [tés·to] *m.* text; quotation; textbook.

tez [tes] *f.* complexion, skin.

ti [ti] *pers. pron.* (*used after prep.*) you; yourself (*fam. sing.*).

tía [tí·a] *f.* aunt; older woman; *Ven.* — **rica** pawnshop; **no hay tu** — there is no use or hope; there is no way out of it; **quedarse una para** — to remain an old maid.

tibio [tí·ßjo] *adj.* tepid, lukewarm; indifferent; *Am.* annoyed, angry.

tiburón [ti·ßu·rón] *m.* shark.

tico [tí·ko] *adj. & m. Am.* Costa Rican (*humorous nickname*).

tictac [tik·ták] *m.* tick-tock.

tiempo [tjém·po] *m.* time; weather; tense; **a** — in time, on time; **a su** — in due time, at the proper time; **a un** — at one and the same time; **andando el** — in time, as time goes on.

tienda [tjén·da] *f.* store; tent; — **de campaña** camping tent, army tent.

tienta [tjén·ta] *f.* probe (*surgical instrument*); **a -s** gropingly, feeling one's way; **andar a -s** to grope, feel one's way.

tiento [tjén·to] *m.* touch; tact; blind man's stick; steady hand; blow; tentacle, feeler (*of an insect*); *Andes, Riopl.* saddle strap, leather strap, thong; *Am.* snack; *Am.* swallow of liquor; **dar un** — to make a trial or attempt; **hacer algo con mucho** — to do something with great care or caution; **perder el** — to lose one's skill; *Andes* **tener a uno a los -s** to keep someone within sight; *Ven.* **tener la vida en un** — to be in great danger.

tierno [tjér·no] *adj.* tender; soft; young; recent, new; sensitive; affectionate; *Am.* green, unripe.

tierra [tjé·rra] *f.* earth; land; ground; soil; native land; — **adentro** inland; — **firme** mainland; solid ground; **dar en** — **con alguien** to overthrow someone; **echar por** — to knock down; to demolish; **tomar** — to land.

tieso [tjé·so] *adj.* stiff, rigid; stuck-up; firm; stubborn.

tiesto [tjés·to] *m. Spain* flowerpot; broken piece of earthenware; *Ch.* pot.

tiesura [tje·sú·ra] *f.* stiffness.

tifo [tí·fo] *m.* typhus; **tifoidea** [ti·foj·ðe·a] *f.* typhoid fever.

tifón [ti·fón] *m.* typhoon; waterspout.

tifus [tí·fus] *m.* typhus.

tigre [tí·ɣre] *m.* tiger.

tijera [ti·xé·ra] *f.* (*usually* **tijeras**) scissors; sawhorse; **silla de** — folding chair; **tener buena** — (*or* **tener buenas -s**) to have a sharp tongue;

to be a gossip.
tijeretada [ti·xe·re·tá·đa] *f.,* **tijeretazo** [ti·xe·re·tá·so] *m.* snip, cut, clip (*with the scissors*).
tijeretear [ti·xe·re·te·ár] *v.* to snip, cut, clip (*with scissors*); to criticize others, gossip.
tila [tí·la] *f.* linden; linden blossom tea.
tildar [til·dár] *v.* to accent (*a word*); to put a tilde over the **n**; to stigmatize.
tilde [til·de] *f.* tilde (*mark over an* **n**); blemish; jot, bit, speck; *Col.* accent mark.
timbrar [tim·brár] *v.* to stamp, mark with a seal.
timbrazo [tim·brá·so] *m.* ring of an electric bell.
timbre [tím·bre] *m.* revenue stamp; seal; crest (*on a coat of arms*); call bell; timbre (*quality of tone, tone color*); merit, fame; glorious deed; *Am.* postage stamp.
timidez [ti·mi·đés] *f.* timidity; shyness.
tímido [tí·mi·đo] *adj.* timid; shy.
timón [ti·món] *m.* helm; rudder; beam of a plow; *Col.* steering wheel.
timonear [ti·mo·ne·ár] *v.* to steer (*a ship*).
timorato [ti·mo·rá·to] *adj.* timorous, timid.
tímpano [tím·pa·no] *m.* eardrum; kettledrum.
tina [tí·na] *f.* large earthen jar; vat, tank, tub; bathtub.
tinaco [ti·ná·ko] *m.* tank, vat, tub.
tinaja [ti·ná·xa] *f.* large earthen jar.
tinglado [tiŋ·glá·đo] *m.* shed.
tinieblas [ti·njé·βlas] *f. pl.* darkness; obscurity; ignorance, confusion; Tenebrae (*Holy Week religious service*).
tino [tí·no] *m.* acumen, keen insight, good judgment; tact; accurate aim; good sense of touch; tank, vat.
tinta [tín·ta] *f.* ink; dye; tint, hue; **-s** paints; **— simpática** invisible ink; **saber de buena —** to know on good authority.
tinte [tín·te] *m.* tint, hue; tinge; color; dye; dyeing.
tinterillo [tin·te·rí·yo] *m.* shyster. *See* **picapleitos.**
tintero [tin·té·ro] *m.* inkwell, inkstand; ink roller (*printing*); *Am.* writing materials, desk set.
tintinear [tin·ti·ne·ár] *v.* to tinkle.
tintineo [tin·ti·né·o] *m.* tinkle, tinkling.
tinto [tín·to] *adj.* tinged; red (*wine*); *Col.* black coffee; *Am.* dark-red; *p.p. irr. of* **teñir.**
tintorería [tin·to·re·rí·a] *f.* cleaner's and dyer's shop.
tintorero [tin·to·ré·ro] *m.* dyer.
tintura [tin·tú·ra] *f.* tincture; tint; color; dye.
tinturar [tin·tu·rár] *v.* to tincture; to tinge; to dye.
tiñoso [ti·ñó·so] *adj.* scabby, mangy; stingy.
tío [tí·o] *m.* uncle; old man; good old man; fellow, guy; *Riopl., Mex., Ven., Andes* **el cuento del —** deceitful story (*told to extract money*).
tiovivo [tí·o·βí·βo] *m.* merry-go-round.
típico [tí·pi·ko] *adj.* typical; *Am.* corrected (*edition*).
tiple [tí·ple] *m. & f.* high soprano singer; *m.* treble; soprano voice; treble guitar.
tipo [tí·po] *m.* type; class; model, standard; fellow, guy; *Am.* rate of interest; *Am.* **— de cambio** rate or exchange; **buen —** good-looking fellow.
tipografía [ti·po·gra·fí·a] *f.* typography, printing; press, printing shop.
tira [tí·ra] *f.* strip; stripe; *Mex.* **estar hecho -s** to be in rags; *Ven.* **sacar a uno las -s** to tan one's hide, beat one to pieces.
tirabuzón [ti·ra·βu·són] *m.* corkscrew.
tirada [ti·rá·đa] *f.* throw; issue, edition, printing; *Am.* tirade, long speech; *Am.* sly trick; *Am.* dash

(*on horseback*); **de una —** all at once, at one fell swoop.
tirador [ti·ra·đór] *m.* shooter; thrower; slingshot; bell cord; handle; printer; *Am.* leather belt with pockets; **— de goma** slingshot.
tiranía [ti·ra·ní·a] *f.* tyranny.
tiránico [ti·rá·ni·ko] *adj.* tyrannical.
tirano [ti·rá·no] *adj.* tyrannical; *m.* tyrant.
tirante [ti·rán·te] *adj.* pulling; stretched, taut; strained; *m.* trace (*of a harness*); brace; **-s** suspenders; supporters (*for stockings*).
tirantez [ti·ran·tés] *f.* tension, tightness; strain; pull.
tirar [ti·rár] *v.* (*lanzar*) to throw; to throw away; to shoot, fire; (*imprimir*) to draw; to print; (*atraer*) to pull; to attract; *Am.* to cart; **— a** to tend toward; to resemble; to aim at; **— de** to pull, tug; **— bien a la espada** to handle a sword well; **ir tirando** to get along; **a todo** (*or* **a más**) **— at** the most; *Am.* **al —** haphazardly; **-se to** throw oneself; to lie down; *Mex., C.A., Col., Ven., Riopl., Andes* **tirársela de** to boast of.
tiritar [ti·ri·tár] *v.* to shiver.
tiro [tí·ro] *m.* (*disparo*) throw; shot; (*pieza*) piece of artillery; (*alcance*) range of a gun; shooting range; (*carga*) charge of a gun; team (*of horses*); chimney draft; mine shaft; *Am.* issue, printing; *Am.* cartage, transport; **-s** *Am.* suspenders; **al blanco** target practice; *Ch., Andes* **al — at** once; *Ven.* **de a** (*or* **de al**) **— all** at once; completely; **caballo de —** draft horse; **ni a -s** absolutely not (*not even if you shoot me*).
tirón [ti·rón] *m.* jerk, sudden pull; **de un —** all at once, with one big pull.
tironear [ti·ro·ne·ár] *v. C.A., Mex., Riopl.* to pull, jerk; *Col.* to attract.
tirotear [ti·ro·te·ár] *v.* to shoot around; to shoot at random; **-se** to exchange shots.
tiroteo [ti·ro·té·o] *m.* shooting; exchange of shots; skirmish.
tirria [tí·rrja] *f.* aversion, grudge; **tenerle — a una persona** to have a strong dislike for someone; to hold a grudge against someone.
tísico [tí·si·ko] *adj.* tubercular, consumptive.
tisis [tí·sis] *f.* tuberculosis, consumption.
titanio [ti·tá·njo] *m.* titanium.
títere [tí·te·re] *m.* puppet; ridiculous little fellow; **-s** puppet show.
titilación [ti·ti·la·sjón] *f.* flicker; twinkle; **titileo** flickering; twinkling; glimmer.
titilar [ti·ti·lár] *v.* to flicker; to twinkle.
titubear [ti·tu·βe·ár] *v.* to hesitate; to totter, stagger; to grope; to stutter, stammer.
titubeo [ti·tu·βé·o] *m.* hesitation, wavering.
titular [ti·tu·lár] *v.* to entitle; to name; **-se** to be called or named; to call oneself; to receive a title; *adj.* titular, in name only; *m.* officer; holder of a title.
título [tí·tu·lo] *m.* (*letrero*) title; heading; label; inscription; (*derecho*) claim, legal right; (*grado*) degree, diploma; credential; titled person; merit; bond, certificate; **a — de** under the pretext of; in the capacity of.
tiza [tí·sa] *f.* chalk.
tiznado [tiz·ná·đo] *adj.* sooty, covered with soot; smutty; dirty; *Ven.* drunk; *p.p. of* **tiznar.**
tiznar [tiz·nár] *v.* to smudge, smut; to smear with soot.
tizne [tíz·ne] *m.* soot; smut; **tiznón** [tiz·nón] *m.* smudge.
tizón [ti·són] *m.* firebrand (*piece of burning wood*);

rust, blight (*on plants*); stain (*on one's honor*).

toalla [to·á·ya] *f*. towel.

tobillo [to·ƀí·yo] *m*. ankle.

tocadiscos [to·ka·đís·kos] *m*. record player; phonograph.

tocado [to·ká·đo] *m*. headdress; hairdo, coiffure; *adj*. "touched", half-crazy; *p.p. of* **tocar.**

tocador [to·ka·đór] *m*. dressing table; boudoir, dressing room; dressing case; player (*of a musical instrument*).

tocar[6] [to·kár] *v*. to touch; to play (*an instrument*); to toll, ring; to knock, rap; — **en** to stop over in; **-le a uno** to fall to one's lot; to be one's share; to be one's turn; to concern one; **-se** to fix one's hair; to become "touched", go slightly crazy.

tocayo [to·ká·yo] *m*. namesake; one who has the same name.

tocino [to·sí·no] *m*. bacon; salt pork; lard.

tocón [to·kón] *m*. stub, stump (*of a tree, arm or leg*).

todavía [to·đa·ƀí·a] *adv*. still; yet; even.

todo [tó·đo] *adj*. all, whole; every, each; — **hombre** every man; **-s los días** every day; **a —** **correr** at full or top speed; *m*. whole; all; everything; **-s** everybody; **ante** — first of all; **así y** — in spite of that; **con** — in spite of that; **del** — wholly.

todopoderoso [to·đo·po·đe·ró·so] *adj*. almighty.

toga [tó·ǥa] *f*. gown, robe (*worn by a judge, professor, etc.*); Roman toga.

toldería [tol·de·rí·a] *f*. *Ríopl*. Indian camp, Indian village.

toldo [tól·do] *m*. awning; pomp, vanity; *Ríopl*. Indian hut.

tolerancia [to·le·rán·sja] *f*. tolerance, toleration; **tolerante** [to·le·rán·te] *adj*. tolerant.

tolerar [to·le·rár] *v*. to tolerate; to allow; to overlook, let pass.

tolete [to·lé·te] *m*. *Col., Mex., Cuba* stick, club, cudgel; *Am*. raft.

toma [tó·ma] *f*. taking; seizure, capture; dose; tap (*of a water main*); *Am*. irrigation ditch; — **de** **corriente** plug, electric outlet.

tomar [to·már] *v*. (*asir*) to take; to grasp, catch; to capture; (*beber*) to drink; — **a pechos** to take to heart, take seriously; **-lo a mal** to take it amiss; — **el pelo a** to make fun of, make a fool of; — **por la derecha** to turn to the right; **-se con** to quarrel with.

tomate [to·má·te] *m*. tomato.

tómbola [tóm·bo·la] *f*. raffle for charity.

tomillo [to·mí·yo] *m*. thyme.

tomo [tó·mo] *m*. tome, volume; *Am*. heavy person; *Am*. dull, silent person; *Am*. **buen** — a heavy drinker; **de** — **y lomo** bulky; important.

ton [ton]: **sin** — **ni son** without rhyme or reason.

tonada [to·ná·đa] *f*. tune, song; *Andes* singsong; *Andes, Mex., Carib., Ríopl*. local accent; **tonadilla** [to·na·đí·ya] *f*. little tune; short popular song.

tonel [to·nél] *m*. keg, cask, barrel.

tonelada [to·ne·lá·đa] *f*. ton.

tonelaje [to·ne·lá·xe] *m*. tonnage.

tónico [tó·ni·ko] *adj. & m*. tonic.

tono [tó·no] *m*. tone; tune; key, pitch; accent; manner; vigor, strength; **de buen** — of good taste, stylish; **subirse de** — to put on airs.

tonsura [ton·sú·ra] *f*. shearing.

tontera [ton·té·ra] = **tontería.**

tontería [ton·te·rí·a] *f*. foolishness; stupidity.

tonto [tón·to] *adj*. foolish; stupid; **a tontas y a** **locas** recklessly, without thought; *m*. fool; dunce; *Col., Ch*. a game of cards.

topar [to·pár] *v*. to collide with, run into, bump into; to encounter; to find; to run across; to butt; *Am*. to gamble; *Col*. to fight with the fists; *Carib., Mex., Ríopl., Andes, Col*. to meet, greet.

tope [tó·pe] *m*. butt, bump, collision; encounter; bumper; dead-end; **hasta el** — up to the top; **estar hasta los -s** to be filled up.

topetada [to·pe·tá·đa] *f*., **topetazo** [to·pe·tá·so] *m*. butt; bump, bump on the head; **topetón** [to·pe·tón] *m*. hard bump, collision; butt.

topetear [to·pe·te·ár] *v*. to butt; to bump.

tópico [tó·pi·ko] *m*. topic, subject.

topo [tó·po] *m*. mole (*small animal*); dunce; awkward person.

topografía [to·po·ǥra·fí·a] *f*. topography.

toque [tó·ke] *m*. touch; ringing; beat (*of a drum*); tap, sound (*of a trumpet, clarinet, etc.*); assay; **piedra de** — touchstone; **¡allí está el** —! there is the difficulty!; there is the real test!

toquilla [to·kí·ya] *f*. triangular handkerchief; ribbon; hatband.

tórax [tó·raks] *m*. thorax.

torbellino [tor·ƀe·yí·no] *m*. whirlwind; rush, bustle, confusion.

torcedura [tor·se·đú·ra] *f*. twist; sprain, strain.

torcer[2, 10] [tor·sér] *v. irr*. to twist; to turn; to bend; to sprain; to distort; **-se** to become twisted, bent, or sprained; to get crooked; to go astray; to turn sour (*said of wine*); *Am*. to get offended, angry.

torcido [tor·sí·đo] *p.p. & adj*. twisted, turned, bent; crooked; angry, resentful; *Am*. unfortunate, unlucky; **estar** — **con** to be on unfriendly terms with; *m*. twisted roll of candied fruit; coarse silk twist; *Mex., Carib*. gesture or look of disdain; *Andes* lasso made of twisted leather.

tordillo [tor·đí·yo] *adj*. greyish, dapple-grey.

tordo [tór·đo] *adj*. dapple-grey; *m*. thrush; dapple-grey horse.

torear [to·re·ár] *v*. to perform in a bullfight; to incite, provoke (*a bull*); to tease.

torero [to·ré·ro] *m*. bullfighter; *adj*. relating to bullfighting

tormenta [tor·mén·ta] *f*. storm, tempest; misfortune.

tormento [tor·mén·to] *m*. torment; torture; rack (*instrument of torture*); anguish; pain.

tornar [tor·nár] *v*. to return; to turn; to change, alter; — **a hacerlo** to do it again.

tornasol [tor·na·sól] *m*. sunflower.

tornasolado [tor·na·so·lá·đo] *adj*. iridescent, rainbow-colored; changeable (*silk*).

tornear [tor·ne·ár] *v*. to turn in a lathe; to do lathe work; to fight in a tournament.

torneo [tor·né·o] *m*. tournament.

tornillo [tor·ní·yo] *m*. screw; clamp, vise; **faltarle a** **uno un** — to have little sense, "have a screw loose".

torniquete [tor·ni·ké·te] *m*. turnbuckle; tourniquet.

torno [tór·no] *m*. turn; lathe; turnstile; revolving server; winch or windlass (*machine for lifting or pulling, turned by a crank*); — **de hilar** spinning wheel; **en** — around.

toro [tó·ro] *m*. bull; *Mex. Col*. difficult question; **-s** bullfight; *Am*. **estar en las astas del** — to be in a predicament.

toronja [to·róŋ·xa] *f.* grapefruit.
torpe [tór·pe] *adj.* stupid, dull; clumsy; slow; lewd.
torpedo [tor·pé·ḍo] *m.* torpedo; **torpedero** [tor·pe·ḍé·ro] *m.* torpedo boat.
torpeza [tor·pé·sa] *f.* stupidity, dullness; clumsiness; slowness; moral turpitude, lewdness.
torre [tó·rre] *f.* tower; turret; castle (*in chess*).
torrencial [to·rren·sjál] *adj.* torrential.
torrente [to·rrén·te] *m.* torrent; flood; — **de voz** powerful voice.
torreón [to·rre·ón] *m.* large tower (*of a fortress, castle, etc.*).
tórrido [tó·rri·ḍo] *adj.* torrid.
torsión [tor·sjón] *f.* twist; sprain.
torta [tór·ta] *f.* torte, round cake; round loaf.
tortilla [tor·tí·ya] *f.* omelet; *Mex., C.A.* tortilla (*flat, thin cornmeal cake*).
tórtola [tór·to·la] *f.* turtledove.
tortuga [tor·tú·ga] *f.* tortoise; turtle.
tortuoso [tor·twó·so] *adj.* tortuous, twisting, winding; sly.
tortura [tor·tú·ra] *f.* torture; grief, affliction.
torturar [tor·tu·rár] *v.* to torture.
torvo [tór·ḅo] *adj.* grim, stern, severe.
tos [tos] *f.* cough; — **ferina** whooping cough.
tosco [tós·ko] *adj.* coarse, harsh, rough.
toser [to·sér] *v.* to cough; *Am.* to brag, boast.
tosquedad [tos·ke·ḍáḍ] *f.* coarseness, crudeness, roughness; rudeness.
tostada [tos·tá·ḍa] *f.* toast, toasted bread; *Am.* boring visit or conversation; *Ven.* toasted **tortilla; dar** (*or* **pegar**) **una — a uno** to play a mean trick on someone; *Am.* to make someone very angry.
tostado [tos·tá·ḍo] *p.p. & adj.* toasted; roasted; tanned; *Am.* worn out, tired out; *m.* toasting; *Am.* roasted corn.
tostador [tos·ta·ḍór] *m.* toaster.
tostar[2] [tos·tár] *v. irr.* to toast; to tan; to overheat; to roast (*coffee*).
tostón [tos·tón] *m.* toast dipped in oil; small roasted pig; *Mex., C.A.* coin worth half a Mexican peso.
total [to·tál] *adj. & m.* total.
totalidad [to·ta·li·ḍáḍ] *f.* entirety, whole.
totalitario [to·ta·li·tá·rjo] *adj.* totalitarian.
totuma [to·tú·ma] *f.* calabash.
tóxico [tók·si·ko] *adj.* toxic.
toxina [tok·si·na] *f.* toxin (*poison produced within animals and plants*).
toza [tó·sa] *f.* wooden block; stump; log; piece of bark.
traba [trá·ḅa] *f.* bond, tie; binding or locking device; fastener, fetter, shackle; hindrance, obstacle
trabado [tra·ḅá·ḍo] *adj. Col., Riopl., Mex.* tongue-tied; *p.p. of* **trabar.**
trabajador [tra·ḅa·xa·ḍor] *adj.* industrious; *m.* worker, laborer.
trabajar [tra·ḅa·xár] *v.* to work; to labor; to strive.
trabajo [tra·ḅá·xo] *m.* work; labor; difficulty, obstacle; trouble; hardship.
trabajoso [tra·ḅa·xó·so] *adj.* laborious, difficult; troublesome; *Am.* unobliging; *Am.* demanding.
trabalenguas [tra·ḅa·lén·gwas] *m.* tongue twister.
trabar [tra·ḅár] *v.* to join, fasten; to clasp; to shackle; to brace; to impede; — **amistad con alguien** to become friends with someone; — **batalla** to join in battle; — **conversación** to be engaged in conversation; to engage in conversation; **-se** *Riopl., Mex., Ven.* to stammer;

-se de palabras to get into an argument.
tracción [trak·sjón] *f.* traction.
tractor [trak·tór] *m.* tractor.
tradición [tra·ḍi·sjón] *f.* tradition.
tradicional [tra·ḍi·sjo·nál] *adj.* traditional.
traducción [tra·ḍuk·sjón] *f.* translation.
traducir[25] [tra·ḍu·sír] *v. irr.* to translate; to interpret.
traductor [tra·ḍuk·tór] *m.* translator.
traer[46] [tra·ér] *v. irr.* to bring; to carry; to lead, conduct; to have; to bring about; to wear; — **a uno inquieto** to keep one disturbed; — **a uno a mal** — to mistreat someone; to bother someone; **-se bien** to dress well; to carry oneself well.
trafagar[7] [tra·fa·gár] *v.* to traffic, trade; to roam about; to bustle, hustle; to toil.
tráfago [trá·fa·go] *m.* trade, commerce; bustle, hustle; toil.
traficante [tra·fi·kán·te] *m.* trader; dealer; tradesman.
traficar[6] [tra·fi·kár] *v.* to traffic, trade; *Ven.* to pass or move back and forth (*as traffic*). *See* **transitar.**
tráfico [trá·fi·ko] *m.* traffic; trade, commerce.
tragaluz [tra·ga·lús] *f.* skylight.
tragar[7] [tra·gár] *v.* to swallow; to gulp; to engulf, swallow up.
tragedia [tra·xé·ḍja] *f.* tragedy.
trágico [trá·xi·ko] *adj.* tragic.
trago [trá·go] *m.* swallow, gulp; misfortune; *Am.* brandy, hard liquor; **a -s** slowly, by degrees; **echar un —** to take a drink; **tragón** *m.* glutton; *adj.* gluttonous.
traición [traj·sjón] *f.* treason; treachery; **a —** treacherously; deceitfully.
traicionar [traj·sjo·nár] *v.* to betray.
traicionero [traj·sjo·né·ro] *adj.* treacherous; deceitful; *m.* traitor.
traído [tra·í·ḍo] *adj.* used, old, worn out; **muy — y llevado** very worn out; *p.p. of* **traer.**
traidor [traj·ḍór] *adj.* treacherous; *m.* traitor; betrayer.
traje [trá·xe] *m.* dress; suit; gown; — **de etiqueta** (— **de çeremonia,** *or Am.* — **de parada**) formal gown; formal suit; dress uniform; — **de luces** bullfighter's costume; *Col., C.A., Mex., Riopl.* — **sastre** woman's tailor-made suit.
trajeado [tra·xe·á·ḍo] *p.p. & adj.* dressed, clothed.
trajín [tra·xín] *m.* traffic, going and coming; hustle, bustle, commotion.
trajinar [tra·xi·nár] *v.* to carry, cart back and forth; to go back and forth; to bustle, hustle.
trama [trá·ma] *f.* plot; scheme; conspiracy; woof (*horizontal threads of a fabric*).
tramar [tra·már] *v.* to weave; to plot; to scheme.
tramitar [tra·mi·tár] *v.* to transact; to take legal steps; to negotiate.
trámite [trá·mi·te] *m.* transaction, procedure, step, formality.
tramo [trá·mo] *m.* stretch, lap, span; short distance; regular interval; flight of stairs.
tramoya [tra·mó·ya] *f.* stage devices and machinery.
trampa [trám·pa] *f.* trap; snare; hatch, trap door; hinged section of a counter; spring door; fraud; trick.
trampear [tram·pe·ár] *v.* to trick, cheat, swindle.
trampista [tram·pís·ta] *m. & f.* cheat, crook, swindler.
trampolín [tram·po·lín] *m.* springboard.
tramposo [tram·pó·so] *adj.* deceitful, tricky; *m.*

swindler, cheat.

tranca [tráŋ·ka] *f*. crossbar, bolt; pole, prop; club, stick; *Mex., Ríopl.* rustic gate; *Ríopl.* fence with gates; *Mex., Ven.* **saltar las -s** to jump over the fence; to lose one's patience, rebel, get angry; *Ch., Ríopl., Andes, Mex.* **tener una** — to be drunk.

trance [trán·se] *m*. critical moment; dangerous situation; **el último** — the last moment of life; **a todo** — at any cost, cost what it may.

tranco [tráŋ·ko] *m*. stride, long step; threshold; **a -s** hurriedly; **en dos -s** in a jiffy; *Ríopl.* **al** — striding, with long steps.

tranquear [traŋ·ke·ár] *v*. to stride along.

tranquera [traŋ·ké·ra] *f*. stockade, wooden fence; *Ríopl., Cuba, Ven.* large gate (*made with* **trancas**).

tranquilidad [traŋ·ki·li·ḍáḍ] *f*. tranquility, peacefulness.

tranquilizar[9] [traŋ·ki·li·sár] *v*. to quiet, calm down; to pacify; **-se** to become tranquil, calm down.

tranquilo [traŋ·kí·lo] *adj*. tranquil, peaceful.

transacción [tran·sak·sjón] *f*. transaction, negotiation; compromise.

transar [tran·sár] *v. Am*. to compromise, yield, give in.

transatlántico [tran·sa·tlán·ti·ko] *adj*. transatlantic; *m*. transatlantic steamer.

transbordar [trans·ḅor·ḍár] = **trasbordar**.

transbordo [trans·ḅór·ḍo] = **trasbordo**.

transcendencia [trans·sen·dén·sja] *f*. consequence, importance; penetration.

transcendental [tran·sen·den·tál] *adj*. consequential, important, far-reaching.

transcribir [trans·kri·ḅír] *v*. to transcribe.

transcurrir [trans·ku·rrír] *v*. to pass elapse.

transcurso [trans·kúr·so] *m*. passing, lapse (*of time*).

transeúnte [tran·se·ún·te] *m*. passer-by; pedestrian; transient; *adj*. transient.

transferencia [trans·fe·rén·sja] *f*. transference, transfer.

transferible [trans·fe·rí·ḅle] *f*. transference, transfer.

transferible [trans·fe·rí·ḅle] *adj*. transferable.

transferir[3] [trans·fe·rír] *v. irr*. to transfer.

transformación [trans·for·ma·sjón] *f*. transformation.

transformador [trans·for·ma·ḍór] *m*. transformer.

transformar [trans·for·már] *v*. to transform.

transfusión [trans·fu·sjón] *f*. transfusion.

transgredir[51] [trans·ḡre·ḍír] *v*. to transgress.

transgresión [trans·ḡre·sjón] *f*. transgression.

transgresor [trans·ḡre·sór] *m*. transgressor, offender.

transición [tran·si·sjón] *f*. transition.

transigente [tran·si·xén·te] *adj*. compromising, yielding, pliable.

transigir[11] [tran·si·xír] *v*. to compromise, yield, make concessions; to settle by compromise.

transistor [tran·sis·tór] *m*. transistor.

transitable [tran·si·tá·ḅle] *adj*. passable (*road*).

transitar [tran·si·tár] *v*. to pass or move back and forth (*as traffic*).

tránsito [trán·si·to] *m*. transit; traffic; passing; passage; transition; **de** — on the way, in transit, passing through.

transitorio [tran·si·tó·rjo] *adj*. transitory.

transmisión [trans·mi·sjón] *f*. transmission; — **automática** automatic transmission.

transmisor [trans·mi·sór] *m*. transmitter; *adj*. transmitting.

transmitir [trans·mi·tír] *v*. to transmit.

transparencia [trans·pa·rén·sja] *f*. transparency.

transparente [trans·pa·rén·te] *adj*. transparent; lucid, clear; *m*. window shade; stained-glass window.

transpirar [trans·pi·rár] *v*. to transpire; to leak out.

transponer[40] [trans·po·nér] *v. irr*. to transpose; to transfer; to transplant; to go beyond, go over to the other side; **-se** to hide from view, go behind; to set, go below the horizon.

transportación [trans·por·ta·sjón] *f*. transportation, transport.

transportar [trans·por·tár] *v*. to transport; to transpose (*music*); **-se** to be transported, carried away by strong feeling; to be in ecstasy.

transporte [trans·pór·te] *m*. transport; transportation; transport vessel; ecstasy; — **de locura** fit of madness.

transpuesto [trans·pwés·to] *p.p. of* **transponer**.

transversal [trans·ḅer·sál] *adj*. transversal, transverse; **sección** — cross section.

transverso [trans·ḅér·so] *adj*. transverse, cross.

tranvía [tram·bí·a] *m*. streetcar; streetcar track.

trapacear [tra·pa·se·ár] *v*. to swindle, cheat; to racketeer.

trapacería [tra·pa·se·rí·a] *f*. racket, fraud, swindle.

trapacero [tra·pa·sé·ro] *m*. racketeer; cheat, swindler; *adj*. cheating, deceiving.

trapacista [tra·pa·sís·ta] *m. & f*. racketeer; swindler, cheat.

trapeador [tra·pe·a·ḍór] *m. Am*. mopper; *Andes, Ven., Col., C.A., Mex., Cuba* mop.

trapear [tra·pe·ár] *v. Am*. to mop; *Am*. to beat up, give (*someone*) a licking.

trapecio [tra·pé·sjo] *m*. trapeze.

trapiche [tra·pí·če] *m*. sugar mill; press (*for extracting juices*); *Andes* grinding machine (*for pulverizing minerals*).

trapisonda [tra·pi·són·da] *f*. escapade, prank; brawl; noisy spree.

trapo [trá·po] *m*. rag; *C.A., Ven., Ur*. cloth; **-s** clothes; **a todo** — at full sail; speedily; **poner a uno como un** — to make one feel like a rag; **sacarle a uno los -s al sol** to exhibit somebody's dirty linen; **soltar el** — to burst out laughing or crying.

traposo [tra·pó·so] *adj. Am*. ragged, tattered, in rags.

tráquea [trá·ke·a] *f*. trachea, windpipe.

traquetear [tra·ke·te·ár] *v*. to rattle; to shake; to jolt; to crack, crackle.

traqueteo [tra·ke·té·o] *m*. rattling; shaking; jolting; cracking, crackling; *Ríopl., Col., Ven., C.A., Mex. Carib., Andes* uproar, din; *Am*. noisy. disorderly traffic.

tras [tras] *prep*. after; in search of; behind, in back of; — **de** behind, after; besides, in addition to; *interj*. ¡ — ! bang!

trasbordar [traz·ḅor·ḍár] *v*. to transfer.

trasbordo [traz·ḅór·ḍo] *m*. transfer.

trascendencia [traz·sen·dén·sja] = **transcendencia**.

trascendental [tra·sen·den·tál] = **transcendental**.

trasegar[1, 7] [tra·se·ḡár] *v. irr*. to upset, overturn; to change from one place to another; to pour from one container to another.

trasero [tra·sé·ro] *adj*. rear, hind, back; *m*. rump.

trasladar [traz·la·ḍár] *v*. to move, remove; to transfer; to postpone; to translate; to transcribe, copy.

traslado [traz·lá·ḍo] *m*. transfer; transcript, written copy.

traslucirse[13] [traz·lu·sír·se] *v. irr*. to be translucent;

to be transparent, clear, evident.

trasnochar [tɾaz·no·čáɾ] *v.* to sit up all night; to stay awake all night; to spend the night out.

traspalar [tɾas·pa·láɾ] *v.* to shovel.

traspapelar [tɾas·pa·pe·láɾ] *v.* to mislay, misplace (*a paper, letter, document, etc.*); **-se** to become mislaid among other papers.

traspasar [tɾas·pa·sáɾ] *v.* to pass over, cross over; to go beyond; to pass through; to pierce; to transfer (*property*); to trespass.

traspaso [tɾas·pá·so] *m.* transfer; transgression, trespass.

traspié [tɾas·pjé] *m.* stumble, slip; **dar un** — to stumble or trip.

trasplantar [tɾas·plan·táɾ] *v.* to transplant.

trasponer⁴⁰ [tɾas·po·néɾ] = **transponer.**

trasquila [tɾas·kí·la], **trasquiladura** [tɾas·ki·la·ɖú·ra] *f.* shearing, clip, clipping; bad haircut.

trasquilar [tɾas·ki·láɾ] *v.* to shear; to clip; to crop; to cut badly (*hair*).

trastazo [tɾas·tá·so] *m.* thump, blow.

traste [tɾás·te] *m.* fret, stop (*of a guitar*); *C.A.* utensil, implement; **dar al** — **con** to destroy, ruin.

trasto [tɾás·to] *m.* household utensil; piece of junk; rubbish, trash; **-s** utensils; implements; **-s de pescar** fishing tackle.

trastornar [tɾas·toɾ·náɾ] *v.* to overturn; to upset; to disturb.

trastorno [tɾas·tóɾ·no] *m.* upset; disorder; disturbance.

trastrocar²,⁶ [tɾas·tɾo·káɾ] *v. irr.* to invert, change; to upset.

trasudar [tɾa·su·ɖáɾ] *v.* to perspire, sweat slightly.

trasudor [tɾa·su·ɖóɾ] *m.* slight perspiration or sweat.

tratable [tɾa·tá·β̞le] *adj.* friendly, sociable; manageable.

tratado [tɾa·tá·ɖo] *m.* treaty; treatise.

tratamiento [tɾa·ta·mjén·to] *m.* treatment; title of courtesy; form of address.

tratante [tɾa·tán·te] *m. & f.* dealer, tradesman, trader.

tratar [tɾa·táɾ] *v.* to treat; to handle; to discuss; to have social relations with; — **con** to have dealings with; — **de** to try to; to treat of, deal with; **-le a uno de** to address someone as; to treat someone as; — **en** to deal in; **-se bien** to treat oneself well; to behave well; **-se de** to be a question of; **no se trata de eso** that isn't the question, that isn't the point.

trato [tɾá·to] *m.* (*acuerdo*) treatment; deal, pact; trade; (*manera*) manner, behavior; social relations; dealings; *Am.* — **pampa** unfair deal; **¡** — **hecho!** it's a deal!; **tener buen** — to be affable, sociable.

traumático [tɾaw·má·ti·ko] *adj.* traumatic.

través [tɾa·β̞és] *m.* crossbeam; reverse, misfortune; **a** (*or* **al**) — **de** through, across; **de** — across; **dar al** — **con** to ruin, destroy; to squander; **mirar de** — to squint in a sinister manner.

travesaño [tɾa·β̞e·sá·ño] *m.* crosspiece, crossbar; bolster, long bedpillow; *Ven., Andes* railway tie.

travesear [tɾa·β̞e·se·áɾ] *v.* to romp, frisk, frolic; to fool around; to misbehave.

travesía [tɾa·β̞e·sí·a] *f.* crossing; sea voyage; wind blowing towards a coast; *Am.* wasteland, desert land; *Am.* partition wall or fence.

travesura [tɾa·β̞e·sú·ra] *f.* mischief; prank; lively wit.

traviesa [tɾa·β̞jé·sa] *f.* railway tie; rafter, crossbeam;

Col. midyear crop.

travieso [tɾa·β̞jé·so] *adv.* mischievous; lively; restless; **a campo** · (*or* **a campo traviesa**) cross-country.

trayecto [tɾa·yék·to] *m.* run, stretch, lap, distance (*traveled over*).

trayectoria [tɾa·yek·tó·rja] *f.* path (*of a bullet, missile, etc.*).

traza [tɾá·sa] *f.* (*plan*) plan; design; plot; invention; (*apariencia*) appearance; semblance; aspect; indication, sign; **darse -s** to use one's wits or ingenuity; **tener -s de** to have the appearance or signs of; **tiene** (*or* **lleva**) **-s de no acabar nunca** it looks as if he would never end.

trazado [tɾa·sá·ɖo] *m.* draft, plan, sketch, outline; drawing; *p.p. & adj.* traced, sketched, outlined.

trazar⁹ [tɾa·sáɾ] *v.* to trace, sketch; to draw, mark out; to plan.

trébol [tɾé·β̞ol] *m.* clover.

trecho [tɾé·čo] *m.* space, distance; lap (*in a race*); **a -s** by or at intervals; **de** — **en** — at certain points or intervals; from time to time.

tregua [tɾé·ɣwa] *f.* truce; rest, respite.

tremedal [tɾe·me·ɖál] *m.* quagmire, bog.

tremendo [tɾe·mén·do] *adj.* tremendous, huge; terrible.

trementina [tɾa·men·tí·na] *f.* turpentine.

tremolar [tɾe·mo·láɾ] *v.* to flutter, wave (*as a flag*).

trémolo [tɾé·mo·lo] *m.* tremolo (*of the voice*), quaver.

trémulo [tɾé·mu·lo] *adj.* tremulous, trembling, quivering; flickering.

tren [tɾen] *m.* train; *Am.* traffic; — **correo** mail train; — **de aterrizaje** landing gear; *Ven., Carib.* — **de lavado** laundry; *Cuba, Ven.* — **de mudadas** moving company; — **de recreo** excursion train; — **mixto** freight and passenger train.

trenza [tɾén·sa] *f.* tress; braid; *Mex., Cuba, Ven.* string (*of garlic, onions, etc.*); **trencilla** *f.* braid.

trenzar⁹ [tɾen·sáɾ] *v.* to braid; **-se** to braid one's hair; *Riopl., Andes, Col.* to fight hand to hand.

trepador [tɾe·pa·ɖóɾ] *adj.* climbing.

trepar [tɾe·páɾ] *v.* to climb; to clamber; **-se** to climb; to clamber; to perch.

trepidación [tɾe·pi·ɖa·sjón] *f.* jar, vibration; trembling, shaking.

trepidar [tɾe·pi·ɖáɾ] *v.* to shape, vibrate, tremble, jar.

treta [tɾé·ta] *f.* trick, wile; **malas -s** bad tricks, bad habits.

triangular [tɾjaŋ·gu·láɾ] *adj.* triangular.

triángulo [tɾján·gu·lo] *m.* triangle.

tribu [tɾí·β̞u] *f.* tribe.

tribulación [tɾi·β̞u·la·sjón] *f.* tribulation, trouble.

tribuna [tɾi·β̞ú·na] *f.* rostrum (*speaker's platform*).

tribunal [tɾi·β̞u·nál] *m.* tribunal; court of justice; body of judges.

tributar [tɾi·β̞u·táɾ] *v.* to pay tribute, pay homage.

tributario [tɾi·β̞u·tá·rjo] *adj. & m.* tributary.

tributo [tɾi·β̞ú·to] *m.* tribute; contribution, tax.

triciclo [tɾi·sí·klo] *m.* tricycle.

trifulca [tɾi·fúl·ka] *f.* fight, quarrel, wrangle, row.

trigo [tɾí·ɣo] *m.* wheat.

trigueño [tɾi·ɣé·ño] *adj.* swarthy; brunet; dark.

trilogía [tɾi·lo·xí·a] *f.* trilogy.

trillado [tɾi·yá·ɖo] *p.p.* beaten; *adj.* trite, hackneyed, commonplace; **camino** — beaten path.

trilladora [tɾi·ya·ɖó·ra] *f.* threshing machine.

trillar [tɾi·yáɾ] *v.* to thresh; to beat, mistreat; *Cuba* to cut a path.

trimestre [tri·més·tre] *m.* quarter, period of three months; quarterly payment, income, or salary; **trimestral** [tri·mes·trál] *adj.* quarterly.

trinar [tri·nár] *v.* to trill (*in singing*); to warble; to quaver (*siad of the voice*); to get furious.

trinchante [trin·čán·te] *m.* carving fork; carving knife; carver.

trinchar [trin·čár] *v.* to carve (*meat*).

trinche [trín·če] *m.* Col., Ven., C.A., Mex. fork; Am. carving table; Am. **plato** — carving platter.

trinchera [trin·čé·ra] *f.* trench; ditch; C.A., Ven., Andes stockade, fence; Am. curved knife.

trinchero [trin·čé·ro] *m.* carving table; **plato** — carving platter.

trineo [tri·né·a] *m.* sleigh; sled.

trino [tri·no] *m.* trill (*in singing*).

tripa [trí·pa] *f.* intestine, bowel; paunch, belly; **-s** entrails, insides.

triple [trí·ple] *adj. & m.* triple.

triplicar[6] [tri·pli·kár] *v.* to triplicate, triple, treble.

tripode [trí·po·de] *m.* tripod.

tripulación [tri·pu·la·sjón] *f.* crew, ship's company.

tripular [tri·pu·lár] *v.* to man (*a ship*).

trique [trí·ke] *m.* crack, snap; Mex. utensil, trinket; Col. clever trick in a game; Am. drink made from barley; **-s** Mex. poor household utensils, goods, etc.

triquinosis [tri·ki·nó·sis] *f.* trichinosis.

triscar[6] [tris·kár] *v.* to romp, frisk, frolic; to stamp or shuffle the feet; Am. to tease, make fun of.

triste [tris·te] *adj.* sad; sorrowful; Mex. bashful, backward; m. Ríopl. melancholy love song.

tristeza [tris·té·sa] *f.* sadness; sorrow; Am. tick fever.

tristón [tris·tón] *adj.* wistful, quite sad, melancholy.

triunfal [trjun·fál] *adj.* triumphal.

triunfante [trjun·fán·te] *adj.* triumphant.

triunfar [trjun·fár] *v.* to triumph; to trump (*at cards*).

triunfo [trjún·fo] *m.* triumph; trump card; trophy.

trivial [tri·bjál] *adj.* trivial, commonplace, trite.

triza [trí·sa] *f.* shred, fragment, small piece; cord, rope (*for sails*); **hacer -s** to tear into shreds; to tear to pieces.

trocar[2, 6] [tro·kár] *v. irr.* to change; to barter, exchange; to do one thing instead of another; **-se** to change; to be transformed; to exchange.

trocha [tró·ča] *f.* path, trail; Ríopl. gauge (*of a railway*); Col. trot; Am. slice or serving of meat.

trofeo [tro·fé·o] *m.* trophy; booty, spoils.

troj [tro], **troje** [tró·xe] *m.* barn, granary.

trole [tró·le] *m.* trolley.

trolebús [tro·le·bús] *m.* trolleybus.

tromba [tróm·ba] *f.* waterspout.

trombón [trom·bón] *m.* trombone.

trompa [tróm·pa] *f.* trumpet; trunk of an elephant; large spinning top; Am. snout; Col. cowcatcher (*of a locomotive*).

trompada [trom·pa·da] *f.* blow with the fist; bump.

trompeta [trom·pé·ta] *f.* trumpet; m. trumpeter; useless individual; Andes drunk, drunkard; Andes bold, shameless fellow.

trompetear [trom·pe·te·ár] *v.* to trumpet, blow the trumpet.

trompo [tróm·po] *m.* spinning top; stupid fellow, dunce.

tronada [tro·na·da] *f.* thunderstorm.

tronar[2] [tro·nár] *v. irr.* to thunder; to explode, burst; Mex., C.A. to execute by shooting; **— los dedos** to snap one's fingers; **por lo que pueda —**

just in case.

tronco [trón·ko] *m.* tree trunk; log; stem; trunk (*of the human body*); team (*of horses*).

tronchar [tron·čár] *v.* to bend or break (*a stalk or trunk*); to chop off; to break off; **-se** to break off or get bent (*said of a stalk or trunk*); Col. to get twisted or bent.

tronera [tro·né·ra] *f.* opening; porthole (*through which to shoot*); small, narrow window; pocket of a billiard table; m. madcap, reckless fellow.

tronido [tro·ní·do] *m.* thunder; detonation; sharp, sudden sound.

trono [tró·no] *m.* throne.

tropa [tró·pa] *f.* troop; crowd; Ríopl. herd of cattle, drove of horses (*often* **tropilla**).

tropel [tro·pél] *m.* throng; bustle, rush; jumble, confusion.

tropezar[1, 9] [tro·pe·sár] *v. irr.* to stumble; to blunder; **— con** to meet, come across, encounter.

tropezón [tro·pe·són] *m.* stumbling; stumble; slip; **a -es** falteringly, stumbling along clumsily; **darse un —** to stumble, trip.

tropical [tro·pi·kál] *adj.* tropical.

trópico [tró·pi·ko] *m.* tropic.

tropiezo [tro·pjé·so] *m.* stumble; stumbling block; slip, fault; dispute.

tropilla [tro·pí·ya] *f.* small troop; Am. drove of horses guided by the **madrina;** Mex. pack of dogs; Am. group of spare saddle horses.

tropillero [tro·pi·yé·ro] *m.* Am. horse wrangler, herdsman.

trotar [tro·tár] *v.* to trot; to hurry.

trote [tró·te] *m.* trot; **al —** quickly.

trovador [tro·ba·dór] *m.* troubadour, minstrel.

troza [tró·sa] *f.* log.

trozar[9] [tro·sár] *v.* to cut off, break off (*a piece*); to break or cut into pieces.

trozo [tro·so] *m.* piece, bit, fragment; passage, selection.

truco [trú·ko] *m.* clever trick; pocketing of a ball (*in the game of pool*); Am. blow with the fist; Andes, Ríopl. a card game; **-s** game of pool (*game similar to billiards*).

truculencia [tru·ku·lén·sja] *f.* cruelty, ferocity, ruthlessness.

truculento [tru·ku·lén·to] *adj.* cruel, fierce, ruthless.

trucha [trú·ča] *f.* trout; Am. vendor's portable stand.

trueno [trwé·no] *m.* thunder; explosion, report of a gun; wild youth, troublemaker; Am. firecracker, rocket.

trueque [trwé·ke], **trueco** [trwé·ko] *m.* exchange; barter; Col., Ven., Andes change, small money; **a** (*or* **en**) **— de** in exchange for.

truhán [tru·án] *m.* scoundrel; swindler; cheat; buffoon, jester.

truncar[6] [truŋ·kár] *v. irr.* to truncate.

tu [tu] *adj.* thy; your (*fam. sing.*).

tú [tu] *pers. pron.* thou; you (*fam. sing.*).

tualet [twa·lét] = **lavabo.**

tuba [tú·ba] *f.* tuba (*instrument*).

tuberculosis [tu·ber·ku·ló·sis] *f.* tuberculosis; **tuberculoso** [tu·ber·ku·ló·so] *adj.* tuberculous, tubercular.

tubería [tu·be·rí·a] *f.* tubing, piping; pipe line.

tubo [tú·bo] *m.* tube; pipe; lamp chimney; **— de ensayo** test tube; **— de escape** tail pipe.

tuerca [twér·ka] *f.* nut (*of a screw*); **llave de -s** wrench.

tuerto [twér·to] *adj.* one-eyed; blind in one eye; *m.*

wrong, injustice; **a — o a derecho** (*or* **a tuertas o a derechas**) rightly or wrongly; thoughtlessly.

tuétano [twé·ta·no] *m.* marrow; pith; innermost part; **mojado hasta los -s** soaked through and through.

tufo [tú·fo] *m.* vapor, fume; disagreeable odor; airs, conceit; **tufillo** [tu·fi·yo] *m.* whiff, pungent odor.

tul [tul] *m.* tulle (*a thin, fine net for veils*); **tul** [tul], **tule** [tú·le] *m. Mex.* a kind of reed or bulrush (*used in the manufacture of seats and backs of chairs*).

tulipán [tu·li·pán] *m.* tulip; *Mex.* hibiscus.

tullido [tu·yí·do] *p.p.* crippled; paralyzed; numb.

tullirse[20] [tu·yír·se] *v. irr.* to become crippled; to become numb or paralyzed.

tumba [túm·ba] *f.* tomb; grave; *Col., Cuba, Mex.* felling of timber; *Ven.* forest clearing.

tumbar [tum·bár] *v.* to knock down; *Col., Mex., Cuba* to fell timber; **-se** to lie down.

tumbo [túm·bo] *m.* tumble; somersault; **dar -s** to jump, bump along.

tumor [tu·mór] *m.* tumor; **tumorcillo** [tu·mor·sí·yo] *m.* boil; small tumor.

tumulto [tu·múl·to] *m.* tumult, uproar; mob, throng.

tumultuoso [tu·mul·twó·so] *adj.* tumultuous.

tuna [tú·na] *f.* prickly pear; *Spain* singing group.

tunante [tu·nán·te] *m. & f.* rascal, rogue, scamp; loafer; *Andes, Ch., C.A.* libertine, licentious or lewd person.

tunco [tún·ko] *m. Sal.*, pig.

tunda [tún·da] *f.* whipping, thrashing; shearing (*the nap of cloth*).

tundir [tun·dír] *v.* to lash, beat, whip; to shear (*the nap of cloth*).

túnel [tú·nel] *m.* tunnel.

túnica [tú·ni·ka] *f.* tunic; gown, robe.

tungsteno [tuns·té·no] *m.* tungsten.

tupido [tu·pí·do] *adj.* dense; compact, thick; blocked, obstructed.

tupir [tu·pír] *v.* to press, pack, squeeze together; to stop up, clog; **-se** to get stopped up; to stuff oneself; to become dense (*as a forest*); *Am.* to get astonished or confused.

turba [túr·ba] *f.* mob, throng.

turbación [tur·ba·sjón] *f.* disturbance, confusion; embarrassment.

turbamulta [tur·ba·múl·ta] *f.* throng, mob, crowd.

turbar [tur·bár] *v.* to perturb; to disturb; to trouble; **-se** to get disturbed, confused, embarrassed.

turbina [tur·bí·na] *f.* turbine.

turbio [túr·bjo] *adj.* muddy; muddled, confused.

turbión [tur·bjón] *m.* thunderstorm; heavy shower.

turbogenerador [tur·bo·xe·ne·ra·dór] *m.* turbogenerator.

turbopropulsor [tur·bo·pro·pul·sór] *m.* turboprop.

turborreactor [tur·bo·rre·ak·tór] *m.* turbojet.

turbulento [tur·bu·lén·to] *adj.* turbulent; restless; disorderly.

turco [túr·ko] *adj.* Turkish; *m.* Turk; Turkish, Turkish language; *Am.* peddler.

turismo [tu·ríz·mo] *m.* tourist travel; touring, sightseeing; **oficina de —** travel bureau; **turista** [tu·rís·ta] *m. & f.* tourist; **turístico** [tu·rís·ti·ko] *adj.* tourist; related to tourism.

tunar [tur·nár] *v.* to alternate; **-se** to alternate; to take turns.

turno [túr·no] *m.* turn, alternate order.

turquesa [tur·ké·sa] *f.* turquoise.

turrón [tu·rrón] *m.* nougat, nut confection; almond

cake; *Mex.* **romper el —** to decide to use the **tú** form of address (*as a mark of close friendship*).

tusa [tú·sa] *f. Am.* corn, corncob; *Cuba, Mex.* corn husk; *Am.* corn silk, tassel of an ear of corn.

tusar [tu·sár] *v. Cuba, Mex., Riopl., Andes* to shear; *Riopl.* to crop, cut badly (*hair*).

tutear [tu·te·ár] *v.* to address familiarly (*using the* **tú** *form*).

tutela [tu·té·la] *f.* guardianship; guidance, protection.

tutelar [tu·te·lár] *v.* to guide, coach, direct; *adj.* guiding, guardian (*used as adj.*).

tutor [tu·tór] *m.* tutor; guardian.

tuyo [tú·yo] *poss. adj.* your, of yours (*fam. sing.*); *poss. pron.* yours.

U:u **u** [u] *conj.* (*before words beginning with* **o** *or* **ho**) *or.*

ubicar[6] [u·bi·kár] *v.* to be located; **-se** *Am.* to situate.

ubre [ú·bre] *f.* udder.

ufanarse [u·fa·nár·se] *v.* to glory (in); to be proud (of).

ufano [u·fá·no] *adj.* proud; gay; self-satisfied.

ujier [u·xjér] *m.* usher, doorman.

úlcera [úl·se·ra] *f.* ulcer; sore.

ulterior [ul·te·rjór] *adj.* ulterior; further; later.

ultimar [ul·ti·már] *v.* to put an end to; *Am.* to give the finishing blow, kill.

último [úl·ti·mo] *adj.* last, final; ultimate; latest; **estar en las últimas** to be on one's last legs; to be at the end of one's rope, be at the end of one's resources.

ultrajar [ul·tra·xár] *v.* to outrage, insult; to scorn.

ultraje [ul·trá·xe] *m.* outrage, insult.

ultramar [ul·tra·már] *m.* country or place across the sea; **de —** overseas, from across the sea; **en** (*or* **a**) **—** overseas.

ultramarinos [ul·tra·ma·rí·nos] *m. pl.* delicatessen; imported foods.

ultratumba [ul·tra·túm·ba] *adv.* beyond the grave.

ultravioleta [ul·tra·bjo·lé·ta] *adj.* ultraviolet.

ulular [u·lu·lár] *v.* to howl, shriek, hoot.

umbral [um·brál] *m.* threshold.

umbrío [um·brí·o] *adj.* shady.

un(o) [ú·no] *indef. art.* a, an; **-s** some, a few; **-s cuantos** a few; **uno** *pron. & num.* one.

unánime [u·ná·ni·me] *adj.* unanimous.

unanimidad [u·na·ni·mi·dád] *f.* unanimity, complete accord.

unción [un·sjón] *f.* unction (*anointing with oil*); religious fervor; spiritual grace; **Extremaunción** [es·tre·mawn·sjón] Extreme Unction (*the Last Sacrament of the Church*).

uncir[10] [un·sír] *v.* to yoke.

ungir[11] [un·xír] *v.* to anoint; to consecrate.

ungüento [un·gwén·to] *m.* ointment; salve.

único [ú·ni·ko] *adj.* only, sole; unique, singular, rare.

unicornio [u·ni·kór·njo] *m.* unicorn.

unidad [u·ni·dád] *f.* unity; unit.

unificar[6] [u·ni·fi·kár] *v.* to unify; to unite.

uniformar [u·ni·for·már] *v.* to standardize; to make uniform; to furnish with uniforms.

uniforme [u·ni·fór·me] *adj. & m.* uniform.

uniformidad [u·ni·for·mi·dád] *f.* uniformity.

unilateral [u·ni·la·te·rál] *adj.* unilateral, one-sided.

unión [u·njón] *f.* union.

unir [uˑnír] *v.* to unite; to join; to bring together; **-se** to unite, join together; to wed.
unísono [uˑníˑsoˑno] *adj.* unison.
universal [uˑniˑƀerˑsál] *adj.* universal.
universidad [uˑniˑƀerˑsiˑđáđ] *f.* university.
universitario [uˑniˑƀerˑsiˑtáˑrjo] *adj.* pertaining to the university; *m. Am.* a university student.
universo [uˑniˑƀérˑso] *m.* universe.
untar [unˑtár] *v.* to anoint; to smear; to oil, grease; to bribe; to corrupt; **-se** to smear oneself; to get smeared.
unto [únˑto] *m.* grease, fat; ointment.
untuosidad [unˑtwoˑsiˑđáđ] *f.* greasiness; **untuoso** *adj.* unctuous; oily, greasy.
uña [úˑña] *f.* fingernail; toenail; claw; hoof; hook (*on a tool*); **a — de caballo** at full gallop, at full speed; **largo de -s** prone to stealing; *Mex., C.A., Ven., Col., Andes* **largas -s** thief; **vivir de sus -s** to live by stealing; *Mex., C.A., Ven., Col., Andes* **echar la —** to steal; **ser — y carne** to be inseparable friends.
uranio [uˑráˑnjo] *m.* uranium.
urbanidad [urˑƀaˑniˑđáđ] *f.* courtesy, politeness; refinement.
urbanizar[9] [urˑƀaˑniˑsár] *v. irr.* to urbanize.
urbano [urˑƀáˑno] *adj.* urban; courteous, polite.
urbe [úrˑƀe] *f.* metropolis, large city.
urdimbre [urˑđímˑbre] *f.* warp (*of a fabric*); scheme.
urdir [urˑđír] *v.* to warp (*in weaving*); to plot, scheme; to invent (*a lie, story, etc.*). ▸
uremia [uˑréˑmja] *f.* uremia.
uretra [uˑréˑtra] *f.* urethra.
urgencia [urˑxénˑsja] *f.* urgency; pressing need.
urgente [urˑxénˑte] *adj.* urgent, pressing.
urgir[11] [urˑxír] *v.* to urge; to be urgent.
úrico [úˑriˑko] *adj.* uric.
urna [úrˑna] *f.* urn; **— electoral** ballot box.
urraca [uˑrráˑka] *f.* magpie.
usado [uˑsáˑđo] *p.p. & adj.* used; accustomed; worn; threadbare.
usanza [uˑsánˑsa] *f.* usage, custom, habit.
usar [uˑsár] *v.* to use; to wear; to wear out; to be accustomed; **-se** to be in use, be in vogue.
uso [úˑso] *m.* (*empleo*) use; usage; wear; (*costumbre*) usage; practice; habit; custom; **al — de la época** according to the custom or usage of the period; **estar en buen —** to be in good condition (*said of a thing*).
usted [usˑté(đ)] *pers. pron.* (*abbreviated as* **Vd., V.,** *or* **Ud.**) you.
usual [uˑswál] *adj.* usual; ordinary, customary.
usufructo [uˑsuˑfrúkˑto] *m.* use, enjoyment; profit.
usufructuar[18] [uˑsuˑfrukˑtwár] *v.* to enjoy the use of; to make use of.
usura [uˑsúˑra] *f.* usury.
usurero [uˑsuˑréˑro] *m.* usurer, loan shark.
usurpar [uˑsurˑpár] *v.* to usurp.
utensilio [uˑtenˑsíˑljo] *m.* utensil; implement, tool.
útero [úˑteˑro] *m.* uterus, womb.
útil [úˑtil] *adj.* useful; profitable; **-es** *m. pl.* tools, instruments.
utilidad [uˑtiˑliˑđáđ] *f.* utility; profit; usefulness.
utilitario [uˑtiˑliˑtáˑrjo] *adj.* utilitarian.
utilizar[9] [uˑtiˑliˑzár] *v.* to utilize; to use.
utopía [uˑtoˑpíˑa] *f.* utopia.
uvula [uˑƀuˑla] *f.* uvula.
uva [úˑƀa] *f.* grape; **— espina** gooseberry; **— pasa** raisin; **estar hecho una —** to be tipsy, drunk.
uvula [uˑƀuˑla] *f.* uvula.
uvular [uˑƀuˑlár] *adj.* uvular.
¡uy! [uj] *interj.* ouch! oh!

V·v

vaca [báˑka] *f.* cow; **carne de —** beef; **cuero de —** cowhide; *Am.* **hacer —** to play hooky, play truant, cut class; to join in a quick business deal.
vacación [baˑkaˑsjón] *f.* vacation (*usually* **vacaciones**).
vacada [baˑkáˑđa] *f.* herd of cows.
vacancia [baˑkánˑsja] *f.* vacancy.
vacante [baˑkánˑte] *adj.* vacant, unfilled; unoccupied; *f.* vacancy.
vaciar[17] [baˑsjár] (*dejar vacío*) to empty; to drain; to flow; (*amoldar*) to cast into a mold; (*ahuecar*) to hollow out; **-se** to spill; to empty; to become empty; to flow (into).
vaciedad [baˑsjeˑđáđ] *f.* emptiness; nonsense, silliness.
vacilación [baˑsiˑlaˑsjón] *f.* hesitation; wavering; doubt.
vacilante [baˑsiˑlánˑte] *adj.* vacillating, hesitating, wavering; unsteady.
vacilar [baˑsiˑlár] *v.* to vacillate, waver, hesitate; to sway.
vacío [baˑsíˑo] *adj.* empty; vacant; unoccupied; hollow; *m.* void; hollow; vacuum; vacancy; gap, blank.
vacuna [baˑkúˑna] *f.* vaccine; vaccination; cowpox (*eruptive disease of the cow*); **vacunación** [baˑkuˑnaˑsjón] *f.* vaccination; **— antipoliomelítica** antipolio inoculation.
vacunar [baˑkuˑnár] *v.* to vaccinate.
vadear [baˑđeˑár] *v.* to ford; to wade; to avoid (*a difficulty*).
vado [báˑđo] *m.* ford; **no hallar —** to find no way out.
vagabundear [baˑgaˑƀunˑdeˑár] *v.* to tramp around, wander, rove; to loiter.
vagabundo [baˑgaˑƀúnˑdo] *adj.* vagabond, wandering; *m.* vagabond, tramp; vagrant; wanderer.
vagar[7] [baˑgár] *v.* to wander, roam; to loiter; to loaf; *m.* leisure; loitering.
vagina [baˑxíˑna] *f.* vagina.
vago [báˑgo] *adj.* vague; roaming; idle; vagrant; *m.* vagrant, tramp.
vagón [baˑgón] *m.* railway car or coach; **vagoneta** [baˑgoˑnéˑta] *f.* small railway car or tram (*used in mines*); **vagonada** [baˑgoˑnáˑđa] *f.* carload.
vaguear [baˑgeˑár] *v.* = **vagar.**
vahído [baˑíˑđo] *m.* dizziness, dizzy spell.
vaho [báˑo] *m.* vapor, steam, fume, mist; odor.
vaina [bájˑna] *f.* sheath, scabbard; case; pod, husk; *Ven., Col., C.A., Mex.* bother, nuisance; *Ven., Col.* luck.
vainilla [bajˑníˑya] *f.* vanilla.
vaivén [bajˑƀén] *m.* sway; fluctuation, wavering; traffic, coming and going; **-es** comings and goings; ups and downs; inconstancy.
vajilla [baˑxíˑya] *f.* tableware; set of dishes; **— de plata** silverware; **— de porcelana** chinaware.
vale [báˑle] *m.* bond, promissory note; voucher; adieu, farewell; *m. & f. Col., Ven., Mes.* comrade, pal, chum.
valedero [baˑleˑđeˑro] *adj.* valid, binding, effective.
valedor [baˑleˑđór] *m.* defender, protector; *Am.* pal, comrade.
valenciano [baˑlenˑsjáˑno] *adj.* Valencian, of or from Valencia, Spain; *m.* Valencian.
valentía [baˑlenˑtíˑa] *f.* courage, valor; exploit; boast.
valentón [baˑlenˑtón] *adj.* blustering, boastful; *m.*

bully, braggart.
valer[47] [ba·lér] *v. irr.* to favor, protect; to cost;
to be worth; to be worthy; to be equivalent to;
to be valid; to prevail; to be useful; *Spain*
¡vale! O.K.; now you're talking; — **la pena** to be
worth while; — **por** to be worth; **-se de** to avail
oneself of, make use of; **más vale** it is better;
¡válgame Dios! heaven help me! good heavens!
valeroso [ba·le·ró·so] *adj.* valiant, brave; valuable.
valía [ba·lí·a] *f.* worth, value; influence.
validez [ba·li·dés] *f.* validity; stability, soundness.
válido [bá·li·ḍo] *adj.* valid.
valiente [ba·ljén·te] *adj.* valiant, brave; powerful;
m. brave man; bully.
valija [ba·lí·xa] *f.* valise, satchel; mailbag.
valimiento [ba·li·mjén·to] *m.* favor, protection;
gozar de — to enjoy protection or favor.
valioso [ba·ljó·so] *adj.* valuable; worthy; wealthy.
valor [ba·lór] *m.* value; worth; price; significance;
valor, courage; boldness; efficacy, power; **-es**
stocks, bonds.
valoración [ba·lo·ra·sjón] *f.* valuation, appraisal.
valorar [ba·lo·rár] *v.* to evaluate, value, appraise.
valorizar[9] [ba·lo·ri·sár] *v. Cuba, Ven., Ríopl., Andes*
to value, appraise; *Am.* to realize, convert into
money.
vals [bals] *m.* waltz.
valsar [bal·sár] *v.* to waltz.
valuación [ba·lwa·sjón] *f.* valuation, appraisal.
valuar[18] [ba·lwár] *v.* to value, price, appraise; to
rate.
válvula [bál·ḅu·la] *f.* valve.
valla [bá·ya] *f.* stockade, fence; barrier;
obstacle; *Cuba, Col.* cockpit (*for cockfights*).
vallado [ba·yá·ḍo] *m.* stockade, fenced-in place;
fence.
valle [bá·ye] *m.* valley; vale.
vampiro [bam·pí·ro] *m.* vampire.
vanadio [ba·ná·ḍjo] *m.* vanadium.
vanagloria [ba·na·ǵló·rja] *f.* vainglory, boastful
vanity.
vanagloriarse[17] [ba·na·ǵlo·rjár·se] *v.* to glory, take
great pride (in), boast (of).
vanaglorioso [ba·na·ǵlo·rjó·so] *adj.* vain, boastful,
conceited.
vándalo [bán·da·lo] *m.* vandal.
vanguardia [baŋ·gwár·ḍja] *f.* vanguard.
vanidad [ba·ni·ḍáḍ] *f.* vanity; conceit; emptiness.
vanidoso [ba·ni·ḍó·so] *adj.* vain, conceited.
vano [bá·no] *adj.* vain; empty; hollow; *m.* opening
in a wall (*for a door or window*).
vapor [ba·pór] *m.* vapor, steam, mist; steamer,
steamship.
vaporoso [ba·po·ró·so] *adj.* vaporous, steamy,
misty; vaporlike.
vapulear [ba·pu·le·ár] *v.* to beat, whip, thrash.
vapuleo [ba·pu·lé·o] *m.* beating, whipping,
thrashing.
vaquería [ba·ke·rí·a] *f.* herd of cows; stable for
cows; dairy.
vaquerizo [ba·ke·rí·so] *m.* herdsman; *adj.*
pertaining to cows; **vaqueriza** [ba·ke·rí·sa] *f.*
stable for cows.
vaquero [ba·ké·ro] *m.* cowherd, herdsman;
cowboy; *Cuba* milkman; *adj.* relating to
cowherds, cowboys, or cattle.
vaqueta [ba·ké·ta] *f.* sole leather; cowhide; *Mex.*
zurrar a uno la — to tan someone's hide, beat
someone up.
vara [bá·ra] *f.* twig; stick; rod; wand; staff;
yard, yardstick; thrust with a picador's lance.

varadero [ba·ra·ḍe·ro] *m.* shipyard.
varar [ba·rár] *v.* to beach (*a boat*); to run aground;
to stop, come to a standstill (*said of business*).
varear [ba·re·ár] *v.* to beat; to whip; to sell by the
yard; to measure with a **vara**; *Am.* to exercise
(*a horse before a race*).
variable [ba·rjá·ḅle] *adj.* variable, unstable,
changeable; *f.* variable.
variación [ba·rja·sjón] *f.* variation.
variado [ba·rjá·ḍo] *p.p.* & *adj.* varied; variegated.
variar[17] [ba·rjár] *v.* to vary; to change; to shift;
to differ.
variedad [ba·rje·ḍáḍ] *f.* variety; variation, change.
varilla [ba·rí·ya] *f.* small rod; wand; long, flexible
twig; rib (*of an umbrella or fan*); corset stay;
Mex. peddler's wares.
varillero [ba·ri·yé·ro] *m. Mex.* peddler.
vario [bá·rjo] *adj.* various; different; changeable;
varied; **-s** various, several.
varón [ba·rón] *m.* male, man; *Am.* long beam,
timber.
varonil [ba·ro·níl] *adj.* manly; strong; brave.
vasallo [ba·sá·yo] *adj.* & *m.* vassal, subject.
vasco [bás·ko], **vascongado** [bas·koŋ·gá·ḍo] *adj.* &
m. Basque.
vascuence [bas·kwén·se] *m.* the Basque language.
vaselina [ba·se·lí·na] *f.* vaseline.
vasija [ba·sí·xa] *f.* vessel, container, receptacle.
vaso [bá·so] *m.* drinking glass; glassful; vase;
vessel; hull of a ship; horse's hoof; — **de**
elección person chosen by God.
vástago [bás·ta·ǵo] *m.* (*de planta*) shoot, sprout;
stem; (*persona*) scion, offspring; *Mex., Col., Ven.*
stem, trunk of a banana tree.
vasto [bás·to] *adj.* vast, extensive, large.
vate [bá·te] *m.* bard, poet.
vaticinar [ba·ti·si·nár] *v.* to prophesy, predict,
foretell.
vaticinio [ba·ti·sí·njo] *m.* prophecy, prediction.
vecindad [be·sin·dáḍ] *f.* vicinity; neighborhood;
neighborliness; **casa de** — tenement.
vecindario [be·sin·dá·rjo] *m.* neighborhood;
neighbors; vicinity.
vecino [be·sí·no] *m.* neighbor; resident; citizen;
adj. neighboring; next, near.
vedar [be·ḍár] *v.* to prohibit; to impede.
vega [bé·ǵa] *f.* fertile lowland or plain; *Cuba,
Ven.* tobacco plantation.
vegetación [be·xe·ta·sjón] *f.* vegetation.
vegetal [be·xe·tál] *adj.* vegetable; *m.* vegetable,
plant.
vegetar [be·xe·tár] *v.* to vegetate.
vegetariano [be·xe·ta·rjá·no] *m.* vegetarian.
vehemente [be·e·mén·te] *adj.* vehement, passionate,
impetuous; violent.
vehículo [be·í·ku·lo] *m.* vehicle.
veintena [bejn·té·na] *f.* score, twenty.
vejamen [be·xá·men] *m.* annoyance, vexation.
vejar [be·xár] *v.* to annoy; to criticize.
vejestorio [be·xes·tó·rjo] *m.* wrinkled old person.
vejete [be·xé·te] *m.* little old man.
vejez [be·xés] *f.* old age.
vejiga [be·xí·ǵa] *f.* bladder; blister; smallpox sore;
— **de la bilis** (*or* — **de la hiel**) gall baldder.
vela [bé·la] *f.* vigil, watch; night watch; candle;
sail; **a toda** — under full sail; at full speed;
en — on watch; without sleep; **hacerse a la** —
to set sail.
velada [be·lá·ḍa] *f.* watch, vigil; evening party;
evening function or meeting.
velador [be·la·ḍór] *m.* night watchman; keeper,

guard; lamp table; bedside table; candlestick; *Ríopl., Mex., Cuba, Col.* lamp shade.

velar [be·lár] *v.* to keep vigil; to stay up at night; to be vigilant; to watch over; to veil; to cover hide.

velatorio [be·la·tó·rjo] *m.* wake (*vigil over a corpse*). *See* **velorio.**

veleidoso [be·lej·ḍó·so] *adj.* inconstant, fickle, changeable.

velero [be·lé·ro] *m.* sailboat; sailmaker; candlemaker; *adj.* swift-sailing; **buque** — sailboat.

veleta [be·lé·ta] *f.* weathervane, weathercock; *m.* & *f.* fickle person.

velis [be·lís] *m. Mex.* valise.

velo [bé·lo] *m.* veil; curtain, covering; — **del paladar** velum, soft palate.

velocidad [be·lo·si·ḍáḍ] *f.* velocity.

velocímetro [be·lo·sí·me·tro] *m.* speedometer.

velorio [be·ló·rjo] *m. Am.* wake (*vigil over a corpse*); *Mex., C.A., Ven., Col., Ch., Andes* dull party.

veloz [be·lós] *adj.* swift, quick, fast.

vello [bé·yo] *m.* hair (*on the body*); down, fuzz; nap (*of cloth*).

vellón [be·yón] *m.* fleece; tuft of wool; sheepskin with fleece; silver and copper alloy; an ancient copper coin.

velloso [be·yó·so] *adj.* hairy; downy, fuzzy.

velludo [be·yú·ḍo] *adj.* hairy; downy; fuzzy; *m.* plush; velvet.

vena [bé·na] *f.* vein; lode, vein of metal ore; mood, disposition; **estar en** — to be in the mood; to be inspired.

venado [be·ná·ḍo] *m.* deer; venison, deer meat; *Mex.* **pintar** — to play hooky.

vencedor [ben·se·ḍór] *adj.* conquering, winning, victorious; *m.* conqueror, winner, victor.

vencer[10] [ben·sér] *v.* to conquer; vanquish; to defeat; to overcome; to surpass; to win; **-se** to control oneself; to mature, fall due; **se venció el plazo** the time limit expired.

vencido [ben·sí·ḍo] *p.p.* & *adj.* conquered; defeated; due, fallen due.

vencimiento [ben·si·mjén·to] *m.* conquering, defeat; maturity (*of a debt*), falling due; expiration (*of a period of time*).

venda [bén·da] *f.* bandage.

vendaje [ben·dá·xe] *m.* bandage.

vendar [ben·dár] *v.* to bandage; to blindfold.

vendaval [ben·da·ḅál] *m.* strong wind, gale.

vendedor [ben·de·ḍór] *m.* vendor, seller, peddler.

vender [ben·dér] *v.* to sell; to betray; **-se** to be sold; to sell oneself; accept a bribe.

vendimia [ben·dí·mja] *f.* vintage; profit.

venduta [ben·dú·ta] *f. Col.* auction; *Cuba* small fruit and vegetable store.

veneno [be·né·no] *m.* venom, poison.

venenoso [be·ne·nó·so] *adj.* poisonous.

venerable [be·ne·rá·ḅle] *adj.* venerable.

veneración [be·ne·ra·sjón] *f.* veneration, reverence.

venerando [be·ne·rán·do] *adj.* venerable, worthy of respect.

venerar [be·ne·rár] *v.* to venerate, revere; to worship.

venero [be·né·ro] *m.* water spring; source, origin; lode, layer, seam (*of mineral*).

venezolano [be·ne·so·lá·no] *adj.* Venezuelan; *m.* Venezuelan; *Ven.* Venezuelan silver coin.

vengador [beŋ·ga·ḍór] *adj.* avenging, revenging; *m.* avenger.

venganza [beŋ·gán·sa] *f.* vengeance, revenge.

vengar[7] [beŋ·gár] *v.* to avenge, revenge; **-se de** to take revenge on.

vengativo [beŋ·ga·ti·ḅo] *adj.* vindictive, revengeful.

venia [bé·nja] *f.* pardon; permission, leave; bow, nod; *C.A., Ven., Ríopl.* military salute.

venida [be·ni·ḍa] *f.* arrival; return; river flood, onrush of water; attack (*in fencing*).

venidero [be·ni·ḍé·ro] *adj.* coming, future; **en lo** — in the future; **-s** *m. pl.* successors.

venir[48] [be·nír] *v. irr.* to come; to arrive; to fit; **-le a uno bien** (*or* **mal**) to be becoming (*or* unbecoming); — **a menos** to decline, decay; — **a pelo** to come just at the right moment; to suit perfectly; to be pat, opportune, to the point; — **en** to agree to; — **sobre** to fall upon; **¿a qué viene eso?** what is the point of that? **-se abajo** to fall down; to collapse; to fail.

venoso [be·nó·so] *adj.* veined; venous (*of or pertaining to the veins; with veins*).

venta [bén·ta] *f.* sale; roadside inn; *Ur.* store, vendor's stand; — **pública** auction.

ventaja [ben·tá·xa] *f.* advantage; gain, profit; bonus; odds.

ventajoso [ben·ta·xó·so] *adj.* advantageous, beneficial, profitable; *Mex.* self-seeking; profiteering.

ventana [ben·tá·na] *f.* window; window shutter; *Col.* clearing (*in a forest*); — (*or* **ventanilla** [ben·ta·ní·ya]) **de la nariz** nostril.

ventarrón [ben·ta·rrón] *m.* gale, strong wind.

ventear [ben·te·ár] *v.* (*oler*) to scent, sniff; (*soplar*) to blow, be windy; (*poner al aire*) to air; (*indagar*) to nose around; *Ven.* to toss in the wind; *Am.* to flee; *Am.* to outrun; **-se** to expel air, break wind; *Col.* to stay outdoors.

ventero [ben·té·ro] *m.* innkeeper.

ventilación [ben·ti·la·sjón] *f.* ventilation.

ventilador [ben·ti·la·ḍór] *m.* ventilator; fan (*for ventilation*).

ventilar [ben·ti·lár] *v.* to ventilate; to air.

ventisca [ben·tís·ka] *f.* blizzard, snowstorm; snowdrift.

ventiscar[6] [ben·tis·kár] *v.* to snow hard and blow (*as in a blizzard*); to drift (*as snow in a blizzard*).

ventisquero [ben·tis·ké·ro] *m.* blizzard, snowstorm; glacier; snowdrift; snow-capped mountain peak.

ventolera [ben·to·lé·ra] *f.* gust of wind; pride, vanity; whim; pin wheel; **darle a uno la** — **de** to take the notion to.

ventoso [ben·tó·so] *adj.* windy.

ventura [ben·tú·ra] *f.* happiness; fortune, chance; risk, danger; **a la** — at random; **buena** — fortune; **por** — perchance.

venturoso [ben·tu·ró·so] *adj.* fortunate, lucky; happy.

ver[49] [ver] *v. irr.* to see; to look; to look at; to look into, examine; — **de** to try to, see to it that; **a más** (*or* **hasta más** — good-bye; **no** — **la hora de** to be anxious to; **no tener nada que** — **con** not to have anything to do with; **-se** to be seen; to be; **-se obligado a** to be obliged to, be forced, to; **a mi modo de** — in my opinion; **de buen** — good-looking; **ser de** — to be worth seeing.

vera [bé·ra] *f.* edge; **a la** — **del camino** at the edge of the road.

veracidad [ve·ra·si·ḍáḍ] *f.* truthfulness.

veraneante [be·ra·ne·án·te] *m.* & *f.* summer resorter, vacationist, or tourist.

veranear [be·ra·ne·ár] *v.* to spend the summer.

VA

veraneo [be·ra·né·o] *m.* summering, summer vacation.

veraniego [be·ra·njé·ǥo] *adj.* summer, of summer.

verano [be·rá·no] *m.* summer.

veras [bé·ras] *f. pl.* reality, truth; **de** — in truth; truly; in earnest.

veraz [be·rás] *adj.* truthful.

verbal [ber·ƀál] *adj.* verbal; oral.

verbena [ber·ƀé·na] *f.* verbena (*a plant*); festival or carnival (*on eve of a religious holiday*).

verbigracia [ber·ƀi·ǥra·sja] *adv.* for instance, for example.

verbo [bér·ƀo] *m.* verb; **el Verbo** the Word (*second person of the Trinity*).

verboso [ber·ƀó·so] *adj.* verbose, wordy.

verdad [ber·dáḍ] *f.* truth; ¿—? really?; is that so?; isn't that so?; — **de Perogrullo** truism, evident truth; **de** (*or* **a la** —) in truth, in earnest; **en** — really, truly.

verdadero [ber·da·dé·ro] *adj.* real; true; truthful; sincere.

verde [bér·de] *adj.* green; unripe; young; offcolor, indecent; *m.* green; verdure; *Ur., Ven.* country, countryside.

verdear [ber·de·ár] *v.* to grow green; to look green.

verdinegro [ber·di·ne·ǥro] *adj.* dark-green.

verdor [ber·dór] *m.* verdure, greenness.

verdoso [ber·dó·so] *adj.* greenish.

verdugo [ber·dú·ǥo] *m.* executioner; cruel person; torment; rapier (*light sword*); lash, whip; welt; shoot of a tree; **verdugón** [ber·du·ǥón] *m.* large welt.

verdulera [ber·du·lé·ra] *f.* woman vendor of green vegetables; **verdulería** [ber·du·le·rí·a] *f.* green vegetable store or stand.

verdura [ber·dú·ra] *f.* verdure; greenness; green vegetables.

vereda [be·ré·da] *f.* path; *Ch., Ríopl., Andes* sidewalk; *Col.* small village; *C.R.* bank of a stream.

veredicto [be·re·dík·to] *m.* verdict.

vergonzoso [ber·ǥon·só·so] *adj.* shameful. disgraceful; shy, bashful; *m.* species of armadillo.

vergüenza [ber·ǥwén·sa] *f.* shame; disgrace; shyness, bashfulness; **tener** — to have shame; to be ashamed.

vericueto [be·ri·kwé·to] *m.* rugged, wild place (*often rocky*).

verídico [be·rí·di·ko] *adj.* truthful; true.

verificar[6] [be·ri·fi·kár] *v.* to verify; to confirm; to test, check; to carry out, fulfill; **-se** to be verified; to take place.

verijas [be·rí·xas] *f. pl. Ríopl., Mex.* groin (*hollow between lower part of abdomen and thigh*); *Am.* flanks of a horse.

verja [bér·xa] *f.* grate, grating.

verónica [be·ró·ni·ka] *f.* veronica; a bullfighting pass executed with the cape held behind the body with both hands.

verruga [be·rrú·ǥa] *f.* wart; nuisance.

versado [ber·sá·do] *adj.* versed, skilled, expert.

versar [ber·sár] *v.* to deal (with), treat (of); **-se en** to become versed in.

versátil [ber·sá·til] *adj.* versatile.

versificar[6] [ber·si·fi·kár] *v. irr.* to versify.

versión [ber·sjón] *f.* version; translation.

verso [bér·so] *m.* verse; meter; — **suelto** (*or* — **libre**) free or blank verse.

vertebrado [ber·te·ƀrá·do] *adj. & m.* vertebrate.

verter[1] [ber·tér] *v. irr.* to pour; to empty; to spill; to translate; to flow down.

vertical [ber·ti·kál] *adj.* vertical.

vértice [bér·ti·se] *m.* top, apex, summit.

vertiente [ber·tjén·te] *f.* slope; watershed; *adj.* flowing.

vertiginoso [ber·ti·xi·nó·so] *adj.* whirling, dizzy, giddy.

vértigo [bér·ti·ǥo] *m.* dizziness, giddiness; fit of madness.

vesícula [be·sí·ku·la] *f.* gall bladder.

vestíbulo [bes·tí·ƀu·lo] *m.* vestibule; lobby.

vestido [bes·tí·do] *m.* clothing, apparel; dress; garment; suit.

vestidura [bes·ti·dú·ra] *f.* vestment; attire, apparel; raiment.

vestigio [bes·tí·xjo] *m.* vestige, sign, trace.

vestir[5] [bes·tír] *v. irr.* (*cubrir*) to dress; to clothe; to put on; to adorn; to cover; (*llevar*) to wear; **-se** to dress, get dressed; to be clothed; to be covered.

vestuario [bes·twá·rjo] *m.* wardrobe, apparel; theatrical costumes; cloakroom; dressing room; vestry (*room for church vestments*).

veta [bé·ta] *f.* vein, seam (*of mineral*); streak, grain (*in wood*); stripe; *Am.* rope.

veteado [be·te·á·do] *adj.* veined; striped; streaked.

veterano [be·te·rá·no] *adj. & m.* veteran.

veterinario [be·te·ri·ná·rjo] *m.* veterinary.

veto [bé·to] *m.* veto.

vetusto [be·tús·to] *adj.* old, ancient.

vez [bes] *f.* time, occasion; turn; **a la** — at the same time; **cada** — **más** more and more; **cada** — **que** whenever; **de** — **en cuando** from time to time; **de una** — all at once; **en** — **de** instead of; **otra** — again; **una que otra** — rarely, once in a while; **tal** — perhaps; **a veces** sometimes; **raras veces** seldom; **hacer las veces de** to take the place of.

vía [bí·a] *f.* way; road; track; railroad track; conduit; **Vía Crucis** the Way of the Cross; **Vía Láctea** the Milky Way.

viaducto [bja·dúk·to] *m.* viaduct.

viajante [bja·xán·te] *m.* traveler; — **de comercio** traveling salesman.

viajar [bja·xár] *v.* to travel.

viaje [bjá·xe] *m.* voyage; trip; travel; — **de ida y vuelta** (*or* — **redondo**) round trip.

viajero [bja·xé·ro] *m.* traveler; *adj.* traveling.

vianda [bján·da] *f.* viands, food; meal.

viandante [bjan·dán·te] *m. & f.* wayfarer, walker, pedestrian; passer-by; vagabond.

viático [bjá·ti·ko] *m.* provisions for a journey; viaticum (*communion given to dying persons*).

víbora [bí·ƀo·ra] *f.* viper.

vibración [bi·ƀra·sjón] *f.* vibration.

vibrante [bi·ƀrán·te] *adj.* vibrant, vibrating.

vibrar [bi·ƀrár] *v.* to vibrate.

vicecónsul [bi·se·kón·sul] *m.* vice consul.

vicepresidente [bi·se·pre·si·dén·te] *m.* vice-president.

viceversa [bi·se·ƀér·sa] *adv.* vice versa, conversely.

viciado [bi·sjá·do] *adj.* contaminated, foul; corrupt; *p.p. of* **viciar.**

viciar [bi·sjár] *v.* to vitiate, corrupt; to adulterate; to falsify; **-se** to become corrupt.

vicio [bí·sjo] *m.* vice; bad habit; fault; craving; **de** — as a habit; **hablar de** — to talk too much; **-s** *Am.* articles and ingredients used for serving mate.

vicioso [bi·sjó·so] *adj.* vicious, evil, wicked; having bad habits; licentious; faulty, incorrect (*grammatical construction, reasoning, etc.*).

vicisitud [bi·si·si·túḏ] *f.* vicissitude; **-es** vicissitudes, ups and downs, changes of fortune or condition.

víctima [bík·ti·ma] *f.* victim.

victoria [bik·tó·rja] *f.* victory, triumph; **victoria** (*carriage*).

victorioso [bik·to·rjó·so] *adj.* victorious.

vicuña [bi·kú·ña] *f.* vicuña (*an Andean animal allied to the alpaca and llama*); vicuña wool; vicuña cloth.

vid [biḏ] *f.* vine, grapevine.

vida [bí·ḏa] *f.* life; living; livelihood; — **mía** dearest; **hacer** — to live together; **pasar a mejor** — to die; **tener la** — **en un hilo** to be in great danger.

vidalita [bi·ḏa·lí·ta] *f. Am.* melancholy song of Argentina and Chile.

vidente [bi·ḏén·te] *m.* seer, prophet; *adj.* seeing.

vidriado [bi·ḏrjá·ḏo] *m.* glaze; glazed earthenware; *p.p.* & *adj.* glazed.

vidriar[17] [bi·ḏrjár] *v.* to glaze (*earthenware*).

vidriera [bi·ḏrjé·ra] *f.* glass window; glass door; *Am.* show case, show window; — **de colores** stained-glass window.

vidriero [bi·ḏrjé·ro] *m.* glazier (*one who installs windowpanes*); glass blower; glass maker; glass dealer.

vidrio [bí·ḏrjo] *m.* glass; any glass article.

vidrioso [bi·ḏrjó·so] *adj.* glassy; brittle; slippery, icy; touchy; irritable.

viejo [bjé·xo] *adj.* old; ancient; worn-out; *m.* old man; — **verde** old man who boasts of his youth and vigor; "dirty" old man; *Am.* **los -s** the youth folks (*applied to one's parents*); **viejota** *f.* old hag.

viento [bjén·to] *m.* wind; scent; **hace** — it is windy; **a los cuatro -s** in all directions; **vientecito** *m.* gentle breeze.

vientre [bjén·tre] *m.* abdomen; belly; bowels; entrails; womb.

viernes [bjér·nes] *m.* Friday.

viga [bi·ga] *f.* beam; rafter.

vigencia [bi·xén·sja] *f.* operation (*of a law*); **entrar en** — to take effect (*said of a law*); **estar en** — to be in force (*said of a law*).

vigente [bi·xén·te] *adj.* effective, in force (*as a law*).

vigía [bi·xí·a] *f.* lookout, watchtower; watch (*act of watching*); reef; *m.* lookout, watchman.

vigilancia [bi·xi·lán·sja] *f.* vigilance.

vigilante [bi·xi·lán·te] *adj.* vigilant, watchful; *m.* watchman.

vigilar [bi·xi·lár] *v.* to keep guard; to watch over.

vigilia [bi·xi·lja] *f.* vigil, watch; wakefulness, sleeplessness; night hours (*spent in study*); eve before certain church festivals; vesper service; **día de** — day of abstinence; **comer de** — to abstain from meat.

vigor [bi·gór] *m.* vigor; **en** — in force (*said of a law*); **entrar en** — to become effective (*as a law, statute, etc.*).

vigorizar[9] [bi·go·ri·sár] *v.* to invigorate, tone up, give vigor to, strengthen.

vigoroso [bi·go·ró·so] *adj.* vigorous.

vihuela [bi·wé·la] *f.* guitar.

vil [bil] *adj.* vile, base, low, mean.

vileza [bi·lé·sa] *f.* villainy; baseness; vile act.

vilipendiar [bi·li·pen·djár] *v.* to revile.

vilo [bí·lo] : **en** — in the air; suspended; undecided; in suspense; **llevar en** — to waft.

villa [bí·ya] *f.* village; villa, country house.

villancico [bi·yan·sí·ko] *n.* carol; Christmas carol.

villanía [bi·ya·ní·a] *f.* villainy; lowliness.

villano [bi·yá·no] *adj.* rustic; uncouth; villainous,

mean, base; *m.* villain; rustic, peasant.

villorrio [bi·yó·rrjo] *m.* small village, hamlet.

vinagre [bi·ná·gre] *m.* vinegar; **vinagrera** [bi·na·gré·ra] *f.* vinegar cruet.

vincular [biŋ·ku·lár] *v.* to tie, bond, unite; to entail (*limit the inheritance of property*); to found, base (on).

vínculo [bíŋ·ku·lo] *m.* bond, tie, chain; entailed inheritance.

vindicar[6] [bin·di·kár] *v.* to vindicate; to avenge; to defend, assert (*one's rights*); **-se** to avenge oneself; to defend oneself.

vino [bí·no] *m.* wine; — **amontillado** good grade of pale sherry (*originally from Montilla*); — **tinto** dark-red wine; **vinería** [bi·ne·rí·a] *f. Ríopl., Andes* wineshop; **vinero** [bi·né·ro] *adj. Am.* pertaining to wine; **vinoso** [bi·nó·so] *adj.* winy.

viña [bí·ña] *f.* vineyard.

viñedo [bi·ñé·ḏo] *m.* vineyard.

viola [bjó·la] *f.* viola.

violación [bjo·la·sjón] *f.* violation.

violado [bjo·lá·ḏo] *adj.* violet; *m.* violet, violet color; *p.p.* violated.

violar [bjo·lár] *v.* to violate; to rape.

violencia [bjo·lén·sja] *f.* violence.

violentar [bjo·len·tár] *v.* to force; to break into (*a house*); **-se** to force oneself; to get angry.

violento [bjo·lén·to] *adj.* violent; impetuous; forced; strained; unnatural.

violeta [bjo·lé·ta] *f.* violet.

violín [bjo·lín] *m.* violin; *m.* & *f.* violinist; *Ven.* **estar hecho un** — to be very thin.

violinista [bjo·li·nís·ta] *m.* & *f.* violinist.

violonchelo [bjo·lon·čé·lo] *m.* violincello, cello.

virada [bi·rá·ḏa] *f.* tack, change of direction, turn.

viraje [bi·rá·xe] *m.* change of direction; turn.

virar [bi·rár] *v.* to turn, turn around, change direction; to tack (*said of a ship*).

virgen [bír·xen] *adj.* & *f.* virgin.

virginal [bir·xi·nál] *adj.* virginal, virgin, pure.

viril [bi·ríl] *adj.* virile, manly.

virilidad [bi·ri·li·dáḏ] *f.* virility, manhood, manly strength, vigor.

virreinal [bi·rrej·nál] *adj.* viceregal.

virreinato [bi·rrej·ná·to] *m.* viceroyalty (*office or jurisdiction of a viceroy*).

virrey [bi·rréj] *m.* viceroy.

virtud [bir·túḏ] *f.* virtue.

virtuoso [bir·twó·so] *adj.* virtuous; *m.* virtuoso (*person skilled in an art*).

viruela [bi·rwé·la] *f.* smallpox; pock (*mark left by smallpox*); **-s locas** (*or* **-s bastardas**) chicken pox.

virtua [bi·rú·ta] *f.* wood shaving.

visado [bi·sá·ḏo] *m.* visa.

visaje [bi·sá·xe] *m.* grimace; wry face; **hacer -s** to make faces.

visar [bi·sár] *v.* to visé; to approve; to O.K.

viscoso [bis·kó·so] *adj.* slimy, sticky.

visera [bi·sé·ra] *f.* visor; eye shade; *Cuba, Mex.* blinder (*on a horse's bridle*).

visible [bi·sí·ble] *adj.* visible; evident; conspicuous; notable.

visigodo [bi·si·gó·ḏo] *adj.* visigothic; *m.* visigoth.

visillo [bi·sí·yo] *m.* window curtain.

visión [bi·sjón] *f.* vision; sight; fantasy; apparition; sight (*ridiculous-looking person or thing*).

visionario [bi·sjo·ná·rjo] *adj.* & *m.* visionary.

visita [bi·sí·ta] *f.* visit, call; visitor; callers, company; — **de cumplimiento** (*or* — **de cumplido**) formal courtesy call, — **domiciliaria** police inspection of a house; home call (*of a* *social worker, doctor, etc.*).

visitación [bi·si·ta·sjón] *f.* visitation, visit.

visitador [bi·si·ta·dór] *m.* visitor, caller; inspector.

visitante [bi·si·tán·te] *m. & f.* caller, visitor; *adj.* visiting.

visitar [bi·si·tár] *v.* to visit; to inspect.

vislumbrar [biz·lum·brár] *v.* to catch a glimpse of; to guess, surmise; **-se** to be faintly visible.

vislumbre [biz·lúm·bre] *f.* glimmer; glimpse; vague idea; faint appearance.

viso [bí·so] *m.* appearance; semblance; pretense, pretext; luster, brilliance, glitter; glass curtain; **a dos -s** with a double view; with a double purpose.

visón [bi·són] *m.* mink.

víspera [bís·pe·ra] *f.* eve, evening or day before; time just before; **-s** vespers; **en -s de** on the eve of; about to.

vista [bís·ta] *f.* (*panorama*) view; landscape; sight; (*sentido*) sight; vision; (*acción*) look, glance; **a — de** in the presence of; in front of, within view of; **pagadero a la —** payable at sight or upon presentation; **¡hasta la —!** good-bye!; **bajar la —** to lower one's eyes; **conocer de —** to know by sight; **hacer la — gorda** to pretend not to see; **pasar la — por** to glance over; **perder de —** to lose sight of; **tener a la —** to have before one; to have received (*a letter*).

vistazo [bis·tá·so] *m.* glance; **dar un — a** to glance over.

visto [bís·to] *p.p. of* **ver** seen; *adj.* evident, clear **bien —** well thought of, proper; **mal —** looked down upon, improper; **— bueno** V⁰.B⁰.) approved (O.K.); **dar el — bueno** to approve, O.K.; **dar el — bueno** to approve, O.K.; **— que** whereas, considering that.

vistoso [bis·tó·so] *adj.* showy; colorful.

vital [bi·tál] *adj.* vital; important, necessary.

vitalicio [bi·ta·lí·sjo] *adj.* for life; *m.* life-insurance policy; lifetime pension.

vitalidad [bi·ta·li·dád] *f.* vitality.

vitamina [bi·ta·mí·na] *f.* vitamin.

vitaminado [bi·ta·mi·ná·do] *adj.* containing vitamins.

vítor [bí·tor] *m.* cheer, applause; **¡—!** hurrah!

vitorear [bi·to·re·ár] *v.* to cheer, applaud.

vitrina [bi·trí·na] *f.* glass case; show case; show window.

vituallas [bi·twá·yas] *f. pl.* victuals, food, provisions.

vituperar [bi·tu·pe·rár] *v.* to revile, insult, call bad names.

vituperio [bi·tu·pé·rjo] *m.* affront, insult; reproach; censure.

viuda [bjú·da] *f.* widow.

viudez [bju·dés] *f.* widowhood.

viudo [bjú·do] *m.* widower.

¡viva! [bí·ba] *interj.* hurrah for; long live!

vivac [bi·bák], **vivaque** [bi·bá·ke] *m.* bivouac, military encampment; *Am.* police headquarters.

vivacidad [bi·ba·si·dád] *f.* vivacity; brightness; liveliness.

vivaracho [bi·ba·rá·čo] *adj.* lively; vivacious, gay.

vivaz [bi·bás] *adj.* vivacious, lively; bright, keen, witty.

víveres [bí·be·res] *m. pl.* food supplies, provisions.

vivero [bi·bé·ro] *m.* fish pond, fish hatchery, tree nursery.

viveza [bi·bé·sa] *f.* vivacity; animation, liveliness; quickness; brilliance, cleverness.

vívido [bí·bi·do] *adj.* vivid; colorful.

vivienda [bi·bjén·da] *f.* dwelling; apartment.

viviente [bi·bjén·te] *adj.* living.

vivir [bi·bír] *v.* to live; to endure, last; **¡viva!** hurrah! long live!; **¿quién vive?** who goes there?; *m.* existence, living.

vivisección [bi·bi·sek·sjón] *f.* vivisection.

vivo [bí·bo] *adj.* (*no muerto*) alive; living; (*ágil*) lively; quick; (*vistoso*) vivid; bright; (*listo*) clever, wide-awake; **tío —** merry-go-round; **al —** vividly; **de viva voz** by word of mouth; **tocar en lo —** to hurt to the quick, touch the most sensitive spot.

vizcacha [bis·ká·ča] *f. Andes, Riopl.* viscacha (*South American rodent about the size of a hare*).

vizcachera [bis·ka·čé·ra] *f. Andes, Riopl.* viscacha burrow or hole; *Am.* room filled with junk; **vizcacheral** [bis·ka·če·rál] *m. Andes, Riopl.* ground full of viscacha burrows.

vizcaíno [bis·ka·í·no] *adj.* Biscayan, of or from Biscay, Spain.

vocablo [bo·ká·blo] *m.* word, term.

vocabulario [bo·ka·bu·lá·rjo] *m.* vocabulary.

vocación [bo·ka·sjón] *f.* vocation; aptness, talent.

vocal [bo·kál] *adj.* vocal; oral; vowel; *f.* vowel; *m.* voter (*in an assembly or council*).

vocear [bo·se·ár] *v.* to shout; to cry out; to hail.

vocecita [bo·se·sí·ta] *f.* sweet little voice.

vocería [bo·se·rí·a] *f.* clamor, shouting.

vocerío [bo·se·rí·o] *m. Am.* clamor, shouting.

vocero *m.* spokesman.

vociferar [bo·si·fe·rár] *v.* to shout, clamor; to yell; to boast loudly of.

vodevil [bo·de·bíl] *m.* vaudeville.

volado [bo·lá·do] *m.* superior letter in printing; *Col.* angry person.

volante [bo·lán·te] *adj.* flying; floating; **papel** (*or* **hoja**) **—** handbill, circular; *m.* ruffle, frill; steering wheel; balance wheel; flywheel.

volar² [bo·lár] *v. irr.* to fly; to fly away; to explode; to irritate, pique; to rouse (*bird game*); **-se** *Carib., Col.* to fly off the handle, lose one's temper.

volátil [bo·lá·til] *adj.* volatile; fickle, changeable; flying.

volcán [bol·kán] *m.* volcano; *Col.* precipice; *Am.* swift torrent; *C.A.* **un — de** many; lots of; a pile of.

volcánico [bol·ká·ni·ko] *adj.* volcanic.

volcar²,⁶ [bol·kár] *v. irr.* to overturn; to capsize; to upset; to make dizzy; **-se** to upset, get upset.

volear [bo·le·ár] *v.* to volley, hit (*a ball*) in the air.

volición [bo·li·sjón] *f.* volition.

voltaje [bol·tá·xe] *m.* voltage.

voltear [bol·te·ár] *v.* to turn, turn around; to revolve; to turn inside out; to overturn; to tumble or roll over; to turn a somersault; *Am.* to go prying around; *Col., Ven., C.A., Mex., Andes* — **la espalda** to turn one's back; **-se** to turn over; to change sides.

voltereta [bol·te·ré·ta] *f.* somersault, tumble.

voltio [ból·tjo], **volt** *m.* volt.

voluble [bo·lú·ble] *adj.* fickle; moody; changeable; twining (*as a climbing vine*).

volumen [bo·lú·men] *m.* volume.

voluminoso [bo·lu·mi·nó·so] *adj.* voluminous, bulky, very large.

voluntad [bo·lun·tád] *f.* will; desire; determination; benevolence, good will; consent; **última —** last will, testament; **de** (*or* **de buena**) **—** willingly, with pleasure.

voluntario [bo·lun·tá·rjo] *adj.* voluntary; willful; *m.*

volunteer.

voluntarioso [bo·lun·ta·rjó·so] *adj.* willful.

voluptuoso [bo·lup·twó·so] *adj.* voluptuous; sensual.

voluta [bo·lú·ta] *f.* scroll, spiral-like ornament; **-s de humo** spirals of smoke.

volver[2,52] [bol·ḅér] *v. irr. (regresar)* to return; *(dar vuelta)* to turn; to turn up, over, or inside out; to restore; — **loco** to drive crazy; — **a** (+ *inf.*) to do again; — **en sí** to come to, recover one's senses; — **por** to return for; to defend; **-se** to become; to turn; to turn around; to change one's ideas; **-se atrás** to go back; to back out, go back to one's word; **-se loco** to go crazy.

vomitar [bo·mi·tár] *v.* to vomit.

vómito [bó·mi·to] *m.* vomit; vomiting.

voracidad [bo·ra·si·ḍáḍ] *f.* voraciousness, greediness.

vorágine [bo·rá·xi·ne] *f.* vortex, whirlpool.

voraz [bo·rás] *adj.* voracious, ravenous, greedy.

vórtice [bór·ti·se] *m.* vortex, whirlpool; whirlwind, tornado; center of a cyclone.

votación [bo·ta·sjón] *f.* voting; vote, total number of votes.

votante [bo·tán·te] *m. & f.* voter.

votar [bo·tár] *v.* to vote; to vow; to curse; **¡voto a tal!** by Jove!

voto [bó·to] *m.* vote; vow; prayer; votive offering; oath; wish; — **de confianza** vote of confidence.

voz [bos] *f. (capacidad)* voice; *(sonido)* shout, outcry; *(palabra)* word; rumor; — **común** common rumor or gossip; **a** — **en cuello** (*or* **a** — **en grito**) shouting; at the top of one's lungs; **en** — **alta** aloud; **a voces** shouting, with shouts; **secreto a voces** open secret; **dar voces** to shout, yell.

vozarrón [bo·sa·rrón] *m.* loud, strong voice.

vuelco [bwél·ko] *m.* upset; overturning; capsizing; tumble.

vuelo [bwé·lo] *m.* flight; width, fullness *(of a dress or cloak)*; frill, ruffle; jut, projection *(of a building)*; **al** (*or* **a**) — on the fly; quickly; **levantar** (*or* **alzar**) **el** — to fly away; to soar.

vuelta [bwél·ta] *f. (giro)* turn; return; repetition; *(parte opuesta)* reverse side; cuff, facing of a sleeve; cloak lining; *(cambio)* change *(money returned)*; **a la** — around the corner; on returning; **a la** — **de los años** within a few years; *Am.* **otra** — again; **dar -s** to turn over and over; to wander about; **dar una** — to take a walk; **estar de** — to be back; **no tiene** — **de hoja** there are no two ways about it.

vuelto [bwél·to] *p.p. of* **volver**; *m. Am.* change *(money returned)*.

vuestro [bwés·tro] *poss. adj.* your, of yours *(fam. pl.)*; *poss. pron.* yours.

vulgar [bul·ḡár] *adj.* common, ordinary; in common use; low, vile, base.

vulgaridad [bul·ḡa·ri·ḍáḍ] *f.* vulgarity, coarseness, commonness.

vulgarismo [bul·ḡa·ríz·mo] *m.* slang, slang expression, vulgar or ungrammatical expression.

vulgo [búl·ḡo] *m.* populace, the common people; *adv.* commonly, popularly.

vulva [búl·ḅa] *f.* external female genitalia.

W:w **water** [gwá·ter] *m. Spain* toilet.

X:x **xilófono** [si·ló·fo·no] *m.* xylophone.

Y:y
y [i] *conj.* and.
ya [ẏa] *adv.* already; now; finally; soon, presently; in time; **¡—!** now I see!; I understand; **enough!; ¡— lo creo!** I should say so!; yes, of course!; — **no** no longer; — **que** since; although; — **se ve** of course; it is clear; — **voy** I am coming.

yacer[50] [ẏa·sér] *v. irr.* to lie *(in the grave)*; to be lying down; to lie, to be situated.

yacimiento [ẏa·si·mjén·to] *m.* bed, layer *(of ore)*; — **de petróleo** oil field.

yanqui [ẏáŋ·ki] *m. & f.* North American, native of the United States; Yankee.

yantar [ẏan·tár] *v.* to eat; *m.* food, meal.

yarará [ẏa·ra·rá] *f. Riopl.* Argentine poisonous snake.

yarda [ẏár·ḍa] *f.* yard *(unit of measure)*.

yate [ẏá·te] *m.* yacht.

yedra [ẏé·ḍra] = **hiedra**.

yegua [ẏé·ḡwa] *f.* mare; *Am.* cigar butt; *adj. Am.* big, large; **yeguada** [ẏe·ḡwá·ḍa] *f.* herd of mares.

yelmo [ẏél·mo] *m.* helmet.

yema [ẏé·ma] *f.* egg yolk; bud, shoot; candied egg yolk; — **del dedo** finger tip.

yerba [ẏér·ḅa] = **hierba**.

yerbabuena [ẏer·ḅa·ḅwé·na] *f.* mint; peppermint.

yerbero [ẏer·ḅé·ro] *m. Mex., Cuba, Ven., Col., Andes* herb vendor.

yermo [ẏér·mo] *m.* desert, wilderness; *adj.* desert uninhabited; uncultivated; sterile.

yerno [ẏér·no] *m.* son-in-law.

yerro [ẏé·rro] *m.* error, fault, mistake.

yerto [ẏér·to] *adj.* stiff, motionless, rigid.

yesca [ẏés·ka] *f.* tinder; anything highly inflammable; incentive *(to passion)*; *Riopl., Mex.* **estar hecho una** — to be in great anger.

yeso [ẏé·so] *m.* gypsum, chalk; plaster; chalk *(for blackboard)*; — **blanco** whitewash; — **mate** plaster of Paris; **yesoso** [ẏe·só·so] *adj.* chalky.

yo [ẏo] *pers. pron.* I.

yod [ẏoḍ] *f.* yod (linguistic symbol).

yodo [ẏó·ḍo] *m.* iodine.

yoduro [ẏo·ḍú·ro] *m.* iodide.

yogi [ẏo·xi] *m* ≡ yogi.

yuca [ẏú·ka] *f.* yucca; cassava.

yugo [ẏú·ḡo] *m.* yoke; marriage tie; burden.

yogur [ẏo·ḡúr] *m.* yogurt.

yoyo [ẏó·ẏo] *m.* yo-yo.

yunga [ẏuŋ·ga] *f.* valley of Peru and Bolivia.

yunque [ẏuŋ·ke] *f.* anvil.

yunta [ẏún·ta] *f.* yoke of oxen; pair of draft animals.

yuyo [ẏú·ẏo] *m. Cuba, Mex., Riopl., Andes* wild grass, weeds; *Am.* an herb sauce; *Am.* garden stuff; *Andes* **estar** — to be lifeless insipid; *Col.* **volverse uno** — to faint.

VI

Z:z **zacate** [sa·ká·te] *m. Mex., C.A.* grass, forage; hay.
zafado [sa·fá·ḍo] *adj.* impudent, brazen, shameless; *Ven.* smart, wide-awake, keen; *Col., Mex., Andes* "touched", half-crazy; *p.p.* of **zafar.**
zafar [sa·fár] *v.* to release, set free; to dislodge; *Am.* to exclude; **-se** to slip away; to dodge; to get rid (of); to get loose; *Col., Ven., Andes* to get dislocated (*said of a bone*); *Col., Mex., Andes* to go crazy; *Col.* to use foul language.
zafio [sá·fjo] *adj.* coarse, uncouth, rude.
zafir [sa·fír], **zafiro** [sa·fi·ro] *m.* sapphire.
zafra [sá·fra] *f.* sugar-making season; sugar making; sugar crop.
zaga [sá·ga] *f.* rear; **a la —** (**a** *or* **en —**) behind.
zagal [sa·gál] *m.* young shepherd; lad; **zagala** [sa·gá·la] *f.* young shepherdess; lass, maiden; **zagalejo** [sa·ga·lé·xo] *m.* young shepherd; short skirt; petticoat.
zaguán [sa·gwán] *m.* vestibule.
zaherir [sa·e·rír] *v. irr.* to hurt (*feelings*); to censure, reprove; to reproach.
zaino [sáj·no] *adj.* treacherous; vicious; chestnut-colored (*horse*).
zalamero [sa·la·mé·ro] *m.* fawner, flatterer, servile person; **zalamería** [sa·la·me·rí·a] *f.* flattery, scraping and bowing.
zalea [sa·lé·a] *f.* pelt, undressed sheepskin.
zamacueca [sa·ma·kwé·ka] *f.* popular dance of Peru and Chile.
zambo [sám·bo] *adj.* knock-kneed; *m. Ríopl., Ven., Andes* Indian and negro half-breed; *Col.* a species of South American monkey.
zambra [sám·bra] *f. Spain* uproar; lively *fiesta.*
zambullida [sam·bu·yí·ḍa] *f.* dive, dip, plunge.
zambullir [sam·bu·yír] *v.* to plunge, dip, duck; **-se** to dive; to plunge.
zambullón [sam·bu·yón] *m.* quick, sudden dip or dive.
zanahoria [sa·na·o·rja] *f.* carrot.
zanca [sáŋ·ka] *f.* long leg of any fowl; long leg; long prop; **zancada** [saŋ·ká·ḍa] *f.* stride, long step.
zanco [sáŋ·ko] *m.* stilt; **andar en -s** to walk on stilts.
zancón [saŋ·kón] *adj.* lanky, long-legged; *Col., Guat., Mex.* too short (*skirt or dress*).
zancudo [saŋ·kú·ḍo] *adj.* long-legged; *m. Mex., C.A., Ven., Col., Andes* mosquito.
zángano [sáŋ·ga·no] *m.* drone; loafer, sponger; *Am.* rogue, rascal.
zangolotear [saŋ·go·lo·te·ár] *v.* to shake, jiggle; **-se** to shake; to waddle; to sway from side to side.
zangoloteo [saŋ·go·lo·té·o] *m.* jiggle, jiggling; shaking; waddling.
zanguanga [saŋ·gwáŋ·ga] *f.* feigned illness; **hacer la —** to pretend to be ill; **zanguango** [saŋ·gwáŋ·go] *adj.* lazy; silly; *m.* fool.
zanja [sáŋ·xa] *f.* ditch; trench; *Am.* irrigation ditch.
zanjar [saŋ·xár] *v.* to excavate; to dig ditches in; to settle (*disputes*).
zapallo [sa·pá·yo] *m. Pan., Col., Ven., Andes* pumpkin; squash.
zapapico [sa·pa·pí·ko] *m.* pickaxe.
zapata [sa·pá·ta] *f.* half-boot; **— de freno** brake shoe.
zapateado [sa·pa·te·á·ḍo] *m.* a Spanish tap dance.
zapatear [sa·pa·te·ár] *v.* to tap with the feet; to tap-dance.
zapateo [sa·pa·té·o] *m.* tapping with the feet; *Am.*

a popular tap dance.
zapatería [sa·pa·te·rí·a] *f.* shoe store; shoemaker's shop.
zapatero [sa·pa·té·ro] *m.* shoemaker; shoe dealer.
zapatilla [sa·pa·tí·ya] *f.* slipper, pump.
zapato [sa·pá·to] *m.* shoe.
zapote [sa·pó·te] *m.* sapodilla.
zaragüeya [sa·ra·gwe·ya] *f.* opossum.
zarandajas [sa·ran·dá·xas] *f. pl.* trifles, trinkets, worthless things.
zarandear [sa·ran·de·ár] *v.* to winnow (*separate the chaff from grain*); to sift; to sift out; to move (*something*) quickly, wiggle, jiggle; *C.A., Ríopl.* to whip, lash, mistreat, abuse; **-se** to wiggle, jiggle; to bump along; to waddle; to strut, swagger.
zarandeo [sa·ran·dé·o] *m.* jiggle, jiggling; sifting; waddling; strutting.
zarcillo [sar·sí·yo] *m.* earring; tendril (*coil of a climbing vine*); *Andes, Mex.* earmark (*on the ear of an animal*).
zarco [sár·ko] *adj.* light-blue (*eyes*).
zarpa [sár·pa] *f.* paw, claw; weighing anchor; **echar la —** to grasp, seize; **zarpada** [sar·pá·ḍa] *f.* pounce; blow with a paw; **zarpazo** [sar·pá·so] *m.* blow with the paw; big blow, thud; hard fall.
zarpar [sar·pár] *v.* to weigh anchor; to set sail.
zarpazo [sar·pá·so] *m.* blow with a claw or paw.
zarza [sár·sa] *f.* bramble; blackberry bush.
zarzamora [sar·sa·mó·ra] *f.* blackberry.
zarzuela [sar·swé·la] *f.* Spanish musical comedy.
¡zas! *interj.* [sas] *interj.* bang!
zigzag [sig·sáġ] *m.* zigzag.
zigzaguear [sig·sa·ge·ár] *v.* to zigzag.
zinc [siŋk] = **cinc.**
zócalo [só·ka·lo] *m.* base (*of a pedestal*); *Mex.* public square.
zodíaco [so·dí·a·ko] *m.* zodiac.
zona [só·na] *f.* zone; band, girdle; shingles (*a disease*).
zonzo [són·so] *adj.* dull, stupid, silly, foolish.
zoología [so·o·lo·xí·a] *f.* zoology.
zoológico [so·o·ló·xi·ko] *adj.* zoological; **jardín —** zoo.
zopenco [so·péŋ·ko] *adj.* studpid, dull, thick-headed *m.* blockhead, dunce.
zopilote [so·pi·ló·te] *m. Mex. C.A.* buzzard.
zoquete [so·ké·te] *m.* (*cosa*) block, chunk of wood; hunk of bread; (*persona*) blockhead, dunce, fool; ugly fat person; *Am.* grease, dirt, filth; *Am.* slap.
zorra [só·rra] *f.* fox; foxy person; drunkenness; prostitute; **pillar una —** to get drunk.
zorro [só·rro] *m.* fox; foxy person; **-s** fox skins; duster made of cloth or leather strips; **estar hecho un —** to be drowsy; **hacerse uno el —** to pretend to be stupid or not to hear; *adj.* foxy; **zorrillo** [so·rrí·yo], **zorrino** [so·rrí·no] *m. Ríopl.* skunk; **zorruno** [so·rrú·no] *adj.* foxy.
zorzal [sor·sál] *m.* thrush; crafty fellow; *Am.* fool, scapegoat, dupe.
zozobra [so·só·ḅra] *f.* foundering; sinking; anxiety, worry.
zozobrar [so·so·ḅrár] *v.* to founder; to capsize; to sink; to be in great danger; to fret, worry.
zumbar [sum·bár] *v.* to buzz; to hum; to ring (*said of the ears*); to scoff at; to strike, hit; *Ven., Col.* to throw out or away; *Andes* to punish; **— una bofetada** to give a slap; **-se** *Am.* to slip away, disappear.
zumbido [sum·bí·ḍo] *m.* buzzing, humming; ringing (*in one's ears*); hit, blow, whack.
zumbón [sum·bón] *adj.* funny, playful; sarcastic;

m. jester.

zumo [sú·mo] *f. Spain* juice; profit; **zumoso** [su·mó·so] *adj.* juicy.

zurcido [sur·sí·ḍo] *m.* darn; darning; *p.p. of* **zurcir.**

zurcir[10] [sur·sír] *v.* to darn; to invent, make up (*lies*).

zurdo [súr·ḍo] *adj.* left-handed; left; **a zurdas** with the left hand; clumsily.

zuro [sú·ro] *m.* cob, corncob.

zurra [sú·rra] *f.* beating, flogging; tanning (*of leather*).

zurrar [su·rrár] *v.* to flog, thrash; to tan (*leather*).

zurrón [su·rrón] *m.* pouch; bag; leather bag; *Ven., Col.* coward.

Zutano [su·tá·no] *m.* so-and-so; a certain person. (*Used often with* **Fulano** *and* **Mengano**).

ZA

A Spanish–English List of 1000 Common Idioms and Proverbs, with Dialectal Variants

The Spanish idioms, proverbs, and sayings are listed alphabetically, followed by American Spanish variants, then English equivalents, some of which are also idiomatic. American Spanish locutions that seem to be fairly common to most of Latin America are listed without regional designation, while local variations are indicated by country or region with the abbreviations employed in the text of the Dictionary. An English index follows the chart of idioms to facilitate the use of the compilation. It is to be noted that the basic element is the Spanish expression and also that the Spanish variants are intentionally more numerous than the English. This is because of the many political entities represented in the Spanish-speaking world, in contrast to American English idiomatic expression which tends to level to a general American form.

Mil Modismos, Refranes, y Dichos Españoles con Variantes Dialectales y Tradducción al Inglés

El cuadro de modismos, refranes, y dichos españoles tiene orden alfabético según la letra inicial de la primera palabra. Siguen variantes hispanoamericanas y luego equivalentes o semejantes del inglés, con ciertas variantes. Los modismos hispanoamericanos que son bastante generales no llevan indicación regional, y se señalan con abreviaturas del texto del Diccionario los que son típicos de ciertos países o regiones. Sigue al cuadro un índice inglés con los números de las locuciones castellanas correspondientes. Se nota que lo básico es la locución española y también que se dan más variantes dialectales en español, con motivo de las numerosas entidades políticas de América. El inglés, por lo visto, ha sufrido más nivelación en este siglo.

	Academy Spanish	*American Spanish Variants*	*English Equivalents*
1.	A aquél loar debemos cuyo pan comemos	No hay que darle patadas al pesebre	Don't bite the hand that feeds you
2.	¡A buenas horas!	¡Qué horitas! (*Mex.*)	Better late than never; It's about time!
3.	A buen hambre no hay pan duro	A buen hambre no hay gordas duras (*Mex.*)	Hunger is the best sauce
4.	A caballo regalado no hay que mirarle el diente	A caballo dado no se le mira el colmillo	Don't look a gift horse in the mouth
5.	A cambio de		In exchange for
6.	A carta cabal		Through and through
7.	A centenares	A cientos	By the hundreds
8.	A ciegas	A tientas	Blindly
9.	A conciencia		Conscientiously
10.	A continuación	Como sigue	Following; as follows
11.	A costa de		By dint of; at the expense of

Academy Spanish	American Spanish Variants	English Equivalents
12. ¿A cuántos estamos?	¿Cuál es la fecha?	What is the date?
13. A decir verdad	Francamente	Frankly
14. A duras penas	Con gran dificultad	With great difficulty
15. A empujones (empellones)	A codazos	By pushing; by shoving; by elbowing
16. A escondidas	Al aguaite (*Ven., Col.*)	Without the knowledge of
17. A ese efecto	Con ese motivo	To that end; for that purpose
18. A falta de		For lack of
19. A favor de	En favor de	In behalf of; in favor of; aided by
20. A fines de		Toward (around) the end of (month, week)
21. A fondo		Thoroughly
22. A fuerza de		By dint of; through; by
23. A grandes rasgos		Briefly; in outline form; in a sketchy way
24. Ahí vamos	Pasándola	(To be) getting along; (to say one) can't complain
25. A juzgar por	Juzgando por	Judging by
26. A la americana; a escote	Al aleluya, cada quien paga la suya; Americanamente (*Col.*)	Dutch treat; go Dutch
27. A la buena de Dios		Casually; as luck would have it
28. A la carrera	Fletado (*Ven., Col.*)	On the run
29. A la corta o a la larga	Tarde o temprano	Sooner or later
30. A la fuerza		By force
31. A la larga	Al fin	In the long run; when all is said and done
32. A la luz de		In light of
33. A la moda	En boga	In style; the "in" thing
34. A la postre	A las cansadas (*Ríopl. Andes*); a la cansada (*Ec.*)	In the end
35. A la vez		At the same time
36. A lo grande	Como gringo (*Mex.*); al olor y flor (*Carib.*)	(To do something) in great style
37. A lo largo de		Along; bordering
38. A lo lejos	Allá lejos	In the distance; away off
39. A lo más	Cuando más	At (the) most
40. A lo mejor	Puede que; a la mejor (*Mex.*)	Like as not; it could be that
41. A lo vivo		Vividly described
42. A mano		By hand; at hand; tied (even)
43. A manos llenas	A Dios dar	By the handful
44. A más no poder	Hasta sacarse los zapatos (*Ch.*)	To the utmost
45. A más tardar	Cuandó más tarde	At the latest
46. A mediados de		About (around) the middle of (month)
47. A medio camino		Halfway
48. A medio hacer		Half done
49. A menos que	A no ser que	Unless
50. A menudo		Often
51. A mi ver	En mi opinión	In my opinion; to my way of thinking
52. A modo de	Una especie de	A kind (sort) of
53. A palabras necias, oídos sordos	A boca de borracho, oídos de cantinero	For foolish talk, deaf ears
54. A pedir de boca		Exactly as desired; just as you want it
55. A pesar de		In spite of
56. A petición de		At the request of
57. A principios de		The early part of; around the first of (month)
58. A propósito		By the way; on purpose
59. A prueba de		Proof against (fire, etc.)
60. A punto fijo	Precisamente	Exactly
61. A que …		I'll bet
62. A quemarropa	A boca de jarro	Point blank; at very close range

Academy Spanish	American Spanish Variants	English Equivalents
63. A quien corresponda		To whom it may concern
64. ¡A quién le importa!	¿Quién te mete, Juan Copete?	Mind your own business; what's it to you?
65. A quien madruga, Dios le ayuda		The early bird catches the worm
66. A ratos perdidos	En los ratos de ocio	In moments of leisure; in (one's) spare time
67. A razón de		At the rate of
68. A rienda suelta		Without restraint
69. A saber	Es decir; o sea	Namely; that is
70. A tal·efecto	Con tal motivo	To that end; for such purpose
71. A tal punto	Hasta tal punto	To such an extent
72. A toda costa	Cueste lo que cueste	At all hazards; whatever the cost
73. A toda prisa	A toda orquesta; a toda vela	At full speed; all out; in high gear
74. A todo correr	Como alma que lleva el diablo; Echando diablos (*Andes*); a todo ful (Andes)	At breakneck speed; like mad
75. A todo trance		At any cost; at all costs
76. A través de		Through, across
77. A última hora		At the last moment; in the nick of time
78. A un paso de aquí	Ahí tras lomita	Just a stone's throw; just a hop, skip, and jump
79. A veces	De repente (pronto) (*Riopl.*)	At times; now and then
80. A ver si como repican doblan	A ver si como roncan duermen	His bark is worse than his bite; all talk and no cider
81. Abandonar la partida	Arrojar la esponja (*Ch.*)	To give up; to say uncle
82. Abierto de par en par		Wide open
83. Abrir la marcha	Hacer la punta	To lead the (pack) parade
84. Abrirse el pecho		To bare one's heart; to let off steam; to get a load off one's chest
85. Abundar como la mala hierba	Ser ajonjolí de todos los moles (*Mex.*)	To be as common as dirt; to be a dime a dozen
86. Abrirse paso (camino)		To make (force) one's way through
87. Acabar de	Venir de (*Col.*); recién (*plus verb*) (*Riopl., Ch.*)	To have just
88. Acerca de	Sobre	Having to do with; about
89. Acusar recibo de		To acknowledge receipt of
90. Además de		In addition to; besides
91. Advertirle algo a alguien		To inform one; to tell someone so
92. Aguzar los oídos	Parar la oreja	To prick up one's ears
93. Ahora bien	Pues; entonces	Now then; so
94. Ahora mismo	Ahorita (*Mex., C.A.*)	Right now
95. Al contrario		On the contrary; on the other hand
96. Al fin	Por fin	At last
97. Al fin y al cabo	Al fin y al fallo (*Ch.*)	In the very end; when all is said and done
98. Al fin se canta la gloria	Nadie diga ¡zape! hasta que no escape; el que quiera huevos, que aguante los cacareos (*Riopl.*)	Don't count your chickens before they're hatched
99. Al gusto		As one wills; to the taste
100. Al mejor cazador se le escapa la liebre	Al mejor mono se le cae el zapote (*C.A.*); A la mejor cocinera se le queman los frijoles	Everyone makes mistakes; it's a good horse that never stumbles
101. Al menos	Cuando menos	At least
102. Al minuto	Al golpe; Al tiro (*Ch., Riopl.*)	Right away; directly (*South*)
103. Al parecer	Por lo visto	Apparently
104. Al pie de la letra		To the letter; thoroughly
105. Al por mayor	Al mayoreo	Wholesale
106. Al por menor		Retail; in detail

Academy Spanish	American Spanish Variants	English Equivalents
107. Al primer golpe de vista	A primera vista	At first glance
108. Al principio	De primero	At first; at the outset
109. Al revés		The opposite; inside out
110. Alegrarse de	Darse por contento con	To be happy (glad) about
111. Algo por el estilo		Something like that; something on that order
112. Amigo del buen tiempo, múdase con el viento	Al nopal lo van a ver sólo cuando tiene tunas (*Mex.*)	Fair-weather friend
113. Andar como loco	Andar como trompo chillador	To run around like a chicken with its head cut off
114. Andar de fiesta en fiesta	Andar de parranda; andar de farras (*Riopl.*); andar de jarana (*Col., Ven., Carib.*)	To lead a fast life; to be a swinger
115. Andar de malas	Tener la de malas	To be out of luck (jinxed)
116. Andar de prisa	Apurarse	To be in a hurry
117. Andarse por las ramas	Andarse con medias tazas; emborrachar la perdiz (*Ch.*)	To beat around the bush
118. Ante todo		Above all
119. Antes doblar que quebrar	Más vale rodear que rodar	Better bend than break; if you can't lick 'em, join 'em
120. Apretar el paso		To hasten; to hurry
121. Aprovecha gaviota, que no hay otra	Atáscate ahora que hay lodo	Gather ye rosebuds while ye may; here's your chance
122. Aprovechar la ocasión		To take advantage of the situation
123. Aquí mismo	Aquí mero (*Mex.*)	Right here
124. Armar un San Quintín	Armar una bronca; revolver el gallinero (*Ch.*)	To start a fight; to raise Cain
125. ¡Arriba los corazones!	¡No le afloje!	Courage! Cheer up! Chin up!
126. Así es la vida	Así es la vida, tango	Such is life; that's the way the ball bounces; that's the way the cookie crumbles
127. A sus órdenes	Para servirle	At your service
128. Atender razones		To listen to reason
129. Atrasado de noticias		Behind the times
130. Aunque la mona se vista de seda, mona se queda		Clothes don't make the man
131. Bajo cuerda	Por debajo del agua	In an underhanded manner; under the table
132. Barrer para adentro	Rascarse para adentro es gran contento; antes mis dientes que mis parientes	To look after oneself first; to take care of number one
133. Beber como una esponja	Beber hasta reventar	To drink like a fish
134. Bien inclinado		Well-disposed; good-natured
135. Bien mirado	Considerándolo bien	On second thought; come to think of it
136. Boca abajo		Face down
137. Boca arriba		Face (up) upward
138. Borracho como una cuba	Borracho perdido	Dead drunk; plastered; tight
139. Buen genio		Good-natured
140. ¡Buen provecho!	¡Que aproveche!	Good appetite!
141. ¡Bueno, bueno! ¡Conforme!	¡De acuerdo!	All right; agreed; O.K.
142. Burlarse de	Reírse de; tener a uno para el fideo (*Ch.*)	To make fun of
143. Buscarle tres pies al gato	Buscarle mangas al chaleco; buscarle cuatro pies al gato (*Ec.*)	To look for knots in a bulrush; to complicate things
144. Buscar pelos en la sopa		To be given to fault finding; to look for an excuse to gripe
145. Cada muerte de obispo	Como visita de obispo	In a month of Sundays; once in a blue moon
146. Cada uno sabe dónde le aprieta el zapato	Cada quien sabe lo que carga su costal	Every man knows best where his own shoe pinches
147. Caer atravesado	Caer gordo; caer mal; caer gacho (*Col.*)	To rub (one) the wrong way; to be a pain in the neck
148. Caer como un balde de agua fría	Caer como un cubetazo de agua fría (*Mex.*)	To be like a dash of cold water; to be a wet blanket
149. Caer de bruces	Dar el azotón; caer de ancho; echarse de boca (*Andes*)	To fall flat; to bite the dust

Academy Spanish	American Spanish Variants	English Equivalents
150. Caer en la cuenta		To realize; to take note of
151. Caer en la red	Caer en la ratonera; pisar el palito (*Ch.*); ensartarse (*Andes*)	To fall into the trap; to fall for it
152. Caerse de su propio peso		To be self-evident (obvious)
153. Calentarse los cascos		To rack one's brains
154. Callarse la boca	Cerrar el pico; no chillar (*Ven., C.A.*)	To keep still; to hold one's tongue
155. Cambiar de opinión		To change one's mind
156. Cambiar de tema	Cambiar el disco	To change the subject; to turn the record over
157. Caminar de arriba abajo	Andar vuelta y vuelta	To pace the floor; to pace up and down
158. Cara a cara		Right to one's face
159. Cara o cruz	Aguila o sol (*Mex.*); cara o sello	Heads or tails
160. Carne de gallina		Goose flesh; goose pimples; burr(brrr) bumps (South)
161. Cerca de		Near; about
162. Colgarle a uno el milagro	Colgarle a uno el muerto	To shift responsibility; to pass the buck
163. Como dijo el otro	Como dice el dicho	As the saying goes; as they say
164. Como Dios manda		As it should be; according to Cocker; according to Hoyle
165. Como dos y dos son cuatro		As sure as two and two are four; as sure as God made little green apples; as sure as shooting
166. Como el más pintado		As (with) the best of them
167. Como llovido del cielo		Like manna from heaven
168. Como perros y gatos	Como dos gatos en un costal	Like cats and dogs
169. Como quiera que sea	Sea lo que sea	However it be; in any case
170. ¿Cómo te (le) va?	¿Qué tal?	How are you? How's it going? What gives?
171. Como una fiera		Furiously
172. Compadecerse de alguien	Compadecerle a alguien	To pity; to sympathize with someone
173. Comprar a ciegas	Comprar potrillo en panza de yegua	To buy blindly; to buy a pig in a poke
174. Comunicarse con		To get in touch with
175. Con destino a		(To be) going to; (to be) bound for
176. Con el ojo y con la fe jamás me burlaré	Aunque te digan que sí, espérate a que lo veas	Seeing is believing; (to say one is) from Missouri
177. Con ese no se juega	A jugar con las muñecas	Don't trifle with that; don't mess with that
178. Con guante blanco	Con mucha mano izquierda	With kid gloves
179. Con intención	Adrede	Deliberately; on purpose
180. Con la condición de que		With the understanding that
181. Con la cuchara que elijas, con ésa comerás	Cada quien se pone la corona que se labra	As you make your bed, so you must lie in it
182. Con las bocas cosidas	¡Chitón!	To keep to oneself; mum's the word; button the lip
183. Con las manos en la masa		To be caught in the act; to be caught red-handed
184. Estar con los pelos de la dehesa	Estar con el pelo del potrero	To be a country bumkin; (hayseed, hick)
185. Con mucho gusto		Gladly
186. Con objeto de	Con el propósito de	With the object of
187. Con permiso		Excuse me; I beg your pardon
188. Con razón		No wonder! Small wonder!
189. Con respecto a		With regard to
190. Con tal que	A condición de que	Provided that; if
191. Con tiempo	Con anticipación; de antemano	In advance; ahead of time
192. Contigo pan y cebolla	Más vale atole con risas que chocolate con lágrimas	Whither thou goest ...; love in a cottage

Academy Spanish	American Spanish Variants	English Equivalents
193. Con todas las de ley	Como Dios manda	According to Cocker (Hoyle)
194. Confiar en	Fiarse de	To rely on; to trust
195. Conforme a	Según	In accordance with
196. Conocerle a uno el juego	Ponerse chango (Mex.)	To be wise to someone; to be onto someone's schemes
197. Constarle a uno		To be evident to one
198. Consultar con la almohada		To think something over; to sleep on something
199. Contar con		To count on; to depend on
200. Contentarse con		To be satisfied with
201. Contra viento y marea		Come what may; come hell or high water
202. Convenirle a uno		To be to one's advantage; to be advisable; to be to one's good
203. Correr la voz	Correr la bola (C.A.); dizque (Col. Andes)	To be rumored; to be noised about; they say; people say
204. Correr peligro		To run a risk; to take a chance
205. Correr riesgo		To run a risk; to take a chance
206. Cortar de raíz		To nip in the bud
207. Cortar el hilo	Cortar la hebra	To interrupt; to cut off
208. Corto de vista		Nearsighted
209. Cosa de		About; more or less; a matter of
210. Cosa de risa	Digno de risa	A laughing matter
211. Cosa de ver		Something worth seeing; something worth to see
212. Cosido a faldas de		To be tied to the apron strings of
213. Costar un ojo de la cara	Costar un huevo (Ven., Col., Andes)	To cost a mint; to cost plenty; to bring a stiff price
214. Cruzarse de brazos		To remain indifferent; to be not interested
215. Cuando quiera		Whenever; any time now
216. Cuanto antes	Tan pronto como posible	As soon as possible; the sooner the better
217. Cuanto más . . . más	Mientras más . . . más; entre más . . . más (C.A., Col., Andes)	The more . . . the more
218. Cuatro letras		A few lines (in a letter)
219. Cuesta abajo		Downhill; easy
220. Cuesta arriba		Uphill; difficult
221. ¡Cuidado!	¡Aguas! ¡Aguila! (Mex.); ¡Hay que pelar el ojo! (Col.)	Look out! Watch out!
222. Dar a entender		To insinuate; to pretend; to give to understand
223. Dar a luz		To give birth
224. Dar al borracho las llaves de la bodega	Poner la iglesia en manos de Lutero	To set the fox to keep the geese; to put the cat among the pigeons
225. Dar ánimo	Animar	To cheer up
226. Dar calabazas	Cortar; dar ayotes (C.A.); dar opio (Andes)	To break off relations; to give (one) the brush-off; to give (one) the mitten (N.E.)
227. Dar cuerda a		To wind (clock, etc.)
228. Dar de baja		To discharge; to drop (from a team, list, etc.)
229. Dar disgustos a		To cause grief to; to distress; to bug
230. Dar el pésame por		To present one's condolences for; to extend one's sympathy for
231. Dar en		To hit; take a notion to
232. Dar en el clavo		Hit the nail on the head
233. Dar forma a		To put in final shape
234. Dar gato por liebre	Hacerle guaje a uno (Mex.); pasársela a uno (Ch.)	To deceive; to cheat

	Academy Spanish	American Spanish Variants	English Equivalents
235.	Dar guerra		To make trouble
236.	Dar (la) lata	Poner gorro (*Mex.*); poner pereque (*Col.*)	To bother; to annoy; to be a nuisance; to bug
237.	Dar la razón a alguien		To acknowledge (a person) to be right; give credit for being right
238.	Dar la vuelta a algo		To go around something; to rotate something
239.	Dar las gracias		To thank; to be grateful
240.	Dar lástima	Dar pena	To arouse pity
241.	Dar mucha pena		To be very embarrassing
242.	Dar muestras de	Dar señales de	To show signs of
243.	Dar parte	Avisar	To inform; to report
244.	Dar por cierto	Estar seguro	To be certain (sure)
245.	Dar por descontado	Tomar por cierto	To take for granted
246.	Dar por hecho	Suponer	To assume; to take for granted
247.	Dar por seguro	Estar seguro	To be certain (sure)
248.	Dar que hacer		To make work; to cause work
249.	Dar rienda suelta a	Dar curso libre	To give free rein to; to let go
250.	Dar salida a	Disponer de	To dispose of; to clear out; to get rid of
251.	Dar señales de		To show signs of
252.	Dar un paseo	Dar una vuelta	To take a walk (stroll)
253.	Dar un paso en falso	Dar una metida de pata	To make a false move; to pull a boner
254.	Dar una mano		To apply (a coat of paint, etc.)
255.	Dar una vuelta		To take a turn (through a place); to turn over
256.	Darle a uno coraje	Darle rabia a uno (*Carib.*);	To make one angry (mad)
257.	Darle a uno en la matadura	Darle a uno en la mera matada (*Mex.*)	To touch to the quick; to strike home
258.	Darle a uno la gana; apetecer	Provocarle a uno (*Col.*)	To feel like; to want to
259.	Darle a uno lo mismo	Serle a uno igual	To be all the same to one; to make no difference to one
260.	Darle a uno una carda	Echarle a uno la viga	To preach at; to give a good talking to; to bawl out; to tell off
261.	Darle a uno vergüenza	Darle a uno mucha pena	To be ashamed; to be shy
262.	Darle a uno una soberana paliza	Darle a uno hasta por debajo de la lengua; aplanchar a uno (*Col.*)	To give one a trouncing; to knock the spots off one
263.	Darse aires; darse tono; ¡cuántos humos!	Darse mucho taco (*Mex.*); Botarse el pucho (*Ch.*); Darse corte; darse paquete (*Ec.*)	To put on airs; to put on the dog; to be stuck up
264.	Darse cuenta de		To realize; to be aware of
265.	Darse la gran vida	Darse vida de rey; darse vida de cachos para arriba (*Ch.*); darse vida de oro (*Col.*)	To live off the fat of the land; to live the life of Riley; to live it up
266.	Darse prisa	Apurarse	To hurry; to move quickly
267.	De acuerdo con		In accordance with
268.	De ahora en adelante	De aquí en adelante	From now on; from here on
269.	De bote en bote	Hasta el tope (*Mex.*)	Full to the brim; full up
270.	De broma	De vacilada (*Mex.*)	As a joke; in jest
271.	De buena gana		Willingly
272.	De buenas a primeras	En un improviso (*Ven., Col.*)	Without warning; suddenly
273.	De cabo a rabo	De punta a punta	From beginning to end; from head to tail
274.	De categoría	De número (*Ríopl.*); de oro (*Col.*); de mentas (*Arg.*)	Of importance; of class
275.	De cuando en cuando	De vez en cuando; de pronto (*C.A.; Ríopl.*)	From time to time
276.	De día en día	De día a día	From day to day
277.	De dirección única	De un solo sentido	One-way

Academy Spanish	American Spanish Variants	English Equivalents
278. De enfrente		(The one) directly opposite; across the way
279. De esta manera		In this way
280. De etiqueta		Formal dress
281. De golpe	En un improviso (*Ven., Col.*)	Suddenly; all of a sudden
282. De gran subida, gran caída	De la subida más alta es la caída más lastimosa	The bigger they are, the harder they fall
283. De hecho	El hecho es que; es que	As a matter of fact
284. De hoy en adelante	De ahora en adelante	From now on
285. De intento	Adrede; a propósito	On purpose
286. De la noche a la mañana		Overnight; all at once
287. De lado		Sideways
288. De lleno		Fully; adequately
289. De lo contrario		Otherwise
290. De mal en peor	De Guatemala en guatepeor	From bad to worse
291. De mala fe		In bad faith
292. De mala gana		Unwillingly
293. De mala muerte	Chafa (*Mex.*)	Worthless; crumby
294. De manera que	Así es que	So that; as a result
295. De memoria		By heart; from memory
296. De modo que		So that; so
297. De ningún modo	Ni modo (*Mex.*)	By no means; not on your life
298. De ninguna manera	Ni loco; ¡qué esperanza!	By no means; no way!
299. De nuevo	Otra vez	Again; anew; once more
300. De paso		In passing; on the way
301. De pronto	De repente	All of a sudden
302. De pura casualidad		Purely by chance
303. De repente	De golpe; en un improviso (*Ven., Col.*)	All of a sudden
304. De tal palo, tal astilla	Cual el cuervo, tal su huevo; de tal jarro, tal tepalcate (*Mex.*)	Like father, like son; a chip off the old block
305. Descubrir el pastel	Hacer aparecer el peine	To let the cat out of the bag; to spill the beans
306. De todas maneras	De toda cuenta (*Col.*)	At any rate; anyway
307. De trecho en trecho		At intervals (space and time)
308. De un día para otro	De día a día	Day by day
309. De un modo u otro		In one way or another
310. De una vez y para siempre	De una vez	Once and for all
311. De un solo sentido		One-way
312. De vuelta a las andadas	Otra vez la burra en el trigo	Back to the old tricks
313. Decidirse a		To make up one's mind to; to decide to
314. Decir a todo amén		To be a yes man
315. Decir agudezas	Tener buenas puntadas	To be witty; to be a wise guy
316. Decir entre dientes		To mumble; to mutter
317. Decir para sí	Decir para sus adentros	To say to oneself
318. Dejar de		To cease; to stop
319. Dejar a uno en la calle	Dejar a uno en la tendida Dejar a uno en un petate (*Col.; Ven.*)	To bleed (one) white; to take (one) to the cleaners
320. Dejar en paz		To leave alone
321. Dejar a uno plantado	Dejar a uno en la estacada; dejar a uno embarcado (*Mex.*)	To stand someone up
322. Dejarse de cuentos	Dejarse de historias; dejarse de rodeos	To come to the point; to stop beating around the bush
323. Del dicho al hecho hay gran trecho		Saying and doing are two different things; there's many a slip twixt the cup and the lip
324. Delante de		In front of; in the presence of
325. Dentro de	Entre (*C.A.*)	Inside; within
326. Dentro de poco	En breve; at rato	Soon; shortly; right away; directly (South)
327. Desde ahora		From now on
328. Desde entonces		Since then

Academy Spanish	American Spanish Variants	English Equivalents
329. Desde fuera		From the outside
330. Desde lejos		From a distance
331. Desde luego		Of course; naturally
332. Desde un principio		Right from the start; from the very beginning
333. Despedirse a la francesa	Irse como burro sin mecate; Pintarse (*Ven.*); emplumárselas (*Col., Ven.*)	To take French leave
334. Después de		After; following
335. Detrás de	Detrás mío (tuyo, etc.) (*Ch., Ríopl.*)	Behind
336. Día hábil		Workday
337. Dicho y hecho		No sooner said than done
338. Digno de confianza		Reliable; trustworthy
339. Dijo la sartén a la caldera, quítate de allá, que me tiznas	El comal le dijo a la olla, qué tiznada estás (*Mex.*)	The pot called the kettle black
340. Dime con quien andas y te diré quién eres	Dime quien es tu junta y te diré si haces yunta	A man is known by the company he keeps; birds of a feather flock together
341. Dios mediante	Si Dios nos da vida; primero Dios (*C.A.*)	God willing; I hope so
342. Dirigir la palabra		To address; to speak to; to talk to
343. Disculparse por		To apologize for
344. Disponer de		To have at one's disposal; to spend; to get rid of
345. Disponerse a		To get ready to
346. Divertirse en grande	Pachanguear (*Mex.*); pasarla a todo dar	To have the time of one's life; to have a ball
347. Doblar la hoja	Cambiar el disco	To change the subject
348. Don de gentes		Winning manners; a way with people
349. Donde hubo fuego hay cenizas	Donde camotes quemaron, cenizas quedaron (*Andes*)	Where there's smoke, there's fire
350. Donde menos se piensa salta la liebre	De cualquier maya salta un ratón (*Ríopl.*)	The unexpected always happens; it happens when least expected
351. Echar a perder		To spoil; to go to waste
352. Echar al correo		To post, mail (letters, etc.)
353. Echar de menos	Extrañar; añorar; hacerle falts a uno (*Andes*)	To feel the absence of; to miss; to long for
354. Echar de ver	Catar de ver (*Col., Ven.*)	To notice; to observe
355. Echar flores	Decir piropos	To flatter; to sweet-talk
356. Echar indirectas		To make insinuations
357. Echar la casa por la ventana		To go all out; to kill the fatted calf; to blow the works
358. Echar la culpa a		To lay (put) the blame on
359. Echar la llave		To lock the door
360. Echar los bofes	¡A darle duro! (*Mex.*)	To work hard; to throw oneself into a job
361. Echar sapos y culebras	Echar tacos (*Mex.*) Echar ajos y cebollas; subir la prima (*Arg.*)	To swear a blue streak; to turn the air blue
362. Echar todo a rodar	Patearle el nido a alguien	To spoil things; to upset everything; to make a mess of everything
363. Echar un sueño (una siesta)	Tomar una siestita; tomar una pestañita (*Mex.*)	To take a nap; to catch a little shut-eye
364. Echar una mano		To lend a hand; to help out
365. Echar un párrafo	Echar guáguara (*Mex.*)	To pass the time of day; to chew the rag (fat)
366. Echarse a		To begin; to suddenly start
367. Echarse para atrás	Rajarse (*Mex.*)	To back out; to back down; to give in
368. Echarse un trago	Echarse un fogonazo (*Mex.*); empinar el codo; empinar el cacho (*Ch.*); pegarse un palo (*Carib., Col.*)	To take a drink (swig); to wet the whistle

Academy Spanish	American Spanish Variants	English Equivalents
369. El día menos pensado	Un día de éstos	One of these fine days
370. El gallito del lugar	El mero mero (*Mex.*)	The cock of the walk; the top banana; the top dog
371. El hombre propone y Dios dispone	El hombre propone, Dios dispone y la mujer descompone	Man proposes, God disposes
372. El mejer día		Some fine day
373. El que no se arriesga no pasa la mar	El que no arriesga no gana	Nothing ventured, nothing gained
374. Empeñarse en		To insist on; to be bent on
375. Empleo de cuello y levita	Empleo de camisa blanca y corbata	White-collar job
376. En aquel entonces		At that time: in those days
377. En breve plazo	Dentro de poco	Within a short time
378. En broma		As a joke; in jest
379. En calidad de		In the capacity of
380. En cambio		On the other hand; but
381. En cierta manera	Hasta cierto punto	In a way
382. En cuanto	Tan pronto como	As soon as
383. En cuanto a		Regarding; as for
384. En cueros	En traje de Adán; en pelota; pila (*Andes*)	Naked; in one's birthday suit; naked as a jay bird
385. En efectivo	En dinero contante y sonante; al chaz-chaz (*Mex.*)	In hard cash; in cold cash; cash on the barrel-head
386. En efecto	El hecho es que	In fact; as a matter of fact
387. En el extranjero		Abroad
388. En el peligro se conoce al amigo	En la cárcel se conocen los amigos	A friend in need is a friend indeed
389. En el fondo		At bottom; at heart; by nature
390. En favor de		On behalf of
391. En fila		In line
392. En fin	Así es que	In short; so
393. En firme	A la segura (*Ch., Andes*); a la fija (*Col.*)	Definite; binding
394. En grande		On a large scale; in a big way
395. En gustos no hay disputa	Sobre gustos se rompen géneros	Every man to his taste; some like it hot; some like it cold
396. En hora buena		Safely; luckily; o.k.
397. En la actualidad	Hoy; estos días	At the present time; nowadays
398. En lo alto de		On top of
399. En lo futuro	En el porvenir	Hereafter; in the future
400. En lugar de		Instead of
401. En mangas de camisa		In shirt sleeves
402. En mi perra vida	En mi cochina vida	Never in all my life; never in all my born days
403. En presencia de		Before; in the presence of; in front of
404. En primer lugar		In the first place
405. En principio		In principle; basically
406. En punto		Exactly (time); on the dot
407. En regla		In order
408. En rueda	Entre pura raza (*Mex.*)	A friendly gathering; among friends
409. En su apogeo		At the height of one's glory; at one's peak
410. En suma	Total	In short; briefly
411. En tal caso		In such a case
412. En todo caso		In any event; anyway
413. En total	Total	In short; to sum up
414. En un abrir y cerrar de ojos		In the twinkling of an eye
415. En un descuido	En un improviso (*Ven., Col.*)	When least expected
416. En un dos por tres	En menos que canta un gallo	When least expected; quick as a wink; in the shake of a lamb's tail
417. En vano	Al ñudo (*Riopl.*)	In vain
418. En vez de		Instead of
419. En voz alta		Out loud

Academy Spanish	American Spanish Variants	English Equivalents
420. En voz baja	Despacio	In a soft (low) voice
421. Encargarse de		To take charge of
422. Encogerse de hombros		To shrug one's shoulders
423. Enfrente de		Opposite; across the way from
424. Enterarse de	Informarse	To find out about; to learn
425. Entrado en años	Ya vetarro	Well along in years; to be no spring chicken
426. Entrar en materia	Llegar al caso	To come to the point; get down to business
427. Entre azul y buenas noches	Entre dos aguas; ni un sí ni un no	To be undecided; to be on the fence
428. Entre bastidores		To be behind the scenes
429. Entre la espada y la pared	Entre dos fuegos	To be between the devil and the deep blue sea
430. Equivocarse de	Salirle a uno gabacho	To be mistaken about
431. Es decir	O sea	That is to say; in other words
432. Es fama que	Dizque (Col.); corre la bola que (C.A.)	It is rumored that; they say that
433. Es harina de otro costal	Es otro cantar; no viene al cuento	That's a horse of a different color
434. Es más bravo que un león	Es un perro; es una fiera	He is a tiger (wildcat)
435. ¡Esto es Jauja!	¡Esta es la tierra de Dios y María Santísima!	This is Seventh Heaven! This is Never-Never Land!
436. Escapársele a uno		To escape one's attention; to get by one
437. Escurrir el bulto	Emplumárselas (Col., Ven.); pelarse	To sneak away; to slip away
438. Esforzarse en (por)	Luchar por	To strive to; to struggle to
439. Está bien (bueno)		All right; o.k.
440. Está hasta en la sopa	Le dicen el diosito	There's no getting away from him; I'm sick of the sight of him
441. Está que pela	Está como para desplumar pollos	It's piping hot; It's as hot as blue blazes
442. Estar a cargo		To be in charge
443. Estar a disgusto		To be ill at ease; to feel awkward
444. Estar a gusto		To be contented; to be comfortable
445. Estar a la expectativa	Catiar la laucha (Ch.)	To be on the lookout for
446. Estar a la merced de		To be at the mercy of
447. Estar a punto de	Estar por	To be about to
448. Estar en su elemento	Estar en su cancha (Ríopl.; Andes); Estar en su mole (Mex.)	To be in one's element
449. Estar con ánimo de		To have a notion to
450. Estar chiflado	Le patina el embrague a uno; tener los alambres pelados (Ch.)	To have a screw loose; not to have all one's marbles
451. Estar de acuerdo		To agree
452. Estar de buen humor		To be in a good humor; to be in a good frame of mind
453. Estar de luto	Estar de duelo	To be in mourning
454. Estar de malas	Tener la de malas; tener el santo a espaldas (Ven., Mex.); estar salado (Col., Andes)	To be out of luck
455. Estar de moda	Estar en boga	To be fashionable; to be popular; to be the "in" thing
456. Estar de sobra		To be superfluous; to be too much
457. Estar de turno		To be on duty; to be on one's shift
458. Estar de viaje		To be traveling; to be on the road
459. Estar en buen uso	Estar en buenas condiciones	To be in good condition; to be in good shape

Academy Spanish	American Spanish Variants	English Equivalents
460. Estar en el pellejo de otro		To be in somebody else's shoes
461. Estar en la luna		To be up in the clouds
462. Estar en las nubes		To daydream; to be high (prices)
463. Estar en lo cierto		To be right; to be correct
464. Estar en lo firme		To be in the right
465. Estar en los huesos	Estar hecho un violín (*Ven.*); no quedarle a uno más que hueso y cuero	To be nothing but skin and bone
466. Estar en plan de		To be in the mood for; to be out for
467. Estar en un error	Estar equivocado	To be mistaken; to be wrong
468. Estar en vigor		To be in effect; to be in force
469. Estar en vísperas de		To be on the eve of; to be about to
470. Estar hecho una furia	Estar como agua para chocolate; estar hecho un chivo; estar hecho un quique (*Ch.*)	To be beside oneself; to be hot under the collar
471. Estar muy metido en		To be deeply involved in
472. Estar para	Estar por	To be about to
473. Estar por	Estar a favor de	To be in favor of; to be for
474. Estar prevenido		To be prepared; to be forewarned
475. Estar quebrado	Estar arrancado; estar bruja (*Mex.*); estar pato (*Ch.*)	To be broke (flat broke)
476. Estar rendido	Estar reventado	To be exhausted; to be all tired out; to be pooped
477. Estar sentido	Estar resentido	To be offended; to be hurt
478. Estar todo patas arriba	Ser todo un verdadero relajo	To be topsy-turvy; to be helter-skelter
479. Estrechar la mano	Chocarla	To shake hands
480. Extrañarle a uno		To seem strange (funny) to one
481. Faltar a		To absent oneself from; to miss
482. Fiarse en (de)		To trust; to rely on
483. Figurarse que	Se me hace que	Imagine that
484. Fijarse en		To pay attention to; to notice
485. Formar parte de		To be a member of; to be a part of
486. Frente a		Facing; opposite; in front of
487. Fuerte como un roble	Bien trabado	As strong as an ox; as strong as a bull moose
488. Fuera de sí		Unconscious; beside oneself
489. Función corrida	Permanencia voluntaria	All-day program; come-and-go function
490. Fulano	Ciertas hierbas (*Col., C.A.*)	Mr. So-and-so; what's-his-name
491. Ganar a uno la mano	Coger a uno la delantera; madrugarle a uno	To get up too early for one; to beat one to it
492. Ganarse la vida	Ganarse el pan de cada día; pegarse para ganar la gorda (*Mex.*)	To work for a living
493. Genio y figura hasta la sepultura	Al que nace barrigón, es al ñudo que lo fajen (*Ríopl.*)	You can't make a silk purse out of a sow's ear; the leopard doesn't change its spots
494. Gente menuda	La chiquillería	Small fry
495. Gracias a		Thanks to
496. Gritar como si le mataran	Gritar como marrano atorado en un caño	To scream bloody murder; to scream like a stuck pig
497. Guardarse de		To guard against; to avoid
498. Guiñar un ojo	Hacer ojos (*Col.*); hacer ojitos (*Mex.*); hacer caras (*Ríopl.*)	To make eyes at; to flirt; to give the glad eye to
499. Haber de		To be expected to; to be scheduled to

Academy Spanish	American Spanish Variants	English Equivalents
500. Haber de todo como en botica		There's a little of everything
501. Haber noros en la costa		The coast is not clear; something's up
502. Habituarse a	Acostumbrarse a; amañarse (Col..)	To accustom oneself to; to get used to
503. Hablar como una cotorra	No pararle la boca a uno (Mex.)	To be a chatterbox; to be a windbag
504. Hablar en voz baja	Hablar despacio; hablar quedito	To speak softly; to speak in a low voice
505. Hablar entre dientes		To mumble; to mutter
506. Hablar hasta por los codos	Ser lengualarga	To chatter; to talk idly; to talk too much
507. Hablar sin rodeos	Cantar claro; Pelar el cobre; Ser claridoso (Ven., C.A.); Hablar a calzón quitado (Col., Ch.)	Not to mince any words; to speak straight from the shoulder; tell it like it is
508. Hacer alarde	Echársela; echar flotas (Col., Ven.); levantarse el tarro (Ch.)	To boast; to brag
509. Hacer algo a medias		To do a halfway job; to do a poor job
510. Hacer arrancar	Dar un empujón	To set the ball rolling; to get the show on the road
511. Hacer buen papel	Jugar buen papel	To make a good showing
512. Hacer buenas migas		To get along well together
513. Hacer caso a uno	Dar boleto a uno	To pay attention to one
514. Hacer cola		To queue up; to stand in line; to line up
515. Hacer comedia	Hacer tango	To put on a show; to make a scene
516. Hacer la vista gorda		To pretend not to see; to wink at
517. Hacer escala		To make a scheduled stop; to stopover
518. Hacer falta		To be necessary; to have need of
519. Hacer frente a		To confront; to face up to
520. Hacer gestos		To make faces (gestures)
521. Hacer gracia	Parecer chistoso	To strike one as funny
522. Hacer hincapié	Poner énfasis; porfiar	To emphasize; to insist upon
523. Hacer juego		To match; to go well with
524. Hacer mal papel	Jugar mal papel	To make a poor showing; to play a poor role
525. Hacer novillos	Pintar venado (Mex.)	To cut classes; to play hooky
526. Hacer presente		To notify; to remind
527. Hacer puente		To take the intervening day off
528. Hacer su agosto		To feather one's nest; to make a killing
529. Hacer un mandado	Hacer un recado	To run an errand
530. Hacerle a uno un flaco servicio	Hacerle a uno la pera; jugar sucio (Ch.)	To do someone a bad turn; to play a dirty trick on someone
531. Hacerle daño a uno		To hurt or harm someone
532. Hacerse de noche		To get dark
533. Hacerse el sordo	Hacerse el cucho (Ch.)	To turn a deaf ear; to refuse to consider
534. Hacerse el tonto	Hacerse el loco; hacerse el menso (Mex.)	To play (act) the fool; to play dumb
535. Hacerse ilusiones		To build castles in Spain; to blow bubbles in the air
536. Hacerse tarde		To become (get) late
537. Hallarse en el pellejo de otro		To be in somebody else's shoes
538. Harto da quien da lo que tiene	El que da lo suyo, harto hace	You can't get blood from a turnip (stone)
539. Hasta aquí		So far; up to now
540. Hasta cierto punto		To a certain point (extent)

Academy Spanish	American Spanish Variants	English Equivalents
541. Hasta el tuétano	Hasta las cachas (*Mex.*)	To the core; to the very center
542. Hasta la fecha		To date; up to now
543. Hasta luego	Ahí nos vemos; hasta lueguito (*Mex.*)	So long; see you later; hurry back
544. Hay que	Es necesario	It is necessary; you have to
545. Hecho a la medida		Custom-made; made to order
546. Hecho y derecho		Mature; grown-up
547. Hincarse de rodillas	Arrodillarse	To kneel down
548. Historias de cuartel	Cuentos colorados; chistes verdes (*Mex.*)	Off-color jokes; pool-room talk
549. Hoy en día	Hoy día; hoy	These days; nowadays
550. Hoy por hoy	Actualmente	Under the present circumstances; for the time being
551. Ida y vuelta		Round-trip
552. Idas y venidas		Comings and goings
553. Impedir el paso		To block the way
554. Imponerse a	Apretar el breque (*Col.*)	To dominate; to command respect
555. Importarle a uno		To be of importance to one; to concern one
556. Incorporarse a		To join (a society or unit)
557. Inocente como una paloma	Como una blanca paloma (*Mex.*)	As harmless as a fly; as innocent as a new-born baby
558. Informarse de		To find out about
559. Ir a medias	Ir mitad mitad	To go fifty-fifty
560. Ir al grano	Ir a lo que truje	To get down to brass tacks; to get to the point
561. Ir de compras	Ir de tiendas	To go shopping
562. Ir del brazo		To walk arm in arm
563. Irle a uno bien (mal)		To be becoming (unbecoming); to be well
564. Irse de juerga	Irse de parranda; irse de tuna (*Col.*); irse de farras (*Riopl.*); irse de jarana (*Ven.*); irse de rumba (*Carib.*)	To go on a spree; to paint the town red
565. Irsele a uno el santo al cielo	Irsele a uno la onda	One's mind goes blank; one clean forgets; to be spacy
566. Jugar con dos barajas	Mamar a dos tetas	To double-cross; to play both ends against the middle
567. Jugarle una mala pasada a uno	Hacerle a uno la cama (*Ch.*)	To play foul with one; to play a dirty trick on one
568. Juntarse con		To associate with; to join
569. La alta sociedad	La gente copetuda	High society; the upper crust; the jet set
570. La esperanz es lo último que se pierde	Como el tiempo dure, lugar tiene la esperanza	Hope springs eternal; while there's life there's hope
571. La mar de	Cantidad de; un montón de; un volcán de (*C.A.*); a patadas (*Ec.*); a ponchadas (*Andes*)	Lots of; loads of; oodles of; right smart of
572. La madeja se enreda	Se enreda la pita	The plot thickens
573. La letra con sangre entra		There's no royal road to learning
574. La mayor parte de	Los más de	The majority of; most of
575. La niña de mis (tus, etc.) ojos		The apple of one's eye
576. La necesidad hace maestro		Necessity is the mother of invention
577. La piedra quieta cría malva	Piedra que rueda no cría moho	A rolling stone gathers no moss
578. La vida no es senda de rosas	No todo es vida y dulzura	Life is not a bed of roses; Life is not all beer and skittles
579. Las verdades amargan	La verdad no peca pero incomoda	Truth begets hatred; the truth hurts

Academy Spanish	American Spanish Variants	English Equivalents
580. Leer entre renglones		To read between the lines
581. Lejos de		Far from
582. Levantar la mesa	Quitar la mesa	To clear the table
583. Levantarse del pie izquierdo	Levantarse de malas	To get up on the wrong side of the bed
584. Librarse de		To get rid of; to escape from
585. Lo de menos		The least of it
586. Lo indicado		What has been stated; that which is stated
587. Lo que el agua trae el agua lleva	Lo del agua, al agua	Easy come, easy go
588. Los estadistas de café		Arm-chair strategists; sidewalk superintendents
589. Los niños y los locos dicen las verdades	Los niños y los borrachos siempre dicen la verdad	Out of the mouths of babes and sucklings
590. Llamar la atención		To attract attention; to reprimand
591. Llegar a las manos	Irse a los moquetes; irse al moño (entre mujeres) (Ch.)	To come to blows; to get into a fight
592. Llegar a ser		To become; to get to be
593. Llevar a cabo		To accomplish; to carry out
594. Llevar la contra		To oppose; to contradict
595. Llevar la delantera		To be ahead
596. Llevar puesto		To be wearing
597. Llevar uno su merecido		To get what's coming (to one)
598. Llevar ventaja		To be ahead; to have a lead
599. Llevarse bien con		To get along well with
600. Llevarse un chasco	Pegarse palo	To be disappointed; to have a setback
601. Llorar a lágrima viva	Llorar como becerro en llano; soltar puchero (Ch.)	To cry like a baby
602. Llover a cántaros	Llover con rabia (Carib.); caer burros aparejados (Carib.)	To rain bucketsful; to pour; to rain cats and dogs
603. Llovido del cielo		Out of a clear blue sky
604. Mal genio	De maleta (Andes)	Bad temper
605. Mal que le pese a uno		Whether one likes it or not
606. Mandar a uno al diablo	Mandar a uno a la porra	(Tell someone to) Go to the devil; (Tell someone to) go jump in the lake
607. Mandar a uno a paseo	Mandar a uno a ver si ya puso la marrana	(Tell someone to) Go fly a kite
608. Más adelante		Farther on; later on
609. ¡Manos a la obra!		Let's get to work
610. Más allá (de)		Farther on; beyond
611. Más bien		Rather
612. Más falso que Judas		As false as a counterfeit penny; worthless as a plugged nickel
613. Más vale pájaro en mano que buitre volando	Más vale pájaro en mano que cien(to) volando; más vale guajito tengo que acocote tendré (Mex.)	A bird in the hand is worth two in the bush
614. Más vale prevenir que lamentar	Un gramo de previsión vale más que una tonelada de curación	An ounce of prevention is worth a pound of cure
615. Más vale tarde que nunca	Nunca es tarde cuando la dicha es buena	Better late than never
616. Matar dos pájaros de un tiro	Matar dos pájaros de una pedrada	To kill two birds with one stone
617. Media naranja		Better half; spouse
618. Mejor dicho		Or rather; better yet
619. Mejor que mejor	Tanto mejor	All the better; so much the better
620. Menos de		Fewer than; less than
621. Menos mal	Date de santos que no fue peor	So much the better; it could have been worse

Academy Spanish	American Spanish Variants	English Equivalents
622. Merecer la pena		To be worthwhile; to be worth the trouble
623. Meter en un puño a uno	Tener a uno agarrado de las greñas	To have someone by the neck; to have someone over a barrel
624. Meter la nariz en todas partes	Meter uno su cuchara en todo	To put one's oar in everywhere; to stick one's nose in others' business
625. Meterlo en el bolsillo	Echarse a uno a la bolsa	To wrap someone around one's little finger
626. Meterse a		To become; to decide to become
627. Meterse con		To pick a fight with
628. Meterse de hoz y coz	Meterse a la brava	To elbow one's way into
629. Mientras más ... más	Entre más ... más (C.A., Col.)	The more ... the more
630. Mientras menos ... menos	Entre menos ... menos (C.A., Col.)	The less ... the less
631. Mirar alrededor		To look around
632. Mirar de hito en hito	Mirar fijamente	To stare at; to eye up and down
633. Mirar de lado		To look askance at; to look at with a side glance
634. Mirar por		To take care of; to look after
635. Molestarse con		To bother about; to take the trouble to
636. Morderse la lengua		To hold one's tongue; to keep quiet
637. ¡Mucho ojo!	Un ojo al gato y otro al garabato	Look out! Watch your step!
638. Mucho ruido, pocas nueces	Tanto cacarear para no poner hueva; más la bulla que la cabuya (Ven.); es más la bulla que las mazorcas (Col.)	Much ado about nothing; his bark is worse than his bite
639. Muchos recuerdos a		Kindest regards to; the best to
640. Muy campante	Como si nada; de muchas correas	Cool as a cucumber
641. Muy de noche		Very late at night
642. Nacer con estrella	Nacer de pie	To be born lucky; to be born with a silver spoon in one's mouth
643. Nada de particular		Nothing unusual; nothing special
644. Nadar en la abundancia	Estar muy pesudo; estar bien parado	To be rolling in money (dough)
645. Negarse a		To refuse to
646. Negocio redondo		Good sound bargain
647. Negro como el carbón	Prieto retinto	As black as ink; as black as the ace of spades
648. ¡Ni a tiros!	¡En absoluto! ¡ni de vainas! (Col.); ¡ni bamba! (Col.)	Not for anything; not for love or money
649. ¡Ni en sueños!	¡Qué esperanza! (Ríopl.; Andes); ¡cuando! (Ec.); ¡frijoles! (Carib.)	By no means! Not on your life!
650. ¡Ni mucho menos!		Far from it! Not by a long shot!
651. Ni siquiera		Not even; not a single
652. ¡Ni soñar!	¡Ni por pienso!	Not even in your dreams! Not by a long shot!
653. Ninguna parte	Ningún lado	Nowhere; no place
654. No andarse por las ramas	No andarse con medias tazas	Not to beat around the bush
655. No cabe duda		There is no doubt; beyond a shadow of a doubt; have (has) got to be (Jones has got to be the best pitcher)
656. No caber en sí de gozo	No caber en el pellejo de gozo	To be beside oneself with joy; to be overcome with joy

Academy Spanish	American Spanish Variants	English Equivalents
657. No caer en la cuenta	No encontrarle el chiste	Not to see the point; not to get it
658. No dar el brazo a torcer	No aflojar un pelo (*Ríopl.*) Andes); hacer pata ancha (*Ríopl.*)	To be stubborn; to be not easily deceived; to be unyielding; to stick to one's guns
659. No dar ni un vaso de agua	Ser muy codo; no darle un grano de arroz al gallo de la Pasión	To be a real Scrooge; to be very stingy
660. No darse por entendido		To pretend not to understand
661. No dejar piedra por mover		To leave no stone unturned
662. No dejarle a uno ni a sol ni a sombra	Seguirlo hasta que se eche	To breathe down someone's neck; to dog someone's footsteps; to bug someone
663. No despegar los labios	No chillar	To keep silent; to keep one's mouth shut
664. No estar para bromas	No estar de humor	To be in no mood for joking; not to be in a laughing mood
665. No hay de qué	De nada; por nada (*Mex.*)	Don't mention it; you're welcome
666. No hay excusa que valga	No hay pero que valga; o la bebes o la derramas	Excuse or no excuse; no buts about it
667. No hay mal que por bien no venga	Una afortunada desgracia	It's an ill wind that blows no good; it's a blessing in disguise
668. ¡No hay que achicarse!	¡No hay que rajarse! (*Mex.*)	Keep your chin up! Keep a stiff upper lip! Don't give in!
669. No hay que darle vueltas		There's no getting around it
670. No importa	No le hace	It doesn't matter; Never mind!
671. No me importa un comino	No me importa un pito; no me importa un cacahuate (*Mex.*); no me importa un cacao (*C.A.*)	I don't care a bit
672. No le suena a uno		It doesn't mean a thing; It doesn't ring a bell
673. No morderse la lengua	Cantar claro; ser claridoso (*Ven., C.A.*)	Not to mince words; to speak straight from the shoulder
674. No poder con	No ser un hueso fácil de roer	Not to be able to stand something (someone); to be too much for one
675. No poder ver a alguien	No poder aguantar a uno; no tragar a uno ni con bombilla de plata (*Ríopl.*)	Not to be able to tolerate (stand) someone
676. No saber dónde meterse	Estar del pin al pon (*Carib.*)	Not to know which way to turn
677. No saber ni jota	No saber ni papa	Not to know a blessed thing; not to know enough to come in out of the rain
678. No se ganó Zamora en una hora	No se ganó Toledo en un credo	Rome wasn't built in a day
679. No ser ni la sombra de uno		Not to be the shadow of one's former self
680. No tener ni en qué caerse muerto	No tener ni segunda camisa; estar arrancado; andar pato (*Ch., Ríopl.*)	Not to have a penny to call one's own; not to have a red cent
681. No tener pelos en la lengua	Ser claridoso (*Ven., C.A.*); hablar a calzón quitado (*Ch., Col.*)	To be outspoken; to speak one's mind
682. No tener pies ni cabeza		Not to make sense
683. No tener precio		To be much esteemed; to be priceless
684. No tener remedio		To be beyond repair (help, recourse); (to say something) can't be helped

Academy Spanish	American Spanish Variants	English Equivalents
685. No todo el monte es orégano	No todo ha de ser chayotes ni vainicas (C.A.)	Things aren't always as we should like them
686. No valer un comino	No valer un cacahuate (Mex.); no valer un cacao; (C.A.); no valer un palo de tabaco (Col.); no valer un taco (Col.); estar para el gato (Ch.)	Not to be worth a brass farthing (cent)
687. Obras son amores, que no buenas razones	Acciones son amores, no besos ni apachurrones	Actions speak louder than words
688. Obstinarse en	Ponerle pino a algo (Ch.); hacer lomo en (Ven.)	To persist in; to insist on
689. Ocurrírsele a uno		To occur to one; to cross one's mind
690. Oír hablar de	Oír mentar	To hear about
691. Ojos que no ven, corazón que no siente	Ojos que no ven tienen menos que sentir	Ignorance is bliss; out of sight, out of mind
692. Oponer resistencia	Pararle el carro a uno; pararle el macho a uno	To offer resistance
693. Otra vez		Again; once more
694. Padre mercader, hijo caballero, nieto limosnero	Padre pulpero, hijo caballero, nieto limosnero (Perú)	Three generations from shirt sleeve to shirt sleeve
695. Pagar a plazos		To pay in installments
696. Pagar en la misma moneda		To get even; tit for tat
697. Pagar los gastos		To pay the expenses; to foot the bill
698. ¡Palabra!	¡Palabra de honor! ¡En serio!	Word of honor! On the level! No fooling! Sure enough!
699. ¡Pamplinas!	¡Pura guasa! ¡Frijoles! (Carib.)	Nonsense! Horsefeathers! Baloney!
700. Para colmo de males	¡No faltaba más!	That's the last straw! That does it! That's the straw that broke the camel's back
701. Parar (la) oreja		To prick up one's ears; to sit up and take notice
702. Pararle los pies a uno	Pararle el carro a uno; pararle el macho a uno	To put an end to something; to put one's foot down
703. Parece mentira		It hardly seems possible; it seems impossible
704. Parecido a		Similar to; like
705. Pares y nones		Odds and evens
706. Participar de		To share in
707. Pasado de moda		Out of style; out of date
708. Pasar de la raya		To go too far
709. Pasar de largo	Pasar de hilo	To pass by (without stopping)
710. Pasar el rato		To pass the time away; to spend the time
711. Pasar estrecheces	Pasar hambres; andar torcido	To feel the pinch
712. Pasar la mano por el lomo	Darle la suave a uno; ser barbero (Mex.)	To butter someone up; to soft-soap someone; to polish the apple; to brown-nose
713. Pasarse sin		To get along without
714. Pasársele a uno		To get over; to forget
715. Pasársele a uno la mano		To overdo; to go too far
716. Paso a paso		Step by step; little by little
717. Pedir prestado	Prestar (C.A., Col.)	To ask (someone) to lend (one something); to borrow
718. Pedirle peras al olmo	Andar buscando guayabas en los magueyes	To try to get blood from a turnip (stone)
719. Pensar de		To have an opinion about; to think of
720. Pensar en		To think about
721. Perder de vista		To lose sight of
722. Perder el hilo de	Perder la hebra de	To lose the thread of
723. Perder la cabeza		To lose one's head (cool)
724. Perder la vista		To go blind

Academy Spanish	American Spanish Variants	English Equivalents
725. Perder los estribos		To lose one's mind; to flip one's lid
726. Perderse de vista		To vanish; to disappear
727. Perro ladrador nunca buen mordedor	Perro que ladra no muerde	Barking dogs seldom bite
728. Pesarle a uno		To be sorry for
729. Plan de estudios		Curriculum; course of study
730. Poco a poco		Little by little; gradually
731. Poco después (de)		A little later; soon after
732. Poco más o menos		More or less; about
733. Poner a uno al corriente	Ponerle al tanto a uno	To inform one; to bring one up to date
734. Poner el grito en el cielo		To make a great fuss; to hit the ceiling
735. Poner en claro		To clear up; to unravel
736. Poner en marcha		To start; to put in motion
737. Poner en ridículo		To humiliate; to make a fool of
738. Poner la mesa		To set the table
739. Poner mucho ojo		To pay close attention
740. Poner pies en polvorosa	Tomar el polvo (Mex., Col.); Emplumárselas (Col.); salir fletado (Ven.)	To run away; to beat it; to take a powder; to hightail it
741. Poner pleito		To sue; to bring charges against
742. Poner reparo(s)		To raise objections
743. Ponerse a	Echarse a	To set about; to begin to
744. Ponerse a la obra		To get to work
745. Ponerse colorado		To blush
746. Ponerse de acuerdo		To come to an agreement
747. Ponerse de pie	Pararse	To get up; to stand
748. Ponerse disgustado	Ponerse bravo; picarse (Col.)	To get angry
749. Ponerse en camino		To start out; to hit the road
750. Ponerse en contra		To oppose
751. Ponérsele a uno carne de gallina		To get gooseflesh; to get goose pimples; to get burr (brrr) bumps
752. Por adelantado	Con anticipación	In advance; beforehand
753. Por ahora	Por el momento	For the present; for right now
754. Por aquí cerca		Around here; close by
755. Por casualidad		By chance; by the way
756. Por consiguiente	Por lo tanto	Therefore; so
757. Por dentro		Inside; within
758. Por detrás		From behind; in back
759. ¿Por dónde?		Which way? Where?
760. Por encima(de)		Above; superficially
761. Por entre		Among; between; through
762. Por extenso		At length; in detail
763. Por fin	A las cansadas (Riopl., Andes); a la cansada (Ec.)	At last; at long last; Finally!
764. Por fórmula		As a matter of form
765. Por fortuna	Por suerte	Fortunately
766. Por fuera		On the outside
767. Por hoy	Por ahora	For the present
768. Por intermedio de		By means of; through
769. Por el hilo se saca el olvillo	Por la hebra se saca el ovillo; En el modo de cortar el queso se conoce al tendero	By their fruits shall ye know them; a fool is known by his laughing
770. Por la mitad		In the middle; in half
771. Por las buenas o por las malas	De mangas o de faldas (Ec.)	Whether one likes it or not; by hook or by crook
772. Por las nubes		Sky-high; up in the clouds
773. Por lo cual	Por cuyo motivo	For which reason; and so
774. Por lo demás		As for the rest; moreover
775. Por fuerza	De juro (Riopl., Andes); juramente (Andes)	Of necessity; necessarily
776. Por lo general	Por regla general; por lo regular	Usually; in general

Academy Spanish	American Spanish Variants	English Equivalents
777. Por lo menos	Cuando menos; al menos	At least
778. Por lo pronto	Por el momento	For the time being
779. Por lo que toca a...		As far as ... is concerned
780. Por lo regular		Ordinarily; as a rule
781. Por lo visto		Apparently; evidently
782. Por más que		However much
783. Por ningún lado		Nowhere; no place
784. Por ningún motivo		Under no circumstances; no way!
785. Por ninguna parte		Nowhere; no place
786. Por otra parte		On the other hand
787. Por poco	Por un pelito de rana; casi, casi	Almost; like(d) to
788. Por primera vez		For the first time
789. Por regla general		Usually; as a rule
790. Por sabido se calla	¡Clarinete!	It goes without saying
791. Por si acaso		Just in case; if by chance
792. Por supuesto	Claro que sí; ¿cómo no?	Of course; certainly
793. Por sus puños		On one's own
794. Por término medio		On the average
795. Por última vez		For the last time
796. Por un lado ... por otro		On one hand ... on the other hand
797. Preguntar por		To inquire about; to ask for (a person)
798. Preguntarse si, cuándo, cómo, etc.		To wonder (if, when, how, etc.)
799. Prender fuego a	Prender candela (Col., Andes)	To set fire to; to set on fire
800. Preocuparse por		To worry about
801. Presentación en sociedad	Fiesta quinceañera	Debutantes' ball; coming-out party
802. Prestar atención		To pay attention; to be alert
803. Prestarse a		To lend itself to; to be used for
804. Presumir de		To consider oneself to be
805. Pretender decir		To mean; to imply
806. Pringar en todas	Ser sjonjolí de todos los moles (Mex.)	To have a finger in every pie
807. Proceder en contra		To take action against
808. Prometer el oro y el moro	Prometer las perlas de la Virgen	To promise wonders (the moon)
809. Pues bien	Pues entonces	All right then; so
810. Puesto que	Ya que	Because of the fact that; since
811. Punto de vista		Point of view; standpoint
812. Punto por punto		Step by step; in detail
813. Puro jarabe de pico	Pura guasa; pura parada (Mex.)	Just talk; lip service; eyewash
814. Que Dios le tenga en la gloria	Que en paz descanse	God rest his soul; may he rest in peace
815. ¿Qué más da?		What's the difference? So what?
816. ¿Qué mosca te picó?		What's the matter with you? What's bugging you?
817. ¿Qué hay de nuevo?	¿Quiubo? (qué hubo) (Mex., Col.)	What's up? What's the good word? How goes it?
818. Quedar bien con		To get along well with; to make a hit with
819. Quedar como postes	Quedarse hecho un idiota	To sit like a bump on a log; to stand there like an idiot
820. Quedar en		To agree (on)
821. Quedar en (de)		To promise to
822. Quedar en los huesos	No quedar más que hueso y cuero	To be a mere skeleton; to be nothing but skin and bones
823. Quedar en paz	Quedar a mano	To be even; to be square
824. Quedar entendido que		To be understood that
825. Quedar mal con		Not to be on good terms with; not to make a hit with

Academy Spanish	American Spanish Variants	English Equivalents
826. Quedarse a la luna de Valencia	Dejarle a uno de a pie; quedarse a la luna de Paita (*Andes*)	To be left holding the bag
827. Quedarse con		To agree to buy (take)
828. Quedarse confundido		To be confused
829. Quedarse para vestir santos	Quedarse para vender estampas y milagros	To be left on the shelf
830. Quemarse las cejas	Quemarse las pestañas; ponerse barbero (*Col.*); machetear (*Mex.*)	To burn the midnight oil; to cram for an exam
831. Querer decir		To mean
832. Quien bien te quiere, te hará llorar	Porque te quiero, te aporreo	Spare the rod and spoil the child
833. Quien fue a Sevilla perdió su silla	El que se fue para la villa perdió su silla	Finders keepers, losers weepers
834. Quien porfía mata venado	Quien mucho porfía logra algún día; hay que hacer collera (*Ch.*)	If at first you don't succeed, try, try again; never say die
835. Quitarse de en medio	Hacerse a un lado; borrarse	To get out of the way
836. Recaer sobre		To devolve upon; to revert to
837. Reducirse a		To amount to; to find oneself forced to
838. Referirse a		To refer to; to have reference to
839. Reflejarse en		To reflect on; to bring credit or discredit to
840. Reflexionar sobre		To reflect on; to think over
841. Rendir cuentas a		To render an accounting to; to present the facts to
842. Reparar en		To notice; to consider
843. Repetir como un perico	El perico dice lo que sabe pero no sabe lo que dice	To parrot (verb); to say by rote
844. Resistirse a		To be unwilling to; to refuse to
845. Responder por		To vouch for; to be responsible for
846. Rezar con	Tener que ver con	To have to do with
847. Risa de conejo	Reír de dientes afuera (*Col., Mex.*); reír a diente pelado (*Ven.*)	Half-hearted laugh
848. Rodearse de		To surround oneself with
849. Romper a		To begin; to suddenly start to; to burst out
850. Ropa blanca	Ropa interior; ropa íntima (feminine)	Underclothes; underwear
851. Saber a		Taste like
852. Saber a (la) gloria		To be delicious
853. Saber al dedillo		To know perfectly; to know in detail
854. Saber de sobra		To be fully aware; to know only too well
855. Saber llevar el compás		To be able to beat time
856. Sacar en limpio		To deduce; to understand
857. Sacar jugo de		To get a lot out of
858. Sacar partido de		To profit (gain) by
859. Sacar ventaja de		To profit by
860. Salir a pedir de boca	Salir al pelo	To be all one could wish for; to suit to a T
861. Salir al encuentro de		To go out to meet
862. Salir de Málaga y entrar en Malagón	Salir de Guatemala y entrar en Guatepeor	Out of the frying pan and into the fire
863. Salir del paso		To manage; to get by
864. Salir ganando		To come out ahead
865. Salirse con la suya		To get one's way; to get away with it
866. Saltar a la vista		To be obvious; not to be able to miss

Academy Spanish	American Spanish Variants	English Equivalents
867. Saludos a todos	Saludes a todos (*Col., Ec.*)	Greetings to all; say hello to everyone; say hey
868. ¡Sea bueno!	¡Tenga corazón! ¡No sea gacho!	Be a sport! Have a heart!
869. Seguir el rastro		To trace; to track down
870. Según el caso		According to the situation; it all depends
871. Según mi entender		As I understand (it)
872. Según parece	Por lo visto	Apparently
873. Sentir en el alma		To be terribly sorry
874. Sentir crecer la hierba	Tener oídos de tísico	To have ears like a fox; to have a sharp ear
875. Sentirse molesto	Embromarse	To be annoyed; to be bothered
876. Sentirse uno así no más	Andar bajo de forma	To feel below par; to be under the weather
877. Ser aficionado a		To be fond of; to be a fan of
878. Ser cabeza de turco		To be the scapegoat; to be the whipping boy; to be a patsy
879. Ser correcto		To be well-mannered
880. Ser de fiar		To be trustworthy; to be dependable
881. Ser de muchas vueltas	Ser muy mañoso	To know a trick (thing) or two
882. Ser de provecho		To be good for
883. Ser de rigor		To be proper; to be indispensable
884. Ser mala pieza	Ser una mala ficha (*Col.*)	To be a misfit (bad penny)
885. Ser mano	Llevar la punta	To lead; to be first
886. Ser menester		To be necessary
887. Ser muy ducho	Ser una trucha	To know the ropes
888. Ser preciso	Ser necesario	To be necessary
889. Ser presentada en sociedad	Cumplir los quince años; celebrar la fiesta quinceañera	To make (one's) social debut; to have a coming-out party
890. Ser una perla		To be a treasure (jewel)
891. Ser un burro; ser un zonzo	Ser un menso (*Mex.*); ser un pendejo (vulgar)	To be an ignoramus (dumbbell, moron)
892. Ser un éxito de taquilla		To be a box-office success (hit)
893. Ser un zángano	Ser un vampiro	To be a parasite (freeloader)
894. Serle a uno igual		To be all the same to one
895. Serle a uno indiferente		To be immaterial to one
896. Servir para	Prestarse a (*C.A.*)	To be used for
897. Sin embargo		Nevertheless
898. Sin falta		Without fail
899. Sin faltar una jota		In minutest detail
900. Sin fin de		Numberless; endless amount
901. Sin novedad		As usual; nothing new
902. Sin parar	De hilo	Endlessly; without a break
903. Sin perjuicio de	Dejando a salvo	Without affecting adversely; setting aside
904. Sin querer		Unintentionally
905. Sin remedio		Beyond solution; hopeless
906. Sin ton ni son		Without rhyme or reason
907. Sobre todo		Especially
908. Sudar la gota gorda	Sudar petróleo	To have a hard time; to sweat blood; to be in a sweat
909. Tal vez	A saber (*C.A.*); ¡quién quita! (*Col.*)	Perhaps; maybe
910. Tan pronto como		As soon as
911. Tanto como		As much as
912. Tanto mejor		So much the better
913. Tanto peor		So much the worse
914. Tarde o temprano		Sooner or later
915. Tener al corriente		To keep someone posted; to keep someone up to date
916. Tener antipatía		To dislike

Academy Spanish	American Spanish Variants	English Equivalents
917. Tener buenas aldabas	Tener buenas agarraderas; tener planca; tener enchufe (*Spain*)	To know the right people; to know influential people; to have a pipeline; to have pull
918. Tener cancha libre	Tener campo y tabla	To have a clear field; to have elbowroom
919. Tener cuidado	Pelar ojo	To be careful; to be watchful
920. Tener deseos de	Provocarle a uno (*Col.*); apetecer (*Spain*)	To be eager to; to want to
921. Tener el riñón bien cubierto	Estar bien parado; tener la canasta baja y el riñón bien cubierto (*Mex.*)	To be well-off; to be well-heeled
922. Tener en cuenta		To consider; to keep in mind
923. Tener en la punta de la lengua		To have on the tip of one's tongue
924. Tener en (la) mente		To have in mind
925. Tener en poco		To hold in low esteem; not to think much of
926. Tener fama de		To have the reputation of
927. Tener fe en		To have faith in
928. Tener ganas de	Apetecer (*Spain*); provocarle a uno (*Col.*)	To feel like; to desire
929. Tener gracia	Ser chistoso	To be funny
930. Tener la culpa		To be to blame
931. Tener la intención de		To mean to; to aim to (*South*)
932. Tener la palabra		To have permission to speak; to have the floor
933. Tener lugar		To take place; to be held
934. Tener mercado con		To trade with
935. Tener mucho mundo		To be sophisticated
936. Tener pesar por	Darle a uno pena	To be sorry about
937. Tener presente		To realize; to bear in mind
938. Tener prisa		To be in a hurry
939. Tener razón		To be right
940. Tener relación con		To have relation (connection) with
941. Tener retraso	Traer retraso; llegar placé (*Ch.*)	To be late
942. Tener sin cuidado		Not to be concerned; to care less
943. Tener trazas		To show signs
944. Tener vara alta	Tener mucha vara	To have far-reaching influence; to carry a big stick
945. Tocante a		Concerning; about; having to do with
946. Tocar de oído		To play by ear
947. Tocar en lo vivo		To hurt deeply; to cut to the quick
948. Tocarle a uno		To concern one; to be one's turn
949. Todas las veces que	Cada que	Whenever; every time that
950. Todavía no	Siempre no	Not yet
951. Todo bicho viviente		Every living soul
952. Todo lo contrario		Just the opposite
953. Todo lo demás		All the rest; everything else
954. Todo lo posible		Everything possible
955. Toma y daca	Dando y dando, pajarito volando	Cash and carry; put your money where your mouth is
956. Tomar a broma		To take as a joke
957. Tomar a pecho		To take to heart
958. Tomar cuerpo		To take shape
959. Tomar el gusto		To begin to like; to take a liking to
960. Tomar el rábano por las hojas		To put the cart before the horse
961. Tomar medidas		To take measures (measurements)

Academy Spanish	American Spanish Variants	English Equivalents
962. Tomar nota de		To take note of; jot down
963. Tomarla con		To pick on; to have a grudge against
964. Tomarle el pelo a uno	Hacerle guaje a uno (Mex.)	To pull someone's leg; to kid someone
965. Tomarle la palabra a uno		To take one at his word
966. Tomarse el trabajo de	Tomarse la molestia de	To take the trouble to
967. Tomarse la libertad de		To take the liberty to
968. Trabajar como una fiera	Trabajar como burro; trabajar como negro	To work like a dog
969. Trabar amistad		To strike up a friendship
970. Traer de cabeza a uno		To drive one crazy
971. Traer retraso		To be behind schedule; to be late
972. ¡Trato hecho!	¡Chóquela! ¡Echeme esos cinco!	It's a deal! Shake on it! Put 'er there!
973. ¡Tres hurras por fulano!	¡Una porra!	Three cheers for
974. Tropezar con	Trompezar con	To encounter; to run into
975. Un bribón de siete suelas	Uno capaz de empeñar la sábana sagrada	An errant rogue; a dirty rat
976. Un no sé qué		A certain something
977. Una comilona	Un banquetazo	A feast fit for a king; quite a spread
978. Una golondrina no hace verano		One swallow does not make a summer
979. Uno que otro		An occasional one; some; a few
980. Unos cuantos		Some; a few
981. Valer la pena		To be worthwhile; to be worth the trouble
982. Valerse de		To avail oneself of; to make use of
983. Variar de opinión		To hold a different opinion; to change one's mind
984. Velar por		To protect; to watch over; to take care of
985. Venir a parar		To turn out; to end up
986. Venirse a tierra		To collapse; to fail
987. Ver visiones		To have false notions; (to be) seeing things
988. ¡Vete a freír espárragos!	¡Vete a freír chongos! (Mex.); ¡vete a freír monos! (Col.); ¡vete a freír mocos! (Andes)	Go peddle your papers! Get lost!
989. Vísteme despacio que tengo prisa	Más vale paso que dure y no que apresure	Haste makes waste; easy does it
990. Volver el estómago	Huacarear (Mex.); echar las migas; dársele vuelta la vianda a uno (Ch.)	To vomit; to have the heaves; to upchuck; to toss one's cookies
991. Voy y vengo	No me tardo un minuto; oritita vengo (Mex.)	I'll be right back; it won't be a minute
992. Y así sucesivamente		And so on
993. Y pico		And some odd; and something
994. Y sanseacabó	Ahí muere	That's final; It's all over with
995. ¡Ya basta!	¡Ya párele! ¡Ya está suave!	That's enough! Hold it!
996. Ya cayó el chivo en el lazo	Este arroz ya se coció	It's in the bag
997. Ya le pasará		He'll get over it
998. Ya lo creo	A la fija (Ríopl.) ¿Cómo no?	Of course; certainly
999. Ya ni llorar es bueno	Nada logras con llorar delante del bien perdido	Don't cry over spilt milk
1000. Zapatero a tus zapatos		Mind your own business

English Index to Spanish Idioms and Proverbs

Parte Segundo Inglés-Español

Al Lector

El auge que desde el principio de la Segunda Guerra Mundial viene cobrando en la América española el aprendizaje del inglés, nos ha movido a recopilar en este breve Diccionario las voces y locuciones más indispensables de esta lengua tal como se habla y escribe en los Estados Unidos de América.

Al igual que en la Sección española-inglesa hemos antepuesto la abreviatura *Am.* y otras de señalados países o regiones a aquellos vocablos o modismos que son de uso exclusivo en alguna región de la América española, o bien de uso frecuentísimo en ésta, aunque ya hayan caído en desuso en la Península. Todo lo cual no excluye la posibilidad de que alguna acepción así designada se oiga en labios de español o sea de uso esporádico en España.

Lo que sí hemos procurado con gran ahinco y anhelamos lograr, presentando al estudioso este caudal indispensable de palabras, es el acercamiento lingüístico de las Américas, como base para nuestra mutua comprensión y como instrumento poderosísimo para nuestra solidaridad.

LOS EDITORES

Lista de Abreviaturas

adj.	adjectivo	*irr.*	irregular
adv.	adverbio	*p.p.*	participio pasado o pasivo
art.	articulo	*pers.*	personal
art. indef.	artículo indefinido	*pl.*	plural
aux.	auxiliar	*pos.*	posesivo
comp.	comparativo	*prep.*	preposición
conj.	conjunción	*pron.*	pronombre
contr.	contracción	*pron. pers.*	pronombre personal
defect.	defectivo	*pron. pos.*	pronombre posesivo
etc.	etcétera	*s.*	sustantivo
ger.	gerundio	*sing.*	singular
gram.	gramatical, gramática	*subj.*	subjuntivo
imperf.	imperfecto	*v.*	verbo
indic.	indicativo	*v. defect.*	verbo defectivo
interj.	interjección	*v. irr.*	verbo irregular
interr.	interrogativo		

Abreviaturas Especiales de Indicación Regional

Am.[1]	Americanismo
Andalucía	
Andes	(Ecuador, Perú, Bolivia)
Arg.	Argentina
Bol.	Bolivia
Carib.	(Cuba, Puerto Rico, República Dominicana)
C.A.	Centroamérica (Guatemala, El Salvador, Honduras, Nicaragua, Costa Rica)

---

[1] Esta abreviatura se emplea para indicar uso general hispanoamericano; se implica a la vez carácter arcaizante en cuanto a España. Se usa también para señalar los vocablos ya poco usados que puedan encontrarse en obras literarias del siglo pasado.

Ch.	Chile
Col.	Colombia
C.R.	Costa Rica
Cuba	
Ec.	El Ecuador
Esp.	España
Guat.	Guatemala
Hond.	Honduras
Méx.	México
N. Esp.	Norte de España
Nic.	Nicaragua
Pan.	Panamá
Par.	Paraguay
Perú	
P.R.	Puerto Rico
Ríopl.	Río de la Plata (La Argentina oriental, el Uruguay)
S.A.	Sudamérica
Sal.	El Salvador
Ur.	El Uruguay
Ven.	Venezuela

Pronunciación Inglesa[2]

I. Vocales

Símbolo fonético	Ortografía inglesa	Ortografía fonética	Explicación de los sonidos
i	see pea	si pi	Equivale a la *i* in *hilo*.
ɪ	bit	bɪt	El sonido más aproximado es la *i* en *virtud*, pero la [ɪ] inglesa es una *i* más abierta tirando a *e* cerrada.
e	late they	lét ðe	Equivale aproximadamente a *ei*; la *i* de este diptongo es muy relajada y más abierta que en español.
ɛ	bet	bɛt	El sonido más aproximado en español es la *e* abierta de *perro*.
æ	sat	sæt	Es una vocal intermedia entre la *a* y la *e*.
ɑ	car	kɑr	Equivale aproximadamente a la *a* en *cargo*.
ɔ	forge	fɔrdʒ	Equivale aproximadamente a la *o* en *corto, corre*.
o	mode	mod	Equivale aproximadamente a *ou*; la *u* de este diptongo es muy relajada y más abierta que en español.
ʊ	pull	pʊl	El sonido más aproximado en español es la *u* en *turrón*, pero la [ʊ] inglesa es todavía más abierta.
u	June moon	dʒun mun	Equivale aproximadamente a la *u* en *uno*.
ə	cudgel apply	kʌdʒəl əplái	Es una *e* muy relajada. No tiene equivalente en español.
ɚ	teacher	titʃɚ	Es una *e* muy relajada, articulada simultáneamente con la *r*. No tiene equivalente en español.

[2] El estudioso puede consultar el importante diccionario de pronunciación norteamericana: Kenyon and Knott, *A Pronouncing Dictionary of American English* (Springfield, Massachusetts: G & C. Merriam Company, Publishers, 1944).

Símbolo fonético	Ortografía inglesa	Ortografía fonética	Explicación de los sonidos
ɜ	earth fur	ɜθ fɜ	Es un sonido intermedio entre la e y la o articulado simultáneamente con la r. Se acerca más a la e que a la o. No tiene equivalente en español.
ʌ	duck	dʌk	Es una vocal intermedia entre la e muy abierta y la o. Se acerca más a la o que a la e. No tiene equivalente en español.

II. Diptongos

aɪ	aisle nice	aɪl naɪs	Equivale aproximadamente a ai en aire.
aʊ	now	naʊ	Equivale aproximadamente a au en causa.
ɔɪ	coy	kɔɪ	Equivale aproximadamente a oy en hoy. El segundo elemento del diptongo es más abierto y débil, tirando a e.
ju	used	juzd	Equivale aproximadamente a iu en ciudad.
jʊ	cure	kjʊr	Equivale aproximadamente al diptongo iu, pero la u es más abierta.

III. Consonantes

p	paper	pépə	Equivale aproximadamente a la p española, pero es aspirada.
b	bat	bæt	La b inglesa es semejante a la b inicial española, pero se pronuncia más explosivamente.
t	tea	ti	Es bastante diferente de la t española. Se articula colocando flojamente la lengua arriba de los dientes incisivos superiores y es aspirada.
d	day	de	Equivale a la d inicial española pronunciada con mayor énfasis.
k	cat kill	kæt kɪl	Equivale aproximadamente a la c española delante de a,o,u pronunciada con aspiracion.
g	go gum ago	go gʌm əgó	Equivale aproximadamente, a la g inicial delante de a,o,u: goma, guerra, gana; sólo que la g inglesa se pronuncia con mayor explosión.
f	fun affair	fʌn əfέr	Equivale aproximadamente a la f española.
v	very	vέrɪ	No tiene equivalente en español. Es una labiodental que se articula con el labio inferior y los dientes incisivos superiores.
θ	thin	θɪn	Equivale aproximadamente a la z en el castellano cazar.
ð	then other	ðɛn ʌðə	Equivale aproximadamente a la d española en pardo.
s	send case cent	sɛnd kes sɛnt	Equivale aproximadamente a la s inicial española de Hispanoamérica; santo.
z	rose these zero	roz ðiz zíro	Equivale aproximadamente a la s sonora en mismo, pero se pronuncia con más sonoridad en inglés.
ʃ	sheet machine nation	ʃit maʃin néʃən	Es una s palatal que no tiene equivalente en español. Suena como la ch francesa; chapeau.
ʒ	vision	vɪʒən	No tiene equivalente en español. Es una palatal fricativa sonora, semejante a la y argentina y uruguaya.
tʃ	chase	tʃes	Equivale aproximadamente a la ch en charla.
dʒ	judge gentle	dʒʌdʒ dʒέntl̩	No tiene equivalente exacto en español. Se parece a la y de inyectar en la pronunciación de uruguayos y argentinos.
m	much	mʌtʃ	Equivale aproximadamente a la m española.
n	none any	nʌn énɪ	Equivale aproximadamente a la n española en nada.

Símbolo fonético	Ortografía inglesa	Ortografía fonética	Explicación de los sonidos
ŋ	eaten button lesson	ítn̩ bʌtn̩ lésn̩	No tiene equivalente en español. Representa la *n* sin la articulación de la vocal anterior.
ŋ	ankle angle ring	æŋkl̩ æŋgl̩ rɪŋ	Equivale a la *n* española en *mango, banco*.
l	late altar fall folly	let ɔ́ltɚ fɔl fɑ́lɪ	La *l* inicial equivale aproximadamente a la *l* española en *lado*. La *l* final de sílaba es más débil que la inicial y semejante a la portuguesa.
l̩	able ankle	ébl̩ æŋkl̩	No tiene equivalente en español. Se pronuncia como la *l* final de sílaba, omitiendo la vocal precedente.
w	weed well wall	wid wɛl wɔl	Equivale a la *u* de los diptongos; *ui, ue, ua, uo*.
h	hat whole	hæt hol	No tiene equivalente exacto en español. Equivale aproximadamente a una *j* suave que se reduce a una simple aspiración.
hw	where	hwɛr	Equivale a una *j* suave seguida de una *w* arriba explicada.
j	year yawn yet	jɪr jɔn jɛt	Equivale a la *i* española en los diptongos *ie, ia, io, iu: hiena*.
r	rose bear	roz bɛr	No tiene equivalente en español. La punta de la lengua se arrolla hacia atrás sin tocar el paladar. A veces se pierde al grado de vocalizarse.

Pronunciación de la *S* del Plural [3]

I. La **-s** del plural es sorda cuando la palabra termina en las consonantes sordas representadas por los símbolos fonéticos [p], [t], [k], [f], [θ]. Pronúnciase como la *s* de *santo:* **caps** [kæps], **gates** [gets], **cats** [kæts], **books** [bʊks], **cliffs** [klɪfs], **lengths** [leŋkθs].
Las excepciones más comunes son: **oath** [oθ], **oaths** [oðz]; **leaf** [lif], **leaves** [livz], **wife** [waɪf], **wives** [waɪvz]; **knife** [naɪf], **knives** [naɪvz]; **calf** [kæf], **calves** [kævz]; **half** [hæf], **halves** [hævz].

II. La **-s** del plural es sonora cuando la palabra termina en vocal (incluyendo la **-y** que se cambia en **-ies**), o en las consonantes sonoras representadas por los símbolos fonéticos [b], [d], [g], [v], [ð], [m], [n], [ŋ], [l]: **cries** [kraɪz], **robes** [robz], **beds** [bɛdz], **logs** [lɔgz], **stoves** [stovz], **lathes** [leðz], **farms** [fɑrmz], **bins** [bɪnz], **kings** [kɪŋz], **falls** [fɔlz], **furs** [fɝz], **papers** [pépɝz], **plows** [plaʊz].

III. Cuando la palabra termina **-en** las consonantes representadas por los símbolos [s], [ʃ], [tʃ], [z], [ʒ], [dʒ], se añade **-es** [ɪz], o **s** [ɪz], si la palabra termina en **-ce, -se, -dge, -ge**: **face** [fes], **faces** [fésɪz]; **kiss** [kɪs], **kisses** [kísɪz]; **ash** [æʃ], **ashes** [æʃɪz]; **lunch** [lʌntʃ], **lunches** [lʌntʃɪz]; **rose** [roz], **roses** [rózɪz]; **judge** [dʒʌdʒ], **judges** [dʒʌdʒɪz].

---

[3] Las mismas reglas se aplican a la pronunciación del genitivo y de la tercera persona del presente de indicativo, singular: **keeps** [kips]; **Kate's** [kets]; **saves** [sevz]; **John's** [dʒɑnz]; **judges** [dʒʌ́dʒɪz]; **Alice's** [ǽlɪsɪz].

El Sustantivo

I. Género

Son masculinos los nombres de varón o animal macho, y son femeninos los nombres de mujer o animal hembra. Los demás son neutros. El artículo definido the se aplica a todos los sustantivos, singular y plural: the man el hombre; the men los hombres; the book el libro; the books los libros; the woman la mujer; the women las mujeres.

En ciertos sustantivos se distingue el género femenino por medio del sufijo -ess: poet poeta; poetess poetisa. A veces es indispensable indicar el género por medio de las palabras male o female, boy o girl, man o woman, she o he: baby boy niño; baby girl niña; woman writer escritora; she-bear osa. En otros casos hay una palabra distinta para cada género; uncle tío; aunt tía.

II. Plural de los Sustantivos[4]

1. Generalmente se forma el plural añadiendo -s al singular: paper, papers papel, papeles; book, books libro, libros; chief, chiefs jefe, jefes.
2. Los sustantivos que terminan en -ch (pronunciada como la ch española), -ss, -x, -sh, -z, y -o añaden -es para formar el plural: arch, arches arco, arcos; kiss, kisses beso, besos; box, boxes caja, cajas; dish, dishes plato, platos; buzz, buzzes zumbido, zumbidos; hero, heroes héroe, héroes. Nótese que los sustantivos terminados en -ch (pronunciada [k]) forman el plural añadiendo -s: monarch, monarchs monarca, monarcas.
3. Los sustantivos que terminan en -fe, y ciertos sustantivos que terminan en -f, cambian estas letras en v y añaden -es: leaf, leaves hoja, hojas; life, lives vida, vidas; wife, wives esposa, esposas; knife, knives cuchillo, cuchillos.
4. Para formar el plural de los sustantivos terminados en -y precedida de consonante cámbiase la -y en -ies: fly, flies mosca, moscas; cry, cries grito, gritos; family, families familia, familias; quantity, quantities cantidad, cantidades. Nótese que los sustantivos terminados en -y precedida de vocal forman el plural añadiendo -s al singular: day, days día, días.
5. Ciertos sustantivos forman el plural de una manera irregular: man, men hombre, hombres; woman, women mujer, mujeres; mouse, mice ratón, ratones; louse, lice piojo, piojos; goose, geese ganso, gansos; tooth, teeth diente, dientes; foot, feet pie, pies; ox, oxen buey, bueyes.
6. Ciertos sustantivos que terminan en -is forman el plural cambiando la i de la terminación en e: axis, axes eje, ejes; the crisis, the crises la crisis, las crisis.

El Adjetivo

El adjetivo inglés es invariable en cuanto a género y número. Normalmente se coloca delante del sustantivo: an interesting book un libro interesante; a large table una mesa grande; beautiful women mujeres hermosas.

[4] Véase las reglas para la pronunciación del plural.

Los comparativos y superlativos. Aunque no hay una regla general, por lo común los adjetivos monosílabos, los adjetivos acentuados en la última sílaba y algunos bisílabos fácilmente pronunciados forman el *comparativo de aumento* y *el superlativo* añadiendo **-er** y **-est**. Los demás adjetivos van precedidos de **more** y **most**.

Nótese que (1) sólo se añaden **-r** y **-st** a los que terminan en -e muda; (2) los adjetivos terminados en -y cambian esta letra en **i**; (3) los adjetivos terminados en consonante precedida de vocal doblan la consonante:

Positivo	Comparativo	Superlativo
tall alto	**taller** más alto	**the tallest** el más alto
wise sabio	**wiser** más sabio	**the wisest** el más sabio
polite cortés	**politer** más cortés	**the politest** el más cortés
happy feliz	**happier** más feliz	**the happiest** el más feliz
fat gordo	**fatter** más gordo	**the fattest** el más gordo
careful cuidadoso	**more careful** más cuidadoso	**the most careful** el más cuidadoso

El superlativo absoluto se forma anteponiendo **very** y a veces **most: very intelligent** muy inteligente; **she is a most beautiful woman** es una mujer hermosísima.

El comparativo y el superlativo de inferioridad se forman con los adverbios **less** y **least: less wise** menos sabio; **the least wise** el menos sabio.

El comparativo de igualdad se forma con el adverbio **as: as poor as** tan pobre como; **as much as** tanto como; **as much money as** tanto dinero como.

Los adjetivos siguientes forman el comparativo y el superlativo de una manera irregular:

good, well	**better**	**best**
bad, ill	**worse**	**worst**
little	**less, lesser**	**least**
far	**farther, further**	**farthest, furthest**
much, many	**more**	**most**
old	**older, elder**	**oldest, eldest**

El Adverbio

Fórmanse muchos adverbios, añadiendo **-ly** al adjetivo: **courteous** cortés, **courteously** cortésmente; **bold** atrevido, **boldly** atrevidamente. Existen las irregularidades siguientes en la formación de los adverbios que terminan en **-ly**: (1) los adjetivos terminados en **-ble** cambian la **-e** en **-y: possible, possibly**; (2) los terminados en **ic** añaden **-ally: poetic, poetically**; (3) los terminados en **-ll** añaden sólo la **-y: full, fully**; (4) los terminados en **-ue** pierden la **-e** final: **true, truly**; (5) los terminados en **-y** cambian la **-y** en **i: happy, happily**.

Como los adjetivos, la mayor parte de los adverbios forman el *comparativo* y el *superlativo* con los adverbios **more** (más), **most** (más), y **very** (muy). Asimismo los adverbios monosílabos añaden **-er** y **-est**:

Positivo	Comparativo	Superlativo	Superlativo Absoluto
boldly	**more boldly**	**most boldly**	**very boldly**
generously	**more generously**	**most generously**	**very generously**

soon	sooner	soonest	very soon
early	earlier	earliest	very early
late	later	latest	very late
near	nearer	nearest	very near
fast	faster	fastest	very fast

Los adverbios siguientes forman el comparativo y el superlativo de una manera irregular:

well	better	best	very well
badly, ill	worse	worst	very badly
little	less	least	very little
much	more	most	very much
far	farther, further	farthest, furthest	very far

Sufijos Comunes en Inglés

-dom denota dominio, jurisdicción, estado, condición, etc.: **kingdom** reino; **martyrdom** martirio; **boredom** aburrimiento; **freedom** libertad.

-ed, -d es la terminación del pretérito y del participio pasivo o pasado de los verbos regulares: **I called** llamé; **called** llamado.

-ee indica la persona que recibe la acción: **addressee** destinatario; **employee** empleado.

-eer denota oficio u ocupación: **engineer** ingeniero; **auctioneer** subastador.

-en a) terminación del participio de muchos verbos irregulares: **fallen, broken, shaken;**
b) sufijo que significa *hecho de*: **golden** dorado, de oro; **wooden** de madera; **leaden** de plomo;
c) terminación verbal equivalente a *hacer*: **whiten** hacer blanco, emblanquecer; **darken** hacer obscuro, obscurecer.

-er a) indica la persona que hace o el agente de la acción del verbo: **player** jugador; **talker** hablador;
b) indica el residente de un lugar: **New Yorker** habitante o residente de Nueva York; **islander** isleño;
c) denota ocupación: **carpenter** carpintero; **baker** panadero.
d) es la terminación del comparativo de adjetivos y adverbios; **taller** más alto; **faster** más aprisa.

-ess úsase para formar el género femenino de ciertos sustantivos: **patroness** patrona; **poetess** poetisa; **countess** condesa.

-est terminación del superlativo: **tallest** el más alto.

-fold sufijo que significa *veces*: **twofold** dos veces; **hundredfold** cien veces.

-ful a) equivale a *lleno*, y tratándose de adjetivos es igual a *-oso*: **hopeful** lleno de esperanzas; **careful** cuidadoso; **wilful** voluntarioso; **merciful** misericordioso; **glassful** un vaso (*lleno*);
b) indica a veces hábito o inclinación: **forgetful** olvidadizo;
c) es a veces equivalente a los sufijos españoles *-ado, -ada*: **handful** puñado; *spoonful* cucharada.

-hood	indica estado, condición, carácter, grupo; a menudo equivale a *-dad*: **motherhood** maternidad; **brotherhood** fraternidad; **childhood** niñez; **falsehood** falsedad.
-ician	denota especialidad en cierto ramo: **musician** músico; **technician** técnico; **electrician** electricista.
-ie	sufijo diminutivo: **birdie** pajarito; **Annie** Anita.
-ing	*a*) sufijo del gerundio: **speaking** hablando; *b*) sufijo del participio activo: **threatening** amenazante; **surprising** sorprendente; *c*) úsase a menudo para formar adjetivos: **running water** agua corriente; **drinking water** agua potable; **waiting room** sala de espera; **washing machine** máquina lavadora; *d*) úsase para formar sustantivos: **understanding** entendimiento; **supplying** abastecimiento; **clothing** ropa; **covering** cobertura; equivale al infinitivo castellano: **swimming is good exercise** el nadar es buen ejercicio.
-ish	*a*) úsase para formar ciertos adjetivos de nacionalidad: **Spanish** español; **English** inglés; **Turkish** turco; *b*) indica semejanza: **boyish** como niño, aniñado; **womanish** como mujer, mujeril, afeminado; **whitish** blancuzco, medio blanco, que tira a blanco.
-less	equivale a *sin, falto de*: **childless** sin hijos; **penniless** sin dinero; en ciertos casos el sufijo inglés se traduce por medio de un prefijo: **countless** innumerable, sin número; **endless** interminable, sin fin.
-like	significa *semejanza*, y equivale a *como, a manera de*: **lifelike** que parece vivo; **childlike** como niño, infantil; **tigerlike** como tigre.
-ly	*a*) sufijo adverbial: **slowly** lentamente; **happily** felizmente; **possibly** posiblemente; *b*) añadido a ciertos sustantivos equivale a *como, a la manera de*: **motherly** como madre, materno; **gentlemanly** como caballero, caballeroso; **friendly** amigable; **manly** varonil; *c*) equivale a *cada* en estos ejemplos: **daily** cada día; diario; **weekly** cada semana, semanal; **monthly** cada mes, mensual; **yearly** cada año, anual.
-ness	úsase para formar sustantivos abstractos: **goodness** bondad; **darkness** obscuridad; **foolishness** tontería; **shamelessness** desvergüenza.
-ship	*a*) úsase para formar sustantivos abstractos: **friendship** amistad; **relationship** relación, parentesco; *b*) denota arte o destreza: **horsemanship** equitación; *c*) expresa dignidad, oficio, cargo, o título: **professorship** profesorado o cátedra; **chairmanship** presidencia (*de un comité, asamblea, etc.*); **lordship** señoría; *d*) a veces expresa tan sólo un estado y su duración: **courtship** galanteo, cortejo, noviazgo.

-some	expresa en alto grado la cualidad representada por el vocablo al cual se añade: **tiresome** que cansa, cansado; **quarrelsome** dado a riñas, pendenciero; **loathsome** que repugna, asqueroso; **burdensome** gravoso.
-th	úsase para formar números ordinales: **fifth** quinto; **tenth** décimo.
-ty	a) terminación de los múltiples de diez: **twenty** veinte; **thirty** treinta; **forty** cuarenta; b) terminación de muchos sustantivos abstractos; equivale frecuentemente al sufijo español -tad o -dad: **beauty** beldad; **paternity** paternidad; **falsity** falsedad.
-ward, -wards	denotan hacia: **homeward** hacia casa; **downward** hacia abajo.
-ways, -wise	expresan manera, dirección, posición, etc.: **edgewise** de lado; **sideways** de lado; **lengthwise** a lo largo.
-y	a) terminación equivalente a los sufijos españoles -ia, -ía: **victory** victoria; **glory** gloria; **courtesy** cortesía; **biology** biología; **astronomy** astronomía; b) sufijo diminutivo: **doggy** perrito; **Johnny** Juanito; c) denota abundancia, y es a menudo equivalente a -udo, -oso, -ado: **rocky** lleno de rocas, rocoso, pedregoso; **rainy** lluvioso; **hairy** lleno de pelo, peludo; **bulky** abultado; **wavy** ondulado; **angry** enojado; d) expresa semejanza: **rosy** rosado, como una rosa, color de rosa.

Números

Consúltese la tabla de la página 35 de la Sección Española-Inglesa para el aprendizaje de los números cardinales y ordinales desde uno hasta un millón.

Verbos Irregulares de la Lengua Inglesa

Se denominan verbos irregulares los que no forman el pretérito o el participio pasivo con la adición de -d o -ed al presente. Obsérvese que en ciertos verbos coexiste la forma regular al lado de la irregular. En otros coexisten dos formas irregulares juntamente con la regular.

Presente	*Pretérito*	*Participio pasivo o pasado*
abide	abode	abode
am, is, are	was, were	been
arise	arose	arisen
awake	awoke, awaked	awaked, awoke
bear	bore	born, borne
beat	beat	beat, beaten
become	became	become
befall	befell	befallen
beget	begat	begotten
begin	began	begun
behold	beheld	beheld
bend	bent	bent
bereave	bereft, bereaved	bereft, bereaved
beseech	besought, beseeched	besought, beseeched
beset	beset	beset
bet	bet	bet

Presente	Pretérito	Participio pasivo o pasado
bid	bid, bade	bidden, bid
bind	bound	bound
bite	bit	bitten, bit
bleed	bled	bled
blow	blew	blown
break	broke	broken
breed	bred	bred
bring	brought	brought
build	built	built
burn	burnt, burned	burnt, burned
burst	burst	burst
buy	bought	bought
can (verbo defectivo)	could	—
cast	cast	cast
catch	caught	caught
chide	chided, chid	chided, chidden
choose	chose	chosen
cleave	cleft, clove, cleaved	cleft, cleaved, cloven
cling	clung	clung
clothe	clad, clothed	clad, clothed
come	came	come
cost	cost	cost
creep	crept	crept
crow	crew, crowed	crowed
cut	cut	cut
deal	dealt	dealt
dig	dug, digged	dug, digged
do	did	done
draw	drew	drawn
dream	dreamt, dreamed	dreamt, dreamed
drink	drank	drunk
drive	drove	driven
dwell	dwelt, dwelled	dwelt, dwelled
eat	ate	eaten
fall	fell	fallen
feed	fed	fed
feel	felt	felt
fight	fought	fought
find	found	found
flee	fled	fled
fling	flung	flung
fly	flew	flown
forbear	forbore	forborne
forbid	forbade	forbidden
foresee	foresaw	foreseen
foretell	foretold	foretold
forget	forgot	forgotten, forgot
forgive	forgave	forgiven
forsake	forsook	forsaken
freeze	froze	frozen
get	got	got, gotten
gild	gilt, gilded	gilt, gilded
gird	girt, girded	girt, girded
give	gave	given
go	went	gone
grind	ground	ground
grow	grew	grown
hang[5]	hung	hung
have, has	had	had
hear	heard	heard
heave	hove, heaved	hove, heaved
hew	hewed	hewn, hewed
hide	hid	hidden, hid
hit	hit	hit
hold	held	held
hurt	hurt	hurt
inlay	inlaid	inlaid

[5] Es regular cuando significa «ahorcar.»

Presente	*Pretérito*	*Participio pasivo o pasado*
keep	kept	kept
kneel	knelt	knelt
knit	knit, knitted	knit, knitted
know	knew	known
lay	laid	laid
lead	led	led
lean	leaned, leant	leaned, leant
leap	leapt, leaped	leapt, leaped
learn	learned, learnt	learned, learnt
leave	left	left
lend	lent	lent
let	let	let
lie[6] (yacer; echarse)	lay	lain
light	lit, lighted	lit, lighted
load	loaded	loaded, laden
lose	lost	lost
make	made	made
may (*verbo defectivo*)	might	—
mean	meant	meant
meet	met	met
melt	melted	melted, molten
mistake	mistook	mistaken
mow	mowed	mown, mowed
must (*verbo defectivo*)	—	—
ought (*verbo defectivo*)	ought	—
pay	paid	paid
put	put	put
quit	quit, quitted	quit, quitted
read [rid]	read [rɛd]	read [rɛd]
rend	rent	rent
rid	rid, ridded	rid, ridded
ride	rode	ridden
ring	rang, rung	rung
rise	rose	risen
run	ran	run
saw	sawed	sawn, sawed
say	said	said
see	saw	seen
seek	sought	sought
sell	sold	sold
send	sent	sent
set	set	set
sew	sewed	sewn, sewed
shake	shook	shaken
shall	should	—
shave	shaved	shaved, shaven
shear	sheared	shorn, sheared
shed	shed	shed
shine[7]	shone	shone
shoe	shod	shod
shoot	shot	shot
show	showed	shown, showed
shred	shred, shredded	shred, shredded
shrink	shrank, shrunk	shrunk, shrunken
shut	shut	shut
sing	sang, sung	sung
sink	sank	sunk
sit	sat	sat
slay	slew	slain
sleep	slept	slept
slide	slid	slid, slidden
sling	slung	slung
slink	slunk	slunk
slit	slit	slit
smell	smelt, smelled	smelt, smelled
smite	smote	smitten

[6] Es regular cuando significa «mentir.»
[7] Es por lo común regular cuando significa «pulir, dar brillo.»

Presente	*Pretérito*	*Participio pasivo o pasado*
sow	sowed	sown, sowed
speak	spoke	spoken
speed	sped, speeded	sped, speeded
spell	spelled, spelt	spelled, spelt
spend	spent	spent
spill	spilled, spilt	spilled, spilt
spin	spun	spun
spit	spit, spat	spit, spat
split	split	split
spread	spread	spread
spring	sprang, sprung	sprung
stand	stood	stood
stave	staved, stove	staved, stove
steal	stole	stolen
stick	stuck	stuck
sting	stung	stung
stink	stank, stunk	stunk
strew	strewed	strewn, strewed
stride	strode	stridden
strike	struck	struck, striken
string	strung	strung
strive	strove, strived	striven, strived
swear	swore	sworn
sweep	swept	swept
swell	swelled	swollen, swelled
swim	swam	swum
swing	swung	swung
take	took	taken
teach	taught	taught
tear	tore	torn
tell	told	told
think	thought	thought
thrive	throve, thrived	thriven, thrived
throw	threw	thrown
thrust	thrust	thrust
tread	trod	trod, trodden
understand	understood	understood
undertake	undertook	undertaken
undo	undid	undone
uphold	upheld	upheld
upset	upset	upset
wake	woke, waked	waked
wear	wore	worn
weave	wove	woven
wed	wedded	wedded, wed
weep	wept	wept
wet	wet, wetted	wet, wetted
will (*verbo auxiliar*)	would	—
win	won	won
wind	wound	wound
withdraw	withdrew	withdrawn
withhold	withheld	withheld
withstand	withstood	withstood
work	worked, wrought	worked, wrought
wring	wrung	wrung
write	wrote	written

A:a

a [ə, e] *art. indef.* un, una; what
— ...! ¡qué ...!; such — tal;
tan.

a·ban·don [əbǽndən] *v.*
abandonar; dejar; *s.* abandono, desahogo,
desenvoltura; entrega.

a·ban·doned [əbǽndənd] *adj.* abandondo; dejado;
perverso; inmoral.

a·ban·don·ment [əbǽndənmənt] *s.* abandono,
abandonamiento; desamparo; desenvoltura,
desembarazo.

a·bashed [əbǽʃt] *adj.* humillado, avergonzado.

a·bate [əbét] *v.* bajar, rebajar; disminuir; acabar
con; mitigar(se); calmarse.

a·bate·ment [əbétmənt] *s.* diminución, merma;
rebaja, descuento; mitigación.

ab·bess [ǽbəs] *s.* abadesa.

ab·bey [ǽbɪ] *s.* abadía, monasterio.

ab·bot [ǽbət] *s.* abad.

ab·bre·vi·ate [əbrívɪet] *v.* abreviar, acortar, reducir.

ab·bre·vi·a·tion [əbriviéʃən] *s.* abreviación,
abreviatura; **initial** — sigla.

ab·di·cate [ǽbdəket] *v.* abdicar, renunciar.

ab·do·men [ǽbdəmən] *s.* abdomen; vientre.

ab·duct [æbdʌkt] *v.* secuestrar, raptar, *Am.* plagiar
(*a alguien*).

ab·duc·tion [æbdʌkʃən] *s.* rapto, robo, secuestro
(*de una persona*).

ab·er·ra·tion [æbəréʃən] *s.* aberración, extravío (*de
la mente*).

a·bet [əbét] *v.* incitar; fomentar.

a·bey·ance [əbéəns] *s.* suspensión; **in** — pendiente.

ab·hor [əbhɔ́r] *v.* aborrecer, odiar, abominar.

ab·hor·rence [əbhɔ́rəns] *s.* aborrecimiento,
aversión.

a·bide [əbáɪd] *v.* quedar, permanecer; morar,
habitar; aguardar; soportar, tolerar; **to** — **by**
conformarse a; atenerse a.

a·bil·i·ty [əbílətɪ] *s.* habilidad, capacidad.

ab·ject [æbdʒékt] *adj.* abatido; vil.

ab·jure [æbdʒúr] *v.* abjurar.

ab·la·tive [ǽblətɪv] *adj.* ablativo.

a·ble [ébl] *adj.* hábil, capaz; competente;
a·ble-bod·ied de cuerpo sano; **to be** — **to** poder;
saber.

a·bly [éblɪ] *adv.* hábilmente.

ab·nor·mal [æbnɔ́rml] *adj.* anormal.

a·board [əbórd] *adv.* a bordo; en el tren; **to go** —
embarcarse; **all** — ! ¡viajeros al tren!; *Méx., C.A.*
¡vámonos!

a·bode [əbód] *s.* morada, domicilio, casa; *pret. &
p.p. de* **to abide.**

a·bol·ish [əbálɪʃ] *v.* abolir; anular.

ab·o·li·tion [æbəlíʃən] *s.* abolición.

a·bom·i·na·ble [əbámnəbl] *adj.* abominable,
aborrecible.

a·bort [əbórt] *v.* abortar.

a·bor·tion [əbórʃən] *s.* aborto.

a·bound [əbáund] *v.* abundar; **to** — **with** abundar
en.

a·bout [əbáut] *prep.* (*concerning*) acerca de, tocante
a, respecto de; (*near, surrounding*) alrededor de,
por; *adv.* (*almost*) casi, poco más o menos; **at** —
ten o'clock a eso de las diez; **to be** — **one's
business** atender a su negocio; **to be** — **to** estar
para, estar a punto de; **to face** — dar media
vuelta; **to have no money** — **one's person** no
llevar dinero consigo.

a·bove [əbʌ́v] *prep.* por encima de; sobre; *adv.*
arriba; — **all** sobre todo; **a·bove-men·tioned**
susodicho, ya mencionado; **from** — de arriba;

del cielo, de Dios.

ab·ra·sive [əbrésɪv] *adj.* abrasivo; tosco.

a·breast [əbrést] *adj., adv.* al lado; **to keep abreast**
ponerse al corriente.

a·bridge [əbrídʒ] *v.* abreviar; compendiar,
condensar; privar (*a uno de sus derechos*).

a·broad [əbrɔ́d] *adv.* en el extranjero; fuera de
casa; **to go** — ir al extranjero; **to spread** —
divulgar o publicar por todas partes.

a·brupt [əbrʌ́pt] *adj.* repentino; precipitado;
áspero, brusco; escarpado; **-ly** *adv.* de repente;
bruscamente.

ab·scess [ǽbsɛs] *s.* absceso.

ab·sence [ǽbsns] *s.* ausencia; falta; — **of mind**
abstracción; **leave of** — licencia (*para
ausentarse*).

ab·sent [ǽbsnt] *adj.* ausente; abstraído, distraído;
ab·sent-mind·ed absorto, abstraído; [æbsént] *v.*
to — **oneself** ausentarse.

ab·sinthe [ǽbsɪnθ] *s.* ajenjo.

ab·so·lute [ǽbsəlut] *adj.* absoluto; **the** — lo
absoluto; **-ly** *adv.* absolutamente; en absoluto.

ab·so·lu·tion [æbsəlúʃən] *s.* absolución.

ab·solve [æbsálv] *v.* absolver, remitir; perdonar,
alzar la pena o el castigo.

ab·sorb [əbsórb] *v.* absorber.

ab·sorb·ent [əbsórbənt] *adj. & s.* absorbente.

ab·sorp·tion [əbsórpʃən] *s.* absorción; abstracción,
embebecimiento.

ab·stain [əbstén] *v.* abstenerse, privarse.

ab·sti·nence [ǽbstənəns] *s.* abstinencia.

ab·stract [ǽbstrækt] *adj.* abstracto; *s.* sumario;
extracto; **in the** — en abstracto; [æbstrǽkt] *v.*
abstraer; considerar aisladamente; separar,
retirar; resumir, compendiar.

ab·strac·tion [æbstrǽkʃən] *s.* abstracción; idea
abstracta.

ab·surd [əbsɑ́d] *adj.* absurdo; insensato; ridículo,
disparatado.

ab·sur·di·ty [əbsɑ́dətɪ] *s.* absurdo, disparate.

a·bun·dance [əbʌ́ndəns] *s.* abundancia, copia.

a·bun·dant [əbʌ́ndənt] *adj.* abundante, copioso.

a·buse [əbjús] *s.* abuso; maltrato; ultraje; [əbjúz] *v.*
abusar de; maltratar; injuriar; ultrajar.

a·bu·sive [əbjúsɪv] *adj.* abusivo; insultante,
injurioso.

a·byss [əbís] *s.* abismo; sima.

ac·a·dem·ic [əkædémɪk] *adj.* académico; escolar.

a·cad·e·my [əkǽdəmɪ] *s.* academia; colegio,
instituto; escuela preparatoria.

ac·cede [æksíd] *v.* acceder, consentir.

ac·cel·er·ate [ækséləret] *v.* acelerar(se).

ac·cel·er·a·tion [ækseləréʃən] *s.* aceleración.

ac·cel·er·a·tor [ækséləretə] *s.* acelerador.

ac·cent [ǽksɛnt] *s.* acento; [æksént] *v.* acentuar;
recalcar.

ac·cen·tu·ate [ækséntʃuet] *v.* acentuar; recalcar;
realzar.

ac·cept [əksépt] *v.* aceptar; admitir; acoger;
aprobar.

ac·cept·a·ble [əkséptəbl] *adj.* aceptable; grato;
acepto.

ac·cep·tance [əkséptəns] *s.* aceptación; aprobación,
buena acogida, recibimiento.

ac·cess [ǽksɛs] *s.* acceso; ataque (*de una
enfermedad*); arrebato (*de furia*).

ac·ces·si·ble [æksésəbl] *adj.* accesible; asequible,
obtenible.

ac·ces·so·ry [æksésərɪ] *adj.* accesorio; adjunto; *s.*
accesorio; cómplice; **ac·ces·so·ries** cosas
accesorias, adornos, adminículos.

ac·ci·dent [æksədənt] s. accidente; percance, contratiempo; **by —** por casualidad.
ac·ci·den·tal [æksədéntl] adj. accidental; casual; **-ly** adv. accidentalmente; por casualidad.
ac·claim [əklém] v. aclamar, aplaudir; s. aclamación, aplauso.
ac·cla·ma·tion [ækləméʃən] s. aclamación, aplauso.
ac·cli·mate [əkláɪmət], [ǽkləmet] v. aclimatar(se); acostumbrar(se).
ac·cli·ma·tize [əkláɪmətaɪz] v. aclimatar(se).
ac·com·mo·date [əkɑmədét] v. (adjust) acomodar, ajustar, ayudar, hacer un favor; (lodge) hospedar, alojar, tener cabida para; **to — oneself** conformarse, adaptarse.
ac·com·mo·da·tion [əkɑmədéʃən] s. favor, ayuda; conveniencia; alojamiento (en un hotel, casa, ect.); cabida; adaptación; ajuste.
ac·com·pa·ni·ment [əkÁmpənɪmənt] s. acompañamiento.
ac·com·pa·nist [əkÁmpənɪst] s. acompañador, acompañante.
ac·com·pa·ny [əkÁmpənɪ] v. acompañar.
ac·com·plice [əkÁmplɪs] s. cómplice.
ac·com·plish [əkÁmplɪʃ] v. cumplir; completar; lograr, conseguir; realizar, efectuar.
ac·com·plished [əkÁmplɪʃt] adj. cumplido; realizado; consumado; establecido; diestro; perfecto.
ac·com·plish·ment [əkÁmplɪʃmənt] s. cumplimiento; logro, realización; habilidad; perfección; mérito, proeza.
ac·cord [əkɔ́rd] s. acuerdo, convenio; armonía, concierto; **of one's own —** voluntariamente; espontáneamente; **in — with** de acuerdo con; **with one —** unánimemente; v. otorgar, conceder, dar; concordar.
ac·cord·ance [əkɔ́rdṇs] s. conformidad, acuerdo; **in — with** de acuerdo con, de conformidad con.
ac·cord·ing [əkɔ́rdɪŋ]: **— to** según; conforme a; de acuerdo con; **— as** según (que), a medida que.
ac·cord·ing·ly [əkɔ́rdɪŋlɪ] adv. en conformidad; así; como tal; por lo tanto; por consiguiente.
ac·cor·di·on [əkɔ́rdɪən] s. acordeón.
ac·cost [əkɔ́st] v. abordar (a alguien) en la calle, acosar; molestar, perseguir.
ac·count [əkáʊnt] s. (bill) cuenta, computación; (story) relato; **on — of** a causa de; con motivo de; por; **on my —** por mí; **on my own —** por mi propia cuenta; **on no —** de ninguna manera; **of no —** de ningún valor o importancia; **to turn to —** aprovechar, hacer útil o provechoso; v. dar cuenta (a); considerar, tener por; **to — for** dar cuenta o razón de; explicar; **how do you — for that?** ¿cómo se explica eso?
ac·count·a·ble [əkáʊntəbl] adj. responsable; explicable.
ac·count·ant [əkáʊntənt] s. contador, tenedor de libros.
ac·count·ing [əkáʊntɪŋ] s. contabilidad, contaduría.
ac·cred·it [əkrédɪt] v. acreditar.
ac·crue [əkrú] v. acumular(se).
ac·cul·tur·ate [əkÁltʃɹet] v. aculturar(se).
ac·cu·mu·late [əkjúmjəlet] v. acumular(se), juntar(se), amontonar(se).
ac·cu·mu·la·tion [əkjumjəléʃən] s. acumulación, amontonamiento.
ac·cu·ra·cy [ǽkjərəsɪ] s. precisión, exactitud, esmero.
ac·cu·rate [ǽkjərɪt] adj. preciso, exacto; correcto; esmerado; cierto; certero; acertado; **-ly** adv. con

exctitud; correctamente; con esmero.
ac·cursed [əkɝ́st] adj. maldito; infame.
ac·cu·sa·tion [ækjəzéʃən] s. acusación.
ac·cu·sa·tive [əkjúzətɪv] adj. acusativo.
ac·cuse [əkjúz] v. acusar; denunciar.
ac·cus·er [əkjúzɚ] s. acusador; delator, denunciador.
ac·cus·tom [əkÁstəm] v. acostumbrar; **to — oneself** acostumbrarse; **to be -ed to** tener la costumbre de, acostumbrar, soler; estar acostumbrado a, estar hecho a.
ace [es] s. as; as, el mejor de su clase (como un aviador excelente); **within an — of** a punto de; muy cerca de.
ac·e·tate [ǽsatet] s. acetato.
a·cet·y·lene [əsétəlin] s. acetileno.
ache [ek] s. dolor; **tooth —** dolor de muelas; v. doler.
a·chieve [ətʃív] v. acabar, llevar a cabo; realizar; conseguir, lograr; alcanzar.
a·chieve·ment [ətʃívmənt] s. logro, realización; proeza, hazaña.
ac·id [ǽsɪd] adj. ácido; agrio; s. ácido.
ac·id·i·ty [əsídətɪ] s. acidez.
ac·knowl·edge [əknálɪdʒ] v. reconocer, admitir; confesar; **to — receipt** acusar recibo.
ac·knowl·edg·ment [əknálɪdʒmənt] s. reconocimiento, expresión de gratitud; confesión, admisión; **— of receipt** acuse de recibo.
a·corn [ékɔrn] s. bellota.
a·cous·tics [əkústɪks] s. acústica.
ac·quaint [əkwént] v. enterar, informar; dar a conocer; familiarizar; **to — oneself with** ponerse al corriente de; enterarse de; **to be -ed with** conocer a (una persona); estar enterado de (algo); conocer (una ciudad, un país, etc.).
ac·quain·tance [əkwéntəns] s. conocimiento; conocido; **-s** amistades.
ac·qui·esce [ækwɪés] v. asentir; consentir, quedar conforme.
ac·qui·es·cence [ækwɪésns] s. asentimiento, consentimiento; conformidad.
ac·quire [əkwáɪr] v. adquirir; obtener, conseguir; contraer (costumbres, vicios).
ac·qui·si·tion [ækwəzíʃən] s. adquisición.
ac·quit [əkwít] v. absolver, exonerar; pagar, redimir, librar de (una obligación); **to — oneself well** quedar bien; portarse bien.
ac·quit·tal [əkwítl] s. absolución.
a·cre [ékɚ] s. acre (medida de superficie).
ac·ro·bat [ǽkrəbæt] s. acróbata.
ac·ro·nym [ǽkrənɪm] s. acrónimo.
a·cross [əkrɔ́s] prep. a través de; al otro lado de; por; por en medio de; adv. a través de; través; **to go —** atravesar; **to come —, run —** encontrarse con; tropezar con.
ac·ryl·ic [əkrílɪk] adj. acrílico.
act [ækt] s. acto, acción, hecho; v. hacer, desempeñar (un papel); representar (en el teatro); obrar; actuar; portarse; funcionar; **to — as** servir de, estar de.
act·ing [ǽktɪŋ] s. representación, desempeño (de un papel dramático); acción, actuación; adj. interino, suplente.
ac·tion [ǽkʃən] s. acción; acto; actuación; funcionamiento.
ac·ti·vate [ǽktəvet] v. activar.
ac·tive [ǽktɪv] adj. activo.
ac·tiv·ism [ǽktəvɪzm] s. activismo.
ac·tiv·ist [ǽktəvɪst] s. activista.
ac·tiv·i·ty [æktívətɪ] s. actividad.

ac·tor [ǽktɚ] *s.* actor.
ac·tress [ǽktrɪs] *s.* actriz.
ac·tu·al [ǽktʃʊəl] *adj.* (*legitimate*) verdadero, real; (*current*) actual, existente; **-ly** *adv.* realmente, en realidad; de hecho, efectivamente.
a·cu·men [əkjúmɪn] *s.* caletre, tino, perspicacia.
a·cute [əkjút] *adj.* agudo; perspicaz; penetrante.
ad·a·mant [ǽdəmænt] *adj.* duro; firme, inflexible.
a·dapt [ədǽpt] *v.* adaptar; **to — oneself** adaptarse, acomodarse.
ad·ap·ta·tion [ædəptéʃən] *s.* adaptación.
add [æd] *v.* sumar; añadir, agregar.
ad·dict [ǽdɪkt] *s.* adicto (*persona adicta al uso de narcóticos*); **drug —** morfinómano.
ad·dic·ted [ədíktɪd] *adj.* adicto, dado, entregado, habituado.
ad·di·tion [ədíʃən] *s.* adición; suma; añadidura, aditamento; **in — to** además de.
ad·di·tion·al [ədíʃənl] *adj.* adicional.
ad·di·tive [ǽdətɪv] *s. & adj.* aditivo.
ad·dress [ədrɛ́] *s.* (*street*) dirección, domicilio, señas; sobrescrito; (*speech*) discurso, arenga, conferencia; **form of —** tratamiento; *v.* dirigir, poner la dirección, señas o sobrescrito a; hablar, dirigir la palabra a; dirigirse a; **to — oneself to a task** aplicarse a una tarea.
ad·dress·ee [ədrɛsí] *s.* destinatario.
ad·duce [ədús] *v.* aducir.
a·dept [ədépt] *adj.* hábil; perito.
ad·e·quate [ǽdəkwɪt] *adj.* adecuado; proporcionado; suficiente.
ad·here [ədhír] *v.* adherirse; pegarse.
ad·her·ence [ədhírəns] *s.* adherencia.
ad·he·sion [ədhíʒən] *s.* adhesión.
ad·he·sive [ədhísɪv] *adj.* adhesivo; pegajoso; — **tape** tela adhesiva, esparadrapo.
ad·ja·cent [ədʒésn̩t] *adj.* adyacente, contiguo.
ad·jec·tive [ǽdʒɪktɪv] *s.* adjetivo.
ad·join [ədʒɔ́ɪn] *v.* estar contiguo o adyacente a, lindar con.
ad·journ [ədʒɝ́n] *v.* aplazar, diferir; **to — the meeting** suspender o levantar la sesión; **meeting -ed** se levanta la sesión.
ad·journ·ment [ədʒɝ́nmənt] *s.* aplazamiento, levantamiento (*de una sesión*).
ad·junct [ǽdʒʌŋkt] *s.* adjunto, aditamento, añadidura; asociado, acompañante; *adj.* adjunto, unido, subordinado.
ad·just [ədʒʌ́st] *v.* ajustar; acomodar; arreglar; graduar; **to — oneself** adaptarse, conformarse.
ad·just·ment [ədʒʌ́stmənt] *s.* ajuste; ajustamiento; arreglo; regulación.
ad-lib [ǽdlíb] *v.* improvisar; expresarse espontáneamente.
ad·min·is·ter [ədmínəstɚ] *v.* administrar; dirigir, regir, gobernar; aplicar (*remedio, castigo, etc.*); **to — an oath** tomar juramento.
ad·min·is·tra·tion [ədmɪnəstréʃən] *s.* administración; dirección, gobierno; gerencia; manejo.
ad·min·is·tra·tive [ədmínəstretɪv] *adj.* administrativo; ejecutivo; gubernativo.
ad·min·is·tra·tor [ədmínəstretɚ] *s.* administrador.
ad·mi·ra·ble [ǽdmərəbl] *adj.* admirable.
ad·mi·ra·bly [ǽdmərəblɪ] *adv.* admirablemente.
ad·mi·ral [ǽdmərəl] *s.* almirante.
ad·mi·ra·tion [ædməréʃən] *s.* admiración.
ad·mire [ədmáɪr] *v.* admirar; estimar.
ad·mir·er [ədmáɪrɚ] *s.* admirador; pretendiente.
ad·mis·si·ble [ədmísabl] *adj.* admisible.
ad·mis·sion [ədmíʃən] *s.* (*entrance*) entrada, precio

de entrada o de ingreso; (*confession*) confesión, admisión.
ad·mit [ədmít] *v.* admitir; aceptar; confesar, reconocer; conceder; dar entrada.
ad·mit·tance [ədmítn̩s] *s.* entrada; derecho de entrar; admisión.
ad·mon·ish [ədmánɪʃ] *v.* amonestar.
ad·mo·ni·tion [ædməníʃən] *s.* amonestación, consejo.
a·do [ədú] *s.* actividad; bulla; disturbio.
a·do·be [ədóbɪ] *s.* adobe; casa de adobe.
ad·o·les·cence [ædlésn̩s] *s.* adolescencia.
ad·o·les·cent [ædlésn̩t] *adj. & s.* adolescente.
a·dopt [ədápt] *v.* adoptar; ahijar, prophijar.
a·dop·tion [ədápʃən] *s.* adopción.
a·dor·a·ble [ədórəbl] *adj.* adorable; encantador.
ad·o·ra·tion [ædəréʃən] *s.* adoración.
a·dore [ədór] *v.* adorar.
a·dorn [ədɔ́rn] *v.* adornar; ornar; embellecer.
a·dorn·ment [ədɔ́rnmənt] *s.* adorno.
ad·re·nal [ədrínl] *adj.* suprarrenal.
ad·ren·a·lin [ədrénəlɪn] *s.* adrenalina.
a·drift [ədríft] *adj. & adv.* a la deriva, flotando, flotante.
a·droit [ədrɔ́ɪt] *adj.* hábil, diestro.
a·dult [ədʌ́lt] *adj. & s.* adulto.
a·dul·ter·ate [ədʌ́ltəret] *v.* adulterar.
a·dul·ter·er [ədʌ́ltərɚ] *s.* adúltero.
a·dul·ter·y [ədʌ́ltərɪ] *s.* adulterio.
ad·vance [ədvǽns] *v.* (*progress*) avanzar, adelantar; progresar; acelerar; (*promote*) promover; proponer; (*pay beforehand*) pagar por adelantado o anticipado; *s.* avance; progreso; adelanto, anticipo; alza aumento de precio; **-s** requerimiento, pretensiones, insinuaciones; **in —** por adelantado, con anticipación.
ad·vanced [ədvǽnst] *adj.* avanzado; adelantado; **— in years** entrado en años, viejo, anciano.
ad·vance·ment [ədvǽnsmənt] *s.* adelantamiento, mejora, progreso; promoción.
ad·van·tage [ədvǽntɪdʒ] *s.* ventaja; beneficio; provecho; **to have the — over** llevar ventaja a; **to take — of** aprovecharse de; **to take — of a person** abusar de la confianza o paciencia de alguien.
ad·van·ta·geous [ædvəntédʒəs] *adj.* ventajoso; provechoso.
ad·vent [ǽdvɛnt] *s.* advenimiento; venida.·
ad·ven·ture [ədvéntʃɚ] *s.* aventura; riesgo.
ad·ven·tur·er [ədvéntʃərɚ] *s.* aventurero.
ad·ven·tur·ous [ədvéntʃərəs] *adj.* aventurero; atrevido; aventurado; arriesgado.
ad·verb [ǽdvɝb] *m.* adverbio.
ad·ver·sar·y [ǽdvɚsɛrɪ] *s.* adversario, antagonista, contrario.
ad·verse [ədvɝ́s] *adj.* adverso; opuesto, contrario; hostil; desfavorable.
ad·ver·si·ty [ədvɝ́səti] *s.* adversidad; infortunio.
ad·ver·tise [ǽdvɚtaɪz] *v.* anunciar; avisar, dar viso.
ad·ver·tise·ment [ædvɚtáɪzmənt] *s.* anuncio, aviso.
ad·ver·tis·er [ǽdvɚtaɪzɚ] *s.* anunciador, anunciante.
ad·ver·tis·ing [ǽdvɚtaɪzɪŋ] *s.* anuncios; arte o negocio de anunciar.
ad·vice [ədváɪs] *s.* aviso, advertencia; consejo; noticia.
ad·vis·a·ble [ədváɪzəbl] *adj.* conveniente; prudente; recomendable.
ad·vise [ədváɪz] *v.* (*counsel*) aconsejar; (*inform*) avisar, informar, advertir; **to — with** consultar con; aconsejarse con.

ad · vis · er, ad · vi · sor [ədváɪzəɾ] *s.* consejero, aconsejador.

ad · vo · cate [ǽdvəkɪt] *s.* abogado; defensor, intercesor; partidario; [ǽdvəket] *v.* abogar por; defender.

aer · i · al [ɛ́rɪəl] *adj.* aéreo; *s.* antena.

aer · o · dy · nam · ic [ɛrodaɪnǽmɪk] *adj.* aerodinámico; aerodynamics; *s.* aerodinámica.

aer · o · plane [ɛ́rəplen] = **airplane.**

aer · o · sol [ɛ́rosol] *s.* aerosol.

aes · thet · ic [ɛsθétɪk] *adj.* estético; **-s** *s.* estética.

a · far [əfáɾ] *adv.* lejos; **from** — desde lejos.

af · fa · ble [ǽfəbl] *adj.* afable, amable.

af · fair [əfɛ́r] *s.* (*social*) función, tertulia, fiesta, convite; (*venture*) asunto; negocio; lance; cosa; **love** — amorío.

af · fect [əfɛ́kt] *v.* afectar; conmover; fingir; hacer ostentación de.

af · fec · ta · tion [æfɪktéʃən] *s.* afectación.

af · fect · ed [əfɛ́ktɪd] *adj.* (*emotion*) afectado, conmovido, enternecido; (*feigned*) fingido, artificioso.

af · fec · tion [əfékʃən] *s.* afecto, cariño; inclinación; afección, dolencia.

af · fec · tion · ate [əfékʃənɪt] *adj.* afectuoso, cariñoso.

af · fi · da · vit [æfədévɪt] *s.* declaración jurada.

af · fil · i · ate [əfíliet] *v.* afiliar; afiliarse, unirse, asociarse.

af · fin · i · ty [əfínətɪ] *s.* afinidad.

af · firm [əfɝ́m] *v.* afirmar, asegurar, aseverar.

af · firm · a · tive [əfɝ́mətɪv] *adj.* afirmativo; *s.* afirmativa.

af · fix [əfíks] *v.* fijar, pegar; **to** — **one's signature** poner su firma, firmar.

af · flict [əflíkt] *v.* afligir; **to be -ed with** padecer de sufrir de, adolecer de.

af · flic · tion [əflíkʃən] *s.* aflicción; pena, dolor; achaque; angustia; infortunio.

af · flu · ent [ǽfluənt] *adj.* acaudalado; abundante.

af · ford [əfórd] *v.* proveer, proporcionar; **I cannot** — **that expense** no puedo hacer ese gasto; **he cannot** — **to waste time** no le conviene perder el tiempo; no tiene tiempo que perder; **I cannot** — **that risk** no puedo (*o* no quiero) exponerme a ese riesgo.

af · fri · cate [ǽfrɪkət] *adj. & s.* africado.

af · front [əfrʌ́nt] *s.* afrenta, agravio, ultraje; *v.* afrentar, agraviar, ultrajar.

a · fire [əfáɪr] *adj.* ardiendo, quemándose.

a · float [əflót] *adj. & adv.* flotante; flotando; a flote; a flor de agua; a bordo; inundado; a la deriva, sin rumbo; **the rumor is** — corre la voz.

a · foot [əfút] *adv.* a pie; en marcha, en movimiento.

a · fore · said [əfórsɛd] *adj.* susodicho, ya dicho.

a · fraid [əfréd] *adj.* miedoso, medroso; atemorizado, amedrentado; **to be** — temer, tener miedo.

a · fresh [əfréʃ] *adv.* de nuevo, desde el principio.

Af · ri · can [ǽfrɪkən] *adj. & s.* africano; negro.

af · ter [ǽftəɾ] *prep.* (*temporal*) después de, tras, tras de; (*position*) detrás de; (*following*) en busca de; *adv.* después; detrás; *conj.* después (de) que; *adj.* subsiguiente; siguiente; — **all** después de todo; de todos modos; **day** — **tomorrow** pasado mañana; **after-dinner** de sobremesa; —**effect** consecuencia, resultado; —**math** consecuencias, resultados (*usualmente desastrosos*); —**thought** idea tardía.

af · ter · noon [æftəɾnún] *s.* tarde.

af · ter · taste [ǽftəɾtest] *s.* dejo, dejillo (*sabor que queda en la boca*).

af · ter · wards [ǽftəɾwəɾdz] *adv.* después.

a · gain [əgén] *adv.* otra vez, de nuevo; además; por otra parte; — **and** — repetidas veces; **never** — nunca jamás; **to come** — volver; **to do it** — volver a hacerlo.

a · gainst [əgénst] *prep.* contra; frente a; en contraste con; — **the grain** a contrapelo, a redopelo; — **a rainy day** para cuando llueva.

age [edʒ] *s.* edad; época; siglo; generación; **of** — mayor de edad; **old** — vejez, ancianidad; **to become of** — llegar a mayor edad; **under** — menor de edad; *v.* envejecer(se).

a · ged [édʒɪd, édʒd] *adj.* viejo, anciano; añejo; envejecido; — **forty years** de cuarenta años; — **in wood** añejado en toneles o barriles (*dícese del vino*).

a · gen · cy [édʒənsɪ] *s.* agencia; medio, intermedio.

a · gen · da [ədʒɛ́ndə] *s.* temario; asuntos que han de tratarse en una reunión.

a · gent [édʒənt] *s.* agente; intermediario, representante; apoderado.

ag · glu · ti · na · tive [əglútɪnətɪv] *adj.* aglutinante.

ag · gran · dize [ǽgrəndaɪz] *v.* engrandecer; agrandar.

ag · gra · vate [ǽgrəvet] *v.* agravar, empeorar; irritar, exasperar.

ag · gre · gate [ǽgrɪgɪt] *s.* agregado, conjunto, colección; *adj.* agregado, unido; **in the** — en conjunto.

ag · gres · sion [əgréʃən] *s.* agresión.

ag · gres · sive [əgrésɪv] *adj.* agresivo; emprendedor.

ag · gres · sor [əgrésəɾ] *s.* agresor.

a · ghast [əgǽst] *adj.* espantado, pasmado.

ag · ile [ǽdʒəl] *adj.* ágil.

a · gil · i · ty [ədʒílətɪ] *s.* agilidad.

ag · i · tate [ǽdʒətet] *v.* agitar; turbar, perturbar; alborotar; discutir acaloradamente; maquinar, tramar.

ag · i · ta · tion [ædʒətéʃən] *s.* agitación; alboroto.

ag · i · ta · tor [ǽdʒətetəɾ] *s.* agitador, alborotador, revoltoso.

ag · nos · tic [ægnástɪk] *adj. s.* agnóstico.

a · go [əgó] *adj. & adv.* pasado; en el pasado; **many years** — hace muchos años; muchos años ha, mucho tiempo ha; **long** — hace mucho tiempo; ha mucho.

ag · o · nize [ǽgənaɪz] *v.* agonizar; sufrir angustiosamente; retorcerse de dolor; luchar.

ag · o · ny [ǽgənɪ] *s.* agonía; angustia; tormento; dolor; lucha.

a · geee [əgrí] *v.* (*accede*) acordar, concordar, consentir, estar de acuerdo, ponerse de acuerdo; (*suit*) sentarle bien a uno (*dícese del clima, del alimento, etc.*).

a · gree · a · ble [əgríəbl] *adj.* agradable, afable; complaciente; conveniente; satisfactorio.

a · gree · ment [əgrímənt] *s.* (*concord*) acuerdo, convenio, conformidad; (*grammatical*) concordancia; **to be in** — estar de acuerdo; **to come to an** — ponerse de acuerdo.

ag · ri · cul · tur · al [ægrɪkʌ́ltʃərəl] *adj.* agrícola.

ag · ri · cul · ture [ǽgrɪkʌltʃəɾ] *s.* agricultura.

ag · ri · cul · tur · ist [ægrɪkʌ́ltʃərɪst] *s.* agricultor.

a · ground [əgráʊnd] *adv.* en o a la costa; encallado; **to go** — encallar.

a · head [əhɛ́d] *adv.* delante, al frente, adelante; — **of time** adelantado; antes de tiempo; **to go** — ir adelante; **to get** — adelantar(se).

aid [ed] *s.* ayuda, auxilio, socorro; ayudante, auxiliar; *v.* ayudar, auxiliar, socorrer.

aide-de-camp [édəkæmp] *s.* edecán.

ail [el] *v.* adolecer, padecer; **what -s you?** ¿qué tienes? ¿qué te aflige?

ai·le·ron [élərən] s. alerón.
ail·ment [élmənt] s. achaque, dolencia.
aim [em] s. (pointing) puntería; tino; (objective) fin, objeto; proposición; v. apuntar (un arma); dirigir, asestar; dirigir la puntería; aspirar (a); **to — to please** proponerse (o tratar de agradar.
aim·less [émlɪs] adj. sin propósito, sin objeto.
air [ɛr] s. (atmosphere) aire, brisa; (music) tonada; **in the —** en el aire; indeciso; incierto; **in the open —** al raso, al aire libre; **to be on the —** emitir, radiodifundir; **to put on -s** darse tono; adj. de aire; aéreo; — **brake** freno neumático; **—line** línea aérea; ruta aérea; — **pocket** bache aéreo; bolsa de aire; **by —mail** por correo aéreo, por avión; **air-conditioned** de aire acondicionado; v. airear; orear; ventilar; publicar, pregonar; ostentar.
air·borne [érborn] aéreo; aerotransportado.
air·craft [érkræft] s. avión, aeroplano; aeronave; aviones; — **carrier** portaaviones.
air·foil [érfɔɪl] s. superficie de control en los aviones.
air·line [érlaɪn] s. aerovía: línea aérea; compañía de transporte aéreo.
air·plane [érplen] s. aeroplano, avión; — **carrier** portaaviones.
air·port [érport] s. aeropuerto, aeródromo.
air·ship [érʃɪp] s. aeronave.
air·tight [értáɪt] adj. hermético.
air·y [ɛ́rɪ] adj. airoso; aireado, ventilado; ligero; tenue.
aisle [aɪl] s. pasillo, pasadizo; nave (de una iglesia).
a·jar [ədʒár] adj. entreabierto, entornado.
al·a·bas·ter [ǽləbæstɚ] s. alabastro.
a·larm [əlárm] s. alarma; rebato; inquietud; — **clock** despertador; v. alarmar; inquietar.
al·bi·no [æbáɪno] s. albino.
al·bum [ǽlbəm] s. álbum.
al·che·my [ǽlkəmɪ] s. alquimia.
al·co·hol [ǽlkəhɔl] s. alcohol.
al·co·hōl·ic [ælkəhɔ́lɪk] adj. alcohólico.
al·cove [ǽlkov] s. alcoba.
al·der·man [ɔ́ldɚmən] s. concejal, regidor.
ale [el] s. cerveza de tipo espeso y amargo.
a·lert [əlɚ́t] adj. alerto, vigilante; despierto; vivo; listo; s. alarma, rebato; **to be on the —** estar alerta.
al·fal·fa [ælfǽlfə] s. alfalfa.
algae [ǽldʒɪ] s. pl. algas.
al·ge·bra [ǽldʒəbrə] s. álgebra.
al·i·bi [ǽləbaɪ] s. coartado; excusa.
a·li·en [éljən] s. extranjero; residente extranjero; adj. extraño, ajeno.
al·ien·ate [éljənet] v. enajenar; apartar, alejar (a una persona de otra).
al·ien·ist [éljənɪst] s. alienista, psiquiatra.
a·light [əláɪt] v. apearse, desmontarse, bajar(de); posarse (dícese de pájaros, mariposas, etc.).
a·lign [əláɪn] v. alinear(se).
a·like [əláɪk] adj. semejante; parecido; **to be —** parecerse, asemejarse; ser iguales; adv. del mismo modo.
al·i·mo·ny [ǽləmonɪ] s. asistencia de divorcio; alimento.
a·live [əláɪv] adj. vivo; con vida; viviente; activo; — **with** lleno de.
al·ka·li [ǽlkəlaɪ] s. álcali.
all [ɔl] adj. todo (el); todos (los); s. todo; todo el mundo, todos; adv. enteramente; — **at once** de una vez; de un tirón; de repente; — **right** bueno; bien; — **the worse** tanto peor; **not at —**

de ninguna manera; no hay de qué; **nothing at —** nada en absoluto; — **told** (o **in —**) en conjunto; **once (and) for —** por última vez; una vez por todas; **to be — in** estar agotado, estar rendido de fatiga; **it is — over** se acabó, ha terminado todo.
al·lay [əlé] v. aliviar; calmar.
al·le·ga·tion [æləgéʃən] s. alegación, alegato; aseveración.
al·lege [əlédʒ] v. alegar; declarar; sostener, asegurar.
al·le·giance [əlídʒəns] s. lealtad, fidelidad; homenaje.
al·le·go·ry [ǽləgorɪ] s. alegoría.
al·ler·gy [ǽlɚdʒɪ] s. alergia (sensibilidad anormal a ciertos alimentos o sustancias).
al·le·vi·ate [əlíviet] v. aliviar.
al·ley [ǽlɪ] s. callejón; callejuela; **blind —** callejón sin salida; **bowling —** boliche, Am. bolera.
al·li·ance [əláɪəns] s. alianza.
al·lied [əláɪd] adj. aliado; relacionado.
al·li·ga·tor [ǽləgetɚ] s. lagarto; caimán; — **pear** aguacate.
al·lot [əlát] v. asignar; repartir.
al·low [əláú] v. permitir, dejar; conceder; admitir; asignar; abonar; **to — for certain errors** tener en cuenta ciertos errores.
al·low·a·ble [əláúəbl] adj. permisible, admisible, lícito.
al·low·ance [əláúəns] s. asignación, abono, pensión; ración; rebaja, descuento; permiso; concesión; **monthly —** mesada, mensualidad; **to make — for** tener en cuenta.
al·loy [ǽlɔɪ] s. aleación, liga, mezcla (de dos o más metales); [əlɔ́ɪ] v. alear, ligar, mezclar (metales).
al·lude [əlúd] v. aludir.
al·lure [əlúr] v. seducir, cautivar; atraer, halagar.
al·lure·ment [əlúrmənt] s. seducción, tentación; atractivo, halago.
al·lur·ing [əlúrɪŋ] adj. seductivo, halagüeño, encantador.
al·lu·sion [əlúʒən] s. alusión; indirecta, insinuación.
al·lu·vi·um [əlúvɪəm] s. aluvión.
al·ly [əláɪ] v. unir; aliarse; **to — oneself (itself) with** aliarse con, unirse con; [ǽlaɪ] s. aliado.
al·ma·nac [ɔ́lmənæk] s. almanaque, calendario.
al·might·y [ɔlmáɪtɪ] adj. todopoderoso, omnipotente.
al·mond [ámənd] s. almendra; — **tree** almendro.
al·most [ɔ́lmost] adv. casi; **I — fell down** por poco me caigo.
alms [amz] s. limosna; — **box** cepo o cepillo, alcancía (para limosnas).
a·lone [əlón] adj. solo; solitario; único; adv. sólo, solamente; **all —** a solas; completamente solo; solito; **to let —** no tocar; no molestar; dejar en paz; no hacer caso de.
a·long [əlɔ́ŋ] prep. a lo largo de; por; al lado de; — **with** junto con; en compañía de; **all —** todo el tiempo; de un extremo a otro; **all — the coast** por toda la costa; **to carry — with one** llevar consigo; **to go — with** acompañar; ir con; bien; **to get — with** llevarse bien con; **get —!** ¡vete! ¡váyase! ¡largo de aquí!
a·long·side [əlɔ́ŋsáɪd] prep. & adv. al lado (de); al costado (de); lado a lado.
a·loof [əlúf] adj. aislado, apartado, retirado; huraño; reservado; adv. aparte; lejos.
a·loof·ness [əlúfnɪs] s. alejamiento, desapego, aislamiento.

a·loud [əláud] *adv*. alto, recio, fuerte, en voz alta.
al·pha·bet [ǽlfəbɛt] *s*. alfabeto.
al·read·y [ɔlrédɪ] *adv*. ya.
al·so [ɔ́lso] *adv*. también, además, igualmente.
al·tar [ɔ́ltə·] *s*. altar; **high** — altar mayor; —**piece** retablo.
al·ter [ɔ́ltə·] *v*. alterar; cambiar; variar.
al·ter·a·tion [ɔltəréʃən] *s*. alteración, cambio; mudanza; modificación.
al·ter·nate [ɔ́ltə·nɪt] *adj*. alternativo; alterno; alternado; *s*. suplente; **-ly** *adv*. alternativamente, por turno; [ɔ́ltə·net] *v*. alternar; variar; turnar.
al·ter·na·tive [ɔltɔ́·nətɪv] *adj*. alternativo; *s*. alternativa.
al·ter·na·tor [ɔltɔ́·nétə·] *s*. alternador.
al·though [ɔlðó] *conj*. aunque, si bien, bien que.
al·tim·e·ter [æltímətə·] *s*. altímetro.
al·ti·tude [ǽltətjud] *s*. altitud, altura, elevación; — **sickness** *Am*. soroche.
al·to [ǽlto] *s*. & *adj*. contralto.
al·to·geth·er [ɔltəgɛ́ðə·] *adv*. del todo, completamente; en conjunto.
a·lu·mi·num [əlúmɪnəm] *s*. aluminio.
a·lum·nus [əlámnəs] *s*. graduado, exalumno.
al·ways [ɔ́lwɪz] *adv*. siempre.
am [æm] *1ª persona del presente de indic. del verbo* **to be**: soy, estoy.
a·mal·ga·mate [əmǽlgəmet] *v*. amalgamar; combinar; unir.
a·mass [əmǽs] *v*. amontonar, acumular, apilar, *Am*. amasar.
am·a·teur [ǽmətʃur] *s*. aficionado; novicio, principiante.
a·maze [əméz] *v*. pasmar, maravillar, asombrar.
a·maze·ment [əmézmənt] *s*. pasmo, admiración, asombro.
a·maz·ing [əmézɪŋ] *adj*. pasmoso, asombroso, maravilloso.
am·bas·sa·dor [æmbǽsədə·] *s*. embajador.
am·ber [ǽmbə·] *s*. ámbar; color de ámbar; *adj*. ambarino; de ámbar.
am·bi·ance [ǽmbiəns] *s*. ambiente.
am·bi·gu·i·ty [æmbɪgjúətɪ] *s*. ambigüedad.
am·big·u·ous [æmbígjuəs] *adj*. ambiguo.
am·bi·tion [æmbíʃən] *s*. ambición, aspiración.
am·bi·tious [æmbíʃəs] *adj*. ambicioso.
am·biv·a·lent [æmbívələnt] *adj*. ambivalente.
am·ble [ǽmbl] *v*. andar, vagar.
am·bu·lance [ǽmbjələns] *s*. ambulancia.
am·bush [ǽmbuʃ] *s*. emboscada; celada; acecho; **to lie in** — estar emboscado, estar al acecho; *v*. emboscar; poner celada a.
a·me·na·ble [əmínəbl] *adj*. dócil; tratable.
a·mend [əménd] *v*. enmendar; rectificar; **-s** *s. pl*. satisfacción, compensación; **to make** — **for** resarcir, dar satisfacción por, compensar por.
a·mend·ment [əméndmənt] *s*. enmienda.
A·mer·i·can [əmɛ́rəkən] *adj*. & *s*. (*continental*) americano; (*U.S.A.*) norteamericano.
A·mer·i·can·ism [əmɛ́rɪkənɪzəm] *s*. americanismo.
am·e·thyst [ǽməθɪst] *s*. amatista.
a·mi·a·ble [émɪəbl] *adj*. amable, afable, amistoso.
am·i·ca·ble [ǽmɪkəbl] *adj*. amigable, amistoso.
a·mid [əmíd] *prep*. en medio de; entre; **amidst** [əmídst] = **amid**.
a·miss [əmís] *adj*. errado, equivocado; impropio; *adv*. mal; fuera de lugar, impropiamente; **to take** — llevar a mal.
am·mo·nia [əmónjə] *s*. amoníaco.
am·mu·ni·tion [æmjəníʃən] *s*. munición.
am·ne·sia [æmníʒə] *s*. amnesia.

am·nes·ty [ǽmnɛstɪ] *s*. amnestía.
a·mong [əmʌ́ŋ] *prep*. entre, en medio de; **amongst** [əmʌ́ŋst] = **among**.
am·o·rous [ǽmərəs] *adj*. amoroso.
a·mor·phous [əmɔ́rfəs] *adj*. amorfo.
am·or·tize [ǽmɔ·taɪz] *v*. amortizar.
a·mount [əmáunt] *s*. suma; cantidad; total; importe; valor; *v*. montar, subir, importar, ascender (a); valer; **that -s to stealing** eso equivale a robar.
am·pere [ǽmpɪr] *s*. amperio.
am·phib·i·ous [æmfíbɪəs] *adj*. anfibio.
am·phi·the·a·ter [ǽmfəθiətə·] *s*. anfiteatro.
am·ple [ǽmpl] *adj*. amplio; abundante; bastante, suficiente.
am·pli·fy [ǽmpləfaɪ] *v*. ampliar; amplificar.
am·pu·tate [ǽmpjətet] *v*. amputar.
a·muck [əmʌ́k] *adv*. con frenesí; **to run** — atacar a ciegas.
a·muse [əmjúz] *v*. divertir, entretener, distraer; **to** — **oneself** divertirse.
a·muse·ment [əmjúzmənt] *s*. diversión, entretenimiento, pasatiempo, recreo, distracción.
a·mus·ing [əmjúzɪŋ] *adj*. divertido, entretenido; gracioso, chistoso.
an [ən, æn] *art. indef*. un, una.
a·nach·ro·nism [ənǽkrɔnɪzm] *s*. anacronismo.
an·al·ge·sic [ænəldʒízɪk] *s*. analgésico.
a·nal·o·gous [ənǽləgəs] *adj*. análogo.
a·nal·o·gy [ənǽlədʒɪ] *s*. analogía, semejanza.
a·nal·y·sis [ənǽləsɪs] *s*. análisis.
an·a·lyt·ic [ænəlítɪk] *adj*. analítico.
an·a·lyze [ǽnlaɪz] *v*. analizar.
an·ar·chist [ǽnə·kɪst] *s*. anarquista.
an·ar·chy [ǽnə·kɪ] *s*. anarquía.
a·nath·e·ma [ənǽθəmə] *s*. anatema.
an·a·tom·i·cal [ænətámɪkl] *adj*. anatómico.
a·nat·o·my [ənǽtəmɪ] *s*. anatomía.
an·ces·tor [ǽnsɛstə·] *s*. antepasado; **-s** abuelos, antepasados.
an·ces·tral [ænsɛ́strəl] *adj*. solariego, de los antepasados; hereditario.
an·ces·try [ǽnsɛstrɪ] *s*. linaje, abolengo, ascendencia.
an·chor [ǽŋkə·] *s*. ancla; **to drop** — anclar, echar anclas, dar fondo, fondear; **to weigh** — levar el ancla; *v*. anclar; echar anclas; fijar, asegurar.
an·cho·vy [ǽntʃovɪ] *s*. anchoa, anchova.
an·cient [énʃənt] *adj*. antiguo; vetusto; **the -s** los antiguos; la antigüedad.
and [ənd, ænd] *conj*. y; e (*delante de i o hi*); — **so forth** etcétera; y así sucesivamente; **let us try** — **do it** tratemos de hacerlo; **let us go** — **see** him vamos a verle.
An·da·lu·sian [ændəlúʒən] *adj*. andaluz.
an·ec·dote [ǽnɪkdot] *s*. anécdota.
a·ne·mi·a [əníḿə] *s*. anemia.
an·es·the·sia [ænɪsθíʒə] *s*. anestesia.
an·es·thet·ic [ænəsθɛ́tɪk] *adj*. & *s*. anestésico.
a·new [ənjú] *adv*. otra vez, de nuevo; nuevamente.
an·gel [éndʒəl] *s*. ángel.
an·gel·ic [ændʒɛ́lɪk] *adj*. angélico.
an·ger [ǽŋgə·] *s*. enojo, enfado, ira, cólera; *v*. enojar, enfadar, encolerizar.
an·gi·na [ændʒáɪnə] *s*. angina; — **pectoris** angina de pecho.
an·gle [ǽŋgl] *s*. ángulo; (*interior*) rincón; (*exterior*) esquina; punto de vista, aspecto; *v*. pescar.
An·glo-Sax·on [ǽŋglosǽksŋ] *adj*. & *s*. anglosajón.
an·gry [ǽŋgrɪ] *adj*. enojado; colérico; airado.
an·guish [ǽŋgwɪʃ] *s*. angustia, ansia, pena, dolor.

an·gu·lar [ǽŋgjǝlǝ] *adj.* angular; anguloso.
an·i·mal [ǽnǝml] *s. & adj.* animal.
an·i·mate [ǽnǝmɪt] *adj.* animado, viviente; **animated cartoon** dibujo animado; [ǽnǝmet] *v.* animar; alentar.
an·i·ma·tion [ænǝméʃǝn] *s.* animación; viveza.
an·i·mos·i·ty [ænǝmásǝtɪ] *s.* animosidad, ojeriza, inquina, rencor.
an·ise [ǽnɪs] *s.* anís.
an·kle [ǽŋkl] *s.* tobillo.
an·nals [ǽnlz] *s. pl.* anales.
an·nex [ǽnɛks] *s.* (*building*) pabellón, ala; (*dependent addition*) anexo; añadidura; [ǝnɛks] *v.* anexar.
an·nex·a·tion [ænɛkséʃǝn] *s.* anexión.
an·ni·hi·late [ǝnáɪǝlet] *v.* aniquilar; anonadar.
an·ni·ver·sa·ry [ænǝvɝsǝrɪ] *s. & adj.* aniversario.
an·no·tate [ǽnotet] *v.* anotar.
an·no·ta·tion [ænotéʃǝn] *s.* anotación, acotación, nota.
an·nounce [ǝnáʊns] *v.* anunciar; proclamar.
an·nounce·ment [ǝnáʊnsmǝnt] *s.* anuncio; aviso; noticia.
an·nounc·er [ǝnáʊnsǝ] *s.* anunciador; **radio —** locutor.
an·noy [ǝnɔ́ɪ] *v.* molestar; fastidiar; incomodar; enfadar.
an·noy·ance [ǝnɔ́ɪǝns] *s.* molestia; fastidio; enfado; vejamen.
an·nu·al [ǽnjʊǝl] *adj.* anual; *s.* anuario; planta anual; **-ly** *adv.* anualmente, cada año, todos los años.
an·nu·i·ty [ǝnúǝtɪ] *s.* anualidad, renta anual.
an·nul [ǝnʌ́l] *v.* anular; abolir.
an·nul·ment [ǝnʌ́lmǝnt] *s.* revocación; anulación.
a·noint [ǝnɔ́ɪnt] *v.* ungir; untar; administrar la Extremaunción.
a·non [ǝnán] *adv.* pronto, luego; otra vez.
a·non·y·mous [ǝnánǝmǝs] *adj.* anónimo.
an·oth·er [ǝnʌ́ðǝ] *adj. & pron.* otro; **one —** uno a otro, unos a otros.
an·swer [ǽnsǝ] *s.* respuesta, contestación; réplica; solución; *v.* responder; contestar; replicar; **to — for** ser responsable de (*o* por); responder de; ser (salir) fiador de; **to — the purpose** ser adecuado, servir para el objeto.
ant [ænt] *s.* hormiga; **—eater** oso hormiguero; **— hill** hormiguero.
ant·ac·id [æntǽsɪd] *s. & adj.* antiácido.
an·tag·o·nism [æntǽgǝnɪzǝm] *s.* antagonismo, oposición, antipatía.
an·tag·o·nist [æntǽgǝnɪst] *s.* antagonista, adversario.
an·tag·o·nize [æntǽgǝnaɪz] *v.* contrariar, oponerse a, hostilizar.
an·te·ce·dent [æntǝsídn̩t] *adj. & s.* antecedente.
an·te·lope [ǽntlop] *s.* antílope.
an·ten·na [ænténǝ] (*pl.* **antennae** [ænténi]) *s.* antena.
an·te·ri·or [æntíríǝ] *adj.* anterior; delantero.
an·te·room [ǽntirum] *s.* antecámara; sala de espera.
an·them [ǽnθǝm] *s.* himno.
an·thol·o·gy [ænθálǝdʒɪ] *s.* antología.
an·thra·cite [ǽnθrǝsaɪt] *s.* antracita.
an·thro·pol·o·gist [ænθrǝpálǝdʒɪst] *s.* antropólogo.
an·thro·pol·o·gy [ænθrǝpálǝdʒɪ] *s.* antropología.
an·ti·air·craft [æntiérkræft] *adj.* antiaéreo.
an·ti·bi·ot·ic [æntɪbaɪátɪk] *s. & adj.* antibiótico.
an·ti·bod·y [ǽntɪbadɪ] *s.* anticuerpo.
an·tic·i·pate [æntísǝpet] *v.* anticipar(se); prever;

esperar.
an·tic·i·pa·tion [æntɪsǝpéʃǝn] *s.* anticipación; expectación; previsión.
an·tics [ǽntɪks] *s. pl.* travesuras, cabriolas.
an·ti·dote [ǽntɪdot] *s.* antídoto.
an·ti·freeze [ǽntɪfriz] *s.* anticongelante.
an·ti·mo·ny [ǽntǝmónɪ] *s.* antimonio.
an·tip·a·thy [æntɪpǝθɪ] *s.* antipatía, repugnancia.
an·ti·quat·ed [ǽntǝkwetɪd] *adj.* anticuado; desusado.
an·tique [æntík] *adj.* antiguo; anticuado; *s.* antigualla.
an·tiq·ui·ty [æntíkwǝtɪ] *s.* antigüedad; vejez, ancianidad.
an·ti·sep·tic [æntǝséptɪk] *adj. & s.* antiséptico.
an·ti·so·cial [æntɪsóʃel] *adj.* antisocial; *s. Am.* criminal.
an·tith·e·sis [æntíθǝsɪs] *s.* antítesis.
ant·ler [ǽntlǝ] *s.* asta, cuerno (*del venado, ciervo, etc.*).
an·vil [ǽnvɪl] *s.* yunque.
anx·i·e·ty [æŋzáɪǝtɪ] *s.* ansiedad, zozobra; ansia, anhelo, afán.
anx·ious [ǽŋkʃǝs] *adj.* ansioso; inquieto, preocupado; anheloso, deseoso; **-ly** *adv.* con ansiedad, con ansia, ansiosamente.
an·y [énɪ] *adj. & pron.* cualquier(a), cualesquier (a); alguno, algunos; **in — case** de todos modos, en todo caso; **I have not — bread** no tengo pan; **she does not sing — more** ya no canta; **he does not want to work — more** no quiere trabajar más.
an·y·bod·y [énɪbadɪ] *pron.* alguien, alguno; cualquiera; **not . . . — no . . .** nadie, no . . . ninguno; **he does not know — no** conoce a nadie.
an·y·how [énɪhaʊ] *adv.* de todos modos; de cualquier modo.
an·y·one [énɪwʌn] *pron.* = **anybody.**
an·y·thing [énɪθɪŋ] *pron.* alguna cosa; cualquier cosa; algo; **not . . . — no . . .** nada; **not to know —** no saber nada; **— you wish** todo lo que quiera Vd.
an·y·way [énɪwe] *adv.* de todos modos; en cualquier caso.
an·y·where [énɪhwɛr] *adv.* dondequiera; en cualquier parte o lugar; en todas partes; **not . . . — no . . .** en (*o* a) ninguna parte; **not to go —** no ir a ninguna parte.
a·part [ǝpárt] *adj.* aparte; separadamente; a un lado; *adj.* aislado, separado; **to take —** desarmar, desmontar; **to tear —** despedazar, hacer pedazos.
a·part·ment [ǝpártmǝnt] *s.* departamento, piso, apartamento; vivienda, habitación.
ap·a·thet·ic [æpǝθétɪk] *adj.* apático.
ap·a·thy [ǽpǝθɪ] *s.* apatía, indiferencia, indolencia.
ape [ep] *s.* mono; *v.* remedar, imitar.
ap·er·ture [ǽpǝtʃǝ] *s.* abertura.
a·pex [épɛks] *s.* ápice, cumbre.
a·pha·sia [ǝfézɪǝ] *s.* afasia.
a·piece [ǝpís] *adv.* cada uno, a cada uno, por persona.
a·poc·o·pe [ǝpákǝpɪ] *s.* apócope.
ap·o·gee [ǽpǝdʒɪ] *s.* apogeo.
a·pol·o·get·ic [ǝpalǝdʒétɪk] *adj.* que se excusa o disculpa.
a·pol·o·gize [ǝpálǝdʒaɪz] *v.* disculparse, excusarse.
a·pol·o·gy [ǝpálǝdʒɪ] *s.* apología; excusa, disculpa, justificación, satisfacción.
ap·o·plex·y [ǽpǝplɛksɪ] *s.* apoplejía.

AL

a·pos·tle [əpás!] *s.* apóstol.
ap·os·tol·ic [æpəstálık] *adj.* apostólico.
a·pos·tro·phe [əpástrəfi] *s.* apóstrofe; (*punctuation*) apóstrofo.
ap·pall [əpól] *v.* aterrorizar, aterrar; asombrar, espantar.
ap·pall·ing [əpólıŋ] *adj.* aterrador; espantoso, asombroso.
ap·pa·ra·tus [æpərétəs] *s.* aparato; aparejo.
ap·par·el [əpǽrəl] *s.* ropa; ropaje; vestidos; indumentaria.
ap·par·ent [əpǽrənt] *adj.* aparente; visible; claro, evidente; patente; **heir** — heredero presunto; **-ly** *adv.* aparentemente, al parecer, por lo visto.
ap·pa·ri·tion [æpərífən] *s.* aparición; aparecido, espectro, fantasma.
ap·peal [əpíl] *s.* (*legal*) apelación, recurso; (*request*) súplica; (*attraction*) atracción, atractivo, llamamiento; *v.* apelar; recurrir, acudir; atraer, despertar interés o simpatía; llamar la atención.
ap·pear [əpír] *v.* aparecer(se); parecer; comparecer.
ap·pear·ance [əpírəns] *s.* apariencia, semblante; porte, facha; aparición; cariz.
ap·pease[əpíz] *v.* apaciguar, aplacar; pacificar; conciliar; sosegar.
ap·pease·ment [əpízmənt] *s.* apaciguamiento; conciliación.
ap·pen·dix [əpéndıks] *s.* apéndice.
ap·per·tain [æpətén] *v.* pertenecer.
ap·pe·tite [ǽpətaıt] *s.* apetito; gana, deseo.
ap·pe·tiz·er [ǽpətaızɚ] *s.* aperitivo.
ap·pe·tiz·ing [ǽpətaızıŋ] *adj.* apetecible; apetitoso.
ap·plaud [əplód] *v.* aplaudir.
ap·plause [əplóz] *s.* aplauso.
ap·ple [ǽpl] *s.* manzana; — **tree** manzano; — **grove** manzanar; **Adam's** — nuez (*de la garganta*); *Ven., C.A., Col.* manzana; — **of my eye** niña de mis ojos.
ap·ple·sauce [ǽplsɔs] *s.* compota de manzana.
ap·pli·ance [əpláıəns] *s.* utensilio, instrumento; herramienta.
ap·pli·ca·ble [ǽplıkəbl] *adj.* aplicable.
ap·pli·cant [ǽpləkənt] *s.* solicitante, aspirante, candidato.
ap·pli·ca·tion [æpləkéfən] *s.* (*dedication*) aplicación; (*petition*) solicitud, petición; *Méx., Carib., Ven.* aplicación.
ap·plied [əpláıd] *adj. & p.p.* aplicado; — **for** pedido, solicitado.
ap·ply [əpláı] *v.* aplicar(se); **to** — **to** dirigirse a, acudir a, recurrir a; **to** — **for** solicitar, pedir; **to** — **oneself** aplicarse, dedicarse; **to** — **on account** acreditar en cuenta.
ap·point [əpóınt] *v.* (*designate*) nombrar, designar, señalar; (*furnish*) amueblar, equipar; **a well -ed house** una casa bien amueblada.
ap·point·ee [əpoıntí] *s.* electo.
ap·point·ment [əpóıntmənt] *s.* (*designation*) nombramiento, designación; (*engagement*) cita, compromiso; **-s** mobiliario, mueblaje; accesorios.
ap·por·tion [əpórfən] *v.* repartir proporcionalmente, prorratear.
ap·por·tion·ment [əpórfənmənt] *s.* prorrateo, distribución, repartimiento.
ap·prais·al [əpréz!] *s.* tasa, valuación.
ap·praise [əpréz] *v.* avaluar, valuar, tasar.
ap·pre·cia·ble [əprífıəb!] *adj.* (*prized*) apreciable; (*perceived*) perceptible; (*quantity*) bastante.
ap·pre·ci·ate [əprífıet] *v.* apreciar; estimar; agradecer; **to** — **in value** subir de valor.

ap·pre·ci·a·tion [əprıfıéfən] *s.* apreciación; aprecio; valuación; agradecimiento; aumento, alza, subida (*de precio*).
ap·pre·hend [æprıhénd] *v.* aprehender, asir, prender; comprender; percibir.
ap·pre·hen·sion [æprıhénfən] *s.* aprehensión, aprensión, recelo, desconfianza, presentimiento; captura.
ap·pre·hen·sive [æprıhénsıv] *adj.* aprensivo.
ap·pren·tice [əpréntıs] *s.* aprendiz; novicio, principiante; *v.* poner de aprendiz.
ap·pren·tice·ship [əpréntısfıp] *s.* aprendizaje.
ap·prise [əprátz] *v.* enterar, informar; apreciar.
ap·proach [əprótf] *s.* acercamiento; aproximación; acceso, entrada; **method of** — técnica o modo de plantear (*un problema*); *v.* acercarse, aproximarse; abordar (*a alguien*).
ap·pro·ba·tion [æprəbéfən] *s.* aprobación.
ap·pro·pri·ate [əprópriıt] *adj.* apropiado, propio, apto, conveniente, a propósito; [əpróprıet] *v.* apropiarse, apoderarse de; asignar (*una suma de dinero*).
ap·pro·pri·a·tion [əproprıéfən] *s.* apropiación; asignación, suma asignada.
ap·prov·al [əprúv!] *s.* aprobación, asentimiento.
ap·prove [əprúv] *v.* aprobar; asentir a.
ap·prox·i·mate [əprákəəmıt] *adj.* aproximado; aproximativo; **-ly** *adv.* aproximadamente, casi, poco más o menos; [əpráksəmet] *v.* aproximar; aproximarse, acercarse.
a·pri·cot [éprıkɑt] *s.* albaricoque; *Am.* chabacano.
A·pril [éprəl] *s.* abril.
a·pron [éprən] *s.* delantal.
ap·ro·pos [æprəpó] *adv.* a propósito; *adj.* oportuno; pertinente; — **of** a propósito de.
apt [æpt] *adj.* apto, capaz; pertinente, a propósito; — **to** propenso a.
ap·ti·tude [ǽptətjud] *s.* aptitud, capacidad; habilidad.
aq·ua·ma·rine [akwəmərín] *s.* aguamarina.
a·quar·i·um [əkwériəm] *s.* acuario; pecera.
a·quat·ic [əkwǽtık] *adj.* acuático.
aq·ue·duct [ǽkwidʌkt] *s.* acueducto.
Ar·ab [ǽrəb] *adj. & s.* árabe.
Ar·a·go·nese [ærəgəniz] *adj. & s.* aragonés.
ar·bi·ter [árbıtɚ] *s.* árbitro, arbitrador, juez árbitro.
ar·bi·trar·y [árbətrɛrı] *adj.* arbitrario; despótico.
ar·bi·trate [árbətret] *v.* arbitrar; decidir; someter al arbitraje.
ar·bi·tra·tion [arbətréfən] *s.* arbitraje, arbitración.
ar·bi·tra·tor [árbətretɚ] *s.* arbitrador, árbitro; medianero.
ar·bor [árbɚ] *s.* emparrado, enramada, glorieta.
arc [ark] *s.* arco; — **lamp** lámpara de arco.
ar·cade [arkéd] *s.* arcada; galería; soportal.
arch [artf] *s.* arco; bóveda; **semicircular** — arco de medio punto; — **enemy** enemigo acérrimo; *v.* arquear(se); enarcar(se).
ar·chae·ol·o·gy [arkıálədʒı] *s.* arqueología.
ar·cha·ic [arkéık] *adj.* arcaico, desusado, anticuado.
arch·bish·op [ártfbífəp] *s.* arzobispo.
arch·bish·op·ric [artfbífəprık] *s.* arzobispado.
arch·er·y [ártfərı] *s.* tiro de flechas.
ar·chi·pel·a·go [arkıpɛləgo] *s.* archipiélago.
ar·chi·tect [árkətɛkt] *s.* arquitecto.
ar·chi·tec·tur·al [arkətɛktfərəl] *adj.* arquitectónico.
ar·chi·tec·ture [árkətɛktfɚ] *s.* arquitectura.
ar·chives [árkaıvz] *s.* archivo.
arch·way [ártfwe] *s.* pasadizo (*bajo un arco*).

arcada, galería abovedada.
arc·tic [árktɪk] *adj.* ártico.
ar·dent [árdn̩t] *adj.* ardiente apasionado.
ar·dor [árdɚ] *s.* ardor; enardecimiento; fervor.
ar·du·ous [árdʒʊəs] *adj.* arduo, trabajoso.
are [ɑr] *2ª persona y pl. del presente de indic. del verbo* to be: eres, estás; somos, estamos; sois, estáis; son, están.
ar·e·a [érɪə] *s.* área, superficie; espacio; región.
a·re·na [ərínə] *s.* arena, redondel, plaza.
Ar·gen·ti·ne [árdʒəntin] *adj. & s.* argentino.
ar·gon [árgan] argón.
ar·gue [árgjʊ] *v.* argüir; debatir; altercar; **to — into** persuadir a.
ar·gu·ment [árgjəmənt] *s.* disputa; polémica; razonamiento; sumario, resumen.
ar·id [ǽrɪd] *adj.* árido.
a·rise [əráɪz] *v.* levantarse; elevarse; surgir; provenir.
a·ris·en [ərízn̩] *p.p. de* to arise.
ar·is·toc·ra·cy [ærəstákrəsɪ] *s.* aristocracia.
a·ris·to·crat [ərístəkræt] *s.* aristócrata.
a·ris·to·crat·ic [ərɪstəkrǽtɪk] *adj.* aristocrático.
a·rith·me·tic [əríθmətɪk] *s.* aritmética.
ark [ɑrk] *s.* arca; **— of the covenant** arca del testamento; **Noah's —** arca de Noé.
arm [ɑrm] *s.* (*anatomy*) brazo; (*weapon*) arma; **— in —** de bracete, de bracero; *Am.* de brazo, de brazos; **at -'s length** a una brazada; **with open -s** con los brazos abiertos; *v.* armar(se).
ar·ma·da [ɑrmádə] *s.* armada, flota.
ar·ma·ment [árməmənt] *s.* armamento.
ar·ma·ture [ármətʃɚ] *s.* armaduar.
arm·chair [ármtʃɛr] *s.* silla de brazos, sillón, butaca.
armed for·ces [ármd fórsəz] *s.* fuerzas armadas.
arm·ful [ármfʊl] *s.* brazada.
ar·mi·stice [árməstɪs] *s.* armisticio.
ar·mor [ármɚ] *s.* armadura; blindaje, coraza; arnés; *v.* blindar, acorazar.
ar·mored [ármɚd] *p.p.* blindado, acorazado.
ar·mor·y [ármərɪ] *s.* armería; arsenal.
arm·pit [ármpɪt] *s.* sobaco.
ar·my [ármɪ] *s.* ejército; muchedumbre; **— doctor** médico militar; **regular —** tropa de línea.
a·ro·ma [ərómə] *s.* aroma; fragancia.
ar·o·mat·ic [ærəmǽtɪk] *adj.* aromático.
a·rose [əróz] *pret. de* to arise.
a·round [əráʊnd] *adv.* alrededor; en redor; a la redonda; en torno, en derredor; cerca; **all —** por todos lados; *prep.* alrededor de; cerca de; **— here** por aquí; **to go — in circles** dar vueltas; **to go — the world** dar la vuelta al mundo.
a·rouse [əráʊz] *v.* despertar, *Riopl., C.A., Ven.* recordar (*al dormido*); excitar; promover.
ar·raign [ərén] *v.* acusar; procesar (*a un criminal*).
ar·range [əréndʒ] *v.* arreglar; disponer, colocar; acomodar; hacer arreglos (para), hacer planes (para).
ar·range·ment [əréndʒmənt] *s.* arreglo; disposición; colocación, orden; convenio.
ar·ray [əré] *s.* arreglo, formación, orden; orden (*de batalla*); pompa; gala, atavío; *v.* formar (*tropas*); poner en orden; ataviar, adornar.
ar·rears [ərírz] *s. pl.* atrasos, pagos o rentas vencidos y no cobrados; **in —** atrasado (*en el pago de una cuenta*).
ar·rest [ərést] *s.* arresto, captura, aprensión, detención; *v.* aprehender o prender, arrestar; detener; llamar, atraer (*la atención*).
ar·ri·val [əráɪvl̩] *s.* llegada; arribo; venida; **the new**

-s los recién llegados.
ar·rive [əráɪv] *v.* llegar; arribar; **to — at a result** lograr (*o* conseguir) un resultado.
ar·ro·gance [ǽrəgəns] *s.* arrogancia.
ar·ro·gant [ǽrəgənt] *adj.* arrogante.
ar·row [ǽro] *s.* saeta, flecha.
ar·se·nal [ársn̩əl] *s.* arsenal.
ar·se·nic [ársn̩ɪk] *s.* arsénico.
ar·son [ársən] *s.* delito de incendio.
art [ɑrt] *s.* arte; destreza; astucia; **fine -s** bellas artes; **master of -s** licenciado en letras, maestro en artes.
ar·ter·y [ártərɪ] *s.* arteria.
art·ful [ártfəl] *adj.* artero, mañero, ladino.
ar·ti·choke [ártɪtʃok] *s.* alcachofa.
ar·ti·cle [ártɪkl̩] *s.* artículo; **— of clothing** prenda de vestir; **— of merchandise** mercancía, mercadería.
ar·tic·u·late [artíkjəlɪt] *adj.* articulado; claro, inteligible; capaz de hablar; [artíkjəlet] *v.* articular; enunciar; enlazar.
ar·tic·u·la·tion [artɪkjəléʃən] *s.* articulación; coyuntura.
ar·ti·fact [ártəfækt] *s.* artefacto.
ar·ti·fice [ártəfɪs] *s.* artificio; ardid.
ar·ti·fi·cial [artəfíʃəl] *adj.* artificial; postizo; afectado, artificioso.
ar·til·ler·y [artílərɪ] *s.* artillería; **— man** artillero.
ar·ti·san [ártəzn̩] *s.* artesano; artífice.
art·ist [ártɪst] *s.* artista.
ar·tis·tic [artístɪk] *adj.* artístico; **-ally** *adv.* artísticamente.
as [æz] *adv., conj., prep.* como; mientras; a medida que, según; en el momento en que; **— far —** hasta, hasta donde; **— for (— to)** en cuanto a; **— if** como si; **— it were** por decirlo así; **— large —** tan grande como; **— much —** tanto como; **— well** tan bien; también; **— yet** hasta ahora, todavía; **— long — you wish** todo el tiempo que Vd. quiera; **— stong — he is** aunque es tan fuerte; **the same —** lo mismo que.
as·bes·tos [æsbéstəs] *s.* asbesto.
as·cend [əsénd] *v.* ascender; subir, elevarse.
as·cen·sion [əsénʃən] *s.* ascensión; subida.
as·cent [əsént] *s.* ascenso; subida; ascensión.
as·cer·tain [æsɚtén] *v.* averiguar, indagar.
as·cet·ic [əsétɪk] *adj.* ascético; *s.* asceta.
as·cribe [əskráɪb] *v.* atribuir, imputar, achacar.
ash [æʃ] *s.* ceniza; **— tray** cenicero; **— tree** fresno; **Ash Wednesday** miércoles de ceniza; **ash-colored** *adj.* ceniciento, cenizo.
a·shamed [əʃémd] *adj.* avergonzado, corrido; **to be —** tener vergüenza; avergonzarse.
a·shore [əʃór] *adv.* a tierra; en tierra; **to go —** desembarcar.
A·si·at·ic [ʒiǽtɪk] *adj. & s.* asiático.
a·side [əsáɪd] *adv.* aparte; a un lado; al lado; *s.* aparte (*en un drama*).
ask [æsk] *v.* (*request*) pedir, rogar, solicitar; (*inquire*) preguntar; (*invite*) invitar; **to — for** pedir; **to — for (about, after)** preguntar por; **to — a question** hacer una pregunta.
a·skance [əskǽns] *adv.* de soslayo; con recelo, recelosamente; **to look —** mirar con recelo; no aprobar.
a·sleep [əslíp] *adj.* dormido; **to fall —** dormirse; **my arm is —** se me ha dormido (entumecido *o* entumido) el brazo.
as·par·a·gus [əspǽrəgəs] *s.* espárrago.
as·pect [ǽspɛkt] *s.* aspecto; cariz.
as·phalt [ǽsfɔlt] *s.* asfalto; chapapote.

as·pi·ra·tion [æspəréʃən] s. aspiración; anhelo.
as·pire [əspáɪr] v. aspirar; anhelar, ambicionar.
as·pi·rin [ǽspʒɪn] s. aspirina.
ass [æs] s. asno, burro; pollino.
as·sail [əsél] v. asaltar, acometer, agredir.
as·sail·ant [əsélənt] s. asaltador, agresor.
as·sas·sin [əsǽsɪn] s. asesino.
as·sas·si·nate [əsǽsņet] v. asesinar.
as·sas·si·na·tion [əsæsņéʃən] s. asesinato.
as·sault [əsɔ́lt] s. asalto, acometida; conato;
ataque; v. asaltar, acometer, atacar; violar.
as·say [əsé] v. ensayar (metales); analizar,
examinar; contrastar (pesas, moneda); s. ensaye
(de metales); contraste (de pesas, moneda).
as·sem·ble [əsémbḷ] v. reunir(se), congregar(se),
juntar(se); convocar; armar, montar
(maquinaria).
as·sem·bly [əsémblɪ] s. asamblea; reunión;
montaje (de maquinaria); — hall salón de
sesiones; paraninfo.
as·sent [əsént] s. asentimiento; consentimiento; v.
asentir; consentir.
as·sert [əsʒ́t] v. aseverar, asegurar, afirmar; to —
oneself hacerse valer; obrar con firmeza;
vindicarse.
as·ser·tion [əsʒ́ʃən] s. aserción, aserto, afirmación.
as·sess [əsés] v. avaluar; tasar; asignar, imponer
(impuestos, multas, contribuciones, etc.).
as·sess·ment [əsésmənt] s. avaluación, tasación;
imposición (de contribuciones, multas, etc.);
contribución, impuesto.
as·set [ǽset] s. cualidad, ventaja; -s capital, fondos,
caudal; haber, activo; personal -s bienes
muebles.
as·sid·u·ous [əsídʒuəs] adj. asiduo, diligente.
as·sign [əsáɪn] v. asignar; señalar, designar;
traspasar, ceder a favor de.
as·sign·ment [əsáɪnmənt] s. asignación;
designación; cesión (de bienes); tarea (asignada);
lección (señalada).
as·sim·i·late [əsímḷet] v. asimilar(se), absorber(se).
as·sist [əsíst] v. asistir, ayudar.
as·sis·tance [əsístəns] s. asistencia, ayuda.
as·sis·tant [əsístənt] s. asistente; ayudante;
auxiliar; adj. subordinado, auxiliar.
as·so·ci·ate [əsóʃɪt] adj. asociado; s. asociado;
socio; compañero; colega; [əsóʃɪet] v.
asociar(se); relacionar.
as·so·ci·a·tion [əsosɪéʃən] s. asociación; sociedad;
conexión, relación.
as·sort [əsɔ́rt] v. ordenar, clasificar.
as·sort·ed [əsɔ́rtɪd] adj. surtido, mezclado, variado,
de todas clases.
as·sort·ment [əsɔ́rtmənt] s. variedad; clasificación;
surtido; colección, grupo.
as·sume [əsúm] v. asumir; tomar; dar por sentado,
dar por supuesto; arrogarse, apropiarse.
as·sump·tion [əsʌ́mpʃən] d. suposición; toma,
apropiación; presunción; asunción (de la
Virgen).
as·sur·ance [əʃúrəns] s. seguridad, certeza;
convicción; confianza; life — seguro de vida.
Véase insurance.
as·sure [əʃúr] v. asegurar; afirmar; infundir
confianza.
as·sur·ed·ly [əʃúrɪdlɪ] adv. seguramente; sin duda,
con seguridad.
as·ta·tine [ǽstətin] s. astato.
as·ter·isk [ǽstərɪsk] s. asterisco.
a·stig·ma·tism [əstígmətɪzəm] s. astigmatismo.
as·ton·ish [əstánɪʃ] v. asombrar, pasmar, espantar.

as·ton·ish·ing [əstánɪʃɪŋ] adj. asombroso, pasmoso,
maravilloso.
as·ton·ish·ment [əstánɪʃmənt] s. asombro, pasmo,
sorpresa.
as·tound [əstáʊnd] v. pasmar; aterrar, aturdir.
a·stray [əstré] adv. fuera de camino; adj. desviado,
extraviado, descaminado; to go — perderse;
errar el camino; extraviarse; to lead — desviar,
extraviar; llevar por mal camino; seducir.
a·stride [əstráɪd] adv. a horcajadas.
as·trin·gent [əstríndʒənt] adj., s. astringente.
as·tro·dome [ǽstrədom] s. astródomo.
as·trol·o·gy [əstrálədʒɪ] s. astrología.
as·tro·naut [ǽstrənɔt] s. astronauta.
as·tron·o·mer [əstránəmɚ] s. astrónomo.
as·tron·o·my [əstránəmɪ] s. astronomía.
as·tro·phys·ics [ǽstrofízɪks] s. astrofísica.
As·tu·ri·an [æstjúrɪən] adj. & s. asturiano.
as·tute [əstjút] adj. astuto, sagaz.
a·sun·der [əsʌ́ndɚ] adj. separado; to cut —
separar, apartar; dividir en dos.
a·sy·lum [əsáɪləm] s. asilo; hospicio; orphan —
orfanato, casa de huérfanos, Méx., C.A., Andes
orfanatorio.
at [æt] prep. a; en; en (la) casa de; — last por fin,
al fin; — once al punto; to be — work estar
trabajando; — that door entrar por
aquella puerta.
at·a·vism [ǽtəvɪzəm] s. atavismo.
ate [et] pret. de to eat.
a·the·ist [éθɪɪst] s. ateo.
ath·lete [ǽθlit] s. atleta.
ath·let·ic [æθlétɪk] adj. atlético.
ath·let·ics [æθlétɪks] s. gimnasia; atletismo;
deportes.
At·lan·tic [ətǽntɪk] adj. atlántico; s. el Atlántico.
at·las [ǽtləs] s. atlas.
at·mos·phere [ǽtməsfɪr] s. atmósfera; ambiente.
at·mos·pher·ic [ætməsfɛ́rɪk] adj. atmosférico.
at·om [ǽtəm] s. átomo; — bomb bomba atómica.
a·tom·ic [ətámɪk] adj. atómico; — age edad
atómica; — energy fuerza atómica; — pile pila
atómica; — weight peso atómico.
a·tone [ətón] v. expiar, purgar; reparar.
a·tone·ment [ətónmənt] s. expiación; reparación.
a·tro·cious [ətróʃəs] adj. atroz.
a·troc·i·ty [ətrásətɪ] s. atrocidad; maldad.
at·ro·phy [ǽtrəfɪ] s. atrofia.
at·tach [ətǽtʃ] v. unir, juntar; sujetar, pegar,
adherir; poner (sello o firma); embargar (bienes);
asignar; atribuir.
at·ta·ché [ætəʃe] s. agregado.
at·tach·ment [ətǽtʃmənt] s. adhesión; apego;
afición, cariño; embargo (de bienes); accesorio.
at·tack [ətǽk] s. ataque, asalto; acceso; v. atacar;
acometer, embestir.
at·tain [ətén] v. lograr, conseguir, alcanzar; llegar
a.
at·tain·ment [əténmənt] s. logro, consecución;
adquisición; dote habilidad.
at·tempt [ətémpt] s. tentativa; prueba, ensayo;
esfuerzo; atentado; v. tentar, intentar; procurar,
tratar (de); probar; to — the life of atentar
contra la vida de.
at·tend [əténd] v. atender, cuidar, mirar por; asistir
a; acompañar.
at·ten·dance [əténdəns] s. asistencia; presencia;
concurrencia.
at·ten·dant [əténdənt] s. acompañante; sirviente,
servidor; asistente; adj. acompañante.
at·ten·tion [əténʃən] s. (care) cuidado; (courtesy)

fineza, urbanidad, atención; **to pay —** hacer caso; prestar atención.

at·ten·tive [ətɛ́ntɪv] *adj.* atento; cortés.

at·test [ətɛ́st] *v.* atestiguar, atestar; certificar; dar fe.

at·tic [ǽtɪk] *s.* desván.

at·tire [ətáɪr] *s.* atavío; vestidura; vestido, traje; *v.* ataviar, adornar.

at·ti·tude [ǽtətjud] *s.* actitud; postura.

at·tor·ney [ətɝ́nɪ] *s.* abogado; procurador; apoderado; **— general** fiscal (*de una nación o estado*); **district —** fiscal de distrito; **power of —** procuración, poder.

at·tract [ətrǽkt] *v.* atraer; cautivar; **to — attention** llamar la atención.

at·trac·tion [ətrǽkʃən] *s.* atracción; atractivo; **-s** diversiones; lugares o sitios de interés.

at·trac·tive [ətrǽktɪv] *adj.* atractivo; seductor; simpático.

at·trac·tive·ness [ətrǽktɪvnɪs] *s.* atracción; atractivo.

at·trib·ute [ǽtrəbjut] *s.* atributo; propiedad; [ətríbjut] *v.* atribuir, achacar.

at·tri·tion [ətríʃən] *s.* agotamiento; atrición.

auc·tion [ɔ́kʃən] *s.* subasta, almoneda, remate, *Am.* venduta; *v.* subastar; rematar.

au·da·cious [ɔdéʃəs] *adj.* audaz, atrevido, osado.

au·dac·i·ty [ɔdǽsətɪ] *s.* audacia, osadía; descaro.

au·di·ble [ɔ́dəbl] *adj.* audible.

au·di·ence [ɔ́dɪəns] *s.* auditorio, concurrencia, público; audiencia.

au·di·o fre·quen·cy [ɔ́dɪofríkwɛnsɪ] *s.* audiofrecuencia.

au·di·o·vis·u·al [ɔ́dɪovíʒuəl] *adj.* audiovisual.

au·dit [ɔ́dɪt] *v.* intervenir [*cuentas*]; asistir a (*una clase*) de oyente; *s.* intervención, comprobación de cuentas.

au·di·tion [ɔdíʃən] *s.* audición.

au·di·tor [ɔ́dɪtɚ] *s.* interventor (*de cuentas*); oyente.

au·di·to·ri·um [ɔdətórɪəm] *s.* salón de conferencias o conciertos; paraninfo.

au·di·to·ry [ɔ́datorɪ] *adj.* auditivo.

au·ger [ɔ́gɚ] *s.* taladro, barrena.

aught [ɔt] *s.* algo.

aug·ment [ɔgmɛ́nt] *v.* aumentar.

au·gur [ɔ́gɚ] *s.* agorero; *v.* augurar, pronosticar; **to — well** (*o* **ill**) ser de buen (*o* mal) agüero.

Au·gust [ɔ́gəst] *s.* agosto.

aunt [ænt] *s.* tía.

aus·pic·es [ɔ́spɪsɪz] *s. pl.* auspicios; protección.

aus·pi·cious [ɔspíʃəs] *adj.* propicio; favorable.

aus·tere [ɔstír] *adj.* austero, adustro, severo.

aus·ter·i·ty [ɔstɛ́rətɪ] *s.* austeridad, severidad.

Aus·tri·an [ɔ́strɪən] *adj.* & *s.* austríaco.

au·then·tic [ɔθɛ́ntɪk] *adj.* auténtico.

au·thor [ɔ́θɚ] *s.* autor; escritor.

au·thor·i·ta·tive [əθɔ́rətetɪv] *adj.* autorizado, que tiene autoridad; autoritario.

au·thor·i·ty [əθɔ́rətɪ] *s.* autoridad; facultad; **to have on good —** saber de buena tinta.

au·thor·ize [ɔ́θəraɪz] *v.* autorizar.

au·to [ɔ́to] *s.* auto, automóvil.

au·to·crat [ɔ́təkræt] *s.* autócrata.

au·to·graph [ɔ́təgræf] *s.* autógrafo.

au·to·mat·ic [ɔtəmǽtɪk] *adj.* automático; **-ally** *adv.* automáticamente.

au·to·mo·bile [ɔ́təməbil] *s.* automóvil.

au·ton·o·my [ɔtánəmɪ] *s.*— autonomía.

au·top·sy [ɔ́tapsɪ] *s.* autopsia.

au·tumn [ɔ́təm] *s.* otoño.

au·tum·nal [ɔtʌ́mnl] *adj.* otoñal.

aux·il·ia·ry [ɔgzíljərɪ] *adj.* & *s.* auxiliar.

a·vail [əvél] *v.* aprovechar; beneficiar; **to — oneself of** aprovecharse de; *s.* provecho; ventaja; **of no —** de ninguna utilidad o ventaja.

a·vail·a·ble [əvéləbl] *adj.* disponible; aprovechable; obtenible.

av·a·lanche [ǽvlæntʃ] *s.* alud; torrente.

av·a·rice [ǽvərɪs] *s.* avaricia.

av·a·ri·cious [ævəríʃəs] *adj.* avaro, avariento.

a·venge [əvɛ́ndʒ] *v.* vengar; vindicar.

a·veng·er [əvɛ́ndʒɚ] *s.* vengador.

av·e·nue [ǽvənu] *s.* avenida.

a·ver [əvɝ́] *v.* afirmar, asegurar.

av·er·age [ǽvrɪdʒ] *s.* promedio, término medio; **on an —** por término medio; *adj.* medio, mediano; ordinario; *v.* promediar, calcular o sacar el promedio; **to — a loss** prorratear una pérdida; **he -s 20 miles an hour** avanza o recorre un promedio de 20 millas por hora.

a·verse [əvɝ́s] *adj.* adverso, renuente.

a·ver·sion [əvɝ́ʒən] *s.* aversión; malquerencia, inquina.

a·vert [əvɝ́t] *v.* apartar, desviar; evitar; impedir.

a·vi·a·tion [evɪéʃən] *s.* aviación.

a·vi·a·tor [évɪetɚ] *s.* aviador.

av·o·ca·do [avəkádo] *s.* aguacate, *Andes* palta.

av·o·ca·tion [ævəkéʃən] *s.* distracción; ocupación de distracción o diversión.

a·void [əvɔ́ɪd] *v.* evitar; eludir.

a·vow [əváʊ] *v.* confesar, reconocer, admitir.

a·vow·al [əváʊəl] *s.* confesión, admisión.

a·wait [əwét] *v.* esperar, aguardar.

a·wake [əwék] *adj.* despierto; alerto; **wide-awake** muy despierto; avispado; *v.* despertar(se).

a·wak·en [əwékən] *v.* despertar(se).

a·ward [əwɔ́rd] *s.* premio; decisión, sentencia; *v.* asignar; otorgar; conferir; adjudicar (*un premio, medalla, etc.*).

a·ware [əwɛ́r] *adj.* consciente; enterado, sabedor; cauto; sobre aviso.

a·way [əwé] *adv.* lejos; fuera; *adj.* ausente; **right —** ahora mismo, ahorita; **ten miles —** a diez millas de aquí; **to give —** regalar; **to go —** irse; **to take —** quitar.

awe [ɔ] *s.* pavor; pasmo; **to stand in —** quedarse, o estar, pasmado; pasmarse; *v.* atemorizar; infundir avor; maravillar.

aw·ful [ɔ́fʊl] *adj.* terrible; horroroso; tremendo; impresionante; **-ly** *adv.* terriblemente; horrosamente; muy.

a·while [əhwáɪl] *adv.* (or) un rato; (por) algún tiempo.

awk·ward [ɔ́kwəd] *adj.* torpe, desmañado; molesto, embarazoso; incómodo; inconveniente.

awl [ɔl] *s.* lezna, punzón.

aw·ning [ɔ́nɪŋ] *s.* toldo.

a·woke [əwók] *pret.* & *p.p. de* **to awake**.

ax, axe [æks] *s.* hacha.

ax·is [ǽksɪs] *pl.* **ax·es** (ǽksiz) *s.* eje.

ax·le [ǽksl] *s.* eje (*de una rueda*); **front —** eje delantero; **rear —** eje trasero.

aye [aɪ] *adv.* si; *s.* voto afirmativo.

Az·tec [ǽztɛk] *adj.* & *s.* azteca.

az·ure [ǽʒɚ] *adj.* azul; *s.* azur, azul celeste.

B:b

bab·ble [bǽbl] s. balbuceo; parloteo, charla; v. balbucear; parlotear, charlar.

babe [beb] = **baby**.

ba·boon [bæbún] s. mandril (especie de mono).

ba·by [bébɪ] s. nene, bebé, criatura; Andes, Ch. guagua; C.A. tierno; adj. infantil; de niño; — **girl** nena; — **sitter** [bébɪsítə] s. cuidaniños, niñera por horas; v. mimar.

bach·e·lor [bǽtʃələ] s. bachiller; soltero.

ba·cil·lus [bəsíləs] s. bacilo.

back [bæk] s. (anatomy) espalda; lomo (de animal); (opposite side) revés; respaldo (de silla), espaldar; **behind one's** — a espaldas de uno, a espaldas vueltas; **in** — **of** detrás de, tras; **to fall on one's** — caer de espaldas, caer boca arriba; **to turn one's** — volver las espaldas; adj. posterior; trasero; retrasado, atrasado, rezagado; — **pay** sueldo atrasado; — **yard** patio interior; corral; adv. atrás, detrás; — **and forth** de aquí para allá; **to come** — volver, regresar; **to give** — devolver; v. respaldar, endosar; sostener, apoyar, retroceder; hacer retroceder; **to** — **down** hacerse (para) atrás; retractarse.

back·bone [bǽkbón] s. espinazo, espina dorsal; firmeza; apoyo, sostén.

back·er [bǽkə] s. fiador; sostenedor, defensor.

back·fire [bǽkfaɪr] s. petardeo.

back·ground [bǽkgraʊnd] s. fondo; educación; experiencia; **to keep in the** — dejar en último término; quedarse en último término; mantenerse retirado.

back·hand [bǽkhænd] s. revés; escritura inclinada a la izquierda; **-ed stroke** revés; **a -ed remark** una ironía; una indirecta.

back·ing [bǽkɪŋ] s. apoyo, garantía; endose, endoso; respaldo.

back·lash [bǽklæʃ] s. contragolpe; culateo.

back·log [bǽklɔg] s. reserva pendiente.

back·stage [bǽkstédʒ] adv. detrás del telón.

back-up [bǽkəp] adj. de reserva.

back·ward [bǽkwəd] adj. atrasado; retrasado; retrógrado; lerdo, tardo; huraño, tímido, esquivo; adv. = **backwards**.

back·ward·ness [bǽkwədnɪs] s. torpeza; atraso; timidez.

back·wards [bǽkwədz] adv. hacia (o para) atrás; de espaldas; **to go** — retroceder, andar hacia (o para) atrás.

ba·con [békən] s. tocino.

bac·te·ri·a [bæktírɪə] s. pl. bacterias.

bac·te·ri·ol·o·gy [bæktɪrɪálədʒɪ] s. bacteriología.

bad [bæd] adj. malo; perverso; dañoso; podrido; **to go from** — **to worse** ir de mal en peor; **to look** — tener mal cariz, tener mala cara o mal aspecto; **-ly** adv. mal, malamente.

bade [bæd] pret. de **to bid**.

badge [bædʒ] s. insignia, divisa; distintivo; Mex. chapa.

bad·ger [bǽdʒə] s. tejón; v. atormentar, acosar, molestar.

bad·ness [bǽdnɪs] s. maldad.

baf·fle [bǽfl] v. desconcertar, confundir; frustrar, impedir.

bag [bæg] s. (sack) saco, bolsa, talega; costal; (baggage) maleta; zurrón, morral; v. ensacar; cazar; agarrar; adueñarse de; inflarse; abolsarse.

bag·gage [bǽgɪdʒ] s. equipaje; bagaje; — **car** furgón, vagón de equipajes; — **check** talón,

contraseña de equipajes; — **tag** marbete, etiqueta.

bag·pipe [bǽgpaɪp] s. gaita.

bail [bel] s. fianza, caución; **to let out on** — poner en libertad bajo fianza; v. dar fianza; salir fiador; achicar (agua), vaciar; **to** — **out of a plane** tirarse (con paracaídas) de un aeroplano.

bait [bet] s. cebo; atractivo, aliciente; v. tentar, atraer; cebar; acosar, perseguir.

bake [bek] v. hornear, cocer al horno; calcinar.

bak·er [békə] s. panadero, pastelero, hornero.

bak·ery [békərɪ] s. panadería, pastelería, tahona.

bak·ing [békɪŋ] s. hornada; cocimiento; — **powder** levadura.

bal·ance [bǽləns] s. (instrument) balanza; (equilibrium) contrapeso, equilibrio, balance; (debit, credit) saldo; — **of payments** balanza de pagos; — **wheel** volante del reloj; — **of trade** balanza comercial; — **of power** equilibrio político; **to lose one's** — perder el equilibrio; v. contrapesar; pesar; balancear(se); equilibrar; saldar (una cuenta).

bal·co·ny [bǽlkənɪ] s. balcón; galería (de teatro).

bald [bɔld] adj. calvo; pelado; pelón; sin vegetación; escueto, sin adornos; — **spot** calva.

bale [bel] s. bala, fardo (de mercancías); v. embalar, enfardar, empacar.

balk [bɔk] v. oponerse, rebelarse, resistirse; pararse de repente; negarse a seguir; encabritarse; **to** — **someone's plans** frustrar los planes de alguien.

ball [bɔl] s. (plaything) pelota, bola; (string, thread) ovillo; (weapon) bala; (dance) baile; — **bearing** cojinete de bolas; — **game** juego de pelota; beisbol; v. ovillar; **to** — **up** enredar, confundir.

bal·lad [bǽləd] s. romance; copla, canción; balada.

bal·last [bǽləst] s. lastre; grava (usada en terraplenes, caminos, etc.); v. lastrar, poner el lastre a (una embarcación).

bal·let [bǽlé] s. ballet.

bal·lis·tics [bəlístɪks] s. balística.

bal·loon [bəlún] s. globo (aerostático).

bal·lot [bǽlət] s. balota, Am. boleta, cédula para votar; voto; — **box** urna electoral; v. balotar, votar.

ball point [bɔlpɔɪnt] s. bolígrafo.

balm [bam] s. bálsamo.

bal·my [bámɪ] adj. balsámico; fragante; refrescante, suave; algo loco, chiflado.

bal·sam [bɔlsəm] s. bálsamo; especie de abeto.

bam·boo [bæmbú] s. bambú.

ban [bæn] s. bando, proclama; excomunión; prohibición; **marriage -s** (o **banns**) amonestaciones; v. proscribir, prohibir; condenar.

ba·nan·a [bənǽnə] s. plátano, banana; C.A. guineo. — **tree** banano; plátano.

band [bænd] s. (group) banda, partida, pandilla, cuadrilla; (musicians) banda; (strip) faja, lista, cinta, tira; partida, pandilla, cuadrilla; **rubber** — liga de goma; v. unit, juntar; atar, ligar; **to** — **together** confederarse, juntarse.

band·age [bǽndɪdʒ] s. venda, vendaje; v. vendar.

ban·dan·na [bændǽnə] s. pañuelo de hierbas.

ban·dit [bǽndɪt] s. bandido, bandolero.

bang [bæŋ] s. golpe, golpazo; estallido; fleco (de pelo); **with a** — de golpe, de golpazo; de repente; con estrépito; —! ¡pum!; v. golpear; hacer estrépito; cortar (el pelo) en fleco; **to** — **the door** dar un portazo.

ban·ish [bǽnɪʃ] *v.* proscribir, desterrar; **to — fear** desechar el temor.
ban·ish·ment [bǽnɪʃmənt] *s.* proscripción; destierro.
ban·is·ter [bǽnɪstəˑ] *s.* balaustre; barandilla, barandal, pasamano.
ban·jo [bǽndʒo] *s.* banjo.
bank [bæŋk] *s.* (*institution*) banco; (*in card game*) banca; (*of a river*) orilla, ribera, banda; escarpa; (*pile*) montón; **savings —** caja de ahorros; *adj.* bancario; de banco; *v.* depositar en un banco; amontonar (*tierra o arena*); cubrir con cenizas, tapar (*el fuego*); ladear (*un aeroplano*); **to — upon** (*o* **on**) contar con.
bank·book [bǽŋkbʊk] *s.* libreta de banco.
bank·er [bǽŋkəˑ] *s.* banquero.
bank·ing [bǽŋkɪŋ] *s.* transacciones bancarias banca; *adj.* bancario, de banca; **— house** banca, casa de banca.
bank·note [bǽŋknot] *s.* billete de banco.
bank·rupt [bǽŋkrʌpt] *adj.* en quiebra, arruinado, insolvente; *v.* quebrar; arruinar.
bank·rupt·cy [bǽŋkrʌptsɪ] *s.* bancarrota, quiebra; **to go into —** decalarse insolvente; quebrar, hacer bancarrota.
ban·ner [bǽnəˑ] *s.* bandera, estandarte, pendón; *adj.* primero, principal, sobresaliente.
ban·quet [bǽŋkwɪt] *s.* banquete; *v.* banquetear.
bap·tism [bǽptɪzəm] *s.* bautismo; bautizo.
Bap·tist [bǽptɪst] *s.* bautista.
bap·tize [bæptáɪz] *v.* bautizar.
bar [bɑr] *s.* (*of iron*) barra; barrote; tranca; (*obstacle*) barrera, obstáculo; (*of justice*) tribunal; foro; (*saloon*) cantina, taberna; (*counter*) mostrador; (*piece*) barra (*de jabón*); pastilla (*de chocolate*); **sand —** banco de arena; **-s** reja; **to be admitted to the —** recibirse de abogado; *v.* atrancar (*la puerta*); estorbar; prohibir; excluir.
barb [bɑrb] *s.* púa.
bar·bar·i·an [bɑrbérɪən] *s.* & *adj.* bárbaro; salvaje.
bar·ba·rous [bɑ́rbərəs] *adj.* bárbaro; salvaje; inculto.
bar·be·cue [bɑ́rbɪkju] *s. Méx., C.A., Col.* barbacoa; *Riopl.* churrasco; *v.* hacer barbacoa; *Riopl.* churrasquear.
barbed [bɑrbd] *adj.* con púas; **— wire** alambre de púas.
bar·ber [bɑ́rbəˑ] *s.* barbero; peluquero.
bar·ber·shop [bɑ́rbəˑʃɑp] *s.* barbería; peluquería.
bard [bɑrd] *s.* bardo, vate, poeta.
bare [ber] *adj.* (*naked*) desnudo; descubierto; pelado; (*evident*) manifiesto, patente; (*unfurnished*) desamueblado, vacío; **— majority** mayoría escasa; **to lay —** poner de manifiesto, hacer patente, revelar; **to ride —back** montar en pelo.
bare·foot [bérfʊt] *adj.* descalzo, con los pies desnudos; **-ed** [bérfʊtɪd] = **barefoot.**
bare·head·ed [bérhédɪd] *adj.* descubierto, sin sombrero.
bare·leg·ged [bérlégɪd] *adj.* con las piernas desnudas; sin medias.
bare·ly [bérlɪ] *adv.* apenas; escasamente; **— three pounds** tres libras escasas.
bare·ness [bérnɪs] *s.* desnudez.
bar·gain [bɑ́rgɪn] *s.* (*agreement*) convenio, pacto; negocio, trato; (*cheap*) ganga; **— sale** ganga, *Méx., C.A., Ven., Andes* barata; **into the —** por añadidura; de ganancia; **to make a —** cerrar un convenio; *v.* regatear; negociar; **to — for**

regatear; contar con, esperar.
barge [bɑrdʒ] *s.* lanchón; barca.
bar·i·tone [bǽrəton] *s.* & *adj.* barítono.
bar·i·um [bǽrɪəm] *s.* bario.
bark [bɑrk] *s.* ladrido; corteza (*de árbol*); barco velero; *v.* ladrar; descortezar, quitar la corteza.
bar·ley [bɑ́rlɪ] *s.* cebada.
barn [bɑrn] *s.* establo, cuadra; granero, troje; pajar; **streetcar —** cobertizo para tranvías.
bar·na·cle [bɑ́rnəkəl] *s.* cirrópodo.
barn·yard [bɑ́rnjɑrd] *s.* corral; **— fowl** aves de corral.
ba·rom·e·ter [bərɑ́mətəˑ] *s.* barómetro.
bar·on [bǽrən] *s.* barón.
ba·roque [bərók] *adj.* & *s.* barroco.
bar·rage [bərɑ́ʒ] *s.* fuego de barrera; presa.
bar·rel [bǽrəl] *s.* barril, barrica, tonel, cuba; cañón (*de fusil, pistola, etc.*); *v.* embarrilar (*meter en barril*).
bar·ren [bǽrən] *adj.* árido; estéril.
bar·ren·ness [bǽrənnɪs] *s.* aridez; esterilidad.
bar·rette [bərét] *s.* broche, prendedor (*para sujetar el pelo*).
bar·ri·cade [bǽrəkéd] *s.* barricada, barrera; *v.* poner barricadas; obstruir el paso con barricadas.
bar·ri·er [bǽrɪəˑ] *s.* barrera, valla; obstáculo.
bar·room [bɑ́rum] *s.* cantina; bar.
bar·ter [bɑ́rtəˑ] *v.* permutar, trocar, cambiar; *s.* permuta, trueque, cambio.
base [bes] *s.* base; basa; fundamento; *adj.* bajo, vil, ruin; inferior; *v.* basar, fundar; establecer.
base·ball [bésbɔ́l] *s.* baseball o beisbol.
base·ment [bésmənt] *s.* sótano.
base·ness [bésnɪs] *s.* bajeza, ruindad, vileza.
bash·ful [bǽʃfəl] *adj.* tímido, encogido, vergonzoso.
bash·ful·ness [bǽʃfəlnɪs] *s.* timidez, vergüenza, cortedad, apocamiento.
ba·sic [bésɪk] *adj.* básico; fundamental.
ba·sin [bésn] *s.* palangana, jofaina; lebrillo; tazón (*de fuente*); estanque, depósito de agua; **river —** cuenca de río.
ba·sis [bésɪs] (*pl.* **bases** [bésɪz]) *s.* base, fundamento.
bask [bæsk] *v.* calentarse (*al sol*); asolearse, tomar el sol.
bas·ket [bǽskɪt] *s.* cesta, cesto, canasta.
bas·ket·ball [bǽskɪtbɔl] *s.* basquetbol.
Basque [bæsk] *adj.* & *s.* (*person*) vasco; (*language*) vascuence, vasco; (*territory*) vascongado, vasco.
bass [bes] *s.* bajo (*en música*); *adj.* bajo, grave; **— drum** tambora, bombo; **— horn** tuba.
bas·tard [bǽstəd] *s.* & *adj.* bastardo.
baste [best] *v.* hilvanar; pringar (*empapar la carne con grasa*); apalear.
bat [bæt] *s.* palo, *Méx., Carib., Ven., C.A.* bate (*de beisbol*); garrote; golpe, garrotazo; murciélago; *v.* apalear; dar palos; *Méx., Carib., Ven., C.A.* batear; **not to — an eye** no pestañear.
batch [bætʃ] *s.* hornada; colección, grupo, conjunto.
bath [bæθ] *s.* baño.
bathe [beð] *v.* bañar(se).
bath·er [béðəˑ] *s.* bañista.
bath·house [bǽθhaʊs] *s.* casa de baños; bañadero.
bath·robe [bǽθrob] *s.* bata de baño.
bath·room [bǽθrum] *s.* baño, cuarto de baño.
bath·tub [bǽθtʌb] *s.* bañera, tina.
bath·y·sphere [bǽθɪsfɪr] *s.* batisfera.
bat·tal·ion [bətǽljən] *s.* batallón.
bat·ter [bǽtəˑ] *s.* batido, masa; *Am.* bateador (*de*

beisbol); *v.* golpear; **to — down** demoler.
bat·ter·y [bǽtərɪ] *s.* batería; acumulador; asalto.
bat·tle [bǽtl̩] *s.* batalla, lucha, combate; *v.* batallar, luchar, combatir.
bat·tle·field [bǽtl̩fɪld] *s.* campo de batalla.
bat·tle·ship [bǽtl̩ʃɪp] *s.* buque de guerra, acorazado.
bawl [bɔl] *s.* aullido; grito; *v.* aullar; gritar; pregonar; **to — out** regañar, reprender.
bay [be] *s.* bahía; ladrido, balido, aullido; **— rum** ron de laurel; **— tree** laurel; **— window** ventana saliente, mirador; **to hold at —** tener a raya; *adj.* bayo; *v.* dar aullidos, ladridos o balidos.
bay·o·net [béənɪt] *s.* bayoneta; *v.* traspasar; herir con bayoneta.
ba·zaar [bəzár] *s.* bazar; feria.
ba·zoo·ka [bəzúka] *s.* bazuca.
be [bi] *v.* (*innately*) ser; (*state or condition*) estar, verse, hallarse, encontrarse; **— that as it may** sea como sea; **to — cold (warm, hungry, right, etc.)** tener frío (calor, hambre, razón, *etc.*); **to — in a hurry** tener prisa; **he is to —** ha de ser; va a ser; **it is cold (hot, windy, etc.)** hace frío (calor, viento, *etc.*).
beach [bitʃ] *s.* playa, ribera; *v.* varar, poner en seco (*una embarcación*), encallar.
beach·head [bítʃhed] *s.* cabeza de playa.
bea·con [bíkən] *s.* faro, fanal; boya luminosa; señal; **aviation —** radiofaro.
bead [bid] *s.* cuenta (*de rosario, collar, etc.*); abalorio; glóbulo; gota (*de sudor*); **-s** rosario; collar de cuentas; *v.* adornar con abalorios o cuentecitas.
beak [bik] *s.* pico (*de ave*); espolón (*de nave*).
beak·er [bíkɚ] *s.* tazon.
beam [bim] *s.* rayo (*de luz o de calor*); sonrisa; viga, vigueta; brazo (*de balanza*); línea de radiación, radiofaro; *v.* emitir (*luz, rayos*); brillar; sonreír, estar radiante de alegría; radiar, transmitir por radio.
beam·ing [bímɪŋ] *adj.* radiante, resplandeciente; sonriente.
bean [bin] *s.* judía, habichuela; *Méx., C.A., Ven., Col.* frijol; *Ch., Ríopl.* poroto; **coffee —** grano de café; **Lima —** haba; **string —** judía o habichuela verde; *Méx., C.A.* ejote; *Ch., Ríopl.* poroto.
bear [bɛr] *s.* oso, osa; bajista (*el que hace bajar los valores en la Bolsa*); *v.* (*stand*) soportar; llevar; sobrellevar; tolerar, aguantar; (*give birth*) parir, dar a luz; producir; **to — down** deprimir; apretar; **to — a grudge** guardar rencor; **to — in mind** tener en cuenta; **to — on a subject** tener relación con un asunto; **to — oneself with dignity** portarse con dignidad; **to — out** confirmar; **to — testimony** dar testimonio.
beard [bɪrd] *s.* barba, barbas; aristas (*de trigo o maíz*); **-ed** *adj.* barbado, barbudo.
bearer [bérɚ] *s.* portador; mensajero. **bearing** [bérɪŋ] *s.* (*posture*) porte, presencia; (*relation*) relación, conexión; (*direction*) rumbo, orientación; (*mechanical*) cojinete; **ball —** cojinete de bolas; **beyond —** inaguantable, insufrible; **to lose one's -s** perder el rumbo, desorientarse; **fruit-bearing** *adj.* fructífero.
beast [bist] *s.* bestia, animal.
beat [bit] *s.* golpe; toque (*de tambor*); latido, palpitación; compás; ronda (*que hace el policía*); *v.* batir; golpear; azotar; vencer, ganar; marcar (*el compás*); pulsar, latir; sonar (*tambores*); **to —**

around the bush andarse por las ramas; valerse de rodeos; *pret. & p.p. de* **to beat.**
beat·en [bítn] *p.p. de* **to beat** & *adj.* batido; vencido; fatigado; **— path** camino trillado.
beat·er [bítɚ] *s.* batidor; molinillo; golpeador; **egg —** batidor de huevos.
be·a·t·if·ic [buɔtɪfɪk] *adj.* beatífico.
beat·ing [bítɪŋ] *s.* paliza, tunda, zurra; latido, pulsación.
be·at·i·tude [bɪǽtətjud] *s.* beatitud, bienaventuranza; **the Beatitudes** las bienaventuranzas.
beau [bo] *s.* galán, pretendiente.
beau·te·ous [bjútɪəs] *adj.* bello, hermoso.
beau·ti·ful [bjútəfəl] *adj.* bello, hermoso.
beau·ti·fy [bjútəfaɪ] *v.* hermosear, embellecer.
beau·ty [bjútɪ] *s.* belleza, hermosura; beldad; **— parlor** salón de belleza.
bea·ver [bívɚ] *s.* castor; **— board** cartón para tabiques.
be·came [bɪkém] *pret. de* **to become.**
be·cause [bɪkɔ́z] *conj.* porque; **— of** *prep.* por, a causa de.
beck·on [békən] *s.* seña, llamada; *v.* llamar a señas.
be·come [bɪkʌ́m] *v.* (*suit*) sentar bien a, quedar bien a; convenir a; (*turn out to be*) hacerse; ponerse; llegar a ser; convertirse en; **to — crazy** volverse loco; enloquecer; **to — angry** enojarse; **to — frightened** asustarse; **to — old** envejecer(se); **what has — of him?** ¿qué ha sido de él?; ¿qué se ha hecho él?; *p.p. de* **to become.**
be·com·ing [bɪkʌ́mɪŋ] *adj.* propio, conveniente; decente, decoroso; **that dress is — to you** le sienta bien ese traje.
bed [bɛd] *s.* cama, lecho; cauce (*de un río*); fondo (*de lago o mar*); cuadro (*de jardín*); yacimiento (*mineral*); **to go to —** acostarse; **to put to —** acostar.
bed·bug [bédʌg] *s.* chinche.
bed·clothes [bédkloz] *s. pl.* ropa de cama.
bed·ding [bédɪŋ] *s.* = **bedclothes.**
bed·pan [bédpæn] *s.* silleta; cómodo.
bed·rid·den [bédrɪdən] *adj.* en cama; postrado.
bed·rock [bédrák] *s.* roca sólida; lecho de roca.
bed·room [bédrum] *s.* cuarto de dormir, alcoba, *Méx., C.A.* recámara.
bed·side [bédsaɪd] *s.* **at the —** al lado de la cama; **— table** velador, mesilla de noche.
bed·spread [bédsprɛd] *s.* colcha, sobrecama.
bed·time [bédtaɪm] *s.* hora de acostarse, hora de dormir.
bee [bi] *s.* abeja; reunión (*para trabajar o competir*); **to have a — in one's bonnet** tener una idea metida en la cabeza.
beech [bitʃ] *s.* haya; **— nut** nuez de haya, hayuco.
beef [bif] *s.* carne de vaca o toro; vaca, toro (*engordados para matar*); **roast —** rosbif.
beef·steak [bífstek] *s.* bistec, biftec o bisté.
bee·hive [bíhaɪv] *s.* colmena; abejera.
been [bɪn, ben] *p.p. de* **to be.**
beer [bɪr] *s.* cerveza; **— tavern** cervecería.
beet [bit] *s.* remolacha, *Am.* betabel.
bee·tle [bítl̩] *s.* escarabajo.
be·fall [bɪfɔ́l] *v.* sobrevenir, acaecer, suceder.
be·fall·en [bɪfɔ́lən] *p.p. de* **to befall.**
be·fell [bɪfél] *pret. de* **to befall.**
be·fit [bɪfít] *v.* convenir.
be·fore [bɪfór] *adv.* (*temporal*) antes; (*spatial*) delante; al frente; *prep.* antes de; delante de; enfrente de; ante; *conj.* antes (de) que.
be·fore·hand [bɪfórhænd] *adv.* de antemano, por

adelantado, con antelación, con anticipación.
be·friend [bɪfrɛnd] v. ofrecer o brindar amistad a;
favorecer; amparar.
beg [bɛg] v. rogar, suplicar, pedir; mendigar,
pordiosear; **to — the question** dar por sentado
lo mismo que se arguye.
be·gan [bɪgǽn] pret. de **to begin.**
be·get [bɪgɛ́t] v. engendrar; causar, producir.
beg·gar [bɛ́gɚ] s. mendigo, pordiosero; pobre;
infeliz, miserable.
be·gin [bɪgín] v. comenzar, empezar, principiar.
be·gin·ner [bɪgínɚ] s. principiante; novicio.
be·gin·ning [bɪgínɪŋ] s. principio; comienzo,
empiezo; origen; **— with** comenzando con (o
por); **a partir de; at the** — al principio.
be·got [bɪgɑ́t] pret. & p.p. de **to beget.**
be·got·ten [bɪgɑ́tn] p.p. de **to beget.**
be·grudge [bɪgrʌ́dʒ] v. envidiar; ceder de mala
gana.
be·guile [bɪgáɪl] v. enganar; defraudar; seducir.
be·gun [bɪgʌ́n] p.p. de **to begin.**
be·half [bɪhǽf]: **in (on) — of** por; en nombre de; a
favor de; en defensa de; **in my** — en mi nombre;
a mi favor; por mi.
be·have [bɪhév] v. portarse, conducirse, obrar,
proceder (bien o mal); **— yourself!** ¡pórtate bien!
be·hav·ior [bɪhévjɚ] s. comportamiento, proceder,
conducta; funcionamiento; reacción.
be·head [bɪhɛ́d] v. decapitar, degollar, descabezar.
be·held [bɪhɛ́ld] pret. & p.p. de **to behold.**
be·hind [bɪháɪnd] adv. detrás; atrás; a la zaga, en
zaga; prep. detrás de, tras; **— one's back** a
espaldas de uno; **— time** atrasado, retrasado
from — por detrás; **to arrive ten minutes — time**
llegar con diez minutos de retraso; **to fall** —
atrasarse; retrasarse.
be·hold [bɪhóld] v. contemplar, mirar; **—! ¡the**
aquí!
be·hoove [bɪhúv] v. serle necesario a uno;
corresponderle a uno; atañerle a uno.
be·ing [bíɪŋ] s. ser; ente; esencia; existencia; ger. de
to be siendo; **for the time** — por ahora; por el
momento.
be·lat·ed [bɪlétɪd] adj. tardío; atrasado.
belch [bɛltʃ] v. eructar; **to — forth** echar, arrojar,
vomitar; s. eructo.
bel·fry [bɛ́lfrɪ] s. campanario.
Bel·gian [bɛ́ldʒɪən] adj. & s. belga.
be·lief [bəlíf] s. creencia; fe; convicción; opinión.
be·liev·a·ble [bəlívəbl] adj. creíble.
be·lieve [bəlív] v. creer; pensar; **to — in** creer en
tener fe en; confiar en.
be·liev·er [bəlívɚ] s. creyente, fiel.
be·lit·tle [bɪlítl] v. menospreciar, apocar,
empequeñecer; dar poca importancia a.
bell [bɛl] s. campana; campanilla; **cow** — cencerro,
esquila; **call** — timbre; **jingle** — cascabel; —
flower campanilla, campánula; **— jar** campana
de cristal.
bell·boy [bɛ́lbɔɪ] s. mozo de hotel, botones.
belle [bɛl] s. beldad, mujer bella.
bel·lig·er·ent [bəlídʒɚrənt] adj. & s. beligerante.
bel·low [bɛ́lo] v. bramido, rugido; v. rugir, bramar,
berrear; gritar.
bel·lows [bɛ́loz] s. (sing. & pl.) fuelle.
bel·ly [bɛ́lɪ] s. barriga, panza, vientre; estómago.
bel·ly·ache [bɛ́liek] s. dolor de barriga (estómago).
be·long [bəlɔ́ŋ] v. pertenecer, corresponder; **it does
not — here** está fuera de su sitio; está mal
colocado.
be·long·ings [bəlɔ́ŋɪŋz] s. pl. posesiones, bienes,

efectos, cosas.
be·lov·ed [bɪlʌ́vɪd] adj. querido, amado.
be·low [bəló] adv. abajo; bajo; debajo; **here** —
aquí abajo; en este mundo, de tejas abajo; prep.
bajo, debajo de.
belt [bɛlt] s. cinturón, cinto; correa; zona; **sword**
— talabarte; v. ceñir, fajar.
belt line [bɛ́ltlaɪn] s. vía de circunvalación.
be·moan [bɪmón] v. lamentarse de, quejarse de.
bench [bɛntʃ] s. banco, banca; tribunal.
bend [bɛnd] s. curva; vuelta, recodo; v. encorvar(se),
doblar(se), Am. enchuecar(se); inclinar(se);
someter(se), ceder; **to — one's efforts** esforzarse
(por), dirigir sus esfuerzos.
be·neath [bɪníθ] prep. debajo de, bajo; indigno de;
inferior a.
ben·e·dic·tion [bɛnədíkʃən] s. bendición.
ben·e·fac·tor [bɛ́nəfæktɚ] s. benefactor, bienhechor;
patrón.
be·nef·i·cent [bənɛ́fəsṇt] adj. benéfico.
ben·e·fi·cial [bɛnəfíʃəl] adj. benéfico; ventajoso,
provechoso.
ben·e·fi·ci·ar·y [bɛnɪfíʃɪɛrɪ] s. beneficiario.
ben·e·fit [bɛ́nəfɪt] s. beneficio; provecho, ventaja;
— performance función de beneficio; v.
beneficiar; hacer bien; **to — by the advice**
aprovecharse del consejo; **he -ed by the medicine**
le hizo bien la medicina.
be·nev·o·lence [bənɛ́vələns] s. benevolencia.
be·nev·o·lent [bənɛ́vələnt] adj. benévolo.
be·nign [bɪnáɪn] adj. benigno; afable.
bent [bɛnt] s. inclinación; tendencia; propensión;
pret. & p.p. de **to bend;** adj. encorvado; inclinado,
doblado; corvo; gacho; **to be — on** estar
resuelto a.
ben·zene [bɛ́nzin] s. benceno.
be·queath [bɪkwíð] v. heredar, legar, dejar en
testamento.
be·quest [bɪkwɛ́st] s. legado, donación.
be·rate [bɪrét] v. regañar, reñir, reprender.
be·ret [bəré] s. boina.
ber·ry [bɛ́rɪ] s. baya (como mora, fresa, etc.); grano
(de café).
berth [bɝθ] s. litera (de un camarote); **to give a
wide** — de sacarle el cuerpo, a hacerse a un lado
para dejar pasar.
be·ryl·li·um [bəríliəm] s. berilio.
be·seech [bɪsít] v. suplicar, rogar.
be·set [bɪsɛ́t] v. atacar; rodear; acosar; pret. &
p.p. de **to beset.**
be·side [bɪsáɪd] prep. (spatial) al lado de; cerca de;
(in addition) además de; fuera de; **to be — oneself**
estar fuera de sí, estar loco; **that is — the
question** eso no hace al caso; no se trata de eso;
adv. además.
be·sides [bɪsáɪdz] adv. además; prep. además de.
be·siege [bɪsídʒ] v. sitiar, cercar; acosar,
importunar.
be·sought [bɪsɔ́t] pret. & p.p. de **to beseech.**
best [bɛst] adj. mejor; adv. mejor; más; **the** — el
mejor; lo mejor; **— girl** novia; querida; **— man**
padrino de boda; **— seller** éxito de venta; de
mayor venta; **at** — a lo más, cuando más; **to do
one's** — hacer todo lo posible; **to get the — of
a person** vencer o ganarle a una persona; **to
make the** — of sacar el mejor partido de
be·stow [bɪstó] v. otorgar, conferir; **to — gifts
upon** hacer regalos (o dádivas) a; **time well -ed**
tiempo bien empleado.
bet [bɛt] s. apuesta; v. apostar; pret. & p.p. de **to
bet.**

be·take [bɪték] *v.* **to — oneself** encaminarse, dirigirse.

be·tak·en [bɪtékən] *p.p. de* **to betake.**

be·took [bɪtúk] *pret. de* **to betake.**

be·tray [bɪtré] *v.* traicionar, vender, hacer tración; revelar, no guardar (*un secreto*); **to one's ignorance** hacer patente su ignorancia.

be·tray·er [bɪtréəʳ] *s.* traidor, traicionera.

be·troth·al [bɪtrɔ́θəl] *s.* esponsales, compromiso, mutua promesa de matrimonio.

be·trothed [bɪtrɔ́θt] *s.* prometido, desposado; novio, novia.

bet·ter [bétəʳ] *adj.* mejor; *adv.* mejor; más; — **half** cara mitad; **so much the** — tanto mejor; **to be** — **off** estar mejor así; estar en mejores condiciones; **to change for the** — mejorar(se); **to get** — (mejorar(se), restablecerse, aliviarse; *v.* mejorar; **to** — **oneself** mejorarse, mejorar de situación.

bet·ter·ment [bétəʳmənt] *s.* mejoramiento, mejora, mejoría.

be·tween [bətwín] *prep.* entre, en medio de; *adv.* en medio.

bev·el [bévəl] *s.* bisel; *adj.* biselado; *v.* biselar.

bev·er·age [bévrɪdʒ] *s.* bebida.

be·wail [bɪwél] *v.* lamentar; quejarse de.

be·ware [btwér] *v.* guardarse (de), cuidarse (de); — ! ¡cuidado! ¡guárdese!

be·wil·der [bɪwíldəʳ] *v.* confundir, turbar, perturbar, dejar perplejo; **to be -ed** estar turbado o perplejo; estar desorientado.

be·wil·der·ment [bɪwíldəʳmənt] *s.* perplejidad. aturdimiento.

be·witch [bɪwítʃ] *v.* hechizar; aojar; encantar, cautivar.

be·yond [bɪjánd] *adv.* más allá, más lejos; *prep.* allende; más allá de; fuera de; — **my reach** fuera de mi alcance; — **the grave** ultratumba.

bi·as [báɪəs] *s.* (*tendency*) prejuicio; inclinación, tendencia; (*diagonal*) sesgo, oblicuidad; **on the** — sesgado, al sesgo, de lado; *adj.* sesgado, oblicuo; *v.* predisponer, inclinar, influir en.

bib [bɪb] *s.* babero; pechera (*de delantal*).

Bi·ble [báɪb] *s.* Biblia.

bib·li·cal [bíblɪk] *adj.* bíblico.

bib·li·og·ra·pher [bɪblɪágrəfəʳ] *s.* bibliógrafo.

bib·li·og·ra·phy [bɪblɪágrəfɪ] *s.* bibliografía.

bi·car·bon·ate [baɪkárbənet] *s.* bicarbonato.

bick·er [bíkəʳ] *v.* disputar, reñir.

bi·cy·cle [báɪsɪkl] *s.* bicicleta; *v.* andar en bicicleta.

bid [bɪd] *v.* postura, oferta; envite (*en naipes*); turno (*para envidar*); invitación; *v.* ofrecer (*precio*); mandar; invitar, convidar; rogar; envidar (*en naipes*); **to** — **fair** parecer muy probable; **to** — **good-bye** decir adiós; despedirse; **to** — **up** alzar, pujar (*la oferta en una subasta*); *pret. & p.p. de* **to bid.**

bid·den [bídn] *p.p. de* **to bid & to bide.**

bide [baɪd] *v.* aguardar; **to** — **one's time** esperar una buena oportunidad.

bi·en·ni·um [baɪénɪəm] *s.* bienio.

bier [bɪr] *s.* féretro.

big [bɪg] *adj.* grande; importante; imponente; — **Dipper** Osa Mayor; — **game** caza mayor; — **sister** hermana mayor; — **with child** encinta; **to talk** — darse bombo, *Am.* darse corte; **big-bellied** panzudo, panzón, barrigón; **big-hearted** magnánimo.

big·a·my [bígəmɪ] *s.* bigamia.

big·ot [bígət] *s.* fanático.

big·ot·ry [bígətrɪ] *s.* fanatismo; intolerancia.

bi·ki·ni [bɪkíni] *s.* traje bikini.

bi·la·bi·al [baɪlébɪəl] *adj.* bilabial.

bile [baɪl] *s.* bilis, hiel, cólera, mal humor.

bi·lin·gual [baɪlíŋgwəl] *adj. & s.* bilingüe.

bill [bɪl] *s.* (*statement*) cuenta; factura; (*poster*) cartel, anuncio; (*bank note*) billete de banco; programa de teatro; (*bird*) pico; (*legislative*) proyecto de ley; — **of exchange** libranza, letra de cambio; — **of fare** lista de platos; — **of lading** conocimiento de embarque; — **of rights** declaración de derechos; — **of sale** escritura o acta de venta; *v.* cargar en cuenta; enviar una cuenta a; **to** — **and coo** acariciarse y arrullar (*como las palomas*).

bill·board [bílbord] *s.* cartelera.

bill·fold [bílfold] *s.* cartera.

bil·liards [bíljəʳdz] *s.* billar.

bill·ing [bílɪŋ] *s.* imortancia relativa de los anuncios de artistas de teatro.

bil·lion [bíljən] *s.* billón, millón de millones; mil millones (*en los Estados Unidos y Francia*).

bil·low [bílo] *s.* oleada; ola grande; *v.* alzarse en olas.

bin [bɪn] *s.* arcón, depósito; **coal** — carbonera; **grain** — granero.

bind [baɪnd] *v.* (*unite*) unir, juntar; (*tie*) ligar; amarrar; vendar; ceñir; (*compel*) restringir; obligar, compeler; (*enclose*) encuadernar, empastar; rivetear.

bind·ing [báɪndɪŋ] *s.* encuadernación; ribete, cinta; **cloth** — encuadernación en tela; **paper** — encuadernación en rústica; *adj.* obligatorio.

binge [bɪndʒ] *s.* jarana; parranda; borrachera.

bi·og·ra·phy [baɪágrəfɪ] *s.* biografía.

bi·ol·o·gy [baɪálədʒɪ] *s.* biología.

bi·par·ti·san [baɪpártəzən] *adj.* de dos partidos; bipartito.

birch [bɜʳtʃ] *s.* abedul.

bird [bɜʳd] *s.* ave; pájaro; persona extraña o mal vista; — **of prey** ave de rapiña; — **seed** alpiste; — **shot** perdigones.

birth [bɜʳθ] *s.* nacimiento; parto; linaje; origen; principio; — **certificate** certificado (o fe) de nacimiento; — **control** control de la natalidad; anticoncepcionismo; limitación de partos; — **rate** natalidad; **to give** — dar a luz, parir.

birth·day [bɜʳθde] *s.* cumpleaños, natalicio.

birth·place [bɜʳθples] *s.* lugar de nacimiento, suelo natal.

birth·right [bɜʳθraɪt] *s.* derechos naturales de nacimiento; naturalidad; primogenitura.

bis·cuit [bískɪt] *s.* bizcocho; galleta; panecillo.

bish·op [bíʃəp] *s.* obispo; alfil (*en ajedrez*).

bish·op·ric [bíʃəprɪk] *s.* obispado.

bis·muth [bízməθ] *s.* bismuto.

bi·son [báɪsn] *s.* bisonte, búfalo.

bit [bɪt] *s.* pedacito, trocito; pizca, miaja, migaja; poquito; bocado (*del freno*); taladro; **I don't care a** — no me importa un ardite; *pret. & p.p. de* **to bite.**

bitch [bɪtʃ] *s.* perra; ramera, prostituta.

bite [baɪt] *s.* mordedura, mordisco, bocado; bocadito; picadura (*de insecto*); *v.* morder; mordiscar; picar.

bit·ten [bítn] *p.p. de* **to bite.**

bit·ter [bítəʳ] *adj.* amargo; agrio, acre; áspero; mordaz; **to fight to the** — **end** luchar hasta morir; **-s** *s. pl.* amargo; **-ly** *adv.* amargamente; con amargura.

bit·ter·ness [bítəʳnɪs] *s.* amargura, amargor; rencor; aspereza.

black [blæk] *adj.* negro; obscuro; sombrío; **black-**

and-blue amoratado, lleno de moretones; —
mark mancha, estigma, marca de deshonra; *s.*
negro; luto; —**out** obscurecimiento; **to put
down in** — **and white** poner por escrito *v.* teñir
de negro; embetunar, dar bola o betún a (*los
zapatos*).
black·ber·ry [blǽkbɛrɪ] *s.* zarzamora; mora.
black·bird [blǽkbɜd] *s.* mirlo.
black·board [blǽkbɔrd] *s.* encerado; pizarrón;
pizarra.
black·en [blǽkən] *v.* ennegrecer; obscurecer; teñir
de negro; denigrar.
black·head [blǽkhɛd] *s.* espinilla.
black·ish [blǽkɪʃ] *adj.* negruzco.
black·jack [blǽkdʒæk] *s.* (*weapon*) cachiporra
flexible; (*card game*) veintiuna.
black·mail [blǽkmel] *s.* chantaje, extorsión; *v.*
ejercer el chantaje, extorsionar.
black·ness [blǽknɪs] *s.* negrura; obscuridad.
black·smith [blǽksmɪθ] *s.* herrero; -'s **shop** herrería.
black·top [blǽktap] *s.* camino de superficie
bituminosa.
blad·der [blǽdɚ] *s.* vejiga.
blade [bled] *s.* hoja (*de navaja, cuchillo, etc.*); hoja
(*de hierba*); espada; pala (*de remo*); aspa (*de
hélice*); **shoulder** — espaldilla o paletilla.
blame [blem] *s.* culpa; *v.* culpar, echar la culpa a;
to be to — tener la culpa.
blame·less [blémlɪs] *adj.* inculpable.
blanch [blæntʃ] *v.* blanquear; palidecer; escaldar
(*almendras*).
bland [blænd] *adj.* blando, suave.
blank [blæŋk] *adj.* (*no writing*) en blanco; (*void*)
vacío; (*confused*) aturdido; — **cartridge** cartucho
vacío; — **face** cara sin expresión; — **form**
blanco, forma en blanco, *Méx., C.A., Ven.*
esqueleto; — **verse** verso suelto o libre; *s.*
blanco; vacío; hueco, intermedio; papel en
blanco; forma en blanco; **application** — forma
(*o blanco*) para memorial o solicitud.
blan·ket [blǽŋkɪt] *s.* manta; frazada; cobertor;
Ríopl., C.A., Méx., Ven., Col. cobija; *Méx.*
sarape, poncho; *adj.* general, inclusivo, que
abarca un grupo o clase.
blare [blɛr] *s.* fragor; son de trompetas; clarinada;
v. trompetear, proclamar; sonar (*las trompetas*);
hacer estruendo.
blas·pheme [blæfím] *v.* blasfemar.
blas·phe·my [blǽsfɪmɪ] *s.* blasfemia.
blast [blæst] *s.* (*wind*) ráfaga de viento, golpe de
viento; soplo repentino; (*trumpet*) trompetazo;
(*whistle*) silbido; (*explosion*) explosión; estallido;
carga de dinamita; — **furnace** alto horno; *v.*
volar (*con dinamita, etc.*); destruir.
blaze [blez] *s.* llama, llamarada, incendio;
resplandor; — **of anger** arranque de ira; *v.*
arder; resplandecer; **to** — **a trail** abrir (*o marcar*)
una senda.
bleach [blitʃ] *s.* blanqueador; blanqueo; *v.*
blasquear(se); desteñir(se).
bleach·ers [blítʃɚz] *s. pl.* graderías.
bleak [blik] *adj.* yermo, desierto; helado.
blear [blɪr] *v.* nublar (*los ojos*).
blear·y [blírɪ] *adj.* nublado, inflamado, lagrimoso,
lagañoso.
bleat [blit] *s.* balido; *v.* balar.
bled [blɛd] *pret. & p.p. de* **to bleed.**
bleed [blid] *v.* sangrar; desangrar; extorsionar.
blem·ish [blɛmɪʃ] *s.* mancha, tacha, defecto; *v.*
manchar; empañar.
blend [blɛnd] *s.* mezcla, entremezcla; gradación (*de

colores, sonidos, etc.); *v.* mezclar, entremezclar;
graduar (*colores o sonidos*); entremezclarse,
fundirse; armonizar.
bless [blɛs] *v.* bendecir; **God** — **you!** ¡que Dios te
bendiga!
bless·ed [blésɪd] *adj.* bendito; santo, beato;
bienaventurado; **the whole** — **day** todo el santo
día; [blɛst] *pret. & p.p. de* **to bless.**
bless·ing [blésɪŋ] *s.* bendición; gracia, don,
beneficio.
blest [blɛst] *adj.* = **blessed.**
blew [blu] *pret. de* **to blow.**
blight [blaɪt] *s.* pulgón (*parásito*); tizón (*honguillo
parásito*); quemadura (*enfermedad de las plantas*);
roña (*de las plantas*); malogro; ruina; *v.* destruir,
arruinar; frustrar (*esperanzas*).
blimp [blɪmp] *s.* dirigible pequeño.
blind [blaɪnd] *adj.* ciego; tapado, oculto; hecho a
ciegas; — **alley** callejón sin salida; — **choice**
selección hecha a ciegas; — **flying** vuelo ciego,
vuelo a ciegas; — **man** ciego; — **man's buff**
juego de la gallina ciega; — **date** [blaɪnddet] *s.*
cita a ciegas; persiana, cortinilla; biombo; venda
(*para los ojos*); anteojera (*para resguardar los
ojos del caballo*); **to be a** — **for someone** ser
tapadera de alguien; *v.* cegar; ofuscar; encubrir,
tapar.
blind·er [blaɪndɚ] *s.* anteojera, *Am.* visera (*para
caballos de tiro*).
blind·fold [blaɪndfold] *v.* vendar (*los ojos*); *adj.*
vendado (*de ojos*); *s.* venda (*para los ojos*).
blind·ly [blaɪndlɪ] *adv.* ciegamente; a ciegas.
blind·ness [blaɪndnɪs] *s.* ceguera, ceguedad.
blink [blɪŋk] *s.* pestañeo; parpadeo; guiño;
guiñada; *v.* pestañear; parpadear; guiñar.
blip [blɪp] *s.* bache de radar.
bliss [blɪs] *s.* beatitud, bienaventuranza, gloria;
felicidad.
blis·ter [blístɚ] *s.* ampolla, vejiga (*en la piel o en
cualquipr superficie*); *v.* ampollar, levantar
ampollas; ampollarse.
blitz [blɪts] *s.* ataque relámpago.
bliz·zard [blízɚd] *s.* ventisca; *v.* ventiscar.
bloat [blot] *v.* inflar(se); abotagarse.
blob [blab] *s.* burbuja.
block [blak] *s.* (*piece*) bloque, trozo de piedra;
zoquete; (*city section*) manzana (*de casas*); *Am.*
cuadra; (*obstacle*) estorbo, obstáculo; (*group*)
grupo, sección (*hat*) horma; — **pulley** polea;
chopping — tajo; *v.* estorbar; tapar; bloquear;
planchar (*sobre horma*); parar (*una pelota, una
jugada*); **to** — **out** esbozar, bosquejar; **to** — **the
door** impedir el paso; **to** — **up a door** tapiar una
puerta.
block·ade [blakéd] *s.* bloqueo, obstrucción *v.*
bloquear.
block·head [blákhɛd] *s.* zoquete, tonto, zopenco.
blond(e) [bland] *adj. & s.* rubio, blondo; *Mex.*
huero, güero; *Guat.* canche; *Sal., Hond.,* chele;
C.R. macho; *Col.* mono; *Ven.* catire.
blood [blʌd] *s.* sangre; — **count** análisis
cuantitativo de la sangre; — **pudding** (*o —
sausage*) morcilla; — **relative** pariente
consanguíneo; — **vessel** vena; arteria; **in cold** —
en sangre fría; — **bank** banco de sangre; —
poisoning septicemia.
blood·shed [blʌdʃɛd] *s.* matanza; derrame,
derramamiento o efusión de sangre.
blood·shot [blʌdʃat] *adj.* inyectado de sangre.
blood·thirst·y [blʌdθɜstɪ] *adj.* sanguinario.
blood·y [blʌdɪ] *adj.* sangriento; ensangrentado;

sanguinario, feroz.

bloom [blum] s. flor; florecimiento floración; lozanía; color rosado (*en las mejillas*) v. florecer, *Am.* florear.

bloom·ing [blúmɪŋ] adj. floreciente; fresco, lozano, vigoroso.

blos·som [blásəm] s. flor; floración, florecimiento; v. florecer.

blot [blɑt] s. mancha, borrón; tacha; v. manchar; borrar; secar (*con papel secante*); emborronar, echar manchas o borrones; **to — out** borrar, tachar; destruir; **this pen -s** esta pluma echa borrones; **blotting paper** papel secante.

blotch [blɑtʃ] v. emborronar o borronear, manchar, cubrir con manchas; s. mancha, borrón.

blot·ter [blɑ́tɚ] s. palel secante; libro borrador.

blouse [blaʊs] s. blusa.

blow [blo] s. (*stroke*) golpe; porrazo; (*shock*) choque, sorpresa, desastre; (*wind*) soplo, soplido; **to come to -s** venir a las manos; v. soplar; ventear; *C.A.* nortear; resoplar; sonar (*una trompeta*); fanfarronear; **to — a fuse** quemar un fusible; **to — one's nose** sonarse; **to — one's brains out** levantarse la tapa de los sesos; **to — open** abrirse; **to — out** apagar(se); estallar, reventar(se) (*un neumático*); **to — over** pasar; disiparse; **to — up** inflar, hinchar; volar (*con dinamita*); estallar, reventar.

blow·er [blóɚ] s. soplador; fuelle; ventilador, aventador.

blown [blon] p.p. de **to blow** & adj. soplado; inflado; **full-blown rose** rosa abierta.

blow·out [blóaʊt] s. reventón (*de neumático*); escape violento de gas, aire, etc.

blow·pipe [blópaɪp] s. soplete.

blow·torch [blótɔrtʃ] s. soplete.

blue [blu] adj. azul; triste, melancólico; s. azul; **light — (ojos)** zarco; **the -s** melancolía, morriña, murria; v. azular, teñir de azul.

blue·bell [blúbɛl] s. campanilla azul (*flor*).

blue·bird [blúbɝd] s. pájaro azul, *Am.* azulejo.

blue·jay [blúdʒe] s. gayo, especie de azulejo (*pájaro*).

bluff [blʌf] s. acantilado, escarpa, risco; fanfarronada; fanfarrón, farsante; v. fanfarronear; alardear, hacer alarde; echar bravatas; embaucar.

bluff·er [blʌ́fɚ] s. farsante, fanfarrón.

blu·ing [blúɪŋ] s. añil (*para ropa blanca*).

blu·ish [blúɪʃ] adj. azulado, azulejo.

blun·der [blʌ́ndɚ] s. disparate, desatino; despropósito; v. disparatar, desatinar; equivocarse.

blunt [blʌnt] adj. despuntado, embotado; brusco, grosero, *Méx.* claridoso; v. despuntar, embotar.

blur [blɝ] s. mancha; tacha; nube, cosa obscura o confusa; v. empañar, borronear, manchar; nublar, ofuscar; empañarse, nublarse.

blush [blʌʃ] s. sonrojo; rubor; v. sonrojarse, ruborizarse, ponerse colorado.

blus·ter [blʌ́stɚ] v. ventear o soplar recio (*el viento*); fanfarronear; s. ventolera, ventarrón, fuerte golpe de viento; jactancia, fanfarronada.

blus·ter·ing [blʌ́stərɪŋ] adj. fanfarrón, hactancioso; **— wind** ventarrón.

boar [bor] s. jabalí.

board [bord] s. (*wood*) tabla, tablero; mesa; (*meals*) comidas; (*directors*) junta, consejo; (*pasteboard*) en pasta; cartón; **the -s** las tablas, el teatro;

room and — cuarto y comida, pensión completa; asistencia; — of directors junta directiva; **bulletin — tabilla para anuncios; free on — (f.o.b.)** franco a bordo; **on — a bordo; en el tren; to go by the — caer en el mar; perderse; ser descartado; v. ir a bordo; subir (*al tren*); entablar, cubrir con tablas; tomar a pupilaje, dar asistencia, pensión o pupilaje; residir o comer (*en casa de huéspedes*).

board·er [bórdɚ] s. huésped, pupilo, pensionista.

board·ing·house [bórdɪŋhaʊs] s. casa de huéspedes, pensión.

boast [bost] s. jactancia; alarde; bravata; gloria, orgullo; v. jactarse, alardear; hacer alarde de; ostentar.

boast·ful [bóstfəl] adj. jactancioso.

boast·ful·ness [bóstfəlnɪs] s. jactancia; ostentación.

boat [bot] s. bote; barco, buque; lancha, chalupa.

boat·house [bóthaʊs] s. casilla o cobertizo para botes.

boat·ing [bótɪŋ] s. paseo en lancha o bote; **to go — pasear en bote.

boat·man [bótmən] (*pl.* **boatmen** [bótmɛn]) s. barquero.

bob [bɑb] s. meneo, sacudida; pesa (*de metal*); **to wear a — llevar el pelo corto (o en melena); v. menearse; **to — one's hair** cortarse el pelo en melena; **to — up** aparecer de repente; **to — up and down** saltar, brincar; cabecear (*dícese de una embarcación*).

bob·bin [bábɪn] s. carrete; bobina.

bob·tail [bábtel] s. rabón.

bob·white [bábhwait] s. cordorniz.

bode [bod] pret. & p.p. de **to bide**.

bod·ice [bádɪs] s. corpiño, jubón.

bod·i·ly [bádlɪ] adj. corpóreo; corporal; adv. todos juntos, colectivamente; **they rose — se levantaron todos a una, se levantaron-todos juntos.

bod·y [bádɪ] s. cuerpo; agregado, conjunto; gremio; carrocería (*de automóvil*); fuselaje (*de aeroplano*); **— of water** extensión de agua; **— politic** grupo político; estado.

bod·y·guard [bádɪgɑrd] s. guardaespaldas; *Am.* pistolero.

bog [bɑg] s. pantano; tremedal; v. hundir(se), atascarse.

Bo·he·mi·an [bohímɪən] adj. & s. bohemio.

boil [bɔɪl] s. hervor; tumorcillo; **to come to a — soltar el hervor, hervir; v. hervir; cocer; bullir; **to — down** hervir hasta evaporar; abreviar.

boil·er [bɔ́ɪlɚ] s. caldera, marmita; caldera de vapor; calorífero central.

boil·ing point [bɔ́ɪlɪŋpɔɪnt] s. punto de ebullición.

bois·ter·ous [bɔ́ɪstərəs] adj. bullicioso; esterpitoso; ruidoso; tumultuoso.

bold [bold] adj. atrevido, osado; arriesgado; audaz; insolente; claro, bien delineado; **— cliff** risco escarpado; **bold-faced** descarado; **bold-faced type** negritas.

bold·ness [bóldnɪs] s. atrevimiento; osadía; audacia; descaro, insolencia.

bo·lo·gna [bəlóní] s. especie de embutido.

Bol·she·vik [bólʃəvik] adj. & s. bolchevique.

bol·ster [bólstɚ] s. travesaño, almohada larga (*para la cabecera de la cama*); refuerzo, sostén, soporte; v. sostener, apoyar; apuntalar; **to — someone's courage** infundirle ánimo a alguien.

bolt [bolt] s. (*door lock*) pestillo, cerrojo; (*pin*) perno, tornillo grande; (*movement*) salida de repente; (*cloth*) rollo; **thunder — rayo; v. cerrar con cerrojo; tragar, engullir; romper con (*un partido político*); echarse a correr, lanzarse de repente; caer como rayo; **to — out** salir de golpe.

bomb [bɑm] *s.* bomba; *v.* bombardear; **— shelter** [bɑmʃɛltɚ] *s.* refugio antiaéreo.

bom·bard [bɑmbárd] *v.* bombardear, cañonear.

bom·bar·dier [bɑmbɚdír] *s.* bombardero.

bom·bard·ment [bɑmbárdmənt] *s.* bombardeo, cañoneo.

bom·bas·tic [bɑmbǽstɪk] *adj.* ampuloso, altisonante.

bom·ber [bɑmɚ] *s.* bombardero, avión de bombardeo.

bo·na fide [bónəfaɪd] *adj.* de buena fe.

bon·bon [bɑnbɑn] *s.* bombón, confite.

bond [bɑnd] *s.* (*tie*) lazo, vínculo; ligadura; (*obligation*) fianza, vale; obligación, bono.

bond·age [bɑndɪdʒ] *s.* servidumbre, esclavitud.

bonds·man [bɑndzmən] *s.* fiador.

bone [bon] *s.* hueso; espina (*de pez*); **-s** restos; osamenta; **— of contention** materia de discordia; **to make no -s about it** no pararse en pelillos; obrar francamente; *v.* deshuesar, quitar los huesos o espinas.

bon·fire [bɑnfaɪr] *s.* hoguera, fogata.

bon·net [bɑnɪt] *s.* gorra; sombrero (*de mujer*).

bo·nus [bónəs] *s.* prima, premio, gratificación.

bon·y [bóni] *adj.* huesudo.

boo [bu] *v.* mofarse, burlarse (*a gritos*); **— !** *interj.* ¡bu!; **-s** *s. pl.* rechifla, gritos de mofa.

boo·by [búbi] *s.* bobo, bobalicón.

book [bʊk] *s.* libro; **The book** la Biblia; **cash —** libro de caja; **memorandum — libreta; on the -s** cargado en cuenta; **to keep -s** llevar los libros o la contabilidad *v.* inscribir, asentar (*en un libro*); **to — passage** reservar pasaje.

book·case [bʊkkes] *s.* estante, estantería, armario para libros.

book·end [bʊkɛnd] *s.* apoyalibros, sujetalibros.

book·keep·er [bʊkkipɚ] *s.* tenedor de libros, contador.

book·keep·ing [bʊkkipɪŋ] *s.* teneduría de libros, contabilidad; **double entry —** partida doble.

book·let [bʊklɛt] *s.* librillo, librito, cuaderno, folleto.

book·sel·ler [bʊksɛlɚ] *s.* librero.

book·shelf [bʊkʃɛlf] *s.* estante, repisa para libros.

book·shop [bʊkʃɑp] *s.* librería.

book·store [bʊkstor] *s.* librería.

boom [bum] *s.* (*noise*) estampido; (*increase*) alza, auge (*en el mercado o bolsa*); bonanza, prosperidad momentánea; *v.* rugir, resonar, hacer estampido; prosperar, medrar, florecer, estar en bonanza; fomentar.

boon [bun] *s.* don; bendición, gracia, favor; *adj.* jovial, congenial.

boor [bʊr] *s.* patán, hombre zafio o grosero.

boor·ish [bʊrɪʃ] *adj.* grosero, zafio.

boost [bust] *s.* empuje, empujón (*de abajo* arriba); **— in prices** alza o auge de precios; *v.* empujar, alzar, levantar; hacer subir.

boost·er [bústɚ] *s.* aumentador; (*rocket*) cohete de lanzamiento; (*electronics*) amplificador.

boot [but] *s.* bota, calzado; **to —** por añadidura, de ganancia, *Méx.* de pilón, *Ven.* de ñapa; *Riopl., Andes* de yapa (*llapa*); *v.* dar un puntapié; **to — out** echar a puntapiés; echar a patadas.

boot·black [bútblæk] *s.* limpiabotas.

booth [buθ] *s.* casilla, puesto.

boot·leg·ger [bútlɛgɚ] *s.* contrabandista (*de licores*).

boot·lick·er [bútlɪkɚ] *s.* servilón, zalamero.

boo·ty [búti] *s.* botín, saqueo.

bo·rax [bóræks] *s.* bórax.

bor·der [bórdɚ] *s.* borde, margen, orilla; orla, franja; ribete; frontera; *v.* ribetear, guarnecer (*el borde*); orlar; **to — on** (*o* **upon**) lindar con, confinar con; rayar en; **it -s on madness** raya en locura.

bor·der·ing [bórdɚɪŋ] *adj.* limítrofe.

bor·der·line [bórdɚlaɪn] *adj.* fronterizo; indefinido.

bore [bor] *s.* taladro, barreno; agujero (*hecho con taladro*); calibre (*de un cañón, cilindro, etc.*); persona o cosa aburrida; *v.* taladrar, horadar, barrenar; aburrir, fastidiar; *pret. de* to **bear.**

bored [bord] *adj.* cansado, aburrido; *p.p. de* to **bore.**

bore·dom [bórdəm] *s.* aburrimiento, tedio, hastío, fastidio.

bo·ric ac·id [bórɪk æsəd] *a.* ácido bórico.

bor·ing [bórɪŋ] *adj.* aburrido, fastidioso, tedioso.

born [bɔrn] *p.p. de* to **bear** & *adj.* nacido; innato; **to be —** nacer.

borne [bɔrn] *p.p.* to **bear.**

bo·ron [bóran] *s.* borón.

bor·ough [bɝo] *s.* villa; distrito de municipio.

bor·row [bóro] *v.* pedir prestado; tomar prestado; tomar fiado.

bor·row·er [bórəwɚ] *s.* el que pide prestado.

bos·om [búzəm] *s.* seno, pecho, corazón; pechera (*de camisa*); **in the — of the family** en el seno de la familia; *adj.* querido; **— friend** amigo íntimo.

boss [bɔs] *s.* jefe; patrón; mayoral, capataz; *Am.* gamonal; **political —** cacique político; *v.* mandar, dominar, dirigir.

boss·y [bɔsɪ] *adj.* mandón, autoritario.

bo·tan·i·cal [bətǽnɪkl] *adj.* botánico.

bot·a·ny [bátnɪ] *s.* botánica.

botch [bɑtʃ] *s.* chapucería.

both [boθ] *adj.* & *pron.* ambos, entrambos, los dos; **— this and that** tanto esto como aquello; **— of them** ambos, ellos dos, los dos; **— (of) his friends** sus dos amigos, ambos amigos.

both·er [báðɚ] *s.* molestia; fastidio; incomodidad; enfado; *v.* molestar(se); fastidiar, enfadar; incomodar; estorbar.

both·er·some [báðɚsəm] *adj.* molesto.

bot·tle [bátl] *s.* botella; *v.* embotellar.

bot·tle·neck [bátlnɛk] *s.* embotellamiento; gollete.

bot·tom [bátəm] *s.* fondo; base; fundamento; asiento (*de silla*); **to be at the — of the class** ser el último de la clase; **what is at the — of all this?** ¿qué hay en el fondo de todo esto?

bou·doir [budwár] *s.* tocador.

bough [baʊ] *s.* rama.

bought [bɔt] *pret.* & *p.p. de* to **buy.**

bouil·lon [búljɑn] *s.* caldo.

boul·der [bóldɚ] *s.* peña, roca, guijarro grande, pedrusco.

boul·e·vard [búləvard] *s.* bulevar.

bounce [baʊns] *s.* bote, rebote (*de una pelota*); salto, brinco; *v.* hacer saltar; saltar, brincar; botar; echar, arrojar (*a alguien*); echar, despedir de un empleo.

bounc·er [baʊnsɚ] *s.* apagabroncas.

bound [baʊnd] *s.* (*jump*) salto, brinco; (*bounce*) bote, rebote; (*limit*) límite, confín; *adj.* ligado; confinado; obligado; ceñido; encuadernado; **to**

be — for ir para, ir con rumbo a; to be — up
in one's work estar absorto en su trabajo; it is
— to happen es seguro que sucederá; I am — to
do it estoy resuelto a hacerlo; v. botar, resaltar;
saltar, brincar; limitar; ceñir, cercar; pret. & p.p.
de to bind.

bound·a·ry [báundərɪ] s. límite, linde; confín;
frontera.

bound·less [báundlɪs] adj. ilimitado, sin límite, sin
término.

boun·ti·ful [báuntəfəl] adj. generoso, liberal;
abundante.

boun·ty [báuntɪ] s. largueza, generosidad; don,
favor, gracia; premio, recompensa.

bou·quet [buké] s. ramillete, ramo de flores;
aroma, fragancia.

bour·geois [burʒwá] adj. & s. burgués.

bout [baut] s. combate, lucha, contienda, asalto;
a — of pneumonia un ataque de pulmonía.

bow [bau] s. (inclination) reverencia; inclinación,
saludo; (of a ship) proa; v. hacer una reverencia,
inclinarse (para saludar); someterse; to — one's
head inclinar la cabeza -ed down agobiado.

bow [bo] s. arco (para tirar flechas); arco (de
violín); curva; lazo, moño (de cintas); bow-
legged adj. patizambo, patituerto; v. arquear;
tocar (un instrumento) con arco.

bow·els [báuəlz] s. pl. intestinos; entrañas; tripas.

bow·er [báuɚ] s. enramada, ramada, glorieta.

bowl [bol] s. cuenco; tazón; jícara; boliche, bola;
wash — palangana, lavamanos; -s juego de
bolos; v. bolear, jugar a los bolos, jugar al
boliche.

box [baks] s. caja; estuche; palco de teatro;
casilla; compartimiento; bofetada; —car furgón;
— office taquilla; — seat asiento de palco; v.
encajonar; meter en una caja; abofetear; boxear.

box·er [báksɚ] s. boxeador, pugilista.

box·ing [báksɪŋ] s. boxeo, pugilato.

boy [bɔɪ] s. niño; muchacho; mozo.

boy·cott [bɔ́ɪkat] v. boicotear; s. boicoteo.

boy·hood [bɔ́ɪhud] s. niñez; mocedad, juventud.

boy·ish [bɔ́ɪʃ] adj. pueril; juvenil; aniñado.

brace [bres] s. traba; tirante; apoyo, refuerzo;
corchete ({}); carpenter's — berbiquí; v. trabar;
apoyar, reforzar; asegurar; estimular, fortalecer;
to — up animarse, cobrar ánimo.

brace·let [bréslɪt] s. brazalete, pulsera.

brack·et [brǽkɪt] s. ménsula, soporte, sostén;
repisa; -s paréntesis cuadrados; v. colocar entre
paréntesis; unir; agrupar.

brag [bræg] s. jactancia; v. jactarse (de); hacer
alarde de.

brag·gart [brǽgɚt] adj. & s. jactancioso,
fanfarrón; matamoros, matamoscas.

braid [bred] s. trenza; galón, trencilla; v. trenzar;
galonear, guarnecer con galones.

brain [bren] s. cerebro; seso; to rack one's -s
devanarse los sesos, romperse la cabeza; v. saltar
la tapa de los sesos; — trust [bréntrʌst] v. grupo
de consejeros; — washing [brénwɔʃɪŋ] s. lavado
cerebral.

brake [brek] s. freno; Ven., Col. retranca; Méx.,
Riopl., C.A., Carib. garrote; — lining forro de
freno; — shoe zapata de freno; — drum tambor
de freno; — fluid flúido de freno; to apply the -s
frenar; v. frenar, enfrenar; Ven., Col. retrancar;
Méx., Riopl., C.A., Carib. dar garrote.

brake·man [brékmən] s. guardafrenos, Ven., Col.
retranquero, Méx., Riopl., C.A., Carib. garrotero.

bram·ble [brǽmbl] s. zarza, breña.

bran [bræn] s. salvado.

branch [bræntʃ] s. rama (de árbol); gajo; ramo
(de la ciencia); sucursal; bifurcación; sección;
tributario (de un río); ramificación; — railway
ramal; v. ramificarse; bifurcarse.

brand [brænd] s. (make) marca; marca de fábrica;
hechura; (cattle mark) hierro; Riopl., Méx. fierro
(de marcar);estigma; brand-new nuevecito,
flamante, acabado de hacer o comprar; v.
marcar; herrar, marcar (con hierro candente);
difamar; to — as motejar de.

bran·dish [brǽndɪʃ] v. blandir; s. floreo, molinete.

bran·dy [brǽndɪ] s. aguardiente; coñac.

brash [bræʃ] adj. insolente; impetuoso; temerario.

brass [bræs] s. (metal) latón, bronce; (actitud)
desfachatez, descaro; -es utensilios de latón;
instrumentos músicos de metal; — band banda
murga.

bras·siere [brəzír] s. corpiño, sostén (para ceñir
los pechos).

brat [bræt] s. mocoso.

bra·va·do [brəvádo] s. bravata; jactancia.

brave [brev] adj. bravo, valiente, valeroso; v.
arrostrar; desafiar, hacer frente a.

brav·ery [brévərɪ] s. valor, valentía.

brawl [brɔl] v. reyerta, pendencia, riña; alboroto;
v. armar una pendencia, alborotar, reñir.

bray [bre] s. rebuzno; v. rebuznar.

bra·zen [brézn] adj. bronceado; de bronce; de
latón; descarado, desvergonzado.

bra·zier [brezjɚ] s. brasero.

breach [britʃ] s. (opening) brecha, abertura;
(infraction) infracción; rompimiento; — of faith
abuso de confianza; — of promise violación de
un compromiso; v. abrir brecha.

bread [bred] s. pan; —box caja para pan; — line
cola del pan; v. Méx., C.A. empanizar; Riopl.,
Ch. empanar.

breadth [bredθ] s. anchura, ancho; extensión;
amplitud.

break [brek] s. rompimiento; rotura; interrupción;
pausa; bajón (en la bolsa o mercado); to have a
bad (good) — tener mala (buena) suerte; to
make a bad — cometer un disparate; v.
romper(se), quebrantar(se), quebrar(se);
amansar, domar; arruinar; to — away fugarse,
escaparse; to — into forzar la entrada en,
allanar (una morada); to — loose escaparse,
desprenderse, soltarse; to — out estallar (una
guerra); to — out of prison escaparse de la cárcel;
to — a promise faltar a la palabra; to — up
desmenuzar, despedazar; disolver; perturbar.

break·a·ble [brékəbl] adj. quebradizo.

break·down [brékdaun] s. parada imprevista;
análisis. (automobile) avería, pane.

break·er [brékɚ] s. rompiente (ola); law —
infractor.

break·fast [brékfəst] s. desayuno; to eat — tomar
el desayuno; v. desayunarse.

break·through [brékθru] s. adelanto repentino;
brecha.

break·wa·ter [brékwɔtɚ] s. rompeolas, malecón.

breast [brest] s. pecho; seno; teta; pechuga (de
ave); to make a clean — of it confesarlo todo.

breath [breθ] s. aliento; resuello; respiro; soplo,
hálito; in the same — al mismo instante, con el
mismo aliento; out of — sin aliento, jadeante;
under one's — en voz baja, entre dientes.

breathe [brið] v. respirar; resollar; tomar aliento;
exhalar; to — into infundir; he -ed his last
exhaló el último suspiro; he did not — a word

no dijo palabra.
breath·less [bɛ́θlıs] *adj.* jadeante; sin aliento.
breath·tak·ing [brɛ́θtekıŋ] *adj.* conmovedor; emocionante.
bred [brɛd] *pret. & p.p. de* **to breed.**
breech·es [brítʃız] *s. pl.* bragas, calzones; **riding —** pantalones de montar.
breed [brid] *s.* casta, raza; ralea, especie; *v.* criar; procrear, engendrar; educar; producirse; multiplicarse.
breed·er [brídɚ] *s.* criador; animal de cría.
breed·ing [brídıŋ] *s.* cría, crianza; educación, modales.
breeze [briz] *s.* brisa, vientecillo.
breez·y [brízı] *adj.* airoso, ventilado; refrescado (*por la brisa*); animado, vivaz; **it is —** hace brisa.
breth·ren [brɛ́ðrın] *s. pl.* hermanos (*los fieles de una iglesia o los miembros de una sociedad*).
brev·i·ty [brɛ́vətı] *s.* brevedad.
brew [bru] *s.* cerveza; mezcla; *v.* fermentar, hacer (*licores*); preparar (*té*); fomentar, tramar; fabricar cerveza; amenazar (*una tormenta, calamidad etc.*).
brew·er·y [brúərı] *s.* cervecería, fábrica de cerveza.
bri·ar, bri·er [bráɚ] *s.* zarza; rosal silvestre.
bribe [braıb] *s.* soborno, cohecho; *v.* sobornar, cohechar.
brib·er·y [bráıbərı] *s.* soborno, choecho.
brick [brık] *s.* ladrillo; ladrillos; *v.* enladrillar.
brick·bat [bríkbæt] *s.* pedazo de ladrillo; insulto.
bri·dal [bráıdl] *adj.* nupcial; de bodas; de novia; **— dress** vestido de novia.
bride [braıd] *s.* novia, desposada.
bride·groom [bráıdgrum] *s.* novio, desposado.
brides·maid [bráıdzmed] *s.* madrina de boda.
bridge [brıdʒ] *a.* puente; caballete de la nariz; **draw —** puente levadizo; **suspension —** puente colgante; *v.* tender un puente; **to — a gap** llenar un vacío.
bri·dle [bráıdl] *s.* brida, freno de caballo; freno, restricción; **— path** camino de harradura; *v.* embridar, enfrenar; reprimir, subyugar; erguirse, erguir la cabeza.
brief [brif] *adj.* breve, corto, conciso; *s.* sumario, resumen; informe, memorial; breve apostólico; **to hold a — for** abogar por; **-ly** *adv.* brevemente; en resumen, en breve.
brief·case [brífkes] *s.* portapapeles, cartera grande.
brief·ing [brífıŋ] *s.* reunión preparatoria.
bri·gade [brıgéd] *s.* brigada.
bright [braıt] *adj.* (*light*) brillante, claro, luciente; radiante; (*smart*) inteligente; (*cheerful*) alegre; listo, vivo; **— color** color subido.
bright·en [bráıtn] *v.* abrillantar, pulir, dar lustre; avivar(se); alegrar(se); animar(se); aclararse; despejarse (*el cielo*).
bright·ness [bráıtnıs] *s.* brillo, lustre, esplendor; claridad; viveza, agudeza, inteligencia.
bril·liance [bríljəns] *s.* brillantez, brillo; lustre; resplandor.
bril·liant [bríljənt] *adj.* brillante; resplandeciente; espléndido; talentoso; *s.* brillante; diamante.
brim [brım] *s.* borde, margen, orilla; ala (*de sombrero*); **to fill to the —** llenar o arrasar hasta el borde; **to be filled to the —** estar hasta los topes; estar de bote en bote; *v.* **to — over** rebosar.
brine [braın] *s.* salmuera.
bring [brıŋ] *v.* traer; llevar; ocasionar, causar; **to — about** producir, efectuar, ocasionar; **to —**

down bajar; **to — forth** dar a luz; producir; **to — to** resucitar; **to — up** criar, educar; **to — up a subject** traer a discusión un asunto.
brink [brıŋk] *s.* borde, orilla, margen; **on the — of** al borde de.
brisk [brısk] *adj.* vivo, animado; fuerte; rápido; **-ly** *adv.* aprisa; fuerte.
bris·tle [brısl] *s.* creda; *v.* erizar(se); **to — with** estar erizado (*o* lleno) de.
bris·tly [brıstı] *adj.* serdoso; erizado.
Brit·ish [brıtıʃ] *adj.* británico; **the —** los ingleses.
brit·tle [brıtl] *adj.* quebradizo; frágil.
broach [brotʃ] *v.* tracer a colación, comenzar a hablar de (*un asunto*).
broad [brɔd] *adj.* ancho; amplio, vasto, extenso; tolerante; **— hint** insinuación clara; **in — daylight** en pleno día; **broad-minded** tolerante; de amplias miras.
broad·cast [brɔ́dkæst] *s.* radiodifusión, difusión, emisión; transmisión; *v.* difundir; radiodifundir, radiar, emitir.
broad·cloth [brɔ́dklɔθ] *s.* paño fino de algodón o de lana.
broad jump [brɔ́ddʒəmp] *s.* salto de longitud.
broad·side [brɔ́dsaıd] *s.* (*guns*) andanada; (*announcement*) hoja suelta de propaganda.
bro·cade [brokéd] *s.* brocado.
broil [brɔıl] *v.* asar(se).
broke [brok] *pret. de* **to break;** *adj.* quebrado, arruinado; pelado; sin dinero; **to go —** quebrar, arruinarse.
bro·ken [brókən] *p.p. de* **to break &** *adj.* roto; rompido; quebrado; quebrantado; arruinado; abatido; **— English** inglés champurrado o champurreado; inglés mal pronunciado.
bro·ker [brókɚ] *s.* corredor, agente; bolsista; **money —** cambista, corredor de cambio.
bro·mide [brómaıd] *s.* bromuro.
bro·mine [brómin] *s.* bromo.
bron·chi·tis [brankáıtıs] *s.* bronquitis.
bron·co, bron·cho [bráŋko] *s.* potro o caballo bronco, *Riopl.* redomón; **— buster** domador.
bronze [branz] *s.* bronce; color de bronce; *v.* broncear.
brooch [brutʃ] *s.* broche (*alfiler de pecho*).
brood [brud] *s.* pollada; nidada; cría; casta; *v.* empollar; encobar; **to — over** cavilar.
brook [bruk] *s.* arroyuelo, riachuelo, *C.A., Col., Ven.* quebrada; *Méx., Riopl.* arroyo, cañada; *v.* tolerar, aguantar.
broom [brum] *s.* escoba; retama (*arbusto*); **—stick** palo o mango de escoba.
broth [brɔθ] *s.* caldo.
broth·er [brʌ́ðɚ]s. hermano; cofrade.
broth·er·hood [brʌ́ðɚhʊd] *s.* hermandad; fraternidad; cofradía.
broth·er-in-law [brʌ́ðɚrınlɔ] *s.* cuñado.
broth·er·ly [brʌ́ðɚlı] *adj.* fraternal.
brought [brɔt] *pret. & p.p. de* **to bring.**
brow [braʊ] *s.* ceja; frente.
brown [braʊn] *adj.* moreno, café; castaño; pardo oscuro; tostado; *v.* tostar(se).
browse [braʊz] *v.* hojear; ramonear, pacer, pastar (*el ganado*).
bruise [bruz] *s.* magulladura, cardenal, magullón, contusión; *v.* magullar(se); estropear(se).
bru·net, bru·nette [brunét] *adj.* moreno, trigueño.
brunt [brʌnt] *s.* fuerza (*de un golpe o ataque*); **the — of the battle** lo más reñido del combate.
brush [brʌʃ] *s.* (*tooth, clothes*) cepillo; (*paint, shaving*) brocha; (*artist's*) pincel; (*vegetation*)

matorral; *(contact)* roce; encuentro; *v.* cepillar, acepillar; rozar; **to — aside** desechar, echar a un lado; **to — up** cepillarse; repasar *(una materia, una técnica, etc.).*

brush·wood [brʌʃwʊd] *s.* broza; maleza, matorral, zarzal.

brusque [brʌsk] *adj.* brusco.

bru·tal [brútl] *adj.* brutal, bruto.

bru·tal·i·ty [brutǽlətɪ] *s.* brutalidad.

brute [brut] *s.* bruto, bestia; *adj.* bruto, brutal; bestial.

bub·ble [bʌbl] *s.* burbuja; borbollón; ampolla; *v.* borbotar; hacer espuma; bullir; **to — over with** joy rebosar de gozo.

bub·ble gum [bʌbl gʌm] *s.* chicle hinchable; chicle de globo.

buck [bʌk] *s.* macho cabrío, cabrón; gamo; macho *(del ciervo, antilope, etc.)*; corveta, respingo *(de un caballo)*; embestida; — **private** soldado raso; **to pass the** — *Ríopl., Andes* pasar el fardo; *v.* cabriolear, respingar; embestir; encabritarse; bregar con *(el viento)*; **to — up** cobrar ánimo; **the horse -ed the rider** el caballo tiró al jinete.

buck·et [bʌkɪt] *s.* cubo, cubeta, balde.

buck·le [bʌkl] *s.* hebilla; *v.* abrochar con hebilla; doblarse; abollarse; **to — down to** aplicarse con empeño a; **to — with** luchar con.

buck·shot [bʌkʃɑt] *s.* posta, perdigón.

buck·skin [bʌkskɪn] *s.* badana; ante.

buck·wheat [bʌkhwit] *s.* trigo sarraceno.

bud [bʌd] *s.* botón, yema; capullo, pimpollo; retoño; *v.* echar botones o retoños; florecer.

bud·dy [bʌdɪ] *s.* camarada, compañero.

budge [bʌdʒ] *v.* mover(se), menear(se), bullir.

bud·get [bʌdʒɪt] *s.* presupuesto.

buff [bʌf] *s.* piel de ante o búfalo; color de ante; pulidor; **blindman's** — juego de la gallina ciega; *v.* pulir, pulimentar.

buf·fa·lo [bʌflo] *s.* búfalo.

buf·fet [bʌfé] *s.* aparador; repostería; mostrador para refrescos; fonda de estación.

buf·fet·ing [bʌfətɪŋ] *s.* golpeteo, bataneo.

buf·foon [bʌfún] *s.* bufón; payaso.

bug [bʌg] *s.* insecto; bicho; microbio.

bug·gy [bʌgɪ] *s.* cochecillo.

bu·gle [bjúgl] *s.* clarín; corneta; trompeta.

build [bɪld] *s.* estructura; talle, forma, hechura; *v.* edificar, construir; fabricar; **to — up one's health** reconstituir su salud.

build·er [bɪldɚ] *s.* constructor.

build·ing [bɪldɪŋ] *s.* edificio; construcción.

build-up [bɪldʌp] *s.* refuerzo paulatino.

built [bɪlt] *pret. & p.p. de* to build.

bulb [bʌlb] *s.* bulbo *(de la cebolla y otras plantas)*; planta bulbosa; **electric light** — bombilla, bujía eléctrica, ampolla, *Méx., C.A., Andes* foco; *Riopl.* bombita.

bulge [bʌldʒ] *s.* bulto; protuberancia; panza; *v.* abultar; combarse.

bulg·y [bʌldʒɪ] *adj.* abultado.

bulk [bʌlk] *s.* bulto, volumen; masa; **the — of the army** el grueso del ejército.

bulk·y [bʌlkɪ] *adj.* abultado, voluminoso, grueso.

bull [bʊl] *s.* toro; alcista *(el que hace subir los valores en la bolsa)*; disparate, error; **Papal** — bula; —**fight** corrida de toros; *adj.* taurino; —**fighter** torero; **bull's-eye** centro del blanco; tiro perfecto.

bull·dog [bʊldɔg] *s.* perro dogo, perro de presa.

bull·doz·er [bʊldozɚ] *s.* topadora; buldózer.

bul·let [bʊlɪt] *s.* bala.

bul·le·tin [bʊlətn] *s.* boletín; — **board** tablilla para fijar anuncios o avisos.

bull·frog [bʊlfrɑg] *s.* rana grande.

bull·head·ed [bʊlhédɪd] *adj.* terco, obstinado.

bul·lion [bʊljən] *s.* oro *(o* plata) en barras; metálico; lingotes de oro o plata.

bul·ly [bʊlɪ] *s.* pendenciero, valentón, fanfarrón, matón; *adj.* excelente, magnífico; *v.* intimidar; echar bravatas.

bul·wark [bʊlwɚk] *s.* baluarte; defensa.

bum [bʌm] *s.* holgazán, vagabundo; gorrón; borracho; **to go on a** — irse de juerga; *adj.* malo, mal hecho, de ínfima calidad; inútil, inservible; **to feel** — estar indispuesto; *v.* holgazanear; vivir de gorra.

bum·ble·bee [bʌmblbi] *s.* abejorro, abejón.

bump [bʌmp] *s. (blow)* tope, choque; golpe; *(lump)* chichón; abolladura; hinchazón; joroba, protuberancia; *v.* topar, topetear; chocar; abollar; **to — along** zarandearse, ir zarandeándose; **to — off** derribar; matar.

bump·er [bʌmpɚ] *s.* parachoques, defensa; tope; *adj.* grande, excelente; — **crop** cosecha abundante.

bun [bʌn] *s.* bollo *(de pan).*

bunch [bʌntʃ] *s.* manojo, puñado; racimo *(de uvas, plátanos, etc.)*; grupo; — **of flowers** ramillete de flores; *v.* juntar(se), agrupar(se).

bun·dle [bʌndl] *s.* lío, bulto, fardo, hato; haz; paquete; *v.* liar, atar; envolver; **to — up** abrigarse, taparse bien.

bun·ga·low [bʌŋgəlo] *s.* casita de un piso.

bun·gle [bʌŋgl] *v.* chapucear; estropear; echar a perder.

bun·ion [bʌnjən] *s.* juanete.

bunk [bʌŋk] *s.* litera, camilla *(fija en la pared)*; embuste, tontería, paparrucha, papa.

bun·ny [bʌnɪ] *s.* conejito.

buoy [bɔɪ] *s.* boya; *v.* boyar, mantener a flote; **to — up** sostener, apoyar.

buoy·ant [bɔɪənt] *adj.* boyante, flotante; vivaz, animado, alegre.

bur·den [bɝdn] *s.* carga, peso; cuidado; gravamen; *v.* cargar; agobiar.

bur·den·some [bɝdnsəm] *adj.* gravoso; pesado.

bu·reau [bjúro] *s.* oficina; despacho; división, ramo; cómoda; **travel** — oficina de turismo; **weather** — oficina de meteorología, observatorio meteorológico.

bu·reauc·ra·cy [bjurákrəsɪ] *s.* burocracia.

bu·reau·crat [bjúrəkræt] *s.* burócrata.

bur·glar [bɝglɚ] *s.* ladrón *(que se mete en casa ajena).*

bur·gla·ry [bɝglərɪ] *s.* robo.

bur·i·al [bérɪəl] *s.* entierro; — **place** cementerio.

bur·lap [bɝlæp] *s.* arpillera, tela burda de cáñamo.

bur·ly [bɝlɪ] *adj.* corpulento, voluminoso, grandote.

burn [bɝn] *s.* quemadura; *v.* quemar(se); incendiar; arder; abrasar(se).

burn·er [bɝnɚ] *s.* quemador; mechero; hornilla.

bur·nish [bɝnɪʃ] *v.* bruñir; pulir; *s.* bruñido, pulimento.

burnt [bɝnt] *pret. & p.p. de* to burn.

bur·row [bɝo] *s.* madriguera, conejera; *v.* hacer madrigueras en; escarbar; socavar, minar; esconderse.

burst [bɝst] *s.* reventón, explosión; estallido; — **of laughter** carcajada; *v.* reventar(se); abrirse; estallar; **to — into** entrar de repente; **to — into tears** prorrumpir en lágrimas; **to — with laughter** estallar o reventar de risa; *pret. & p.p.*

de to burst.
bur·y [bérɪ] *v.* enterrar; sepultar; soterrar; **to be buried in thought** estar absorto, meditabundo o pensativo.
bus [bʌs] *s.* autobús, ómnibus, *Méx.* camión; *C.A.* camioneta; *Ríopl.* colectivo; *Ch.* micro; *Carib.* guagua.
bus·boy [bʌ́sbɔi] *s.* ayudante de camarero.
bush [buʃ] *s.* arbusto; mata; matorral, breñal; **rose** — rosal; **to beat around the** — andarse por las ramas.
bush·el [búʃəl] *s.* fanega (*medida de áridos*).
bush·ing [buʃɪŋ] *s.* buje.
bush·y [búʃɪ] *adj.* matoso, espeso; lleno de arbustos.
bus·i·ly [bízḷɪ] *adv.* diligentemente.
busi·ness [bíznɪs] *s.* negocio; ocupación; comercio; asunto; — **house** casa de comercio, establecimiento mercantil; — **transaction** negocio, transacción comercial; **to do** — **with** negociar con, comerciar con; **he has no** — **doing it** no tiene derecho a hacerlo; **not to be one's** — no concernirle a uno, no importarle a uno; **to make a** — **deal** hacer un trato.
busi·ness·like [bíznɪslaɪk] *adj.* eficaz, eficiente, práctico; formal.
busi·ness·man [bíznɪsmæn] *s.* hombre de negocios, comerciante.
bust [bʌst] *s.* busto; pecho (*de mujer*); **to go out on a** — salir o ir de parranda; *v.* reventar; quebrar; domar (*un potro*).
bus·tle [bʌ́sl] *s.* bulla, bullicio, trajín, alboroto; polisón (*para abultar las caderas*); *v.* bullir(se); menearse; trajinar.
bus·y [bízɪ] *adj.* ocupado; activo; —**body** entremetido; — **street** calle de mucho tráfico; *v.* **to** — **oneself** ocuparse.
but [bʌt] *conj., prep. & adv.* pero, mas; sino; menos, excepto; sólo, no … más que; — **for you** a no ser por Vd.; **not only** … — **also** no sólo … sino (que) también; **I cannot help** — no puedo menos de; **she is** — **a child** no es más que una niña.
bu·tane [bjutén] *s.* butano.
butch·er [bútʃɚ] *s.* carnicero; **-'s shop** carnicería; *v.* matar (*reses*); hacer una matanza o carnicería; destrozar.
butch·er·y [bútʃɚɪ] *s.* carnicería, matanza.
but·ler [bʌ́tlɚ] *s.* despensero, mayordomo; **-'s pantry** despensa.
butt [bʌt] *s.* culata (*de rifle*); colilla (*de cigarro*); tope; topetazo; cabezada; **the** — **of ridicule** el blanco de las burlas; *v.* topetear, embestir; **to** — **in** entremeterse; **to** — **into a conversation** meter baza, *Am.* meter su cuchara.
but·ter [bʌ́tɚ] *s.* manteca, mantequilla; *v.* enmantecar, untar con manteca o mantequilla.
but·ter·cup [bʌ́tɚkʌp] *s.* botón de oro (*flor*).
but·ter·fly [bʌ́tɚflaɪ] *s.* mariposa; — **stroke** brazada mariposa.
but·ter·milk [bʌ́tɚmɪlk] *s.* suero de mantequilla.
but·ter·scotch [bʌ́tɚskátʃ] *s.* confite o jarabe de azúcar y mantequilla.
but·tocks [bʌ́təks] *s. pl.* nalgas, asentaderas.
but·ton [bʌ́tṇ] *s.* botón; — **hook** abotonador; *v.* abotonar(se).
but·ton·hole [bʌ́tṇhol] *s.* ojal; *v.* hacer ojales; **to** — **someone** detener, demorar a uno (*charlando*).
but·tress [bʌ́trɪs] *s.* contrafuerte; refuerzo, sostén; *v.* sostener, reforzar, poner contrafuerte.
buy [baɪ] *v.* comprar; **to** — **off** sobornar; **to** — **up**

acaparar.
buy·er [báɪɚ] *s.* comprador.
buzz [bʌz] *s.* zumbido; murmullo; *v.* zumbar; murmurar; **to** — **the bell** tocar el timbre.
buz·zard [bʌ́zɚd] *s.* buitre, *Am.* aura, *Méx., C.A.* zopilote, *Ríopl.* carancho; *Col., Andes* gallinazo.
by [baɪ] *prep.* por; cerca de; al lado de; junto a; según; — **and** — luego, pronto; — **dint of** fuerza de; — **far** con mucho; — **night** de noche; — **the way** de paso; a propósito; entre paréntesis; — **this time** ya; a la hora de ésta; — **two o'clock** para las dos; **days gone** — días pasados.
by·gone [báɪgɔn] *adj.* pasado; **let -s be -s** lo pasado pasado, lo pasado pisado.
by·law [báɪlɔ] *s.* estatuto; reglamento.
by·pass [báɪpæs] *s.* desviación.
by·path [báɪpæθ] *s.* atajo, vereda.
by-prod·uct [báɪprɑdəkt] *s.* producto secundario o accessorio.
by·stand·ers [báɪstændɚz] *s.* circunstantes, presentes; mirones.

C:c **cab** [kæb] *s.* coche de alquiler; taxímetro, taxi; casilla (*de una locomotora*); — **driver** cochero; chófer.
cab·bage [kǽbɪdʒ] *s.* col, repollo, berza.
cab·in [kǽbɪn] *s.* cabaña, choza; bohío, *Mex.* jacal; *Carib.* barraca; camarote (*de buque*); **airplane** — cabina de aeroplano.
cab·i·net [kǽbənɪt] *s.* gabinete; armario; escaparate, vitrina; (*dept. heads*) gabinete.
cab·i·net·ma·ker [kǽbənɪtmékɚ] *s.* ebanista.
ca·ble [kébḷ] *s.* cable, amarra; cablegrama; — **address** dirección cablegráfica; *v.* cablegrafiar.
ca·ble·gram [kéblgræm] *s.* cablegrama.
cab·man [kǽbmən] *s.* cochero; chófer.
cack·le [kǽkḷ] *s.* cacareo; charla; risotada; *v.* cacarear; parlotear, charlar.
cac·tus [kǽktəs] *s.* (*pl.* **cacti** [kǽktaɪ]) *s.* cacto.
cad [kæd] *s.* canalla (*m.*); malcriado.
cad·die [kǽdɪ] *s.* muchacho que lleva los palos de golf; caddy.
ca·dence [kédṇs] *s.* cadencia.
ca·det [kədét] *s.* cadete.
cad·mi·um [kǽdmɪəm] *s.* cadmio.
ca·fé [kəfé] *s.* café, restaurante.
caf·e·te·ri·a [kæfətíriə] *s.* restaurante (*en donde se sirve uno mismo*).
caf·fein [kǽfiɪn] *s.* cafeína.
cage [kedʒ] *s.* jaula; *v.* enjaular.
ca·jole [kədʒol] *v.* halagar para conseguir algo.
cake [kek] *s.* pastel; bizcocho; bollo; torta; *Ven., Col.* panqué; pastilla (*de jabón*); — **of ice** témpano de hielo; *v.* apelmazarse, formar masa compacta.
cal·a·bash [kǽləbæʃ] *s.* totuma.
ca·lam·i·ty [kəlǽmətɪ] *s.* calamidad.
cal·ci·um [kǽlsɪəm] *s.* calcio.
cal·cu·late [kǽlkjəlet] *v.* calcular; **to** — **on** contar con.
cal·cu·la·tion [kælkjəléʃən] *s.* cálculo; cómputo, cuenta.
cal·cu·lus [kǽlkjələs] *s.* cálculo.
cal·en·dar [kǽləndɚ] *s.* calendario, almanaque; — **year** año corriente.
calf [kæf] *s.* (*pl.* **calves** [kævz]) *s.* ternero, ternera,

becerro, becerra; pantorrilla (*de la pierna*); —
skin piel de becerro o becerrillo.
cal·i·ber [kǽlǝbǝ] *s.* calibre.
cal·i·co [kǽlǝko] *s.* calicó (*tela de algodón*).
call [kɔl] *s.* (*summons*) llamada; llamamiento; (*visit*)
visita; (*demand*) demanda, pedido; **within** — al
alcance de la voz; *v.* llamar; gritar; hacer una
visita; pasar (*lista*); **to** — **at a port** hacer escala
en un puerto; **to** — **for** ir por; demandar,
pedir; **to** — **on** visitar a; acudir a (*en busca de
auxilio*); **to** — **to order a meeting** abrir la sesión;
to — **together** convocar; **to** — **up on the phone**
llamar por teléfono.
cal·ler [kɔ́lǝ] *s.* visita, visitante; llamador (*el que
llama*).
cal·lous [kǽlǝs] *adj.* calloso; duro.
cal·lus [kǽlǝs] *s.* callo.
calm [kɑm] *s.* calma; sosiego; *adj.* calmo,
tranquilo, quieto, sosegado; *v.* calmar,
tranquilizar, sosegar; desenfadar; **to** — **down**
calmarse; **-ly** *adv.* tranquilamente, con calma.
calm·ness [kɑ́mnɪs] *s.* calma, sosiego, tranquilidad.
cal·o·rie [kǽlǝrɪ] *s.* caloría.
cal·um·ny [kǽlǝmnɪ] *s.* calumnia.
cam [kæm] *s.* leva.
came [kem] *pret. de* **to come**.
cam·el [kǽml] *s.* camello.
cam·e·o [kǽmɪo] *s.* camafeo.
cam·er·a [kǽmǝrǝ] *s.* cámara fotográfica.
cam·ou·flage [kǽmǝflɑʒ] *s.* camuflaje; disfraz; *v.*
encubrir, disfrazar.
camp [kæmp] *s.* campo, campamento; — **chair**
silla de tijera; **political** — partido político; *v.*
acampar.
cam·paign [kæmpén] *s.* campaña; *v.* hacer
campaña; hacer propaganda.
cam·phor [kǽmfǝ] *s.* alcanfor.
cam·pus [kǽmpǝs] *s.* campo (*de una universidad*).
can [kæn] *s.* lata, bote, envase; — **opener** abrelatas;
v. envasar, enlatar; *v. defect. y aux.* (*usado sólo
en las formas* **can** *y* **could**) poder, saber.
Ca·na·di·an [kǝnédɪǝn] *adj. & s.* canadiense.
ca·nal [kǝnǽl] *s.* canal; **irrigation** — acequia.
ca·nar·y [kǝnérɪ] *s.* canario.
can·cel [kǽnsl] *v.* cancelar; anular; revocar; techar.
can·cel·er [kǽnsǝlǝ] *s.* matasellos.
can·cel·la·tion [kænsléʃǝn] *s.* cancelación;
anulación; revocación.
can·cer [kǽnsǝ] *s.* cáncer.
can·de·la·brum [kændǝlǽbrǝm] *s.* candelabro.
can·did [kǽndɪd] *adj.* cándido, franco, sincero.
can·di·da·cy [kǽndǝdǝsɪ] *s.* candidatura.
can·di·date [kǽndǝdet] *s.* candidato; aspirante.
can·dle [kǽndl] *s.* candela, vela; bujía; cirio; —
power potencia lumínica (*en bujías*).
can·dle·stick [kǽndlstɪk] *s.* candelero; palmatoria.
can·dor [kǽndǝ] *s.* candor, sinceridad.
can·dy [kǽndɪ] *s.* dulce, confite, bombón; — **shop**
confitería, dulcería; *v.* confitar, azucarar;
almibarar, garapiñar; cristalizarse (*el almibar*);
candied almonds almendras garapiñadas.
cane [ken] *s.* caña; — **plantation** (*o* —**field**)
cañaveral; C.A. cañal; — **chair** silla de bejuco;
sugar — caña de azúcar; **walking** — bastón;
chuzo (*de sereno*); **to beat with a** — bastonear,
apalear.
ca·nine [kénaɪn] *adj.* canino, perruno.
can·ker [kǽnkǝ] *s.* úlcera, llaga (*de la boca*).
canned [kænd] *adj.* enlatado, envasado, conservado
(*en lata o en vidrio*); — **goods** conservas
alimenticias.

can·ner·y [kǽnǝrɪ] *s.* fábrica de conservas
alimenticias.
can·ni·bal [kǽnǝbl] *s.* caníbal.
can·non [kǽnǝn] *s.* cañón.
can·non·ade [kænǝnéd] *s.* cañoneo; *v.* cañonear.
can·not [kǽnɑt] = **can not** no puedo, no puede, no
podemos, etc.
can·ny [kǽnɪ] *adj.* sagaz; astuto.
ca·noe [kǝnú] *s.* canoa, *Ríopl.* piragua, *Méx.*
chalupa.
can·on [kǽnǝn] *s.* canon; ley, regla; criterio,
norma; canónigo.
can·o·py [kǽnǝpɪ] *s.* dosel, pabellón; (*airplane*)
capota, cúpula.
can·ta·loupe [kǽntlop] *s.* melón.
can·teen [kæntín] *s.* cantina; cantimplora.
can·ton [kǽntǝn] *s.* cantón, región, distrito.
can·vas [kǽnvǝs] *s.* lona; lienzo; toldo; cañamazo.
can·vass [kǽnvǝs] *s.* inspección; escrutinio;
indagación, encuesta, pesquisa; solicitación (*de
votos*); *v.* examinar, escudriñar; recorrer (*un
distrito solicitando algo*); hacer una encuesta;
solicitar votos o pedidos comerciales.
can·yon [kǽnjǝn] *s.* cañón, garganta.
cap [kæp] *s.* (*head covering*) gorro, gorra, boina;
Mex. cachucha; (*academic*) birrete; (*bottle,
wheel*) tapa, tapón; (*mountain*) cima, cumbre;
percussion — cápsula fulminante; *v.* tapar,
poner tapón a; **that -s the climax** eso es el
colmo.
ca·pa·bil·i·ty [kepǝbílǝtɪ] *s.* capacidad, aptitud.
ca·pa·ble [képǝbl] *adj.* capaz; hábil; competente.
ca·pa·cious [kǝpéʃǝs] *adj.* capaz, amplio, espacioso.
ca·pac·i·ty [kǝpǽsǝtɪ] *s.* capacidad; cabida;
habilidad; aptitud; **in the** — **of a teacher** en
calidad de maestro.
cape [kep] *s.* capa; capote; cabo, promontorio.
ca·per [képǝ] *s.* cabriola; voltereta, brinco; **to cut
-s** cabriolar, retozar, hacer travesuras; *v.*
cabriolar, retozar, juguetear, brincar.
cap·il·lar·y [kǽpɪlɛrɪ] *s. & adj.* capilar.
cap·i·tal [kǽpǝtl] *s.* capital (*f.*), ciudad principal;
capital (*m.*), caudal; chapitel (*de una columna*);
letra mayúscula; **to make** — **of** sacar partido
de, aprovecharse de; *adj.* capital; principal;
excelente; —**punishment** pena capital, pena de
muerte.
cap·i·tal·ism [kǽpǝtlɪzǝm] *s.* capitalismo.
cap·i·tal·ist [kǽpǝtlɪst] *s.* capitalista; -**ic** *adj.*
capitalista.
cap·i·tal·i·za·tion [kæpǝtlǝzéʃǝn] *s.* capitalización.
cap·i·tal·ize [kǽpǝtlaɪz] *v.* capitalizar; sacar
provecho de; escribir con mayúscula.
cap·i·tol [kǽpǝtl] *s.* capitolio.
ca·pit·u·late [kǝpítʃǝlet] *v.* capitular.
ca·price [kǝprís] *s.* capricho.
ca·pri·cious [kǝpríʃǝs] *adj.* caprichoso.
cap·size [kæpsáɪz] *v.* zozobrar, volcar(se).
cap·sule [kǽpsl] *s.* cápsula.
cap·tain [kǽptɪn] *s.* capitán; *v.* capitanear, mandar;
servir de capitán.
cap·ti·vate [kǽptǝvet] *v.* cautivar.
cap·tive [kǽptɪv] *s. & adj.* cautivo, prisionero.
cap·tiv·i·ty [kæptívǝtɪ] *s.* cautiverio, prisión.
cap·tor [kǽptǝ] *s.* aprehensor o aprensor.
cap·ture [kǽptʃǝ] *s.* captura; aprensión; presa;
toma; *v.* capturar; prender; tomar (*una ciudad*).
car [kɑr] *s.* coche, automóvil, auto, *Am.* carro;
(*de ferrocarril*); camarín (*de ascensor*), ascensor,
Am. elevador; **dining** — coche comedor; **freight**
— furgón, vagón de carga.

car·a·mel [kǽrəml̩] s. caramelo.
car·at [kǽrət] s. quilate.
car·a·van [kǽrəvæn] s. caravana.
car·bol·ic [karbálɪk] adj. carbólico.
car·bon [kárbən] s. carbono; — **copy** copia en papel carbón; — **paper** papel carbón; — **monoxide** monóxido de carbono; — **dioxide** dióxido de carbono.
car·bu·re·tor [kárbəretɚ] s. carburador.
car·cass [kárkəs] s. esqueleto; cuerpo descarnado, despojo; res (muerta); casco (de un buque).
card [kard] s. (missive) tarjeta; (playing) naipe, carta; carda (para cardar lana); — **index** índice de fichas; fichero; —**sharp** fullero; **file** — ficha, papeleta; **post**— tarjeta postal; **pack of -s** baraja, naipes; **to play -s** jugar a la baraja, jugar a los naipes; v. cardar (lana).
card·board [kárdbord] s. cartón; **fine** — cartulina.
car·di·ac [kárdɪæk] adj. cardiaco, cardíaco.
car·di·nal [kárdn̩əl] adj. cardinal; principal, fundamental; rojo, bermellón; — **number** número cardinal; s. cardenal (dignatario eclesiástico); — **bird** cardenal.
care [kɛr] s. (worry) cuidado; aflección; ansiedad; (caution) cuidado, cautela, esmero; (responsibility) cargo, custodia; **to take** — **of** cuidar de; v. tener interés (por); **to** — **about** tener interés en (o por); preocuparse de; importarle a uno; **to** — **for** cuidar de; estimar, tenerle cariño a; gustarle a uno; simpatizarle a uno (una persona); **to** — **to** querer, desear, tener ganas de; **what does he** —? ¿a él qué le importa?
ca·reen [kərín] v. moverse con rapidez y sin control; volcar (un buque).
ca·reer [kərír] s. carrera, profesión.
care·free [kérfri] adj. libre de cuidado, sin cuidados, despreocupado.
care·ful [kérfəl] adj. cuidadoso; esmerado; cauteloso; **to be** — tener cuidado; **-ly** adv. cuidadosamente, con cuidado; con esmero.
care·ful·ness [kérfəlnɪs] s. cuidado; esmero; cautela.
care·less [kérlɪs] adj. descuidado; negligente; indiferente; **-ly** adv. sin cuidado; sin esmero; descuidadamente.
care·less·ness [kérlɪsnɪs] s. descuido; falta de esmero; desaliño; negligencia.
ca·ress [kərés] s. caricia; v. acariciar.
care·tak·er [kértekɚ] s. cuidador, guardián, vigilante, celador.
car·fare [kárfɛr] s. pasaje de tranvía.
car·go [kárgo] s. carga, cargamento; flete.
car·i·ca·ture [kǽrɪkətʃɚ] s. caricatura; v. caricaturar o caricaturizar.
car·load [kárlod] s. furgonada, vagonada, carga de un furgón o vagón.
car·nal [kárn̩l] adj. carnal.
car·na·tion [karnéʃən] s. clavel; color encarnado o rosado.
car·ni·val [kárnəvl̩] s. carnaval; fiesta, holgorio; feria, verbena.
car·niv·o·rous [karnívərəs] adj. carnívoro, carnicero.
car·ol [kǽrəl] s. villancico; **Christmas** — villancico de Navidad; v. cantar villancicos; celebrar con villancicos.
car·om [kǽrəm] s. carambola; rebote.
ca·rouse [kəráuz] v. andar de parranda, Ríopl., Ch. andar de farra; embriagarse.
car·pen·ter [kárpəntɚ] s. carpintero.

car·pen·try [kárpəntrɪ] s. carpintería.
car·pet [kárpɪt] s. alformbra; **small** — tapete; v. tapizar.
car·riage [kǽrɪdʒ] s. carruaje, coche; acarreo, transporte; porte; — **paid** porte pagado; **good** — buen porte, garbo, manera airosa.
car·ri·er [kǽrɪɚ] s. portador; mensajero; carretero, trajinante; transportador; Am. cargador; **airplane** — portaaviones; **disease** — transmisor de gérmenes contagiosos; **mail** — cartero.
car·rot [kǽrət] s. zanahoria.
car·ry [kǽrɪ] v. llevar; acarrear, transportar; Am. cargar; sostener (una carga); traer consigo; ganar, lograr (una elección, un premio, etc.); **to** — **away** llevarse; cargar con; entusiasmar, encantar; **to** — **on** continuar; no parar; **to** — **oneself well** andar derecho, airoso, garboso; **to** — **out** llevar a cabo, realizar; sacar.
cart [kart] s. carro, carreta, vagoncillo; v. acarrear.
cart·age [kártɪdʒ] s. carretaje, acarreo.
cart·er [kártɚ] s. carretero; àcarreador.
car·ton [kártn̩] s. caja de cartón.
car·toon [kartún] s. caricatura.
car·toon·ist [kartúnɪst] s. caricaturista.
car·tridge [kártrɪdʒ] s. cartucho; — **belt** cartuchera canana; — **box** cartuchera; — **shell** cápsula.
carve [karv] v. tallar; labrar; cincelar; esculpir; trinchar, tajar (carne).
carv·er [kárvɚ] s. trinchador; trinchante (cuchillo); entallador, escultor.
carv·ing [kárvɪŋ] s. talla, obra de escultura, entalladura; — **knife** trinchante.
cas·cade [kæskéd] s. cascada, salto de agua.
case [kes] s. (instance) caso; (box) caja; (pillow) funda, cubierta; (scabbard) vaina; **window** — marco de ventana; **in** — **that** caso que, en caso de que, dado que; **in any** — en todo caso; **just in** — por si acaso; — **work** trabajo con casos.
case·ment [késmənt] s. puerta ventana.
cash [kæʃ] s. dinero contante; — **box** cofre; — **payment** pago al contado; — **on delivery (c.o.d.)** contra reembolso, cóbrese al entregar; — **register** caja registradora (de dinero); **to pay** — pagar al contado; v. cambiar, cobrar (un cheque).
ca·shew [kǽʃju] s. anacardo; marañón.
cash·ier [kæʃír] s. cajero.
cask [kæsk] s. tonel, barril, cuba.
cas·ket [kǽskɪt] s. ataúd; **jewel** — joyero, cofrecillo.
cas·se·role [kǽsərol] s. cacerola.
cas·sette [kəsét] s. carrete pequeña de cinta magnetofónica; pequeña grabadora.
cas·sock [kǽsək] s. sotana.
cast [kæst] s. tirada (al pescar); molde; matiz; apariencia; defecto (del ojo); reparto (de papeles dramáticos); actores; — **iron** hierro fundido o colado; v. echar; tirar; arrojar; lanzar; moldear; repartir (papeles dramáticos); escoger (para un papel dramático); **to** — **a ballot** votar; **to** — **a statue in bronze** vaciar una estatua en bronce; **to** — **about** buscar; hacer planes; **to** — **aside** desechar; **to** — **lots** echar suertes; **to be** — **down** estar abatido; pret. & p.p. de **to cast**.
cas·ta·nets [kǽstənɛts] s. pl. castañuelas.
caste [kæst] s. casta; **to lose** — perder el prestigio social.
Cas·til·ian [kæstíljən] s. & adj. castellano.
cas·tle [kǽsl̩] s. castillo; alcázar; fortaleza; torre, roque (en ajedrez).

CA

cas·tor oil [kǽstɚ ɔɪl] s. aceite de ricino.
cas·trate [kǽstret] v. capar, castrar.
cas·u·al [kǽʒʊəl] adj. casual; accidental.
cas·u·al·ty [kǽʒʊəltɪ] s. baja o pérdida (en el ejército); accidente.
cat [kæt] s. gato; gata.
cat·a·log [kǽtlɔg] s. catálogo; v. catalogar.
cat·a·lyst [kǽtəlɪst] s. catalizador.
cat·a·ract [kǽtərækt] s. catarata.
ca·tarrh [kətár] s. catarro.
ca·tas·tro·phe [kətǽstrəfɪ] s. catástrofe.
catch [kætʃ] s. presa; botín; presa; pestillo (de la puerta); trampa; cogida (de la pelota); — **phrase** frase llamativa; — **question** pregunta tramposa; **he is a good** — es un buen partido; **to play** — jugar a la pelota; v. coger; prender; asir; alcanzar; enganchar; comprender; ser contagioso, pegarse; **to** — **a glimpse of** vislumbrar; **to** — **cold** coger un resfriado, resfriarse; **to** — **on** comprender, caer en la cuenta; **to** — **one's eye** llamarle a uno la atención; **to** — **sight of** avistar; **to** — **unaware** sorprender, coger desprevenido; **to** — **up with** alcanzar a, emparejarse con.
catch·er [kǽtʃɚ] s. cogedor, agarrador; parador, cácher o receptor (en béisbol).
catch·ing [kǽtʃɪŋ] adj. pegajoso, contagioso; atractivo.
cat·e·chism [kǽtəkɪzəm] s. catecismo.
cat·e·go·ry [kǽtəgorɪ] s. categoría.
ca·ter [kétɚ] v— surtir, abastecer, proveer los alimentos (para banquetes, fiestas, etc.) **to** — **to** proveer a las necesidades o al gusto de; **to** — **to the taste of** halagar el gusto de.
cat·er·pil·lar [kǽtəpɪlɚ] s. oruga; — **tractor** tractor.
ca·the·dral [kəθídrəl] s. catedral.
cath·ode [kǽθod] s. cátodo; — **rays** rayos católicos.
Cath·o·lic [kǽθəlɪk] s. & adj. católico.
Ca·thol·i·cism [kəθáləsɪzəm] s. catolicismo.
cat·sup [kǽtsəp] s. salsa de tomate.
cat·tle [kǽtl] s. ganado, ganado vacuno; — **raiser** ganadero, Ríopl. estanciero; — **raising** ganadería; — **ranch** hacienda de ganado, Méx., C.A. rancho, Ríopl. estancia; Ven., Col. hato.
caught [kɔt] pret. & p.p. de **to catch**.
cau·li·flow·er [kóləflaʊɚ] s. coliflor.
cause [kɔz] s. causa; v. causar; originar; **to** — **to** hacer; inducir a.
caus·tic [kóstɪk] adj. cáustico.
cau·ter·ize [kótɚraɪz] v. cauterizar.
cau·tion [kóʃən] s. precaución, cautela; aviso, advertencia; —! ¡cuidado! ¡atención!; v. prevenir, avisar, advertir.
cau·tious [kóʃəs] adj. cauto; cauteloso, cuidadoso; precavido.
cav·a·lier [kævəlír] s. caballero; galán; adj. orgulloso, altivo, desdeñoso.
cav·al·ry [kǽvlrɪ] s. caballería.
cave [kev] s. cueva; caverna; v. **to** — **in** hundirse; desplomarse.
cav·ern [kǽvɚn] s. caverna.
cav·i·ty [kǽvətɪ] s. cavidad, hueco; (tooth) carie.
ca·vort [kəvórt] v. cabriolar.
caw [kɔ] s. graznido; v. graznar.
cease [sis] v. cesar; parar, desistir; dejar de.
cease·less [síslɪs] adj. incesante.
ce·dar [sídɚ] s. cedro.
cede [sid] v. ceder.
ce·dil·la [sɪdɪlə] s. cedilla.

ceil·ing [sílɪŋ] s. techo (interior); cielo máximo (en aviación); altura máxima (en aviación); — **price** precio máximo.
cel·e·brate [sǽləbret] v. celebrar.
cel·e·brat·ed [sǽləbretɪd] adj. célebre, renombrado.
cel·e·bra·tion [sɛləbréʃən] s. celebración; fiesta.
ce·leb·ri·ty [səlébrətɪ] s. celebridad; renombre.
cel·er·y [sélərɪ] s. apio.
ce·les·tial [səléstʃəl] adj. celestial, celeste.
cell [sɛl] s. (enclosure) celda; (structural) célula; (battery) pila eléctrica.
cel·lar [sélɚ] s. bodega, sótano.
cel·lu·loid [séljəlɔɪd] s. celuloide.
ce·ment [səmént] s. cemento; hormigón; **reinforced** — cemento armado; — **mixer** hormigonera; v. unir, cementar, pegar con cemento; cubrir con cemento.
cem·e·ter·y [sémətɛrɪ] s. cementerio.
cen·sor [sénsɚ] s. censor; censurador, crítico; v. censurar (cartas, periódicos, etc.).
cen·sor·ship [sénsɚʃɪp] s. censura.
cen·sure [sénʃɚ] s. censura, crítica, reprobación; v. censurar, criticar, reprobar.
cen·sus [sénsəs] s. censo.
cent [sɛnt] s. centavo (de peso o dólar); **per** — por ciento.
cen·ten·ni·al [sɛntɛnɪəl] adj. & s. centenario.
cen·ter [séntɚ] s. centro; v. centrar; colocar en el centro; concentrar(se).
cen·ti·grade [séntəgred] adj. centígrado.
cen·ti·pede [séntəpid] s. ciempiés, cientopiés.
cen·tral [séntrəl] adj. central; céntrico; s. (la) central de teléfonos.
cen·tral·ize [séntrəlaɪz] v. centralizar.
cen·trif·u·gal [sɛntrífjʊgl] adj. centrífugo.
cen·trip·e·tal [sɛntrípətl] adj. centrípeto.
cen·tu·ry [séntʃərɪ] s. siglo.
ce·ram·ic [sərǽmɪk] adj. cerámico; **ceramics** s. cerámica.
ce·re·al [sírɪəl] adj. cereal; s. cereal; grano.
cer·e·mo·ni·al [sɛrəmónɪəl] adj. ceremonial; s. ceremonial; rito.
cer·e·mo·ni·ous [sɛrəmónɪəs] adj. ceremonioso.
cer·e·mo·ny [sérəmonɪ] s. ceremonia; ceremonial.
cer·tain [sɑ́tn] adj. cierto, seguro; **-ly** adv. ciertamente; por cierto; de cierto; seguramente; de seguro.
cer·tain·ty [sɑ́tntɪ] s. certeza; certidumbre; seguridad.
cer·tif·i·cate [sɚtífəkɪt] s. certificado; documento; testimonio; — **of stock** bono, obligación; **birth** — partida de nacimiento; **death** — partida (o certificado) de defunción.
cer·ti·fi·ca·tion [sɚtɪfɪkéʃən] s. certificación.
cer·ti·fy [sɑ́təfaɪ] v. certificar; dar fe, atestiguar.
ces·sa·tion [sɛséʃən] s. suspensión, paro.
cess·pool [séspul] s. cloaca, rezumadero.
chafe [tʃef] s. rozadura; irritación, molestia; v. rozar(se); frotar; irritar(se).
chaff [tʃæf] s. hollejo, cáscara; v. embromar, bromear.
cha·grin [ʃəgrín] s. mortificación, desazón, pesar; **-ed** p.p. mortificado, afligido.
chain [tʃen] s. cadena; — **of mountains** cordillera; — **store** tienda sucursal (una entre muchas de una misma empresa); — **reaction** reacción en cadena; reacción eslabonada; — **saw** aserradora de cadena; — **smoker** el que fuma cigarro tras cigarro; v. encadenar.
chair [tʃɛr] s. silla; cátedra; presidencia; **arm** —

sillón (de brazos); **easy** — butaca, poltrona; **folding** — silla de tijera; **rocking** — mecedora.
chair·man [tʃérmən] *s.* presidente, director (*de una junta o de departamento*).
chair·man·ship [tʃérmənʃɪp] *s.* presidencia (*de una junta*).
chal·ice [tʃælɪs] *s.* cáliz (*vaso sagrado*).
chalk [tʃɔk] *s.* tiza, yeso; greda; *v.* enyesar; marcar con tiza o yeso; **to** — **down** apuntar con tiza o yeso (*en el pizarrón*); **to** — **out** bosquejar, esbozar con tiza.
chalk·y [tʃɔkɪ] *adj.* yesoso; blanco.
chal·lenge [tʃælɪndʒ] *s.* desafío; reto; demanda; *v.* desafiar, retar; disputar, poner a prueba; dar el quienvive.
cham·ber [tʃémbɚ] *s.* cámara; aposento; — **of commerce** cámara de comercio.
cham·ber·maid [tʃémbɚmed] *s.* camarera, sirvienta.
cham·ois [ʃǽmɪ] *s.* gamuza.
cham·pi·on [tʃǽmpɪən] *s.* campeón; defensor; *v.* defender.
cham·pi·on·ship [tʃǽmpɪənʃɪp] *s.* campeonato.
chance [tʃæns] *s.* (*opportunity*) oportunidad, ocasión; (*possibility*) posibilidad, probabilidad; (*fortune*) suerte, fortuna; casualidad, azar; (*risk*) riesgo; billete de rifa o lotería; **by** — por casualidad; **game of** — juego de azar; **to run a** — correr riesgo; *adj.* casual, accidental; *v.* arriesgar; **to** — **to** acertar a, hacer (*algo*) por casualidad.
chan·cel·lor [tʃænsəlɚ] *s.* canciller; primer ministro; magistrado; rector de universidad.
chan·de·lier [ʃændlír] *s.* araña de luces, *Am.* candil.
change [tʃendʒ] *s.* (*money*) cambio; vuelta, *Am.* vuelto; suelto; *Méx.* feria; (*fresh clothes*) muda de ropa; (*switch*) mudanza; **the** — **of life** la menopausia; *v.* cambiar; mudar; alterar; **to** — **clothes** mudar de ropa; **to** — **trains** transbordar(se), cambiar de tren.
change·a·ble [tʃéndʒəbl] *adj.* mudable, variable; inconstante; tornadizo; — **silk** seda tornasolada.
chan·nel [tʃænl] *s.* canal; cauce; canal (*de televisión*).
chant [tʃænt] *s.* canto llano o gregoriano; sonsonete; *v.* cantar (*psalmos, himnos, etc.*).
cha·os [kéas] *s.* caos; desorden.
cha·ot·ic [keɑ́tɪk] *adj.* caótico.
chap [tʃæp] *s.* grieta, raja, rajadura (*en la piel*); chico; **what a fine** — **he is!** ¡qué buen tipo (*o* sujeto) es!; *v.* agrietarse, rajarse (*la piel*).
chap·el [tʃǽpl] *s.* capilla.
chap·er·on(e) [ʃǽpərɔn] *s.* acompañante, persona de respeto; **to go along as a** — *Am.* ir de moscón; *v.* acompañar, servir de acompañante.
chap·lain [tʃæplɪn] *s.* capellán; **army** — capellán castrense.
chap·ter [tʃǽptɚ] *s.* capítulo; cabildo (*de una catedral*).
char [tʃɑr] *v.* requemar, carbonizar.
char·ac·ter [kærɪktɚ] *s.* carácter; personaje.
char·ac·ter·is·tic [kærɪktərístɪk] *adj.* característico; típico; *s.* característica, rasgo característico; distintivo; peculiaridad.
char·ac·ter·ize [kærɪktəraɪz] *v.* caracterizar.
cha·rade [ʃəréd] *s.* charada.
char·coal [tʃɑ́rkol] *s.* carbón; carboncillo (*para dibujar*); — **drawing** dibujo al carbón.
charge [tʃɑrdʒ] *s.* (*custody*) cargo; custodia; cuidado; (*order*) mandato, encargo; (*accusation*) cargo, acusación; (*load*) carga; peso; (*cost*) precio, coste; (*attack*) embestida, asalto, ataque;

chargé d'affaires agregado; — **account** cuenta abierta; — **prepaid** porte pagado; **under my** —a mi cargo; **to be in** — **of** estar encargado de; *v.* cargar; cargar en cuenta; cobrar (*precio*); mandar; exhortar; atacar, embestir, asaltar; **to** — **with murder** acusar de homicidio.
charg·er [tʃɑ́rdʒɚ] *s.* cargador (*de batería*); caballo de guerra, corcel.
char·i·ot [tʃǽrɪət] *s.* carroza; carruaje.
cha·ris·ma [kərɪ́zmə] *s.* carisma.
char·i·ta·ble [tʃǽrətəbl] *adj.* caritativo.
char·i·ty [tʃǽrətɪ] *s.* caridad; limosna; beneficencia.
char·la·tan [ʃɑ́rlətn] *s.* charlatán; farsante.
charm [tʃɑrm] *s.* encanto; atractivo; hechizo; talismán; **watch** — dije; *v.* encantar; cautivar; hechizar.
charm·ing [tʃɑ́mɪŋ] *adj.* encantador, atractivo.
chart [tʃɑrt] *s.* carta (*hidrográfica o de navegar*); mapa; gráfica, representación gráfica; *v.* cartografiar, delinear mapas o cartas; **to** — **a course** trazar o planear una ruta o derrotero.
char·ter [tʃɑ́rtɚ] *s.* carta constitucional, constitución, código; título; carta de privilegio; — **member** socio fundador; *v.* fletar (*un barco*); alquilar (*un ómnibus*).
chase [tʃes] *s.* caza; persecución; *v.* cazar; perseguir; **to** — **away** ahuyentar.
chasm [kæzəm] *s.* abismo; vacío.
chaste [tʃest] *adj.* casto; honesto; puro.
chas·tise [tʃæstáɪz] *v.* castigar.
chas·tise·ment [tʃæstáɪzmənt] *s.* castigo, escarmiento.
chas·ti·ty [tʃæstətɪ] *s.* castidad; honestidad; pureza.
chat [tʃæt] *s.* charla, *Mex.* plática; *v.* charlar, *Mex.* platicar.
chat·tels [tʃǽtlz] *s. pl.* enseres, bienes muebles.
chat·ter [tʃǽtɚ] *s.* charla, parloteo; castañeteo (*de los dientes*); chirrido (*de aves*); *v.* charlar, parlotear, cotorrear; castañetear (*los dientes*).
chauf·feur [ʃófɚ] *s.* chófer, cochero de automóvil.
cheap [tʃip] *adj.* barato; cursi, de mal gusto; **to feel** — sentir vergüenza; **-ly** *adv.* barato, a poco precio.
cheap·en [tʃípən] *v.* abaratar.
cheap·ness [tʃípnɪs] *s.* baratura; cursilería.
cheat [tʃit] *s.* fraude, engaño; trampa; trampista, tramposo; estafador; embaucador; *v.* engañar; trampear; embaucar; estafar.
check [tʃek] *s.* cheque (*de banco*); talón, marbete, contraseña (*de equipajes, etc.*); marca, señal; cuenta (*de restaurante*); restricción, represión; cuadro (*de un tejido o tela*); comprobación; jaque (*en ajedrez*); —**room** vestuario; guardarropa; consigna (*equipajes*); — **point** punto de inspección; — **list** lista comprobante. *v.* refrenar, reprimir, restringir; facturar, depositar (*equipajes*); inspeccionar; confrontar, comprobar; marcar (*con una señal*); dar jaque (*en ajedrez*); **to** — **out of a hotel** desocupar el cuarto o alojamiento de un hotel.
check·book [tʃékbʊk] *s.* libreta de cheques; libro talonario.
check·er [tʃékɚ] *s.* cuadro; casilla (*de un tablero de ajedrez, etc.*); pieza (*del juego de damas*); comprobador; inspector; **-s** juego de damas; —**board** tablero; *v.* cuadricular, marcar con cuadritos; **-ed career** vida azarosa, vida llena de variedad; **-ed cloth** paño o tela a cuadros.
check·mate [tʃékmet] *s.* jaque mate.
cheek [tʃik] *s.* mejilla, carrillo; cachete; descaro, desfachatez; **fat** — mejilla gorda, moflete; —

bone pómulo; red — chapetón.

cheer [tʃɪr] s. alegría; buen ánimo, jovialidad; consuelo; -s aplausos, vivas; v. alegrar, alentar, animar; refocilar; aplaudir, vitorear; **to — up** alentar, dar ánimo; cobrar ánimo, animarse.

cheer·ful [tʃɪrfəl] adj. animado, alegre, jovial; -ly adv. alegremente, con alegría, con júbilo; de buena gana, de buen grado.

cheer·ful·ness [tʃɪrfəlnɪs] s. jovialidad, alegría; buen humor.

cheer·i·ly [tʃɪrəlɪ] = **cheerfully.**

cheer·less [tʃɪrlɪs] adj. abatido, desalentado, desanimado; triste, sombrío.

cheer·y [tʃɪrɪ] = **cheerful.**

cheese [tʃiz] s. queso; **cottage** — requesón.

chef [ʃɛf] s. cocinero.

chem·i·cal [kɛmɪkl] adj. químico; s. producto químico.

chem·ist [kɛmɪst] s. químico.

chem·is·try [kɛmɪstrɪ] s. química.

cher·ish [tʃɛrɪʃ] v. acariciar, abrigar (una esperanza, un ideal, etc.); apreciar.

cher·ry [tʃɛrɪ] s. cereza; — **tree** cerezo.

cher·ub [tʃɛrəb] s. querubín.

chess [tʃɛs] s. ajedrez; —**board** tablero de ajedrez.

chest [tʃɛst] s. cofre, arca; caja; pecho; — **of drawers** cómoda.

chest·nut [tʃɛsnət] s. castaña; — **tree** castaño; adj. castaño; — **horse** caballo zaino.

chev·ron [ʃɛvrən] s. galón.

chew [tʃu] s. mascada, mordisco, bocado; v. mascar, masticar.

chew·ing gum [tʃúɪŋ gʌm] s. goma de mascar; Am. chicle.

chick [tʃɪk] s. polluelo, pollito; pajarito; **chick-pea** garbanzo.

chick·en [tʃɪkɪn] s. pollo; polluelo; — **pox** viruelas locas; **chicken-hearted** cobarde, gallina.

chic·o·ry [tʃɪkərɪ] s. achicoria.

chide [tʃaɪd] v. regañar, reprender, reprobar.

chief [tʃif] s. jefe, caudillo; cacique (de una tribu); **commander in** — comandante en jefe; adj. principal; — **clerk** oficial mayor; — **justice** presidente de la corte suprema; -ly adv. principalmente, mayormente; sobre todo.

chif·fon [ʃɪfán] s. gasa.

chig·ger [tʃɪgɚ] s. nigua.

chil·blain [tʃɪlblen] s. sabañón.

child [tʃaɪld] s. niño, niña; hijo, hija; -'s **play** cosa de niños; **to be with** — estar encinta.

child·birth [tʃaɪldbɜθ] s. parto, alumbramiento.

child·hood [tʃaɪldhʊd] s. niñez, infancia.

child·ish [tʃaɪdɪʃ] adj. pueril; infantil; — **action** niñería, niñada.

child·less [tʃaɪdlɪs] adj. sin hijos.

child·like [tʃaɪldlaɪk] adj. como niño, aniñado, pueril.

chil·dren [tʃɪldrən] pl. de **child.**

Chil·e·an [tʃɪliən] adj. & s. chileno.

chil·i [tʃɪlɪ] s. Méx., C.A. chile, Carib., S.A. ají.

chill [tʃɪl] s. frío, resfrío; enfriamiento; escalofrío; calofrío; -s **and fever** escalofríos; adj. frío; v. resfriar(se); enfriar(se); **to become -ed** resfriarse, escalofriarse.

chill·y [tʃɪlɪ] adj. frío; friolento.

chime [tʃaɪm] s. repique, campaneo; -s órgano de campanas, juego de campanas; v. repicar, campanear; tocar, sonar, tañer (las campanas); **to** — **with** estar en armonía con.

chim·ney [tʃɪmnɪ] s. chimenea; **lamp** — tubo de lámpara, Am. bombilla.

chin [tʃɪn] s. barba.

chi·na [tʃáɪnə] s. loza de china, porcelana, loza fina; vajilla de porcelana; — **closet** chinero.

chi·na·ware [tʃáɪnəwɛr] = **china.**

Chi·nese [tʃaɪníz] adj. chino; s. chino; idioma chino.

chink [tʃɪŋk] s. grieta, hendidura.

chip [tʃɪp] s. astilla, brizna; fragmento; desconchadura; desportilladura; ficha (de pócar); v. astillar; desconchar(se); descascarar(se); desportillar(se); picar, tajar (con cincel o hacha); **to** — **in** contribuir con su cuota.

chip·munk [tʃɪpmʌŋk] s. especie de ardilla.

chi·ro·prac·tic [kaɪrəpræktɪk] adj. quiropráctico.

chirp [tʃɝp] s. chirrido; pío; gorjeo; v. chirriar; piar; pipiar; gorjear.

chis·el [tʃɪzl] s. cincel; v. cincelar; sisar, estafar.

chiv·al·rous [ʃɪvlrəs] adj. caballeresco, caballeroso, galante, cortés.

chiv·al·ry [ʃɪvlrɪ] s. caballería; caballerosidad.

chlo·ride [klóraɪd] s. cloruro.

chlo·rine [klórɪn] s. cloro.

chlo·ro·form [klórəfɔrm] s. cloroformo.

chlo·ro·phyll [klórəfɪl] s. clorofila.

choc·o·late [tʃɔklɪt] s. chocolate; — **pot** chocolatera.

choice [tʃɔɪs] s. selección; preferencia; escogimiento; cosa elegida; favorito, preferido; alternativa; **to have no other** — no tener otra alternativa; adj. selecto; bien escogido; excelente.

choir [kwaɪr] s. coro.

choke [tʃok] s. sofoco, ahogo; tos ahogada; estrangulación; estrangulador, obturador (de automóvil); v. sofocar(se), ahogar(se); estrangular(se); obstruir, tapar; regularizar (el motor).

chol·er·a [kálərə] s. cólera (m.).

cho·les·ter·ol [kəléstəvol] s. colesterol.

choose [tʃuz] v. escoger; elegir; seleccionar; **to** — **to** optar por; preferir; **I do not** — **to do it** no se me antoja (o no es mi gusto) hacerlo.

chop [tʃap] s. chuleta, costilla, tajada (de carne); -s quijadas (usualmente de animal); v. tajar, cortar; picar, desmenuzar (carne).

chop·py [tʃápɪ] adj. picado, agitado.

cho·ral [kórəl] s. coral.

chord [kɔrd] s. cuerda; acorde.

chore [tʃor] s. tarea; quehacer.

cho·re·og·ra·phy [koriágrəfɪ] s. coreografía.

cho·rus [kórəs] s. coro; v. cantar o hablar en coro; contestar a una voz.

chose [tʃoz] pret. de **to choose.**

cho·sen [tʃózn] p.p. de **to choose.**

chris·ten [krɪsn] v. bautizar.

chris·ten·ing [krɪnɪŋ] s. bautizo, bautismo.

Chris·tian [krɪstʃən] s. & adj. cristiano; — **name** nombre de pila bautismal.

Chris·ti·an·i·ty [krɪstʃɪænətɪ] s. cristiandad; cristianismo.

Christ·mas [krɪsməs] s. Navidad, Pascua de Navidad; adj. navideño; — **Eve** Nochebuena; — **gift** regalo de Navidad; aguinaldo; **Merry** —! ¡Felices Navidades! ¡Felices Pascuas!

chrome [krom] s. cromo; adj. cromado.

chro·mi·um [krómɪəm] s. cromo.

chro·mo·some [króməsom] s. cromosoma.

chron·ic [kránɪk] adj. crónico.

chron·i·cle [kránɪkl] s. crónica; v. relatar; escribir la crónica de.

323

chr-cle

chron·i·cler [kránɪklə-] *s.* cronista.
chron·o·log·i·cal [krɑnəládʒɪkl̩] *adj.* cronológico.
chro·nom·e·ter [krɑnámətə-] *s.* cronómetro.
chry·san·the·mum [krɪsǽnθəməm] *s.* crisantema, crisantemo.
chub·by [tʃʌ́bɪ] *adj.* rechoncho; gordiflón.
chuck [tʃʌk] *s.* mamola, golpecito, caricia (*debajo de la barba*); *v.* echar, tirar (*lo que no sirve*); **to — under the chin** hacer la mamola.
chuck·le [tʃʌ́kl̩] *s.* risita; *v.* reír entre dientes.
chum [tʃʌm] *s.* compañero, camarada, compinche.
chunk [tʃʌŋk] *s.* trozo; zoquete.
church [tʃɜt] *s.* iglesia.
church·man [tʃɜ́tʃmən] *s.* clérigo, eclesiástico, sacerdote; (*parishoner*) feligrés.
church·yard [tʃɜ́tʃjɑrd] *s.* patio de iglesia; camposanto, cementerio.
churn [tʃɜn] *s.* mantequera (*para hacer manteca*); *v.* batir (*en una mantequera*); agitar, revolver.
ci·der [sáɪdə-] *s.* sidra.
ci·gar [sɪgár] *s.* puro; *Carib., Col., Ven.* tabaco; **— store** tabaquería, estanquillo.
cig·a·rette [sɪgərét] *s.* cigarrillo, pitillo, *Méx., C.A., Ven., Col.* cigarro; **— case** cigarrera, pitillera; **— holder** boquilla; **— lighter** encendedor.
cinch [sɪntʃ] *s.* cincha; ganga, cosa fácil; *v.* cinchar; apretar.
cin·der [síndə-] *s.* ceniza; carbón, brasa, ascua; cisco; **-s** cenizas; rescoldo.
cin·na·mon [sínəmən] *s.* canela; **— tree** canelo.
ci·pher [sáɪfə-] *s.* cifra; número; cero.
cir·cle [sɜ́kl̩] *s.* círculo; cerco, rueda; *v.* cercar, circundar; circular, dar vueltas.
cir·cuit [sɜ́kɪt] *s.* circuito; rode o, vuelta.
cir·cu·lar [sɜ́kjələ-] *adj.* circular; redondo; *s.* circular; hoja volante.
cir·cu·late [sɜ́kjəlet] *v.* circular; poner en circulación.
cir·cu·la·tion [sɜkjəléʃən] *s.* circulación.
cir·cum·fer·ence [sə-kʌ́mfərəns] *s.* circunferencia.
cir·cum·flex [sɜ́kəmflɛks] *adj.* circunflejo.
cir·cum·lo·cu·tion [sɜkəmlokjúʃən] *s.* circunlocución, rodeo.
cir·cum·scribe [sɜ́kəmskráɪb] *v.* circunscribir, limitar.
cir·cum·spect [sɜ́kəmspɛkt] *adj.* circunspecto; prudente.
cir·cum·spec·tion [sɜkəmspékʃən] *s.* circunspección, miramiento, prudencia.
cir·cum·stance [sɜ́kəmstæns] *s.* circunstancia; incidente; ceremonia, pompa.
cir·cum·vent [sɜkəmvént] *v.* evitar; embaucar.
cir·cus [sɜ́kəs] *s.* circo.
cir·rho·sis [sɪrósɪs] *s.* cirrosis.
cis·tern [sístə-n] *s.* cisterna.
cit·a·del [sítədl̩] *s.* ciudadela.
ci·ta·tion [saɪtéʃən] *s.* citación; cita; mención.
cite [saɪt] *v.* citar; citar a juicio; mencionar.
cit·i·zen [sítəzn̩] *s.* ciudadano, paisano.
cit·i·zen·ship [sítəzn̩ʃɪp] *s.* ciudadanía.
cit·ron [sítrən] *s.* acitrón.
cit·rus [sítrəs] *s.* cidro.
cit·y [sítɪ] *s.* ciudad, población; municipio; *adj.* municipal; urbano; **— council** ayuntamiento; **— hall** ayuntamiento, casa municipal.
civ·ic [sívɪk] *adj.* cívico.
civ·ics [sívɪks] *s.* derecho político.
civ·il [sívl̩] *adj.* civil; cortés; **— engineer** ingeniero civil; **— rights** derechos civiles; **— disobedience** desobediencia civil.
ci·vil·ian [səvíljən] *s.* civil; paisano (*persona no militar*).
ci·vil·i·ty [səvílətɪ] *s.* civilidad, cortesía, urbanidad.
civ·i·li·za·tion [sɪvl̩əzéʃən] *s.* civilización.
civ·i·lize [sívlaɪz] *v.* civilizar.
civ·i·lized [sívlaɪzd] *adj.* civilizado.
clad [klæd] *pret. & p.p. de* **to clothe.**
claim [klem] *s.* demanda; reclamación, reclamo; derecho, título; pretensión; **miner's** — denuncia; *v.* reclamar; demandar; pedir, exigir; afirmar, sostener; **to — a mine** denunciar una mina; **to — to be** pretender ser.
claim·ant [klémənt] *s.* reclamante o reclamador; pretendiente (*a un trono*).
clair·voy·ant [klervóɪənt] *adj.* clarividente.
clam [klæm] *s.* almeja.
clam·ber [klǽmbə-] *v.* trepar, encaramarse, subir a gatas, subir gateando.
clam·my [klǽmɪ] *adj.* frío y húmedo.
clam·or [klǽmə-] *s.* clamor; clamoreo; gritería, vocería; *v.* clamar; vociferar, gritar.
clam·or·ous [klǽmərəs] *adj.* clamoroso.
clamp [klæmp] *s.* grapa; tornillo de banco; *v.* afianzar, sujetar; pisar recio.
clan [klæn] *s.* clan; tribu.
clan·des·tine [klændéstɪn] *adj.* clandestino.
clang [klæŋ] *s.* tantán, retintín; campanada, campanillazo; —! —! ¡tan! ¡tan!; *v.* sonar, repicar (*una campana o timbre*); hacer sonar, tocar fuerte.
clap [klæp] *s.* palmada; golpe seco; **— of thunder** trueno; *v.* palmear, palmotear, aplaudir, dar palmadas; cerrar de golpe (*un libro*); dar una palmada, *Am.* palmear (*sobre la espalda*); **to — in jail** meter (*o* encajar) en la cárcel.
clap·per [klǽpə-] *s.* badajo.
clar·i·fy [klǽrəfaɪ] *v.* aclarar.
clar·i·net [klǽrənɛt] *s.* clarinete.
clar·i·ty [klǽrətɪ] *s.* claridad, luz.
clash [klæʃ] *s.* choque, encontrón, colisión; riña, conflicto; estruendo; *v.* chocar; darse un encontrón; hacer crujir; oponerse, estar en conflicto.
clasp [klæsp] *s.* (*fastener*) broche; hebilla; cierre; traba; (*grip*) apretón, apretón de manos; *v.* abrochar; asir; agarrar; sujetar, asegurar; abrazar; apretar (*la mano*).
class [klæs] *s.* clase; *v.* clasificar.
clas·sic [klǽsɪk] *adj. & s.* clásico; **— scholar** humanista, erudito clásico.
clas·si·cal [klǽsɪkl̩] *adj.* clásico.
clas·si·cism [klǽsɪsɪzm] *s.* clasicismo.
clas·si·fi·ca·tion [klæsəfəkéʃən] *s.* clasificación.
clas·si·fy [klǽsəfaɪ] *v.* clasificar.
class·mate [klǽsmet] *s.* compañero de clase, condiscípulo.
class·room [klǽsrum] *s.* clase, aula.
clat·ter [klǽtə-] *s.* estrépito, boruca; traqueteo; bullicio; alboroto; *v.* hacer estrépito o boruca; traquetear; meter bulla o alboroto.
clause [klɔz] *s.* cláusula.
claw [klɔ] *s.* garra; zarpa; uña; pinza (*de langosta, cangrejo, etc.*); orejas (*de un martillo*); arañazo; *v.* desgarrar; arañar; rasgar.
claw·ing [klɔ́ɪŋ] *s.* zarpazo.
clay [kle] *s.* barro; arcilla, greda.
clean [klin] *adj.* limpio; puro; *adv.* limpiamente; **clean-cut** bien tallado, de buen talle, de buen parecer; *v.* limpiar; asear; desempañar; **to — up** limpiar(se), asear(se).
clean·er [klínə-] *s.* limpiador; quitamanchas.
clean·li·ness [klénlɪnɪs] *s.* limpieza; aseo.

clean·ly [klénlɪ] *adj.* limpio; aseado; [klínlɪ] *adv.* limpiamente.

clean·ness [klínnɪs] *s.* limpieza; aseo.

cleanse [klɛnz] *v.* limpiar; asear; purificar, depurar.

cleans·er [klénzɚ] *s.* limpiador.

clear [klɪr] *adj.* (*evident*) claro; patente, manifiesto; (*clean*) límpido; despejado; libre (*de culpa, estorbos, deudas, etc.*); — **profit** ganancia neta; **clear-cut** *adj.* bien delineado; clarividente; **to pass — through** atravesar, traspasar de lado a lado; **to be in the** — estar sin deudas; estar libre de culpa; *v.* aclarar(se); despejar(se); escampar; clarificar; quitar (*estorbos*); desmontar (*un terreno*); salvar, saltar por encima de; librar (*de culpa, deudas, etc.*); sacar (*una ganancia neta*); pasar (*un cheque*) por un banco de liquidación; liquidar (*una cuenta*); **to — the table** levantar la mesa; **to — up** aclarar(se).

clear·ance [klírəns] *s.* espacio (*libre entre dos objetos*); despacho de aduana; — **sale** saldo, venta (*de liquidación*), *Am.* barata.

clear·ing [klírɪŋ] *s.* aclaramiento; claro, terreno desmontado o desarbolado; liquidación de balances; — **house** banco de liquidación.

clear·ness [klírnɪs] *s.* claridad.

cleav·age [klívɪdʒ] *s.* hendedura.

cleave [kliv] *v.* hender(se); tajar; rajar, partir.

cleav·er [klívɚ] *s.* cuchilla o hacha (*de carnicero*).

clef [klɛf] *s.* clave (*en música*).

cleft [klɛft] *s.* grieta, hendedura; *adj.* hendido, partido, rajado; *pret. & p.p. de* **to cleave.**

clem·en·cy [klémənsɪ] *s.* clemencia.

clem·ent [klémənt] *adj.* clemente.

clench [klɛntʃ] *s.* agarro, agarrada, agarrón; apretón; *v.* agarrar, asir; apretar (*los dientes, el puño*).

cler·gy [klɝdʒɪ] *s.* clero.

cler·gy·man [klɝdʒɪmən] *s.* clérigo, eclesiástico; pastor, sacerdote.

cler·i·cal [klérɪkl] *adj.* clerical, eclesiástico; oficinesco, de oficina; de dependientes.

clerk [klɝk] *s.* dependiente; empleado (*de oficina*); escribiente; archivero (*de municipio*); **law** — escribano; *v.* estar de dependiente.

clev·er [klévɚ] *adj.* diestro, hábil; listo; talentoso; mañoso; **-ly** *adv.* hábilmente; con destreza; con maña.

clev·er·ness [klévɚnɪs] *s.* destreza, habilidad, maña; talento.

clew [klu] *s.* indicio (*que indica el camino para resolver un misterio o problema*).

cli·ché [kliʃé] *s.* (*plate*) clisé; *Am.* cliché; (*phrase*) cliché.

click [klɪk] *s.* golpecito; chasquido (*de la lengua*); gatillazo (*sonido del gatillo de una pistola*); taconeo (*sonido de tacones*); *v.* sonar (*un pestillo, un broche, un gatillo, etc.*); chasquear (*la lengua*); **to — the heels** cuadrarse (*militarmente*); taconear.

cli·ent [kláɪənt] *s.* cliente.

cli·en·tele [klaɪəntél] *s.* clientela.

cliff [klɪf] *s.* risco, precipicio, peñasco, escarpa.

cli·mate [kláɪmɪt] *s.* clima.

cli·max [kláɪmæks] *s.* clímax, culminación; *v.* culminar; llegar al clímax.

climb [klaɪm] *s.* subida, ascenso; *v.* subir; trepar; encaramarse; **to — down** bajar a gatas; desprenderse (*de un árbol*).

climb·er [kláɪmɚ] *s.* trepador; enredadera, planta trepadora.

clime [klaɪm] *s.* clima.

clinch [klɪntʃ] *v.* remachar, redoblar (*un clavo*); afianzar, sujetar, asegurar bien; cerrar (*un trato*); abrazarse fuertemente; *s.* remache; abrazo; agarrón; **to be in a** — estar agarrados o abrazados.

cling [klɪŋ] *v.* pegarse, adherirse.

clin·ic [klínɪk] *s.* clínica.

clink [klɪŋk] *s.* tintín.

clip [klɪp] *s.* (*fastener*) broche, presilla; (*cutting*) tijeretada (*corte con tijeras*); trasquila, trasquiladura; **paper** — sujetapapeles; **to go at a good** — ir a paso rápido; andar de prisa; *v.* recortar; cortar; trasquilar (*el pelo o lana de los animales*); **to — together** sujetar.

clip·per [klípɚ] *s.* clíper (*velero o avión de gran velocidad*); trasquilador; recortador; **-s** tijeras; maquinilla (*para recortar el pelo*).

clip·ping [klípɪŋ] *s.* recorte.

cloak [klok] *s.* capa; manto; *v.* tapar, embozar, encubrir.

cloak·room [klókrum] *s.* guardarropa, vestuario.

clock [klɑk] *s.* reloj; **alarm** — despertador; *v.* marcar; cronometrar.

clock·wise [klákwaɪz] *adv.* en el sentido de las manecillas de reloj.

clock·work [klákwɝk] *s.* maquinaria de reloj; **like** — con precisión, puntualmente; sin dificultad.

clod [klɑd] *s.* terrón; tonto, necio.

clog [klɑg] *s.* estorbo, obstáculo; zueco (*zapato de suela gruesa o de madera*); — **dance** zapateado; *v.* estorbar, embarazar; obstruir, atorar, tapar; obstruirse, atascarse, azolvarse (*Am.* enzolvarse), atorarse (*un caño, acequia, etc.*).

clois·ter [klɔ́ɪstɚ] *s.* claustro; monasterio; convento; *v.* enclaustrar.

close [kloz] *s.* fin, terminación, conclusión; *v.* cerrar(se); concluir; **to — an account** saldar una cuenta; **to — in upon** cercar, rodear; **to — out** liquidar, vender en liquidación.

close [klos] *adj.* (*near*) cercano, próximo; aproximado; íntimo; (*tight*) estrecho, ajustado; (*stingy*) cerrado; tacaño, mezquino; (*suffocating*) opresivo; sofocante; — **attention** suma atención; — **questioning** interrogatorio detallado o minucioso; — **translation** traducción fiel; **at** — **range** de cerca; *adv.* cerca; **-ly** *adv.* aproximadamente; estrechamente; apretadamente; con sumo cuidado o atención.

closed cir·cuit [klozd sɝkɔt] *s. & adj.* circuito cerrado.

close·ness [klósnɪs] *s.* cercanía, proximidad; aproximación; estrechez; intimidad; tacañería, avaricia; mala ventilación, falta de aire; fidelidad (*de una traducción*).

clos·et [klázɪt] *s.* ropero; alacena, armario; gabinete, retrete, excusado; *v.* encerrar en un cuarto (*para una entrevista secreta*); **to** — **oneself** (*themselves*) encerrarse.

clot [klɑt] *v.* coagular(se), cuajar(se); *s.* coágulo, cuajarón.

cloth [klɔθ] *s.* tela, paño, género; trapo; *adj.* de paño; — **binding** encuadernación de tela.

clothe [kloð] *v.* vestir; cubrir; revestir; investir.

clothes [kloz] *s. pl.* ropa, ropaje, vestidos; **suit of** — terno, traje, *Carib., Ven.* flux; **—line** tendedero; **—pin** pinzas, gancho (*para tender la ropa*).

cloth·ier [klóðjɚ] *s.* comerciante en ropa o paño; ropero, pañero.

cloth·ing [klóðɪŋ] *s.* ropa; ropaje, vestidos.

cloud [klaʊd] s. nube; **storm —** nubarrón; v. nublar(se), anublar(se); obscurecer; manchar.

cloud·burst [kláʊdbɵst] s. chaparrón, aguacero.

cloud·less [kláʊdlɪs] adj. claro, despejado; sin nubes.

cloud·y [kláʊdɪ] adj. nublado; Esp. nuboso; sombrío.

clove [klov] s. clavo (especia); **—** **of garlic** diente de ajo.

clo·ven [klóvən] adj. hendido; s. & adj. **— hoof** patihendido, pie hendido.

clo·ver [klóvɵ] s. trébol; **to be in —** estar o vivir en la abundancia; sentirse próspero.

clo·ver·leaf [klóvɵlif] s. (highway) cruce en trébol.

clown [klaʊn] s. payaso, bufón; v. payasear, bufonear, hacer el payaso.

cloy [klɔɪ] v. empalagar; hastiar.

club [klʌb] s. club, círculo; casino; garrote, porra; palo; basto (de la baraja); v. golpear, aporrear, apalear; **to — together** formar club; escotar, pagar la cuota que le toca a cada uno, Am. cotizar.

club·house [klʌ́bhaʊs] s. club, casino.

cluck [klʌk] s. cloqueo; v. cloquear.

clue = clew.

clump [klʌmp] s. terrón; pisada fuerte; **— of bushes** matorral; **— of trees** grupo de árboles, arboleda; v. apiñar, amontonar; **to — along** andar pesadamente.

clum·sy [klʌ́mzɪ] adj. torpe, desmañado; incómodo; difícil de manejar; mal hecho.

clung [klʌŋ] pret. & p.p. de **to cling.**

clus·ter [klʌ́stɵ] s. racimo; grupo; v. agrupar(se); arracimarse (formar racimo).

clutch [klʌtʃ] s. apretón fuerte; agarro, agarrón; embrague (de automóvil); **-es** garras; uñas; **— pedal** palanca del embrague; **to step on the —** pisar el embrague; desembragar, soltar el embrague; **to throw in the —** embragar; v. agarrar, asir; apretar.

clut·ter [klʌ́tɵ] v. obstruir; atestar (de cosas); poner en desorden; s. desorden, confusión.

coach [kotʃ] s. coche; entrenador (en deportes); maestro particular; v. aleccionar; guiar, adiestrar, Am. entrenar; **to — with** ser instruido o entrenado por.

coach·man [kótʃmən] s. cochero.

co·ag·u·late [koǽgjəlet] v. coagular(se), cuajar(se).

coal [kol] s. carbón; ascua, brasa; **hard —** carbón de piedra, antracita; **soft —** hulla; **— bin** carbonera; **— dealer** carbonero; **— oil** kerosina; **— tar** alquitrán de carbón; v. cargar de carbón, echar carbón; proveer(se) de carbón.

co·a·li·tion [koəlíʃən] s. coalición.

coarse [kors] adj. (crude) burdo, basto; tosco; áspero; (rude) rudo; grosero; vulgar; tosco; **— sand** arena gruesa.

coarse·ness [kórsnɪs] s. tosquedad; vulgaridad, grosería, rudeza.

coast [kost] s. costa, litoral; **— guard** guardacostas, guarda de costas; v. costear, navegar por la costa; deslizar(se), resbalar(se) cuesta abajo.

coast·al [kóstl] adj. costero, costanero, de la costa; **— traffic** cabotaje.

coast·line [kóstlaɪn] s. costa, litoral.

coat [kot] s. chaqueta, americana; Am. saco; lana, pelo (de un animal); **lady's —** abrigo de señora; **— hanger** colgador; **— of arms** escudo de armas; **— of paint** capa de pintura; v. cubrir; revestir, dar una mano (de pintura); **to — with**

sugar azucarar, bañar en azúcar.

coat·ing [kótɪŋ] s. capa.

coat·tail [kóttel] s. faldón.

coax [koks] v. rogar o persuadir con halagos, halagar, tentar.

cob [kɑb] s. carozo, zuro (de la mazorca del maíz), Ven., Col., Carib. tusa, Méx., C.A. olote.

co·balt [kóbɔlt] s. cobalto.

cob·bler [kάblɵ] s. remendón (zapatero); pudin de bizcocho y fruta.

cob·ble·stone [kάblston] s. guijarro; adj.

cob·web [kάbwɛb] s. telaraña.

co·caine [kokén] s. cocaína.

cock [kɑk] s. gallo; macho de ave; espita, grifo; martillo (de armas de fuego); **—sure** muy seguro de sí mismo; v. amartillar (un arma de fuego); ladear (la cabeza), ladearse (el sombrero).

cock·fight [kάkfaɪt] s. pelea de gallos, riña de gallos.

cock·pit [kάkpɪt] s. gallera; (airplane) cabina.

cock·roach [kάkrotʃ] s. cucaracha.

cock·tail [kάktel] s. coctel; aperitivo (de ostras), almejas, frutas, etc.).

cock·y [kάkɪ] adj. arrogante, Am. retobado.

co·coa [kóko] s. cacao; bebida de cacao, chocolate.

co·co·nut [kókənət] s. coco (fruta).

co·coon [kəkún] s. capullo (del gusano de seda, etc.).

cod [kɑd] s. N.Esp. abadejo; Andalucía, Am. bacalao; **cod-liver oil** aceite de hígado de bacalao.

cod·dle [kάdl] v. mimar, consentir.

code [kod] s. código; clave; **— message** comunicación en clave; **signal —** código de señales.

co·dex [kódɛks] s. codice.

cod·fish [kάdfɪʃ] = **cod.**

co·erce [koɵs] v. forzar, obligar.

co·er·cion [koɵʃən] s. coacción.

co·ex·is·tence [koegzístəns] s. coexistencia.

cof·fee [kɔ́fɪ] s. café; **— shop** café; **— tree** cafeto; **black —** café solo; Col. tinto.

cof·fee·pot [kɔ́fɪpɑt] s. cafetera.

cof·fer [kɔ́fɵ] s. cofre, arca.

cof·fin [kɔ́fɪn] s. ataúd, féretro.

cog [kɑg] s. diente; **— wheel** rueda dentada.

cog·nate [kάgnet] s. cognato.

co·her·ent [kohírənt] adj. coherente; conexo.

co·he·sion [kohíʒən] s. cohesión.

coif·fure [kwafjúr] s. tocado, peinado.

coil [kɔɪl] s. rollo; rosca; espiral de alambre; **electric —** bobina; v. arrollar(se), enrollar(se); enroscar(se).

coin [kɔɪn] s. moneda; v. acuñar; inventar, forjar (una frase o palabra).

coin·age [kɔ́ɪnɪdʒ] s. acuñación; sistema monetario; moneda, monedas; invención (de una palabra o frase).

co·in·cide [koɪnsáɪd] v. coincidir.

co·in·ci·dence [koɪnsάdəns] s. coincidencia; casualidad.

coke [kok] s. cok, coque (combustible).

cold [kold] adj. frío; **— cream** crema cosmética; **— meat** fiambre; **— wave** ola de frío; **— war** guerra fría; **to be —** tener frío; **it is — today** hace frío hoy; s. frío; catarro, resfriado; **to catch a —** resfriarse, acatarrarse.

cold·ness [kóldnɪs] s. frialdad; indiferencia, despego.

col·ic [kálɪk] s. cólico.
col·lab·o·rate [kəlǽbəret] v. colaborar.
col·lab·o·ra·tion [kəlæbəréʃən] s. colaboración.
col·lapse [kəlǽps] s. desplome, derrumbe, derrumbamiento; hundimiento; postración; v. doblar(se), plegar(se); contraer (el volumen); hundirse, derrumbarse, desplomarse; sufrir una postración.
col·lar [kálə] s. collar; cuello (de vestido, camisa, etc.); collera (para mulas o caballos de tiro); v. acollarar, poner collar a; coger o agarrar por el cuello; prender.
col·late [kəlét, kólet] v. cotejar; colacionar.
col·lat·er·al [kəlǽtərəl] adj. colateral; auxiliar, subsidiario, accesorio; s. garantía (para un préstamo bancario).
col·league [kálig] s. colega.
col·lect [kəlékt] v. recoger; coleccionar; cobrar; recaudar (impuestos); reunir(se); congregarse; **to — oneself** calmarse; sosegarse, reportarse.
col·lec·tion [kəlékʃən] s. colección; agrupación (de gente); recolección, cobranza, cobro, recaudación, colecta.
col·lec·tive [kəléktɪv] adj. colectivo.
col·lec·tiv·ism [kəléktəvɪzm] s. colectivismo.
col·lec·tor [kəléktə] s. colector; coleccionista (de sellos, objetos artísticos, etc.); cobrador (de billetes, deudas, etc.); recaudador (de impuestos).
col·lege [kálɪdʒ] s. universidad; **— of engineering** facultad de ingeniería; **— of medicine** escuela (facultad) de medicina.
col·lide [kəláɪd] v. chocar; estar en conflicto, oponerse.
col·lie [kálɪ] s. perro de pastor.
col·li·sion [kəlíʒən] s. choque, colisión; oposición, pugna (de intereses, ideas, etc.).
col·lo·qui·al [kəlókwɪəl] adj. familiar; — **expression** locución o frase familiar.
col·lu·sion [kəlúʒɪən] s. confabulación.
co·lon [kólən] s. colon (del intestino); dos puntos (signo de puntuación).
colo·nel [kɝnl] s. coronel.
co·lo·ni·al [kəlónɪəl] adj. colonial.
col·o·nist [kálənɪst] s. colono, colonizador.
col·o·ni·za·tion [kalənəzéʃən] s. colonización.
col·o·nize [kálənaɪz] v. colonizar; establecerse en colonia.
col·o·ny [kálənɪ] s. colonia.
col·or [kʌlə] s. color; colorido; **the -s** la bandera; v. colorar; colorear; dar colorido; pintar; teñir; iluminar (una fotografía, grabado, etc.); ruborizarse.
col·ored [kʌləd] adj. colorado, teñido, colorido, pintado; de color; coloreado; — **person** persona de color.
col·or·ful [kʌləfəl] adj. lleno de color; colorido; vistoso; vívido; pintoresco.
col·or·ing [kʌlərɪŋ] s. colorido; coloración; colorante.
col·or·less [kʌləlɪs] adj. incoloro; descolorido.
co·los·sal [kəlásl] adj. colosal.
colt [kolt] s. potro.
Co·lum·bi·an [kəlʌmbɪən] adj. colombiano, de Colombia; colombino, referente a Cristóbal Colón.
col·umn [káləm] s. columna.
co·ma [kómə] s. coma.
comb [kom] s. peine; peineta (de mujer); cresta (de gallo); rastrillo, carda (para lana); almohaza (para caballos); panal (de miel); v. peinar; rastrillar, cardar (lana); escudriñar; **to — one's**

hair peinarse.
com·bat [kámbæt] s. combate, pelea; v, combatir.
com·bat·ant [kámbətənt] adj. & s. combatiente.
com·bi·na·tion [kambənéʃən] s. combinación.
com·bine [kəmbáɪn] v. combinar(se), unir(se).
com·bo [kámbo] s. batería de jazz.
com·bus·ti·ble [kəmbástəbl] adj. & s. combustible.
com·bus·tion [kəmbástʃən] s. combustión.
come [kʌm] v. venir; llegar; provenir; **to — about** suceder; **to — again** volver, volver a venir; **to — back** volver, regresar; **to — downstairs** bajar; **to — in** entrar; **to — out** salir; **to — of age** llegar a mayor edad; **to — off** soltarse, zafarse; **to — to** volver en sí; **to — to terms** ponerse de acuerdo, ajustarse; **to — up** subir; surgir (una cuestión); p.p. de **to come**.
co·me·di·an [kəmídɪən] s. cómico, comediante.
com·e·dy [kámədɪ] s. comedia.
come·ly [kámlɪ] adj. agradable a la vista, gentil, bien parecido.
com·et [kámɪt] s. cometa.
com·fort [kámfət] s. comodidad; bienestar; alivio, consuelo; v. consolar, confortar, aliviar.
com·fort·a·ble [kámfətəbl] adj. cómodo; confortable; — **life** vida holgada; — **income** un buen pasar, renta suficiente; **comfortably** adv. cómodamente; con comodidad; holgadamente.
com·fort·er [kámfətə] s. consolador; edredón, cobertor acolchado.
com·fort·less [kámfətlɪs] adj. incómodo; desconsolado.
com·ic [kámɪk] adj. cómico; chistoso, gracioso; **-s** s. pl. caricaturas, historietas cómicas.
com·i·cal [kámɪkl] adj. cómico, gracioso.
com·ing [kámɪŋ] adj. que viene, que llega; próximo; venidero; s. venida, llegada; — **Christ** advenimiento de Cristo.
com·ma [kámə] s. coma.
com·mand [kəmǽnd] s. (order) mando; mandato, orden; mandamiento; (post) comandancia; (dominance) dominio; **at your —** a la orden de Vd., a la disposición de Vd.; **he has a good —** **of English** domina bien el inglés; v, mandar; ordenar; dominar; comandar; **to — respect** inspirar respeto, imponerse.
com·mand·er [kəmǽndə] s. jefe; comandante; teniente de navío; comendador (de ciertas órdenes); — **in chief** comandante en jefe; general en jefe.
com·mand·ment [kəmǽndmənt] s. mandamiento; mandato, orden.
com·man·do [kəmǽndo] s. comando.
com·mem·o·rate [kəmǽmoret] v. conmemorar.
com·mence [koméns] v. comenzar.
com·mence·ment [kəménsmənt] s. comienzo, principio; acto de distribución de diplomas.
com·mend [kəménd] v. alabar, elogiar; encomendar, encargar; recomendar.
com·men·da·tion [kaməndéʃən] s. encomio, alabanza.
com·ment [kámɛnt] s. comentario, observación, nota; v. comentar; hacer observaciones; hacer comentarios.
com·men·tar·y [káməntɛrɪ] s. comentario.
com·men·ta·tor [káməntetə] s. comentador; comentarista; **radio —** comentarista radial.
com·merce [kámɝs] s. comercio.
com·mer·cial [kəmɝʃəl] adj. comercial.
com·mis·er·a·tion [kəmɪzəréʃən] s. compasión.
com·mis·sar [kámɪsar] s. comisario.
com·mis·sar·y [káməsɛrɪ] s. comisario.

com·mis·sion [kəmíʃən] *s.* comisión; encargo; junta; nombramiento; **to put out of** — inutilizar; descomponer, quebrar; retirar del servicio (*un navío*); *v.* comisionar; encargar; nombrar; poner en servicio (*un navío*); **-ed officer** oficial comisionado (*alférez u oficial superior a éste*).

com·mis·sion·er [kəmíʃənɚ] *s.* comisionado; comisario; **police** — comisario de policía.

com·mit [kəmít] *v.* (*perpetrate*) cometer; (*entrust*) encargar; **to** — **to memory** aprender de memoria **to** — **to prison** encarcelar; **to** — **oneself** dar o expresar su opinión, expresarse abiertamente, comprometerse.

com·mit·tee [kəmítɪ] *s.* comité; comisión, junta; — **of one** comisionado o delegado único.

com·mod·i·ty [kəmádətɪ] *s.* mercancía; género; mercadería, artículo de comercio, producto.

com·mon [kámən] *adj.* común; general; corriente; vulgar, ordinario; público; — **law** derecho consuetudinario; — **sense** sentido común; — **soldier** soldado raso; — **market** mercado común; **-s** *s. pl.* refectorio (*de un colegio o universidad*); ejido, campo común; **-ly** *adv.* comúnmente, por lo común.

com·mon·ness [kámənnɪs] *s.* vulgaridad, ordinariez; frecuencia.

com·mon·place [kámənples] *adj.* común, trivial; *s.* lugar común.

com·mon·wealth [kámənwɛlθ] *s.* estado; república; pueblo, colectividad.

com·mo·tion [kəmóʃən] *s.* conmoción; tumulto; bullicio; levantamiento.

com·mune [kəmjún] *v.* comunicarse (con); comulgar.

com·mu·ni·cate [kəmjúnəket] *v.* comunicar(se); transmitir.

com·mu·ni·ca·tion [kəmjunəkéʃən] *s.* comunicación.

com·mu·ni·ca·tive [kəmjúnəketɪv] *adj.* comunicativo.

com·mun·ion [kəmjúnjən] *s.* comunión.

com·mu·nism [kámjʊnɪzəm] *s.* comunismo.

com·mu·nist [kámjʊnɪst] *s.* & *adj.* comunista.

com·mu·ni·ty [kəmjúnətɪ] *s.* comunidad; sociedad; vecindario, barrio; — **chest** caja de beneficencia, fondos de beneficencia.

com·mute [kəmjút] *v.* conmutar; viajar diario de una población a otra.

com·pact [kəmpǽkt] *adj.* compacto; denso; apretado; conciso; sucinto; [kámpækt] *s.* pacto, trato, convenio; polvera.

com·pact·ness [kəmpǽktnɪs] *s.* solidez; densidad; concisión.

com·pan·ion [kəmpǽnjən] *s.* compañero; acompañante.

com·pan·ion·ship [kəmpǽnjənʃɪp] *s.* compañerismo, camaradería; compañía.

com·pany [kámpənɪ] *s.* compañía; sociedad; visita; **ship's** — tripulación; **to keep** — **with** acompañar a; cortejar a; tener relaciones con, frecuentar la compañía de.

com·pa·ra·ble [kámpərəbl] *adj.* comparable.

com·par·a·tive [kəmpǽrətɪv] *adj.* comparativo.

com·pare [kəmpɛ́r] *v.* comparar; cotejar; confrontar; contrastar; **beyond** — incomparable, sin par, sin igual, sin comparación.

com·par·i·son [kəmpǽrəsn] *s.* comparación; símil; **beyond** — incomparable, sin comparación; **in** — **with** comparado con.

com·part·ment [kəmpártmənt] *s.* compartimiento, sección, división; departamento.

com·pass [kámpəs] *s.* compás (*para dibujar*); brújula; área, ámbito; alcance.

com·pas·sion [kəmpǽʃən] *s.* compasión, lástima.

com·pas·sion·ate [kəmpǽʃənɪt] *adj.* compasivo, misericordioso.

com·pat·i·ble [kəmpǽtəbl] *adj.* compatible.

com·pa·tri·ot [kəmpétrɪət] *s.* compatriota.

com·pel [kəmpél] *v.* compeler, obligar; exigir.

com·pen·sate [kámpənset] *v.* compensar; recompensar; remunerar.

com·pen·sa·tion [kampənséʃən] *s.* compensación; recompensa; remuneración.

com·pete [kəmpít] *v.* competir.

com·pe·tence [kámpətəns] *s.* competencia, aptitud, capacidad.

com·pe·tent [kámpətənt] *adj.* competente; calificado; capaz.

com·pe·ti·tion [kampətíʃən] *s.* competencia; concurso, certamen; contienda.

com·pet·i·tive [kəmpétətɪv] *adj.* en competencia; — **examination** oposición, concurso.

com·pet·i·tor [kəmpétətɚ] *s.* competidor; rival; opositor.

com·pile [kəmpáɪl] *v.* compilar, recopilar.

com·pla·cen·cy [kəmplésn̩sɪ] *s.* complacencia, contentamiento.

com·pla·cent [kəmplésn̩t] *adj.* complaciente, satisfecho.

com·plain [kəmplén] *v.* quejarse; querellarse.

com·plaint [kəmplént] *s.* queja; quejido, lamento; dolencia, enfermedad; **to lodge a** — hacer una reclamación.

com·ple·ment [kámpləmənt] *s.* complemento; [kámpləmənt] *v.* complementar, completar.

com·plete [kəmplít] *adj.* completo; *v.* completar; terminar; **-ly** *adv.* completamente, por completo.

com·plete·ness [kəmplítnɪs] *s.* perfección; minuciosidad; lo completo; lo cabal; lo acabado.

com·ple·tion [kəmplíʃən] *s.* completamiento, terminación, conclusión; cumplimiento.

com·plex [kámpleks] *s.* complejo; [kámplɛks] *adj.* complejo; compuesto; complicado.

com·plex·ion [kəmplékʃən] *s.* cutis, tez; aspecto.

com·plex·i·ty [kəmpléksətɪ] *s.* complejidad.

com·pli·ance [kəmpláɪəns] *s.* complacencia; condescendencia; conformidad; cumplimiento; **in** — **with** en conformidad con; de acuerdo con, conforme a.

com·pli·cate [kámpləket] *v.* complicar.

com·pli·cat·ed [kámpləketɪd] *adj.* complicado.

com·pli·ca·tion [kampləkéʃən] *s.* complicación.

com·plic·i·ty [kəmplísətɪ] *s.* complicidad.

com·pli·ment [kámpləmənt] *s.* cumplido, cumplimiento; requiebro; lisonja, galantería; **to send one's -s** enviar saludos; [kámpləmənt] *v.* cumplimentar; requebrar; lisonjear; alabar.

com·ply [kəmpláɪ] *v.* consentir, conformarse (con), obrar de acuerdo (con); cumplir (con).

com·po·nent [kəmpónənt] *adj.* & *s.* componente.

com·pose [kəmpóz] *v.* componer; **to** — **oneself** sosegarse, serenarse, calmarse.

com·posed [kəmpózd] *adj.* compuesto; tranquilo, sereno, sosegado; **to be** — **of** estar compuesto de, componerse de, constar de.

com·pos·er [kəmpózɚ] *s.* compositor; autor.

com·pos·ite [kəmpázɪt] *adj.* compuesto; *s.* compuesto; mezcla.

com·po·si·tion [kampəzíʃən] *s.* composición; arreglo; compuesto.

com·po·sure [kəmpóʒɚ] *s.* compostura, calma,

com·pound [kámpaʊnd] *adj.* & *s.* compuesto; [kampáʊnd] *v.* componer; mezclar, combinar; **to — interest** calcular el interés compuesto.

com·pre·hend [kamprɪhénd] *v.* comprender; abarcar, abrazar, incluir.

com·pre·hen·si·ble [kamprɪhénsəbl] *adj.* comprensible, inteligible.

com·pre·hen·sion [kamprɪhénʃən] *s.* comprensión.

com·pre·hen·sive [kamprɪhénsɪv] *adj.* comprensivo; inclusivo.

com·press [kámprɛs] *s.* compresa; [kəmprés] *v.* comprimir, apretar, condensar.

com·pres·sion [kəmpréʃən] *s.* compresión.

com·prise [kəmpráɪz] *v.* comprender, abarcar, incluir, abrazar; constar de.

com·pro·mise [kámprəmaɪz] *s.* compromiso; arreglo; avenencia; término medio; *v.* comprometer; avenirse, transigir; *Am.* transar.

comp·trol·ler [kəntrólɚ] *s.* interventor, *Am.* contralor.

com·pul·sion [kəmpʌ́lʃən] *s.* compulsión, coacción.

com·pul·so·ry [kəmpʌ́lsərɪ] *adj.* obligatorio.

com·pu·ta·tion [kampjətéʃən] *s.* cómputo, cálculo.

com·pute [kəmpjút] *v.* computar.

com·put·er [kəmpjútɚ] *s. Esp.* calculadora electrónica; *Arg.* computadora; programadora.

com·put·er·ize [kəmpjútɚaɪz] *v.* someter datos a la calculadora electrónica; suplir con sistema computadora.

com·rade [kámræd] *s.* camarada, compañero.

con·cave [kankév] *adj.* cóncavo.

con·ceal [kənsíl] *v.* encubrir, ocultar, esconder.

con·ceal·ment [kənsílmənt] *s.* encubrimiento.

con·cede [kənsid] *v.* conceder; otorgar: admitir, reconocer.

con·ceit [kənsít] *s.* presunción, amor propio, vanagloria; concepto, agudeza.

con·ceit·ed [kənsítɪd] *adj.* presuntuoso, presumido, vanidoso, engreído.

con·ceiv·a·ble [kənsívəbl] *adj.* concebible, imaginable, comprensible.

con·ceive [kənsív] *v.* concebir; imaginar.

con·cen·trate [kánsṇtret] *v.* concentrar(se), reconcentrar(se).

con·cen·tra·tion [kansṇtréʃən] *s.* concentración; reconcentración; — **camp** reconcentración de presos.

con·cept [kánsɛpt] *s.* concepto, idea; opinión.

con·cep·tion [kənsɛ́pʃən] *s.* concepción; concepto, idea.

con·cern [kənsɝ́n] *s.* (*business*) compañía, negociación; negocio; establecimiento mercantil; (*interest*) cuidado; interés; preocupación; **to be of no** — no ser de consecuencia; *v.* concernir, importar, interesar; preocupar; **in all that -s him** en cuanto le atañe, en cuanto le concierne; **to whom it may** — a quien corresponda.

con·cerned [kənsɝ́nd] *adj.* interesado; preocupado, intranquilo, inquieto, ansioso; **to be — about** interesarse por, preocuparse por; **as far as I am** — por lo que me concierne, por lo que me toca, en cuanto a mí me atañe.

con·cern·ing [kənsɝ́nɪŋ] *prep.* tocante a, respecto a, acerca de.

con·cert [kánsɝt] *s.* concierto; [kənsɝ́t] *v.* concertar, arreglar (*un plan*).

con·ces·sion [kənsɛ́ʃən] *s.* concesión.

con·cil·i·ate [kənsíliet] *v.* conciliar, poner en armonía; ganar la voluntad de.

con·cise [kənsáɪs] *adj.* conciso, sucinto.

con·cise·ness [kənsáɪsnɪs] *s.* concisión, brevedad.

con·clude [kənklúd] *v.* concluir; acabar, terminar; deducir; decidir.

con·clu·sion [kənklúʒən] *s.* conclusión.

con·clu·sive [kənklúsɪv] *adj.* conclusivo, concluyente.

con·coct [kankákt] *v.* confeccionar; preparar (*combinando diversos ingredientes*); inventar, urdir.

con·coc·tion [kankákʃən] *s.* cocimiento, menjurje; mezcla.

con·cord [kánkɔrd] *s.* concordia, conformidad, acuerdo; convenio, pacto.

con·crete [kankrít] *adj.* concreto; de hormigón, de cemento; *s.* hormigón, cemento, *Am.* concreto.

con·cu·bine [kɑ́ŋkjubaɪn] *s.* concubina.

con·cur [kənkɝ́] *v.* estar de acuerdo, ser del mismo parecer; unirse.

con·cus·sion [kənkʌ́ʃən] *s.* concusión.

con·demn [kəndém] *v.* condenar; **to — a building** condenar un edificio.

con·dem·na·tion [kandɛmnéʃən] *s.* condenación.

con·den·sa·tion [kandɛnséʃən] *s.* condensación; resumen, compendio.

con·dense [kəndɛ́ns] *v.* condensar(se).

con·de·scend [kandɪsɛ́nd] *v.* condescender.

con·de·scen·sion [kandɪsɛ́nʃən] *s.* condescendencia.

con·di·ment [kándəmənt] *s.* condimento.

con·di·tion [kəndíʃən] *s.* condición; estado; nota o calificación provisional; **on — that** a condición de que, con tal que; *v.* acondicionar; poner en buena condición; estipular; reprobar provisionalmente (*a un estudiante*).

con·di·tion·al [kəndíʃənl] *adj.* condicional.

con·dole [kəndól] *v.* condolerse; **to — with** dar el pésame a; consolar a.

con·do·lence [kəndóləns] *s.* pésame.

con·do·min·i·um [kandəmínɪəm] *s.* condominio.

con·done [kəndón] *v.* dispensar; perdonar; condonar.

con·duce [kəndjús] *v.* conducir.

con·du·cive [kəndjúsɪv] *adj.* conducente.

con·duct [kándʌkt] *s.* (*behavior*) conducta; comportamiento, proceder; (*handling*) dirección; manejo; [kəndʌ́kt] *v.* conducir; dirigir; manejar; **to — oneself** well portarse bien.

con·duc·tor [kəndʌ́ktɚ] *s.* conductor; guía; **orchestra** — director de orquesta; **train** — revisor; cobrador, *Am.* conductor.

con·duit [kánduɪt] *s.* conducto; caño; cañería, tubería.

cone [kon] *s.* cono; **paper** — cucurucho; **pine** — piña.

con·fec·tion [kənfɛ́kʃən] *s.* confección; confitura; confite, dulce.

con·fec·tion·er·y [kənfɛ́kʃənɛrɪ] *s.* confitería; dulcería; confites, dulces.

con·fed·er·a·cy [kənfédərəsɪ] *s.* confederación.

con·fed·er·ate [kənfédərɪt] *adj.* & *s.* confederado; [kənfédəret] *v.* confederar(se).

con·fed·er·a·tion [kənfɛdəréʃən] *s.* confederación.

con·fer [kənfɝ́] *v.* conferir, conceder; conferenciar, consultar.

con·fer·ence [kánfərəns] *s.* conferencia; congreso; consulta, junta, sesión.

con·fess [kənfés] *v.* confesar(se); reconocer, admitir.

con·fes·sion·al [kənféʃənl] *s.* confesionario.

con·fes·sor [kənfésɚ] *s.* confesor.

con·fi·dant [kɑnfədǽnt] *s.* confidente.

con·fide [kənfáɪd] *v.* confiar; fiar.

con·fi·dence [kánfədəns] *s.* confianza; confidencia; — **game** estafa; — **man** estafador.

con·fi·dent [kánfədənt] *adj.* confiado; seguro, cierto; **-ly** *adv.* confiadamente, con toda seguridad.

con·fi·den·tial [kɑnfədɛ́nʃəl] *adj.* confidencial; íntimo; secreto; **-ly** *adv.* en confianza.

con·fine [kánfaɪn] *s.* confín; [kənfáɪn] *v.* confinar; encerrar; **to — oneself to** limitarse a; **to be -ed in bed** estar encamado, guardar cama.

con·fine·ment [kənfáɪnmənt] *s.* encerramiento; encierro; prisión, encarcelación.

con·firm [kənfɜ́m] *v.* confirmar.

con·fir·ma·tion [kɑnfɚméʃən] *s.* confirmación.

con·fis·cate [kánfɪsket] *v.* confiscar.

con·fla·gra·tion [kɑnfləgréʃən] *s.* conflagración, incendio.

con·flict [kánflɪkt] *s.* conflicto, oposición, choque; lucha, combate; [kənflíkt] *v.* chocar, oponerse, estar en conflicto.

con·form [kənfɔ́rm] *v.* conformar(se).

con·form·i·ty [kənfɔ́rməti] *s.* conformidad.

con·found [kɑnfáʊnd] *v.* confundir, perturbar, desconcertar, aturdir; — **it!** ¡caramba!

con·front [kənfrʌ́nt] *v.* confrontar; carear, poner cara a cara (*a dos reos*); encararse con, afrontar, hacer frente a, arrostrar.

con·fuse [kənfjúz] *v.* confundir; trastornar; embrollar; desconcertar.

con·fused [kənfjúzd] *adj.* confuso; revuelto; desconcertado, perplejo; **to become —** confundirse; desconcertarse.

con·fus·ing [kənfjúzɪŋ] *adj.* confuso, revuelto; desconcertante.

con·fu·sion [kənfjúʒən] *s.* confusión; desorden; tumulto; perplejidad.

con·geal [kəndʒíl] *v.* congelar(se), helar(se), cuajar(se).

con·gen·ial [kəndʒínjəl] *adj.* congenial; simpático; **to be — with** congeniar con, simpatizar con.

con·ges·tion [kəndʒɛ́stʃən] *s.* congestión; aglomeración.

con·glom·er·a·tion [kənglɑməréʃən] *s.* aglomeración.

con·grat·u·late [kəngrǽtʃəlet] *v.* congratular, felicitar, dar el parabién.

con·grat·u·la·tion [kəngrǽtʃəléʃən] *s.* congratulación, felicitación, parabién, enhorabuena.

con·gre·gate [káŋgrɪget] *v.* congregar(se), juntar(se), reunir(se).

con·gre·ga·tion [kɑŋgrɪgéʃən] *s.* congregación; asamblea, reunión; colección, agregado; fieles, feligreses (*de una iglesia*).

con·gress [káŋgrəs] *s.* congreso; asamblea.

con·gres·sion·al [kəngréʃənl] *adj.* perteneciente al congreso.

con·gress·man [káŋgrəsmən] *s.* congresista, diputado, representante.

con·ic [kánɪk] *adj.* cónico.

con·jec·ture [kəndʒɛ́ktʃɚ] *s.* conjetura, suposición; *v.* conjeturar, suponer.

con·ju·gate [kándʒəget] *v.* conjugar.

con·ju·ga·tion [kɑndʒəgéʃən] *s.* conjugación.

con·junc·tion [kəndʒʌ́ŋkʃən] *s.* conjunción.

con·jure [kándʒɚ] *v.* conjurar; **to — up** evocar; [kəndʒúr] rogar, implorar.

con·nect [kənɛ́kt] *v.* conectar; unir(se), juntar(se); enlazar(se); relacionar(se); acoplar.

con·nect·ing rod [kənɛ́ktɪŋ rad] *s.* biela.

con·nec·tion [kənɛ́kʃən] *s.* conexión; enlace;

vínculo; unión; relación; **-s** parientes; amigos, amistades.

con·nip·tion [kənípʃən] *s.* pataleta; **to have a —** darle a uno una pataleta.

con·nive [kənáɪv] *v.* conspirar; disimular; hacerse cómplice.

con·nois·seur [kɑnəsɝ́] *s.* conocedor, perito.

con·quer [káŋkɚ] *v.* conquistar; vencer.

con·quer·or [káŋkərɚ] *s.* conquistador; vencedor.

con·quest [káŋkwɛst] *s.* conquista.

con·science [kánʃəns] *s.* conciencia.

con·sci·en·tious [kɑnʃiénʃəs] *adj.* concienzudo.

con·scious [kánʃəs] *adj.* consciente; sabedor; **-ly** *adv.* conscientemente; a sabiendas.

con·scious·ness [kánʃəsnɪs] *s.* consciencia, estado consciente; **to lose —** perder el sentido o conocimiento.

con·script [kənskrípt] *v.* reclutar; [kánskrɪpt] *s.* recluta.

con·se·crate [kánsɪkret] *v.* consagrar; dedicar.

con·se·cra·tion [kɑnsɪkréʃən] *s.* consagración; dedicación.

con·sec·u·tive [kənsékjətɪv] *adj.* consecutivo.

con·sen·sus [kənsénsəs] *s.* consenso.

con·sent [kənsɛ́nt] *s.* consentimiento; permiso, asentimiento; *v.* consentir; permitir, asentir.

con·se·quence [kánsəkwɛns] *s.* consecuencia.

con·se·quent [kánsəkwɛnt] *adj.* consecuente; consiguiente; *s.* consecuente, consiguiente, consecuencia; **-ly** *adv.* por consiguiente, por consecuencia.

con·se·quen·tial [kɑnsəkwéntʃl] *adj.* de consecuencia.

con·ser·va·tion [kɑnsɚvéʃən] *s.* conservación; preservación.

con·ser·va·tive [kənsɝ́vətɪv] *adj.* conservador; conservativo; *s.* conservador.

con·ser·va·to·ry [kənsɝ́vətorɪ] *s.* conservatorio; invernadero.

con·serve [kánsɝv] *s.* conserva, dulce; *v.* [kənsɝ́v] conservar; preservar.

con·sid·er [kənsídɚ] *v.* considerar.

con·sid·er·a·ble [kənsídərəbl] *adj.* considerable; cuantioso; **considerably** *adv.* considerablemente; **considerably older** bastante más viejo.

con·sid·er·ate [kənsídərɪt] *adj.* considerado.

con·sid·er·a·tion [kənsɪdəréʃən] *s.* (*respect*) respeto; consideración; importancia; (*pay*) remuneración; **in — of** en atención a, teniendo en cuenta, en razón de, en vista de.

con·sid·er·ing [kənsídərɪŋ] *prep.* en razón de; vista de; en atención a, en consideración de.

con·sign [kənsáɪn] *v.* consignar; enviar; entregar.

con·sign·ee [kɑnsaɪní] *s.* consignatario.

con·sign·ment [kənsáɪnmənt] *s.* consignación.

con·sist [kənsíst] *v.* consistir (en); constar (de).

con·sis·ten·cy [kənsístənsi] *s.* consecuencia; consistencia, firmeza, solidez.

con·sis·tent [kənsístənt] *adj.* consecuente, lógico; compatible; consistente, coherente.

con·so·la·tion [kɑnsəléʃən] *s.* consolación; consuelo.

con·sole [kənsól] *v.* consolar.

con·sol·i·date [kənsáladət] *v.* consolidar(se); unir(se), combinar(se).

con·so·nant [kánsənənt] *adj.* consonante; conforme; *s.* consonante.

con·sort [kánsɔrt] *s.* consorte; [kənsɔ́rt] *v.* **to — with** asociarse con.

con·spic·u·ous [kənspíkjʊəs] *adj.* conspicuo, notorio; manifiesto, sobresaliente.

con·spir·a·cy [kənspírəsı] *s.* conspiración, conjuración.
con·spir·a·tor [kənspírətə] *s.* conspirador, conjurado.
con·spire [kənspáɪr] *v.* conspirar; tramar, maquinar.
con·sta·ble [kánstəbl] *s.* alguacil, policía; condestable (*titulo*).
con·stan·cy [kánstənsı] *s.* constancia.
con·stant [kánstənt] *adj.* constante; *s.* constante, cantidad constante; **-ly** *adv.* constantemente, continuamente, siempre; a menudo.
con·stel·la·tion [kanstəleʃən] *s.* constelación.
con·ster·na·tion [kanstənéʃən] *s.* consternación.
con·sti·pate [kánstəpet] *v.* estreñir.
con·sti·pa·tion [kanstəpéʃən] *s.* estreñimiento.
con·stit·u·ent [kənstítʃʊənt] *adj.* constituyente; constitutivo; componente; *s.* componente, elemento; elector, votante.
con·sti·tute [kánstətjut] *v.* constituir; componer; establecer.
con·sti·tu·tion [kanstətjúʃən] *s.* constitución.
con·sti·tu·tion·al [kanstətjúʃənl] *adj.* constitucional; *s.* paseo a pie, caminata (*para hacer ejercicio*).
con·strain [kənstrén] *v.* constreñir; obligar, forzar; apretar, comprimir.
con·strict [kənstríkt] *v.* apretar; estrechar.
con·struct [kənstrʌkt] *v.* construir, fabricar.
con·struc·tion [kənstrʌktʃən] *s.* construcción; estructura; interpretación.
con·struc·tive [kənstrʌktıv] *adj.* constructivo; de utilidad positiva; provechoso.
con·strue [kənstrú] *v.* interpretar, explicar.
con·sul [kánsl] *s.* cónsul.
con·su·late [kánslıt] *s.* consulado.
con·sult [kənsʌlt] *v.* consultar.
con·sult·ant [kənsʌltənt] *s.* consultante.
con·sul·ta·tion [kans|téʃən] *s.* consulta.
con·sume [kənsúm] *v.* consumir; gastar; perder (*el tiempo*).
con·sum·er [kənsúmə] *s.* consumidor.
con·sum·mate [kánsəmet] *v.* consumar, completar; [kənsʌmıt] *adj.* consumado, perfecto, completo.
con·sump·tion [kənsʌmpʃən] *s.* consumo, gasto; consunción; tisis, tuberculosis.
con·sump·tive [kənsʌmptıv] *adj.* tísico.
con·tact [kántækt] *s.* contacto; *v.* tocar; poner(se) en contacto con; estar en contacto con.
con·ta·gion [kəntédʒən] *s.* contagio.
con·ta·gious [kəntédʒəs] *adj.* contagioso.
con·tain [kəntén] *v.* contener; encerrar; tener cabida para; reprimir, refrenar; **to — oneself** contenerse, refrenarse.
con·tain·er [kənténə] *s.* envase, caja, recipiente.
con·tam·i·nate [kəntǽmənet] *v.* contaminar, viciar, inficionar.
con·tam·i·na·tion [kəntǽmənéʃən] *s.* contaminación; cruce.
con·tem·plate [kántəmplet] *v.* contemplar; meditar; tener la intención de; proyectar.
con·tem·pla·tion [kantəmpléʃən] *s.* contemplación; meditación; intención, propósito.
con·tem·po·rar·y [kəntémpərɛrı] *adj.* contemporáneo; coetáneo.
con·tempt [kəntémpt] *s.* desdén, menosprecio; desprecio; **— of court** contumacia.
con·tempt·i·ble [kəntémptəbl] *adj.* despreciable, vil.
con·temp·tu·ous [kəntémptʃʊəs] *adj.* desdeñoso.
con·tend [kənténd] *v.* contender; competir; argüir; altercar; sostener, afirmar.

con·tent [kántɛnt] *s.* contenido; sustancia; capacidad, volumen; **-s** contenido; **table of -s** tabla de materias, índice general.
con·tent [kəntént] *adj.* contento; satisfecho; *s.* contento; satisfacción; **to one's heart's — a** pedir de boca; hasta saciarse; a su entera satisfacción; *v.* contentar; satisfacer.
con·tent·ed [kənténtıd] *adj.* contento, satisfecho.
con·ten·tion [kənténʃən] *s.* contención, contienda; disputa, controversia; tema, argumento; aseveración.
con·tent·ment [kənténtmənt] *s.* contentamiento, contento.
con·test [kántɛst] *s.* concurso, certamen; debate; contienda; torneo; [kəntɛst] *v.* contender; disputar; luchar por; **to — with** competir con.
con·text [kántɛkst] *s.* contexto.
con·tig·u·ous [kəntígjʊəs] *adj.* contiguo; adyacente.
con·ti·nent [kántənənt] *s.* continente; *adj.* continente, casto, moderado.
con·ti·nen·tal [kantənéntl] *adj.* & *s.* continental.
con·tin·gen·cy [kəntíndʒənsı] *s.* contingencia, eventualidad.
con·tin·gent [kəntíndʒənt] *adj.* & *s.* contingente.
con·tin·u·al [kəntínjʊəl] *adj.* continuo; frecuente; **-ly** *adv.* de continuo, continuamente, frecuentemente.
con·tin·u·ance [kəntínjʊəns] *s.* continuación; aplazamiento.
con·tin·u·a·tion [kəntınjʊéʃən] *s.* continuación.
con·tin·ue [kəntínju] *v.* continuar.
con·ti·nu·i·ty [kantənúıtı] *s.* continuidad.
con·tin·u·ous [kəntínjʊəs] *adj.* continuo, sin parar, sin cesar.
con·tor·tion [kəntórʃən] *s.* contorsión.
con·tour [kántur] *s.* contorno; perímetro.
con·tra·band [kántrəbænd] *s.* contrabando.
con·tract [kántrækt] *s.* contrato, pacto, convenio; contrata; **marriage —** esponsales; [kəntrǽkt] *v.* contratar; contraer(se), encoger(se); **to — an illness** contraer una enfermedad; **to — :he brows** fruncir las cejas.
con·trac·tion [kəntrǽkʃən] *s.* contracción.
con·trac·tor [kəntrǽktə] *s.* contratista.
con·tra·dict [kantrədíkt] *v.* contradecir; contrariar.
con·tra·dic·tion [kantrədíkʃən] *s.* contradicción; contrariedad.
con·tra·dic·to·ry [kantrədíktərı] *adj.* contradictorio; opuesto, contrario.
con·tra·ry [kántrɛrı] *adj.* contrario; opuesto; testarudo, obstinado; *s.* contrario; **on the —** al contrario.
con·trast [kántræst] *s.* contraste; [kəntrǽst] *v.* contrastar.
con·tra·vene [kantrəvín] *v.* contravenir a; oponerse a.
con·trib·ute [kəntríbjut] *v.* contribuir.
con·tri·bu·tion [kantrəbjúʃən] *s.* contribución; aportación; cuota; dádiva.
con·trib·u·tor [kəntríbjətə] *s.* contribuidor; colaborador.
con·trib·u·to·ry [kəntríbjutərı] *adj.* contribuidor.
con·trite [kántraıt] *adj.* contrito.
con·tri·vance [kəntráıvəns] *s.* traza, maquinación; artificio, invención; designio; artefacto, aparato, máquina.
con·trive [kəntráıv] *v.* tramar, maquinar; inventar; idear; proyectar; **to — to** buscar el medio de, tratar de, procurar.
con·trol [kəntról] *s.* (*authority*) mando, manejo; dirección; (*instrument*) freno, regulador;

restricción; *Am.* control; **-s** mandos, controles; — **stick** palanca *(de un aeroplano)*; — **tower** torre de mando; — **experiment** experimento controlado; **to lose — of one's temper** perder la paciencia; *v.* gobernar, manejar, *Am.* controlar; regular, regularizar; restringir; contener, reprimir; tener a raya; **to — oneself** contenerse dominarse.

con·trol·ler [kəntrólæ] *s.* interventor, registrador, *Ríopl., C.A., Andes, Ven., Col.* contralor, *Ch., Méx.* controlador; regulador; aparato de manejo y control.

con·tro·ver·sy [kántrəvɜsɪ] *s.* controversia, debate, disputa; polémica.

co·nun·drum [kənʌ́ndrəm] *s.* adivinanza, acertijo.

con·va·lesce [kanvəlés] *v.* convalescer.

con·vene [kənvín] *v.* juntar, convocar; reunirse.

con·ven·ience [kənvínjəns] *s.* conveniencia, comodidad; **at one's** — cuando le convenga a uno, cuando tenga oportunidad, cuando buenamente pueda.

con·ven·ient [kənvínjənt] *adj.* conveniente; oportuno; cómodo; a propósito; **-ly** *adv.* convenientemente, cómodamente.

con·vent [kánvɛnt] *s.* convento.

con·ven·tion [kənvɛ́nʃən] *s.* convención; congreso, asamblea; convenio; costumbre, regla.

con·ven·tion·al [kənvɛ́nʃənl] *adj.* convencional; tradicional.

con·ven·tion·eer [kənvɛnʃənír] *s.* congresista.

con·verge [kənvɜ́dʒ] *v.* converger o convergir.

con·ver·sant [kánvəsṇt] *adj.*: — **with** versado en.

con·ver·sa·tion [kanvəséʃən] *s.* conversación.

con·verse [kənvɜ́s] *v.* conversar, hablar, platicar.

con·ver·sion [kənvɜ́ʒən] *s.* conversión,

con·vert [kánvɜt] *s.* converso, persona convertida; catecúmeno *(converso reciente)*; [kənvɜ́t] *v.* convertir(se).

con·vex [kanvéks] *adj.* convexo.

con·vey [kənvé] *v.* llevar; transportar; transferir; traspasar; transmitir; comunicar; **to — thanks** expresar agradecimiento, dar las gracias.

con·vey·ance [kənvéəns] *s.* vehículo; transporte; transmisión; entrega; comunicación; traspaso; escritura de propiedad o traspaso.

con·vey·er [kənvéæ] *s.* correa de transmisión.

con·vict [kánvɪkt] *s.* presidiario; reo; [kənvíkt] *v.* convencer *(de un delito)*, declarar culpable; probar la culpabilidad de.

con·vic·tion [kənvíkʃən] *s.* convicción; convencimiento; prueba de culpabilidad.

con·vince [kənvíns] *v.* convencer.

con·vinc·ing [kənvínsɪŋ] *adj.* convincente.

con·vo·ca·tion [kanvəkéʃən] *s.* convocación; asamblea.

con·voke [kənvók] *v.* convocar.

con·voy [kánvɔɪ] *s.* convoy, escolta, guardia; [kənvɔ́ɪ] *v.* convoyar.

con·vulse [kənvʌ́ls] *v.* crispar; agitar; convulsionar.

con·vul·sion [kənvʌ́lʃən] *s.* convulsión, agitación.

coo [ku] *s.* arrullo; *v.* arrullar.

cook [kʊk] *s.* cocinero, cocinera; *v.* cocinar, guisar; cocer; **to — up a plan** urdir un plan.

cook·er·y [kʊ́kərɪ] *s.* cocina, arte de cocinar.

cook·ie, cook·y [kʊ́kɪ] *s.* bizcochito, bollito.

cook·ing [kʊ́kɪŋ] *s.* cocina, arte culinaria; — **stove** cocina de gas, cocina eléctrica, estufa; — **utensils** batería de cocina, trastos de cocina.

cool [kul] *adj.* fresco; frío, indiferente; calmo, sereno; *s.* fresco, frescura; *v.* refrescar; enfriar; templar, calmar; **to — off** enfriarse; calmarse.

cool·ant [kúlənt] *s.* líquido refrigerador.

cool·ness [kúlnɪs] *s.* fresco, frescura: frialdad, indiferencia.

coon [kun] *s.* coatí *(cuadrúpedo carnívoro)*; negro; **a -'s age** una eternidad, mucho tiempo.

coop [kup] *s.* jaula; **chicken** — gallinero; *v.* enjaular; **to — up** encerrar.

co·op·er·ate [koápəret] *v.* cooperar.

co·op·er·a·tion [koapəréʃən] *s.* cooperación.

co·op·er·a·tive [koápəretɪv] *adj.* cooperativo; *s.* cooperativa, sociedad cooperativa.

co·or·di·nate [koórdṇet] *v.* coordinar; [koórdṇɪt] *adj.* coordinado.

co·or·di·na·tion [koordṇéʃən] *s.* coordinación.

cop [kap] *s.* polizonte, policía.

cope [kop] *v.* **to — with** tener suficiente fuerza para; **I cannot — with this** no puedo con esto, no puedo dar abasto a esto.

co·pi·ous [kópɪəs] *adj.* copioso, abundante.

cop·per [kápæ] *s.* cobre; polizonte, policía; — **coin** moneda de cobre, centavo; — **kettle** marmita o caldera de cobre; *adj.* cobrizo.

cop·y [kápɪ] *s.* copia; ejemplar *(de un libro)*; manuscrito *(para el impresor)*; *v.* copiar; imitar; remedar.

cop·y·right [kápɪraɪt] *s.* derecho de propiedad literaria; *v.* registrar, obtener patente de propiedad literaria.

co·quette [kokét] *s.* coqueta.

cor·al [kórəl] *s.* coral; *adj.* coralino, de coral; — **reef** arrecife de coral.

cord [kɔrd] *s.* cuerda; cordón, cordel; cuerda *(medida de leña)*; tendón; **-s** pantalones de pana; **spinal** — espinazo, espina dorsal.

cor·dial [kórdʒəl] *adj. & s.* cordial.

cor·du·roy [kɔrdərɔ́ɪ] *s.* pana; **-s** pantalones de pana; — **road** camino de troncos o maderos.

core [kor] *s.* corazón, centro; núcleo; esencia; *v.* cortar el centro o corazón de; despepitar *(una manzana)*.

cork [kɔrk] *s.* corcho; tapón; — **tree** alcornoque; *v.* tapar con corcho.

cork·screw [kórkskru] *s.* tirabuzón, sacacorchos; *adj.* espiral, de forma espiral.

corn [kɔrn] *s.* maíz; grano, cereal; callo *(de los pies o manos)*; — **bread** pan de maíz; — **meal** harina de maíz; — **cob** *Esp.* zuro; *Am.* tusa; *v.* salar, curar, acecinar.

corned beef [kórnd bif] *s.* carne de vaca curada *(en salmuera y salitre)*.

cor·ner [kórnæ] *s.* *(interior)* rincón; rinconada; ángulo; *(exterior)* esquina; ángulo; *(monopoly)* monopolio; — **stone** piedra angular; — **table** (— **shelf,** — **bracket)** rinconera; *v.* arrinconar; acorralar; acaparar, monopolizar.

cor·net [kɔrnét] *s.* corneta.

corn·field [kórnfild] *s.* maizal, *Am.* milpa.

cor·nice [kórnɪs] *s.* cornisa.

cor·ol·lar·y [kórəlɛrɪ] *s.* corolario; consecuencia natural.

cor·o·na·tion [kɔrənéʃən] *s.* coronación.

cor·o·ner [kórənæ] *s.* juez de guardia.

cor·o·net [kórənɪt] *s.* coronilla, guirnalda.

cor·po·ral [kórpərəl] *adj.* corporal; corpóreo; *s.* cabo *(militar)*.

cor·po·ra·tion [kɔrpəréʃən] *s.* corporación; sociedad mercantil.

corps [kor] *s.* cuerpo *(grupo organizado)*; **air** — cuerpo de aviación; **army** — cuerpo de ejército.

corpse [kɔrps] *s.* cadáver.

cor·pu·lent [kórpjələnt] *adj.* corpulento.

cor·pus·cle [kɔ́rpəsļ] *s.* corpúsculo; glóbulo.
cor·ral [kəráel] *s.* corral; *v.* acorralar.
cor·rect [kərékt] *v.* corregir; *adj.* correcto; **it is —** está bien; **-ly** *adv.* correctamente; **-ly done** bien hecho.
cor·rec·tion [kərékʃən] *s.* corrección.
cor·rect·ness [kəréktnıs] *s.* corrección.
cor·rec·tor [kəréktɚ] *s.* corregidor, corrector.
cor·re·late [kɔ́rəlet] *v.* correlacionar.
cor·re·spond [kɔrəspánd] *v.* corresponder; corresponderse, cartearse, escribirse.
cor·re·spon·dence [kɔrəspándəns] *s.* correspondencia.
cor·re·spon·dent [kɔrəspándənt] *adj.* correspondiente; *s.* correspondiente; corresponsal.
cor·re·spond·ing [kɔrəspándıŋ] *adj.* correspondiente; conforme.
cor·ri·dor [kɔ́rədɚ] *s.* corredor, pasillo, pasadizo.
cor·rob·o·rate [kərábəret] *v.* corroborar.
cor·rode [kəród] *v.* corroer(se).
cor·ru·gat·ed i·ron [kɔ́rəgetəd aiɚn] *s.* hierro acanalado.
cor·rupt [kərápt] *adj.* corrompido; perverso, depravado; **to become —** corromperse; *v.* corromper; pervertir; sobornar.
cor·rup·tion [kərápʃən] *s.* corrupción; soborno; descomposición.
cor·set [kɔ́rsıt] *s.* corsé.
cor·ti·sone [kɔ́rtəzon] *s.* cortisono.
cos·met·ic [kazmétık] *adj.* & *s.* cosmético.
cos·mic [kázmık] *adj.* cósmico.
cos·mo·naut [kázmənɔt] *s.* cosmonauta.
cos·mo·pol·i·tan [kazməpálətņ] *adj.* cosmopolita.
cost [kɔst] *s.* coste, costa o costo; **at all -s** a toda costa; **to sell at —** vender al costo; *v.* costar; *pret.* & *p.p. de* **to cost.**
cost·ly [kɔ́stlı] *adj.* costoso.
cos·tume [kástjum] *s.* vestuario, traje, vestido; atavío; indumentaria.
cot [kat] *s.* catre; **folding —** catre de tijera.
cot·tage [kátıdʒ] *s.* casita, caseta; casa de campo; **— cheese** requesón.
cot·ter pin [kátɚ pın] *s.* chaveta.
cot·ton [katņ] *s.* algodón; **—seed** semilla de algodón; **— wool** algodón en rama; **— yarn** hilaza.
couch [kautʃ] *s.* canapé, diván; *v.* expresar; estar escondido o en acecho; **-ed in difficult language** expresado en lenguaje difícil.
cough [kɔf] *s.* tos; **— drop** pastilla para la tos; **whooping —** tos ferina; *v.* toser; **to — up** expectorar.
could [kud] *pret. del. v. defect.* **can.**
coun·cil [káunsļ] *s.* concilio; consejo; **city —** consejo muncipal.
coun·cil·man [káunsļmən] *s.* concejal.
coun·cil·or [káunsļɚ] *s.* concejal.
coun·sel [káunsļ] *s.* (*advice*) consejo; parecer; dictamen; (*lawyer*) abogado consultor; *v.* aconsejar; recomendar.
coun·sel·or [káunsļɚ] *s.* consejero; abogado consultor.
count [kaunt] *s.* (*reckoning*) cuenta, cálculo; cómputo; (*charge*) cargo, acusación; (*noble*) conde; *v.* contar; valer, tener importancia; **to — on** contar con, confiar en.
count·down [káuntdaun] *s.* recuento descendiente hasta cero.
coun·te·nance [káuntənəns] *s.* semblante, aspecto; **to give — to** favorecer, apoyar; aprobar; *v.*

aprobar; favorecer, apoyar; tolerar.
count·er [káuntɚ] *s.* contador; mostrador; tablero; ficha; *adj.* contrario, opuesto; *adv.* al contrario; **to run —** to ser contrario a, oponerse a; *v.* oponerse; contradecir; **to — a blow** devolver un golpe.
coun·ter·act [kauntɚǽkt] *v.* contrarrestar, neutralizar.
coun·ter·bal·ance [kauntɚbǽləns] *v.* contrapesar; equilibrar; [káuntɚbæləns] *s.* contrapeso.
coun·ter·feit [káuntɚfıt] *s.* falsificación; *adj.* falso; falsificado, falseado; contrahecho; **— money** moneda falsa; *v.* contrahacer, falsificar, falsear.
coun·ter·mand [káuntɚmænd] *s.* contraorden; contramando, revocación, cancelación; [káuntɚmænd] *v.* contramandar, revocar, cancelar.
coun·ter·part [káuntɚpart] *s.* contraparte.
coun·ter·poise [káuntɚpɔız] *s.* contrapeso; *v.* contrapesar.
coun·ter·rev·o·lu·tion [kauntɚrɛvəlúʃən] *s.* contrarrevolución.
coun·ter·sign [káuntɚsaın] *s.* contraseña.
count·ess [káuntıs] *s.* condesa.
count·less [káuntlıs] *adj.* incontable, innumerable.
coun·try [kántrı] *s.* país; tierra; patria; campo; *adj.* campestre; rural; rústico; campesino.
coun·try·man [kántrımən] *s.* compatriota, paisano; (*rural type*) campesino, *Méx., C.A.* ranchero, *P.R.* jíbaro; *Cuba* guajiro; *Ch.* huaso; *Arg.* gaucho; *Ec., Col.* paisa.
coun·try·side [kántrısaıd] *s.* campiña, campo.
coun·ty [káuntı] *s.* condado (*división de un estado*).
coup d'é·tat [ku detá] *s.* golpe de estado; cuartelazo.
cou·pé [kupé, kup] *s.* cupé.
cou·ple [kápļ] *s.* par; pareja; *v.* parear; unir; acoplar.
cou·plet [káplıt] *s.* copla, versos pareados.
cou·pling [káplıŋ] *s.* unión, conexión; acoplamiento; enganche.
cou·pon [kúpan] *s.* cupón; talón.
cour·age [kɝıdʒ] *s.* coraje, ánimo, valor.
cou·ra·geous [kərédʒəs] *adj.* valeroso, valiente, animoso.
cou·ri·er [kúrıɚ] *s.* mensajero.
course [kors] *s.* (*way*) curso; rumbo, trayecto; (*advance*) marcha, progreso; (*mode*) método; (*study*) asignatura; (*dish*) plato (*de una comida*); **— of conduct** conducta, proceder; **golf —** campo o cancha de golf; **race —** hipódromo, pista; **in the — of a year** en el transcurso de un año; **of —** claro, por supuesto; **to follow a straight —** seguir una línea recta.
court [kort] *s.* patio; plazuela, plazoleta; juzgado, tribunal de justicia; corte; **tennis —** cancha para tenis; **— plaster** tela adhesiva, tafetán inglés, esparadrapo; **to pay —** to hacer la corte a, cortejar; galantear; galantear; buscar; **to — danger** exponerse al peligro.
cour·te·ous [kɝtıəs] *adj.* cortés.
cour·te·sy [kɝtəsı] *s.* cortesia; fineza, atención; reverencia.
court·i·er [kɔ́rtıɚ] *s.* cortesano, palaciego.
court·mar·tial [kɔ́rtmarʃəl] *s.* consejo de guerra; *v.* someter a consejo de guerra.
court·ship [kɔ́rtʃıp] *s.* cortejo, galanteo.
court·yard [kɔ́rtjard] *s.* patio.
cous·in [kázņ] *s.* primo; prima; **first —** primo hermano, primo carnal.
cove [kov] *s.* cala, ensenada.

cov·e·nant [kʌvənənt] *s.* convenio, pacto; contrato.

cov·er [kʌvɚ] *s.* (*lid*) cubierta, tapa, tapadera; (*blanket*) cobija; cobertor; (*binding*) encuadernación; envoltura; (*pillow*) funda; (*shelter*) albergue, abrido; **table** — tapete; — **charge** precio fijo que se agrega a la cuenta por servicios; **to send under separate** — enviar por separado; *v.* cubrir; tapar; encubrir; abrigar, proteger; abarcar; **to** — **a distance** recorrer una distancia.

cov·er·age [kʌvərɪdʒ] *s.* alcance; (*journalism*) reportaje.

cov·er·ing [kʌvrɪŋ] *s.* cubierta; cobertura; envoltura; cobija, abrigo.

cov·et [kʌvɪt] *v.* codiciar; ambicionar.

cov·et·ous [kʌvɪtəs] *adj.* codicioso.

cow [kaʊ] *s.* vaca; hembra (*de elefante y otros cuadrúpedos*); *v.* atemorizar, acobardar.

cow·ard [káʊəd] *adj.* & *s.* cobarde.

cow·ard·ice [káʊədɪs] *s.* cobardía.

cow·ard·li·ness [káʊədlɪnɪs] *s.* cobardía.

cow·ard·ly [káʊədlɪ] *adj.* cobarde; *adv.* cobardemente.

cow·boy [káʊbɔɪ] *s.* vaquero, *Riopl.* resero, gaucho; *Ven., Col.* llanero.

cow·er [káʊɚ] *v.* agacharse (*de miedo o vergüenza*), achicarse, encogerse (*de miedo*), acobardarse.

cow·hide [káʊhaɪd] *s.* cuero de vaca, vaqueta.

cowl [kaʊl] *s.* capucha.

cox·swain [kɑksən] *s.* timonel.

coy [kɔɪ] *adj.* recatado, esquivo, modesto; tímido; gazmoño.

coy·o·te [káɪot, kaɪótɪ] *s.* coyote.

co·zy [kózɪ] *adj.* cómodo y abrigado; cómodo y agradable.

crab [kræb] *s.* cangrejo; cascarrabias (*persona de mal genio*); — **apple** manzana silvestre.

crack [kræk] *s.* (*space*) raja, grieta, rendija; (*sound*) crujido; estallido; trueno, estampido; (*blow*) golpe; (*joke*) pulla, chanza; **at the** — **of dawn** al romper el alba; *adj.* excelente; *v.* rajar(se), hender(se), agrietarse; crujir; estallar; **to** — **a joke** soltar un chiste; **to** — **nuts** cascar nueces.

crack·down [krækdaʊn] *s.* represión severa.

cracked [krækt] *adj.* agrietado, rajado; quebrado; chiflado, loco.

crack·er [krækɚ] *s.* galleta.

crack·le [krækl̩] *s.* crujido; crepitación; chasquido; *v.* crujir, crepitar.

crack·pot [krækpat] *s.* eccéntrico.

cra·dle [krédl̩] *s.* cuna.

craft [kræft] *s.* (*skill*) maña, destreza; astucia, artificio, cautela; (*occupation*) arte, oficio; (*boat*) embarcación; embarcaciones.

crafts·man [kræftsmən] *s.* artesano, artífice.

craft·y [kræftɪ] *adj.* mañoso, astuto, cauteloso, taimado.

crag [kræg] *s.* risco, peñasco.

cram [kræm] *v.* rellenar; atestar; atracar(se), hartar(se); engullir.

cramp [kræmp] *s.* calambre; grapa; *v.* comprimir, apretar, estrechar; afianzar, sujetar (*con grapa*).

cran·ber·ry [krǽnbɛrɪ] *s.* arándano.

crane [kren] *s.* grulla (*ave*); grúa (*máquina para levantar pesos*); *v.* **to** — **one's neck** estirar el cuello.

cra·ni·um [krénɪəm] *s.* cráneo.

crank [kræŋk] *s.* cigüeña, manubrio, manija, manivela; **he is a** — es un maniático; *v.* voltear el manubrio o la cigüeña.

crank·case [krǽŋkes] *s.* cárter del motor.

crank·shaft [krǽŋkʃæft] *s.* cigüeñal.

crank·y [krǽŋkɪ] *adj.* cascarrabias; maniático; enojadizo.

cran·ny [krǽnɪ] *s.* grieta, rendija.

crape [krep] *s.* crespón;·crespón negro.

crash [kræʃ] *s.* (*noise*) estallido, golpazo. estruendo; (*collision*) choque; (*failure*) fracaso; quiebra; bancarrota; — **landing** aterrizaje violento; aterrizaje de barriga; *v.* estrellar(se); estallar; chocar; **to** — **an airplane** aterrizar de golpe un aeroplano; **to** — **into** chocar con, estrellarse contra.

crate [kret] *s.* canasto, cesta, jaula (*para el transporte de mercancías, etc.*); *Am.* huacal; *v.* embalar en jaula.

cra·ter [krétɚ] *s.* cráter.

cra·vat [krəvǽt] *s.* corbata.

crave [krev] *v.* ansiar, anhelar, apetecer; **to** — **mercy** (**pardon**) pedir misericordia (perdón).

crawl [krɔl] *s.* marcha lenta; natación a la marinera; *v.* arrastrarse; gatear, andar a gatas; marchar lentamente; **to be -ing with ants** hormiguear, estar lleno de hormigas.

cray·on [kréən] *s.* lápiz de color, *Am.* creyón; pastel; tiza, yeso.

craze [krez] *s.* manía, locura; moda; antojo; *v.* enloquecer.

cra·zy [krézɪ] *adj.* loco; trastornado; **to go** — volverse loco, perder el juicio.

creak [krik] *s.* crujido, rechino, rechinamiento; *v.* crujir, rechinar.

cream [krim] *s.* crema; nata; — **of tomato soup** puré de tomate; **cold** — crema cosmética; **ice** — helado; *v.* desnatar; batir, mezclar (*azúcar y mantequilla*); preparar (*legumbres*) con salsa de crema.

cream·er·y [krímərɪ] *s.* lechería, quesería, *Am.* mantequillería.

cream·y [krímɪ] *adj.* natoso; lleno de crema o nata.

crease [kris] *s.* pliegue; arruga; *v.* plegar, hacer pliegues; arrugar.

cre·ate [kriét] *v.* crear.

cre·a·tion [kriéʃən] *s.* creación; obra.

cre·a·tive [kriétɪv] *adj.* creativo, creador.

cre·a·tor [kriétɚ] *s.* creador.

crea·ture [krítʃɚ] *s.* criatura; ser viviente; animalejo.

cre·dence [krídn̩s] *s.* creencia, crédito.

cre·den·tials [krɪdénʃəlz] *s. pl.* credenciales.

cred·i·ble [krédəbl̩] *adj.* creíble.

cred·it [krédɪt] *s.* crédito; buena fama; — **and debit** haber y deber; activo y pasivo; — **card** tarjeta de crédito; — a crédito, al fiado, a plazo; **to give** — dar crédito, creer; acreditar, abonar; **that does him** — eso le acredita; *v.* acreditar; abonar en cuenta; creer, dar crédito; atribuir.

cred·it·a·ble [krédɪtəbl̩] *adj.* loable.

cred·i·tor [krédɪtɚ] *s.* acreedor.

cred·u·lous [krédʒələs] *adj.* crédulo.

creed [krid] *s.* credo; creencia.

creek [krik, krɪk] *s.* riachuelo, arroyo.

creep [krip] *v.* arrastrarse; gatear, andar a gatas; trepar (*las plantas*); andar lentamente; deslizarse; sentir hormigueo (*en le cuerpo*); *s. pl.* hormigueo; aprensión, horror.

creep·er [krípɚ] *s.* enredadera, planta trepadora.

cre·mate [krímet] *v.* incinerar.

Cre·ole [kríol] *s.* criollo; descendiente de los franceses de Luisiana; persona de sangre mestiza.

CO

cre·o·sote [kriəsot] s. creosota.
crepe [krep] = **crape**.
crept [krɛpt] pret. & p.p. de to creep.
cres·cent [krɛsn̩t] adj. creciente; s. luna creciente; media luna (emblema de turcos y mahometanos).
crest [krɛst] s. cresta; penacho; copete; cima, cumbre; timbre (de un escudo de armas).
crest·fall·en [krɛstfɔlən] adj. cabizbajo, alicaído, abatido.
cre·tonne [krɪtán] s. cretona.
crev·ice [krɛvɪs] s. grieta, hendedura.
crew [kru] s. tripulación; cuadrilla (de obreros); pret. de to crow.
crib [krɪb] s. camita de niño; pesebre; granero, arcón; armazón (usado en la construcción de edificios); traducción o clave fraudulenta (en un examen); v. enjaular; usar traducción o clave fraudulenta (en un examen).
crick·et [krɪkɪt] s. grillo; vilorta (juego).
crime [kraɪm] s. crimen.
crim·i·nal [krímən̩l] adj. & s. criminal.
crimp [krɪmp] v. rizar; s. rizo.
crim·son [krímzn̩] adj. & s. carmesí.
cringe [krɪndʒ] v. encogerse; arrastrarse.
crip·ple [krípl̩] s. cojo, manco; tullido, baldado, inválido; v. estropear; mutilar, derrengar; baldar; incapacitar.
cri·sis [kráɪsɪs] s. crisis.
crisp [krɪsp] adj. (brittle) quebradizo; tieso; bien tostado; (curly) crespo, encrespado; — answer contestación aguda; — wind brisa refrescante; v. encrespar.
cri·te·ri·on [kraɪtíriən] s. criterio.
crit·ic [krítɪk] s. crítico; criticón.
crit·i·cal [krítɪkl̩] adj. crítico; criticador, criticón.
crit·i·cism [krítəsɪzəm] s. crítica; criticismo.
crit·i·cize [krítəsaɪz] v. criticar; censurar.
croak [krok] v. croar; graznar; s. canto de ranas; graznido.
cro·chet [kroʃé] s. labor de gancho; — hook aguja de gancho; v. hacer labor de gancho.
crock [krɑk] s. vasija de loza, jarra.
crock·er·y [krákərɪ] s. loza.
croc·o·dile [krákədaɪl] s. cocodrilo, Am. caimán.
cro·ny [krónɪ] s. compadre, compinche, camarada, compañero.
crook [krʊk] s. (thief) falsario; estafador, maleante, pícaro; (curve) curva, vuelta; recodo; gancho; **shepherd's** — cayado; v. torcer(se); **to** — **one's arm** doblar el brazo o codo.
crook·ed [krʊkɪd] adj. torcido; curvo, encorvado, Am. chueco; Riopl. chingado; falso, fraudulento.
croon [krun] v. cantar «tristes» (con exagerado patetismo y exagerando los sonidos nasales).
crop [krɑp] s. cosecha; buche (de ave); látigo, Am. cuarta; — **of hair** cabellera; v. segar; recortar; rapar; to — **out** aparecer, asomar; to — **up** brotar, manifestarse inesperadamente.
cross [krɔs] s. cruz; cruce; cruzamiento (de razas); mezcla; v. cruzar(se); atravesar(se); santiguar(se); encontrarse; contrariar; adj. en cruz, cruzado, transversal; malhumorado; **cross-country** a campo traviesa; **cross-examine** v. interrogar, repreguntar; **cross-eyed** bizco; —**word puzzle** crucigrama; — **walk** cruce para transeúntes.
cross·bar [krɔsbar] s. travesaño.
cross·ing [krɔsɪŋ] s. cruce; cruzamiento; encrucijada, crucero; travesía; **railroad** — cruce; **river** — vado.
cross·road [krɔsrod] s. vía transversal, encrucijada,

crucero.
cross sec·tion [krɛs sékʃən] s. corte transversal; sección transversal.
crouch [krautʃ] v. agacharse, agazaparse.
crow [kro] s. cuervo; canto del gallo; **crow's-foot** pata de gallo (arrugas en el rabo del ojo); v. cantar (el gallo); cacarear; jactarse, hacer alarde.
crow·bar [króbar] s. barra, palanca de hierro.
crowd [kraud] s. muchedumbre; gentío, gente; cuadrilla, pandilla; grupo; v. agolparse, apiñar(se); estrujar, empujar.
crowd·ed [kráudɪd] adj. atestado, lleno, apiñado.
crown [kraun] s. corona; copa (de sombrero); cima; v. coronar.
cru·ci·ble [krúsəbl̩] s. crisol.
cru·ci·fix [krúsəfɪks] s. crucifijo.
cru·ci·fy [krúsəfaɪ] v. crucificar.
crude [krud] adj. basto, tosco, rudo; inculto; — **oil** petróleo crudo; — **sugar** azúcar bruto, azúcar crudo.
cru·el [krúəl] adj. cruel.
cru·el·ty [krúəltɪ] s. crueldad.
cru·et [krúɪt] s. ampolla (pequeña vasija de cristal); vinajera (para servir vino en la misa); **oil** — aceitera; **vinegar** — vinagrera.
cruise [kruz] s. travesía, viaje por mar; excursión; v. navegar.
cruis·er [krúzə] s. crucero (buque).
crumb [krʌm] s. migaja; miga; mendrugo; v. desmenuzar, desmigajar.
crum·ble [krʌmbl̩] v. desmenuzar(se); desmoronarse.
crum·ple [krʌmpl̩] v. arrugar(se); ajar, apabullar.
crunch [krʌntʃ] v. crujir; mascullar.
cru·sade [kruséd] s. cruzada; v. hacer una campaña; hacer una cruzada.
cru·sad·er [krusédə] s. cruzado.
crush [krʌʃ] s. compresión, presión; estrujamiento, apiñamiento de gente; v. estrujar; aplastar; majar; subyugar; **to** — **stone** moler piedra.
crust [krʌst] s. corteza (de pan, queso, etc.); costra; mendrugo; v. encostrarse, cubrir(se) de costra.
crust·y [krʌstɪ] adj. costroso.
crutch [krʌtʃ] s. muleta.
cry [kraɪ] s. grito; lloro, lamento; **a far** — **from** muy distante de, muy lejos de; v. gritar; llorar; clamar; exclamar; vocear; **to** — **for help** pedir socorro.
crys·tal [krístl̩] s. cristal; — **clear** cristalino.
crys·tal·line [krístl̩ɪn] adj. cristalino.
crys·tal·lize [krístl̩aɪz] v. cristalizar(se).
cub [kʌb] s. cachorro (de oso, tigre, lobo, león); — **reporter** reportero novato.
Cu·ban [kjúbən] adj. & s. cubano.
cub·by·hole [kábihol] s. chiribitil.
cube [kjúb] s. cubo; — **root** raíz cúbica.
cu·bic [kjúbɪk] adj. cúbico.
cu·bism [kjúbɪzm̩] s. cubismo.
cuck·old [kákold] s. cornudo.
cuck·oo [kúku] s. cuco, cuclillo; adj. tocado, chiflado, medio loco.
cu·cum·ber [kjúkʌmbə] s. pepino.
cud [kʌd] s. rumia; **to chew the** — rumiar.
cud·dle [kʌdl̩] v. abrazar, tener en brazos; estar abrazados.
cudg·el [kádʒəl] s. garrote; porra; v. aporrear, apalear.
cue [kju] s. señal, indicación; pie (últimas palabras de un parlamento que sirven de señal en el teatro); **billiard** — taco de billar.
cuff [kʌf] s. puño (de camisa o de vestido); doblez

(*del pantalón*); bofetada; *v.* bofetear, dar de
bofetadas.
cull [kʌl] *v.* entresacar; extraer.
cul·mi·nate [kʌlmənet] *v.* culminar.
cul·prit [kʌlprɪt] *s.* reo, delincuente, culpable.
cult [kʌlt] *s.* culto; secta religiosa.
cul·ti·vate [kʌltəvet] *v.* cultivar; labrar, barbechar.
cul·ti·vat·ed [kʌltəvetɪd] *adj.* cultivado; culto.
cul·ti·va·tion [kʌltəvéʃən] *s.* cultivación, cultivo;
cultura.
cul·ti·va·tor [kʌltəvetə˞] *s.* cultivador; máquina
cultivadora.
cul·ture [kʌltʃə˞] *s.* (*societal*) cultura; (*tillage*)
cultivo.
cul·tured [kʌltʃəd] *adj.* culto; cultivado.
cum·ber·some [kʌmbə˞səm] *adj.* engorroso,
embarazoso, incómodo.
cu·mu·la·tive [kjúmjələtɪv] *adj.* acumulativo.
cun·ning [kʌnɪŋ] *adj.* astuto, socarrón, sagaz,
taimado; diestro; cuco, mono, gracioso; *s.*
astucia, maña, sagacidad.
cup [kʌp] *s.* taza, pocillo; copa (*trofeo*).
cup·board [kʌbə˞d] *s.* armario, aparador; alacena.
cur [kɜ] *s.* perro mestizo, *Am.* perro chusco;
villano, vil, cobarde.
cu·rate [kjúrɪt] *s.* cura.
cu·ra·tor [kjúretə˞] *s.* conservador.
curb [kɜb] *s.* reborde, encintado (*de la acera*);
Ríopl. cordón de la acera; freno, restricción;
barbada (*del freno de un caballo*); brocal (*de
pozo*); *v.* refrenar, reprimir.
curd [kɜd] *s.* cuajada; *v.* cuajar(se), coagular(se).
cur·dle [kɜdl] *v.* cuajar(se), coagular(se).
cure [kjʊr] *s.* cura, curación; remedio; *v.* curar(se);
sanar.
cur·few [kɜfju] *s.* queda.
cu·ri·o [kjúrɪo] *s.* curiosidad, objeto raro y curioso.
cu·ri·os·i·ty [kjʊrɪásətɪ] *s.* curiosidad; rareza.
cu·ri·ous [kjúrɪəs] *adj.* curioso; extraño, raro.
curl [kɜl] *s.* rizo, bucle; espiral (*de humo*); *v.*
rizar(se); ensortijar(se); enroscar(se); retorcerse,
alzarse en espirales (*el humo*).
curl·y [kɜlɪ] *adj.* rizo, rizoso, rizado, crespo, *Am.*
chino.
cur·rant [kɜənt] *s.* grosella; — **bush** grosellero.
cur·ren·cy [kɜənsɪ] *s.* moneda corriente;
circulación; **paper** — papel moneda.
cur·rent [kɜənt] *adj.* corriente; común,
prevaleciente, en boga; *s.* corriente.
cur·ric·u·lum [kərikjələm] *s.* programa de estudios.
curse [kɜs] *s.* maldición; calamidad; *v.* maldecir.
cursed [kɜst] *adj.* maldito.
curs·ing [kɜsɪŋ] *adj.* maldiciente.
cur·sive [kɜsɪv] *adj.* cursivo.
curt [kɜt] *adj.* corto; brusco.
cur·tail [kɜtél] *v.* cercenar; acortar; restringir,
reducir.
cur·tain [kɜtn] *s.* cortina; telón (*de teatro*); *v.*
poner cortinas.
cur·va·ture [kɜvətʃə˞] *s.* curvatura.
curve [kɜv] *s.* curva; *v.* encorvar(se); torcer(se);
doblar(se).
curved [kɜvd] *adj.* encorvado; torcido; curvo,
corvo, *Méx.*, *C.A.* chueco.
cush·ion [kúʃən] *s.* cojín; almohadilla; almohadón;
amortiguador (*para amortiguar un sonido o
golpe*); *v.* acojinar; amortiguar (*un choque*).
cus·tard [kʌstəd] *s.* flan, natillas.
cus·to·dy [kʌstədɪ] *s.* custodia, cargo, cuidado; **to
hold in** — custodiar.
cus·tom [kʌstəm] *s.* costumbre, hábito, uso, usanza;

-s derechos de aduana; — **made** hecho a la
medida; — **tailor** maestro sastre; — **built**
construido según pedido.
cus·tom·ar·y [kʌstəmɛrɪ] *adj.* acostumbrado,
habitual, usual, de costumbre.
cus·tom·er [kʌstəmə˞] *s.* parroquiano, cliente,
marchante.
cus·tom·house [kʌstəmhaʊs] *s.* aduana; — **official**
aduanero; — **mark** marchamo.
cut [kʌt] *s.* corte (*m.*); cortadura, *Am.* cortada;
rebanada, tajada; rebaja, reducción (*de precios,
sueldos*); hechura (*de un traje*); ausencia (*de la
clase*); grabado; **short** — atajo, camino corto; *v.*
cortar; tajar; truncar; talar (*árboles*) labrar,
tallar; segar; rebajar, reducir (*precios, sueldos*);
negar el saludo a; alzar (*los naipes*); **to** — **across**
cruzar, atravesar; **to** — **capers** hacer cabriolas,
cabriolar; **to** — **class** faltar a la clase; **to** — **out**
recortar; excluir; **to be** — **out for** estar hecho
para, tener vocación para; *pret. & p.p. de* **to cut.**
cut-and-dried [kʌtænddráɪd] *adj.* ya determinado;
ordinario.
cut·back [kʌtbæk] *s.* reducción.
cute [kjut] *adj.* mono, cuco; astuto.
cu·ti·cle [kjútɪkl] *s.* cutícula.
cut·ler·y [kʌtlərɪ] *s.* cuchillería, cuchillos.
cut·let [kʌtlɪt] *s.* chuleta.
cut·off [kʌtɔf] *s.* límite ya indicado.
cut·ter [kʌtə˞] *s.* cortador; máquina para cortar;
trineo; **wood** — leñador; **coast guard** — barco
guardacostas.
cut·ting [kʌtɪŋ] *adj.* cortante; penetrante;
mordaz, sarcástico.
cy·ber·net·ics [saɪbə˞nétɪks] *s.* cibernética.
cy·cle [sáɪkl] *s.* ciclo.
cy·clone [sáɪklon] *s.* ciclón; huracán.
cy·clo·tron [sáɪklətran] *s.* ciclotrón.
cyl·in·der [sɪlɪndə˞] *s.* cilindro; — **head** émbolo.
cy·lin·dri·cal [sɪlíndrɪkl] *adj.* ciíndrico.
cym·bal [sɪmbl] *s.* címbalo, platillo; **to play the -s**
tocar los platillos.
cyn·ic [sɪnɪk] *s.* cínico.
cyn·i·cal [sɪnɪkl] *adj.* cínico.
cyn·i·cism [sínəsɪzəm] *s.* cinismo.
cy·press [sáɪprəs] *s.* ciprés.
cyst [sɪst] *s.* quiste.

D:d

dab·ble [dæbl] *v.* chapotear;
trabajar superficialmente.
dad [dæd] *s.* papá, tata; **daddy** *s.*
papaíto o papacito, tata, tatita,
Am. taita.
daf·fo·dil [dæfədɪl] *s.* narciso.
dag·ger [dægə˞] *s.* daga; puñal; **to look -s at**
traspasar con la mirada.
dahl·ia [dæljə] *s.* dalia.
dai·ly [délɪ] *adj.* diario; *adv.* diariamente; *s.* diario,
periódico.
dain·ty [déntɪ] *adj.* delicado, fino, primoroso,
exquisito; *s.* golosina, manjar exquisito.
dair·y [dérɪ] *s.* lechería, vaquería; quesería, quesera.
dai·sy [dézɪ] *s.* margarita, maya.
dale [del] *s.* cañada.
dal·ly [dælɪ] *v.* juguetear; holgazanear; entretenerse,
tardar; malgastar el tiempo.
dam [dæm] *s.* presa, represa; *v.* represar, estancar.
dam·age [dæmɪdʒ] *s.* daño; perjuicio; avería; **to
pay for -s** indemnizar, pagar los daños y

perjuicios; *v.* dañar(se); averiar(se).
Dam·a·scene [dǽməsin] *adj. s.* damasquinado.
dame [dem] *s.* dama, señora; **old** — vieja.
damn [dæm] *v.* maldecir; condenar; blasfemar; —
it ¡maldito sea!
dam·na·tion [dæmnéʃən] *s.* condenación, perdición.
damp [dæmp] *adj.* húmedo; mojado; *s.* humedad;
v. humedecer, mojar.
damp·en [dǽmpən] *v.* mojar, humedecer;
desalentar; amortiguar.
damp·ness [dǽmpnɪs] *s.* humedad.
dam·sel [dǽmzl] *s.* damisela.
dance [dæns] *s.* baile; danza; — **music** música de
baile; *v.* bailar; danzar.
danc·er [dǽnsɚ] *s.* bailador; bailarín, bailarina;
danzante.
dan·de·li·on [dǽndlaɪən] *s.* diente de león.
dan·druff [dǽndrəf] *s.* caspa.
dan·dy [dǽndɪ] *s.* currutaco, majo, afectado; chulo;
adj. elegante, excelente.
dan·ger [déndʒɚ] *s.* peligro, riesgo.
dan·ger·ous [déndʒɚəs] *adj.* peligroso;
arriesgado; **-ly** *adv.* peligrosamente; **-ly ill**
gravemente enfermo.
dan·gle [dǽŋgl] *v.* pender, colgar, bambolear(se)
(*en el aire*).
dap·ple(d) [dǽpl(d)] *adj.* rodado, con manchas
(*dícese de los caballos*); **dapple-grey** rucio rodado,
tordo, tordillo.
dare [dɛr] *s.* desafío, reto, provocación; – **devil**
atrevido, osado; *v.* atreverse, osar; desafiar.
dar·ing [dérɪŋ] *s.* atrevimiento, osadía; *adj.* osado,
atrevido, arrojado.
dark [dɑrk] *adj.* obscuro; sombrío; — **horse** caballo
desconocido (*que gana inesperadamente en la
carrera*); candidato nombrado inesperadamente;
— **secret** secreto profundo; enigma;
darkskinned moreno, trigueño; *s.* obscuridad;
sombra.
dark·en [dárkən] *v.* obscurecer(se); nublarse.
dark·ness [dárknɪs] *s.* obscuridad; tinieblas;
sombra.
dark·y [dárkɪ] *s.* negro (*persona*).
dar·ling [dárlɪŋ] *adj. & s.* amado, querido; **my** —
vida mía (*o* mi vida), amor mío.
darn [dɑrn] *s.* zurcido; **it is not worth a** — no vale
un comino, no vale un pito; *v.* zurcir; —!
¡caramba! ¡canastos!; **-ing needle** aguja de zurcir.
dart [dɑrt] *s.* dardo, flecha; sisa (*en un vestido*);
movimiento rápido; *v.* lanzar(se); flechar; **to** —
out salir como una flecha; **to** — **in and out**
entrar y salir precipitadamente.
dash [dæʃ] *s.* (*line*) raya; (*run*) carrera corta; (*vigor*)
ímpetu; (*grace*) garbo; pizca (*de sal, azúcar, etc.*);
rociada (*de agua*); —**board** tablero de
instrumentos; **with a** — **of the pen** de una
plumada; *v.* lanzar(se); echar(se); estrellar(se);
salpicar; frustrar (*esperanzas*); **to** — **by** pasar
corriendo; **to** — **out** salir a la carrera; **to** — **off**
a letter escribir de prisa una carta.
da·ta [détə] *s. pl.* datos.
date [det] *s.* (*time*) fecha; (*statement*) data;
(*appointment*) cita, compromiso; (*fruit*) dátil; **out
of** — anticuado, desusado; fuera de moda; **up to**
— al día, moderno; **up to this** — hasta ahora,
hasta la fecha; *v.* fechar; **to** — **from** datar de;
remontarse a.
daub [dɔb] *v.* embarrar, untar; pintarrajear.
daugh·ter [dótɚ] *s.* hija; **daughter-in-law** nuera.
daunt [dɔnt] *v.* intimidar, asustar, espantar;
desanimar.

daunt·less [dóntlɪs] *adj.* denodado, intrépido.
dav·en·port [dǽvənport] *s.* sofá.
dawn [dɔn] *s.* alba; amanecer, madrugada; *v.*
amanecer; alborear, rayar (*el día*); **it just -ed
upon me** acabo de darme cuenta.
day [de] *s.* día; — **after tomorrow** pasado
mañana; — **before yesterday** anteayer o antier;
— **laborer** jornalero; **by** — de día; **by the** — por
día; **eight-hour** — jornada de ocho horas; **to win
the** — genar la jornada, triunfar; *adj.* diurno.
day·break [débrek] *s.* amanecer, alba; **at** — al
amanecer, al romper el día, al rayar el día.
day·light [délaɪt] *s.* luz del día.
day·time [détaɪm] *s.* día (*tiempo de luz natural*); **in
the** — durante el día; de día.
daze [dez] *s.* aturdimiento; deslumbramiento; **to be
in a** — estar aturdido; *v.* aturdir; ofuscar;
deslumbrar.
daz·zle [dǽzl] *s.* brillantez; *v.* deslumbrar; ofuscar.
dea·con [díkən] *s.* diácono.
dead [dɛd] *adj.* muerto; – **air** aire viciado o
estancado; – **letter** carta no reclamada; — **loss**
pérdida absoluta; *adv.* completamente,
absolutamente; sumamente, muy; — **sure**
completamente seguro; — **tired** muerto de
cansancio; *s.* **the** — los muertos; **in the** — **of the
night** en el sigilo de la noche; **in the** — **of winter**
en lo más crudo del invierno.
dead·en [dɛdn] *v.* amortiguar.
dead·head [dédhɛd] *s.* persona que no paga la
entrada; colado.
dead·ly [dédlɪ] *adj.* mortal; fatal; como la muerte,
cadavérico; *adv.* mortalmente; — **dull** sumamente
aburrido.
deaf [dɛf] *adj.* sordo; **deaf-mute** *s. & adj.*
sordomudo.
deaf·en [défən] *v.* ensordecer; amortiguar, apagar
(*un sonido*).
deaf·en·ing [défənɪŋ] *adj.* ensordecedor,
estruendoso.
deaf·ness [défnɪs] *s.* sordera.
deal [dil] *s.* trato, negocio; mano (*en el juego de
naipes*); distribución, reparto (*de los naipes*); **a
great** — **of** una gran cantidad de, mucho; **to
give a square** — tratar con equidad; *v.* tallar (*en
juegos de naipes*); distribuir, repartir; dar (*un
golpe*); **to** — **in** comerciar en; **to** — **with** tratar
de (*un asunto*); tratar con; negociar con.
deal·er [dílɚ] *s.* negociante, comerciante, tratante;
tallador (*en el juego de naipes*).
deal·ings [dílɪŋz] *s. pl.* relaciones (*comerciales o
amistosas*); comercio, tratos; negocios.
dealt [dɛlt] *pret. & p.p.* de **to deal**.
dean [din] *s.* deán (*dignidad eclesiástica*); decano
(*de universidad*).
dear [dɪr] *adj.* (*beloved*) querido, amado; (*expensive*)
caro; costoso; *adv.* caro; —**me!** ¡Dios mío!; **oh
—!** ¡ay!; **my** — querido mío; **Dear Sir** Muy
señor mío; **-ly** *adv.* cariñosamente; a precio alto;
my -ly beloved muy amado mío; muy amados
míos.
dearth [dɝθ] *s.* escasez, carestía, insuficiencia.
death [dɛθ] *s.* muerte; mortandad; — **rate**
mortalidad.
death·bed [déθbɛd] *s.* lecho de muerte.
de·base [dɪbés] *v.* rebajar el valor de; degradar,
humillar, envilecer.
de·bat·a·ble [dɪbétəbl] *adj.* discutible, disputable.
de·bate [dɪbét] *s.* debate, discusión; *v.* debatir,
discutir; considerar; deliberar.
de·bil·i·tate [dəbílətet] *v.* debilitar.

deb·it [débɪt] s. débito, adeudo, cargo; debe (de una cuenta); pasivo (en contabilidad); v. adeudar, cargar en cuenta.

de·brief·ing [dibrífɪŋ] s. informe de vuelo bajo interrogación; informe.

de·bris [dəbrí] s. escombros; ruinas.

debt [dɛt] s. deuda; adeudo; débito; **bad** — cuenta incobrable; **to run into** — adeudarse, entramparse, cargarse de deudas.

bedt·or [détə·] s. deudor.

de·bunk [dibʌŋk] s. desbaratar; desenmascarar.

de·but [dɪbjú] s. estreno; **to make a** — debutar, estrenarse.

de·cade [déked] s. década, decenio.

de·ca·dence [dɪkédns̩] s. decadencia.

de·cant·er [dɪkǽntə·] s. garrafa; **large** — garrafón.

de·cay [dɪké] s. decaimiento; decadencia, ruina; podredumbre; caries (de la dentadura); v. decaer; venir a menos; pudrir(se) o podrir(se).

de·cease [dɪsís] s. muerte, fallecimiento; v. morir, fallecer.

de·ceased [dɪsíst] adj. & s. muerto, difunto.

de·ceit [dɪsít] s. engaño; fraude; trampa.

de·ceit·ful [dɪsítfəl] adj. engañador; tramposo; engañoso.

de·ceive [dɪsív] v. engañar.

De·cem·ber [dɪsɛmbə·] s. diciembre.

de·cen·cy [dísn̩sɪ] s. decencia.

de·cent [dísn̩t] adj. decente; decoroso.

de·ci·bel [désɪbɛl] s. decibelio; decibel.

de·cide [dɪsáɪd] v. decidir, resolver, determinar; **to** — to resolverse a, decidirse a.

de·cid·ed [dɪsáɪdɪd] adj. decidido, resuelto.

dec·i·mal [désəml̩] adj. decimal; s. decimal, fracción decimal.

dec·i·mate [désɪmet] v. diezmar.

de·ci·pher [dɪsáɪfə·] v. descifrar.

de·ci·sion [dɪsíʒən] s. decisión, resolución.

de·ci·sive [dɪsáɪsɪv] adj. decisivo; terminante.

deck [dɛk] s. cubierta (de un buque); baraja; v. cubrir; ataviar; **to** — oneself out emperifollarse.

dec·la·ra·tion [dɛkləréʃən] s. declaración.

de·clare [dɪklǽr] v. declarar; afirmar.

de·cline [dɪkláɪn] s. declinación; decadencia; mengua; baja (de precios); v. declinar; decaer; rehusar; **to** — to do something negarse a hacer algo.

de·cliv·i·ty [dɪklívətɪ¹] s. declive.

de·col·le·te [dekɑlté] adj. escotado.

de·com·pose [dikəmpóz] v. descomponer(se); corromper(se), pudrir(se).

dec·o·rate [dékəret] v. decorar, adornar; condecorar.

dec·o·ra·tion [dɛkəréʃən] s. decoración; adorno; insignia, condecoración.

dec·o·ra·tive [dékəretɪv] adj. decorativo; ornamental.

de·co·rum [dɪkórəm] s. decoro; circunspección.

de·coy [dɪkɔ́ɪ] s. reclamo, señuelo, figura de ave (que sirve para atraer aves); cebo (artificio para atraer con engaño); trampa, lazo; v. atraer con señuelo o engaño.

de·crease [dikrís] s. disminución o diminución; merma; mengua; [dɪkrís] v. disminuir(se); mermar; menguar.

de·cree [dɪkrí] s. decreto; v. decretar; mandar.

de·crep·it [dɪkrépɪt] adj. decrépito.

ded·i·cate [dédəket] v. dedicar.

ded·i·ca·tion [dɛdəkéʃən] s. dedicación; dedicatoria.

de·duce [dɪdjús] v. deducir, inferir.

de·duct [dɪdʌkt] v. deducir, descontar, rebajar.

de·duc·tion [dɪdʌkʃən] s. deducción; rebaja, descuento.

deed [did] s. hecho, acción, acto; hazaña; escritura (de venta o compra).

deem [dim] v. juzgar, creer, considerar.

deep [dip] adj. (down) hondo; profundo; (obscure) oscuro; (tone) grave, bajo; — **in debt** cargado de deudas; — **in thought** absorto; — **mourning** luto riguroso; **to go off the** — end echarse a pique; caer en el abismo; — **into the night** en las tinieblas de la noche; s. **the** — el mar; **-lv** adv. profundamente, hondamente; intensamente

deep·en [dípən] v. ahondar, profundizar.

deer [dɪr] s. ciervo, venado; —**skin** piel o cuero ci venado.

de·face [dɪfés] v. desfigurar, estropear, mutilar.

de·fame [dɪfém] v. difamar, calumniar, denigrar.

de·fault [dɪfɔ́lt] s. falla, falta, negligencia (de un deber, pago, obligación); deficiencia; v. fallar, faltar (en el cumplimiento de un deber, pago, obligación); no comparecer a la cita de un tribunal.

de·feat [dɪfít] s. derrota, vencimiento; frustración (de un plan); v. vencer, derrotar; frustrar.

de·fect [dɪfékt] s. defecto.

de·fec·tive [dɪféktɪv] adj. defectuoso; incompleto; subnormal, falto de inteligencia; — **verb** verbo defectivo.

de·fend [dɪfénd] v. defender.

de·fen·dant [dɪféndənt] s. acusado, demandado, procesado.

de·fend·er [dɪféndə·] s. defensor; abogado defensor.

de·fense [dɪféns] s. defensa.

de·fense·less [dɪfénslɪs] adj. indefenso, inerme.

de·fen·sive [dɪfénsɪv] adj. defensivo; s. defensiva.

de·fer [dɪfɚ́] v. diferir, posponer, aplazar; **to** — to another's opinion remitirse o ceder al dictamen de otro.

de·fi·ance [dɪfáɪəns] s. reto, desafío, provocación; oposición; **in** — of en abierta oposición con, a despecho de.

de·fi·cien·cy [dɪfíʃənsɪ] s. deficiencia; defecto; déficit.

de·fi·cient [dɪfíʃənt] adj. deficiente; defectuoso.

def·i·cit [défəsɪt] s. déficit.

de·file [dɪfáɪl] v. viciar, corromper; profanar; manchar, ensuciar.

de·fine [dɪfáɪn] v. definir.

def·i·nite [défənɪt] adj. definido; claro, preciso; fijo; —**article** artículo determinado o definido; **ly** adv. definidamente; claramente; **-ly not** terminantemente no.

def·i·ni·tion [dɛfəníʃən] s. definición.

de·fin·i·tive [dɪfínətɪv] adj. definitivo.

de·flate [dɪflét] v. desinflar.

de·flect [dɪflékt] v. desviar(se).

de·form [dɪfɔ́rm] v. deformar; desfigurar, afear.

de·formed [dɪfɔ́rmd] adj. deforme, disforme; deformado; desfigurado.

de·form·i·ty [dɪfɔ́rmətɪ] s. deformidad; deformación.

de·fraud [dɪfrɔ́d] v. defraudar.

de·fray [dɪfré] v. sufragar, costear, pagar (gastos).

deft [dɛft] adj. diestro, ágil.

de·funct [dɪfʌŋkt] adj. difunto.

de·fy [dɪfáɪ] v. desafiar; retar; oponerse a, resistirse a.

de·gen·er·ate [dɪdʒénərɪt] adj. & s. degenerado; [dɪdʒénəret] v. degenerar.

deg·ra·da·tion [dɛgrədéʃən] s. degradación; envilecimiento.

de·grade [dɪgréd] *v.* degradar; envilecer, rebajar.

de·gree [dɪgrí] *s.* grado; rango; **by -s** gradualmente; **to get a—**graduarse.

de·hu·man·ize [dihjúmənaɪz] *v.* deshumanizar.

de·hy·drate [dɪháɪdret] *v.* deshidratar(se).

deign [den] *v.* dignarse, condescender.

de·i·ty [díətɪ] *s.* deidad.

de·ject·ed [dɪdʒéktɪd] *adj.* abatido.

de·jec·tion [dɪdʒékʃən] *s.* abatimiento, melancolía, depresión.

de·lay [dɪlé] *s.* demora, tardanza, dilación, retraso; *v.* demorar; retardar, dilatar; diferir; tardarse.

de·layed ac·tion [dɪléd ǽkʃən] *adj.* atrasado; retardado.

del·e·gate [déləget] *s.* delegado, representante; *v.* delegar, diputar.

del·e·ga·tion [déləgéʃən] *s.* delegación diputación.

de·le·tion [dɪlíʃən] *s.* suspensión.

de·lib·er·ate [dɪlíbərɪt] *adj.* deliberado. premeditado; cauto, prudente; lento; **-ly** *adv.* deliberadamente; con premeditación; [dɪlíbəret] *v.* deliberar.

de·lib·er·a·tion [dɪlɪbəréʃən] *s.* deliberación.

del·i·ca·cy [déləkəsɪ] *s.* delicadeza; sensibilidad; finura; golosina.

del·i·cate [déləkət] *adj.* delicado; frágil; exquisito.

del·i·ca·tes·sen [dɛləkətésṇ] *s.* tienda de fiambres. queso, ensaladas, ultramarinos, etc.

de·li·cious [dɪlíʃəs] *adj.* delicioso.

de·light [dɪláɪt] *s.* deleite; delicia; *v.* deleitar(se); encantar; agradar; **to — in** gozarse en, deleitarse en.

de·light·ed [dɪláɪtɪd] *adj.* encantado; **to be — to** alegrarse de, tener mucho gusto en (*o* de).

de·light·ful [dɪláɪtfəl] *adj.* deleitoso; delicioso; ameno, agradable.

de·lin·e·ate [dɪlínɪet] *v.* delinear, trazar.

de·lin·quent [dɪlíŋkwənt] *adj. & s.* delincuente.

de·lir·i·ous [dɪlírɪəs] *adj.* delirante; **to be —** delirar, desvariar.

de·lir·i·um [dɪlírɪəm] *s.* delirio, desvarío.

de·liv·er [dɪlívɚ] *v.* entregar; librar, libertar; pronunciar (*un discurso*); dar (*un golpe*).

de·liv·er·ance [dɪlívərəns] *s.* liberación, rescate.

de·liv·er·er [dɪlívərɚ] *s.* libertador; portador, mansajero.

de·liv·er·y [dɪlívərɪ] *s.* (*giving*) entrega; (*saving*) liberación; (*birth*) parto; (*speaking*) elocuencia; manera de hacer una conferencia; **— service** servicio de entrega; **— truck** camión (*o* camioneta) de reparto; **mail —** reparto de carreo.

dell [dɛl] *s.* cañada, hondonada.

del·ta wing [délta wɪŋ] *s.* ala en delta.

de·lude [dɪlúd] *v.* engañar.

del·uge [déljudʒ] *s.* diluvio; *v.* inundar; abrumar.

de·lu·sion [dɪlúʒən] *s.* ilusión; engaño, error.

de·mand [dɪmǽnd] *s.* demanda; exigencia; solicitud; **on — a** solicitud; *v.* demandar, reclamar; exigir.

de·mand·ing [dɪmǽndɪŋ] *adj.* exigente.

de·mean·or [dɪmínɚ] *s.* conducta, comportamiento, proceder.

de·ment·ed [dɪméntɪd] *adj.* demente.

dem·i·john [démɪdʒan] *s.* damajuana.

de·mise [dɪmáɪz] *s.* fallecimiento.

de·mo·bil·ize [dimóbḷaɪz] *v.* demovilizar.

de·moc·ra·cy [dəmákrəsɪ] *s.* democarcia.

dem·o·crat [déməkræt] *s.* demócrata.

dem·o·crat·ic [dɛməkrǽtɪk] *adj.* democrático.

de·mol·ish [dɪmálɪʃ] *v.* demoler.

de·mon [dímən] *s.* demonio.

dem·on·strate [démənstret] *v.* demostrar.

dem·on·stra·tion [dɛmənstréʃən] *s.* demostración; prueba; (*protest*) manifestación.

de·mon·stra·tive [dɪmánstrətɪv] *adj.* demostrativo; efusivo.

den [dɛn] *s.* guarida; escondrijo; cueva, lugar de retiro.

de·ni·al [dɪnáɪəl] *s.* negación; negativa; **self-denial** abnegación.

den·i·grate [dénɪgret] *v.* calumniar; ennegrecer.

de·nom·i·na·tion [dɪnamənéʃən] *s.* (*name*) denominación; nombre; título, designación; (*sect*) secta religiosa.

de·note [dɪnót] *v.* denotar.

de·nounce [dɪnáʊns] *v.* denunciar; delatar, acusar.

dense [dɛns] *adj.* denso; espeso, apretado; estúpido.

den·si·ty [dénsətɪ] *s.* densidad; estupidez.

dent [dɛnt] *s.* abolladura; mella; *v.* abollar; mellar.

den·tal [déntḷ] *adj.* dental; *s.* dental, consonante dental.

den·ti·frice [déntɪfrɪs] *s.* pasta dentífrica; dentífrico.

den·tist [déntɪst] *s.* dentista.

de·nun·ci·a·tion [dɪnʌnsiéʃən] *s.* denuncia, acusación.

de·ny [dɪnáɪ] *v.* negar; rehusar; **to — oneself** sacrificarse, abnegarse; **to — oneself to callers** negarse a recibir visitas.

de·o·dor·ant [diódərənt] *s.* desodorante.

de·ox·i·dize [diáksədaɪz] *v.* desoxidar.

de·part [dɪpárt] *v.* partir, salir, irse; desviarse, apartarse.

de·part·ed [dɪpártɪd] *adj.* ido; ausente; difunto.

de·part·ment [dɪpártmənt] *s.* departamento; distrito; ramo, división; **— store** almacén.

de·par·ture [dɪpártʃɚ] *s.* salida, partida; desviación.

de·pend [dɪpénd] *v.* depender; **to — on** depender de; contar con, confiar en.

de·pend·a·ble [dɪpéndəbḷ] *adj.* seguro, fidedigno, digno de confianza.

de·pen·dence [dɪpéndəns] *s.* dependencia; confianza.

de·pen·den·cy [dɪpéndənsɪ] *s.* dependencia; sucursal.

de·pen·dent [dɪpéndənt] *adj.* dependiente; subordinado; *s.* dependiente, familiar.

de·pict [dɪpíkt] *v.* pintar, describir; representar.

dep·i·late [dépəlet] *v.* depilar.

de·pil·a·to·ry [dɪpílətorɪ] *s.* depilatorio.

de·plete [dɪplít] *v.* agotar; vaciar.

de·plor·a·ble [dɪplórəbḷ] *adj.* deplorable, lamentable.

de·plore [dɪplór] *v.* deplorar.

de·port [dɪpórt] *v.* deportar; **to — oneself well** portarse bien.

de·port·ment [dɪpórtmənt] *s.* comportamiento, conducta.

de·pose [dɪpóz] *v.* deponer; declarar, atestiguar.

de·pos·it [dɪpázɪt] *s.* depósito; *v.* depositar.

dep·o·si·tion [dɛpəzíʃən] *s.* deposición, declaración.

de·pos·i·tor [dɪpázɪtɚ] *s.* depositador.

de·pot [dípo] *s.* depósito; almacén; estación de ferrocarril.

dep·re·cate [déprɪket] *v.* desaprobar.

de·pre·ci·ate [dɪpríʃiet] *v.* depreciar; bajar de precio; abaratar(se); menospreciar.

de·press [dɪprés] *v.* deprimir; abatir; desanimar; depreciar, rebajar el valor de.

de·pressed [dɪprést] *adj.* abatido, decaído.
de·press·ing [dɪprésɪŋ] *adj.* deprimente.
de·pres·sion [dɪpréʃən] *s.* depresión; decaimiento, abatimiento; rebaja (*de precios*).
de·prive [dɪpráɪv] *v.* privar.
depth [dɛpθ] *s.* profundidad; hondura; fondo; longitud (*de un solar*); gravedad (*de los sonidos*); viveza (*de los colores*); **in the — of the night** en las tinieblas de la noche; **in the — of winter** en lo más crudo del invierno.
dep·u·ta·tion [dɛpjətéʃən] *s.* diputación, delagación; comisión.
de·pute [dɪpjút] *v.* diputar, delegar.
dep·u·ty [dépjətɪ] *s.* diputado; agente; delegado.
de·range [dɪréndʒ] *v.* trastornar, desordenar.
der·by [dɜ́bɪ] *s.* sombrero hongo, *Méx., Ven., Col.* sombrero de bola.
der·e·lict [dérɪlɪkt] *adj.* abandonado; negligente.
de·ride [dɪráɪd] *v.* escarnecer, ridiculizar, mofarse de, burlarse de.
de·ri·sion [dɪríʒən] *s.* mofa, escarnio.
de·rive [dəráɪv] *v.* derivar(se); provenir; sacar (*provecho*); recibir (*placer*).
der·ma·tol·o·gy [dɚmətáledʒɪ] *s.* dermatología.
der·rick [dérɪk] *s.* grúa; armazón (*para la explotación del petróleo*).
de·scend [dɪsénd] *v.* descender; bajar; **to — upon** caer sobre, acometer.
de·scen·dant [dɪséndənt] *adj. & s.* descendiente.
de·scent [dɪsént] *s.* descenso; bajada; descendencia, linaje; descendimiento; declive.
de·scribe [dɪskráɪb] *v.* describir; trazar.
de·scrip·tion [dɪskrípʃən] *s.* descripción; **of all -s** de todas clases.
de·scrip·tive [dɪskríptɪv] *adj.* descriptivo; **— linguistics** lingüística descriptiva.
des·ert [dézɚt] *adj.* desierto, despoblado; estéril; *s.* desierto, yermo; páramo; [dɪzɜ́t] *v.* abandonar, desamparar; desertar.
de·sert·er [dɪzɜ́tɚ] *s.* desertor.
de·ser·tion [dɪzɜ́ʃən] *s.* deserción, abandono, desamparo.
de·serve [dɪzɜ́v] *v.* merecer.
de·serv·ing [dɪzɜ́vɪŋ] *adj.* meritorio; merecedor.
de·sign [dɪzáɪn] *s.* (*sketch*) dibujo, diseño; (*plan*) designio, propósito, intención; plan, proyecto; *v.* diseñar, trazar; proyectar; idear.
des·ig·nate [dézɪgnet] *v.* designar; señalar, indicar, nombrar.
de·sign·er [dɪzáɪnɚ] *s.* diseñador; dibujante; proyectista; intrigante.
de·sir·a·bil·i·ty [dɪzaɪrəbílətɪ] *s.* conveniencia, utilidad.
de·sir·a·ble [dɪzáɪrəbl] *adj.* deseable; agradable; conveniente.
de·sire [dɪzáɪr] *s.* deseo; anhelo, ansia; *v.* desear; anhelar, ansiar.
de·sir·ous [dɪzáɪrəs] *adj.* deseoso.
de·sist [dɪzíst] *v.* desistir.
desk [dɛsk] *s.* escritorio, bufete, pupitre, mesa de escribir.
des·o·late [déslɪt] *adj.* desolado; despoblado, desierto; solitario; [déslet] *v.* desolar; asolar, arrasar; despoblar.
des·o·la·tion [dɛsléʃən] *s.* desolación; soledad.
de·spair [dɪspér] *s.* desesperación; desesperanza; *v.* desesperarse, perder la esperanza.
de·spair·ing [dɪspérɪŋ] *adj.* desesperado, sin esperanza.
des·patch [dɪspǽtʃ] = **dispatch**.
des·per·ate [désprɪt] *adj.* desesperado; arriesgado,

temerario; **— illness** enfermedad gravísima; **-ly** *adv.* desesperadamente; **-ly ill** gravísimamente enfermo.
des·per·a·tion [dɛspəréʃən] *s.* desesperación; temeridad.
des·pi·ca·ble [déspɪkəbl] *adj.* despreciable; desdeñable.
de·spise [dɪspáɪz] *v.* despreciar; desdeñar; menospreciar.
de·spite [dɪspáɪt] *s.* despecho; *prep.* a despecho de, a pesar de.
de·spoil [dɪspóɪl] *v.* despojar.
de·spon·den·cy [dɪspándənsɪ] *s.* abatimiento desaliento, descaecimiento o decaimiento del ánimo.
de·spon·dent [dɪspándənt] *adj.* abatido, descaecido o decaído de ánimo, desalentado, desesperanzado.
des·pot [déspət] *s.* déspota.
des·pot·ic [dɪspátɪk] *adj.* despótico.
des·pot·ism [déspətɪzəm] *s.* despotismo.
des·sert [dɪzɜ́t] *s.* postre.
des·ti·na·tion [dɛstənéʃən] *s.* destinación, destino; paradero.
des·tine [déstɪn] *v.* destinar; **-ed for** con rumbo a, con destinación a; destinado a.
des·ti·ny [déstənɪ] *s.* destino, sino, hado.
des·ti·tute [déstətjut] *adj.* destituido, necesitado; falto, desprovisto.
de·stroy [dɪstróɪ] *v.* destruir.
de·stroy·er [dɪstróɪɚ] *s.* destruidor; destructor, cazatorpedero, destroyer.
de·struc·ti·ble [dɪstrʌ́ktəbl] *adj.* destructible.
de·struc·tion [dɪstrʌ́kʃən] *s.* destrucción; ruina.
de·struc·tive [dɪstrʌ́ktɪv] *adj.* destructivo.
de·tach [dɪtǽtʃ] *v.* separar, despegar, desprender; destacar (*una porción de tropa*).
de·tach·ment [dɪtǽtʃmənt] *s.* separación; desprendimiento; desapego, despego, alejamiento; destacamento (*militar*).
de·tail [dítel] *s.* detalle; pormenor; destacamento (*militar*); **to go into —** detallar, pormenorizar; [dɪtél] *v.* detallar; pormenorizar; destacar, asignar.
de·tain [dɪtén] *v.* detener; entretener, demorar, retardar.
de·tect [dɪtékt] *v.* descubrir.
de·tec·tive [dɪtéktɪv] *s.* detective, detectivo, policía secreto.
de·ten·tion [dɪténʃən] *s.* detención.
de·ter·gent [dɪtɜ́dʒənt] *s.* detergente.
de·te·ri·o·rate [dɪtírɪəret] *v.* deteriorar(se).
de·te·ri·o·ra·tion [dɪtɪrɪəréʃən] *s.* deterioro.
de·ter·mi·na·tion [dɪtɜmənéʃən] *s.* determinación; decisión; resolución, firmeza.
de·ter·mine [dɪtɜ́mɪn] *v.* determinar; decidir; **to — to** determinarse a, decidirse a, resolverse a.
de·ter·mined [dɪtɜ́mɪnd] *adj.* determinado, decidido, resuelto.
de·test [dɪtést] *v.* detestar, aborrecer.
de·tour [dítʊr] *s.* rodeo, desvío, desviación, vuelta; *v.* dar o hacer un rodeo.
dev·as·tate [dévəstet] *v.* devastar, arruinar, asolar.
de·vel·op [dɪvéləp] *v.* desarrollar(se); desenvolver(se); revelar (*una película o placa fotográfica*); explotar (*una mina*).
de·vel·op·ment [dɪvéləpmənt] *s.* (*evolution*) desarrollo; desenvolvimiento; evolución; crecimiento; (*generation*) fomento; explotación; (*photo*) revelado.
de·vi·ate [díviet] *v.* desviar(se).

de·vi·a·tion [dɪvɪéʃən] s. desviación; desvío, extravío.

de·vice [dɪváɪs] s. artificio; mecanismo, aparato; ardid, recurso; divisa; **left to one's own -s** abandonado a sus propios recursos.

dev·il [dévl] s. diablo; demonio.

dev·il·ish [dévlɪʃ] adj. diabólico; endiablado; travieso.

dev·il·try [dévltrɪ] s. diablura.

de·vi·ous [dívɪəs] adj. desviado; tortuoso; indirecto.

de·vise [dɪváɪz] v. idear, trazar, urdir.

de·void [dɪvóɪd] adj. exento, libre, falto, privado, desprovisto.

de·vote [dɪvót] v. dedicar; consagrar; **to — oneself to** dedicarse a, consagrarse a, aplicarse a.

de·vot·ed [dɪvótɪd] adj. dedicado, consagrado; apegado; **— friend** amigo fiel o leal.

de·vo·tion [dɪvóʃən] s. devoción; piedad; afecto; lealtad.

de·vour [dɪváʊr] v. devorar.

de·vout [dɪváʊt] adj. devoto, piadoso; sincero.

dew [dju] s. rocío, sereno; v. rociar; caer (el rocío).

dew·drop [djúdrɑp] s. gota de rocío.

dew·y [djúɪ] adj. rociado, húmedo de rocío.

dex·ter·i·ty [dɛkstérətɪ] s. destreza.

dex·ter·ous [dékstrəs] adj. diestro.

dex·trose [dékstros] s. dextrosa.

di·a·dem [dáɪədɛm] s. diadema.

di·ag·nose [daɪəgnós] v. diagnosticar.

di·ag·o·nal [daɪǽgən] adj. diagonal, oblicuo; s. diagonal.

di·a·gram [dáɪəgræm] s. diagrama.

di·al [dáɪəl] s. esfera; muestra (del reloj), Méx., C.Á. carátula; — **telephone** teléfono automático; v. sintonizar o captar (una estación radiotelefónica).

di·a·lect [dáɪəlɛkt] s. dialecto.

di·a·lec·tol·o·gy [daɪəlɛktálədʒɪ] dialectología.

di·a·logue [dáɪəlɔg] s. diálogo; v. dialogar.

di·am·e·ter [daɪǽmətəˑ] s. diámetro.

dia·mond [dáɪmənd] s. diamante; rombo (figura geométrica).

di·a·per [dáɪəpəˑ] s. pañal.

di·ar·rhe·a [daɪəríə] s. diarrea.

di·a·ry [dáɪərɪ] s. diario.

dice [daɪs] s. pl. de **die** dados; v. cuadricular, cortar en cuarterones o cubos.

di·chot·o·my [daɪkátəmɪ] s. dicotomía.

dic·tate [díktet] s. dictado, precepto; v. dictar.

dic·ta·tion [dɪktéʃən] s. dictado; mando absoluto; **to take** — escribir al dictado.

dic·ta·tor [díktetəˑ] s. dictador.

dic·ta·tor·ship [dɪktétəˑʃɪp] s. dictadura.

dic·tion [díkʃən] s. dicción.

dic·tion·ar·y [díkʃənɛrɪ] s. diccionario.

did [dɪd] pret. de **to do**.

die [daɪ] s. (pl. **dice**) dado (para jugar); (pl. **dies**) matriz, molde; cuño (sello para acuñar moneda).

die [daɪ] v. morir(se); marchitarse; secarse (las flores, plantas, etc.); **to — out** morirse, extinguirse, apagarse.

di·er·e·sis [daɪérəsɪs] s. diéresis.

di·et [dáɪət] s. dieta; régimen; **to be on a —** estar a dieta; **to put on a —** adietar, poner a dieta; v. ponerse a dieta; estar a dieta.

dif·fer [dífəˑ] v. diferir, diferenciarse, distinguirse; disentir, **to — with** no convenir con, no estar de acuerdo con.

dif·fer·ence [dífrəns] s. diferencia; distinción; discordia, controversia; **it makes no — no** importa, es igual, da lo mismo.

dif·fer·ent [dífrənt] adj. diferente; distinto.

dif·fer·en·tial [dɪfɜˑénʃəl] s. diferencial.

dif·fer·en·ti·ate [dɪfɜˑénʃɪet] v. diferenciar(se); distinguir(se).

dif·fi·cult [dífəkʌlt] adj. difícil; dificultoso, trabajoso, penoso.

dif·fi·cul·ty [dífəkʌltɪ] s. dificultad: apuro, aprieto.

dif·fi·dence [dífədəns] s. timidez; desconfianza de sí propio.

dif·fi·dent [dífədənt] adj. huraño; tímido.

dif·fuse [dɪfjús] adk. difuso; prolijo; [dɪfjúz] v. difundir.

dif·fu·sion [dɪfjúʒən] s. difusión; diseminación.

dig [dɪg] v. cavar; excavar; ahondar; escarbar; trabajar duro; **to — under** socavar; **to — up** desenterrar; s. piquete; pulla, sarcasmo.

di·gest [dáɪdʒɛst] s. sumario, compendio; recopilación; código; [dədʒést] v. digerir; recopilar.

di·gest·i·ble [dədʒéstəbl] adj. digestible, digerible.

di·ges·tion [dədʒéstʃən] s. digestión.

di·ges·tive [dədʒéstɪv] adj. digestivo.

dig·ni·fied [dígnəfaɪd] adj. digno, mesurado; serio, grave.

dig·ni·tar·y [dígnətɛrɪ] s. dignatario.

dig·ni·ty [dígnətɪ] s. dignidad.

di·graph [dáɪgræf] s. dígrafo.

di·gress [dəgrés] v. divagar.

di·gres·sion [dəgréʃən] s. digresión, divagación.

dike [daɪk] s. dique, represa; zanja.

di·late [daɪlét] v. dilatar(se), extender(se), ensanchar(se).

dil·i·gence [dílədʒəns] s. diligencia; aplicación; esmero.

dil·i·gent [dílədʒənt] adj. diligente, activo, aplicado.

di·lute [dɪlút] v. diluir, desleír; aguar; adj. diluido.

dim [dɪm] adj. penumbroso, obscuro; nublado; confuso; indistinto; deslustrado, sin brillo; v. obscurecer; anublar, ofuscar; atenuar.

dime [daɪm] s. moneda de diez centavos.

di·men·sion [dəménʃən] s. dimensión.

di·min·ish [dəmínɪʃ] v. disminuir; rebajar.

di·min·u·tion [dɪmənjúʃən] s. diminución, mengua.

di·min·u·tive [dəmínjətɪv] adj. diminutivo; diminuto; s. diminutivo.

dim·ness [dímnɪs] s. semi-obscuridad, penumbra; ofuscamiento.

dim·ple [dímpl] s. hoyuelo.

din [dɪn] s. estruendo, fragor, estrépito.

dine [daɪn] v. comer; festejar u obsequiar con una comida.

din·er [dáɪnəˑ] s. coche-comedor; comensal (persona que come a la mesa).

din·gy [díndʒɪ] adj. negruzco; manchado, sucio.

din·ing [dáɪnɪŋ] ger. de **to dine**; — **car** coche-comedor; — **room** comedor.

din·ner [dínəˑ] s. comida; — **coat** smoking o esmoquin.

dint [dɪnt] s. **by — of** a fuerza de.

di·o·ram·a [daɪərǽmə] s. diorama.

dip [dɪp] v. zambullída; sumergir; bajada; declive; depresión; v. meter(se); zambullirse; mojar (la pluma en el tintero); teñir; agachar (la cabeza); saludar (con la bandera); inclinarse (un camino); dar un bajón (un avión); hundirse (el sol en el horizonte); **to — out** vaciar (con cucharón o cazo).

diph·the·ri·a [dɪfθírɪə] s. difteria.

diph·thong [dífθɔŋ] s. diptongo.

di·plo·ma [dɪplómə] s. diploma.

di·plo·ma·cy [dɪplóməsɪ] *s.* diplomacia.
dip·lo·mat [dɪpləmæt] *s.* diplomático.
dip·lo·mat·ic [dɪpləmætɪk] *adj.* diplomático.
dip·per [dɪpə·] *s.* cucharón, cazo; **the Big Dipper** la Osa Mayor.
dire [daɪr] *adj.* extremo; horrendo; fatal, de mal agüero.
di·rect [dərékt] *adj.* (*straight*) directo; derecho, en línea recta; *C.A.* recto; (*immediate*) inmediato; — **current** corriente continua; — **object** acusativo; *adv.* directamente; **-ly** *adv.* directamente; inmediatamente; en seguida; *v.* dirigir; guiar; encaminar; dar direcciones u órdenes.
di·rec·tion [dərékʃən] *s.* dirección; administración; gerencia; rumbo.
di·rec·tion·al an·ten·na [dərékʃən| ænténə] *s.* antena direccional.
di·rec·tion·al sig·nal [dərékʃən| sígnl] *s.* señal direccional.
di·rec·tive [déréktɪv] *adj.* directivo; *s.* orden, mandato.
di·rect·ness [déréktnɪs] *s.* derechura; franqueza; lo directo; **with** — sin rodeos.
di·rec·tor [dérékta·] *s.* director; gerente.
di·rec·to·ry [dérékterɪ] *s.* directorio; junta directiva; **telephone** — guía telefónica.
dir·i·gi·ble [dírədʒəbl] *adj. & s.* dirigible.
dirt [dɜrt] *s.* suciedad; mugre; tierra, polvo, lodo.
dirt·y [dɜ́rtɪ] *adj.* sucio; mugriento; cochino; enlodado; manchado; *v.* ensuciar; manchar; enlodar.
dis·a·ble [dɪsébl] *v.* incapacitar.
dis·ad·van·tage [dɪsədvǽntɪdʒ] *s.* desventaja; **to be at a** — estar en una situación desventajosa.
dis·a·gree [dɪsəgrí] *v.* (*dissent*) diferir, disentir; no convenir, no estar de acuerdo; (*bad effect*) no sentarle bien a uno (*el clima, la comida, etc.*).
dis·a·gree·a·ble [dɪsəgríəbl] *adj.* desagradable; áspero, de mal genio.
dis·a·gree·ment [dɪsəgrímənt] *s.* desavenencia, desacuerdo; disensión; discordia; discordancia.
dis·al·low [dɪsəlaʊ] *v.* desaprobar; rechazar.
dis·ap·pear [dɪsəpír] *v.* desaparecer.
dis·ap·pear·ance [dɪsəpírəns] *s.* desaparición.
dis·ap·point [dɪsəpóɪnt] *v.* chasquear; contrariar; decepcionar; faltar a lo prometido; desilusionar; **to be -ed** estar desilusionado o decepcionado; estar desengañado; quedar contrariado.
dis·ap·point·ing [dɪsəpóɪntɪŋ] *adj.* desilusionante, desengañador, decepcionante.
dis·ap·point·ment [dɪsəpóɪntmənt] *s.* desilusión, desengaño, decepción; chasco; contrariedad.
dis·ap·prov·al [dɪsəprúvl] *s.* desaprobación.
dis·ap·prove [dɪsəprúv] *v.* desaprobar.
dis·arm [dɪsárm] *v.* desarmar(se).
dis·ar·ma·ment [dɪsárməmənt] *s.* desarme.
dis·ar·ray [dɪsəré] *s.* desarreglo, confusión, desorden; *v.* desarreglar, desordenar.
dis·as·ter [dizǽstə·] *s.* desastre.
dis·as·trous [dɪzǽstrəs] *adj.* desastroso.
dis·band [dɪsbǽnd] *v.* dispersar; licenciar (*las tropas*); desbandarse.
dis·be·lieve [dɪsbəlív] *v.* descreer, no creer.
dis·burse [dɪsbɜ́s] *v.* desembolsar.
dis·burse·ment [dɪsbɜ́smənt] *s.* desembolso; gasto.
disc [dɪsk] = **disk**.
dis·card [dískard] *s.* descarte; desecho, cosa desechada; [dɪskárd] *v.* descartar; desechar.
dis·cern [dɪsɜ́rn] *v.* discernir, distinguir; percibir.
dis·cern·ment [dɪsɜ́rnmənt] *s.* discernimiento.

dis·charge [dɪstʃárdʒ] *s.* descarga (*de artillería*); descargo (*de una obligación*); desempeño (*de un deber*); exoneración; despedida; licencia (*militar*); pago (*de una deuda*); derrame, desagüe; supuración; *v.* descargar; exonerar; poner en libertad; despedir; echar, deponer; dar de baja (*a un soldado*); pagar (*una deuda*); arrojar, supurar; desaguar.
dis·ci·ple [dɪsáɪpl] *s.* discípulo.
dis·ci·pline [dísəplɪn] *s.* disciplina; *v.* disciplinar.
dis·close [dɪsklóz] *v.* descubrir; revelar.
dis·col·or [dɪskʌ́lə·] *v.* descolorar(se), desteñir(se).
dis·com·fort [dɪskʌ́mfə·t] *s.* incomodidad; malestar.
dis·con·cert [dɪskənsɜ́t] *v.* desconcertar.
dis·con·nect [dɪskənékt] *v.* desconectar; desacoplar; desunir, separar.
dis·con·nect·ed [dɪskənéktɪd] *p.p. & adj.* desconectado; desunido; inconexo, incoherente.
dis·con·so·late [dɪskánslɪt] *adj.* desconsolado.
dis·con·tent [dɪskəntént] *s.* descontento; *v.* descontentar.
dis·con·tent·ed [dɪskənténtɪd] *adj.* descontento; descontentadizo.
dis·con·tin·ue [dɪskəntínju] *v.* descontinuar; parar; suspender, interrumpir; abandonar.
dis·cord [dískɔrd] *s.* discordia; disonancia; discordancia; desavenencia.
dis·count [dískaʊnt] *s.* descuento; rebaja; — **rate** tipo de descuento; *v.* descontar; rebajar.
dis·cour·age [dɪskɜ́rɪdʒ] *v.* desanimar, desalentar, abatir; **to** — **from** disuadir de.
dis·cour·age·ment [dɪskɜ́rɪdʒmənt] *s.* desaliento, abatimiento.
dis·course [dískors] *s.* discurso; conversación; [dɪskórs] *v.* disertar, discurrir, hablar.
dis·cour·te·ous [dɪskɜ́tɪəs] *adj.* descortés, desatento.
dis·cour·te·sy [dɪskɜ́təsɪ] *s.* descortesía, desatención.
dis·cov·er [dɪskʌ́və·] *v.* descubrir.
dis·cov·er·er [dɪskʌ́vərə·] *s.* descubridor.
dis·cov·er·y [dɪskʌ́vrɪ] *s.* descubrimiento.
dis·cred·it [dɪskrédɪt] *s.* descrédito; deshonra; *v.* desacreditar; deshonrar; no creer.
dis·creet [dɪskrít] *adj.* discreto, prudente.
dis·crep·an·cy [dɪskrépənsɪ] *s.* discrepancia, diferencia; variación.
dis·cre·tion [dɪskréʃən] *s.* discreción; prudencia; **at one's own** — a discreción.
dis·crim·i·nate [dɪskrímənet] *v.* discernir; distinguir; hacer distinciones, hacer favoritismos; dar trato de inferioridad con motivos de prejuicio; **to** — **against** hacer favoritismos en perjuicio de.
dis·cuss [dɪskʌ́s] *v.* discutir.
dis·cus·sion [dɪskʌ́ʃən] *s.* discusión.
dis·dain [dɪsdén] *s.* desdén, menosprecio; *v.* desdeñar, menospreciar; desdeñarse de.
dis·dain·ful [dɪsdénfəl] *adj.* desdeñoso.
dis·ease [dɪzíz] *s.* enfermedad.
dis·eased [dɪzízd] *adj.* enfermo.
dis·em·bark [dɪsɪmbárk] *v.* desembarcar.
dis·en·tan·gle [dɪsɪntǽŋgl] *v.* desenredar, desenmarañar, deshacer (*una maraña o enredo*).
dis·fig·ure [dɪsfígjə·] *v.* desfigurar; afear; desencajar.
dis·fran·chise [dɪsfrǽntʃaɪz] *v.* privar de derecho de voto o de ciudadanía.
dis·grace [dɪsgrés] *s.* ignominia; deshonra; vergüenza; **to be in** — estar desacreditado, haber perdido la gracia o el favor; *v.* deshonrar; degradar; desacreditar; avergonzar.

dis·grace·ful [dɪsgrésfəl] *adj.* vergonzoso.

dis·guise [dɪsgáɪz] *s.* disfraz; *v.* disfrazar.

dis·gust [dɪsgʌ́st] *s.* asco; repugnancia; disgusto; *v.* disgustar, dar asco; repugnar.

dis·gust·ed [dɪsgʌ́stɪd] *adj.* disgustado; descontento; asqueado.

dis·gust·ing [dɪsgʌ́stɪŋ] *adj.* asqueroso, repugnante.

dish [dɪʃ] *s.* plato; manjar, vianda; -es vajilla; *v.* servir.

dis·heart·en [dɪshártŋ] *v.* desalentar, desanimar, descorazonar.

di·shev·el [dɪʃévl] *v.* desgreñar.

di·shev·eled [dɪʃévld] *adj.* desgreñado; desaliñado, desaseado; revuelto.

dis·hon·est [dɪsánɪst] *adj.* engañoso, falso, tramposo, falto de honradez, fraudulento.

dis·hon·es·ty [dɪsánɪstɪ] *s.* fraude, falta de honradez.

dis·hon·or [dɪsánɚ] *s.* deshonra; afrenta; *v.* deshonrar; recusar (*un giro o cheque*).

dis·hon·or·a·ble [dɪsánɚəbl] *adj.* deshonroso; infame.

dish·wash·er [dɪ́ʃwɔʃɚ] *s.* (*person*) lavaplatos; (*machine*) máquina de lavar platos.

dis·il·lu·sion [dɪsɪlúʒən] *v.* desilusión, decepción, desengaño; *v.* desilusionar, decepcionar, desengañar.

dis·in·fect [dɪsɪnfékt] *v.* desinfectar.

dis·in·fec·tant [dɪsɪnféktənt] *s.* desinfectante.

dis·in·ter·est·ed [dɪsíntərəstɪd] *adj.* desinteresado.

disk [dɪsk] *s.* disco; — **brake** freno de disco.

dis·like [dɪsláɪk] *s.* antipatía, aversión; *v.* sentir o tener aversión por; **I — it** me repugna, no me gusta, me desagrada.

dis·lo·cate [dɪ́sloket] *v.* dislocar, descoyuntar; desencajar.

dis·lodge [dɪslád͡ʒ] *v.* desalojar.

dis·loy·al [dɪslóɪəl] *adj.* desleal.

dis·mal [dɪ́zml] *adj.* lúgubre, sombrío, tétrico.

dis·man·tle [dɪsmǽntl] *v.* desmantelar; desmontar, desarmar.

dis·may [dɪsmé] *s.* desmayo, desaliento, pavor; *v.* desalentar, desanimar; atemorizar.

dis·miss [dɪsmís] *v.* (*discharge*) despedir, expulsar, destituir; (*dispel*) desechar; (*allow to leave*) licenciar, dar de baja; (*close*) dar por terminado (*un pleito o caso jurídico*); **to — the meeting** disolver la junta, levantar la sesión.

dis·miss·al [dɪsmís] *s.* despedida, expulsión, destitución (*de un cargo*).

dis·mount [dɪsmáunt] *v.* desmontar; apear(se); desarmar (*un cañón, una máquina*); desengastar (*joyas*).

dis·o·be·di·ence [dɪsəbídɪəns] *s.* desobediencia.

dis·o·be·di·ent [dɪsəbídɪənt] *adj.* desobediente.

dis·o·bey [dɪsəbé] *v.* desobedecer.

dis·or·der [dɪsɔ́rdɚ] *s.* (*confusion*) desorden; trastorno; confusión; (*illness*) enfermedad; *v.* desordenar; trastornar; desarreglar.

dis·or·der·ly [dɪsɔ́rdɚlɪ] *adj.* desordenado; desarreglado; revoltoso; escandaloso; *adv.* desordenadamente.

dis·own [dɪsón] *v.* repudiar; desconocer, negar.

dis·par·age [dɪspǽrɪd͡ʒ] *v.* desacreditar; desdorar.

dis·pas·sion·ate [dɪspǽʃənɪt] *adj.* desapasionado.

dis·patch [dɪspǽtʃ] *s.* despacho; envío; parte (*m.*), comunicación, mensaje; prontitud, expedición; *v.* despachar; enviar, expedir; matar.

dis·pel [dɪspél] *v.* disipar, dispersar.

dis·pen·sa·ry [dɪspénsərɪ] *s.* dispensario.

dis·pen·sa·tion [dɪspənséʃən] *s.* dispensa, exención;

dispensación; distribución.

dis·pense [dɪspéns] *v.* (*give*) dispensar, dar; repartir; distribuir; administrar (*la justicia*); despachar (*recetas, medicamentos*); **to — from** eximir de dispensar de; **to — with** omitir; pasarse sin, prescindir de.

dis·per·sal [dɪspɚ́sl] *s.* dispersión; desbandada.

dis·perse [dɪspɚ́s] *v.* dispersar(se), disipar(se), esparcir(se).

dis·place [dɪsplés] *v.* desalojar; desplazar; poner fuera de su lugar; suplantar.

dis·placed per·son [dɪsplést pɚ́sən] *s.* persona desplazada.

dis·play [dɪsplé] *s.* manifestación, exhibición; ostentación; *v.* exhibir; mostrar, manifestar; desplegar.

dis·please [dɪsplíz] *v.* desagradar; disgustar, fastidiar.

dis·pleas·ure [dɪsplɛ́ʒɚ] *s.* desagrado, disgusto, descontento.

dis·pos·al [dɪspózl] *s.* disposición; arreglo; venta (*de bienes*).

dis·pose [dɪspóz] *v.* disponer; arreglar; influir; **to — of** deshacerse de.

dis·po·si·tion [dɪspəzíʃən] *s.* disposición; arreglo; aptitud, inclinación; venta; **good (bad) — buen (mal) genio.

dis·pos·ses [dɪspozés] *v.* desposeer; despojar.

dis·prove [dɪsprúv] *v.* refutar.

dis·pute [dɪspjút] *s.* disputa; *v.* disputar.

dis·qual·i·fy [dɪskwɑləfaɪ] *v.* inhabilitar, incapacitar, descalificar.

dis·re·gard [dɪsrɪgárd] *s.* desatención, falta de atención, negligencia, descuido; falta de respeto o consideración; *v.* desatender, no hacer caso de, desentenderse de.

dis·re·spect [dɪsrɪspékt] *s.* desacato, falta de respeto.

dis·re·spect·ful [dɪsrɪspéktfəl] *adj.* irrespetuoso.

dis·rupt [dɪsrʌ́pt] *v.* desbaratar; romper.

dis·sat·is·fied [dɪssǽtɪsfaɪd] *adj.* descontento, malcontento, mal satisfecho.

dis·sat·is·fy [dɪssǽtɪsfaɪ] *v.* descontentar, no satisfacer.

dis·sect [dɪsékt] *v.* disecar, hacer una disección; analizar.

dis·sem·ble [dɪsémbl] *v.* disimular, fingir.

dis·sen·sion [dɪsénʃən] *s.* disensión, discordia.

dis·sent [dɪsént] *v.* disentir; *s.* desacuerdo; disensión, desavenencia.

dis·ser·ta·tion [dɪsɚtéʃən] *s.* disertacion; tratado; tesis.

dis·sim·u·la·tion [dɪsɪmjəléʃən] *s.* disimulo.

dis·si·pate [dɪsəpet] *v.* disipar(se).

dis·si·pa·tion [dɪsəpéʃən] *s.* disipación.

dis·so·lute [dɪsəlut] *adj.* disoluto.

dis·so·lu·tion [dɪsəlúʃən] *s.* disolución.

dis·solve [dɪzálv] *v.* disolver(se); anular.

dis·suade [dɪswéd] *v.* disuadir.

dis·taff [dɪstæf] *s.* rueca.

dis·tance [dɪstəns] *s.* distancia; lejanía; alejamiento; **in the —** a lo lejos, en lontananza.

dis·tant [dɪstənt] *adj.* (*far*) distante; apartado, lejano, remoto; (*aloof*) esquivo; **to be — from** distar de; **-ly** *adv.* de lejos; remotamente; a distancia; en lontananza.

dis·taste [dɪstést] *s.* disgusto, aversión, repugnancia.

dis·taste·ful [dɪstéstfəl] *adj.* desagradable, repugnante.

dis·tem·per [dɪstémpɚ] *s.* moquillo; pepita (*de las*

gallinas).
dis·tend [dɪsténd] v. dilatar, ensanchar.
dis·til [dɪstíl] v. destilar.
dis·til·la·tion [dɪstléʃən] s. destilación.
dis·till·er·y [dɪstíləri] s. destilería.
dis·tinct [dɪstíŋkt] adj. distinto, claro; diferente; **-ly** adv. distintamente, claramente, con claridad.
dis·tinc·tion [dɪstíŋkʃən] s. distinction.
dis·tinc·tive [dɪstíŋktɪv] adj. distintivo.
dis·tin·guish [dɪstíŋgwɪʃ] v. distinguir; discernir.
dis·tin·guished [dɪstíŋgwɪʃt] adj. distinguido.
dis·tin·guish·ing [dɪstíŋgwɪʃɪŋ] adj. distintivo, característico.
dis·tort [dɪstóry] v. desfigurar, deformar, torcer, falsear; tergiversar.
dis·tract [dɪstrǽkt] v. distraer; perturbar.
dis·trac·tion [dɪstrǽkʃən] s. distracción, diversión; perturbación; **to drive to** — volver loco.
dis·tress [dɪstrés] s. angustia, aflicción, congoja; dolor; **to be in** — tener una aflicción; estar apurado; estar en zozobra (un navío); v. angustiar, acongojar, afligir; **to be -ed** estar afligido o apurado.
dis·trib·ute [dɪstríbjut] v. distribuir, repartir.
dis·tri·bu·tion [dɪstrəbjúʃən] s. distribución; repartimiento.
dis·trib·u·tor [dɪstríbjətɚ] s. distribuidor.
dis·trict [dístrɪkt] s. distrito; — **attorney** fiscal de distrito.
dis·trust [dɪstrʌ́st] s. deconfianza; recelo; v. desconfiar; recelar.
dis·trust·ful [dɪstrʌ́stfəl] adj. desconfiado, sospechoso, receloso.
dis·turb [dɪstɝ́b] v. turbar, perturbar, inquietar; desarreglar; incomodar, molestar; **don't** — **yourself!** ¡no se moleste Vd.!
dis·tur·bance [dɪstɝ́bəns] s. disturbio; perturbación; desorden; alboroto; molestia.
dis·use [dɪsjús] s. desuso; **to fall into** — caer en desuso; caducar.
ditch [dɪtʃ] s. zanja; foso; **irrigation** — acequia; v. zanjar, abrir zanjas; meter en la zanja; **to** — **someone** deshacerse de alguien.
dit·to [díto] s. ídem, lo mismo.
di·u·ret·ic [daɪjʊrétɪk] adj. & s. diurético.
di·van [dáɪvæn] s. diván.
dive [daɪv] s. zambullida (echándose de cabeza), buceada, chapuz; picada (descenso rápido de un avión); Méx. clavado; garito, leonera; v. echarse de cabeza; zambullirse (de cabeza); bucear; sumergirse (un submarino); **to** — **into someone** abalanzarse sobre alguien.
div·er [dáɪvɚ] s. buzo; zambullidor.
di·verge [dəvɝ́dʒ] v. divergir, irse apartando, separarse; diferir.
di·ver·gence [dəvɝ́dʒəns] s. divergencia; diferencia (de opiniones).
di·vers [dáɪvɚz] adj. diversos, varios.
di·verse [dəvɝ́s] adj. diverso; diferente.
di·ver·sion [dəvɝ́ʒən] s. diversión, recreo; desviación.
di·ver·si·ty [dəvɝ́sətɪ] s. diversidad, diferencia, variedad.
di·vert [dəvɝ́t] v. divertir, entretener; distraer; desviar, apartar.
di·vide [dəváɪd] v. dividir(se), partir.
div·i·dend [dívədɛnd] s. dividendo.
di·vid·ing [dɪváɪdɪŋ] adj. divisorio.
di·vine [dəváɪn] adj. divino; v. adivinar.
di·vin·i·ty [dəvínətɪ] s. divinidad; deidad; teología.
di·vi·sion [dəvíʒən] s. división.

di·vorce [dəvórs] s. divorcio; v. divorciar(se).
di·vulge [dəvʌ́ldʒ] v. divulgar.
diz·zi·ness [dízɪnɪs] s. vahido o vaguido, desvanecimiento, mareo, vértigo.
diz·zy [dízɪ] adj. desvanecido, mareado; confuso; aturdido; — **speed** velocidad vertiginosa.
do [du] v. hacer; **to** — **away with** deshacerse de; prescindir de; **to** — **a lesson** estudiar una lección; **to** — **one's hair** peinarse, arreglarse el pelo; **to** — **the dishes** lavar los platos; **to** — **up** envolver; limpiar, arreglar; lavar o planchar; **to** — **well in business** prosperar en los negocios; **to** — **without** pasarse sin; **to have nothing to** — **with** no tener nada que ver con; **that will** — basta, bastará; **that won't** — eso no sirve; eso no resultará bien; **this will have to** — habrá que conformarse con esto; **how** — **you** —? ¿cómo está Vd.?; — **you hear me?** ¿me oye Vd.?; **yes, I** — si, le oigo; **I** — **say it** sí lo digo.
doc·ile [dásl] adj. dócil.
dock [dɑk] s. muelle, desembarcadero; dársena; **dry** — carenero, dique de carena; v. entrar en el muelle; atracar, meter (una embarcación) en el muelle o dique; **to** — **the wages** rebajar la paga.
doc·tor [dáktɚ] s. doctor; médico, facultativo; v. medicinar, curar; **to** — **oneself** medicinarse, tomar medicinas.
doc·trine [dáktrɪn] s. doctrina.
doc·u·ment [dákjəmənt] s. documento; [dákjəment] v. documentar.
dod·der [dádɚ] v. tambalear; temblar.
dodge [dadʒ] s. evasión, evasiva; v. evadir(se); escabullirse; hurtar el cuerpo; **to** — **around a corner** dar un esquinazo.
doe [do] s. cierva; hembra (del antílope, del gamo, de la liebre).
dog [dɔg] s. perro, perra; can; **hot** — salchicha caliente, Ch., C.A. perro caliente; Ríopl. pancho; **to put on a lot of** — emperifollarse; darse mucho tono, Ríopl. darse mucho corte; v. seguir la pista de, perseguir, acosar; adv. sumamente, completamente; **dog-tired** cansadísimo.
dog·ma [dɔ́gmə] s. dogma.
dog·mat·ic [dɔgmǽtɪk] adj. dogmático.
doi·ly [dóɪlɪ] s. mantelito (para platos, vasos, lámparas, etc.).
do·ings [dúɪŋz] s. pl. hechos, acciones, acontecimientos; **great** — mucha actividad, fiesta, función.
do-it-your·self [duɪtjʊrsélf] adj. proyectado para que uno pueda hacer sus propios trabajos manuales en casa; autodidáctico.
dole [dol] s. reparto gratuito (de dinero o alimento); ración, limosna; v. repartir gratuitamente.
dole·ful [dólfəl] adj. lúgubre, triste, lastimoso.
doll [dɑl] s. muñeca, muñeco; v. **to** — **up** emperifollarse, ataviarse; **dolly** s. muñequita.
dol·lar [dálɚ] s. dólar.
dol·phin [dólfɪn] s. delfín.
do·main [domén] s. dominio; heredad.
dome [dom] s. cúpula; media naranja (de iglesia).
do·mes·tic [dəméstɪk] adj. doméstico; hogareño; nacional, del país, Am. criollo; s. criado, sirviente.
do·mi·cile [dáməsaɪl] s. domicilio.
dom·i·nant [dámənənt] adj. dominante.
dom·i·nate [dámənet] v. dominar.
dom·i·na·tion [dɑmənéʃən] s. dominación, dominio.
dom·i·neer [dɑmənír] v. dominar, señorear.
dom·i·neer·ing [dɑmənírɪŋ] adj. dominador,

DI

mandón, imperioso, tiránico.

do·min·ion [dəmínjən] s. dominio.

dom·i·no [dámǝno] s. dominó, traje de máscara; disfraz; ficha (de dominó); **dominoes** dominó (juego).

don [dɑn] s. don (título); caballero; v. ponerse, vestirse.

do·nate [dónet] v. donar, regalar, hacer donación.

do·na·tion [donéʃən] s. donación; regalo, dádiva.

done [dʌn] p.p. de **to do** hecho; terminado, acabado; **to be — in** estar rendido de cansancio; **the meat is well —** está bien asada la carne.

don·key [dáŋkɪ] s. burro, asno.

doo·dad [dúdæd] s. chuchería, chisme.

doom [dum] s. hado, sino, destino; mala suerte, perdición, ruina; **the day of —** el día del juicio final; v. condenar, sentenciar; predestinar; **to be -ed to failure** estar predestinado al fracaso.

door [dor] s. puerta; entrada.

door·bell [dórbɛl] s. campanilla o timbre (de llamada).

door·knob [dórnɑb] s. tirador de puerta, perilla, manija.

door·man [dórmæn] s. portero.

door·step [dórstɛp] s. escalón de la puerta; umbral.

door·way [dórwe] s. puerta, entrada; vano (de la puerta).

dope [dop] s. (narcotic) narcótico; opio; droga; menjurje, medicamento; (information) información; **— fiend** morfinómano; **he is a —** es un zoquete; v. narcotizar; **to — out** adivinar, conjeturar; **to — oneself up** medicinarse demasiado.

dor·mi·to·ry [dɔ́rmǝtorɪ] s. dormitorio.

dose [dos] s. dosis; v. medicinar; **to — oneself** medicinarse.

dos·si·er [dásie] s. expediente; legajo.

dot [dɑt] s. punto; **on the —** en punto; v. marcar con puntos; poner el punto (sobre la i).

do·tage [dótɪdʒ] s. chochez; **to be in one's —** chochear.

dote [dot] v. chochear; **to — on** estar loco por.

dou·ble [dʌ́bl] adj. doble; doblado; **— boiler** baño de María; **— deal** trato doble; **— entry** partida doble; **— standard** norma de conducta sexual mas restringida para la mujer; s. doble; -s juego de dobles (en tenis); adv. doblemente; **doublebreasted** cruzado; **double-faced** de dos caras; v. doblar(se); duplicar(se); **to — up** doblarse; **doubly** adv. doblemente; por duplicado.

doubt [daʊt] s. duda; v. dudar.

doubt·ful [dáʊtfǝl] adj. dudoso; dudable.

doubt·less [dáʊtlɪs] adj. indudable, cierto, seguro; adv. sin duda; indudablemente; probablemente.

douche [duʃ] s. ducha vaginal.

dough [do] s. pasta, masa; dinero.

dough·nut [dónǝt] s. bollito o buñuelo en rosca.

dove [dʌv] s. paloma.

dove [dov] pret. de **to dive.**

down [daʊn] adv. abajo, hacia abajo; **— to** hasta; **— East** en el este; **— the street** calle abajo; **to cut —** prices reducir o rebajar precios; **to get — to work** aplicarse; **to go** (o come) **—** bajar; **to pay —** pagar al contado; **to put —** poner; anotar, apuntar, poner por escrito; adj. abatido, descorazonado; **— grade** declive, pendiente; **prices are —** han bajado los precios; **to be — on someone** tenerle ojeriza a alguien; s. plumón; vello; pelusa; v. echar por tierra, derribar; rebajar (precios).

down·cast [dáʊnkæst] adj. cabizbajo, abatido; **with — eyes** con los ojos bajos.

down·fall [dáʊnfɔl] s. caída; ruina.

down·pour [dáʊnpor] s. aguacero, chaparrón.

down·right [dáʊnraɪt] adj. claro, positivo, categórico, absoluto; **— foolishness** solemne disparate; adv. enteramente; absolutamente.

down·stairs [dáʊnstérz] adv. abajo; en el piso bajo; adj. del piso bajo; s. piso bajo, piso inferior.

down·stream [dáʊnstrím] adv. río abajo, aguas abajo; con la corriente.

down-to-earth [daʊntǝɜ́θ] adj. sensato; practico.

down·town [dáʊntáʊn] adv. al centro, en el centro (de una población); adj. del centro; s, centro.

down·ward [dáʊnwɚd] adj. descendente; inclinado; adv. (= **downwards**) hacia abajo.

dow·ny [dáʊnɪ] adj. suave, blando; velloso; plumoso.

dow·ry [dáʊrɪ] s. dote.

doze [doz] s. siestecita, sueño ligero; v. dormitar.

doz·en [dʌ́zn] s. docena.

drab [dræb] adj. pardo, pardusco; monótono.

draft [dræft] s. corriente de aire; trago; libranza, letra de cambio, giro bancario; trazado; plan; leva (militar), conscripción; tiro (de estufa, hogar, etc.); calado (de un barco); **— beer** cerveza de barril; **— horse** caballo de tiro; **rough —** croquis, borrador; v. trazar, dibujar, delinear, reclutar, echar leva; redactar (un documento).

drafts·man [drǽftsmǝn] s. dibujante.

drag [dræg] s. rastra, traba, obstáculo; **to have a — with someone** tener buenas aldabas con alguien; v. arrastrar(se); rastrear; moverse despacio; **to — on and on** prolongarse demasiado, prolongarse hasta el fastidio.

drag·on [drǽgǝn] s. dragón.

drain [dren] s. (channel) desagüe; desaguadero, conducto; (exhaust) agotamiento; consumo; v. desaguar(se); apurar (un vaso); agotar, consumir; escurrir(se), secar(se); desecar (un terreno), Am. drenar.

drain·age [drénɪdʒ] s. desagüe, Am. drenaje; desaguadero; sistema de desaguaderos; desecamiento, desecación (de un terreno, laguna, etc.).

drake [drek] s. pato.

dra·ma [drámǝ] s. drama.

dra·mat·ic [drǝmǽtɪk] adj. dramático.

dra·ma·tist [drǽmǝtɪst] s. dramaturgo, dramático.

dra·ma·tize [drǽmǝtaɪz] v. dramatizar.

drank [dræŋk] pret. de **to drink.**

drape [drep] s. colgadura, cortina, tapiz; v. colgar, entapizar, adornar con tapices; cubrir, revestir.

drap·er·y [drépǝrɪ] s. tapicería, colgaduras, cortinas; pañería, paños, géneros.

dras·tic [drǽstɪk] adj. extremo, fuerte, violento; **to take — steps** tomar medidas enérgicas.

draught [dræft] véase **draft.**

draw [drɔ] v. (pull) tirar; estirar; jalar (halar); (attract) atraer; sacar; (design) debujar, trazar; (withdraw) girar, librar (una libranza); hacer (una comparación); correr (la cortina); **to — aside** apartar(se); **to — a breath** aspirar, tomar aliento; **to — lots** echar suertes, sortear; **to — near** acercarse; **to — out** sacar; sonsacar (a una persona); alargar, prolongar; **to — up** acercar(se); redactar (un documento); s. empate (en deportes o juegos); número sacado (en una rifa); atracción; **—bridge** puente levadizo.

draw·back [dró bæk] s. desventaja; obstáculi,

inconveniente.

drawer [drɔr] *s.* cajón, gaveta; **-s** calzoncillos.

draw·er [drɔ́ɚ] *s.* librador, girador; dibujante.

draw·ing [drɔ́ɪŋ] *s.* (*design*) dibujo; delineación, trazado; (*raffle*) sorteo; — **paper** papel de dibujo; — **room** sala de recibo, recibidor, recibimiento.

drawn [drɔn] *p.p. de* to draw.

dread [drɛd] *s.* pavor, temor, aprensión; *adj.* terrible; temido; *v.* temer; sentir aprensión de.

dread·ful [drɛ́dfəl] *adj.* horrendo; espantoso.

dream [drim] *s.* sueño; ensueño; *v.* soñar; **to — of** soñar con, soñar en.

dream·er [drímɚ] *s.* soñador.

dream·land [drímlænd] *s.* tierra del ensueño; región de los sueños.

dreamt [drɛmpt] = **dreamed**.

drea·my [drímɪ] *adj.* soñoliento; soñador; melancólico; como un sueño; **a — recollection** un vago recuerdo.

drea·ry [drírɪ] *adj.* sombrío; melancólico.

dredge [drɛdʒ] *s.* draga; *v.* dragar.

dregs [drɛgz] *s. pl.* heces, sedimento.

drench [drɛntʃ] *s.* mojada, mojadura, empapada; *v.* empapar; mojar; remojar.

dress [drɛs] *s.* vestido, traje; vestidura, ropaje, atavío; — **rehearsal** ensayo general y último (*antes de una función*); — **suit** traje de etiqueta; *v.* vestir(se); arreglarse, componerse; aderezar; adobar (*carne o pieles*); curar (*heridas*); alinear, formar (*las tropas*); **to — down** reprender, regañar; **to — up** emperifollarse, acicalarse, ataviarse.

dress·er [drɛ́sɚ] *s.* tocador, cómoda (*con espejo*); **she is a good —** viste con elegancia o buen gusto.

dress·ing [drɛ́sɪŋ] *s.* aderezo; salsa (*para ensaladas*); relleno (*para carne, pollo, etc.*); medicamento, vendajes (*para heridas*); **a — down** regaño; — **gown** bata; — **room** tocador; — **table** tocador.

dress·mak·er [drɛ́smekɚ] *s.* modista.

drew [dru] *pret. de* to draw.

drib·ble [dríbl] *v.* gotear; dejar caer en gotas; babear; *s.* goteo; chorrito.

drib·let [dríblɪt] *s.* gota, gotita; **in -s** gota a gota; en pequeñas cantidades.

dried [draɪd] *pret. & p.p. de* to dry; *adj.* seco; paso; — **fig** higo paso.

drift [drɪft] *s.* (*direction*) rumbo, dirección, tendencia, deriva; (*pile*) montón, amontonamiento (*de arena, nieve, etc.*); (*off course*) desvío (*de un barco o avión*); **to get the — of a conversation** enterarse a medias de una conversación; *v.* flotar; ir(se) a la deriva; dejarse llevar por la corriente; amontonarse (*la nieve, la arena*); esparcirse (*la arena, la nieve, las nubes*).

drift·wood [dríftwʊd] *s.* madera o leña flotante; madera de playa.

drill [drɪl] *s.* (*tool*) taladro; barrena; (*training*) ejercicio; adiestramiento; *Am.* entrenamiento; dril (*tela*); *v.* taladrar, barrenar, perforar; hacer ejercicio; aleccionar; disciplinar (*un ejército*); adiestrar(se), *Am.* entrenar(se).

dri·ly [dráɪlɪ] *adv.* secamente.

drink [drɪŋk] *s.* bebida; trago; *v.* beber; **to — a toast** beber a la salud de, brindar por; — **it down** ¡bébaselo! ¡trágueselo!

drink·a·ble [dríŋkəbl] *adj.* potable.

drip [drɪp] *s.* goteo; *v.* gotear, caer gota a gota; dejar caer gota a gota.

drive [draɪv] *s.* (*ride*) paseo en coche; (*road*) calzada, carretera, paseo; (*campaign*) campaña; (*impulse*) empuje; tiro, tirada (*de una pelota*); *v.* impulsar,

impeler, empujar; arrear (*animales*); conducir, guiar o manejar (*un auto*); forzar; encajar, clavar (*una estaca, cuña, o clavo*); tirar, lanzar (*una pelota*); dar un paseo en auto; llevar (*a alguien*) en auto; cavar (*un pozo, túnel, etc.*); **to — away** ahuyentar; **to — a good bargain** hacer un buen trato; **to — mad** volver loco; **what are you driving at?** ¿qué quieres decir con eso?

drive-in [dráɪvɪn] *s. adj.* establecimiento como tienda, banco, teatro que tiene pista automovilística que permite al cliente permanecer en su coche; automovilístico.

driv·el [drívl] *s.* baba; ñoñería, tontería; *v.* babear; chochear, decir ñoñerías.

driv·el·ing [drívlɪŋ] *adj.* baboso.

driv·en [drívən] *p.p. de* to drive.

driv·er [dráɪvɚ] *s.* cochero, chófer, mecánico, conductor (*de automóvil*); arriero (*de animales*); uno de los palos de golf; **pile —** martinete (*para clavar pilotes*); **slave —** mandón, tirano; **truck —** carretero, camionero.

drive·way [dráɪvwe] *s.* calzada de entrada, carretera de entrada.

driz·zle [drízl] *v.* lloviznar; *s.* llovizna.

drone [dron] *s.* zángano; holgazán; zumbido; *v.* zumbar; hablar con monotonía; holgazanear, perder el tiempo.

droop [drup] *v.* doblarse, andar o estar alicaído, estar abatido; languidecer; marchitarse; bajar (*los hombros, los párpados*); **his shoulders —** tiene los hombros caídos; **-ing eyelids** párpados caídos.

drop [drɑp] *s.* (*liquid*) gota; (*descent*) baja; caída; (*incline*) declive; **cough —** pastilla para la tos; **letter —** buzón; **curtain —** telón (*de teatro*); **hammer —** martinete; **— out** dimitente; *v.* dejar caer, soltar; gotear; caer; dejar (*un asunto, una amistad*); **to — a line** ponar unos renglones; **to — asleep** quedarse dormido, dormirse; **to — behind** dejar atrás; quedarse atrás; **to — in** hacer una visita inesperada, *Am.* descolgarse; **to — in a mailbox** echar al buzón; **to — out** retirarse; desaparecer; **to — the curtain** bajar el telón.

drought [draʊt] *s.* sequía.

drove [drov] *s.* manada, recua, rebaño; tropel; *pret. de* to drive.

drown [draʊn] *v.* ahogar(se), anegar(se); apagar, ahogar (*un sonido*).

drowse [draʊz] *v.* dormitar; estar amodorrado.

drows·i·ness [dráʊzɪnɪs] *s.* modorra, somnolencia.

drow·sy [dráʊzɪ] *adj.* soñoliento; adormilado, amodorrado; **to become —** amodorrarse.

drudge [drʌdʒ] *v.* afanarse, atarearse; *s.* trabajador, esclavo del trabajo.

drug [drʌg] *s.* droga; narcótico; **to be a — on the market** ser invendible (*una mercancía*); *v.* jaropar (*administrar drogas en demasía*); narcotizar.

drug·gist [drʌ́gɪst] *s.* boticario, droguista, droguero, farmacéutico.

drug·store [drʌ́gstor] *s.* botica, droguería, farmacia.

drum [drʌm] *s.* tambor; tímpano (*del oído*); barril, tonel; **bass —** tambora, bombo; **—stick** bolillo de tambor; — **major** tambor mayor; *v.* tocar el tambor; tamborilear; **to — a lesson into someone** meterle a uno la lección en la cabeza; **to — up trade** solicitar o fomentar ventas.

drum·mer [drʌ́mɚ] *s.* tambor, tamborilevo; viajante de comercio, agente.

drunk [drʌŋk] *p.p. de* to drink; *adj.* borracho, ebrio, emborrachado, bebido; *Riopl.* mamado; *C.A.*

bolo; *Ch.* cufifo; **to get** — emborracharse, embriagarse.

drunk·ard [drʌ́ŋkəd] *s.* borracho, borrachón, beodo, bebedor.

drunk·en [drʌ́ŋjən] *adj.* borracho, ebrio.

drunk·en·ness [drʌ́ŋkənnɪs] *s.* borrachera, embriaguez.

dry [draɪ] *adj.* seco; árido; **a** — **book** un libro aburrido; — **cleaner** quitamanchas; tintorero; — **cleaning** lavado o limpieza al seco; — **goods** lencería, géneros, tejidos, telas; — **measure** medida para áridos; — **run** ejercicio de ensayo; ensayo. — **wash** ropa lavada pero no planchada. *v.* secar(se); enjugar; **to** — **up** secarse, resecarse.

dry·ness [dráɪnɪs] *s.* sequedad; aridez.

dub [dʌb] *v.* doblar (*una película*).

du·bi·ous [djúbɪəs] *adj.* dudoso.

duch·ess [dʌ́tʃɪs] *s.* duquesa.

duck [dʌk] *s.* pato, pata; ánade; dril (*género*); zambullida, chapuz; agachada rápida (*para evitar un golpe*); *v.* zambullir(se), chapuzar(se); agachar(se); agachar (*la cabeza*).

duck·ling [dʌ́klɪŋ] *s.* patito, añadeja.

duc·tile [dʌ́ktɪl] *adj.* dúctil.

dud [dʌd] *s.* bomba que no estalla.

dude [dud] *s.* caballerete; novato.

due [dju] *adj.* debido; vencido, pagadero; **in** — **time** a su debido tiempo; **the bill is**— se ha vencido la cuenta; **the train is—at two o'clock** el tren debe llegar a las dos; *adv.* directamente; — **east** hacia el este, rumbo al oriente; *s.* derecho, privilegio; **-s** cuota.

du·el [djúəl] *s.* duelo, desafío, combate; *v.* batirse en duelo.

du·et [djuét] *s.* duo, dueto.

dug [dʌg] *pret. & p.p. de* **to dig.**

dug·out [dʌ́gaʊt] *s.* piragua.

duke [djuk] *s.* duque.

duke·dom [djúkdəm] *s.* ducado.

dull [dʌl] *adj.* (*dim*) opaco, empañado, mate; sin brillo; (*boring*) aburrido; (*blunt*) embotado, sin punta, sin filo; (*stupid*) torpe; tardo; — **pain** dolor sordo; — **sound** sonido sordo o apagado; *v.* embotar(se); empañar(se); ofuscar; amortiguar (*un dolor o sonido*).

dull·ness [dʌ́lnɪs] *s.* (*dimness*) falta de brillo; (*sluggishness*) estupidez, torpeza; (*bluntness*) falta de punta o filo; (*monotony*) aburrimiento; (*heaviness*) pesadez.

du·ly [djúlɪ] *adv.* debidamente.

dumb [dʌm] *adj.* (*silent*) mudo; silencioso, callado; (*dull*) estúpido, torpe; —**creature** animal.

dumb·found·ed [dʌmfáʊndəd] *adj.* patitieso.

dumb·ness [dʌ́mnɪs] *s.* mudez; mutismo; estupidez.

dum·my [dʌ́mɪ] *s.* (*figure*) maniquí, figurón, muñeco; (*fool*) zoquete, tonto; *adj.* falso, fingido.

dump [dʌmp] *s.* montón (*de tierra, carbón, etc.*); terrero, vaciadero, escorial; **garbage**—muladar; basurero; **to be in the -s** estar abatido; *v.* echar, vaciar, descargar; echar a la basura.

dunce [dʌns] *s.* zopenco, zoquete, tonto.

dune [djun] *s.* duna o médano.

dung [dʌŋ] *s.* boñiga, estiércol.

dun·geon [dʌ́ndʒən] *s.* mazmorra, calabozo.

dung·hill [dʌ́ŋhɪl] *s.* muladar, estercolero.

dupe [djup] *s.* inocentón, incauto, víctima (*de un engaño*); *v.* embaucar.

du·pli·cate [djúpləkɪt] *adj. & s.* doble, duplicado; [djúpləkət] *v.* duplicar, copiar.

du·plic·i·ty [djuplísətɪ] *s.* duplicidad, doblez.

du·ra·ble [djúrəbl] *adj.* durable, duradero.

du·ra·tion [djʊréʃən] *s.* duración.

dur·ing [dúrɪŋ] *prep.* durante.

dusk [dʌsk] *s.* crepúsculo (*vespertino*), anochecida; caída de la tarde; sombra, oscuridad; **at**—al atardecer.

dusk·y [dʌ́skɪ] *adj.* obscuro, negruzco; sombrío.

dust [dʌst] *s.* polvo; tierra; **cloud of**—polvareda; *v.* sacudir el polvo, desempolvar, quitar el polvo; empolvar, llenar de polvo; espolvorear.

dust·er [dʌ́stə] *s.* limpiador; quitapolvo; **feather** — plumero.

dust·y [dʌ́stɪ] *adj.* polvoriento; empolvado, lleno de polvo.

Dutch [dʌtʃ] *adj. & s.* holandés; — **treat** convite a escote.

Dutch·man [dʌ́tʃmən] *s.* holandés.

du·ty [djútɪ] *s.* deber, obligación; derechos aduanales; impuesto; —**free** libre de derechos aduanales.

dwarf [dwɔrf] *s. & adj.* enano; *v.* achicar, empequeñecer; impedir el desarrollo o crecimiento de.

dwell [dwɛl] *v.* residir, morar, habitar vivir; **to** — **on a subject** espaciarse o dilatarse en un asunto.

dwell·er [dwɛ́lə] *s.* habitante, morador.

dwell·ing [dwɛ́lɪŋ] *s.* morada, habitación, domicilio.

dwelt [dwɛlt] *pret. & p.p. de* **to dwell.**

dwin·dle [dwíndl] *v.* menguar, mermar; disminuir(se); gastarse.

dye [daɪ] *s.* tinte, tintura; *v.* teñir, tinturar.

dy·er [dáɪə] *s.* tintorero; **-'s shop** tintorería.

dy·ing [dáɪŋ] *adj.* moribundo; agonizante.

dy·nam·ic [daɪnǽmɪk] *adj.* dinámico; enérgico; **-s** *s.* dinámica.

dy·na·mite [dáɪnəmaɪt] *s.* dinamita; *v.* dinamitar, volar con dinamita.

dy·na·mo [dáɪnəmo] *s.* dínamo.

dy·nas·ty [dáɪnəstɪ] *s.* dinastía.

dys·en·ter·y [dísn̩tɛrɪ] *s.* disentería.

E:e

each [itʃ] *adj.* cada; *pron.* cada uno; — **other** el uno al otro, uno(s) a otro(s).

ea·ger [ígə] *adj.* anhelante, ansioso; **-ly** *adv.* con anhelo; con ahínco; ansiosamente.

ea·ger·ness [ígənɪs] *s.* anhelo, ansia, deseo vehemente; ahinco; ardor.

ea·gle [ígl] *s.* águila.

ear [ɪr] *s.* (*outer*) oreja; (*hearing*) oído; —**drum** tímpano; — **muff** orejera; — **of corn** mazorca; — **of wheat** espiga; **by** — de oído; **within**—**shot** al alcance del oído.

earl [ɝl] *s.* conde.

ear·ly [ɝ́lɪ] *adv.* temprano; *adj.* temprano; primitivo, remoto; — **riser** madrugador, tempranero, mañanero; **at an** — **date** en fecha a próxima.

earn [ɝn] *v.* ganar; merecer.

ear·nest [ɝ́nɪst] *adj.* serio, formal; ardiente; **in** — en serio, con toda formalidad; de buena fe; **-ly** *adv.* seriamente; con ahínco; encarecidamente; ansiosamente.

ear·nest·ness [ɝ́nɪstnɪs] *s.* seriedad; celo; solicitud; sinceridad; **in all** — con todo ahínco; con toda formalidad; con toda sinceridad.

earn·ings [ɝ́nɪŋz] *s.* ganancias; sueldo, salario,

paga.
ear·ring [írrɪŋ] *s.* arete, zarcillo, pendiente, arracada; *C.A.* arito; *P.R.* pantalla.
earth [ʒθ] *s.* tierra; suelo.
earth·en [ʒθən] *adj.* de tierra; de barro.
earth·en·ware [ʒθənwɛr] *s.* loza de barro; trastos, cacharros.
earth·ly [ʒθlɪ] *adj.* terrenal, terrestre, mundano; terreno; **to be of no — use** no servir para nada.
earth·quake [ʒθkwek] *s.* terremoto, temblor de tierra.
earth·shak·ing [ʒθʃekɪŋ] *adj.* desmedido.
earth·worm [ʒθwʒm] *s.* lombriz.
ease [iz] *s.* (*facility*) facilidad; naturalidad; soltura; (*comfort*) comodidad; tranquilidad; **at —** tranquilo; cómodo; *v.* facilitar; aliviar; mitigar; tranquilizar; aligerar (*el peso*); aflojar.
ea·sel [ízl] *s.* caballete (*de pintor*).
eas·i·ly [ízəlɪ] *adv.* fácilmente; sin dificultad; cómodamente.
east [ist] *s.* este; oriente, levante; *adj.* del este, oriental; *adv.* al este, hacia el este; en el este.
East·er [ístəʳ] *s.* Pascuas, Pascua Florida; **— Sunday** Domingo de Resurrección o de Pascuas.
east·ern [ístəʳn] *adj.* oriental; del este.
east·ward [ístwəʳd] *adv.* & *adj.* hacia el este u oriente.
eas·y [ízɪ] *adj.* (*simple*) fácil; (*comfortable*) cómodo; tranquilo; **— chair** silla cómoda, poltrona, butaca; **easy-going man** hombre cachazudo o calmo; **at an — pace** a paso moderado; **within — reach** al alcance; a la mano.
eat [it] *v.* comer; **to — away** corroer, destruir; **to — breakfast** desayunarse, tomar el desayuno; **to — dinner** tomar la comida, comer; **to — supper** tomar la cena, cenar; **to — one's heart out** sufrir en silencio; **to — one's words** retractarse.
eat·en [ítn] *p.p.* de **to eat**.
eaves [ivz] *s. pl.* alero (*de un tejado*).
ebb [ɛb] *s.* reflujo; decadencia; **— tide** marea menguante; **to be at a low —** estar decaído; *v.* menguar, decaer.
eb·on·y [ɛbənɪ] *s.* ébano.
ec·cen·tric [ɪksɛntrɪk] *adj.* & *s.* excéntrico.
ec·cle·si·as·tic [ɪklizɪǽstɪk] *adj.* & *s.* eclesiástico.
ech·e·lon [ɛʃəlɑn] *s.* escalón.
ech·o [ɛko] *s.* eco; *v.* hacer eco, repetir; resonar, repercutir.
ec·lec·tic [ɪklɛktɪk] *adj.* ecléctico.
e·clipse [ɪklíps] *s.* eclipse; *v.* eclipsar.
ec·o·nom·ic [ɪkɑnámɪk] *adj.* económico.
ec·o·nom·i·cal [ɪkɑnámɪkl] *adj.* económico.
ec·o·nom·ics [ɪkɑnámɪks] *s.* economía política.
e·con·o·mist [ɪkɑnəmɪst] *s.* economista.
e·con·o·mize [ɪkɑnəmaɪz] *v.* economizar.
e·con·o·my [ɪkɑnəmɪ] *s.* economía; parsimonia.
e·con·o·my class [ɪkɑnəmɪ klæs] *s.* segunda clase en las líneas aéreas.
ec·sta·sy [ɛkstəsɪ] *s.* éxtasis.
ec·u·men·i·cal [ɛkjuménəkl] *adj.* ecuménico.
ed·dy [ɛdɪ] *s.* remolino; *v.* arremolinarse.
E·den [ídn] *s.* Edén; paraíso.
edge [ɛdʒ] *s.* orilla, borde; filo; **to be on —** estar nervioso.
edge·wise [ɛdʒwaɪz] *adv.* de lado; de filo.
ed·i·ble [ɛdəbl] *adj.* & *s.* comestible.
ed·i·fice [ɛdəfɪs] *s.* edificio.
ed·i·fy [ɛdəfaɪ] *v.* edificar (*moral, espiritualmente*).
ed·it [ɛdɪt] *v.* redactar; preparar o corregir (*un manuscrito*) para la imprenta; cuidar (*una edición*).

e·di·tion [ɪdíʃən] *s.* edición.
ed·i·tor [ɛdɪtəʳ] *s.* redactor; director de un periódico; revisor (*de manuscritos*).
ed·i·to·ri·al [ɛdətóriəl] *adj.* editorial; *s.* editorial (*m.*), artículo de fondo.
ed·i·to·ri·al·ize [ɛdɪtóriəlaɪz] *v.* expresar opiniones como en artículo de fondo; editorializar.
ed·u·cate [ɛdʒəket] *v.* educar; instruir.
ed·u·ca·tion [ɛdʒəkéʃən] *s.* educación; crianza; instrucción, enseñanza; pedagogía.
ed·u·ca·tion·al [ɛdʒəkéʃənl] *adj.* educativo, docente; pedagógico.
ed·u·ca·tor [ɛdʒəketəʳ] *s.* educador.
eel [il] *s.* anguila.
ef·fect [əfɛkt] *s.* efecto; **-s** bienes, efectos; **to go into —** hacerse vigente, ponerse en operación (*una ley*); *v.* efectuar; ejecutar; realizar.
ef·fec·tive [əfɛktɪv] *adj.* efectivo, eficaz; vigente (*una ley*); **-ly** *adv.* eficazmente.
ef·fec·tu·al [əfɛktʃʊəl] *adj.* eficaz.
ef·fem·i·nate [əfɛmənɪt] *adj.* afeminado.
ef·fete [ɪfít] *adj.* gastado; estéril; decadente.
ef·fi·ca·cy [ɛfəkəsɪ] *s.* eficacia.
ef·fi·cien·cy [əfíʃəsɪ] *s.* eficiencia; eficacia.
ef·fi·cient [əfíʃənt] *adj.* eficiente; eficaz.
ef·fi·gy [ɛfɪdʒɪ] *s.* efigie; **to burn in —** quemar en efigie.
ef·fort [ɛfəʳt] *s.* esfuerzo; empeño; conato.
ef·front·er·y [əfrántərɪ] *s.* descaro, desvergüenza, desfachatez.
ef·fu·sive [ɛfúsɪv] *adj.* efusivo, demostrativo, expansivo.
egg [ɛg] *s.* huevo; **fried —** huevo frito o estrellado; **hard-boiled —** huevo cocido, huevo duro; **scrambled -s** huevos revueltos; **soft-boiled —** huevo pasado por agua; *Mex.* huevo tibio; *v.* **to — on** incitar.
egg·nog [ɛgnag] *s.* rompopo.
egg·plant [ɛgplænt] *s.* berenjena.
e·go·cen·tric [igoséntrɪk] *adj.* egocéntrico.
e·go·tism [ígətɪzəm] *s.* egotismo; egoísmo.
E·gyp·tian [ɪdʒípʃən] *adj.* & *s.* egipcio.
ei·ther [íðəʳ] *adj.* & *pron.* uno u otro; **— of the two** cualquiera de los dos; **in — case** en ambos casos; *adv.* tampoco; **nor I —** ni yo tampoco; *conj.* o.
e·jac·u·late [ɪdʒǽkjulet] *v.* eyacular.
e·ject [ɪdʒɛkt] *v.* echar, arrojar, expulsar.
e·jec·tion [ɪdʒɛkʃən] *s.* expulsión; **— seat** asiento lanzable.
e·lab·o·rate [ɪlǽbərɪt] *adj.* elaborado, primoroso; esmerado; [ɪlǽbəret] *v.* elaborar.
e·lapse [ɪlǽps] *v.* transcurrir, pasar.
e·las·tic [ɪlǽstɪk] *adj.* elástico; *s.* elástico; goma elástica; cordón elástico; liga elástica.
e·las·tic·i·ty [ɪlæstísətɪ] *s.* elasticidad.
e·lat·ed [ɪlétɪd] *adj.* exaltado, gozoso, alborozado.
el·bow [ɛlbo] *s.* codo; recodo, ángulo; **to be within — reach** estar a la mano; *v.* codear, dar codazos; **to — one's way through** abrirse paso a codazos.
eld·er [ɛldəʳ] *adj.* mayor, más grande, más viejo, de más edad; *s.* mayor; anciano; dignatario (*en ciertas iglesias*); **our -s** nuestros mayores; nuestros antepasados.
el·der·ly [ɛldəʳlɪ] *adj.* viejo, anciano.
el·dest [ɛldɪst] *adj.* mayor.
e·lect [ɪlɛkt] *adj.* & *s.* electo; elegido; *v.* elegir.
e·lec·tion [ɪlɛkʃən] *s.* elección.
e·lec·tor [ɪlɛktəʳ] *s.* elector.
e·lec·tor·al [ɪlɛktərəl] *adj.* electoral.
e·lec·tric [ɪlɛktrɪk] *adj.* eléctrico; **— meter**

electrómetro, contador eléctrico; — **storm** tronada, tempestad; — **eye** ojo eléctrico; s. tranvía o ferrocarril eléctrico.

e·lec·tri·cal [ɪléktrɪkl̩] *adj.* eléctrico; — **engineering** electrotecnia, ingeniería eléctrica; — **engineer** ingeniero electricista; electrotécnico.

e·lec·tri·cian [ɪlektríʃən] *s.* electricista.

e·lec·tric·i·ty [ɪlektrísətɪ] *s.* electricidad.

e·lec·tri·fy [ɪléktrəfaɪ] *v.* electrizar; electrificar.

e·lec·tro·car·di·o·graph [ɪlektrokárdɪəgræf] *s.* electrocardiógrafo.

e·lec·tro·cute [ɪléktrəkjut] *v.* electrocutar.

e·lec·trol·y·sis [ilektrálɪsɪs] *s.* electrolisis.

e·lec·tro·mag·net [ɪlektromǽgnət] *s.* electroimán.

e·lec·tron [ɪléktrɑn] *s.* electrón; — **microscope** microscopio electrónico.

e·lec·tron·ics [ɪlektrɑ́nɪks] *s.* electrónica.

el·e·gance [ɛ́ləgəns] *s.* elegancia.

el·e·gant [ɛ́ləgənt] *adj.* elegante.

el·e·ment [ɛ́ləmənt] *s.* elemento.

el·e·men·tal [ɛləméntl̩] *adj.* elemental.

el·e·men·ta·ry [ɛləméntərɪ] *adj.* elemental.

el·e·phant [ɛ́ləfənt] *s.* elefante.

el·e·vate [ɛ́ləvet] *v.* elevar; alzar, levantar.

el·e·va·tion [ɛləvéʃən] *s.* elevación; altura; exaltación.

el·e·va·tor [ɛ́ləvetɚ] *s.* ascensor, *Am.* elevador; **grain** — almacén de granos.

e·lic·it[ɪlísɪt] *v.* extraer, sonsacar; **to** — **admiration** despertar admiración; **to** — **applause** suscitar el aplauso o los aplausos.

el·i·gi·ble [ɛ́lɪdʒəbl̩] *adj.* elegible.

e·lim·i·nate [ɪlímənet] *v.* eliminar.

e·lim·i·na·tion [ɪlɪmənéʃən] *s.* eliminación.

e·lite [ɛlít] *s.* lo selecto; los selectos; los escogidos.

elk [ɛlk] *s.* ante.

el·lip·tic [ɪlíptɪk] *adj.* elíptico.

elm [ɛlm] *s.* olmo.

e·lope [ɪlóp] *v.* fugarse (*con su novio*).

el·o·quence [ɛ́ləkwəns] *s.* elocuencia.

el·o·quent [ɛ́ləkwənt] *adj.* elocuente.

else [ɛls] *adj.* & *adv.* otro (*úsase sólo en ciertas combinaciones*); más, además; **or** — de otro modo; si no; **nobody** — ningún otro; **nothing** — nada más; **somebody** — algún otro, otra persona; **what** —? ¿ qué más?

else·where [ɛ́lshwɛr] *adv.* en otra parte, a otra parte.

e·lu·ci·date [ɪlúsədet] *v.* elucidar, esclarecer, aclarar, clarificar.

e·lu·ci·da·tion [ɪlusədéʃən] *s.* elucidación, esclarecimiento, explicación.

e·lude [ɪlúd] *v.* eludir, evadir.

e·lu·sive [ɪlúsɪv] *adj.* evasivo; que elude.

e·ma·ci·at·ed [ɪméʃietɪd] *v.* demacrado, escuálido, macilento.

em·a·nate [ɛ́mənet] *v.* emanar, brotar.

em·a·na·tion [ɛmənéʃən] *s.* emanación; efluvio.

e·man·ci·pate [ɪmǽnsəpet] *v.* emancipar.

e·man·ci·pa·tion [ɪmǽnsəpéʃən] *s.* emancipación.

em·balm [ɪmbám] *v.* embalsamar.

em·bank·ment [ɪmbǽŋkmənt] *s.* terraplén; dique.

em·bar·go [ɪmbárgo] *s.* embargo; prohibición; **to put an** — **on** embargar.

em·bark [ɪmbárk] *v.* embarcar(se).

em·bar·rass [ɪmbǽrəs] *v.* turbar, desconcertar; apenar; avergonzar; embarazar; **to be financially** -**ed** encontrarse escaso de fondos.

em·bar·rass·ing [ɪmbǽrəsɪŋ] *adj.* embarazoso, penoso; desconcertante; angustioso.

em·bar·rass·ment [ɪmbǽrəsmənt] *s.* turbación,

vergüenza, desconcierto; aprieto, apuro, dificultad; estorbo, embarazo.

em·bas·sy [ɛ́mbəsɪ] *s.* embajada.

em·bel·lish [ɪmbélɪʃ] *v.* embellecer, hermosear.

em·ber [ɛ́mbɚ] *s.* ascua; -**s** ascuas, rescoldo.

em·bez·zle [ɪmbézl̩] *v.* desfalcar.

em·bez·zle·ment [ɪmbézl̩mənt] *s.* desfalco, peculado.

em·bit·ter [ɪmbítɚ] *v.* amargar.

em·blem [ɛ́mbləm] *s.* emblema.

em·bod·y [ɪmbádɪ] *v.* encarnar, dar cuerpo a; incorporar, abarcar.

em·boss [ɪmbɔ́s] *v.* realzar, grabar en relieve.

em·brace [ɪmbrés] *s.* abrazo; *v.* abrazar(se); abarcar.

em·broi·der [ɪmbrɔ́ɪdɚ] *v.* bordar; recamar; ornar, embellecer.

em·broi·der·y [ɪmbrɔ́ɪdərɪ] *s.* bordado; bordadura; recamo.

em·bry·o [ɛ́mbrɪo] *s.* embrión.

em·er·ald [ɛ́mərəld] *s.* esmeralda.

e·merge [ɪmɚ́dʒ] *v.* emerger; surtir.

e·mer·gen·cy [ɪmɚ́dʒənsɪ] *s.* caso fortuito; aprieto; urgencia; emergencia.

em·i·grant [ɛ́məgrənt] *adj.* & *s.* emigrante.

em·i·grate [ɛ́məgret] *v.* emigrar.

em·i·gra·tion [ɛməgréʃən] *s.* emigración.

em·i·nence [ɛ́mənəns] *s.* eminencia.

em·i·nent [ɛ́mənənt] *adj.* eminente.

e·mit [ɪmít] *v.* emitir; exhalar, arrojar; despedir (*olor, humo, etc.*).

e·mo·tion [ɪmóʃən] *s.* emoción.

e·mo·tion·al [ɪmóʃənl̩] *adj.* emocional; emotivo; sentimental; sensible.

em·pa·thy [ɛ́mpəθɪ] *s.* empatía.

em·per·or [ɛ́mpərɚ] *s.* emperador.

em·pha·sis [ɛ́mfəsɪs] *s.* énfasis.

em·pha·size [ɛ́mfəsaɪz] *v.* dar énfasis; hacer hincapié en; subrayar, recalcar; acentuar.

em·phat·ic [ɪmfǽtɪk] *adj.* enfático; recalcado; -**ally** *adv.* enfáticamente.

em·phy·se·ma [ɛmfəsímə] *s.* enfisema.

em·pire [ɛ́mpaɪr] *s.* imperio.

em·pir·i·cal [ɛmpírəkl̩] *adj.* empírico.

em·ploy [ɪmplɔ́ɪ] *v.* emplear; dar empleo a; ocupar; **to be in his** — ser su empleado; trabajar a sus órdenes.

em·ploy·ee [ɪmplɔ́ɪ] *s.* empleado.

em·ploy·er [ɪmplɔ́ɪɚ] *s.* patrón, amo, principal.

em·ploy·ment [ɪmplɔ́ɪmənt] *s.* empleo; ocupación.

em·pow·er [ɪmpáuɚ] *v.* autorizar; apoderar (*dar poder a un abogado*).

em·press [ɛ́mprɪs] *s.* emperatriz.

emp·ti·ness [ɛ́mptɪnɪs] *s.* vaciedad; futilidad, vanidad.

emp·ty [ɛ́mptɪ] *adj.* vacío; vacante, desocupado; vano; *v.* vaciar; desaguar, desembocar.

emp·ty-hand·ed [ɛmptɪhǽndɪd] *adj.* con las manos vacías; sin posesión.

em·u·late [ɛ́mjʊlet] *v.* emular.

en·a·ble [ɪnébl̩] *v.* capacitar, hacer capaz; habilitar; dar poder; facilitar; hacer posible.

en·act [ɪnǽkt] *v.* decretar, promulgar; hacer el papel de.

en·am·el [ɪnǽml̩] *s.* esmalte; *v.* esmaltar.

en·am·or [ɪnǽmɚ] *v.* enamorar, mover a amar; encantar; **to be** -**ed of** estar enamorado de.

en·camp [ɪnkǽmp] *v.* acampar.

en·chant [ɪntʃǽnt] *v.* encantar; embelesar; hechizar.

en·chant·er [ɪntʃǽntɚ] *s.* encantador; hechicero, mago, brujo.

en·chant·ment [ɪntʃǽntmənt] *s.* encanto;

encantamiento; hechicería.
en·chant·ress [ɪntʃǽntrɪs] s. encantadora;
  hechicera, bruja.
en·cir·cle [ɪnsɚ́kl̩] v. cercar, rodear, ceñir.
en·clit·ic [enklítɪk] adj. enclítico.
en·close [ɪnklóz] v. encerrar; cercar, rodear,
  circundar; incluir.
en·clo·sure [ɪnklóʒɚ] s. recinto, cercado, vallado;
  remesa, lo remitido (dentro de una carta), lo
  adjunto; encerramiento.
en·com·pass [ɪnkʌ́mpəs] v. abarcar; encuadrar;
  rodear, ceñir, circundar.
en·coun·ter [ɪnkáʊntɚ] s. encuentro; combate; v.
  encontrar(se); encontrarse con; tropezar con.
en·cour·age [ɪnkɚ́ɪdʒ] v. alentar, animar; fomentar.
en·cour·age·ment [ɪnkɚ́ɪdʒmənt] s. aliento, ánimo;
  estímulo; fomento.
en·croach [ɪnkrótʃ] v. **to — upon** usurpar, invadir,
  meterse en; quitar (el tiempo).
en·cum·ber [ɛnkʌ́mbɚ] v. impedir; estorbar.
en·cy·clo·pe·di·a [ɪnsaɪkləpídɪə] s. enciclopedia.
end [ɛnd] s. (temporal) fin; cabo; término; (spatial)
  término; extremo; **no — of things** un sin fin de
  cosas; **odds and -s** retazos; **on —** de punta; **to
  put an — to** acabar con, poner fin a; v. acabar;
  terminar; concluir, dar fin.
en·dan·ger [ɪndéndʒɚ] v. poner en peligro,
  arriesgar.
en·dear [ɪndír] v. hacer amar, hacer querer; **to —
  oneself** hacerse querer.
en·deav·or [ɪndévɚ] s. esfuerzo, empeño; tentativa;
  tarea; v. procurar, tratar de, intentar; esforzarse
  por o en.
en·dem·ic [ɛndémɪk] adj. endémico.
end·ing [éndɪŋ] s. final; terminación; conclusión.
end·less [éndlɪs] adj. sin fin, interminable,
  inacabable; eterno.
en·dorse [ɛndórs] v. endosar; repaldar; apoyar,
  garanitzar.
en·dorse·ment [ɛndórsmənt] s. (signature) endose,
  endoso; (backing) respaldo; garantía, apoyo.
en·dors·er [ɛndórsɚ] s. endosante.
en·dow [ɪndáʊ] v. dotar.
en·dow·ment [ɪndáʊmənt] s. dotación; dote, don.
en·dur·ance [ɪndjúrəns] s. resistencia, aguante;
  paciencia; duración.
en·dure [ɪndjúr] v. aguantar, soportar, sufrir; durar,
  perdurar.
en·e·ma [énəmə] s. lavativa.
en·e·my [énəmɪ] s. enemigo.
en·er·get·ic [enɚdʒétɪk] adj. enérgico.
en·er·gy [énɚdʒɪ] s. energía.
en·er·vate [énɚvet] v. enervar, debilitar.
en·fold = **infold.**
en·force [ɪnfórs] v. dar fuerza a; hacer cumplir
  (una ley); **to — obedience** hacer obedecer,
  imponer obediencia.
en·force·ment [ɪnfórsmənt] s. coacción;
  cumplimiento forzoso (de una ley).
en·gage [ɪngédʒ] v. (employ) ocupar; emplear;
  contratar; (reserve) alquilar; (attract) atraer;
  (mesh) engranar, acoplar; **to — in battle** trabar
  batalla; **to — (oneself) to do it** comprometerse a
  hacerlo; **to be -ed in something** estar ocupado en
  algo; **to be -ed to be married** estar comprometido
  para casarse.
en·gage·ment [ɪngédʒmənt] s. compromiso; cita;
  noviazgo; convenio, contrato; pelea; traba,
  engrane, acoplamiento (de maquinaria).
en·gen·der [ɪndʒéndɚ] v. engendrar, producir.
en·gine [éndʒən] s. máquina; motor; locomotora.

en·gi·neer [endʒənír] s. ingeniero; maquinista (de
  locomotora); v. dirigir, planear.
en·gi·neer·ing [endʒəníriŋ] s. ingeniería; manejo,
  planeo.
Eng·lish [íŋglɪʃ] adj. inglés; s. inglés, idioma inglés;
  the — los ingleses.
Eng·lish·man [íŋglɪʃmən] s. inglés.
en·grave [ɪngrév] v. grabar, esculpir.
en·grav·ing [ɪngrévɪŋ] s. grabado; estampa, lámina;
  wood — grabado en madera.
en·gross [ɛngrós] v. absorber; redactar en limpio.
en·grossed [ɪngróst] adj. absorto, ensimismado.
en·gulf [ɪngʌ́lf] v. engolfar, absorber, tragar.
en·hance [ɪnhǽns] v. realzar; engrandecer.
e·nig·ma [ɪnígmə] s. enigma.
en·join [ɪndʒóɪn] v. mandar, ordenar; **to — from**
  prohibir, vedar.
en·joy [ɪndʒóɪ] v. gozar de; disfrutar de; **to —
  oneself** divertirse, gozar, deleitarse; **to — the use
  of** usufructuar.
en·joy·a·ble [ɪndʒóɪəbl̩] adj. agradable, deleitable.
en·joy·ment [ɪndʒóɪmənt] s. placer, goce; disfrute;
  usufructo.
en·large [ɪnlárdʒ] v. agrandar(se); ensanchar;
  ampliar; **to — upon** explayarse en, extenderse
  en; comentar.
en·large·ment [ɪnlárdʒmənt] s. (photo) ampliación;
  ensanchamiento.
en·light·en [ɪnláɪtn̩] v. alumbrar; iluminar; ilustrar,
  instruir.
en·list [ɪnlíst] v. alistar(se); sentar plaza (de
  soldado); reclutar.
en·list·ment [ɪnlístmənt] s. reclutamiento;
  alistamiento.
en·li·ven [ɪnláɪvən] v. avivar, animar, alegrar.
en·mi·ty [énmətɪ] s. enemistad.
en·no·ble [ɪnóbl̩] v. ennoblecer.
e·nor·mous [ɪnórməs] adj. enorme.
e·nough [ənʌ́f] adj. & adv. bastante; s. lo bastante,
  lo suficiente; **that is —** eso basta, con eso basta;
  —! ¡basta!
en·quire = **inquire.**
en·rage [ɪnrédʒ] v. enrabiar, hacer rabiar; enfurecer.
en·rap·ture [ɪnrǽptʃɚ] v. extasiar, embelesar,
  enajenar.
en·rich [ɪnrítʃ] v. enriquecer.
en·roll [ɪnról] v. alistar(se); matricular(se);
  inscribir(se); hacerse miembro.
en·roll·ment [ɪnrólmənt] s. alistamiento; registro,
  matrícula.
en·sem·ble [ansámbl̩] s. (music) conjunto musical;
  (dress) traje armonioso.
en·sign [énsn̩] s. alférez (de la marina); [énsaɪn]
  bandera; insignia.
en·slave [ɪnslév] v. esclavizar.
en·snare [ɪnsnér] v. enredar, entrampar, embaucar.
en·sue [ɛnsú] v. sobrevenir, seguir(se), resultar.
en·tail [ɪntél] v. envolver, ocasionar; vincular (una
  herencia).
en·tan·gle [ɪntǽŋgl̩] v. enredar, enmarañar,
  embrollar.
en·ter [éntɚ] v. entrar; ingresar en; asentar (una
  partida, cantidad, etc.); registrar; salir (al
  escenario).
en·ter·prise [éntɚpraɪz] s. empresa.
en·ter·pris·ing [éntɚpraɪzɪŋ] adj. emprendedor.
en·ter·tain [entɚtén] v. divertir; agasajar;
  obsequiar; banquetear; acariciar (una idea);
  abrigar (una esperanza, un rencor); **she -s a great
  deal** es muy fiestera u obsequiosa.
en·ter·tain·ing [entɚténɪŋ] adj. entretenido,

EL

divertido, chistoso.

en·ter·tain·ment [ɛntərténmənt] *s.* entretenimiento; pasatiempo; diversión; fiesta; convite.

en·thu·si·asm [ɪnθjúzɪæzəm] *s.* entusiasmo.

en·thu·si·ast [ɪnθjúzɪæst] *s.* entusiasta.

en·thu·si·as·tic [ɪnθjuzɪǽstɪk] *adj.* entusiasta, entusiástico; **to be** — estar entusiasmado.

en·tice [ɪntáɪs] *v.* atraer, tentar, seducir, halagar.

en·tire [ɪntáɪr] *adj.* entero, cabal; **the** — **world** todo el mundo; **-ly** *adv.* enteramente, por entero.

en·tire·ty [ɪntáɪrtɪ] *s.* totalidad, entereza; conjunto; todo.

en·ti·tle [ɪntáɪtl̩] *v.* titular, intitular; autorizar, dar derecho.

en·ti·ty [ɛntətɪ] *s.* entidad; ente, ser.

en·trails [ɛntrəlz] *s. pl.* entrañas; tripas.

en·trance [ɛntrəns] *s.* entrada; ingreso.

en·treat [ɪntrít] *v.* suplicar, rogar; instar.

en·treat·y [ɪntrítɪ] *s.* súplica, ruego; instancia.

en·trench = **intrench.**

en·trust [ɪntrʌst] *v.* confiar; depositar, entregar.

en·try [ɛntrɪ] *s.* entrada; ingreso; partida, registro, anotación; **double** — partida doble (*en teneduría*).

e·nu·mer·ate [ɪnjúməret] *v.* enumerar.

e·nun·ci·ate [ɪnʌ́nsɪet] *v.* articular; enunciar, declarar.

en·vel·op [ɪnvéləp] *v.* envolver.

en·ve·lope [ɛnvəlop] *s.* sobre, cubierta (*de una carta*).

en·vi·a·ble [ɛnvɪəbl̩] *adj.* envidiable.

en·vi·ous [ɛnvɪəs] *adj.* envidioso.

en·vi·ron·ment [ɪnváɪrənmənt] *s.* ambiente, medio ambiente.

en·vi·rons [ɪnváɪrənz] *s. pl.* cercanías, contornos, alrededores.

en·vis·age [ɛnvízɪdʒ] *v.* prever; encararse con.

en·voy [ɛnvɔɪ] *s.* enviado.

en·vy [ɛnvɪ] *v.* envidia; *v.* envidiar.

e·phem·er·al [ɪfémərəl] *adj.* efímero.

ep·ic [ɛ́pɪk] *s.* epopeya, poema, épico; *adj.* épico.

ep·i·dem·ic [ɛpədémɪk] *s.* epidemia; peste; *adj.* epidémico.

ep·i·logue [ɛ́pəlɔg] *s.* epílogo.

E·piph·a·ny [ɪpífənɪ] *s*— Epifanía.

ep·i·sode [ɛ́pəsod] *s.* episodio.

e·pis·tle [ɪpísl̩] *s.* epístola, carta.

ep·i·taph [ɛ́pətæf] *s.* epitafio.

e·pit·o·me [ɪpítəmɪ] *s.* epítome.

ep·och [ɛ́pək] *s.* época.

e·qual [íkwəl] *adj.* igual; **to be** — **to a task** ser competente (*o* tener suficientes fuerzas) para una tarea; *s.* igual, cantidad igual; *v.* igualar; ser igual a; **-ly** *adv.* igualmente; por igual.

e·qual·i·ty [íkwálətɪ] *s.* igualdad.

e·qual·ize [íkwəlaɪz] *v.* igualar; emparejar; equilibrar; nivelar.

e·qua·tion [ɪkwéʒən] *s.* ecuación.

e·qua·tor [ɪkwétə·] *s.* ecuador.

e·qui·lib·ri·um [ikwəlíbrɪəm] *s.* equilibrio.

e·quip [ɪkwíp] *v.* equipar; proveer; habilitar.

e·quip·ment [ɪkwípmənt] *s.* equipo; aparatos; avíos; habilitación.

eq·ui·ta·ble [ɛ́kwɪtəbl̩] *adj.* equitativo.

eq·ui·ty [ɛ́kwətɪ] *s.* equidad; justicia.

e·quiv·a·lent [ɪkwívələnt] *adj. & s.* equivalente.

e·quiv·o·cal [ɪkwívəkl̩] *adj.* equívoco, ambiguo.

e·ra [írə] *s.* era, época.

e·rad·i·cate [ɪrǽdɪket] *v.* desarraigar, extirpar.

e·rase [ɪrés] *v.* borrar; tachar.

e·ras·er [ɪrésə·] *s.* goma, *Am.* borrador; **blackboard** — cepillo.

e·ra·sure [ɪréʃə·] *s.* borradura, raspadura.

ere [ɛr] *prep.* antes de; *conj.* antes (de) que.

e·rect [ɪrɛ́kt] *adj.* erguido; derecho; levantado; *Am.* parado; *v.* erigir; levantar, alzar.

er·mine [ɝ́mɪn] *s.* armiño.

e·rode [ɪród] *v.* erosionar.

e·ro·sion [ɪróʒən] *s.* erosión; desgaste.

e·rot·ic [ɪrátɪk] *adj.* erótico.

err [ɝ] *v.* errar; equivocarse; descarriarse.

er·rand [ɛ́rənd] *s.* mandado, recado, encargo; — **boy** mandadero.

er·rant [ɛ́rənt] *adj.* errante; **knight-errant** caballero andante.

er·rat·ic [ɛrǽtɪk] *adj.* inconstante errático; vagabundo.

er·ro·ne·ous [ərónɪəs] *adj.* erróneo, errado.

er·ror [ɛ́rə·] *s.* error.

er·u·di·tion [ɛrʊdíʃən] *s.* erudición.

e·rupt [ɪrʌ́pt] *v.* arrojar.

e·rup·tion [ɪrʌ́pʃən] *s.* erupción.

es·ca·late [ɛ́skəlet] *v.* aumentar; intensificar.

es·ca·pade [ɛ́skəped] *s.* trapisonda, travesura.

es·cape [əskép] *s.* escape; fuga, huída; escapada; escapatoria; *v.* escapar(se); fugarse; huir(se); eludir, evadir; **it** — **s me** se me escapa.

es·cort [ɛ́skɔrt] *s.* escolta; acompañante; convoy; [ɪskɔ́rt] *v.* escoltar; convoyar; acompañar.

es·cutch·eon [ɪskʌ́tʃən] *s.* escudo de armas, blasón.

Es·ki·mo [ɛ́skəmo] *s.* esquimal.

es·pe·cial [əspéʃəl] *adj.* especial; **-ly** *adv.* especialmente.

es·pi·o·nage [ɛ́spɪənɪdʒ] *s.* espionaje.

es·pouse [əspáʊs] *v.* patrocinar; casarse.

es·say [ɛ́se] *s.* ensayo; [ɛsé] *v.* ensayar.

es·sence [ɛ́sn̩s] *s.* esencia.

es·sen·tial [əsɛ́nʃəl] *adj.* esencial.

es·tab·lish [əstǽblɪʃ] *v.* establecer.

es·tab·lish·ment [əstǽblɪʃmənt] *s.* establecimiento.

es·tate [əstét] *s.* hacienda, heredad; bienes, propiedades; estado, condición; **country** — finca rural.

es·teem [əstím] *s.* estima, estimación, aprecio; *v.* estimar, apreciar; considerar, juzgar.

es·ti·ma·ble [ɛ́stəməbl̩] *adj.* estimable.

es·ti·mate [ɛ́stəmɪt] *s.* (*calculation*) tasa, cálculo aproximado; presupuesto; (*judgment*) opinión; [ɛ́stəmet] *v.* estimar, tasar, calcular aproximadamente; hacer un presupuesto; juzgar, opinar.

es·ti·ma·tion [ɛstəméʃən] *s.* juicio, opinión; estima; estimación.

es·trange [əstréndʒ] *v.* enajenar; apartar.

es·tu·ar·y [ɛ́stʃʊɛrɪ] *s.* estuario o estero, desembocadura de un rio.

etch [ɛtʃ] *v.* grabar al agua fuerte.

etch·ing [ɛ́tʃɪŋ] *s.* agua fuerte, grabado al agua fuerte.

e·ter·nal [ɪtɝ́nl̩] *adj.* eterno.

e·ter·ni·ty [ɪtɝ́nətɪ] *s.* eternidad.

e·ther [íθə·] *s.* éter.

e·the·re·al [ɪθírɪəl] *adj.* etéreo.

eth·i·cal [ɛ́θɪkl̩] *adj.* ético, moral.

eth·ics [ɛ́θɪks] *s.* ética, moral.

eth·nic [ɛ́θnɪk] *adj.* étnico.

eth·nol·o·gy [ɛθnáptədʒɪ] *s.* etnología.

et·i·quette [ɛ́tɪkɛt] *s.* etiqueta (*regla de conducta social*).

et·y·mol·o·gy [ɛtəmáladʒɪ] *s.* etimología.

eu·ca·lyp·tus [jukəlíptəs] *s.* eucalipto.

Eu·cha·rist [júkərɪst] *s.* Eucaristía.

eu·phe·mism [júfəmɪzm̩] *s.* eufemismo.

eu·pho·ri·a [jufórɪə] s. euforia.
Eu·ro·pe·an [jʊrəpíən] adj. & s. europeo.
e·vac·u·ate [ɪvǽkjʊet] v. evacuar; desocupar.
e·vade [ɪvéd] v. evadir.
e·val·u·ate [ɪvǽljʊet] v. valorar, avaluar.
e·vap·o·rate [ɪvǽpəret] v. evaporar(se).
e·vap·o·ra·tion [ɪvæpəréʃən] s. evaporación.
e·va·sion [ɪvéʒən] s. evasión, evasiva.
e·va·sive [ɪvésɪv] adj. evasivo.
eve [iv] s. víspera, vigilia; **Christmas Eve**
   Nochebuena; **New Year's Eve** víspera del Año
   Nuevo; **on the — of** en vísperas de.
e·ven [ívən] adj. (level) liso, plano, llano, a nivel;
   (same) parejo; uniforme; igual; — **dozen** docena
   cabal; — **number** número par; — **temper** genio
   apacible; **to be — with someone** estar mano a
   mano (o estar a mano) con alguien; **to get —**
   with someone desquitarse de alguien; adv. aun,
   hasta; — **if** (o — **though**) aun cuando; — **so** aun
   así; **not** — ni siquiera, ni aun; v. allanar;
   nivelar(se); igualar(se); emparejar; **-ly** adv.
   igualmente; de un modo igual; con uniformidad;
   con suavidad.
eve·ning [ívnɪŋ] s. tarde; atardecer; noche (las
   primeras horas); — **gown** vestido de etiqueta; —
   star estrella vespertina, lucero de la tarde.
e·ven·ness [ívənnɪs] s. lisura; igualdad; — **of**
   temper apacibilidad o suavidad de genio.
e·vent [ɪvént] s. suceso, acontecimiento; incidente,
   evento; resultado, coneecuencia; **in any** — en
   todo caso; **in the — of** en caso de.
e·vent·ful [ɪvéntfəl] adj. lleno de sucesos;
   importante, memorable.
e·ven·tu·al [ɪvéntʃʊəl] adj. eventual; último, final,
   terminal; **-ly** adv. finalmente, por fin, con el
   tiempo; eventualmente.
ev·er [ɛvɚ] adv. siempre; jamás; alguna vez; — **so**
   much muchísimo; **for** — **and** — por (o para)
   siempre jamás; **hardly** — casi nunca, apenas; **if**
   — si alguna vez; **more than** — más que nunca;
   the best friend I — **had** el mejor amigo que en
   mi vida he tenido.
ev·er·green [ɛvɚgrin] s. siempreviva, sempiterna;
   adj. siempre verde.
ev·er·last·ing [ɛvɚlǽstɪŋ] adj. sempiterno, eterno,
   perpetuo; duradero; s. eternidad; sempiterna;
   (planta); siempreviva; perpetua, flor perpetua.
ev·er·more [ɛvɚmór] adv. para siempre; **for** —
   para siempre jamás.
eve·ry [ɛvrɪ] adj. cada; todo; todos los, todas las;
   — **bit of it** todo, todito; — **day** todos los días;
   — **once in a while** de vez en cuando; — **one of**
   them todos ellos; — **other day** cada dos días, un
   día sí y otro no.
eve·ry·bod·y [ɛvrɪbadɪ] pron. todos, todo el
   mundo.
eve·ry·day [ɛvrɪdé] adj. diario, cuotidiano, de todos
   los días; ordinario.
eve·ry·one [ɛvrɪwʌn] pron. todos; todo el mundo;
   cada uno.
eve·ry·thing [ɛvrɪθɪŋ] pron. todo.
eve·ry·where [ɛvrɪhwɛr] adv. por (o en) todas
   partes; a todas partes.
e·vict [ɪvíkt] v. desalojar; expulsar.
ev·i·dence [ɛvədəns] s. evidencia; prueba;
   demostración, señal; testimonio; **to be in** —
   mostrarse; v. hacer evidente, evidenciar;
   patentizar, revelar, mostrar.
ev·i·dent [ɛvədənt] adj. evidente, patente.
e·vil [ívl] adj. malo, malvado, maligno; aciago, de
   mal agüero; **to cast the** — **eye** aojar; **the Evil**

One el Diablo; s. mal; maldad; adv. mal.
e·vil·do·er [ívldúɚ] s. malhechor.
e·voke [ɪvók] v. evocar; **to — laughter** provocar a
   risa.
ev·o·lu·tion [ɛvəlúʃən] s. evolución.
e·volve [ɪválv] v. desarrollar(se), desenvolver(se);
   urdir; evolucionar.
ewe [ju] s. oveja.
ex·act [ɪgzǽkt] adj. exacto; v. exigir; **-ly** adv.
   exactamente; en punto.
ex·act·ing [ɪgzǽktɪŋ] adj. exigente.
ex·ag·ger·ate [ɪgzǽdʒəret] v. exagerar.
ex·alt [ɪgzólt] v. exaltar, ensalzar.
ex·al·ta·tion [ɛgzɔltéʃən] s. exaltación.
ex·am·i·na·tion [ɪgzæmənéʃən] s. examen;
   reconocimiento (médico).
ex·am·ine [ɪgzǽmɪn] v. examinar; reconocer (dícese
   del médico).
ex·am·ple [ɪgzǽmpl] s. ejemplo.
ex·as·per·ate [ɪgzǽspəret] v. exasperar, irritar.
ex·ca·vate [ɛkskəvet] v. excavar.
ex·ca·va·tor [ɛkskəvetɚ] s. excavadora.
ex·ceed [ɪksíd] v. exceder; sobrepasar; propasarse.
ex·ceed·ing·ly [ɪksídɪŋlɪ] adv. sumamente,
   extremamente; — **well** extremamente bien.
ex·cel [ɪksɛl] v. sobresalir (en o entre); sobrepujar
   (a).
ex·cel·lence [ɛksləns] s. excelencia.
ex·cel·len·cy [ɛkslənsɪ] s. excelencia.
ex·cel·lent [ɛkslənt] adj. excelente.
ex·cept [ɪksɛpt] prep. excepto, menos; v. exceptuar.
ex·cept·ing [ɪksɛptɪŋ] prep. excepto, salvo, menos,
   exceptuando.
ex·cep·tion [ɪksɛpʃən] s. (exclusion) excepción;
   (opposition) objeción; **with the — of** a excepción
   de, con excepción de; **to take** — objetar;
   ofenderse.
ex·cep·tion·al [ɪksɛpʃənl] adj. exceptional.
ex·cess [ɪksɛs] s. exceso; sobrante; — **baggage**
   (weight) exceso de equipaje (de peso); **to drink to**
   — beber en exceso.
ex·ces·sive [ɪksɛsɪv] adj. excesivo; desmedido; **-ly**
   adv. excesivamente, en exceso, demasiado.
ex·change [ɪkstʃéndʒ] s. (money) cambio;
   (interchange) trueque; intercambio, canje (de
   publicaciones, prisioneros); (stock) lonja, bolsa;
   rate of — cambio, Am. tipo de cambio;
   telephone — central de teléfonos; **foreign** —
   divisa. v. cambiar; trocar; canjear (publicaciones,
   prisioneros); **to — greetings** saludarse; mandarse
   felicitaciones.
ex·cise [ɪksáɪz] v. excitar; acalorar; agitar.
ex·cit·ed [ɪksáɪtɪd] adj. excitado, acalorado,
   animado; **to get** — entusiasmarse;
   sobreexcitarse; acalorarse; **-ly** adv.
   acaloradamente, agitadamente.
ex·cite·ment [ɪksáɪtmənt] s. excitación;
   acaloramiento; agitación, alboroto; animación.
ex·cit·ing [ɪksáɪtɪŋ] adj. excitante, excitador;
   estimulante.
ex·claim [ɪksklém] v. exclamar.
ex·cla·ma·tion [ɛkskləméʃən] s. exclamación; —
   point punto de admiración.
ex·clude [ɪksklúd] v. excluir.
ex·clu·sion [ɪksklúʒən] s. exclusión.
ex·clu·sive [ɪksklúsɪv] adj. exclusivo; privativo; —
   of sin contar.
ex·com·mu·ni·cate [ɛkskəmjúnəket] v.
   excomunicar.
ex·com·mu·ni·ca·tion [ɛkskəmjunəkéʃən] s.
   excomunión.

ex·cre·ment [ékskrɪmənt] s. excremento; caca.
ex·cur·sion [ɪkskɜ́ʒən] s. excursión; correría; expedición.
ex·cus·a·ble [ɪkskjúzəbl] adj. excusable, disculpable.
ex·cuse [ɪkskjús] s. excusa; disculpa; [ɪkskjúz] v. excusar; disculpar; perdonar, dispensar; eximir; — me! ¡dispense Vd.! ¡perdone Vd.!
ex·e·cute [éksɪkjut] v. ejecutar; fusilar; adjusticiar; llevar a cabo.
ex·e·cu·tion [èksɪkjúʃən] s. ejecución; desempeño; — wall paredón.
ex·e·cu·tion·er [èksɪkjúʃənɚ] s. verdugo.
ex·ec·u·tive [ɪgzékjʊtɪv] adj. ejecutivo; s. ejecutivo, poder ejecutivo; gerente, administrador.
ex·ec·u·tor [ɪgzékjətɚ] s. albacea, ejecutor testamentario; [éksɪkjutɚ] ejecutor.
ex·em·pla·ry [ɪgzémplərɪ] adj. ejemplar.
ex·empt [ɪgzémpt] adj. exento, libre; v. eximir, exentar.
ex·emp·tion [ɪgzémpʃən] s. exención.
ex·er·cise [éksɚsaɪz] s. ejercicio; v. ejercitar(se); ejercer (poder o autoridad); hacer ejercicio, hacer gimnasia; to be -d about something estar preocupado o sobreexcitado por algo.
ex·ert [ɪgzɜ́t] v. ejercer; to — oneself esforzarse, hacer esfuerzos, empeñarse.
ex·er·tion [ɪgzɜ́ʃən] s. ejercicio; esfuerzo, empeño.
ex·hale [ɛkshél] v. exhalar, emitir; espirar, soplar.
ex·haust [ɪgzɔ́st] s. escape (de gas o vapor); v. agotar; consumir; debilitar, fatigar; I am -ed no puedo más; estoy agotado.
ex·haus·tion [ɪgzɔ́stʃən] s. agotamiento; fatiga, postración.
ex·haus·tive [ɛgzɔ́stɪv] adj. comprensivo; detallado.
ex·hib·it [ɪgzíbɪt] v. exhibir; mostrar, exponer.
ex·hi·bi·tion [èksəbíʃən] s. exhibición; exposición; manifestación.
ex·hil·a·rate [ɪgzíləret] v. alborozar, excitar, animar, entusiasmar; refocilar.
ex·hort [ɪgzɔ́rt] v. exhortar.
ex·ile [égzaɪl] s. destierro, exilio; desterrado; v. desterrar; expatriar.
ex·ist [ɪgzíst] v. existir.
ex·is·tence [ɪgzístəns] s. existencia.
ex·is·tent [ɪgzístənt] adj. existente.
ex·it [égzɪt] s. salida; salida (del foro); v. vase o vanse (un personaje o personajes al fin de una escena).
ex·o·dus [éksədəs] s. éxodo.
ex·on·er·ate [ɪgzánəret] v. exonerar.
ex·or·bi·tant [ɪgzɔ́rbətənt] adj. exorbitante.
ex·or·cism [éksɔrsɪzəm] s. exorcismo; conjuro.
ex·ot·ic [ɪgzátɪk] adj. exótico; raro, extraño.
ex·pand [ɪkspǽnd] v. ensanchar(se); dilatar(se); extender(se); agrandar(se); desarrollar (una ecuación).
ex·panse [ɪkspǽns] s. espacio, extensión.
ex·pan·sion [ɪkspǽnʃən] s. expansión; ensanche; desarrollo (de una ecuación).
ex·pan·sive [ɪkspǽnsɪv] adj. expansivo; efusivo.
ex·pect [ɪkspékt] v. esperar; contar con; I — so supongo que sí.
ex·pec·ta·tion [èkspɛktéʃən] s. expectación; expectativa; esperanza.
ex·pec·to·rate [ɪkspéktəret] v. expectorar, desgarrar.
ex·pe·di·ent [ɪkspídɪənt] adj. conveniente, oportuno; ventajoso; prudente; s. expediente, medio.
ex·pe·dite [ékspədaɪt] v. facilitar; despachar.
ex·pe·di·tion [èkspɪdíʃən] s. expedición.

ex·pe·di·tion·ary [èkspɪdíʃənɛrɪ] adj. expedicionario.
ex·pel [ɪkspél] v. expeler; expulsar.
ex·pend [ɪkspénd] v. gastar; consumir.
ex·pen·di·ture [ɪkspéndɪtʃɚ] s. gasto; desembolso.
ex·pense [ɪkspéns] s. gasto; coste, costa o costo.
ex·pen·sive [ɪkspénsɪv] adj. costoso.
ex·pen·sive·ness [ɪkspénsɪvnɪs] s. precio subido, coste elevado.
ex·pe·ri·ence [ɪkspírɪəns] s. experiencia; aventura, lance; v. experimentar; pasar (penas, sufrimientos); sentir.
ex·pe·ri·enced [ɪkspírɪənst] adj. experimentado; ducho, perito, experto.
ex·per·i·ment [ɪkspérəmənt] s. experimento, prueba; v. experimentar, hacer un experimento.
ex·per·i·men·tal [ɪkspɛrəméntl] adj. experimental.
ex·pert [ékspɝt] s. experto, perito; [ɪkspɝt] adj. experto, perito, experimentado.
ex·pi·ra·tion [èkspəréʃən] s. terminación; vencimiento (de un plazo); espiración (del aire).
ex·pire [ɪkspáɪr] v. expirar, morir; acabar; vencerse (un plazo); expeler (el aire aspirado).
ex·plain [ɪksplén] v. explicar.
ex·plain·a·ble [ɪksplénəbl] adj. explicable.
ex·pla·na·tion [èksplənéʃən] s. explicación.
ex·plan·a·to·ry [ɪksplǽnətorɪ] adj. explicativo.
ex·plic·it [ɪksplísɪt] adj. explícito.
ex·plode [ɪksplód] v. estallar, hacer explosión, Am. explotar; reventar; volar (con dinamita); desacreditar (una teoría).
ex·ploit [ɪksplɔ́ɪt] s. hazaña, proeza; [ɪksplɔ́ɪt] v. explotar; sacar partido de, abusar de.
ex·ploi·ta·tion [èksplɔɪtéʃən] s. explotación.
ex·plo·ra·tion [èkspləréʃən] s. exploración.
ex·plore [ɪksplór] v. explorar.
ex·plor·er [ɪksplórɚ] s. explorador.
ex·plo·sion [ɪksplóʒən] s. explosión, estallido.
ex·plo·sive [ɪksplósɪv] adj. & s. explosivo.
ex·port [éksport] s. exportación; artículo exportado, mercancía exportada; [ɪkspórt] v. exportar.
ex·por·ta·tion [èksportéʃən] s. exportación.
ex·pose [ɪkspóz] v. exponer; exhibir, mostrar; poner a la vista; revelar; desenmascarar.
ex·po·si·tion [èkspəzíʃən] s. exposición; exhibición.
ex·po·sure [ɪkspóʒɚ] s. exposición; revelación; to die of — morir a efecto de la intemperie.
ex·pound [ɪkspáund] v. exponer, explicar.
ex·press [ɪksprés] adj. (rapid) expreso; (explicit) explícito, claro; — company compañía de expreso; expreso, Am. exprés; — train tren expreso; adv. por expreso, por exprés; s. expreso; tren expreso, Am. exprés; v. expresar; enviar por expreso (o por exprés).
ex·pres·sion [ɪksspréʃən] s. expresión.
ex·pres·sive [ɪksprésɪv] adj. expresivo.
ex·pul·sion [ɪkspʌ́lʃən] s. expulsión.
ex·qui·site [ɪkskwízɪt] adj. exquisito.
ex·qui·site·ness [ɪkskwízɪtnɪs] s. exquisitez; primor.
ex·stant [ɪkstǽnt] adj. existente.
ex·tem·po·ra·ne·ous [ɛkstɛmpəréniəs] adj. improvisado.
ex·tend [ɪksténd] v. extender(se); tender; prolongar(se); alargar(se); agrandar; dilatar, prorrogar (un plazo); dar (el pésame, el parabién, ayuda, etc.).
ex·tend·ed [ɪksténdɪd] adj. extenso; prolongado; extendido.
ex·ten·sion [ɪksténʃən] s. extensión; prolongación;

prórroga (*de un plazo*); añadidura, anexo.
ex·ten·sive [ɪksténsɪv] *adj.* extenso, ancho, dilatado; extensivo; **-ly** *adv.* extensamente, por extenso; extensivamente; **-ly** used de uso general o común.
ex·tent [ɪkstént] *s.* extensión; grado; **to a great —** en gran parte, generalmente; **to such an — that** a tal grado que; **to the — one's ability** en proporción a su habilidad; **up to a certain —** hasta cierto punto.
ex·ten·u·ate [ɪksténjʊet] *v.* atenuar, mitigar.
ex·te·ri·or [ɪkstírɪɚ] *adj.* exterior; externo; *s.* exterioridad; exterior, porte, aspecto.
ex·ter·mi·nate [ɪkstɝmənet] *v.* exterminar, destruir por completo, extirpar.
ex·ter·mi·na·tion [ɪkstɝmənéʃən] *s.* exterminio.
ex·ter·nal [ɪkstɝnl] *adj.* externo; exterior; *s.* exterioridad; lo externo.
ex·tinct [ɪkstíŋkt] *adj.* extinto; extinguido, apagado.
ex·tin·guish [ɪkstíŋgwɪʃ] *v.* extinguir; apagar.
ex·tol [ɪkstól] *v.* enaltecer; ensalzar.
ex·tort [ɪkstɔrt] *v.* obtener por fuerza o amenaza, exigir (*dinero, promesa, etc.*), *Am.* extorsionar.
ex·tor·tion [ɪkstɔrʃən] *s.* extorsión.
ex·tra [ékstrə] *adj.* extraordinario; de sobra, de más, adicional; suplementario; **— tire** neumático de repuesto o de recambio; **— workman** obrero supernumerario; *adv.* extraordinariamente; *s.* extra; extraordinario (*de un periódico*); suplemento; gasto extraordinario; recargo (*cargo adicional*); actor suplente o supernumerario.
ex·tract [ékstrækt] *s.* extracto; cita, trozo (*entresacado de un libro*); resumen; [ɪkstrǽkt] *v.* extraer; seleccionar; citar.
ex·traor·di·nar·y [ɪkstrɔ́rdnɛrɪ] *adj.* extraordinario; **extraordinarily** *adv.* extraordinariamente; de manera extraordinaria.
ex·trav·a·gance [ɪkstrǽvəgəns] *s.* despilfarro, derroche, gasto excesivo; lujo excesivo; extravagancia, capricho.
ex·trav·a·gant [ɪkstrǽvəgənt] *adj.* gastador, despilfarrado; extravagante, disparatado; **— praise** elogios excesivos; **— prices** precios exorbitantes.
ex·treme [ɪkstrím] *adj.* (*last*) último; extremo; más remoto; (*excessive*) excesivo; riguroso; radical; **— opinions** opiniones extremadas; *s.* extremo; cabo; **to go to -s** extremar, exagerar; hacer extremos; tomar las medidas más extremas; **-ly** *adv.* extremamente, en extremo.
ex·trem·i·ty [ɪkstrémətɪ] *s.* extremidad, extremo; medida extrema; **in —** en gran peligro; en un apuro.
ex·u·ber·ant [ɪgzjúbərənt] *adj.* exuberante.
ex·ult [ɪgzʌ́lt] *v.* alborozarse, regocijarse.
eye [aɪ] *s.* ojo; **— shade** visera; **in a twinkling of an —** en un abrir y cerrar de ojos; **hook and —** macho y hembra; **to catch one's —** llamar la atención; **to have good -s** tener buena vista; **to have before one's -s** tener a (o tener ante) la vista; **to keep an — on** cuidar, vigilar; **to see — to —** estar completamente de acuerdo; *v.* mirar, observar.
eye·ball [áɪbɔl] *s.* globo del ojo.
eye·brow [áɪbraʊ] *s.* ceja.
eye·glass [áɪglæs] *s.* lente, cristal (*de anteojo*); ocular (*de microscopio o telescopio*); **-es** lentes, anteojos.
eye·lash [áɪlæʃ] *s.* pestaña.

eye·lid [áɪlɪd] *s.* párpado.
eye·sight [áɪsaɪt] *s.* vista; **poor —** mala vista.

F·f

fa·ble [fébl] *s.* fábula.
fab·ric [fǽbrɪk] *s.* género, tela; tejido; textura; estructura.
fab·u·lous [fǽbjələs] *adj.* fabuloso.
fa·çade [fəsád] *s.* fachada.
face [fes] *s.* (*human*) cara, rostro; (*building*) fachada, frente; (*surface*) haz, superficie; (*watch*) muestra; *Riopl.* esfera; *Méx., C.A., Ven., Col.* carátula; — **value** valor nominal; **in the—of** en presencia de, ante, frente a; **to lose —** perder prestigio; **to make -s** hacer muecas o gestos; **to save one's —** salvar el amor propio; *v.* encararse con; enfrentarse con; hacer frente a; mirar hacia; forrar; **to — about** volverse, *Méx., C.A., Ven., Col., Andes* voltearse; **to — danger** afrontar o arrostrar el peligro; **to — with marble** revestir de mármol; **it -s the street** da a la calle.
fac·et [fǽsɪt] *s.* faceta.
fa·cil·i·tate [fəsílətet] *v.* facilitar.
fa·cil·i·ty [fəsílətɪ] *s.* facilidad.
fact [fækt] *s.* hecho; dato; verdad, realidad; **in —** de hecho; en realidad.
fac·tion [fǽkʃən] *s.* facción, bando, partido, pandilla.
fac·tor [fǽktɚ] *s.* factor; elemento; agente; *v.* decomponer en factores.
fac·to·ry [fǽktrɪ] *s.* fábrica.
fac·ul·ty [fǽkltɪ] *s.* facultad; (*college*) profesorado; cuerpo docente.
fad [fæd] *s.* novedad; manía; moda.
fade [fed] *v.* descolorar(se), desteñir(se); marchitar(se); apagarse (*un sonido*); desvanecerse.
fagged [fægd] *adj.* agotado, rendido de cansancio.
fail [fel] *v.* (*not effect*) faltar; fallar; fracasar; no tener éxito; (*wane*) decaer; debilitarse; (*go broke*) quebrar, hacer bancarrota; **to — in an examination** fallar en un examen, salir mal en un examen; **to — a student** reprobar o suspender a un estudiante; **to — to do it** dejar de hacerlo, no hacerlo; **don't — to come** no deje Vd. de venir; **without —** sin falta.
fail·ure [féljɚ] *s.* fracaso; malogro; falta; descuido; negligencia; quiebra, bancarrota, debilitamiento.
faint [fent] *adj.* (*weak*) débil, lánguido; (*indistinct*) imperceptible, tenue, vago, indistinto; **to feel —** sentirse desvanecido; **—hearted** tímido, cobarde; *s.* desmayo; *v.* desmayarse, languidecer; **-ly** *adv.* débilmente; lánguidamente; indistintamente, vagamente, tenuemente; apenas.
faint·ness [féntnɪs] *s.* languidez, debilidad, desfallecimiento; falta de claridad o vaguedad.
fair [fɛr] *adj.* (*just*) justo, recto, honrado; imparcial; equitativo; (*mediocre*) regular, mediano; (*complexion*) rubio, blondo; *Méx.* huero; *Guat.* canche; *C.R.* macho; *Pan.* fulo; *Col.* mono; *Ven.* catire; (*Sal.*) chele; (*weather*) claro, despejado; **— chance of success** buena probabilidad de éxito; **— complexion** tez blanca; **— hair** pelo rubio; **— name** reputación sin mancilla; **— play** juego limpio; **— sex** sexo bello; **— weather** buen tiempo, tiempo bonancible; **to act —** obrar con imparcialidad (o con equidad); **to play —** jugar limpio; *s.* feria; mercado; exposición; (*Valencia*) falla; **-ly** *adv.*

justamente; imparcialmente; medianamente; -ly
difficult medianamente difícil; -ly well regular,
bastante bien.
fair·ness [fέrnɪs] s. justicia, equidad, imparcialidad;
blancura (de la tez); belleza.
fair·y [fέrɪ] s. hada; — godmother hada madrina;
— tale cuento de hadas.
fair·y·land [fέrɪlænd] s. tierra de las hadas.
faith [feθ] s. fe; fidelidad; in good — de buena fe;
to have — in tener fe o confianza en; to keep —
cumplir con la palabra.
faith·ful [féθfəl] adj. fiel; leal; -ly adv. fielmente;
con fidelidad; puntualmente; -ly yours suyo
afectísimo; siempre suyo.
faith·ful·ness [féθfəlnɪs] s. fidelidad; lealtad;
exactitud.
faith·less [féθlɪs] adj. infiel; sin fe; desleal; falso.
fake [fek] s. fraude, trampa; falsedad; embustero;
adj. falso, fingido; v. falsear; fingir; simular.
fal·con [fɔlkən] s. halcón.
fall [fɔl] s. (drop) caída; bajada; (collapse) ruina;
baja (de precios); (season) otoño; -s cascada,
catarata, salto de agua; v. caer(se); decaer;
bajar; to — asleep dormirse, quedarse dormido;
to — back retroceder; to — behind atrasarse,
rezagarse, quedarse atrás; to — in love
enamorarse; to — out with reñir con, enemistarse
con; to — to one tocarle a uno, corresponderle a
uno; his plans fell through fracasaron (o se
malograron) sus planes.
fal·la·cy [fǽləsɪ] s. falsedad; error.
fall·en [fɔlən] p.p. de to fall.
fall·out [fɔlaʊt] s. precipitación radiactiva.
fal·low [fǽlo] adj. baldío; s. barbecho; v. barbechar.
false [fɔls] adj. falso; postizo (dientes, barba, etc.);
fingido, simulado.
false·hood [fɔlshʊd] s. falsedad, mentira.
false·ness [fɔlsnɪs] s. falsedad.
fal·si·fy [fɔleəfaɪ] v. falsificar, falsear; mentir.
fal·si·ty [fɔlsətɪ] s. falsedad; mentira.
fal·ter [fɔltə] v. vacilar; titubear; tambalearse;
bambolearse; to — an excuse balbucear una
excusa; s. temblor, vacilación.
fame [fem] s. fama.
famed [femd] adj. afamado, famoso, renombrado.
fa·mil·iar [fəmíljə] adj. familiar, íntimo;
confianzudo; to be — with a subject conocer bien,
estar versado en o ser conocedor de una materia;
s. familiar.
fa·mil·i·ar·i·ty [fəmɪlɪǽrətɪ] s. familiaridad;
confianza, franqueza.
fam·i·ly [fǽmlɪ] s. familia; — name apellido; — tree
árbol genealógico; to be in the — way estar
encinta.
fam·ine [fǽmɪn] s. hambre; escasez, carestía.
fam·ished [fǽmɪʃt] adj. hambriento, muerto de
hambre; to be — morirse de hambre.
fa·mous [féməs] adj. famoso.
fan [fæn] s. abanico; aventador; ventilador;
aficionado (a deportes); admirador; v. abanicar;
ventilar.
fa·nat·ic [fənǽtɪk] adj. & s. fanático.
fa·nat·i·cism [fənǽtəsɪzəm] s. fanatismo.
fan·ci·ful [fǽnsɪfəl] adj. fantástico; caprichoso;
imaginario.
fan·cy [fǽnsɪ] s. fantasía, antojo, capricho;
imaginación; afición, gusto; to have a — for tener
afición a; to strike one's — antojársele a uno; to
take a — to a person caerle a uno bien (o
simpatizarle a uno) una persona; adj. fantástico,
de fantasía; de adorno; elegante; — ball baile de

fantasía o disfraces; — free libre de cuidados;
—work labor; bordado fino; v. imaginar(se);
fantasear; forjar, concebir (una idea); to —
oneself imaginarse; just — the idea! ¡figúrate qué
idea! I don't — the idea of no me gusta la idea
de.
fang [fæŋ] s. colmillo (de ciertos animales).
fan·tas·tic [fæntǽstɪk] adj. fantástico; extravagante.
fan·ta·sy [fǽntəsɪ] s. fantasía.
far [fɑr] adv. lejos; — away muy lejos; — and wide
por todas partes; — better mucho mejor; — off
muy lejos; a lo lejos; by — con mucho; as — as
hasta; en cuanto a; as — as I know según
parece; a lo que parece; que yo sepa; so —
hasta ahora; hasta aquí; hasta entonces; how
—? ¿hasta dónde?; adj. lejano, distante, remoto;
— journey largo viaje; it is a — cry from dista
mucho de.
far·a·way [fɑrəwé] adj. muy lejano, distante,
remoto; abstraído.
farce [fɑrs] s. farsa.
fare [fɛr] s. pasaje, tarifa de pasajes; pasajero;
comida, alimento; v. pasarla (bien o mal); irle a
uno (bien o mal); to — forth salir.
fare·well [fɛrwél] s. despedida, adiós; to bid — to
despedirse de; —! ¡adiós!
far·fetched [fɑrfɛtʃt] adj. traído de muy lejos;
forzado; traído por los cabellos; que no hace al
caso; improbable, poco creíble.
far·flung [fɑrflʌ́ŋ] adj. extenso, de gran alcance.
farm [fɑrm] s. hacienda, granja, Riopl. estancia,
Méx. rancho; — hand peón; — produce
productos agrícolas; v. cultivar, labrar (la tierra);
to — out dar en arriendo; repartir.
farm·er [fɑ́rmə] s. labrador; granjero; agricultor;
Méx. ranchero, Riopl. estanciero, Am.
hacendado.
farm·house [fɑ́rmhaʊs] s. alquería, finca.
farm·ing [fɑ́rmɪŋ] s. labranza, agricultura, cultivo
de los campos; adj. agrícola.
farm·yard [fɑ́rmjɑrd] s. corral (de una alquería).
far·off [fɑ́rɔ́f] adj. distance, remoto.
far·sighted [fɑrsáɪtɪd] adj. (sight) présbite;
(foresighted) precavido.
far·ther [fɑ́rðə] adv. más lejos; más; — on más
adelante; más remoto, más lejano.
far·thest [fɑ́rðɪst] adj. más lejano; más remoto;
adv. más lejos.
fas·ci·nate [fǽsɪnet] v. fascinar.
fas·ci·na·tion [fæsɪnéʃən] s. fascinación.
fas·cism [fǽʃɪzm] s. fascismo.
fas·cist [fǽʃɪst] s. fascista.
fash·ion [fǽʃən] s. (style) moda, boga, estilo; (way)
manera, modo; — plate figurín; the latest — la
última moda (o novedad); after a —
medianamente, no muy bien; to be in — estar de
moda; estilarse; v. forjar, hacer, formar; idear.
fash·ion·a·ble [fǽʃnəbl] adj. de moda; de buen
tono; elegante.
fast [fæst] adj. rápido, veloz; adelantado (dícese del
reloj); firme; fiel (amigo); fijo; disipado,
disoluto; adv. aprisa, de prisa; firmemente,
fijamente; — asleep profundamente dormido; s.
ayuno; v. ayunar.
fas·ten [fǽsṇ] v. fijar(se); sujetar(se), asegurar(se);
atar, unir; abrochar(se).
fas·ten·er [fǽsṇə] s. broche, abrochador.
fas·tid·i·ous [fæstídɪəs] adj. melindroso.
fat [fæt] adj. gordo; grasiento; mantecoso; —
profits ganancias pingües; s. grasa, manteca;
gordura; the — of the land lo mejor y más rico

de la tierra.
fa·tal [fétl] *adj.* fatal.
fa·tal·i·ty [fətǽlətɪ] *s.* fatalidad; muerte.
fate [fet] *s.* hado, sino, destino; fortuna, suerte.
fa·ther [fáðɚ] *s.* padre.
fa·ther·hood [fáðɚhʊd] *s.* paternidad.
fa·ther-in-law [fáðɚrɪnlɔ] *s.* suegro.
fa·ther·land [fáðɚlænd] *s.* patria.
fa·ther·ly [fáðɚlɪ] *adv.* paternal.
fath·om [fǽðəm] *v.* sondar, sondear; penetrar; *s.* braza *(medida de profundidad)*.
fath·om·less [fǽðəmlɪs] *adj.* insondable.
fa·tigue [fətíg] *s.* fatiga, cansancio; *v.* fatigar(se), cansar(se).
fat·ness [fǽtnɪs] *s.* gordura.
fat·ten [fǽtn] *v.* engordar.
fat·ty [fǽtɪ] *adj.* grasiento; seboso.
fau·cet [fɔsɪt] *s.* grifo, llave, espita, canilla, *Am.* bitoque.
fault [fɔlt] *s.* *(defect)* falta; defecto, tacha; *(blame)* culpa; *(geological)* falla; **to a** — excesivamente; **to be at** — ser, culpable; **to find** — **with** criticar a.
fault·find·er [fɔltfaɪndɚ] *s.* criticón, criticador.
fault·less [fɔltlɪs] *adj.* intachable, sin tacha, perfecto.
fault·y [fɔltɪ] *adj.* defectuoso, imperfecto.
fa·vor[févɚ] *s.* favor; **your** — **of the ...** su grata (carta) del ...; *v.* favorecer.
fa·vor·able [févrəbl] *adj.* favorable; **favorably** *adv.* favorablemente.
fa·vor·ite [févrɪt] *adj.* & *s.* favorito.
fa·vor·it·ism [févrɪtɪzəm] *s.* favoritismo.
fawn [fɔn] *s.* cervato; color de cervato; *v.* adular; halagar.
fear [fɪr] *s.* temor, miedo; pavor; *v.* temer.
fear·ful [fírfəl] *adj.* terrible, espantoso; temible, temeroso; miedoso.
fear·less [fírlɪs] *adj.* sin temor, intrépido, atrevido, arrojado.
fear·less·ness [fílɪsnɪs] *s.* intrepidez, arrojo, osadía, atrevimiento.
fea·si·ble [fízəbl] *adj.* factible, hacedero, dable.
feast [fist] *s.* fiesta; festín, banquete; *v.* festejar, obsequiar; banquetear; **to** — **one's eyes on** deleitar la vista en.
feat [fit] *s.* proeza, hazaña; acto de destreza; suerte *(en el circo)*.
feath·er [féðɚ] *s.* pluma; **-s** plumaje; **a** — **in one's cap** un triunfo para uno; — **weight** de peso mínimo; *v.* emplumar.
feath·er·y [féðɚɪ] *adj.* plumoso; ligero, como una pluma.
fea·ture [fítʃɚ] *s.* facción, rasgo distintivo; película principal *(en el cine)*; **-s** facciones *(de la cara)*; — **article** articulo sobresaliente o principal; *v.* destacar, hacer sobresalir; dar realce a; mostrar, exhibir *(como cosa principal)*, hacer resaltar.
Feb·ru·ar·y [fébrʊɛrɪ] *s.* febrero.
fed [fed] *pret.* & *p.p. de* **to feed; to be** — **up** estar harto; estar hasta la coronilla, estar hasta el copete.
fed·er·al [fédərəl] *adj.* federal.
fed·er·a·tion [fedəréʃən] *s.* federación, confederación, liga.
fee [fi] *s.* honorario (honorarios); derechos; cuota; **admission** — derechos de entrada; precio de entrada.
fee·ble [fíbl] *adj.* débil, endeble; **feebly** *adv.* débilmente.
feed [fid] *s.* forraje, pasto, pienso *(para los*

caballos); comida; *v.* alimentar(se); dar de comer; pacer, pastar; **to** — **coal** echar carbón.
feed·back [fídbæk] *s.* regeneración.
feel [fil] *v.* sentir; tocar, tentar; palpar; **to** — **better** **(sad, happy,** *etc.)* sentirse mejor (triste, feliz, *etc*); **to** — **one's way** tantear el camino; **to** — **for** someone compadecer a alguien; **it -s soft** está suave; **it -s hot in here** se siente calor aquí; *s.* tacto, sentido del tacto; **this cloth has a nice** — esta tela es suave al tacto.
feel·er [fílɚ] *s.* tentáculo, antena *(de los insectos)*; tiento; propuesta *(para averiguar la inclinación o pensamiento de alguien)*.
feel·ing[fílɪŋ] *s.* *(touch)* tacto; sensación *(emotion)* sentimiento; emoción; pasión; *(pity)* compasión; ternura; **to hurt someone's -s** ofender la sensibildad de alguien; *adj.* sensible, compasivo.
feet [fit] *pl. de* **foot.**
feign [fen] *v.* fingir.
fell [fel] *v.* derribar, echar abajo; talar *(un árbol)*; *pret. de* **to fall.**
fel·low [félo] *s.* socio, miembro *(de una sociedad, colegio, etc.)*; becario *(estudiante que disfruta una beca)*; camarada; compañero; individuo, tipo, sujeto, hombre; — **citizen** conciudadano; — **man** prójimo; — **member** consocio; colega; — **student** condiscípulo.
fel·low·ship [féloʃɪp] *s.* compañerismo; unión; confraternidad; sociedad; beca; **to get a** — obtener una beca.
fel·o·ny [félənɪ] *s.* crimen.
felt [felt] *s.* fieltro; *adj.* de fieltro; *pret.* & *p.p. de* **to feel.**
fe·male [fímel] *s.* hembra; *adj.* hembra; femenino, mujeril, de la mujer; — **cat (dog,** *etc.)* gata (perra, *etc.*); — **screw** tuerca, hembra de tornillo.
fem·i·nine [fémənɪn] *adj.* femenino, femenil.
fem·i·nin·i·ty [femɪnínɪtɪ] *s.* feminidad.
fe·mur [fímɚ] *s.* fémur.
fence [fens] *s.* cerca, valla, vallado; receptor de cosas robadas; **to be on the** — estar indeciso; *v.* esgrimir; **to** — **in** cercar, rodear con cerca.
fenc·ing [fénsɪŋ] *s.* esgrima; cercado.
fend·er [féndɚ] *s.* guardabarros, guardafango; *Am.* trompa *(de locomotora)*; *Riopl.* parrilla.
fer·ment [fɚmɛnt] *s.* fermento; fermentación; [fɚmɛnt] *v.* fermentar; hacer fermentar.
fer·men·ta·tion [fɚməntéʃən] *s.* fermentación.
fern [fɚn] *s.* helecho.
fe·ro·cious [fɚóʃəs] *adj.* feroz, fiero.
fe·roc·i·ty [fɚrásətɪ] *s.* ferocidad, fiereza.
fer·ret [férɪt] *v.* **to** — **out** buscar, cazar; escudriñar, indagar.
fer·ry [férɪ] *s.* barca de pasaje *(a través de un rio o bahía)*; embarcadero; *v.* transportar de una orilla a otra; atravesar *(un rio)* en barca de pasaje.
fer·tile[fɚtl] *adj.* fértil; fecundo.
fer·til·i·ty [fɚtílətɪ] *s.* fertilidad.
fer·til·ize [fɚtlaɪz] *v.* fertilizar; abonar; fecundar.
fer·til·iz·er [fɚtlaɪzɚ] *s.* abono *(para la tierra)*.
fer·vent [fɚvənt] *adj.* ferviente; fervoroso.
fer·vor [fɚvɚ] *s.* fervor; ardor.
fes·ter [féstɚ] *v.* supurar; enconarse *(una llaga)*; *s.* llaga, úlcera.
fes·ti·val [féstəvl] *s.* fiesta.
fes·tive [féstɪv] *adj.* festivo; alegre.
fes·tiv·i·ty [festívətɪ] *s.* júbilo, regocijo; festividad.
fetch [fetʃ] *v.* ir a buscar; coger; traer.
fete [fet] *s.* fiesta; *v.* festejar; agasajar.
fet·ish [fétɪʃ] *s.* fetiche.

fet·ter [fɛ́tɚ] v. engrillar, meter en grillos encadenar; **-s** s. pl. grillos, cadenas, trabas.

fe·tus [fítəs] s. feto.

feud [fjud] s. riña, pelea, contienda; old — enemistad antigua (entre dos personas o familias).

feu·dal [fjúdl] adj. feudal.

fe·ver [fívɚ] s. fiebre, calentura.

fe·ver·ish [fívɚɪʃ] adj. calenturiento, febril.

fe·ver·ish·ness [fívɚɪʃnɪs] s. calentura; agitación febril.

few [fju] adj. & pron. pocos; a — unos pocos, unos cuantos.

fi·an·cé [fiɑnsé] s. novio; **fiancée** f. novia.

fi·as·co [fiǽsko] s. fiasco.

fib [fɪb] s. bola, mentirilla, paparrucha, papa; v. echar papas, decir o contar paparruchas.

fib·ber [fíbɚ] s. paparruchero, cuentero, mentirosillo.

fi·ber [fáɪbɚ] s. fibra.

fi·brous [fáɪbrəs] adj. fibroso.

fick·le [fíkl] adj. inconstante, voluble, veleidoso, mudable; tornadizo.

fic·tion [fíkʃən] s. ficción.

fic·tion·al [fíkʃənl] adj. novelesco; ficticio.

fic·ti·tious [fɪktíʃəs] adj. ficticio.

fid·dle [fídl] s. violín; v. tocar el violín; **to** — **around** malgastar el tiempo; juguetear.

fi·del·i·ty [faɪdéləti] s. fidelidad.

fid·get [fídʒɪt] v. estar inquieto; agitarse, menearse nerviosamente.

field [fild] s. campo; campo o cancha (de deportes); — **artillery** artillería de campaña; — **glasses** anteojos de larga vista; — **work** trabajo de investigación en el campo.

fiend [find] s. demonio, diablo; **dope** — morfinómano.

fiend·ish [fíndɪʃ] adj. diabólico.

fierce [fɪrs] adj. feroz, fiero; furioso, espantoso.

fierce·ness [fírsnɪs] s. ferocidad; fiereza; vehemencia.

fier·y [fáɪrɪ] adj. fogoso; ardiente; vehemente.

fife [faɪf] s. pífano.

fig [fɪg] s. higo; — **tree** higuera.

fight [faɪt] s. lucha; pelea; riña, pleito; **he has a lot of** — **left** le sobra fuerza para luchar; v. luchar (con) pelear; combatir; reñir; batirse; **to** — **it out** decidirlo a golpes o con argumentos; **to** — **one's way through** abrirse camino a la fuerza.

fight·er [fáɪtɚ] s. luchador; combatiente; guerrero; — **airplane** avión de caza.

fight·ing [fáɪtɪŋ] s. lucha, combate pelea; adj. combatiente; luchador.

fig·ure [fígjɚ] s. (form) figura; forma; talle (de una persona); (numerical) cifra, número; valor; precio; **-s** cuentas, cálculos; — **of speech** figura de dicción; **to be good at -s** saber hacer bien las cuentas; ser listo en aritmética; **to cut a poor** — tener mala facha, hacer el ridículo; v. figurar; imaginarse, figurarse; adornar con dibujos; calcular; **to** — **on** contar con, confiar en; tener la intención de, proponerse; tomar en cuenta; **to** — **out** descifrar, resolver.

fil·a·ment [fíləmənt] s. filamento.

file [faɪl] s. (records) fichero; archivo; registro, lista; legajo; (cabinet) guardapapeles; (line) fila; (tool) lima; — **card** ficha, papeleta; v. archivar; guardar en el fichero; registrar, asentar en el registro; limar; desfilar, marchar en fila.

fil·i·al [fíliəl] adj. filial.

fil·i·gree [fíligri] s. filigrana.

fill [fɪl] v. llenar(se); ocupar (un puesto); empastar

(un diente); servir, atender, despachar (un pedido); inflar (un neumático); tapar (un agujero); **to** — **out a blank** llenar un formulario (forma o esqueleto); **her eyes -ed with tears** se le arrasaron los ojos de lágrimas.

fil·let [fɪlé] s. filete; [fíllt] cinta, lista de adorno.

fill·ing [fílɪŋ] s. relleno; empaste (dental); **gold** — orificación.

fil·ly [fíll] s. potranca.

film [fɪlm] s. película; membrana; tela (formada sobre la superficie de un líquido); nube (en el ojo); v. filmar (cinematografiar).

fil·ter [fíltɚ] s. filtro; v. filtrar(se).

filth [fɪlθ] s. suciedad; porquería; mugre.

filth·i·ness [fílθɪnɪs] s. suciedad, porquería.

filth·y [fílθɪ] adj. sucio; puerco, cochino; mugriento.

fin [fɪn] s. aleta (de pez).

fi·nal [fáɪnl] adj. final; terminante; definitivo; **-ly** adv. finalmente; en fin, por fin.

fi·nance [fənǽns] s. teoría bancaria, Am. finanza; **-s** fondos, recursos monetarios; negocios bancarios, Am. finanzas; v. hacer operaciones bancarias; fomentar (un negocio o empresa), Am. financiar.

fi·nan·cial [fənǽnʃəl] adj. financiero; monetario.

fi·nan·cier [fɪnənsír] s. financiero, Am. financista.

fi·nanc·ing [fənǽnsɪŋ] s. Am. financiamiento.

find [faɪnd] v. hallar; encontrar; declarar; **to** — **fault with** criticar a, censurar a; **to** — **guilty** declarar o encontrar culpable; **to** — **out** descubrir; averiguar; s. hallazgo.

find·ing [fáɪndɪŋ] s. descubrimiento; hallazgo; fallo, decisión; **-s** resultados, datos (de una investigación).

fine [faɪn] adj. fino; perfecto, excelente; superior; primoroso; — **arts** bellas artes; — **sand** arena fina o menuda; —**weather** tiempo claro o despejado; **to feel** — sentirse muy bien de salud; **to have a** — **time** pasar un rato muy divertido; **fine-looking** bien parecido, guapo; s. multa; **in** — finalmente, en fin, en resumen; v. multar; **-ly** adv. finamente; con primor; excelentemente; muy bien, perfectamente.

fine·ness [fáɪnnɪs] s. finura; fineza; primor; excelencia, perfección.

fin·er·y [fáɪnərɪ] s. galas; atavíos, adornos.

fi·nesse [fɪnés] s. sutileza; artificio; soltura.

fin·ger [fíŋgɚ] s. dedo (de la mano); —**print** impresión digital; **the little** — el dedo meñique; **middle** — el dedo del corazón, dedo de enmedio; **ring** — dedo anular; v. tocar; manosear.

fin·ger·nail [fíŋgɚnel] s. uña.

fin·ick·y [fíniki] adj. melindroso.

fin·ish [fíniʃ] s. fin, término, conclusión; (varnish) acabado; pulimiento; **to have a rough** — estar sin pulir, sin pulimento o al natural; v. acabar, acabar con, terminar, finalizar; pulir, pulimentar.

fin·ished [fíniʃt] adj. acabado; pulido, pulimentado, excelente.

fir [fɚ] s. abeto.

fire [faɪr] s. (flame) fuego; lumbre; (destructive) quemazón; incendio; — **alarm** alarma de incendios; — **department** cuerpo o servicio de bomberos; servicio de incendios; — **engine** bomba (para incendios); — **escape** escalera de salvamento; — **insurance** seguro contra incendios; **to be on** — estar ardiendo, estar quemándose; **to catch** — incendiarse, quemarse; **to set on** — pegar fuego, incendiar; **to be under enemy** — estar expuesto al fuego del enemigo; v. incendiar; pegar fuego; inflamar; disparar; **to** — **an employee** despedir (o expulsar) a un empleado.

fire·arm [fáɪrɑrm] s. arma de fuego.

fire·brand [fáɪrbrænd] s. tizón; pavesa.

fire·crack·er [fáɪrkrækɚ] s. triquitraque.

fire·fly [fáɪrflaɪ] s. luciérnaga.

fire·man [fáɪrmən] s. bombero; fogonero.

fire·place [fáɪrples] s. chimenea, hogar.

fire·proof [fáɪrpruf] adj. incombustible; a prueba de incendio; v. hacer incombustible.

fire·side [fáɪrsaɪd] s. hogar.

fire·wood [fáɪrwʊd] s. leña.

fire·works [fáɪrwɝks] s. fuegos artificiales; pirotecnia.

fir·ing pin [fáɪrɪŋ pɪn] s. percusor.

firm [fɝm] adj. firme; fijo; estable; s. firma, razón social (nombre de una casa comercial); compañía (comercial o industrial); **-ly** adv. firmemente, con firmeza.

fir·ma·ment [fɝməmənt] s. firmamento.

firm·ness [fɝmnɪs] s. firmeza; estabilidad.

first [fɝst] adj. primero; adv. primero, en primer lugar, al principio, **from the** — desde el principio; **first-born** primogénito; **first-class** de primera clase; **first-cousin** primo hermano; **first-rate** de primera clase; muy bien; **—hand** de primera mano.

first aid [fɝst éd] s. primeros auxilios.

fish [fɪʃ] s. pez; C.A. peje; pescado; — **market** pescadería; — **story** patraña, cuento extravagante o increíble; **neither** — **nor fowl** ni chicha ni limonada; v. pescar.

fish·er [fíʃɚ] s. pescador.

fish·er·man [fíʃɚmən] s. pescador.

fish·er·y [fíʃɚɪ] s. pesquera; pesquería, pesca.

fish·hook [fíʃhʊk] s. anzuelo.

fish·ing [fíʃɪŋ]s. pesca, pesquería; — **rod** caña de pescar; — **tackle** avíos o enseres de pescar; **to go** — ir de pesca.

fis·sure [fíʃɚ] s. grieta, hendedura, Am. rajadura.

fist [fɪst] s. puño; **to shake one's** — **at** amenazar con el puño.

fit [fɪt] adj. (proper) apto; a propósito, propio, conveniente; (healthy) sano, de buena salud, en buen estado; capaz; — **to be tied** frenético; **not to see** — **to do it** no tener a bien hacerlo; s. talle (de un traje); ajuste; encaje (de una pieza en otra); ataque, convulsión; — **of anger** acceso, arrebato o arranque de cólera; **by -s and starts** espasmódicamente; **that suit is a good** — ese traje le entalla (o le viene) bien; v. ajustar(se); adaptar; encajar(se), caber (en); acomodar; entallar (un vestido); venir bien (un vestido, zapatos, sombrero, etc.); ser a propósito para, ser propio para; capacitar, preparar; **to** — **in with** armonizar con; llevarse bien con; **to** — **out** equipar, proveer; **it does not** — **the facts** no está de acuerdo con los hechos; no hace al caso.

fit·ness [fítnɪs] s. aptitud; capacidad; conveniencia; propiedad (de una idea, de una palabra, etc.); **physical** — buena salud.

fit·ting [fítɪŋ] adj. propio, apropiado; a propósito, conveniente; s. ajuste; **dress** — prueba de un traje o vestido; **-s** avíos, guarniciones, accesorios.

fix [fɪks] v. (repair) remendar; componer; reparar; ajustar; arreglar; (prearrange) fijar; asegurar; **to** — **up** arreglar(se); componer(se); s. apuro, aprieto.

fixed [fɪkst] adj. fijo, firme.

fix·ed·ly [fíksɪdlɪ] adv. de hito en hito; fijamente.

fix·ture [fíksʃɚ] s. (thing) accesorio fijo; (person)

persona firmemente establecida (en un sitio o empleo); **electric light -s** instalaciones eléctricas (como brazos de lámparas, arañas).

flab·by [flǽbɪ] adj. blanducho.

flag [flæg] s. bandera; banderola; — **lily** flor de lis; v. hacer señas con banderola; adornar con banderas; decaer, debilitarse, menguar, flaquear.

fla·grant [flǽgrənt] adv. flagrante, notorio, escandaloso.

flag·staff [flǽgstæf] s. asta de bandera.

flag·stone [flǽgston] s. losa.

flair [flɛr] s. instinto, penetración, cacumen; disposición o aptitud natural.

flak [flæk] s. fuego antiaéreo; crítica abusiva.

flake [flek] s. copo (de nieve); escama; hojuela; **corn -s** hojuelas de maíz; v. descostrarse, descascararse.

flam·boy·ant [flæmbɔ́jənt] adj. rimbombante; flameante.

flame [flem] s. llama; flama; — **thrower** lanzallamas; v. llamear, flamear, echar llamas; inflamar(se); enardecer(se).

flam·ing [flémɪŋ] adj. llameante; flameante; encendido; ardiente, apasionado; — **red** rojo encendido.

flank [flæŋk] s. flanco; costado; lado; ijar (de un animal); v. flanquear; rodear.

flan·nel [flǽnl] s. franela.

flap [flæp] s. (thing) aleta; cubierta (del bolsillo); (action) golpeteo; aleteo; v. golpetear; aletear, batir (las alas); hojear con violencia (las páginas).

flare [flɛr] s. llamarada; llama; arranque (de ira); vuelo (de una falda); v. llamear, echar llamaradas; tener vuelo (una falda); **to** — **up** enfurecerse; encenderse; **the illness -ed up** recrudeció la enfermedad.

flash [flæʃ] s. rayo; destello, llamarada; fogonazo; — **of hope** rayo de esperanza; — **of lightning** relámpago; — **of wit** agudeza; —**bulb** bombilla de destello; bombilla flash; **in a** — en un instante; **news** — última noticia (enviada por radio o telégrafo); v. relampaguear; destellar; brillar; centellear; radiar o telegrafiar (noticias); **to** — **by** pasar como un relámpago.

flash·ing [flǽʃɪŋ] s. relampagueo, centello; adj. relumbrante; flameante.

flash·light [flǽʃlaɪt] s. linterna eléctrica.

flash·y [flǽʃɪ] adj. relumbrante; llamativo, de relumbrón, ostentoso; chillante, chillón (dícese de los colores).

flask [flæsk] s. frasco.

flat [flæt] adj. (no curves) plano, llano, chato; aplastado; (tasteless) insípido; monótono; (without air) desinflado; — **denial** negativa terminante; — **note** nota desentonada; — **rate** precio o número redondo; **D** — re bemol (nota musical); — **car** vagón de plataforma; **to be** — **broke** estar completamente pelado, estar sin dinero; **to fall** — caer de plano; caer mal (un discurso, chiste, etc.); **to sing** — desafinarse, cantar desentonadamente; **to refuse -ly** negarse absolutamente; s. plano; palma (de la mano); apartamento, departamento, piso; bemol (en música).

flat·i·ron [flǽtaɪən] s. plancha.

flat·ness [flǽtnɪs] s. llanura; lisura; insipidez; desafinamiento (en música).

flat·ten [flǽtn] v. aplastar(se); aplanar(se); allanar(se).

flat·ter [flǽtɚ] v. lisonjear; adular.

FE

flat·ter·er [flǽtərə˞] s. lisonjero, adulador.
flat·ter·ing [flǽtərɪŋ] adj. lisonjero, halagüeño, adulador.
flat·ter·y [flǽtərɪ] s. lisonja, halago; adulación.
flat·u·lence [flǽtjʊləns] s. hinchazón, flatulencia.
flaunt [flɔnt] v. ostentar; hacer gala de.
fla·vor [flévə˞] s. sabor; gusto; condimento; v. sazonar; dar sabor a; condimentar.
fla·vor·less [flévə˞lɪs] adj. insípido, sin sabor.
flaw [flɔ] s. defecto; falta; tacha; imperfección.
flaw·less [flɔ́lɪs] adj. sin tacha; intachable, irreprochable; perfecto.
flax [flæks] s. lino.
flay [fle] s. desollar.
flea [fli] s. pulga.
fled [flɛd] pret. & p.p. de to flee.
flee [fli] v. huir; huir de.
fleece [flis] s. vellón, lana; v. trasquilar, esquilar; despojar, estafar, defraudar.
fleet [flit] s. flota; armada; adj. veloz.
fleet·ing [flitɪŋ] adj. fugaz, transitorio, pasajero, efímero.
Flem·ish [flémɪʃ] adj. flamenco; s. flamenco, idioma flamenco; the — los flamencos.
flesh [flɛʃ] s. carne; — and blood carne y hueso; — color color encarnado; in the — en persona.
flesh·y [flɛʃɪ] adj. carnoso; gordo, gordiflón.
flew [flu] pret. de to fly.
flex·i·bil·i·ty [flɛksəbɪlətɪ] s. flexibilidad.
flex·i·ble [flɛksəbl] adj. flexible.
flick·er [flíkə˞] s. titilación, parpadeo, luz trémula; temblor momentáneo (de emoción); aleteo; especie de pájaro carpintero; v. titilar; temblar; parpadear; vacilar; aletear; to — one's eyelash pestañear.
fli·er [fláɪə˞] s. volador; aviador; tren rápido.
flight [flaɪt] s. vuelo; bandada (de pájaros); escuadrilla (de aviones); fuga, huída; — of stairs tramo de escalera; to put to — poner en fuga.
flim·sy [flímzɪ] adj. endeble, débil; tenue; quebradizo; frágil; baladí; a — excuse una excusa baladí.
fling [flɪŋ] v. arrojar(se), lanzar(se); tirar; echar; to — open (shut) abrir (cerrar) de golpe; s. tiro; tirada, lanzamiento; tentativa; to go out on a — irse a echar una cana al aire.
flint [flɪnt] s. pedernal.
flip [flɪp] v. arrojar, lanzar al aire; sacudir; dar un dedazo.
flip·pan·cy [flípənsɪ] s. ligereza; frivolidad; impertinencia; petulancia.
flip·pant [flípənt] adj. ligero (en sus acciones y modales), ligero de cascos; frívolo; inpertinente; petulante.
flirt [flɜt] s. coqueta; coquetón, coquetona; v. coquetear.
flir·ta·tion [flɜtéʃən] s. coquetería; to carry on a — coquetear.
flit [flɪt] v. pasar velozmente; volar; revolotear.
float [flot] s. boya; cosa flotante, flotador; corcho (de una caña de pescar); balsa; carro o carroza (de procesiones, fiestas, etc.); v. flotar; sobrenadar; boyar; poner a flote; lanzar al mercado (una nueva emisión de valores, bonos, etc.).
flock [flak] s. bandada (de pájaros, niños, etc.); rebaño, grey; manada (de animales); grupo; — of people gentío, muchedumbre; v. agruparse; congregarse; to — to acudir juntos (o en bandadas) a; to — together andar juntos, volar en bandadas, ir en grupo.

flog [flag] v. azotar.
flood [flʌd] s. inundación; diluvio; avenida (de agua), crecida; creciente; torrente; —gate compuerta (de una presa); esclusa (de un canal); — light reflector; proyector de luz; — tide flujo (o marea ascendiente); v. inundar.
floor [flor] s. (surface) suelo; piso; (story) piso; (bottom) fondo; to have the — tener la palabra; v. solar; entarimar, enladrillar, enlosar; echar al suelo, derribar; asombrar.
flop [flap] v. (flap) caer o colgar flojamente; aletear; menearse; (throw) lanzar; dejar caer; (fail) fracasar; fallar; to — down dejarse caer; desplomarse, tumbarse; to — over voltear(se); dar vueltas; s. fracaso.
flo·rist [flórɪst] s. florero, florera; -'s shop florería.
floss [flɔs] s. seda floja; pelusa; fibra sedosa; dental — seda dental.
flound·er [fláʊndə˞] v. patalear (en el lodo, nieve, etc.); forcejear (por salir del lodo, nieve, o cualquier aprieto); revolcarse; tropezar, cometer errores; s. lenguado (pez).
flour [flaʊr] s. harina.
flour·ish [flɜ́ɪʃ] v. (prosper) florecer, prosperar, medrar; (blandish) blandir; agitar en el aire; s. floreo; adorno o rasgo caprichoso; ostentación; (with the signature) rúbrica.
flour·y [fláʊrɪ] adj. harinoso.
flow [flo] s. flujo; corriente; — of words torrente de palabras; v. fluir; correr; flotar, ondear; to — into desembocar en; to be -ing with riches nadar en la abundancia.
flow·er [fláʊə˞] s. flor; — bed cuadro de jardín; — vase florero; v. florecer, Am. florear.
flow·er·pot [fláʊrpat] s. N. Spain tiesto, And. Am. maceta.
flow·er·y [fláʊrɪ] adj. florido.
flow·ing [flóɪŋ] adj. fluído, corriente, fluente; suelto, ondeante.
flown [flon] p.p. de to fly.
flu [flu] s. influenza, gripe.
fluc·tu·ate [flʌ́ktʃʊet] v. fluctuar.
fluc·tu·a·tion [flʌktʃʊéʃən] s. fluctuación.
flue [flu] s. cañón (de chimenea); tubo de escape.
flu·en·cy [flúənsɪ] s. fluidez; labia.
flu·ent [flúənt] adj. fluente, flúido; to speak -ly hablar con facilidad.
fluff [flʌf] v. mullir; esponjar.
fluff·y [flʌ́fɪ] adj. mullido, suave, blando; cubierto de vello o plumón; — hair pelo esponjado o esponjoso.
flu·id [flúɪd] adj. & s. flúido.
flung [flʌŋ] pret. & p.p. de to fling.
flunk [flʌŋk] s. reprobación (en un examen o asignatura); v. reprobar, suspender (en un examen); salir mal, fracasar o fallar (en un examen).
flun·ky [flʌ́ŋkɪ] s. lacayo; ayudante servil; zalamero, persona servil.
flu·o·rine [flúərin] s. fluor.
flur·ry [flɜ́ɪ] s. (weather) ráfaga; nevisca; (action) agitación.
flush [flʌʃ] s. sonrojo, rubor; bochorno; flujo rápido; flux (de naipes); adj. lleno; rico; parejo, al mismo nivel; — with a flor de, a ras de; v. sonrojar(se), ruborizar(se), poner(se) colorado; hacer rebosar (de agua); to — out vaciar (un depósito), enjuagar.
flute [flut] s. flauta; estría (de una columna); v. acanalar, estriar (una columna).
flut·ter [flʌ́tə˞] s. aleteo; agitación; alboroto; vuelco

(*del corazón*); *v.* aletear; revolotear; agitar(se); palpitar; menear(se); tremolar (*una bandera*).

flux [flʌks] *s.* flujo.

fly [flaɪ] *s.* mosca; pliegue (*para cubrir botones*); bragueta (*abertura de los pantalones*); **on the** — al vuelo; **to hit a** — pegar una planchita o elevar una palomita (*en béisbol*); — **swatter** matamoscas; *v.* volar; pasar velozmente; huir; ondear; enarbolar (*una bandera*); **to** — **at** lanzarse sobre; **to** — **away** volar, irse, escaparse; **to** — **off the handle** perder los estribos (*o* la paciencia); **to** — **open (shut)** abrirse (cerrarse) de repente; **to** — **up in anger** montar en cólera.

fly·er = **flier**.

fly·leaf [flaɪlif] *s.* guarda (*hoja en blanco al principio y al fin de un libro*).

foam [fom] *s.* espuma; *v.* espumar, hacer espuma.

fo·cus [fókəs] *s.* foco; distancia focal; *v.* enfocar(se).

fod·der [fɑdɚ] *s.* forraje.

foe [fo] *s.* enemigo.

fog [fɑg] *s.* niebla, neblina, bruma; velo, nube (*en una película o fotografía*); —**horn** sirena; *v.* anublar, ofuscar, obscurecer; ponerse brumoso; velar(se) (*una película*).

fog·gy [fɑgɪ] *adj.* brumoso, nublado; obscuro, confuso.

foil [fɔɪl] *s.* oropel, hojuela, laminita de metal; florete (*de esgrima*); realce, contraste; **tin** — hojuela de estaño; *v.* frustrar.

fold [fold] *s.* (*double over*) pliegue, doblez; (*enclosure*) redil; grey; **three** — tres veces; **hundred** — cien veces; *v.* doblar(se); plegar(se); envolver; **to** — **one's arms** cruzarse de brazos.

fold·er [fóldɚ] *s.* (*pamphlet*) folleto, circular; (*holder*) papelera; plegadera (*máquina para plegar*).

fold·ing [fóldɪŋ] *adj.* plegadizo; — **chair** silla plegadiza, silla de tijera; — **machine** plegadora, máquina plegadora; — **screen** biombo.

fo·li·age [fólɪdʒ] *s.* follaje, fronda.

fo·li·o [fólɪo] *s.* folio; infolio, libro en folio; pliego; — **edition** edición en folio.

folk [fok] *s.* gente; pueblo; **-s** parientes, allegados; familia; personas; amigos (*vocativo familiar*); *adj.* popular, del pueblo; — **dance** danza o baile tradicional; —**lore** folklore; cuentos, leyendas y tradiciones populares; — **song** canción popular, canción típica o tradicional; — **music** música del pueblo; música tradicional.

fol·low [fálo] *v.* seguir; ejercer (*un oficio o profesión*); seguir el hilo de (*un argumento*); seguirse (*como consecuencia*); **to** — **suit** jugar el mismo palo (*en naipes*); seguir el ejemplo, imitar.

fol·low·er [fáləwɚ] *s.* seguidor; imitador; partidario.

fol·low·ing [fáləwɪŋ] *s.* séquito, comitiva, partidarios; *adj.* siguiente; subsiguiente.

fol·ly [fálɪ] *s.* locura; necedad, tontería; desatino.

fo·ment [fomént] *v.* fomentar.

fond [fɑnd] *adj.* aficionado (a); amigo (de); amante (de), encariñado (con); cariñoso, afectuoso; tierno; **to be** — **of** querer a (*una persona*); estar encariñado con, ser aficionado a; gustar de (*algo*); **-ly** *adv.* cariñosamente, afectuosamente.

fon·dle [fándl] *v.* acariciar.

fond·ness [fándnɪs] *s.* cariño, afecto; afición.

font [fɑnt] *s.* pila bautismal; fuente.

food [fud] *s.* alimento, sustento; comida.

food·stuff [fúdstʌf] *s.* alimento; producto

alimenticio; comestibles.

fool [ful] *s.* tonto, necio, zonzo; payaso; **to play the** — payasear, hacer el payaso; *v.* chasquear, chancear(se); bromear, embromar; engañar; **to** — **away the time** malgastar el tiempo.

fool·ish [fúlɪʃ] *adj.* tonto; necio, bobo, zonzo.

fool·ness [fúlɪʃnɪs] *s.* tontería, necedad, bobería.

foot [fut] *s.* pie; pata (*de animal*); **on** — a pie; — **soldier** soldado de infantería; **to put one's** — **in** it meter la pata; *v.* andar a pie; **to** — **it** andar a pie; **to** — **the bill** pagar la cuenta; sufragar los gastos.

foot·ball [fútbɔl] *s.* fútbol, football.

foot·hold [fúthold] *s.* arraigo; puesto establecido.

foot·ing [fútɪŋ] *s.* base; posición firme; **to be on a friendly** — **with** tener relaciones amistosas con; **to lose one's** — perder pie.

foot·lights [fúlaɪts] *s. pl.* candilejas (*dei teatro*); tablas, teatro.

foot·man [fútmən] *s.* lacayo.

foot·note [fútnot] *s.* nota al pie de una página.

foot·path [fútpæθ] *s.* vereda, senda, trocha (*para gente de a pie*).

foot·print [fútprɪnt] *s.* huella, pisada.

foot·step [fútstɛp] *s.* (*action*) pisada, paso; (*trace*) huella; **to follow in the -s of** seguir las pisadas o huellas de.

foot·stool [fútstul] *s.* banquillo, taburete, escabel.

fop [fɑp] *s.* currutaco.

for [fɔr] *prep.* por; para; — **all of her intelligence** a pesar de su inteligencia; — **feat that** por miedo (de) que; — **the present** por el presente, por ahora; **as** — **him** en cuanto a él; **to know** — **a fact** saber de cierto, saber de hecho; **to pay** — **it** pagárselo; **to thank him** — **it** agradecérselo; *conj.* porque, pues.

for·age [fɔrɪdʒ] *s.* forraje; *v.* forrajear; dar forraje a.

for·ay [fóre] *s.* correría, incursión; saqueo; *v.* pillar, saquear.

for·bade [fɚbǽd] *pret. de* **to forbid.**

for·bear [fɔrbɛr] *s.* antepasado; [fɔrbér] *v.* abstenerse de; tener paciencia.

for·bid [fɚbíd] *v.* prohibir; vedar.

for·bid·den [fɚbídn] *adj.* prohibido; vedado; *p.p. de* **to forbid.**

for·bid·ding [fɚbídɪŋ] *adj.* austero, reservado; pavoroso; impenetrable.

for·bore [fɔrbór] *pret. de* **to forbear.**

for·borne [fɔrbórn] *p.p. de* **to forbear.**

force [fors] *s.* fuerza; cuerpo (*de policía, de empleados, etc.*); **in** — en vigor, vigente; **armed -s** fuerzas armadas; *v.* forzar, obligar; **to** — **one's way** abrirse paso por fuerza; **to** — **out** echar por fuerza, echar a la fuerza.

forced [forst] *adj.* forzado.

force·ful [fórsfəl] *adj.* vigoroso; enérgico.

for·ceps [fórsəps] *s.* gatillo (*tenazas para sacar muelas*); pinzas.

for·ci·ble [fórsəbl] *adj.* (*strong*) fuerte, enérgico; potente; eficaz; (*by force*) violento; hecho a la fuerza; **forcibly** *adv.* fuertemente, con energía; forzosamente; por fuerza.

ford [ford] *s.* vado; *v.* vadear.

fore [for] *adj.* anterior, delantero; de proa; *s.* frente; puesto delantero; *adv.* delante, hacia adelante; *interj.* ¡cuidado! (*dícese en el campo de golf*).

fore·arm [fórarm] *s.* antebrazo.

fore·bode [forbód] *v.* presagiar; presentir.

FL

fore·bod·ing [forbódɪŋ] *s.* presentimiento; presagio.
fore·cast [fórkæst] *s.* pronóstico; [forkǽst] *v.* pronosticar; predecir; *pret. & p.p. de* **to forecast.**
fore·fa·ther [fórfɑðɚ] *s.* antepasado.
fore·fin·ger [fórfɪŋgɚ] *s.* (dedo) índice.
fore·foot [fórfʊt] *s.* pata delantera, mano (*de cuadrúpedo*).
fore·go [forgó] *v.* abstenerse de.
fore·gone [forgón] *p.p. de* **to forego; a —** **conclusion** una conclusión inevitable.
fore·ground [fórgraʊnd] *s.* frente, primer plano, primer término.
fore·head [fɔ́rɪd] *s.* frente (*f.*).
for·eign [fɔ́rɪn] *adj.* extranjero; foráneo; extraño; **— to his nature** ajeno a su índole; **— office** ministerio de relaciones exteriores; departamento de negocios extranjeros; **— trade** comercio exterior; **foreign-born** extranjero de nacimiento.
for·eign·er [fɔ́rɪnɚ] *s.* extranjero; forastero.
fore·lock [fórlɑk] *s.* guedeja.
fore·man [fórmən] *s.* capataz; presidente (*de un jurado*); *Méx., C.A., Ven., Col.* caporal (*de un rancho o hacienda*); *Riopl.* capataz.
fore·most [fórmost] *adj.* (*first*) primero; delantero; (*most important*) principal, más notable, más distinguido.
fore·noon [fornún] *s.* (la) mañana.
fore·run·ner [forrʌ́nɚ] *s.* precursor; presagio.
fore·saw [forsɔ́] *pret. de* **to foresee.**
fore·see [forsí] *s.* prever.
fore·seen [forsín] *p.p. de* **to foresee** previsto.
fore·sight [fórsaɪt] *s.* previsión.
for·est [fɔ́rɪst] *s.* bosque, selva; **— ranger** guardabosques; *v.* arbolar, plantar de árboles.
fore·stall [forstɔ́l] *v.* prevenir; madrugar.
for·est·er [fɔ́rɪstɚ] *s.* guardabosques; silvicultor; ·habitante de un bosque.
for·est·ry [fɔ́rɪstrɪ] *s.* silvicultura.
fore·tell [fortél] *v.* precedir, pronosticar, presagiar.
fore·told [fortóld] *pret. & p.p, de* **foretell.**
for·ev·er [fɚévɚ] *adv.* por (*o* para) siempre.
for·feit [fɔ́rfɪt] *s.* multa; pena; prenda perdida; **game of -s** juego de prendas; *v.* perder, perder el derecho a.
for·gave [fɚgév] *pret. de* **to forgive.**
forge [fordʒ] *s.* fragua; forja; *v.* fraguar; forjar; falsear, falsificar; **to — ahead** abrirse paso; avanzar.
for·ger·y [fórdʒɚɪ] *s.* falsificación.
for·get [fɚgét] *v.* olvidar; olvidarse de; **to — oneself** cometer un desmán impensadamente; perder el tino o la paciencia.
for·get·ful [fɚgétfəl] *adj.* olvidadizo; negligente.
for·get·ful·ness [fɚgétfəlnɪs] *s.* olvido; negligencia.
for·get-me-not [fɚgétmɪnɑt] *s.* nomeolvides.
for·give [fɚgív] *v.* perdonar.
for·giv·en [fɚgívən] *p.p. de* **to forgive.**
for·give·ness [fɚgívnɪs] *s.* perdón.
for·giv·ing [fɚgívɪŋ] *adj.* perdonador, misericordioso, de buen corazón.
for·got [fɚgát] *pret. & p.p. de* **to forget.**
for·got·ten [fɚgátn] *p.p. de* **to forget.**
fork [fork] *s.* tenedor, *Méx., Col., Ven., Andes* trinche; horquilla (*para heno*); horcón; bifurcación; *v.* bifurcarse; levantar o arrojar (*heno*) con horquilla.
for·lorn [fɚlórn] *adj.* desamparado, desdichado.
form [form] *s.* forma; condición, estado; **blank —** blanco, forma en blanco, *Méx., Ven.* esqueleto; *v.* formar(se).

for·mal [fɔ́rml] *adj.* formal, perteneciente a la forma; convencional, ceremonioso; **— party** reunión de etiqueta; **-ly** *adv.* formalmente, con ceremonia, solemnemente.
for·mal·i·ty [formǽlətɪ] *s.* formalidad, ceremonia; formalismo.
for·ma·tion [forméʃən] *s.* formación.
for·ma·tive [fɔ́rmətɪv] *adj.* formativo.
for·mer [fɔ́rmɚ] *adj.* primero, precedente, anterior; antiguo; **in — times** en otro tiempo, en días de antaño, antiguamente, anteriormente; **the —** aquél (aquèlla, aquéllos, aquéllas); **-ly** *adv.* anterioremente; antes, en tiempos pasados.
for·mi·da·ble [fɔ́rmɪdəbl] *adj.* formidable.
for·mu·la [fɔ́rmjələ] *s.* fórmula.
for·mu·late [fɔ́rmjəlet] *v.* formular.
for·sake [fɚsék] *v.* desamparar; abandonar.
for·sak·en [fɚsékən] *p.p. de* **to forsake** *& adj.* desamparado, abandonado.
for·sook [fɚsʊ́k] *pret. de* **to forsake.**
for·swear [forswέr] *v.* abjurar.
fort [fort] *s.* fuerte, fortín, fortaleza.
forth [forθ] *adv.* adelante; hacia adelante; **to go —** salir; **and so —** etcétera, y así succesivamente.
forth·com·ing [fórθkʌ́mɪŋ] *adj.* venidero, próximo; **funds will not be — until** no habrá fondos disponibles hasta.
forth·with [forθwíθ] *adv.* en seguida, pronto, al punto.
for·ti·fi·ca·tion [fortəfəkéʃən] *s.* fortificación.
for·ti·fy [fɔ́rtəfaɪ] *v.* fortificar; fortalecer.
for·ti·tude [fɔ́rtətjud] *s.* fortaleza.
fort·night [fɔ́rtnaɪt] *s.* quincena, quince días, dos semanas.
for·tress [fɔ́rtrɪs] *s.* fortaleza, fuerte.
for·tu·i·tous [fortjúətəs] *adj.* fortuito; inopinado, inesperado.
for·tu·nate [fɔ́rtʃənɪt] *adj.* afortunado; **-ly** *adv.* afortunadamente, por fortuna.
for·tune [fɔ́rtʃən] *s.* fortuna; **—teller** agorero, adivino.
fo·rum [fórəm] *s.* foro; tribunal; ateneo.
for·ward [fɔ́rwəd] *adj.* (*leading*) delantero; (*progressive*) precoz; progresista; (*daring*) atrevido; descarado; *adv.* adelante, hacia adelante; *v.* transmitir; despachar; reenviar; reexpedir, **to — a plan** fomentar un plan.
fos·sil [fásl] *adj.* fósil; anticuado; *s.* fósil.
fos·ter [fóstɚ] *v.* criar, nutrir; fomentar; promover; *adj.* putativo; adoptivo.
fought [fɔt] *pret. & p.p. de* **to fight.**
foul [faʊl] *adj.* sucio; asqueroso; puerco, cochino; fétido; vil; injusto; **— air** aire viciado; **— ball** pelota foul (*en béisbol*); **—mouthed** mal hablado, obsceno; **— play** juego sucio; fraude; violencia; **— weather** mal tiempo; *s.* mala jugada (*contraria a las reglas del juego*), trampa, *Am.* chapuza, foul; *Am.* pegar un foul (*en béisbol*).
found [faʊnd] *v.* fundar, establecer; *pret. & p.p. de* **to find.**
foun·da·tion [faʊndéʃən] *s.* fundación; base, fundamento; dotación.
foun·der [fáʊndɚ] *s.* fundador; fundidor (*de metales*); *v.* zozobrar, irse a pique; fracasar; tropezar; hacer zozobrar.
foun·dry [fáʊndrɪ] *s.* fundición.
foun·tain [fáʊntɪn] *s.* fuente; manatial; **— pen** pluma (de) fuente, pluma estilográfica.
four·score [fórskór] *adj.* cuatro veintenas, ochenta.
fourth [forθ] *adj.* cuarto; *s.* cuarto, cuarta parte;

the — of July el cuarto de julio.
fowl [faul] s. ave; gallo, gallina; pollo.
fox [faks] s. zorra; zorro; persona astuta.
fox·y [fáksı] adj. zorro, zorruno, astuto.
frac·tion [frǽkʃən] s. fracción; quebrado.
frac·ture [frǽktʃəʴ] s. fractura; quiebra; rotura; v. fracturar; quebrar, romper.
frag·ile [frǽdʒəl] adj. frágil.
frag·ment [frǽgmənt] s. fragmento.
fra·grance [frégrəns] s. fragancia.
fra·grant [frégrənt] adj. fragante, oloroso.
frail [frel] adj. frágil; endeble, débil.
frail·ty [fréltı] s. debilidad, flaqueza.
frame [frem] s. armazón, armadura, esqueleto; estructura; marco (de un cuadro, ventana, puerta, etc.); disposición (de ánimo); **embroidery —** bastidor para bordar; **— house** casa con armazón de madera; v. formar, forjar; fabricar; enmarcar (poner en marco); inventar; **to — someone** conspirar contra una persona; **to — up a charge** forjar un cargo o acusación.
frame·work [frémwəʴk] s. armazón, esqueleto; estructura.
franc [frǽŋk] s. franco (moneda francesa).
fran·chise [frǽntʃaız] s. (privilege) franquicia; derecho o privilegio político; (vote) sufragio, voto.
fran·ci·um [frǽnsıəm] s. francio.
frank [frǽŋk] adj. franco, sincero; **very —** francote; s. sello de franqueo; franquicia de correos; v. franquear, despachar, enviar (carta) exenta de franqueo.
frank·furt·er [frǽŋkfəʴtəʴ] s. salchicha.
frank·ness [frǽŋknıs] s. franqueza, sinceridad.
fran·tic [frǽntık] adj. frenético; **-ally** adv. frenéticamente.
fra·ter·nal [frətɜ́ʴnl] adj. fraternal.
fra·ter·ni·ty [frətɜ́ʴnətı] s. fraternidad; confraternidad.
frat·er·nize [frǽtəʴnaız] v. fraternizar.
fraud [frɔd] s. fraude, engaño; trampa, Am. chapuza; trampista, tramposo.
fraud·u·lent [frɔ́dʒələnt] adj. fraudulento.
fray [fre] s. reyerta, riña, pelea, alboroto; raedura; v. raer(se); deshilacharse.
frayed [fred] adj. raído, deshilachado.
freak [frik] s. capricho; rareza, hombre o cosa rara; monstruosidad, fenómeno.
freck·le [frékl] s. peca; v. ponerse pecoso.
freck·led [frékld] adj. pecoso.
freck·ly [fréklı] adj. pecoso.
free [fri] adj. (not bound) libre; suelto; (gratis) gratuito; exento; (generous) liberal, generoso; **— of charge** gratis; **— on board (f.o.b.)** libre a bordo; **— port** puerto franco; **postage —** franco de porte; **to give someone a — hand** dar rienda suelta o libertad de acción a una persona; **— hand drawing** dibujo a pulso, dibujo a mano; **— thinker** libre pensador; adv. libremente; gratis, de balde; v. librar; libertar; soltar; eximir; **-ly** adv. libremente; con soltura.
free·dom [frídəm] s. libertad; libre uso; exención.
freeze [friz] v. helar(se); congelar(se).
freez·ing [frízıŋ] adj. helado, glacial; **— point** punto de congelación.
freight [fret] s. flete; carga; **— train** tren de carga, tren de mercancías; **by —** por carga; v. fletar, cargar; enviar por carga.
French [frɛntʃ] adj. francés; **to take — leave** marcharse a la francesa, irse sin despedirse; s. francés, idioma francés; **the —** los franceses.

French·man [frɛ́ntʃmən] s. francés.
fren·zy [frɛ́nzı] s. frenesí.
fre·quen·cy [fríkwənsı] s. frecuencia.
fre·quent [fríkwənt] adj. frecuente; v. frecuentar; **-ly** adv. frecuentemente, a menudo.
fresh [frɛʃ] adj. (not stale) fresco; (new) reciente; nuevo; (bold) impertinente, entremetido; **— water** agua dulce; **-ly** adv. frescamente; con frescura; nuevamente, recientemente; **-ly painted** recién pintado, acabado de pintar.
fresh·en [frɛ́ʃən] v. refrescar(se).
fresh·man [frɛ́ʃmən] s. novato, novicio, estudiante del primer año.
fresh·ness [frɛ́ʃnıs] s. frescura; frescor, fresco; descaro.
fret [frɛt] v. irritar(se); apurarse; estar nervioso; agitarse; s. agitación, apuro, preocupación; traste (de guitarra, mandolina, etc.); **—work** calado.
fret·ful [frɛ́tfəl] adj. descontentadizo. malhumorado, enojadizo; nervioso.
fri·ar [fráıəʴ] s. fraile ≡
fric·tion [fríkʃən] s. fricción; rozamiento; frotación; desavenencia.
Fri·day [fráıdı] s. viernes.
fried [fraıd] adj. frito; freído; p.p. de **to fry.**
friend [frɛnd] s. amigo, amiga.
friend·less [frɛ́ndlıs] adj. sin amigos, solo.
friend·li·ness [frɛ́ndlınıs] s. afabilidad; amistad.
friend·ly [frɛ́ndlı] adj. amistoso, afable, amigable; propicio, favorable; adv. amistosamente.
friend·ship [frɛ́nʃıp] s. amistad.
frig·ate [frígət] s. fragata.
fright [fraıt] s. espanto, susto; terror; espantajo; **she is a —** es un adefesio.
fright·en [fráıtn] v. espantar, asustar, atemorizar; **to — away** espantar, ahuyentar; **to get -ed** espantarse, asustarse.
fright·ened [fráıtnd] adj. espantado, asustado.
fright·ful [fráıtfəl] adj. espantoso, terrible; horroroso.
frig·id [frídʒıd] adj. frígido, frío.
fringe [frındʒ] s. fleco; flequillo; orla; v. adornar con fleco; orlar.
frip·per·y [frípərı] s. perifollos, moños, perejiles; cursilería.
frisk [frısk] v. retozar, cabriolar, saltar, brincar; registrar (los bolsillos), Ven., Méx. exculcar.
frisk·y [frískı] adj. retozón, juguetón.
frit·ter [frítəʴ] s. fritura, fruta de sartén; v. **to — away** malgastar, desperdiciar poco a poco.
fri·vol·i·ty [frıválətı] s. frivolidad.
friv·o·lous [frívələs] adj. frívolo.
fro [fro]: **to and —** de una parte a otra; de aquí para allá.
frock [frak] s. vestido (de mujer); **— coat** levita.
frog [frɔg] s. rana; broche (de cordoncillos o galones); **— in the throat** gallo en la garganta.
frol·ic [frálık] s. retozo, juego; holgorio, diversión; v. retozar, travesear, juguetear.
from [frɑm, frʌm] prep. de; desde; **to take something away — a person** quitarle algo a una persona.
front [frʌnt] s. frente (m.); fachada; frontispicio; **in — of** enfrente de; delante de; **— shirt** pechera; adj. delantero; frontal; frontero; v. hacer frente a; **to — towards** mirar hacia; dar a, caer a.
fron·tier [frʌntír] s. frontera; adj. fronterizo.
frost [frɔst] s. escarcha; helada; v. escarchar; helar; cubrir de escarcha.

frost·ing [frɔ́stɪŋ] s. escarcha, confitura (*para cubrir un pastel*).
frost·y [frɔ́stɪ] adj. escarchado, cubierto de escarcha; helado.
froth [frɔθ] s. espuma; v. espumar, hacer espuma; echar espuma o espumarajos; **to — at the mouth** echar espumarajos por la boca; enfurecerse.
frown [fraʊn] s. ceño; entrecejo; v. fruncir el ceño o las cejas; **to — at** mirar con ceño; desaprobar (*algo*).
froze [froz] pret. de **to freeze**.
fro·zen [frózn̩] p.p. de **to freeze**.
fru·gal [frúgl̩] adj. frugal.
fruit [frut] s. fruto (*en general*); fruta (*comestible*); **to eat —** comer fruta; **tree** árbol frutal; v. fructificar, producir frutas.
fruit·ful [frútfəl] adj. fructuoso; productivo; provechoso.
fruit·less [frútlɪs] adj. infructuoso, improductivo, estéril.
frus·trate [frʌ́stret] v. frustrar.
frus·tra·tion [frʌstréʃən] s. frustración.
fry [fraɪ] v. freír(se); s. fritada; **small —** pececillos; gente menuda; **French fries** patatas fritas a la francesa; **-ing pan** sartén.
fudge [fʌdʒ] s. dulce (*usualmente de chocolate y nueces*).
fu·el [fjúəl] s. combustible; incentivo.
fu·gi·tive [fjúdʒətɪv] adj. fugitivo; transitorio; s. fugitivo, prófugo.
ful·fill [fʊlfíl] v. cumplir; cumplir con; realizar; llevar a cabo; llenar (*un requisito*).
ful·fill·ment [fʊlfílmənt] s. cumplimiento.
full [fʊl] adj. lleno; completo; harto; pleno; **— dress** traje de etiqueta; **— moon** plenilunio, luna llena; **— skirt** falda de vuelo entero; **— of fun** muy divertido, muy chistoso; **at — speed** a toda velocidad; **in —** completamente; por completo; **to the —** por completo, por entero, totalmente; adv. completamente, enteramente; **to know — well** saber perfectamente, saber a ciencia cierta; **full-blooded** de raza pura; **full-fledged** hecho y derecho; maduro; completo; **-y** adv. completamente, enteramente, por completo.
full·ness [fʊ́lnɪs] s. plenitud; llenura.
fum·ble [fʌ́mbl̩] v. tentalear, buscar a tientas; chapucear, no coger la pelota o soltarla al correr.
fume [fjum] v. exhalar vapor o gas; rabiar; **-s** s. pl. vapores, emanaciones, gases.
fu·mi·gate [fjúməget] v. fumigar, sahumar, Riopl. humear.
fun [fʌn] s. diversión; burla, broma, chanza, Carib., Méx., C.A. choteo; **for —** en (o de) broma; de chanza; de chiste; **full of —** muy divertido; **to have —** divertirse; **to make — of** burlarse de, chancearse con, Carib., Méx., C.A. chotear, chotearse con; Riopl. jorobar.
func·tion [fʌ́ŋkʃən] s. función; v. funcionar.
fund [fʌnd] s. fondo, caudal; **-s** fondos, recursos; v. consolidar (*una deuda*); prorrogar el plazo de (*una deuda*).
fun·da·men·tal [fʌndəméntl̩] adj. fundamental; s. fundamento, principio.
fu·ner·al [fjúnərəl] adj. funeral, fúnebre; s. funeral, exequias, funerales.
fun·gus [fʌ́ŋgəs] s. hongo; fungosidad.
fun·nel [fʌ́nl̩] s. embudo; humero (*cañón de chimenea*).
fun·ny [fʌ́nɪ] adj. (*comical*) chistoso, cómico, gracioso, divertido; (*odd*) extraño, raro; **the**

funnies la sección cómica (*de un periódico*).
fur [fɜ] s. piel (*de animales peludos o lanudos*); sarro (*en la lengua*); **— coat** abrigo de pieles; v. forrar, cubrir o adornar con pieles.
fur·bish [fɜ́bɪʃ] v. acicalar, pulir.
fu·ri·ous [fjúrɪəs] adj. furioso.
furl [fɜl] v. arrollar, enrollar; plegar.
fur·lough [fɜ́lo] s. licencia militar; s. dar licencia militar.
fur·nace [fɜ́nɪs] s. calorífero; **blast —** alto horno.
fur·nish [fɜ́nɪʃ] v. (*equip*) equipar; amueblar; (*provide*) proveer, suministrar, surtir; **to — a room** amueblar un cuarto.
fur·ni·ture [fɜ́nɪtʃɚ] s. muebles, mobiliario, moblaje, mueblaje.
fur·row [fɜ́o] s. surco; arruga; v. surcar; arar.
fur·ther [fɜ́ðɚ] adj. adicional; más lejano, más remoto; adv. además; más; más lejos; v. promover, fomentar, adelantar.
fur·ther·more [fɜ́ðɚmor] adv. además.
fur·thest [fɜ́ðɪst] adj. (el) más lejano, (el) más remoto; adv. más lejos.
fur·tive [fɜ́tɪv] adj. furtivo.
fu·ry [fjúrɪ] s. furia; frenesí.
fuse [fjuz] s. fusible; mecha; v. fundir(se).
fu·se·lage [fjúzlɪdʒ] s. fuselaje.
fu·sion [fjúʒən] s. fusión; **nuclear —** fusión nuclear.
fuss [fʌs] s. melindre, preocupación inútil; bulla innecesaria; **to make a — over someone** darle a alguien demasiada importancia, desvivirse por alguien; v. hacer melindres, inquietarse (*por bagatelas*).
fuss·y [fʌ́sɪ] adj. melindroso; minucioso (*en demasía*); inquieto, nervioso; **— dress** vestido con demasiados adornos.
fu·tile [fjútl̩] adj. fútil; vano.
fu·ture [fjútʃɚ] adj. futuro; s. futuro; porvenir.
fuzz [fʌz] s. vello; pelusa.
fuzz·y [fʌ́zɪ] adj. velloso; cubierto de plumón fino; cubierto de pelusa.

G:g

gab [gæb] v. charlar, parlotear; s. charla; **gift of —** labia, facundia.
gab·ar·dine [gǽbɚdin] s. gabardina (*paño*).
gab·ble [gǽbl̩] s. charla, cotorreo; v. charlar, cotorrear.
ga·ble [gébl̩] s. gablete (*de un tejado*); **— roof** tejado de caballete o de dos aguas; **— window** ventana con gablete.
gad [gæd] v. vagar, callejear; andar de aquí para allá.
gadg·et [gǽdʒɪt] s. adminículo, artefacto, chisme.
gag [gæg] s. (*obstacle*) mordaza; (*joke*) broma, burla; morcilla, chiste (*improvisado por un actor*); v. amordazar; dar náuseas, hacer vomitar, basquear; interpolar chistes (*en la escena*).
gage véase **gauge**.
gai·e·ty [géətɪ] s. alegría, viveza, alborozo.
gai·ly [gélɪ] adv. alegremente; vistosamente.
gain [gen] s. ganancia, provecho; v. ganar.
gain·ful [génfl̩] adj. ganancioso.
gait [get] s. paso, andadura, marcha.
gale [gel] s. ventarrón; **— of laughter** risotada, carcajada, risada.
gall [gɔl] s. (*bile*) bilis, hiel; (*bitterness*) amargura; odio; descaro; **— bladder** vesícula; v. irritar.

gal·lant [gǽlənt] *adj.* valiente; noble; vistoso; [gəlǽnt] *adj.* galante, atento, cortés; galanteador; *s.* galán.

gal·lant·ry [gǽləntrɪ] *s.* galantería; gallardía, valor.

gal·ler·y [gǽlərɪ] *s.* galería; paraíso, gallinero *del (teatro)*.

gal·ley [gǽlɪ] *s.* galera; cocina *(de un buque)*; — **proof** galerada; — **slave** galeote.

gal·lium [gǽliəm] *s.* galio.

gal·lon [gǽlən] *s.* galón *(aproximadamente cuatro litros)*.

gal·lop [gǽləp] *s.* galope; *v.* galopar, galopear; ir a galope.

gal·lows [gǽloz] *s.* horca.

gal·losh·es [gəlɑ́ʃɪz] *s. pl.* chanclos, zapatos fuertes, zapatones.

gal·va·nom·e·ter [gælvənámətɚ] *s.* galvanómetro.

gam·ble [gǽmbl] *v.* jugar, apostar, aventurar *(algo)* en el juego; **to** — **away** perder en el juego; **to** — **everything** jugar el todo por el todo; arriesgarlo todo; *s.* jugada *(en juegos de azar)*, apuesta; riesgo.

gam·bol [gǽmbəl] *v.* retozar; cabriolar; juguetear; *s.* retozo, cabriola.

game [gem] *s.* juego; deporte; caza *(animales de caza y su carne)*; **to make** — **of** mofarse de, burlarse de; *adj.* valiente, atrevido; resuelto; — **bird** ave de caza.

gam·ut [gǽmət] *s.* gama.

gan·der [gǽndɚ] *s.* ánsar, ganso.

gang [gǽŋ] *s.* cuadrilla; pandilla; juego *(de herramientas o máquinas)*; *v.* agrupar(se); **to** — **up against** conspirar contra.

gang·plank [gǽŋplæŋk] *s.* plancha, pasamano *(de un buque)*, pasarela.

gan·grene [gǽŋgrin] *s.* gangrena; *v.* gangrenar(se).

gang·ster [gǽŋstɚ] *s.* bandolero, bandido, maleante, atracador.

gang·way [gǽŋwe] *s.* paso, pasadizo; plancha, pasamano; portalón *(de un barco)*; —! ¡a un lado! ¡ábranse!

gant·let = **gauntlet**.

gap [gǽp] *s.* brecha, abertura; boquete; hueco; intervalo.

gape [gep] *s. (breach)* brecha, abertura; *(open jaws)* bostezo; boqueada; *v.* boquear, abrir la boca; estar boquiabierto *(mirando)*; estar embobado; bostezar.

ga·rage [gərɑ́ʒ] *s.* garaje.

garb [gɑrb] *s.* vestido; vestidura; aspecto, apariencia; *v.* vestir, ataviar.

gar·bage [gɑ́rbɪdʒ] *s.* desperdicios, basura.

gar·den [gɑ́rdn̩] *s.* jardín; huerta; huerto; *v.* cultivar un jardín.

gar·den·er [gɑ́rdnɚ] *s.* jardinero, hortelano; horticultor.

gar·gle [gɑ́rgl̩] *s.* gargarismo, *Am.* gárgaras; *v.* gargarizar, hacer gárgaras, *Am.* gargarear.

gar·land [gɑ́rlənd] *s.* guirnalda.

gar·lic [gɑ́rlɪk] *s.* ajo.

gar·ment [gɑ́rmənt] *s.* prenda *(de vestir)*.

gar·net [gɑ́rnɪt] *s.* granate.

gar·nish [gɑ́rnɪʃ] *s.* aderezo; adorno; *v.* aderezar; adornar; guarnecer.

gar·ret [gǽrɪt] *s.* desván, buhardilla.

gar·ri·son [gǽrəsn̩] *s.* guarnición; *v.* guarnecer o guarnicionar *(una fortaleza)*.

gar·ter [gɑ́rtɚ] *s.* liga *(para sujetar las medias)*; *v.* sujetar con liga.

gas [gǽs] *s. (gaseous)* gas; *(petroleum)* gasolina; — **burner** mechero; — **stove** estufa o cocina de gas; **tear** — gas lacrimante o lacrimógeno; *v.* asfixiar con gas; envenenar con gas.

gas·e·ous [gǽsɪəs] *adj.* gaseoso.

gash [gǽʃ] *s.* cuchillada, herida, incisión; *v.* dar una cuchillada, acuchillar.

gas·o·line [gǽslɪn] *s.* gasolina.

gasp [gǽsp] *s.* boqueada; grito sofocado; *v.* boquear; jadear; sofocarse; abrir la boca *(de asombro)*.

gas·tric [gǽstrɪk] *adj.* gástrico.

gas·tro·in·tes·ti·nal [gǽstrointéstɪnl̩] *adj.* gastrointestinal.

gate [get] *s.* portón, entrada; puerta; *Ven., Col.* tranquera *(puerta de trancas)*.

gate·way [gétwe] *s.* paso, entrada.

gath·er [gǽðɚ] *v.* recoger; coger; reunir(se), juntar(se); deducir, colegir; fruncir *(en pliegues)*; cobrar *(fuerzas)*; **to** — **dust** llenarse de polvo, empolvarse; *s.* pliegue.

gath·er·ing [gǽðrɪŋ] *s.* asamblea, reunión; muchedumbre; pliegue.

gaud·y [gɔ́dɪ] *adj.* vistoso, llamativo, chillón, chillante.

gauge [gedʒ] *s.* calibrador; indicador; medidor; instrumento para medir; medida; calibre *(de un cañón, pistola, etc.)*; ancho *(del ferrocarril)*, *Ven.* trocha; *v.* medir; calibrar; estimar, calcular.

gaunt [gɔnt] *adj.* macilento, demacrado, flaco.

gaunt·let [gɔ́ntlɪt] *s.* guantelete; manopla; **to throw down the** — retar, desafiar.

gauze [gɔz] *s.* gasa; cendal.

gave [gev] *pret. de* **give**.

gav·el [gǽvl̩] *s.* mazo del que preside.

gawk [gɔk] *v.* bobear, mirar embobado; *s.* simplón, bobo.

gawk·y [gɔ́kɪ] *adj.* torpe, desmañado; bobo.

gay [ge] *adj.* alegre; vivo; vistoso; festivo.

gay·e·ty *véase* **gaiety**.

gaze [gez] *s.* mirada (fija); *v.* contemplar, mirar con fijeza, clavar la mirada.

ga·zette [gəzét] *s.* gaceta.

gear [gɪr] *s. (equipment)* aperos; herramientas; aparejo; equipo; *(wheel)* rueda dentada; *(assembly)* engranaje *(de ruedas dentadas)*; **foot**— calzado; **low** — primera velocidad; **steering** — mecanismo de dirección; **to be in** — estar engranado; **to shift** — cambir de engrane o velocidad; **to throw in** — engranar; **to throw out of** — desengranar; —**shift lever** palanca de engrane, palanca de cambios; *v.* engranar.

geese [gis] *pl. de* **goose**.

Gei·ger count·er [gáɪgɚkáʊntɚ] *s.* contador (de) Geiger.

gel·a·tin [dʒélətn] *s.* gelatina, jaletina.

gem [dʒɛm] *s.* gema, piedra preciosa; joya, alhaja, panecillo, bollo.

gem·i·nate [dʒémənet] *v.* geminar(se).

gen·der [dʒéndɚ] *s.* género.

gene [dʒin] *s.* gene.

ge·ne·al·o·gy [dʒiniælədʒɪ] *s.* genealogía.

gen·er·al [dʒénərəl] *adj. & s.* general; **in** — en general, por lo común, por lo general; — **delivery** lista de correos.

gen·er·al·i·ty [dʒenərǽləti] *s.* generalidad.

gen·er·al·ize [dʒénərəlaɪz] *v.* generalizar.

gen·er·ate [dʒénəret] *v.* engendrar; producir; originar.

gen·er·a·tion [dʒenəréʃən] *s.* generación; producción.

gen·er·a·tor [dʒénɚetɚ] *s.* generador.

ge·ner·ic [dʒənérɪk] *adj.* genérico.

gen·er·os·i·ty [dʒɛnərásətɪ] *s.* generosidad.
gen·er·ous [dʒɛnərəs] *adj.* generoso; magnánimo, liberal; amplio; abundante.
ge·net·ics [dʒənétɪks] *s.* genética.
gen·ial [dʒɪ́njəl] *adj.* genial, afable.
gen·i·tive [dʒɛ́nətɪv] *adj. & s.* genitivo.
gen·ius [dʒɪ́njəs] *s.* genio; ingenio, talento.
gen·teel [dʒɛntíl] *adj.* gentil, cortés; elegante; gallardo.
gen·tile [dʒɛ́ntaɪ] *adj. & s.* gentil.
gen·tle [dʒɛ́ntl] *adj.* suave; afable; apacible; manso; gentil.
gen·tle·man [dʒɛ́ntlmən] *s.* caballero; **gentlemen** *pl.* caballeros; señores.
gen·tle·man·ly [dʒɛ́ntlmənlɪ] *adj.* caballeroso, caballero, cortés.
gen·tle·ness [dʒɛ́ntlnɪs] *s.* suavidad, dulzura, apacibilidad; mansedumbre.
gen·tly [dʒɛ́ntlɪ] *adv.* suavemente; despacio; dulcemente; con ternura; mansamente.
gen·u·ine [dʒɛ́njʊɪn] *adj.* genuino; sincero.
ge·o·graph·i·cal [dʒɪəgrǽfɪkl] *adj.* geográfico.
ge·og·ra·phy [dʒɪágrəfɪ] *s.* geografía.
ge·o·log·i·cal [dʒɪəládʒɪkl] *adj.* geológico.
ge·ol·o·gy [dʒɪáldʒɪ] *s.* geología.
ge·o·met·ric [dʒɪəmétrɪk] *adj.* geométrico.
ge·om·e·try [dʒɪámətrɪ] *s.* geometría.
ge·o·phys·ics [dʒɪofɪ́zɪks] *s.* geofísica.
ge·ra·ni·um [dʒəréniəm] *s.* geranio.
germ [dʒɜm] *s.* germen; microbio.
Ger·man [dʒɜ́mən] *adj. & s.* alemán.
ger·mane [dʒɚmén] *adj.* pertinente, relacionado.
ger·ma·ni·um [dʒɜ́ménɪəm] *s.* germanio.
ger·mi·nate [dʒɜ́mənet] *v.* germinar.
ger·und [dʒɛ́rənd] *s.* gerundio.
ges·ta·tion [dʒɛstéʃən] *s.* gestación.
ges·tic·u·late [dʒɛstíkjəlet] *v.* gesticular, hacer gestos o ademanes, accionar, manotear.
ges·ture [dʒɛ́stʃɚ] *s.* gesto; ademán; **a mere —** una pura formalidad; *v.* gesticular, hacer gestos.
get [gɛt] *v.* (*obtain*) obtener, adquirir, lograr, conseguir; (*earn*) recibir, ganar; (*reach*) llegar (a); traer; (*catch*) coger, atrapar; preparar (*la lección, la comida, ɛtc.*); **to — along** llevarse bien (*con alguien*); ir pasándolo (*o* ir pasándola); **to — angry** ponerse enojado, enojarse; **to — away** escaparse; irse; **to — down** bajar; **to — ill** ponerse enfermo, enfermar(se); **to — in** entrar; meter(se); llegar; **to — married** casarse; **to — off** **the train** bajar del tren; apearse del tren; **to — old** envejecer(se); **to — on** subir a; montar; **to — out** salir; irse; sacar; divulgarse (*un secreto*); **to — over** pasar por encima de; recuperarse de (*una enfermedad*); olvidar (*una ofensa*); pasársele a uno (*el susto*); **to — ready** preparar(se); alistar(se); **to — rich** enriquecerse, hacerse rico; **to — rid of** deshacerse de, desprenderse de; **to — through** pasar; terminar; **to — together** juntar(se), reunir(se); ponerse de acuerdo; **to — up** levantarse; **I got him to do it** le persuadí a que lo hiciese; **I (have) got to do it** tengo que hacerlo; **I don't — it** no lo comprendo; **that's what -s me** (*ɔr* -s **my goat**) eso es lo que me irrita.
ghast·ly [gǽstlɪ] *adj.* horrible; pálido, lívido, cadavérico.
ghost [gost] *s.* espectro, fantasma; **the Holy Ghost** el Espíritu Santo; **not to have the — of a notion of** no tener la más remota idea de; **— writer** colaborador anónimo.
ghost·ly [góstlɪ] *adj.* como un espectro, de

espectros, de aparecidos.
gi·ant [dʒáɪənt] *s.* gigante; *adj.* gigantesco; enorme.
gid·dy [gídɪ] *adj.* ligero de cascos, frívolo; voluble, inconstante; desvanecido; **— speed** velocidad vertiginosa.
gift [gɪft] *s.* regalo; dádiva; don; dote, talento, prenda; donación.
gift·ed [gíftɪd] *adj.* talentoso, de talento.
gi·gan·tic [dʒaɪgǽntɪk] *adj.* gigantesco.
gig·gle [gígl] *s.* risita, risilla; risa falsa; *v.* reírse falsamente; reírse sofocando la voz; reír con una risilla afectada.
gild [gɪld] *v.* dorar.
gill [gɪl] *s.* agalla (*de pez*).
gilt [gɪlt] *adj. & s.* dorado; *pret. & p.p. de* to **gild.**
gim·mick [gímɪk] *s.* adminículo.
gin [dʒɪn] *s.* ginebra (*licor*).
gin·ger [dʒíndʒɚ] *s.* jengibre; **— ale** cerveza de jengibre.
gin·ger·bread [dʒíndʒɚbrɛd] *s.* pan de jengibre; ornato de mal gusto.
ging·ham [gíŋəm] *s.* guinga (*tela de algodón*).
gip·sy *véase* **gypsy.**
gi·raffe [dʒɚǽf] *s.* jirafa.
gird [gɝd] *v.* ceñir; rodear; **to — oneself for** prepararse para.
gir·dle [gɝdl] *s.* ceñidor; cinto; faja; *v.* ceñir; fajar; cercar.
girl [gɝl] *s.* niña; muchacha; joven, chica, moza; criada.
girl·hood [gɝ́lhʊd] *s.* niñez; mocedad, juventud.
girl·ish [gɝ́lɪʃ] *adj.* pueril; de niña, de muchacha; juvenil.
girt [gɝt] *pret. & p.p. de* to **gird;** *v. véase* **gird.**
girth [gɝθ] *s.* circunferencia; cincha (*para caballos*); faja; *v.* cinchar; ceñir.
gist [dʒɪst] *s.* substancia, esencia.
give [gɪv] *v.* dar; regalar; ceder; dar de sí; **to — away** regalar; entregar; revelar (*un secreto*); **to — back** devolver; **to — birth** dar a luz, parir; **to — in** ceder; darse por vencido; **to — off** emitir; **to — out** divulgar; repartir; agotarse; **to — up** abandonar; desistir; renunciar a; perder la esperanza; rendir(se); ceder, darse por vencido; *s.* elasticidad.
giv·en [gívən] *p.p. de* to **give;** *adj.* (*presented*) (dado); regalado; (*inclined*) adicto, entregado; dispuesto, inclinado; **— name** nombre de pila, nombre de bautismo; **— time** hora determinada; **— that** dada que supuesto que.
giv·er [gívɚ] *s.* dador, donador.
gla·cial [gléʃəl] *adj.* glacial.
gla·cier [gléʃɚ] *s.* glaciar, helero.
glad [glæd] *adj.* contento; alegre; **to be — to** alegrarse de, tener mucho gusto en (*o* de); **-ly** *adv.* alegremente, con mucho gusto; de buena gana.
glad·den [glǽdn̩] *v.* regocijar, alegrar.
glade [gled] *s.* claro herboso (*en un bosque*).
glad·ness [glǽdnɪs] *s.* alegría, gozo.
glam·our [glǽmɚ] *s.* encanto, hechizo; fascinación, embrujo; **— girl** niña hechicera.
glam·or·ous [glǽmərəs] *adj.* fascinador, hechicero.
glance [glæns] *s.* mirada, vistazo, ojeada; vislumbre; *v.* echar (*o* dar) un vistazo; vislumbrar; pegar de soslayo, **to — off** rebotar de soslayo (*o* de lado).
gland [glænd] *s.* glándula.
glare [glɛr] *s.* (*light*) resplandor, relumbre; (*stare*) mirada furiosa; *v.* resplandecer, relumbrar; **to — at** mirar enfurecido a.

glass [glæs] *s.* (*substance*) vidrio; cristal; (*receptacle*) vaso; copa (*de cristal*); (*eye*) lente; **looking — ** espejo; **-es** anteojos, lentes, gafas; *adj.* de vidrio; — **blower** vidriero, soplador de vidrio; — **case** escaparate.
glass·ware [glǽswɛr] *s.* vajilla de cristal, cristalería; — **shop** cristalería.
glass·y [glǽsɪ] *adj.* vidrioso.
glau·co·ma [glɔkómə] *s.* glaucoma.
glaze [glez] *s.* vidriado; lustre; superficie lustrosa o glaseada; *v.* vidriar; glasear; lustrar; poner vidrios a.
gla·zier [gléʒə·] *s.* vidriero.
gleam [glim] *s.* destello, rayo, fulgor, viso; *v.* destellar, fulgurar, centellear.
glean [glin] *v.* recoger; espigar.
glee [gli] *s.* regocijo; júbilo; — **club** orfeón, masa coral.
glib [glɪb] *adj.* locuaz; de mucha labia; — **excuse** excusa fácil.
glide [glaɪd] *s.* deslizamiento; ligadura (*en música*); planeo (*de un aeroplano*); *v.* deslizarse; resbalarse; planear (*un aeroplano*).
glid·er [gláɪdə·] *s.* deslizador, planeador (*aeroplano*).
glim·mer [glímə·] *s.* vislumbre; viso; titileo; — **of hope** rayo de esperanza; *v.* titilar, centellear.
glimpse [glɪmps] *s.* vislumbre; vistazo, ojeada; **to catch a — of** vislumbrar; *v.* vislumbrar.
glint [glɪnt] *s.* fulgor, rayo, destello.
glis·ten [glísn] *v.* relucir, brillar.
glit·ter [glítə·] *s.* lustre, brillo, resplandor; *v.* relumbrar, relucir, brillar.
gloat [glot] *v.* gozarse (en), deleitarse (en); relamerse (*de gusto*).
globe [glob] *s.* globo; esfera.
glob·ule [glábjul] *s.* glóbulo.
gloom [glum] *s.* lobreguez, sombra; abatimiento, tristeza, melancolía.
gloom·y [glúmɪ] *adj.* lóbrego, sombrío; triste, melancólico; abatido.
glo·ri·fy [glórəfaɪ] *v.* glorificar.
glo·ri·ous [glórɪəs] *adj.* glorioso; espléndido.
glo·ry [glórɪ] *s.* gloria; *v.* gloriarse; vanagloriarse.
gloss [glɔs] *s.* (*shine*) lustre, brillo; pulimento; (*note*) glosa, comentario; *v.* lustrar, dar brillo a; pulir; glosar, comentar; **to — over** encubrir, dar colorido de bueno (*a algo que no lo es*).
glos·sa·ry [glásərɪ] *s.* glosario.
gloss·y [glɔ́sɪ] *adj.* lustroso; pulido.
glove [glʌv] *s.* guante; *v.* enguantar, poner guantes.
glow [glo] *s.* incandescencia; brillo (*de un ascua*); calor vivo; fosforescencia; *v.* lucir, brillar (*como un ascua*); fosforescer; estar encendido o enardecido.
glow·ing [glóɪŋ] *adj.* encendido, ardiente.
glow·worm [glówʒm] *s.* luciérnaga.
glue [glu] *s.* cola (*para pegar*); *v.* encolar, pegar (*con cola*).
glum [glʌm] *adj.* hosco.
glut·ton [glʌ́tn] *s.* glotón.
glut·ton·ous [glʌ́tnəs] *adj.* glotón; goloso.
glut·ton·y [glʌ́tnɪ] *s.* gula, glotonería.
glyc·er·in [glísəɪn] *s.* glicerina.
gnarled [narld] *adj.* nudoso, torcido.
gnash [næʃ] *v.* crujir, rechinar (*los dientes*).
gnat [næt] *s.* jején (*insecto*).
gnaw [nɔ] *v.* roer.
gnu [ñu] *s.* nu.
go [go] *v.* (*move*) ir(se); andar; (*function*) marchar, funcionar, servir; **to — around** andar alrededor

de; dar vueltas; **to — away** irse; **to — back on one's word** faltar a la palabra; **to — by** pasar por; guiarse por (*una regla*); **to — down** bajar; **to — insane** volverse loco; **to — into** entrar en; investigar; caber en; **to — off** hacer explosión; dispararse; irse, salir disparado; **to — on** proseguir, continuar; **to — out** salir; apagarse; **to — over** pasar por encima de; examinar con cuidado; releer; repasar; recorrer; **to — to sleep** dormirse; **to — under** ir o pasar por debajo de; hundirse; **to — up** subir; **to let — ** soltar; **there is not enough to — around** no hay (bastante) para todos; *s.* empuje, energía; **it is a — ** trato hecho; **to be on the — ** estar en continuo movimiento.
goad [god] *s.* aguijón; puya; *v.* aguijonear; aguijar, incitar.
goal [gol] *s.* meta; fin, objetivo.
goat [got] *s.* cabra; **male — ** macho cabrío; **to be the — ** ser la víctima, pagar el pato.
goat·ee [gotí] *s.* perilla.
goat·herd [góthəd] *s.* cabrero.
gob·ble [gɑbl] *v.* tragar, engullir; **to — up** engullirse.
gob·bler [gáblə·] *s.* pavo.
go-be·tween [góbətwin] *s.* medianero.
gob·let [gáblɪt] *s.* copa grande.
gob·lin [gáblɪn] *s.* duende.
god [gɑd] *s.* dios; **God** Dios.
god·child [gádtʃaɪld] *s.* ahijado, ahijada.
god·dess [gádɪs] *s.* diosa.
god·fa·ther [gádfɑðə·] *s.* padrino.
god·less [gádlɪs] *adj.* impío, ateo.
god·like [gádlaɪk] *adj.* como Dios; divino.
god·ly [gádlɪ] *adj.* pío, devoto; divino.
god·moth·er [gádmʌðə·] *s.* madrina.
gog·gles [gáglz] *s. pl.* antiparras, gafas.
go·ing [góɪŋ] *ger.* & *adj.* que anda, marcha o funciona bien; **to be — in**, ir, irse; *s.* ida, partida; **comings and -s** idas y venidas.
goi·ter [gɔ́ɪtə·] *s.* papera; bocio; *Riopl.*, *Méx.*, *C.A.* buche; *C.A.* güecho.
gold [gold] *s.* oro; — **standard** patrón de oro.
gold·en [góldn] *adj.* de oro; áureo; dorado.
gold·finch [góldfɪntʃ] *s.* jilguero amarillo.
gold·fish [góldfɪʃ] *s.* carpa dorada.
gold·smith [góldsmɪθ] *s.* orfebre; — **shop** orfebrería.
golf [gɑlf] *s.* golf.
gon·do·la [gándələ] *s.* góndola; cabina (*de una aeronave*); — **car** vagón de mercancías (*sin techo*), *Am.* jaula.
gone [gɔn] *p.p.* de **to go** & *adj.* ido; perdido; **he is — ** se fué; **it is all — ** se acabó; ya no hay más.
gong [gɔŋ] *s.* gong, batintín.
good [gʊd] *adj.* bueno; válido; valedero; — **afternoon** buenas tardes; — **day** buenos días; adiós; — **evening** buenas noches; — **morning** buenos días; — **night** buenas noches; **Good Friday** Viernes Santo; **for — ** para siempre, permanentemente; **to have a — time** pasar un buen rato; divertirse; **to make — ** pagar, compensar; cumplir (*una promesa*); salir bien, tener buen éxito; *s.* bien; beneficio, provecho, ventaja; **-s** bienes, efectos; mercancías.
good-bye [gʊdbáɪ] *s.* & *interj.* adiós.
good-look·ing [gúdlúkɪŋ] *adj.* bien parecido, guapo.
good·ly [gúdlɪ] *adj.* grande, considerable; de buena apariencia.
good-na·tured [gúdnétʃəd] *adj.* de buen genio, bonachón, afable.

good·ness [gúdnɪs] s. bondad; —! ¡Dios mío! ¡cielos!

good·y [gúdɪ] s. golosina, bonbón, dulce; *interj.* ¡qué gusto!; **goody-goody** beatuco (*el que afecta virtud*), papanatas.

goof [guf] v. chapucear.

goose [gus] s. ganso; bobo, tonto; — **flesh** carne de gallina.

goose·ber·ry [gúsbɛrɪ] s. grosella; grosellero (*arbusto*).

go·pher [gófɚ] s. roedor semejante a la ardilla.

gore [gor] s. (*blood*) cuajarón de sangre; sangre; (*cloth*) cuchillo (*Am.* cuchilla), sesga (*tira de lienzo en figura de cuchilla*); v. acornear, herir con los cuernos; hacer una sesga en (*un traje*).

gorge [gɔrdʒ] s. cañada, barranco, barranca; v. engullir(se), atracarse.

gor·geous [gɔ́rdʒəs] adj. primoroso, vistoso, hermosísimo.

go·ril·la [gərílə] s. gorila.

go·ry [górɪ] adj. sangriento, ensangrentado.

gos·pel [gáspl] s. evangelio; **it is the — truth** es la pura verdad.

gos·sip [gásɪp] s. (*rumors*) chisme, chismería; murmuración, hablilla; (*person*) murmurador, chismero, chismoso; v. chismear, murmurar.

gos·sip·y [gásəpɪ] adj. chismero, chismoso.

got [gɑt] pret. & p.p. de **to get**.

Goth·ic [gáθɪk] adj. gótico; s. gótico (*idioma de los godos*); estilo gótico.

got·ten [gátṇ] p.p. de **to get**.

gouge [gaUdʒ] s. gubia (*especie de formón o escoplo curvo*); v. excavar con gubia, formón o escoplo; **to — someone's eyes out** sacarle los ojos a alguien.

gourd [gord] s. calabaza.

gour·met [gUrmé] s. gastrónomo.

gout [gaUt] s. gota (*enfermedad*).

gov·ern [gʌ́vɚn] v. gobernar; regir.

gov·ern·ess [gʌ́vɚnɪs] s. institutriz.

gov·ern·ment [gʌ́vɚmənt] s. gobierno.

gov·ern·ment·al [gʌ́vɚméntl] adj. gubernativo.

gov·er·nor [gʌ́vɚnɚ] s. gobernador; regulador (*de una máquina*).

gown [gaUn] s. vestido (*de mujer*); toga (*de un juez, profesor, etc.*); **dressing — bata.**

grab [græb] v. agarrar asir; arrebatar; s. arrebatiña; agarro, agarrón; presa.

grace [gres] s. gracia; favor; donaire, garbo; **to say — bendecir la mesa, dar gracias; to be in the good -s of someone** gozar del favor de uno; v. agraciar, adornar.

grace·ful [grésfəl] adj. gracioso, agraciado, garboso; **-ly** adv. graciosamente, con gracia, con garbo.

grace·ful·ness [grésfəlnɪs] s. gracia, donaire, gallardía, garbo.

gra·cious [gréʃəs] adj. afable; cortés; —! ¡válgame Dios!

gra·da·tion [gredéʃən] s. graduación; gradación; grado.

grade [gred] s. (*degree*) grado; (*mark*) nota, calificación; (*slope*) cuesta, declive, pendiente; *Am.* gradiente; — **crossing** cruce a nivel (*de un ferrocarril con una carretera*); **the -s** la escuela primaria; v. graduar, clasificar; calificar, dar una calificación; nivelar (*un camino*).

grad·u·al [grǽdʒUəl] adj. gradual; **-ly** adv. gradualmente, poco a poco.

grad·u·ate [grǽdʒUɪt] adj. graduado, que ha recibido un grado académico; **to do — work**

cursar asignaturas superiores (*al bachillerato*); s. estudiante graduado (*que estudia para licenciado o doctor*); [grǽdʒUet] v. graduar(se).

grad·u·a·tion [grædʒUéʃən] s. graduación.

graft [græft] s. (*insertion*) injerto; tejido injertado; (*extortion*) sisa, malversación (*de caudales públicos*); ganancia ilegal, *Am.* mordida; v. injertar; malversar fondos ajenos; sisar, exigir pago ilegal, *Am.* morder.

graft·er [grǽftɚ] s. malversador (*de fondos públicos*), estafador, *C.A.* coyote, *Méx.* mordelón.

grain [gren] s. (*cereal*) grano; (*markings*) fibra (*de la madera*), veta (*del mármol o madera*); **against the — a** (*o* al) redopelo, a contrapelo.

gram [græm] s. gramo.

gram·mar [grǽmɚ] s. gramática; — **school** escuela primaria.

gram·mat·i·cal [grəmǽtɪkl] adj. gramatical, gramático.

gran·a·ry [grǽnərɪ] s. granero.

grand [grænd] adj. grande; grandioso, admirable; magnífico.

grand·child [grǽntʃaɪld] s. nieto.

grand·chil·dren [grǽntʃɪldrən] s. pl. nietos.

grand·daugh·ter [grǽndɔtɚ] s. nieta.

gran·deur [grǽndʒɚ] s. grandeza, grandiosidad; majestad.

grand·fa·ther [grǽnfɑðɚ] s. abuelo.

gran·di·ose [grǽndɪos] adj. grandioso, magnífico.

grand·ma [grǽnmɑ] s. abuela, abuelita, *Am.* mamá grande.

grand·moth·er [grǽnmʌðɚ] s. abuela.

grand·ness [grǽndnɪs] s. grandeza; grandiosidad; magnificencia.

grand·pa [grǽnpɑ] s. abuelo, abuelito, *Am.* papá grande.

grand·par·ent [grǽnpɛrənt] s. abuelo, abuela; **-s** abuelos.

grand·son [grǽnsʌn] s. nieto.

grand·stand [grǽnstænd] s. andanada, gradería cubierta.

grange [grendʒ] s. granja; asociación de agricultores.

gran·ite [grǽnɪt] s. granito (*roca*).

gran·ny [grǽnɪ] s. abuelita; viejecita, viejita.

grant [grænt] s. concesión; subvención; donación; transferencia de propiedad (*mediante escritura*); v. conceder; otorgar; ceder, transferir (*derechos, propiedad, etc.*); **to take for -ed** dar por supuesto, dar por sentado.

gran·u·late [grǽnjəlet] v. granular(se).

grape [grep] s. uva.

grape·fruit [grépfrut] s. toronja; *Esp.* pomelo.

grape·vine [grépvaɪn] s. vid; parra.

graph [græf] s. diagrama, gráfica; v. hacer una gráfica o diagrama.

graph·ic [grǽfɪk] adj. gráfico.

graph·ite [grǽfaɪt] s. grafito.

grap·ple [grǽpl] v. luchar, pelear cuerpo a cuerpo; aferrar, agarrar.

grasp [græsp] v. (*seize*) agarrar; asir; apretar; (*understand*) comprender; abarcar; s. agarro, asimiento; apretón de manos; **to be within one's — estar** al alcance de uno; **to have a good — of a subject** estar fuerte en una materia, saber a fondo una materia.

grass [græs] s. hierba; césped; pasto; *Méx.* zacate; *Méx., Ven., Col.* grama.

grass·hop·per [grǽshapɚ] s. saltamontes, saltón; *Méx., C.A.* chapulín.

grass·roots [græsruts] *adj.* del pueblo; de la gente.
grass·y [græsɪ] *adj.* herboso, *Am.* pastoso.
grate [gret] *s.* (*window*) reja, verja, enrejado; (*grill*) parrilla, brasero; *v.* enrejar, poner enrejado; crujir, rechinar (*los dientes*); rallar (*queso*); **to — on** molestar, irritar.
grate·ful [grétfəl] *adj.* agradecido; grato, agradable.
grat·er [grétə▸] *s.* rallador.
grat·i·fy [grǽtəfaɪ] *v.* complacer, dar gusto, agradar; satisfacer.
grat·ing [grétɪŋ] *s.* reja, enrejado, verja; *adj.* rechinante; molesto, áspero.
gra·tis [grétɪs] *adv.* gratis, de balde.
grat·i·tude [grǽtətjud] *s.* gratitud.
gra·tu·i·tous [grətjúətəs] *adj.* gratuito; sin fundamento; **— statement** afirmación arbitraria.
grave [grev] *adj.* grave; serio; *s.* tumba sepulcro, sepultura; acento grave; **—stone** losa o lápida sepulcral.
grave·dig·ger [grévdɪgə▸] *s.* sepulturero.
grav·el [grǽvl] *s.* grava, guijo, cascajo, *Am.* maicillo; cálculos (*en los riñones, la vejiga, etc.*); mal de piedra; *v.* cubrir con grava.
grave·yard [grévjɑrd] *s.* cementerio.
grav·i·ta·tion [grævɪtéʃən] *s.* atracción; gravitación.
grav·i·ty [grǽvətɪ] *s.* gravedad; seriedad.
gra·vy [grévɪ] *s.* salsa; jugo (*de carne*).
gray [gre] *adj.* gris; cano; pelicano; entrecano (*que empieza a encanecer*); **— horse** rucio, tordo, tordillo; **— matter** seso; **gray-headed** canoso; *s.* gris, color gris; *v.* encanecer; poner(se) gris.
gray·ish [gréɪʃ] *adj.* grisáceo, pardusco; **— hair** pelo entrecano.
gray·ness [grénɪs] *s.* grisura, gris, calidad de gris; encanecimiento.
graze [grez] *v.* (*feed*) pacer; apacentar, *Am.* pastear, pastar; (*brush*) rozar; raspar; *s.* roce, rozón, raspadura.
grease [gris] *s.* grasa; *v.* engrasar; untar; lubricar; **to — the palm** untar la mano, sobornar.
greas·y [grísɪ] *adj.* grasiento, grasoso; pringoso.
great [gret] *adj.* gran(de); eminente; magnífico, excelente; **a — deal** una gran cantidad; muchos; mucho; **a — many** muchos; **a — while** un largo rato o tiempo; **-ly** *adv.* grandemente; mucho; muy; en gran parte; sobremanera.
great-grand·child [grétgrǽntʃaɪld] *s.* biznieto.
great-grand·fa·ther [grétgrǽnfɑðə▸] *s.* bisabuelo.
great-grand·moth·er [grétgrǽnmʌðə▸] *s.* bisabuela.
great·ness [grétnɪs] *s.* grandeza.
Gre·cian [gríʃən] *adj. & s.* griego.
greed [grid] *s.* codicia; avaricia; gula.
greed·i·ly [grídlɪ] *adv.* vorazmente; con avaricia; con gula.
greed·i·ness [grídɪnɪs] *s.* codicia; avaricia; gula; voracidad.
greed·y [grídɪ] *adj.* codicioso; avaro; goloso; voraz.
Greek [grik] *adj. & s.* griego.
green [grin] *adj.* (*color*) verde; (*novice*) novato, inexperto; **to grow —** verdear; **the fields look —** verdean los campos; *s.* verde, verdor; césped, prado; campo de golf; **-s** verduras, hortalizas.
green·horn [grínhɔrn] *s.* novato, pipiolo.
green·house [grínhaʊs] *s.* invernáculo, invernadero.
green·ish [grínɪʃ] *adj.* verdoso.
green·ness [grínnɪs] *s.* (*color*) verdor, verdura; (*experience*) inmadurez; impericia.
greet [grit] *v.* saludar; **to — each other** saludarse.
greet·ing [grítɪŋ] *s.* saludo; salutación, **-s!** ¡salud! ¡saludos!
gre·nade [grɪnéd] *s.* granada, bomba pequeña.

grew [gru] *pret. de* **to grow**.
grey = **gray.**
grey·ish = **gray.**
grey·ness = **grayness.**
grey·hound [gréhaʊnd] *s.* lebrel, galgo.
grid·dle [grídl] *s.* tartera; plancha (*para tapar el hornillo*).
grief [grif] *s.* dolor, pesar; **to come to —** sobrevenirle a uno una desgracia; fracasar.
griev·ance [grívəns] *s.* queja; resentimiento; motivo de queja, injusticia, ofensa.
grieve [griv] *v.* afligir(se); lamentar(se), acongojar(se).
grieved [grivd] *adj.* penado.
griev·ous [grívəs] *adj.* doloroso, penoso; grave, altroz.
grill [grɪl] *s.* parrilla; **men's —** restaurante para hombres; *v.* asar en parrillas; interrogar (*a un sospechoso*).
grim [grɪm] *adj.* austero, áspero; fiero; torvo, siniestro.
gri·mace [grɪmés] *s.* mueca, gesto; *v.* hacer muecas o gestos.
grime [graɪm] *s.* mugre; *v.* ensuciar.
grim·y [gráɪmɪ] *adj.* mugriento.
grin [grɪn] *s.* sonrisa abierta; sonrisa maliciosa; sonrisa canina; *v.* sonreír (*mostrando mucho los dientes*).
grind [graɪnd] *v.* (*crush*) moler; machacar; (*sharpen*) afilar, amolar; (*study hard*) afanarse demasiado; estudiar con empeño; **to — a hand organ** tocar el organillo; **to — one's teeth** rechinar los dientes; *s.* molienda; faena, trabajo penoso; estudiante tesonero; **the daily —** la rutina diaria.
grind·er [gráɪndə▸] *s.* moledor; molinillo (*para moler café*); amolador, afilador; muela (*piedra para afilar*); muela (*diente molar*).
grind·stone [gráɪndston] *s.* piedra de amolar.
grip [grɪp] *v.* (*seize*) agarrar; asir; apretar; empuñar; (*impress*) impresionar; conmover; *s.* agarro; asimiento; apretón; asidero, asa; (*suitcase*) valija, maletín; *Méx.*, velís; **to have a — on someone** tener agarrado a alguien.
grippe [grɪp] *s.* gripe, influenza.
grit [grɪt] *s.* (*gravel*) arenilla, arena; piedra arenisca; (*pluck*) firmeza, tesón; **-s** maíz, avena, o trigo a medio moler; *v.* rechinar, crujir.
grit·ty [grítɪ] *adj.* arenoso; valeroso, firme.
griz·zly [grízlɪ] *adj.* grisáceo, pardusco; **— bear** oso pardo.
groan [gron] *s.* gemido, quejido; *v.* gemir; quejarse; crujir (*por exceso de peso*).
gro·cer [grósə▸] *s.* abacero, *Méx.* abarrotero, *Carib.*, *C.A.* bodeguero; *Ríopl.* almacenero.
gro·cer·y [grósərɪ] *s.* abacería, tienda de comestibles, *Méx.* abarrotería, *Méx.* tienda de abarrotes; *Carib.*, *C.A.* bodega; **groceries** comestibles, *Méx.* abarrotes.
groom [grum] *s.* (*bridegroom*) novio; (*stable groom*) caballerizo, mozo de caballeriza; establero; *v.* almohazar, limpiar con la almohaza (*a los caballos*), cuidar (*a los caballos*); **to — oneself** asearse, peinarse, componerse; **well-groomed** bien vestido, aseado, limpio.
groove [gruv] *s.* estría, ranura, acanaladura; surco (*en un camino*); muesca, encaje; *v.* acanalar, estriar.
grope [grop] *v.* tentalear, tentar, andar a tientas; **to — for** buscar tentando, buscar a tientas.
gross [gros] *adj.* grueso; burdo; tosco; grosero;

— **earnings** ganancias totales; — **ignorance**
ignorancia crasa; — **weight** peso bruto; *s.*
grueso, totalidad; gruesa (*doce docenas*).
gro·tesque [grotésk] *adj. & s.* grotesco.
grot·to [gráto] *s.* gruta.
grouch [graʊtʃ] *s.* mal humor; gruñón, refunfuñón,
cascarrabias; **to have a — against someone**
tenerle ojeriza (*o* mala voluntad) a una persona;
guardarle rencor a alguien; *v.* grunñir,
refunfuñar; estar de mal humor.
grouch·y [gráʊtʃı] *adj.* gruñón, refunfuñón,
malhumorado, cascarrabias.
ground [graʊnd] *s.* (*earth*) suelo, tierra; terreno;
(*motive*) motivo, rezón; base, fundamento; —
crew personal de tierra; **-s** heces, desperdicios,
sedimento; — **floor** piso bajo, planta baja, **to
break** — roturar, arar; cavar; **to give** —
retroceder, ceder; **to hold one's** — mantenerse
firme; *v.* conectar (*un alambre*) con la tierra;
encallar (*una embarcación*); aterrizar (*un
aeroplano*); **to be well -ed** poseer las bases o
principios fundamentales; *pret. & p.p. de* **to
grind.**
ground·less [gráʊndlıs] *adj.* infundado.
group [grup] *s.* grupo; — **insurance** seguros
sociales; *v.* agrupar.
grove [grov] *s.* arboleda, bosquecillo.
grow [gro] *v.* crecer; brotar; cultivar; criar;
producir; **to** — **angry** ponerse enojado o
enfadado, enfadarse, enojarse; **to** — **better**
ponerse mejor, mejorar; **to** — **difficult**
dificultarse, hacerse difícil; **to** — **late** hacerse
tarde; **to** — **old** ponerse viejo, envejecer; **to** —
out of a habit perder la costumbre; **to** — **pale**
ponerse pálido, palidecer; **to** — **tired** cansarse.
growl [graʊl] *s.* gruñido; *v.* gruñir.
growl·er [gráʊlɚ] *s.* gruñón; regañón.
grown [gron] *p.p. de* **to grow** & *adj.* crecido;
desarrollado; — **man** hombre maduro, hombre
hecho; — **with trees** poblado de árboles.
grown-up [grónʌp] *adj.* crecido, adulto; *s.* adulto.
growth [groθ] *s.* (*increase*) crecimiento,
acrecentamiento; aumento; (*development*)
desarrollo; (*vegetation*) vegetación; (*tissue*)
tumor, lobanillo, excrecencia.
grub·by [grʌ́bı] *adj.* roñoso; sucio.
grudge [grʌdʒ] *s.* inquina, rencor, resentimiento,
mala voluntad; *v.* tener inquina, evidia o mala
voluntad; dar de mala gana.
gruff [grʌf] *adj.* áspero, rudo; grosero.
grum·ble [grʌ́mbl] *s.* refunfuño, gruñido, queja; *v.*
refunfuñar, gruñir, quejarse.
grum·bler [grʌ́mblɚ] *s.* gruñón; regañón.
grump·y [grʌ́mpı] *adj.* malhumorado; gruñón.
grunt [grʌnt] *s.* gruñido, *Méx., C.A., Col., Ven.*
pujido; *v.* gruñir, *Riopl., Méx., C.A., Ven., Andes*
pujar.
guar·an·tee [gærəntí] *s.* garantía; fianza; fiador; *v.*
garantizar; dar fianza; salir fiador de.
guar·an·tor [gǽrəntɚ] *s.* fiador.
guar·an·ty [gǽrəntı] *s.* garantía; fianza; fiador; *v.*
véase **guarantee.**
guard [gard] *s.* guarda; guardia; resguardo; **to be
on** — estar alerta; estar en guardia; **to keep** —
vigilar; *v.* guardar; resguardar; vigilar; **to** —
(**oneself**) **against** guardarse de.
guard·i·an [gárdıən] *s.* guardián, custodio; tutor;
— **angel** ángel custodio, ángel de la guarda.
guard·i·an·ship [gárdıənʃıp] *s.* tutela; guarda,
custodia.
guard·rail [gárdrel] *s.* baranda.

Gua·te·ma·lan [gwɑtəmálən] *adj. & s.*
guatemalteco.
guess [ges] *s.* conjetura, suposición; adivinación;
v. adivinar; suponer, creer.
guest [gest] *s.* convidado; visita; huésped,
pensionista, inquilino.
guf·faw [gʌfɔ́] *s.* risotada, carcajada.
gui·dance [gáıdn̩s] *s.* guía, dirección.
guide [gaıd] *s.* guía.
guide·book [gáıdbʊk] *s.* guía del viajero; **railway**
— guía de ferrocarriles.
guide·line [gáıdlaın] *s.* norma; precepto.
guild [gıld] *s.* gremio; cofradía; asociación.
guile [gaıl] *s.* engaño, astucia.
guilt [gılt] *s.* culpa, delito; culpabilidad.
guilt·less [gíltlıs] *adj.* libre de culpa; inocente.
guilt·y [gíltı] *adj.* culpable; reo, delincuente.
guise [gaız] *s.* aspecto, apariencia; modo; **under the**
— **of** so capa de; disfrazado de.
gui·tar [gıtár] *s.* guitarra.
gulf [gʌlf] *s.* golfo; abismo.
gull [gʌl] *s.* gaviota.
gul·let [gʌ́lıt] *s.* gaznate.
gul·ly [gʌ́lı] *s.* barranco, barranca; hondonada.
gulp [gʌlp] *s.* trago; *v.* tragar; engullir; **to** — **it
down** tragárselo.
gum [gʌm] *s.* (*product*) goma; (*of mouth*) encía;
chewing — goma de mascar, *Am.* chicle; —
tree árbol gomífero, *Col.* gomero; *v.* engomar,
pegar con goma.
gun [gʌn] *s.* (*cannon*) cañón; (*rifle*) fusil, rifle;
(*shotgun*) escopeta; pistola, revólver; **a 21** —
salute una salva de 21 cañonazos.
gun·boat [gʌ́nbot] *s.* cañonero, lancha cañonera.
gun·ner [gʌ́nɚ] *s.* artillero, cañonero; ametrallador.
gun·pow·der [gʌ́npaʊdɚ] *s.* pólvora.
gur·gle [gɝ́gl] *v.* borbotar, hacer borbollones; *s.*
borbollón, borbotón.
gush [gʌʃ] *s.* chorro; borbollón, borbotón; efusión
(*de cariño o entusiasmo*); *v.* chorrear, borbotar,
borbollar, borbollonear; brotar; ser demasiado
efusivo.
gust [gʌst] *s.* ráfaga, ventolera.
gut [gʌt] *s.* tripa, intestino; cuerda de tripa; **to have
-s** tener agallas (*ánimo*).
gut·ter [gʌ́tɚ] *s.* arroyo (*de la calle o de un
camino*); gotera (*del techo*); zanja.
guy [gaı] *s.* (*person*) sujeto, tipo, individuo; (*wire*)
tirante, alambre, cadena (*para sostener algo*); *v.*
sostener (*algo*) con tirantes; burlarse de, mofarse
de.
gym·na·si·um [dʒımnézıəm] *s.* gimnasio.
gym·nas·tics [dʒımnǽstıks] *s. pl.* gimnasia.
gy·ne·col·o·gy [gaınəkálədʒı] *s.* ginecología.
gyp·sy [dʒípsı] *s. & adj.* gitano.
gy·rate [dʒáıret] *v.* girar.
gy·ro·scope [dʒáırəskop] *s.* giroscopio.

H:h

hab·it [hǽbıt] *s.* hábito,
costumbre; **drinking** — vicio de
la bebida; **riding** — traje de
montar.
ha·bit·u·al [həbítʃʊəl] *adj.* habitual; acostumbrado.
hack [hæk] *s.* (*cut*) tajo; (*cough*) tos seca; (*horse*)
caballo de alquiler; rocín; (*writer*) escritor
mercenario; *v.* tajar, picar; toser con tos seca.
hack·neyed [hǽknıd] *adj.* trillado, muy común.
had [hæd] *pret. & p.p. de* **to have**; **you** — **better**

do it es bueno que Vd. lo haga; sería bueno que Vd. lo hiciese; **I — rather go than stay** preferiría irme a quedarme.

haf·ni·um [hǽfniəm] s. hafnio.

hag [hæg] s. hechicera, bruja; viejota.

hag·gard [hǽgəd] adj. macilento, flaco.

hag·gle [hǽgl] v. regatear.

hail [hel] s. (*storm*) granizo; (*greeting*) saludo; llamada, grito; **Hail Mary** Ave María; *interj.* ¡salud!; ¡salve!; v. granizar; saludar; llamar; aclamar; **to — from** proceder de, ser oriundo de.

hail·storm [hélstɔrm] s. granizada.

hair [hɛr] s. pelo; cabello; vello; filamento (*de las plantas*); — **net** red para el cabello.

hair·brush [hɛ́rbrʌʃ] s. cepillo para el cabello.

hair·cut [hɛ́rkʌt] s. corte de pelo; **close — rape**; **to have a —** hacerse cortar el pelo.

hair·do [hɛ́rdu] s. peinado.

hair·dress·er [hɛ́rdrɛsə] s. peluquero; peinadora.

hair·less [hɛ́rlɪs] adj. sin pelo, pelado; lampiño.

hair·pin [hɛ́rpɪn] s. horquilla, *Am.* gancho (*para el pelo*).

hair·y [hɛ́rɪ] adj. peludo, cabelludo; hirsuto, velloso, velludo.

hale [hel] adj. sano, fuerte, robusto; v. llevar (*a una persona*) por fuerza.

half [hæf] s. mitad; — **an apple** media manzana; adj. medio; — **brother** hermanastro; — **cooked** a medio cocer, medio cocido; **half-past one** la una y media; **half-baked** a medio cocer; a medio planear.

half-breed [hǽfbrid] adj. & s. mestizo.

half-hour [hǽfáʊr] s. media hora; adj. de media hora.

half-mast [hǽfmæst] s. media asta; v. poner a media asta (*la bandera*).

half-o·pen [hǽfópən] adj. entreabierto; medio abierto, entornado.

half·way [hǽfwe] adj. & adv. a medio camino; parcial, incompleto; — **between** equidistante de; — **finished** a medio acabar; **to do something —** hacer algo a medias.

half-wit·ted [hǽfwítɪd] adj. imbécil, zonzo.

hal·i·but [hǽləbət] s. mero, hipogloso (*pez*).

hall [hɔl] s. salón (*para asambleas, funciones, etc.*); edificio (*de un colegio o universidad*); vestíbulo; corredor, pasillo; **town —** ayuntamiento.

hall·mark [hɔ́lmɑrk] s. distintivo.

hal·lo = hello.

hal·low [hǽlo] v. santificar; consagrar.

Hal·low·een [hæloín] s. víspera de Todos los Santos.

hall·way [hɔ́lwe] s. corredor, pasillo; zaguán.

ha·lo [hélo] s. halo; aureola.

halt [hɔlt] s. alto, parada; v. parar(se), detener(se); hacer alto; vacilar.

hal·ter [hɔ́ltə] s. ronzal, cabestro.

halt·ing [hɔ́ltɪŋ] adj. vacilante; **-ly** adv. con vacilación.

halve [hæv] v. partir por la mitad; partir en dos.

halves [hævz] pl. de **half**; **to go —** ir a medias.

ham [hæm] s. jamón.

ham·burg·er [hǽmbɜgə] s. carne picada de vaca; bocadillo o emparedado de carne picada, *Am.* hamburguesa.

ham·let [hǽmlɪt] s. caserío, aldehuela.

ham·mer [hǽmə] s. martillo; martinete (*de piano*); **sledge —** macho; v. martillar; machacar; clavar.

ham·mock [hǽmək] s. hamaca, *Ven., Col.* chinchorro; *Riopl.* mangangá; coy.

ham·per [hǽmpə] s. canasto, cesto grande,

cuévano; v. estorbar, impedir, embarazar.

hand [hænd] s. mano; manecilla; aguja (*de reloj*); obrero; letra (*modo de escribir*); — **and glove** uña y carne; — **in —** (cogidos) de la mano; **at —** a la mano, cerca; **made by —** hecho a mano; **on —** disponible; en existencia; listo; a la mano, presente; **on the other —** en cambio, por otra parte; **to have one's -s full** estar ocupadísimo; v. entregar, dar; **to — down** bajar (*una cosa para dársela a alguien*); transmitir (*de una a otra generación*); pronunciar (*un fallo*); **to — in** entregar; **to — over** entregar.

hand·bag [hǽndbæg] s. bolsa o bolso; saco de noche, maletín.

hand·ball [hǽndbɔl] s. pelota; juego de pelota.

hand·bill [hǽndbɪl] s. hoja volante (*anuncio*).

hand·cuff [hǽndkʌf] v. maniatar; **-s** s. pl. esposas, manillas de hierro.

hand·ful [hǽndfəl] s. manojo, puñado.

hand·i·cap [hǽndɪkæp] s. desventaja, estorbo, impedimento, obstáculo; ventaja o desventaja (*impuesta en ciertas contiendas*); — **race** carrera de handicap; v. estorbar, poner trabas a.

hand·i·work [hǽndɪwɜk] s. labor, trabajo hecho a mano; artefacto.

hand·ker·chief [hǽŋkətʃɪf] s. pañuelo.

han·dle [hǽndl] s. mango, asa; tirador (*de puerta o cajón*); puño (*de espada*); manubrio (*de bicicleta, organillo, etc.*); v. manejar; manipular; manosear, tocar; comerciar en; **-s easily** se maneja con facilidad, es muy manuable.

hand·made [hǽndméd] adj. hecho a mano.

hand·saw [hǽndsɔ] s. serrucho.

hand·shake [hǽndʃek] s. apretón de manos.

hand·some [hǽnsəm] adj. (*good-looking*) hermoso, guapo, bien parecido; (*generous*) generoso; **a — sum** una suma considerable.

hand·writ·ing [hǽndraitɪŋ] s. letra (*modo de escribir*), escritura.

hand·y [hǽndɪ] adj. a la mano, próximo; hábil, diestro; manuable, fácil de manejar.

hang [hæŋ] v. colgar; suspender; ahorcar; inclinar (*la cabeza*); **sentenced to —** condenado a la horca; **to — around** andar holgazaneando por un sitio; rondar; esperar sin hacer nada; **to — on** colgarse de; depender de; estar pendiente de; persistir; **to — paper on a wall** empapelar una pared; **to — with tapestries** entapizar; s. modo de caerle la ropa a una persona; modo de manejar (*un mecanismo*); modo de resolver (*un problema*); significado (*de un argumento*); **I don't care a —** no me importa un ardite.

han·gar [hǽŋə] s. hangar, cobertizo.

hang·er [hǽŋə] s. colgadero; percha, clavijero; **paper —** empapelador.

hang·ing [hǽŋɪŋ] s. muerte en la horca; **-s** colgaduras; adj. colgante; colgado.

hang·man [hǽŋmən] s. verdugo.

hang·nail [hǽŋnel] s. padrastro (*pedacito de pellejo que se levanta junto a las uñas*).

hang·o·ver [hǽŋovə] s. sobrante, remanente, resto; **to have a — *Ven., Col., Andes*** tener un ratón o estar enratonado (*tras una borrachera*), *Méx.* estar crudo o tener una cruda; *Ch.* la mona; *C.A.* de goma; *Riopl.* resaca.

hap·haz·ard [hæphǽzəd] adv. al azar, al acaso, a la ventura, a la buena de Dios; adj. casual; impensado.

hap·haz·ard·ly [hæphǽzədlɪ] adv. = **haphazard**.

hap·less [hǽplɪs] adj. desventurado, desgraciado.

GR

hap·pen [hǽpən] *v.* suceder, pasar, acontecer, sobrevenir, acaecer; **to — to hear (do, be,** *etc.***)** oír (hacer, estar, *etc.*); **) por** casualidad; **to — to pass by** acertar a pasar; **to — on (upon)** encontrarse con, tropezar con.

hap·pen·ing [hǽpənɪŋ] *s.* acontecimiento, suceso.

hap·pi·ly [hǽplɪ] *adv.* felizmente; afortunadamente.

hap·pi·ness [hǽpɪnɪs] *s.* felicidad, dicha, contento.

hap·py [hǽpɪ] *adj.* feliz; dichoso, alegre; afortunado; **to be — to** alegrarse de.

ha·rangue [hərǽŋ] *s.* arenga, perorata; *v.* arengar, perorar.

har·ass [hǽrəs] *v.* acosar, hostigar, molestar.

har·bor [hárbɚ] *s.* puerto; asilo, refugio, abrigo; *v.* abrigar; hospedar; albergar.

hard [hard] *adj.* (*firm*) duro; (*stiff*) tieso; (*difficult*) arduo, difícil; — **cash** dinero contante y sonante, metálico; — **coal** antracita; — **liquor** licor espiritoso (*aguardiente, ron, etc.*); — **luck** mala suerte; — **of hearing** medio sordo; — **water** agua cruda; *adv.* fuerte, recio, con fuerza; con empeño, con ahinco; — **by** muy cerca; — **core** núcleo resistente (*de un grupo*); —**hearted** de corazón duro; **hard-working** muy trabajador, industrioso, aplicado.

hard·en [hárdn̩] *v.* endurecer(se).

hard·en·ing [hárdnɪŋ] *s.* endurecimiento.

hard·ly [hárdlɪ] *adv.* apenas; a duras penas; difícilmente; duramente; con aspereza; probablemente no.

hard·ness [hárdnɪs] *s.* dureza; aspereza; dificultad.

hard·ship [hárdʃɪp] *s.* apuro, aflicción; trabajo, penalidad.

hard·ware [hárdwɛr] *s.* quincalla, quincallería; — **shop** quincallería, ferretería.

har·dy [hárdɪ] *adj.* robusto, fuerte, recio, atrevido.

hare [hɛr] *s.* liebre.

hare·brained [hɛrbrénd] *adj.* atolondrado, ligero de cascos.

hare·lip [hɛrlɪp] *s.* labio leporino.

har·em [hɛrəm] *s.* harén.

har·lot [harlət] *s.* ramera, prostituta.

harm [harm] *s.* daño, mal; perjuicio; *v.* dañar; hacer mal, hacer daño; perjudicar.

harm·ful [hármfəl] *adj.* dañoso; dañino, nocivo, perjudicial.

harm·less [hármlɪs] *adj.* innocuo; inofensivo; no dañoso, inocente.

harm·less·ness [hármlɪsnɪs] *s.* innocuidad; inocencia, falta de malicia.

har·mon·ic [harmánɪk] *adj.* armónico.

har·mo·ni·ous [harmónɪəs] *adj.* armonioso.

har·mo·nize [hármənaɪz] *v.* armonizar; concordar; congeniar.

har·mo·ny [hármənɪ] *s.* armonía.

har·ness [hárnɪs] *s.* guarniciones (*de caballerías*); jaez, aparejo; **to get back in —** volver al servicio activo, volver a trabajar; volver a la rutina; *v.* enjaezar, poner guarniciones a (*un caballo, mula, etc.*).

harp [harp] *s.* arpa; *v.* tocar el arpa; **to — on** repetir constantemente (*una nota, palabra, tema, etc.*); porfiar en.

har·poon [harpún] *s.* arpón; *v.* arponear, pescar con arpón.

har·row [hǽro] *s.* rastro, rastrillo, grada; *v.* rastrear, rastrillar; atormentar; horrorizar.

har·row·ing [hǽrəwɪŋ] *adj.* horrendo, horripilante, que pone los cabellos de punta; espeluznante.

har·ry [hǽrɪ] *v.* acosar, molestar; asolar.

harsh [harʃ] *adj.* tosco, áspero; severo, austero.

harsh·ness [hárʃnɪs] *s.* aspereza; tosquedad; severidad.

har·vest [hárvɪst] *s.* cosecha; siega, agosto; recolección; recogida; *v.* cosechar; segar.

hash [hæʃ] *s.* picadillo.

haste [hest] *s.* prisa; apresuramiento; **in —** de prisa; **to make —** darse prisa, apresurarse; *Am.* apurarse.

has·ten [hésn̩] *v.* apresurar(se), precipitar(se); darse prisa.

hast·i·ly [héstlɪ] *adv.* aprisa, de prisa, apresuradamente, precipitadamente.

hast·y [héstɪ] *adj.* apresurado; precipitado.

hat [hæt] *s.* sombrero.

hatch [hætʃ] *v.* empollar; criar pollos; idear, maquinar; *s.* cría, nidada, pollada; escotillón, trampa (*puerta en el suelo*); —**way** escotilla.

hatch·et [hǽtʃɪt] *s.* hacha; **to bury the —** echar pelillos a la mar, olvidar rencores o enemistades.

hate [het] *s.* odio; aborrecimiento; *v.* odiar; aborrecer; detestar.

hate·ful [hétfəl] *adj.* odioso, aborrecible.

ha·tred [hétrɪd] *s.* odio, aversión.

haugh·ti·ly [hótɪlɪ] *adv.* con altivez, altaneramente, arrogantemente.

haugh·ti·ness [hótɪnɪs] *s.* altanería, altivez.

haugh·ty [hótɪ] *adj.* altivo, altanero, arrogante.

haul [hɔl] *v.* (*transport*) acarrear, transportar; (*pull*) jalar (*halar*); tirar de; (*drag*) arrastrar; **to — down the flag** arriar (*o* bajar) la bandera; *s.* acarreo; transporte; tirón, estirón; buena pesca; ganancia, botín; (*round-up*) redada.

haunch [hɔntʃ] *s.* anca.

haunt [hɔnt] *v.* frecuentar a menudo; andar por, vagar por (*como fantasma o espectro*); **that idea -s me** me persigue esa idea; **-ed house** casa de espantos, fantasmas o aparecidos; *s.* guarida.

have [hæv] *v.* tener; poseer; haber (*v. aux.*); **to — a suit made** mandar hacer un traje; **to — a look at** dar un vistazo a, echar una mirada a; **to — to** tener que; deber; **I'll not — it** so no lo toleraré, no lo permitiré; **what did she — on?** ¿qué vestido llevaba (puesto)?

ha·ven [hévən] *s.* asilo, abrigo, refugio; puerto.

hav·oc [hǽvək] *s.* estrago, estropicio, ruina; **to cause —** hacer estragos.

hawk [hɔk] *s.* halcón; *v.* pregonar (*mercancías*).

haw·thorn [hɔ́θɔrn] *s.* espino.

hay [he] *s.* heno, paja, hierba seca; — **fever** catarro asmático.

hay·loft [hélɔft] *s.* henil, pajar.

hay·stack [héstæk] *s.* montón de heno o paja.

haz·ard [hǽzɚd] *s.* azar; riesgo, peligro; estorbo, obstáculo (*en el campo de golf*); *v.* arriesgar, aventurar.

haz·ard·ous [hǽzɚdəs] *adj.* peligroso.

haze [hez] *s.* bruma, neblina, niebla; *v.* atormentar, hostigar (*con bromas estudiantiles*).

ha·zel [hézl] *s.* avellano; —**nut** avellana; *adj.* de avellano; avellanado, color de avellana.

haz·y [hézɪ] *adj.* (*weather*) nublado, brumoso; (*mind*) confuso.

he [hi] *pron. pers.* él; — **who** el que, quien; **he-goat** macho cabrío.

head [hed] *s.* cabeza; cabecera (*de cama*); jefe; — **of hair** cabellera; **game of -s or tails** juego de cara y cruz, juego de las chapas, *Ven., Col., Andes, Ch.* juego de cara y sello; *Méx.* juego de águila y sol; **to be out of one's —** delirar, estar delirante; **to come to a —** madurar; supurar (*un absceso*); **to keep one's —** conservar la calma, no

perder la cabeza; **it goes to his** — le desvanece;
se le sube a la cabeza; *adj.* principal, primero;
de proa, de frente; **head-on** de frente; *v.*
encabezar; ir a la cabeza de; acaudillar; mandar,
dirigir; **to** — **off** atajar; detener, refrenar; **to** —
towards dirigirse a, encaminarse a.
head·ache [hédek] *s.* dolor de cabeza.
head·dress [héddrɛs] *s.* tocado, adorno para la
cabeza.
head·gear [hédgɪr] *s.* sombrero, gorro, gorra;
tocado, toca (*de mujer*); cabezada (*de
guarnición para caballo*).
head·ing [hédɪŋ] *s.* encabezamiento, título.
head·land [hédlənd] *s.* cabo, promontorio.
head·light [hédlaɪt] *s.* linterna delantera, faro
delantero.
head·line [hédlaɪn] *s.* título, encabezado.
head·long [hédlɔ́ŋ] *adv.* de cabeza;
precipitadamente.
head·quar·ters [hédkwɔ́rtɚz] *s.* cuartel general;
jefatura; oficina principal.
head·set [hédsɛt] *s.* receptor de cabeza.
head·strong [hédstrɔŋ] *adj.* testarudo, porfiado,
obstinado.
head·way [hédwe] *s.* progreso, avance; **to make** —
avanzar, adelantar, progresar.
heal [hil] *v.* curar; sanar; cicatrizar.
health [hɛlθ] *s.* salud; sanidad; salubridad.
health·ful [hɛ́lθfəl] *adj.* sano; salubre; saludable.
health·ful·ness [hɛ́lθfəlnɪs] *s.* salubridad; sanidad.
health·y [hɛ́lθɪ] *adj.* sano; saludable.
heap [hip] *s.* montón; pila; *v.* amontonar; apilar.
hear [hɪr] *v.* (*listen*) oír; escuchar; (*get news*) tener
noticias; **to** — **about someone** oír hablar de
alguien; **to** — **from someone** tener noticias de
alguien; **to** — **of** saber de, tener noticias de, oír
hablar de; **I -d that ...** oí decir que ...
heard [hɜd] *pret.* & *p.p. de* **to hear.**
hear·er [hɪrɚ] *s.* oyente.
hear·ing [hírɪŋ] *s.* (*sense*) oído; (*trial*) audiencia;
examen de testigos; **hard of** — medio sordo,
algo sordo; **within** — al alcance del oído; — **aid**
aparato auditivo.
hear·say [hírse] *s.* habilla, rumor; **by** — de oídas.
hearse [hɜs] *s.* carroza fúnebre.
heart [hɑrt] *s.* (*organ*) corazón; (*spirit*) ánimo; **at**
— **en realidad**, en el fondo; **from the bottom of
one's** — de corazón, con toda el alma; con toda
sinceridad; **to learn by** — aprender de memoria;
to take — cobrar ánimo; **to take to** — tomar
en serio; tomar a pechos; — **attack** ataque
cardíaco; — **of lettuce, cabbage** cogollo.
heart·ache [hártek] *s.* dolor del corazón; angustia,
pesar, congoja.
heart·bro·ken [hártbrokən] *adj.* traspasado de
dolor, acongojado, angustiado; desengañado.
heart·en [hártn̩] *v.* animar.
heart·felt [hártfɛlt] *adj.* sentido, cordial, sincero;
my — **sympathy** mi más sentido pésame.
hearth [hɑrθ] *s.* hogar; fogón.
heart·i·ly [hártlɪ] *adv.* de corazón; cordialmente;
de buena gana; **to eat** — comer con apetito;
comer bien (*o mucho*).
heart·less [hártlɪs] *adj.* de mal corazón; cruel;
insensible.
heart·rend·ing [hártrɛndɪŋ] *adj.* angustioso; agudo.
heart·y [hártɪ] *adj.* sincero, cordial; sano, fuerte;
— **food** alimento nutritivo; **a** — **laugh** una
buena carcajada; — **meal** comida abundante.
heat [hit] *s.* (*hot*) calor; ardor; (*emotion*)
vehemencia; celo (*ardor sexual de la hembra*);

calefacción (*para las habitaciones*); corrida,
carrera (*de prueba*); *v.* calentar(se); acalorar(se).
heat·er [hítɚ] *s.* calentador; calorífero.
hea·then [híðən] *s.* pagano, gentil, idólatra;
paganos; *adj.* pagano; irreligioso.
heat·ing [hítɪŋ] *s.* calefacción.
heave [hiv] *v.* levantar, alzar (*con esfuerzo*); arrojar,
lanzar; exhalar (*un suspiro*); jalar (*un cable*);
jadear; basquear, hacer esfuerzos por vomitar.
heav·en [hévən] *s.* cielo.
heav·en·ly [hévənlɪ] *adj.* celeste; celestial; divino.
heav·i·ly [hévlɪ] *adv.* pesadamente, lentamente;
copiosamente, excesivamente.
heav·i·ness [hévɪnɪs] *s.* pesadez, pesantez; opresión,
abatimiento.
heav·y [hévɪ] *adj.* (*weight*) pesado; (*thick*) grueso;
(*coarse*) burdo; (*oppressive*) opresivo; — **rain**
aguacero recio o fuerte; **with a** — **heart** abatido,
acongojado.
heav·y·weight [hévɪwet] *s.* & *adj.* peso pesado
(*fuerte*).
hectare [hɛktɚ] *s.* hectárea.
hec·tic [hɛktɪk] *adj.* febril; inquieto.
hedge [hɛdʒ] *s.* seto; vallado, barrera; *v.* cercar;
poner valla o seto a; evitar o evadir
contestaciones.
hedge·hog [hédʒhɑg] *s.* erizo.
he·don·ism [hídənɪzm] *s.* hedonismo.
heed [hid] *v.* atender; hacer caso; prestar atención;
s. atención, cuidado; **to pay** — **to** prestar
atención a; hacer caso de.
heed·less [hídlɪs] *adj.* descuidado; desatento.
heel [hil] *s.* talón (*del pie o de una media*); tacón
(*del zapato*); **head over -s** patas arriba; *v.* poner
tacón a; poner talón a.
he·gem·o·ny [hɪdʒémənɪ] *s.* hegemonía.
heif·er [héfɚ] *s.* novilla, vaquilla.
height [haɪt] *s.* altura; elevación; — **of folly** colmo
de la locura.
height·en [háɪtn̩] *v.* avivar; aumentar(se); realzar.
hei·nous [hénəs] *adj.* aborrecible, odioso; malvado.
heir [ɛr] *s.* heredero.
heir·ess [ɛrɪs] *s.* heredera.
held [hɛld] *pret.* & *p.p. de* **to hold.**
hel·i·cop·ter [hélɪkaptɚ] *s.* helicóptero.
he·li·um [hiliəm] *s.* helio.
hell [hɛl] *s.* infierno.
hel·lo [hɛló] *interj.* ¡hola!; ¡halo!
helm [hɛlm] *s.* timón.
hel·met [hɛ́lmɪt] *s.* yelmo.
help [hɛlp] *s.* (*aid*) ayuda; auxilio; remedio; alivio;
(*employee*) criado o criados, empleado o
empleados; *v.* ayudar, asistir; auxiliar; remediar;
servir (*algo de comer*); **to** — **down** ayudar a
bajar; — **yourself** sírvase Vd. (*de comer o beber*);
tómelo Vd., está a la disposición de Vd.; **he
cannot** — **it** no puede evitarlo; **he cannot** —
doing it no puede menos de hacerlo; **he cannot**
— **but come** no puede menos de venir.
help·er [hélpɚ] *s.* ayudante, asistente.
help·ful [hélpfəl] *adj.* útil, servicial; provechoso.
help·ing [hélpɪŋ] *s.* ayuda; porción (*que se sirve en
la mesa*).
help·less [hélplɪs] *adj.* (*defenseless*) desamparado;
(*handicapped*) desvalido; imposibilitado;
incapaz; (*confused*) perplejo, indeciso (*sin saber
qué hacer*); **a** — **situation** una situación
irremediable.
help·less·ness [hélplɪsnɪs] *s.* incapacidad;
incompetencia; impotencia, debilidad; abandono;
desamparo.

HA

hem [hɛm] s. dobladillo, bastilla; v. dobladillar, bastillar, hacer dobladillos en (la ropa); **to — in** rodear, cercar; **to — and haw** toser y retoser (fingidamente); tartamudear, vacilar.

hem·i·sphere [hémǝsfɪr] s. hemisferio.

hem·lock [hémlɑk] s. cicuta (hierba venenosa); abeto americano.

he·mo·glo·bin [hímoglobɪn] s. hemoglobina.

hem·or·rhage [hémǝrɪdʒ] s. hemorragia.

hemp [hɛmp] s. cáñamo, Am. sisal.

hem·stitch [hémstɪtʃ] s. dobladillo de ojo; v. hacer (o echar) dobladillo de ojo.

hen [hɛn] s. gallina; ave hembra.

hence [hɛns] adv. de (o desde) aquí; desde ahora; por lo tanto, por consiguiente; **a week —** de hoy en ocho días; de aquí a una semana.

hence·forth [hɛnsfórθ] adv. de aquí en adelante; de hoy en adelante; desde ahora.

hep·a·ti·tis [hɛpǝtáɪtɪs] s. hepatitis.

her [hɝ] pron. la; le, a ella; ella (con preposición); adj. su (sus), de ella.

her·ald [hérǝld] s. heraldo; anunciador, proclamador; precursor; v. anunciar, proclamar, publicar.

her·ald·ry [hérǝldrɪ] s. heráldica.

herb [ɝb] s. hierba (yerba).

herd [hɝd] s. (animals) hato; rebaño; manada; tropel; tropilla; (cattle) ganado; (people) muchedumbre; **the common —** el populacho, la chusma; v. reunir, juntar (el ganado); ir en manadas, ir juntos.

herds·man [hɝdzmǝn] s. vaquero, vaquerizo; pastor.

here [hɪr] adv. aquí; acá; **— it is** aquí está, helo aquí, aquí lo tiene Vd., **— is to you!** ¡a la salud de Vd.!; **that is neither — nor there** eso no viene al caso; (to call a dog) ¡cuz! ¡toma! (a cat) ¡misi! ¡mis!

here·af·ter [hɪræftǝ] adv. de aquí (o de hoy) en adelante; desde ahora en adelante; en lo futuro; s. **the —** la otra vida.

here·by [hɪrbáɪ] adv. por este medio; mediante la presente, por la presente; con estas palabras.

he·red·i·tar·y [hǝrédǝtɛrɪ] adj. hereditario.

he·red·i·ty [hǝrédǝtɪ] s. herencia.

here·in [hɪrín] adv. aquí dentro; en esto.

her·e·sy [hérǝsɪ] s. herejía.

her·e·tic [hérǝtɪk] s. hereje.

here·to·fore [hɪrtǝfór] adv. hasta ahora, hasta el presente.

here·with [hɪrwíθ] adv. aquí dentro, con esto, adjunto, incluso.

her·i·tage [hérǝtɪdʒ] s. herencia.

her·met·ic [hǝmétɪk] adj. hermético.

her·mit [hɝmɪt] s. ermitaño.

her·ni·a [hɝnɪǝ] s. hernia, ruptura, relajamiento.

he·ro [híro] s. héroe; protagonista.

he·ro·ic [hɪróɪk] adj. heroico.

her·o·in [héroɪn] s. heroína.

her·o·ine [héroɪn] s. heroína.

her·o·ism [héroɪzǝm] s. heroísmo.

her·on [hérǝn] s. garza.

her·ring [hérɪŋ] s. arenque.

hers [hɝz] pron. pos. suyo (suya, suyos, suyas), de ella; el suyo (la suya, los suyos, las suyas); el (la, los, las) de ella; **a friend of —** un amigo suyo.

her·self [hǝsélf] pron. ella misma; se (como reflexivo); **by —** sola; por sí (sola); **she — did it** ella misma lo hizo; **she talks to —** ella habla para sí, habla consigo misma, habla para sus adentros, habla sola.

hes·i·tant [hézǝtǝnt] = **hesitating.**

hes·i·tate [hézǝtet] v. vacilar; titubear; dudar.

hes·i·tat·ing [hésǝtetɪŋ] adj. vacilante; indeciso; irresoluto; **-ly** adv. con vacilación.

hes·i·ta·tion [hɛzǝtéʃǝn] s. vacilación; titubeo, duda.

het·er·o·ge·ne·ous [hɛtǝǝdʒínɪǝs] adj. heterogeneo.

hew [hju] v. tajar, cortar; picar (piedra); labrar (madera, piedra).

hewn [hjun] p.p. de **to hew.**

hey [he] interj. ¡he!; ¡oiga!; ¡oye!

hi·a·tus [haɪétǝs] s. hiato.

hi·ber·nate [háɪbǝnet] v. invernar.

hic·cup, hic·cough [híkʌp] s. hipo; v. hipar, tener hipo.

hick·o·ry [híkǝrɪ] s. nogal americano; **— nut** nuez (del nogal americano).

hid [hɪd] pret. & p.p. de **to hide.**

hid·den [hídn] p.p. de **to hide;** adj. oculto, escondido.

hide [haɪd] v. ocultar(se); esconder(se); **to — from** esconderse de, recatarse de; s. cuero, piel; **to play — and seek** jugar al escondite.

hid·e·ous [hídɪǝs] adj. horrendo, horripilante, feote.

hi·er·ar·chy [háɪǝrɑrkɪ] s. jerarquía.

hi·er·o·glyph·ic [haɪǝroglífɪk] adj. & s. jeroglífico.

high [haɪ] adj. alto; **— altar** altar mayor; **— and dry** enjuto; en seco; solo, abandonado; **— antiquity** antigüedad remota; **— explosive** explosivo de gran potencia; **— tide** pleamar; **— wind** ventarrón, viento fuerte; **in — gear** en directa, en tercera velocidad; **two feet —** dos pies de alto; **it is — time that** ya es hora de que; **to be in — spirits** estar muy animado; adv. alto; a precio subido; en alto; **to look — and low** buscar por todas partes; **high-grade** de calidad superior; **high-handed** arbitrario, despótico; **high-minded** magnánimo; orgulloso; **high-sounding** altisonante, rimbombante; **high-strung** muy tenso.

high·land [háɪlǝnd] s. tierra montañosa; **the Highlands** las montañas de Escocia.

high·light [háɪlaɪt] s. lo más notable.

high·ly [háɪlɪ] adv. altamente; sumamente; muy; — **paid** muy bien pagado.

high·ness [háɪnɪs] s. altura; elevación; Alteza (título).

high·way [háɪwe] s. camino real; carretera, calzada.

high·way·man [háɪwemǝn] s. forajido, salteador de caminos, bandido.

hike [haɪk] s. caminata, paseo largo, Am. andada; v. dar (o echar) una caminata.

hill [hɪl] s. colina, collado, cerro; montoncillo de tierra; Andes, Am. loma; **— ant —** hormiguero; **down —** cuesta abajo; **up —** cuesta arriba.

hill·ock [hílǝk] s. collado, otero, montecillo.

hill·side [hílsaɪd] s. ladera.

hill·top [híltɑp] s. cumbre, cima (de una colina).

hill·y [hílɪ] adj. montuoso; accidentado.

hilt [hɪlt] s. empuñadura, puño (de una espada o daga).

him [hɪm] pron. le; lo; él (con preposición).

him·self [hɪmsélf] pron. él mismo; se (como reflexivo); a sí mismo; véase **herself.**

hind [haɪnd] adj. trasero; posterior; s. cierva; **—most** adj. último, postrero.

hin·der [híndǝ] v. estorbar, impedir, obstruir.

hin·drance [híndrǝns] s. estorbo, obstáculo, impedimento.

hinge [hɪndʒ] s. gozne; bisagra; v. engoznar, poner goznes; **to — on** girar sobre; depender de.

hint [hɪnt] s. indirecta, insinuación; sugestión; **not to take the —** no darse por entendido; v. insinuar, intimar, sugerir indirectamente.

hip [hɪp] s. cadera.

hip·po·pot·a·mus [hɪpəpátəməs] s. hipopótamo.

hire [haɪr] s. (rent) alquiler; (pay) paga, sueldo; v. alquilar; emplear, dar empleo, C.A., Ven., Col. enganchar, Am. conchabar; **to — out** alquilarse, ponerse a servir a otro.

his [hɪz] pron. pos. suyo (suya, suyos, suyas), de él; el suyo (la suya, los suyos, las suyas); el (la, los, las) de él; **a friend of —** un amigo suyo; adj. su (sus), de él.

hiss [hɪs] s. silbido, chiflido; siseo; v. sisear, silbar, chiflar.

his·ta·mine [hístəmin] s. histamina.

his·to·ri·an [hɪstɔ́rɪən] s. historiador.

his·tor·ic [hɪstɔ́rɪk] adj. histórico.

his·tor·i·cal [hɪstɔ́rɪkḷ] adj. histórico.

his·to·ry [hístrɪ] s. historia.

his·tri·on·ics [hɪstrɪɑ́nɪks] s. histrionismo.

hit [hɪt] v. pegar, golpear; dar (un golpe); dar en (o con); chocar; **they — it off well** se llevan bien, congenian; **to — the mark** acertar, atinar, dar en el blanco; **to — upon** dar con; encontrarse con, encontrar por casualidad; pret. & p.p. de **to hit**; s. golpe; choque; golpe de fortuna; pulla, dicharacho; **to be a great —** ser un gran éxito; **to make a — with someone** caerle en gracia a una persona; **hit-and-run** adj. que abandona a su víctima atropellada.

hitch [hɪtʃ] v. atar, amarrar; enganchar; uncir (bueyes); dar un tirón; **to — one's chair nearer** acercar su silla a; s. tirón; obstáculo, impedimento, tropiezo; enganche, enganchamiento.

hitch·hike [hítʃhaɪk] v. viajar de gorra (en automóvil), Méx. irse o viajar de mosca; Ch., Ríopl. hacer dedo, ir a dedo; Esp. viajar por auto-stop.

hith·er [híðɚ] adv. acá; **— and thither** acá y allá.

hith·er·to [híðɚtú] adv. hasta aquí, hasta ahora, hasta hoy.

hive [haɪv] s. colmena; enjambre; **-s** ronchas (de la piel).

hoard [hord] s. tesoro escondido; acumulamiento secreto de provisiones; v. atesorar, guardar (con avaricia); acumular secretamente.

hoarse [hors] adj. bronco, áspero, ronco.

hoarse·ness [hórsnɪs] s. ronquera; carraspera.

hoar·y [hórɪ] adj. cano, encanecido, canoso.

hob·ble [hábḷ] v. (limp) cojear, renquear; (tie) maniatar o manear (un animal); (impede) impedir, estorbar; s. cojera; traba, maniota o manea (cuerda con que se atan las manos de una bestia).

hob·by [hábɪ] s. afición; trabajo hecho por afición (no por obligación).

ho·bo [hóbo] s. vagabundo.

hodge·podge [hádʒpadʒ] s. mezcolanza, baturrillo.

hoe [ho] s. azada, azadón; v. cavar, escardar, limpiar con azadón.

hog [hag] s. puerco, cerdo, cochino; chancho; adj. porcino; v. apropiárselo todo.

hoist [hɔɪst] v. alzar, levantar; izar (la bandera, las velas); s. elevador, Am. malacate.

hold [hold] v. tener(se); retener; detener; tener cabida para; sostener; mantener(se); opinar; celebrar (una reunión, etc.); ocupar (un puesto); ser válido (un argumento o regla); **to — back** someone detener (o refrenar) a alguien; **to —**

forth perorar, hablar largamente; **to — in place** sujetar; **to — off** mantener(se) a distancia; mantenerse alejado; **to — on** agarrar(se); asir(se); persistir; **— on!** ¡agárrese bien!; ¡deténgase! ¡pare!; **to — someone responsible** hacerle a uno responsable; **to — someone to his word** obligar a uno a cumplir su palabra; **to — oneself erect** tenerse o andar derecho; **to — one's own** mantenerse firme; **to — one's tongue** callarse; **to — out** continuar, durar; mantenerse firme; **to — over** aplazar; durar; continuar en un cargo; **to — still** estarse quieto o callado; **to — tight** apretar; **to — to one's promise** cumplir con la promesa; **to — up** levantar, alzar; detener; asaltar, atracar (para robar); **how much does it —?** ¿cuánto le cabe? s. agarro; dominio; influencia; autoridad; bodega (de un barco); cabina de carga (de un aeroplano); **to get — of** asir, agarrar; atrapar; **to take — of** coger, agarrar, asir.

hold·er [hóldɚ] s. (person) tenedor, posesor; (device) receptáculo; cojinillo (para coger un trasto caliente); **cigarette —** boquilla; **pen—** portaplumas.

hold·up [hóldʌp] s. asalto, atraco.

hole [hol] s. agujero; abertura; hoyo, hueco, cavidad; bache (de un camino); **swimming —** charco, remanso; **to be in a —** hallarse en un apuro o aprieto.

hol·i·day [háləde] s. día de fiesta, día festivo, festividad; **-s** días de fiesta; vacaciones.

ho·li·ness [hólɪnɪs] s. santidad.

hol·low [hálo] adj. (empty) hueco; vacío; (concave) cóncavo; hundido; (insincere) falso; s. hueco; hoyo; cavidad; concavidad; depresión; cañada, hondonada; v. ahuecar; excavar; ahondar.

hol·ly [hálɪ] s. agrifolio, acebo.

hol·ster [hólstɚ] s. pistolera, funda (de pistola).

ho·ly [hólɪ] adj. santo; sagrado, sacro; **— water** agua bendita.

hom·age [hámɪdʒ] s. homenaje; reverencia, acatamiento; **to do —** acatar, rendir homenaje, honrar.

home [hom] s. casa, hogar; habitación; domicilio; **at —** en casa; adj. doméstico; casero; **— office** oficina matriz o central; **— rule** autonomía; **— run** Méx., C.A., Ven., Col. jonrón (en béisbol); **— stretch** último trecho (de una carrera); adv. a casa; en casa; **to strike —** herir en lo vivo; dar en el clavo o en el blanco.

home·land [hómlænd] s. tierra natal, suelo patrio.

home·less [hómlɪs] adj. sin casa; destituido.

home·like [hómlaɪk] adj. hogareño, cómodo.

home·ly [hómlɪ] adj. feo; llano; sencillo; casero, doméstico.

home·made [hómméd] adj. hecho en casa; doméstico, nacional, del país.

home·sick [hómsɪk] adj. nostálgico.

home·sick·ness [hómsɪknɪs] s. nostalgia.

home·stead [hómstɛd] s. heredad; casa y terrenos adyacentes.

home·ward [hómwɚd] adv. a casa; hacia la patria; **— voyage** retorno, viaje de vuelta.

home·work [hómwɝk] s. trabajo de casa; trabajo hecho en casa.

hom·i·cide [háməsaɪd] s. homicidio; homicida, asesino.

ho·mo·ge·ne·ous [homədʒínɪəs] adj. homogéneo.

ho·mog·e·nize [homándʒənaɪz] v. homogenizar.

ho·mo·sex·u·al [homəsékʃjʊl] adj. & s. homosexual.

HE

hone [hon] *v.* amolar, asentar, afilar; *s.* piedra de afilar.

hon·est [ánɪst] *adj.* honrado, recto; genuino; — **goods** mercancías genuinas; **-ly** *adv.* honradamente; de veras.

hon·es·ty [ánɪstɪ] *s.* honradez, rectitud.

hon·ey [hʌnɪ] *s.* miel; dulzura; querido, querida.

hon·ey·comb [hʌnɪkom] *s.* panal.

hon·eyed [hʌnɪd] *adj.* meloso; dulce; melifluo.

hon·ey·moon [hʌnɪmun] *s.* luna de miel; viaje de novios, viaje de bodas; *v.* pasar la luna de miel.

hon·ey·suck·le [hʌnɪsʌkl] *s.* madreselva.

honk [hɔŋk] *s.* pitazo (*de automóvil*); graznido (*voz del ganso*); *v.* donar la bocina; graznar.

hon·or [ánɚ] *s.* honor; honra; señoría (*título*); **upon my** — sobre mi palabra; *v.* honrar; dar honra.

hon·or·a·ble [ánɚəbl] *adj.* honorable; honroso; honrado.

hon·or·ar·y [ánɚɛrɪ] *adj.* honorario, honorífico.

hood [hʊd] *s.* capucha, caperuza; capirote, cubierta (*del motor*); *v.* encapuchar, encapirotar.

hood·lum [húdləm] *s.* maleante; antisocial.

hoof [hʊf] *s.* casco, pezuña; pata (*de caballo, toro, etc.*); (*half of cloven hoof*) pesuño.

hook [hʊk] *s.* gancho, garfio; anzuelo (*para pescar*); — **and eye** corchete; macho y hembra, **by** — **or crook** por la buena o por la mala, por angas o por mangas; **on his own** — por su propia cuenta; *v.* enganchar(se); abrochar(se); pescar, coger con anzuelo; robar, hurtar.

hook·y [húkɪ]: **to play** — hacer novillos, *Carib.* capear la escuela, *Méx.* pintar venado, *C.A., Ven., Col.* jubilarse; *Ríopl.* hacerse la rata (*la rabona*).

hoop [hup] *s.* aro; argolla; *v.* poner aro a; ceñir, cercar.

hoot [hut] *v.* ulular (*dícese del buho, lechuza, etc.*); rechiflar, ridiculizar; *s.* alarido, chillido.

hoot·ing [hútɪŋ] *s.* grita, rechifla.

hop [hɑp] *s.* salto, brinco; baile; *v.* saltar; brincar.

hope [hop] *s.* esperanza; *v.* esperar; **to** — **for** esperar; **to** — **against** — esperar desesperando; esperar lo que no puede ser, esperar lo imposible.

hope·ful [hópfəl] *adj.* esperanzado, lleno de esperanza; **a young** — un joven prometedor; **-ly** *adv.* con esperanza; con ansia; lleno de esperanza.

hope·less [hóplɪs] *adj.* sin esperanza, falto de esperanza, desesperanzado; desesperado; irremediable; — **cause** causa perdida; — **illness** enfermedad incurable; **it is** — no tiene remedio; **-ly** *adv.* sin esperanza, sin remedio.

hope·less·ness [hóplɪsnɪs] *s.* falta de esperanza; falta de remedio; desesperanza, desaliento.

horde [hord] *s.* horda; muchedumbre, gentío; enjambre.

ho·ri·zon [həráɪzn] *s.* horizonte.

hor·i·zon·tal [hɔrəzántl] *adj.* horizontal.

hor·mone [hɔ́rmon] *s.* hormona.

horn [hɔrn] *s.* (*animal*) cuerno; asta; cacho; (*automobile*) bocina, klaxon, trompa; (*musical*) corneta; trompeta; — **of plenty** cuerno de la abundancia; *v.* acornear, dar cornadas; **to** — **in** entremeterse; — tip piton.

hor·net [hɔ́rnɪt] *s.* avispón; —**'s nest** avispero.

hor·o·scope [hɔ́rəskop] *s.* horóscopo.

hor·ri·ble [hɔ́rəbl] *adj.* horrible; **horribly** *adv.* horriblemente.

hor·rid [hɔ́rɪd] *adj.* horrendo, horrible.

hor·ri·fy [hɔ́rəfaɪ] *v.* horrorizar, aterrorizar, espantar.

hor·ror [hɔ́rɚ] *s.* horror.

hors d'oeuvre [ɔrdǽvrə] *s.* entremés; bocadillos.

horse [hɔrs] *s.* caballo; caballete (*de madera*), borriquete (*de carpinteros*); **saddle** — caballo de silla; — **dealer** chalán; — **race** carrera de caballos; — **sense** sentido común.

horse·back [hɔ́rsbæk] *s.* lomo de caballo; **to ride** — montar a caballo, cabalgar, jinetear.

horse·fly [hɔ́rsflaɪ] *s.* tábano, mosca de caballo.

horse·laugh [hɔ́rslæf] *s.* carcajada, risotada.

horse·man [hɔ́rsmən] *s.* jinete.

horse·man·ship [hɔ́rsmənʃɪp] *s.* equitación.

horse·pow·er [hɔ́rspauɚ] *s.* caballo de fuerza.

horse·rad·ish [hɔ́rsrædɪʃ] *s.* rábano picante.

horse·shoe [hɔ́rsʃu] *s.* herradura.

hose [hoz] *s.* medias; manga o manguera (*para regar*); **men's** — calcetines.

ho·sier·y [hóʒrɪ] *s.* medias; calcetines; calcetería (*negocio*); — **shop** calcetería.

hos·pi·ta·ble [háspɪtəbl] *adj.* hospitalario.

hos·pi·tal [háspɪtl] *s.* hospital.

hos·pi·tal·i·ty [háspɪtǽlətɪ] *s.* hospitalidad.

host [host] *s.* huésped (*el que hospeda*), anfitrión (*el que convida*); hospedero, mesonero; hueste; ejército, multitud; hostia; **sacred** — hostia consagrada.

hos·tage [hástɪdʒ] *s.* rehén (*persona que queda como prenda en poder del enemigo*).

hos·tel·ry [hástəlrɪ] *s.* hostería.

host·ess [hóstɪs] *s.* huéspeda (*la que hospeda o convida*).

hos·tile [hástl] *adj.* hostil.

hos·til·i·ty [hastílətɪ] *s.* hostilidad.

hot [hat] *adj.* caliente; caluroso; cálido; picante (*como el pimentón, chile, ají, etc.*); furioso; fresco, reciente; — **bed** semillero; **hot-headed** enojadizo, impetuoso; exaltado; — **house** invernáculo, invernadero; **it is** — **today** hace calor hoy.

ho·tel [hotél] *s.* hotel.

ho·tel·keep·er [hotélkipɚ] *s.* hotelero.

hot·ly [hátlɪ] *adv.* calurosamente, con vehemencia.

hound [haʊnd] *s.* perro de busca, lebrel, galgo, sabueso, podenco; *v.* acosar, perseguir; azuzar, incitar.

hour [aʊr] *s.* hora; — **hand** horario.

hour·ly [áʊrlɪ] *adv.* por horas; a cada hora; a menudo; *adj.* frecuente; por horas.

house [haʊs] *s.* (*residence*) casa; domicilio; (*legislature*) cámara, asamblea legislativa; **country** — casa de campo; **a full** — un lleno completo (*en el teatro*); [haʊz] *v.* alojar; hospedar.

house·hold [háʊshold] *s.* casa, familia; *adj.* casero; doméstico.

house·keep·er [háʊskipɚ] *s.* casera; ama de llaves; **to be a good** — ser una mujer hacendosa.

house·keep·ing [háʊskipɪŋ] *s.* gobierno de casa; quehaceres domésticos.

house·top [háʊstɑp] *s.* techumbre, tejado.

house·wife [háʊswaɪf] *s.* mujer de su casa; madre de familia; ama de casa.

house·work [háʊswɝk] *s.* trabajo de casa; quehaceres domésticos.

hous·ing [háʊzɪŋ] *s.* viviendas; programa de construcción de viviendas.

hove [hov] *pret. & p.p. de* **to heave**.

hov·el [hʌ́vl] *s.* choza, cabaña, *Carib., Ven.* bohío, *Méx.* jacal; cobertizo; *Ríopl.* tapera.

hov·er [hʌ́vɚ] *v.* cernerse (*como un pájaro*); vacilar;

to — around revolotear; rondar.

how [haʊ] adv. cómo; — beautiful! ¡qué hermoso!; — early (late, soon)? ¿cuándo? ¿a qué hora?; — far is it? ¡a qué distancia está? ¿cuánto dista de aquí?; — long? ¿cuánto tiempo?; — many? ¿cuántos?; — much is it? ¿cuánto es? ¿a cómo se vende? ¿cuál es el precio?; — old are you? ¿cuántos años tiene Vd.?; — no matter — much por mucho que; he knows — difficult it is él sabe lo difícil que es; él sabe cuán difícil es.

how·ev·er [haʊévəʳ] adv. & conj. sin embargo, no obstante, con todo, empero; — difficult it may be por muy difícil que sea; — much por mucho que.

howl [haʊl] s. aullido, alarido, chillido, grito; v. aullar; chillar, dar alaridos; gritar.

hub [hʌb] s. cubo (de una rueda); eje, centro de actividad.

hub·bub [hʌbʌb] s. ajetreo; barullo.

huck·ster [hʌkstəʳ] s. vendedor ambulante.

hud·dle [hʌdl] s. montón, confusión, tropel; to be in a — estar agrupados (en futbol para planear una jugada); to get in a — agruparse (para aconsejarse o planear algo); v. amontonar(se); acurrucarse.

hue [hju] s. tinte, matiz.

huff [hʌf] s. enojo, rabieta; to get into a — enojarse.

hug [hʌg] v. abrazar, estrechar; to — the coast costear; s. abrazo fuerte.

huge [hjudʒ] adj. enorme; descomunal.

hull [hʌl] s. casco (de una nave); armazón (de una aeronave); vaina, hollejo (de ciertas legumbres); v. mondar, pelar desvainar, deshollejar.

hum [hʌm] v. canturrear (o canturriar), tararear; zumbar (dícese de insectos, maquinaria, etc.); to — to sleep arrullar; s. canturreo, tarareo; zumbido; interj. ¡hum!; ¡ejém!

hu·man [hjúmən] adj. humano; s. ser humano.

hu·mane [hjumén] adj. humano; humanitario.

hu·man·ism [hjúmənɪzm] s. humanismo.

hu·man·i·tar·i·an [hjumænətériən] adj. humanitario; s. filántropo.

hu·man·i·ty [hjumǽnɪtɪ] s. humanidad; -ies humanidades.

hum·ble [hʌmbl] adj. humilde; v. humillar; humbly adv. humildemente, con humildad.

hum·ble·ness [hʌmblnɪs] s. humildad.

hu·mid [hjúmɪd] adj. húmedo.

hu·mid·i·fy [hjumídəfaɪ] v. humedecer.

hu·mid·i·ty [hjumídətɪ] d. humedad.

hu·mil·i·ate [hjumíliet] v. humillar.

hu·mil·i·a·tion [hjumɪliéʃən] s. humillación.

hu·mil·i·ty [hjumílətɪ] s. humildad.

hum·ming·bird [hʌmɪŋbɜʳd] s. colibrí, pájaro mosca, Méx. chuparrosa, Am. chupaflor, Am. guainumbí; Riopl., Ch. picaflor.

hu·mor [hjúməʳ] s. humor, humorismo, gracia; capricho; out of — de mal humor, malhumorado, disgustado; v. seguir el humor (a una persona), complacer; mimar.

hu·mor·ous [hjúmərəs] adj. humorístico, gracioso, cómico, chistoso.

hump [hʌmp] s. joroba, corcova, giba; v. encorvar.

hump·back [hʌmpbæk] = hunchback.

hunch [hʌntʃ] s. joroba, corcova, giba; presentimiento, corazonada; v. encorvar (la espalda).

hunch·back [hʌntʃbæk] s. joroba; jorobado.

hun·dred [hʌndrəd] adj. cien(to); s. ciento; -s centenares, cientos.

hun·dredth [hʌndrədθ] adj. centésimo.

hung [hʌŋ] pret. & p.p. de to hang.

hun·ger [hʌŋgəʳ] s. hambre; v. tener hambre, estar hambriento; to — for ansiar, anhelar.

hun·gri·ly [hʌŋgrɪlɪ] adv. con hambre, hambrientamente.

hun·gry [hʌŋgrɪ] adj. hambriento; to be — tener hambre.

hunk [hʌŋk] s. pedazo grande; mendrugo (de pan).

hunt [hʌnt] v. cazar; perseguir; buscar; escudriñar; to — down dar caza a; seguir la pista de; to — for buscar; s. caza, cacería; busca, búsqueda; perseguimiento.

hunt·er [hʌntəʳ] s. cazador; buscador; perro de caza, perro de busca.

hunts·man [hʌntsmən] s. cazador.

hurl [hɜʳl] v. arrojar, lanzar.

hur·rah [hərɔ́] interj. ¡hurra! ¡viva!; ¡ole!; v. vitorear.

hur·ri·cane [hɜʳɪken] s. huracán.

hur·ried [hɜʳɪd] adj. apresurado; -ly adv. de prisa, apresuradamente, a escape.

hur·ry [hɜʳɪ] v. apresurar(se); precipitar(se); dar(se) prisa; apurarse; correr; to — in (out) entrar (salir) de prisa; to — up apresurar(se); dar(se) prisa; s. prisa; precipitación; to be in a — tener prisa, ir de prisa, estar de prisa.

hurt [hɜʳt] v. hacer daño; dañar; perjudicar; herir; lastimar; doler; to — one's feelings darle a uno que sentir; lastimar a uno; my tooth -s me duele la muela; pret. & p.p. de to hurt; s. daño; herida; lesión; dolor.

hus·band [hʌzbənd] s. marido, esposo.

hush [hʌʃ] v. acallar, aquietar; callar(se); —! ¡chitón! ¡silencio! ¡cállese! ¡quieto!; to — up a scandal encubrir un escándalo; s. silencio, quietud.

husk [hʌsk] s. cáscara, hollejo, vaina; v. mondar, pelar, deshollejar.

husk·y [hʌskɪ] adj. ronco; forzudo, fuerte; cascarudo.

hus·tle [hʌsl] v. apresurar(se); apurarse; menear(se); atropellar; s. prisa, apresuramiento, meneo; actividad; — and bustle vaivén.

hut [hʌt] s. choza, cabaña, Carib. bohío.

hy·a·cinth [háɪəsɪnθ] s. jacinto.

hy·brid [háɪbrɪd] adj. híbrido.

hy·drate [háɪdret] s. hidrato.

hy·drau·lic [haɪdrɔ́lɪk] adj. hidráulico.

hy·dro·e·lec·tric [haɪdroɪléktrɪk] adj. hidroeléctrico.

hy·dro·gen [háɪdrədʒən] s. hidrógeno.

hy·dro·pho·bi·a [haɪdrofóbɪə] s. hidrofobia.

hy·dro·plane [háɪdrəplen] s. hidroplano, hidroavión.

hy·giene [háɪdʒin] s. higiene.

hymn [hɪm] s. himno.

hy·phen [háɪfən] s. guión.

hyp·no·sis [hɪpnósɪs] s. hipnosis.

hy·poc·ri·sy [hɪpákrəsɪ] s. hipocresía.

hyp·o·crite [hípəkrɪt] s. hipócrita.

hyp·o·crit·i·cal [hɪpəkrítɪkl] adj. hipócrita.

hy·poth·e·sis [haɪpáθəsɪs] s. hipótesis.

hys·ter·i·cal [hɪstérɪkl] adj. histérico.

HO

I:i **I** [aɪ] *pron. pers.* yo.

I·be·ri·an [aɪbírɪən] *adj.* ibérico, ibero.

ice [aɪs] *s.* (*solid*) hielo; (*food*) helado; mantecado; sorbete; — **cream** helado; **icecream parlor** *Am.* heladería; nevería; — **skates** patines de cuchilla; — **water** agua helada; *v.* helar; escarchar, alfeñicar, cubrir con escarcha (*un pastel*).

ice·berg [áɪsbɜɡ] *s.* montaña de hielo, témpano.

ice·box [áɪsbɑks] *s.* nevera, *Am.* refrigerador.

ice·man [áɪsmæn] *s.* vendedor de hielo.

i·ci·cle [áɪsɪkḷ] *s.* carámbano.

i·con·o·clasm [aɪkánəklæzəm] *s.* iconoclasmo.

i·con·o·clast [aɪkánəklæst] *s.* iconoclasta.

i·cy [áɪsɪ] *adj.* helado, frío; congelado; cubierto de hielo.

i·de·a [aɪdíə] *s.* idea.

i·de·al [aɪdíəl] *adj. & s.* ideal.

i·de·al·ism [aɪdíəlɪzəm] *s.* idealismo.

i·de·al·ist [aɪdíəlɪst] *s.* idealista.

i·de·al·is·tic [aɪdiəlístɪk] *adj.* idealista.

i·den·ti·cal [aɪdɛ́ntɪkḷ] *adj.* idéntico.

i·den·ti·fi·ca·tion [aɪdɛntəfikéʃən] *s.* identificación; **I.D. card** carnet.

i·den·ti·fy [aɪdɛ́ntəfaɪ] *v.* identificar.

i·den·ti·ty [aɪdɛ́ntətɪ] *s.* identidad.

i·de·ol·o·gy [aɪdɪáləd͡ʒɪ] *s.* ideología.

id·i·o·cy [Ídiəsɪ] *s.* idiotez.

id·i·om [Ídɪəm] *s.* modismo, idiotismo.

id·i·o·syn·cra·sy [ɪdɪosínkrəsɪ] *s.* idiosincrasia.

id·i·ot [ídɪət] *s.* idiota.

id·i·ot·ic [ɪdɪátɪk] *adj.* idiota.

i·dle [áɪdḷ] *adj.* ocioso; perezoso, holgazán; vano; desocupado; *v.* holgazanear; perder el tiempo; funcionar (*el motor solo, sin engranar*); **idly** *adv.* ociosamente; inútilmente; perezosamente.

i·dle·ness [áɪdḷnɪs] *s.* ociosidad; ocio, desocupación; pereza, holgazanería.

i·dler [áɪdlɚ] *s.* holgazán, haragán.

i·dol [áɪdḷ] *s.* ídolo.

i·dol·a·try [aɪdálətrɪ] *s.* idolatría.

i·dol·ize [áɪdḷaɪz] *v.* idolatrar.

i·dyl [áɪdḷ] *s.* idilio.

if [ɪf] *conj.* si.

ig·nite [ɪgnáɪt] *v.* encender(se), inflamar(se); prender, pegar fuego a.

ig·ni·tion [ɪgníʃən] *s.* ignición, encendido (*de un motor*); — **switch** interruptor de encendido, *Méx., C.A., Ven., Carib.* switch de ignición.

ig·no·ble [ɪgnóbḷ] *adj.* innoble; bajo, vil.

ig·no·rance [ígnərəns] *s.* ignorancia.

ig·no·rant [ígnərənt] *adj.* ignorante.

ig·nore [ɪgnór] *v.* no hacer caso de, desatender; desairar.

ill [ɪl] *adj.* enfermo; malo; — **nature** mal genio, mala índole; — **will** mala voluntad, ojeriza, inquina; *s.* mal; enfermedad; calamidad, infortunio; *adv.* mal, malamente; — **at ease** inquieto, intranquilo; **ill-bred** mal criado; **ill-clad** mal vestido; **ill-humored** malhumorado; **ill-mannered** descortés, grosero; **ill-natured** de mala índole, *Ven., Col., Méx.* mal genioso; **ill-advised** mal aconsejado.

il·le·gal [ɪlíɡḷ] *adj.* ilegal; ilícito.

il·le·git·i·mate [ɪlɪd͡ʒítəmɪt] *adj.* ilegítimo; bastardo.

il·lic·it [ɪlísɪt] *adj.* ilícito.

il·lit·er·a·cy [ɪlítərəsɪ] *s.* analfabetismo.

il·lit·er·ate [ɪlítərɪt] *adj. & s.* analfabeto.

ill·ness [ɪlnɪs] *s.* mal, enfermedad.

il·lu·mi·nate [ɪlúmənət] *v.* iluminar; alumbrar;

esclarecer.

il·lu·mi·na·tion [ɪlumənéʃən] *s.* iluminación; alumbrado.

il·lu·sion [ɪlúʒən] *s.* ilusión.

il·lu·sive [ɪlúsɪv] *adj.* ilusorio, ilusivo, falaz.

il·lu·so·ry [ɪlúsərɪ] *adj.* ilusorio, ilusivo, engañoso.

il·lus·trate [ɪləstrét] *v.* ilustrar; esclarecer.

il·lus·tra·tion [ɪləstréʃən] *s.* ilustración; grabado, estampa; aclaración, esclarecimiento.

il·lus·tra·tor [ɪləstretɚ] *s.* ilustrador.

il·lus·tri·ous [ɪlʌ́strɪəs] *adj.* ilustre.

im·age [ímɪd͡ʒ] *s.* imagen.

im·age·ry [ímɪd͡ʒrɪ] *s.* conjunto de imágenes, figuras; fantasía.

im·ag·i·nar·y [ɪmǽd͡ʒənɛrɪ] *adj.* imaginario.

im·ag·i·na·tion [ɪmæd͡ʒənéʃən] *s.* imaginación; imaginativa.

im·ag·i·na·tive [ɪmǽd͡ʒənetɪv] *adj.* imaginativo.

im·ag·ine [ɪmǽd͡ʒɪn] *v.* imaginar(se); figurarse.

im·be·cile [ímbəsɪl] *adj. & s.* imbécil.

im·bibe [ɪmbáɪb] *v.* embeber, absorber; beber.

im·bue [ɪmbjú] *v.* imbuir, infundir; impregnar, empapar.

im·i·tate [ímətet] *v.* imitar; remedar.

im·i·ta·tion [ɪmətéʃən] *s.* imitación; remedo; *adj.* imitado, de imitación.

im·i·ta·tor [ímətetɚ] *s.* imitador; remedador.

im·mac·u·late [ɪmǽkjəlɪt] *adj.* inmaculado, sin mancha.

im·ma·te·ri·al [ɪmətírɪəl] *adj.* inmaterial, espiritual; **it is** — to me es indiferente.

im·me·di·ate [ɪmídɪɪt] *adj.* inmediato; próximo; **-ly** *adv.* inmediatamente; en seguida; al punto, en el acto, al instante.

im·mense [ɪmɛ́ns] *adj.* inmenso.

im·men·si·ty [ɪmɛ́nsətɪ] *s.* inmensidad.

im·merse [ɪmɚ́s] *v.* sumergir, sumir.

im·mi·grant [íməgrənt] *adj. & s.* inmigrante.

im·mi·grate [íməgret] *v.* inmigrar.

im·mi·gra·tion [ɪməgréʃən] *s.* inmigración.

im·mi·nent [ímənənt] *adj.* inminente.

im·mo·bile [ɪmóbɪl] *adj.* inmóbil.

im·mod·est [ɪmádɪst] *adj.* deshonesto, impúdico, indecente.

im·mor·al [ɪmɔ́rəl] *adj.* inmoral; licencioso.

im·mor·al·i·ty [ɪmərǽlətɪ] *s.* inmoralidad.

im·mor·tal [ɪmɔ́rtḷ] *adj. & s.* inmortal.

im·mor·tal·i·ty [ɪmɔrtǽlətɪ] *s.* inmortalidad.

im·mov·a·ble [ɪmúvəbḷ] *adj.* inmovible (*o* inamovible); inmóvil; inmutable.

im·mune [ɪmjún] *adj.* inmune.

im·mu·ni·ty [ɪmjúnətɪ] *s.* inmunidad.

im·mu·ta·ble [ɪmjútəbḷ] *adj.* inmutable.

imp [ɪmp] *s.* diablillo.

im·pair [ɪmpér] *v.* dañar, perjudicar, menoscabar, desvirtuar, debilitar.

im·pair·ment [ɪmpérmənt] *s.* menoscabo; perjuicio; deterioro.

im·part [ɪmpárt] *v.* impartir, dar, comunicar.

im·par·tial [ɪmpárʃəl] *adj.* imparcial.

im·par·ti·al·i·ty [ɪmparʃǽlətɪ] *s.* imparcialidad.

im·pas·si·ble [ɪmpǽsəbḷ] *adj.* impasible.

im·pas·sioned [ɪmpǽʃənd] *adj.* apasionado, vehemente, ardiente.

im·pas·sive [ɪmpǽsɪv] *adj.* impasible.

im·pa·tience [ɪmpéʃəns] *s.* impaciencia.

im·pa·tient [ɪmpéʃənt] *adj.* impaciente.

im·peach [ɪmpítʃ] *v.* demandar o acusar formalmente (*a un alto funcionario de gobierno*); **to** — **a person's honor** poner en tela de juicio el honor de uno.

im·pede [ɪmpíd] v. impedir, estorbar, obstruir.
im·ped·i·ment [ɪmpédəmənt] s. impedimento, obstáculo, estorbo; traba.
im·pel [ɪmpél] v. impeler, impulsar.
im·pend·ing [ɪmpéndɪŋ] adj. inminente, amenazador.
im·per·a·tive [ɪmpérətɪv] adj. imperativo; imperioso, urgente; s. imperativo.
im·per·cep·ti·ble [ɪmpɚséptəbl] adj. imperceptible.
im·per·fect [ɪmpɚ́fɪkt] adj. imperfecto; defectuoso; s. imperfecto (tiempo del verbo).
im·pe·ri·al [ɪmpírɪəl] adj. imperial.
im·pe·ri·al·ism [ɪmpírɪəlɪzm] s. imperialismo.
im·per·il [ɪmpérəl] v. poner en peligro, arriesgar.
im·pe·ri·ous [ɪmpírɪəs] adj. imperioso; urgente.
im·per·son·al [ɪmpɚ́sn̩l] adj. impersonal.
im·per·son·ate [ɪmpɚ́snet] v. representar (un personaje); remedar, imitar; fingirse otro, pretender ser otro.
im·per·ti·nence [ɪmpɚ́tn̩əns] s. impertinencia; insolencia, descaro.
im·per·ti·nent [ɪmpɚ́tn̩ənt] adj. impertinente; insolente, descarado.
im·per·vi·ous [ɪmpɚ́vɪəs] adj. impermeable; impenetrable; — to reason refractario, testarudo.
im·pet·u·ous [ɪmpétʃʊəs] adj. impetuoso.
im·pe·tus [ímpətəs] s. ímpetu.
im·pi·ous [ímpɪəs] adj. impío.
im·pla·ca·ble [ɪmplékəbl] adj. implacable.
im·plant [ɪmplǽnt] v. implantar, plantar; inculcar, infundir.
im·ple·ment [ímpləmənt] s. herramienta, instrumento; -s utensilios, aperos, enseres.
im·pli·cate [ímplɪket] v. implicar, envolver, enredar.
im·plic·it [ɪmplísɪt] adj. implícito.
im·plore [ɪmplór] v. implorar, rogar; suplicar.
im·ply [ɪmpláɪ] v. implicar; querer decir; insinuar.
im·po·lite [ɪmpəláɪt] adj. descortés.
im·port [ímport] s. significado, significación, sentido; importancia; importación; -s artículos importados; [ɪmpórt] v. importar; significar, querer decir.
im·por·tance [ɪmpórtn̩s] s. importancia.
im·por·tant [ɪmpórtn̩t] adj. importante.
im·pose [ɪmpóz] v. imponer; to — upon abusar de (la amistad, hospitalidad, confianza de alguien); engañar.
im·pos·ing [ɪmpózɪŋ] adj. imponente; impresionante.
im·po·si·tion [ɪmpəzíʃən] s. imposición; carga, impuesto; abuso (de confianza).
im·pos·si·bil·i·ty [ɪmpasəbílətɪ] s. imposibilidad.
im·pos·si·ble [ɪmpásəbl] adj. imposible.
im·pos·tor [ɪmpástɚ] s. impostor, embaucador.
im·pos·ture [ɪmpástʃɚ] s. impostura, fraude, engaño.
im·po·tence [ímpətəns] s. impotencia.
im·po·tent [ímpətənt] adj. impotente.
im·pov·er·ish [ɪmpávərɪʃ] v. empobrecer.
im·preg·nate [ɪmprégnet] v. impregnar; empapar; empreñar.
im·press [ɪmprɛs] s. impresión, marca, señal, huella; [ɪmprés] v. imprimir, estampar, marcar, grabar; impresionar.
im·pres·sion [ɪmpréʃən] s. impresión; marca.
im·pres·sive [ɪmprésɪv] adj. impresionante; imponente.
im·print [ímprɪnt] s. impresión; pie de imprenta; [ɪmprínt] v. imprimir; estampar.

im·pris·on [ɪmprísn̩] v. aprisionar, encarcelar.
im·pris·on·ment [ɪmprízn̩mənt] s. prisión, encarcelación o encarcelamiento.
im·prob·a·ble [ɪmprábəbl] adj. improbable.
im·promp·tu [ɪmprámptu] adv. de improviso.
im·prop·er [ɪmprápɚ] adj. impropio.
im·prove [ɪmprúv] v. mejorar(se); to — upon mejorar; to — one's time aprovechar el tiempo.
im·prove·ment [ɪmprúvmənt] s. mejoramiento; mejora; progreso, adelanto; mejoría (de una enfermedad).
im·pro·vise [ímprəvaɪz] v. improvisar.
im·pru·dent [ɪmprúdn̩t] adj. imprudente.
im·pu·dence [ímpjədəns] s. impudencia, descaro, insolencia.
im·pu·dent [ímpjədənt] adj. impudente, descarado, insolente.
im·pulse [ímpʌls] s. impulso; ímpetu; inclinación; to act on — obrar impulsivamente.
im·pul·sive [ɪmpʌ́lsɪv] adj. impulsivo.
im·pu·ni·ty [ɪmpjúnətɪ] s. impunidad, falta o exención de castigo.
im·pure [ɪmpjʊr] adj. impuro; sucio; adulterado.
im·pu·ri·ty [ɪmpjʊ́rətɪ] s. impureza.
im·pute [ɪmpjút] v. imputar, achacar, atribuir.
in [ɪn] prep. en; dentro de; de (después de un superlativo); — haste de prisa; — the morning por (o en) la mañana; — writing por escrito; at two — the morning a las dos de la mañana; dressed — white vestido de blanco; the tallest — his class el más alto de su clase; to come — a week venir de hoy en ocho días, venir dentro de ocho días; adv. dentro; adentro; en casa; to be — and out estar entrando y saliendo; to be all — no poder más, estar rendido de cansancio; to be — with someone estar asociado con alguien; disfrutar del aprecio de una persona; to come — entrar; to have it — for someone tenerle ojeriza a una persona; to put — meter; is the train —? ¿ha llegado el tren?
in·a·bil·i·ty [ɪnəbílətɪ] s. inhabilidad, incapacidad.
in·ac·ces·si·ble [ɪnəksésəbl] adj. inaccesible; inasequible.
in·ac·cu·rate [ɪnǽkjərɪt] adj. inexacto, impreciso, incorrecto.
in·ac·tive [ɪnǽktɪv] adj. inactivo; inerte.
in·ac·tiv·i·ty [ɪnæktívətɪ] s. inactividad, inacción, inercia.
in·ad·e·quate [ɪnǽdəkwɪt] adj. inadecuado; insuficiente.
in·ad·ver·tent [ɪnədvɚ́tn̩t] adj. inadvertido; descuidado; -ly adv. inadvertidamente; descuidadamente.
in·ad·vis·a·ble [ɪnədváɪzəbl] adj. imprudente.
in·an·i·mate [ɪnǽnəmɪt] adj. inanimado.
in·as·much [ɪnəzmʌ́tʃ]: — as visto que, puesto que; en cuanto.
in·at·ten·tive [ɪnətɛ́ntɪv] adj. desatento.
in·au·gu·rate [ɪnɔ́gjəret] v. inaugurar, iniciar; investir de una dignidad o cargo.
in·au·gu·ra·tion [ɪnɔgjəréʃən] s. inauguración.
in·board [ínbord] adj. interior.
in·born [ínbórn] adj. innato, connatural.
in·can·des·cent [ɪnkəndésn̩t] adj. incandescente, candente.
in·can·ta·tion [ɪnkæntéʃən] s. conjuro.
in·ca·pa·ble [ɪnképəbl] adj. incapaz.
in·ca·pac·i·tate [ɪnkəpǽsɪtet] v. incapacitar.
in·cen·di·ar·y [ɪnséndɪɛrɪ] adj. incendiario; — bomb bomba incendiaria.
in·cense [ínsɛns] s. incienso; [ɪnséns] v. inflamar,

in·cen·tive [ɪnséntɪv] *s.* incentivo, estímulo.
in·ces·sant [ɪnsésn̩t] *adj.* incesante, continuo.
inch [ɪntʃ] *s.* pulgada (*2.54 centímetros*); **by -es** poco a poco, gradualmente; **every — a man** nada menos que todo un hombre; **to be within an — of** estar a dos pulgadas de, estar muy cerca de; *v.* avanzar muy despacio (*por pulgadas*).
in·ci·dence [ɪ́nsɪdəns] *s.* incidencia.
in·ci·dent [ɪ́nsədənt] *s.* incidente, suceso, acontecimiento.
in·ci·den·tal [ɪnsədéntl̩] *adj.* incidental; accidental; contingente; **-s** *s. pl.* gastos imprevistos; **-ly** *adv.* incidentalmente; de paso.
in·cip·i·ent [ɪnsípɪənt] *adj.* incipiente.
in·ci·sion [ɪnsíʒən] *s.* incisión.
in·ci·sive [ɪnsáɪsɪv] *adj.* incisivo.
in·cite [ɪnsáɪt] *v.* incitar.
in·clem·ent [ɪnklɛmənt] *adj.* inclemente.
in·cli·na·tion [ɪnklənéʃən] *s.* inclinación.
in·cline [ɪ́nklaɪn] *s.* declive, pendiente, cuesta; [ɪnkláɪn] *v.* inclinar(se).
in·close = **enclose.**
in·clo·sure = **enclosure.**
in·clude [ɪnklúd] *v.* incluir, encerrar; abarcar.
in·clu·sive [ɪnklúsɪv] *adj.* inclusivo; **from Monday to Friday —** del lunes al viernes inclusive.
in·co·her·ent [ɪnkohírənt] *adj.* incoherente, inconexo.
in·come [ɪnkʌm] *s.* renta, rédito, ingreso, entrada; **— tax** impuesto sobre rentas.
in·com·pa·ra·ble [ɪnkámpərəbl̩] *adj.* incomparable, sin par, sin igual.
in·com·pat·i·ble [ɪnkəmpǽtəbl̩] *adj.* incompatible.
in·com·pe·tent [ɪnkámpətənt] *adj.* incompetente.
in·com·plete [ɪnkəmplít] *adj.* incompleto.
in·com·pre·hen·si·ble [ɪnkəmprɪhénsəbl̩] *adj.* incomprensible.
in·con·ceiv·a·ble [ɪnkənsívəbl̩] *adj.* inconcebible.
in·con·clu·sive [ɪnkənklúsɪv] *adj.* inconcluso.
in·con·sid·er·ate [ɪnkənsídərɪt] *adj.* inconsiderado, falto de miramiento.
in·con·sis·ten·cy [ɪnkənsístənsɪ] *s.* inconsecuencia; falta de uniformidad (*en la aplicación de una regla o principio*).
in·con·sis·tent [ɪnkənsístənt] *adj.* inconsecuente; falto de uniformidad.
in·con·spic·u·ous [ɪnkənspíkjuəs] *adj.* poco llamativo.
in·con·stan·cy [ɪnkánstənsɪ] *s.* inconstancia, mudanza.
in·con·stant [ɪnkánstənt] *adj.* inconstante, mudable, voluble.
in·con·test·a·ble [ɪnkəntéstəbl̩] *adj.* incontestable.
in·con·ven·ience [ɪnkənvínjəns] *s.* inconveniencia; molestia; *v.* incomodar; molestar.
in·con·ven·ient [ɪnkənvínjənt] *adj.* inconveniente, inoportuno.
in·cor·po·rate [ɪnkórpərɪt] *adj.* incorporado; asociado; [ɪnkórpəret] *v.* incorporar; incorporarse, asociarse (*para formar un cuerpo*).
in·cor·rect [ɪnkərékt] *adj.* incorrecto.
in·cor·ri·gi·ble [ɪnkórɪdʒəbl̩] *adj.* incorregible.
in·crease [ɪnkris] *s.* aumento; acrecentamiento; crecimiento; incremento; [ɪnkrís] *v.* aumentar(se); acrecentar(se), crecer; recargar.
in·creas·ing·ly [ɪnkrísɪŋlɪ] *adv.* más y más; cada vez más.
in·cred·i·ble [ɪnkrédəbl̩] *adj.* increíble.
in·cre·du·li·ty [ɪnkrədúlətɪ] *s.* incredulidad.
in·cred·u·lous [ɪnkrédʒələs] *adj.* incrédulo, descreído.

in·cre·ment [ɪ́nkrəmənt] *s.* incremento.
in·crim·i·nate [ɪnkrímənet] *v.* acriminar.
in·cu·ba·tor [ɪnkjubetə] *s.* incubadora.
in·cul·cate [ɪnkʌ́lket] *v.* inculcar, infundir.
in·cur [ɪnkə́] *v.* incurrir en.
in·cur·a·ble [ɪnkjúrəbl̩] *adj.* incurable, irremediable; *s.* incurable.
in·debt·ed [ɪndétɪd] *adj.* adeudado, endeudado; obligado, agradecido.
in·debt·ed·ness [ɪndétɪdnɪs] *s.* deuda; obligación.
in·de·cen·cy [ɪndísn̩sɪ] *s.* indecencia.
in·de·cent [ɪndísn̩t] *adj.* indecente.
in·de·ci·sion [ɪndəsíʒən] *s.* indecisión.
in·deed [ɪndíd] *adv.* en verdad, a la verdad; de veras; realmente.
in·de·fen·si·ble [ɪndɪfénsəbl̩] *adj.* indefendible.
in·def·i·nite [ɪndéfənɪt] *adj.* indefinido.
in·del·i·ble [ɪndéləbl̩] *adj.* indeleble.
in·del·i·cate [ɪndéləkət] *adj.* indelicado, indecoroso.
in·dem·ni·fy [ɪndémnəfaɪ] *v.* indemnizar.
in·dem·ni·ty [ɪndémnətɪ] *s.* indemnización.
in·dent [ɪndént] *v.* dentar, endentar; sangrar (*comenzar un renglón más adentro que los otros*).
in·de·pend·ence [ɪndɪpéndəns] *s.* independencia.
in·de·pend·ent [ɪndɪpéndənt] *adj.* independiente.
in·de·scrib·a·ble [ɪndɪskráɪbəbl̩] *adj.* indescriptible.
in·dex [ɪ́ndɛks] *s.* índice; *v.* alfabetizar, ordenar alfabéticamente; poner en un índice; **— finger** índice.
In·di·an [ɪ́ndɪən] *adj. & s.* indio; **— Ocean** Océano Indico.
in·di·cate [ɪ́ndəket] *v.* indicar.
in·di·ca·tion [ɪndəkéʃən] *s.* indicación.
in·dic·a·tive [ɪndíkətɪv] *adj. & s.* indicativo.
in·dict [ɪndáɪt] *v.* procesar, demandar (*ante un juez*); enjuiciar, formar causa a.
in·dict·ment [ɪndáɪtmənt] *s.* acusación (*hecha por el Gran Jurado*), denuncia, proceso judicial.
in·dif·fer·ence [ɪndífrəns] *s.* indiferencia; apatía.
in·dif·fer·ent [ɪndífrənt] *adj.* indiferente; apático.
in·dig·e·nous [ɪndídʒənəs] *adj.* indígena, autóctono, nativo.
in·di·gent [ɪndədʒənt] *adj. & s.* indigente.
in·di·ges·tion [ɪndədʒéstʃən] *s.* indigestión.
in·dig·nant [ɪndígnənt] *adj.* indignado; **-ly** *adv.* con indignación.
in·dig·na·tion [ɪndɪgnéʃən] *s.* indignación.
in·dig·ni·ty [ɪndígnətɪ] *s.* indignidad, afrenta.
in·di·go [ɪ́ndɪgo] *s.* índigo, añil; **— blue** azul de añil.
in·di·rect [ɪndərékt] *adj.* indirecto.
in·dis·creet [ɪndɪskrít] *adj.* indiscreto.
in·dis·cre·tion [ɪndɪskréʃən] *s.* indiscreción.
in·dis·pen·sa·ble [ɪndɪspénsəbl̩] *adj.* indispensable.
in·dis·pose [ɪndɪspóz] *v.* indisponer.
in·dis·posed [ɪndɪspózd] *adj.* indispuesto.
in·dis·po·si·tion [ɪndɪspəzíʃən] *s.* indisposición; malestar.
in·dis·tinct [ɪndɪstíŋkt] *adj.* indistinto.
in·di·um [ɪ́ndɪəm] *s.* indio.
in·di·vid·u·al [ɪndəvídʒʊəl] *adj.* individual; *s.* individuo, sujeto, persona.
in·di·vid·u·al·ism [ɪndəvídʒʊəlɪzm] *s.* individualismo.
in·di·vid·u·al·ist [ɪndəvídʒʊəlɪst] *s.* individualista.
in·di·vid·u·al·i·ty [ɪndəvɪdʒʊǽlətɪ] *s.* individualidad, personalidad, individuo, persona.
in·di·vis·i·ble [ɪndəvízəbl̩] *adj.* indivisible.
in·doc·tri·nate [ɪndáktrɪnet] *v.* adoctrinar.
in·do·lence [ɪ́ndələns] *s.* indolencia, desidia, apatía.
in·do·lent [ɪ́ndələnt] *adj.* indolente, desidioso,

apático.
in·dom·i·ta·ble [ɪndámətəbl] *adj.* indomable.
in·door [índor] *adj.* interior, de casa.
in·doors [indórz] *adv.* dentro, en casa; adentro; **to go** — entrar; ir adentro.
in·dorse = endorse.
in·dorse·ment = endorsement.
in·dors·er = endorser.
in·duce [ɪndjús] *v.* inducir.
in·duce·ment [ɪndjúsmənt] *s.* aliciente, incentivo.
in·duct [ɪndʌ́kt] *v.* introducir; iniciar; instalar (*en un cargo*).
in·duc·tion [ɪndʌ́kʃən] *s.* inducción; instalación (*en un cargo*).
in·dulge [ɪndʌ́ldʒ] *v.* gratificar, complacer; seguir el humor a (*una persona*); mimar, consentir (*a un niño*); **to** — **in** darse a, entregarse a (*un placer*); darse el lujo de, permitirse el placer de.
in·dul·gence [ɪndʌ́ldʒəns] *s.* indulgencia; complacencia (*en el vicio o placer*).
in·dul·gent [ɪndʌ́ldʒənt] *adj.* indulgente.
in·dus·tri·al [ɪndʌ́strɪəl] *adj.* industrial.
in·dus·tri·al·ist [ɪndʌ́strɪəlɪst] *s.* industrial; fabricante.
in·dus·tri·ous [ɪndʌ́strɪəs] *adj.* industrioso, aplicado, diligente.
in·dus·try [índəstrɪ] *s.* industria; aplicación, diligencia.
in·ed·i·ble [ɪnédəbl] *adj.* incomestible.
in·ef·fa·ble [ɪnéfəbl] *adj.* inefable.
in·ef·fec·tive [ɪnəféktɪv] *adj.* inefectivo, ineficaz.
in·ef·fi·cient [ɪnɪfíʃənt] *adj.* ineficaz.
in·el·i·gi·ble [ɪnélədʒəbl] *adj.* inelegible.
in·e·qual·i·ty [ɪnɪkwálətɪ] *s.* desigualdad; disparidad.
in·ert [ɪnɝ́t] *adj.* inerte.
in·er·tia [ɪnɝ́ʃə] *s.* inercia.
in·es·cap·a·ble [ɪnəsképəbl] *adj.* forzoso, inevitable.
in·es·ti·ma·ble [ɪnéstəməbl] *adj.* inestimable.
in·ev·i·ta·ble [ɪnévətəbl] *adj.* inevitable.
in·ex·haust·i·ble [ɪnɪgzɔ́stəbl] *adj.* inagotable.
in·ex·o·ra·ble [ɪnéksərəbl] *adj.* inexorable; severo.
in·ex·pe·di·ent [ɪnɛkspídjənt] *adj.* inoportuno; imprudente.
in·ex·pen·sive [ɪnɪkspénsɪv] *adj.* económico, barato.
in·ex·pe·ri·ence [ɪnɪkspírɪəns] *s.* inexperiencia, falta de experiencia.
in·ex·pe·ri·enced [ɪnɪkspírɪənst] *adj.* inexperto, falto de experiencia.
in·ex·pli·ca·ble [ɪnéksplɪkəbl] *adj.* inexplicable.
in·ex·press·i·ble [ɪnɪkprésəbl] *adj.* inexpresable, indecible, inefable.
in·fal·li·ble [ɪnfǽləbl] *adj.* infalible.
in·fa·mous [ínfəməs] *adj.* infame, ignominioso.
in·fa·my [ínfəmɪ] *s.* infamia.
in·fan·cy [ínfənsɪ] *s.* infancia.
in·fant [ínfənt] *s.* infante, bebé, criatura, nene.
in·fan·tile [ínfəntaɪl] *adj.* infantil.
in·fan·try [ínfəntrɪ] *s.* infantería.
in·fect [ɪnfékt] *v.* infectar, inficionar; contagiar; contaminar.
in·fec·tion [ɪnfékʃən] *s.* infección; contagio.
in·fec·tious [ɪnfékʃəs] *adj.* infeccioso; contagioso.
in·fer [ɪnfɝ́] *v.* inferir, deducir, colegir.
in·fer·ence [ínfərəns] *s.* inferencia, deducción.
in·fe·ri·or [ɪnfírɪɚ] *adj.* & *s.* inferior.
in·fe·ri·or·i·ty [ɪnfɪrɪɔ́rətɪ] *s.* inferioridad; — **complex** complejo de inferioridad.
in·fer·nal [ɪnfɝ́nl] *adj.* infernal.
in·fer·no [ɪnfɝ́no] *s.* infierno.
in·fest [ɪnfést] *v.* infestar, plagar.

in·fi·del [ínfədl] *adj.* & *s.* infiel.
in·fil·trate [ɪnfíltret] *v.* infiltrar(se).
in·fi·nite [ínfənɪt] *adj.* & *s.* infinito.
in·fin·i·tive [ɪnfínətɪv] *adj.* & *s.* infinitivo.
in·fin·i·ty [ɪnfínətɪ] *s.* infinidad; infinito.
in·firm [ɪnfɝ́m] *adj.* enfermizo, achacoso, débil.
in·fir·ma·ry [ɪnfɝ́mərɪ] *s.* enfermería.
in·fir·mi·ty [ɪnfɝ́mətɪ] *s.* enfermedad, achaque; flaqueza.
in·flame [ɪnflém] *v.* inflamar(se); enardecer(se).
in·flam·ma·tion [ɪnfləméʃən] *s.* inflamación.
in·flate [ɪnflét] *v.* inflar; hinchar.
in·fla·tion [ɪnfléʃən] *s.* inflación; hinchazón.
in·flec·tion [ɪnflékʃən] *s.* inflexión.
in·flict [ɪnflíkt] *v.* infligir, imponer.
in·flu·ence [ínfluəns] *s.* influencia, influjo; *v.* influir en; ejercer influencia o influjo sobre.
in·flu·en·tial [ɪnfluénʃəl] *adj.* influyente.
in·flu·en·za [ɪnfluénzə] *s.* influenza, gripe.
in·flux [ínflʌks] *s.* entrada, afluencia (*de gente*).
in·fold [ɪnfóld] *v.* envolver; abrazar; abarcar.
in·form [ɪnfɔ́rm] *v.* informar; enterar; avisar; **to** — **against** delatar a, denunciar a.
in·for·mal [ɪnfɔ́rml] *adj.* informal, sin ceremonia; — **visit** visita de confianza; **-ly** *adv.* informalmente, sin ceremonia, de confianza.
in·form·ant [ɪnfɔ́rmənt] *s.* informante.
in·for·ma·tion [ɪnfɚméʃən] *s.* (*service*) información; (*details*) informes; (*news*) noticias; (*knowledge*) conocimientos, saber.
in·frac·tion [ɪnfrǽkʃən] *s.* infracción.
in·fringe [ɪnfríndʒ] *v.* infringir, violar; **to** — **upon** violar.
in·fu·ri·ate [ɪnfjúriet] *v.* enfurecer.
in·fuse [ɪnfjúz] *v.* infundir; inculcar.
in·gen·ious [ɪndʒínjəs] *adj.* ingenioso.
in·ge·nu·i·ty [ɪndʒənúətɪ] *s.* ingeniosidad.
in·grat·i·tude [ɪngrǽtətjud] *s.* ingratitud.
in·gre·di·ent [ɪngrídɪənt] *s.* ingrediente.
in·hab·it [ɪnhǽbɪt] *v.* habitar, vivir en, residir en.
in·hab·i·tant [ɪnhǽbətənt] *s.* habitante.
in·hale [ɪnhél] *v.* inhalar, aspirar, inspirar.
in·her·ent [ɪnhírənt] *adj.* inherente.
in·her·it [ɪnhérɪt] *v.* heredar.
in·her·i·tance [ɪnhérətəns] *s.* herencia.
in·hib·it [ɪnhíbɪt] *v.* inhibir, cohibir, refrenar; reprimir; impedir.
in·hi·bi·tion [ɪnɪbíʃən] *s.* inhibición, cohibición, prohibición, restricción.
in·hos·pi·ta·ble [ɪnháspɪtəbl] *adj.* inhospitalario.
in·hu·man [ɪnhjúmən] *adj.* inhumano.
in·im·i·ta·ble [ɪnímətəbl] *adj.* inimitable.
in·iq·ui·ty [ɪníkwətɪ] *s.* iniquidad, maldad.
in·i·tial [ɪníʃəl] *adj.* & *s.* inicial; — **abbreviation** sigla; *v.* marcar o firmar con iniciales.
in·i·ti·ate [ɪníʃɪet] *v.* iniciar.
in·i·ti·a·tive [ɪníʃɪetɪv] *s.* iniciativa.
in·ject [ɪndʒékt] *v.* inyectar; injerir, introducir.
in·jec·tion [ɪndʒékʃən] *s.* inyección.
in·junc·tion [ɪndʒʌ́ŋkʃən] *s.* mandato, orden; entredicho.
in·jure [índʒɚ] *v.* dañar; herir, lesionar; lastimar.
in·ju·ri·ous [ɪndʒúrɪəs] *adj.* dañoso, dañino, perjudicial.
in·ju·ry [índʒərɪ] *s.* daño; herida, lesión; perjuicio.
in·jus·tice [ɪndʒʌ́stɪs] *s.* injusticia.
ink [ɪŋk] *s.* tinta; *v.* entintar; teñir o manchar con tinta.
ink·ling [íŋklɪŋ] *s.* indicación, indicio, idea, sospecha, noción vaga.
ink·stand [íŋkstænd] *s.* tintero.

ink·well [íŋkwɛl] s. tintero.

in·laid [ɪnléd] adj. incrustado, embutido; — **work** embutido, incrustación; pret. & p.p. de to inlay.

in·land [ínlənd] s. interior (de un país); adj. interior, del interior de un país; adv. tierra adentro.

in·lay [ɪnlé] v. incrustar, embutir; [ínle] s. embutido.

in·mate [ínmet] s. residente, asilado (de un hospicio, asilo, casa de corrección, etc.); presidiario; hospiciano.

in·most [ínmost] adj. más interior, más íntimo, más secreto o recóndito; más profundo.

inn [ɪn] s. posada, mesón, fonda.

in·nate [ɪnét] adj. innato, connatural.

in·ner [ínɚ] adj. interior; íntimo, recóndito; —most = inmost.

in·ning [ínɪŋ] s. entrada, cuadro (en béisbol); turno (del bateador en béisbol y otros juegos).

inn·keep·er [ínkipɚ] s. ventero, mesonero, posadero.

in·no·cence [ínəsns] s. inocencia.

in·no·cent [ínəsnt] adj. & s. inocente.

in·noc·u·ous [ɪnákjuəs] adj. innocuo, inofensivo.

in·no·va·tion [ɪnəvéʃən] s. innovación.

in·nu·en·do [ɪnjuéndo] s. insinuación, indirecta.

in·nu·mer·a·ble [ɪnjúmərəbl] adj. innumerable.

in·oc·u·late [ɪnákjəlet] v. inocular; contaminar.

in·of·fen·sive [ɪnəfɛ́nsɪv] adj. inofensivo.

in·op·por·tune [ɪnapətjún] adj. inoportuno.

in·put [ínpʊt] s. potencia consumida; (electric) entrada.

in·quire [ɪnkwáɪr] v. inquirir, indagar; preguntar; **to** — **about** preguntar por; **to** — **into** indagar, investigar.

in·qui·ry [ɪnkwáɪrɪ] s. indagación, investigación; pregunta; interrogatorio.

in·qui·si·tion [ɪnkwəzíʃən] s. inquisición; indagación.

in·quis·i·tive [ɪnkwízətɪv] adj. inquisitivo, investigador; preguntón; curioso.

in·road [ínrod] s. incursión, invasión, ataque; **to make -s upon** atacar; mermar.

in·sane [ɪnsén] adj. insano, loco; — **asylum** manicomio, casa de locos.

in·san·i·ty [ɪnsǽnətɪ] s. locura.

in·sa·tia·ble [ɪnséʃɪəbl] adj. insaciable.

in·scribe [ɪnskráɪb] v. inscribir.

in·scrip·tion [ɪnskrípʃən] s. inscripción; letrero.

in·sect [ínsɛkt] s. insecto.

in·se·cure [ɪnsɪkjúr] adj. inseguro.

in·sen·si·ble [ɪnsɛ́nsəbl] adj. insensible.

in·sen·si·tive [ɪnsɛ́nsətɪv] adj. insensible.

in·sep·a·ra·ble [ɪnsɛ́pərəbl] adj. inseparable.

in·sert [ínsɝt] s. inserción; intercalación; hoja (insertada en un libro); circular, folleto (insertado en un periódico); [ɪnsɝt] v. insertar; intercalar; encajar; meter.

in·ser·tion [ɪnsɝ́ʃən] s. inserción; introducción.

in·side [ínsáɪd] s. interior; -s entrañas; adj. interior, interno; secreto; adv. dentro; adentro; **to turn** — **out** volver(se) al revés; prep. dentro de.

in·sight [ínsaɪt] s. penetración, discernimiento; intuición; perspicacia; comprensión.

in·sig·ni·a [ɪnsígnɪə] s. pl. insignias.

in·sig·nif·i·cant [ɪnsɪgnífəkənt] adj. insignificante.

in·sin·u·ate [ɪnsínjuet] v. insinuar.

in·sin·u·a·tion [ɪnsɪnjuéʃən] s. insinuación, indirecta.

in·sip·id [ɪnsípɪd] adj. insípido.

in·sist [ɪnsíst] v. insistir en; empeñarse(en); porfiar,

persistir.

in·sis·tence [ɪnsístəns] s. insistencia, empeño, porfía.

in·sis·tent [ɪnsístənt] adj. insistente; porfiado, persistente.

in·so·lence [ínsələns] s. insolencia.

in·so·lent [ínsələnt] adj. insolente.

in·sol·u·ble [ɪnsáljəbl] adj. insoluble.

in·spect [ɪnspɛ́kt] v. inspeccionar; examinar, registrar.

in·spec·tion [ɪnspɛ́kʃən] s. inspección; registro.

in·spec·tor [ɪnspɛ́ktɚ] s. inspector.

in·spi·ra·tion [ɪnspəréʃən] s. inspiración.

in·spire [ɪnspáɪr] v. inspirar.

in·stall [ɪnstɔ́l] v. instalar.

in·stal·la·tion [ɪnstəléʃən] s. instalación.

in·stall·ment, in·stal·ment [ɪnstɔ́lmənt] s. instalación; abono (pago); entrega o continuación (semanal o mensual de una novela); **to pay in -s** pagar por plazos; pagar en abonos.

in·stance [ínstəns] s. ejemplo, caso; vez, ocasión; instancia; **for** — por ejemplo.

in·stant [ínstənt] s. instante; adj. inmediato; urgente; **the 10th** — el 10 del (mes) corriente; -ly adv. al instante, inmediatamente.

in·stan·ta·ne·ous [ɪnstənténɪəs] adj. instantáneo.

in·stead [ɪnstɛ́d] adv. en lugar de ello (eso, él, ella, etc.); — **of** en lugar de, en vez de.

in·step [ínstɛp] s. empeine (del pie, del zapato).

in·sti·gate [ínstəget] v. instigar.

in·still [ɪnstíl] v. inculcar, infundir.

in·stinct [ínstɪŋkt] s. instinto.

in·stinc·tive [ɪnstíŋktɪv] adj. instintivo.

in·sti·tute [ínstətjut] s. instituto; v. instituir.

in·sti·tu·tion [ɪnstətjúʃən] s. institución.

in·struct [ɪnstrʌ́kt] v. instruir; dar instrucciones.

in·struc·tion [ɪnstrʌ́kʃən] s. instrucción; enseñanza; **lack of** — falta de saber o conocimientos; -s órdenes, instrucciones.

in·struc·tive [ɪnstrʌ́ktɪv] adj. instructivo.

in·struc·tor [ɪnstrʌ́ktɚ] s. instructor.

in·stru·ment [ínstrəmənt] s. instrumento; — **panel** salpicadero.

in·stru·men·tal [ɪnstrəméntl] adj. instrumental; **to be** — in ayudar a, servir de instrumento para.

in·sub·or·di·nate [ɪnsəbɔ́rdɪnət] adj. insubordinado.

in·suf·fer·a·ble [ɪnsʌ́frəbl] adj. insufrible, inaguantable.

in·suf·fi·cien·cy [ɪnsəfíʃənsɪ] s. insuficiencia; incompetencia; falta, escasez.

in·suf·fi·cient [ɪnsəfíʃənt] adj. insuficiente; inadecuado.

in·su·late [ínsəlet] v. aislar.

in·su·la·tion [ɪnsəléʃən] s. aislamiento; aislación.

in·su·la·tor [ínsəletɚ] s. aislador.

in·su·lin [ínsəlɪn] s. insulina.

in·sult [ínsʌlt] s. insulto; [ɪnsʌ́lt] v. insultar.

in·sur·ance [ɪnʃúrəns] s. aseguramiento; seguro; prima, premio (de una póliza de seguro); — **agent** agente de seguros; · **company** cómpañía de seguros; — **policy** póliza de seguro; **accident** — seguro contra accidentes; **fire** — seguro contra incendios; **life** — seguro sobre la vida.

in·sure [ɪnʃúr] v. asegurar; asegurarse de.

in·sur·gent [ɪnsɝ́dʒəbl] adj. & s. insurgente, insurrecto.

in·sur·mount·a·ble [ɪnsɚmáʊntəbl] adj. insuperable.

in·sur·rec·tion [ɪnsəɾékʃən] s. insurrección, rebelión, alzamiento.

in·tact [ɪntǽkt] adj. intacto.

in·te·gral [íntəgrəl] *adj.* integral; integrante; *s.* integral.

in·te·grate [íntəgret] *v.* integrar.

in·teg·ri·ty [ɪntégrətɪ] *s.* integridad, entereza.

in·tel·lect [íntlɛkt] *s.* intelecto; entendimiento.

in·tel·lec·tu·al [ɪntlɛktʃuəl] *adj. & s.* intelectual.

in·tel·li·gence [ɪntélədʒəns] *s.* inteligencia; información, noticias; policía secreta.

in·tel·li·gent [ɪntélədʒənt] *adj.* inteligente.

in·tel·li·gi·ble [ɪntélədʒəbl] *adj.* inteligible.

in·tem·per·ance [ɪntémpərəns] *s.* intemperancia.

in·tend [ɪnténd] *v.* intentar, pensar, tener la intención de; proponerse; destinar; **to — to do it** pensar hacerlo.

in·tense [ɪnténs] *adj.* intenso.

in·ten·si·fy [ɪnténsɪfaɪ] *v.* intensificar.

in·ten·si·ty [ɪnténsətɪ] *s.* intensidad.

in·ten·sive [ɪnténsɪv] *adj.* intenso; intensivo.

in·tent [ɪntént] *s.* intento, intención, propósito; significado; **to all -s and purposes** en todo caso, en todos sentidos; en realidad; *adj.* atento; **— on** absorto en, reconcentrado en; resuelto a, decidido a.

in·ten·tion [ɪnténʃən] *s.* intención.

in·ten·tion·al [ɪnténʃənl] *adj.* intencional; **-ly** *adv.* intencionalmente, adrede, a propósito.

in·ter [ɪntʃ́] *v.* enterrar, sepultar.

in·ter·cede [ɪntəsíd] *v.* interceder.

in·ter·cept [ɪntəsépt] *v.* interceptar; atajar.

in·ter·cep·tion [ɪntəsépʃən] *s.* interceptación.

in·ter·ces·sion [ɪntəséʃən] *s.* intercesión.

in·ter·change [íntətʃendʒ] *s.* intercambio; cambio, trueque; [ɪntətʃéndʒ] *v.* cambiar, trocar; permutar; alternar.

in·ter·course [íntəkors] *s.* comunicación; comercio, trato; intercambio (*de ideas, sentimientos, etc.*).

in·ter·den·tal [ɪntədéntl] *adj.* interdental.

in·ter·est [íntərɪst] *s.* interés; rédito; participación (*en un negocio*); *v.* interesar.

in·ter·est·ed [íntərɪstɪd] *adj.* interesado; **to be** (*o become*) **— in** interesarse en (*o por*).

in·ter·est·ing [íntərɪstɪŋ] *adj.* interesante.

in·ter·fere [ɪntəfír] *v.* intervenir; interponerse, entremeterse; estorbar; **to — with** estorbar, frustrar; dificultar.

in·ter·fer·ence [ɪntəfírəns] *s.* intervención; obstáculo; interferencia (*en la radio*).

in·te·ri·or [ɪntíriə] *adj.* interior; interno; *s.* interior.

in·ter·jec·tion [ɪntədʒékʃən] *s.* interjección; exclamación; intercalación.

in·ter·lace [ɪntəlés] *v.* entrelazar, enlazar, entretejer.

in·ter·lin·e·ar [ɪntərlíniə] *adj.* interlineal.

in·ter·lock [ɪntəlák] *v.* entrelazar(se); trabar(se).

in·ter·lude [íntəlud] *s.* intervalo.

in·ter·me·di·ate [ɪntəmídɪt] *adj.* intermedio.

in·ter·mi·na·ble [ɪntʃ́mɪnəbl] *adj.* interminable, inacabable.

in·ter·min·gle [ɪntəmíŋgl] *v.* entremezclar(se), entreverar(se); mezclar(se).

in·ter·mis·sion [ɪntəmíʃən] *s.* intermisión; intermedio, entreacto.

in·ter·mit·tent [ɪntəmítņt] *adj.* intermitente.

in·tern [ɪntʃ́n] *v.* internar, confinar, encerrar; [íntʃn] *s.* practicante (*de medicina en un hospital*).

in·ter·nal [ɪntʃ́nl] *adj.* interno; interior.

in·ter·na·tion·al [ɪntənǽʃənl] *adj.* internacional.

in·ter·o·ce·an·ic [ɪntəoʃiǽnɪk] *adj.* interoceánico.

in·ter·pose [ɪntəpóz] *v.* interponer(se).

in·ter·pret [ɪntʃ́prɪt] *v.* interpretar.

in·ter·pre·ta·tion [ɪntʃprɪtéʃən] *s.* interpretación.

in·ter·pret·er [ɪntʃ́prɪtə] *s.* intérprete.

in·ter·ro·gate [ɪntérəget] *v.* interrogar.

in·ter·ro·ga·tion [ɪntɛrəgéʃən] *s.* interrogación.

in·ter·o·ga·tive [ɪntərágətɪv] *adj.* interrogativo; *s.* pronombre o palabra interrogativa.

in·ter·rupt [ɪntərʌ́pt] *v.* interrumpir.

in·ter·rup·tion [ɪntərʌ́pʃən] *s.* interrupción.

in·ter·sect [ɪntəsɛ́kt] *v.* cortar(se); cruzar(se).

in·ter·sec·tion [ɪntəsɛ́kʃən] *s.* intersección; **street —** bocacalle.

in·ter·sperse [ɪntəspʃ́s] *v.* entremezclar, esparcir.

in·ter·stice [ɪntʃ́rstɪs] *s.* intersticio.

in·ter·twine [ɪntətwáɪn] *v.* entrelazar, entretejer, trenzar.

in·ter·val [íntəvl] *s.* intervalo.

in·ter·vene [ɪntəvín] *v.* intervenir; interponerse; mediar.

in·ter·ven·tion [ɪntəvénʃən] *s.* intervención.

in·ter·view [íntəvju] *s.* entrevista; *v.* entrevistar, entrevistarse con.

in·tes·tine [ɪntéstɪn] *s.* intestino; *adj.* intestino, interno.

in·ti·ma·cy [íntəməsɪ] *s.* intimidad.

in·ti·mate [íntəmɪt] *adj.* íntimo; *s.* amigo íntimo; [íntəmet] *v.* intimar, insinuar; indicar, dar a entender.

in·ti·ma·tion [ɪntəméʃən] *s.* intimación, insinuación.

in·tim·i·date [ɪntímədet] *v.* intimidar, acobardar; infundir miedo.

in·to [íntu, íntə] *prep.* en; dentro de; hacia el interior. .

in·tol·er·a·ble [ɪntálərəbl] *adj.* intolerable, inaguantable.

in·tol·er·ance [ɪntálərəns] *s.* intolerancia.

in·tol·er·ant [ɪntálərənt] *adj.* intolerante.

in·to·na·tion [ɪntonéʃən] *s.* entonación.

in·tox·i·cate [ɪntáksəket] *v.* embriagar, emborrachar.

in·tox·i·ca·tion [ɪntaksəkéʃən] *s.* embriaguez; envenenamiento, intoxicación (*estado tóxico o envenenamiento parcial*).

in·tran·si·gent [ɪntrǽnsədʒənt] *adj.* intransigente.

in·tra·ve·nous [ɪntrəvínəs] *adj.* intravenoso.

in·trench [ɪntréntʃ] *v.* atrincherar; **to — oneself** atrincherarse; **to — upon another's rights** infringir los derechos ajenos; **to be -ed** estar atrincherado; estar firmemente establecido.

in·trep·id [ɪntrépɪd] *adj.* intrépido.

in·tri·cate [íntrɪkɪt] *adj.* intrincado, enredado.

in·trigue [ɪntríg] *s.* intriga; enredo; trama; lío, embrollo; *v.* intrigar; tramar, maquinar.

in·tri·guer [ɪntrígə] *s.* intrigante.

in·tro·duce [ɪntrədjús] *v.* introducir; presentar.

in·tro·duc·tion [ɪntrədʌ́kʃən] *s.* introducción; presentación.

in·tro·spec·tion [ɪntrospékʃən] *s.* introspección.

in·tro·vert [íntrovʃt] *adj.* introvertido.

in·trude [ɪntrúd] *v.* entremeterse (*o entrometerse*); introducir, meter.

in·trud·er [ɪntrúdə] *s.* intruso, entremetido.

in·tru·sion [ɪntrúʒən] *s.* intrusión, entremetimiento.

in·tru·sive [ɪntrúsɪv] *adj.* intruso.

in·trust = entrust.

in·tu·i·tion [ɪntuíʃən] *s.* intuición.

in·un·date [ínəndet] *v.* inundar.

in·ure [ɪnjúr] *v.* habituar, acostumbrar.

in·vade [ɪnvéd] *v.* invadir.

in·vad·er [ɪnvédə] *s.* invasor.

in·va·lid [ɪnvǽlɪd] *adj.* inválido (*que no vale*), nulo, de ningún valor.

in·va·lid [ínvəlɪd] *adj.* inválido, enfermizo,

achacoso; — **diet** dieta para inválidos; *s.* inválido.

in·val·u·a·ble [ɪnvǽljebl] *adj.* de gran precio o valor, inapreciable, inestimable.

in·var·i·a·ble [ɪnvǽrɪəbl] *adj.* invariable; **invariably** *adv.* invariablemente; sin falta, sin excepción.

in·va·sion [ɪnvéʒən] *s.* invasión.

in·vent [ɪnvént] *v.* inventar.

in·ven·tion [ɪnvénʃən] *s.* invención; invento; inventiva, facultad para inventar.

in·ven·tive [ɪnvéntɪv] *adj.* inventivo.

in·ven·tive·ness [ɪnvéntɪvnɪs] *s.* inventiva.

in·ven·tor [ɪnvéntə] *s.* inventor.

in·ven·to·ry [ínvəntorɪ] *s.* inventario; *v.* inventariar.

in·verse [ɪnvэ́s] *adj.* inverso.

in·vert [ɪnvэ́t] *v.* invertir; trastrocar; volver al revés.

in·vest [ɪnvést] *v.* invertir, colocar (*fondos*); investir (*de una dignidad o cargo*); revestir (*de autoridad*); sitiar.

in·ves·ti·gate [ɪnvéstəget] *v.* investigar, indagar.

in·ves·ti·ga·tion [ɪnvɛstəgéʃən] *s.* investigación; indagación.

in·ves·ti·ga·tor [ɪnvéstəgetə] *s.* investigador; indagador.

in·vest·ment [ɪnvéstmənt] *s.* inversión (*de fondos*).

in·ves·tor [ɪnvéstə] *s.* el que invierte fondos.

in·vig·o·rate [ɪnvígəret] *v.* vigorizar, fortalecer.

in·vin·ci·ble [ɪnvínsəbl] *adj.* invencible.

in·vis·i·ble [ɪnvízəbl] *adj.* invisible.

in·vi·ta·tion [ɪnvətéʃən] *s.* invitación.

in·vite [ɪnváɪt] *v.* invitar; convidar.

in·vit·ing [ɪnváɪtɪŋ] *adj.* atractivo; seductivo, tentador.

in·vo·ca·tion [ɪnvəkéʃən] *s.* invocación.

in·voice [ínvɔɪs] *s.* factura; envío, mercancías enviadas; *v.* facturar.

in·voke [ɪnvók] *v.* invocar.

in·vol·un·tar·y [ɪnvάlənterɪ] *adj.* involuntario.

in·volve [ɪnvάlv] *v.* complicar, enredar; envolver; implicar; comprometer; **to get -d in difficulties** embrollarse, meterse en embrollos.

in·ward [ínwэd] *adj.* interior; interno; secreto; *adv.* hacia el interior; hacia dentro, adentro, para dentro; **-s** *adv.* = **inward.**

i·o·dide [áɪədaɪd] *s.* yoduro.

i·o·dine [áɪədaɪn] *s.* yodo.

i·on [áɪən] *s.* ion.

i·on·ize [áɪənaɪz] *v.* ionizar.

ire [aɪr] *s.* ira.

ir·i·des·cent [ɪrədésn̩t] *adj.* iridiscente, tornasolado, irisado.

i·rid·i·um [ɪrídɪəm] *s.* iridio.

i·ris [áɪrɪs] *s.* iris; arco iris; flor de lis.

I·rish [áɪrɪʃ] *adj.* irlandés; *s.* irlandés, idioma irlandés; **the** — los irlandeses.

irk·some [э́ksəm] *adj.* fastidioso, engorroso, molesto, tedioso.

i·ron [áɪэn] *s.* hierro; plancha (*de planchar ropa*); *adj.* férro, de hierro; —**work** herraje, trabajo en hierro; —**works** herrería; fábrica de hierro; *v.* planchar; **to** — **out a difficulty** allanar una dificultad.

i·ron·ic·al [aɪrάnɪkl̩] *adj.* irónico.

i·ron·ing [áɪэnɪŋ] *s.* planchado.

i·ro·ny [áɪrənɪ] *s.* ironía.

ir·ra·di·ate [ɪrédɪet] *v.* irradiar.

ir·ra·tion·al [ɪrǽʃənl̩] *adj.* irracional.

ir·re·fut·a·ble [ɪrɛfjútəbl̩] *adj.* irrefutable.

ir·reg·u·lar [ɪrégjələ] *adj.* irregular.

ir·rel·e·vant [ɪréləvənt] *adj.* fuera de propósito,

inaplicable al caso, inoportuno, que no viene (*o* no hace) al caso.

ir·re·li·gious [ɪrɪlídʒəs] *adj.* irreligioso, impío.

ir·re·me·di·a·ble [ɪrɪmídɪəbl̩] *adj.* irremediable; incurable.

ir·re·proach·a·ble [ɪrɪprótʃəbl̩] *adj.* irreprochable, intachable.

ir·re·sis·ti·ble [ɪrɪzístəbl̩] *adj.* irresistible.

ir·res·o·lute [ɪrézəlut] *adj.* irresoluto, indeciso.

ir·re·triev·a·ble [ɪrɪtrívəbl̩] *adj.* inapelable.

ir·rev·er·ence [ɪrévərəns] *s.* irreverencia, desacato.

ir·rev·er·ent [ɪrévərənt] *adj.* irreverente.

ir·ri·gate [írəget] *v.* regar; irrigar, bañar.

ir·ri·ga·tion [ɪrəgéʃən] *s.* riego; irrigación; — **canal** acequia, canal de irrigación.

ir·ri·ta·ble [írətəbl̩] *adj.* irritable; colérico.

ir·ri·tate [írətet] *v.* irritar.

ir·ri·tat·ing [írətetɪŋ] *adj.* irritante.

ir·ri·ta·tion [ɪrətéʃən] *s.* irritación.

ir·rupt [ɪrápt] *v.* irrumpir.

is·land [áɪlənd] *s.* isla.

is·land·er [áɪləndə] *s.* isleño.

isle [aɪl] *s.* isla, ínsula.

i·so·bar [áɪsəbɑr] *s.* isobara.

i·so·late [áɪslet] *v.* aislar.

i·so·la·tion [aɪsléʃən] *s.* aislamiento.

i·so·la·tion·ism [aɪsoléʃənɪzəm] *s.* aislamiento.

i·so·met·ric [aɪsométrɪk] *adj.* isométrico.

Is·ra·el [ízrɪəl] *s.* Israel.

is·sue [íʃU] *s.* (*printing*) tirada, impresión; (*stock, bonds*) emisión (*de valores*); (*problem*) problema, tema; (*result*) resultado, consecuencia; **without** — sin prole, sin sucesión; **to take** — **with** disentir o diferir de; *v.* publicar, dar a luz; dar, promulgar (*un decreto*); emitir (*valores, acciones, etc.*); emanar; fluir; salir; brotar; provenir.

isth·mus [ísməs] *s.* istmo.

it [ɪt] *pron.* neutro lo, la (*acusativo*); ello, él, ella (*después de una preposición*); por lo general no se traduce cuando es sujeto del verbo; — **is there** está allí; — **I** soy yo; — **is raining** llueve, está lloviendo; **what time is** —? ¿qué hora es?; — **is two o'clock** son las dos; **how goes** —? ¿qué tal?

I·tal·ian [ɪtǽljən] *adj. & s.* italiano.

i·tal·ic [ɪtǽlɪk] *adj.* itálico; **-s** *s.* letra bastardilla.

i·tal·i·cize [ɪtǽləsaɪz] *v.* poner en letra bastardilla.

itch [ɪtʃ] *s.* comezón; picazón; sarna (*enfermedad de la piel*); *v.* picar, darle a uno comezón; sentir comezón; **to be** — **ing to** tener ansias de.

itch·y [ítʃɪ] *adj.* sarnoso, Méx., Ven. sarniento; **to feel** — sentir comezón.

i·tem [áɪtəm] *s.* artículo; detalle; noticia, suelto (*de un periódico*); partida (*de una lista*).

i·tem·ize [áɪtəmaɪz] *v.* pormenorizar detallar; hacer una lista de.

i·tin·er·ant [aɪtínərənt] *adj.* ambulante.

i·tin·er·ar·y [aɪtínərɛrɪ] *s.* itinerario; ruta; guía de viajeros.

its [ɪts] *pos. neutro* su (sus), de él, de ella, de ellos.

it·self [ɪtsélf] *pron. neutro* mismo, misma; **by** — por sí, de por sí, por sí solo; solo, aislado; **in** — en sí.

i·vo·ry [áɪvrɪ] *s.* marfil; —**tower** torre de marfil.

i·vy [áɪvɪ] *s.* hiedra (yedra).

J·j

jab [dʒæb] v. picar; pinchar; s. piquete, pinchazo.

jack [dʒæk] s. gato (para alzar cosas pesadas); sota (en naipes); macho (del burro y otros animales); bandera de proa; — of all trades aprendiz de todo y oficial de nada; — pot premio gordo, premio mayor; — rabbit liebre americana; v. to — up solevantar, alzar con gato (un objeto pesado).

jack·ass [dʒǽkæs] s. asno, burro.

jack·et [dʒǽkɪt] s. chaqueta; envoltura; forro (de un libro); hollejo (de la patata).

jack·knife [dʒǽknaɪf] s. navaja.

jag·ged [dʒǽgɪd] adj. serrado, dentado.

jag·uar [dʒǽgwar] s. jaguar.

jail [dʒel] s. cárcel; v. encarcelar.

jail·er [dʒélə] s. carcelero.

ja·lop·y [dʒalápɪ] s. fotingo.

jam [dʒæm] v. estrujar, apachurrar; atorar(se); obstruir(se), atascar(se); apiñar(se); agolpar(se); to — on the brakes frenar de golpe; to — one's fingers machucarse los dedos; to — through forzar por, meter a la fuerza; s. conserva, compota; apretura; atascamiento; traffic — aglomeración de transeúntes o automóviles, Am. bola; to be in a — estar en un aprieto.

jan·i·tor [dʒænətə] s. conserje; portero; casero (encargado de un edificio).

Jan·u·ar·y [dʒǽnjuɛrɪ] s. enero.

Jap·a·nese [dʒæpəníz] adj. & s. japonés.

jar [dʒɑr] s. jarra, jarro; tarro; choque; sacudida; trepidación, vibración; large earthen — tinaja; v. trepidar; hacer vibrar; hacer temblar; menear; to — one's nerves ponerle a uno los nervios de punta.

jar·gon [dʒárgən] s. jerga, jerigonza.

jas·mine [dʒǽzmɪn] s. jazmín.

jas·per [dʒǽspə] s. jaspe.

jaunt [dʒɔnt] s. caminata, excursión; v. dar un paseíto, hacer una corta caminata.

jaw [dʒɔ] s. quijada, mandíbula, Am. carretilla; -s grapa (de herramienta).

jaw·bone [dʒɔ́bón] s. mandíbula, quijada.

jay [dʒe] s. grajo; rústico, bobo; blue — azulejo; —walker el que cruza las bocacalles descuidadamente.

jazz [dʒæz] s. jazz (cierta clase de música sincopada); v. tocar el jazz; bailar el jazz; to — up sincopar; animar, alegrar.

jeal·ous [dʒéləs] adj. celoso; envidioso; to be — of someone tener celos de una persona, tenerle celos a una persona.

jeal·ou·sy [dʒéləsɪ] s. celos; envidia.

jeer [dʒɪr] s. mofa, befa, escarnio, Carib. choteo; v. mofar, befar, Carib. chotear; to — at mofarse de.

jel·ly [dʒélɪ] s. jalea; v. convertir(se) en jalea, hacer(se) gelatinoso.

jeop·ar·dy [dʒépədɪ] s. riesgo.

jerk [dʒɚk] s. tirón; sacudida, Méx., C.A., Ven., Col. jalón; espasmo muscular; v. sacudir(se); dar un tirón; atasajar (la carne); to — out sacar de un tirón; -ed beef tasajo, Am. charqui.

jerk·wa·ter [dʒɚkwɔtə] adj. de mala muerte.

jer·sey [dʒɚ́zɪ] s. tejido de punto, tejido elástico, Am. jersey; chaqueta, blusa, camisa (de punto), Am. jersey.

jest [dʒɛst] s. broma; chanza; chiste; v. bromear; chancearse.

jest·er [dʒéstə] s. chancero, burlón; bufón.

Jes·u·it [dʒéʒuɪt] s. jesuita.

jet [dʒɛt] s. chorro; surtidor (de fuente); — airplane avión de reacción; — engine motor de reacción; motorreactor; gas — mechero de gas; adj. de azabache; jet-black negro como el azabache; v. chorrear, salir en chorro.

Jew [dʒu] s. judío.

jew·el [dʒúəl] s. joya, alhaja; gema; — box estuche, joyero.

jew·el·er [dʒúələ] s. joyero; -'s shop joyería.

jew·el·ry [dʒúəlrɪ] s. joyas, alhajas, pedrería; — store joyería.

Jew·ish [dʒúɪʃ] adj. judío.

jif·fy [dʒífɪ] s. instante; in a — en un instante, en dos paletas; en un decir Jesús, en un santiamén.

jig [dʒɪg] s. jiga (música y baile); — saw sierra mecánica (para recortar figuras); —saw puzzle rompecabezas (de recortes); v. tocar una jiga; bailar una jiga; bailotear; menear(se).

jig·gle [dʒígl] v. zangolotear(se), zarandear(se), menear(se); s. zarandeo, meneo, zangoloteo.

jilt [dʒɪlt] v. desairar, dar calabazas, dejar plantado.

jin·gle [dʒíŋgl] s. retintín; verso o rima infantil; — bell cascabel; v. hacer retintín.

job [dʒɑb] s. tarea, faena; trabajo; empleo; ocupación; to be out of a — estar sin trabajo; estar desocupado.

jock·ey [dʒákɪ] s. jockey; v. maniobrar (para sacar ventaja o ganar un puesto).

join [dʒɔɪn] v. juntar(se); enlazar(se); acoplar; unirse a, asociarse a.

joint [dʒɔɪnt] s. (point) juntura, coyuntura; (function) articulación; conexión; bisagra; (public place) garito (casa de juego); fonducho, restaurante de mala muerte; out of — descoyuntado; desunido; adj. unido, asociado; copartícipe; colectivo; — account cuenta en común; — action acción colectiva; — committee comisión mixta; — creditor acreedor copartícipe; — heir coheredero; — session sesión plena; -ly adv. juntamente, juntos, unidamente, colectivamente.

joke [dʒok] s. broma; chiste, chanza; v. bromear; chancear(se), Carib. chotear; Ríopl. farrear; jorobar.

jok·er [dʒókə] s. bromista, chancero, guasón, Carib. choteador; (card) comodín.

jok·ing·ly [dʒókɪŋlɪ] adv. en (o de) chanza, en (o de) broma; de chiste.

jol·ly [dʒálɪ] adj. jovial; alegre; festivo; v. bromear, chancearse.

jolt [dʒolt] s. sacudida; sacudimiento; choque; v. sacudir.

jos·tle [dʒásl] v. rempujar o empujar, dar empellones; codear; s. rempujón, empujón, empellón.

jot [dʒɑt] v. to — down apuntar, tomar apuntes; s. jota, pizca.

jour·nal [dʒɚ́nl] s. diario; periódico; revista; acta (de una junta o concilio).

jour·nal·ism [dʒɚ́nlɪzəm] s. periodismo.

jour·nal·ist [dʒɚ́nlɪst] s. periodista.

jour·nal·is·tic [dʒɚnlístɪk] adj. periodístico.

jour·ney [dʒɚ́nɪ] s. viaje; jornada; v. viajar; peregrinar.

joy [dʒɔɪ] s. júbilo, regocijo; alegría, gusto, deleite; felicidad.

joy·ful [dʒɔ́ɪfəl] adj. regocijado, jubiloso; alegre; -ly adv. con regocijo, regocijadamente, con júbilo, alegremente.

joy·ous [dʒɔ́ɪəs] *adj.* jubiloso, alegre, gozoso.
ju·bi·lant [dʒúbḷənt] *adj.* jubiloso, alegre.
ju·bi·lee [dʒúblɪ] *s.* jubileo; júbilo.
judge [dʒʌdʒ] *s.* juez; — **advocate** auditor de un consejo militar; *v.* juzgar.
judg·ment [dʒʌ́dʒmənt] *s.* juicio; sentencia, fallo; opinión; discernimiento; — **day** día del juicio final.
ju·di·cial [dʒudíʃəl] *adj.* judicial.
ju·di·cious [dʒudíʃəs] *adj.* juicioso, cuerdo.
jug [dʒʌg] *s.* cántaro; jarro, jarra; botija; chirona (*cárcel*) *Am.* chirola.
jug·gle [dʒʌ́gḷ] *v.* hacer juegos de manos; hacer suertes; **to — the accounts** barajar (*o* manipular) las cuentes; *s.* juego de manos, suerte; trampa.
jug·gler [dʒʌ́glɚ] *s.* prestidigitador, malabarista.
juice [dʒus] *s.* jugo; zumo.
juic·i·ness [dʒúsɪnɪs] *s.* jugosidad.
juic·y [dʒúsɪ] *adj.* jugoso, zumoso; suculento; **a — story** un cuento picante.
juke box [dʒúkbɑks] *s.* tragamonedas; tragaquintos.
Ju·ly [dʒulái] *s.* julio.
jum·ble [dʒʌ́mbḷ] *s.* revolver(se), barajar; mezclar(se); *s.* mezcolanza, revoltijo; confusión.
jump [dʒʌmp] *v.* saltar; brincar; salvar (*de un salto*); hacer saltar; comerse una pieza (*en el juego de damas*); **to — at the chance** asir o aprovechar la oportunidad; **to — bail** perder la fianza por evasión; **to — over** saltar por encima de, salvar de un salto; **to — the track** descarrilarse; **to — to conclusions** hacer deducciones precipitadas; *s.* salto; brinco; subida repentina (*del precio*); **to be always on the — andar siempre de aquí para allá; trajinar, trafagar, ser muy activo.
jump·er [dʒʌ́mpɚ] *s.* saltador; chaquetón holgado (*de obrero*); vestido sin mangas (*puesto sobre la blusa de mujer*); **-s** traje de juego (*para miños*).
jump·y [dʒʌ́mpɪ] *adj.* saltón; asustadizo, nervioso.
junc·tion [dʒʌ́ŋkʃən] *s.* unión, juntura; confluencia (*de dos ríos*); empalme (*de ferrocarriles*).
junc·ture [dʒʌ́ŋktʃɚ] *s.* juntura; coyuntura; **at this — a** esta sazón, en esta coyuntura.
June [dʒun] *s.* junio.
jun·gle [dʒʌ́ŋgḷ] *s.* selva; matorral; *Am.* jungla; *Carib.* manigua.
ju·nior [dʒúnjɚ] *adj.* menor, más joven; — **college** colegio para los dos primeros años del bachillerato; **John Smith, Junior (Jr.)** John Smith, hijo; *s.* estudiante del tercer año (*en escuela superior, colegio o universidad*).
ju·ni·per [dʒúnɪpɚ] *s.* junípero; enebro.
junk [dʒʌŋk] *s.* basura, desperdicios; trastos viejos; cosa inservible; **Chinese —** junco chino (*embarcación pequeña*); *v.* desechar, echar a la basura.
ju·ris·dic·tion [dʒʊrɪsdíkʃən] *s.* jurisdicción.
ju·ris·pru·dence [dʒʊrɪsprúdn̩s] *s.* jurisprudencia, derecho.
ju·ror [dʒúrɚ] *s.* jurado, miembro de un jurado.
ju·ry [dʒúrɪ] *s.* jurado; **grand —** jurado de acusación.
just [dʒʌst] *adj.* justo; recto; exacto; *adv.* ni más ni menos, exactamente, justamente; precisamente; sólo, no más, nada más; apenas; — **now** ahora mismo; **he — left** acaba de salir, *Riopl.* salió recién; **she is — a little girl** no es más que una niña, es una niña no más; **to have —** acabar de.
jus·tice [dʒʌ́stɪs] *s.* justicia; juez; magistrado.
jus·ti·fi·ca·tion [dʒʌstəfəkéʃən] *s.* justificación.

jus·ti·fy [dʒʌ́stəfaɪ] *v.* justificar.
just·ly [dʒʌ́stlɪ] *adv.* justamente; con razón.
jut [dʒʌt] *v.* sobresalir, proyectarse, extenderse; *s.* salidizo, proyección.
ju·ve·nile [dʒúvənḷ] *adj.* juvenil.

K:k

kan·ga·roo [kæŋgərú] *s.* canguro.
keel [kil] *s.* quilla; *v.* dar de quilla (*voltear un barco*); **to — over** volcar(se); zozobrar; caerse patas arriba, desplomarse.
keen [kin] *adj.* agudo; afilado; perspicaz; ansioso.
keen·ness [kínnɪs] *s.* agudeza; perspicacia; anhelo, ansia.
keep [kip] *v.* guardar; tener guardado; tener; retener; conservar(se); preservar(se); mantener(se); **to — accounts** llevar las cuentas; **to — at it** persistir, seguir dale que dale; **to — away** mantener(se) alejado; **to — back** tener a raya; detener; reprimir, restringir; **to — from** impedir; guardar(se) de; abstenerse de; **to — going** seguir andando, seguir adelante; seguir viviendo; **to — off** no arrimarse, no acercarse; no entrar; mantener(se) a distancia; **to — one's hands off** no tocar; **to — one's temper** contenerse, refrenarse, reprimirse; **to — quiet** estarse quieto o callado; **to — something up** seguir o continuar haciendo algo; **to — to the right** seguir a la derecha; mantenerse a la derecha; **to — track of** llevar la cuenta de; no perder de vista; *s.* manutención, subsistencia; **for -s** para siempre; para guardar; dado, no prestado.
keep·er [kípɚ] *s.* guardián, custodio; **jail —** carcelero.
keep·ing [kípɪŋ] *s.* custodia; mantenimiento; preservación, conservación; **in — with** en armonía con.
keep·sake [kípsek] *s.* prenda, recuerdo, regalo.
keg [keg] *s.* tonel, barril.
ken·nel [kɛ́nl̩] *s.* perrera.
kept [kɛpt] *pret. & p.p. de* **keep**.
ker·chief [kɝtʃɪf] *s.* pañuelo, pañolón.
ker·nel [kɝnl̩] *s.* simiente; grano (*de trigo o maíz*); meollo (*de ciertas frutas como la nuez*); núcleo.
ker·o·sene [kɛ́rəsin] *s.* kerosina, petróleo para lámparas.
ket·tle [kɛ́tl̩] *s.* caldera; —**drum** tímpano; **tea—** marmita, tetera, *Am.* pava (*para el mate*).
key [ki] *s.* (*lock*) llave; (*music*) clave; (*instrument*) tecla; (*land*) cayo; isleta; — **ring** llavero; **to be in —** estar a tono, estar templado; estar en armonía; *v.* poner a tono, afinar, templar (*con llave*); armonizar; **to — up** elevar el tono de; **to be -ed up** estar sobreexcitado, estar en tensión nerviosa.
key·board [kíbord] *s.* teclado.
key·hole [kíhol] *s.* ojo de la cerradura.
key·note [kínot] *s.* nota tónica; idea o principio fundamental.
key·stone [kíston] *s.* clave (*de un arco*); base, fundamento principal.
kha·ki [kɑ́kɪ] *s.* caqui, kaki; *adj. de* kaki.
kick [kɪk] *s.* (*foot*) *Esp.* coz; puntapié; *Am.* patada; (*complaint*) queja; protesta; fuerza (*de una bebida*); estímulo; **to have a —** *Am.* patear (*dícese del licor*); *v.* cocear; dar coces o patadas;

dar puntapiés; patear; quejarse, protestar; **to —
out** echar a patadas; echar, expulsar; **to — the
bucket** estirar la pata, morir, *Am.* patear el
balde; **to — up a lot of dust** levantar una
polvareda.
kid [kɪd] *s.* cabrito; cabritilla (*piel curtida de
cabrito*); niño, niña; — **gloves** guantes de
cabritilla; *v.* bromear, embromar; chancearse
con, *Carib., Méx.* chotear.
kid·nap [kídnæp] *v.* secuestrar, raptar.
kid·nap·per [kídnæpɚ] *s.* secuestrador; robachicos,
ladrón de niños.
kid·nap·ping [kídnæpɪŋ] *s.* rapto, secuestro.
kid·ney [kídnɪ] *s.* riñon; — **bean** judía, frijol; —
stones cálculos.
kill [kɪl] *v.* matar; destruir; amortiguar; parar (*el
motor*); *s.* animal o animales matados (*en la
caza*).
kill·er [kílɚ] *s.* matador; asesino.
kiln [kɪln], [kɪl] *s.* horno.
ki·lo [kílo], **ki·lo·gram** [kíləgræm] *s.* kilo,
kilogramo.
ki·lo·cy·cle [kíləsaɪkl] *s.* kilociclo.
kil·o·me·ter [kíləmitɚ] *s.* kilómetro.
kil·o·watt [kíləwat] *s.* kilovatio.
ki·mo·no [kəmónə] *s.* quimono; bata.
kin [kɪn] *s.* parentela, parientes, familia; **to notify
the nearest of** — avisar al pariente o deudo
más cercano.
kind [kaɪnd] *adj.* bondadoso; benévolo; amable;
to send one's — **regards to** enviar afectuosos
saludos a; **kindhearted** de buen corazón; — **of
tired** algo cansado; *s.* clase, especie, género;
to pay in — pagar en especie; pagar en la
misma moneda.
kin·der·gar·ten [kíndɚgartṇ] *s.* escuela de
párvulos.
kin·dle [kíndl] *v.* encender(se); inflamar(se);
incitar; prender (*el fuego*).
kin·dling [kíndlɪŋ] *s.* encendimiento; leña ligera,
astillas, *Andes* charamuscas.
kind·ly [káɪndlɪ] *adj.* bondadoso; benigno;
benévolo; amable, apacible; *adv.*
bondadosamente, ambablemente; con
benevolencia; por favor; **not to take** — **to
criticism** no aceptar de buen grado las
correcciones.
kind·ness [káɪndnɪs] *s.* bondad, amabilidad;
gentileza; benevolencia; favor.
kin·dred [kíndrɪd] *adj.* emparentado; allegado;
semejante; — **facts** hechos relacionados; —
spirits espiritus afines.
ki·nes·ics [kaɪnízɪks] *s.* kinésica; quinésica.
king [kɪŋ] *s.* rey; rey (*en ajedrez*); dama (*en el
juego de damas*).
king·dom [kíŋdəm] *s.* reino.
king·ly [kíŋlɪ] *adj.* regio; real; majestuoso; *adv.*
regiamente; majestuosamente.
kink [kɪŋk] *s.* (*bend*) enroscadura; (*pain*) torticólis.
kink·y [kíŋkɪ] *adj.* crespo, ensortijado, *Am.* grifo.
kin·ship [kínʃɪp] *s.* parentesco; afinidad;
semejanza.
kins·man [kínzmən] *s.* pariente, deudo.
kiss [kɪs] *s.* beso; *v.* besar.
kit [kɪt] *s.* estuche, caja de herramientas; saco,
evoltura (*para guardar instrumentos,
herramientas, etc.*); gatito; **medicine** — botiquín;
soldier's — mochila.
kitch·en [kítʃɪn] *s.* cocina; —**ware** trastos de
cocina.
kite [kaɪt] *s.* cometa (*f.*), *Méx.* papalote; *Ch.*

volantín; *Arg.* barrilete; milano (*pájaro*).
kit·ten [kítṇ] *s.* gatito.
kit·ty [kítɪ] *s.* gatito, minino.
knack [næk] *s.* destreza, maña, habilidad.
knap·sack [næpsæk] *s.* mochila, morral, alforja.
knave [nev] *s.* bribón, bellaco, pícaro; sota (*de
naipes*).
knead [nid] *v.* amasar, sobar.
knee [ni] *s.* rodilla; **knee-deep** hasta la rodilla;
metido hasta las rodillas.
kneel [nil] *v.* arrodillarse; hincarse.
knell [nɛl] *s.* doble (*toque de campanas por los
difuntos*); *v.* doblar, tocar a muerto.
knelt [nɛlt] *pret. & p.p. de* **to kneel.**
knew [nju] *pret. de* **to know.**
knick·knack [níknæk] *s.* chuchería, baratija,
chisme.
knife [naɪf] *s.* cuchillo; cuchilla; **carving** —
trinchante; **pocket** — cortaplumas; navaja; *v.*
acuchillar.
knight [naɪt] *s.* caballero; campeón; caballo (*en
ajedrez*); — **errant** caballero andante; *v.* armar
caballero.
knight·hood [náɪthʊd] *s.* caballería, orden de la
caballería.
knit [nɪt] *v.* tejer (*a punto de aguja*); hacer calceta
o malla; enlazar; soldarse (*un hueso*) **to** — **one's
brow** fruncir las cejas, arrugar la frente; *pret.
& p.p. de* **to knit.**
knit·ting [nítɪŋ] *s.* labor de punto; — **needle** aguja
de media.
knives [naɪvz] *pl. de* **knife.**
knob [nɑb] *s.* perilla, botón, tirador (*de puerta,
cajón, etc.*); protuberancia.
knock [nɑk] *v.* (*pound*) golpear, golpetear; llamar
o tocar a la puerta; (*criticize*) criticar, censurar
o hablar mal de; **to** — **down** derribar;
desmontar (*una máquina o aparato*); **to** — **off**
suspender (*el trabajo*); rebajar (*del precio*);
derribar, echar abajo; **to** — **out** aplastar de un
golpe, poner fuera de combate; dejar sin
sentido; *s.* golpe; golpeteo; toque, llamada,
aldabonazo; crítica, censura; **knock-kneed**
zambo, patizambo.
knock·er [nákɚ] *s.* llamador, aldaba, aldabón;
criticón, murmurador.
knoll [nol] *s.* colina, loma; eminencia.
knot [nɑt] *s.* nudo; lazo; *v.* anudar(se).
knot·ty [nátɪ] *adj.* nudoso; dificultoso, enredado.
know [no] *v.* (*to be acquainted with*) conocer; (*to
have knowledge of; to know how to*) saber; (*to
recognize*) reconocer; distinguir; **to** — **how to
swim** saber nadar; **to** — **of** saber de; tener
conocimiento de; tener noticias de; estar
enterado de.
know·ing·ly [nóɪŋlɪ] *adv.* a sabiendas; adrede.
knowl·edge [nálɪdʒ] *s.* conocimiento; saber,
sabiduría; pericia; **not to my** — no que yo sepa.
known [non] *p.p. de* **to know.**
knuck·le [nʌkl] *s.* nudillo; coyuntura, articulación;
artejo; *v.* someterse; **to** — **down** someterse;
aplicarse con empeño al trabajo.
kryp·ton [kríptan] *s.* criptón.

JO

L:1

la·bel [lébl] *s.* marbete, etiqueta, rótulo; *v.* marcar, rotular; apodar, llamar.

la·bor [lébɚ] *s.* trabajo; labor; obra; mano de obra; la clase obrera; — **union** sindicato; — **gang** peonaje; — **party** Partido Laborista; **to be in** — estar de parto; *v.* trabajar; afanarse; estar de parto; elaborar (*un punto*).

lab·o·ra·to·ry [lǽbrətorɪ] *s.* laboratorio.

la·bor·er [lébərɚ] *s.* trabajador, obrero; jornalero, peón.

la·bo·ri·ous [ləbórɪəs] *adj.* laborioso, trabajoso, penoso; industrioso.

lab·y·rinth [lǽbərɪnθ] *s.* laberinto.

lace [les] *s.* (*cloth*) encaje; (*cord*) cordón, cordoncillo, cinta (*de corsé, etc.*); **gold** — galón de oro (*para guarnecer uniformes*); *v.* atar con cinta o cordón; guarnecer con encajes; enlazar, entrelazar.

lack [læk] *s.* falta; escasez, carencia; deficiencia; *v.* carecer de, faltarle a uno; necesitar; **he -s courage** le falta ánimo.

lack·ey [lǽkɪ] *s.* lacayo.

lack·ing [lǽkɪŋ] *adj.* falto, carente.

lac·quer [lǽkɚ] *s.* laca; *v.* barnizar con laca.

lad [læd] *s.* rapaz, chico.

lad·der [lǽdɚ] *s.* escalera de mano.

lad·en [lédn] *adj.* cargado; agobiado, abrumado; *v.* cargar; agobiar.

la·dies [lédɪz] *pl. de* **lady**.

la·dle [lédl] *s.* cucharón; *v.* servir (*sopa*) con cucharón.

la·dy [lédɪ] *s.* señora; dama; —**like** como señora, muy fina, elegante; — **love** amada, querida.

lag [læg] *v.* rezagarse, quedarse atrás, atrasarse; andar lentamente; *s.* retardo o retardación, retraso.

la·goon [ləgún] *s.* laguna.

laid [led] *pret. & p.p. de* **to lay**; **to be** — **up** estar incapacitado o estropeado.

lain [len] *p.p. de* **to lie**.

lair [lɛr] *s.* guarida; cueva de fieras.

lake [lek] *s.* lago.

lamb [læm] *s.* cordero; —**kin** corderito.

lame [lem] *adj.* cojo; lisiado; estropeado; — **excuse** disculpa falsa; *v.* hacer cojo; estropear, incapacitar.

la·ment [ləmént] *s.* lamento; *v.* lamentar(se).

lam·en·ta·ble [lǽməntəbl] *adj.* lamentable; doloroso.

lam·en·ta·tion [læməntéʃən] *s.* lamentación, lamento.

lam·i·nate [lǽmənet] *v.* laminar.

lamp [læmp] *s.* lámpara; linterna; farol; —**post** poste (de farol); —**shade** pantalla de lámpara.

lance [læns] *s.* lanza; *v.* alancear, lancear, herir con lanza; picar con bisturí.

land [lænd] *s.* tierra; terreno; suelo; *v.* desembarcar; aterrizar (*un avión*); llegar; coger (*un pez*); **to** — **a job** conseguir una colocacion, lograr un empleo.

land-grant [lǽndgrænt] *adj.* mediante donación federal de tierras.

land·hold·er [lǽndholdɚ] *s.* terrateniente, propietario, hacendado.

land·ing [lǽndɪŋ] *s.* (*act*) desembarco, desembarque; aterrizaje (*de un avión*); (*place*) desembarcadero; descanso (*de escalera*); — **field** campo de aterrizaje; aeropuerto; — **strip** pista de aterrizaje.

land·la·dy [lǽndledɪ] *s.* patrona, casera, dueña (*de la casa*).

land·lord [lǽndlɔrd] *s.* amo, patrón, propietario, dueño; casero.

land·mark [lǽndmɑrk] *s.* mojón, señal (*para fijar los confines*); marca; suceso culminante.

land·own·er [lǽndonɚ] *s.* terrateniente, propietario, hacendado.

land·scape [lǽndskep] *s.* paisaje.

land·slide [lǽndslaid] *s.* derrumbe, derrumbamiento, desplome; gran mayoría de votos.

lane [len] *s.* senda, vereda; callejuela; ruta, derrotero (*de vapores o aviones*).

lan·guage [lǽŋgwidʒ] *s.* lengua; idioma; lenguaje.

lan·guid [lǽŋgwid] *adj.* lánguido.

lan·guish [lǽŋgwiʃ] *v.* languidecer.

lan·guor [lǽŋgɚ] *d.* languidez.

lank [læŋk] *adj.* alto y delgado, largucho.

lank·y [lǽŋkɪ] *adj.* largucho, zancón, zancudo.

lan·tern [lǽntɚn] *s.* linterna; farol.

lan·tha·nides [lǽnθənaidz] *s.* lantánidos.

lap [læp] *s.* falda, regazo; aleta; etapa, trecho (*de una carrera*); *v.* lamer; **to** — **over** cruzar(se) sobre, entrecruzar(se).

la·pel [ləpél] *s.* solapa.

lap·i·da·ry [lǽpidɛri] *s. & adj.* lapidario.

lapse [læps] *s.* lapso; transcurso; desliz; error; *v.* deslizarse; pasar, transcurrir; caer en un desliz; decaer (*el entusiasmo, el interés, etc.*); caducar (*un plazo, un contrato, etc.*).

lar·board [lárbɚd] *s.* babor; *adj.* de babor; — **side** banda de babor.

lar·ce·ny [lársn̩ɪ] *s.* latrocinio, hurto; ratería.

lard [lɑrd] *s.* lardo, manteca de puerco; *v.* mechar.

large [lɑrdʒ] *adj.* grande; **at** — suelto, libre; sin trabas; en general; **-ly** *adv.* grandemente, en gran parte.

large-scale [lárdʒskél] *adj.* en grande escala.

lar·i·at [lǽrɪət] *s.* reata.

lark [lɑrk] *s.* (*bird*) alondra; (*fun*) diversión, holgorio, jarana; **to go on a** — ir o andar de jarana.

lar·va [lúrvə] *s.* larva.

lar·ynx [lǽrɪŋks] *s.* laringe.

las·civ·i·ous [ləsíviəs] *adj.* lascivo.

lash [læʃ] *s.* látigo; azote, latigazo; pestaña; *v.* fustigar; azotar; censurar, reprender; amarrar.

lass [læs] *s.* moza, muchacha, doncella.

las·si·tude [lǽsətjud] *s.* dejadez, flojedad, decaimiento de fuerzas.

las·so [lǽso] *s.* lazo, reata, mangana; *v.* lazar, *Am.* enlazar.

last [læst] *adj.* (*in a series*) último; final; (*just passed*) pasado; — **night** anoche; — **year** el año pasado; **at** — por fin, finalmente, al fin; **next to the** — penúltimo; **to arrive** — llegar el último; *s.* fin, término; horma (*de zapato*); *v.* durar; perdurar; **-ly** *adv.* finalmente, en conclusión.

last·ing [lǽstɪŋ] *adj.* duradero; perdurable.

latch [lætʃ] *s.* pestillo, picaporte, aldaba, cerrojo; *v.* cerrar con aldaba.

late [let] *adj.* (*tardy*) tardío; tardo; (*recent*) reciente; último; —**comer** recién llegado; rezagado; **a** — **hour** una hora avanzada; **the** — **Mr. X** el finado (*o difunto*) Sr. X; **to have a** — **supper** cenar tarde; *adv.* tarde; — **afternoon** atardecer; — **in the night** a una hora avanzada de la noche; — **into the night** a deshoras de la noche; — **in the week** a fines de la semana; **of** — últimamente, recientemente; hace poco; **to**

be — ser tarde; llegar tarde; estar atrasado, venir o llegar con retraso (*el tren*); **the train was ten minutes** — el tren llegó con diez minutos de retraso; **-ly** últimamente, recientemente; hace poco, poco ha.

la·tent [létṇt] *adj*. latente.

lat·er [létɚ] *adv*. & *adj*. (*comp. de* late) más tarde; después, luego; más reciente; posterior.

lat·er·al [lǽtərəl] *adj*. lateral.

lat·est [létɪst] *adv*. & *adj*. (*superl. de* late) más tarde; más reciente, más nuevo; último; **the** — **fashion** la última moda, las últimas novedades; **the** — **news** las últimas novedades, las noticias más recientes; **at the** — a más tardar.

lathe [leð] *s*. torno (*de carpintero o mecánico*).

lath·er [lǽðɚ] *s*. jabonadura, espuma de jabón; *v*. jabonar, enjabonar; espumar, hacer espuma.

Lat·in [lǽtṇ] *adj*. latino; *s*. latín.

lat·i·tude [lǽtətjud] *s*. latitud; libertad; amplitud.

lat·ter [lǽtɚ] *adj*. último; **towards the** — **part of the week** a (*o* hacia) fines de la semana; **the** — éste (ésta, esto, etc.).

lat·tice [lǽtɪs] *s*. celosía; enrejado, rejilla.

laud [lɔd] *v*. loar, encomiar, alabar.

laud·a·ble [lɔ́dəbl] *adj*. laudable, loable.

laugh [læf] *v*. reír(se); **to** — **at** reírse de; **to** — **loudly** reírse a carcajadas; **to** — **in one's sleeve** reírse para sus adentros; **she -ed in his face** se rió en sus barbas; *s*. risa; **loud** — risotada, carcajada, risada.

laugh·a·ble [lǽfəbl] *adj*. risible; ridículo.

laugh·ing·stock [lǽfɪŋstak] *s*. hazmerreír.

laugh·ter [lǽftɚ] *s*. risa.

launch [lɔntʃ] *v*. (*put into water*) botar o echar (*un barco*) al agua; (*a rocket*) lanzar; (*begin*) empezar, poner en operación; **to** — **forth** lanzarse; **to** — **forth on a journey** emprender un viaje; *s*. lancha.

laun·der [lɔ́ndɚ] *v*. lavar y planchar (*la ropa*).

laun·dress [lɔ́ndrɪs] *s*. lavandera.

laun·dry [lɔ́ndrɪ] *s*. lavandería; lavado; ropa (lavada).

lau·rel [lɔ́rəl] *s*. laurel; gloria, honor.

la·va [lávə] *s*. lava.

lav·a·to·ry [lǽvətorɪ] *s*. lavabo; lavamanos; lavatorio.

lav·en·der [lǽvəndɚ] *s*. espliego, lavándula; *adj*. lila, morado claro.

lav·ish [lǽvɪʃ] *adj*. gastador, pródigo, dadivoso; abundante, copioso; profuso; lujoso; *v*. prodigar; malgastar, despilfarrar; **to** — **praise upon** colmar de alabanzas a; **-ly** pródigamente; copiosamente; lujosamente.

law [lɔ] *s*. ley; derecho, jurisprudencia; regla; — **student** estudiante de leyes, estudiante de derecho; **law-abiding** observante de la ley.

law·break·er [lɔ́brekɚ] *s*. infactor, transgresor.

law·ful [lɔ́fəl] *adj*. legal; lícito; válido; permitido.

law·less [lɔ́lɪs] *adj*. sin ley; ilegal; desenfrenado; revoltoso; licencioso.

law·mak·er [lɔ́mekɚ] *s*. legislador.

lawn [lɔn] *s*. césped, prado; *Am*. pasto, grama; linón (*tela de hilo o algodón*); — **mower** cortadora de césped.

law·suit [lɔ́sut] *s*. pleito, litigio.

law·yer [lɔ́jɚ] *s*. abogado, jurisconsulto.

lax [læks] *adj*. flojo; suelto; relajado.

lax·a·tive [lǽksətɪv] *adj*. & *s*. laxante, purgante.

lax·i·ty [lǽksətɪ] *s*. flojedad, flojera; relajamiento (*de una regla, ley, etc.*).

lay [le] *pret. de to* lie.

lay [le] *v*. colocar; poner; tender, extender; poner (*huevos*); echar (*la culpa*); atribuir (*la responsabilidad*); presentar, exponer; asentar (*el polvo*); **to** — **a wager** apostar; **to** — **aside** poner a un lado; ahorrar; **to** — **away** (*o* by) guardar; **to** — **bare** revelar; exponer; **to** — **down** poner, colocar; rendir (*las armas*); **to** — **down the law** mandar, dictar; **to** — **hold of** asir, agarrar; **to** — **off a workman** suspender a un obrero; **to** — **open** exponer a la vista; **to** — **out a plan** trazar un plan; **to** — **up** almacenar; guardar, ahorrar; **to be laid up** estar incapacitado o estropeado; **to** — **waste** asolar; *s*. lay, balada, canción; situación, orientación (*del terreno*); *adj*. lego, laico; profano (*no iniciado en una ciencia*).

lay·er [léɚ] *s*. capa; estrato; gallina ponedora.

lay·man [lémən] *s*. lego, seglar, laico.

la·zi·ly [lézɪlɪ] *adv*. perezosamente.

la·zi·ness [lézɪnɪs] *s*. pereza.

la·zy [lézɪ] *adj*. perezoso, holgazán.

lead [lɛd] *s*. plomo; plomada, pesa de plomo.

lead [lid] *v*. (*guide*) guiar, dirigir; llevar; conducir; mandar (*un ejército*); (*precede*) ir a la cabeza de; sobresalir entre; ser mano (*en el juego de naipes*); **to** — **an orchestra** dirigir una orquesta, llevar la batuta; **to** — **astray** llevar por mal camino, extraviar, descarriar; **to** — **the way** ir por delante, mostrar el camino; *s*. delantera; primer lugar; mando, dirección; indicio; papel principal; primer actor.

lead·en [lɛ́dṇ] *adj*. plomizo; aplomado, color de plomo; pesado.

lead·er [lídɚ] *s*. jefe, caudillo; *Am*. líder; director; guía; caballo delantero; **-s** puntos suspensivos.

lead·er·ship [lídɚʃɪp] *s*. dirección, mando; iniciativa.

lead·ing [lidɪŋ] *adj*. principal; delantero; — **man** primer actor.

lead·off [lídɔf] *adj*. delantero; puntero.

leaf [lif] *s*. hoja; *v*. echar hojas (*un árbol*), cubrirse de hojas; **to** — **through a book** hojear un libro.

leaf·less [líflɪs] *adj*. sin hojas, deshojado.

leaf·let [líflɪt] *s*. hojilla; folleto, hoja volante, papel volante, circular.

leaf·y [lífɪ] *adj*. frondoso.

league [lig] *s*. (*alliance*) liga, confederación; sociedad; (*distance*) legua; *v*. asociar(se); ligarse, coligarse.

leak [lik] *s*. gotera (*en un techo*); agujero, grieta (*por donde se escapa el agua o el gas*); escape (*de gas, vapor, electricidad, etc.*); *v*. gotear(se); rezumar(se); hacer agua (*dícese de un barco*); salirse, escaparse (*el gas, el vapor, etc.*).

lean [lin] *v*. (*incline*) inclinar(se); recostar(se), reclinar(se); (*support*) apoyar(se); *adj*. magro; flaco; — **year** año estéril, año improductivo.

leant [lɛnt] = **leaned**.

leap [lip] *v*. saltar; brincar; *s*. salto, brinco; — **year** año bisiesto.

leapt [lɛpt] *pret*. & *p.p. de to* leap.

learn [lɝn] *v*. aprender; saber, averiguar, enterarse de.

learn·ed [lɝnɪd] *adj*. erudito; docto.

learn·er [lɝnɚ] *s*. aprendedor; estudiante, estudioso.

learn·ing [lɝnɪŋ] *s*. erudición, saber; aprendizaje.

learnt [lɝnt] *pret*. & *p.p. de to* learn.

lease [lis] *v*. arrendar, dar o tomar en arriendo; *s*. arriendo, contrato de arrendamiento.

leash [liʃ] *s*. traílla; cuerda.

least [list] *adj*. (el) mínimo, (el) más pequeño; *adv*.

LA

menos; **at** — al menos, a lo menos, por lo menos; **the** — lo (el, la) menos.
leath·er [lέðɚ] s. cuero, piel; *adj.* de cuero, de piel; — **strap** correa.
leave [liv] *v.* dejar; abandonar; salir (de); partir; irse; **to** — **out** dejar fuera; omitir; *s.* permiso, licencia; — **of absence** licencia; **to take** — **of** despedirse de.
leav·en [lέvən] *s.* levadura, fermento; *v.* fermentar (*la masa*).
leaves [livz] *pl. de* **leaf**.
leav·ings [lívɪŋz] *s.* sobras, desperdicios.
lec·ture [lέktʃɚ] *s.* conferencia, discurso; reprensión; *v.* dar un a conferencia; explicar; reprender.
lec·tur·er [lέktʃərɚ] *s.* conferenciante; lector (*de universidad*).
led [lɛd] *pret. & p.p. de* **to lead**.
ledge [lɛdʒ] *s.* borde; salidizo.
ledg·er [lέdʒɚ] *s.* libro mayor (*en contabilidad*).
leech [litʃ] *s.* sanguijuela.
leer [lɪr] *s.* mirada de soslayo, mirada lujuriosa; *v.* mirar de soslayo; mirar con lujuria.
lee·ward [líwɚd] *s. & adv.* sotavento.
left [lɛft] *pret. & p.p. de* **to leave; I have two books** — me quedan dos libros; *adj.* izquierdo; *s.* izquierda; mano izquierda; **at (on, to) the** — a la izquierda.
left-hand·ed [lέfthændɪd] *adj.* zurdo; a la izquierda; torpe; malicioso, insincero; — **compliment** alabanza irónica.
left·ist [lέftɪst] *s.* izquierdista.
left·o·ver [lέftovɚ] *adj.* sobrante; **-s** *s. pl.* sobras.
left-wing [lέftwɪŋ] *adj.* izquierdista.
leg [lɛg] *s.* pierna; pata (*de animal, mesa, etc.*); pie o pata (*de banquillo, silla, etc.*); etapa, trecho (*de una carrera o viaje*); **to be on one's last -s** estar en las últimas.
leg·a·cy [lέgəsɪ] *s.* legado, herencia.
le·gal [lígl] *adj.* legal; lícito.
le·gal·ize [líglaɪz] *v.* legalizar; sancionar, autorizar.
leg·ate [lέgɪt] *s.* legado; delegado.
le·ga·tion [lɪgéʃən] *s.* legación; embajada.
leg·end [lέdʒənd] *s.* leyenda; letrero, inscripción.
leg·en·dar·y [lέdʒəndɛrɪ] *adj.* legendario.
leg·gings [lέgɪŋz] *s. pl.* polainas.
leg·i·ble [lέdʒəbl] *adj.* legible.
le·gion [lídʒən] *s.* legión.
leg·is·late [lέdʒɪslet] *v.* legislar.
leg·is·la·tion [lɛdʒɪsléʃən] *s.* legislación.
leg·is·la·tive [lέdʒɪsletɪv] *adj.* legislativo.
leg·is·la·tor [lέdʒɪsletɚ] *s.* legislador.
leg·is·la·ture [lέdʒɪsletʃɚ] *s.* legislatura, asamblea legislativa.
le·git·i·mate [lɪdʒítəmɪt] *adj.* legítimo.
lei·sure [líʒɚ] *s.* ocio; — **hours** horas de ocio; **to be at** — estar ocioso; estar libre o desocupado; **do it at your** — hágalo Vd. cuando pueda o le convenga; hágalo Vd. en sus ratos de ocio.
lei·sure·ly [líʒɚlɪ] *adj.* lento, deliberado, pausado; *adv.* sin prisa, despacio, a sus (mis, tus, *etc.*) anchas.
lem·on [lέmən] *s.* limón; — **tree** limonero; *adj.* de limón; — **color** cetrino.
lem·on·ade [lɛmənéd] *s.* limonada.
lend [lɛnd] *v.* prestar.
lend·er [lέndɚ] *s.* prestador; **money** — prestamista.
length [lɛŋkθ] *s.* largo, largor, largura, longitud; duración; cantidad (*de una sílaba*); **at** —

largamente, detenidamente; **al fin; to go to any** — hacer cuanto esté de su parte.
length·en [lέŋkθən] *v.* alargar(se); prolongar(se).
length·wise [lέŋkθwaɪz] *adv.* a lo largo; longitudinalmente; *adj.* longitudinal.
length·y [lέŋkθɪ] *adj.* largo, prolongado.
le·ni·ent [líniənt] *adj.* indulgente, clemente, poco severo.
lens [lɛnz] *s.* lente; cristalino (*del ojo*).
lent [lɛnt] *pret. & p.p. de* **to lend**.
Lent [lɛnt] *s.* cuaresma.
leop·ard [lέpɚd] *s.* leopardo.
lep·ro·sy [lέprəsɪ] *s.* lepra.
less [lɛs] *adj.* menor; *adv. & prep.* menos; — **and** — cada vez menos.
less·en [lέsn] *v.* aminorar(se), disminuir(se), reducir(se); mermar.
less·er [lέsɚ] *adj.* menor, más pequeño.
les·son [lέsn] *s.* lección.
lest [lɛst] *conj.* no sea que, por miedo de que.
let [lɛt] *v.* (*permit*) dejar, permitir; (*rent*) alquilar, arrendar; — **us** (*o* **let's**) **do it** vamos a hacerlo, hagámoslo; — **him come** que venga; **to** — **be** no molestar, dejar en paz; no tocar; **to** — **down** nar; **to** — **go** soltar; **to** — **in** dejar entrar, admitir; **to** — **know** avisar, enterar, hacer saber; **to** — **off** soltar; dejar libre; **to** — **through** dejar pasar; **to** — **up** disminuir; *pret. & p.p. de* **to let**.
let·down [lέtdaʊn] *s.* aflojamiento; desilusión.
le·thal [líθəl] *adj.* letal.
leth·ar·gy [lέθɚdʒɪ] *s.* letargo; **to fall into a** — aletargarse.
let·ter [lέtɚ] *s.* (*alphabet*) letra; (*missive*) carta; — **box** buzón; — **carrier** cartero; **—head** membrete; *v.* rotular, hacer a mano letras de molde.
let·tuce [lέtɪs] *s.* lechuga.
lev·el [lέvl] *adj.* llano, plano; a nivel; igual; parejo; **level-headed** bien equilibrado, sensato; *adv.* a nivel; a ras; *s.* nivel; **to be on the** — obrar rectamente, obrar sin engaño; ser o decir la pura verdad; *v.* nivelar; igualar; allanar; apuntar, asestar (*un arma*); **to** — **to the ground** arrasar, echar por tierra.
le·ver [lέvɚ] *s.* palanca; **control** — palanca de mando.
lev·i·ty [lέvɪtɪ] *s.* frivolidad; levedad.
lev·y [lέvɪ] *s.* imposición, recaudación (*de tributos, impuestos, etc.*); leva, enganche, reclutamiento; embargo (*de propiedad*); *v.* imponer, exigir, recaudar (*tributos o multas*); reclutar; **to** — **on someone's property** embargar la propiedad de alguien.
lewd [lud] *adj.* lujurioso, lascivo, deshonesto.
lewd·ness [lúdnɪs] *s.* lascivia, lujuria.
lex·i·cal [lέksɪkl] *adj.* léxico.
lex·i·cog·ra·phy [lɛksɪkágrəfɪ] *s.* lexicografía.
lex·i·con [lέksɪkən] *s.* léxico.
li·a·bil·i·ty [laɪəbílətɪ] *s.* responsabilidad, obligación; desventaja; **li·a·bil·i·ties** obligaciones, deudas; pasivo.
li·a·ble [láɪəbl] *adj.* responsable, obligado; sujeto, expuesto; propenso; probable.
li·ai·son [liezán] *s.* enlace; unión.
li·ar [láɪɚ] *s.* mentiroso, embustero.
li·bel [láɪbl] *s.* libelo; difamación; *v.* difamar.
lib·er·al [líbərəl] *adj. & s.* liberal.
lib·er·al·ism [líbɚəlɪzm] *s.* liberalismo.
lib·er·al·i·ty [lɪbərǽlətɪ] *s.* liberalidad; largueza, generosidad.

lib·er·al·ize [líbərəlaɪz] v. liberalizar(se).
lib·er·ate [líbəret] v. libertar, librar; soltar.
lib·er·a·tion [lıbəréʃən] s. liberación.
lib·er·a·tor [líbəretə·] s. libertador.
lib·er·tine [líbətin] adj. & s. libertino.
lib·er·ty [líbətɪ] s. libertad; **at** — libre.
li·bi·do [lıbído] s. libido.
li·brar·i·an [laɪbrérɪən] s. bibliotecario.
li·brar·y [láɪbrɛrɪ] s. biblioteca.
li·bret·to [lıbréto] s. libreto.
lice [laɪs] pl. de **louse**.
li·cense, licence [láɪsɲs] s. licencia; permiso; título; **driver's** — licencia (pase, certificado o patente) de chófer; título de conductor; licencia para manejar; — **plate** placa (o chapa) de numeración, chapa de circulación, chapa de matrícula; v. licenciar, dar licencia a; permitir, autorizar.
li·cen·tious [laɪsɛnʃəs] adj. licencioso, disoluto.
lick [lɪk] v. (tongue) lamer; (thrash) dar una tunda o zurra; vencer; **to** — **someone's boots** adular a uno con servilismo; **to** — **the dust** morder el polvo; adular; s. lamedura, Am. lamida; lengüetada; C.A. lambida; **salt** — lamedero (lugar salino donde lame el ganado); **not to do a** — **of work** no hacer absolutamente nada.
lick·ing [lɪkɪŋ] s. zurra, tunda.
lid [lɪd] s. tapadera, tapa; **eye**— párpado.
lie [laɪ] s. mentira; embuste; **to give the** — **to** desmentir, dar un mentís; v. mentir (pret. & p.p. **lied**); tenderse, acostarse; yacer; estar; estar situado; consistir (en); **to** — **back** recostarse, echarse hacia atrás; **to** — **down** acostarse, echarse, tenderse; **to** — **in wait** acechar, espiar.
lieu·ten·ant [luténənt] s. teniente; **second** — subteniente.
life [laɪf] s. vida; **from** — del natural; **still** — naturaleza muerta; —**boat** bote de salvamento, lancha salvavidas; — **imprisonment** prisión perpetua; — **insurance** seguro sobre la vida; — **pension** pensión vitalicia; — **preserver** salvavidas, cinto o chaqueta de salvamento.
life·less [láɪflɪs] adj. sin vida; muerto; exánime; inanimado; desanimado.
life·less·ness [láɪflɪsnɪs] s. falta de vida; inercia; falta de animación.
life·like [láɪflaɪk] adj. como la vida; natural, que parece vivo.
life·long [láɪflɔ̀ŋ] adj. perpetuo, de toda la vida.
life·time [láɪftaɪm] s. vida, transcurso de la vida.
lift [lɪft] v. levantar; alzar; elevar; disiparse (las nubes, la niebla, las tinieblas); **to** — **one's hat** quitarse el sombrero (para saludar); s. elevación; exaltación de ánimo; alzamiento, levantamiento; carga; ayuda (para levantar una carga); alza (de un zapato); ascensor, Am. elevador; **to give someone a** — **in a car** llevar a alguien en el auto.
lig·a·ture [lígətʃur] s. ligadura.
light [laɪt] s. luz; lumbre; **tail** — Am. farito trasero, Am. farol de cola, Méx. calavera; adj. claro; con luz; de tez blanca; ligero; leve; frívolo; — **drink** bebida suave; —**headed** frívolo, ligero de cascos; —**hearted** alegre; — **opera** opereta; **to make** — **of** dar poca importancia a; v. encender(se); iluminar, alumbrar; **to** — **upon** caer sobre; posarse en (dícese de los pájaros, mariposas, etc.).
light·en [láɪtn̩] v. aligerar; iluminar; aclarar; relampaguear; alegrar.
light·er [láɪtə·] s. encendedor.
light·house [láɪthaUs] s. faro.

light·ing [láɪtɪŋ] s. iluminación; alumbrado.
light·ly [láɪtlɪ] adv. ligeramente; levemente; frívolamente; sin seriedad.
light·ness [láɪtnɪs] s. ligereza; frivolidad; claridad.
light·ning [láɪtnɪŋ] s. relampagueo; relámpago; — **rod** pararrayos.
light·weight [láɪtwet] s. peso liviano; peso ligero.
lik·a·ble [láɪkəbl] adj. agradable, simpático, placentero.
like [laɪk] adv. & prep. como; del mismo modo que; semejante a; adj. semejante, parecido; **in** — **manner** de manera semejante, del mismo modo; **to feel** — **going** tener ganas de ir; **to look** — someone parecerse a alguien; **it looks** — **rain** parece que va a llover, quiere llover; s. semejante, igual; **-s gustos**; preferencias; v. gustarle a uno; **he -s books** le gustan los libros; **do whatever you** — haz lo que gustes.
like·ly [láɪklɪ] adj. probable, creíble; prometedor; — **place** lugar a propósito; **it is** — **to happen** es probable que suceda; adv. probablemente.
lik·en [láɪkən] v. asemejar, comparar.
like·ness [láɪknɪs] s. semejanza; parecido; retrato.
like·wise [láɪkwaɪz] adv. igualmente, asimismo; del mismo modo; también.
lik·ing [láɪkɪŋ] s. simpatía; afición; preferencia, gusto.
li·lac [láɪlək] s. lila; adj. lila, morado claro.
lil·y [lílɪ] s. lirio; azucena.
lil·y-white [lílɪwáɪt] adj. blanquísimo; puro; racialmente segregado.
limb [lɪm] s. rama (de árbol); miembro (del cuerpo), pierna, brazo.
lim·ber [límbə·] adj. flexible; ágil; v. hacer flexible; **to** — **up** agilitar(se), hacer(se) flexible.
lime [laɪm] s. cal; lima (fruta); Am. limón; — **tree** limonero; liga (para cazar pájaros).
lime·light [láɪmlaɪt] s. luz de calcio; proscenio; **to be in the** — estar a la vista del público.
lime·stone [láɪmston] s. piedra caliza.
lim·it [límɪt] s. límite; confín; v. limitar.
lim·i·ta·tion [lɪmɪtéʃən] s. limitación; restricción.
lim·it·ed [límɪtɪd] adj. limitado; restringido.
lim·it·less [límɪtlɪs] adj. ilimitado, sin límites; desmedido.
limp [lɪmp] s. cojera; v. cojear; renquear; adj. flojo; flexible.
lim·pid [límpɪd] adj. límpido; claro, transparente.
line [laɪn] s. (mark) línea; renglón; raya; (cord) cuerda; (business) ramo; giro (de negocios); especialidad; — **of goods** surtido, línea (Am. renglón) de mercancías; **branch railway** — ramal; **pipe** — cañería, tubería; **to bring into** — alinear; obligar a proceder de acuerdo con un plan; poner de acuerdo; **to get in** — meterse en fila, hacer (o formar) cola; v. linear, rayar; alinear; forrar; **to** — **up** alinear(se); formarse, formar fila.
lin·e·age [línɪɪdʒ] s. linaje.
lin·e·ar [línɪə·] adj. lineal.
lined [laɪnd] adj. rayado; forrado.
lin·en [línɪn] s. lino; ropa blanca.
lin·er [láɪnə·] s. vapor; buque; **air** — avión, transporte aéreo.
line·up [láɪnəp] s. formación.
lin·ger [língə·] v. tardar(se), demorarse, dilatarse; andar ocioso, vagar; perdurar; prolongarse.
lin·ge·rie [læ̃nʒərí] s. ropa interior de mujer.
lin·guist [língwɪst] s. lingüista.
lin·guis·tics [lɪŋgwístɪks] s. lingüística.

LE

lin·ing [láɪnɪŋ] s. forro.
link [lɪŋk] s. eslabón; enlace; **cuff -s** gemelos; v. eslabonar(se); enlazar(se).
lin·net [línɪt] s. jilguero.
li·no·le·um [lɪnólɪəm] s. linóleo (tela impermeable para cubrir el suelo).
lin·seed [línsid] s. linaza; — **oil** aceite de linaza.
lint [lɪnt] s. hilas; hilachas.
li·on [láɪən] s. león.
li·on·ess [láɪənɪs] s. leona.
lip [lɪp] s. labio.
lip·stick [lípstɪk] s. lápiz para los labios.
liq·uid [líkwɪd] adj. líquido; — **assets** valores líquidos (o realizables); — **measure** medida para líquidos; s. líquido.
liq·ui·date [líkwɪdet] v. liquidar, saldar (cuentas); poner término a.
liq·ui·da·tion [lɪkwɪdéʃən] s. liquidación; saldo de cuentas.
liq·uor [líkɚ] s. licor; bebida espiritosa (como aguardiente, ron, etc.).
lisp [lɪsp] s. ceceo; v. cecear; balbucir.
list [lɪst] s. lista; registro; escora (inclinación de un barco); v. alistar, registrar poner o apuntar en una lista; hacer una lista de; escorar, inclinarse a la banda.
lis·ten [lísn̩] v. escuchar; atender, dar oídos, prestar atención; —! ¡oye! ¡escucha!; ¡oiga! ¡escuche!; **to** — **in** escuchar por radio; escuchar a hurtadillas (una conversación).
lis·ten·er [lísnɚ] s. escuchador, oyente; **radio** — radioescucha, radioyente.
list·less [lístlɪs] adj. abstraído; indiferente; indolente; desatento.
list·less·ness [lístlɪsnɪs] s. indiferencia, inatención, abstracción.
lit [lɪt] pret. & p.p. de **to light**; adj. alumbrado; algo borracho.
lit·er·al [lítərəl] adj. literal; -**ly** adv. al pie de la letra, literalmente.
lit·er·ar·y [lítərɛrɪ] adj. literario.
lit·er·a·ture [lítərətʃʊr] s. literatura; impresos, folletos, circulares.
lith·i·um [líθɪəm] s. litio.
lit·i·ga·tion [lɪtəgéʃən] s. litigio, pleito.
lit·ter [lítɚ] s. (young animals) camada, cría; (stretcher) litera; camilla; cama de paja para animales; (disorder) cosas esparcidas; desorden; revoltillo; v. desarreglar, revolver, esparcir cosas.
lit·tle [lítl̩] adj. pequeño; poco; — **Bear** Osa Menor; **a** — **coffee** un poco de café; **a** — **while** un ratito (o ratico), un poco; adv. & s. poco; — **by** — poco a poco.
live [lɪv] v. vivir; **to** — **down** hacer olvidar, borrar (el pasado); **to** — **up to** vivir en conformidad con, vivir de acuerdo con.
live [laɪv] adj. (not dead) vivo; (lively) enérgico; vivo, activo; — **coal** ascua encendida; — **oak** encina; — **question** cuestión palpitante, cuestión de actualidad; — **wire** alambre cargado; persona muy activa.
live·li·hood [láɪvlɪhʊd] s. vida, alimento, subsistencia, manutención.
live·li·ness [láɪvlɪnɪs] s. viveza, animación; agilidad.
live·long [lívlɔŋ] adj. todo; absolutamente todo.
live·ly [láɪvlɪ] adj. vivo; vivaz; animado, alegre; airoso; — **horse** caballo brioso; adv. vivamente; de prisa.
liv·er [lívɚ] s. hígado; vividor.
liv·er·y [lívərɪ] s. librea; caballeriza (para caballos de alquiler); **auto** — garage para autos de alquiler.

lives [laɪvz] pl. de **life**.
live·stock [láɪvstɑk] s. ganado.
live wire [láɪvwáɪr] s. persona alerta y vivaz.
liv·id [lívɪd] adj. lívido; amoratado.
liv·ing [lívɪŋ] s. (state) vida; (means) manutención, subsistencia; adj. vivo; viviente; — **room** sala; — **wage** sueldo suficiente para vivir; **the** — los vivos.
liz·ard [lízəd] s. lagarto; **small** — lagartija.
load [lod] s. carga; **ship** — cargamento; -**s of** gran cantidad de; montones de; v. cargar; agobiar; colmar.
loaf [lof] s. hogaza de pan; **sugar** — azúcar de pilón; v. holgazanear, haraganear.
loaf·er [lófɚ] s. holgazán, haragán, zángano.
loan [lon] s. préstamo; empréstito; — **shark** usurero; — **word** préstamo semántico; v. prestar (dinero).
loath [loθ] adj. maldispuesto, renuente; **to be** — **to** repugnarle a uno.
loathe [loð] v. repugnarle a uno; abominar.
loath·some [lóðsəm] adj. repugnante, asqueroso; aborrecible.
loaves [lovz] pl. de **loaf**.
lob [lɑb] v. volear.
lob·by [lábɪ] s. (place) vestíbulo; antecámara; salón de entrada; hall; (influence) camarilla (que busca ventajas ante un cuerpo legislativo); **hotel** — vestíbulo o patio del hotel, hall; v. cabildear (procurar ventajas o partidarios en una asamblea).
lobe [lob] s. lóbulo.
lob·ster [lábstɚ] s. langosta de mar.
lo·cal [lókl] adj. local; — **train** tren ordinario.
lo·cal·i·ty [lokǽlətɪ] s. localidad; comarca.
lo·cal·ize [lókaɪz] v. localizar.
lo·cate [lóket] v. situar, establecer; localizar, averiguar la posición de; avecindarse, radicarse, establecerse.
lo·ca·tion [lokéʃən] s. situación; sitio, localidad.
lock [lɑk] s. (door) cerradura; (canal) esclusa (de un canal); llave (de un arma de fuego); guedeja (de pelo); bucle, rizo; v. cerrar con llave; trabar(se), juntar(se); entrelazar(se); **to** — **in** encerrar; **to** — **out** cerrar la puerta (a alguien), dejar afuera; **to** — **up** encerrar; encarcelar.
lock·er [lákɚ] s. alacena; armario.
lock·et [ákɪt] s. guardapelo.
lock·out [lákaʊt] s. paro (suspensión del trabajo por parte de los empresarios); cierre de fábrica.
lock·smith [láksmɪθ] s. cerrajero.
lo·co·mo·tive [lokəmótɪv] s. locomotora; — **engineer** maquinista.
lo·cust [lókəst] s. langosta, saltamontes; cigarra; — **tree** algarrobo; acacia falsa.
lodge [lɑdʒ] s. logia; casita accesoria; casa de campo; v. alojar(se); hospedar(se); colocar; **to** — **a complaint** presentar una queja.
lodg·er [lɑdʒɚ] s. huésped, inquilino.
lodg·ing [lɑdʒɪŋ] s. alojamiento, hospedaje; vivienda.
loft [lɔft] s. desván; galería, balcón interior (de un templo); **choir** — coro; **hay** — pajar.
loft·y [lɔftɪ] adj. elevado; sublime; altivo.
log [lɔg] s. leño, troza, tronco aserrado; corredera (aparato para medir las millas que anda la nave); diario de navegación; — **cabin** cabaña de troncos; v. cortar (árboles); cortar leños y transportarlos; registrar (en el diario de navegación).
log·ic [lɑdʒɪk] s. lógica.

log·i·cal [ládʒɪkl] *adj.* lógico.
log·roll [lógrol] *v.* lograr aprobación de leyes mediante favores.
loin [lɔɪn] *s.* ijada, ijar, lomo.
loi·ter [lɔ́ɪtɚ] *v.* holgazanear, vagar, malgastar el tiempo; **to — behind** rezagarse.
loll [lɑl] *v.* arrellanarse o repantigarse, recostarse con toda comodidad.
lone [lon] *adj.* solo, solitario.
lone·li·ness [lónlɪnɪs] *s.* soledad.
lone·ly [lónlɪ] *adj.* solo, solitario; triste, desamparado.
lone·some [lónsəm] *adj.* solo, solitario; triste, nostálgico.
long [lɔŋ] *adj.* largo; **the whole day —** todo el santo día; **three feet —** tres pies de largo; **to be — in coming** tardar en venir; *adv.* mucho, mucho tiempo; **— ago** hace mucho tiempo; **— live!** ¡viva! **as** (*o* **so**) **—** as en tanto que mientras que; **how — is it since ... ?** ¿cuánto tiempo hace que ... ?; **so —!** ¡hasta luego! ¡adiós!; **long-suffering** sufrido, paciente; **long-winded** prolijo, largo (*en hablar*); **long-distance** de larga distancia; *v.* anhelar; ansiar; **to — for** anhelar; suspirar por.
long·er [lóŋgɚ] *adj.* más largo; *adv.* más, más tiempo; **no —** ya no; **not ... any —** ya no; **no ... más.**
lon·gev·i·ty [lándʒévətɪ] *s.* longevidad.
long·ing [lóŋɪŋ] *s.* anhelo, añoranza, nostalgia; *adj.* anhelante, anheloso, nostálgico; **-ly** *adv.* con anhelo, anhelosamente, con ansia.
lon·gi·tude [lándʒətjud] *s.* longitud.
long·shore·man [lóŋʃormən] *s.* estibador (*de barco o muelle*), cargador.
long-term [lóŋtɚm] *adj.* a largo plazo.
look [lʊk] *v.* (*see*) mirar; (*seem*) parecer; **it -s well on you** le cae (*o* le sienta) bien; **to — after** atender, cuidar; **to — alike** parecerse; asemejarse; **to — down on a person** mirar con desprecio (*o* menospreciar) a alguien; **to — for** buscar; esperar; **to — forward to** anticipar con placer; **to — into** examinar, investigar; **— out!** ¡cuidado!; ¡tenga cuidado!; **to — out of** asomarse a; **to — over** examinar; dar un vistazo a; **to — up** levantar la vista; buscar; **to — up to** admirar, mirar con respeto; *s.* mirada, vistazo; **-s** apariencia, aspecto; **to have good -s** ser bien parecido.
look·ing glass [lúkɪŋglæs] *s.* espejo.
look·out [lúkaʊt] *s.* vigía; atalaya; mirador; vista, perspectiva; **that is your — ** ¡eso a usted!; **to be on the —** estar alerta.
loom [lum] *s.* telar; *v.* destacarse, descollar; asomar(se), aparecer.
loop [lup] *s.* (*closed*) lazo, gaza, presilla; (*road*) vuelta, curva; (*electric*) circuito; *v.* hacer una gaza (con *o* en); atar con gaza o presilla; hacer un circuito.
loop·hole [lúphol] *s.* agujero, abertura; salida; escapatoria.
loose [lus] *adj.* (*slack*) suelto; flojo; (*unfettered*) desatado; (*licentious*) disoluto; **— change** suelto, moneda suelta; **— jointed** de articulaciones flojas; **to let —** soltar; *v.* soltar, desatar; aflojar; **-ly** *adv.* sueltamente; flojamente; con poca exactitud, sin fundamento.
loos·en [lúsn̩] *v.* soltar(se); aflojar(se); desatar(se); **to — one's hold** desasirse, soltarse.
loose·ness [lúsnɪs] *s.* (*limberness*) soltura; flojedad; (*laxness*) flojera; holgura; relajación; (*of bowel*)

flujo.
loot [lut] *s.* botín, pillaje, saqueo; *v.* saquear, pillar, robar.
lop [lɑp] *v.* tronchar, desmochar (*Am.* mochar).
lo·qua·cious [lokwéʃəs] *adj.* locuaz, hablador, lenguaraz.
lo·quat [lókwat] *s.* níspero.
lord [lɔrd] *s.* señor; dueño, amo; lord; **Lord's Prayer** Padre Nuestro; **Our Lord** Nuestro Señor; *v.* señorear, mandar; **to — it over** señorear, dominar.
lord·ly [lórdlɪ] *adj.* señoril; noble; altivo; despótico; *adv.* altivamente, imperiosamente.
lord·ship [lórdʃɪp] *s.* señoría (*título*); señorío, dominio.
lose [luz] *v.* perder; **to — sight of** perder de vista.
loss [lɔs] *s.* pérdida; **to be at a —** estar perplejo; no saber qué hacer; **to sell at a —** vender con pérdida.
lost [lɔst] *pret.* & *p.p. de* **to lose**; *adj.* perdido; extraviado; **— in thought** absorto, abstraído; **to get —** perderse extraviarse.
lot [lɑt] *s.* (*land*) lote; (*section*) parte, porción; (*luck*) suerte; solar, porción de terreno; **a — of** (*o* **-s of**) una gran cantidad de; mucho; muchos; **to draw -s** echar suertes; **to fall to one's —** tocarle a uno, caerle en suerte; *adv.* mucho; **a — better** mucho mejor.
lo·tion [lóʃən] *s.* loción.
lot·ter·y [látərɪ] *s.* lotería.
loud [laʊd] *adj.* ruidoso; recio, fuerte; chillón (*dícese también de los colores*); *adv.* ruidosamente, fuerte, recio; alto, en voz alta.
loud-speak·er [láʊdspíkɚ] *s.* altavoz, altoparlante.
lounge [laʊndʒ] *s.* sala de descanso; sofá, diván, canapé; *v.* arrellanarse, repantigarse, recostarse cómodamente; sestear; holgazanear.
louse [laʊs] *s.* piojo.
lous·y [láʊzɪ] *adj.* piojoso; asqueroso.
lov·a·ble [lávəbl] *adj.* amable.
love [lʌv] *s.* (*affection*) amor; cariño; (*fondness*) afición; **— affair** amorío; **to be in —** estar enamorado; **to fall in — with** enamorarse de; **to make — to** enamorar a; *v.* amar, querer; gustar mucho de, gustarle a uno mucho; encantarle a uno algo.
love·li·ness [lávlɪnɪs] *s.* belleza, hermosura; amabilidad.
love·ly [lávlɪ] *adj.* amable; lindo, bello; exquisito; encantador; ameno.
lov·er [lávɚ] *s.* amante; **music —** aficionado a (*o* amante de) la música.
lov·ing [lávɪŋ] *adj.* amante, amoroso, cariñoso, afectuoso; **-ly** *adv.* cariñosamente, afectuosamente.
low [lo] *adj.* (*not high*) bajo; (*base*) vil; (*humble*) humilde; (*downcast*) abatido; débil; (*lacking*) deficiente; (*sick*) gravemente enfermo; **— comedy** farsa, sainete; **— gear** primera velocidad; **— Mass** misa rezada; **— key** de intensidad mínima; **dress with a — neck** vestido escotado (*o* con escote); **to be — on something** estar escaso de algo; **to be in — spirits** estar abatido o desanimado; *adv.* bajo; en voz baja, quedo, quedito; con bajeza, a precio bajo vilmente; *s.* mugido; *v.* mugir.
low·er [lóɚ] *adj.* más bajo; inferior; **— case letter** letra minúscula; **— classman** estudiante de los dos primeros años; **— house** cámara de diputados; *v.* bajar; disminuir; rebajar; abatir; humillar.

LI

low·land [lólænd] s. tierra baja.
low·li·ness [lólɪnɪs] s. bajeza; humildad.
low·ly [lólɪ] adj. bajo, humilde; inferior; adv. humildemente.
low·ness [lónɪs] s. bajeza; humildad; abatimiento; gravedad (de tono); debilidad (de un sonido); baratura.
loy·al [lɔ́ɪəl] adj. leal, fiel.
loy·al·ty [lɔ́ɪəltɪ] s. lealtad, fidelidad.
lu·bri·cant [lúbrɪkənt] adj. & s. lubricante.
lu·bri·cate [lúbrɪket] v. lubricar.
lu·cid [lúsɪd] adj. lúcido; claro; luciente.
luck [lʌk] s. suerte; fortuna; **in** — de buena suerte; **in bad** — de mala suerte.
luck·i·ly [lʌklɪ] adv. afortunadamente, por fortuna.
luck·y [lʌkɪ] adj. afortunado, feliz; **to be** — tener suerte, tocarle a uno la suerte.
lu·cra·tive [lúkrətɪv] adj. lucrativo.
lu·di·crous [lúdɪkrəs] adj. ridículo.
lug [lʌg] v. llevar, traer, Am. carger; **to** — **away** cargar con, llevarse (una cosa pesada).
lug·gage [lʌgɪdʒ] s. equipaje.
luke·warm [lúkwɔ́rm] adj. tibio, templado; indiferente.
lull [lʌl] v. arrullar; sosegar; calmar(se); s. calma, momento de calma.
lul·la·by [lʌ́ləbaɪ] s. arrullo, canción de cuna.
lum·ber [lʌ́mbɚ] s. madera, maderaje; —**man** maderero, negociante en madera; —**yard** depósito de maderas; — **jack** leñador; v. cortar y aserrar madera; explotar los bosques; moverse pesadamente.
lu·mi·nous [lúmənəs] adj. luminoso.
lump [lʌmp] s. (mass) terrón; bulto; (swelling) hinchazón, chichón; protuberancia; — **of sugar** terrón de azúcar; v. amontonar; consolidar (gastos); apelotonarse, aterronarse, formar terrones.
lump·y [lʌ́mpɪ] adj. aterronado.
lu·na·tic [lúnətɪk] adj. & s. lunático, loco.
lunch [lʌntʃ] s. almuerzo; merienda; —**room** merendero, Méx., Ven., Carib. lonchería; Ríopl. confitería; Spain cafetería; v. almorzar; merendar; Am. tomar el lonche.
lun·cheon [lʌ́ntʃən] s. almuerzo; merienda.
lung [lʌŋ] s. pulmón.
lurch [lɝtʃ] s. sacudida; tambaleo repentino; **to give a** — tambalearse; **to leave someone in the** — dejar a uno plantado, dejar a uno a buenas noches; v. tambalearse; dar un tambaleo repentino.
lure [lʊr] s. aliciente, atractivo; tentación; cebo o reclamo (para atraer); v. atraer; seducir; atraer (con cebo o reclamo).
lurk [lɝk] v. estar oculto; estar en acecho; moverse furtivamente.
lus·cious [lʌ́ʃəs] adj. exquisito, delicioso, sabroso.
lust [lʌst] s. lujuria; deseo vehemente; codicia; v. **to** — **after** codiciar.
lus·ter [lʌ́stɚ] s. lustre, brillo.
lus·trous [lʌ́strəs] adj. lustroso.
lust·y [lʌ́stɪ] adj. vigoroso, fornido, robusto.
lute [lut] s. laúd.
lux·u·ri·ant [lʌgʒúrɪənt] adj. lozano, frondoso, exuberante.
lux·u·ri·ous [lʌgʒúrɪəs] adj. lujoso; dado al lujo; frondoso.
lux·u·ry [lʌ́kʃərɪ] s. lujo.
lye [laɪ] s. lejía.
ly·ing [láɪɪŋ] ger. de **to lie**; adj. mentiroso; **lying-in hospital** casa de maternidad.

lymph [lɪmf] s. linfa.
lynch [lɪntʃ] v. linchar.
lynx [lɪŋks] s. lince.
lyre [laɪr] s. lira.
lyr·ic [lɪ́rɪk] s. poema lírico; adj. lírico.
lyr·i·cal [lɪ́rɪkl] adj. lírico.
lyr·i·cism [lɪ́rəsɪzəm] s. lirismo.

M:m

mac·a·ro·ni [mækərónɪ] s. macarrón o macarrones.
mac·a·roon [mækərún] s. macarrón, almendrado, bollito de almendra.
ma·chine [məʃín] s. máquina; automóvil; — **gun** ametralladora; — **made** hecho a máquina; —**pistol** metralleta; **political** — camarilla politica; **sewing** — mácamarilla política; **sewing** — máquina para coser.
ma·chin·er·y [məʃínərɪ] s. maquinaria.
ma·chin·ist [məʃínɪst] s. mecánico, maquinista.
mack·er·el [mǽkərəl] s. escombro, caballa (pez).
mad [mæd] adj. loco; rabioso; furioso, enojado; **to drive** — enloquecer; volver loco; **to get** — encolerizarse; **to go** — volverse loco, enloquecerse; -**ly** adv. locamente.
mad·am [mǽdəm] s. madama, señora.
mad·cap [mǽdkæp] s. calavera (m.), adj. temerario; temerario; atolondrado.
mad·den [mǽdn] v. enloquecer(se).
made [med] pret. & p.p. de **to make**; **to be** — **of** estar hecho de; ser de; **to have something** — mandar hacer algo; **made-up** fingido, falso; artificial, pintado (con afeites).
made-to-or·der [medtuɔ́rdɚ] adj. hecho a la medida.
mad·man [mǽdmæn] s. loco.
mad·ness [mǽdnɪs] s— locura; rabia.
mag·a·zine [mǽgəzín] s. revista; almacén (especialmente para provisiones militares); **powder** — polvorín.
mag·ic [mǽdʒɪk] s. magia; adj. mágico.
ma·gi·cian [mədʒíʃən] s. mágico; prestidigitador; brujo.
mag·is·trate [mǽdʒɪstret] s. magistrado.
mag·nan·i·mous [mægnǽnəməs] adj. magnánimo.
mag·ne·sia [mægnízə] s. magnesia.
mag·ne·si·um [mægnízɪəm] s. magnesio.
mag·net [mǽgnɪt] s. imán.
mag·net·ic [mægnétɪk] adj. magnético; — **pole** polo magnético; — **tape** cinta magnetofónica.
mag·net·ize [mǽgnətaɪz] v. magnetizar; imantar; cautivar.
mag·nif·i·cence [mægnífəsn̩s] s. magnificencia.
mag·nif·i·cent [mægnífəsn̩t] adj. magnífico.
mag·ni·fy [mǽgnəfaɪ] v. agrandar, engrandecer; amplificar; exagerar.
mag·ni·tude [mǽgnətjud] s. magnitud.
mag·pie [mǽgpaɪ] s. urraca; cotorra, hablador, habladora.
ma·hog·a·ny [məhágənɪ] s. caoba.
maid [med] s. criada, sirvienta, camarera, Méx. recamarera, Ríopl., Andes mucama; doncella; — **of honor** doncella de honor; **old** — solterona.
maid·en [médn̩] s. doncella; virgen; mozuela; soltera; — **lady** mujer soltera; — **voyage** primer viaje (de un vapor).
mail [mel] s. correo; correspondencia; **air** — correo aéreo; **coat of** — malla; —**bag** valija;

—train tren correo; *v.* echar al correo.
mail·box [mélbɑks] *s.* buzón.
mail·man [mélmæn] *s.* cartero.
maim [mem] *v.* mutilar, estropear.
main [men] *adj.* principal, mayor, de mayor importancia; *s.* tubería, cañería principal (*de agua o gas*); alta mar, océano; **in the —** en su mayor parte; en general, en conjunto; **-ly** *adv.* principalmente.
main·land [ménlænd] *s.* continente, tierra firme.
main·spring [ménsprɪŋ] *s.* muelle real; origen.
main·tain [mentén] *v.* mantener; sostener, afirmar; guardar.
main·te·nance [méntənəns] *s.* mantenimiento; sustento; manutención; sostén, sostenimiento.
maize [mez] *s.* maíz.
ma·jes·tic [mədʒéstɪk] *adj.* majestuoso.
maj·es·ty [mædʒɪstɪ] *s.* majestad.
ma·jor [médʒɚ] *adj.* (*greater*) mayor, más grande; (*principal*) principal; **— key** tono mayor; *s.* comandante; mayor, mayor de edad; curso o asignatura de especialización (*en la universidad*); **— league** liga mayor; *v.* especializarse (*en un curso de estudios*).
ma·jor·i·ty [mədʒórətɪ] *s.* mayoría; mayor edad.
make [mek] *v.* (*do*) hacer; (*create*) fabricar; formar; (*deliver*) pronunciar (*un discurso*); **to — a clean breast of** confesar; **to — a train** alcanzar un tren; **to — a turn** dar vuelta; **to — away with** llevarse, robar; matar; **to — fast** asegurar, afianzar; **to — headway** progresar, adelantar, avanzar; **to — much of** dar mucha importancia a; **to — neither head nor tail of** no comprender nada de; **to — nothing out of** no comprender nada de, no sacar nada en limpio; **to — out in the distance** distinguir a lo lejos; **to — over** rehacer, alterar (*un traje*); **to — sure** asegurarse; **to — toward** dirigirse a, encaminarse a; **to — up a story** inventar un cuento; **to — up after a quarrel** hacer las paces; **to — up for a loss** compensar por una pérdida; **to — up one's face** pintarse la cara; **to — up one's mind** resolverse, decidirse; *s.* hechura, forma; marca (*de fábrica*); manufactura.
mak·er [mékɚ] *s.* hacedor; fabricante; artífice.
make·shift [mékʃɪft] *adj.* provisional.
make-up [mékʌp] *s.* (*composition*) compostura, composición, hechura; (*character*) naturaleza, carácter; **facial —** afeite, cosmético; maquillaje.
mal·a·chite [mǽləkaɪt] *s.* malaquita.
mal·a·dy [mǽlədɪ] *s.* mal, enfermedad.
ma·lar·i·a [məlérɪə] *s.* malaria, fiebre palúdica, paludismo.
mal·con·tent [mǽlkɑntɛnt] *adj.* & *s.* malcontento.
male [mel] *adj.* macho; varón; masculino; varonil; de hombres, de varones; *s.* macho; varón; hombre.
mal·ice [mǽlɪs] *s.* malicia.
ma·li·cious [məlíʃəs] *adj.* malicioso, perverso; malévolo.
ma·lign [məláɪn] *v.* calumniar, difamar; *adj.* maligno; pernicioso.
ma·lig·nant [məlígnənt] *adj.* maligno; malévolo.
mal·le·a·ble [mǽlɪəbl] *adj.* maleable; manejable.
mal·let [mǽlɪt] *s.* mazo, maceta.
mal·nu·tri·tion [mælnutríʃən] *s.* desnutrición.
malt [mɔlt] *s.* malta; **-ed milk** leche malteada.
ma·ma, mam·ma [mámə] *s.* mamá.
mam·mal [mǽml] *s.* mamífero.
mam·moth [mǽməθ] *adj.* gigantesco, enorme.
mam·my [mǽmɪ] *s.* mamita; niñera negra; criada

negra.
man [mæn] *s.* hombre; varón; pieza (*de ajedrez*); **— and wife** marido y mujer; **to a —** unánimente, todos a una; **officers and men** oficiales y soldados; **man-of-war** buque de guerra; **— cook** cocinero; *v.* armar, proveer de gente armada; guarnecer (*una fortaleza*); tripular (*una embarcación*).
man·age [mǽnɪdʒ] *v.* manejar; gobernar, dirigir; gestionar; **to — to do something** arreglárselas para hacer algo.
man·age·a·ble [mǽnɪdʒəbl] *adj.* manejable; domable, dócil.
man·age·ment [mǽnɪdʒmənt] *s.* manejo; dirección; gobierno, administración; gerencia.
man·ag·er [mǽnɪdʒɚ] *s.* gerente; director. administrador; empresario.
man·date [mǽndet] *s.* mandato; *v.* asignar por mandato.
man·do·lin [mǽndəlɪn] *s.* mandolina.
mane [men] *s.* melena (*del león*), crin (*del caballo*).
ma·neu·ver [mɔnúvɚ] *s.* maniobra; gestión; *v.* maniobrar; manipular, manejar.
man·ful [mǽnfəl] *adj.* varonil; viril.
man·ga·nese [mǽŋɡənɪs] *s.* manganeso.
mange [mendʒ] *s.* sarna, roña.
man·ger [méndʒɚ] *s.* pesebre.
man·gle [mǽŋɡl] *v.* magullar, mutilar, destrozar, estropear; planchar en máquina de planchar; *s.* planchadora (*máquina de planchar*).
man·grove [mǽŋɡrov] *s.* mangle.
man·gy [méndʒɪ] *adj.* sarnoso, *Am.* sarniento.
man·hood [mǽnhʊd] *s.* virilidad; edad viril; hombres.
ma·ni·a [ménɪə] *s.* manía.
man·i·cure [mǽnɪkjʊr] *s.* manicura; *v.* manicurar.
man·i·fest [mǽnəfɛst] *adj.* manifiesto; *s.* manifiesto (*lista de la carga de un buque*); *v.* manifestar; poner de manifiesto; declarar.
man·i·fes·ta·tion [mænəfɛstéʃən] *s.* manifestación.
man·i·fes·to [mænɪfésto] *s.* manifiesto, bando, proclama.
man·i·fold [mǽnəfold] *adj.* múltiple; numeroso, diverso.
man·i·kin [mǽnəkɪn] *s.* maniquí; muñeco; hombrecillo.
ma·nil·a [mənílə] *s.* abacá (*cáñamo de Manila*); **— paper** papel de Manila.
man·i·oc [mǽnɪak] *s.* mandioca.
ma·nip·u·late [mənípjəlet] *v.* manipular; manejar.
ma·nip·u·la·tion [mənɪpjəléʃən] *s.* manipulación.
man·kind [mǽnkaɪnd] *s.* humanidad, género humano; los hombres.
man·like [mǽnlaɪk] *adj.* hombruno; varonil; (*mujer*) marimacho.
man·ly [mǽnlɪ] *adj.* varonil; viril; *adv.* varonilmente.
man·ner [mǽnɚ] *s.* (*way*) manera; modo; género; (*air*) aire, ademán, **-s** manejas, modales; costumbres; **after the —** of a la manera de; **by no — of means** de ningún modo.
man·ner·ism [mǽnɚɪzm] *s.* costumbre; amaneramiento.
man·nish [mǽnɪʃ] *adj.* hombruno.
ma·noeu·vre = **maneuver**.
man·or [mǽnɚ] *s.* solar, casa solariega.
man·sion [mǽnʃən] *s.* mansión; palacio.
man·slaugh·ter [mǽnslɔtɚ] *s.* homicidio impremeditado o casual.
man·tel [mǽntl] *s.* manto (*de una chimenea*); repisa de chimenea.

man·tle [mǽntl] s. manto; capa.
man·u·al [mǽnjʊəl] adj. manual; — **training school** escuela de artes y oficios; s. manual; teclado de órgano.
man·u·fac·ture [mænjəfǽktʃɚ] s. fabricación; manufactura; v. fabricar, manufacturar.
man·u·fac·tur·er [mænjəfǽktʃərɚ] s. fabricante.
man·u·fac·tur·ing [mænjəfǽktʃərɪŋ] s. fabricación; adj. fabril, manufacturero.
ma·nure [mənʊ́r] s. estiércol, abono; v. estercolar, abonar (la tierra).
man·u·script [mǽnjəskrɪpt] adj. & s. manuscrito.
man·y [mɛ́nɪ] adj. muchos; — **a time** muchas veces; **a great** — muchísimos; **as** — **as** tantos como; cuantos; **as** — **as five** hasta cinco; **how** —? ¿cuántos?; **three books too** — tres libros de más; **too** — demasiados.
map [mæp] s. mapa; v. trazar un mapa de; **to** — **out** proyectar, planear.
ma·ple [mépl] s. arce, Méx. meple; Ríopl. maple.
mar [mɑr] v. desfigurar, estropear.
mar·ble [mɑ́rbl] s. mármol; canica (para jugar); **to play -s** jugar a las canicas; adj. de mármol; marmóreo.
march [mɑrtʃ] s. marcha; v. marchar, caminar; hacer marchar; **to** — **in** entrar marchando; **to** — **out** marcharse; salirse marchando.
March [mɑrtʃ] s. marzo.
mare [mɛr] s. yegua.
mar·ga·rine [mɑ́rdʒərɪn] s. margarina.
mar·gin [mɑ́rdʒɪn] s. margen; orilla; sobrante; reserva (fondos).
mar·gin·al [mɑ́rdʒɪnl] adj. marginal; — **note** nota marginal, acotación.
mar·i·gold [mǽrəgold] s. caléndula, maravilla.
ma·rine [mərín] adj. marino; marítimo; — **corps** cuerpo de marinos; s. marino; soldado de marina; **merchant** — marina mercante.
mar·i·ner [mǽrənɚ] s. marinero.
mar·i·time [mǽrətaɪm] adj. marítimo.
mark [mɑrk] s. marca; señal, seña; nota, calificación; **question** — punto de interrogación; **to come up to the** — alcanzar la norma requerida; **to hit the** — dar en el blanco; **to make one's** — distinguirse; **to miss one's** — fallar; errar el tiro; fracasar; v. marcar; señalar; notar; observar; calificar; — **my words!** ¡advierte lo que te digo!; **to** — **down** anotar, apuntar; rebajar el precio de.
mark·er [mɑ́rkɚ] s. marcador; marca, señal; jalón.
mar·ket [mɑ́rkɪt] s. mercado, plaza; — **place** mercado, plaza; — **price** precio corriente; **meat** — carnicería; **stock** — mercado de valores, bolsa; v. vender; vender o comprar en el mercado; **to go -ing** ir de compras.
mar·ma·lade [mɑ́rmled] s. mermelada.
ma·roon [mərún] s. & adj. rojo obscuro.
ma·rooned [mərúnd] adj. abandonado (en lugar desierto); aislado; **to get** — encontrarse aislado, perdido o incomunicado.
mar·quis [mɑ́rkwɪs] s. marqués.
mar·quise [mɑrkíz] s. marquesa.
mar·riage [mǽrɪdʒ] s. matrimonio; casamiento, boda; unión, enlace; — **license** licencia para casarse.
mar·riage·a·ble [mǽrɪdʒəbl] adj. casadero.
mar·ried [mǽrɪd] adj. casado; conyugal; — **couple** matrimonio, cónyuges; pareja de casados; **to get** — casarse.
mar·row [mǽro] s. meollo, tuétano, medula (de los huesos).

mar·ry [mǽrɪ] v. casar; casarse; casarse con.
marsh [mɑrʃ] s. pantano; ciénaga.
mar·shal [mɑ́rʃəl] s. mariscal; alguacil; jefe de policía (en ciertas regiones); maestro de ceremonia; **fire** — jefe de bomberos; v. ordenar, arreglar; guiar, conducir con ceremonia.
marsh·mal·low [mɑ́rʃmælo] s. pastilla o bombón de altea.
marsh·y [mɑ́rʃɪ] adj. pantanoso, cenagoso.
mart [mɑrt] s. mercado.
mar·tial [mɑ́rʃəl] adj. marcial; — **law** estado de sitio.
mar·tin [mɑ́rtɪn] s. avión pájaro).
mar·tyr [mɑ́rtɚ] s. mártir; v. martirizar, torturar, atormentar.
mar·tyr·dom [mɑ́rtədəm] s. martirio.
mar·vel [mɑ́rvl] s. maravilla; v. maravillarse.
mar·vel·ous [mɑ́rvləs] adj. maravilloso.
Marx·ism [mɑ́rksɪzəm] s. marxismo.
mas·cot [mǽskɑt] s. mascota.
mas·cu·line [mǽskjəlɪn] adj. masculino; varonil; hombruno.
mash [mæʃ] v. majar, amasar; machacar, magullar; **-ed potatoes** puré de papas (o patatas); patatas majadas.
mask [mæsk] s. máscara; disfraz; careta; v. disfrazar, enmascarar; encubrir; **-ed ball** baile de máscaras.
ma·son [mésn] s. albañil; **Mason** masón, francmasón.
ma·son·ry [mésnɪ] s. albañilería; mampostería; **Masonry** masonería, francmasonería.
mas·quer·ade [mæskəréd] s. mascarada; disfraz, máscara; v. enmascararse, disfrazarse; andar disfrazado.
mass [mæs] s. masa; montón; mole; mayoría, mayor parte; misa; — **meeting** mitin popular; — **communication** comunicación extensa; — **media** los medios de comunicarse con el público (radio, televisión, periódicos, etc.); **the -es** las masas, el pueblo; v. juntar(se) en masa.
mas·sa·cre [mǽsəkɚ] s. hecatombe, matanza, carnicería, destrozo; v. hacer matanza o hecatombe, destrozar.
mas·sage [məsáʒ] v. friccionar, dar masaje; s. masaje.
mas·sive [mǽsɪv] adj. sólido, macizo; voluminoso, imponente.
mast [mæst] s. mástil, palo.
mas·ter [mǽstɚ] s. (head) amo, dueño, señor; maestro; patrón; (skilled) experto, perito; **band** — director de la banda; — **of arts** maestro en artes, licenciado; **-'s degree** licenciatura, grado de licenciado; — **builder** maestro de obras; — **key** llave maestra; v. dominar; domar; gobernar; **to** — **a language** dominar un idioma.
mas·ter·ful [mǽstɚfəl] adj. magistral; dominante.
mas·ter·ly [mǽstɚlɪ] adj. magistral; adv. magistralmente.
mas·ter·piece [mǽstɚpis] s. obra maestra.
mas·ter·y [mǽstərɪ] s. maestría, arte, destreza; dominio.
mas·tiff [mǽstɪf] s. mastín, alano.
mat [mæt] s. (covering) estera, esterilla, felpudo, tapete; (gymnasium) colchoncillo (de gimnasia); borde de cartón (para hacer resaltar una pintura).
match [mætʃ] s. (pair) pareja, (game) partida, contienda, juego; (light) fósforo, cerilla; Méx. cerillo; **he has no** — no tiene igual; **he is a**

good — es un buen partido; **the hat and coat are a good** — el abrigo y el sombrero hacen juego; *v.* igualar; aparear; hacer juego, armonizar; **to** — **one's strength** medir uno sus fuerzas; **these colors do not** — **well** estos colores no casan bien.

match·less [mǽtʃlɪs] *adj.* sin par, sin igual, incomparable.

mate [met] *s.* compañero, compañera; consorte; macho o hembra (*entre animales o aves*); piloto (*el segundo de un buque mercante*); oficial subalterno (*en la marina*); *v.* aparear(se).

ma·te·ri·al [mǝtírɪǝl] *adj.* material; esencial; *s.* material; tejido, género; materia; **raw** — materia prima.

ma·ter·nal [mǝtɝ́nl] *adj.* maternal, materno.

ma·ter·ni·ty [mǝtɝ́nǝtɪ] *s.* maternidad.

math·e·mat·i·cal [mæθǝmǽtɪkl] *adj.* matemático.

math·e·mati·cian [mæθǝmǝtíʃǝn] *s.* matemático.

math·e·mat·ics [mæθǝmǽtɪks] *s*) matemáticas.

mat·i·née [mǽtṇé] *s.* función de la tarde, *Am.* matiné.

ma·tri·arch [métrɪɑrk] *s.* matriarca.

ma·tric·u·late [mǝtríkjǝlet] *v.* matricular(se).

ma·tric·u·la·tion [mǝtrɪkjǝléʃǝn] *s.* matriculación, matrícula.

mat·ri·mo·ny [mǽtrǝmonɪ] *s.* matrimonio, casamiento.

ma·trix [métrɪks] *s.* matriz; molde.

ma·tron [métrǝn] *s.* matrona, madre de familia; ama de llaves; vigilante, cuidadora (*de un asilo, cárcel par mujeres, etc.*).

mat·ter [mǽtɚ] *s.* (*substance*) material, materia; sustancia; (*affair*) asunto, cuestión; cosa; (*discharge*) pus; — **for complaint** motivo de queja; — **of two minutes** cosa de dos minutos; **as a** — **of fact** de hecho; en verdad, en realidad; **business -s** negocios; **printed** — impresos; **serious** — cosa seria; **it is of no** — no tiene importancia; **to do something as a** — **of course** hacer algo por rutina; **what is the** —? ¿qué tiene Vd.?; **matter-of-fact person** persona de poca imaginación; *v.* importar; supurar; **it does not** — no importa, no le hace.

mat·tress [mǽtrɪs] *s.* colchón; **spring** — colchón de muelles.

ma·ture [mǝtʃúr] *adj.* maduro; **a** — **note** un pagaré vencido; *v.* madurar(se); vencerse, hacerse cobrable o pagadero (*un pagaré, una deuda*).

ma·tur·i·ty [mǝtʃúrǝɪ] *s.* madurez; vencimiento (*de una deuda u obligación*).

maul [mɔl] *v.* magullar; maltratar; manejar rudamente; golpear.

mav·er·ick [mǽvɚɪk] *s.* animal sin marca; becerro suelto.

max·im [mǽksɪm] *s.* máxima.

max·i·mum [mǽksǝmǝm] *adj. & s.* máximo.

may [me] *v. irr. y. defect.* (*able*) poder; (*permitted*) tener permiso para; (*possible*) ser posible; — **I sit down?** ¿puedo sentarme?; — **you have a good time** que se divierta Vd., **it** — **be that** puede ser que, tal vez sea que; **it** — **rain** puede (ser) que llueva, es posible que llueva; **she** — **be late** puede (ser) que llegue ella tarde.

May [me] *s.* mayo, mes de mayo; — **Day** primero de mayo; —**pole** mayo; — **Queen** maya (*reina de la fiesta del primero de mayo*).

may·be [mébɪ] *adv.* quizás, tal vez, acaso.

may·on·naise [meǝnéz] *s.* mayonesa.

may·or [méǝ] *s.* alcalde, alcalde mayor.

maze [mez] *s.* laberinto; confusión; **to be in a** — estar confuso o perplejo.

me [mi] *pron. pers.* me; mí (*después de preposición*); **give it to** — démelo (a mí); **for** — para mí; **with** — conmigo.

mead·ow [médo] *s.* pradera, prado; — **lark** alondra de los prados.

mea·ger [mígɚ] *adj.* escaso, insuficiente; magro, flaco.

meal [mil] *s.* comida; harina (*a medio moler*); **corn** — harina de maíz; —**time** hora de comer.

mean [min] *adj.* (*malicious*) ruin, bajo; vil; (*humble*) humilde; (*stingy*) mezquino, tacaño; (*difficult*) de mal genio; (*sick*) malo, indispuesto; (*middle*) mediano; medio; intermedio; — **distance** distancia media; *s.* medio; término medio; -**s** medios; recursos; **a man of -s** un hombre pudiente o rico; **by -s of** por medio de; **by all -s** de todos modos; a toda costa; por supuesto; **by no -s** de ningún modo; *v.* querer decir, significar; pensar, proponerse, tener la intención de; intentar; destinar; **he -s well** tiene buenas intenciones.

me·an·der [mɪǽndɚ] *v.* serpentear.

mean·ing [mínɪŋ] *s.* (*sense*) significado, sentido; significación; (*intent*) propósito, intención; *adj.* significativo; **well-meaning** bien intencionado.

mean·ing·less [mínɪŋlɪs] *adj.* sin sentido, vacío de sentido.

mean·ness [mínnɪs] *s.* ruindad, vileza, bajeza; mezquindad.

meant [mɛnt] *pret. & p.p. de* **to mean.**

mean·time [míntaɪm] *adv.* mientras tanto, entretanto; *s.* ínterin, entretanto; **in the** — en el ínterin, mientras tanto.

mean·while [mínhwaɪl] = **meantime.**

mea·sles [mízlz] *s.* sarampión.

mea·sur·a·ble [méʒrǝbl] *adj.* medible, mensurable; **mea·sur·a·bly** *adv.* marcadamente.

mea·sure [méʒɚ] *s.* (*dimension*) medida; compás (*de música*); cadencia, ritmo; (*law*) proyecto de ley; ley; **beyond** — sobremanera; con exceso; **dry** — medida para áridos; **in large** — en gran parte, en gran manera; *v.* medir.

mea·sured [méʒɚd] *adj.* medido; moderado; acompasado.

mea·sure·ment [méʒɚmǝnt] *s.* medida; dimensión; tamaño; medición.

meat [mit] *s.* carne; meollo, sustancia; — **ball** albóndiga; — **market** carnicería; **cold** — fiambre.

meat·y [mítɪ] *adj.* carnoso; sustancioso.

me·chan·ic [mǝkǽnɪk] *adj. & s.* mecánico; -**s** *s.* mecánica.

me·chan·i·cal [mǝkǽnɪkl] *adj.* mecánico; maquinal.

mech·a·nism [mékǝnɪzǝm] *s.* mecanismo.

med·al [médl] *s.* medalla.

med·dle [médl] *v.* entrometerse o entremeterse; meterse.

med·dler [médlɚ] *s.* entremetido.

med·dle·some [médlsǝm] *adj.* entremetido.

me·di·an [mídɪǝn] *adj.* mediano, del medio; *s.* punto, línea o número del medio; mediana.

me·di·ate [mídɪet] *v.* mediar; intervenir; arbitrar.

me·di·a·tion [midɪéʃǝn] *s.* mediación, intervención, intercesión.

me·di·a·tor [mídɪetɚ] *s.* mediador, medianero, árbitro.

med·i·cal [médɪkl] *adj.* médico; — **school** escuela de medicina.

MA

med·i·ca·tion [mɛdɪkéʃən] *s.* medicación.
med·i·cine [médəsṇ] *s.* medicina; medicamento; — **ball** pelota grande de cuero; — **cabinet** botiquín; — **man** curandero indio.
me·di·e·val [midíívḷ] *adj.* medioeval o medieval.
me·di·o·cre [midióka-] *adj.* mediocre, mediano; ordinario.
me·di·oc·ri·ty [midiákrətɪ] *s.* mediocridad, medianía.
med·i·tate [médətet] *v.* meditar.
med·i·ta·tion [mɛdətéʃən] *s.* meditación.
me·di·um [mídɪəm] *s.* medio; medio ambiente; *adj.* mediano; intermedio; a medio cocer, a medio asar; — **of exchange** mediador de cambio.
med·ley [médlɪ] *s.* baturrillo, mezcla, mezcolanza.
meek [mik] *adj.* manso, dócil, paciente, sufrido.
meek·ness [míknɪs] *s.* mansedumbre, docilidad.
meet [mit] *v.* encontrar(se); reunirse; conocer *(personalmente)*, ser presentado a; ir a esperar *(un tren, vapor, o a alguien)*; satisfacer *(deseos, requisitos, etc.)*; pagar *(una deuda)*; sufragar *(gastos)*; responder a *(una acusación)*; **to — in battle** trabar batalla; **to — with** encontrarse con; tropezar con; topar con; reunirse con; *s.* concurso; contienda *(tratándose de deportes)*; **track** — competencia de atletas.
meet·ing [mítɪŋ] *s.* reunión; mitin; sesión; asamblea; encuentro.
meg·a·phone [mégəfon] *s.* megáfono, portavoz, bocina.
meg·a·ton [mégətʌn] *s.* megatón.
mel·an·chol·y [mélənkalɪ] *s.* melancolía; *adj.* melancólico.
me·lee [méle] *s.* reyerta; zafarrancho.
mel·low [mélo] *adj.* maduro, sazonado; dulce, blando, suave; *v.* madurar(se), sazonar(se); ablandar(se), suavizar(se).
me·lo·di·ous [məlódɪəs] *adj.* melodioso.
mel·o·dra·ma [mélodramə] *s.* melodrama.
mel·o·dy [mélədɪ] *s.* melodía.
mel·on [mélən] *s.* melón.
melt [mɛlt] *v.* derretir(se); disolver(se); fundir(se).
mem·ber [mémbə-] *s.* miembro; socio.
mem·ber·ship [mémbə-ʃɪp] *s.* número de miembros o socios; asociación; *(los)* miembros *(de un club o sociedad)*.
mem·brane [mémbren] *s.* membrana.
me·men·to [mɪménto] *s.* memento, memoria; recuerdo.
mem·oir [mémwar] *s.* memoria, apuntaciones; **-s** memorias; autobiografía.
mem·o·ra·ble [mémərəbḷ] *adj.* memorable.
mem·o·ran·dum [mɛmərǽndəm] *s.* memorándum; memoria, apunte; — **book** memorándum, librito de apuntes, memorial.
me·mor·i·al [məmórɪəl] *s. (monument)* monumento conmemorativo; *(occasion)* obra o fiesta conmemorativa; memorial, petición; *adj.* conmemorativo.
mem·o·rize [méməraɪz] *v.* aprender de memoria.
mem·o·ry [mémərɪ] *s.* memoria; recuerdo.
men [mɛn] *pl. de* **man.**
men·ace [ménɪs] *s.* amenaza; *v.* amenazar.
mend [mɛnd] *v.* remendar; reparar, componer; enmendar; **to — one's ways** enmendarse, reformarse; *s.* remiendo; reparación; **to be on the** — ir mejorando.
me·ni·al [mínɪəl] *adj.* servil, bajo.
men·stru·a·tion [mɛnstruéʃən] *s.* menstruo o menstruación.

men·tal [mɛ́ntḷ] *adj.* mental.
men·tal·i·ty [mɛntǽlətɪ] *s.* mentalidad, ingenio.
men·tion [ménʃən] *s.* mención; alusión; *v.* mencionar, mentar; **don't** — **it** no hay de qué *(contestación a* "thank you"*)*.
men·u [ménju] *s.* menú, lista de platos.
me·ow [mjaʊ] = **mew.**
mer·can·tile [má-kəntɪl] *adj.* mercantil.
mer·ce·nar·y [má-sṇɛrɪ] *adj.* mercenario.
mer·chan·dise [má-tʃəndaɪz] *s.* mercancías, mercaderías; **piece of** — mercancía.
mer·chant [má-tʃənt] *s.* comerciante; negociante; mercader; *adj.* mercante, mercantil; — **marine** marina mercante.
mer·ci·ful [má-sɪfəl] *adj.* misericordioso, piadoso.
mer·ci·less [má-sɪlɪs] *adj.* sin piedad, despiadado, incompasivo.
mer·cu·ry [má-kjəri] *s.* mercurio; azogue.
mer·cy [má-sɪ] *s. (favor)* merced; favor, gracia; *(compassion)* misericordia, piedad, compasión; **to be at the** — **of** estar a merced de.
mere [mɪr] *adj.* mero; simple, puro; **a** — **formality** una pura formalidad, no más que una formalidad, una formalidad no más; **a** — **trifle** una nonada; **-ly** *adv.* meramente; sólo, solamente; simplemente.
merge [mʒdʒ] *v.* combinar(se), unir(se); absorber(se); fundirse.
merg·er [má-dʒa-] *s.* amalgamación comercial.
me·rid·i·an [mərídɪən] *adj. & s.* meridiano.
mer·it [mérɪt] *s.* mérito; *v.* merecer.
mer·i·to·ri·ous [mɛrətórɪəs] meritorio.
mer·maid [má-med] *s.* ninfa marina.
mer·ri·ly [mérəlɪ] *adv.* alegremente, con regocijo.
mer·ri·ment [mérɪmənt] *s.* alegría, regocijo, júbilo.
mer·ry [mérɪ] *adj.* alegre; jovial; divertido; festivo; —**Christmas** Felices Navidades, Felices Pascuas; **to make** — divertirse.
mer·ry-go-round [mérɪgəraʊnd] *s.* tío vivo, *Méx.,* *C.A.* los caballitos; *Ríopl.* calesita.
mer·ry·mak·er [mérɪmeka-] *s.* fiestero; juerguista.
mer·ry·mak·ing [mérɪmekɪŋ] *s.* regocijo; jaleo, juerga, jolgorio; *adj.* regocijado, alegre, festivo, fiestero.
mesh [mɛʃ] *s.* malla; red; **-es** red, redes; *v.* enredar, coger con red; **to** — **gears** engranar.
mess [mɛs] *s. (food)* rancho, comida *(en el ejército o la marina)*; *(confusion)* lío, confusión; *(dirt)* suciedad; — **of fish** plato o ración de pescado; **to make a** — **of** revolver, confundir; ensuciar; echar a perder; *v.* revolver, confundir; ensuciar, echar a perder *(generalmente:* **to** — **up)**; **to** — **around** revolver o mezclar las cosas; entrometerse; meterse.
mes·sage [mésɪdʒ] *s.* mensaje; parte *(m.),* comunicación; recado.
mes·sen·ger [mésṇdʒa-] *s.* mensajero; mandadero.
met [mɛt] *pret. & p.p. de* **to meet.**
me·tab·o·lism [mətǽbəlɪzm] *s.* metabolismo.
met·al [métḷ] *s.* metal; *adj.* de metal, metálico.
me·tal·lic [mətǽlɪk] *adj.* metálico.
met·al·lur·gy [métḷ́ɜ-dʒɪ] *s.* metalurgia.
met·a·mor·pho·sis [mɛtəmórfəsɪs] *s.* metamorfosis.
met·a·phor [métəfa-] *s.* metáfora.
me·tath·e·sis [mətǽθəsɪs] *s.* metátesis.
me·te·or [mítɪa-] *s.* meteoro; estrella fugaz.
me·te·or·ic [mítɪorɪt] *s.* meteorito.
me·te·or·o·lo·gy [mitɪərálədʒɪ] *s.* meteorología.
me·ter [míta-] *s.* metro; contador *(de gas, agua,*

electricidad, etc.); *Am.* medidor.
meth·od [mέθəd] *s.* método; técnica.
me·thod·i·cal [məθádɪk|] *adj.* metódico.
me·tre = **meter**.
met·ric [métrɪk] *adj.* métrico; — **system** sistema métrico.
me·trop·o·lis [mətrɑ́plɪs] *s.* metrópoli.
met·ro·pol·i·tan [mɛtrəpálətn] *adj.* metropolitano.
met·tle [métl] *s.* temple, brío, ánimo, valor.
mew [mju] *s.* maullido, maúllo, miau; *v.* maullar.
Mex·i·can [méksɪkən] *adj.* & *s.* mejicano o mexicano.
mez·za·nine [mézənin] *s.* entresuelo.
mice [maɪs] *pl. de* **mouse**.
mi·crobe [máɪkrob] *s.* microbio.
mi·cro·bus [máɪkrobʌs] *s.* microbús.
mi·cro·film [máɪkrəfɪlm] *s.* microfilm.
mi·cro·phone [máɪkrəfon] *s.* micrófono.
mi·cro·scope [máɪkrəskop] *s.* microscopio.
mi·cro·scop·ic [maɪkrəskápɪk] *adj.* microscópico.
mid [mɪd] *adj.* medio (*úsase por lo general en composición*); **in** — **air** en el aire; *prep.* en medij de, entre.
mid·day [mídde] *s.* mediodía; *adj.* del mediodía.
mid·dle [mídl] *adj.* medio; intermedio; **Middle Ages** Edad Media; — **finger** dedo de en medio, dedo del corazón; — **size** tamaño mediano; *s.* medio, centro, mitad; **in the** — **of** en medio de, a la mitad de **towards the** — **of the month** a mediados del mes; — **class** clase media.
mid·dle-aged [mídlédʒd] *adj.* de edad mediana, de edad madura.
mid·dle·man [mídlmæn] *s.* revendedor; medianero, corredor, agente.
mid·dle-sized [mídlsáɪzd] *adj.* de mediano tamaño, de mediana estatura.
mid·dy [mídɪ] *s.* guardiamarina (*m.*); — **blouse** blusa a la marinera.
midg·et [mídʒɪt] *s.* enanillo.
mid·night [mídnaɪt] *s.* medianoche; *adj.* de (la) medianoche; — **blue** azul oscuro; — **Mass** misa de gallo.
mid·riff [mídrɪf] *s.* diafragma.
mid·ship·man [mídʃɪpmən] *s.* guardiamarina (*m.*).
midst [mɪdst] *s.* medio, centro; **in the** — **of** en medio de, entre; **in our** — entre nosotros.
mid·stream [mídstrim] *s.* el medio (*o* el centro) de la corriente.
mid·sum·mer [mídsʌ́mɚ] *s.* pleno verano, solsticio estival, la mitad del verano.
mid·term [mídtȝm]; — **examination** examen a mitad del curso.
mid·way [mídwé] *adj.* situado a medio camino; equidistante; *adv.* a medio camino; en medio del camino.
mid·wife [mídwaɪf] *s.* partera, comadrona.
mien [min] *s.* facha, aspecto.
might [maɪt] *imperf. de* **may** podía; podría; pudiera, pudiese; *s.* poder, poderío, fuerza.
might·y [máɪtɪ] *adj.* poderoso, potente, fuerte; *adv.* muy, sumamente.
mi·grant [máɪgrənt] *adj.* migratorio.
mi·grate [máɪgret] *v.* emigrar.
mi·gra·tion [maɪgréʃən] *s.* migración.
mike [maɪk] = **microphone**.
mild [maɪld] *adj.* (*gentle*) suave; blando; apacible; (*moderate*) templado, moderado.
mil·dew [míldu] *s.* moho; enmohecimiento.
mild·ness [máɪldnɪs] *s.* suavidad; mansedumbre; apacibilidad; templanza, dulzura.
mile [maɪl] *s.* milla; —**stone** mojón.

mile·age [máɪlɪdʒ] *s.* millaje, número de millas; recorrido (*en millas*). *Compárese* kilometraje, número de kilómetros.
mil·i·tant [mílɪtənt] *s.* militante; belicoso.
mil·i·tar·y [mílətɛrɪ] *adj.* militar; de guerra; *s.* **the** — el ejército; los militares.
mi·li·tia [məlíʃə] *s.* milicia.
milk [mɪlk] *s.* leche; — **diet** régimen lácteo; *v.* ordeñar.
milk·maid [mílkmed] *s.* lechera.
milk·man [mílkmən] *s.* lechero, *Am.* vaquero.
milk·y [mílkɪ] *adj.* lácteo; lechoso; **Milky Way** Vía Láctea.
mill [mɪl] *s.* (*grinder*) molino; (*factory*) fábrica; (*money*) la milésima parte de un dólar; **saw** — aserradero; **spinning** — hilandería; **sugar** — ingenio de azúcar; **textile** — fábricar; acordonar (*el* moler; aserrar (*madera*); fabricar; acordonar (*el canto de la moneda*); **to** — **around** arremolinarse (*una muchedumbre*).
mill·er [mílɚ] *s.* molinero; mariposa nocturna.
mil·li·gram [mílɪgræm] *s.* miligramo.
mil·li·me·ter [míləmitɚ] *s.* milímetro.
mil·li·ner [mílənɚ] *s.* modista (*de sombreros para señoras*).
mil·li·ner·y [mílənɛrɪ] *s.* sombreros de señora; artículos para sombreros de señora; oficio de modista; — **shop** sombrerería.
mil·lion [míljən] *s.* millón; **a** — **dollars** un millón de dólares.
mil·lion·aire [mɪljənɛ́r] *adj.* & *s.* millonario.
mil·lionth [míljənθ] *adj.* & *s.* millonésimo.
mill·stone [mílston] *s.* muela de piedra de molino; carga pesada.
mim·ic [mímɪk] *adj.* mímico, imitativo; — **battle** simulacro; *s.* imitador, remedador; *v.* imitar, remedar.
mince [mɪns] *v.* picar, desmenuzar; **not to** — **words** hablar con toda franqueza.
mince·meat [mínsmit] *s.* picadillo (*especialmente el de carne, pasas, manzanas y especias*).
mind [maɪnd] *s.* (*brain*) mente; (*thought*) pensamiento; inteligencia; (*spirit*) ánimo, espíritu; (*purpose*) propósito, intención; (*opinion*) parecer, opinión; **to be out of one's** — estar loco, haber perdido el juicio; **to change one's** — cambiar de parecer; **to give someone a piece of one's** — cantarle a alguien la verdad; echarle a alguien un buen regaño; **to have a** — **to** estar por; sentir ganas de; **to make up one's** — decidirse, resolverse; **to my** — a mi modo de ver; **to speak one's** — **freely** hablar con toda franqueza; *v.* cuidar; atender a, hacer caso de; obedecer; **I don't** — no tengo inconveniente en ello; **never** — no importa; no se preocupe; no se moleste; no haga Vd. caso; **to** — **one's own business** atender a lo suyo, no meterse en lo ajeno.
mind·ful [máɪndfəl] *adj.* atento (a); cuidadoso (de).
mine [maɪn] *pron. pos.* mío (mía, míos, mías); **el** mío (la mía, los míos, las mías); **a book of** — un libro mío.
mine [maɪn] *s.* mina; — **sweeper** dragaminas; *v.* minar; explotar (*una mina*); extraer (*mineral*).
min·er [máɪnɚ] *s.* minero.
min·er·al [mínərəl] *adj.* & *s.* mineral.
min·gle [míngl] *v.* mezclar(se); entremezclar(se); confundir(se); juntarse.
min·i·a·ture [mínɪtʃɚ] *s.* miniatura; *adj.* en miniatura; diminuto.
min·i·mal [mínəml] *adj.* mínimo.

min·i·mize [mínəmaɪz] *v.* empequeñecer.

min·i·mum [mínəməm] *adj. & s.* mínimo.

min·ing [máɪnɪŋ] *s.* minería, explotación de minas; *adj.* minero; — **engineer** ingeniero de minas.

min·i·skirt [míniskə·t] *s.* minifalda.

min·is·ter [mínɪstə·] *s.* ministro; pastor, clérigo; *v.* ministrar; atender; proveer, socorrer.

min·is·try [mínɪstrɪ] *s.* ministerio; socorro, ayuda.

mink [mɪŋk] *s.* visón.

min·now [míno] *s.* pececillo de río.

mi·nor [máɪnə·] *adj.* (*young*) menor; de menor edad; (*secondary*) secundario; — **key** tono menor; *s.* menor de edad; premisa menor (*de un silogismo*); tono menor; curso o asignatura menor.

mi·nor·i·ty [mənɔ́rətɪ] *s.* minoría; minoridad, menor edad; menor parte.

min·strel [mínstrəl] *s.* trovador; bardo, vate; actor cómico que remeda al negro norteamericano.

mint [mɪnt] *s.* (*flavor*) menta, hierbabuena (*yerbabuena*); (*candy*) pastilla o bombón de menta; (*money*) casa de moneda; **a** — **of money** un montón de dinero, la mar de dinero; *v.* acuñar.

mint·age [míntədʒ] *s.* acuñación; moneda acuñada.

min·u·et [mɪnjuét] *s.* minué.

mi·nus [máɪnəs] *adj.* negativo; sin, falto de; **seven** — **four** siete menos cuatro; *s.* menos, signo menos.

min·ute [mínɪt] *s.* minuto; **-s** acta (*de una junta*); — **hand** minutero.

mi·nute [mənjút] *adj.* menudo, diminuto; minucioso, detallado.

mir·a·cle [mírəkl] *s.* milagro.

mi·rac·u·lous [mərǽkjələs] *adj.* milagroso.

mi·rage [məráʒ] *s.* espejismo.

mire [maɪr] *s.* cieno, fango, lodo; *v.* atascar(se) en el fango; enlodar(se).

mir·ror [mírə·] *s.* espejo; *v.* reflejar.

mirth [mɝθ] *s.* júbilo, regocijo, alegría.

mirth·ful [mɝθfəl] *adj.* jubiloso, regocijado, gozoso, alegre.

mir·y [máɪrɪ] *adj.* cenagoso, fangoso, lodoso.

mis·ad·ven·ture [mɪsədvéntʃə·] *s.* desgracia; contratiempo.

mis·be·have [mɪsbihév] *v.* portarse mal, obrar mal.

mis·car·riage [mɪskǽrɪdʒ] *s.* aborto, malparto; mal éxito; extravío (*de una carta, papel, etc.*).

mis·car·ry [mɪskǽrɪ] *v.* (*fail*) malograrse, frustrarse; extraviarse (*una carta*); (*abort*) abortar.

mis·cel·la·ne·ous [mɪslénɪəs] *adj.* misceláneo, diverso.

mis·chief [místʃɪf] *s.* travesura; diablura; mal, daño; diablillo, persona traviesa.

mis·chie·vous [místʃɪvəs] *adj.* travieso; malicioso; dañino; revoltoso.

mis·con·cep·tion [mɪskənsépʃən] *s.* concepto erróneo.

mis·con·duct [mɪskándʌkt] *s.* mala conducta; mala administración; [mɪskəndʌ́kt] *v.* maladministrar, manejar mal; **to** — **oneself** portarse mal, conducirse mal.

mis·cue [mɪskjú] *s.* pifia.

mis·deed [mɪsdíd] *s.* fechoría, mala acción.

mis·de·mean·or [mɪsdɪmínə·] *s.* mal comportamiento; fechoría.

mi·ser [máɪzə·] *s.* avaro, avariento.

mis·er·a·ble [mízrəbl] *adj.* miserable; infeliz, desdichado.

mi·ser·ly [máɪzə·lɪ] *adj.* avariento, avaro; tacaño, mezquino.

mis·er·y [mízrɪ] *s.* miseria, desgracia; estrechez, pobreza; dolor.

mis·for·tune [mɪsfɔ́rtʃən] *s.* infortunio, desgracia, desastre.

mis·giv·ing [mɪsgívɪŋ] *s.* mal presentimiento, aprensión, recelo, temor.

mis·guid·ed [mɪsgáɪdəd] *adj.* mal aconsejado.

mis·hap [míshæp] *s.* desgracia, contratiempo, accidente.

mis·judge [mɪsdʒʌ́dʒ] *v.* juzgar mal.

mis·laid [mɪsléd] *pret. & p.p. de* **to mislay.**

mis·lay [mɪslé] *v.* extraviar, perder; poner fuera de su sitio, colocar mal; traspapelar (*una carta, documento, etc.*).

mis·lead [mɪslíd] *v.* guiar por mal camino; extraviar, descarriar; engañar.

mis·led [mɪsléd] *pret. & p.p. de* **to mislead.**

mis·man·age [mɪsmǽnɪdʒ] *v.* administrar mal.

mis·place [mɪsplés] *v.* extraviar, poner fuera de su sitio, colocar mal; traspapelar (*una carta, documento, etc.*).

mis·print [mɪsprínt] *s.* errata, error tipográfico, error de imprenta.

mis·pro·nounce [mɪsprənɑuns] *v.* pronunciar mal.

mis·rep·re·sent [mɪsrɛprɪzént] *v.* falsear, falsificar; tergiversar.

miss [mɪs] *v.* (*not hit*) errar, no acertar; fallar; (*omit*) equivocar; perder; faltar a; (*feel absence of*) echar de menos; *Am.* extrañar; **he just -ed being killed** por poco lo matan; *s.* error; falla, falta.

miss [mɪs] *s.* señorita; **Miss Smith** la señorita Smith.

mis·sile [mísl] *s.* proyectil; arma arrojadiza; *adj.* arrojadizo, que se puede arrojar o tirar.

miss·ing [mísɪŋ] *adj.* ausente; perdido; **one book is** — falta un libro.

mis·sion [míʃən] *s.* misión.

mis·sion·ar·y [míʃənɛrɪ] *adj. & s.* misionero.

mis·spell [mɪsspél] *v.* escribir con mala ortografía, deletrear mal.

mist [mɪst] *s.* neblina, niebla; llovizna, *Ven., Col., Andes* garúa; *v.* lloviznar; anublar.

mis·take [məsték] *s.* error, yerro, equivocación; errata (*de imprenta*); **to make a** — equivocarse; *v.* equivocar.

mis·tak·en [məstékən] *p.p. de* **to mistake** & *adj.* equivocado; errado; erróneo, incorrecto; **to be** — estar equivocado, equivocarse, errar.

mis·ter [místə·] *s.* señor.

mis·took [mɪstúk] *pret. de* **mistake.**

mis·treat [mɪstrít] *v.* maltratar.

mis·tress [místrɪs] *s.* señora; ama, dueña; querida, amante; **school—** maestra.

mis·tri·al [mɪstráɪl] *v.* pleito viciado de nulidad.

mis·trust [mɪstrʌ́st] *s.* desconfianza; *v.* desconfiar de.

mis·trust·ful [mɪstrʌ́stfəl] *adj.* desconfiado; sospechoso, receloso.

mist·y [místɪ] *adj.* brumoso; nublado, empañado; vago, indistinto.

mis·un·der·stand [mɪsʌndə·stǽnd] *v.* comprender mal; entender mal; interpretar mal; no comprender.

mis·un·der·stand·ing [mɪsʌndə·stǽndɪŋ] *s.* equivocación; mala interpretación, mala inteligencia; desavenencia.

mis·un·der·stood [mɪsʌndə·stúd] *pret. & p.p. de* **misunderstand.**

mis·use [mɪsjús] *s.* abuso, mal uso; malversación (*de fondos*); [mɪsjúz] *v.* abusar de; maltratar;

usar o emplear mal; malversar (*fondos*).
mite [maɪt] s. óbolo, friolera, pequeñez; criatura.
mi·ter [máɪtə·] s. mitra; dignidad de obispo.
mit·i·gate [mítəget] v. mitigar.
mit·ten [mítṇ] s. mitón (*guante de una pieza y sin dedos*).
mix [mɪks] v. mezclar(se); unir(se), juntar(se), asociar(se); **to — someone up** confundir a uno; s. mezcla; confusión, lío.
mix·ture [míkstʃə·] s. mezcla; mezcolanza.
mix·up [míksʌp] s. equívoco; enredo.
moan [mon] s. quejido, gemido; v. gemir; quejarse; lamentar(se).
moat [mot] s. foso.
mob [mɑb] s. populacho; muchedumbre, gentío, *Am.* bola (*de gente*); v. atropellar; apiñarse o agolparse alrededor de.
mo·bile [móbḷ] adj. móvil; movible; movedizo.
mo·bi·li·za·tion [mobḷəzéʃən] s. movilización.
mo·bi·lize [móbḷaɪz] v. movilizar.
moc·ca·sin [mákəsṇ] s. *Am.* mocasín (*zapato burdo de cuero*); *Am.* mocasín (*víbora venenosa*).
mock [mɔk] v. (*ridicule*) mofar, mofarse de; (*imitate*) remedar, imitar; **to — at** mofarse de; burlarse de; s. mofa, burla, escarnio; mímica; remedo; adj. falso, ficticio, imitado; **— battle** simulacro, batalla fingida.
mock·er·y [mókərɪ] s. burla, mofa, escarnio; remedo.
mock·up [mákʌp] s. maqueta; modelo.
mode [mod] s. modo, manera; moda.
mod·el [mádḷ] s. (*guide*) modelo; (*pattern*) patrón; (*figure*) figurín, maniquí; adj. ejemplar; modelo; **— school** escuela modelo ; v. modelar; moldear, formar; posar, servir de modelo.
mod·er·ate [mádərɪt] adj. moderado; templado; módico; (máderət) v. moderar(se); templar(se).
mod·er·a·tion [madəréʃən] s. moderación; templanza.
mod·ern [mádəˑn] adj. moderno.
mod·ern·ize [mádəˑnaɪz] v. modernizar.
mod·est [mádɪst] adj. modesto.
mod·es·ty [mádəstɪ] s. modestia.
mod·i·fi·ca·tion [madəfəkéʃən] s. modificación.
mod·i·fy [mádəfaɪ] v. modificar.
mod·u·late [mádʒəlet] v. modular.
mo·hair [móhɛr] s. moer.
Mo·ham·med·an [mohǽmədən] adj. & s. mahometano.
moist [mɔɪst] adj. húmedo; mojado.
mois·ten [mɔ́ɪsṇ] v. humedecer, mojar.
mois·ture [mɔ́ɪstʃə·] s. humedad.
mo·lar [mólə·] adj. molar; s. muela.
mo·las·ses [məlǽsɪz] s. melaza, miel de caña.
mold [mold] s. (*form*) molde, matriz; (*substance*) moho; tierra vegetal; v. moldear, amoldar; modelar; enmohecer(se), cubrir(se) de moho.
mold·er [móldə·] v. desmoronarse.
mold·ing [móldɪŋ] s. moldura; moldeamiento.
mold·y [móldɪ] adj. mohoso.
mole [mol] s. lunar; topo (*animal*); dique, malecón, rompeolas.
mol·e·cule [máləkjul] s. molécula.
mo·lest [məlést] v. molestar.
mol·li·fy [máləfaɪ] v. apaciguar.
mol·ten [móltṇ] adj. derretido, fundido, en fusión.
mo·lyb·de·num [məlíbdənəm] s. molibdeno.
mo·ment [mómənt] s. momento; importancia, consecuencia.
mo·men·tar·y [mómənterɪ] adj. momentáneo.

mo·men·tous [moméntəs] adj. importante.
mo·men·tum [moméntəm] s. momento (*de una fuerza*); ímpetu.
mon·arch [mánə·k] s. monarca.
mon·ar·chy [mánə·kɪ] s. monarquía.
mon·as·ter·y [mánəsterɪ] s. monasterio.
Mon·day [mándɪ] s. lunes.
mon·e·tar·y [mánətɛrɪ] adj. monetario.
mon·ey [mánɪ] s. dinero; **— changer** cambista; **— order** giro postal; **paper — paper** papel moneda; **silver — moneda de plata; money-making** lucrativo, provechoso, ganancioso.
mon·ger [mángə·] s. traficante; defensor.
mon·grel [máŋgrəl] adj. & s. mestizo, mixto, cruzado, *Am.* chusco (*perro*).
monk [mʌŋk] s. monje.
mon·key [máŋkɪ] s. mono; **—shine** monada, monería; **— wrench** llave inglesa; v. juguetear; hacer monerías; payasear; entremeterse; **to — with** juguetear con; meterse con.
mon·o·gram [mánəgræm] s. monograma.
mon·o·graph [mánəgræf] s. monografía.
mon·o·logue [mánḷɔg] s. monólogo, soliloquio.
mo·nop·o·lize [mənápḷaɪz] v. monopolizar, acaparar.
mo·nop·o·ly [mənápḷɪ] s. monopolio.
mon·o·syl·la·ble [mánəsɪləbḷ] s. monosílabo.
mon·o·tone [mánəton] adj. monótono.
mo·not·o·nous [mənátṇəs] adj. monótono.
mo·not·o·ny [mənátṇɪ] s. monotonía.
mon·ster [mánstə·] s. monstruo; adj. enorme.
mon·stros·i·ty [manstrásətɪ] s. monstruosidad; monstruo.
mon·strous [mánstrəs] adj. monstruoso.
month [mʌnθ] s. mes.
month·ly [mánθlɪ] adj. mensual; s. publicación mensual; adv. mensualmente.
mon·u·ment [mánjəmənt] s. monumento.
mon·u·men·tal [manjəméntḷ] adj. monumental; colosal, grandioso.
moo [mu] s. mugido; v. mugir.
mood [mud] s. humor, disposición de ánimo; modo (*del verbo*); **to be in a good —** estar de buen humor; **to be in the — to** estar dispuesto a, tener gana de.
mood·y [múdɪ] adj. (*changing*) caprichoso, voluble, mudable; (*sad*) melancólico, mohino.
moon [mun] s. luna; mes lunar; **once in a blue —** de Pascuas a San Juan, muy rara vez, *Am.* por campanada de vacante, *Am.* a cada muerte de (o por la muerte de un) obispo.
moon·light [múnlaɪt] s. luz de la luna; **— dance** baile a la luz de la luna; **— night** noche de luna.
moor [mʊr] v. amarrar, atracar (*un buque*); anclar; estar anclado; s. terreno inculto o baldío.
Moor [mʊr] s. moro.
Moor·ish [múrɪʃ] adj. morisco, moro.
mop [mɑp] s. *Am.* trapeador; **dust —** limpiapolvo; **— of hair** greñas, cabellera abundante; v. limpiar (*el suelo*), *Am.* trapear; **to — one's brow** limpiarse (o secarse) la frente; **to — up** limpiar; vencer; acabar con.
mope [mop] v. andar quejumbroso o abatido.
mor·al [mɔ́rəl] adj. moral; **— philosophy** ética, moral; s. moraleja, -s moral, ética.
mo·rale [mərǽl] s. moral, entereza de ánimo.
mor·al·ist [mɔ́rəlɪst] s. moralista.
mo·ral·i·ty [mərǽlətɪ] s. moralidad.
mor·al·ize [mɔ́rəlaɪz] v. moralizar.
mor·bid [mɔ́rbɪd] adj. mórbido, morboso; malsano.
mor·dant [mɔ́rdənt] adj. mordaz.

more [mor] *adj.* & *adv.* más; — **and** — cada vez más, más y más; — **or less** poco más o menos; **there is no** — no hay más, ya no hay; se acabó.

more·o·ver [moróvə] *adv.* además.

morn·ing [mɔ́rnɪŋ] *s.* mañana; **good** —! ¡buenos días!; **tomorrow** — mañana por la mañana; *adj.* de la mañana; matutino, matinal; **morning-glory** dondiego de día; — **star** lucero del alba.

mor·phine [mɔ́rfin] *s.* morfina.

mor·phol·o·gy [mɔrfálədʒɪ] *s.* morfología.

mor·row [mɔ́ro]: **on the** — el día de mañana; mañana.

mor·sel [mɔ́rsl] *s.* bocado; manjar sabroso.

mor·tal [mɔ́rtl] *adj.* & *s.* mortal.

mor·tal·i·ty [mɔrtǽlətɪ] *s.* mortalidad; mortandad.

mor·tar [mɔ́rtə] *s.* mortero; argamasa, mezcla; **metal** — almirez.

mort·gage [mɔ́rgɪdʒ] *s.* hipoteca, gravamen; *v.* hipotecar; *adj.* hipotecario.

mor·ti·fy [mɔ́rtəfaɪ] *v.* mortificar; avergonzar.

mo·sa·ic [mozéɪk] *adj.* & *s.* mosaico.

Mos·lem [mázləm] *adj.* & *s.* musulmán.

mosque [mɔsk] *s.* mezquita.

mos·qui·to [məskíto] *s.* mosquito; — **net** mosquitero.

moss [mɔs] *s.* musgo; **moss-grown** musgoso, cubierto de musgo; anticuado.

moss·y [mɔ́sɪ] *adj.* musgoso.

most [most] *adv.* más; sumamente, muy; *s.* la mayoría, la mayor parte, el mayor número o cantidad; los más; — **people** la mayoría (*o* la mayor parte) de la gente; **at the** — a lo más, a lo sumo; **for the** — **part** por la mayor parte; generalmente, mayormente; **the** — **that I can do** lo más que puedo hacer; **the** — **votes** el mayor número de votos, los más votos.

most·ly [móstlɪ] *adv.* por la mayor parte; mayormente, principalmente.

moth [mɔθ] *s.* polilla; mariposa nocturna; —**ball** bolita de naftalina; **moth-eaten** apolillado.

moth·er [mʌ́ðə] *s.* madre; **mother-of-pearl** madreperla, nácar; *adj.* de madre; materno, maternal; nativo, natal; — **country** madre patria; país natal; — **Superior** superiora; — **tongue** lengua materna; *v.* servir de madre a, cuidar de.

moth·er·hood [mʌ́ðəhʊd] *s.* maternidad.

moth·er-in-law [mʌ́ðərɪnlɔ] *s.* suegra.

moth·er·ly [mʌ́ðəlɪ] *adj.* maternal, materno.

mo·tif [motíf] *s.* motivo, tema.

mo·tion [móʃən] *s.* (*movement*) moción; 'movimiento; (*signal*) ademán, señal, seña; — **sickness** mareo; *v.* hacer una seña o señas; indicar.

mo·tion·less [móʃənlɪs] *adj.* inmóvil, inmoble.

mo·tion pic·ture [móʃənpíktʃə] *s.* cine o cinematógrafo; película; fotografía cinematográfica; **motion-picture** *adj.* cinematográfico.

mo·tive [mótɪv] *s.* motivo; tema; *adj.* motriz.

mot·ley [mátlɪ] *adj.* abigarrado, multicolor, de diversos colores; variado, mezclado; *s.* mezcla, mezcolanza.

mo·tor [mótə] *s.* motor; automóvil; *v.* pasear o ir en automóvil.

mo·tor·bike [mótəbaɪk] *s.* motocicleta pequeña; moto.

mo·tor·boat [mótəbot] *s.* autobote, lancha de gasolina, bote de motor.

mo·tor·car [mótəkar] *s.* automóvil.

mo·tor·coach [mótəkotʃ] *s.* autobús, ómnibus; *Méx.* camión, *Carib.* guagua; *Ríopl., Ch.* micro; *C.A.* bus.

mo·tor·cy·cle [mótəsaɪkl] *s.* motocicleta.

mo·tor·ist [mótərɪst] *s.* motorista, automovilista.

mo·tor·man [mótəmən] *s.* motorista.

mo·tor scoot·er [mótəskutə] *s.* motoneta.

mot·tled [mátld] *adj.* moteado; jaspeado, manchado.

mot·to [máto] *s.* mote, divisa, lema.

mould = mold.

mould·er = molder.

mould·ing = molding.

mould·y = moldy.

mound [maʊnd] *s.* montecillo, montículo, montón de tierra.

mount [maʊnt] *s.* (*elevation*) monte; (*horse*) montura, cabalgadura, caballo; *v.* montar; montar a caballo; subir, ascender; armar (*una máquina*); engastar (*joyas*).

moun·tain [máʊntn̩] *s.* montaña; *adj.* montañés; de montaña; — **goat** cabra montés; — **lion** puma; — **range** cordillera, cadena de montañas.

moun·tain climb·er [máʊntənklaɪmə] *s.* alpinista.

moun·tain·eer [maʊntn̩ír] *s.* montañés.

moun·tain·ous [máʊntn̩əs] *adj.* montañoso.

mourn [morn] *v.* lamentar; deplorar; **to** — **for** llorar a; estar de duelo por.

mourn·ful [mórnfəl] *adj.* fúnebre; lúgubre; lastimero; triste.

mourn·ing [mórnɪŋ] *s.* luto; duelo; lamentación; **to be in** — estar de luto, estar de duelo; *adj.* de luto.

mouse [maʊs] *s.* ratón; — **trap** ratonera.

mous·tache = mustache.

mouth [maʊθ] *s.* boca; abertura; desembocadura, embocadura (*de un río*).

mouth·ful [máʊθfəl] *s.* bocado.

mouth·piece [máʊθpis] *s.* boquilla (*de un instrumento de viento*); portavoz.

mov·a·ble [múvəbl] *adj.* movible, móvil; -**s** *s. pl.* muebles, bienes muebles.

move [muv] *v.* (*motion*) mover(se); (*change*) mudar(se), mudar de casa; (*propose*) proponer, hacer la moción de; (*game*) hacer una jugada (*en ajedrez o damas*); (*emotion*) conmover; inducir; — **away** irse; alejarse; apartarse; **to** — **forward** avanzar; **to** — **on** seguir adelante, caminar; **to** — **out** irse, mudarse, mudar de casa; *s.* movimiento; mudanza (*de una casa a otra*); paso, trámite (*para conseguir algo*); jugada, turno (*en juegos*); **get a** — **on there!** ¡ande! ¡dése prisa!; *Am.* ¡ándele!

move·ment [múvmənt] *s.* (*motion*) movimiento; maniobra; meneo; acción; (*mechanism*) mecanismo, movimiento (*de un reloj*); (*bowel*) evacuación.

mov·ie [múvɪ] *s.* cine, película; -**s** cine.

mow [mo] *v.* segar; cortar (*césped*).

mow·er [móə] *s.* segador; segadora, cortadora mecánica; máquina segadora.

mown [mon] *adj.* & *p.p.* segado.

Mr. [místə] Sr., señor; **Mrs.** [mísɪz] Sra., señora.

much [mʌtʃ] *adj., adv.* & *s.* mucho; — **the same** casi lo mismo; **as** — **as** tanto como; **how** —? ¿cuánto?; **not** — **of a book** un libro de poco valor; **not** — **of a poet** un poetastro; **so** — **that** tanto que; **too** — demasiado; **very** — muchísimo; **to make** — **of** dar mucha importancia a.

muck [mʌk] *s.* (*manure*) estiércol húmedo; (*mire*) cieno; (*filth*) porquería, suciedad.

mu·cous [mjúkəs] *adj.* mucoso; — **membrane** membrana mucosa.

mud [mʌd] *s.* lodo, fango, cieno; — **wall** tapia.

mud·dle [mʌdl] *v.* enturbiar; confundir; embrollar; *s.* confusión, embrollo, lío, desorden.

mud·dy [mʌdɪ] *adj.* fangoso, lodoso; turbio; confuso; *v.* enlodar, ensuciar; enturbiar.

muff [mʌf] *s.* manguito (*para las manos*); falla, error (*en ciertos juegos*); *v.* no coger, dejar escapar (*la pelota*).

muf·fin [mʌfɪn] *s.* bollo, panecillo.

muf·fle [mʌfl] *v.* embozar; tapar; apagar, amortiguar (*un sonido*).

muf·fler [mʌfləˑ] *s.* bufanda; silenciador (*para maquinaria*); mofle.

mug [mʌg] *s.* pichel, vaso con asa.

mu·lat·to [məlǽto] *s.* mulato.

mul·ber·ry [mʌlbɛrɪ] *s.* mora; — **tree** moral.

mule [mjul] *s.* mulo, mula; **muleteer** [mjulətír] *s.* arriero.

mull [mʌl] *v.* meditar, ponderar, revolver en la mente; calentar (*vino, sidra, etc.*) con azúcar y especias.

mul·ti·ple [mʌltəpl] *s.* múltiplo; *adj.* múltiple.

mul·ti·pli·ca·tion [mʌltəpləkéʃən] *s.* multiplicación; — **table** tabla de multiplicar.

mul·ti·plic·i·ty [mʌltəplísətɪ] *s.* multiplicidad.

mul·ti·ply [mʌltəplaɪ] *v.* multiplicar(se).

mul·ti·tude [mʌltətjud] *s.* multitud.

mum [mʌm] *adj.* callado, silencioso; **to keep —** estarse (*o* quedarse) callado.

mum·ble [mʌmbl] *v.* murmurar, hablar entre dientes; mascullar; *s.* murmullo; **to talk in a —** mascullar las palabras, hablar entre dientes.

mum·my [mʌmɪ] *s.* momia.

mumps [mʌmps] *s.* parótidas, paperas.

munch [mʌntʃ] *v.* mascar ruidosamente, mascullar.

mun·dane [məndén] *adj.* mundano.

mu·nic·i·pal [mjunísəpl] *adj.* municipal.

mu·nic·i·pal·i·ty [mjunɪsəpǽlətɪ] *s.* municipio; municipalidad.

mu·ni·tion [mjunɪʃən] *s.* munición; — **plant** fábrica de municiones, arsenal; *v.* guarnecer, abastecer de municiones.

mu·ral [mjúrəl] *adj.* & *s.* mural.

mur·der [mɝdəˑ] *s.* asesinato, homicidio; *v.* asesinar.

mur·der·er [mɝdərəˑ] *s.* asesino, homicida.

mur·der·ess [mɝdərɪs] *s.* asesina, homicida.

mur·der·ous [mɝdərəs] *adj.* asesino, homicida.

mur·mur [mɝməˑ] *s.* (*noise*) murmullo; susurro; (*complaint*) queja; *v.* murmurar; susurrar; quejarse.

mus·cle [mʌsl] *s.* músculo.

mus·cu·lar [mʌskjələˑ] *adj.* muscular; musculoso.

muse [mjuz] *v.* meditar; *s.* meditación; **Muse** musa.

mu·se·um [mjuzíəm] *s.* museo.

mush [mʌʃ] *s.* potaje espeso de maíz; masa de maíz; cualquier masa blanda; sentimentalismo.

mush·room [mʌʃrum] *s.* seta, hongo.

mu·sic [mjúzɪk] *s.* música; — **stand** atril.

mu·si·cal [mjúzɪkl] *adj.* musical, músico; melodioso; armonioso; aficionado a la música; — **comedy** zarzuela, comedia musical.

mu·si·cian [mjuzíʃən] *s.* músico.

musk·mel·on [mʌskmelən] *s.* melón.

musk·rat [mʌskræt] *s.* almizclera (*roedor semejante a la rata*).

mus·lin [mʌzlɪn] *s.* muselina.

muss [mʌs] *v.* desarreglar, desordenar; arrugar.

must [mʌst] *v. defect.* (*por lo general se usa sólo en

el presente*) deber; deber de, haber de; tener que.

mus·tache [mʌstæʃ] *s.* bigote, mostacho.

mus·tard [mʌstəd] *s.* mostaza; — **plaster** sinapismo.

mus·ter [mʌstəˑ] *v.* pasar lista o revista; juntarse para una formación militar; reunir(se); **to — out** dar de baja; **to — up one's courage** cobrar valor o ánimo; **to — pass** — pasar lista o revista; ser aceptable (*en una inspección*).

must·y [mʌstɪ] *adj.* mohoso; rancio, añejo.

mu·ta·tion [mjutéʃən] *s.* mutación.

mute [mjut] *adj.* mudo; *s.* mudo; letra muda; sordina (*de violín*).

mu·ti·late [mjútlet] *v.* mutilar.

mu·ti·ny [mjútnɪ] *s.* motín; *v.* amotinarse.

mut·ter [mʌtəˑ] *v.* murmurar, refunfuñar; hablar entre dientes; *s.* murmullo, refunfuño.

mut·ton [mʌtn] *s.* carne de carnero; — **chop** chuleta de carnero.

mu·tu·al [mjútʃuəl] *adj.* mutuo.

muz·zle [mʌzl] *s.* hocico; bozal (*para el hocico*); boca (*de arma de fuego*); *v.* abozalar, poner bozal a; amordazar; hacer callar.

my [maɪ] *adj.* mi (mis).

myr·i·ad [mírɪəd] *s.* miríada, diez mil; millares, gran cantidad.

myrrh [mɝ] *s.* mirra.

myr·tle [mɝtl] *s.* mirto, arrayán.

my·self [maɪsélf] *pron.* yo mismo; me (*como reflexivo*); a mí mismo; **by —** solo; **I — did it** yo mismo lo hice; **I talk to —** hablo conmigo mismo, hablo para mis adentros.

mys·te·ri·ous [mɪstírɪəs] *adj.* misterioso.

mys·ter·y [místrɪ] *s.* misterio.

mys·tic [místɪk] *adj.* & *s.* místico.

mys·ti·cal [místɪkl] *adj.* místico.

myth [mɪθ] *s.* mito, fábula.

my·thol·o·gy [mɪθálədʒɪ] *s.* mitología.

MO

N:n
nab [næb] *v.* agarrar, coger; arrestar.
nag [næg] *s.* rocin, caballejo, jaco; *v.* importunar, irritar (*con repetidos regaños*).

nail [nel] *s.* clavo; uña (*del dedo*); — **file** lima (*para las uñas*); *v.* clavar; clavetear; agarrar, atrapar.

na·ive [naív] *adj.* simple, ingenuo, cándido.

na·ked [nékɪd] *adj.* desnudo.

na·ked·ness [nékɪdnɪs] *s.* desnudez.

name [nem] *s.* (*designation*) nombre; (*fame*) renombre, fama; — **sake** tocayo; **by the — of** nombrado, llamado; apellidado; **family —** apellido; **to call someone -s** motejar o decirle groserías a uno; ponerle apodos a uno; **to make a — for oneself** ganar fama; **what is your —?** ¿cómo se llama Vd.?; *v.* nombrar; mentar, mencionar; llamar; *adj.* onomástico.

name·less [némlɪs] *adj.* sin nombre; anónimo.

name·ly [némlɪ] *adv.* a saber, esto es, es decir.

nap [næp] *s.* siesta; pelo (*de un tejido*); **to take a —** echar un sueño, echar una siesta; *v.* dormitar; echar un sueño; sestear.

nape [nep] *s.* nuca, cogote.

naph·tha [næfθə] *s.* nafta.

nap·kin [næpkɪn] *s.* servilleta.

nar·cis·sus [narsísəs] *s.* narciso.

nar·cot·ic [narkátɪk] *adj.* & *s.* narcótico.

nar·rate [nærét] v. narrar.

nar·ra·tion [næréʃən] s. narración.

nar·ra·tive [nǽrətɪv] adj. narrativo; s. narración; narrativa; relato.

nar·row [nǽro] adj. (cramped) estrecho; angosto; limitado (intolerant) intolerante; — **escape** trance difícil, escapada difícil; — **search** búsqueda esmerada; **narrow-minded** fanático, intolerante; **-s** s. pl. desfiladero, paso; estrecho o estrechos; v. angostar(se), estrechar(se); limitar, restringir, reducir; **-ly** adv. estrechamente; **he -ly escaped** por poco no se escapa.

nar·row·ness [nǽrənɪs] s. (cramped) estrechez, estrechura, angostura; limitación; (intolerance) intolerancia.

na·sal [nézl] adj. nasal.

nas·ti·ness [nǽstɪnɪs] s. suciedad, porquería; grosería.

na·stur·tium [næstʒ́ʃəm] s. mastuerzo.

nas·ty [nǽstɪ] adj. (foul) sucio, asqueroso; feo (indecent) grosero; indecente; **a** — **fall** una caída terrible; **a** — **disposition** un genio horrible.

na·tal [nétl] adj. natal.

na·tion [néʃən] s. nación.

na·tion·al [nǽʃənl] adj. nacional; s. nacional, ciudadano.

na·tion·al·ism [nǽʃənəlɪzm] s. nacionalismo.

na·tion·al·i·ty [næʃənǽlətɪ] s. nacionalidad; **adjective of** — gentilicio.

na·tive [nétɪv] adj. nativo; natal; natural; indígena; del país, Am. criollo; — **of** oriundo de, natural de; s. nativo, natural, indígena; habitante.

na·tiv·i·ty [nətívətɪ] s. nacimiento; natividad (de la Virgen María); **the Nativity** la Navidad.

nat·u·ral [nǽtʃərəl] adj. natural; sencillo, sin afectación; s. becuadro (signo musical); **he is a** — **for that job** tiene aptitud natural para ese puesto; **-ly** adv. naturalmente; con naturalidad.

nat·u·ral·ism [nǽtʃərəlɪzəm] s. naturalismo.

nat·u·ral·ist [nǽtʃərəlɪst] s. naturalista.

nat·u·ral·i·za·tion [nætʃərələzéʃən] s. naturalización.

nat·u·ral·ize [nǽtʃərəlaɪz] v. naturalizar.

nat·u·ral·ness [nǽtʃərəlnts] s. naturalidad.

na·ture [nétʃɚ] s. naturaleza; natural, genio, índole; instinto; especie; **to copy from** — copiar del natural.

naught [nɔt] s. cero; nada.

naugh·ty [nɔ́tɪ] adj. malo, desobediente; travieso, pícaro; malicioso.

nau·se·a [nɔ́zɪə] s. náusea.

nau·se·ate [nɔ́zɪet] v. dar náuseas, dar bascas, asquear, dar asco; sentir náusea; **to be -ed** tener náuseas.

nau·se·at·ing [nɔ́zɪetɪŋ] adj. nauseabundo, asqueroso.

nau·ti·cal [nɔ́tɪkl] adj. náutico, naval.

na·val [névl] adj. naval; — **officer** oficial de marina.

nave [nev] s. nave (de una iglesia).

na·vel [névl] s. ombligo; — **orange** naranja california (sin semillas).

nav·i·ga·ble [nǽvəgəbl] adj. navegable.

nav·i·gate [nǽvəget] v. navegar.

nav·i·ga·tion [nævəgéʃən] s. navegación; náutica.

nav·i·ga·tor [nǽvəgetɚ] s. navegador, navegante.

na·vy [névɪ] s. marina de guerra; armada; — **blue** azul marino; — **yard** astillero, arsenal.

nay [ne] adv. no; no sólo ... sino (que) también; s. no, voto negativo.

near [nɪr] adv. (space, time) cerca; (almost) casi; — **at hand** cerca, a la mano; **I came** — **forgetting to do it** por poco se me olvida hacerlo; **to come (go, draw)** — acercarse; — **sighted** miope; prep. cerca de; — **the end of the month** hacia fines del mes; adj. cercano, próximo; estrecho, íntimo; — **silk** seda imitada; **I had a** — **accident** por poco me sucede un accidente; v. acercarse (a).

near·by [nírbáɪ] adv. cerca, a la mano; adj. cercano, próximo.

near·ly [nírlɪ] adv. casi, cerca de; aproximadamente, próximamente; **I** — **did it** estuve al punto de hacerlo, estuve para hacerlo.

near·ness [nírnɪs] s. cercanía, proximidad.

neat [nit] adj. pulcro, aseado, limpio; ordenado; esmerado; hábil, diestro; **-ly** adv. aseadamente; esmeradamente; ordenadamente; hábilmente.

neat·ness [nítnɪs] s. pulcritud, aseo; limpieza; esmero; claridad.

neb·u·lous [nébjʊləs] adj. nebuloso.

nec·es·sar·i·ly [nesəsérəlɪ] adv. necesariamente; forzosamente.

nec·es·sar·y [nèsəserɪ] adj. necesario; forzoso; **nec·es·sar·ies** s. pl. necesidades, requisitos.

ne·ces·si·tate [nəsésətet] v. necesitar, precisar.

ne·ces·si·ty [nəsésətɪ] s. necesidad.

neck [nek] s. cuello; pescuezo; cerviz; garganta; — **of land** istmo; **low** — escote; — **and** — parejos (en una carrera).

neck·lace [néklɪs] s. collar; gargantilla.

neck·tie [néktaɪ] s. corbata.

ne·crol·o·gy [nɛkrɑ́lədʒɪ] s. necrología.

need [nid] s. (lack) necesidad; (poverty) pobreza; **for** — **of** por falta de; **if** — **be** si fuere menester, en caso de necesidad; v. necesitar; tener necesidad de; hacerle falta a uno; tener que.

need·ful [nídfəl] adj. necesario; necesitado.

nee·dle [nídl] s. aguja.

nee·dle·point [nídlpɔɪnt] s. encaje de mano.

need·less [nídlɪs] adj. innecesario, inútil.

nee·dle·work [nídlwʒk] s. labor, bordado; costura.

need·y [nídɪ] adj. necesitado, menesteroso.

ne'er [nɛr] adv. contr. de never; **ne'er-do-well** s. persona incompetente; haragán.

ne·ga·tion [nɪgéʃən] s. negación; negativa.

neg·a·tive [négətɪv] adj. negativo; s. negativa; negación, partícula o voz negativa; negativa (de una fotografía).

ne·glect [nɪglékt] v. negligencia; descuido; abandono; v. descuidar; desatender; abandonar; **to** — **to** dejar de, olvidar, olvidarse de.

ne·glect·ful [nɪgléktfəl] adj. negligente, descuidado.

neg·li·gence [néglədʒəns] s. negligencia.

neg·li·gent [néglədʒənt] adj. negligente, descuidado.

ne·go·ti·ate [nɪgóʃɪet] v. negociar; agenciar; vencer (un obstáculo o dificultad), dar cima a.

ne·go·ti·a·tion [nɪgoʃɪéʃən] s. negociación.

Ne·gro [nígro] s. & adj. negro.

Ne·groid [nígrɔɪd] adj. negroide.

neigh [ne] s. relincho; v. relinchar.

neigh·bor [nébɚ] s. vecino; prójimo; adj. vecino; cercano.

neigh·bor·hood [nébɚhʊd] s. vecindad; vecindario; inmediación; **in the** — **of a hundred dollars** cerca de cien dólares.

neigh·bor·ing [nébərɪŋ] adj. vecino; cercano; colindante.

nei·ther [níðɚ] pron. ninguno, ni (el) uno ni (el) otro; — **of the two** ninguno de los dos; adj. ninguno; — **one of us** ninguno de nosotros; conj. ni; — ... — **nor** ni ... ni; — **will I** tampoco yo, ni yo tampoco.

ne·ol·o·gism [nɪɑ́lədʒɪzm] s. neologismo.

ne·on [nían] *s.* neón.
ne·o·phyte [níofaɪt] *s.* neófito.
neph·ew [néfju] *s.* sobrino.
ne·phri·tis [nəfráɪtɪs] *s.* nefritis.
nep·o·tism [népətɪzm] *s.* nepotismo.
nerve [nɜv] *s.* (*anatomy*) nervio; (*courage*) valor,
ánimo; audacia; (*effrontery*) descaro; **-s** nervios;
nerviosidad; **to strain every** — esforzarse hasta
más no poder, poner el mayor empeño posible.
nerv·ous [nɜvəs] *adj.* nervioso.
nerv·ous·ness [nɜvəsnɪs] *s.* nerviosidad; agitación.
nest [nɛst] *s.* nido; nidada; — **egg** nidal; ahorros;
— **of baskets (boxes, tables)** juego graduado de
cestas (cajas, mesitas); **wasp's** — avispero; *v.*
anidar.
nes·tle [nésl] *v.* acurrucarse; abrigar(se); anidar.
net [nɛt] *s.* red; malla; tejido de mallas; *adj.* de
mallas, de punto de malla; *v.* redar, enredar,
coger con red; cubrir con una red.
net [nɛt] *adj.* neto; — **price** precio neto; — **profit**
ganancia neta o líquida; *v.* producir una
ganancia neta o líquida; obtener una ganancia
líquida.
net·tle [nétl] *s.* ortiga; *v.* picar, irritar, enfadar.
net·work [nétwɜk] *s.* red; malla; **radio** — red de
estaciones radiofónicas.
neu·ral·gia [nuræld͡ʒə] *s.* neuralgia.
neu·ras·the·ni·a [nurəsθíniə] *s.* neurastenia.
neu·rot·ic [njurátɪk] *adj.* & *s.* neurótico.
neu·ter [njútə] *adj.* neutro.
neu·tral [njútrəl] *adj.* neutral; neutro.
neu·tral·i·ty [njutrælətɪ] *s.* neutralidad.
neu·tral·ize [njútrəlaɪz] *v.* neutralizar.
neu·tron [nútran] *s.* neutrón.
nev·er [névə] *adv.* nunca, jamás; — **mind** no
importa; no haga Vd. caso; no se moleste Vd.;
never-ending perpetuo, eterno; de nunca acabar.
nev·er·the·less [nevəðəlés] *adv.* & *conj.* sin
embargo, no obstante, con todo, empero.
new [nju] *adj.* (*not old*) nuevo; moderno; (*fresh*)
fresco; reciente; *adv.* recién; **—born baby** criatura
recién nacida.
new·com·er [njúkʌmə] *s.* recién llegado.
new·ly [njúlɪ] *adv.* nuevamente, recientemente; —
arrived recién llegado; — **wed** recién casado.
new·ness [njúnɪs] *s.* novedad, calidad de nuevo.
news [njuz] *s.* noticias, nuevas; novedades; **piece of**
— noticia, nueve; **—boy** vendedor de periódicos;
— **reel** película noticiera; película de noticias
mundiales; **—stand** puesto de periódicos.
news·mong·er [njúzmʌŋgə] *s.* chismoso, chismero,
gacetilla.
news·pa·per [njúzpepə] *s.* periódico.
next [nɛkst] *adj.* (*future*) próximo; entrante, que
viene; (*following*) siguiente; contiguo; **in the** —
life en la otra vida; **to be** — **in turn** tocarle a
uno, ser su turno; *adv.* después, luego; — **best**
segundo en cualidad o importancia; *prep.*; — **to**
junto a; al lado de; después de.
nib·ble [níbl] *s.* mordisco; *v.* mordiscar,
mordisquear; picar, morder.
nice [naɪs] *adj.* (*attractive*) fino; bueno; amable,
simpático; lindo; primoroso; (*refined*) refinado;
esmerado; preciso, exacto; **-ly** *adv.* con esmero;
con finura o primor; sutilmente, con delicadeza;
amablemente; bien; **to get along -ly with** llevarse
bien con.
ni·ce·ty [náɪsətɪ] *s.* fineza, finura; delicadeza;
exactitud.
niche [nɪtʃ] *s.* nicho.
nick [nɪk] *s.* mella, desportilladura; **in the** — **of**

---

time en el momento crítico; *v.* mellar,
desportillar.
nick·el [níkl] *s.* níquel; moneda de cinco centavos;
nickel-plated niquelado.
nick·name [níknem] *s.* mote, apodo; *v.* apodar,
poner apodo a.
nic·o·tine [níkətɪn] *s.* nicotina.
niece [nis] *s.* sobrina.
nig·gard·ly [nígədlɪ] *adj.* mezquino, ruin, tacaño;
adv. mezquinamente, ruinmente.
night [naɪt] *s.* noche; **good** —! ¡buenas noches!;
tomorrow — mañana por la noche; *adj.*
nocturno; de noche; — **owl** buho; trasnochador;
— **watchman** sereno, vigilante nocturno.
night·fall [náɪtfɔl] *s.* anochecer, caída de la tarde,
anochecida.
night·gown [náɪtgaʊn] *s.* camisa de dormir, camisa
de noche, *Am.* camisón.
night·in·gale [náɪtɪŋgel] *s.* ruiseñor.
night·ly [náɪtlɪ] *adv.* cada noche, todas las noches;
adj. nocturno, de noche.
night·mare [náɪtmer] *s.* pesadilla.
ni·hil·ism [náɪɪlɪzm] *s.* nihilismo.
nim·ble [nímbl] *adj.* ágil, ligero; listo.
ni·o·bi·um [naɪóbiəm] *s.* niobio.
nip [nɪp] *v.* (*pinch*) pellizcar; (*bite*) mordiscar;
(*frostbite*) marchitar, helar (*por la acción del
frío*); **to** — **in the bud** cortar en germen, destruir
al nacer; **to** — **off** despuntar; podar; *s.* pellizco;
mordisco; trago.
nip·ple [nípl] *s.* teta, tetilla, pezón; pezón de goma.
ni·trate [náɪtret] *s.* nitrato.
ni·tric·a·cid [náɪtrɪkæsɪd] *s.* ácido nítrico.
ni·tro·gen [náɪtrəd͡ʒən] *s.* nitrógeno.
ni·tro·glyc·er·in [naɪtroglísɜɪn] *s.* nitroglicerina.
no [no] *adv.* no; — **longer** ya no; **there is** — **more**
no hay más; *adj.* ningun(o); — **matter how much**
por mucho que; — **one** ninguno, nadie; —
smoking se prohibe fumar; **I have** — **friend** no
tengo ningún amigo; **of** — **use** inútil, sin
provecho; *s.* no, voto negativo.
no·bil·i·ty [nobílətɪ] *s.* nobleza.
no·ble [nóbl] *s.* & *adj.* noble.
no·ble·man [nóblmən] *s.* noble.
no·ble·ness [nóblnɪs] *s.* nobleza.
no·bly [nóblɪ] *adv.* noblemente.
no·bod·y [nóbadɪ] *pron.* nadie, ninguno.
noc·tur·nal [naktɜnl] *adj.* nocturno.
nod [nad] *v.* inclinar la cabeza (*para hacer una
seña, saludar, o asentir*); cabecear, dar cabezadas
(*dormitando*); *s.* inclinación de cabeza, saludo;
señal de asentimiento (*con la cabeza*).
noise [nɔɪz] *s.* ruido; barullo; sonido; *v.* divulgar;
it is being -d about that corre el rumor que.
noise·less [nɔ́ɪzlɪs] *adj.* sin ruido, silencioso, quieto;
-ly *adv.* sin ruido, silenciosamente.
nois·i·ly [nɔ́ɪzɪlɪ] *adv.* ruidosamente.
nois·y [nɔ́ɪzɪ] *adj.* ruidoso.
no·men·cla·ture [nómənklefə] *s.* nomenclatura.
nom·i·nal [námənl] *adj.* nominal.
nom·i·nate [námənet] *v.* nombrar, designar.
nom·i·na·tion [namənéfən] *s.* nombramiento,
nominación.
non·con·form·ist [nankənfɔ́rmɪst] *adj.* & *s.*
disidente.
none [nʌn] *pron.* ninguno; ningunos; nada; **I want**
— **of that** no quiero nada de eso; **that is** — **of**
his business no le importa a él eso; *adv.* no, de
ningún modo; — **the less** no menos; **to be** — **the**
happier for that no estar por eso más contento.
non·en·ti·ty [nanéntətɪ] *s.* nulidad, persona o cosa

inútil.

non·in·ter·ven·tion [nɑnɪntəvénʃən] s. no intervención.

non·par·ti·san [nɑnpártəzən] *adj.* imparcial; independiente.

non·sense [nánsɛns] s. tontería, necedad; disparate, desatino; **to talk** — pavear.

noo·dle [núdl] s. tallarín, fideo, pasta (*para sopa*).

nook [nʊk] s. rincón; **breakfast** — desayunador.

noon [nun] s. mediodía.

noon·day [núnde] s. mediodía; *adj.* meridiano, de mediodía; — **meal** comida de mediodía.

noon·tide [núntaɪd] s. mediodía.

noon·time [núntaɪm] s. mediodía.

noose [nus] s. dogal; lazo, nudo corredizo, *Am.* gaza; *v.* lazar, coger con lazo; hacer un lazo corredizo en.

nor [nɔr] *conj.* ni; **neither** ... — ni ... ni.

Nor·dic [nɔ́rdɪk] *adj.* nórdico.

norm [nɔrm] s. norma.

nor·mal [nɔ́ml] *adj.* normal; s. norma; normal, línea perpendicular.

north [nɔrθ] s. norte; *adj.* septentrional; norteño; del norte; — **pole** polo norte, polo ártico; — **wind** cierzo, norte; **North American** norteamericano; *adv.* al norte, hacia el norte.

north·east [nɔrθíst] *adj.* & s. nordeste; *adv.* hacia el nordeste, rumbo al nordeste.

north·east·ern [nɔrθístən] *adj.* del nordeste, nordeste.

north·ern [nɔ́rðən] *adj.* septentrional; norteño; del norte; hacia el norte; — **lights** aurora boreal.

north·ern·er [nɔ́rðənə] s. norteño, habitante del norte.

north·ward [nɔ́rθwəd] *adv.* hacia el norte, rumbo al norte.

north·west [nɔrθwést] *adj.* & s. noroeste; *adv.* hacia el noroeste.

north·west·ern [nɔrθwéstən] *adj.* noroeste, del noroeste.

Nor·we·gian [nɔrwídʒən] *adj.* & s. noruego.

nose [noz] s. nariz; proa (*de un barco*); — **dive** picada (*de un avión*); *v.* olfatear; **to** — **around** husmear, curiosear.

nos·tal·gi·a [nɑstǽldʒɪə] s. nostalgia, añoranza.

nos·trils [nástrəlz] s. *pl.* narices, ventanas de la nariz.

not [nɑt] *adv.* no; — **at all** de ningún modo; de nada (*contestación a* "thank you"); — **at all sure** nada seguro; — **even a word** ni siquiera una palabra.

no·ta·ble [nótəbl] *adj.* notable.

no·ta·ry [nótərɪ] s. notario.

no·ta·tion [notéʃən] s. notación; apunte; anotación.

notch [nɑtʃ] s. muesca, ranura; hendidura; *v.* ranurar, hacer una ranura en.

note [not] s. nota; apunte, apuntación; **bank** — billete de banco; **promissory** — pagaré, abonaré; *v.* notar, observar, reparar; **to** — **down** apuntar.

note·book [nótbʊk] s. libreta, cuaderno, libro de apuntes.

not·ed [nótɪd] *adj.* notable, célebre, famoso.

note·worth·y [nótwɜðɪ] *adj.* notable, célebre.

noth·ing [nʌ́θɪŋ] s. nada; cero; **for** — por nada; inútilmente; de balde, gratis.

no·tice [nótɪs] s. noticia; aviso; advertencia, anuncio; mención; **to give a short** — avisar a última hora; **to take** — **of** hacer caso de, prestar atención a; *v.* notar, observar; prestar atención a; hacer caso a (*o* de); notificar.

no·tice·a·ble [nótɪsəbl] *adj.* notable; conspicuo;

perceptible.

no·ti·fy [nótəfaɪ] *v.* notificar, avisar.

no·tion [nóʃən] s. noción; idea; capricho; **-s** mercería, artículos menudos (*como alfileres, botones, etc.*), chucherías.

no·to·ri·ous [notórɪəs] *adj.* notorio.

not·with·stand·ing [nɑtwɪθstǽndɪŋ] *prep.* a pesar de; *adv.* & *conj.* no obstante, sin embargo; — **that** a pesar (de) que.

nought = **naught**.

noun [naʊn] s. nombre, sustantivo.

nour·ish [nɜ́ɪʃ] *v.* nutrir, alimentar.

nour·ish·ing [nɜ́ɪʃɪŋ] *adj.* nutritivo, alimenticio.

nour·ish·ment [nɜ́ɪʃmənt] s. nutrimento, sustento, alimento; nutrición.

nov·el [návl] s. novela; *adj.* novel, nuevo; raro, original.

nov·el·ist [návlɪst] s. novelista.

nov·el·ty [návltɪ] s. novedad; innovación; **nov·el·ties** novedades.

No·vem·ber [novémbə] s. noviembre.

nov·ice [návɪs] s. novicio; novato, principiante.

now [naʊ] *adv.* ahora; ya; — **...** — ya ... ya, ora **...** ora; — **and than** de vez en cuando, de cuando en cuando; — **that** ahora que; — **then** ahora bien; **he left just** — salió hace poco, *Riopl., Ch., Andes* recién salió.

now·a·days [náʊədez] *adv.* hoy día.

no·where [nóhwɛr] *adv.* en ninguna parte, a ninguna parte.

nox·ious [nákʃəs] *adj.* nocivo.

nu·cle·us [njúklɪəs] s. núcleo.

nude [njud] *adj.* desnudo.

nudge [nʌdʒ] *v.* codear, tocar con el codo; s. codazo ligero.

nudge [nʌdʒ] *v.* codear, tocar con el codo; s. codzao ligero.

nug·get [nʌ́gɪt] s. pepita; pedazo.

nui·sance [njúsṇs] s. molestia; lata, fastidio; persona o cosa fastidiosa.

null [nʌl] *adj.* nulo; — **and void** nulo e inválido.

nul·li·fy [nʌ́lɪfaɪ] *v.* invalidar; anular.

numb [nʌm] *adj.* entumecido o entumido, aterido; **to become** — entumecerse, entumirse, aterirse; *v.* entumecer.

num·ber [nʌ́mbə] s. número; *v.* numerar; ascender a (*cierto número*); **to** — **him among one's friends** contarle entre sus amigos.

num·ber·less [nʌ́mbəlɪs] *adj.* innumerable, sin número.

nu·mer·al [njúmrəl] s. número, cifra; guarismo; *adj.* numeral.

nu·mer·i·cal [njumérɪk] *adj.* numérico.

nu·mer·ous [njúmrəs] *adj.* numeroso; numerosos, muchos.

nu·mis·mat·ics [numɪsmǽtɪks] s. numismática.

nun [nʌn] s. monja.

nup·tial [nʌ́pʃəl] *adj.* nupcial; **-s** s. *pl.* nupcias, bodas.

nurse [nɜs] s. (*for the sick*) enfermera, enfermero; (*for children*) niñera, ama; *Méx., Ven., Col., Andes* nana, *Am.* manejadora, *Andes* pilmama; *C.A.* china; **wet** — ama de cría; *v.* criar, amamantar, dar de mamar, lactar; mamar; cuidar (*a un enfermo*); abrigar (*rencor*).

nurs·er·y [nɜ́srɪ] s. cuarto para niños; criadero, semillero (*de plantas*); **day** — sala donde se cuida y divierte a los niños.

nur·ture [nɜ́tʃə] s. crianza; nutrimento; *v.* criar; nutrir; cuidar; fomentar.

nut [nʌt] s. nuez (*nombre genérico de varias frutas como la almendra, la castaña, la avellana, etc.*);

tuerca; loco, tipo raro o extravagante.
nut·crack·er [nʌ́tkrækəˑ] *s.* cascanueces.
nut·meg [nʌ́tmɛg] *s.* nuez moscada.
nu·tri·ent [nútrɪənt] *s.* nutritivo.
nu·tri·tion [njuríʃən] *s.* nutrición; nutrimento, alimento.
nu·tri·tious [njutríʃəs] *adj.* nutritivo, alimenticio.
nu·tri·tive [njútrɪtɪv] *adj.* nutritivo.
nut·shell [nʌ́tʃɛ] *s.* cáscara de nuez (*o de otro fruto semejante*); **in a** — en suma, en breve, en pocas palabras.
nymph [nɪmf] *s.* ninfa.

O:o   **oak** [ok] *s.* roble; encina; — **grove** robledo o robledal; **live** — encina siempreverde.
oar [or] *s.* remo; *v.* remar, bogar.
o·a·sis [oésɪs] *s.* oasis.
oat [ot] *s.* avena (*planta*); **-s** avena, granos de avena.
oath [oθ] *s.* juramento; blasfemia, reniego.
oat·meal [ótmɪl] *s.* harina de avena; gachas de avena.
o·be·di·ence [əbídɪəns] *s.* obediencia.
o·be·di·ent [əbídɪənt] *adj.* obediente.
ob·e·lisk [áblɪsk] *s.* obelisco.
o·be·si·ty [obisətɪ] *s.* obesidad, gordura.
o·bey [əbé] *v.* obedecer.
ob·ject [ábdʒɪkt] *s.* objeto; cosa; complemento (*del verbo*); [əbdʒékt] *v.* objetar; oponerse; tener inconveniente.
ob·jec·tion [əbdʒékʃən] *s.* objeción, reparo; inconveniente.
ob·jec·tive [əbdʒéktɪv] *adj.* objetivo; — **case** caso complementario; *s.* objetivo; fin, propósito.
ob·li·gate [ábləget] *v.* obligar, constreñir; comprometer.
ob·li·ga·tion [abləgéʃən] *s.* (*duty*) obligación; deber (*debt*) deuda; **to be under** — to estar obligado a; estar agradecido a, deber favores a.
o·blig·a·to·ry [əblígətorɪ] *adj.* obligatorio.
o·blige [əbláidʒ] *v.* obligar; complacer; **much -ed!** ¡muchas gracias! ¡muy agradecido!; **to be very much -ed to someone** quedar muy agradecido con alguien.
o·blig·ing [əbláidʒɪŋ] *adj.* complaciente, obsequioso, comedido, cortés.
o·blique [əblík] *adj.* oblicuo.
o·blit·er·ate [əblítəret] *v.* borrar; arrasar, destruir.
o·bliv·i·on [əblívɪən] *s.* olvido.
o·bliv·i·ous [əblívɪəs] *adj.* olvidado, abstraído.
ob·long [ábloŋ] *adj.* cuadrilongo; oblongo.
ob·nox·ious [əbnákʃəs] *adj.* ofensivo; molesto; odioso.
o·boe [óbo] *s.* oboe.
ob·scene [əbsín] *adj.* obsceno.
ob·scen·i·ty [əbsénətɪ] *s.* obscenidad, indecencia.
ob·scure [əbskjúr] *adj.* obscuro; *v.* obscurecer; ofuscar.
ob·scu·ri·ty [əbskjúrətɪ] *s.* obscuridad.
ob·se·quies [ábsɪkwiz] *s.* exequias, honras, funerales.
ob·se·qui·ous [əbsíkwɪəs] *adj.* obsequioso; servil, zalamero.
ob·serv·a·ble [əbzɚvəbl] *adj.* observable.
ob·ser·vance [əbzɚvəns] *s.* observancia; ceremonia, rito.
ob·ser·vant [əbzɚvənt] *adj.* observador; observante.

ob·ser·va·tion [abzɚvéʃən] *s.* observación.
ob·ser·va·to·ry [əbzɚvətorɪ] *s.* observatorio; mirador.
ob·serve [əbzɚv] *v.* observar; guardar (*las fiestas religiosas*); celebrar (*una fiesta*).
ob·serv·er [əbzɚvɚ] *s.* observador.
ob·sess [əbsɛs] *v.* obsesionar, causar obsesión.
ob·ses·sion [əbsɛ́ʃən] *s.* obsesión; idea fija.
ob·so·lete [ábsəlit] *adj.* anticuado; desusado.
ob·sta·cle [ábstəkl] *s.* obstáculo.
ob·stet·rics [abstɛ́trɪks] *s.* obstetricia.
ob·sti·na·cy [ábstənəsɪ] *s.* obstinación, terquedad, porfía.
ob·sti·nate [ábstənɪt] *adj.* obstinado, terco, porfiado.
ob·strep·er·ous [əbstrɛ́pɚəs] *adj.* estrepitoso, turbulento.
ob·struct [əbstrʌ́kt] *v.* obstruir.
ob·struc·tion [əbstrʌ́kʃən] *s.* obstrucción; impedimento, estorbo.
ob·tain [əbtén] *v.* obtener, conseguir, alcanzar, adquirir.
ob·tain·a·ble [əbténəbl] *adj.* obtenible, asequible.
ob·tru·sive [əbtrúsɪv] *adj.* intruso, entremetido.
ob·vi·ate [ábvɪet] *v.* obviar; allanar (*una dificultad*).
ob·vi·ous [ábvɪəs] *adj.* obvio, evidente.
oc·ca·sion [əkéʒən] *s.* (*timely*) ocasión; (*chance*) oportunidad; (*cause*) motivo, causa; (*event*) acontecimiento; *v.* ocasionar, causar.
oc·ca·sion·al [əkéʒənl] *adj.* ocasional; infrecuente; poco frecuente; **-ly** *adv.* de vez en cuando, a veces.
oc·ci·den·tal [aksədéntl] *adj.* & *s.* occidental.
oc·clu·sive [oklúsɪv] *adj.* & *s.* oclusivo.
oc·cult [əkʌ́lt] *adj.* oculto, misterioso.
oc·cu·pant [ákjəpənt] *s.* ocupante; inquilino.
oc·cu·pa·tion [akjəpéʃən] *s.* ocupación; trabajo, empleo, oficio.
oc·cu·py [ákjəpaɪ] *v.* ocupar.
oc·cur [əkɚ́] *v.* ocurrir, suceder; **to** — **to one** ocurrírsele a uno, venirle a la mente.
oc·cur·rence [əkɚ́əns] *s.* ocurrencia, suceso, caso, acontecimiento.
o·cean [óʃən] *s.* océano.
o·cean·og·ra·phy [oʃənágrəfɪ] *s.* oceanografía.
o·cher [okɚ] *s.* ocre.
o'clock [əklák] *contr. de* **of the clock; it is two** — son las dos.
oc·tave [áktɪv] *s.* octava.
Oc·to·ber [aktóbɚ] *s.* octubre.
oc·u·list [ákəlɪst] *s.* oculista.
odd [ad] *adj.* (*rare*) extraño, singular, raro; (*not even*) non, impar; — **change** suelto, cambio sobrante; — **moments** momentos libres, momentos de ocio; — **shoe** zapato suelto (*sin compañero*); — **volume** tomo suelto; **thirty** — treinta y tantos, treinta y pico; **-ly** *adv.* extrañamente, de un modo raro.
odd·i·ty [ádətɪ] *s.* rareza.
odds [adz] *s. pl. o sing.* diferencia, disparidad (*en apuestas*); ventaja, puntos de ventaja (*en apuestas*); — **and ends** retazos, trozos sobrantes, pedacitos varios; **the** — **are against me** la suerte me es contraria, estoy de mala suerte; **to be at -s with** estar reñido o enemistado con.
ode [od] *s.* oda.
o·di·ous [ódɪəs] *adj.* odioso.
o·dor [odɚ] *s.* olor; **bad** — mal olor, hedor.
o·dor·ous [ódərəs] *adj.* oloroso.
o'er [or] *contr. de* **over.**
of [ɑv, ʌv] *prep.* de; — **course** por supuesto, claro,

ya se ve; — late últimamente; a quarter — five
las cinco menos cuarto; to smell — oler a; to
taste — saber a.

off [ɔf] adv. (distant) lejos, fuera, a distancia; (not
attached) suelto; apagado (la luz); (equivale al
reflexivo se en ciertos verbos: marcharse, irse,
etc.); — and on de vez en cuando; a intervalos;
ten cents — rebaja de diez centavos; ten miles
— a una distancia de diez millas; to take a day
— ausentarse por un día; descansar por un día;
adj. ausente; distante, más remoto; quitado; the
— side el lado más remoto; with his hat — con el
sombrero quitado; the electricity is — está
cortada la electricidad; to be — in one's
accounts estar errado en sus cuentas; to be — to
war haberse ido a la guerra; to be well — ser
persona acomodada, estar en buenas
circunstancias; prep. lejos de; offcolor de mal
color; verde (indecente); — shore a vista de la
costa; — standard de calidad inferior; — the
road deviado, descarriado; a un lado del camino;
to be — duty no estar de turno; estar libre.
of·fend [əfɛnd] v. ofender.
of·fend·er [əfɛndəʳ] s. ofensor; transgresor,
delincuente.
of·fense [əfɛns] s. ofensa; agravio; delito, culpa; no
— was meant lo hice (o lo dije) sin malicia;
weapon of — arma ofensiva.
of·fen·sive [əfɛnsɪv] adj. ofensivo; s. ofensiva.
of·fer [ɔfəʳ] v. ofrecer; to — to do it ofrecerse a
hacerlo; s. oferta; ofrecimiento; promesa;
propuesta.
of·fer·ing [ɔfərɪŋ] s. ofrenda; oferta, ofrecimiento.
off·hand [ɔfhænd] adv. de improviso, por el
momento, sin pensarlo, impensadamente; adj.
impensado, hecho de improviso; in an —
manner con indiferencia; descuidadamente; sin
plan.
of·fice [ɔfɪs] s. (function) oficio; cargo; función;
(place) oficina, despacho; — building edificio
para oficinas; post — correo; box — taquilla,
Ch., Riopl. boletería; through the good -s of por
el intermedio de.
of·fi·cer [ɔfəsəʳ] s. (office holder) oficial; funcionario;
(police) policía, gendarme; agente de policía; v.
comandar, dirigir (como oficial); proveer de
oficiales.
of·fi·cial [əfɪʃəl] adj. oficial; s. oficial, funcionario;
empleado público.
of·fi·ci·ate [əfɪʃɪet] v. oficiar.
of·fi·cious [əfɪʃəs] adj. oficioso, intruso,
entremetido.
off·set [ɔfsɛt] v. compensar por; contrapesar.
off·shore [ɔfʃór] adj. & adv. (land) terral; (at sea)
lejos de la playa.
off·spring [ɔfˌsprɪŋ] s. prole, hijos, descendientes;
hijo, vástago; resultado, consecuencia.
off·stage [ɔfstédʒ] adv. & adj. entre bastidores.
oft [ɔft] = often.
of·ten [ɔfən] adv. muchas veces, con frecuencia,
frecuentemente, a menudo; how —? ¿cuántas
veces?; ¿cada cuándo?
o·gre [ógəʳ] s. ogro, gigante, monstruo.
oil [ɔɪl] s. aceite; óleo; petróleo; — can alcuza;
— painting pintura al óleo; — well pozo de
petróleo; motor — aceite para motores; v.
aceitar, engrasar, lubricar; untar.
oil·cloth [ɔɪlklɔθ] s. hule, tela de hule.
oil·y [ɔɪlɪ] adj. aceitoso, oleoso; grasiento.
oint·ment [ɔɪntmənt] s. ungüento.
O.K. [óké] adj. bueno; corriente, convenido; adv.

bien; it's — está bien; to give one's — dar el
V°. B°. (visto bueno); v. dar el V°. B°., aprobar.
old [old] adj. viejo; antiguo; añejo; — maid
solterona; — man anciano, viejo; — wine vino
añejo; days of — días de antaño; how — are
you? ¿cuántos años tiene Vd.? ¿qué edad tiene
Vd.?; to be — enough to ... tener bastante edad
para ...; to be an — hand at ser ducho en, ser
muy perito o experto en.
old·en [óldn] adj. viejo, antiguo, de antaño.
old-fash·ioned [óldfæʃənd] adj. pasado de moda;
anticuado; chapado a la antigua.
old-time [óldtáɪm] adj. vetusto, de tiempos
antiguos; de antaño.
old-tim·er [óldtáɪməʳ] s. antiguo residente.
o·le·an·der [óliændəʳ] s. adelfa.
ol·fac·to·ry [ɔlfæktərɪ] adj. olfatorio.
ol·ive [álɪv] s. oliva, aceituna; — grove olivar;
— oil aceite de oliva; — tree olivo; — branch
ramo de olivo; adj. aceitunado, verde aceituna.
O·lym·pi·ad [olímpiæd] s. olimpiada.
O·lym·pic [olímpɪk] adj. olímpico.
om·e·let [ámlɪt] s. tortilla de huevos.
o·men [ómən] s. agüero, presagio.
om·i·nous [ámənəs] adj. siniestro, de mal agüero,
amenazador.
o·mis·sion [omíʃən] s. omisión.
o·mit [omít] v. omitir; dejar de.
om·nip·o·tent [amnípətənt] adj. omnipotente,
todopoderoso.
on [ɑn] prep. en; a; sobre, encima de; — all sides
por todos lados; — arriving al llegar; — board
a bordo; en el tren; — condition that con la
condición de que; — credit al fiado; — foot a
pie; — horseback a caballo; — Monday el lunes;
— purpose a propósito, adrede; — sale de venta;
— time a tiempo; a plazo; adv. adelante;
farther — más adelante; later — después; —
and — sin parar, sin cesar, continuamente; adj.
puesto; his hat is — lleva puesto el sombrero;
the light is — está encendida la luz.
once [wʌns] adv. una vez; en otro tiempo; — and
for all una vez por todas, definitivamente; in
a while de vez en cuando; — upon a time
érase que se era; en otro tiempo; at — al punto;
a un mismo tiempo; just this — siquiera esta
vez, sólo esta vez; conj. una vez que, cuando;
luego que.
one [wʌn] adj. un, uno; — hundred cien, ciento;
— thousand mil; his — chance su única
oportunidad; the — and only el único; s.
one-armed manco; one-eyed tuerto; one-sided de
un solo lado; unilateral; parcial; desigual;
one-way de un sentido; s. & pron. uno; —
another uno a otro; — by — uno a uno; uno
por uno; the — who el que, la que; the green —
el verde; this — éste, ésta.
one·self [wʌnsɛlf] pron. se (reflexivo); to speak to
— hablar consigo mismo; by — solo; por sí, por
sí solo.
on·go·ing [ángoɪŋ] adj. que está haciéndose;
corriente; que cursa.
on·ion [ánjən] s. cebolla; — patch cebollar.
on·look·er [ánlʊkəʳ] s. espectador, mirón.
on·ly [ónlɪ] adj. solo, único; adv. sólo, solamente;
conj. sólo que.
on·set [ánsɛt] s. embestida, ataque, impulso inicial,
primer ímpetu; attanque.
on·to [ántu] prep. a; sobre.
on·ward [ánwəd] adv. adelante; hacia adelante.
on·yx [ánɪks] s. onix, ónice.

ooze [uz] *v.* rezumar(se), escurrir(se).

o·pal [ópl] *s.* ópalo.

o·paque [opék] *adj.* opaco; mate.

o·pen [ópən] *v.* abrir(se); **to** — **into** comunicarse con, tener paso a; **to** — **onto** dar a, caer a, mirar a; *adj.* abierto; franco, sincero; expuesto (a); — **country** campo raso, campo abierto; — **question** cuestión discutible; — **to temptation** expuesto a caer en la tentación; — **winter** invierno sin nieve; **in the** — **air** al (o en el) aire libre; **open-minded** receptivo; de amplias miras; —**mouthed** boquiabierto, con la boca abierta; **open-end** [ópənénd] sin límites; sin trabas; *s.* campo raso, aire libre.

o·pen·ing [ópənɪŋ] *s.* (*hole*) abertura; (*beginning*) apertura, comienzo; (*clearing*) claro (*en un bosque*); (*vacancy*) puesto vacante; oportunidad; *adj.* primero; — **night of a play** estreno de una comedia; **the** — **number** el primer número (*de un programa*).

op·er·a [ápərə] *s.* ópera; — **glasses** gemelos; — **house** ópera, teatro de la ópera; **comic** — ópera cómica, zarzuela.

op·er·ant [ápʒənt] *adj.* operante.

op·er·ate [ápəret] *v.* (*function*) operar; funcionar; obrar; (*manage*) maniobrar; manejar; **to** — **on a person** operar a una persona.

op·er·a·tion [apəréʃən] *s.* (*function*) operación; funcionamiento; (*management*) manipulación; manejo; maniobra; **to be in** — funcionar, estar funcionando.

op·er·a·tor [ápəretɚ] *s.* operador, cirujano; maquinista, mecánico, operario; especulador (*en la Bolsa*); **mine** — explotador de minas; **telegraph** — telegrafista; **telephone** — telefonista.

op·e·ret·ta [apərétə] *s.* opereta, zarzuela.

o·pin·ion [əpínjən] *s.* opinión, parecer.

o·pi·um [ópiəm] *s.* opio.

o·pos·sum [əpásəm] *s.* zarigüeya.

op·po·nent [əpónənt] *s.* contrario, adversario, antagonista.

op·por·tune [apətjún] *adj.* oportuno; a propósito.

op·por·tun·ist [apətúnıst] *s.* oportunista.

op·por·tu·ni·ty [apətjúnətɪ] *s.* oportunidad; ocasión.

op·pose [əpóz] *v.* oponer(se); oponerse a.

op·pos·ing [əpózɪŋ] *adj.* opuesto, contrario.

op·po·site [ápəzɪt] *adj.* (*contrary*) opuesto; contrario; (*facing*) frontero, de enfrente; — **to** frente a; *prep.* frente a, en frente de; *s.* contrario; **the** — lo opuesto, lo contrario.

op·po·si·tion [apəzíʃən] *s.* oposición; resistencia.

op·press [əprɛs] *v.* oprimir; agobiar.

op·pres·sion [əpréʃən] *s.* opresión.

op·pres·sive [əprɛsıv] *adj.* (*harsh*) opresivo; (*distressing*) abrumador; gravoso; bochornoso, sofacante.

op·pres·sor [əprésɚ] *s.* opresor.

op·tic [áptık] *adj.* óptico; **-s** *s.* óptica.

op·ti·cal [áptık] *adj.* óptico.

op·ti·cian [aptíʃən] *s.* óptico.

op·ti·mism [áptəmizəm] *s.* optimismo.

op·ti·mist [áptəmıst] *s.* optimista.

op·ti·mis·tic [aptəmístık] *adj.* optimista.

op·tion [ápʃən] *s.* opción, derecho de escoger; alternativa.

op·tion·al [ápʃənl] *adj.* discrecional.

op·u·lence [ápjələns] *s.* opulencia, riqueza, abundancia.

op·u·lent [ápjələnt] *adj.* opulento, rico; abundante.

or [ɔr] *conj.* o; u (*delante de o, ho*).

or·a·cle [ɔ́rəkl] *s.* oráculo.

o·ral [ɔ́rəl] *adj.* oral; bucal.

or·ange [ɔ́rɪndʒ] *s.* naranja; — **blossom** azahar; — **grove** naranjal; — **tree** naranjo; *adj.* de naranja; anaranjado.

or·ange·ade [ɔrɪndʒéd] *s.* naranjada.

o·ra·tion [oréʃən] *s.* discurso, peroración, arenga.

or·a·tor [ɔ́rətɚ] *s.* orador.

or·a·to·ry [ɔ́rətorɪ] *s.* oratoria, elocuencia; oratorio, capilla.

orb [ɔrb] *s.* orbe.

or·bit [ɔ́rbɪt] *s.* órbita; *v.* moverse en órbita.

or·bit·al [ɔ́rbɪtl] *adj.* orbital.

or·chard [ɔ́rtʃɚd] *s.* huerto.

or·ches·tra [ɔ́rkɪstrə] *s.* orquesta; — **seat** butaca, luneta, *Am.* platea (*de orquesta*).

or·ches·trate [ɔ́rkɪstret] *v.* orquestar.

or·chid [ɔ́rkɪd] *s.* orquídea.

or·dain [ɔrdén] *v.* ordenar; decretar.

or·deal [ɔrdíl] *s.* prueba penosa.

or·der [ɔ́rdɚ] *s.* (*request*) orden (*s.*); pedido; (*group*) clase; orden; (*arrangement*) orden (*m.*); **holy -s** órdenes sagradas; **in** — en orden; **in** buen estado; en regla; **in** — **to** para, a fin de; **in** — **that** para que, a fin de que; **made to** — mandado hacer, hecho a la medida; **to be out of** — estar descompuesto; estar desordenado; no estar en regla; *v.* ordenar; mandar; arreglar; pedir (*hacer un pedido*); **to** — **away** echar, despedir, expulsar.

or·der·ly [ɔ́rdɚlı] *adj.* ordenado; en orden, bien arreglado; bien disciplinado; *s.* ordenanza (*soldado*); asistente de hospital.

or·di·nal [ɔ́rdɪnl] *adj.* ordinal; — **number** número ordinal.

or·di·nance [ɔ́rdnəns] *s.* ordenanza, ley, reglamento.

or·di·nar·i·ly [ɔrdŋérəlɪ] *adv.* ordinariamente, por lo común.

or·di·nar·y [ɔ́rdŋɛrɪ] *adj.* ordinario.

ore [or] *s.* mineral.

or·gan [ɔ́rgən] *s.* órgano; **hand** — organillo.

or·gan·ic [ɔrgǽnɪk] *adj.* orgánico; constitutivo, fundamental.

or·gan·ism [ɔ́rgənizəm] *s.* organismo.

or·gan·ist [ɔ́rgənıst] *s.* organista.

or·gan·i·za·tion [ɔrgənəzéʃən] *s.* organización; organismo; entidad; sociedad.

or·gan·ize [ɔ́rgənaɪz] *v.* organizar(se).

or·gan·iz·er [ɔ́rgənaɪzɚ] *s.* organizador.

or·gy [ɔ́rdʒɪ] *s.* orgía.

o·ri·ent [ɔ́rɪɛnt] *s.* oriente; *v.* orientar.

o·ri·en·tal [ɔrɪéntl] *adj.* & *s.* oriental.

o·ri·en·tate [ɔ́rɪɛntet] *v.* orientar.

o·ri·en·ta·tion [ɔrɪɛntéʃən] *s.* orientación.

or·i·fice [ɔ́rəfıs] *s.* orificio.

or·i·gin [ɔ́rədʒɪn] *s.* origen; procedencia.

or·ig·i·nal [ərídʒənl] *adj.* & *s.* original; **-ly** *adv.* originalmente, originariamente; en el principio, al principio.

or·ig·i·nal·i·ty [ərıdʒənǽlətɪ] *s.* originalidad.

or·ig·i·nate [ərídʒənet] *v.* originar(se).

o·ri·ole [ɔ́rɪol] *s.* oriol (*pájaro*).

Or·lon [ɔ́rlan] *s.* orlón.

or·na·ment [ɔ́rnəmənt] *s.* ornamento, adorno; [ɔ́rnəmɛnt] *v.* ornamentar, adornar, ornar.

or·na·men·tal [ɔrnəméntl] *adj.* ornamental, de adorno, decorativo.

or·nate [ɔrnét] *adj.* ornado, adornado en exceso; — **style** estilo florido.

or·ni·thol·o·gy [ɔrnəθálədʒɪ] *s.* ornitología.

or·phan [ɔ́rfən] *adj.* & *s.* huérfano; — **asylum** hospicio, orfanato, asilo de huérfanos; *v.* dejar huérfano a.

or·tho·dox [ɔ́rθədɑks] *adj.* ortodoxo.

or·thog·ra·phy [ɔrθɑ́grəfɪ] *s.* ortografía.

os·cil·late [ɑ́sələt] *v.* oscilar.

os·cil·la·to·ry [ɑ́sələtɔrɪ] *adj.* oscilatorio.

os·mi·um [ázmɪəm] *s.* osmio.

os·ten·ta·tion [ɑstəntéʃən] *s.* ostentación, boato.

os·ten·ta·tious [ɑstəntéʃəs] *adj.* ostentoso.

os·trich [ɔ́strɪtʃ] *s.* avestruz.

oth·er [ʌ́ðɚ] *adj.* & *s.* otro; — **than** otra cosa que; más que; **every** — **day** cada dos días, un día sí y otro no; **some** — **day** otro día.

oth·er·wise [ʌ́ðɚwaɪz] *adv.* de otro modo; en otros respetos; *adj.* otro, diferente.

ot·ter [ɑ́tɚ] *s.* nutria; piel de nutria.

ought [ɔt] *v. defect.* (*por lo general se traduce por el presente y el condicional de* deber) debo, debes, etc.; debería, deberías, etc.; debiera, debieras, etc.

ounce [aʊns] *s.* onza.

our [aʊr] *adj.* nuestro (nuestra, nuestros, nuestras).

ours [aʊrz] *pron. pos.* nuestro (nuestra, nuestros, nuestras); el nuestro (la nuestra, los nuestros, las nuestras); **a friend of** — un amigo nuestro.

our·selves [aʊrsélvz] *pron.* nosotros mismos; nos (*reflexivo*); a nosotros mismos; **we** — nosotros mismos; **by** — solos; por nosotros; *véase* **herself.**

oust [aʊst] *v.* echar, expulsar.

out [aʊt] *adv.* fuera; afuera; hacia fuera; — **of fear** por miedo, de miedo; — **of humor** malhumorado; — **of money** sin dinero; — **of print** agotado; — **of touch with** aislado de, sin contacto con; — **of tune** desentonado; **made** — **of** hecho de; **to fight it** — decidirlo luchando; **to have it** — **with** habérselas con; **to speak** — hablar francamente; *adj.* ausente; apagado; — **and** — **criminal** criminal empedernido; — **and** — **refusal** una negativa redonda; — **size** tamaño poco común o extraordinario; **before the week is** — antes de que termine la semana; **the book is just** — acaba de publicarse el libro; **the secret is** — se ha divulgado el secreto.

out·break [áʊtbrek] *s.* (*eruption*) erupción; (*revolt*) motin, insurrección, tumulto; (*attack*) ataque, arranque (*de ira*); **at the** — **of the war** al estallar la guerra.

out·burst [áʊtbɜst] *s.* explosión; estallido; arranque (*de pasión*); erupción.

out·cast [áʊtkæst] *adj.* excluido, desechado; desterrado; *s.* paria (*persona excluida de la sociedad*).

out·come [áʊtkʌm] *s.* resultado, consecuencia.

out·cry [áʊtkraɪ] *s.* grito; clamor.

out·door [áʊtdor] *adj.* externo; fuera de la casa; — **games** juegos al aire libre.

out·doors [aʊtdórz] *adv.* puertas afuera, fuera de casa, al aire libre, al raso; *s.* aire libre, campo raso, campiña.

out·er [áʊtɚ] *adj.* exterior, externo.

out·fit [áʊtfɪt] *s.* equipo; pertrechos; *v.* equipar, habilitar, aviar.

out·go·ing [áʊtgoɪŋ] *adj.* (*leaving*) saliente; (*extrovert*) extrovertido.

out·guess [aʊtgés] *v.* anticipar; madrugar.

out·ing [áʊtɪŋ] *s.* excursión, gira (jira), caminata.

out·law [áʊtlɔ] *s.* forajido, bandido; prófugo, fugitivo; *v.* proscribir, declarar ilegal.

out·lay [áʊtle] *s.* gasto, desembolso; [áʊtlé] *v.* gastar, desembolsar.

out·let [áʊtlet] *s.* salida; desaguadero, desagüe; escurridero.

out·line [áʊtlaɪn] *s.* (*abstract*) bosquejo, esbozo; (*boundary*) contorno; *v.* bosquejar, esbozar; delinear.

out·live [aʊtlív] *v.* sobrevivir.

out·look [áʊtlʊk] *s.* vista; perspectiva.

out·ly·ing [áʊtlaɪɪŋ] *adj.* circundante, exterior, remoto (*del centro*).

out-of-date [áʊtəvdét] *adj.* fuera de moda, anticuado.

out·post [áʊtpost] *s.* avanzada.

out·put [áʊtpʊt] *s.* rendimiento; producción total.

out·rage [áʊtredʒ] *s.* ultraje; *v.* ultrajar.

out·ra·geous [aʊtrédʒəs] *adj.* afrentoso; atroz.

out·ran [aʊtrǽn] *pret. de* **to outrun.**

out·right [aʊtráɪt] *adv.* & *adj.* sin rodeo; cabal; completo.

out·run [aʊtrʌ́n] *v.* aventajar (*en una carrera*); dejar atrás; *p.p. de* **to outrun.**

out·set [áʊtset] *s.* comienzo, principio.

out·shine [aʊtʃáɪn] *v.* eclipsar, sobrepasar (*en brillo o lucidez*).

out·shone [aʊtʃón] *pret.* & *p.p. de* **to outshine.**

out·side [áʊtsáɪd] *adj.* (*external*) exterior; externo; (*foreign*) foráneo, extranjero; *adv.* fuera, afuera; fuera de casa; *prep.* fuera de; *s.* exterior, parte exterior; superficie; lado de afuera; **in a week, at the** — en una semana, a lo sumo; **to close on the** — cerrar por fuera.

out·sid·er [aʊtsáɪdɚ] *s.* foráneo, persona de fuera; extraño.

out·skirts [áʊtskɜts] *s. pl.* alrededores, arrabales, cercanías.

out·spo·ken [áʊtspókən] *adj.* franco, francote, *Ven., Méx., C.A., Carib.* claridoso.

out·stand·ing [áʊtstǽndɪŋ] *adj.* sobresaliente; destacado, notable; — **bills** cuentas por cobrar; — **debts** deudas por pagar.

out·stretched [aʊtstrétʃt] *adj.* extendido; **with** — **arms** con los brazos abiertos.

out·ward [áʊtwəd] *adj.* (*external*) exterior, externo; (*apparent*) aparente; superficial; *adv.* fuera, hacia fuera; — **bound** que sale, de salida; para fuera, para el extranjero; **-ly** *adv.* exteriormente; por fuera; aparentemente.

out·weigh [aʊtwé] *v.* exceder en peso o valor; sobrepujar.

o·val [óvl] *adj.* oval, ovalado; *s.* óvalo.

o·va·ry [óvərɪ] *s.* ovario.

o·va·tion [ovéʃən] *s.* ovación.

ov·en [ʌ́vən] *s.* horno.

o·ver [óvɚ] *prep.* sobre; por; por encima de; encima de; a través de; al otro lado de; más de; — **night** por la noche, durante la noche; (*véase* **overnight**); — **to a; all** — **the city** por toda la ciudad; *adv.* encima; al otro lado; otra vez, de nuevo; — **again** otra vez, de nuevo; — **against** en contraste con; — **and** — una y otra vez, repetidas veces; — **curious** demasiado curioso; — **generous** demasiado generoso; — **here** acá, aquí; — **there** allá, allí; **two years and** — más de dos años; **to do it** — hacerlo otra vez, volver a hacerlo; *adj.* excesivo; **it is all** — ya se acabó, se ha acabado; ha pasado.

o·ver·alls [óvɚɔlz] *s. pl. Am.* overol, overoles (*pantalones de trabajo*).

o·ver·ate [ovɚét] *pret. de* **to overeat.**

o·ver·board [óvɚbord] *adv.* al mar, al agua.

o·ver·came [ovɚkém] *pret. de* **to overcome.**

o·ver·cast [óvəkæst] *adj.* encapotado, nublado; **to become** — encapotarse, nublarse; [ovəkæst] *v.* nublar o anublar; sobrehilar (*dar puntadas sobre el borde de una tela*); *pret.* & *p.p. de* **to overcast.**

o·ver·charge [ovətʃárdʒ] *v.* cargar demasiado; cobrar demasiado.

o·ver·coat [óvəkot] *s.* sobretodo, abrigo.

o·ver·come [ovəkʌ́m] *v.* vencer; rendir; *p.p.* & *adj.* vencido; rendido; agobiado; **to be** — **by weariness** estar rendido de fatiga.

o·ver·due [ovədú] *adj.* atrasado; vencido sin pago.

o·ver·eat [ovəít] *v.* hartarse.

o·ver·eat·en [ovəítn] *p.p. de* **to overeat.**

o·ver·ex·cite [óvəriksáit] *v.* sobreexcitar.

o·ver·flow [óvəflo] *s.* derrame, desbordamiento; inundación; superabundancia; [ovəfló] *v.* derramarse, desbordarse; rebosar; inundar.

o·ver·grown [óvəgrón] *adj.* denso, frondoso, poblado (*de follaje, herbaje, etc.*); — **boy** muchachón, muchacho demasiado crecido para su edad.

o·ver·hang [ovəhǽŋ] *v.* colgar por encima de; proyectarse o sobresalir por encima de; adornar con colgaduras; amenazar (*dícese de un desastre o calamidad*).

o·ver·haul [ovəhól] *v.* reparar (*de cabo a rabo*); remendar; alcanzar (*en una carrera*).

o·ver·head [óvəhɛd] *s.* gastos generales (*renta, seguro, alumbrado, calefacción, etc.*); *adj. de* arriba; elevado; — **expenses** gastos generales; [óvəhɛ́d] *adv.* encima de la cabeza, arriba; en lo alto.

o·ver·hear [ovəhír] *v.* oír por casualidad, alcanzar a oír, acertar a oír.

o·ver·heard [ovəhɜ́d] *pret.* & *p.p. de* **to overhear.**

o·ver·heat [óvəhít] *v.* recalentar(se); calentar(se) demasiado.

o·ver·hung [ovəhʌ́ŋ] *pret.* & *p.p. de* **to overhang.**

o·ver·land [óvələænd] *adv.* & *adj.* por tierra.

o·ver·lap [ovəlǽp] *v.* solapar.

o·ver·lay [ovəlé] *v.* cubrir; incrustar.

o·ver·load [ovəlód] *v.* sobrecargar; [óvəlod] *s.* sobrecarga.

o·ver·look [ovəlúk] *v.* mirar a (*desde lo alto*); dar a, tener vista a; pasar por alto, omitir; perdonar (*faltas*); descuidar, no notar; inspeccionar, examinar.

o·ver·ly [óvəli] *adv.* excesivamente.

o·ver·night [óvənáit] *adv.* durante la noche; toda la noche; *adj. de* noche; nocturno; — **bag** saco de noche; — **trip** viaje de una noche.

o·ver·pass [óvəpǽs] *v.* viaducto.

o·ver·pow·er [ovəpáuə] *v.* subyugar, abrumar, vencer.

o·ver·ran [ovəfǽn] *pret. de* **to overrun.**

o·ver·ride [ovəráid] *v.* anular; invalidar.

o·ver·rule [ovərúl] *v.* anular.

o·ver·run [ovərʌ́n] *v.* desbordarse, mundar; sobrepasar; infestar, invadir; *p.p. de* **overrun.**

o·ver·seas [óvəsíz] *adv.* en ultramar, allende los mares; *adj. de* ultramar.

o·ver·see [ovəsí] *v.* dirigir; vigilar.

o·ver·se·er [óvəsir] *s.* sobrestante, capataz; inspector, superintendente.

o·ver·shoe [óvəʃu] *s.* chanclo; zapato de goma, caucho o hule.

o·ver·sight [óvəsait] *s.* inadvertencia, negligencia, descuido.

o·ver·step [ovəstép] *v.* sobrepasarse, propasarse; traspasar; **to** — **the bounds** traspasar los límites;

propasarse.

o·ver·take [ovəték] *v.* alcanzar.

o·ver·tak·en [ovətékən] *p.p. de* **to overtake.**

o·ver·threw [ovəθrú] *pret. de* **to overthrow.**

o·ver·throw [óvəθro] *s.* (*overturn*) derrocamiento; (*defeat*) derrota, destrucción; caída; [ovəθró] *v.* derrocar; derribar, echar abajo, volcar; destronar.

o·ver·thrown [ovəθrón] *p.p. de* **to overthrow.**

o·ver·time [óvətaim] *adv.* & *adj.* en exceso de las horas estipuladas; — **pay** sobresueldo.

o·ver·took [ovətúk] *pret. de* **to overtake.**

o·ver·ture [óvətʃə] *s.* obertura, preludio; propuesta, proposición.

o·ver·turn [ovətɜ́n] *v.* volcar(se); trastornar; derribar; echar abajo.

o·ver·whelm [ovəhwɛ́lm] *v.* abrumar, agobiar; oprimir; arrollar.

o·ver·whelm·ing [ovəhwɛ́lmiŋ] *adj.* abrumador; opresivo; arrollador, irresistible, poderoso.

o·ver·work [óvəwɜ́k] *v.* atarearse, afanarse más de lo debido, trabajar demasiado; *s.* exceso de trabajo.

owe [o] *v.* deber, adeudar.

ow·ing [óıŋ] *adj.* debido; — **to** debido a.

owl [aul] *s.* lechuza, buho, *Méx., C.A.* tecolote.

own [on] *adj.* propio; **a house of his** — una casa suya; **his** — **people** los suyos; **to be on one's** — no estar a merced ajena; trabajar por su propia cuenta; **to come into one's** — entrar en posesión de lo suyo; **to hold one's** — mantenerse firme; *v.* poseer, tener; admitir, reconocer; **to** — **to** confesar; **to** — **up** confesar.

own·er [ónə] *s.* dueño, amo; propietario; poseedor.

own·er·ship [ónəʃɪp] *s.* posesión, propiedad.

ox [aks] (*pl* ox·en [áksn]) *s.* buey.

ox·ide [áksaid] *s.* óxido.

ox·i·dize [áksədaiz] *v.* oxidar.

ox·y·gen [áksədʒən] *s.* oxígeno.

oys·ter [ɔ́istə] *s.* ostra, ostión.

o·zone [ózon] *s.* ozono.

P:p pace [pes] *s.* paso; *v.* pasear, andar; andar al paso; marchar; medir a pasos.

pace·mak·er [pésmekə] *s.* marcapaso.

pa·cif·ic [pəsífik] *adj.* pacífico.

pac·i·fy [pǽsəfai] *v.* pacificar, apaciguar; calmar.

pack [pæk] *s.* fardo, lío, carga; manada (*de lobos*); cuadrilla, pandilla (*de ladrones*); jauría (*de perros*); muchedumbre; baraja (*de naipes*); — **animal** acémila, bestia de carga; *v.* empacar, empaquetar; embalar; enlatar; envasar; apiñar(se); cargar (*una bestia*); hacer (*el baúl, la maleta*); **to** — **off** despedir de repente; echar a la calle; largarse, irse.

pack·age [pǽkidʒ] *s.* paquete; fardo, bulto; cajetilla (*de cigarrillos*).

pack·er [pǽkə] *s.* empacador; embalador, envasador.

pack·et [pǽkit] *s.* paquetito; cajetilla.

pack·ing [pǽkiŋ] *s.* (*covering*) embalaje; envase; (*filling*) relleno; — **box** caja para embalar o empacar; — **house** establecimiento frigorífico, fábrica para envasar o enlatar comestibles.

pact [pækt] *s.* pacto, convenio.

pad [pæd] *s.* almohadilla, cojincillo; tableta, block

de papel; *v.* rellenar; forrar; acolchar.
pad·ding [pǽdɪŋ] *s.* relleno (*de pelo, algodón, paja, etc.*), *Andes* guata; ripio, palabras o frases inútiles.
pad·dle [pǽdl̩] *s.* pala; remo de canoa; — **wheel** rueda de paleta; *v.* remar con pala; apalear; chapotear (*en el agua*).
pad·dock [pǽdək] *s.* dehesa.
pad·lock [pǽdlɑk] *s.* candado; *v.* cerrar con candado.
pa·gan [pégən] *s.* & *adj.* pagano.
pa·gan·ism [pégənɪzəm] *s.* paganismo.
page [pedʒ] *s.* página; paje; "botones" (*de hotel*), mensajero; *v.* paginar; vocear, llamar a voces.
pag·eant [pǽdʒənt] *s.* (*parade*) manifestación, desfile, procesión, pompa; (*drama*) representación al aire libre.
paid [ped] *pret.* & *p.p.* de **to pay.**
pail [pel] *s.* balde, cubo, cubeta.
pain [pen] *s.* dolor; sufrimiento; **-s** esmero; **on (under)** — **of** so pena de; **to be in** — estar sufriendo, tener dolores; **to take -s** esmerarse, extremarse; *v.* doler; causar dolor; afligir.
pain·ful [pénfəl] *adj.* doloroso; penoso; arduo.
pain·less [pénlɪs] *adj.* sin dolor; libre de dolor.
pains·tak·ing [pénztekɪŋ] *adj.* esmerado, cuidadoso; aplicado.
paint [pent] *s.* (*mixture*) pintura, color; (*rouge*) colorete; *v.* pintar; pintarse (*la cara*); **to** — **the town red** irse de juerga o de parranda, *Ríopl.* irse de farra.
paint·brush [péntbrʌʃ] *s.* (*art*) pincel; (*house*) brocha.
paint·er [péntə] *s.* pintor.
paint·ing [péntɪŋ] *s.* pintura.
pair [pɛr] *s.* par; pareja; **a** — **of scissors** unas tijeras; *v.* aparear(se); hacer pareja, hacer pares; **to** — **off** aparear(se).
pa·jam·as [pədʒǽməz] *s. pl.* pijama.
pal [pæl] *s.* compañero, camarada.
pal·ace [pǽlɪs] *s.* palacio.
pal·ate [pǽlɪt] *s.* paladar.
pa·la·tial [pəléʃl] *adj.* suntuoso.
pale [pel] *adj.* pálido; descolorido; *v.* palidecer, ponerse pálido o descolorido.
pale·ness [pélnɪs] *s.* palidez.
pal·i·sade [pæləséd] *s.* palizada, estacada; **-s** riscos, acantilados.
pall [pɔl] *v.* empalagar; aburrir; **it -s on me** me empalaga; me aburre; *s.* paño de ataúd; palia (*lienzo que pone encima del cáliz*).
pal·la·di·um [pəlédiəm] *s.* paladio.
pal·li·a·tive [pǽljətɪv] *adj.* & *s.* paliativo.
pal·lid [pǽlɪd] *adj.* pálido.
pal·or [pǽlə] *s.* palidez.
palm [pɑm] *s.* palma; palmera; — **Sunday** Domingo de Ramos; — **tree** palma, palmera; *v.* **to** — **something off on someone** pasar o dar algo indeseable a una persona (*sin que se dé cuenta de ello*).
pal·pa·ble [pǽlpəbl] *adj.* palpable, tangible; evidente.
pal·pi·tate [pǽlpətet] *v.* palpitar, latir.
pal·pi·ta·tion [pælpətéʃən] *s.* palpitación; latido.
pal·try [pɔ́ltrɪ] *adj.* mezquino, miserable, despreciable, insignificante.
pam·per [pǽmpə] *v.* mimar, consentir (*a un niño*).
pam·phlet [pǽmflɪt] *s.* folleto, *Am.* panfleto.
pan [pæn] *s.* cazuela, cacerola; cazo; platillo (*de balanza*); **dish** — cazo para lavar platos; **frying** — sartén; *v.* **to** — **out (well)** salir bien, dar buen

resultado.
Pan-A·mer·i·can [pænəmérəkən] *adj.* panamericano.
pan·cake [pǽnkek] *s.* tortita de harina, *Ven., Col.* panqué; *Ríopl.* panqueque.
pan·der [pǽndə] *s.* alcahuete, encubridor *v.* alcahuetear, servir de alcahuete.
pane [pen] vidrio, cristal (*de ventana o puerta*); cuadro (*de vidrio*).
pan·el [pǽnl] *s.* panel, tablero; cuarterón (*de puerta, ventana, etc.*); tabla (*doble pliegue de una falda o vestido*); **jury** — jurado; *v.* proveer de (*o adornar con*) paneles.
pang [pæŋ] *s.* dolor agudo; angustia, tormento.
pan·han·dle [pǽnhændl] *s.* mango de sartén; territorio en forma de mango; *v.* mendigar.
pan·ic [pǽnɪk] *adj.* & *s.* pánico; **pan·ic-strick·en** sobrecogido de pánico.
pan·o·ram·a [pænərǽmə] *s.* panorama.
pan·sy [pǽnzɪ] *s.* pensamiento (*flor*).
pant [pænt] *v.* jadear; palpitar; **to** — **for** anhelar, ansiar.
pan·ther [pǽnθə] *s.* pantera.
pant·ing [pǽntɪŋ] *s.* jadeo, palpitación; *adj.* jadeante.
pan·to·mime [pǽntəmaɪm] *s.* pantomima.
pan·try [pǽntrɪ] *s.* despensa.
pants [pænts] *s. pl.* pantalones.
pa·pa [pɑ́pə] *s.* papá.
pa·pa·cy [pépəsɪ] *s.* papado.
pa·pal [pépl] *adj.* papal.
pa·per [pépə] *s.* (*material*) papel; (*daily*) periódico; (*essay*) tema, ensayos; **-s** papeles, documentos, credenciales; **naturalization -s** carta de naturaleza, certificado de ciudadanía; **scholarly** — **ponencia**; — **of pins** cartón de alfileres; **on** — escrito; por escrito; *adj.* de papel; para papel; — **doll** muñeca de papel; — **money** papel moneda; **—weight** pisapapeles; *v.* empapelar.
pa·per·back [pépəbæk] *s.* & *adj.* libro en rústica.
pa·per·work [pépəwək] *s.* preparación de escritos; papeleo.
pa·pri·ka [pæpríkə] *s.* pimentón.
par [pɑr] *s.* (*equality*) paridad, igualdad; (*standard*) valor nominal; — **value** valor a la par; **above** — sobre par, a premio, con prima; **at** — a la par; **below** — bajo par, a descuento; **on a** — **with** al par de, al nivel de, igual a; **to feel above** — sentirse mejor que de ordinario; **to feel below** — sentirse menos bien que de ordinario.
par·a·ble [pǽrəbl] *s.* parábola (*alegoría bíblica*).
par·a·chute [pǽrəʃut] *s.* paracaídas.
par·a·chut·ist [pǽrəʃutɪst] *s.* paracaidista.
pa·rade [pəréd] *s.* (*procession*) desfile, procesión, manifestación; paseo; (*review*) parada; — **ground** campo de maniobras; **to make a** — **of** ostentar, hacer ostentación de; *v.* desfilar, pasar en desfile; marchar en parada; hacer ostentación de.
par·a·digm [pǽrədɪm], [pǽrədaɪm] *s.* paradigma.
par·a·dise [pǽrədaɪs] *s.* paraíso.
par·a·dox·i·cal [pærədáksɪk] *adj.* paradójico.
par·a·dox [pǽrədaks] *s.* paradoja.
par·af·fin [pǽrəfɪn] *s.* parafina.
par·a·graph [pǽrəgræf] *s.* párrafo; *v.* dividir en párrafos.
Par·a·guay·an [pærəgwáɪən] *adj.* & *s.* paraguayo.
par·al·lel [pǽrəlɛl] *adj.* & *s.* paralelo; *v.* ser (*o correr*) paralelo a; comparar, cotejar.
pa·ral·y·sis [pərǽləsɪs] *s.* parálisis.
par·a·lyt·ic [pærəlítɪk] *adj.* paralítico.
par·a·lyze [pǽrəlaɪz] *v.* paralizar.

pa·ram·e·ter [pərǽmətə˞] s. parámetro.
par·a·mount [pǽrəmaʊnt] adj. importantísimo, superior, supremo, máximo.
par·a·noi·a [pærənɔ́ja] s. paranoia.
par·a·pet [pǽrəpɪt] s. parapeto.
par·a·phrase [pǽrəfrez] v. parafrasear.
par·a·site [pǽrəsaɪt] s. parásito.
par·a·sol [pǽrəsɔl] s. parasol, sombrilla.
par·a·troops [pǽrətrups] s. tropas paracaidistas.
par·cel [pársl] s. paquete; parcela, porción, lote (de terreno); — **post** paquete postal; v. parcelar, dividir en porciones o parcelas; hacer paquetes; **to — out** repartir.
parch [partʃ] v. resecar(se); tostar(se).
parch·ment [pártʃmənt] s. pergamino.
par·don [párdn] s. perdón; indulto; **I beg your —** perdone Vd.; dispense Vd.; v. perdonar; dispensar; indultar.
pare [pɛr] v. mondar, pelar (manzanas, patatas, etc.); cortar, recortar; **to — down expenditures** reducir gastos.
par·ent [pérənt] s. padre, madre; origen; **-s** padres.
par·ent·age [pérəntɪdʒ] s. linaje; padres.
pa·ren·tal [pərɛ́ntl] adj. parental.
pa·ren·the·sis [pərɛ́nθəsɪs] (pl. **pa·ren·the·ses** [pərɛ́nθəsiz]) s. paréntesis.
par·ish [pǽrɪʃ] s. parroquia.
par·ish [pərɪ́ʃənə˞] s. parroquiano, feligrés; **-s** fieles, feligreses.
park [park] s. parque; v. estacionar, dejar (un automóvil); estacionarse; **-ing lot** Ch., Ríopl. playa de estacionamiento; Mex., Ven. estacionamiento; Col. parqueadero; **-ing space** sitio o lugar para estacionarse; **free -ing** estacionamiento gratis; **no -ing** se prohibe estacionarse; no estacionarse.
par·lance [párləns] s. lenguaje.
par·ley [párlɪ] s. parlamento, discusión, conferencia; v. parlamentar, discutir.
par·lia·ment [párləmənt] s. parlamento.
par·lia·men·ta·ry [parləméntərɪ] adj. parlamentario.
par·lor [párlə˞] s. sala, salón; sala de recibo; — **car** coche salón; **beauty —** salón de belleza.
pa·ro·chi·al [pərókɪəl] adj. parroquial.
par·o·dy [pǽrədɪ] s. parodia; v. parodiar.
pa·role [pəról] s. palabra de honor; **to put on —** dejar libre (a un prisionero) bajo palabra de honor; v. dejar libre bajo palabra de honor.
par·rot [pǽrət] s. cotorra, loro, perico, papagayo; v. remedar, repetir como loro.
par·ry [pǽrɪ] v. parar, quitar o reparar (un golpe); s. quite, reparo.
pars·ley [párslɪ] s. perejil.
pars·nip [pársnəp] s. chirivía (legumbre).
par·son [pársn] s. pastor, clérigo.
part [part] s. parte (f.); papel (dramático); raya (del cabello); — **and parcel** parte esencial o inherente; — **owner** condueño, dueño en parte; — **time** parte del tiempo; **in foreign -s** en el extranjero, en países extranjeros; **spare -s** piezas accesorias, piezas de repuesto (o de refacción); **do your —** haga Vd. cuanto esté de su parte; v. partir(se); separar(se); **to — company** separarse; **to — from** separarse de, despedirse de; **to — one's hair** hacerse la raya; **to — with** separarse de, despedirse de, deshacerse de.
par·take [párték] v. tomar parte, tener parte, participar.
par·tak·en [partékən] p.p. de **to partake**.
par·tial [párʃəl] adj. parcial; **-ly** adv. parcialmente, en parte; con parcialidad.

par·ti·al·i·ty [parʃǽlətɪ] s. parcialidad.
par·tic·i·pant [pətísəpənt] adj. & s. participante, partícipe, copartícipe.
par·tic·i·pate [pətísəpet] v. participar.
par·tic·i·pa·tion [pətɪsəpéʃən] s. participación.
par·ti·ci·ple [pártəsɪpl] s. participio; **present —** gerundio.
par·ti·cle [pártɪl] s. partícula.
par·tic·u·lar [pətíkjələ˞] adj. (single) particular; peculiar; (special) esmerado, exacto; escrupuloso; (demanding) quisquilloso; exigente; s. particular, detalle, circunstancia; **in —** en particular, especialmente; **-ly** adv. particularmente; en particular.
part·ing [pártɪŋ] (departure) despedida; (division) separación; bifurcación; **the — of the ways** encruijada, bifurcación, cruce de caminos; adj. de despedida, último.
par·ti·san [pártəzn] adj. partidario; parcial; s. partidario; secuaz, seguidor.
par·ti·tion [pətíʃən] s. (division) partición; división; separación; (wall) tabique; Am. medianía; v. partir, dividir; repartir.
par·ti·tive [pártɪtɪv] adj. partitivo.
part·ly [pártlɪ] adv. en parte.
part·ner [pártnə˞] s. socio, consocio; compañero; **dancing —** pareja de baile.
part·ner·ship [pártnə˞ʃɪp] s. sociedad, compañía.
par·took [partúk] pret. de **to partake**.
par·tridge [pártrɪdʒ] s. perdiz.
par·ty [pártɪ] s. (get-together) tetulia, reunión, fiesta; (group) grupo, partida (de gente); (legal) parte; **hunting —** partida de caza; **political —** partido político.
pass [pæs] s. paso; pase, permiso de entrar; aprobación (en un examen); trance, situación; — **key** llave maestra; **to come to —** suceder; v. pasar; pasar por; pronunciar (sentencia), dar (un juicio o parecer); aprobar (a un estudiante); adoptar (una ley); ser aprobado en (un examen); **to — away** pasar a mejor vida, morir; desaparecer; pasar (el tiempo).
pass·a·ble [pǽsəbl] adj. (penetrable) transitable; (acceptable) pasadero, regular, mediano.
pas·sage [pǽsɪdʒ] s. pasaje; paso, tránsito; transcurso (del tiempo); pasillo, pasadizo; travesía, viaje por mar; aprobación (de un proyecto de ley); adopción (de una ley).
pass·age·way [pǽsədʒwe] s. corredor; pasaje.
pass·book [pǽsbʊk] s. libreta de banco.
pas·sen·ger [pǽsndʒə˞] s. pasajero; **the -s** los pasajeros; el pasaje.
pas·ser·by [pǽsə˞bái] s. transeúnte, viandante.
pas·sion [pǽʃən] s. pasión; **Passion play** drama de la Pasión; **to fly into a —** montar en cólera, encolerizarse.
pas·sion·ate [pǽʃənɪt] adj. apasionado.
pas·sive [pǽsɪv] adj. pasivo; s. voz pasiva.
pass·port [pǽsport] s. pasaporte.
pass·word [pǽswɜ˞d] s. consigna, contraseña, santo y seña.
past [pæst] adj. pasado; último; — **master** perito; **the — president** el expresidente, el último presidente; — **tense** tiempo pasado; pretérito; **for some time —** desde hace algún tiempo, de poco tiempo a esta parte; prep. más allá; insoportable; — **understanding** incomprensible; **half — two** las dos y media; **woman — forty** cuarentona, mujer de más de cuarenta años; **to go — the house** pasar por (o por enfrente de) la casa; s. pasado; pretérito; pretérito imperfecto;

man with a — hombre de dudosos antecedentes.
paste [pest] *s.* pasta; engrudo; *v.* pegar *(con engrudo)*.
paste·board [péstbord] *s.* cartón; — **box** caja de cartón.
pas·teur·ize [pǽstəraɪz] *v.* pasterizar *(o pasteurizar)*.
pas·time [pǽstaɪm] *s.* pasatiempo.
pas·tor [pǽstə·] *s.* pastor, clérigo, cura.
pas·tor·al [pǽstərəl] *adj.* pastoril; pastoral; *s.* pastoral, carta pastoral; écloga; pastorela, idilio.
pas·try [péstrɪ] *s.* pastelería, pasteles; — **cook** pastelero; — **shop** pastelería; repostería.
pas·ture [pǽstʃə·] *s.* pastura, pasto; dehesa; *v.* pastar, pacer; apacentar(se).
pat [pæt] *adj.* apto, oportuno; **to have a lesson** — saber al dedillo la lección; **to stand** — mantenerse firme; *adv.* a propósito; oportunamente; de molde; *s.* palmadita, caricia, golpecito; — **of butter** cuadrito de mantequilla; *v.* dar palmaditas a; acariciar; pasar la mano *(para alisar o acariciar)*.
patch [pæt] *s. (repair)* remiendo; parche; mancha; *(plot)* pedazo *(de terreno)*; sembrado; *v.* remendar; **to** — **up a quarrel** hacer las paces.
pate [pet] *s.* coronilla *(de la cabeza)*; **bald** — calva.
pat·ent [pǽtnt] *adj.* patente, evidente, manifiesto; de patente; — **leather** charol; — **medicine** medicina de patente; — **right** patente; *s.* patente; *v.* patentar.
pa·ter·nal [pətɜ́nl] *adj.* paternal, paterno.
pa·ter·ni·ty [pətɜ́nətɪ] *s.* paternidad.
path [pæθ] *s.* senda, sendero; vereda; ruta; trayectoria *(de una bala)*.
pa·thet·ic [pəθέtɪk] *adj.* patético.
path·o·log·i·cal [pæθəládʒɪkl] *adj.* patológico.
pa·thol·o·gy [pæθáləɖʒɪ] *s.* patología.
pa·thos [péθɑs] *s.* patetismo, cualidad patética.
path·way [pǽθwe] *s.* senda, vereda, vía.
pa·tience [péʃəns] *s.* paciencia.
pa·tient [péʃənt] *adj.* paciente; pacienzudo; *s.* paciente, enfermo.
pa·tri·arch [pétrɪɑrk] *s.* patriarca.
pa·tri·ar·chal [petrɪárkl] *adj.* patriarcal.
pa·tri·cian [pətríʃən] *s.* patricio.
pat·ri·mo·ny [pǽtrəmonɪ] *s.* patrimonio.
pa·tri·ot [pétrɪət] *s.* patriota.
pa·tri·ot·ic [petrɪátɪk] *adj.* patriótico.
pa·tri·ot·ism [pétrɪətɪzəm] *s.* patriotismo.
pa·trol [pət ról] *s.* patrulla; ronda; *v.* patrullar, rondar.
pa·tron [pétrən] *s.* patrón, patrono; benefactor; cliente, parroquiano; — **saint** santo patrón.
pa·tron·age [pétrənɪdʒ] *s. (support)* patrocinio, amparo; *(clientele)* clientela; *(manner)* condescendencia — **control de** nombramientos políticos.
pa·tron·ess [pétrənɪs] *s.* patrona, protectora.
pa·tron·ize [pétrənaɪz] *v.* patrocinar, amparar; tratar con condescendencia; favorecer; ser parroquiano de.
pat·ter [pǽtə·] *v.* golpetear ligeramente; talonear; charlar, parlotear; *s.* golpeteo; golpecitos; taloneo; charla, parloteo.
pat·tern [pǽtə·n] *s. (model)* modelo; dechado; muestra; ejemplo; patrón, molde; *(design)* diseño, dibujo *(en tejidos, telas, etc.)*; *v.* **to** — **oneself after** seguir el ejemplo de; **to** — **something after (on, upon)** forjar o modelar algo a imitación de.
pau·ci·ty [pósɪtɪ] *s.* escasez; falta.

paunch [pɔntʃ] *s.* panza, barriga.
pause [pɔz] *s.* pausa; *s.* pausar, hacer pausa; detenerse, parar.
pave [pev] *v.* pavimentar; **to** — **the way for** preparar o abrir el camino para; **to** — **with bricks** enladrillar; **to** — **with flagstones** enlosar.
pave·ment [pévmənt] *s.* pavimento; **brick** — enladrillado.
pa·vil·ion [pəvíljən] *s.* pabellón.
paw [pɔ] *s.* garra, zarpa; *v.* echar la zarpa; arañar; manosear; **to** — **the ground** patear la tierra *(dícese del caballo)*.
pawn [pɔn] *s.* prenda, empeño; peón *(de ajedrez)*; —**broker** prestamista, prendero; —**shop** empeño, casa de empeños, montepío; **in** — en prenda; *v.* empeñar, dejar en prenda.
pay [pe] *v. (remit)* pagar; *(pay for)* costear; *(profit)* ser provechoso; *(worthwhile)* valer la pena; **to** — **attention** prestar atención; **to** — **back** restituir, devolver; **to** — **court** hacer la corte; **to** — **down** pagar al contado; **to** — **homage** hacer o rendir homenaje; **to** — **one's respects** presentar sus respetos; **to** — **a visit** hacer una visita; *s.* pago; recompensa; paga; sueldo; — **day** día de pagos, *Am.* día de raya; — **master** pagador, *Am.* rayador; — **roll** nómina.
pay·a·ble [péəbl] *adj.* pagadero.
pay·ment [pémənt] *s.* pago; paga; — **in full** pago total.
pay·off [péɔf] *s.* arreglo; pago.
pea [pi] *s.* guisante, chícharo; **sweet** — guisante de olor.
peace [pis] *s.* paz.
peace·a·ble [písəbl] *adj.* pacífico, tranquilo.
peace·ful [písfəl] *adj.* pacífico; tranquilo, quieto, sosegado.
peach [pitʃ] *s.* melocotón, durazno; persona bella o admirable; — **tree** durazno, duraznero, melocotonero.
pea·cock [píkɑk] *s.* pavón, pavo real; **to act like a** — pavonearse, hacer ostentación.
peak [pik] *s.* pico, cumbre, cima; cúspide; punto máximo.
peal [pil] *s.* repique *(de campanas)*; — **of laughter** carcajada, risotada; — **of thunder** trueno; *v.* repicar *(las companas)*.
pea·nut [pínət] *s.* cacahuate, *Carib., Ven., Col., Ch., Ríopl., Andes* maní.
pear [pɛr] *s.* pera; — **tree** peral; **alligator** — aguacate, *Ch., Andes, Ríopl.* palta *(variedad sudamericana)*.
pearl [pɜl] *s.* perla; — **nucklace** collar de perlas; **mother-of-pearl** nácar, madreperla.
pear·ly [pɜ́lɪ] *adj.* perlino; nacarado; aperlado.
peas·ant [pézɳt] *adj. & s.* campesino, rústico, *P.R.* jíbaro, *Cuba* guajiro; *Col.* paisa; *Ch.* guaso; *Ríopl.* gaucho.
peb·ble [pέbl] *s.* guija, china, guijarro, piedrecilla.
pe·can [pɪkán] *s.* pacana.
peck [pɛk] *v.* picar, picotear; *s.* picotazo, picotada; medida de áridos *(aproximadamente 9 litros)*; **a** — **of trouble** la mar de disgustos o molestias.
pe·cu·liar [pɪkúljə·] *adj.* peculiar; raro, singular, extraño.
pe·cu·li·ar·i·ty [pɪkjulɪǽrətɪ] *s.* peculiaridad; particularidad; rareza.
ped·a·gogue [pédəgɑg] *s.* pedagogo, dómine.
ped·a·go·gy [pédəgodʒɪ] *s.* pedagogía.
ped·al [pédl] *s.* pedal; *v.* pedalear, mover los pedales.
ped·ant [pédɳt] *s.* pedante.

pe·dan·tic [pɪdǽntɪk] adj. pedante, pedantesco.
ped·dle [pédl] v. ir vendiendo de puerta en puerta;
to — gossip chismear.
ped·dler [pédlə·] s. buhonero; vendedor ambulante.
ped·es·tal [pédɪstl] s. pedestal.
pe·des·tri·an [pədéstrɪən] s. peatón, transeúnte,
viandante; adj. pedestre.
pe·di·at·rics [pidɪǽtrɪks] s. pediatría.
ped·i·gree [pédəgri] s. linaje, genealogía.
peek [pik] v. atisbar, espiar; s. atisbo.
peel [pil] s. corteza, cáscara (de algunas frutas);
pellejo (de patatas); v. pelar(se), descortezar(se),
deshollejar(se); to keep one's eye -ed tener los
ojos muy abiertos, estar alerta.
peep [pip] v. atisbar, espiar; asomar(se); pipiar,
piar; s. atisbo; ojeada; pío (de pollo o ave).
peer [pir] s. (equal) par, igual; (noble) noble; v.
mirar con atención, atisbar; asomar; to — into
other people's business fisgar, curiosear.
peer group [pɪrgrup] s. conjunto de personas de la
misma edad y condiciones.
peer·less [pírlɛs] adj. incomparable; sin par.
peeve [piv] v. irritar, poner de mal humor; to get -d
amoscarse, ponerse de mal humor.
pee·vish [pívɪʃ] adj. enojadizo; malhumorado.
peg [pɛg] s. espiga, clavo de madera, estaquilla;
clavija (de violín); to take a person down a —
rebajar o humillar a alguien; v. clavar, clavetear;
poner estaquillas; to — along atarearse, trabajar
con tesón.
pe·jor·a·tive [pədʒɔ́rətɪv] adj. peyorativo;
despectivo.
pel·i·can [pélɪkən] s. pelícano.
pel·let [pélɪt] s. (ball) pelotilla; bola; (pill) píldora.
pell-mell [pélmél] adj. confuso, tumultuoso; adv. a
trochemoche, atropelladamente, en tumulto.
pelt [pɛlt] s. zalea, cuero (especialmente de oveja);
piel; v. golpear; to — with stones apedrear,
arrojar piedras a.
pel·vis [pélvɪs] s. pelvis.
pen [pɛn] s. pluma (para escribir); corral; redil;
—holder mango de pluma, portapluma; —name
nombre de pluma; fountain — pluma fuente,
pluma estilográfica; ballpoint — bolígrafo; pig —
pocilga; v. escribir (con pluma); acorralar,
encerrar.
pe·nal [pínl] adj. penal.
pe·nal·ize [pínəlaɪz] v. penar; aplicar sanción.
pen·al·ty [pénlti] s. pena, castigo; multa.
pen·ance [pénəns] s. penitencia.
pen·cil [pénsl] s. lápiz; lapicero; — sharpener
tajalápiz.
pen·dant [péndənt] s. pendiente (ardorno que
cuelga); adj. pendiente.
pend·ing [péndɪŋ] adj. pendiente; colgado; prep.
durante.
pen·du·lum [péndʒələm] s. péndulo.
pen·e·trate [pénətret] v. penetrar.
pen·e·trat·ing [pénətretɪŋ] adj. penetrante.
pen·a·tra·tion [pɛnətréʃən] s. penetración.
pen·guin [péngwɪn] s. pingüino.
pen·i·cil·lin [pɛnəsílɪn] s. penicilina.
pen·in·su·la [pənínsələ] s. península.
pe·nis [pínɪs] s. pene.
pen·i·tent [pénətənt] adj. arrepentido, penitente; s.
penitente.
pen·i·ten·tia·ry [pɛnətéʃərɪ] s. penitenciaría,
presidio.
pen·knife [pénnaɪf] s. cortaplumas; navaja.
pen·man·ship [pénmənʃɪp] s. escritura, caligrafía.
pen·nant [pénənt] s. banderola, gallardete.

pen·ni·less [pénɪlɪs] adj. pobre, sin dinero.
pen·ny [pénɪ] s. centavo (de dólar); to cost a pretty
— costar un ojo de la cara, costar un dineral.
pen·sion [pénʃən] s. pensión, retiro (de un militar);
v. pensionar.
pen·sive [pénsɪv] adj. pensativo.
pent [pɛnt] adj. encerrado; acorralado; pent-up
emotions sentimientos reprimidos.
pent·house [pénthaʊs] s. casa de azotea; colgadizo.
peo·ple [pípl] s. gente; pueblo v. poblar.
pep·per [pépə·] s. pimienta; — plant pimentero; —
shaker pimentero; green -s pimientos verdes; red
— pimentón, chile, Carib., Col., Ven., Andes, Ch.,
Ríopl. ají; v. sazonar con pimienta; to — with
bullets acribillar a balazos.
pep·per·mint [pépə·mɪnt] s. menta; pastilla o
bombón de menta.
per [pə·] prep. por; — capita por cabeza; — cent
por ciento; — year al año; ten cents — dozen
diez centavos por docena (o diez centavos la
docena).
per·cale [pə·kél] s. percal.
per·ceive [pə·sív] v. percibir.
per·cent·age [pə·séntɪdʒ] s. porcentaje, tanto por
ciento.
per·cep·ti·ble [pə·séptəbl] adj. perceptible.
per·cep·tion [pə·sépʃən] s. percepción.
per·cep·tive [pə·séptɪv] adj. perceptivo; sensible.
perch [pɜtʃ] s. percha (para pájaros); perca (pez); v.
encaramar(se); posarse (en una percha o rama).
per·chance [pə·tʃǽns] adv. por ventura, acaso,
quizás, tal vez.
per·co·late [pə·kəlet] v. filtrar(se), colar(se);
rezumarse; penetrar.
per·cus·sion [pə·kʌ́ʃən] s. percusión.
per·di·tion [pə·díʃən] s. perdición.
per·en·ni·al [pərénɪəl] adj. perenne; continuo;
perpetuo.
per·fect [pə·fɪkt] adj. perfecto; completo; s. tiempo
perfecto (del verbo); [pə·fékt] v. perfeccionar.
per·fec·tion [pə·fékʃən] s. perfección.
per·fid·i·ous [pə·fídɪəs] adj. pérfido.
per·fi·dy [pə·fədɪ] s. perfidia.
per·fo·rate [pə·fəret] v. perforar.
per·force [pə·fɔ́rs] adj. necesariamente; por fuerza.
per·form [pə·fɔ́rm] v. ejecutar; llevar a cabo,
cumplir, hacer; funcionar (una máquina);
desempeñar o representar un papel.
per·form·ance [pə·fɔ́rməns] s. ejecución; desempeño,
cumplimiento; funcionamiento (de una máquina
o motor); función, representación; acto, acción.
per·fume [pə·fjum] s. perfume; [pə·fjúm] v.
perfumar.
per·fum·er·y [pə·fjúmərɪ] s. perfumería; perfumes.
per·haps [pə·hǽps] adv. acaso, tal vez, quizá (o
quizás), puede ser.
per·i·gee [pérədʒi] s. perigeo.
per·il [pérəl] s. peligro; riesgo; v. poner en peligro.
per·il·ous [pérələs] adj. peligroso.
pe·ri·od [pírɪəd] s. período; punto final; fin,
término.
pe·ri·od·i·cal [pɪrɪádɪk] adj. periódico.
pe·ri·od·i·cal [pɪrɪádɪkl] adj. periódico; s. revista,
publicación periódica.
pe·riph·er·y [pərífərɪ] s. periferia.
per·ish [périʃ] v. perecer.
per·ish·a·ble [périʃəbl] adj. perecedero; deleznable.
per·i·to·ne·um [pɛrətəniəm] s. peritoneo.
per·i·to·ni·tis [pɛrətənáɪtɪs] s. peritonitis.
per·jure [pə·dʒə·] v. to — oneself perjurar.

PA

per·ju·ry [pɝ́dʒrɪ] s. perjurio, juramento falso.
per·ma·nence [pɝ́mənəns] s. permanencia.
per·ma·nent [pɝ́mənənt] adj. permanente; duradero.
per·me·ate [pɝ́mɪet] v. penetrar, saturar; difundirse por, filtrarse por.
per·mis·si·ble [pəmísəbl] adj. lícito.
per·mis·sion [pəmíʃən] s. permiso, licencia.
per·mis·sive [pəmísɪv] adj. permisivo.
per·mit [pɝ́mɪt] s. permiso, pase; licencia; [pəmít] v. permitir.
per·mu·ta·tion [pɝmjutéʃən] s. permutación.
per·ni·cious [pəníʃəs] adj. pernicioso.
per·ox·ide [pəráksaɪd] s. peróxido.
per·pen·dic·u·lar [pɝpəndíkjələ] adj. & s. perpendicular.
per·pe·trate [pɝ́pətret] v. perpetrar, cometer.
per·pet·u·al [pəpétʃuəl] adj. perpetuo.
per·pet·u·ate [pəpétʃuet] v. perpetuar.
per·plex [pəpléks] v. confundir, turbar, aturdir.
per·plexed [pəplékst] adj. perplejo, confuso.
per·plex·i·ty [pəpléksətɪ] s. perplejidad, confusión.
per·se·cute [pɝ́sɪkjut] v. perseguir, acosar.
per·se·cu·tion [pɝsɪkjúʃən] s. persecución.
per·se·cu·tor [pɝ́sɪkjutə] s. perseguidor.
per·se·ver·ance [pɝsəvírəns] s. perseverancia.
per·se·vere [pɝsəvír] v. perseverar; persistir.
per·sist [pəzíst] v. persistir; porfiar.
per·sist·ence [pəzístəns] s. persistencia; porfía.
per·sist·ent [pəzístənt] adj. persistente; porfiado.
per·son [pɝ́sṇ] s. persona.
per·son·a·ble [pɝ́sənəbl] adj. presentable; bien parecido.
per·son·age [pɝ́sṇɪdʒ] s. personaje.
per·son·al [pɝ́sṇl] adj. personal; en persona.
per·son·al·ism [pɝ́sənəlɪzm] s. personalismo.
per·son·al·i·ty [pɝsṇǽlətɪ] s. personalidad; persona, personaje; alusión personal.
per·son·nel [pɝsṇél] s. personal.
per·spec·tive [pəspɛ́ktɪv] s. perspectiva; — drawing dibujo en perspectiva.
per·spi·ca·cious [pɝspɪkéʃəs] adj. perspicaz.
per·spi·ra·tion [pɝspəréʃən] s. sudor.
per·spire [pəspáɪr] v. sudar.
per·suade [pəswéd] v. persuadir.
per·sua·sion [pəswéʒən] s. persuasión; creencia.
per·sua·sive [pəswésɪv] adj. persuasivo.
pert [pɝt] adj. insolente, descarado, atrevido, Am. retobado.
per·tain [pətén] v. pertenecer; atañer.
per·ti·nent [pɝ́tṇənt] adj. pertinente, a propósito, al caso.
per·turb [pətɝ́b] v. perturbar.
pe·rus·al [pərúzl] s. lectura.
pe·ruse [pərúz] v. leer con cuidado.
Pe·ru·vi·an [pərúviən] adj. & s. peruano.
per·vade [pəvéd] v. llenar, penetrar, difundirse por.
per·verse [pəvɝ́s] adj. perverso; terco, obstinado.
per·vert [pəvɝ́t] v. pervertir; falsear; [pɝ́vɝt] s. perverso.
pes·si·mism [pɛ́səmɪzm] s. pesimismo.
pes·si·mist [pɛ́səmɪst] s. pesimista; -ic adj. pesimista.
pest [pɛst] s. peste, plaga; pestilencia.
pes·ter [pɛ́stə] v. importunar, molestar.
pes·ti·cide [pɛ́stəsaɪd] s. & adj. insecticida.
pes·ti·lence [pɛ́stləns] s. pestilencia.
pet [pɛt] s. animal mimado, animal casero o doméstico; niño mimado; favorito; adj. favorito; mimado; — name nombre de cariño (por lo general diminutivo); v. mimar, acariciar.

pet·al [pɛ́tl] s. pétalo.
pet·cock [pɛ́tkɑk] s. llave de desagüe (purga).
pe·ti·tion [pətíʃən] s. petición, súplica; instancia, memorial, solicitud, Am. ocurso; v. solicitar, pedir, dirigir una instancia o memorial a; suplicar, rogar.
pet·ri·fy [pɛ́trɪfaɪ] v. petrificar.
pe·tro·le·um [pətrólɪəm] s. petróleo.
pet·ti·coat [pɛ́tɪkot] s. enaguas.
pet·ty [pɛ́tɪ] adj. insignificante, pequeño; nezquino, inferior, subordinado; — cash fondos para gastos menores; — larceny ratería; — officer oficial subordinado (en la marina); — treason traición menor.
pe·tu·nia [pətúnjə] s. petunia.
pew [pju] s. banco de iglesia.
pha·lanx [félæŋks] s. falanje.
phan·tom [fǽntəm] s. fantasma.
phar·ma·cist [fárməsɪst] s. farmacéutico, boticario.
phar·ma·cy [fárməsɪ] s. farmacia, botica.
phar·ynx [fǽrɪŋks] s. faringe.
phase [fez] s. fase.
pheas·ant [fézənt] s. faisán.
phe·nom·e·na [fənámənə] pl. de phenomenon.
phe·nom·e·non [fənámənən] s. fenómeno.
phi·lan·thro·py [fɪlǽnθrəpɪ] s. filantropía.
phi·lat·e·ly [fɪlǽtlɪ] s. filatelia.
phil·har·mon·ic [fɪlharmánɪk] adj. filarmónico.
phi·lol·o·gy [fɪláədʒɪ] s. filología.
phi·los·o·pher [fəlásəfə] s. filósofo.
phil·o·soph·i·cal [fɪləsáfɪk] adj. filosófico.
phi·los·o·phy [fəlásəfɪ] s. filosofía.
phlegm [flɛm] s. flema.
phone [fon] s. teléfono; v. telefonear.
pho·neme [fónim] s. fonema.
pho·net·ics [fonétɪks] s. fonética.
pho·no·graph [fónəgræf] s. fonógrafo.
pho·nol·o·gy [fonálədʒɪ] s. fonología.
phos·phate [fásfet] s. fosfato.
phos·pho·rous [fásfərəs] s. fósforo (elemento químico).
pho·to [fóto] s. fotografía, retrato; foto.
pho·to·e·lec·tric [fotoɪlɛ́ktrɪk] fotoeléctrico.
pho·to·graph [fótəgræf] s. fotografía, retrato; v. fotografiar, retratar.
pho·tog·ra·pher [fətágrəfə] s. fotógrafo.
pho·tog·ra·phy [fətágrəfɪ] s. fotografía.
pho·to·syn·the·sis [fotosínθəsɪs] fotosíntesis.
phrase [frez] s. frase; expresión, locución; v. frasear; espresar, formular.
phys·ic [fízɪk] s. purga, purgante; v. purgar.
phys·i·cal [fízɪk] adj. físico.
phy·si·cian [fəzíʃən] s. médico.
phys·i·cist [fízəsɪst] s. físico.
phys·ics [fízɪks] s. física.
phys·i·o·log·i·cal [fɪziəládʒɪk] adj. fisiológico.
phys·i·ol·o·gy [fɪzɪálədʒɪ] s. fisiología.
phy·sique [fɪzík] s. físico, constitución física, talle, cuerpo.
pi·an·o [pɪǽno] s. piano; — bench banqueta de piano; — stool taburete de piano; grand — piano de cola; upright — piano vertical.
pic·a·resque [pɪkərɛ́sk] adj. picaresco.
pick [pɪk] v. (choose) escoger; coger; (break) picar; (clean) mondarse, limpiarse (los dientes); desplumar (un ave); roer (un hueso); falsear (una cerradura); armar (una pendencia); to — flaws criticar, censurar; to — out escoger; to — pockets ratear; to — up recoger; to — up speed acelerar la marcha; s. pico (herramienta); selección, lo selecto, lo mejor; recolección,

cosecha; **ice** — punzón para romper hielo;
tooth— mondadientes, palillo de dientes.
pick·ax [píkæks] *s.* pico, zapapico.
pick·et [píkɪt] *s.* piquete (*estaca o palo clavado en
la tierra*); piquete (*vigilante huelguista*); piquete
de soldados; *v.* estacionar piquetes cerca de (*una
fábrica, campamento, etc.*); vigilar (*por medio de
piquetes*); estar de guardia.
pick·le [píkl] *s.* encurtido; **to be in a** — hallarse
en un aprieto; *v.* encurtir, escabechar; **-ed**
cucumbers pepinillos encurtidos; **-ed fish**
excabeche, pescado en escabeche.
pick·pock·et [píkpɑkɪt] *s.* rata (*m.*), ratero; *Méx.*,
Ven., *Col.* carterista.
pic·nic [píknɪk] *s.* partida de campo, día de campo,
comida campestre, *Am.* picnic; *v.* hacer una
comida campestre; ir a un picnic.
pic·ture [píktʃɚ] *s.* (*painting*) cuadro, pintura;
(*portrait*) retrato; (*photo*) fotografía; (*engraving*)
grabado; (*movie*) película; — **frame** marco; —
gallery museo o galería de pinturas; *v.* pintar,
dibujar; describir; imaginar(se).
pic·tur·esque [pɪktʃɚrésk] *adj.* pintoresco.
pie [paɪ] *s.* pastel; empanada.
piece [pis] *s.* (*section*) pieza; pedazo; parte;
sección; (*passage*) trozo; — **of advice** consejo;
— **of land** parcela; — **of money** moneda; — **of**
news noticia; — **of nonsense** tontería; —**meal** en
pedazos, a, pedazos, por partes; *v.* remendar;
to — **between meals** comer a deshoras; **to** — **on**
to juntar a, pegar a; **to** — **together** unir, pegar,
juntar.
pier [pɪr] *s.* muelle, embarcadero; rompeolas; pilar
(*de puente o arco*).
pierce [pɪrs] *v.* atravesar, traspasar; taladrar,
agujerar, perforar.
pi·e·ty [páɪətɪ] *s.* piedad, religiosidad.
pig [pɪg] *s.* puerco, cerdo, cochino; *S.A.* chancho;
C.A. tunco; cuchi; *adj.* porcino; — **iron** hierro
en lingotes; —**headed** cabezón, testarudo; **guinea**
— conejillo de Indias; **suckling** — gorrino.
pi·geon [pídʒən] *s.* pichón; paloma.
pi·geon·hole [pídʒənhol] *s.* casilla; *v.* encasillar.
pig·ment [pígmənt] *s.* pigmento, color.
pig·my [pígmɪ] *s.* pigmeo.
pike [paɪk] *s.* pica, lanza; lucio (*pez*).
pile [paɪl] *s.* pila, montón; pelo (*de ciertos tejidos*);
pilote; **-s** almorranas (*enfermedad*); — **driver**
martinete (*para clavar pilotes*); *v.* apilar(se),
amontonar(se); acumular(se).
pil·fer [pílfɚ] *v.* pillar, ratear, hurtar, sisar.
pil·grim [pílgrɪm] *s.* peregrino, romero.
pil·grim·age [pígrəmɪdʒ] *s.* peregrinación, romería.
pill [pɪl] *s.* píldora; persona fastidiosa.
pil·lage [pílɪdʒ] *v.* pillar, saquear; *s.* pillaje, saqueo.
pil·lar [pílɚ] *s.* pilar, columna; **to go from** — **to**
post ir de Ceca en Meca.
pil·low [pílo] *s.* almohada; cojín.
pil·low·case [pílokes] *s.* funda de almohada.
pi·lot [páɪlət] *s.* piloto; guía; — **light** (*o* —
burner) mechero, encendedor (*de una cocina o
estufa de gas*); **harbor** — prático de puerto; *v.*
pilotar o pilotear; dirigir, guiar.
pim·ple [pímpl] *s.* grano, barro.
pin [pɪn] *s.* alfiler; prendedor; espiga; bolo (*del
juego de bolos*); — **money** dinero para alfileres;
— **wheel** molinete, *Am.* remolino; **breast** —
broche, **safety** — imperdible; *v.* prender (*con
alfiler*); asegurar, fijar, clavar; **to** — **down** fijar,
inmovilizar; hacer dar una contestación
definitiva; **to** — **one's hope to** poner toda su

esperanza en; **to** — **up** prender con alfileres;
colgar (*un dibujo o retrato*), fijar con tachuelas.
pin·cers [pínsɚz] *s. pl.* pinzas; tenazas; **small** —
tenacillas.
pinch [pɪntʃ] *v.* (*squeeze*) pellizcar; apretar;
(*economize*) economizar; (*arrest*) prender,
arrestar; **to** — **one's finger in the door**
machucarse el dedo en la puerta; *s.* pellizco;
pizca, porción pequeña; punzada, dolor agudo;
aprieto, apuro; — **hitter** suplente, sustituto.
pin·chers [píntʃɚz] = **pincers**.
pine [paɪn] *s.* pino; — **cone** piña; — **grove** pinar;
— **nut** piñon; *v.* languidecer; **to** — **away**
consumirse; **to** — **for** anhelar, suspirar por.
pine·ap·ple [páɪnæpl] *s.* piña, ananá o ananás.
pin·ion [pínjən] *s.* piñón.
pink [pɪŋk] *s.* clavel; color de rosa; **in the** — **of**
condition en la mejor condición; *adj.* rosado,
color de rosa.
pin·na·cle [pínəkl] *s.* pináculo, cumbre.
pint [paɪnt] *s.* pinta (*aproximadamente medio litro*).
pi·o·neer [paɪənír] *s.* explorador, colonizador;
fundador, iniciador, precursor; pionero; *v.*
explorar, colonizar; fundar, promover.
pi·ous [páɪəs] *adj.* pío, piadoso.
pipe [paɪp] *s.* pipa (*de fumar*); tubo, caño; cañón
(*de órgano*); caramillo, flauta; — **line** cañería,
tubería; oleoducto (*petróleo*); *v.* conducir por
cañerías; desaguar por cañería; proveer de
tuberías o cañerías; chillar; **to** — **down** bajar la
voz.
pip·er [páɪpɚ] *s.* gaitero, flautista.
pip·ing [páɪpɪŋ] *s.* cañería, tubería; cordoncillo (*de
adorno para costuras*); chillido, silbido; *adj.*
agudo, chillón; — **hot** muy caliente; hirviendo.
pip·pin [pípɪn] *s.* camuesa.
pique [pik] *s.* enojo, resentimiento; *v.* picar, excitar;
enojar, irritar; **to** — **oneself on** picarse de,
preciarse de.
pi·rate [páɪrət] *s.* pirata; *v.* piratear; plagiar.
pis·tol [pístl] *s.* pistola; revólver.
pis·ton [pístn] *s.* pistón, émbolo; — **ring** aro de
pistón; — **rod** vástago del émbolo.
pit [pɪt] *s.* hoyo; foso; hueso (*de ciertas frutas*);
— **of the stomach** boca del estómago.
pitch [pɪtʃ] *s.* (*throw*) tiro, lanzamiento (*de una
pelota*); cabezada (*de un barco*); (*music*)
diapasón, tono; (*inclination*) grado, declive,
grado de inclinación; pez (*f.*), brea; resina;
— **dark** oscurísimo; *v.* tirar, lanzar, arrojar;
cabecear (*un barco*); graduar el tono de (*un
instrumento o voz*); echarse de cabeza; inclinarse;
to — **a tent** armar una tienda de campaña;
acampar; **to** — **into** arremeter contra; reprender,
regañar; — **in!** ¡manos a la obra!
pitch·er [pítʃɚ] *s.* cántaro, jarro o jarra; tirador,
lanzador (*en béisbol*).
pitch·fork [pítʃfɔrk] *s.* horca, horquilla (*para
hacinar las mieses, levantar la paja, etc.*).
pit·e·ous [pítɪəs] *adj.* lastimero, lastimoso.
pith [pɪθ] *s.* meollo, médula; esencia, sustancia.
pit·i·ful [pítɪfəl] *adj.* lastimoso; lamentable;
miserable.
pit·i·less [pítɪlɪs] *adj.* despiadado, incompasivo,
cruel.
pit·y [pítɪ] *s.* piedad; lástima; compasión; **for -'s**
sake por piedad, por Dios; **what a** —! ¡qué
lástima!; *v.* compadecer; tener lástima por;
apiadarse de, tener piedad de.
plac·ard [plǽkard] *s.* letrero, cartel; *v.* fijar carteles.
place [ples] *s.* (*site*) lugar, sitio; localidad;

(*position*) puesto; empleo; posición; *Col.* cupo;
— **of business** oficina, despacho; — **of worship**
templo, iglesia; **market** — plaza, mercado; **in** —
of en lugar de, en vez de; **it is not my** — **to do**
it no es mi deber hacerlo, no me toca a mí
hacerlo; *v.* colocar; situar; poner; acomodar, dar
empleo a.
plac·id [plǽsɪd] *adj.* plácido, apacible, sosegado.
pla·gia·rism [plédʒərɪzəm] *s.* plagio.
plague [pleg] *s.* plaga; peste, pestilencia;
calamidad; *v.* plagar, infestar; importunar.
plaid [plæd] *s.* tartán, tela a cuadros; manta
escocesa a cuadros; diseño a cuadros; *adj.* a
cuadros.
plain [plen] *adj.* (*flat*) llano; (*simple*) sencillo;
claro; franco; ordinario; — **fool** tonto de
capriote; — **woman** mujer sin atractivo; **in** —
sight en plena vista; **plain-clothes man** detectivo;
adv. claramente; — **stupid** completamente
estúpido; **plain-spoken** franco, francote, sincero;
s. llano, llanura.
plain·tiff [pléntɪf] *s.* demandante.
plain·tive [pléntɪv] *adj.* lastimero, triste.
plan [plæn] *s.* plan; proyecto; plano (*dibujo o*
mapa); *v.* planear; proyectar, idear; pensar,
proponerse.
plane [plen] *s.* (*airplane*) avión; aeroplano;
(*surface*) plano, superficie plana; cepillo (*de*
carpintero); *adj.* plano, llano; — **tree** plátano
falso; *v.* acepillar, alisar con cepillo (*la madera o*
los metales).
plan·et [plǽnɪt] *s.* planeta.
plan·e·tar·i·um [plænətériəm] *s.* planetario.
plank [plæŋk] *s.* table, tablón; principio, base (*del*
programa de un partido político); *v.* entablar,
entarimar, cubrir con tablas; asar (*carne*) en una
tabla.
plank·ton [plǽŋktən] *s.* plancton.
plant [plænt] *s.* (*vegetation*) planta; (*industry*)
fábrica; taller; *v.* plantar; sembrar; implantar;
establecer.
plan·ta·tion [plæntéʃən] *s.* plantación; haciendo;
plantío; sembrado; **coffee** — cafetal; **cotton** —
algodonal; **rubber** — cauchal; **sugar** — ingenio
de azúcar.
plant·er [plǽntɚ] *s.* plantador, cultivador.
plaque [plæk] *s.* placa.
plas·ma [plǽzmə] *s.* plasma.
plas·ter [plǽstɚ] *s.* yeso; emplasto; — **of Paris**
yeso, yeso mate; **court** — esparadrapo, tafetán
inglés; **mustard** — sinapismo; *v.* enyesar;
emplastar, poner emplastos a; pegar (*carteles*,
anuncios); embarrar.
plas·tic [plǽstɪk] *adj.* plástico.
plat [plæt] *s.* plano; parcela; *v.* levantar o trazar
un plano.
plate [plet] *s.* (*eating*) plato; (*metal*) placa;
plancha; lámina; **dental** — dentadura postiza;
v. platear; dorar; niquelar; blindar, proteger con
planchas de metal; laminar.
pla·teau [plætó] *s.* antiplanicie, mesa, meseta.
plat·ed [plétəd] *adj.* chapeado; blindado.
plate·ful [plétfʊl] *s.* plato, plato lleno.
plat·form [plǽtfɔrm] *s.* plataforma; tablado;
programa de un partido político; **railway** —
andén.
plat·i·num [plǽtnəm] *s.* platino.
plat·i·tude [plǽtətjud] *s.* lugar común,
perogrullada.
plat·ter [plǽtɚ] *s.* platel, platón.
play [ple] *v.* (*game*) jugar; juguetear; (*instrument*)

tocar; (*drama*) representar; hacer, desempeñar
(*un papel*); manipular (*un instrumento, radio,*
fonógrafo, etc.); **to** — **a joke** hacer una broma,
dar un chasco; **to** — **cards** jugar a los naipes,
jugar a la baraja; **to** — **havoc** hacer estragos,
causar daño; **to** — **tennis** jugar al tenis; **to** —
the fool hacerse el tonto, fingirse tonto; **to be**
all -ed out no poder más, estar agotado; *s.*
juego; jugada (*acción, movimiento en un juego*);
pieza, drama, comedia, representación;
recreación, diversión; — **on words** juego de
palabras, equívoco; **to give full** — **to** dar rienda
suelta a.
play·er [pléɚ] *s.* (*games*) jugador; (*music*) músico;
(*plays*) cómico, actor; artista; — **piano** piano
mecánico, pianola; **piano** — pianista; **violin** —
violinista.
play·ful [pléfəl] *adj.* juguetón, retozón; bromista.
play·ground [plégraʊnd] *s.* campo o patio de
recreo.
play·mate [plémet] *s.* compañero de juego.
play·thing [pléθɪŋ] *s.* juguete.
play·wright [pléraɪt] *s.* dramático, dramaturgo.
plea [pli] *s.* súplica; ruego; alegato, defensa;
pretexto; **on the** — **that** con el pretexto de que.
plead [plid] *v.* abogar; suplicar; argüir; alegar;
defender (*una causa*); **to** — **guilty** declararse o
confesarse culpable.
pleas·ant [pléznt] *adj.* grato; agradable; simpático.
pleas·ant·ry [plézntri] *s.* chanza, broma, chiste,
humorada.
please [pliz] *v.* agradar, gustar, dar gusto a;
complacer; — **do it** haga Vd. el favor de hacerlo,
tenga Vd. la bondad de hacerlo, sírvase hacerlo;
as you — como Vd. quiera, como Vd. guste; **if**
you — si me hace Vd. (el) favor; **to be -ed to**
complacerse en, tener gusto en; alegrarse de; **to**
be -ed with gustarle a uno, estar satisfecho de
(*o con*).
pleas·ing [plízɪŋ] *adj.* agradable.
pleas·ure [pléʒɚ] *s.* placer, gusto; deleite, alegría,
gozo; — **trip** viaje de recreo; **what is your** —?
¿qué desea Vd.? ¿en qué puedo servirle?
pleat [plit] *s.* pliegue, doblez; *v.* plegar, hacer
pliegues (en).
ple·be·ian [plɪbíən] *adj. & s.* plebeyo.
pledge [plɛdʒ] *s.* promesa; prenda (*garantía*);
fianza; **as a** — **of** en prenda de; *v.* prometer;
empeñar, dar en prenda; hacer firmar una
promesa; **to** — **one's word** empeñar (*o dar*) su
palabra; **to** — **to secrecy** exigir promesa de
sigilo.
ple·na·ry [plénəri] *adj.* plenario.
plen·i·po·ten·ti·ar·y [plɛnəpəténʃəri] *adj. & s.*
plenipotenciario.
plen·ti·ful [pléntɪfəl] *adj.* abundante, copioso.
plen·ty [plénti] *s.* abundancia, copia; — **of time**
bastante tiempo; **that is** — con eso basta; basta.
pleu·ri·sy [plúrəsi] *s.* pleuresía.
pli·a·ble [plátəbl] *adj.* flexible; manejable, dócil;
transigente.
pli·ant [plátənt] *adj.* flexible, dócil, sumiso.
pli·ers [plátɚz] *s. pl.* alicates, tenazas.
plight [plaɪt] *s.* apuro, aprieto, situación difícil.
plod [plɑd] *v.* bregar, trafagar, afanarse, trabajar
asiduamente.
plo·sive [plósɪv] *adj. & s.* oclusivo.
plot [plɑt] *s.* (*outline*) trama, enredo; argumento;
(*conspiracy*) complot, conspiración; (*land*)
parcela (*de tierra*), solar; (*plan*) plano, diagrama;
v. tramar, urdir; maquinar, conspirar; hacer el

plano o diagrama de; **to — a curve** hacer una gráfica.

plot·ter [plátə·] *s.* conspirador; tramador; conjurado.

plough = **plow**.

plow [plaʊ] *s.* arado; —**share** reja de arado; *v.* arar; surcar.

pluck [plʌk] *v.* coger; arrancar; desplumar (*un ave*); puntear (*las cuerdas de una guitarra*); **to — at** tirar de; **to — up** arrancar; cobrar ánimo; *s.* ánimo, valor; tirón.

pluck·y [plʌkɪ] *adj.* valeroso, animoso.

plug [plʌg] *s.* (*stopper*) taco, tapón; (*horse*) caballejo, penco; (*boost*) elogio incidental (*de un producto comercial o de una persona*); **— of tobacco** tableta de tabaco; **electric —** clavija de conexión; **fire —** boca de agua para incendios; **spark —** bujía; *v.* tapar; **to — along** afanarse, atarearse; **to — in** enchufar, conectar; **to — up** tapar, obstruir.

plum [plʌm] *s.* (*fruit*) ciruela; (*prize*) la cosa mejor; la mejor colocación; **— pudding** pudín inglés con pasas; **— tree** ciruelo.

plum·age [plúmɪdʒ] *s.* plumaje.

plumb [plʌm] *s.* plomo, pesa de plomo; sonda; **out of —** no vertical; *adj.* vertical, a plomo, recto; **— bob** plomo, plomada; *adv.* a plomo, verticalmente; **— crazy** completamente loco; *v.* sondear; aplomar (*una pared*).

plumb·er [plʌmə·] *s.* plomero.

plumb·ing [plʌmɪŋ] *s.* plomería; cañerías (*de un edificio*); oficio de plomero.

plume [plum] *s.* pluma; plumaje; penacho; *v.* adornar con plumas; **to — its wing** alisarse o componerse el plumaje del ala.

plump [plʌmp] *adj.* rechoncho, regordete, rollizo; *adv.* de golpe; *v.* **to — down** dejar(se) caer; desplomarse, sentarse de golpe.

plun·der [plʌndə·] *s.* pillaje, saqueo; botín; *v.* pillar; saquear.

plunge [plʌndʒ] *v.* zambullir(se), sumergir(se); hundir(se); lanzar(se), arrojar(se), precipitar(se); **to — headlong** echarse de cabeza; *s.* zambullida; salto (*de arriba abajo*).

plunk [plʌŋk] *v.* (*instrument*) puntear; (*place*) arrojar.

plu·ral [plúrəl] *adj. & s.* plural.

plu·ral·i·ty [plʊrǽlɪtɪ] *s.* pluralidad.

plus [plʌs] *s.* más, signo más; **— quantity** cantidad positiva; **two — three** dos más tres.

plush [plʌʃ] *s.* felpa; velludo.

Plu·to [plúto] *s.* Plutón.

plu·ton·ic [plutánɪk] *adj.* plutónico.

ply [plaɪ] *v.* manejar con tesón (*un instrumento o herramienta*); importunar (*con preguntas*); hacer con regularidad un recorrido (*entre dos puntos*); **to — a trade** seguir o ejercer un oficio; **to — oneself with** saturarse de, rellenarse de; *s.* doblez, pliegue; capa (*de tejido, goma, etc.*).

pneu·mat·ic [njumǽtɪk] *adj.* neumático.

pneu·mo·nia [njumónjə] *s.* pulmonía.

poach [potʃ] *v.* escalfar (*huevos*); invadir (*un vedado*); cazar o pescar en vedado; robar caza o pesca (*de un vedado*).

pock·et [pákɪt] *s.* bolsillo, faltriquera, *C.A.* bolsa; tronera (*de billar*); cavidad; hoyo; *v.* embolsarse; apropiarse; ocultar (*el orgullo o rencor*); aguantar (*un insulto*).

pock·et·book [pákɪtbʊk] *s.* cartera; portamonedas; **woman's —** bolsa.

pock·et·knife [pákɪtnaɪf] *s.* navaja; cortaplumas.

pod [pɑd] *s.* vaina (*de guisante, frijol, etc.*).

po·di·um [pódɪəm] *s.* podio.

po·em [póɪm] *s.* poema, poesía.

po·et [póɪt] *s.* poeta; vate.

po·et·ess [póɪtɪs] *s.* poetisa.

po·et·ic [poétɪk] *adj.* poético; **-s** *s.* arte poética, poética.

po·et·i·cal [poétɪkl] *adj.* poético.

po·et·ry [póɪtrɪ] *s.* poesía.

poign·ant [póɪnjənt] *adj.* intenso; picante.

point [pɔɪnt] *s.* punto; punta (*de lápiz, espada, tierra, etc.*); **it is not to the —** no viene al caso; **not to see the —** no caer en la cuenta; no ver el chiste, propósito o intención; **on the — of** a punto de; *v.* apuntar; señalar; indicar; **to — out** señalar, mostrar, indicar.

point·blank [pɔɪntblǽŋk] *adj.* a quema ropa.

point·ed [póɪntɪd] *adj.* puntiagudo, agudo; satírico; apto; a propósito, al caso; **— arch** arco apuntado, arco ojival.

point·er [póɪntə·] *s.* (*indicator*) puntero; indicador, señalador; (*dog*) perro de punta y vuelta; (*advice*) indicación, consejo.

poise [pɔɪz] *s.* equilibrio; porte, compostura; *v.* equilibrar(se); balancear(se).

poi·son [póɪzn] *s.* veneno; ponzoña; *v.* envenenar, emponzoñar.

poi·son·ous [póɪznəs] *adj.* venenoso, ponzoñoso.

poke [pok] *v.* atizar, remover (*el fuego*); picar (*con el dedo o cualquier objeto puntiagudo*); **to — along** andar perezosamente; **to — around** husmear, curiosear; **to — fun at** burlarse de; **to — into** meter en; **to — out** sacar; proyectarse; *s.* pinchazo; piquete; codazo; aguijonada; **slow —** tardón.

po·lar [pólə·] *adj.* polar; **— bear** oso blanco.

po·lar·i·ty [polǽrɪtɪ] *s.* polaridad.

po·lar·i·za·tion [polərɪzéʃən] *s.* polarización.

pole [pol] *s.* poste; pértiga, palo largo; asta (*de bandera*); garrocha; polo; **Pole** polaco; **north —** polo norte, polo ártico; **south —** polo sur, polo antártico; **— vault** salto con garrocha (*pértiga*).

po·lem·ics [polémɪks] *s.* polémica.

po·lice [pəlís] *s.* policía; *v.* vigilar; guardar el orden; *adj.* policíaco.

po·lice·man [pəlísmən] *s.* policía (*m.*), guardia de policía, polizonte, *Ven., Col.* vigilante, *Méx.* gendarme; *Ch.* carabinero.

pol·i·cy [pálɔsɪ] *s.* política; **insurance —** póliza de seguro.

Po·lish [pólɪʃ] *adj.* polaco; *s.* polaco, idioma polaco.

pol·ish [pálɪʃ] *s.* pulimento; lustre, brillo; urbanidad, cultura; **shoe —** betún, bola; *v.* pulir, pulimentar; dar brillo o lustre a; embolar, dar bola o brillo a (*zapatos*); *adj.* pulidor.

po·lite [pəláɪt] *adj.* cortés, fino, urbano, político.

po·lite·ness [pəláɪtnɪs] *s.* cortesía; fineza, urbanidad.

pol·i·tic [pálətɪk] *adj.* político, prudente; conveniente.

po·lit·i·cal [pəlítɪkl] *adj.* político.

pol·i·ti·cian [pɑlətíʃən] *s.* político; politicastro.

pol·i·tics [pálətɪks] *s.* política.

poll [pol] *s.* votación; lista electoral; **-s** comicios; urnas electorales; casilla (*donde se vota*); **— tax** impuesto (*de tanto por cabeza*); *v.* registrar los votos de; votar; recibir (*votos*).

pol·len [pálən] *s.* polen.

pol·li·nate [pálənet] *v.* polinizar.

po·lo [pólo] *s.* polo.

po·lo·ni·um [pəlóniəm] s. polonio.
pol·y·glot [páliglat] s. políglota.
pome·gran·ate [pʌmgrænɪt] s. granada; — tree granado.
pomp [pamp] s. pompa, boato.
pom·pous [pámpəs] adj. pomposa, ostentoso.
pond [pand] s. charca; estanque; fish — vivero.
pon·der [pándəˑ] v. ponderar, pesar, examinar; to — over reflexionar.
pon·der·ous [pándəres] adj. ponderoso; pesado.
pon·toon [pantún] s. pontón, chata, barco chato; flotador (de hidroavión); — bridge pontón, puente flotante.
po·ny [póni] s. caballito, potrillo; clave o traducción (usada ilícitamente en un examen).
poo·dle [púdl] s. perro de lanas.
pool [pul] s. charco; charca; trucos (juego parecido al billar); polla o puesta (en ciertos juegos); fondos en común, combinación de fondos (para una empresa o para especular); "trust"; swimming — piscina; v. formar una polla; combinar fondos.
poor [pʊr] adj. pobre; malo; de mala calidad; — student estudiante pobre; mal estudiante; — little thing pobrecito; the — los pobres; -ly adv. pobremente; mal.
poor·house [pʊrhaʊs] s. hospicio, casa de probes.
pop [pap] s. tronido, trueno, estallido; detonación; — of a cork taponazo; soda — gaseosa; v. reventar, estallar; detonar; saltar (un tapón); to — a question espetar una pregunta; to — corn hacer palomitas de maíz, hacer rosetas de maíz; to — in and out entrar y salir de sopetón; to — one's head out sacar o asomar de repente la cabeza.
pop·corn [pápkɔrn] s. rosetas, palomitas de maíz, Andes alborotos; Ch. cabritas; Méx. esquite.
Pope [pop] s. Papa.
pop·eyed [pápaɪd] adj. de ojos saltones, Am. desorbitado.
pop·lar [páplə˞] s. álamo; black — chopo; — grove alameda.
pop·py [pápɪ] s. amapola.
pop·u·lace [pápjəlɪs] s. pueblo, populacho.
pop·u·lar [pápjələ˞] adj. popular.
pop·u·lar·i·ty [papjelǽrɪtɪ] s. popularidad.
pop·u·late [pápjələt] v. poblar.
pop·u·la·tion [papjeléʃən] s. población.
pop·u·lous [pápjələs] adj. populoso.
por·ce·lain [pórslɪn] s. porcelana.
porch [pórtʃ] s. pórtico, porche; galería.
por·cu·pine [pɔ́kjəpaɪn] s. puerco espín.
pore [pɔr] s. poro; v. to — over a book engolfarse en la lectura.
pork [pɔrk] s. puerco, carne de puerco — chop chuleta de puerco; salt — tocino salado.
por·nog·ra·phy [pɔrnágrəfɪ] s. pornografía.
po·rous [pórəs] adj. poroso.
por·ridge [pórɪdʒ] s. potaje, gachas.
port [pɔrt] s. (harbor) puerto; (wine) oporto; (left side) babor (de un barco); —hole porta, portilla.
port·a·ble [pórtəbl] adj. portátil.
por·tal [pórtl] s. portal.
por·tent [pórtɛnt] s. portento, presagio, agüero.
por·ten·tous [pɔrténtəs] adj. portentoso; prodigioso; de mal agüero.
por·ter [pórtə˞] s. mozo de cordel, Méx., C.A. cargador; Riopl. changador; camarero (en un coche-cama); portero.
port·fo·li·o [pɔrtfólio] s. portafolio, cartera; carpeta; ministerio.

por·tion [pórʃən] s. porción; v. repartir.
port·ly [pórtlɪ] adj. corpulento.
por·trait [pórtret] s. retrato.
por·tray [pɔrtré] v. retratar, pintar, dibujar, representar.
por·tray·al [pɔrtreəl] s. retrato, delineación, delineamiento, representación.
Por·tu·guese [pórtʃəgiz] adj. & s. portugués.
pose [poz] s. (posture) postura, actitud; (affected attitude) afectación; v. posar (como modelo); colocar(se) en cierta postura; afectar una actitud o postura; proponer, plantear (una cuestión o problema); to — as fingirse, hacerse pasar por.
po·si·tion [pəzíʃən] s. posición; postura; situación, empleo, puesto.
pos·i·tive [pázətɪv] adj. positivo; cierto, seguro; categórico; dogmático.
pos·sess [pəzǽs] v. poseer.
pos·ses·sion [pəzéʃən] s. posesión.
pos·ses·sive [pəzésɪv] adj. & s. posesivo.
pos·ses·sor [pəzésə˞] s. poseedor, posesor, dueño.
pos·si·bil·i·ty [pasəbílətɪ] s. posibilidad.
pos·si·ble [pásəbl] adj. posible; possibly adv. posiblemente; acaso, tal vez.
post [post] s. (pole) poste, pilar; (position) puesto; empleo; army — guarnición militar; — haste por la posta, rápidamente; — office correo, casa de correos; post-office box apartado, casilla postal; —paid porte pagado, franco de porte; v. fijar (anuncios, carteles); anunciar; poner en lista; apostar, situar; echar al correo; to — an entry asentar o hacer un asiento (en teneduría); to be well -ed estar al corriente, estar bien enterado.
post·age [póstɪdʒ] s. porte, franqueo; — stamp sello de correo, Am. estampilla, Méx., Riopl. timbre.
post·al [póstl] adj. postal; — card tarjeta postal; — money order giro postal.
post·card [póstkard] s. tarjeta postal.
post·er [póstə˞] s. cartel, cartelón; fijador de carteles.
pos·te·ri·or [pastírɪə˞] adj. posterior; trasero.
pos·ter·i·ty [pastérətɪ] s. posteridad.
post·hu·mous [pástʃuməs] adj. póstumo.
post·man [póstmən] s. cartero.
post·mas·ter [póstmæstə˞] s. administrador de correos.
post·pone [postpón] v. posponer; aplazar, diferir; postergar.
post·pone·ment [postpónmənt] s. aplazamiento.
post·script [pósskrɪpt] s. posdata.
pos·ture [pástʃə˞] s. postura, actitud; posición; v. adoptar una postura.
po·sy [pózɪ] s. flor.
pot [pat] s. pote; olla; puchero, cacharro (de cocina); bacín, bacinica (de cámara o recámara); flower — tiesto, maceta; —bellied panzudo, barrigón; — hole bache.
po·tas·si·um [pətǽsɪəm] s. potasio.
po·ta·to [pətéto] s. patata, papa; sweet — batata, Méx., C.A., Ch., Andes camote, Carib., Riopl. boniato.
po·ten·cy [pótṇsɪ] s. potencia, poder, fuerza.
po·tent [pótṇt] adj. potente, poderoso, fuerte.
po·ten·tial [pəténʃəl] adj. & s. potencial.
pot·pour·ri [popurí] s. popurrí.
pot·tage [pátɪdʒ] s. potaje.
pot·ter [pátə˞] s. alfarero, fabricante de vasijas o cacharros de barro; -'s field cementerio de

pobres y desconocidos.
pot·ter·y [pátərɪ] *s.* cerámica, alfarería; vasijas de barro.
pouch [pautʃ] *s.* bolsa, saquillo; **mail** — valija; **tobacco** — tabaquera, petaca.
poul·tice [póltɪs] *s.* emplasto.
poul·try [póltrɪ] *s.* aves de corral.
pounce [pauns] *s.* salto (*para agarrar*); zarpada; *v.* **to** — **into** entrar de sopetón; **to** — **upon** abalanzarse sobre, saltar sobre, agarrar.
pound [paund] *s.* libra; golpazo; — **sterling** libra esterlina; *v.* golpear; machacar, martillar.
pour [por] *v.* vaciar, verter; servir (*una taza*); fluir; llover a cántaros, llover recio.
pout [paut] *v.* hacer pucheros, lloriquear; poner cara de enfado; *s.* puchero, pucherito.
pov·er·ty [pávətɪ] *s.* pobreza.
pow·der [páudə] *s.* polvo; pólvora (*explosivo*); polvos (*de tocador*); — **compact** polvera; — **magazine** polvorín; — **puff** polvera, borla, *Riopl.*, *Ch.* cisne, *Méx.*, *Andes* mota; *v.* empolvar(se); polvorear, espolvorear; pulverizar(se); **to** — **one's face** empolvarse la cara, ponerse polvos.
pow·er [páuə] *s.* poder; poderío; potencia; fuerza; **motive** — fuerza motriz; — **of attorney** poder; — **plant** planta de fuerza motriz.
pow·er·ful [páuəfəl] *adj.* poderoso.
pow·er·less [páuəlɪs] *adj.* impotente.
prac·ti·ca·ble [prǽktɪkəbl] *adj.* practicable; factible, hacedero; práctico; — **road** camino transitable.
prac·ti·cal [prǽktɪkl] *adj.* práctico; — **joke** chasco, burla pesada; **-ly** *adv.* casi, virtualmente; realmente, en realidad; prácticamente.
prac·tice [prǽktɪs] *s.* práctica; ejercicio (*de una profesión*); método; regla, costumbre; clientela; *v.* practicar; ejercer (*una profesión*); ejercitarse.
prac·ticed [prǽktɪst] *adj.* práctico, experimentado; experto, perito.
prac·ti·tion·er [prǽktɪʃənə] *s.* profesional; práctico.
prai·rie [prɛrɪ] *s.* pradera, llanura.
praise [prez] *s.* alabanza; elogio; encomio; *v.* alabar; elogiar; encomiar.
praise·wor·thy [prézwɜði] *adj.* laudable.
prance [præns] *v.* cabriolar, hacer cabriolas.
prank [præŋk] *s.* travesura, burla; **to play -s** hacer travesuras.
prate [pret] *v.* parlotear, charlar; *s.* parloteo, charla.
prat·tle [prǽtl] *v.* parlotear, charlar; *s.* parloteo, charla.
pray [pre] *v.* orar, rezar; rogar, suplicar; — **tell me** dígame por favor, le ruego que me diga.
prayer [prɛr] *s.* oración, rezo; ruego, súplica; — **book** devocionario; **Lord's** — Padre Nuestro.
preach [pritʃ] *v.* predicar; sermonear.
preach·er [prítʃə] *s.* predicador.
preach·ing [prítʃɪŋ] *s.* predicación; sermón; sermoneo.
pre·am·ble [príæmbl] *s.* preámbulo.
pre·ar·ranged [priəréndʒd] *adj.* arreglado de antemano.
pre·car·i·ous [prɪkɛrɪəs] *adj.* precario; inseguro.
pre·cau·tion [prɪkɔ́ʃən] *s.* precaución.
pre·cede [prɪsíd] *v.* preceder.
pre·ce·dence [prɪsídn̩s] *s.* precedencia; prioridad.
pre·ce·dent [présədənt] *s.* precedente.
pre·ced·ing [prisídɪŋ] *adj.* precendente, anterior.
pre·cept [prísɛpt] *s.* precepto.
pre·cinct [prísɪŋkt] *s.* distrito; recinto; **-s** límites, inmediaciones.
pre·cious [préʃəs] *adj.* precioso; querido, amado,

caro; — **little** poquísimo, muy poco.
prec·i·pice [présəpɪs] *s.* precipicio.
pre·cip·i·tate [prɪsípətet] *v.* precipitar(se); *adj.* precipitado, apresurado, atropellado; *s.* precipitado.
pre·cip·i·ta·tion [prɪsɪpətéʃən] *s.* precipitación; lluvia (*o* nieve, rocío, granizo, *etc.*); cantidad de agua pluvial.
pre·cip·i·tous [prɪsípətəs] *adj.* precipitoso, excarpado; precipitado.
pre·cise [prɪsáɪs] *adj.* preciso, exacto.
pre·ci·sion [prɪsíʒən] *s.* precisión, exactitud.
pre·clude [prɪklúd] *v.* excluir; impedir.
pre·co·cious [prɪkóʃəs] *adj.* precoz.
pre·cur·sor [prikɜsə] *s.* precursor.
pred·e·ces·sor [prɛdɪsésə] *s.* predecesor.
pre·des·tine [prɪdéstɪn] *v.* predestinar.
pre·dic·a·ment [prɪdíkəmənt] *s.* aprieto, apuro, dificultad.
pred·i·cate [prédɪkɪt] *adj.* & *s.* predicado.
pre·dict [prɪdíkt] *v.* predicir, vaticinar.
pre·dic·tion [prɪdíkʃən] *s.* predicción, pronóstico, vaticinio.
pre·di·lec·tion [pridlɛkʃən] *s.* predilección, preferencia.
pre·dis·pose [pridɪspóz] *v.* predisponer.
pre·dom·i·nance [prɪdámənəns] *s.* predominio; ascendiente.
pre·dom·i·nant [prɪdámənənt] *adj.* predominante.
pre·dom·i·nate [prɪdámənet] *v.* predominar.
pref·ace [préfɪs] *s.* prefacio; prólogo; *v.* prologar.
pre·fect [prífɛkt] *s.* prefecto.
pre·fer [prɪfɜ́] *v.* preferir; **to** — **a claim** presentar una demanda.
pref·er·a·ble [préfrəbl] *adj.* preferible; preferente.
pref·er·a·bly *adv.* preferiblemente; preferentemente, de preferencia.
pref·er·ence [préfrəns] *s.* preferencia.
pre·ferred [prɪfɜ́d] *p.p.* & *adj.* preferido; — **shares** acciones preferentes.
pre·fix [prífɪks] *s.* prefijo; [prifíks] *v.* prefijar, anteponer.
preg·nan·cy [prégnənsɪ] *s.* preñez, embarazo.
preg·nant [prégnənt] *adj.* preñado; embarazada, encinta; lleno, repleto.
pre·hen·sile [prihénsɪl] *adj.* prensil.
pre·judge [pridʒʌ́dʒ] *v.* prejuzgar.
prej·u·dice [prédʒədɪs] *s.* (*preconception*) prejuicio, prevención; (*harm*) daño; *v.* predisponer, prevenir; perjudicar.
prel·ate [prélɪt] *s.* prelado.
pre·lim·i·nar·y [prɪlímənɛrɪ] *adj.* & *s.* preliminar.
prel·ude [préljud] *s.* preludio; *v.* preludiar.
pre·ma·ture [primətjúr] *adj.* prematuro.
pre·med·i·tat·ed [prɪmédətetɪd] *adj.* premeditado.
pre·mier [prímɪə] *s.* primer ministro; *adj.* primero; principal.
prem·ise [prémɪs] *s.* premisa, **-s** terrenos; local.
pre·mi·um [prímɪəm] *s.* premio; **at a** — muy escaso, muy caro; **insurance** — prima de seguro.
pre·na·tal [prinétl] *adj.* prenatal.
pre·oc·cu·py [priákjəpaɪ] *v.* preocupar; ocupar de antemano.
pre·or·bit·al [príɔrbɪtl] *adj.* preorbital.
pre·paid [pripéd] *adj.* pagado de antemano; **to send** — enviar porte pagado, enviar franco de porte.
prep·a·ra·tion [prepəréʃən] *s.* preparación; preparativo.
pre·par·a·to·ry [prɪpǽrətorɪ] *adj.* preparatorio.
pre·pare [prɪpɛr] *v.* preparar(se).
pre·par·ed·ness [prɪpɛrɪdnɪs] *s.* preparación,

PO

prevención.

pre·pon·der·ance [prɪpándɜrəns] *s.* preponderancia.

pre·pon·der·ant [prɪpándrənt] *adj.* preponderante.

prep·o·si·tion [prɛpəzíʃən] *s.* preposición.

pre·pos·sess [pripozɛ́s] *v.* preocupar; predisponer.

pre·pos·ter·ous [prɪpástrəs] *adj.* absurdo, insensato.

pre·req·ui·site [prirɛ́kwəzit] *s.* requisito previo.

pre·rog·a·tive [prɪrɑ́gətɪv] *s.* prerrogativa.

pres·age [présɪdʒ] *s.* presagio; [prɪsédʒ] *v.* presagiar.

pre·scribe [prɪskáɪb] *v.* prescribir; recetar.

pre·scrip·tion [prɪskrípʃən] *s.* recata; prescripción, precepto, mandato.

pres·ence [prézŋs] *s.* presencia; — **of mind** aplomo, serenidad.

pres·ent [prézŋt] *s.* (*time*) presente; (*gift*) regalo; **at** — **al presente**, ahora; **for the** — por ahora; *adj.* presente; corriente, actual; — **company excepted** mejorando lo presente; — **participle** gerundio; **to be** — asistir, estar presente; [prɪzɛ́nt] *v.* presentar; regalar, obsequiar.

pres·en·ta·tion [prɛzŋtéʃən] *s.* presentación; regalo, obsequio.

pre·sen·ti·ment [prɪzɛ́ntəmənt] *s.* presentimiento; corazonada.

pres·ent·ly [prézŋtlɪ] *adv.* luego, pronto, dentro de poco.

pres·er·va·tion [prɛzəvéʃən] *s.* preservación; conservación.

pre·serve [prɪzɜ́v] *v.* preservar, guardar; conservar; mantener; *s.* conserva, compota; **forest** — vedado.

pre·side [prɪzáɪd] *v.* presidir; **to** — **at** (— **over**) **a meeting** presidir una junta.

pres·i·den·cy [prézədənsɪ] *s.* presidencia.

pres·i·dent [prézədənt] *s.* presidente.

pres·i·den·tial [prɛzədénʃəl] *adj.* presidencial.

press [prɛs] *v.* (*bear down*) prensar; apretar; comprimir; planchar (*ropa*); (*force*) forzar; apremiar; urgir; empujar; **to** — **forward** empujar hacia adelante; avanzar, ganar terreno; **to** — **one's point** porfiar; insistir en su argumento; **to** — **through the crowd** abrirse paso por entre la multitud; **to be hard -ed by work** estar abrumado de trabajo; **to be hard -ed for money** estar esacaso de fondos; *s.* prensa; imprenta.

press·ing [présɪŋ] *adj.* apremiante, urgente.

pres·sure [préʃɚ] *s.* presión; apremio, urgencia; — **cooker** cocinilla de presión; — **gauge** manómetro.

pres·sur·ize [préʃɚaɪz] *v.* sobrecargar.

pres·tige [prɛstíʒ] *s.* prestigio.

pre·sum·a·ble [prɪsúməbl] *adj.* presumible, probable.

pre·sume [prɪzúm] *v.* presumir; suponer; **to** — **on** (**upon**) abusar de; **to** — **to** atreverse a.

pre·sump·tion [prɪzʌ́mpʃən] *s.* presunción; pretensión; suposición.

pre·sump·tu·ous [prɪzʌ́mptʃuəs] *adj.* presuntuoso, pretencioso, presumido.

pre·sup·pose [prisəpóz] *v.* presuponer.

pre·tend [prɪténd] *v.* pretender; fingir.

pre·tense [prɪténs] *s.* pretensión; presunción; ostentación; apariencia; pretexto; **under** — **of so** pretexto de.

pre·ten·sion [prɪténʃən] *s.* pretensión; pretexto.

pre·ten·tious [prɪténʃəs] *adj.* pretencioso.

pre·text [prítɛkst] *s.* pretexto.

pret·ti·ly [prítɪlɪ] *adv.* lindamente; agradablemente.

pret·ti·ness [prítɪnɪs] *s.* lindeza, gracia.

pret·ty [prítɪ] *adj.* lindo, bonito, bello, *Am.* chulo; *adv.* medianamente; bastante; un poco, algo; —

well regular, así así; bastante bien, medianamente.

pre·vail [prɪvél] *v.* prevalecer; **to** — **on** (**upon**) persuadir.

pre·vail·ing [prɪvélɪŋ] *adj.* predominante; en boga.

prev·a·lent [prévələnt] *adj.* prevaleciente; común, corriente.

pre·vent [prɪvént] *v.* prevenir, evitar; impedir; estorbar.

pre·ven·tion [prɪvénʃən] *s.* prevención; precaución.

pre·ven·tive [prɪvéntɪv] *adj.* impeditivo.

pre·view [prívju] *s.* vista previa (*anticipada*).

pre·vi·ous [prívɪəs] *adj.* previo; **-ly** *adv.* previamente; antes; de antemano.

prey [pre] *s.* presa; victima; **birds of** — aves de rapiña; *v.* **to** — **on** cazar; rapiñar, pillar; robar; **it -s upon my mind** me tiene preocupado, me tiene en zozobra.

price [praɪs] *s.* precio; valor; costo (coste *o* costa); **at any** — a toda costa, a todo trance; *v.* apreciar, valuar, fijar el precio de; averiguar el precio de.

price·less [práɪslɪs] *adj.* sin precio, inapreciable.

prick [prɪk] *v.* picar; pinchar; punzar; sentir comezón; sentir picazón; **to** — **up one's ears** aguzar las orejas; *s.* picadura; punzada; pinchazo; piquete; aguijón; púa.

prick·ly [príklɪ] *adj.* espinoso, lleno de espinas; lleno de púas; — **heat** picazón causada por el calor; — **pear** tuna (*de nopal*).

pride [praɪd] *s.* orgullo; soberbia; *v.* **to** — **oneself on** (**upon**) enorgullecerse de, preciarse de.

priest [prist] *s.* sacerdote.

priest·hood [prísthʊd] *s.* sacerdocio.

prim [prɪm] *adj.* remilgado; repulido; peripuesto; estirado.

pri·mar·i·ly [praɪmérəlɪ] *adv.* primariamente, principalmente; en primer lugar.

pri·ma·ry [práɪmɛrɪ] *adj.* (*first*) primario; primero; (*basic*) fundamental; principal; — **colors** colores elementales; — **election** elección primaria; — **school** escuela primaria.

prime [praɪm] *adj.* (*main*) principal, primario, primero; (*select*) selecto, de primera calidad; — **minister** primer ministro; — **number** número primo; *s.* flor (*de la vida o de la edad*); la flor y nata (*lo mejor*); plenitud; número primo; **to be in one's** — estar en la flor de la edad; *v.* preparar, informar, instruir de atemano; cebar (*un carburador, bomba o arma de fuego*).

prim·er [prímɚ] *s.* abecedario, cartilla de lectura; compendio.

pri·me·val [praɪmívl] *adj.* primitivo.

prim·i·tive [prímətɪv] *adj.* primitivo.

prim·ness [prímnɪs] *s.* remilgo, tiesura, demasiada formalidad, dengue, afectación.

primp [prɪmp] *v.* acicalar(se), adornar(se), arreglar(se).

prim·rose [prímroz] *s.* prímula o primavera (*flor*); color amarillo pálido.

prince [prɪns] *s.* príncipe.

prince·ly [prínslɪ] *adj.* noble, regio, magnífico, propio de un príncipe.

prin·cess [prínsɪs] *s.* princesa.

prin·ci·pal [prínsəpl] *adj.* principal; *s.* principal, capital; principal, jefe, director.

prin·ci·ple [prínsəpl] *s.* principio; regla, ley; fundamento, base.

print [prɪnt] *s.* (*type*) tipo, letra de molde; (*art*) lámina, grabado; estampado (*tejido estampado*); diseño (*estampado*); impresión; **in** — impreso,

publicado; **out of** — agotado; *v.* imprimir; estampar; escribir en letra de molde; **-ed fabric** estampado.
print·er [prínta·] *s.* impresor.
print·ing [príntɪŋ] *s.* imprenta; impresión; tipografía; — **office** imprenta; — **press** prensa.
pri·or [práɪa·] *adj.* previo, anterior, precedente; — **to** anterior a, con antelación a; *s.* prior (*de un monasterio*).
pri·or·i·ty [praɪɔ́rətɪ] *s.* prioridad, precedencia, antelación.
prism [prízəm] *s.* prisma.
pris·on [prízn̩] *s.* prisión, cárcel; *v.* encarcelar.
pris·on·er [prízṇa·] *s.* prisionero, preso.
pri·va·cy [práɪvəsɪ] *s.* secreto, reserva; retiro; **to have no** — carecer de sitio privado; estar a la vista del público.
pri·vate [práɪvɪt] *adj.* privado; personal; particular; secreto; confidencial; **a** — **citizen** un particular; — **school** escuela particular; *s.* soldado raso; **in** — en secreto; a solas, privadamente.
pri·va·tion [praɪvéʃən] *s.* privación.
priv·i·lege [prívlɪdʒ] *s.* privilegio.
priv·i·leged [prívlɪdʒd] *adj.* privilegiado; **to be** — **to** tener el privilegio de.
priv·y [prívɪ] *adj.* privado; enterado de; *s.* excusado exterior.
prize [praɪz] *s.* (*reward*) premio, galardón; (*booty*) presa, botín de guerra; — **fight** boxeo público, pugilato; — **fighter** boxeador, pugilista; — **medal** medalla de premio; *v.* apreciar, estimar, tener en gran estima.
prob·a·bil·i·ty [prɑbəbílətɪ] *s.* probabilidad.
prob·a·ble [prɑ́bəbl̩] *adj.* probable; **prob·a·bly** *adv.* probablemente.
pro·ba·tion [probéʃən] *s.* probación; noviciado; prueba; **to put a prisoner on** — poner a un prisionero en libertad bajo la vigilancia de un juez.
probe [prob] *v.* tentar, reconocer, sondear (*una herida*); escudriñar, examinar a fondo; indagar; *s.* tienta (*instrumento de cirujano*); indagación.
prob·lem [prɑ́bləm] *s.* problema.
prob·lem·at·i·cal [prɑbləmǽtɪkl̩] *adj.* problemático.
pro·ce·dure [prəsídʒa·] *s.* procedimiento; proceder.
pro·ceed [prəsíd] *v.* proceder; proseguir; seguir adelante; **to** — **to** proceder a, comenzar a, ponerse a.
pro·ceed·ing [prəsídɪŋ] *s.* procedimiento; transacción; **-s** transacciones; actas; proceso.
pro·ceeds [prósidz] *s. pl.* producto, ganancia.
proc·ess [prɑ́sɛs] *s.* (*series*) proceso; (*method*) procedimiento, método; **in** — **of time** con el transcurso del tiempo, con el tiempo, andando el tiempo; **in the** — **of being made** en vía de preparación; *v.* preparar mediante un procedimiento especial, someter a un procedimiento; procesar (*ante un juez*).
pro·ces·sion [prəsɛ́ʃən] *s.* procesión; desfile; **funeral** — cortejo fúnebre.
pro·claim [proklém] *v.* proclamar; promulgar.
proc·la·ma·tion [prɑkləméʃən] *s.* proclamación; proclama.
pro·cliv·i·ty [proklívɪtɪ] *s.* inclinación.
pro·cure [prokjúr] *v.* procurar, conseguir, obtener.
prod [prɑd] *v.* aguijonear; picar.
prod·i·gal [prɑ́dɪgl̩] *adj. & s.* pródigo, gastador.
pro·di·gious [prədídʒəs] *adj.* prodigioso.
prod·i·gy [prɑ́dədʒɪ] *s.* prodigio.
pro·duce [prɑ́djus] *s.* producto; productos agrícolas; [prədjús] *v.* producir.

pro·duc·er [prədjúsa·] *s.* productor; **theatrical** — empresario.
prod·uct [prɑ́dəkt] *s.* producto.
pro·duc·tion [prədʌ́kʃən] *s.* producción; producto; obra, composición; representación teatral.
pro·duc·tive [prədʌ́ktɪv] *adj.* productivo.
pro·fa·na·tion [prɑfənéʃen] *s.* profanación, desacato.
pro·fane [prəfén] *adj.* profano; *v.* profanar.
pro·fess [prəfɛ́s] *v.* profesar; pretender.
pro·fes·sion [prəfɛ́ʃən] *s.* profesión.
pro·fes·sion·al [prəfɛ́ʃənl̩] *adj.* profesional; *s.* profesional, *Méx.* profesionista.
pro·fes·sor [prəfɛ́sa·] *s.* profesor, catedrático.
prof·fer [prɑ́fa·] *s.* oferta, propuesta; *v.* ofrecer, proponer.
pro·fi·cien·cy [prəfíʃənsɪ] *s.* pericia, destreza.
pro·fi·cient [prəfíʃənt] *adj.* proficiente, perito, experto.
pro·file [prófaɪl] *s.* perfil; contorno.
prof·it [prɑ́fɪt] *s.* (*gain*) ganancia; lucro; (*usefulness*) provecho, utilidad, beneficio; — **and loss** pérdidas y ganancias; **net** — ganancia neta o líquida; *v.* aprovechar; ganar, sacar provecho; **to** — **by** aprovecharse de, sacar provecho de.
prof·it·a·ble [prɑ́fɪtəbl̩] *adj.* provechoso; lucrativo.
prof·i·teer [prɑfətír] *s.* extorsionista, carero, explotador, logrero; *v.* extorsionar, explotar, cobrar más de lo justo.
pro·found [prəfáʊnd] *adj.* profundo.
pro·fuse [prəfjús] *adj.* profuso, abundante; pródigo.
prog·e·ny [prɑ́dʒɛnɪ] *s.* prole.
prog·no·sis [prɑgnósɪs] *s.* pronóstico.
pro·gram [prógræm] *s.* programa; plan.
prog·ress [prɑ́grɛs] *s.* progreso; [prəgrɛ́s] *v.* progresar.
pro·gres·sive [prəgrɛ́sɪv] *adj.* progresivo; progresista; *s.* progresista.
pro·hib·it [prohíbɪt] *v.* prohibir; vedar.
pro·hi·bi·tion [proəbíʃən] *s.* prohibición.
proj·ect [prɑ́dʒɛkt] *s.* proyecto, plan; [prədʒɛ́kt] *v.* proyectar(se); extender(se) sobresalir.
pro·jec·tile [prədʒɛ́ktɪl] *s.* proyectil; *adj.* arrojadizo; — **weapon** arma arrojadiza.
pro·jec·tion [prədʒɛ́kʃən] *s.* proyección; saliente, salidizo.
pro·jec·tor [prədʒɛ́kta·] *s.* proyector.
pro·le·tar·i·an [prolətɛ́rɪən] *adj. & s.* proletario.
pro·le·tar·i·at [prolətɛ́rɪət] *s.* proletariado.
pro·lif·ic [prolífɪk] *adj.* prolífico.
pro·logue [prólɔg] *s.* prólogo.
pro·long [prəlɔ́ŋ] *v.* prolongar.
pro·lon·ga·tion [prolɔŋgéʃən] *s.* prolongación.
prom·e·nade [prɑmɛnéd] *s.* paseo; baile (*usualmente* **prom**); *v.* pasearse.
prom·i·nent [prɑ́mɛnənt] *adj.* prominente; notable; saliente; conspicuo.
pro·mis·cu·ous [prəmískjʊəs] *adj.* promiscuo.
prom·ise [prɑ́mɪs] *s.* promesa; *v.* prometer; **Promised Land** Tierra de Promisión.
prom·is·ing [prɑ́mɪsɪŋ] *adj.* prometedor.
prom·is·so·ry [prɑ́məsorɪ] *adj.* promisorio; — **note** pagaré.
prom·on·to·ry [prɑ́məntorɪ] *s.* promontorio.
pro·mote [prəmót] *v.* (*favor*) promover; fomentar; explotar; adelantar; (*raise*) ascender; elevar.
pro·mot·er [prəmóta·] *s.* promotor, promovedor.
pro·mo·tion [prəmóʃən] *s.* promoción; ascenso; adelantamiento.
prompt [prɑmpt] *adj.* pronto, puntual; listo; presto; *v.* mover, incitar, inducir; apuntar (*servir*

PR

de apuntador en el teatro); soplar (*sugerir a otro lo que debe decir en una clase o junta*).
prompt·ly [prámptlı] *adv.* pronto, prontamente, presto; puntualmente; con prontitud, con presteza.
prompt·ness [prámptnıs] *s.* prontitud, presteza; puntualidad.
prom·ul·gate [prəmʌlget] *v.* promulgar.
prone [pron] *adj.* inclinado; propenso, dispuesto; boca abajo; postrado.
prong [prɔŋ] *s.* púa, punta.
pro·noun [prónaʊn] *s.* pronombre.
pro·nounce [prənáʊns] *v.* pronunciar; declarar.
pro·nounced [prənáʊnst] *adj.* pronunciado; marcado; — **opinions** opiniones decididas.
pro·nun·ci·a·tion [prənʌnsıéʃən] *s.* pronunciación.
proof [pruf] *s.* prueba; comprobación; *adj.* impenetrable, resistente; — **against** a prueba de; —**reader** corrector de pruebas de imprenta; — **sheet** prueba, pliego de prueba; **galley** — galerada; **bomb**— a prueba de bomba; **fire** — a prueba de incendios; **water**— impermeable.
prop [prɑp] *s.* puntal; sostén, apoyo; *v.* apuntalar, sostener.
prop·a·gan·da [prɑpəgǽndə] *s.* propaganda.
prop·a·gate [prápəget] *v.* propagar(se).
prop·a·ga·tion [prɑpəgéʃən] *s.* propagación; diseminación.
pro·pel [prəpél] *v.* populsar, impeler.
pro·pel·ler [prəpélə·] *s.* hélice (*de un buque o avión*); propulsor, impulsor.
prop·er [prápə·] *adj.* propio; conveniente a propósito; justo; correcto; — **noun** nombre propio; **-ly** *adv.* propiamente; con propiedad, correctamente.
prop·er·ty [prápə·tı] *s.* propiedad; posesión; posesiones, bienes.
proph·e·cy [práfəsı] *s.* profecía.
proph·e·sy [práfəsaı] *v.* profetizar, predecir, pronosticar, augurar.
proph·et [práfıt] *s.* profeta.
pro·phet·ic [prəfétık] *adj.* profético.
pro·pi·ti·ate [prəpíʃıet] *v.* propiciar.
pro·pi·tious [prəpíʃəs] *adj.* propicio, favorable.
pro·por·tion [prəpórʃən] *s.* proporción; **out of** — desproporcionado; *v.* proporcionar; **well -ed** bien proporcionado.
pro·pos·al [prəpózl] *s.* propuesta; proposición; declaración (*de amor*).
pro·pose [prəpóz] *v.* proponer; declararse, hacer propuesta de matrimonio; **to** — **to do something** proponerse hacer algo.
prop·o·si·tion [prɑpəzíʃən] *s.* proposición; propuesta; asunto.
pro·pri·e·tor [prəpráıətə·] *s.* propietario, dueño.
pro·pri·e·ty [prəpráıətı] *s.* propiedad, corrección; decoro.
pro·pul·sion [propʌlʃən] *s.* propulsión.
pro·rate [prorét] *v.* prorratear, repartir proporcionalmente.
pro·sa·ic [prozéık] *adj.* prosaico.
prose [proz] *s.* prosa; *adj.* prosaico.
pros·e·cute [prásıkjut] *v.* procesar, enjuidiar, demandar ante un juez; llevar adelante (*un negocio, empresa, demanda, etc.*).
pros·e·cu·tion [prɑsıkjúʃən] *s.* prosecución, seguimiento; parte acusadora (*en un pleito*).
pros·e·cu·tor [prásıkjutə·] *s.* fiscal; acusador.
pros·e·lyte [prásəlaıt] *s.* prosélito.
pros·pect [práspɛkt] *s.* (*hope*) perspectiva, vista; esperanza; espectativa; (*candidate*) cliente;

(*chances*) probabilidad de éxito; *v.* explorar, andar en busca de.
pro·spec·tive [prəspéktıv] *adj.* probable, posible, esperado; presunto.
pros·pec·tor [prəspéktə·] *s.* explorador, buscador (*de minas, petróleo, etc.*).
pros·per [práspə·] *v.* prosperar, medrar.
pros·per·i·ty [praspérətı] *s.* prosperidad.
pros·per·ous [prásprəs] *adj.* próspero.
pros·tate [prástet] *s.* próstata.
pros·ti·tute [prástətjut] *s.* ramera, prostituta; *v.* prostituir.
pros·trate [prástret] *adj.* postrado; abatido; *v.* postrar; abatir.
pro·tag·o·nist [protǽgənıst] *s.* protagonista.
pro·tect [prətɛkt] *v.* proteger.
pro·tec·tion [prətɛ́kʃen] *s.* protección; amparo.
pro·tec·tive [prətɛ́ktıv] *adj.* protector; — **tariff** tarifa proteccionista.
pro·tec·tor [prətɛ́ktə·] *s.* protector.
pro·tec·tor·ate [prətɛ́ktrıt] *s.* protectorado.
pro·té·gé [prótəge] *s.* protegido.
pro·tein [prótiın] *s.* proteína.
pro·test [prótɛst] *s.* protesta, protestación; [prətɛst] *v.* protestar.
prot·es·tant [prátıstənt] *adj.* & *s.* protestante.
prot·es·ta·tion [pratəstéʃən] *s.* protestación, protesta.
pro·to·col [prótəkɔl] *s.* protocol.
pro·to·plasm [prótəplæzəm] *s.* protoplasma.
pro·to·type [prótotaıp] *s.* prototipo.
pro·tract [protrǽkt] *v.* alargar, extender, prolongar.
pro·trude [protrúd] *v.* sobresalir; resaltar; proyectar(se).
pro·tu·ber·ance [protjúbərəns] *s.* protuberancia.
proud [praʊd] *adj.* orgulloso; soberbio.
prove [pruv] *v.* probar; demostrar; comprobar; resultar.
prov·erb [právɜb] *s.* proverbio; refrán.
pro·vide [prəváıd] *v.* proveer; abastecer; suplir; estipular; **to** — **for** hacer provisión para; **to** — **with** proveer de.
pro·vid·ed [prəváıdıd] *conj.* con tal (de) que, a condición (de) que; — **that** con tal (de) que.
prov·i·dence [právədəns] *s.* providencia.
prov·i·den·tial [pravədénʃəl] *adj.* providencial.
pro·vid·er [prəváıdə·] *s.* proveedor.
prov·ince [právıns] *s.* provincia; jurisdicción; **it isn't within my** — no está dentro de mi jurisdicción; no es de mi incumbencia.
pro·vin·cial [prəvínʃəl] *adj.* provincial; *s.* provinciano.
pro·vi·sion [prəvíʒən] *s.* (*goods*) provision; abastecimiento; (*plan*) estipulación; **-s** provisiones; víveres; **to make the necessary -s** tomar las medidas (*o precauciones*) necesarias.
pro·vi·so [prəváızo] *s.* condición, estipulación.
prov·o·ca·tion [pravəkéʃən] *s.* provocación.
pro·voke [prəvók] *v.* provocar; irritar; enfadar.
prow [praʊ] *s.* proa.
prow·ess [práʊıs] *s.* proeza.
prowl [praʊl] *v.* rondar en acecho; fisgonear.
prox·im·i·ty [praksímətı] *s.* proximidad.
prox·y [práksı] *s.* apoderado, substituto, delegado; **by** — mediante apoderado.
prude [prud] *s.* mojigato, persona gazmoña.
pru·dence [prúdns] *s.* prudencia.
pru·dent [prúdnt] *adj.* prudente.
prud·er·y [prúdərı] *s.* mojigatería, gazmoñería, remilgo.

prud·ish [prúdɪʃ] *adj.* gazmoño, remilgado.
prune [prun] *s.* ciruela; ciruela pasa; *v.* podar, recortar.
pry [praɪ] *v.* atisbar, espiar; fisgar, fisgonear; curiosear; **to — a secret out** extraer (*o* arrancar) un secreto; **to — apart** separar por fuerza; **to — into other people's affairs** entremeterse en lo ajeno; **to — open** abrir a la fuerza; **to — up** .levantar con una palanca.
psalm [sɑm] *s.* salmo.
pseu·do·nym [sjúdṇɪm] *s.* seudónimo.
psit·ta·co·sis [sɪtəkósɪs] *s.* psitacósis.
psy·chi·a·trist [saɪkáɪətrɪst] *s.* psiquiatra, alienista.
psy·chi·a·try [saɪkáɪətrɪ] *s.* psiquiatría.
psy·cho·log·i·cal [saɪkəládʒɪkl] *adj.* psicológico.
psy·chol·o·gist [saɪkálədʒɪst] *s.* psicólogo.
psy·chol·o·gy [saɪkálədʒɪ] *s.* psicología.
psy·cho·sis [saɪkósɪs] *s.* sicosis.
pto·maine [tómen] *s.* ptomaína.
pub·lic [pʌblɪk] *adj.* público; **— prosecutor** fiscal; *s.* público.
pub·li·ca·tion [pʌblɪkéʃən] *s.* publicación.
pub·lic·i·ty [pʌblísətɪ] *s.* publicidad, propaganda.
pub·lish [pʌblɪʃ] *v.* publicar; editar; **-ing house** editorial o editora.
pub·lish·er [pʌblɪʃɚ] *s.* publicador; editor.
puck·er [pʌkɚ] *v.* fruncir.
pud·ding [púdɪŋ] *s.* budín, pudín.
pud·dle [pʌdl] *s.* charco.
puff [pʌf] *s.* resoplido; bocanada (*de numo, vapor, etc.*); bullón (*de vestido*); **— of wind** ráfaga, soplo; **— paste** hojaldre; **cream —** bolo de crema; **powder —** polvera, borla, *Méx.* mota; *Ríopl.* cisne; *v.* resoplar, jadear; echar bocanadas; **to — up** inflar(se); ahuecar(se); hinchar(se).
pug [pʌg] *s.* perro dogo; **— nose** nariz chata, ñata o respingada.
pull [pʊl] *v.* (*tug*) tirar de; jalar (halar); (*extract*) sacar; arrancar; (*stretch*) estirar; **to — apart** desgarrar; despedazar; descomponer; desmontar; **to — down the curtain** bajar la cortinilla; **to — oneself together** componerse, serenarse; **to — over to the right** hacerse a la derecha, desviarse hacia la derecha; **to — up** parar (*un caballo, un auto*); parar, hacer alto; **to — through** salir de un apuro; sacar (*a alguien*) de un apuro; **the train -ed into the station** el tren llegó a la estación; **to — out** desatascar; *s.* tirón; estirón; ascenso difícil; esfuerzo (*para subir*); **to have —** tener buenas aldabas, tener influencia (palanca).
pul·let [pʊlɪt] *s.* polla.
pul·ley [pʊlɪ] *s.* polea; garrucha.
pulp [pʌlp] *s.* pulpa.
pul·pit [pʊlpɪt] *s.* púlpito.
pul·sate [pʌlset] *v.* pulsar, latir.
pulse [pʌls] *s.* pulso; pulsación.
pul·ver·ize [pʌlvəraɪz] *v.* pulverizar.
pum·ice [pʌmɪs] *s.* piedra pómez.
pump [pʌmp] *s.* bomba (*para sacar agua*); zapatilla; **gasoline —** bomba de gasolina; **hand —** bomba de mano; **tire —** bomba para neumáticos; *v.* manejar la bomba, *Am.* bombear; inflar (*un neumático*); **to — someone** sacarle (*o* sonsacarle) a una persona la verdad o un secreto.
pump·kin [pʌmpkɪn] *s.* calabaza.
pun [pʌn] *s.* equívoco, retruécano, juego de palabras; *v.* decir retruécanos o equívocos, jugar del vocablo.
punch [pʌntʃ] *s.* (*blow*) puñetazo, puñada; (*drink*) ponche; (*drill*) punzón, sacabocados; (*vitality*)

fuerza, empuje; vitalidad; **— bowl** ponchera; *v.* dar un puñetazo, dar una puñada; punzar, horadar, perforar; **to — a hole** hacer un agujero o perforación.
punc·tu·al [pʌŋktʃʊəl] *adj.* puntual.
punc·tu·al·i·ty [pʌŋktʃʊælətɪ] *s.* puntualidad.
punc·tu·ate [pʌŋktʃuet] *v.* puntuar.
punc·tu·a·tion [pʌŋktʃuéʃən] *s.* puntuación.
punc·ture [pʌŋktʃɚ] *v.* picar, punzar, pinchar; agujerear, perforar; **-d tire** neumático picado; *s.* picadura; pinchazo; perforación; **to have a tire —** tener un neumático picado, tener una llanta o goma picada.
pun·ish [pʌnɪʃ] *v.* castigar.
pun·ish·ment [pʌnɪʃmənt] *s.* castigo.
punt [pʌnt] *s.* puntapié, patada.
pu·ny [pjúnɪ] *adj.* endeble, débil, flaco, enfermizo; insignificante.
pup [pʌp] *s.* cachorro.
pu·pil [pjúpl] *s.* discípulo; **— of the eye** pupila, niña del ojo.
pup·pet [pʌpɪt] *s.* títere, muñeco, monigote; **— show** títeres.
pup·py [pʌpɪ] *s.* cachorrito.
pur·chase [pɝtʃəs] *v.* comprar; mercar; *s.* compra; merca; **to get a — upon** agarrarse fuerte a.
pur·chas·er [pɝtʃəsɚ] *s.* comprador, marchante.
pure [pjʊr] *adj.* puro; **-ly** *adv.* puramente, meramente.
pu·ree [pjʊré] *s.* puré.
pur·ga·tive [pɝgətɪv] *adj.* purgante; *s.* purga, purgante.
pur·ga·to·ry [pɝgətorɪ] *s.* purgatorio.
purge [pɝdʒ] *v.* purgar(se); limpiar; purificar(se); *s.* purga, purgante.
pu·ri·fy [pjʊrəfaɪ] *v.* purificar(se); depurar.
pur·ist [pjʊrɪst] *s.* purista.
pu·ri·ty [pjʊrətɪ] *s.* pureza.
pur·ple [pɝpl] *s.* púrpura; *adj.* purpúreo, morado.
pur·port [pɝport] *s.* significado; tenor, sustancia; [pɚpórt] *v.* pretender, aparentar.
pur·pose [pɝpəs] *s.* (*intention*) propósito, intención; (*goal*) fin, objeto; **for no —** sin objeto, inútilmente, en vano, para nada; **on —** adrede, de propósito; *v.* proponerse.
purr [pɝ] *s.* ronroneo (*del gato*); zumbido (*del motor*); *v.* ronronear (*el gato*).
purse [pɝs] *s.* bolsillo, portamonedas, bolsa; *v.* **to — one's lips** fruncir los labios.
pur·su·ant [pɚsúənt] *adv.* conforme; de acuerdo con.
pur·sue [pɚsú] *v.* perseguir; seguir; dedicarse a (*una carrera, un estudio*).
pur·su·er [pɚsúɚ] *s.* perseguidor.
pur·suit [pɚsút] *s.* perseguimiento; caza, acoso; ocupación; ejercicio (*de una profesión, cargo, etc.*); **in — of** a caza de, en seguimiento de, en busca de.
pus [pʌs] *s.* pus, podre.
push [pʊʃ] *v.* (*shove*) empujar; (*promote*) fomentar, promover; (*hurry*) apresurar; **to — aside** hacer a un lado, rechazar, apartar; **to — forward** empujar, abrirse paso; avanzar; **to — through** encajar (*por un agujero o rendija*); abrirse paso a empujones; *s.* empuje; empujón, empellón; **— button** botón eléctrico.
push·cart [pʊʃkɑrt] *s.* carretilla de mano.
puss·y [pʊsɪ] *s.* minino, gatito; **— willow** especie de sauce americano.
put [pʊt] *v.* poner; colocar; **to — a question** hacer una pregunta; **to — across an idea** darse a

entender bien; hacer aceptar una idea; **to —
away** apartar; guardar; **to — before** poner
delante, anteponer; proponer ante; **to — by
money** ahorrar o guardar dinero; **to — down**
apuntar, anotar; sofocar (*una revolución*); rebajar
(*los precios*); **to — in words** expresar; **to — in
writing** poner por escrito; **to — off** aplazar,
posponer; diferir; **to — on** ponerse (*ropa*); **to —
on airs** darse tono o ínfulas; **to — on weight**
engordar; **to — out** apagar, extinguir; **to —
someone out** echar o expulsar a alguien;
molestar o incomodar a alguien; **to — to shame**
avergonzar; **to — up** enlatar, envasar (*frutas,
legumbres*); apostar (*dinero*); alojar(se); erigir; **to
— up for sale** poner de venta; **to — up with**
aguantar, tolerar; *pret. & p.p. de* **to put.**
pu·tre·fy [pjútrəfaɪ] *v.* podrir (*o* pudrir), corromper.
pu·trid [pjútrɪd] *adj.* putrefacto, podrido.
put·ter [pʌ́tə] *v.* trabajar sin orden ni sistema;
ocuparse en cosas de poca monta; malgastar el
tiempo.
put·ty [pʌ́tɪ] *s.* masilla; *v.* tapar o rellenar con
masilla.
puz·zle [pʌ́zl] *s.* rompecabezas, acertijo; enigma ·
crossword — crucigrama; *v.* embrollar, poner
perplejo, confundir; **to — out** desenredar,
descifrar; **to — over** ponderar; tratar de resolver
o descifrar; **to be -d** estar perplejo.
pyr·a·mid [pírəmɪd] *s.* pirámide.

Q:q

quack [kwæk] *s.* graznido (*del
pato*); curandero, matasanos,
medicastro; charlatán; *adj.*
falso; *v.* graznar.
quag·mire [kwǽgmaɪr] *s.* tremedal, cenagal.
quail [kwel] *s.* codorniz.
quaint [kwent] *adj.* raro, extraño; pintoresco.
quake [kwek] *s.* temblor; terremoto; *v.* temblar.
qual·i·fi·ca·tion [kwɑləfəkéʃən] *s.* (*condition*)
calificación; cualidad, calidad; (*requirement*)
requisito; aptitud.
qual·i·fy [kwɑ́ləfaɪ] *v.* calificar; capacitar; **to — for
a position** estar capacitado para una posición;
his studies — him for the job sus estudios le
capacitan para el puesto.
qual·i·ty [kwɑ́lətɪ] *s.* cualidad; calidad.
qualm [kwɑm] *s.* escrúpulo.
quan·ti·fy [kwɑ́ntɪfaɪ] *v.* cuantificar.
quan·ti·ty [kwɑ́ntətɪ] *s.* cantidad.
quar·an·tine [kwɔ́rəntɪn] *s.* cuarentena; *v.* poner en
cuarentena, aislar.
quar·rel [kwɔ́rəl] *s.* riña, reyerta, pendencia;
querella; *v.* reñir; pelear, disputar.
quar·rel·some [kwɔ́rəlsəm] *adj.* reñidor,
pendenciero.
quar·ry [kwɔ́rɪ] *s.* cantera; presa, caza (*animal
perseguido*); *v.* explotar (*una cantera*); trabajar
en una cantera.
quart [kwɔrt] *s.* cuarto de galón (*0.9463 de un
litro*).
quar·ter [kwɔ́rtə] *s.* (*one-fourth*) cuarto, cuarta
parte; (*coin*) moneda de 25 centavos; (*district*)
barrio, distrito; **-s** morada, vivienda;
alojamiento; **from all -s** de todas partes; **to give
no — to the enemy** no dar cuartel al enemigo;
adj. cuarto; *v.* cuartear, dividir en cuartos;
descuartizar; acuartelar, acantonar, alojar
(*tropas*).

quar·ter·ly [kwɔ́rtəⁱlɪ] *adv.* trimestralmente, por
trimestres; *adj.* trimestral; *s.* publicación
trimestral.
quar·tet [kwɔrtét] *s.* cuarteto.
quartz [kwɔrts] *s.* cuarzo.
qua·ver [kwévə] *v.* temblar; *s.* temblor; trémolo
(*de la voz*).
quay [ki] *s.* muelle, embarcadero.
queen [kwin] *s.* reina.
queer [kwɪr] *adj.* raro, extraño, singular; excéntrico;
to feel — sentirse raro, no sentirse bien; *v.* poner
en ridículo, comprometer; **to — oneself with**
quedar mal con, ponerse mal con.
quell [kwɛl] *v.* reprimir; sofocar (*una revuelta*);
calmar.
quench [kwɛntʃ] *v.* apagar (*el fuego, la sed*);
reprimir, sofocar, ahogar, templar el ardor de.
que·ry [kwírɪ] *s.* (*interrogation*) pregunta;
interrogación, signo de interrogación; (*doubt*)
duda; *v.* preguntar, expresar duda; marcar con
signo de interrogación.
quest [kwɛst] *s.* busca; pesquisa.
ques·tion [kwéstʃən] *s.* (*interrogation*) pregunta;
(*issue*) cuestión; problema; duda; proposición;
— **mark** signo de interrogación; **that is out of the —** ¡imposible!; ¡ni
pensar en ello!; *v.* preguntar; interrogar; dudar.
ques·tion·a·ble [kwéstʃənəbl] *adj.* dudoso;
discutible.
ques·tion·er [kwéstʃənə] *s.* interrogador,
preguntador.
ques·tion·ing [kwéstʃənɪŋ] *s.* interrogatorio; *adj.*
interrogador.
ques·tion·naire [kwɛstʃənɛ́r] *s.* cuestionario, lista de
preguntas, interrogatorio.
quib·ble [kwíbl] *v.* sutilizar, valerse de argucias o
sutilezas; andar en dimes y diretes; *s.* sutileza,
argucia.
quick [kwɪk] *adj.* (*soon*) pronto, presto; (*smart*)
listo; (*speedy*) rápido, veloz; agudo; — **temper**
genio violento; — **wit** mente aguda; *adv.*
rápidamente, de prisa, con prisa, pronto; *s.*
carne viva; **to cut to the —** herir en lo vivo,
herir en el alma.
quick·en [kwíkən] *v.* acelerar(se); avivar(se);
aguzar (*la mente, el entendimiento*).
quick·ly [kwíklɪ] *adv.* pronto, presto, de prisa,
aprisa, rápidamente.
quick·ness [kwíknɪs] *s.* (*speed*) rapidez; presteza,
prontitud; (*alertness*) vivezal; agudeza (*de
ingenio*).
quick·sand [kwíksænd] *s.* arena movediza.
quick·sil·ver [kwíksɪlvə] *s.* mercurio, azogue.
qui·et [kwáɪət] *adj.* quieto; callado; tranquilo; en
calma; reposado; *s.* quietud; sosiego, reposo;
calma; silencio; *v.* aquietar; sosegar; calmar,
tranquilizar; **to — down** aquietarse; calmarse;
-ly *adv.* quietamente, con quietud;
calladamente; tranquilamente.
qui·et·ness [kwáɪətnɪs] *s.* quietud; sosiego, calma.
quill [kwɪl] *s.* pluma; cañón (*de pluma de ave*);
púa (*de puerco espín*).
quilt [kwɪlt] *s.* colcha; *v.* acolchar.
quince [kwɪns] *s.* membrillo.
qui·nine [kwáɪnaɪn] *s.* quinina.
quip [kwɪp] *s.* pulla, dicharacho; agudeza.
quirk [kwɜk] *s.* chifladura, extravagancia,
capricho; peculiaridad mental.
quit [kwɪt] *v.* (*abandon*) dejar, abandonar; irse;
(*cease*) parar, cesar; **to — doing something** dejar
de hacer algo; **-s** *adj.* desquitado; **we are -s** no

nos debemos nada, estamos desquitados, *Am.*
estamos a mano; *pret. & p.p. de* **to quit.**
quite [kwaɪt] *adv.* bastante; del todo, enteramente;
— **a person** una persona admirable; — **so así es,**
en efecto; **it's** — **the fashion** está muy en boga.
quit·ter [kwítɚ] *s.* el que deja fácilmente lo
empezado, el que se da fácilmente por vencido;
evasor; desertor.
quiv·er [kwívɚ] *v.* temblar; estremecerse; *s.*
temblor; estremecimiento.
quix·ot·ic [kwiksátɪk] *adj.* quijotesco.
quiz [kwɪz] *s.* examen; interrogatorio; cuestionario;
v. examinar, interrogar, hacer preguntas.
quiz·zi·cal [kwízəkl] *adj.* curioso; burlón.
quo·ta [kwótə] *s.* cuota.
quo·ta·tion [kwotéʃen] *s.* citación, cita; cotización
(de precios); — **marks** comillas.
quote [kwot] *v.* citar; cotizar *(precios);* **to** — **from**
citar a, entresacar una cita de; *s.* cita, citación;
-s comillas; **in -s** entre comillas.
quo·tient [kwóʃənt] *s.* cociente.

R.r   **rab·bi** [rǽbaɪ] *s.* rabí, rabino.
     rab·bit [rǽbɪt] *s.* conejo.
     rab·ble [rǽbl] *s.* populacho, plebe;
     canalla.
rab·id [rǽbəd] *adj.* rabioso.
ra·bies [rébiz] *s.* rabia, hidrofobia.
rac·coon [rækún] *s. Méx., C.A., Andes* mapache.
race [res] *s. (lineage)* raza; *(competition)* corrida,
carrera; contienda; —**track** *(o* —**course)** pista;
boat — regata; *v.* correr; competir en una
carrera; ir corriendo; regatear *(competir en una
regata);* acelerar *(un motor).*
rac·er [résɚ] *s.* corredor; caballo de carrera; auto
de carrera.
ra·cial [réʃəl] *adj.* racial.
ra·cism [résɪzm] *s.* racismo.
rack [ræk] *s. (framework)* percha, colgadero,
clavijero; *(torture)* potro de tormento; **baggage**
— red; **towel** — toallero; **to fall into** — **and
ruin** caer en un estado de ruina total; — **and
pinion** cremallera; *v.* atormentar; **to** — **one's
brain** devanarse los sesos, quebrarse una la
cabeza.
rack·et [rǽkɪt] *s. (instrument)* raqueta *(de tenis);*
(noise) boruca, estrépito, baraúnda; bullicio;
trapacería.
rack·et·eer [rækɪtír] *s.* trapacista, trapacero,
extorsionista; *v.* trapacear, extorsionar.
ra·dar [rédar] *s.* radar.
ra·di·al [rédɪəl] *adj.* radial.
ra·di·ance [rédɪəns] *s.* resplandor, brillo.
ra·di·ant [rédɪənt] *adj.* radiante; resplandeciente,
brillante.
ra·di·ate [rédɪet] *v.* irradiar; radiar.
ra·di·a·tor [rédɪetɚ] *s.* radiador; calorífero.
rad·i·cal [rǽdɪkl] *adj. & s.* radical.
rad·i·cal·ism [rǽdɪkəlɪzm] *s.* extremismo.
ra·di·o [rédɪo] *s.* radio *(m. o f.);* radio-telefonía;
radiotelegrafía; — **commentator** comentarista
radial; — **listener** radioescucha, radioyente; —
program programa radiofónico; **by** — por radio;
v. radiar, emitir, transmitir, radioifundir o
difundir.
ra·di·o·ac·tive [redɪoǽktɪv] *adj.* radiactivo.
ra·di·ol·o·gy [redɪáládʒɪ] *s.* radiología.
rad·ish [rǽdɪʃ] *s.* rábano.

ra·di·um [rédɪəm] *s.* radio *(elemento químico).*
ra·di·us [rédɪəs] *s.* radio *(de un círculo).*
ra·don [rédan] *s.* radón.
raf·fle [rǽfl] *s.* rifa, sorteo; tombola; *v.* rifar,
sortear.
raft [ræft] *s.* balsa; **a** — **of things** un montón *(o* la
mar) de cosas.
raft·er [rǽftɚ] *s.* viga *(del techo).*
rag [ræg] *s.* trapo; harapo, andrajo, *Am.* hilacho;
— **doll** muñeca de trapo; **to be in -s** estar
hecho andrajos, *Am.* estar hecho tiras.
rag·a·muf·fin [rǽgəmʌfɪn] *s.* pelagatos, golfo;
granuja, pilluelo.
rage [redʒ] *s.* rabia, furor; ira; **to be all the** — estar
en boga, estar de moda; *v.* rabiar; enfurecerse;
estar enfurecido; bramar; **to** — **with anger**
bramar de ira.
rag·ged [rǽgɪd] *adj.* andrajoso, haraposo,
harapiento, desharrapado, roto; — **edge** borde
radio o deshilachado; **to be on the** — **edge** estar
al borde del precipicio; estar muy nervioso.
raid [red] *s.* incursión, invasión repentina;
allanamiento *(de un local);* **air** — ataque aéreo,
bombardeo aéreo; *v.* hacer una incursión,
invadir de repente; caer sobre; allanar *(un local),*
entrar a la fuerza.
rail [rel] *s. (steel bar)* riel, carril; *(railroad)*
ferrocarril; *(railing)* barandal, barandilla; —
fence empalizada, estacada; **by** — por
ferrocarril.
rail·ing [rélɪŋ] *s.* baranda, barandilla; pasamano
(de escalera), balaustrada, barrera; rieles.
rail·road [rélrod] *s.* ferrocarril; *adj.* ferroviario; de
ferrocarril.
rail·way [rélwe] *s.* ferrocarril; *adj.* ferroviario; de
ferrocarril; — **crossing** cruce, crucero.
rai·ment [rémənt] *s.* vestidura, ropaje.
rain [ren] *s.* lluvia; — **or shine** que llueva o no; llueva o
truene; a todo trance.
rain·bow [rénbo] *s.* arco iris.
rain·coat [rénkot] *s.* impermeable; *Ch.* capa de
agua, *Méx.* manga o capa de hule; *Riopl.* piloto.
rain·drop [réndrap] *s.* gota de agua.
rain·fall [rénfɔl] *s.* lluvia, lluvias; cantidad de agua
pluvial; aguacero.
rain·y [rénɪ] *adj.* lluvioso.
raise [rez] *v. (lift)* levantar, alzar; subir; eregir;
(cultivate) criar; cultivar; *(collect)* reunir;
reclutar; **to** — **a question** hacer una observación
o suscitar una duda; **to** — **a racket** armar un
alboroto; *s.* aumento de sueldo.
rai·sin [rézn] *s.* pasa, uva seca.
ra·jah [rádʒə] *s.* rajá.
rake [rek] *s.* rastro, rastrillo, libertino, perdulario;
v. rastrear, rastrillar *(la tierra);* raspar; barrer
(con rastrillo); atizar *(el fuego).*
ral·ly [rǽlɪ] *v. (unite)* reunir(se); juntar(se);
(improve) recobrar(se); mejorar *(de salud);*
fortalecerse; revivir; tomar nueva vida; **to** — **to
the side of** acudir al lado de; *s.* junta
popular, junta libre; recuperación.
ram [ræm] *s. (animal)* carnero; *(tool)* ariete o
martillo hidráulico; espolón de buque; **battering**
— ariete; *v.* apisonar, aplanar a golpes; aplastar
de un choque; rellenar atestar; **to** — **a boat**
chocar con un barco; arremeter contra un
barco.
ram·ble [rǽmbl] *v.* vagar; divagar; callejear; *s.*
paseo, andanza.
ram·page [rǽmpedʒ] *s.* alboroto.

ram·pant [rǽmpənt] *adj.* extravagante; desenfrenado.

ram·part [rǽmpɑrt] *s.* baluarte, muralla.

ran [ræn] *pret. de* **to run.**

ranch [ræntʃ] *s.* hacienda, *Méx., C.A.* rancho; **cattle —** hacienda de ganado, *Méx., C.A.* rancho, *Ríopl.* estancia; *Ch.* fundo; *Ven., Col.* hato.

ran·cid [rǽnsɪd] *adj.* rancio, acedo.

ran·cor [rǽŋkə] *s.* rencor, encono.

ran·dom [rǽndəm] *adj.* impensado; fortuito, al azar; **at —** al azar, a la ventura.

rang [ræŋ] *pret. de* **to ring.**

range [rendʒ] *v.* *(align)* alinear; poner en fila; arreglar; *(wander)* vagar por; rondar; fluctuar; **to — ten miles** tener un alcance de diez millas *(un arma de fuego)*; *s.* fila, hilera; alcance; extensión; fluctuación, variación *(dentro de ciertos* límites); distancia; pastizal, *C.A.* pastal; estufa; **gas —** cocina de gas; **— of mountains** cordillera, cadena de montañas; **— of vision** campo de visión; **in — with** en línea con; **shooting —** campo de práctica para tirar.

range find·er [réndʒfaɪndə] *s.* telémetro.

rank [ræŋk] *s.* *(position)* rango, categoría; orden; calidad; grado; *(line)* fila; línea, hilera; **the — and file** el pueblo, la gente ordinaria; la tropa; *v.* poner en fila; ordenar, arreglar; clasificar; **to — above** sobrepasar a; ser de grado superior a; **to — high** tener un alto rango, categoría o renombre; ser tenido en alta estima; **to — second** tener el segundo lugar; **to — with** estar al nivel de, tener el mismo grado que; **he -s high in athletics** sobresale en los deportes.

ran·sack [rǽnsæk] *v.* escudriñar; saquear.

ran·som [rǽnsəm] *s.* rescate; *v.* rescatar; redimir.

rant [rænt] *v.* desvariar; disparatar, gritar necedades.

rap [ræp] *v.* *(strike)* golpear, dar un golpe; *(censure)* criticar, censurar; **to — on the door** llamar o tocar a la puerta; *s.* golpe; **not to care a —** no importarle a uno un ardite.

ra·pa·cious [rəpéʃəs] *adj.* rapaz.

rape [rep] *s.* estupro, violación *(de una mujer)*; *v.* forzar, violar *(a una mujer).*

rap·id [rǽpɪd] *adj.* rápido; **-s** *s. pl.* raudal, rápidos *(de un río).*

ra·pid·i·ty [rəpídətɪ] *s.* rapidez, velocidad.

rap·port [rəpór] *s.* relación de confianza mutua.

rapt [ræpt] *adj.* extasiado; absorto.

rap·ture [rǽptʃə] *s.* éxtasis, rapto.

rare [rer] *adj.* *(strange)* extraordinario, extraño; raro; *(precious)* raro; precioso; *(not well-done)* a medio asar, a medio freír, medio crudo; **-ly** *adv.* rara vez, raras veces; raramente; extraordinariamente.

rar·i·ty [rérətɪ] *s.* rareza, enrarecimiento *(de la atmósfera).*

ras·cal [rǽskl] *s.* bribón, bellaco, pícaro.

rash [ræʃ] *adj.* temerario, atrevido; precipitado; imprudente; *s.* salpullido, erupción *(de la piel).*

rash·ness [rǽʃnɪs] *s.* temeridad.

rasp [ræsp] *v.* chirriar; irritar; *s.* chirrido, sonido áspero; ronquera, carraspera.

rasp·ber·ry [rǽzbɛrɪ] *s.* frambuesa; **— bush** frambueso.

rasp·y [rǽspɪ] *adj.* ronco; áspero.

rat [ræt] *s.* rata; postizo *(para el pelo).*

rate [ret] *s.* proporción; porcentaje, tanto por ciento, *Am.* tipo *(de interés)*; tarifa; precio; **— of exchange** cambio, *Am.* tipo de cambio; **— of**

increase incremento proporcional; **at any —** en todo caso, de todos modos; **at that —** a ese paso; en esa proporción; **at the — of** a razón de; **first —** de primera clase o calidad; muy bien; *v.* calificar, clasificar, considerar; tasar, valuar; **he -s as the best** se le considera como el mejor; **he -s high** se le tiene en alta estima.

rath·er [rǽðə] *adv.* algo, un poco, un tanto; más bien; mejor; mejor dicho; **— than** más bien que; **I would — die than** prefiero antes la muerte que; **I would — not go** preferiría no ir.

rat·i·fy [rǽtəfaɪ] *s.* ratificar.

rat·ing [rétɪŋ] *s.* clasificación; rango, grado; clase.

ra·tio [réʃo] *s.* razón, proporción; relación.

ra·tion [réʃən] *s.* ración; *v.* racionar.

ra·tio·nal [rǽʃənl] *adj.* racional.

ra·tio·nal·ize [rǽʃənlaɪz] *v.* buscar excusas.

ra·tion·ing [réʃənɪŋ] *s.* racionamiento.

rat·tle [rǽtl] *v.* traquetear; golpetear; sacudir ruidosamente; confundir, desconcertar; **to — off** decir de corrido *(o* decir muy aprisa); *s.* traqueteo; golpeteo; **child's —** sonaja, sonajero; **death —** estertor de la muerte.

rat·tle·snake [rǽtlsnek] *s.* culebra de cascabel, *Ríopl., Ch.* cascabel o cascabela.

rau·cous [rókəs] *adj.* ronco; estentóreo.

rav·age [rǽvɪdʒ] *s.* estrago, ruina, destrucción; asolamiento; saqueo, pillaje; *v.* asolar, arruinar; pillar, saquear.

rave [rev] *v.* desvariar, delirar, disparatar; bramar; **to — about someone** deshacerse en elogios de alguien.

ra·ven [révən] *s.* cuervo; *adj.* negro lustroso.

rav·en·ous [rǽvənəs] *adj.* voraz; devorador; **to be —** tener un hambre canina.

ra·vine [rəvín] *s.* quebrada, hondonada, barranco *(o* barranca).

rav·ish [rǽvɪʃ] *v.* encantar; arrebatar; violar *(a una mujer).*

raw [rɔ] *adj.* *(crude)* crudo; áspero; pelado, descarnado; *(untrained)* inexperto, nuevo; **— material** materia prima; **— recruit** recluta nuevo; **— silk** seda en rama, seda cruda; **— sugar** azúcar bruto, azúcar crudo.

raw·hide [róhaɪd] *s.* cuero crudo; **— whip** rebenque.

ray [re] *s.* rayo; raya *(especie de pez).*

ray·on [réɑn] *s.* rayón, seda artificial.

raze [rez] *v.* arrasar, asolar.

ra·zor [rézə] *s.* navaja de afeitar; **— blade** hoja de afeitar; **safety —** navaja de seguridad.

reach [ritʃ] *v. (go as far as)* llegar a; alcanzar; *(touch)* tocar; *(extend)* extenderse; **to — for** tratar de coger; echar mano a; **to — into** meter la mano en; penetrar en; **to — out one's hand** alargar o tender la mano; *s.* alcance; extensión; **beyond his —** fuera de su alcance; **within his —** a su alcance.

re·act [rɪǽkt] *v.* reaccionar.

re·ac·tion [rɪǽkʃən] *s.* reacción.

re·ac·tion·ar·y [rɪǽkʃənɛrɪ] *adj. & s.* reaccionario.

read [rid] *v.* leer; indicar *(dícese de un contador, termómetro, etc.)*; **to — law** estudiar derecho; **it -s thus** dice así, reza así; **it -s easily** se lee fácilmente, se lee sin esfuerzo.

read [rɛd] *pret. & p.p. de* **to read.**

read·er [rídə] *s.* lector; libro de lectura.

read·i·ly [rédlɪ] *adv.* pronto, con presteza; fácilmente, sin esfuerzo.

read·i·ness [rédɪnɪs] *s.* prontitud, presteza, facilidad; buena disposición; **to be in —** estar

preparado, estar listo.
read·ing [rídɪŋ] *s.* lectura; indicación (*de un barómetro, termómetro, etc.*); — **room** sala o salón de lectura.
re·ad·just [riədʒʌ́st] *v.* reajustar, ajustar de nuevo; arreglar de nuevo; readaptar.
re·ad·just·ment [riədʒʌ́stmənt] *s.* reajuste; readaptación; nuevo arreglo.
read·y [rédɪ] *adj.* pronto, listo; preparado; propenso; dispuesto; — **cash** fondos disponibles; dinero a la mano.
read·y-made [rédɪméd] *adj.* hecho, ya hecho.
re·al [ríəl] *adj.* real, verdadero; — **estate** bienes raíces, bienes inmuebles; **-ly** *adv.* realmente, verdaderamente.
re·al·ism [ríəlɪzəm] *s.* realismo.
re·al·ist [ríəlɪst] *s.* realista; **-ic** *adj.* realista, vivo, natural.
re·al·i·ty [riǽlətɪ] *s.* realidad.
re·al·i·za·tion [riəlezéʃən] *s.* realización; comprensión.
re·al·ize [ríəlaɪz] *v.* (*comprehend*) darse cuenta de, hacerse cargo de; (*achieve*) realizar, efectuar; convertir en dinero.
realm [rɛlm] *s.* reino; dominio, región.
re·al·tor [ríəltə] *s.* corredor de bienes raíces.
reap [rip] *v.* segar; cosechar; recoger; obtener; sacar (*provecho, fruto, etc.*).
reap·er [rípə] *s.* segador; segadora, máquina segadora.
re·ap·pear [riəpír] *v.* reaparecer.
rear [rɪr] *adj.* trasero, posterior; de atráa; — **admiral** contraalmirante; — **guard** retaguardia; *s.* espalda, parte de atrás; trasero; fondo (*de una sala, salón, etc.*); cola (*de una fila*); **in the** — detrás, atrás, a la espalda; *v.* criar, educar; encabritarse, empinarse (*el caballo*).
rea·son [rízṇ] *s.* razón; causa, motivo; **by** — **of a** causa de; **it stands to** — es razonable; *v.* razonar; **to** — **out** discurrir, razonar.
rea·son·a·ble [ríznəbḷ] *adj.* razonable; justo; racional; módico, moderado; **rea·son·a·bly** *adv.* razonablemente; con razón; bastante.
rea·son·ing [ríznɪŋ] *s.* razonamiento, raciocinio.
re·as·sure [riəʃúr] *v.* tranquilizar, restaurar la confianza a; asegurar de nuevo.
re·bate [ríbet] *s.* rebaja (*de precio*); *v.* rebajar (*precio*).
reb·el [rébḷ] *s. & adj.* rebelde; [rɪbɛ́l] *v.* rebelarse.
re·bel·lion [rɪbɛ́ljən] *s.* rebelión.
re·bel·lious [rɪbɛ́ljəs] *adj.* rebelde.
re·birth [ribɝ́θ] *s.* renacimiento.
re·bound [rɪbáʊnd] *v.* rebotar; repercutir; [ríbaʊnd] *s.* rebote; **on the** — de rebote.
re·buff [rɪbʌ́f] *s.* desaire; repulsa; *v.* desairar; rechazar.
re·build [ribíld] *v.* reconstruir, reedificar.
re·built [ribílt] *pret. & p.p. de* **to rebuild**.
re·buke [rɪbjúk] *s.* represión, reproche, reprimenda, repulsa; *v.* reprender, reprochar.
re·call [rɪkɔ́l] *s.* llamada, aviso (*para hacer volver*); retirada (*de un diplomático*); revocación; [rɪkɔ́l] *v.* recordar; retirar; revocar.
re·ca·pit·u·late [rikəpítʃəlet] *v.* recapitular.
re·cede [rɪsíd] *v.* retroceder; retirarse.
re·ceipt [rɪsít] *s.* recibo; fórmula, receta; **-s** entradas, ingresos; **on** — **of** al recibo de; **we are in** — **of your kind letter . . .** obra en nuestro poder su grata . . .; *v.* sellar (*con el recibí*), dar recibo.
re·ceive [rɪsív] *v.* recibir.

re·ceiv·er [rɪsívə] *s.* receptor; recibidor, depositario, síndico; recipiente, receptáculo.
re·cent [rísṇt] *adj.* reciente; **-ly** *adv.* recientemente, *Ch., Ríopl.* recién (*como en salió recién*); **-ly** **married** recién casados.
re·cep·ta·cle [rɪsɛ́ptəkḷ] *s.* receptáculo.
re·cep·tion [rɪsɛ́pʃən] *s.* recepción; recibimiento; acogida, acogimiento.
re·cess [rɪsɛ́s] *s.* (*niche*) nicho, hueco; (*cessation*) tregua, intermisión; (*period*) hora de recreo o asueto; **in the -es of** en lo más recóndito de; *v.* suspender el trabajo; levantar (*por corto tiempo*) una sesión; hacer un hueco o nicho en (*la pared*).
re·ces·sion [rɪsɛ́ʃən] *s.* retroceso; contracción económica.
rec·i·pe [résəpɪ] *s.* receta, fórmula.
re·cip·i·ent [rɪsípɪənt] *s.* recipiente, recibidor; *adj.* receptivo.
re·cip·ro·cal [rɪsíprəkḷ] *adj.* recíproco, mutuo.
re·cip·ro·cate [rɪsíprəket] *v.* corresponder.
re·cit·al [rɪsáɪtḷ] *s.* recitación; relación; narración; recital (*músico*).
rec·i·ta·tion [rɛsətéʃən] *s.* recitación.
re·cite [rɪsáɪt] *v.* recitar; relatar; decir o dar la lección.
reck·less [réklɪs] *adj.* temerario, atrevido, precipitado; descuidado; — **with one's money** derrochador.
reck·less·ness [réklɪsnɪs] *s.* temeridad, osadía, descuido.
reck·on [rékən] *v.* contar, computar, calcular; juzgar; suponer; **to** — **on** contar con.
reck·on·ing [rékənɪŋ] *s.* cuenta; ajuste de cuentas; cálculo; **the day of** — el día del juicio.
re·claim [rɪklém] *v.* recobrar, aprovechar (*tierras baldías*); aprovechar o utilizar (*el hule usado*); pedir la devolución de, tratar de recobrar.
re·cline [rɪkláɪn] *v.* reclinar(se), recostar(se).
re·cluse [rɪklús] *adj.* recluso, solitario; *s.* recluso, solitario, ermitaño.
rec·og·ni·tion [rɛkəgníʃən] *s.* reconocimiento.
rec·og·nize [rékəgnaɪz] *v.* reconocer.
re·coil [rɪkɔ́ɪl] *v.* recular, *Am.* patear (*un arma de fuego*); retroceder, retirarse; *s.* reculada; rebote.
rec·ol·lect [rɛkəlékt] *v.* recordar (*rɪkəlékt*) recobrar, volver a cobrar; recoger, reunir.
rec·ol·lec·tion [rɛkəlékʃən] *s.* recuerdo.
rec·om·mend [rɛkəménd] *v.* recomendar.
rec·om·men·da·tion [rɛkəmendéʃən] *s.* recomendación.
rec·om·pense [rékəmpɛns] *v.* recompensar; *s.* recompensa.
rec·on·cile [rékənsaɪl] *v.* reconciliar; ajustar, conciliar; **to** — **oneself to** resignarse a, conformarse con.
rec·on·cil·i·a·tion [rɛkənsɪliéʃən] *f.* reconciliación; ajuste, conciliación; conformidad, resignación.
re·con·noi·ter [rikənɔ́ɪtə] *v.* reconocer, explorar; hacer un reconocimiento o exploración.
re·con·sid·er [rikənsídə] *v.* reconsiderar.
re·con·struct [rikənstrʌ́kt] *v.* reconstruir, reedificar.
re·con·struc·tion [rikənstrʌ́kʃən] *s.* reconstrucción.
rec·ord [rékəd] *s.* registro; copia oficial de un documento; memoria; historial (*de una persona*); hoja de servicios; disco (*fonográfico*); record (*en deportes*); **to break the speed** — batir el record de velocidad; **an off-the-record remark** una observación que no ha de constar en el acta; observación hecha en confianza; *adj.* notable, extraordinario; sobresaliente; [rɪkɔ́rd] *v.*

registrar; asentar, apuntar; inscribir; grabar en disco fonográfico.

re·cord·ing [rikɔ́rdɪŋ] s. grabación.

re·count [ríkaʊnt] s. recuento, segunda cuenta; [rɪkáʊnt] v. contar, narrar, relatar, referir; [rikáʊnt] recontar, volver a contar.

re·course [ríkors] s. recurso, refugio, auxilio; **to have — to** recurrir a.

re·cov·er [rɪkávɚ] v. recobrar(se), recuperar(se); recobrar la salud; reponerse; [rikávɚ] volver a cubrir.

re·cov·er·y [rɪkávrɪ] s. recobro; recuperación; cobranza; reivindicación.

rec·re·a·tion [rɛkrɪéʃən] s. recreación, recreo.

re·crim·i·nate [rɪkrímənet] v. recriminar.

re·cruit [rɪkrút] v. reclutar; alistar; s. recluta; novato, nuevo miembro (de una organización).

rec·tan·gle [rɛ́ktæŋgl] s. rectángulo.

rec·ti·fy [rɛ́ktəfaɪ] v. rectificar.

rec·tor [rɛ́ktɚ] s. rector.

rec·tum [rɛ́ktəm] s. recto.

re·cu·per·ate [rɪkjúpəret] v. recuperar, recobrar; recobrar la salud.

re·cur [rɪkɝ́] v. volver a ocurrir; repetirse; **to — to a matter** volver a un asunto.

red [rɛd] adj. rojo; colorado, encarnado; **red-hot** candente; enfurecido, furioso; muy caliente; — **tape** formalismo, trámites enojosos; — **wine** vino tinto; **to see** — enfurecerse; s. color rojo; rojo.

red·den [rɛ́dn̩] v. enrojecer(se); ruborizarse, ponerse rojo; teñir de rojo.

red·dish [rɛ́dɪʃ] adj. rojizo.

re·deem [rɪdím] v. redimir; rescatar; desempeñar (una prenda); cumplir (una promesa).

re·deem·er [rɪdímɚ] s. salvador, redentor; **the Redeemer** el Redentor.

re·demp·tion [rɪdɛ́mpʃən] s. redención; rescate; — **of a note** pago de una obligación.

red·ness [rɛ́dnɪs] s. rojez o rojura; inflamación.

re·dou·ble [rɪdábl] v. redoblar; repetir; repercutir.

re·dound [rɪdáʊnd] v. redundar.

re·dress [rídrɛs] s. reparación, enmienda; compensación; desagravio; [rɪdrés] v. enmendar, rectificar, remediar, reparar; desagraviar.

red snap·per [rɛdsnǽpɚ] s. pargo; Mex. huachinango.

re·duce [rɪdjús] v. reducir; mermar, rebajar; adelgazar(se); subyugar.

re·duc·tion [rɪdákʃən] s. reducción; merma; rebaja.

re·dun·dant [rɪdándənt] adj. redundante.

red·wood [rɛ́dwʊd] s. Am. secoya o secuoya (árbol gigantesco de California); madera roja de la secoya.

reed [rid] s. caña; junco, junquillo; lengüeta, boquilla (de ciertos instrumentos de viento); caramillo.

reef [rif] s. arrecife, escollo; banco de arena (en el mar).

reek [rik] v. (fume) exhalar, echar (vaho o vapor); (stink) heder, oler mal; s. hedor, mal olor.

reel [ril] s. (spool) carrete; carrete!; (film) cinta cinematográfica; v. aspɛr, enredar (en carretel); bambolearse, tambalearse; **to — off stories** ensartar cuento tras cuento.

re·e·lect [riəlɛ́kt] v. reelegir.

re·e·lec·tion [riəlɛ́kʃən] s. reelección.

re·en·ter [riɛ́ntɚ] v. volver a entrar.

re·es·tab·lish [riəstǽblɪʃ] v. restablecer.

re·fer [rɪfɝ́] v. referir; transmitir, remitir; dejar

al juicio o decisión de; referirse, aludir; acudir, recurrir (a un tratado, diccionario, etc.).

ref·er·ee [rɛfərí] s. árbitro; v. arbitrar.

ref·er·ence [rɛ́frəns] s. (mention) referencia; mención, alusión; (sponsor) fiador, el que recomienda a otro; — **book** libro de referencia, libro de consulta; **commercial -s** fiadores, referencias comerciales; **letter of** — carta de recomendación; **with** — **to** con respecto a, respecto de, en cuanto a.

re·fill [rifíl] v. rellenar.

re·fine [rɪfáɪn] v. refinar, purificar; pulir; perfeccionar.

re·fined [rɪfáɪnd] adj. refinado; pulido, fino, culto.

re·fine·ment [rɪfáɪnmənt] s. refinamiento, finura; buena crianza; refinación, purificación; perfeccionamiento.

re·fin·er·y [rɪfáɪnərɪ] s. refinería.

re·flect [rɪflɛ́kt] v. reflejar (luz, calor); reflexionar; meditar; **to** — **on one's character** desdecir del carácter de uno.

re·flec·tion [rɪflɛ́kʃən] s. reflexión; reflejo, imagen; tacha, discrédito; **on** — después de reflexionarlo.

re·flec·tive [rɪflɛ́ktɪv] adj. reflexivo.

re·flex [ríflɛks] adj. reflejo; s. reflejo; acción refleja.

re·flex·ive [rɪflɛ́ksɪv] adj. reflexivo.

re·form [rɪfɔ́rm] v. reformar(se); s. reforma.

ref·or·ma·tion [rɛfəméʃən] s. reforma.

re·for·ma·to·ry [rɪfɔ́rmətorɪ] adj. reformatorio.

re·form·er [rɪfɔ́rmɚ] s. reformador; reformista.

re·frac·tion [rɪfrǽkʃən] s. refracción.

re·frac·to·ry [rɪfrǽktorɪ] adj. refractario; terco, obstinado, rebelde.

re·frain [rɪfrén] v. refrenarse, abstenerse; s. estribillo.

re·fresh [rɪfrɛ́ʃ] v. refrescar(se); renovar.

re·fresh·ing [rɪfrɛ́ʃɪŋ] adj. refrescante; renovador, que renueva; placentero.

re·fresh·ment [rɪfrɛ́ʃmənt] s. refresco.

re·frig·er·a·tion [rɪfrɪdʒəréʃən] s. refrigeración, enfriamiento.

re·frig·er·a·tor [rɪfrídʒəretɚ] s. nevera, Am. refrigerador.

ref·uge [rɛ́fjudʒ] s. refugio, asilo, amparo.

ref·u·gee [rɛfjʊdʒí] s. refugiado.

re·fund [rɪfánd] s. reembolso, reintegro; [rɪfánd] v. reembolsar, restituir, reintegrar; [rifánd] consolidar (una deuda).

re·fur·bish [rɪfɝ́bɪʃ] v. retocar.

re·fus·al [rɪfjúzl] s. negativa; desaire; opción (derecho de recusar un convenio provisional).

re·fuse [rɪfjúz] v. rehusar; negar; desechar; rechazar; **to** — **to** rehusarse a, negarse a.

ref·use [rɛ́fjus] s. desechos, basura, sobras, desperdicios.

re·fute [rɪfjút] v. refutar.

re·gain [rɪgén] v. recobrar; ganar de nuevo.

re·gal [rígl] adj. regio, real.

re·gale [rɪgél] v. regalar, agasajar; recrear.

re·ga·lia [rɪgélɪə] s. pl. galas, decoraciones, insignias.

re·gard [rɪgárd] v. (look) mirar; (consider) considerar; juzgar; estimar; **as -s this** tocante a esto, en cuanto a esto; por lo que toca a esto; s. miramiento, consideración; respeto; estima; mirada; **-s** recuerdos, memorias; **in** (o **with**) — **to** con respecto a, tocante a, respecto de.

re·gard·ing [rɪgárdɪŋ] prep. tocante a, con respecto a, respecto de, relativo a.

re·gard·less [rɪgárdlɪs]: — **of** sin hacer caso de, prescindiendo de.

re·gen·cy [rídʒənsɪ] s. regencia.
re·gent [rídʒənt] s. regente.
re·gime [rɪʒím] s. régimen.
reg·i·ment [rédʒəmənt] s. regimiento.
re·gion [rídʒən] s. región.
reg·is·ter [rédʒɪstə] s. (*recording*) registro; matrícula; (*entry*) archivo; lista; (*machine*) contador; indicador; (*voice*) registro; **cash** — caja registradora; *v.* registrar; matricular(se); inscribir(se); marcar, indicar; mostrar, manifestar; certificar (*una carta*).
reg·is·trar [rédʒɪstrɑr] s. registrador, archivero.
reg·is·tra·tion [rɛdʒɪstréʃən] s. registro; asiento (*en un libro*); matrícula; inscripción.
re·gret [rɪgrét] s. pesadumbre, dolor; sentimiento, remordimiento; **to send -s** enviar sus excusas (*al rehusar una invitación*); *v.* sentir, lamentar; arrenpentirse de.
re·gret·ful [rɪgrétfʊl] *adj.* deplorable.
re·gret·ta·ble [rɪgrétəbl] *adj.* lamentable.
reg·u·lar [régjələ] *adj.* regular; metódico; ordenado; **a — fool** un verdadero necio, un tonto de capirote; **— price** precio corriente; **— soldier** soldado de línea.
reg·u·lar·i·ty [rɛgjəlǽrɪtɪ] s. regularidad.
reg·u·late [régjəlet] *v.* regular, regularizar.
reg·u·la·tion [rɛgjəléʃən] s. regulación; regla, orden; **-s** reglamento; **— uniform** uniforme de regla, uniforme de ordenanza.
reg·u·la·tor [régjəletə] s. regulador; registro (*de reloj*).
re·ha·bil·i·tate [rihæbílətet] *v.* rehabilitar.
re·hears·al [rɪhɝsl] s. ensayo (*de un drama*; *concierto, etc.*); enumeración, repetición.
re·hearse [rɪhɝs] *v.* ensayar; repetir, repasar.
reign [ren] s. reino, reinado; *v.* reinar.
re·im·burse [riɪmbɝs] *v.* reembolsar.
re·im·burse·ment [riɪmbɝsmənt] s. reembolso, reintegro.
rein [ren] s. rienda; *v.* guiar, gobernar; refrenar (*un caballo*).
re·in·car·nate [riɪnkárnet] *v.* reencarnar.
rein·deer [réndɪr] s. reno (*especie de ciervo*).
re·in·force [riɪnfórs] *v.* reforzar.
re·in·force·ment [riɪnfórsmənt] s. refuerzo.
re·it·er·ate [riítəret] *v.* reiterar, repetir.
re·ject [rɪdʒékt] *v.* rechazar; desechar; descartar; rehusar.
re·joice [rɪdʒɔ́ɪs] *v.* regocijar(se).
re·joic·ing [rɪdʒɔ́ɪsɪŋ] s. regocijo, júbilo.
re·join [rɪdʒɔ́ɪn] *v.* reunirse con; volver(se) a unir; [rɪdʒɔ́ɪn] replicar.
re·ju·ve·nate [rɪdʒúvənet] *v.* rejuvenecer.
re·lapse [rɪlǽps] s. recaída; *v.* recaer, reincidir.
re·late [rɪlét] *v.* relatar, narrar; relacionar; **it -s to** se relaciona con, se refiere a.
re·lat·ed [rɪlétɪd] *adj.* relatado, narrado; relacionado; **to become — by marriage** emparentar; **we are —** somos parientes; estamos emparentados.
re·la·tion [rɪléʃən] s. (*association*) relación; (*story*) narración; (*kinship*) parentesco; pariente; **-s** parientes, parentela; **with — to** con relación a, con respecto a, tocante a.
re·la·tion·ship [rɪléʃənʃɪp] s. relación; parentesco.
rel·a·tive [rélətɪv] *adj.* relativo; s. relativo, pronombre relativo; pariente, deudo; **— to** relativo a; tocante a; referente a.
re·lax [rɪlǽks] *v.* relajar; aflojar; mitigar(se); esparcirse, recrearse.
re·lax·a·tion [rilækséʃən] s. (*loosening*) expansión,

esparcimiento; aflojamento o relajamiento; (*recreation*) solaz, recreo; **— of discipline** relajación de la disciplina; **— of one's mind** esparcimiento del ánimo.
re·lay [rile] s. relevo, remuda **— race** carrera de relevo; **electric —** relevador; [rɪlé] *v.* transmitir, despachar; hacer cundir (*una noticia*); **to — a broadcast** reemitir (*o* redifundir) un programa de radio.
re·lease [rɪlís] *v.* soltar; librar; poner en libertad; relevar, aliviar; **to — a piece of news** hacer pública una nueva; **to — from blame** exonerar; s. liberación; alivio; exoneración; escape.
rel·e·gate [réləget] *v.* relegar; **to — to a corner** arrinconar, arrumbar.
re·lent [rɪlént] *v.* mitigar(se); ceder; aplacarse.
re·lent·less [rɪléntlɪs] *adj.* implacable.
rel·e·vant [réləvənt] *adj.* pertinente; a propósito.
re·li·a·bil·i·ty [rɪlaɪəbílətɪ] s. formalidad; puntualidad; integridad.
re·li·a·ble [rɪláɪəbl] *adj.* formal; puntual; digno de confianza.
re·li·ance [rɪláɪəns] s. confianza; **self-reliance** confianza en sí, confianza en sus propias fuerzas.
rel·ic [rélɪk] s. reliquia.
re·lief [rɪlíf] s. (*ease*) alivio; descanso; consuelo; (*help*) ayuda, socorro; (*projection*) relieve, realce; **low —** bajo relieve; **to be on —** recibir manutención gratuita; **to put in —** realzar, poner en relieve.
re·lieve [rɪlív] *v.* relevar; librar; ayudar; aliviar; mitigar.
re·li·gion [rɪlídʒən] s. religión.
re·li·gious [rɪlídʒəs] *adj.* & s. religioso.
re·lin·quish [rɪlíŋkwɪʃ] *v.* abandonar, dejar.
rel·ish [rélɪʃ] s. (*zest*) buen sabor; gusto; apetito; goce; (*condiment*) condimento; entremés; *v.* saborear, paladear; gustarle a uno, agradarle a uno.
re·lo·cate [rɪlóket] *v.* restablecer.
re·luc·tance [rɪlʌ́ktəns] s. repugnancia, renuencia, aversión, desgana.
re·luc·tant [rɪlʌ́ktənt] *adj.* renuente, refractario, opuesto; **-ly** *adv.* renuentemente, con renuencia, de mala gana; a redopelo.
re·ly [rɪláɪ] *v.* **to — on** contar con, confiar en, fiarse en.
re·main [rɪmén] *v.* quedar(se), permanecer, estarse; restar, faltar.
re·main·der [rɪméndə] s. resto; restante; residuo.
re·mains [rɪménz] s. *pl.* restos; reliquias; sobras.
re·mark [rɪmárk] s. observación, nota, reparo; *v.* notar, observar; **to — on** comentar; aludir a.
re·mark·a·ble [rɪmárkəbl] *adj.* notable; extraordinario; **remarkably** *adv.* notablemente, extraordinariamente.
rem·e·dy [rémədɪ] s. remedio; cura; *v.* remediar; curar.
re·mem·ber [rɪmémbə] *v.* recordar; acordarse; **me to him** déle Vd. recuerdos (*o* memorias) de mi parte.
re·mem·brance [rɪmémbrəns] s. recuerdo; recordación; memoria; **-s** recuerdos, saludos.
re·mind [rɪmáɪnd] *v.* recordar.
re·mind·er [rɪmáɪndə] s. recordatorio, recordativo, memorándum, memoria; advertencia.
rem·i·nis·cence [rɛmənísns] s. reminiscencia, memoria, recuerdo.
re·miss [rɪmís] *adj.* descuidado, negligente.
re·mis·sion [rɪmíʃən] s. remisión, perdón.

RE

re·mit [rɪmít] v. remitir; remesar, enviar una remesa; perdonar, absolver.

re·mit·tance [rɪmítn̩s] s. remisión, envío, remesa (de fondos).

rem·nant [rémnənt] s. resto; residuo; retazo (de tela, paño, etc.); vestigio.

re·mod·el [rimádl] v. rehacer, reconstruir; modelar de nuevo.

re·morse [rɪmɔ́rs] s. remordimiento.

re·mote [rɪmót] adj. remoto; lejano; s. — control telecontrol; comando a distancia.

re·mov·al [rɪmúvl] s. mudanza, traslado; deposición (de un empleo); eliminación; extracción; alejamiento.

re·move [rɪmúv] v. remover; mudar(se), trasladar(se); quitar; eliminar; extirpar; sacar, extraer; deponer (de un empleo); apartar; alejar.

re·moved [rɪmúvd] adj. remoto, distante.

re·nais·sance [renəsáns] s. renacimiento.

re·na·scence [rɪnǽsn̩s] s. renacimiento.

rend [rend] v. desgarrar, rasgar; rajar.

ren·der [réndɚ] v. dar; entregar; hacer; ejecutar, interpretar (música o un papel dramático); traducir; **to — an account of** rendir o dar cuenta de; **to — homage** rendir homenaje; **to — thanks** rendir gracias, dar las gracias; **to — useless** inutilizar, incapacitar.

ren·di·tion [rendíʃən] s. (surrender) rendición; (version) traducción, ejecución.

re·new [rɪnjú] v. renovar; restaurar; reanudar; prorrogar (un préstamo).

re·new·al [rɪnjúəl] s. renovación; reanudación; prórroga.

re·nounce [rɪnáuns] v. renunciar.

ren·o·vate [rénəvet] v. renovar.

re·nown [rɪnáun] s. renombre.

re·nowned [rɪnáund] adj. renombrado.

rent [rent] s. alquiler; renta, arrendamiento; **it is for** — se alquila, se arrienda; v. alquilar, arrendar.

rent [rent] pret. & p.p. de **to rend**; s. grieta, hendidura; rasgadura, rotura.

rent·al [réntl] s. renta, alquiler.

re·o·pen [riópən] v. reabrir(se), volver a abrir(se).

re·pair [rɪpér] v. reparar; remendar; componer; restaurar; **to — to** dirigirse a; s. reparo, reparación; remiendo; compostura; **in — en** buen estado; compuesto.

rep·a·ra·tion [repəréʃən] s. reparación; desagravio.

rep·ar·tee [repartí] s. respuesta viva; agudeza en el diálogo.

re·pay [rɪpé] v. resarcir; compensar; reembolsar; pagar.

re·pay·ment [rɪpémənt] s. reintegro, pago, devolución, restitución.

re·peal [rɪpíl] v. derogar, abrogar, revocar, abolir (una ley); s. abrogación, derogación, revocación, abolición (de una ley).

re·peat [rɪpít] v. repetir; s. repetición.

re·peat·ed [rɪpítɪd] adj. repetido; **-ly** adv. repetidamente; repetidas veces, una y otra vez.

re·pel [rɪpél] v. repeler; rechazar; repugnar; **that idea -s me** me repugna (o me es repugnante) esa idea.

re·pel·lent [rɪpélənt] s. repelente; (water) impermeable.

re·pent [rɪpént] v. arrepentirse (de).

re·pen·tance [rɪpéntəns] s. arrepentimiento.

re·pen·tant [rɪpéntənt] adj. arrepentido; penitente.

rep·er·toire [répətwar] s. repertorio.

rep·e·ti·tion [repɪtíʃən] s. repetición.

re·place [rɪplés] v. reponer, volver a colocar; reemplazar; restituir; remudar.

re·place·a·ble [rɪplésəbl] adj. reemplazable; substituible.

re·place·ment [rɪplésmənt] s. reposición; reemplazo; devolución, restitución; substitución.

re·plen·ish [rɪpléniʃ] v. reabastecer; rellenar, llenar.

re·plete [rɪplít] adj. repleto, atestado.

rep·li·ca [réplɪkə] s. reproducción, copia exacta.

re·ply [rɪplái] v. replicar, contestar, responder; s. réplica, contestación, respuesta.

re·port [rɪpórt] v. dar cuenta de; avisar; informar; presentar un informe; rendir informe; hacer un reportaje, Am. reportar; denunciar, delatar; presentarse; **to — for duty** presentarse; **it is -ed that** dizque, se dice que, corre la voz que; s. noticia, reporte; informe; memorial; relación; rumor; estallido, disparo; **news** — reportaje.

re·port·er [rɪpórtɚ] s. reportero, repórter.

re·pose [rɪpóz] v. reposar, decansar; **to — one's confidence in** confiar en; depositar su confianza en; s. reposo.

re·pos·i·to·ry [rɪpázətorɪ] s. depósito; almacén.

rep·re·sent [reprɪzént] v. representar.

rep·re·sen·ta·tion [reprɪzentéʃən] s. representación.

rep·re·sen·ta·tive [reprɪzéntətɪv] adj. representativo; típico; s. representante; delegado, diputado.

re·press [rɪprés] v. reprimir; refrenar, restringir; cohibir.

re·pres·sion [rɪpréʃən] s. represión.

re·prieve [rɪpriv] v. suspensión temporal de pena; alivio.

rep·ri·mand [réprəmænd] v. reprender, regañar; s. reprensión, regaño.

re·pri·sal [rɪpráɪzl] s. represalia.

re·proach [rɪprótʃ] v. reprochar; censurar, criticar; echar en cara; s. reproche, reprimenda; censura.

re·pro·duce [riprədjús] v. reproducir.

re·pro·duc·tion [riprədʌ́kʃən] s. reproducción.

re·proof [rɪprúf] s. reprensión, reproche, regaño.

re·prove [rɪprúv] v. reprobar; reprender, censurar.

rep·tile [réptl] s. reptil.

re·pub·lic [rɪpʌ́blɪk] s. república.

re·pub·li·can [rɪpʌ́blɪkən] adj. & s. republicano.

re·pu·di·ate [rɪpjúdɪet] v. repudiar.

re·pug·nance [rɪpʌ́gnəns] s. repugnancia; aversión.

re·pug·nant [rɪpʌ́gnənt] adj. repugnante; antipático.

re·pulse [rɪpʌ́ls] v. repulsar, repeler; rechazar; s. repulsa; desaire.

re·pul·sive [rɪpʌ́lsɪv] adj. repulsivo, repugnante.

rep·u·ta·ble [répjətəbl] adj. de buena reputación.

rep·u·ta·tion [repjətéʃən] s. reputación, renombre.

re·pute [rɪpjút] v. reputar; estimar, considerar; s. reputación; renombre, fama; **of ill** — de mala fama.

re·quest [rɪkwést] s. solicitud, petición, demanda; súplica, ruego; **at the** — **of** a solicitud de, a instancias de; v. solicitar, pedir, rogar, suplicar.

re·quire [rɪkwáɪr] v. requerir; exigir, demandar.

re·quire·ment [rɪkwáɪrmənt] s. requerimiento, requisito; exigencia; necesidad.

req·ui·site [rékwəzɪt] s. requisito; adj. requerido, necesario.

req·ui·si·tion [rekwəzíʃən] s. requisición, demanda, orden; v. demandar, pedir, ordenar.

re·scind [rɪsínd] v. rescindir.

res·cue [réskju] v. rescatar; librar; salvar; s. rescate, salvamento, salvación, socorro; **to go to the** — **of** acudir al socorro de, a salvar a.

re·search [rísɜrtʃ] s. rebusca, búsqueda,

investigación; [rɪsɜ́tʃ] v. rebuscar, investigar.
re·sem·blance [rɪzémbləns] s. semejanza, parecido.
re·sem·ble [rɪzémbl] v. asemejarse a, semejar, parecerse a.
re·sent [rɪzént] v. resentirse de, sentirse de, darse por agraviado de.
re·sent·ful [rɪzéntfəl] adj. resentido; rencoroso.
re·sent·ment [rɪzéntmənt] s. resentimiento.
res·er·va·tion [rɛzɚvéʃən] s. reservación; reserva.
re·serve [rɪzɜ́v] v. reservar; s. reserva.
re·served [rɪzɜ́vd] adj. retraido.
res·er·voir [rézɚvwɔr] s. depósito (de agua, aceite, gas, provisiones, etc.); receptáculo; water — alberca, aljibe, tanque, estanque.
re·side [rɪzáɪd] v. residir, vivir.
res·i·dence [rézədəns] s. residencia; domicilio.
res·i·dent [rézədənt] adj. & s. residente.
res·i·den·tial [rɛzɪdéntʃəl] adj. residencial.
res·i·due [rézədju] s. residuo; resto.
re·sign [rɪzáɪn] v. renunciar; dimitir; to — oneself to resignarse a.
res·ig·na·tion [rɛzɪgnéʃən] s. renuncia, dimisión; resignación.
re·sil·ience [rɪzíljəns] s. elasticidad.
res·in [rézɪn] s. resina.
re·sist [rɪzíst] v. resistir; oponerse, resistirse a.
re·sis·tance [rɪzístəns] s. resistencia.
re·sis·tant [rɪzístənt] adj. resistente.
res·o·lute [rézəlut] adj. resuelto.
res·o·lu·tion [rɛzəlúʃən] s. resolución; acuerdo.
re·solve [rɪzálv] v. resolver(se); to — into resolverse en, reducirse a, transformarse en; to — to acordar; proponerse, resolverse a.
res·o·nance [rézənəns] s. resonancia.
res·o·nant [rézənənt] adj. resonante.
re·sort [rɪzɔ́rt] v. recurrir, acudir; to — to force recurrir a la fuerza; s. refugio; morada; as a last — como último recurso; summer — lugar de veraneo; vice — garito; casa de mala fama; to have — to recurrir a.
re·sort·er [rɪzɔ́rtɚ] s. summer — veraneante.
re·sound [rɪzáʊnd] v. resonar; repercutir; retumbar.
re·source [rɪsórs] s. recurso; natural -s recursos o riquezas naturales.
re·spect [rɪspékt] v. respectar; as -s por lo que respecta a, por lo que toca a, tocante a; s. respeto; consideración; with — to (con) respecto a, respecto de; por lo que atañe a.
re·spect·a·ble [rɪspéktəbl] adj. respetable.
re·spect·ful [rɪspéktfəl] adj. respetuoso.
re·spect·ing [rɪspéktɪŋ] prep. con respecto a, tocante a.
re·spec·tive [rɪspéktɪv] adj. respectivo.
res·pi·ra·tion [rɛspəréʃən] s. respiración, respiro.
re·spite [réspɪt] s. tregua, pausa, descanso; intervalo; prórroga.
re·splen·dent [rɪspléndənt] adj. resplandeciente.
re·spond [rɪspánd] v. responder; corresponder; reaccionar.
re·sponse [rɪspáns] s. respuesta, contestación; reacción.
re·spon·si·bil·i·ty [rɪspansəbílətɪ] s. responsabilidad.
re·spon·si·ble [rɪspánsəbl] adj. responsable; formal, digno de confianza.
rest [rɛst] s. (repose) descanso; reposo; quietud; tregua; pausa; (support) apoyo; at — en paz; en reposo; tranquilo; the — el resto; los demás; v. descansar; reposar; apoyar; to — on descansar sobre; apoyar(se) en; basar(se) en; contar con, confiar en, depender de.

res·tau·rant [réstərənt] s. restaurante. Am. restorán.
rest·ful [réstfəl] adj. reposado, sosegado, tranquilo.
res·ti·tu·tion [rɛstətjúʃən] s. restitución; devolución.
res·tive [réstɪv] adj. intranquilo.
rest·less [réstlɪs] adj. inquieto, intranquilo.
rest·less·ness [réstlɪsnɪs] s. inquietud, desasosiego, intranquilidad.
res·to·ra·tion [rɛstəréʃən] s. restauración; restitución; renovación.
re·store [rɪstór] v. restaurar; renovar; restituir; restablecer.
re·strain [rɪstrén] v. refrenar, contener, cohibir, reprimir, coartar; restringir.
re·straint [rɪstrént] s. restricción; reserva, circunspección; moderación; cohibición.
re·strict [rɪstríkt] v. restringir, limitar.
re·stric·tion [rɪstríkʃən] s. restricción.
re·sult [rɪzʌ́lt] v. resultar; to — from resultar de; to — in parar en; causar; dar por resultado; s. resulta, resultado; as a — de resultas, como resultado.
re·sume [rɪzúm] v. reasumir, volver a tomar; recomenzar; reanudar, continuar.
ré·su·mé [rɛzʊmé] s. resumen, sumario.
re·sur·gent [rɪsɜ́dʒənt] adj. resurgente.
res·ur·rec·tion [rɛzərékʃən] s. resurrección.
re·sus·ci·tate [rɪsʌ́sətet] v. resucitar; revivir.
re·tail [rítel] s. venta al por menor; at — al por menor; — merchant detallista, comerciante al por menor; — price precio al por menor; v. detallar; vender al menudeo (o vender al por menor), Méx., C.A., Ven., Col. menudear.
re·tail·er [rítelɚ] s. detallista, revendedor, comerciante al por menor.
re·tain [rɪtén] v. retener; emplear.
re·tal·i·ate [rɪtǽliet] v. desquitarse, vengarse.
re·tal·i·a·tion [rɪtæliéʃən] s. desquite; desagravio; represalia, venganza.
re·tard [rɪtárd] v. retardar, retrasar, atrasar.
re·ten·tion [rɪténʃən] s. retención.
ret·i·cence [rétəsəns] s. reserva.
ret·i·nue [rétnju] s. comitiva, séquito, acompañamiento.
re·tire [rɪtáɪr] v. retirar(se); jubilar(se); acostarse; apartarse.
re·tire·ment [rɪtáɪrmənt] s. retiro; jubilación.
re·tort [rɪtɔ́rt] v. replicar; redargüir; s. réplica.
re·touch [rɪtʌ́tʃ] v. retocar; s. retoque.
re·trace [rɪtrés] v. repasar; volver a trazar; to — one's steps volver sobre sus pasos, retroceder.
re·tract [rɪtrǽkt] v. retractar, retractarse de; desdecirse (de); retraer.
re·treat [rɪtrít] s. retiro, refugio, asilo; retirada; retreta (toque de retirada); v. retirarse; retroceder.
re·trench [rɪtréntʃ] v. cercenar, reducir, disminuir; economizar.
re·trieve [rɪtrív] v. cobrar (la caza); recobrar, recuperar; reparar (una pérdida).
ret·ro·ac·tive [rɛtroǽktɪv] adj. retroactivo.
ret·ro·flex [rɛtrofléks] adj. retroflejo.
ret·ro·rock·et [rétrorakɪt] s. retrocohete.
ret·ro·spect [rétrospɛkt] s. retrospección; in — retrospectivamente.
re·turn [rɪtɜ́n] v. volver, regresar; retornar; devolver; replicar; redituar; producir; restar (la pelota en tenis); to — a favor corresponder a un favor; to — a report rendir un informe; s. vuelta, regreso; retorno; recompensa; restitución, devolución; réplica; resto (en un juego de pelota);

RE

rédito, ganancia; informe; — **game** desquite, juego de desquite; — **ticket** boleto de vuelta; **by** — **mail** a vuelta de correo; **election -s** reportaje de elecciones; **in** — en cambio; **in** — **for** a cambio de, a trueque de; **income tax** — declaración de rentas; **many happy -s** muchas felicidades (en su día).

re·un·ion [rijúnjən] s. reunión; junta.

re·u·nite [rijʊnáit] v. reunir(se), volver a unirse; reconciliar(se).

re·veal [rɪvíl] v. revelar.

rev·el [révl] v. deleitarse, gozarse; parrandear, Am. farrear; andar de parranda, Ríopl. andar de farra; s. parranda, juerga, jarana.

rev·e·la·tion [rɛvļéʃən] s. revelación; **Revelation(s)** Apocalipsis.

rev·el·ry [révlrɪ] s. jaleo, juerga, jarana.

re·venge [rɪvéndʒ] v. vengar, vindicar; s. venganza; desquite.

re·venge·ful [rɪvéndʒfəl] adj. vengativo.

rev·e·nue [révənju] s. renta; rédito; rentas públicas, ingresos.

re·vere [rɪvír] v. venerar.

rev·er·ence [révrəns] s. reverencia; veneración; v. reverenciar, venerar.

rev·er·end [révrənd] adj. reverendo; venerable.

rev·er·ent [révrənt] adj. reverente.

rev·er·ie, rev·er·y [révərɪ] s. ensueño; arrobamiento.

re·verse [rɪvɝs] adj. inverso, invertido; contrario, opuesto; s. revés; reverso, dorso; lo contrario; contratiempo; v. invertir; voltear; revocar (una sentencia).

re·vert [rɪvɝt] v. revertir, volver atrás, retroceder.

re·view [rɪvjú] v. (study) repasar, revisar; revistar; (inspect) pasar revista a (las tropas); (criticize) reseñar, hacer una reseña de (un libro); s. revista; repaso; reseña, crítica (de un libro, drama, etc.); revisión (de un caso jurídico, sentencia, etc.).

re·vile [rɪváɪl] v. vilipendiar, vituperar, denigrar.

re·vise [rɪváɪz] v. revisar, repasar, releer (para corregir); corregir, enmendar.

re·vi·sion [rɪvíʒən] s. revisión; enmienda; edición enmendada o mejorada.

re·viv·al [rɪváɪvļ] s. (renewal) renovación; revivificación; (repeating) renacimiento; nueva presentación (teatral); — **meeting** junta para revivir el fervor religioso; **religious** — despertamiento (o nuevo fervor) religioso.

re·vive [rɪváɪv] v. revivir, resucitar; volver en sí; renacer; reavivar, reanimar(se); avivar.

re·voke [rɪvók] v. revocar, abrogar, anular; renunciar (en los juegos de naipes).

re·volt [rɪvólt] s. revuelta, rebelión, sublevación; v. rebelarse, sublevarse; **it -s me** me da asco, me repugna.

re·volt·ing [rɪvóltɪŋ] adj. repugnante; asqueroso.

rev·o·lu·tion [rɛvəlúʃən] s. revolución; vuelta (que da una rueda).

rev·o·lu·tion·ar·y [rɛvəlúʃənɛrɪ] adj. & s. revolucionario.

rev·o·lu·tion·ist [rɛvəlúʃənɪst] s. revolucionario.

re·volve [rɪválv] v. girar, dar vueltas; rodar; voltear, dar vueltas a; **to** — **in one's mind** revolver en la mente, ponderar, reflexionar.

re·volv·er [rɪválvɚ] s. revólver.

re·ward [rɪwórd] v. premiar; recompensar; s. premio, gratificación, recompensa, galardón; albricias (por haber hallado algún objeto perdido).

re·write [rɪráɪt] v. volver a escribir; refundir (un

escrito).

rhap·so·dy [ræpsədɪ] s. rapsodia.

rhe·ni·um [ríniəm] s. renio.

rhet·o·ric [rétərɪk] s. retórica.

rheu·ma·tism [rúmətɪzəm] s. reumatismo, reuma.

rhi·noc·er·os [raɪnásərəs] s. rinoceronte.

rho·di·um [ródiəm] s. rodio.

rho·do·den·dron [rodədéndrən] s. rododendro.

rhu·barb [rúbarb] s. ruibarbo.

rhyme [raɪm] s. rima; **without** — **or reason** sin ton ni son; v. rimar.

rhythm [ríðəm] s. ritmo.

rhyth·mi·cal [ríðmɪkļ] adj. rítmico, acompasado, cadencioso.

rib [rɪb] s. costilla; varilla (de paraguas); cordoncillo (de ciertos tejidos).

rib·bon [ríbən] s. cinta; listón, banda; moña; tira.

rice [raɪs] s. arroz; — **field** arrozal.

rich [rɪtʃ] adj. rico; costoso, suntuoso; sabroso; — **color** color vivo; — **food** alimento muy mantecoso o dulce.

rich·es [rítʃɪz] s. pl. riqueza, riquezas.

rick·et·y [ríkɪtɪ] adj. desvencijado; raquítico.

rid [rɪd] v. librar, desembarazar; **to get** — **of** librarse de, deshacerse de, desembarazarse de; pret. & p.p. **de to rid.**

rid·den [rídŋ] p.p. de to ride.

rid·dle [rídļ] acertijo, adivinanza, enigma; v. acribillar, perforar; **to** — **with bullets** acribillar a balazos.

ride [raɪd] v. (horse) cabalgar, montar; (vehicle) pasear; ir en (tranvía, tren); **to** — **a bicycle** andar o montar en bicicleta; **to** — **a horse** montar un caballo; **to** — **horseback** montar a caballo; **to** — **over a country** pasar o viajar por un país (en auto, a caballo o por tren); **to** — **someone** dominar a alguien; burlarse de alguien; s. paseo (a caballo o en automóvil); viaje (a caballo, en automóvil, por ferrocarril, etc.).

rid·er [ráɪdɚ] s. jinete; pasajero (de automóvil); biciclista; motociclista; aditamento, cláusula añadida (a un proyecto de ley).

ridge [rɪdʒ] s. espinazo; lomo (entre dos surcos); arista, intersección (de dos planos); cordillera; cerro, caballete (de tejado); cordoncillo (de ciertos tejidos).

rid·i·cule [rídɪkjul] s. ridículo; burla, mofa; v. ridiculizar, poner en ridículo.

ri·dic·u·lous [rɪdíkjələs] adj. ridículo.

ri·fle [ráɪfl] s. rifle; v. pillar, robar; despojar.

rift [rɪft] s. (opening) raja; abertura; (disagreement) desacuerdo.

rig [rɪg] v. aparejar, equipar; enjarciar (un barco de vela); **to** — **oneself up** emperifollarse, ataviarse; s. aparejo, equipo; aparato; atavío, traje.

rig·ging [rɪ́gɪŋ] — jarcia, aparejo.

right [raɪt] adj. (not left) derecho; diestro; (proper) recto; justo; propio; adecuado; correcto; — **angle** ángulo recto; — **side** lado derecho; derecho (de un tejido, traje, etc.); **it is** — **that** está bien que, es justo que; **to be** — **tener razón; **to be all** — estar bien; estar bien de salud; **to be in one's** — **mind** estar en sus cabales; adv. derecho, directamente; rectamente; justamente; bien; correctamente; a la derecha; — **about-face** media vuelta; — **hungry** muy hambriento; — **now** ahora mismo, inmediatamente; — **there** allí mismo, Am. allí mero; **go** — **home!** ¡vete derechito a casa!; **it is** — **where you left it** está exactamente (o en el mero lugar) donde lo dejaste; **to to hit** — **in the eye** dar de lleno en el ojo, *Am.* dar en el mero ojo; *s.* derecho; *s.* derecho; autoridad; privilegio; — **of way** derecho de vía; **by** — **(by -s)** justamente, con justicia; según la ley; **from** — **to left** de derecha a izquierda; **to the** — a la derecha; **to be in the** — tener razón; *v.* enderezar; corregir.

righ·teous [ráitʃəs] *adj.* recto, justo, virtuoso.

righ·teous·ness [ráitʃəsnis] *s.* rectitud, virtud.

right·ful [ráitfəl] *adj.* justo; legítimo.

right-hand [ráithǽnd] *adj.* derecho, de la mano derecha; — **man** brazo derecho.

right·ist [ráitist] *s.* derechista.

right·ly [ráitli] *adv.* con razón; justamente, rectamente; propiamente, aptamente, debidamente.

right-wing [ráitwiŋ] *adj.* derechista.

rig·id [ridʒid] *adj.* rígido.

ri·gid·i·ty [ridʒídəti] *s.* rigidez; tiesura.

rig·or [rígə] *s.* rigor; rigidez; severidad.

rig·or·ous [rígəəs] *adj.* rigoroso (*o* riguroso), severo.

rim [rim] *s.* borde, orilla; aro.

rime = **rhyme.**

rind [raind] *s.* corteza, cáscara; mondadura.

ring [riŋ] *s.* (*finger*) anillo, sortija; argolla; aro; (*circle*) arena; pista; (*sound*) toque; tañido; repique; (*telephone*) timbrazo; telefonazo; —**leader** cabecilla; — **of defiance** tono de reto; — **of shouts** gritería; — **of a telephone** llamada de teléfono; **ring-shaped** en forma de anillo, anular; **key**— llavero; **sarcastic** — retintín; *v.* tocar (*un timbre, una campanilla o campana*); sonar; tañer, repicar; resonar; zumbar (*los oídos*); **to** — **for something** llamar para pedir algo; **to** — **the nose of an animal** ponerle una argolla en la nariz a un animal; **to** — **up on the phone** llamar por teléfono.

ring·let [ríŋlit] *s.* rizo, bucle; pequeña sortija.

rink [riŋk] *s.* patinadero (*cancha para patinar*).

rinse [rins] *v.* enjuagar; lavar; aclarar (*la ropa*); *s.* enjuague.

ri·ot [ráiət] *s.* motín, desorden, alboroto, tumulto; — **of color** riqueza o exceso de colores chillantes; *v.* amotinarse, alborotar, armar un tumulto.

ri·ot·ous [ráiətəs] *adj.* revoltoso.

rip [rip] *v.* rasgar(se), romper(se); descoser(se); **to** — **off** rasgar, arrancar, cortar; **to** — **out a seam** descoser una costura; *s.* rasgón, rasgadura, rotura; descosido.

ripe [raip] *adj.* maduro, sazonado; en sazón; — **for** maduro para, sazonado para; bien preparado para, listo para.

rip·en [ráipən] *v.* madurar(se), sazonar(se).

ripe·ness [ráipnis] *s.* madurez, sazón.

rip·ple [rípl] *v.* rizar(se), agitar(se), ondear, temblar (*la superficie del agua*); murmurar (*un arroyo*); *s.* onda, temblor, ondulación (*en la superficie del agua*); murmullo (*de un arroyo*).

rise [raiz] *v.* subir; ascender; alzarse, levantarse; elevarse; surgir; salir (*el sol, la luna, un astro*); hincharse (*la masa del pan*); **to** — **up in rebellion** sublevarse, levantarse, alzarse (en rebelión); *s.* subida; ascenso; pendiente; elevación; salida (*del sol, de la luna, etc.*); subida, alza (*de precios*).

ris·en [rízn] *p.p. de* **to rise.**

risk [risk] *s.* riesgo; *v.* arriesgar, aventurar, poner en peligro; exponerse a; **to** — **defeat** correr el riesgo de perder, exponerse a perder.

risk·y [ríski] *adj.* arriesgado, peligroso, aventurado.

ris·qué [riské] *adj.* escabroso.

rite [rait] *s.* rito, ceremonia.

rit·u·al [rítʃuəl] *adj. & s.* ritual, ceremonial.

ri·val [ráivl] *s.* rival, competidor, émulo; *adj.* competidor; **the** — **party** el partido opuesto; *v.* rivalizar con, competir con.

ri·val·ry [ráivl̩ri] *s.* rivalidad.

riv·er [rívə] *s.* río.

riv·et [rívit] *s.* remache; *v.* remachar; fijar.

riv·u·let [rívjəlit] *s.* riachuelo, arroyuelo.

road [rod] *s.* camino; carretera; vía.

road·side [ródsaid] *s.* borde del camino.

road·way [ródwe] *s.* camino, carretera.

roam [rom] *v.* vagar, errar, andar errante.

roar [ror] *v.* rugir, bramar; **to** — **with laughter** reír a carcajadas; *s.* rugido, bramido; — **of laughter** risotada, carcajada.

roast [rost] *v.* asar(se); tostar (*café, maíz, etc.*); ridiculizar, criticar; *s.* asado, carne asada; *adj.* asado; — **beef** rosbif, rosbí.

rob [rɑb] *v.* robar, hurtar; **to** — **someone of something** robarle algo a alguien.

rob·ber [rábə] *s.* ladrón; **highway** — salteador.

rob·ber·y [rábri] *s.* robo, hurto.

robe [rob] *s.* manto, traje talar, túnica, toga (*de un juez, letrado, etc.*); bata; **automobile** — manta de automóvil.

rob·in [rábin] *s.* petirrojo.

ro·bust [róbʌst] *adj.* robusto, fuerte.

rock [rɑk] *s.* roca, peña; peñasco; — **crystal** cristal de roca; — **salt** sal de piedra, sal gema o sal mineral; **to go on the -s** tropezar en un escollo, *Am.* escollar; *v.* mecer(se), balancear(se); bambolear(se); estremecer; **to** — **to sleep** adormecer (*meciendo*), arrullar.

rock·er [rákə] *s.* mecedora; arco de una mecedora o cuna.

rock·et [rákit] *s.* cohete.

rock·et·ry [rákətri] *s.* cohetería.

rock·ing [rákiŋ] *s.* balanceo; *adj.* oscilante; — **chair** silla mecedora.

rock·y [ráki] *adj.* roqueño, rocoso, rocalloso; peñascoso; pedregoso; movedizo; tembloroso; débil, desvanecido.

rod [rɑd] *s.* vara, varilla; medida de longitud (*aproximadamente 5 metros*); **fishing** — caña de pescar.

rode [rod] *pret. de* **to ride.**

ro·dent [ródənt] *s.* roedor.

rogue [rog] *s.* pícaro, bribón, tunante, pillo; **-s' gallery** colección policíaca de retratos de criminales.

ro·guish [rógiʃ] *adj.* pícaro, pillo, picaresco; travieso.

role [rol] *s.* papel, parte.

roll [rol] *v.* (*move*) rodar; girar; balancearse (*un barco*); bambolearse; ondular, retumbar (*el trueno, un cañón*); aplanar, alisar con rodillo; arrollar, enrollar, hacer un rollo o bola; envolver; redoblar (*un tambor*); pronunciar (*la rr doble*); **to** — **over in the snow** revolverse o revolcarse en la nieve; **to** — **up** arrollar, enrollar, envolver; *s.* rollo (*de papel, paño, tela, etc.*); balanceo (*de un barco*); retumbo (*del trueno, de cañón*); redoble (*de un tambor*); lista ondulación; oleaje; bollo, rosca, panecillo; **to call the** — pasar lista.

roll·er [rólə] *s.* rodillo, cilindro (*para aplanar o alisar*); apisonadora; rollo (*rodillo de pastelero*); oleada; — **coaster** montaña rusa; — **skate** patín de ruedas.

Ro·man [rómən] *adj. & s.* romano; — **nose** nariz aguileña.

ro·mance [románs] *s.* (*literature*) romance; novela; cuento; fábula; (*affair*) aventura romántica; amorío, lance amoroso; *v.* contar o fingir fábulas; andar en amoríos o aventuras; **Ro·mance** *adj.* romance, románico, neolatino.

ro·man·tic [romǽntɪk] *adj.* romántico; novelesco.

ro·man·ti·cism [romǽntəsɪzəm] *s.* romanticismo.

ro·man·ti·cist [romǽntəsɪst] *s.* romántico, escritor romántico.

romp [rɑmp] *v.* triscar, juguetear, retozar, travesear.

roof [ruf] *s.* techo, techumbre, techado; tejado; — **garden** azotea-jardín; — **of the mouth** paladar; **flat** — azotea; *v.* techar.

room [rum] *s.* (*in building*) cuarto, pieza, sala, habitación; (*space*) espacio; lugar, sitio; **there is no** — **for more** no cabe(n) más, no hay lugar o cabida para más; **to make** — hacer lugar; —**mate** compañero de cuarto; *v.* vivir, hospedarse, alojarse.

room·er [rúmɚ] *s.* inquilino.

room·i·ness [rúmɪnɪs] *s.* holgura.

room·y [rúmɪ] *adj.* espacioso, amplio, holgado.

roost [rust] *s.* gallinero; peroha de gallinero; *v.* acurrucarse (*las aves en la percha*); pasar la noche.

roost·er [rústɚ] *s.* gallo.

root [rut] *s.* raíz; *v.* arraigar(se); echar raíces; hocicar, hozar (*dícese de los cerdos*); **to** — **for** vitorear, aclamar; **to** — **out** (*o* — **up**) desarraigar, arrancar de raíz; **to become -ed** arraigarse.

rope [rop] *s.* (*cord*) soga, cuerda; (*lasso*) reata, lazo; **to be at the end of one's** — haber agotado el último recurso; estar (*o* andar) en las últimas; no saber qué hacer; **to know the -s** saber todas las tretas de un asunto o negocio; *v.* amarrar; lazar, enlazar; **to** — **off** acordelar, poner cuerdas tirantes alrededor de (*un sitio*); **to** — **someone in** embaucar a alguien.

ro·sa·ry [rózərɪ] *s.* rosario.

rose [roz] *pret. de* **to rise.**

rose [roz] *s.* rosa; color de rosa; —**bush** rosal; — **window** rosetón.

rose·bud [rózbʌd] *s.* capullo o botón de rosa, yema, pimpollo.

ros·ette [rozét] *s.* roseta; rosetón.

ros·ter [rástɚ] *s.* registro; lista.

ros·trum [rástrəm] *s.* tribuna.

ros·y [rózɪ] *adj.* (*color*) rosado; color de rosa; (*condition*) alegre, risueño; — **future** porvenir risueño.

rot [rɑt] *v.* pudrir(se); corromperse; *s.* podre, podredumbre, putrefacción.

ro·ta·ry [rótərɪ] *adj.* rotatorio, giratorio, rotativo.

ro·tate [rótet] *v.* girar, dar vueltas; hacer girar; turnarse; cultivar en rotación.

ro·ta·tion [rotéʃən] *s.* rotación, vuelta; — **of crops** rotación de cultivos.

rote [rot] *s.* rutina, repetición maquinal; **by** — maquinalmente.

rot·ten [rátṇ] *adj.* podrido, putrefacto; hediondo; corrompido, corrupto.

rouge [ruʒ] *s.* colorete; *v.* pintar(se), poner(se) colorete.

rough [rʌf] *adj.* (*coarse*) áspero; tosco; fragoso; escabroso; (*rude*) brusco; grosero; (*stormy*) borrascoso, tempestuoso; — **diamond** diamante en bruto; — **draft** borrador; bosquejo; — **estimate** cálculo aproximativo, tanteo; — **ground** terreno escabroso; — **idea** idea aproximada; — **sea** mar picado; — **weather** tiempo borrascoso;

adv. véase **roughly**; *v.* **to** — **it** vivir sin lujos ni comodidades, hacer vida campestre.

rough·en [rʌfən] *v.* hacer o poner áspero; picar, rascar (*una superficie*); rajarse, agrietarse (*la piel*).

rough·ly [rʌflɪ] *adv.* ásperamente; groseramente, rudamente; aproximadamente; **to estimate** — tantear.

rough·ness [rʌfnɪs] *s.* aspereza; escabrosidad; rudeza; tosquedad; **the** — **of the sea** lo picado del mar; **the** — **of the weather** lo borrascoso del tiempo.

round [raund] *adj.* redondo; rotundo; circular; — **trip** viaje redondo, viaje de ida y vuelta; **round-trip ticket** boleto (*o* billete) de ida y vuelta; *s.* vuelta, rotación, revolución; ronda; vuelta (*en el juego de naipes*); tanda, turno (*en ciertos deportes*); escalón, travesaño (*de escalera de mano*); danza en rueda; — **of ammunition** carga de municiones; descarga; — **of applause** explosión de aplausos; — **of pleasures** sucesión de placeres; **to make the -s** rondar; *prep. & adv. véase* **around**; — **about** a la redonda; por todos lados, **round-shouldered** cargado de espaldas; **to come** — **again** volver otra vez; **to go** — **a corner** doblar una esquina; *v.* redondear; dar vuelta a; **to** — **a corner** doblar una esquina; **to** — **out** redondear; completar; **to** — **up cattle** juntar el ganado, *Am.* rodear el ganado.

round·a·bout [ráundəbaut] *adj.* indirecto.

round·ness [ráundnɛs] *s.* redondez.

round·up [ráundʌp] *s.* rodeo (*de ganado*); redada (*de criminales*); *v.* reputar.

rouse [rauz] *v.* despertar(se), *Riopl.* recordar; excitar; incitar, provocar; levantar (*la caza*).

rout [raut] *s.* derrota, fuga desordenada; *v.* derrotar; poner en fuga; **to** — **out** echar, hacer salir a toda prisa.

route [rut] *s.* ruta, camino, vía; itinerario; *v.* dirigir o enviar por cierta ruta.

rou·tine [rutín] *s.* rutina.

rove [rov] *v.* vagar, errar, andar errante.

rov·er [róvɚ] *s.* vagabundo.

row [rau] *s.* riña, pelea, pelotera; *v.* pelearse, reñir; armar una riña o pelotera.

row [ro] *s.* fila, hilera; paseo en lancha; *v.* remar, bogar; llevar en lancha o bote.

row·boat [róbot] *s.* bote de remos, lancha.

row·er [róɚ] *s.* remero.

roy·al [rɔ́ɪəl] *adj.* real, regio.

roy·al·ist [rɔ́ɪəlɪst] *s.* realista.

roy·al·ty [rɔ́ɪəltɪ] *s.* realeza, soberanía real; persona o personas reales; derechos (*pagados a un autor o inventor*).

rub [rʌb] *v.* (*apply friction*) frotar; restregar; fregar; (*scrape*) raspar; irritar; **to** — **out** borrar; **to** — **someone the wrong way** irritar, contrariar, llevarle a uno la contraria; *s.* fricción, friega, frotación; roce; sarcasmo; **there is the** — allí está la dificultad.

rub·ber [rʌbɚ] *s.* caucho, goma, *Méx., C.A.* hule; goma elástica; goma de borrar; partida (*en ciertos juegos de naipes*); jugada decisiva (*en ciertos juegos de naipes*); **-s** chanclos, zapatos de goma o hule; *adj.* de caucho, de goma, *Méx., C.A.* de hule; — **band** faja o banda de goma; — **plantation** cauchal, *Am.* caucho, *Am.* gomero.

rub·bish [rʌbɪʃ] *s.* basura, desechos, desperdicios; tonterías.

rub·ble [rʌbḷ] *s.* escombros; ripio, cascajo,

fragmentos de ladrillos o piedras; piedra en bruto, piedra sin labrar.

ru·bid·i·um [rubídiəm] *s.* rubidio.

ru·bric [rúbrɪk] *s.* rúbrica.

ru·by [rúbɪ] *s.* rubí.

rud·der [rʌ́dəʳ] *s.* timón.

rud·dy [rʌ́dɪ] *adj.* rojo; rojizo; rubicundo.

rude [rud] *adj.* rudo; grosero; áspero; brusco; tosco.

rude·ness [rúdnɪs] *s.* rudeza; grosería, descortesía; tosquedad.

rue·ful [rúfəl] *adj.* triste; lastimoso, lamentable.

ruf·fi·an [rʌ́fɪən] *s.* rufián, hombre brutal.

ruf·fle [rʌ́fl] *v.* rizar, fruncir (*tela*); arrugar; desarreglar; rizar (*la superficie del agua*); perturbar; molestar; *s.* volante (*de un traje*); frunce, pliegue; ondulación (*en al agua*).

rug [rʌg] *s.* alfombra, tapete.

rug·ged [rʌ́gɪd] *adj.* escabroso, fragoso; áspero; recio, robusto; tosco; borrascoso, tempestuoso.

ru·in [rúɪn] *s.* ruina; **to go to —** arruinarse, caer en ruinas, venir a menos; *v.* arruinar; echar a perder; estropear.

ru·in·ous [rúɪnəs] *adj.* ruinoso; desastroso.

rule [rul] *s.* (*regulation*) regla; reglamento; precepto; (*control*) mando, gobierno; **as a —** por regla general; *v.* regir, gobernar; mandar; dirigir, guiar; dominar; fallar, decidir; rayar (*con regla*); **to — out** excluir; **to — over** regir, gobernar.

rul·er [rúlə-] *s.* gobernante; soberano; regla (*para medir o trazar líneas*).

rul·ing [rúlɪŋ] *s.* fallo, decisión; gobierno; *adj.* predominante, prevaleciente; principal.

rum [rʌm] *s.* ron.

rum·ble [rʌ́mbl] *v.* retumbar, hacer estruendo, rugir; *s.* retumbo, estruendo, rumor, ruido sordo; **— seat** asiento trasero (*de cupé*).

ru·mi·nant [rúmənənt] *s.* rumiante.

ru·mi·nate [rúmənet] *v.* rumiar; reflexionar, meditar.

rum·mage [rʌ́mɪdʒ] *v.* escudriñar revolviéndolo todo; *s.* búsqueda desordenada; **— sale** venta de prendas usadas (*para beneficencia*).

ru·mor [rúmə-] *s.* rumor; runrún; *v.* murmurar; **it is -ed that** corre la voz que.

rump [rʌmp] *s.* anca; trasero.

rum·ple [rʌ́mpl] *v.* estrujar, ajar; arrugar; *s.* arruga (*en un traje*).

rum·pus [rʌ́mpəs] *s.* barullo, alharaca, boruca, batahola.

run [rʌn] *v.* (*on foot*) correr; (*function*) andar; marchar; funcionar; (*flow*) fluir; chorrear; (*go over*) recorrer; (*direct*) dirigir, manejar; (*un negocio, empresa, máquina, casa, etc.*); extenderse (*de un punto a otro*); correrse (*los colores*); ser candidato (*a un puesto político*); **to — a fever** tener calentura; **to — away** huir; fugarse, escaparse; **to — across a person** encontrarse o tropezar con una persona; **to — down** dejar de funcionar (*una máquina, reloj, etc.*); aprehender a (*un criminal*); hablar mal de; atropellar; **to get — down in health** quebrantársele a uno la salud; **to — dry** secarse; **to — into** tropezar con, encontrarse con; chocar con; **— around with** asociarse con; tener amores con; **to — into debt** adeudarse; **to — something into** meter algo en, clavar algo en; **to — out** salirse; **to — out of money** acabársele a uno el dinero; **to — over** derramarse (*un líquido*); atropellar, pasar por encima de; repasar, echar un vistazo a (*la

lección, un libro, etc.); **to — through a book** hojear un libro; **the play ran for three months** se dió la comedia durante tres meses; *s.* carrera, corrida; curso, marcha; recorrido; manejo; **— of good luck** serie de repetidos éxitos; **— of performances** serie de representaciones; **— on a bank** corrida, demanda extraordinaria de fondos bancarios; **in the long —** a la larga; **stocking —** carrera; **the common — of mankind** el común de las gentes; **to have the — of** tener el libre uso de; *p.p. de* **to run.**

run·a·way [rʌ́nəwe] *adj.* fugitivo; **— horse** caballo desbocado; **— marriage** casamiento de escapatoria; *s.* fugitivo; caballo desbocado; fuga.

rung [rʌŋ] *s.* barrote, travesaño (*de silla, escalera de mano, etc.*); *pret. & p.p. de* **to ring.**

run·ner [rʌ́nə-] *s.* corredor; tapete (*para un pasillo o mesa*), Ríopl. pasillo; carrera (*en una media*); cuchilla (*de patín o de trineo*); contrabandista.

run·ning [rʌ́nɪŋ] *s.* (*race*) corrida, carrera; (*direction*) manejo, dirección; (*flow*) flujo; **to be out of the —** estar fuera de combate; *adj.* corriente; **— board** estribo; **— expenses** gastos corrientes; **— knot** nudo corredizo; **— water** agua corriente; **in — condition** en buen estado; **for ten days —** por diez días seguidos.

runt [rʌnt] *s.* enano; hombrecillo.

run·way [rʌ́nwe] *s.* senda; vía; pista (*de aterrizaje*).

rup·ture [rʌ́ptʃə-] *s.* ruptura; rompimiento, rotura; hernia; *v.* romper(se); reventar.

ru·ral [rúrəl] *adj.* rural, campestre.

rush [rʌʃ] *v.* (*hurry*) apresurar(se); *Am.* apurarse; despachar con prisa; (*attack*) lanzar(se), precipitar(se); abalanzarse; acometer; **to — out** salir a todo correr; **to — past** pasar a toda prisa; *s.* precipitación, prisa; acometida; junco; **— chair** silla de junco; **— of business** gran movimiento comercial; **— of people** tropel de gente; **— order** pedido urgente.

Rus·sian [rʌ́ʃən] *adj. & s.* ruso.

rust [rʌst] *s.* moho, orín; herrumbre; tizón (*enfermedad de las plantas*); **— color** color rojizo; *v.* enmohecer(se), oxidar(se).

rus·tic [rʌ́stɪk] *adj. & s.* rústico, campesino.

rus·tle [rʌ́sl] *v.* susurrar, crujir; menear; **to — cattle** robar ganado; *s.* susurro, crujido.

rust·proof [rʌ́stpruf] *adj.* inoxidable.

rust·y [rʌ́stɪ] *adj.* mohoso, cubierto de orín, oxidado; rojizo; entorpecido, falto de uso; falto de práctica.

rut [rʌt] *s.* rodada; rutina, método rutinario; **to be in a —** hacer una cosa por rutina, ser esclavo de la rutina.

ru·the·ni·um [ruθíniəm] *s.* rutenio.

ruth·less [rúθlɪs] *adj.* despiadado, cruel, brutal.

ruth·less·ness [rúθlɪsnɪs] *s.* fiereza, falta de miramiento, truculencia, crueldad.

rye [raɪ] *s.* centeno.

S.s **sa·ber** [sébə-] *s.* sable.

sab·o·tage [sæbətɑʒ] *s.* sabotaje; *v.* sabotear.

sack [sæk] *s.* (*bag*) saco; costal; (*looting*) saqueo, pillaje; *v.* ensacar, meter en un saco; saquear, pillar.

sac·ra·ment [sǽkrəmənt] *s.* sacramento.

sa·cred [sékrɪd] *adj.* sagrado, sacro.

sa·cred·ness [sékrɪdnɪs] *s.* santidad; lo sagrado.

sac·ri·fice [sǽkrəfaɪs] *s.* sacrificio; **to sell at a —** vender con pérdida; *v.* sacrificar.

sac·ri·lege [sǽkrəlɪdʒ] *s.* sacrilegio.

sac·ri·le·gious [sækrɪlídʒəs] *adj.* sacrílego.

sac·ro·sanct [sǽkrosænkt] *adj.* sacrosanto.

sad [sæd] *adj.* triste.

sad·den [sǽdn̩] *v.* entristecer(se).

sad·dle [sǽdl̩] *s.* silla de montar; silla de bicicleta o motocicleta; **—bag** alforja; **— horse** caballo de silla **—tree** arzón; *v.* ensillar; **to — someone with responsibilities** cargar a alguien de responsabilidades.

sa·dis·tic [sədístɪk] *adj.* sádico, cruel.

sad·ness [sǽdnɪs] *s.* tristeza.

safe [sef] *adj.* (*secure*) seguro; salvo; sin riesgo, sin peligro; (*trustworthy*) digno de confianza; **— and sound** sano y salvo; **safe-conduct** salvo-conducto; **to be —** no correr peligro, estar a salvo; *s.* caja fuerte; **-ly** *adv.* seguramente; con seguridad; sin peligro; **to arrive -ly** llegar bien, llegar sin contratiempo alguno.

safe·guard [séfgɑrd] *s.* salvaguardia; resguardo, defensa; *v.* resguardar, proteger, salvaguardar.

safe·ty [séftɪ] *s.* seguridad; protección; **in —** con seguridad; sin peligro; *adj.* de seguridad; **— device** mecanismo de seguridad; **— pin** imperdible, alfiler de seguridad.

saf·fron [sǽfrən] *s.* azafrán; *adj.* azafranado, color de azafrán.

sag [sæg] *v.* combarse, pandearse; doblegarse; deprimirse, hundirse (*en el centro*); encorvarse; **his shoulders —** tiene las espaldas caídas; *s.* pandeo, flexión, depresión; concavidad.

sa·ga·cious [səgéʃəs] *adj.* sagaz, ladino, astuto.

sa·gac·i·ty [segǽsətɪ] *s.* sagacidad; astucia.

sage [sedʒ] *adj.* sabio; cuerdo, prudente; *s.* sabio; salvia (*planta*).

said [sed] *pret. & p.p. de* **to say.**

sail [sel] *s.* (*canvas*) vela (*de barco*); (*trip*) viaje o paseo en barco de vela; **under full —** a toda vela; **to set —** hacerse a la vela; *v.* navegar; hacerse a la vela; zarpar, salir (*un buque*); viajar, ir (*en barco, bote, etc.*); pasear en bote de vela; **to — a kite** volar una cometa o papalote; **to — along** deslizarse; navegar; ir bien; **to — along the coast** costear.

sail·boat [sélbot] *s.* bote o barco de vela.

sail·or [sélɚ] *s.* marinero; marino.

saint [sent] *s.* santo; *adj.* santo; san (*delante de nombres masculinos excepto: Santo Tomás, Santo Domingo, Santo Toribio*); *v.* canonizar.

saint·ly [séntlɪ] *adj.* santo; pío, devoto.

sake [sek]: **for the — of** por; por amor a; por consideración a; **for my —** por mí; **for pity's —** por piedad; ¡caramba!; **for the — of argument** por vía de argumento.

sa·la·cious [səléʃəs] *adj.* salaz.

sal·ad [sǽləd] *s.* ensalada; **— dressing** aderezo (*para ensalada*).

sal·a·ry [sǽlərɪ] *s.* salario, sueldo.

sale [sel] *s.* venta; saldo, *Méx., C.A., Andes* barata; *Ríopl., Andes* realización; **— by auction** almoneda, subasta; **-s tax** impuesto sobre ventas; **for (on) —** de venta.

sales·man [sélzmən] *s.* vendedor; dependiente (*de tienda*); **traveling —** agente viajero, viajante de comercio.

sales·wom·an [sélzwʊmən] *s.* vendedora; dependiente (*de tienda*).

sa·li·ent [sélɪənt] *adj.* saliente, sobresaliente; prominente.

sa·line [sélin] *adj.* salino.

sa·li·va [səláɪvə] *s.* saliva.

sal·low [sǽlo] *adj.* amarillento, pálido.

sal·ly [sǽlɪ] *s.* salida; agudeza, chiste agudo; *v.* salir, hacer una salida; **to — forth** salir.

salm·on [sǽmən] *s.* salmón.

sa·loon [səlún] *s.* salón (*de un vapor*); taberna, *Am.* cantina; *Ríopl.* bar; **dining — of a ship** salón-comedor de un vapor.

salt [sɔlt] *s.* (*sodium chloride*) sal; (*wit*) chiste, agudeza; **smelling -s** sales aromáticas; **the — of the earth** la flor y nata de la humanidad; *adj.* salado; salobre; **—cellar** salero; **— mine** salina; **— pork** tocino salado; **— shaker** salero; **— water** agua salada, agua de mar; *v.* salar; **to — one's money away** guardar o ahorrar su dinero.

salt·pe·ter [sɔ́ltpítɚ] *s.* salitre, nitro; **— mine** salitral, salitrera.

salt·y [sɔ́ltɪ] *adj.* salado; salobre.

sal·u·tar·y [sǽljʊtɛrɪ] *adj.* saludable.

sal·u·ta·tion [sæljətéʃən] *s.* salutación, saludo.

sa·lute [səlút] *s.* saludo; **gun —** salva; *v.* saludar; cuadrarse (*militarmente*).

sal·vage [sǽlvɪdʒ] *s.* salvamento.

sal·va·tion [sælvéʃən] *s.* salvación.

salve [sæv] *s.* untura, ungüento; alivio; *v.* aliviar, aquietar, calmar; untar.

sal·vo [sǽlvo] *s.* salva.

same [sem] *adj.* mismo; igual; idéntico; **it is all the — to me** me es igual, me da lo mismo; **the —** lo mismo; el mismo (la misma, los mismos, las mismas).

sam·ple [sǽmpl̩] *s.* muestra, prueba; **book of -s** muestrario; *v.* probar; calar.

san·a·to·ri·um [sænətorɪəm] *s.* sanatorio.

sanc·ti·fy [sǽŋktəfaɪ] *v.* santificar.

sanc·tion [sǽŋkʃən] *s.* sanción; aprobación; autorización;·*v.* sancionar; facultar; aprobar, autorizar.

sanc·ti·ty [sǽŋktətɪ] *s.* santidad.

sanc·tu·ar·y [sǽŋktʃʊɛrɪ] *s.* santuario; asilo.

sand [sænd] *s.* arena; **— pit** arenal; *v.* enarenar; cubrir de arena; mezclar con arena; refregar con arena.

san·dal [sǽndl̩] *s.* sandalia; alpargata; *Méx.* guarache (huarache); *Andes* ojota.

sand·pa·per [sǽndpepɚ] *s.* papel de lija; *v.* lijar, pulir o alisar con papel de lija.

sand·stone [sǽndston] *s.* piedra arenisca.

sand·wich [sǽndwɪtʃ] *s.* bocadillo, emparedado, sandwich; *v.* intercalar, meter (entre).

sand·y [sǽndɪ] *adj.* arenoso; arenisco; **— hair** pelo rojizo.

sane [sen] *adj.* sano, sensato; cuerdo.

sang [sæŋ] *pret. de* **to sing.**

san·i·tar·i·um [sænətérɪəm] *s.* sanatorio.

san·i·tar·y [sǽnətɛrɪ] *adj.* sanitario.

san·i·ta·tion [sænətéʃən] *s.* saneamiento; salubridad; sanidad.

san·i·ty [sǽnətɪ] *s.* cordura.

sank [sæŋk] *pret. de* **to sink.**

sap [sæp] *s.* savia; tonto, bobo; *v.* agotar, debilitar, minar.

sap·ling [sǽplɪŋ] *s.* vástago, renuevo; arbolillo.

sap·phire [sǽfaɪr] *s.* zafiro; color de zafiro.

sar·casm [sárkæzəm] *s.* sarcasmo.

sar·cas·tic [sɑrkǽstɪk] *adj.* sarcástico.

sar·coph·a·gus [sɑrkɔ́fəgəs] *s.* sarcófago.

sar·dine [sɑrdín] *s.* sardina.

sar·don·ic [sɑrdɑ́nɪk] *adj.* burlón; sarcástico.

sash [sæʃ] s. faja (*cinturón de lana, seda o algodón*); banda, cinta ancha; **window** — bastidor (*o marco*) de ventana.

sat [sæt] *pret. & p.p. de* **to sit.**

satch·el [sǽtʃəl] s. valija, maletín, maleta, saco.

sate [set] v. saciar.

sa·teen [sætín] s. satén o rasete (*raso de inferior calidad*).

sat·el·lite [sǽtlaɪt] s. satélite.

sa·ti·ate [séʃɪet] v. saciar, hartar.

sat·in [sǽtn̩] s. raso.

sat·ire [sǽtaɪr] s. sátira.

sa·tir·i·cal [sətírɪkl̩] *adj.* satírico.

sat·i·rize [sǽtəraɪz] v. satirizar.

sat·is·fac·tion [sætɪsfǽkʃən] s. satisfacción.

sat·is·fac·to·ri·ly [sætɪsfǽktrəlɪ] *adv.* satisfactoriamente.

sat·is·fac·to·ry [sætɪsfǽktrɪ] *adj.* satisfactorio.

sat·is·fied [sǽtɪsfaɪd] *adj.* satisfecho, contento.

sat·is·fy [sǽtɪsfaɪ] v. satisfacer.

sat·u·rate [sǽtʃəret] v. saturar, empapar.

Sat·ur·day [sǽtədɪ] s. sábado.

sauce [sɔs] s. salsa; — **dish** salsera; v. aderezar con salsa; sazonar, condimentar; insolentarse con.

sauce·pan [sɔ́spæn] s. cacerola.

sau·cer [sɔ́sə] s. platillo.

sau·ci·ness [sɔ́sɪnɪs] s. descaro, insolencia.

sau·cy [sɔ́sɪ] *adj.* descarado, respondón, insolente, *Am.* retobado.

saun·ter [sɔ́ntə] v. pasearse, vagar.

sau·sage [sɔ́sɪdʒ] s. salchicha, salchichón; longaniza; chorizo.

sav·age [sǽvɪdʒ] *adj.* salvaje; fiero; bárbaro, brutal, feroz; s. salvaje.

sav·age·ry [sǽvɪdʒrɪ] s. salvajismo; crueldad, fiereza.

sa·vant [səvánt] s. sabio.

save [sev] v. (*rescue*) salvar; (*hoard*) ahorrar; economizar; (*keep*) guardar; resguardar; **to** — **from** librar de; **to** — **one's eyes** cuidarse la vista; *prep.* salvo, menos, excepto.

sav·er [sévə] s. salvador; libertador; ahorrador; **life**— salvavidas.

sav·ing [sévɪŋ] *adj.* (*rescuer*) salvador; (*economizing*) ahorrativo, económico; frugal; s. ahorro, economía; **-s** ahorros; **-s bank** caja o banco de ahorros; *prep.* salvo, excepto, con excepción de.

sav·ior [sévjə] s. salvador.

sa·vor [sévə] s. sabor; dejo; v. saborear; sazonar; **to** — **of** saber a, tener el sabor de; **it -s of treason** huele a traición.

sa·vor·y [sévərɪ] *adj.* sabroso.

saw [sɔ] s. sierra; —**horse** caballete; v. aserrar, serrar; **it -s easily** es fácil de aserrar; *pret. de* **to see.**

saw·dust [sɔ́dʌst] s. aserrín, serrín.

saw·mill [sɔ́mɪl] s. aserradero.

sawn [sɔn] *p.p. de* **to saw.**

Sax·on [sǽksn̩] *adj. & s.* sajón.

sax·o·phone [sǽksəfon] s. saxófono; saxofón.

say [se] v. decir; declarar; —! ¡diga! ¡oiga usted!; **that is to** — es decir; **to** — **one's prayers** rezar, decir o recitar sus oraciones; **to** — **the least** por lo menos; **it is said that** dizque, se dice que, dicen que; s. afirmación, aserto; **the final** — la autoridad decisiva; **to have a** — **in a matter** tener voz y voto en un asunto; **to have one's** — expresarse, dar su opinión.

say·ing [séɪŋ] s. dicho, refrán; aserto; **as the** — **goes** como dice el refrán.

scab [skæb] s. costra (*de una herida*); roña;

esquirol (*obrero que sustituye a un huelguista*); obrero que acepta un jornal inferior; v. encostrarse (*una herida*), cubrirse de una costra.

scab·bard [skǽbəd] s. vaina, funda (*de espada, puñal, etc.*).

scab·by [skǽbɪ] *adj.* costroso; roñoso, sarnoso, tiñoso.

scab·rous [skébrəs] *adj.* escabroso.

scaf·fold [skǽfld] s. andamio, tablado; patíbulo, andamiaje, andamios.

scald [skɔld] v. escaldar; **to** — **milk** calentar la leche hasta que suelte el hervor; s. escaldadura, quemadura.

scale [skel] s. escala; platillo de balanza; balanza; escama (*de pez o de la piel*); costra; **pair of -s** balanza; **platform** — báscula; v. escalar; subir, trepar por; graduar (*a escala*); medir según escala; pesar; escamar, quitar las escamas a; pelarse, despellejarse; descostrar(se); **to** — **down prices** rebajar proporcionalmente los precios.

scal·lop [skáləp] s. onda, pico (*adorno*); molusco bivalvo; **-s** festón (*recortes en forma de ondas o picos*); v. festonear, recortar en forma de ondas o picos; asar con salsa o migas de pan.

scalp [skælp] s. cuero cabelludo; v. desollar el cráneo; revender (*boletos, billetes*) a precio subido.

scal·y [skélɪ] *adj.* escamoso, lleno de escamas; — **with rust** mohoso.

scamp [skæmp] s. pícaro, bribón, bellaco.

scam·per [skǽmpə] v. correr, escabullirse, escaparse; s. escabullida, carrera, corrida.

scan [skæn] v. escudriñar; examinar, mirar detenidamente; echar un vistazo a (*en el habla popular*); medir (*el verso*).

scan·dal [skǽndl] s. escándalo; maledicencia, murmuración.

scan·dal·ize [skǽndlaɪz] v. escandalizar, dar escándalo.

scan·dal·ous [skǽndləs] *adj.* escandaloso; difamatorio; vergonzoso.

scan·di·um [skǽndiəm] s. escandio.

scant [skænt] *adj.* escaso; corto; insuficiente; v. escatimar, limitar.

scant·y [skǽntɪ] *adj.* escaso; insuficiente.

scar [skar] s. (*skin blemish*) cicatriz; costurón; (*mark*) raya, marca (*en una superficie pulida*); v. marcar, rayar; hacer o dejar una cicatriz en.

scarce [skɛrs] *adj.* escaso; raro; **-ly** *adv.* escasamente; apenas.

scar·ci·ty [skɛ́rsətɪ] s. escasez; carestía; insuficiencia.

scare [skɛr] v. espantar, asustar; alarmar; sobresaltar; **he -s easily** se asusta fácilmente; **to** — **away** ahuyentar, espantar; s. susto, sobresalto.

scare·crow [skɛ́rkro] s. espantajo; espantapájaros.

scarf [skɑrf] s. bufanda; mantilla; pañuelo (*para el cuello de la cabeza*); tapete (*para una mesa, tocador, etc.*).

scar·let [skɑ́rlɪt] *adj.* escarlata; *adj.* de color escarlata; — **fever** escarlata, escarlatina.

scar·y [skɛ́rɪ] *adj.* espantadizo, asustadizo, miedoso.

scat [skæt] *interj.* ¡zape!

scat·ter [skǽtə] v. esparcir(se); desparramar(se); dispersar(se); —**brained** ligero de cascos, aturdido.

scene [sin] s. escena; escenario; decoración; vista; **to make a** — causar un escándalo.

scen·er·y [sínərɪ] *s.* paisaje, vista; **stage** — decoraciones.

scent [sɛnt] *s.* (*odor*) olor; (*substance*) perfume; (*trace*) pista, rastro; **to be on the** — **of** seguir el rastro de; **to have a keen** — tener buen olfato; *v.* oler, olfatear, ventear, husmear; perfumar.

scep·ter [sɛ́ptɚ] *s.* cetro.

scep·tic [skɛ́ptɪk] *adj.* & *s.* escéptico.

scep·ti·cism [skɛ́ptəsɪzəm] *s.* escepticismo.

sched·ule [skɛ́dʒʊl] *s.* horario; itinerario (*de trenes*); lista, inventario (*adjunto a un documento*); *v.* fijar el día y la hora (*para una clase, conferencia, etc.*); establecer el itinerario para (*un tren o trenes*).

scheme [skim] *s.* (*plan*) esquema, plan, proyecto; empresa; (*plot*) ardid, trama, maquinación; **color** — combinación de colores; **metrical** — sistema de versificación; *v.* proyectar, urdir; maquinar, intrigar, tramar.

schem·er [skímɚ] *s.* maquinador, intrigante; proyectista.

schem·ing [skímɪŋ] *adj.* maquinador, intrigante; *s.* maquinación.

schism [sɪzəm] *s.* cisma.

schiz·o·phre·ni·a [skɪzofrínɪə] *s.* esquizofrenia.

schol·ar [skálɚ] *s.* escolar, estudiante; becario (*el que disfruta una beca*); erudito, docto.

schol·ar·ly [skálɚlɪ] *adj.* erudito, sabio, docto; *adv.* eruditamente, doctamente.

schol·ar·ship [skálɚʃɪp] *s.* saber; erudición; beca; **to have a** — disfrutar una beca.

scho·las·tic [skolǽstɪk] *adj.* escolástico; escolar.

school [skul] *s.* escuela; — **of fish** banco de peces; *adj.* de escuela; — **day** día de escuela; — **board** consejo de enseñanza; *v.* enseñar, educar, instruir, aleccionar.

school·boy [skúlbɔɪ] *s.* muchacho de escuela.

school·girl [skúlgɚl] *s.* muchacha de escuela.

school·house [skúlhaʊs] *s.* escuela.

school·ing [skúlɪŋ] *s.* instrucción; enseñanza, educación.

school·mas·ter [skúlmæstɚ] *s.* maestro de escuela.

school·mate [skúlmet] *s.* condiscípulo, compañero de escuela.

school·room [skúlrum] *s.* clase, aula.

school·teach·er [skúltitʃɚ] *s.* maestro de escuela.

schoo·ner [skúnɚ] *s.* goleta; vaso grande para cerveza; **prairie** — galera con toldo.

sci·ence [sáɪəns] *s.* ciencia.

sci·en·tif·ic [saɪəntífɪk] *adj.* científico; **-ally** *adv.* científicamente.

sci·en·tist [sáɪəntɪst] *s.* científico, hombre de ciencia.

scin·til·late [síntəlet] *v.* centellear; chispear.

sci·on [sáɪən] *s.* vástago.

scis·sors [sízɚz] *s. pl.* tijeras.

scle·ro·sis [sklərósɪs] *s.* esclerosis.

scoff [skɔf] *s.* mofa, burla, befa, escarnio; *v.* escarnecer; mofarse; **to** — **at** mofarse de, burlarse de, escarnecer a.

scold [skold] *v.* reñir, reprender, regañar; *s.* regañona, persona regañona.

scold·ing [skóldɪŋ] *s.* regaño, reprensión; *adj.* regañón.

scoop [skup] *s.* (*tool*) cuchara, cucharón; pala; (*quantity*) palada, cucharada; (*winnings*) buena ganancia; **newspaper** — primera publicación de una noticia; *v.* cavar, excavar; ahuecar; cucharear, sacar con cucharón o pala; achicar (*agua*); **to** — **in a good profit** sacar buena ganancia.

scoot [skut] *v.* escabullirse, correr, irse a toda prisa; —! ¡largo de aquí!

scoot·er [skútɚ] *s.* motoneta (*de motor*); monopatín.

scope [skop] *s.* alcance, extensión; esfera, campo.

scorch [skɔrtʃ] *v.* chamuscar; resecar, agostar; *s.* chamusquina, *Am.* chamuscada o chamuscadura.

score [skor] *s.* cuenta; escor (*en el juego*); raya, línea; calificación (*expresada numéricamente*); veintena; **musical** — partitura; **on that** — a ese respecto; **on the** — **of** a causa de, con motivo de; **to keep the** — llevar el escor, llevar la cuenta; **to settle old -s** desquitarse; *v.* marcar el escor, señalar los tantos en un juego; calificar (*numéricamente*); instrumentar (*música*); rayar, marcar con rayas; **to** — **a point** ganar un punto o tanto; **to** — **a success** lograr éxito, obtener un triunfo.

scorn [skɔrn] *s.* desdén, menosprecio; *v.* desdeñar, menospreciar.

scorn·ful [skɔ́rnfəl] *adj.* desdeñoso.

scor·pi·on [skɔ́rpɪən] *s.* escorpión, alacrán.

Scotch [skatʃ] *adj.* escocés; **the** — los escoceses, el pueblo escocés.

scoun·drel [skáʊndrəl] *s.* bellaco, bribón, pícaro.

scour [skaʊr] *v.* fregar, restregar, limpiar; pulir; **to** — **the country** recorrer la comarca (*en busca de algo*).

scourge [skɝdʒ] *s.* azote; *v.* azotar; castigar.

scout [skaʊt] *s.* explorador (*usualmente militar*); **a good** — un buen explorador; una buena persona, un buen compañero; *v.* explorar; reconocer.

scowl [skaʊl] *v.* ceño; *v.* fruncir el ceño, mirar con ceño; poner mala cara.

scram·ble [skrǽmbl] *v.* (*move*) gatear; (*eggs*) hacer un revoltillo; (*mix up*) revolver, mezclar; **to** — **for something** forcejear por coger algo; pelearse por coger algo; **to** — **up** trepar o subir a gatas (*una cuesta*); **-d eggs** revoltillo, huevos revueltos; *s.* revoltillo, confusión; pelea.

scrap [skræp] *s.* (*fragment*) fragmento, pedacito; migaja; (*fight*) riña, reyerta; **-s** sobras; desperdicios; desechos; retales; **—book** álbum de recortes; — **iron** recortes o desechos de hierro; *v.* desechar; tirar a la basura; descartar; pelear, reñir.

scrape [skrep] *v.* (*abrasively*) raspar; rasguñar; rascar; (*rub*) raer; rozar; **to** — **along** ir tirando, ir pasándola; **to** — **together** recoger o acumular poco a poco; **to bow and** — ser muy servil; *s.* raspadura; rasguño; aprieto, dificultad, lío.

scrap·er [skrépɚ] *s.* (*tool*) raspador; (*scrimping person*) tacaño.

scratch [skrætʃ] *v.* (*mark*) arañar, rasguñar; (*rub*) rascar; raspar; (*line*) rayar; escarbar; (*write badly*) hacer garabatos; **to** — **out** borrar, tachar; sacar (*los ojos*) con las uñas; *s.* arañazo, araño, rasguño; raya, marca; **to start from** — empezar sin nada; empezar desde el principio; empezar sin ventaja.

scrawl [skrɔl] *s.* garabato; *v.* hacer garabatos, escribir mal.

scraw·ny [skrɔ́nɪ] *adj.* huesudo, flaco.

scream [skrim] *s.* chillido, alarido, grito; **he's a** — es muy cómico o chistoso; *v.* chillar, gritar.

screech [skritʃ] *s.* chillido; — **owl** lechuza; *v.* chillar.

screen [skrin] *s.* (*projection*) pantalla; (*divider*) biombo; mampara; resguardo; (*sifter*) tamiz, cedazo; **—door** antepuerta de tela metálica;

motion-picture — pantalla de cinematógrafo; **wire** — pantalla de tela metálica; *v.* tapar; resguardar, proteger con una pantalla o biombo; cerner; proyectar sobre la pantalla, filmar; **to — windows** proteger las ventanas con tela metálica.

screw [skru] *s.* tornillo; — **eye** armella; — **nut** tuerca; — **propeller** hélice; — **thread** rosca; *v.* atornillar; torcer, retorcer; **to — a lid on** atornillar una tapa; **to — up one's courage** cobrar ánimo.

screw·driv·er [skrúdraɪvɚ] *s.* destornillador.

scrib·ble [skríbl] *v.* garrapatear, hacer garabatos, borronear, escribir mal o de prisa; *s.* garabato.

script [skrɪpt] *s.* letra cursiva, escritura; manuscrito (*de un drama, de una película*).

scrip·ture [skríptʃɚ] *s.* escritura sagrada; **the Scriptures** la Sagrada Escritura, la Biblia.

scroll [skrol] *s.* rollo de pergamino o papel; voluta, adorno en espiral; rúbrica (*de una firma*).

scrub [skrʌb] *v.* fregar; restregar; *s.* friega, fregado; *adj.* achaparrado; bajo, inferior; — **oak** chaparro; — **pine** pino achaparrado; — **team** equipo de jugadores suplentes o menos bien entrenados; — **woman** fregona.

scru·ple [skrúpl] *s.* escrúpulo; *v.* escrupulizar, tener escrúpulos.

scru·pu·lous [skrúpjələs] *adj.* escrupuloso.

scru·ti·nize [skrútṇaɪz] *v.* escudriñar, escrutar.

scru·ti·ny [skrútṇɪ] *s.* escrutinio.

scuff [skʌf] *v.* raspar; arrastrar los pies.

scuf·fle [skʌfl] *s.* refriega, riña, pelea; *v.* forcejear; luchar, pelear; arrastrar los pies.

sculp·tor [skʌlptɚ] *s.* escultor.

sculp·ture [skʌlptʃɚ] *s.* escultura; *v.* esculpir, cincelar, tallar.

scum [skʌm] *s.* nata, capa, espuma; escoria; residuo, desechos; canalla, gente baja; *v.* espumar.

scur·ry [skɚ́ɪ] *v.* escabullirse; echar a correr; apresurarse; *s.* apresuramiento; corrida, carrera.

scut·tle [skʌtl] *v.* echar a correr; barrenar (*un buque*); echar a pique; *s.* escotilla, escotillón; balde (*para carbón*).

scythe [saɪð] *s.* guadaña.

sea [si] *s.* mar; **to be at** — estar en el mar; estar perplejo o confuso; **to put to** — hacerse a la mar; *adj.* marino, marítimo, de mar; — **biscuit** galleta; — **green** verdemar; — **gull** gaviota; — **level** nivel del mar; — **lion** león marino, foca; — **power** potencia naval.

sea·board [síbord] *s.* costa, litoral; *adj.* costanero, litoral.

sea·coast [síkost] *s.* costa, litoral.

seal [sil] *s.* (*stamp*) sello; timbre; (*animal*) foca, león marino; **to set one's** — **to** sellar; aprobar; *v.* sellar; estampar; cerrar; tapar; **to** — **in** encerrar, cerrar herméticamente; **to** — **with sealing wax** lacrar.

seal·ing wax [sílɪŋ wæks] *s.* lacre.

seam [sim] *s.* costura; juntura; cicatriz; filón, veta; *v.* echar una costura, coser.

sea·man [símən] *s.* marino, marinero.

seam·stress [símstrɪs] *s.* costurera.

sea·plane [síplen] *s.* hidroavión.

sea·port [síport] *s.* puerto de mar.

sear [sɪr] *v.* chamuscar(se), tostar(se); resecar(se); herrar, marcar con hierro candente; *adj.* reseco, marchito.

search [sɝtʃ] *v.* buscar; escudriñar; registrar; examinar; **to** — **a prisoner** registrar a un prisionero; **to** — **for something** buscar algo; **to**

— **into** investigar, indagar; *s.* busca, búsqueda; registro, inspección; investigación, pesquisa, indagación; — **warrant** mandato judicial de practicar un registro; **in** — **of** en busca de.

search·light [sɝtʃlaɪt] *s.* reflector.

sea·shore [síʃor] *s.* costa, playa, orilla o ribera del mar.

sea·sick [sísɪk] *adj.* mareado; **to get** — marearse.

sea·sick·ness [sísɪknɪs] *s.* mareo.

sea·side [sísaɪd] *s.* costa, litoral; playa.

sea·son [sízṇ] *s.* estación (*del año*); temporada; sazón, ocasión, tiempo; — **ticket** billete de abono; **Christmas** — navidades; **harvest** — siega, tiempo de la cosecha; **opera** — temporada de la ópera; **to arrive in good** — llegar en sazón, llegar a tiempo; *v.* sazonar; condimentar; aclimatar.

sea·son·ing [sízṇɪŋ] *s.* condimento; salsa; desecación (*de la madera*).

seat [sit] *s.* (*furniture*) asiento; silla; (*site*) sitio; (*headquarters*) residencia; sede (*episcopal, del gobierno, etc.*); (*body*) nalgas; fondillos, parte trasera (*de los pantalones o calzones*); — **of learning** centro de estudios, centro de erudición; *v.* sentar; asentar; dar asiento a; **to** — **oneself** sentarse; **it -s a thousand people** tiene cabida para mil personas.

sea·weed [síwid] *s.* alga marina.

se·cede [sisíd] *v.* separarse (*de una federación o unión*).

se·clude [sɪklúd] *v.* recluir, apartar, aislar; **to** — **oneself from** recluirse de, apartarse de.

se·clud·ed [sɪklúdɪd] *adj.* apartado, aislado; solitario.

se·clu·sion [sɪklúʒən] *s.* apartamiento, soledad, aislamiento; retiro.

sec·ond [sékənd] *adj.* segundo; inferior; — **hand** segundero (*de reloj*); — **lieutenant** subteniente; **second-rate** de segunda clase; mediocre, inferior; **on** — **thought** después de pensarlo bien; *s.* segundo; padrino (*en un desafío*); ayudante; mercancía de segunda calidad; mercancía defectuosa; — **child** segundón; *v.* secundar (*o segundar*), apoyar; apadrinar.

sec·on·dar·y [sékəndɛrɪ] *adj.* secundario; — **education** segunda enseñanza; — **school** escuela secundaria, escuela de segunda enseñanza.

sec·ond-hand [sékəndhænd] *adj.* de segunda mano; usado; de ocasión; indirecto, por intermedio de otro.

sec·ond·ly [sékəndlɪ] *adv.* en segundo lugar.

se·cre·cy [síkrəsɪ] *s.* secreto, sigilo, reserva.

se·cret [síkrɪt] *s.* secreto; *adj.* secreto; escondido, oculto; — **service** policía secreta; **-ly** *adv.* secretamente, en secreto.

sec·re·tar·i·at [sɛkrətɛ́riət] *s.* secretaría.

sec·re·tar·y [sékrətɛrɪ] *s.* secretario; escritorio (*con estantes para libros*).

se·crete [sɪkrít] *v.* secretar (*una secreción*); esconder, ocultar.

se·cre·tion [sɪkríʃən] *s.* secreción.

se·cre·tive [sɪkrítɪv] *adj.* reservado, callado; — **gland** glándula secretoria.

sect [sɛkt] *s.* secta.

sec·tion [sékʃən] *s.* sección; trozo; tajada; región; barrio; *v.* seccionar, dividir en secciones.

sec·u·lar [sékjələ] *adj. & s.* secular.

se·cure [sɪkjúr] *adj.* seguro; firme; *v.* asegurar; afianzar; obtener; resguardar; **-ly** *adv.* seguramente, con seguridad, firmemente.

se·cu·ri·ty [sɪkjúrətɪ] *s.* seguridad; fianza, garantía,

SC

prenda; resguardo, protección; **securities** bonos, obligaciones, acciones, valores.

se·dan [sɪdǽn] *s.* sedán.

se·date [sɪdét] *adj.* sosegado; tranquilo, sereno; serio.

se·da·tion [sədéʃən] *d.* sedación.

sed·a·tive [sédətɪv] *adj. & s.* calmante, sedativo.

sed·en·tar·y [sédntɛrɪ] *adj.* sedentario; inactivo.

sed·i·ment [sédəmənt] *s.* sedimento, heces, residuo.

se·di·tion [sɪdíʃən] *s.* sedición.

se·di·tious [sɪdíʃəs] *adj.* sedicioso.

se·duce [sɪdjús] *v.* seducir.

se·duc·tion [sɪdʌkʃən] *s.* seducción.

see [si] *v.* ver; — **that you do it** no deje Vd. de hacerlo; **tenga** Vd. cuidado de hacerlo; **I'll — to it** me encargaré de ello; **let me — a** ver; **to — a person home** acompañar a una persona a casa; **to — a person off** ir a la estación para despedir a una persona; **to — a person through a difficulty** ayudar a una persona a salir de un apuro; **to — through a person** adivinar lo que piensa una persona, darse cuenta de sus intenciones; **to — to one's affairs** atender a sus asuntos; **to have seen military service** haber servido en el ejército; *s.* sede, silla; **Holy See** Santa Sede.

seed [sid] *s.* (*grains*) semilla; (*semen*) simiente; (*fruit*) pepita; **to go to — producir semillas;** decaer, declinar; descuidar de su persona, andar desaseado; *v.* sembrar; despepitar, quitar las pepitas o semillas de; producir semillas.

seed·er [sídə] *s.* sembradora.

seed·ling [sídlɪŋ] *s.* planta de semillero; arbolillo (*de menos de tres pies de altura*).

seed·y [sídɪ] *adj.* semilloso, lleno de semillas; raído; desaseado.

seek [sik] *v.* buscar; pedir, solicitar; **to — after** buscar; **to — to** tratar de, esforzarse por.

seem [sim] *v.* parecer; **it -s to me** me parece.

seem·ing·ly [símɪŋlɪ] *adv.* aparentemente, en apariencia, al parecer.

seem·ly [símlɪ] *adj.* propio, decente, decoroso.

seen [sin] *p.p. de* **to see.**

seep [sip] *v.* escurrirse, rezumarse, colarse, filtrarse.

seer [sɪr] *s.* vidente, adivino, profeta.

seethe [sið] *v.* bullir, hervir; burbujear.

seg·ment [ségmənt] *s.* segmento.

seg·re·gate [ségrəget] *v.* segregar.

seize [siz] *v.* (*grasp*) asir, coger, agarrar; apoderarse de; (*arrest*) prender o aprehender; (*take advantage of*) aprovecharse de; (*capture*) embargar, secuestrar; **to — upon** asir; **to become -d with fear** sobrecogerse de miedo.

sei·zure [síʒə] *s.* cogida; captura; aprehensión (*de un criminal*); secuestro, embargo (*de bienes*); ataque (*de una enfermedad*).

sel·dom [séldəm] *adv.* rara vez, raras veces, raramente.

se·lect [səlékt] *adj.* selecto, escogido; *v.* elegir, escoger; entresacar.

se·lec·tion [səlékʃən] *s.* selección, elección.

se·le·ni·um [sɪlíniəm] *s.* selenio.

self [sɛlf]: **by one— por sí, por sí mismo; for one—** para sí; **one's other —** su otro yo; **his wife and —** su esposa y él (*véase* **herself, himself, ourselves, themselves,** *etc.*); **self-centered** egoísta, egocéntrico; **self-conscious** consciente de sí, cohibido, tímido; **self-control** dominio de sí mismo (*o* de sí propio); **self-defense** defensa propia; **self-denial** abnegación; **self-evident** patente, manifiesto; **self-esteem** respeto de sí mismo; amor propio; **self-government** gobierno

autónomo, autonomía; gobierno democrático; **self-interest** propio interés; egoísmo; **self-love** amor propio; **self-possessed** sereno, dueño de sí, tranquilo; **self-sacrifice** abnegación; **self-serv·ice** [sɛlfsɚ́vɪs] *s.* autoservicio; **self-satisfied** pagado de sí, satisfecho de sí.

self-ish [sɛ́lfɪʃ] *adj.* egoísta; **-ly** *adv.* con egoísmo, por egoísmo.

self·ish·ness [sɛ́lfɪʃnɪs] *s.* egoísmo.

self·same [sɛ́lfsém] *adj.* mismo, idéntico, mismísimo.

sell [sɛl] *v.* vender; venderse, estar de venta; **to — at auction** vender en almoneda o subasta, subastar; **to — out** venderlo todo.

sell·er [sɛ́lə] *s.* vendedor.

selves [sɛlvz] *pl. de* **self.**

se·man·tics [səmǽntɪks] *s.* semántica.

sem·blance [sémbləns] *s.* semejanza; apariencia.

se·mes·ter [səmɛ́stə] *s.* semestre.

sem·i·cir·cle [séməsɚ̀kl] *s.* semicírculo.

sem·i·co·lon [séməkolən] *s.* punto y coma.

sem·i·nar·y [sémənɛrɪ] *s.* seminario.

Se·mit·ic [səmɪ́tɪk] *adj.* semítico.

sen·ate [sénɪt] *s.* senado.

sen·a·tor [sénɪtɚ] *s.* senador.

send [sɛnd] *v.* enviar; mandar; despachar; remitir, expedir; lanzar (*una flecha, pelota, etc.*); **to — away** despedir, despachar; **to — forth** despachar, enviar; emitir; exhalar; echar; **to — someone up for 15 years** condenar a un reo a 15 años de prisión; **to — word** avisar, mandar decir, mandar recado.

send·er [sɛ́ndɚ] *s.* remitente; transmisor.

se·nile [sínaɪl] *adj.* senil, caduco; chocho.

se·nil·i·ty [sənílətɪ] *s.* senectud; chochera o chochez.

sen·ior [sínjɚ] *adj.* (*older*) mayor, de más edad; más antiguo; (*superior*) superior; — **class** clase del cuarto año; *s.* persona o socio más antiguo; estudiante del último año; **to be somebody's — by two years** ser dos años mayor que alguien.

sen·sa·tion [sɛnséʃən] *s.* sensación.

sen·sa·tion·al [sɛnséʃənl] *adj.* sensacional; emocionante.

sense [sɛns] *s.* (*function*) sentido; (*sentiment*) sentimiento; sensación; (*judgment*) juicio, sensatez; (*meaning*) significado; **common — sentido común; to make — tener sentido; to be out of one's -s** estar fuera de sí, estar loco; *v.* percibir, sentir; darse cuenta de.

sense·less [sénslɪs] *adj.* sin sentido; insensato, absurdo; insensible, privado de sentido.

sen·si·bil·i·ty [sɛnsəbílətɪ] *s.* sensibilidad.

sen·si·ble [sénsəbl] *adj.* (*aware*) sensato, razonable, cuerdo; (*appreciable*) sensible, perceptible; **sensibly** *adv.* sensatamente, con sensatez, con sentido común; sensiblemente, perceptiblemente.

sen·si·tive [sénsɪtɪv] *adj.* sensitivo; sensible; quisquilloso, susceptible.

sen·si·tive·ness [sénsətɪvnɪs] *s.* sensibilidad.

sen·si·tize [sénsətaɪz] *v.* sensibilizar.

sen·su·al [sénʃuəl] *adj.* sensual, carnal, lujurioso.

sen·su·al·i·ty [sɛnʃuǽlətɪ] *s.* sensualidad; lujuria.

sent [sɛnt] *pret. & p.p. de* **to send.**

sen·tence [séntəns] *s.* sentencia, fallo, decisión; oración (*grammatical*); **death —** pena capital; *v.* sentenciar.

sen·ti·ment [séntəmənt] *s.* sentimiento, sentido.

sen·ti·men·tal [sɛntəméntl] *adj.* sentimental.

sen·ti·men·tal·i·ty [sɛntəmɛntǽlətɪ] *s.* sentimentalismo, sentimentalidad.

sen·ti·nel [séntənl] s. centinela.

sen·try [séntrɪ] s. centinela.

sep·a·rate [séprɪt] adj. (apart) separado; apartado; solitario; (different) distinto, diferente; **-ly** adv. separadamente, por separado; aparte; [sépəret] v. separar(se); apartar(se).

sep·a·ra·tion [sepəréʃən] s. separación.

Se·phar·dic [səfárdɪk] adj. sefardí, sefardita.

Sep·tem·ber [septémbə·] s. setiembre.

sep·ul·cher [sépḷkə·] s. sepulcro, sepultura.

se·quel [síkwəl] s. secuela; continuación, consecuencia; resultado.

se·quence [síkwəns] s. (continuity) secuencia, sucesión; serie, continuación; (result) consecuencia, resultado; runfla (serie de tres o más naipes de un mismo palo).

ser·e·nade [serənéd] s. serenata; v. dar serenata a.

se·rene [sərín] adj. sereno; tranquilo; claro, despejado.

se·ren·i·ty [sərénətɪ] s. serenidad; calma.

ser·geant [sárdʒənt] s. sargento; — at arms oficial que guarda el orden (en un cuerpo legislativo).

se·ri·al [sírɪəl] s. cuento o novela por entregas; adj. consecutivo, en serie; — novel novela por entregas.

se·ries [síriz] s. serie; series.

se·ri·ous [sírɪəs] adj. serio; grave; **-ly** adv. seriamente, con seriedad, en serio; gravemente.

se·ri·ous·ness [sírɪəsnɪs] s. seriedad; gravedad.

ser·mon [sə́mən] s. sermón.

ser·pent [sə́pənt] s. serpiente; sierpe.

se·rum [sírəm] s. suero.

ser·vant [sə́vənt] s. sirviente; criado; servidor; — girl criada, Ríopl. mucama; Andes, Col., Ven. muchacha de servicio.

serve [sɜv] v. (wait on) servir; (supply) surtir, abastecer; **to — a term in prison** cumplir una condena; **to — as** servir de; **to — for** servir de, servir para; **to — notice on** notificar, avisar, advertir; **to — one's purpose** servir para el caso o propósito; **it -s me right** bien me lo merezco; s. saque (de la pelota en tenis).

serv·er [sə́və·] s. servidor; saque (el que saca la pelota en el juego de tenis); bandeja; mesa de servicio.

ser·vice [sə́vɪs] s. servicio; saque (de la pelota en tenis); entrega (de una citación judicial); **at your** — a la disposición de Vd., servidor de Vd.; funeral — honras fúnebres, funerales, exequias; mail — servicio de correos; table — servicio de mesa, vajilla; tea — juego o servicio de té; — entrance entrada para el servicio; — man militar; — station estación de servicio; v. servir; reparar; surtir (una tienda).

ser·vice·a·ble [sə́vɪsəbl] adj. servible; útil; duradero.

ser·vile [sə́vl] adj. servil.

ser·vi·tude [sə́vətjud] s. servidumbre; esclavitud.

ses·sion [séʃən] s. sesión.

set [set] v. (place) poner; colocar, asentar; (fix) fijar; establecer; ajustar; engastar (piedras preciosas); solidificar(se), endurecer(se) (el cemento, yeso, etc.); ponerse (el sol, la luna); empollar; **to — a bone** componer un hueso dislocado; **to — a trap** armar una trampa; **to — about** ponerse a; **to — an example** dar ejemplo; **to — aside** poner a un lado, poner aparte; apartar; ahorrar; **to — back** retrasar, atrasar; **to — forth** exponer, expresar; manifestar; **to — forth on a journey** ponerse en camino; **to — off**

disparar, hacer estallar (un explosivo); hacer resaltar; salir; **to — on fire** pegar o poner fuego a, incendiar; **to — one's jaw** apretar las quijadas; **to — one's heart on** tener la esperanza puesta en; **to — one's mind on** resolverse a, aplicarse a; **to — out for** partir para, salir para; **to — out** to empezar a; **to — right** colocar bien; enderezar; rectificar; **to — sail** hacerse a la vela; **to — the brake** frenar, apretar el freno; **to — up** erigir, levantar; armar, montar (una máquina); parar (tipo de imprenta); establecer, poner (una tienda, un negocio); **to — upon** someone acometer, asaltar a alguien; pret. & p.p. de **to set;** adj. fijo; firme; sólido; resuelto; rígido; puesto; establecido; engastado; — to go listo para partir; s. juego, colección; serie; grupo, clase; partida (de tenis); — of dishes servicio de mesa, vajilla; — of teeth dentadura; radio — radio, radiorreceptor; tea — servicio para té.

set·back [sétbæk] s. atraso, revés, retroceso inesperado.

set·tee [setí] s. canapé.

set·ting [sétɪŋ] s. engaste (de una joya); escena, escenario; puesta (del sol, de un astro); — sun sol poniente.

set·tle [sétl] v. (colonize) colonizar, poblar; establecer(se); fijar(se); asentar(se); (solve) arreglar, poner en orden, ajustar (cuentas); zanjar (una disputa); pagar, liquidar, saldar; to — down formalizarse; asentarse; calmarse; poner casa; **to — on a date** fijar o señalar una fecha; **to — property on (upon)** asignar bienes o propiedad (de propiedad); ajuste, arreglo; pago; saldo, finiquito, liquidación; — house casa de beneficencia; marriage — dote.

set·tle·ment [sétḷmənt] s. (community) establecimiento; colonia; poblado; población; colonización; (arrangement) asignación o traspaso (de propiedad); ajuste, arreglo o saldo, finiquito, liquidación; — house casa de beneficencia; marriage — dote.

set·tler [sétlə·] s. colono, poblador; — of disputes zanjador de disputas.

set·up [sétəp] s. arreglo; organización.

sev·er [sévə·] v. desunir(se), partir(se), dividir(se), separar(se); cortar, romper.

sev·er·al [sévrəl] adj. varios, diversos; distintos, diferentes.

se·vere [səvír] adj. severo; áspero; austero; rígido; riguroso; grave; recio, fuerte.

se·ver·i·ty [səvérətɪ] s. severidad; austeridad; rigidez; gravedad; rigor.

sew [so] v. coser.

sew·er [sjúə·] s. albañal, cloaca.

sew·ing [sóɪŋ] s. costura; modo de coser; — machine máquina de coser; — room cuarto de costura.

sewn [son] p.p. de **to sew.**

sex [seks] s. sexo; — appeal atracción sexual.

sex·tant [sékstənt] s. sextante.

sex·ton [sékstən] s. sacristán.

sex·u·al [sékʃʊəl] adj. sexual.

shab·by [ʃǽbɪ] adj. raído, gastado; andrajoso; mal vestido; vil, injusto; **to treat someone shabbily** tratar a uno injustamente o con menosprecio.

shack [ʃæk] s. cabaña, choza, Am. bohío, Am. jacal.

shack·le [ʃǽkl] v. encadenar; trabar, echar trabas a, poner grillos; estorbar; **-s** s. pl. cadenas, trabas, grillos, esposas; estorbo.

shad [ʃæd] s. sábalo.

SE

shade [ʃed] *s.* (*shadow*) sombra; (*nuance*) tinte, matiz; (*cover*) visillo, cortinilla; pantalla (*de lámpara*); visera (*para los ojos*); **a — longer** un poco más largo; **— of meaning** matiz; **in the — of** a la sombra de; *v.* sombrear; dar sombra; resguardar de la luz; matizar.

shad·ow [ʃǽdo] *s.* (*darkness*) sombra; oscuridad; (*phantom*) espectro; **under the — of** al abrigo de, a la sombra de; **without a — of doubt** sin sombra de duda; *v.* sombrear; obscurecer; **to —** someone espiarle a alguien los pasos, seguirle por todas partes.

shad·ow·y [ʃǽdəwɪ] *adj.* lleno de sombras, tenebroso; vago, indistinto.

shad·y [ʃédɪ] *adj.* sombrío, sombreado, umbrío; **— business** negocio sospechoso; **— character** persona de carácter dudoso, persona de mala fama.

shaft [ʃæft] *s.* pozo o tiro (*de mina, de elevador*); cañón de chimenea; columna; eje, árbol (*de maquinaria*); flecha.

shag·gy [ʃǽgɪ] *adj.* peludo, velludo; lanudo; desaseado; áspero.

shake [ʃek] *v.* menear(se); estremecer(se); temblar; sacudir(se); agitar(se); titubear, vacilar; hacer vacilar; dar, estrechar (*la mano*); **to — hands** dar un apretón de manos, darse la mano; **to — one's head** mover o menear la cabeza; cabecear; **to — with cold** tiritar de frío, estremecerse de frío; **to — with fear** temblar de miedo, estremecerse de miedo; *s.* sacudida; sacudimiento; estremecimiento, temblor; apretón (*de manos*); **hand—** apretón de manos.

shak·en [ʃékən] *p.p. de* **to shake.**

shake-up [ʃékəp] *s.* reorganización.

shak·y [ʃékɪ] *adj.* tembloroso; vacilante.

shall [ʃæl] *v. aux. del futuro del indicativo en las primeras personas* (**I, we**); *en las demás expresa mayor énfasis, mandato u obligación*; **he — not do it** no lo hará, no ha de hacerlo; **thou shalt not steal** no hurtarás.

shal·low [ʃǽlo] *adj.* bajo, poco profundo; superficial; ligero de cascos.

shal·low·ness [ʃǽlonɪs] *s.* poca hondura, poca profundidad; superficialidad; ligereza de juicio.

sham [ʃæm] *s.* fingimiento, falsedad, farsa; *adj.* fingido, simulado; falso; **— battle** simulacro, batalla fingida; *v.* fingir, simular.

sham·bles [ʃǽmblz] *s.* desorden.

shame [ʃem] *s.* vergüenza; deshonra; **— on you!** ¡qué vergüenza!; **it is a —** es una vergüenza; es una lástima; **to bring — upon** deshonrar; *v.* avergonzar; deshonrar.

shame·ful [ʃémfəl] *adj.* vergonzoso.

shame·less [ʃémlɪs] *adj.* desvergonzado, descarado.

shame·less·ness [ʃémlɪsnɪs] *s.* desvergüenza; descaro, desfachatez.

sham·poo [ʃæmpú] *s.* champú, lavado de la cabeza; *v.* dar un champú, lavar (*la cabeza*).

sham·rock [ʃǽmrɑk] *s.* trébol.

shank [ʃæŋk] *s.* canilla (*parte inferior de la pierna*); zanca.

shan·ty [ʃǽntɪ] *s.* choza, cabaña, casucha.

shape [ʃep] *s.* (*form*) forma; (*figure*) figura; (*condition*) estado, condición; **to be in a bad —** estar mal; **to put into —** arreglar, poner en orden, ordenar; *v.* formar, dar forma a; tomar forma; **to — one's life** dar forma a, ajustar o disponer su vida; **his plan is shaping well** va desarrollándose bien su plan.

shape·ly [ʃéplɪs] *adj.* informe, sin forma.

share [ʃɛr] *s.* (*portion*) proción, parte; (*participation*) participación; acción (*participación en el capital de una compañía*); *v.* compartir; repartir; participar; **to — in** participar en, tener parte en; **to — a thing with** compartir una cosa con.

share·hold·er [ʃɛrholdɚ] *s.* accionista.

shark [ʃɑrk] *s.* (*fish*) tiburón; (*usurer*) estafador; (*expert*) perito, experto; **loan —** usurero; **to be a — at** ser un águila (*o* ser muy listo) para.

sharp [ʃɑrp] *adj.* (*acute*) agudo, puntiagudo; cortante; punzante; (*biting*) mordaz; picante; (*bright*) astuto; (*clear*) claro, distinto, bien marcado; (*sudden*) repentino; **— curve** curva abrupta, curva pronunciada o muy cerrada; **— ear** oídofino; **— features** facciones bien marcadas; **— struggle** lucha violenta; **— taste** sabor acre; **— temper** genio áspero; **— turn** vuelta repentina; *s.* sostenido (*en música*); **— card** tahur, fullero; *adv. véase* **sharply; at ten o'clock —** a las diez en punto.

sharp·en [ʃárpən] *v.* afilar(se); sacar punta a; aguzar(se); amolar.

sharp·ly [ʃárplɪ] *adv.* agudamente; mordazmente, ásperamente; repentinamente; claramente; **to arrive —** llegar en punto.

sharp·ness [ʃárpnɪs] *s.* agudeza; sutileza; mordacidad; rigor; aspereza; acidez.

shat·ter [ʃǽtɚ] *v.* estrellar(se), astillar(se), hacer(se) añicos; quebrar(se), romper(se); **to — one's hopes** frustrar sus esperanzas; **his health was -ed** se le quebrantó la salud; **-s** *s. pl.* pedazos, trozos, añicos, fragmentos; **to break into —** hacer(se) añicos.

shave [ʃev] *v.* afeitar(se), rasurar(se); rapar(se); acepillar (*madera*); *s.* rasura, *Am.* afeitada; **he had a close —** por poco no se escapa; se salvó por milagro.

shav·en [ʃévən] *p.p. de* **to shave; clean-shaven** bien afeitado.

shav·ing [ʃévɪŋ] *s.* rasura, *Am.* afeitada; **wood -s** virutas; **— brush** brocha de afeitar; **— soap** jabón de afeitar.

shawl [ʃɔl] *s.* mantón, chal.

she [ʃi] *pron. pers.* ella; **— who** la que; *s.* hembra; **she-bear** osa; **she-goat** cabra.

sheaf [ʃif] *s.* haz, gavilla, manojo; lío; *v.* hacer gavillas.

shear [ʃir] *v.* trasquilar, esquilar (*las ovejas*); cortar (*con tijeras grandes*).

shear·ing [ʃírɪŋ] *s.* tonsura.

shears [ʃɪrz] *s. pl.* tijeras grandes.

sheath [ʃiθ] *s.* vaina; funda, envoltura.

sheathe [ʃið] *v.* envainar.

sheaves [ʃivz] *pl. de* **sheaf.**

shed [ʃed] *s.* cobertizo; tejadillo; tinglado; *Ríopl., Andes* galpón (*de una estancia*); *v.* derramar; difundir; esparcir; mudar (*de piel plumas, etc.*); ser impermeable (*un paño, abrigo, sombrero, etc.*); **to — leaves** deshojarse; *pret. & p.p. de* **shed.**

sheen [ʃin] *s.* lustre, viso.

sheep [ʃip] *s.* oveja; carnero; ovejas; **— dog** perro de pastor; **—fold** redil; **—skin** zalea; badana; pergamino; diploma (*de pergamino*).

sheep·ish [ʃipɪʃ] *adj.* vergonzoso, encogido, tímido.

sheer [ʃir] *adj.* (*pure*) puro; completo; (*thin*) fino, delgado, transparente, diáfano; (*steep*) escarpado; **by — force** a pura fuerza.

sheet [ʃit] *s.* (*bed*) sábana; (*paper*) hoja, pliego (*de papel*); lámina (*de metal*); extensión (*de agua, hielo*); **— lightning** relampagueo.

shelf [ʃɛlf] *s.* estante, anaquel; repisa; saliente de roca.

shell [ʃɛl] *s.* concha; cáscara (*de huevo, nuez, etc.*); vaina (*de guisantes, frijoles, garbanzos, etc.*); casco (*de una embarcación*); armazón (*de un edificio*); granada, bomba; cápsula (*para cartuchos*); *v.* cascar (*nueces*); desvainar, quitar la vaina a, pelar; desgranar (*maíz, trigo, etc.*); bombardear.

shel·lac [ʃəlǽk] *s.* laca; *v.* barnizar con laca.

shell·fish [ʃɛ́lfiʃ] *s.* marisco; mariscos.

shel·ter [ʃɛ́ltɚ] *s.* abrigo, refugio, asilo; resguardo, protección; **to take** — refugiarse, abrigarse; *v.* abrigar, refugiar, guarecer; proteger, amparar.

shelve [ʃɛlv] *v.* poner o guardar en un estante; poner a un lado, arrinconar, arrumbar.

shelves [ʃɛlvz] *s. pl.* estantes, anaqueles; estantería.

shep·herd [ʃɛ́pɚd] *s.* pastor; zagal; — **dog** perro de pastor.

sher·bet [ʃɚ́bɪt] *s.* sorbete.

sher·iff [ʃɛ́rɪf] *s.* alguacil mayor (*de un condado en los Estados Unidos*).

sher·ry [ʃɛ́rɪ] *s.* jerez, vino de Jerez.

shield [ʃild] *s.* escudo, rodela, broquel; resguardo, defensa; *v.* escudar, resguardar, proteger.

shift [ʃɪft] *v.* (*change*) cambiar; mudar(se); alternar(se); variar; desviar(se); (*transfer*) trasladar, transferir; **to** — **for oneself** valerse o mirar por sí mismo; **to** — **gears** cambiar de marcha; **to** — **the blame** echar a otro su propio culpa; *s.* cambio; desvío, desviación; tanda, grupo de obreros; turno; **gear**— cambio de marcha.

shift·less [ʃíftlɪs] *adj.* negligente; holgazán.

shil·ling [ʃílɪŋ] *s.* chelín.

shim·my [ʃími] *s.* (*dance*) shimmy; (*vibration*) abaniqueo.

shin [ʃɪn] *s.* espinilla (*de la pierna*); *v.* **to** — **up** trepar.

shine [ʃaɪn] *v.* (*beam*) brillar, resplandecer, lucir; (*polish*) pulir; dar brillo, lustre o bola, embolar (zapatos); *s.* brillo, lustre, resplandor; **rain or** — llueva o truene; **to give a shoe** — dar bola (brillo *o* lustre) a los zapatos; embolar o embetunar los zapatos; limpiar el calzado.

shin·gle [ʃíŋgl] *s.* ripia, tabla delgada, *Méx.* tejamanil o tejamaní; pelo corto escalonado; letrero de oficina; **-s** zona (*erupcion de la piel*); *v.* cubrir con tejamaniles; techar con tejamaniles.

shin·ing [ʃáɪnɪŋ] *adj.* brillante; resplandeciente.

shin·y [ʃáɪnɪ] *adj.* brillante; lustroso.

ship [ʃɪp] *s.* (*naval*) buque, barco, navío, nave; (*air*) aeronave, avión; —**builder** ingeniero naval, constructor de buques; —**mate** camarada de a bordo; —**yard** astillero; **on** —**board** a bordo; *v.* embarcar(se); despachar, enviar; remesar; transportar; alistarse como marino.

ship·ment [ʃípmənt] *s.* embarque; cargamento; despacho, envío; remesa.

ship·per [ʃípɚ] *s.* embarcador; remitente.

ship·ping [ʃípɪŋ] *s.* embarque; despacho, envío; — **charges** gastos de embarque; — **clerk** dependiente de muelle; dependiente encargado de embarques.

ship·wreck [ʃíprɛk] *s.* naufragio; *v.* echar a pique, hacer naufragar; naufragar, irse a pique.

ship·yard [ʃípyard] *s.* astillero.

shirk [ʃɚk] *v.* evadir, evitar.

shirt [ʃɚt] *s.* camisa; *C.A.* cotón; —**waist** blusa; **in** — **sleeves** en camisa, en mangas de camisa.

shiv·er [ʃívɚ] *v.* tiritar; temblar; estremecerse; *s.* escalofrío, temblor, estremecimiento.

shoal [ʃol] *s.* bajío, banco de arena; banco (*de peces*).

shock [ʃak] *s.* (*blow*) choque; sacudida; Dn< sacudimiento; golpe; (*surprise*) sobresalto; — **absorber** amortiguador; — **of grain** hacina o gavilla de mieses; — **of hair** guedeja, greña; — **troops** tropas de asalto; *v.* chocar, ofender; escandalizar; causar fuerte impresión; horrorizar; sacudir; conmover; hacinar, hacer gavillas de (*mieses*).

shock·ing [ʃákɪŋ] *adj.* chocante, ofensivo, repugnante; espantoso, escandaloso.

shod [ʃad] *pret. & p.p. de* **to shoe.**

shoe [ʃu] *s.* zapato; botín; **brake** — zapata de freno; **horse**— herradura; — **blacking** betún, bola; — **polish** brillo, lustre, bola; — **store** zapatería; *v.* calzar; herrar (*un caballo*).

shoe·black [ʃúblæk] *s.* limpiabotas.

shoe·horn [ʃúhɔrn] *s.* calzador.

shoe·lace [ʃúles] *s.* lazo, cinta, cordón de zapato.

shoe·mak·er [ʃúmekɚ] *s.* zapatero.

shoe·string [ʃústrɪŋ] *s.* lazo, cinta, cordón de zapato.

shone [ʃon] *pret. & p.p. de* **to shine.**

shook [ʃʊk] *pret. de* **to shake.**

shoot [ʃut] *v.* (*firearm*) tirar, disparar, descargar; hacer fuego; fusilar; dar un balazo; (*throw*) lanzar, disparar (*una instantánea*); fotografiar, filmar (*una escena*); echar (*los dados*); brotar (*las plantas*); **to** — **by** pasar rápidamente; **to** — **forth** brotar, salir; germinar; lanzarse; **to** — **it out** pelearse a balazos; **to** — **up a place** entrarse a balazos por un lugar; *s.* vástago, retoño, renuevo; **to go out for a** — salir a tirar; ir de caza.

shoot·er [ʃútɚ] *s.* tirador.

shoot·ing [ʃútɪŋ] *s.* tiroteo; — **match** certamen de tiradores (*o* de tiro al blanco); — **pain** punzada, dolor agudo; — **star** estrella fugaz.

shop [ʃap] *s.* tienda; taller; — **window** escaparate, vitrina, aparador, *Ríopl., Andes* vidriera; **barber**— barbería; **beauty** — salón de belleza; **to talk** — hablar uno de su oficio o profesión; *v.* ir de tiendas; ir de compras, comprar.

shop·keep·er [ʃapkipɚ] *s.* tendero.

shop·per [ʃápɚ] *s.* comprador.

shop·ping [ʃápɪŋ] *s.* compra, compras; **to go** — ir de compras, ir de tiendas.

shore [ʃor] *s.* costa, playa, orilla, ribera; puntal; **ten miles off** — a diez millas de la costa; *v.* **to** — **up** apuntalar, poner puntales.

shorn [ʃorn] *p.p. de* **to shear.**

short [ʃɔrt] *adj.* (*duration*) corto; breve; (*height*) bajo; *Méx.* chaparro; escaso; brusco; — **cut** atajo; — **circuit** cortocircuito; — **wave** onda corta; método corto; **short-legged** de piernas cortas; — **loan** préstamo a corto plazo; **for** — para abreviar; **in** — en resumen, en suma, en conclusión; **in** — **order** rápidamente, prontamente; **in a** — **time** en poco tiempo; al poco tiempo; **to be** — **of** estar falto o escaso de; **to cut** — acortar, abreviar, terminar de repente; **to run** — **of something** acabársele (írsele acabando) a uno algo; **to stop** — parar de repente, parar en seco.

short·age [ʃɔ́rtɪdʒ] *s.* escasez, carestía; déficit; falta.

short·com·ing [ʃɔ́rtkʌmɪŋ] *s.* falta, defecto.

short·en [ʃɔ́rtn̩] *v.* acortar(se), abreviar(se), disminuir(se).

short·en·ing [ʃɔ́rtnɪŋ] *s.* manteca, grasa (*para hacer pasteles*); acortamiento; abreviación.

SH

short·hand [ʃɔ́rthænd] *s.* taquigrafía.
short·ly [ʃɔ́rtlɪ] *adj.* brevemente; en breve; al instante, pronto, luego; bruscamente, secamente.
short·ness [ʃɔ́rtnɪs] *s.* cortedad; brevedad; pequeñez; escasez, deficiencia.
shorts [ʃɔrts] *s. pl.* calzoncillos, calzones cortos.
short·sight·ed [ʃɔ́rtsáɪtɪd] *adj.* miope; corto de vista.
shot [ʃɑt] *pret. & p.p. de* **to shoot; s.** (*discharge*) tiro; disparo; balazo; cañonazo; (*pellet*) bala; balas; (*injection*) inyección; (*throw*) tirada; — **of liquor** trago de aguardiente; **buck**— municiones, postas; **not by a long** — ni con mucho, ni por pienso, nada de eso; **he is a good** — es buen tirador, tiene buen tino; **to take a** — **at** disparar un tiro a; hacer una tentativa de; **within rifle** — a tiro de rifle.
shot·gun [ʃɑ́tgʌn] *s.* escopeta.
should [ʃʊd] *v. aux. del condicional en las primeras personas* (**I, we**): **I said that I** — **go** dije que iría; *equivale al imperfecto de subjuntivo*; **if it** — **rain** si lloviera; *se usa con la significación de deber*: **you** — **not do it** no debiera (*o* no debería) hacerlo.
shoul·der [ʃóldɚ] *s.* (*person*) hombro; (*animal*) lomo, pernil (*de puerco, cordero*); borde, saliente (*de un camino*); **-s** espalda, espaldas; — **blade** espaldilla, paletilla; **straight from the** — con toda franqueza; **to turn a cold** — **to** volver las espaldas a, tratar fríamente; *v.* cargar al hombro, echarse sobre las espaldas; cargar con, asumir; empujar con el hombro.
shout [ʃaʊt] *v.* gritar; vocear; *s.* grito.
shove [ʃʌv] *v.* empujar, dar empellones; **to** — **aside** echar a un lado, rechazar; **to** — **off** partir, zarpar (*un buque*); salir, irse; *s.* empujón, empellón; empuje.
shov·el [ʃʌ́vl] *s.* pala; *v.* traspalar.
show [ʃo] *v.* (*exhibit*) mostrar, enseñar; exhibir; (*prove*) probar, demostrar; indicar; (*appear*) verse; asomarse; — **him in** que pase, hágale entrar; **to** — **off** alardear, hacer ostentación de; lucirse; **to** — **up** aparecer, presentarse; **to** — **someone up** hacer subir a alguien; mostrarle el camino (*para subir*); desenmascarar a alguien, poner a alguien en la evidencia; *s.* exhibición; demostración; ostentación; espectáculo; representación, función; apariencia; — **window** escaparate, vitrina, aparador, *Am.* vidriera; **to go to the** — ir al teatro, ir al cine; **to make a** — **of** oneself exhibirse, hacer ostentación.
show·case [ʃókes] *s.* vitrina, aparador.
show·down [ʃódaun] *s.* arreglo terminante.
show·er [ʃáuɚ] *s.* aguacero, chubasco, chaparrón, lluvia; ducha, baño de ducha; *Méx.* regadera; **bridal** — tertulia para obsequiar a una novia; *v.* llover; caer un aguacero.
shown [ʃon] *p.p. de* **to show.**
show·y [ʃóɪ] *adj.* ostentoso; vistoso, chillón.
shrank [ʃræŋk] *pret. de* **to shrink.**
shred [ʃred] *s.* tira, triza; andrajo; fragmento; pizca; **to be in -s** estar raído; estar andrajoso; estar hecho trizas; **to tear to -s** hacer trizas; *v.* desmenuzar; hacer trizas, hacer tiras; *pret. & p.p. de* **to shred.**
shrew [ʃru] *s.* arpía, mujer brava, mujer de mal genio.
shrewd [ʃrud] *adj.* astuto, sagaz, agudo.
shriek [ʃrik] *v.* chillar, gritar; *s.* chillido, grito.
shrill [ʃrɪl] *adj.* agudo, penetrante, chillón; *v.* chillar.

shrimp [ʃrɪmp] *s.* camarón; *Esp.* gamba; hombrecillo insignificante.
shrine [ʃraɪn] *s.* santuario; altar; lugar venerado.
shrink [ʃrɪŋk] *v.* encoger(se); contraer(se); disminuir; **to** — **back** retroceder; **to** — **from** retroceder ante, apartarse de; huir de, rehuir.
shrink·age [ʃrínkɪdʒ] *s.* encogimiento; contracción; merma.
shriv·el [ʃrívl] *v.* encoger(se); fruncir(se), marchitar(se); disminuir(se).
shroud [ʃraud] *s.* mortaja; *v.* amortajar; cubrir, ocultar.
shrub [ʃrʌb] *s.* arbusto.
shrub·ber·y [ʃrʌ́bərɪ] *s.* arbustos.
shrug [ʃrʌg] *v.* encogerse de hombros; *s.* encogimiento de hombros.
shrunk [ʃrʌŋk] *pret. & p.p. de* **to shrink.**
shrunk·en [ʃrʌ́nkən] *p.p. de* **to shrink.**
shuck [ʃʌk] *s.* hollejo; cáscara.
shud·der [ʃʌ́dɚ] *v.* temblar, estremecerse; *s.* temblor, estremecimiento.
shuf·fle [ʃʌ́fl] *v.* barajar; revolver, mezclar; arrastrar (*los pies*); **to** — **along** ir arrastrando los pies; *s.* mezcla, confusión; evasiva; — **of feet** arrastramiento de pies; **it is your** — **a** Vd. le toca barajar.
shun [ʃʌn] *v.* esquivar, evadir, rehuir, evitar.
shut [ʃʌt] *v.* cerrar(se); **fo** — **down** parar el trabajo; cerrar (*una fábrica*); **to** — **in** encerrar; **to** — **off** cortar (*el gas, la electricidad, el agua, etc.*); **to** — **off from** incomunicar, aislar de, cortar la communicación con; excluir; **to** — **out** impedir la entrada de; cerrar la puerta a; **to** — **up** cerrar bien; tapar; encerrar; tapar la boca, hacer callar; callarse; *pret. & p.p. de* **to shut;** *adj.* cerrado.
shut·ter [ʃʌ́tɚ] *s.* contraventana; postigo (*de ventana*); cerrador; obturador (*de una cámara fotográfica*).
shut·tle [ʃʌ́tl] *s.* lanzadera; *v.* ir y venir acompasadamente (*como una lanzadera*).
shy [ʃaɪ] *adj.* tímido, apocado, retraído; vergonzoso; asustadizo; esquivo; **to be** — **on** estar escaso de; **to be** — **two cents** faltarle a uno dos centavos; *v.* esquivarse, hacerse a un lado; asustarse; **to** — **at something** retroceder ante algo; respingar (*un caballo*) al ver algo; espantarse con algo; **to** — **away** esquivarse de repente; respingar (*un caballo*); desviarse, apartarse.
shy·ness [ʃáɪnɪs] *s.* apocamiento, timidez, vergüenza.
shy·ster [ʃáɪstɚ] *s.* leguleyo, abogadillo tramposo, picapleitos.
sib·i·lant [síbələnt] *s.* sibilante.
sick [sɪk] *adj.* enfermo, malo; nauseado; angustiado; — **leave** licencia por enfermedad; **to be** — **for** languidecer por, suspirar por; **to be** — **of** estar cansado de; estar harto de; **to be** — **to** (*o at*) one's **stomach** tener náuseas; **to make** — enfermar; dar pena, dar lástima; *s.* **the** — los enfermos; *v.* incitar, azuzar (*a un perro*) — **him** ¡síguele!
sick·en [síkən] *v.* enfermar(se), poner(se) enfermo; dar asco; tener asco; sentir náuseas.
sick·en·ing [síknɪŋ] *adj.* nauseabundo, repugnante; lastimoso.
sick·le [síkl] *s.* hoz.
sick·ly [síklɪ] *adj.* enfermizo; achacoso, enclenque; malsano.
sick·ness [síknɪs] *s.* enfermedad; malestar; náuseas.

side [saɪd] *s.* (*surface*) lado; cara; costado; ladera; falda (*de una colina*); (*faction*) partido, facción; — **by** — lado a lado; **by his** — a su lado; **by the** — **of** al lado de; **on all -s** por todos lados; **to take -s with** ser partidario de, ponerse al lado de; *adj.* lateral; de lado; oblicuo; incidental; secundario, de menos importancia; — **glance** mirada de soslayo, de través o de reojo; — **issue** cuestión secundaria; — **light** luz lateral; noticia, detalle o ilustración incidental; *v.* **to** — **with** estar por, ser partidario de, apoyar a, opinar con.

side·board [sáɪdbord] *s.* aparador; *Col., Ven.* seibó.

side·slip [sáɪdslɪp] *s.* deslizamiento.

side·track [sáɪdtræk] *v.* desviar; echar a un lado.

side·walk [sáɪdwɔk] *s.* acera, *Méx.* banqueta, *Riopl., Ch., Andes* vereda; *C.A., Col.,* andén.

side·ways [sáɪdwez] *adv.* de lado, de costado; oblicuamente; hacia un lado; *adj.* lateral, de lado, oblicuo.

siege [sidʒ] *s.* cerco, sitio, asedio; **to lay** — **to** sitiar, cercar.

sieve [sɪv] *s.* tamiz, cedazo; criba; *v. véase* **sift**.

sift [sɪft] *v.* cerner, tamizar; cribar.

sigh [saɪ] *v.* suspirar; *s.* suspiro.

sight [saɪt] *s.* (*sense*) vista; (*view*) visión; espectáculo, escena; (*gun*) mira (*de un arma de fuego*); **in** — **of** a vista de; **payable at** — pagadero a la vista; **he is a** — es un adefesio o mamarracho; **this room is a** — este cuarto es un horror; **to catch** — **of** vislumbrar, avistar; **to know by** — conocer de vista; **to lose** — **of** perder de vista; **to see the -s** ver of visitar los puntos de interés; *v.* avistar; ver.

sight·see·ing [sáɪtsiɪŋ] *s.* turismo; — **tour** paseo en auto para ver puntos de interés.

sign [saɪn] *s.* (*signal*) signo; seña, señal; (*indication*) muestra; (*placard*) letrero; —**board** cartel; tablero (*para fijar anuncios*); *v.* firmar; contratar, hacer firmar; **to** — **over property** ceder una propiedad mediante escritura, hacer cesión legal de propiedad; **to** — **up for a job** firmar el contrato para un empleo; contratar para un empleo.

sig·nal [sígnl] *s.* señal, seña; *v.* señalar, indicar, hacer seña, dar la señal; *adj.* señalado, notable; extraordinario; — **beacon** faro; — **code** código de señales.

sig·na·ture [sígnətʃɚ] *s.* firma.

sign·er [sáɪnɚ] *s.* firmante.

sig·nif·i·cance [sɪgnífəkəns] *s.* significación; significado.

sig·nif·i·cant [sɪgnífəkənt] *adj.* significativo.

sig·ni·fy [sígnəfaɪ] *v.* significar.

si·lence [sáɪləns] *s.* silencio; *v.* acallar; apagar (*un sonido*); aquietar, sosegar.

si·lent [sáɪlənt] *adj.* silencioso; callado; tácito; — **partner** socio comanditario (*que no tiene voz ni voto*).

sil·hou·ette [sɪluét] *s.* silueta; *v.* perfilar; **to be -d against** perfilarse contra.

sil·i·con [sɪləkən] *s.* silicio.

silk [sɪlk] *s.* seda; *adj.* de seda; — **industry** industria sedera; — **ribbon** cinta de seda.

silk·en [sɪlkən] *adj.* sedoso; de seda.

silk·worm [sɪlkwɝm] *s.* gusano de seda.

silk·y [sɪlkɪ] *adj.* sedoso, sedeño; de seda.

sill [sɪl] *s.* umbral; **window** — antepecho de ventana.

sil·ly [sɪlɪ] *adj.* necio, tonto, bobo, simple; absurdo, insensato.

si·lo [sáɪlo] *s.* silo.

silt [sɪlt] *s.* cieno.

sil·ver [sílvɚ] *s.* (*metal*) plata; (*tableware*) cubierto; (*dishes*) vajilla de plata; (*color*) color de plata; *adj.* de plata; plateado; argentino; — **wedding** bodas de plata; *v.* platear; argentar; **to** — **a mirror** azogar un espejo.

sil·ver·smith [sílvɚsmɪθ] *s.* platero.

sil·ver·ware [sílvɚwer] *s.* vajilla de plata, vajilla plateada; cuchillos, cucharas y tenedores (*por lo general de plata o plateados*).

sil·ver·y [sílvɚɪ] *adj.* plateado; argentino.

sim·i·lar [sɪmələ] *adj.* semejante; similar; -**ly** *adv.* semejantemente; de la misma manera.

sim·i·lar·i·ty [sɪməlǽrətɪ] *s.* semejanza, parecido.

sim·i·le [sɪməlɪ] *s.* símil.

sim·mer [sɪmɚ] *v.* hervir a fuego lento.

sim·ple [sɪmpl] *adj.* simple; sencillo; llano; tonto, mentecato; **simpleminded** ingenuo, simple, simplón; *s.* simple.

sim·ple·ton [sɪmpltən] *s.* simplón, papanatas, papamoscas.

sim·plic·i·ty [sɪmplísətɪ] *s.* sencillez; simplicidad; simpleza; ingenuidad.

sim·pli·fy [sɪmpləfaɪ] *v.* simplificar.

sim·ply [sɪmplɪ] *adv.* simplemente; sencillamente; solamente.

sim·u·late [sɪmjəlet] *v.* simular.

si·mul·ta·ne·ous [saɪmltḗnɪəs] *adj.* simultáneo.

sin [sɪn] *s.* pecado, culpa; *v.* pecar.

since [sɪns] *conj.* desde que; después (de) que; puesto que, como, visto que; dado que; *prep.* desde, despues de; *adv.* desde entonces; **ever** — desde entonces; **he died long** — murió hace mucho tiempo; **we have been here** — **five** estamos aquí desde las cinco.

sin·cere [sɪnsír] *adj.* sincero.

sin·cer·i·ty [sɪnsérətɪ] *s.* sinceridad.

si·ne·cure [sɪnɪkjur] *s.* sinecura (*trabajo fácil y bien pagado*).

sin·ew [sɪnju] *s.* tendón; fibra, vigor.

sin·ew·y [sɪnjəwɪ] *adj.* nervudo, nervioso o nervoso; fuerte, vigoroso.

sin·ful [sɪnfəl] *adj.* pecaminoso; pecador.

sing [sɪŋ] *v.* cantar; **to** — **out of tune** desentonar(se), desafinar; **to** — **to sleep** arrullar.

singe [sɪndʒ] *v.* chamuscar; *s.* chamusquina, *Am.* chamuscada, *Am.* chamuscadura.

sing·er [sɪŋɚ] *s.* cantor; cantora, cantatriz.

sin·gle [sɪŋgl] *adj.* (*unique*) solo; (*distinct*) individual; particular; (*unmarried*) soltero; — **entry bookkeeping** teneduría por partida simple; — **room** cuarto para uno; — **woman** mujer soltera; **not a** — **word** ni una sola palabra; *s.* billete de un dólar; *v.* **to** — **out** singularizar, distinguir, escoger; entresacar.

sin·gle·handed [sɪŋglhǽndɪd] *adj.* solo, sin ayuda.

sing·song [sɪŋsɔŋ] *s.* sonsonete, cadencia monótona.

sin·gu·lar [sɪŋgjələ] *adj.* singular; raro, extraordinario; *s.* singular, número singular.

sin·is·ter [sɪnɪstɚ] *adj.* siniestro, aciago, funesto.

sink [sɪŋk] *v.* hundir(se); sumir(se), sumergir(se); echar a pique; irse a pique, naufragar; cavar (*un pozo*); enterrar, clavar (*un puntal o poste*); **to** — **into one's mind** grabarse en la memoria; **to** — **one's teeth into** clavar el diente en; **to** — **to sleep** caer en el sueño; *s.* sumidero; fregadero.

sin·ner [sínɚ] *s.* pecador.

sin·u·ous [sínjʊəs] *adj.* sinuoso, tortuoso; con vueltas y rodeos.

si·nus [sáɪnəs] s. seno, cavidad (en un hueso); **frontal —** seno frontal.

sip [sɪp] v. sorber; chupar; s. sorbo.

si·phon [sáɪfən] s. sifón; v. sacar (agua) con sifón.

sir [sɜ] s. señor.

si·ren [sáɪrən] s. sirena.

sir·loin [sɜlɔɪn] s. solomillo, solomo.

sir·up [sírəp] s. jarabe.

sis·sy [sísɪ] adj. & s. afeminado, maricón.

sis·ter [sístɚ] s. hermana; **Sister Mary** Sor María.

sis·ter-in-law [sístərɪnlɔ] s. cuñada, hermana política.

sit [sɪt] v. sentar(se); colocar, asentar; posarse (un pájaro); estar sentado; estar situado; empollar (las gallinas); apoyarse; reunirse, celebrar sesión (un cuerpo legislativo, un tribunal); sentar, venir o caer (bien o mal un traje); **to — down** sentarse; **to — out a dance** quedarse sentado durante una pieza de baile; **to — still** estarse quieto; **to — tight** mantenerse firme en su puesto; **to — up** incorporarse; **to — up all night** velar toda la noche; **to — up and take notice** despabilarse.

site [saɪt] s. sitio, local, situación.

sit·ting [sítɪŋ] s. sesión (de un cuerpo legislativo, tribunal, etc.); sentada; **at one —** de una sentada; adj. sentado; **— hen** gallina ponedora; **— room** sala (de descanso); sala de espera; antesala.

sit·u·at·ed [sítʃuetɪd] adj. situado, sito, ubicado, colocado.

sit·u·a·tion [sɪtʃuéʃən] s. (location) situación, colocación; (employment) empleo; posición; (status) situación.

size [saɪz] s. tamaño; medida; talla; v. clasificar según el tamaño, ajustar a tamaño; **to — up** tantear, formarse una idea de, juzgar.

siz·zle [sízl] v. chirriar (aplícase al sonido que hace la carne al freírse); s. chirrido (de la carne al freírse).

skate [sket] s. patín; **ice —** patín de hielo, patín de cuchilla; **roller —** patín de ruedas; v. patinar.

skein [sken] s. madeja.

skel·e·ton [skélətn] s. esqueleto; osamenta; armazón; **— key** llave maestra.

skep·tic = **sceptic.**

sketch [skɛtʃ] s. (drawing) boceto; diseño; croquis; (outline) esbozo; bosquejo; v. bosquejar; delinear; esbozar, dibujar.

ski [ski] s. esquí; v. esquiar, patinar con esquís.

skid [skɪd] v. patinar, resbalar(se); patinar (una rueda); deslizarse.

skill [skɪl] s. destreza, maña, habilidad, pericia.

skilled [skɪld] adj. experto, práctico, experimentado, hábil.

skil·let [skílɪt] s. sartén; cacerola.

skill·ful, skil·ful [skílfəl] adj. experto, diestro, ducho, hábil, perito.

skim [skɪm] v. (remove layer) desnatar, quitar la nata a; espumar, quitar la espuma a; (read) leer superficialmente; **to — over the surface** rozar la superficie.

skimp [skɪmp] v. escatimar; economizar; ser tacaño; hacer (las cosas) con descuido.

skimp·y [skímpɪ] adj. escaso; tacaño.

skin [skɪn] s. piel; cutis; pellejo; cuero; cáscara, hollejo; **to save one's —** salvar el pellejo; **skin-deep** superficial; v. desollar; pelar; **to — someone (out of his money)** desplumar a una persona, quitarle a uno el dinero.

skin·ny [skínɪ] adj. flaco; descarnado.

skip [skɪp] v. saltar; brincar; saltarse (unos renglones, un párrafo, etc.), omitir; saltar por encima de, salvar de un brinco; **to — out** salir a escape, escabullirse, escaparse, s. salto, brinco; omisión.

skip·per [skípɚ] s. patrón (de barco); capitán; saltador, brincador.

skir·mish [skɜmɪʃ] s. escaramuza; v. escaramuzar, sostener una escaramuza.

skirt [skɜt] s. falda, Riopl. pollera; orilla, borde; **under—** enaguas; v. bordear, orillar, ir por la orilla de; circundar; **to — along a coast** costear.

skit [skɪt] s. parodia, juguete o paso cómico; boceto satírico o burlesco.

skull [skʌl] s. cráneo; calavera.

skunk [skʌŋk] s. C.A., Méx., Riopl. zorrillo o zorrino, Ven., Col. mapurite.

sky [skaɪ] s. cielo; **— blue** azul celeste.

sky·lark [skáɪlɑrk] s. alondra, calandria.

sky·light [skáɪlaɪt] s. claraboya, tragaluz.

sky·rock·et [skáɪrɑkɪt] s. cohete.

sky·scrap·er [skáɪskrepɚ] s. rascacielos.

slab [slæb] s. tabla, plancha, losa; tajada gruesa; **marble —** losa de mármol.

slack [slæk] adj. (not taut) flojo; (sluggish) tardo, lento; inactivo; **— season** temporada muerta; s. flojedad, flojera; inactividad; **to take up the —** apretar, estirar; **-s** pantalones anchos con pliegues, v. véase **slacken.**

slack·en [slǽkən] v. aflojar(se); flojear; retardar(se); disminuir.

slag [slæg] s. escoria.

slain [slen] p.p. de **to slay.**

slam [slæm] v. cerrar(se) de golpe; dejar caer de golpe; **to — someone** decirle a alguien una claridad o grosería; **to — the door** dar un portazo; s. golpazo; claridad, grosería; **— of a door** portazo; **to make a grand —** ganar todas las bazas (en el juego de bridge).

slan·der [slǽndɚ] s. calumnia, maledicencia; v. calumniar.

slan·der·ous [slǽndərəs] adj. calumnioso; maldiciente.

slang [slæŋ] s. jerga, jerigonza; vulgarismo.

slant [slænt] s. sesgo; inclinación; punto de vista; adj. sesgado; inclinado; oblicuo; v. sesgar, inclinar(se); ladear.

slap [slæp] s. palmada, manazo, manotada; insulto, desaire; v. dar una palmada a, dar un manazo a.

slap·stick [slǽpstɪk] adj. de golpe y porrazo.

slash [slæʃ] v. acuchillar; dar cuchilladas o tajos; cortar; truncar; hacer fuerte rebaja de (precios, sueldos); s. cuchillada; tajo, tajada, cortadura.

slat [slæt] s. tabla, tablilla.

slate [slet] s. pizarra; color de pizarra; lista de candidatos; **— pencil** pizarrín.

slaugh·ter [slótɚ] s. carnicería, matanza, Riopl. carneada; **—house** matadero, Méx., C.A. rastro; v. matar; Riopl. carnear; hacer una matanza; destrozar.

slave [slev] s. esclavo; **— driver** capataz de esclavos; persona que agobia de trabajo a otra; **— labor** trabajo de esclavos; trabajadores forzados; **— dealer** negrero; v. trabajar como esclavo.

slav·er [slǽvɚ] s. baba; v. babosear, babear.

slav·er·y [slévrɪ] s. esclavitud.

slav·ish [slévɪʃ] adj. servil.

slay [sle] v. matar.

sled [slɛd] s. trineo, rastra.

sleek [slik] adj. liso; pulido, resbaloso; suave;

artero, mañoso; *v.* alisar; pulir.
sleep [slip] *v.* dormir; **to — it off** dormir la mona;
to — off a headache curarse con sueño un dolor
de cabeza; **to — on it** consultarlo con la
almohada; *s.* sueño; — **walker** sonámbulo; **to go
to** — dormirse, quedarse dormido; **to put to** —
adormecer; arrullar (*al nene*).
sleep·er [slípæ] *s.* durmiente; cochecama,
coche-dormitorio.
sleep·i·ly [slípɪlɪ] *adv.* con somnolencia.
sleep·i·ness [slípɪnɪs] *s.* sueño, modorra,
somnolencia.
sleep·ing [slípɪŋ] *adj.* durmiente; dormido; — **car**
coche-cama, coche-dormitorio; — **pills** píldoras
para dormir; — **sickness** encefalitis letárgica.
sleep·less [slíplɪs] *adj.* desvelado, insomne, sin
sueño.
sleep·y [slípɪ] *adj.* soñoliento; amodorrado; **to be
— tener sueño.**
sleet [slit] *s.* cellisca; *v.* cellisquear.
sleeve [sliv] *s.* manga.
sleigh [sle] *s.* trineo; — **bell** cascabel; *v.* pasearse
en trineo.
sleight [slaɪt]: — **of hand** juego de manos;
prestidigitación, escamoteo.
slen·der [slɛndæ] *adj.* delgado; tenue; escaso,
insuficiente.
slept [slɛpt] *pret.* & *p.p.* de **to sleep.**
sleuth [sluθ] *s.* detective (*o detectivo*).
slew [slu] *pret. de* **to slay.**
slice [slaɪs] *s.* rebanada, tajada; lonja; *v.* rebanar,
tajar; cortar.
slick [slɪk] *v.* alisar; pulir; **to — up** alisar bien,
pulir bien; pulirse, acicalarse, componerse; *adj.*
liso; meloso, suave; aceitoso; astuto, mañoso.
slick·er [slíkæ] *s.* impermeable de hule (*o de*
caucho); embaucador.
slid [slɪd] *pret.* & *p.p.* de **to slide.**
slid·den [slɪdn] *p.p. de* **to slide.**
slide [slaɪd] *v.* resbalar(se); deslizar(se); hacer
resbalar; patinar; **to — into** meter(se) en; **to —
out** (*o* — **away**) deslizarse, colarse, escabullirse,
escaparse; **to let something** — dejar pasar algo;
no hacer caso de algo; *s.* resbalón; resbaladero,
lugar resbaladizo; ligado (*en música*); *véase*
landslide; — **cover** tapa corrediza; — **rule** regla
de cálculo; **microscope** — platina.
slight [slaɪt] *s.* desaire, menosprecio, desdén;
desatención; *v.* desairar, menospreciar; descuidar,
desatender; *adj.* delgado; delicado; leve, ligero;
pequeño; insignificante; escaso; **-ly** *adv.*
escasamente; ligeramente; un poco, apenas.
slim [slɪm] *adj.* delgado; esbelto; escaso.
slime [slaɪm] *s.* limo, cieno, fango; baba, secreción
viscosa.
slim·y [slaɪmɪ] *adj.* viscoso, mucoso, fangoso;
baboso.
sling [slɪŋ] *s.* honda (*para tirar piedras*); cabestrillo
(*para sostener el brazo*); eslinga (*maroma provista
de ganchos para levantar pesos*); —**shot** tirador
de goma o hule; *v.* tirar, arrojar; **to — a rifle
over one's shoulder** echarse el rifle al hombro.
slink [slɪŋk] *v.* andar furtivamente; **to — away**
escurrirse, escabullirse, deslizarse.
slip [slɪp] *v.* (*slide*) deslizar(se); resbalar(se); (*err*)
cometer un desliz; equivocarse; **to — away**
escaparse, escabullirse, escurrirse; **to — in**
meter(se); **to — one's dress on** ponerse de prisa
el vestido; **to — out** salirse; sacar a hurtadillas;
to — out of joint dislocarse, *Am.* zafarse (*un
hueso*); **to — something off** quitar(se) algo; **to let**

an opportunity — dejar pasar una oportunidad;
it slipped my mind se me olvidó, se me pasó. **it
slipped off** se zafó; *s.* desliz; resbalón. error.
equivocación; funda (*de muebles, de almohada*);
combinación-enagua; pedazo (*de papel*
papeleta; embarcadero; guía, sarmiento (*para
transplantar*); — **knot** nudo corredizo
slip·per [slípæ] *s.* zapatilla; babucha; pantufla.
slip·per·y [slíprɪ] *adj.* resbaloso, resbaladizo;
evasivo.
slit [slɪt] *v.* cortar, hacer una rendija, abertura o
incisión; **to — into strips** cortar en tiras; *pret.* &
p.p. de **to slit;** *s.* abertura, hendedura, rendija;
cortada, incisión.
slob·ber [slábæ] *s.* baba; *v.* babosear, babear.
slob·ber·ing [slábərɪŋ] *adj.* baboso.
slo·gan [slógən] *s.* lema, mote.
sloop [slup] *s.* balandra.
slop [slɑp] *v.* (*soil*) ensuciar; (*splash*) salpicar;
(*spill*) derramar(se); *s.* fango suciedad; **-s**
lavazas, agua sucia; desperdicios.
slope [slop] *v.* inclinar(se); *s.* inclinación; declive;
falda, ladera; cuesta, bajada; vertiente.
slop·py [slápɪ] *adj.* puerco, sucio, cochino;
desaseado; mal hecho.
slot [slɑt] *s.* (*opening*) abertura, hendedura; (*groove
for coins*) ranura (*en que se introduce una
moneda*); — **machine** máquina automática que
funciona por medio de una moneda
«traganíqueles,» «tragamonedas»; *v.* hacer una
abertura o hendedura.
sloth [slɔθ] *s.* pereza; perezoso (*cuadrúpedo*).
slouch [slaʊtʃ] *s.* (*posture*) postura muy relajada
o floja; (*person*) persona perezosa o desaseada;
— **hat** sombrero gacho; **to walk with a** —
andar con los hombros caídos y la cabeza
inclinada; *v.* andar agachado; andar caído de
hombros; andar alicaído; arrellanarse,
repantigarse (*en una silla*).
slov·en·li·ness [slávənlɪnɪs] *s.* desaseo, desaliño;
suciedad.
slov·en·ly [slávənlɪ] *adj.* desaseado, desaliñado;
desarreglado.
slow [slo] *adj.* (*low speed*) lento, despacio; (*late*)
tardo; atrasado; (*sluggish*) lerdo; torpe; *adv.*
lentamente, despacio; *v.* **to — down** (*o* — **up**)
retardar disminuir (*el paso, la marcha, la
velocidad*); aflojar el paso; **-ly** *adv.* despacio,
lentamente.
slow·ness [slónɪs] *s.* lentitud; torpeza; cachaza.
slug [slʌg] *s.* bala; porrazo, puñetazo; babosa
(*molusco sin concha*); haragán; trago (*de
aguardiente*); lingote (*de imprenta*); *c.* aporrear,
abofetear, dar puñetazos.
slug·gard [slʌgəd] *s.* holgazán, haragán.
slug·gish [slʌgɪʃ] *adj.* tardo; inactivo.
sluice [slus] *s.* compuerta; caño, canal; —**gate**
compuerta.
slum [slʌm] *s.* barrio bajo; *v.* visitar los barrios
bajos.
slum·ber [slʌmbæ] *v.* dormitar; dormir; *s.* sueño,
sueño ligero.
slump [slʌmp] *v.* hundirse; desplomarse; bajar
repentinamente (*los precios o valores*); *s.*
desplome, hundimiento, bajón, baja repentina
(*de precios, valores, etc.*).
slung [slʌŋ] *pret.* & *p.p. de* **to sling.**
slunk [slʌŋk] *pret.* & *p.p. de* **to slink.**
slush [slʌʃ] *s.* (*snow*) nieve a medio derretir; (*mud*)
lodazal, fango; (*refuse*) desperdicios; (*drivel*)
sentimentalismo.

SI

sly [slaı] *adj.* astuto, socarrón, zorro, taimado; **on the —** a hurtadillas, a escondidas.

sly·ness [sláınıs] *s.* disimulo, astucia.

smack [smæk] *s.* (*taste*) sabor, dejo; (*kiss*) beso ruidoso; (*crack*) chasquido (*de látigo*); (*slap*) palmada, manotada; **a — of something** una pizca de algo; *v.* dar un beso ruidoso; chasquear (*un látigo*); dar un manazo; **to — of** saber a, tener el sabor de; oler a; **to — one's lips** chuparse los labios, saborearse, rechuparse, relamerse.

small [smɔl] *adj.* (*size*) pequeño, chico; bajo; (*insignificant*) insignificante; mezquino; **— change** dinero menudo, suelto; **— hours** primeras horas de la mañana; **— letters** letras minúsculas; **— talk** conversación insubstancial, charladuría; **— voice** vocecita; **to feel —** sentirse pequeño o insignificante.

small·ness [smɔ́lnıs] *s.* pequeñez; bajeza.

small·pox [smɔ́lpɑks] *s.* viruelas.

smart [smɑrt] *adj.* (*intelligent*) listo, inteligente; (*astute*) ladino; astuto; agudo; (*stylish*) elegante; **— remark** observación aguda o penetrante; **— set** gente de buen tono; *s.* escozor, *Ríopl., C.A., Méx.* ardor; *v.* picar, escocer, *Ríopl., C.A., Méx.* arder.

smash [smæʃ] *v.* quebrantar, quebrar, romper; destrozar; aplastar; **to — into** chocar con; topar con, darse un tope contra; *s.* quebrazón, quiebra; fracaso; choque o tope violento; derrota completa.

smat·ter·ing [smǽtərıŋ] *s.* conocimiento superficial y rudimental.

smear [smır] *v.* embarrar, untar, manchar; **to — with paint** pintorrear, pintarrajear; *s.* mancha.

smell [smɛl] *v.* oler; **to — of** oler a; *s.* olor; olfato; **— of** olor a; **to take a —** oler.

smell·y [smɛ́lı] *adj.* oloroso; hediondo.

smelt [smɛlt] *v.* fundir (*metales*); *pret. & p.p. de* **to smell.**

smile [smaıl] *v.* sonreír(se); *s.* sonrisa.

smil·ing [smáılıŋ] *adj.* risueño, sonriente; **-ly** *adv.* sonriendo, con cara risueña.

smite [smaıt] *v.* golpear; herir; castigar; afligir; *véase* **smitten.**

smith [smıθ] *s.* forjador; *véase* **blacksmith, goldsmith, silversmith.**

smith·y [smíθı] *s.* herrería, fragua, forja.

smit·ten [smítn] *p.p. de* **to smite &** *adj.* afligido; castigado; enamorado; **to be — with a disease** darle a uno una enfermedad.

smock [smɑk] *s.* bata corta, batín.

smoke [smok] *s.* humo; **— screen** cortina de humo; **cloud of —** humareda; **to have a —** dar una fumada, fumar; *v.* fumar, *Am.* chupar (*un cigarro*); humear; ahumar; **to — out** ahuyentar o echar fuera con humo.

smok·er [smókər] *s.* fumador; vagón de fumar; reunión o tertulia de fumadores.

smoke·stack [smókstæk] *s.* chimenea.

smok·ing [smókıŋ] *adj.* humeante; de fumar; para fumadores; **— car** vagón de fumar; **— room** fumadero, cuarto de fumar.

smok·y [smókı] *adj.* humeante; humoso, lleno de humo; ahumado.

smooth [smuð] *adj.* (*even*) liso; terso; igual, parejo; plano, llano; (*serene*) tranquilo; (*pleasant*) suave; (*wise*) sagaz; **— disposition** genio afable; **— manners** maneras o modales afables; **— style** estilo flúido y fácil; **— talker** hablador melifluo y sagaz; *v.* alisar; allanar; pulir; emparejar; **to**

— over allanar, alisar, arreglar; **-ly** *adv.* suavemente; blandamente; fácilmente, con facilidad.

smooth·ness [smúðnıs] *s.* (*evenness*) lisura; igualdad, uniformidad; (*pleasantness*) suavidad; afabilidad; tranquilidad; facilidad, fluidez.

smote [smot] *pret. de* **to smite.**

smoth·er [smʌ́ðər] *v.* ahogar(se); sofocar(se); asfixiar(se).

smudge [smʌdʒ] *v.* tiznar, manchar o ensuciar con tizne; ahumar; *s.* tiznón, mancha (*hecha con tizne*); humareda, nube espesa de humo.

smug·gle [smʌ́gl] *v.* contrabandear, hacer contrabando; **to — in** meter de contrabando; **to — out** sacar de contrabando.

smug·gler [smʌ́glər] *s.* contrabandista.

smut [smʌt] *s.* (*smudge*) tizne; suciedad, mancha; (*obscenity*) obscenidad, dicho obseno o indecente; tizón (*enfermedad de ciertas plantas*); *v.* tiznar; ensuciar, manchar.

smut·ty [smʌ́tı] *adj.* tiznado, manchado de tizne; sucio.

snack [snæk] *s.* bocado, bocadillo, tentempié, bocadito; merienda, comida ligera.

snag [snæg] *s.* (*protuberance*) tocón; raigón; (*obstacle*) tropiezo, obstáculo; **to hit a —** tropezar con un obstáculo; *v.* rasgar; enredar.

snail [snel] *s.* caracol.

snake [snek] *s.* culebra, víbora; *v.* culebrear.

snap [snæp] *v.* (*make sound*) chasquear, dar un chasquido; estallar; (*break*) quebrar(se); (*photograph*) fotografiar instantáneamente; **his eyes —** le chispean los ojos; **to — at** echar una mordida o mordisco a; dar una tarascada a, morder; asir (*una oportunidad*); **to — back at** tirar una mordida a; dar una respuesta grosera a; **to — off** soltarse, saltar; quebrar(se); **to — one's fingers** tronar los dedos, castañetear con los dedos; **to — shut** cerrar(se) de golpe; **to — together** apretar, abrochar; **to — up** agarrar, asir; morder; *s.* chasquido; estallido; mordida, mordisco, dentellada; broche de presión; energía, vigor; galleta; cosa fácil, ganga; **cold —** nortazo; repentino descenso de temperatura; **not to care a —** no importarle a uno un ardite o un comino; *adj.* hecho de prisa, impensado; instantáneo; **— fastener** broche de presión; **— judgment** decisión atolondrada; **— lock** cerradura de golpe.

snap·py [snǽpı] *adj.* mordedor, *Ven., C.A., Andes* mordelón; enojadizo, *Méx.* enojón; violento, vivo; elegante; **— cheese** queso acre o picante; **— eyes** ojos chispeantes.

snap·shot [snǽpʃɑt] *s.* instantánea, fotografía instantánea; *v.* sacar una instantánea.

snare [snɛr] *s.* (*trap*) trampa, lazo; (*ambush*) acechanza; red; *v.* enredar; atrapar, coger con trampa; tender lazos a.

snarl [snɑrl] *v.* gruñir; enmarañar(se), enredar(se); *s.* gruñido; maraña, enredo; pelo enmarañado.

snatch [snætʃ] *v.* arrebatar; agarrar; **to — at** tratar de asir o agarrar; *s.* arrebatiña, arrebatamiento; trozo, pedacito; **to make a — at** tratar de arrebatar, tratar de agarrarse a.

sneak [snik] *v.* andar furtivamente; obrar solapadamente; **to — in** meter(se) a escondidas; colarse; **to — out** escurrirse, salirse a hurtadillas; sacar, llevarse (*algo*) a escondidas; *s.* persona solapada.

sneer [snır] *v.* (*smile*) sonreír con sorna; (*gesture*) hacer un gesto de desdén; (*ridicule*) mofarse; **to — at** mofarse de; *s.* sorna, mofa, rechifla; gesto

desdeñoso.
sneeze [sniz] *v.* estornudar; *s.* estornudo.
sniff [snɪf] *v.* husmear, olfatear; sorber (*por las narices*); resollar para adentro; **to — at** husmear; menospreciar; *s.* husmeo, olfateo; sorbo (*por las narices*).
snif·fle [snɪfl] *v.* sorber por las narices.
snip [snɪp] *v.* tijeretear; **to — off** cortar de un tijeretazo, recortar; *s.* tijeretada, tijeretazo; pedacito, recorte.
snipe [snaɪp] *v.* tirar, disparar desde un escondite.
snip·er [snáɪpɚ] *s.* francotirador; tirador emboscado.
snitch [snɪtʃ] *v.* arrebatar; ratear, hurtar.
sniv·el [snɪvl] *v.* moquear; gimotear.
snob [snɑb] *s.* esnob.
snoop [snup] *v.* fisgar, fisgonear, curiosear; *s.* curioso, fisgón.
snooze [snuz] *v.* dormitar, sestear; *s.* siestecita, siestita; **to take a —** echar un sueñecito o siestita; descabezar el sueño.
snore [snor] *v.* roncar; *s.* ronquido.
snor·kel [snɔ́rkl] *s.* tubo esnorkel.
snort [snɔrt] *v.* resoplar; bufar; *s.* resoplido, bufido.
snout [snaʊt] *s.* hocico, jeta.
snow [sno] *s.* nieve; *v.* nevar; **to be -ed under** estar totalmente cubierto por la nevada.
snow·ball [snóbɔl] *s.* bola de nieve; *v.* tirar bolas de nieve.
snow-drift [snódrɪft] *s.* ventisca, ventisquero, montón de nieve.
snow·fall [snófɔl] *s.* nevada.
snow·flake [snóflek] *s.* copo de nieve.
snow·storm [snóstɔrm] *s.* fuerte nevada, nevasca.
snow·y [snóɪ] *adj.* nevado; níveo, blanco como la nieve.
snub [snʌb] *v.* desairar, menospreciar; *s.* desaire; **snub-nosed** chato, *Am.* ñato.
snuff [snʌf] *v.* olfatear, husmear, ventear; aspirar (*por la nariz*); despabilar (*una candela*); **to — at** olfatear, ventear; **to — out** apagar, extinguir; **to — up** sorber (*por las narices*); *s.* sorbo (*por la nariz*); rapé, tabaco en polvo; pabilo, mecha quemada (*de una vela*).
snuf·fle [snʌfl] *v.* ganguear; husmear.
snug [snʌg] *adj.* (*squeezed*) apretado; ajustado; compacto; (*comfortable*) abrigado; cómodo.
so [so] *adv.* así; tan, muy; tanto; **so-so** regular; **so-and-so** Fulano (de tal); **— as to** para; **— far** tan lejos; hasta ahora, hasta aquí; **— many** tantos; **— much** tanto; **— much for that** basta por ese lado; **— much the better** tanto mejor; **— that** de modo que; para que; a fin de que; de suerte que; **— then** conque, pues bien, así pues; **— long!** ¡hasta luego!; **and — forth** etcetera; y así sucesivamente; **I believe —** así lo creo; **is that —?** ¿de veras? ¿de verdad?; ¡no diga!; **ten minutes or —** poco más o menos diez minutos, como diez minutos.
soak [sok] *v.* remojar(se); empapar(se); **to — up** absorber, embeber; chupar; **— in grease** pringar; **to be -ed through** estar empapado; estar calado hasta los huesos; *s.* remojo, mojada; borrachín; golpe, puñetazo.
soap [sop] *s.* jabón; **— bubble** pompa de jabón, *Ven., Col.* bombita; *Andes, Méx.* burbuja de jabón; **— dish** jabonera; **soft —** jabón blando; lisonja, adulación; *v.* enjabonar.
soap·y [sópɪ] *adj.* lleno de jabón.
soar [sor] *v.* remontarse; encumbrarse; subir muy alto; remontar el vuelo.

sob [sɑb] *v.* sollozar; *s.* sollozo.
so·ber [sóbɚ] *adj.* (*temperate*) sobrio; moderado, templado; (*serious*) serio, grave; (*sane*) cuerdo, sensato; (*calm*) tranquilo, sereno; **to be — estar** en su juicio; no estar borracho; *v.* **to — down** sosegar(se), calmar(se); formalizarse; **to — up** desembriagarse, desemborracharse; bajársele a uno la borrachera.
so·ber·ly [sóbɚlɪ] *adv.* sobriamente; cuerdamente, con sensatez; seriamente.
so·ber·ness [sóbɚnɪs] *s.* sobriedad; seriedad.
so·bri·e·ty [sʌbráɪɪtɪ] *s.* sobriedad; cordura.
so-called [sókɔ́ld] *adj.* así llamado, llamado.
soc·cer [sákɚ] *s.* fútbol.
so·cia·ble [sóʃəbl] *adj.* sociable, social, tratable.
so·cial [sóʃəl] *adj.* social; sociable; tratable, de buen trato; *s.* reunión social; tertulia.
so·cial·ism [sóʃəlɪzəm] *s.* socialismo.
so·cial·ist [sóʃəlɪst] *adj.* & *s.* socialista.
so·cial·ize [sóʃəlaɪz] *v.* socializar.
so·ci·e·ty [səsáɪətɪ] *s.* sociedad; compañía.
so·ci·ol·o·gy [soʃɪálədʒɪ] *s.* sociología.
sock [sɑk] *s.* (*garment*) calcetín; (*blow*) porrazo, golpe, puñetazo; *v.* pegar, apalear, golpear; *Am.* batear (*una pelota*).
sock·et [sákɪt] *s.* cuenca (*del ojo*); portalámparas, enchufe, *Carib.* sóquet.
sod [sɑd] *s.* césped; terrón (*de tierra sembrada de* céaped); *v.* cubrir de césped.
so·da [sódə] *s.* soda, sosa; **— fountain** *Am.* fuente de soda; **— water** agua gaseosa; **baking —** bicarbonato de sodio.
so·di·um [sódɪəm] *s.* sodio.
sod·om·y [sádəmɪ] *s.* sodomía.
so·fa [sófə] *s.* sofá.
soft [sɔft] *adj.* (*bland*) blando; muelle; suave; (*gentle*) tierno; dulce; **soft-boiled eggs** huevos pasados por agua; **— coal** carbón bituminoso; **— drink** bebida no alcohólica; **— metal** metal dulce, metal maleable; **— soap** jabón blando; adulación; **— water** agua dulce; *adv. véase* softly.
sof·ten [sɔ́fən] *v.* ablandar(se); suavizar(se); enternecer(se); templar(se); **to — one's voice** bajar la voz, hablar quedo (*o* quedito).
soft-heart·ed [sɔfthártəd] *adj.* de buen corazón.
soft·ly [sɔ́ftlɪ] *adv.* blandamente; suavemente; quedo, quedito.
soft·ness [sɔ́ftnɪs] *s.* blandura; molicie; suavidad; ternura; dulzura.
sog·gy [ságɪ] *adj.* remojado; empapado.
soil [sɔɪl] *s.* suelo, terreno, tierra; mancha; **native —** terruño; *v.* ensuciar(se); manchar(se).
so·journ [sódʒɝn] *s.* estada, estancia, permanencia, *Andes, Méx., Riopl.* estadía; [sodʒɝ́n] *v.* permanecer; estarse, residir por una temporada.
sol·ace [sálɪs] *s.* solaz; *v.* solazar.
so·lar [sólɚ] *adj.* solar, del sol; **— plexis** plexo solar.
sold [sold] *pret.* & *p.p. de* **to sell**; **to be — on an idea** estar bien convencido de una idea.
sol·der [sáldɚ] *v.* soldar; *s.* soldadura.
sol·dier [sóldʒɚ] *s.* soldado.
sole [sol] *adj.* solo, único; exclusivo; *s.* suela (*del zapato*); planta (*del pie*); lenguado (*pez*); *v.* solar, echar suelas a; **to half-sole** echar o poner medias suelas a.
sole·ly [sóllɪ] *adv.* sólamente, únicamente.
sol·emn [sáləm] *adj.* solemne.
so·lem·ni·ty [səlémnətɪ] *s.* solemnidad.
sol-fa·ing [solfáɪŋ] *s.* solfeo.

sol·lic·it [səlísɪt] *v.* solicitar.
so·lic·i·tor [səlísətə·] *s.* solicitador, agente.
so·lic·i·tous [səlísɪtəs] *adj.* solícito.
so·lic·i·tude [səlísətjud] *s.* solicitud, cuidado.
sol·id [sálɪd] *s.* sólido; *adj.* sólido; firme; macizo; sensato; unánime; — **blue** todo azul; — **gold** oro puro; **for one — hour** por una hora entera, · por una hora sin parar; **the country is — for** el país está firmemente unido en favor de.
sol·i·dar·ty [saladǽratɪ] *s.* solidaridad.
so·lid·i·fy [səlídəfaɪ] *v.* solidificar(se).
so·lid·i·ty [səlídatɪ] *s.* solidez.
sol·id-state [saladstét] *adj.* física del estado sólido.
so·lil·o·quy [səlíləkwɪ] *s.* soliloquio.
sol·i·tar·y [sálətɛrɪ] *adj.* solitario; solo; *s.* solitario, ermitaño.
sol·i·tude [sálətjud] *s.* soledad.
so·lo [sólo] *s.* solo.
so·lo·ist [sóloɪst] *s.* solista.
sol·stice [sálstəs] *s.* solsticio.
sol·u·ble [sáljəbl] *adj.* soluble, que se disuelve fácilmente.
so·lu·tion [səlúʃən] *s.* solución.
solve [salv] *v.* resolver; explicar, aclarar, desenredar; solucionar.
som·ber [sámbə·] *adj.* sombrío.
some [sʌm] *adj.* algún, alguno; algunos, unos; algo de, un poco de; —**one** alguien, alguno; — **twenty people** unas veinte personas; *pron.* algunos, unos; algo, un poco; una parte.
some·bod·y [sámbadɪ] *pron.* alguien; **a** — un personaje de importancia.
some·how [sámhaʊ] *adv.* de algún modo, de alguna manera; — **or other** de una manera u otra; por alguna razón.
some·one [sámwʌn] *pron.* alguno, alguien.
som·er·sault [sámərsɔlt] *s.* voltereta; *v.* dar una voltereta.
some·thing [sámθɪŋ] *s.* algo, alguna cosa; un poco; — **else** alguna otra cosa, otra cosa.
some·time [sámtaɪm] *adv.* algún día; alguna vez; **-s** *adv.* a veces, algunas veces, de vez en cuando.
some·what [sámhwat] *s.* algo, alguna cosa, un poco; *adv.* algo, un tanto.
some·where [sámhwɛr] *adv.* en alguna parte; — **else** en alguna otra parte.
son [sʌn] *s.* hijo.
song [sɔŋ] *s.* canción; canto; **the Song of Songs** el Cantar de los Cantares; — **bird** ave canora, pájaro cantor; **to buy something for a** — comprar algo muy barato.
son·ic bar·ri·er [sanɪkbǽrɪə·] *s.* barrera sónica.
son-in-law [sánɪnlɔ] *s.* yerno, hijo político.
son·net [sánɪt] *s.* soneto.
so·no·rous [sənórəs] *adj.* sonoro.
soon [sun] *adv.* pronto, presto; luego; — **after** poco después (de); al poco tiempo; **as — as** tan pronto como; luego que, así que; **how** —? ¿cuándo?
soot [sʊt] *s.* hollín; tizne.
soothe [suð] *v.* calmar, sosegar; aliviar.
sooth·say·er [súθseə·] *s.* adivino.
soot·y [sútɪ] *adj.* tiznado, cubierto de hollín.
sop [sap] *v.* empapar; **to — up** absorber; **to be sopping wet** estar hecho una sopa, estar mojado hasta los huesos; *s.* sopa *(pan u otra cosa empapada en leche, caldo, etc.)*; soborno, regalo *(para acallar, conciliar, o sobornar).*
so·phis·ti·cat·ed [səfístəketəd] *adj.* mundano; exento de simplicidad.

soph·o·more [sáfəmor] *s.* estudiante de segundo año.
so·pran·o [səprǽno] *s.* soprano; **high** — tiple; — **voice** voz de soprano.
sor·cer·er [sɔ́rsərə·] *s.* brujo, hechicero.
sor·did [sɔ́rdɪd] *adj.* sórdido; vil, indecente; mezquino.
sore [sor] *adj. (painful)* dolorido; inflamado, enconado; *(grevious)* afligido, apenado; *(injured)* lastimado; picado; *(offended)* ofendido; — **eyes** mal de ojos; **to be — at** estar enojado con; **to have a — throat** tener mal de garganta, dolerle a uno la garganta; *s.* úlcera, llaga; inflamación; lastimadura; pena, aflicción; **-ly** *adv.* dolorosamente, penosamente; **to be -ly in need of** necesitar con urgencia.
sore·ness [sórnɪs] *s.* dolor, dolencia; inflamación.
sor·rel [sɔ́rəl] *adj.* alazán *(rojo canela)*; *s.* color alazán; caballo alazán.
sor·row [sáro] *s. (sadness)* dolor, pena, pesar; *(grieving)* pesadumbre; *(repentance)* arrepentimiento; *v.* apenarse, afligirse, sentir pena.
sor·row·ful [sárəfəl] *adj.* pesaroso, doloroso, lastimoso, afligido; **-ly** *adv.* tristemente, dolorosamente, con pena, desconsoladamente.
sor·ry [sɔ́rɪ] *adj.* triste, pesaroso, afligido, arrepentido; lastimoso; **I am** — lo siento; me pesa; **I am — for her** la compadezco.
sort [sort] *s.* suerte, clase, especie; — **of tired** algo cansado, un tanto cansado; **all -s of** toda suerte de, toda clase de; **out of -s** de mal humor, malhumorado; indispuesto; *v.* clasificar, ordenar, arreglar; **to — out** separar, clasificar; entresacar; escoger.
sought [sɔt] *pret. & p.p.* de **to seek.**
soul [sol] *s.* alma; **not a** — nadie, ni un alma.
sound [saʊnd] *adj. (healthy)* sano; cuerdo; sensato; *(firm)* firme, sólido; ileso; **a — beating** una buena zurra o tunda; — **business** buen negocio, negocio bien oganizado; — **reasoning** raciocinio sólido; — **sleep** sueño profundo; — **title** título válido o legal; **of — mind** en su juicio cabal; **safe and** — sano y salvo; **to sleep** — dormir profundamente; *s.* son, sonido; tono; brazo de mar; — **wave** onda sonora; *v.* sonar, tocar; sondear; tantear; auscultar *(el pecho, los pulmones)*; cantar, entonar *(alabanzas)*; **to — out** tantear, sondear.
sound·ness [sáʊndnɪs] *s. (firmness)* solidez; *(healthiness)* cordura, buen juicio; *(validity)* rectitud; validez; — **of body** buena salud corporal.
soup [sup] *s.* sopa; **cold vegetable** — gazpacho; — **tureen** sopera; — **dish** sopero.
sour [saʊr] *adj. (acid-like)* agrio; acre; ácido; desabrido; rancio; *(peevish)* malhumorado; — **milk** leche cortada; *v.* agriar(se); cortarse *(la leche)*; fermentar; poner(se) de mal humor.
source [sors] *s.* origen; manantial, fuente.
sour·ness [sáʊrnɪs] *s.* acidez, agrura, desabrimiento.
souse [saʊs] *v.* zambullir; chapuzar.
south [saʊθ] *s.* sur, sud; *adj.* meridional, del sur; austral; **South American** sudamericano; suramericano; — **pole** polo sur, polo antártico; *adv.* hacia el sur.
south·east [saʊθíst] *s. & adj.* sudeste; *adv.* hacia el sudeste.
south·east·ern [saʊθístən·] *adj.* del sudeste, sudeste.
south·ern [sʌ́ðən] *adj.* meridional, del sur, austral, sureño; — **Cross** Cruz del Sur.

south·ern·er [sáðənəʳ] *s.* sureño, meridional, habitante del sur.
south·ward [sáuθwəd] *adv.* hacia el sur, rumbo al sur.
south·west [sauθwést] *s. & adj.* sudoeste (*o* suroeste); *adv.* hacia el sudoeste.
south·west·ern [sauθwéstən] *adj.* sudoeste (*o* suroeste), del sudoeste.
sou·ve·nir [suvənír] *s.* recuerdo, memoria.
sov·er·eign [sávrɪn] *s. & adj.* soberano.
sov·er·eign·ty [sávrɪntɪ] *s.* soberanía.
so·vi·et [sóvɪɪt] *s.* sóviet; *adj.* soviético.
sow [sau] *s.* puerca.
sow [so] *v.* sembrar.
sown [son] *p.p. de* **to sow**.
space [spes] *s.* espacio; — **science** ciencia del espacio; ciencia espacial; — **station** estación espacial; — **suit** traje espacial; *v.* espaciar.
space·craft [spéskræft] *s.* nave espacial; astronave.
space·man [spésmæn] *s.* astronauta.
spa·cious [spéʃəs] *adj.* espacioso; dilatado, vasto.
spade [sped] *s.* azada, azadón; espada (*del juego de naipes*); *v.* cavar con la azada.
span [spæn] *s.* palmo; espacio; tramo; arco u ojo (*de puente*); envergadura (*de un aeroplano*); — **of life** longevidad; *v.* medir a palmos; atravesar.
span·gle [spǽŋgl] *s.* lentejuela; *v.* adornar con lentejuelas; brillar, centellear; **-d with stars** estrellado, sembrado (*o* tachonado) de estrellas.
Span·iard [spǽnjəd] *s.* español.
span·iel [spǽnjəl] *s.* perro de aguas.
Span·ish [spǽnɪʃ] *adj.* español; *s.* español, idioma español.
spank [spæŋk] *v.* zurrar, dar una tunda, dar nalgadas; *s.* palmada, nalgada.
spank·ing [spǽŋkɪŋ] *s.* zurra, tunda, nalgadas.
spar [spɑr] *v.* boxear, pelear.
spare [spɛr] *v.* ahorrar; evitar (*molestias, trabajo, etc.*); perdonar; **I cannot** — **another dollar** no dispongo de otro dólar, no tengo más dinero disponible; **I cannot** — **the car today** no puedo pasarme hoy sin el automóvil; **to** — **no expense** no escatimar gastos; **to** — **the enemy** usar de clemencia con el enemigo; **to have time to** — tener tiempo de sobra; *adj.* flaco, descarnado; escaso, frugal; mezquino; sobrante; de sobra; de repuesto; — **cash** dinero disponible o de sobra; — **time** tiempo libre, tiempo disponible; — **tire** neumático de repuesto.
spark [spɑrk] *s.* chispa; — **plug** bujía; *v.* chispear, echar chispas, chisporrotear.
spar·kle [spárkl] *s.* (*flash*) chispa, centella; brillo, centelleo; (*spirit*) viveza, animación; *v.* centellear; chispear; relucir, brillar.
spark·ling [spárklɪŋ] *adj.* centelleante; reluciente; chispeante; — **wine** vino espumoso.
spar·row [spǽro] *s.* gorrión, pardal.
sparse [spɑrs] *adj.* escaso; esparcido; poco denso, poco poblado; — **hair** pelo ralo.
spasm [spǽzəm] *s.* espasmo.
spas·tic [spǽstɪk] *adj.* espástico.
spat [spæt] *pret. & p.p. de* **to spit**; *v.* reñir, disputar; dar un manazo o sopapo; *s.* sopapo, manotada; riña, desavenencia; **-s** polainas cortas.
spat·ter [spǽtəʳ] *v.* salpicar; rociar; manchar; *s.* salpicadura; rociada.
speak [spik] *v.* hablar; decir; recitar; — **to the point!** ¡vamos al grano!; **so to** — por decirlo así; **to** — **for** hablar por, hablar en nombre o en favor de; pedir, solicitar; apalabrar, reservar; **to**

— **one's mind** hablar sin rodeos, decir claramente lo que se piensa; **to** — **out** (*o* — **up**) hablar claro; hablar con toda franqueza; hablar en voz alta.
speak·er [spínkəʳ] *s.* orador; conferenciante, conferencista; el que habla; — **of the House** presidente de la cámara de representantes; **loud-speaker** altavoz, altoparlante.
spear [spɪr] *s.* lanza; arpón (*para pescar*); brote, retoño, hoja· (*de hierba*); *v.* alancear, lancear, herir con lanza.
spear·mint [spírmɪnt] *s.* yerbabuena (hierbabuena), menta.
spe·cial [spéʃəl] *adj.* especial; particular; — **delivery** entrega especial de correo; *s.* tren o autobús especial; carta urgente, entrega especial; **-ly** *adv.* especialmente; en especial; sobre todo.
spe·cial·ist [spéʃəlɪst] *s.* especialista.
spe·cial·i·za·tion [spɛʃəlɪzéʃən] *s.* especialización.
spe·cial·ize [spéʃəlaɪz] *v.* especializarse.
spe·cial·ty [spéʃəltɪ] *s.* especialidad.
spe·cies [spíʃɪz] *s.* especie; especies.
spe·cif·ic [spɪsífɪk] *adj.* específico; peculiar, característico; — **gravity** peso específico; *s.* específico; **-ally** *adv.* específicamente; especificadamente; particularmente, en particular.
spec·i·fy [spésəfaɪ] *v.* especificar; estipular.
spec·i·men [spésəmən] *s.* espécimen, muestra, ejemplar.
speck [spɛk] *s.* mota; manchita; partícula; **not a** — ni pizca; *v. véase* **speckle**.
speck·le [spékl] *s.* manchita; mota; *v.* motear, salpicar de motas o manchas; manchar.
speck·led [spékld] *adj.* moteado; — **with freckles** pecoso.
spec·ta·cle [spéktəkl] *s.* espectáculo; **-s** gafas, anteojos; **to make a** — **of oneself** ponerse en la evidencia, ponerse en ridículo.
spec·tac·u·lar [spɛktǽkjələʳ] *adj.* espectacular, ostentoso, aparatoso.
spec·ta·tor [spéktetəʳ] *s.* espectador.
spec·ter [spéktəʳ] *s.* espectro, fantasma, aparecido.
spec·tro·graph [spéktrogræf] *s.* espectrógrafo.
spec·trum [spéktrəm] *s.* espectro.
spec·u·late [spékjəlet] *v.* especular; reflexionar.
spec·u·la·tion [spɛkjəléʃən] *s.* especulación; reflexión.
spec·u·la·tive [spékjəletɪv] *adj.* especulativo; teórico.
spec·u·la·tor [spékjəletəʳ] *s.* especulador.
sped [sped] *pret. & p.p. de* **to speed**.
speech [spitʃ] *s.* habla; lenguaje, idioma; discurso, arenga; conferencia; parlamento (*de un actor*); **to make a** — pronunciar un discurso, hacer una perorata.
speech·less [spítʃlɪs] *adj.* sin habla; mudo; estupefacto.
speed [spid] *s.* velocidad; rapidez; presteza, prontitud; — **limit** velocidad máxima; **at full** — a toda velocidad; *v.* apresurar(se), acelerar(se), dar(se) prisa; correr; ir con exceso de velocidad; despachar.
speed·i·ly [spídɪlɪ] *adv.* velozmente, rápidamente; a todo correr, de prisa, con prontitud.
speed·om·e·ter [spidámətəʳ] *s.* velocímetro.
speed·y [spídɪ] *adj.* veloz, rápido.
spell [spɛl] *s.* (*charm*) hechizo, encanto; (*period*) temporada, corto período; (*sickness*) ataque (*de una enfermedad*); **to put under a** — aojar; hechizar, encantar; *v.* deletrear; significar,

SO

indicar; **how is it -ed?** ¿cómo se escribe?
spell·er [spέlə·] *s.* silabario; deletreador.
spell·ing [spέlıŋ] *s.* ortografía; deletreo; — **book** silabario.
spelt [spεlt] *pret. & p.p. de* **to spell.**
spend [spεnd] *v.* gastar; usar, agotar, consumir; **to — a day** pasar un día.
spend·thrift [spέndθrıft] *s.* derrochador, gastador, pródigo.
spent [spεnt] *pret. & p.p. de* **to spend.**
sperm [spɔ·m] *s.* esperma.
sphere [sfır] *s.* esfera; globo, orbe.
spher·i·cal [sfέrıkl] *adj.* esférico.
sphynx [sfıŋks] *s.* esfinge.
spice [spaıs] *s.* especia; picante; aroma; *v.* condimentar, sazonar con especias.
spic·y [spáısı] *adj.* sazonado con especias; picante; aromático.
spi·der [spáıdə·] *s.* araña; sartén; — **web** telaraña.
spig·ot [spígət] *s.* espita, grifo, canilla.
spike [spaık] *s.* espiga; perno; clavo largo; alcayata; pico; *v.* clavar; clavetear.
spill [spıl] *v.* verter; derramar(se); desparramar(se); hacer caer (*de un caballo*); revelar (*una noticia, un secreto*); *s.* derrame, derramamiento; vuelco; caída (*de un caballo*).
spilt [spılt] *pret. & p.p. de* **to spill.**
spin [spın] *v.* hilar; girar, dar vueltas, rodar; bailar (*un trompo*); **to — out** prolongar, alargar; **to — yarns** contar cuentos; *s.* giro, vuelta; paseo (*en automóvil, bicicleta, etc.*); barrena (*hablando de aeroplanos*).
spin·ach [spínıtʃ] *s.* espinaca.
spi·nal [spáınl] *adj.* espinal; — **column** columna vertebral, espina dorsal.
spin·dle [spíndl] *s.* huso; eje.
spine [spaın] *s.* espina; espinazo, espina dorsal, columna vertebral.
spin·ner [spínə·] *s.* hilandero, hilandera; máquina de hilar.
spin·ning [spínıŋ] *s.* hilandería, arte de hilar; — **machine** aparato para hilar, máquina de hilar; — **mill** hilandería; — **top** trompo; — **wheel** torno de hilar.
spin·ster [spínstə·] *s.* soltera; solterona.
spi·ral [spáırəl] *adj.* espiral; — **staircase** caracol, escalera espiral; *s.* espiral.
spire [spaır] *s.* aguja, chapitel de torre; cúspide, ápice; punto más alto; — **of grass** brizna de hierba.
spir·it [spírıt] *s.* (*essence*) espíritu; temple; (*animation*) viveza, animación; ánimo; **low -s** abatimiento; **to be in good -s** estar de buen humor; **to be out of -s** estar triste o abatido; *v.* **to — away** llevarse misteriosamente.
spir·it·ed [spírıtıd] *adj.* vivo, brioso, fogoso.
spir·i·tu·al [spírıtʃυɛl] *adj.* espiritual; *s.* espiritual (*tonada religiosa de los negros del sur de los Estados Unidos*).
spit [spıt] *v.* escupir; expectorar; *pret. & p.p. de* **spit;** *s.* esputo, saliva; asador.
spite [spaıt] *s.* despecho, rencor, inquina, ojeriza; **in — of** a despecho de, a pesar de; **out of —** por despecho; *v.* picar, irritar, hacer rabiar.
spite·ful [spáıtfəl] *adj.* rencoroso.
splash [splæʃ] *v.* salpicar; rociar; enlodar, manchar; chapotear (*en el agua*); *s.* salpicadura; rociada; chapoteo.
spleen [splin] *s.* bazo; mal humor, rencor.
splen·did [splέndıd] *adj.* espléndido.
splen·dor [splέndə·] *s.* esplendor; esplendidez.

splice [splaıs] *v.* empalmar, unir, juntar; *s.* empalme; junta.
splint [splınt] *s.* tablilla; astilla; *v.* entablillar.
splin·ter [splíntə·] *s.* astilla; raja; *v.* astillar(se), hacer(se) astillas; romper(se) en astillas.
split [splıt] *v.* hender(se), rajar(se); resquebrajar(se); partir(se), dividir(se); **to — hairs** pararse en pelillos; **to — one's dies with laughter** desternillarse de risa, reventar de risa; **to — the difference** partir la diferencia; *pret. & p.p. de* **to split;** *adj.* partido, hendido, rajado; dividido; resquebrajado; *s.* raja, hendedura, grieta; cisma, rompimiento.
splurge [splə·dʒ] *s.* ostentación; fachenda.
spoil [spɔıl] *v.* (*decay*) dañar(se); echar(se) a perder, podrir(se), corromper(se); (*harm*) estropear(se); arruinar; (*overindulge*) consentir, mimar; *s.* botín, presa; **-s of war** botín o despojos de guerra.
spoke [spok] *s.* rayo (*de rueda*); *pret. de* **to speak.**
spo·ken [spókən] *p.p. de* **to speak.**
spokes·man [spóksmən] *s.* portavoz, vocero.
sponge [spʌndʒ] *s.* (*absorbent*) esponja; (*dependent person*) gorrón, parásito; *v.* lavar o limpiar con esponja; vivir de gorra, vivir a costa ajena; **to — up** chupar, absorber.
sponge·cake [spʌ́ndʒkek] *s.* bizcocho esponjoso.
spong·er [spʌ́ndʒə·] *s.* esponja, gorrón, pegote, parásito; *Am.* pavo.
spon·gy [spʌ́ndʒı] *adj.* esponjoso, esponjado.
spon·sor [spʌ́nsə·] *s.* padrino, madrina; patrón (*el que patrocina una empresa*); defensor; fiador; fomentador, promovedor; *v.* apadrinar; promover, fomentar; patrocinar; ser fiador de.
spon·ta·ne·i·ty [spantənίıtı] *s.* espontaneidad.
spon·ta·ne·ous [spantένıəs] *adj.* espontáneo.
spook [spuk] *s.* espectro, fantasma, aparecido.
spool [spul] *s.* carrete, carretel; *v.* devanar, enredar (*hilo*) en carrete.
spoon [spun] *s.* cuchara; *v.* cucharear, sacar con cuchara.
spoon·ful [spúnfəl] *s.* cucharada.
sport [sport] *s.* deporte; **in —** en broma, de burla; **to make — of** reírse de, burlarse de; **to be a good —** ser buen perdedor (*en el juego*); ser un buen compañero; *v.* jugar; divertirse; bromear, chancearse; **to — a new dress** lucir un traje nuevo; **-s** *adj.* deportivo; — **clothes** trajes deportivos.
sports car [spórtskar] *s.* coche (*carro*) deportivo.
sports·man [spórtsmən] *s.* deportista; jugador generoso, buen perdedor (*en deportes*).
spot [spat] *s.* (*blemish*) mancha, mota; (*place*) sitio, lugar; **in -s** aquí y allí; aquí y allá; **on the —** allí mismo; al punto; **to pay — cash** pagar al contado; *v.* manchar, ensuciar; motear; echar de ver, distinguir; avistar; localizar.
spot·less [spátlıs] *adj.* sin mancha, limpio.
spot·light [spátlaıt] *s.* faro giratorio.
spot·ted [spátıd] *adj.* manchado; moteado.
spouse [spauz] *s.* esposo, esposa.
spout [spaut] *v.* chorrear; brotar; salir en chorro; emitir; declamar, perorar; hablar mucho; *s.* chorro; surtidor; pico (*de tetera, cafetera, jarra, etc.*); espita.
sprain [spren] *v.* torcer (*una coyuntura o músculo*); **to — one's ankle** torcerse el tobillo; *s.* torsión, torcedura.
sprang [spræŋ] *pret. de* **to spring.**
sprawl [sprɔl] *v.* despatarrarse; estar despatarrado; tenderse; **to — one's legs** abrir las piernas; *s.*

postura floja (*abiertos los brazos y piernas*).
spray [spre] *s.* (*liquid*) rocío, rociada; liquido para rociar; (*branch*) ramita; **sea —** espuma del mar; *v.* rociar.
spread [sprɛd] *v.* extender(se); desparramar(se); esparcir(se); difundir(se), diseminar(se), dispersar(se); propalar(se) (*noticias, rumores, etc.*), propagar(se); **to — apart** abrir(se), separar(se); **to — butter on** poner mantequilla en; **to — out the tablecloth** tender el mantel; **to — paint on** dar una mano de pintura a; **to — with** cubrir de; untar con; *s.* extensión; amplitud, anchura; envergadura (*de un aeroplano*); difusión; diseminación; propagación; cubierta, sobrecama; comilitona, festín; mantequilla, queso, etc., que se le unta al pan; *pret. & p.p. de* **to spread.**
spree [spri] *s.* juerga, parranda, holgorio; **to go on a —** andar (*o* ir) de parranda o juerga, *Ríopl.* ir de farra.
sprig [sprɪg] *s.* ramita.
spright·ly [spráɪtlɪ] *adj.* vivo, animado, brioso; alegre.
spring [sprɪŋ] *v.* saltar; brincar; hacer saltar; **to — a leak** hacer agua (*un barco*); comenzar a gotearse (*la cañería, el techo, etc.*); formarse una gotera; **to — a trap** hacer saltar una trampa; **to — at** abalanzarse sobre; **to — from** salir de, nacer de, brotar de; **to — news of a surprise** dar de sopetón una noticia o sorpresa; **to — something open** abrir algo a la fuerza; **to — to one's feet** levantarse de un salto; **to — up** brotar; surgir; crecer; levantarse de un salto; *s.* primavera; muelle (*de metal*); resorte; elasticidad; salto, brinco; manantial, fuente; origen; *adj.* primaveral; **— board** trampolín; **— mattress** colchón de muelles; **— water** agua de manantial.
spring·time [sprɪŋtaɪm] *s.* primavera.
sprink·le [sprɪŋkl] *v.* (*scatter*) rociar; regar; espolvorear; salpicar; (*rain*) lloviznar; *s.* rociada, rocío; llovizna; **— of salt** pizca de sal.
sprint [sprɪnt] *v.* echar una carrera; *s.* carrera, carrerilla, corrida corta.
sprout [spraʊt] *v.* brotar; retoñar, germinar; hacer germinar o brotar; *s.* retoño, renuevo; **Brussels -s** bretones, coles de Bruselas.
spruce [sprus] *s.* abeto; *adj.* pulcro, aseado, pulido; elegante; *v.* **to — up** asearse, componerse, emperifollarse.
sprung [sprʌŋ] *pret. & p.p. de* **to spring.**
spun [spʌn] *pret. & p.p. de* **to spin.**
spur [spɝ] *s.* espuela; acicate; aguijón, estímulo; espolón (*del gallo*); estribación (*de una montaña*); **— track** ramal corto (*de ferrocarril*); **on the — of the moment** impensadamente, sin la reflexión debida; por el momento; *v.* espolear, aguijar, picar, incitar; **to — on** animar, incitar a obrar o a seguir adelante.
spu·ri·ous [spúrɪəs] *adj.* espurio.
spurn [spɝn] *v.* rechazar, desdeñar, menospreciar.
spurt [spɝt] *v.* salir a borbotones; chorrear; echar chorros; hacer un repentino esfuerzo (*para ganar una carrera*); *s.* borbotón, chorrazo, chorro repentino; esfuerzo repentino; **— of anger** arranque de ira; **-s of flame** llamaradas.
sput·ter [spʌtɚ] *v.* chisporrotear; refunfuñar; *s.* chisporroteo; refunfuño.
spu·tum [spjútəm] *s.* esputo.
spy [spaɪ] *s.* espía; *v.* espiar; acechar; atisbar; **to — on** espiar, atisbar.

spy·glass [spáɪglæs] *s.* anteojo de larga vista.
squab [skwɑb] *s.* pichón.
squab·ble [skwábl] *s.* reyerta; *v.* reñir, disputar.
squad [skwɑd] *s.* escuadra, patrulla, partida.
squad·ron [skwádrɑn] *s.* escuadra; escuadrón.
squal·id [skwálɪd] *adj.* escuálido.
squall [skwɔl] *s.* chubasco; chillido; *v.* chillar.
squan·der [skwándɚ] *v.* despilfarrar, derrochar, malgastar, disipar.
square [skwɛr] *s.* (*rectangle*) cuadro; cuadrado; (*central park*) plaza; (*block*) manzana de casas; *Am.* cuadra; escuadra (*de carpintero*); casilla (*de tablero de ajedrez, damas, etc.*); **he is on the —** obra de buena fe; *v.* cuadrar; ajustar, arreglar, saldar (*cuentas*); justificar; cuadricular; **to — one's shoulders** enderezar los hombros; cuadrarse; **to — oneself with** sincerarse con, justificarse ante; **to — a person with another** poner bien a una persona con otra; *adj.* cuadrado, en cuadro, a escuadra, en ángulo recto; saldado; justo, recto, equitativo; franco; **— corner** esquina en ángulo recto; **— meal** comida completa, comida en regla; **— mile** milla cuadrada; **— root** raíz cuadrada; **— dance** danza de figuras; cuadrilla; **to be — with someone** estar en paz con alguien, no deberle nada, *Am.* estar a mano; *adv.* véase **squarely.**
square·ly [skwɛrlɪ] *adv.* equitativamente, honradamente; firmemente; de buena fe; derecho, derechamente; **to hit the target — in the middle** pegar de lleno en el blanco.
squash [skwɑʃ] *s.* calabaza; *v.* aplastar, despachurrar o apachurrar.
squat [skwɑt] *v.* agazaparse, sentarse en cuclillas; agacharse; ocupar tierras baldías para ganar título de propietario; *adj.* agazapado, sentado en cuclillas; (*short*) rechoncho, achaparrado, *Méx., C.A., Andes* chaparro.
squawk [skwɔk] *v.* (*noise*) graznar; chillar; (*complain*) quejarse; *s.* graznido; chillido; queja.
squeak [skwik] *v.* rechinar, chirriar; chillar; *s.* rechinamiento; chirrido, chillico.
squeal [skwil] *v.* chillar; quejarse, protestar; soplar, delatar; *s.* chillido.
squea·mish [skwímɪʃ] escrupuloso; delicado; remilgado.
squeeze [skwiz] *v.* estrujar; despachurrar o apachurrar; exprimir; prensar; apretar; **to — into** meter(se) a estrujones, encajar(se) en; **to — out the juice** exprimir el jugo; **to — through a crowd** abrirse paso a estrujones por entre la muchedumbre; *s.* estrujón; apretón; abrazo fuerte; apretura.
squelch [skwɛltʃ] *v.* aplastar; acallar, imponer silencio; reprender; **to — a revolt** sofocar o apagar una revuelta.
squid [skwɪd] *s.* calamar.
squint [skwɪnt] *v.* mirar de través; mirar de soslayo; mirar achicando los ojos; mirar furtivamente; bizquear (*mirar bizco*); *s.* mirada de soslayo; mirada bizca, mirada furtiva; **squint-eyed** *adj.* bisojo o bizco.
squire [skwaɪr] *s.* escudero; *v.* acompañar, escoltar.
squirm [skwɝm] *v.* retorcerse; **to — out of a difficulty** forcejear para salir de un aprieto.
squir·rel [skwɝəl] *s.* ardilla.
squirt [skwɝt] *v.* jeringar; echar un chisguete; salir a chorritos (*o* a chisguetes); *s.* jeringazo; chisguete.
stab [stæb] *v.* apuñalar, dar una puñalada, dar de puñalada, acuchillar; pinchar; *s.* puñalada,

cuchillada, estocada; pinchazo.

sta·bil·i·ty [stəbílətɪ] *s.* estabilidad.

sta·ble [stébḷ] *adj.* estable; *s.* establo, cuadra; caballeriza; *v.* poner (*los animales*) en la caballeriza.

stack [stæk] *s.* pila, montón, rimero; hacina (*de paja o heno*); chimenea, cañón de chimenea; **library -s** estanterías o anaqueles de biblioteca; *v.* amontonar, apilar.

sta·di·um [stédɪəm] *s.* estadio.

staff [stæf] *s.* (*stick*) báculo, cayado, bastón, vara; (*pole*) asta (*de bandera, de lanza*); (*group*) cuerpo, consejo administrativo; — **of life** sostén de la vida; — **officer** oficial de estado mayor; **army** — estado mayor; **editorial** — redacción; **musical** — pentagrama; **teaching** — cuerpo docente; *v.* proveer de funcionarios y empleados (*una organización*).

stag [stæg] *s.* venado, ciervo; macho, hombre; — **dinner** banquete exclusivo para hombres.

stage [stedʒ] *s.* (*platform*) tablado; tablas, escenario; escena; (*theater*) teatro; (*period*) etapa, tramo; período; (*stop*) parada; —**coach** ómnibus, autobús; — **hand** tramoyista; **by easy -s** por grados, gradualmente; *v.* representar, poner en escena; **to — a hold-up** hacer un asalto, atracar; **to — a surprise** dar una sorpresa.

stag·ger [stǽgɚ] *v.* (*totter*) tambalearse, tratabillar, bambolearse; hacer tambalear; (*overwhelm*) azorar, asombrar; **to — working hours** escalonar las horas de trabajo; *s.* tambaleo, bamboleo.

stag·nant [stǽgnənt] *adj.* estancado; **to become —** estancarse.

staid [sted] *adj.* grave, serio.

stain [sten] *v.* manchar; teñir; colorar; **stained-glass window** vidriera de colores; *s.* mancha, mancilla; tinte, tintura; materia colorante.

stain·less [sténlɪs] *adj.* sin mancha, inmaculado, limpio; — **steel** acero inempañable o inoxidable.

stair [stɛr] *s.* peldaño, escalón; **-s** escalera.

stair·case [stérkes] *s.* escalera.

stair·way [stɛ́rwe] *s.* escalera.

stake [stek] *s.* estaca; puesta, apuesta; **his future is at** — su porvenir está en peligro o riesgo; **to die at the** — morir en la hoguera; **to have a —in the future of** tener interés en el porvenir de; **to have much at** — irle a uno mucho en una cosa; haber aventurado mucho; *v.* estacar; atar a una estaca; apostar; arriesgar, aventurar; **to — off** señalar con estacas (*un perímetro*).

sta·lac·tite [stəlǽktaɪt] *s.* estalactita.

sta·lag·mite [stəlǽgmaɪt] *s.* estalagmita.

stale [stel] *adj.* viejo; rancio; gastado, improductivo.

stale·mate [stélmet] *s.* punto muerto; estancación.

stalk [stɔk] *s.* tallo; caña.

stall [stɔl] *s.* casilla, puesto (*de un mercado o feria*); casilla o sección de un establo; *v.* encasillar, meter en casilla; atascarse (*un auto*); pararse (*el motor*); **he is -ing** está haciendo la pala; **to be -ed in the mud** estar atascado en el lodo.

stal·lion [stǽljən] *s.* caballo de cría, caballo padre, *Ven., Col., Riopl.* padrillo; *Méx., C.A.* garañón.

stam·mer [stǽmɚ] *v.* tartamudear, balbucear; *s.* tartamudeo, balbuceo.

stam·mer·er [stǽmərɚ] *s.* tartamundo.

stam·mer·ing [stǽmərɪŋ] *s.* tartamudeo; *adj.* tartamundo.

stamp [stæmp] *v.* (*affix*) sellar; timbrar; poner un sello a; estampar; (*mark*) marcar, imprimir; señalar; (*with foot*) patear, patalear; **to — one's**

foot dar patadas en el suelo; **to — out** extirpar, borrar; *s.* sello; timbre, estampilla; estampa; marca, impresión; patada (*en el suelo*); **postage** — sello, *Am.* estampilla, *Am.* timbre; **revenue** — timbre.

stam·pede [stæmpíd] *s.* estampida; huída en desorden; tropel; éxodo repentino; *v.* arrancar, huir en tropel; ir en tropel; ahuyentar, hacer huir en desorden.

stanch [stɑntʃ] *v.* restañar, estancar; *adj.* fuerte, firme; leal, constante, fiel.

stand [stænd] *v.* poner derecho, colocar verticalmente; (*rise*) ponerse de pie, levantarse; *Am.* parar(se); (*be erect*) estar de pie; *Am.* estar parado; (*withstand*) augantar, sufrir, tolerar; **to — a chance of** tener probabilidad de; **to — an expense** sufragar un gasto; **to — aside** apartarse; mantenerse apartado; **to — back of** colocarse detrás de; salir fiador de, garantizar a, respaldar a; **to — by** mantenerse a corta distancia; apoyar, defender; estar alerta; **to — for** significar; estar por, apoyar; tolerar; **to — in the way** estorbar; **to — on end** poner(se) de punta; erizarse (*el pelo*); **to — one's ground** mantenerse firme; **to — out** resaltar, destacarse; sobre-salir; **to — six feet** tener seis pies de altura; **to — up for** apoyar, defender; **it -s to reason** es razonable, es lógico; *s.* puesto; mesilla; pedestal; posición; actitud; alto, parada (*para resistir*); quiosco; **grand** — andanada, gradería cubierta (*para espectadores*); **music** — atril; **umbrella —** paragüero.

stan·dard [stǽndɚd] *s.* (*norm*) norma; nivel normal; criterio; (*model*) modelo, patrón; *Am.* estándar; (*base*) base, pedestal; (*banner*) estandarte; **gold** — patrón de oro; **to be up to** — satisfacer las normas requeridas; *adj.* normal, que sirve de norma; de uso general; corriente; **standard-bearer** portaestandarte.

stan·dard·i·za·tion [stændədəzéʃən] *s.* normalización, igualación, igualación.

stan·dard·ize [stǽndɚdaɪz] *v.* normalizar, uniformar, *Méx., C.A., Carib.* estandardizar.

stand·by [stǽndbaɪ] *s.* sustituto.

stand·ing [stǽndɪŋ] *s.* (*position*) posición; (*fame*) fama, reputación; **of long** — que ha prevalecido largo tiempo; muy antiguo; *adj.* derecho, en pie; de pie; establecido, permanente; — **water** agua estancada; **there is — room only** no quedan asientos.

stand·point [stǽndpɔɪnt] *s.* punto de vista.

stand·still [stǽndstɪl] *s.* alto; pausa; **to come to a —** pararse; hacer alto.

stank [stæŋk] *pret. de* **to stink.**

stan·za [stǽnzə] *s.* estrofa.

sta·ple [stépḷ] *s.* broche de alambre (*para sujetar papeles*); grapa, argolla, armella; artículo principal; **-s** artículos de necesidad prima; *adj.* principal; de uso corriente; indispensable; *v.* asegurar (*papeles*) con broche de alambre; sujetar con armellas.

star [stɑr] *s.* estrella; asterisco; **star-spangled** estrellado; *adj.* sobresaliente, excelente; *v.* estrellar, adornar o señalar con estrellas; marcar con asterisco; presentar como estrella (*a un actor*); lucir(se) en las tablas o el cine, hacer el papel principal

star·board [stárbord] *s.* estribor; *adj.* de estribor; — **side** banda de estribor; *adv.* a estribor.

starch [stɑrtʃ] *s.* almidón; fécula; *v.* almidonar.

stare [stɛr] *v.* mirar, mirar con fijeza o curiosidad;

mirar azorado; clavar la mirada, fijar la vista; *s.* mirada fija, mirada persistente.

star·fish [stárfıʃ] *s.* estrella de mar.

stark [stɑrk] *adj.* (*utter*) tieso; (*grim*) escueto; — **folly** pura tontería; — **in death** tieso, muerto; — **narrative** narración escueta, sin adornos; *adv.* completamente, totalmente; — **mad** loco de remate; — **naked** enteramente desnudo, en cueros, *Am.* encuerado.

star·light [stárlaıt] *s.* luz estelar, luz de las estrellas.

star·ry [stárı] *adj.* estrellado, sembrado de estrellas; como estrellas, brillante.

start [stɑrt] *v.* comenzar, empezar, principiar; poner(se) en marcha; partir, salir; dar un salto, sobresaltarse; **the motor -s** el motor arranca; **to — after someone** salir en busca de alguien; **to — off** salir, partir; dar principio a; **to — out on a trip** empezar una jornada, emprender un viaje; **to — the motor** hacer arrancar el motor; *s.* comienzo, empiezo, principio; sobresalto; respingo (*de un caballo*); arranque; ventaja (*en una carrera*).

start·er [stártɚ] *s.* (*automobile*) arranque; (*person*) arrancador; iniciador; (*first*) primero de la serie; **self-starter** arranque automático.

star·tle [stártl] *v.* asustar(se), sobresaltar(se), espantar(se).

start·ling [stártlıŋ] *adj.* sobresaltante, pasmoso, asombroso, sorprendente.

star·va·tion [stɑrvéʃən] *s.* inanición, hambre.

starve [stɑrv] *v.* morir(se) de hambre; hambrear; matar de hambre.

state [stet] *s.* estado; condición, situación; **in great** — con gran pompa; *adj.* de estado; del estado; de ceremonia; *v.* declarar, decir; expresar, exponer.

state·ly [stétlı] *adj.* majestuoso, imponente.

state·ment [stétmənt] *s.* (*declaration*) declaración; exposición; (*information*) informe, relato; (*bill*) cuenta, estado de cuentas.

state·room [strétrum] *s.* camarote (*de un buque*).

states·man [stétsmən] *s.* estadista, hombre de estado.

stat·ic [stǽtık] *adj.* estático; *s.* estática.

sta·tion [stéʃən] *s.* (*operations point*) estación; (*post*) paradero; puesto; (*condition*) estado, posición social; **broadcasting** — transmisora o emisora; *v.* estacionar, colocar, apostar; — **wagon** *Esp.* rubia; *Méx.* camioneta, huayin; *C.A.* camionetilla.

sta·tion·ar·y [stéʃənɛrı] *adj.* estacionario; fijo.

sta·tion·er·y [stéʃənɛrı] *s.* papelería.

sta·tis·tics [stətístıks] *s.* estadística; datos estadísticos.

stat·u·ar·y [stǽtʃuɛrı] *s.* estatuaria, arte de hacer estatuas; colección de estatuas.

stat·ue [stǽtʃu] *s.* estatua.

stat·ure [stǽtʃɚ] *s.* estatura.

stat·us [stétəs] *s.* estado, condición; posición social o profesional.

stat·ute [stǽtʃut] *s.* estatuto, ordenanza.

staunch = stanch.

stave [stev] *s.* duela de barril; *v.* poner duelas (*a un barril*); **to — off** mantener a distancia; evitar; rechazar.

stay [ste] *v.* (*remain*) quedarse, permanecer; parar(se); detener(se); (*sojourn*) hospedarse, alojarse; (*check*) resistir; **to — an execution** diferir o aplazar una ejecución; **to — one's hunger** engañar el hambre; **to — up all night** velar toda la noche; *s.* estada, estancia,

permanencia; suspensión; sostén, apoyo; varilla o ballena de corsé; **to grant a** — conceder una prórroga.

stead [stɛd]: **in her** (**his**) — en su lugar; **to stand one in good** — servirle a uno, ser de provecho para uno.

stead·fast [stɛdfæst] *adj.* fijo, firme; constante.

stead·i·ly [stɛdılı] *adv.* constantemente; firmemente; sin parar, de continuo; sin vacilar.

stead·i·ness [stɛdınıs] *s.* firmeza; constancia; estabilidad.

stead·y [stɛdı] *adj.* firme; estable; invariable, constante; continuo; *v.* afianzar, mantener firme, asegurar; calmar (*los nervios*).

steak [stek] *s.* biftec o bisté; tajada (*para asar o freír*).

steal [stil] *v.* (*rob*) robar, hurtar; (*move*) andar furtivamente; **to — away** colarse, escabullirse, escaparse; **to — into a room** meterse a hurtadillas en un cuarto; **to — out of a room** salirse a escondidas de un cuarto, colarse, escabullirse; *s.* robo, hurto.

stealth [stɛlθ]: **by** — a hurtadillas, a escondidas, con cautela.

stealth·y [stɛlθı] *adj.* cauteloso, furtivo, secreto.

steam [stim] *s.* vapor; vaho; *adj.* de vapor; por vapor; — **engine** máquina de vapor; — **heat** calefacción por vapor; — **shovel** excavadora; *v.* cocer al vapor; dar un baño de vapor; saturar de vapor; echar vapor; **to — into port** llegar a puerto (*un vapor*).

steam·boat [stímbot] *s.* buque de vapor.

steam·er [stímɚ] *s.* vapor, buque de vapor.

steam·ship [stímʃıp] *s.* vapor, buque de vapor.

steed [stid] *s.* corcel, caballo de combate; caballo brioso.

steel [stil] *s.* acero; — **industry** siderurgía; *adj.* acerado, de acero; *v.* acerar, revestir de acero; **to — oneself against** fortalecerse contra.

steep [stip] *adj.* empinado, escarpado, pendiente; muy alto; — **price** precio alto o excesivo; *v.* remojar, empapar; saturar; poner o estar en infusión.

stee·ple [stípl] *s.* aguja, chapitel; cúspide.

steep·ness [stípnıs] *s.* inclinación abrupta; lo empinado, lo escarpado; altura (*de precios*).

steer [stır] *s.* novillo; buey; *v.* guiar, conducir, manejar, gobernar; timonear; **to — a course** seguir un rumbo; **the car -s easily** se maneja fácilmente el auto, es de fácil manejo.

steer·ing wheel [stírıŋhwil] *s.* volante; *Col.* timón.

stel·lar [stɛlɚ] *adj.* estelar.

stem [stɛm] *s.* tallo; tronco; pedúnculo (*de hoja, flor o fruto*); raíz (*de una palabra*); pie (*de copa*); cañón (*de pipa de fumar*); proa; *v.* estancar, represar; resistir, refrenar; contraponerse a; **from** — provenir de.

stench [stɛntʃ] *s.* hedor, hediondez.

sten·cil [stɛnsıl] *s.* patrón picado; esténcil.

ste·nog·ra·pher [stənágrəfɚ] *s.* estenógrafo, taquígrafo, mecanógrafo.

step [stɛp] *s.* (*walking*) paso; pisada; (*staircase*) peldaño, escalón, grada; (*degree*) grado; (*effort*) gestión; — **by** — paso a paso; **to be in** — **with** marchar a compás con; estar de acuerdo con; **to take -s** dar pasos; tomar medidas; gestionar; *v.* andar, caminar; dar un paso; **to — aside** hacerse a un lado, apartarse; **to — back** dar un paso o pasos atrás; retroceder; **to — down** bajar; **to — off a distance** medir a pasos una distancia; **to — on** pisar, pisotear; **to — on the**

off

ST

gas pisar el acelerador; darse prisa; **to — out** salir; **to — up** subir; acelerar.
step·fa·ther [stépfaðɚ] s. padrastro.
step·mo·ther [stépmʌðɚ] s. madrastra.
steppe [stɛp] s. estepa.
ster·e·o·type [stírɪotaɪp] s. estéreotipo.
ster·ile [stérəl] adj. estéril.
ste·ril·i·ty [stərílətɪ] s. esterilidad.
ster·il·ize [stérəlaɪz] v. esterilizar.
ster·ling [stɚlɪŋ] s. vajilla de plata esterlina; adj. genuino; de ley; — **silver** plata de ley, plata esterlina; **pound** — libra esterlina.
stern [stɚn] adj. austero, severo; firme; s. popa.
stern·ness [stɚnnɪs] s. austeridad, severidad; firmeza.
steth·o·scope [stéθəskop] s. estetoscopio.
ste·ve·dore [stívədor] s. estibador, cargador.
stew [stju] v. estofar; preocuparse, apurarse; s. estofado, guisado; cocido, puchero, sancocho; **to be in a —** estar preocupado o apurado.
stew·ard [stjúwɚd] s. mayordomo; camarero (de buque o avión).
stew·ard·ess [stjúwɚdɪs] s. camarera (de buque o avión); Esp. azafata.
stick [stɪk] s. palo; vara; garrote; raja de leña; — **of dynamite** barra de dinamita; **control —** palanca (de aeroplano); **walking —** bastón; chuzo (de sereno); **stick-up** atraco (para robar), asalto; v. pegar(se), adherir(se); permanecer; estar pegado; picar, pinchar; herir (con cuchillo, puñal, etc.); fijar (con clavos, alfileres, tachuelas, etc.); atascarse (en el fango un carro, auto, etc.); **to — something in** (o **into**) clavar o meter algo en; encajar en; **to — out** salir, sobresalir; proyectarse; **to — out one's head** asomar la cabeza; **to — out one's tongue** sacar la lengua; **to — to a job** perseverar (o persistir) en una tarea; **to — up** sobresalir, destacarse; estar de punta (el pelo); **to — one's hands up** alzar las manos; **to — someone up** asaltar o atracar a alguien (para robar); véase **stuck.**
stick·er [stíkɚ] s. marbete engomado; etiqueta.
stick·y [stíkɪ] adj. pegajoso.
stiff [stɪf] adj. tieso; rígido; entumido; duro; terco; fuerte; — **climb** subida ardua o difícil; — **price** precio alto o subido; **stiff-necked** terco, obstinado; **scared —** yerto, muerto de miedo; s. cadáver.
stiff·en [stífən] v. atiesar(se), poner(se) tieso; entumir(se); endurecer(se); espesar(se); subir de punto, aumentar (la resistencia).
stiff·ness [stífnɪs] s. tiesura; rigidez; dureza; rigor; terquedad.
sti·fle [stáɪfl] v. ahogar(se), asfixiar(se), sofocar(se); apagar, extinguir.
stig·ma [stígmə] s. estigma; baldón.
stig·ma·tize [stígmətaɪz] v. estigmatizar.
still [stɪl] adj. (quiet) quieto; callado, silencioso; (at ease) tranquilo; inmóvil; —**born** nacido muerto; — **life** naturaleza muerta; v. aquietar; calmar; acallar; adv. todavía, aún; conj. empero, no obstante, sin embargo; s. destiladera, alambique; silencio.
still·ness [stílnɪs] s. quietud, calma, silencio.
stilt [stɪlt] s. zanco; pilote, puntal, soporte.
stilt·ed [stíltɪd] adj. tieso, afectado, pomposo.
stim·u·lant [stímjələnt] adj. & s. estimulante.
stim·u·late [stímjəlet] v. estimular.
stim·u·la·tion [stímjəléʃən] s. estimulación, estímulo.
stim·u·lus [stímjələs] s. estímulo.

sting [stɪŋ] v. (pierce) picar; pinchar, aguijonear; (irritate) escocer; Am. arder; (cheat) embaucar; estafar; s. picadura, piquete, mordedura, picazón; aguijón; escozor; — **of remorse** remordimiento.
stin·gi·ness [stíndʒɪnɪs] s. tacañería, mezquindad.
stin·gy [stíndʒɪ] adj. mezquino, ruin, tacaño; escaso; Riopl., Méx. codo.
stink [stɪŋk] v. heder, oler mal; apestar; s. hedor, mal olor, hediondez.
stint [stɪnt] v. escatimar; ser frugal o económico; **to — oneself** privarse de lo necasario, economizar demasiado; s. tarea, faena; **without —** sin límite; sin escatimar; generosamente.
stip·u·late [stípjəlet] v. estipular.
stip·u·la·tion [stɪpjəléʃən] s. estipulación, condición.
stir [stɝ] v. menear(se); mover(se), bullir(se); atizar (el fuego); incitar; conmover; perturbar; revolver; **to — up** incitar; conmover; revolver; suscitar (un argumento, pelea, etc.); s. meneo, agitación, movimiento; alboroto.
stir·ring [stɝɪŋ] adj. conmovedor.
stir·rup [stírəp] s. estribo.
stitch [stɪtʃ] v. coser; dar puntadas; s. puntada; punzada; **to be in -es** desternillarse de risa.
stock [stak] s. (supply) surtido; existencias, provisión; (cattle) ganado; (lineage) cepa, linaje, estirpe; (shares) acciones, valores; **in —** en existencia; **live—** ganado; **meat —** caldo de carne; adj. en existencia, esistente, disponible; común, trivial; — **answer** contestación corriente, común o trivial; — **company** sociedad anónima; compañía teatral; — **exchange** bolsa; — **farm** hacienda de ganado, Am. rancho, Am. estancia; — **market** mercado de valores, bolsa; — **room** almacén; — **size** tamaño ordinario (regularmente en existencia); —**yard** matadero; v. surtir, abastecer; tener en existencia (para vender); **to — a farm** surtir o proveer de ganado un rancho; **to — up with** surtirse de, acumular.
stock·ade [stakéd] s. estacada, empalizada; vallado; v. empalizar, rodear de empalizadas.
stock·bro·ker [stákbrokɚ] s. bolsista, corredor de bolsa.
stock·hold·er [stákholdɚ] s. accionista.
stock·ing [stákɪŋ] s. media.
sto·ic [stóɪk] adj. & s. estoico.
stoke [stok] v. atizar (el fuego); cebar, alimentar (un horno).
stole [stol] pret. de **steal.**
sto·len [stólən] p.p. de **steal.**
stol·id [stálɪd] adj. estólido, insensible.
stom·ach [stʌmək] s. estómago; v. aguantar, tolerar.
stomp [stamp] v. pisar violentamente.
stone [ston] s. piedra; hueso (de las frutas); **within a -'s throw** a tiro de piedra; adj. pétreo, de piedra; **Stone Age** Edad de Piedra; **stone-deaf** totalmente sordo, sordo como una tapia; v. apedrear; deshuesar (las frutas).
ston·y [stónɪ] adj. pedregoso; pétreo, de piedra; duro.
stood [stʊd] pret. & p.p. de **to stand.**
stool [stul] s. (furniture) taburete; C.A. banquillo; (toilet) bacín, bacinica; (excrement) excremento; — **pigeon** soplón (el que delata a otro).
stoop [stup] v. agacharse; doblarse, inclinarse; encorvarse; andar encorvado o caído de hombros; rebajarse, humillarse, abajarse; s. encorvamiento, inclinación (de espaldas); **to walk**

with a — andar encorvado o caído de hombros;
stoop-shouldered cargado de espaldas encorvado.

stop [stɑp] *v.* (*pause*) parar(se), hacer alto,
detener(se); (*cease*) acabar(se); cesar; parar de,
dejar de; (*block*) atajar; reprimir; suspender;
obstruir, tapar; **to — at a hotel** hospedarse o
alojarse en un hotel; **to — at nothing** no pararse
en escrúpulos; **to — from** impedir; **to — over at**
hacer escala en; **to — short** parar(se) de sopetón,
parar(se) en seco; **to — up** tapar, obstruir;
atascar; *s.* parada; alto, pausa; estada, estancia;
detención; suspensión; llave (*de instrumento de
viento*); traste (*de guitarra*); registro (*de órgano*);
— consonant consonante explosiva.

stop·o·ver [stápovɚ] *s.* parada, escala; **to make a
— in** hacer escala en.

stop·page [stápidʒ] *s.* detención; obstrucción; **work
— paro**.

stop·per [stápɚ] *s.* tapón.

stor·age [stóridʒ] *s.* almacenaje; **— battery**
acumulador; **to keep in** — almacenar.

store [stor] *s.* (*shop*) tienda; almacén; (*supply*)
depósito; acopio; **-s** provisiones; bastimentos;
víveres; **department** — almacén; **dry-goods** —
lencería, *Méx.*, *Ríopl.*, *Andes* mercería, *Am.* cajón
de ropa; **fruit** — frutería; **hat** — sombrerería;
grocery — abacería, tienda de comestibles, *Méx.*,
C.A. tienda de abarrotes, *Carib.* bodega; **shoe** —
zapatería; **to have in** — tener guardado; *v.*
almacenar; guardar; abastecer; **to — up**
acumular.

store·house [stórhaᴜs] *s.* almacén, depósito.

store·keep·er [stórkipɚ] *s.* tendero; almacenista;
guardalmacén.

store·room [stórrum] *s.* almacén; bodega;
despensa.

stork [stɔrk] *s.* cigüeña.

storm [stɔrm] *s.* (*weather*) tormenta, tempestad,
borrasca, temporal; (*disturbance*) tumulto;
asalto; **— troops** tropas de asalto; **hail** —
granizada; **snow**— nevasca; **wind**— vendaval; *v.*
asaltar, atacar; rabiar; **it is -ing** hay tormenta,
hay tempestad.

sto·ry [stóri] *s.* (*tale*) cuento, historia, historieta;
relato; (*gossip*) chisme; rumor; bola; (*plot*)
argumento, trama; (*floor*) piso (*de un edificio*);
newspaper — artículo de periódico, gacetilla.

stout [staᴜt] *adj.* corpulento, robusto, fornido;
fuerte; firme; leal; valiente.

stove [stov] *s.* estufa; concina de gas, cocina
eléctrica; *pret.* & *p.p. de* **to stave.**

stow [sto] *v.* meter, guardar; esconder; estibar,
acomodar la carga de un barco; rellenar; **to —
away on a ship** embarcarse clandestinamente,
esconderse en un barco.

strad·dle [strǽdl] *v.* ponerse o estar a horcajadas;
ponerse a caballo, cabalgar; favorecer ambos
lados (*de un pleito, controversia, etc.*).

strafe [stref] *v.* ametrallar; *Am.* abalear.

strag·gle [strǽgl] *v.* vagar, desviarse; extraviarse;
andar perdido; dispersarse; **to — behind**
rezagarse.

straight [stret] *adj.* (*direction*) recto; derecho;
directo; (*proper*) honrado; franco; erguido;
correcto; en orden; **— face** cara seria; **— hair**
pelo lacio; **— hand of five cards** runfla de cinco
naipes del mismo palo; **— rum** ron puro, sin
mezcla; **for two hours** — por dos horas seguidas,
por dos horas sin parar; **to set a person** — dar

consejo a una persona; mostrarle el camino,
modo o manera de hacer algo; *adv.*
directamente, derecho, en línea recta;
francamente; honradamente; **—away** (*o* **— off**)
en seguida, al punto; **to talk** — **from the
shoulder** hablar con toda franqueza o sinceridad.

straight·en [strétn] *v.* enderezar(se); arreglar,
poner en orden.

straight·for·ward [stretfɔrwɚd] *adj.* derecho, recto;
honrado; franco, sincero; *adv.* directamente, en
línea recta.

straight·ness [strétnɪs] *s.* derechura; rectitud;
honradez.

straight·way [strétwe] *adv.* luego, inmediatamente,
en seguida.

strain [stren] *v.* (*force*) estirar demasiado, hacer
fuerza; poner tirante; violentar, forzar (*los
músculos, los nervios, la vista, etc.*); (*sift*) colar,
tamizar; **to — one's wrist** torcerse la muñeca; *s.*
tensión excesiva; tirantez; torcedura; esfuerzo
excesivo; linaje, rasgo racial; aire, tonada.

strain·er [strénɚ] *s.* coladera; cedazo.

strait [stret] *s.* estrecho; **-s** estrecho; aprieto,
apuro; **—jacket** camisa de fuerza.

strait·laced [strétlest] *adj.* estricto.

strand [strænd] *v.* encallar; dejar perdido (*sin
medios de salir*), dejar aislado, extraviar; **to be
-ed** estar encallado; estar extraviado (*sin medios
de salir*), estar aislado, andar perdido; *s.* ribera,
playa; ramal (*de cuerda, cable, etc.*); hebra, hilo;
— of hair guedeja; trenza; **— of pearls** hilera de
perlas.

strange [strendʒ] *adj.* extraño; raro, singular;
desconocido.

strange·ness [stréndʒnɪs] *s.* extrañeza, rareza.

stran·ger [stréndʒɚ] *s.* extraño, desconocido;
forastero.

stran·gle [strǽŋgl] *v.* estrangular(se).

strap [stræp] *s.* correa; tira de cuero o de tela;
correón; tirante; **metal** — banda de metal; *v.*
amarrar o atar con correas; azotar (*con correa*);
véase **strop.**

strat·a·gem [strǽtədʒəm] *s.* estratagema.

stra·te·gic [strətídʒɪk] *adj.* estratégico.

strat·e·gy [strǽtədʒɪ] *s.* estrategia.

strat·o·sphere [strǽtəsfɪr] *s.* estratosfera.

straw [strɔ] *s.* paja; **I don't care a** — no me
importa un comino; *adj.* de paja; pajizo;
straw-colored pajizo, color de paja; **— hat**
sombrero de paja; **— vote** voto no oficial (*para
averiguar la opinion pública*).

straw·ber·ry [strɔ́berɪ] *s.* fresa.

stray [stre] *v.* extraviarse, descarriarse, desviarse;
perderse, errar el camino; vagar; *adj.* extraviado,
perdido; **— remark** observación aislada; *s.*
animal perdido o extraviado.

streak [strik] *s.* (*line*) raya, línea, lista; (*vein*) vena;
(*trace*) rasgo; (*beam*) rayo (*de luz*); **— of
lightning** relámpago, rayo; *v.* rayar, *Am.* listar,
hacer rayas o listas en.

stream [strim] *s.* corriente; chorro; río, arroyo,
arroyuelo; **— of cars** desfile de autos; **down**—
río abajo, agua abajo, con la corriente; **up**— río
arriba, agua arriba, contra la corriente; *v.* correr
(*el agua*), fluir; brotar, manar; derramarse; flotar
(*en el viento*), ondear; **to — out of** salir a
torrentes de.

stream·er [strímɚ] *s.* banderola; gallardete; listón,
cinta (*que flota en el aire*).

stream·lined [strímlaɪnd] *adj.* aerodinámico.

street [strit] *s.* calle.

street·car [strítkɑr] *s.* tranvía.
strength [strɛŋkθ] *s.* fuerza; poder; potencia; fortaleza; **on the — of his promise** fundado en su promesa.
strength·en [strɛ́ŋkθən] *v.* fortalecer(se); reforzar(se).
stren·u·ous [strɛ́njʊəs] *adj.* arduo; enérgico, vigoroso.
strep·to·my·cin [strɛptomáɪsɪn] *s.* estreptomicina.
stress [strɛs] *s.* (*force*) fuerza, esfuerzo; tensión, torsión, compresión; (*importance*) urgencia; énfasis; (*intensity*) acento; *v.* acentuar; recalcar, dar énfasis a, hacer hincapié en.
stretch [strɛtʃ] *v.* estirar(se); alargar(se); tender(se); ensanchar; **to — oneself** estirarse, desperezarse; **to — out one's hand** tender o alargar la mano; *s.* trecho, distancia; extension; período de tiempo; elasticidad; tensión; esfuerzo (*de la imaginación*); estirón; **home — último** trecho (*de una carrera*).
stretch·er [strɛ́tʃɚ] *s.* estirador, ensanchador, dilatador; camilla (*para los heridos*).
strew [stru] *v.* regar, esparcir.
strewn [strun] *p.p.* *de* **to strew;** — **with** regado de, cubierto de.
strick·en [stríkən] *p.p.* *de* **to strike;** *adj.* herido; afligido; agobiado; atacado.
strict [strɪkt] *adj.* estricto; **in — confidence** en absoluta confianza, con toda reserva.
strid·den [strídn̩] *p.p.* *de* **to stride.**
stride [straɪd] *v.* tranquear, caminar a paso largo, dar zancadas, andar a trancos; *s.* zancada, tranco, paso largo.
strife [straɪf] *s.* refriega, contienda, pleito.
strike [straɪk] *v.* (*hit*) dar, golpear, pegar; azotar; herir; atacar; (*collide with*) chocar con; dar con, encontrar (*oro, petróleo, etc.*); ocurrírsele a uno (*una idea*); asumir, afectar (*una postura, una actitud*); dar (*la hora un reloj*); encender (*un fósforo*); acuñar (*moneda*); declararse o estar en huelga; **to — at** amagar; acometer; **to — off** borrar, tachar; cortar; **to — one's attention** atraer o llamar la atención; **to — one's fancy** antojársele a uno; **to — one's head against** darse un cabezazo contra; **to — out in a certain direction** tomar cierto rumbo, encaminarse o irse en cierta dirección; **to — someone for a loan** darle un sablazo a alguien; **to — up a friendship** trabar amistad; **to — with terror** sobrecoger de terror; **how does she — you?** ¿qué tal le parece?; ¿qué piensa Vd. de ella;? *s.* golpe; huelga; descubrimiento repentino (*de petróleo, de una mina, etc*); **—breaker** esquirol (*obrero que sustituye a un huelguista*).
strik·er [stráɪkɚ] *s.* (*person on strike*) huelguista; (*device*) golpeador.
strik·ing [stráɪkɪŋ] *adj.* notable; llamativo; conspicuo, manifiesto; sorprendente; extraordinario; (*on strike*) que está de huelga; que está en huelga.
string [strɪŋ] *s.* cuerda; cordel, cinta, cordón; sarta (*de perlas, cuentas, etc.*); fibra (*de habichuelas, porotos, etc.*); fila, hilera; — **bean** habichuela, judía verde, *Méx.* ejote, *Ch., Riopl.* poroto; — **of lies** sarta de mentiras; *v.* ensartar; tender (*un cable, un alambre*); desfibrar, quitar las fibras a; encordar (*una raqueta, un violín*); encordelar, atar con cordeles, lazos o cuerdas; tomar el pelo, engañar; **to — out** extender(se), prolongar(se); **to — up** colgar.
strip [strɪp] *v.* despojar; robar; desnudar(se); desvestir(se), desmantelar; **to — the gears**

estropear el engranaje; **to — the skin from** desollar, pelar; *s.* tira, lista, listón; — **of land** faja de tierra.
stripe [straɪp] *s.* (*band*) franja, raya, lista, tira; banda, galón; (*kind*) tipo, índole; *v.* rayar, *Am.* listar, adornar con listas.
striped [straɪpt, stráɪpɪd] *adj.* listado.
strive [straɪv] *v.* esforzarse; luchar, forcejear; hacer lo posible; **to — to** esforzarse por.
striv·en [strívən] *p.p.* *de* **to strive.**
strode [strod] *pret.* *de* **to stride.**
stroke [strok] *s.* golpe; ataque, apoplejía; — **of a bell** campanada; — **of a painter's brush** pincelada; — **of lightning** rayo; — **of the hand** caricia; — **of the pen** plumada; **at the — of ten** al dar las diez; *v.* frotar suavemente, pasar suavemente la mano, acacriciar; alisar.
stroll [strol] *v.* dar un paseo, pasearse; vagar; **to — the streets** callejear; *s.* paseo, paseíto.
strong [strɔŋ] *adj.* fuerte; forzudo, fornido; vigoroso; recio; enérgico; firme; bien marcado; acérrimo; — **chance** buena probabilidad; — **coffee** café cargado; — **market** mercado firme; **strong-willed** de voluntad fuerte, decidido; **strong-arm** violento; *adv.* fuertemente; firmemente.
strong·hold [strɔ́ŋhold] *s.* fuerte, plaza fuerte.
stron·ti·um [strántʃɪəm] *s.* estroncio.
strop [strɑp] *v.* asentar (*navajas de afeitar*); *s.* asentador de navajas.
strove [strov] *pret.* *de* **to strive.**
struck [strʌk] *pret.* & *p.p.* *de* **to strike; to be — with a disease** darle a uno una enfermedad; **to be — with terror** estar o quedar sobrecogido de terror.
struc·tu·ral [strʌ́ktʃərəl] *adj.* estructural, relativo a la estructura.
struc·ture [strʌ́ktʃɚ] *s.* estructura; construcción; edificio.
strug·gle [strʌ́gl̩] *v.* bregar, luchar, pugnar; forcejear; esforzarse; *s.* esfuerzo; contienda, lucha, pugna.
strung [strʌŋ] *pret.* & *p.p.* *de* **to string.**
strut [strʌt] *v.* pavonearse, contonearse; *s.* contoneo; tirante, puntal.
stub [stʌb] *s.* trozo, fragmento, pedazo mochado; tocón (*de árbol*); talón (*de libro talonario, boleto, etc.*); — **book** libro talonario; — **pen** pluma de punta mocha; *v.* **to — one's foot** dar(se) un tropezón.
stub·ble [stʌ́bl̩] *s.* rastrojo; cañones (*de la barba*).
stub·born [stʌ́bɚn] *adj.* terco, testarudo, obstinado, porfiado, cabezón.
stub·born·ness [stʌ́bɚnɪs] *s.* terquedad, testarudez, porfía, obstinación.
stuc·co [stʌ́ko] *s.* estuco; *v.* estucar, cubrir de estuco.
stuck [stʌk] *pret.* & *p.p.* *de* **to stick** pegado; atorado; atascado; — **full of holes** agujereado; **stuck-up** tieso, estirado, orgulloso.
stud [stʌd] *s.* (*knob*) tachón, tachuela de adorno; (*button*) botón postizo para camisa; (*bolt*) perno; — **horse** caballo padre; *v.* tachonar; clavetear.
stu·dent [stjúdn̩t] *s.* estudiante; *adj.* estudiantil.
stud·ied [stʌ́dɪd] *adj.* estudiado.
stu·di·o [stjúdɪo] *s.* estudio, taller.
stu·di·ous [stjúdɪəs] *adj.* estudioso; aplicado; estudiado.
stud·y [stʌ́dɪ] *s.* estudio; cuidado, solicitud; gabinete de estudio; *v.* estudiar.

stuff [stʌf] s. (*material*) materia; material; (*cloth*) género, tela; (*thing*) cosa; (*medicine*) menjurje, medicina; (*junk*) cachivaches, baratijas; **of good** — de buena estofa; *v.* rellenar; henchir; hartar(se), atracar(se), atiborrar(se).

stuf·fing [stʌfɪŋ] s. relleno; material para rellenar.

stum·ble [stʌmbl] *v.* tropezar, dar(se) un tropezón; dar un traspié; hablar o recitar equivocándose a cada paso; **to — upon** tropezar con; s. tropiezo, tropezón, traspié.

stump [stʌmp] s. tocón (*tronco que queda de un árbol*); raigón (*de muela*); muñón (*de brazo o pierna cortada*); — **of a tail** rabo; **to be up a** — hallarse en un apuro, estar perplejo; *v.* trozar el tronco de (*un árbol*); renquear, cojear; dejar confuso, confundir; **to — the country** recorrer el país pronunciando discursos políticos.

stump·y [stʌmpɪ] *adj.* rechoncho, *Am.* chaparro; lleno de tocones.

stun [stʌn] *v.* aturdir, pasmar; atolondrar.

stung [stʌŋ] *pret.* & *p.p. de* **to sting.**

stunk [stʌŋk] *pret.* & *p.p. de* **to stink.**

stun·ning [stʌnɪŋ] *adj.* aplastante; elegante, bellísimo.

stunt [stʌnt] *v.* achaparrar, impedir el desarrollo de, no dejar crecer; hacer suertes; hacer piruetas; s. suerte; pirueta, suerte acrobática, maniobra gimnástica; hazaña sensacional.

stu·pe·fy [stjúpəfaɪ] *v.* atontar; entorpecer; aturdir, atolondrar, pasmar, dejar estupefacto.

stu·pen·dous [stjupéndəs] *adj.* estupendo.

stu·pid [stjúpɪd] *adj.* estúpido; atontado.

stu·pid·i·ty [stjupídətɪ] s. estupidez.

stu·por [stjúpɚ] s. letargo, modorra; sopor; aturdimiento; **in a** — aletargado.

stur·dy [stɝdɪ] *adj.* fornido, fuerte, robusto; firme.

stut·ter [stʌtɚ] *v.* tartamudear; s. tartamudeo; tartamudez.

stut·er·er [stʌtərɚ] s. tartamudo.

stut·ter·ing [stʌtərɪŋ] *adj.* tartamudo; s. tartamudeo.

sty [staɪ] s. pocilga; orzuelo (*en el párpado*), *Méx.* perilla; *Ríopl.* chiquero.

style [staɪl] s. estilo; moda; **to be in** — estar de moda, estilarse; *v.* intitular, nombrar; **to — a dress** cortar un vestido a la moda.

styl·ish [stáɪlɪʃ] *adj.* elegante; a la moda.

styl·ize [stáɪlaɪz] *v.* estilizar.

sub·con·scious [sʌbkánʃəs] *adj.* subconsciente.

sub·di·vi·sion [sʌbdəvíʒən] s. subdivisión; parcelación de terrenos.

sub·due [səbdjú] *v.* subyugar, someter; sujetar, dominar; amansar, domar.

sub·dued [səbdjúd] *p.p. de* **to subdue;** *adj.* sumiso; sujeto; manso; suave; tenue; — **light** luz tenue.

sub·ject [sʌ́bdʒɪkt] s. súbdito; sujeto; asunto, tema, materia; *adj.* sujeto; sometido; inclinado, propenso; expuesto; [səbdʒékt] *v.* sujetar; someter; subyugar, sojuzgar.

sub·jec·tion [səbdʒékʃən] s. sujeción; dominación; sumisión.

sub·jec·tive [səbdʒéktɪv] *adj.* subjetivo.

sub·ju·gate [sʌ́bdʒəget] *v.* subyugar, sojuzgar.

sub·li·mate [sʌ́bləmet] *v.* sublimar.

sub·lime [səbláɪm] *adj.* sublime.

sub·ma·rine [sʌbmərín] *adj.* submarino; [sʌ́bmərin] s. submarino.

sub·merge [səbmɝdʒ] *v.* sumergir(se), hundir(se), sumir(se).

sub·mis·sion [səbmíʃən] s. sumisión, sometimiento.

sub·mis·sive [səbmísɪv] *adj.* sumiso.

sub·mit [səbmít] *v.* someter; **to — a report** someter (presentar *o* rendir) un informe; **to — to punishment** someterse a un castigo.

sub·or·di·nate [səbɔ́rdṇɪt] *adj.* & s. subordinado; subalterno; dependiente; [səbɔ́rdṇet] *v.* subordinar.

sub·scribe [səbskráɪb] *v.* subscribir(se); firmar; **to — five dollars** prometer una cuota o subscripción de cinco dólares; **to — for** subscribirse a, abonarse a; **to — to a plan** subscribirse a (*o* aprobar) un plan.

sub·scrib·er [səbskráɪbɚ] s. suscritor, abonado; infrascrito (*que firma un documento*), firmante.

sub·scrip·tion [səbskrípʃən] s. subscripción, abono.

sub·se·quent [sʌ́bsɪkwɛnt] *adj.* subsiguiente, subsecuente, posterior; **-ly** *adv.* después, posteriormente, subsiguientemente.

sub·ser·vi·ent [sʌbsɝ́vɪənt] *adj.* servil, servilón.

sub·side [səbsáɪd] *v.* menguar, disminuir; bajar (*de nivel*); calmarse, aquietarse.

sub·sid·i·ar·y [səbsídɪɛrɪ] *adj.* subsidiario; sucursal.

sub·si·dize [sʌ́bsədaɪz] *v.* subvencionar.

sub·si·dy [sʌ́bsədɪ] s. subvención.

sub·sist [səbsíst] *v.* subsistir.

sub·stance [sʌ́bstəns] s. substancia (sustancia).

sub·stan·tial [səbstǽnʃəl] *adj.* substancial, substancioso; sólido; considerable; importante; **to be in — agreement** estar en substancia de acuerdo.

sub·stan·ti·ate [səbstǽnʃɪet] *v.* comprobar; verificar.

sub·stan·tive [sʌ́bstəntɪv] *adj.* & s. sustantivo.

sub·sti·tute [sʌ́bstətjut] *v.* sustituir (substituir); reemplazar; s. sustituto, suplente; reemplazo.

sub·sti·tu·tion [sʌbstətjúʃən] s. sustitución (substitución); reemplazo.

sub·stra·tum [sʌ́bstrætəm] s. sustrato.

sub·ter·fuge [sʌ́btɚfjudʒ] s. escapatoria; subterfugio.

sub·ter·ra·ne·an [sʌbtərénɪən] *adj.* subterráneo.

sub·tle [sʌ́tl] *adj.* sutil.

sub·tle·ty [sʌ́tl̩tɪ] *adj.* sutileza; agudeza.

sub·tract [səbtrǽkt] *v.* sustraer (substraer); restar.

sub·trac·tion [səbtrǽkʃən] s. sustracción (substracción), resta.

sub·urb [sʌ́bɝb] s. suberbio, arrabal.

sub·ur·ban [səbɝ́bən] *adj.* & s. suburbano.

sub·ver·sive [səbvɝ́sɪv] *adj.* subversivo (*en contra de la autoridad constituida*); trastornador, destructivo.

sub·way [sʌ́bwe] s. subterráneo, túnel; metro, ferrocarril subterráneo.

suc·ceed [səksíd] *v.* suceder a; medrar, tener buen éxito, salir bien.

suc·cess [səksés] s. éxito, buen éxito; triunfo.

suc·cess·ful [səksésfəl] *adj.* afortunado; próspero; **to be** — tener buen éxito; **-ly** *adv.* con buen éxito, próspermente.

suc·ces·sion [səkséʃən] s. sucesión.

suc·ces·sive [səksésɪv] *adj.* sucesivo.

suc·ces·sor [səksésɚ] s. sucesor; heredero.

suc·cor [sʌ́kɚ] s. socorro; *v.* socorrer.

suc·cumb [səkʌ́m] *v.* sucumbir.

such [sʌtʃ] *adj.* tal; semejante; — **a tal**, semejante; — **a good man** un hombre tan bueno; — **as tal** como, tales como; **at — an hour** a tal hora; **at — and — a place** en tal o cual lugar.

suck [sʌk] *v.* chupar; mamar; **to — up** chupar; sorber; s. chupada; mamada.

suck·er [sʌ́kɚ] s. chupador; mamón, mamantón; dulce (*que se chupa*); primo (*persona demasiado*

ST

crédula).

suck·le [sʌk!] v. mamar; amamantar, dar de mamar.

suc·tion [sʌkʃən] s. succión; chupada, aspiración.

sud·den [sʌdn̩] adj. súbito, repentino; precipitado; inesperado; **all of a** — de súbito, de repente, de sopetón; **-ly** adv. de súbito, de repente, de sopetón.

sud·den·ness [sʌdn̩nɪs] s. precipitación; rapidez.

suds [sʌdz] s. espuma, jabonadura.

sue [su] v. demandar; **to** — **for damages** demandar por daños y perjuicios; **to** — **for peace** pedir la paz.

su·et [súɪt] s. sebo, gordo, grasa.

suf·fer [sʌfə] v. sufrir; padecer.

suf·fer·er [sʌfərə] s. sufridor.

suf·fer·ing [sʌfərɪŋ] s. sufrimiento, padecimiento; adj. doliente; sufrido, paciente.

suf·fice [səfáɪs] v. bastar, ser bastante o suficiente.

suf·fi·cient [səfíʃənt] adj. suficiente, bastante; **-ly** adv. suficientemente, bastante.

suf·fix [sʌfɪks] s. sufijo.

suf·fo·cate [sʌfəket] v. sofocar(se), ahogar(se), asfixiar(se).

suf·fo·ca·tion [sʌfəkéʃən] s. asfixia, sofoco.

suf·frage [sʌfrɪdʒ] s. sufragio; voto.

sug·ar [ʃúgə] s. azúcar; — **bowl** azucarera; — **cane** caña de azúcar; **lump of** — terrón de azúcar; v. azucarar; cristalizarse (el almíbar), Am. azucararse.

sug·gest [səgdʒést] v. sugerir, indicar.

sug·ges·tion [səgdʒéstʃən] s. sugestión, Am. sugerencia; indicación.

sug·ges·tive [səgdʒéstɪv] adj. sugestivo.

su·i·cide [súəsaɪd] s. suicidio; suicida; **to commit** — suicidarse.

suit [sut] s. traje, terno, Carib., Ven. flux (o flus); palo (de la baraja); demanda, pleito; petición; galanteo; v. adaptar, acomodar; agradar; satisfacer; sentar bien, venir bien; caer bien; convenir; set a propósito; — **yourself** haz lo que quieras, haga Vd. lo que guste.

suit·a·ble [sútəbl] adj. propio, conveniente, debido, a propósito, apropiado, adecuado.

suit·a·bly [sútəblɪ] adv. propiamente, adecuadamente, convenientemente.

suit·case [sútkes] s. maleta, valija.

suite [swit] s. serie; comitiva, acompañamiento; — **of rooms** vivienda, apartamento, habitación; **bedroom** — juego de muebles para alcoba.

suit·or [sútə] s. pretendiente, galán; demandante (en un pleito).

sulk [sʌlk] v. tener murria; estar hosco o malhumorado; s. murria.

sulk·y [sʌlkɪ] adj. malcontento, hosco, malhumorado; **to be** — tener murria.

sul·len [sʌlɪn] adj. hosco, sombrío, tétrico; malhumorado, taciturno.

sul·ly [sʌlɪ] v. manchar, ensuciar; empañar.

sul·phate [sʌlfet] s. sulfato.

sul·phide [sʌlfaɪd] s. sulfuro.

sul·phur [sʌlfə] s. azufre.

sul·phur·ic [sʌlfjúrɪk] adj. sulfúrico.

sul·tan [sʌltn̩] s. sultán.

sul·try [sʌltrɪ] adj. bochornoso, sofocante; — **heat** bochorno, calor sofocante.

sum [sʌm] s. suma; cantidad; esencia, substancia; — **total** total; v. sumar; **to** — **up** resumir, recapitular.

sum·ma·rize [sʌməraɪz] v. resumir, compendiar.

sum·ma·ry [sʌmərɪ] s. sumario, resumen;

compendio; adj. sumario; breve.

sum·mer [sʌmə] s. verano; estío; adj. veraniego, estival de verano; — **resort** balneario, lugar de veraneo; v. veranear.

sum·mit [sʌmɪt] s. cima, cúspide, cumbre.

sum·mon [sʌmən] v. citar; convocar, llamar; **-s** s. notificación; cita judicial, citación, emplazamiento.

sump·tu·ous [sʌmptʃʊəs] adj. suntuoso.

sun [sʌn] s. sol; — **bath** baño de sol; — **lamp** lámpara de rayos ultravioletas; — **porch** solana; v. asolear; **to** — **oneself** asolearse, tomar el sol.

sun·beam [sʌnbim] s. rayo de sol.

sun·burn [sʌnbɜn] s. quemadura de sol; v. asolear(se); quemar(se) al sol, tostar(se) al sol.

Sun·day [sʌndɪ] s. domingo.

sun·di·al [sʌndaɪəl] s. cuadrante solar, reloj de sol.

sun·down [sʌndaʊn] s. puesta del sol.

sun·dry [sʌndrɪ] adj. varios, diversos.

sun·flow·er [sʌnflaʊə] s. girasol; tornasol.

sung [sʌŋ] pret. & p.p. de **to sing**.

sun·glass·es [sʌnglæsəz] s. gafas (anteojos) del sol.

sunk [sʌŋk] pret. & p.p. de **to sink**.

sunk·en [sʌŋkən] adj. hundido, sumido.

sun·light [sʌnlaɪt] s. luz del sol, luz solar.

sun·ny [sʌnɪ] adj. asoleado o soleado; alegre, risueño, resplandeciente; — **day** día de sol.

sun·rise [sʌnraɪz] s. salida del sol, amanecer, amanecida.

sun·set [sʌnset] s. puesta del sol.

sun·shine [sʌnʃaɪn] s. luz del sol, solana.

sun·stroke [sʌnstrok] s. insolación.

sup [sʌp] v. cenar.

su·perb [supɜb] adj. soberbio.

su·per·fi·cial [supəfíʃəl] adj. superficial.

su·per·flu·ous [supɜfluəs] adj. superfluo.

su·per·hu·man [supəhjúmən] adj. sobrehumano.

su·per·in·tend [suprɪnténd] v. dirigir, inspeccionar, vigilar.

su·per·in·ten·dent [suprɪnténdənt] s. superintendente; inspector; capataz.

su·pe·ri·or [səpírɪə] adj. & s. superior; — **letter** volado.

su·pe·ri·or·i·ty [səpɪrɪórətɪ] s. superioridad.

su·per·la·tive [səpɜ́lətɪv] adj. & s. superlativo.

su·per·mar·ket [súpəmarkət] s. supermercado.

su·per·nat·u·ral [supənǽtʃrəl] adj. sobrenatural; **the** — lo sobrenatural.

su·per·sede [supəsíd] v. reemplazar.

su·per·sti·tion [supəstíʃən] s. superstición.

su·per·sti·tious [supəstíʃəs] adj. supersticioso.

su·per·vise [supəváɪz] v. dirigir, inspeccionar, vigilar.

su·per·vi·sion [supəvíʒən] s. inspección, vigilancia.

su·per·vi·sor [supəváɪzə] s. superintendente, inspector; interventor.

sup·per [sʌpə] s. cena.

sup·plant [səplǽnt] v. suplantar; reemplazar.

sup·ple [sʌpl] adj. flexible; dócil.

sup·ple·ment [sʌpləmənt] s. suplemento; apéndice; [sʌpləmənt] v. suplementar, completar.

sup·pli·ant [sʌplɪənt] adj. & s. suplicante.

sup·pli·ca·tion [sʌplɪkéʃən] s. súplica, plegaria; ruego.

sup·ply [səplái] v. proveer; abastecer, surtir; suplir; dar, suministrar; s. provisión, abastecimiento; bastimento; abasto; surtido; **supplies** provisiones; materiales; víveres; pertrechos; — **pipe** cañería o caño de abastecimiento, tubería o tubo de suministro.

sup·port [səpórt] v. (keep from falling) sostener;

apoyar; (*provide for*) mantener; sustentar; (*bear*) soportar, aguantar; *s.* apoyo; sostén, soporte, puntal; sustento, manutención; amparo.

sup·port·er [səpórtəʳ] *s.* defensor; partidario; mantenedor; sostén, apoyo; tirante (*para medias*).

sup·pose [səpóz] *v.* suponer.

sup·posed [səpózd] *adj.* supuesto; presunto; -ly *adv.* supuestamente.

sup·po·si·tion [sʌpəzíʃən] *s.* suposición.

sup·press [səprés] *v.* suprimir; reprimir; parar, suspender; **to — a revolt** sofocar una revuelta o motín.

sup·pres·sion [səpréʃən] *s.* supresión; represión.

su·prem·a·cy [səpréməsɪ] *s.* supremacía.

su·preme [səprím] *adj.* supremo.

sure [ʃʊr] *adj.* seguro; cierto; estable; *adv.* véase **surely; be — to do it** hágalo sin falta, no deje Vd. de hacerlo; -ly *adv.* seguramente; ciertamente; con toda seguridad; sin falta.

sure·ty [ʃúrtɪ] *s.* seguridad; garantía, fianza; fiador.

surf [sɝf] *s.* oleaje, rompientes; resaca.

sur·face [sɝfɪs] *s.* superficie; cara; *v.* alisar, allanar; poner superficie a.

surf·board [sɝfbord] *s.* patín de mar.

sur·feit [sɝfɪt] *s.* hastío, exceso; *v.* hastiar; empalagar.

surge [sɝdʒ] *s.* oleada, oleaje; *v.* agitarse, hinchar(se) (*el mar*); surgir.

sur·geon [sɝdʒən] *s.* cirujano.

sur·ger·y [sɝdʒərɪ] *s.* cirujía.

sur·gi·cal [sɝdʒɪkl] *adj.* quirúrgico.

sur·ly [sɝlɪ] *adj.* rudo, hosco, malhumorado.

sur·mise [səʳmáɪz] *v.* conjeturar, suponer, presumir; *s.* conjetura, suposición.

sur·mount [səʳmáʊnt] *v.* superar, vencer; coronar.

sur·name [sɝnem] *s.* sobrenombre, apellido; *v.* apellidar, llamar.

sur·pass [səʳpǽs] *v.* sobrepasar, superar, sobrepujar, exceder, aventajar.

sur·pass·ing [səʳpǽsɪŋ] *adj.* sobresaliente, excelente.

sur·plus [sɝplʌs] *s.* sobra, sobrante, exceso, excedente; superávit; *adj.* sobrante, excedente, de sobra.

sur·prise [səʳpráɪz] *s.* sorpresa; *v.* sorprender.

sur·pris·ing [səʳpráɪzɪŋ] *adj.* sorprendente.

sur·ren·der [səréndəʳ] *v.* rendir(se), entregar(se), darse; ceder; *s.* rendición; entrega; cesión; sumisión.

sur·round [səráʊnd] *v.* rodear, cercar, circundar.

sur·round·ing [səráʊndɪŋ] *adj.* circundante, circunvecino, circunstante.

sur·round·ings [səráʊndɪŋz] *s. pl.* alrededores, inmediaciones, cercanías; ambiente.

sur·vey [sɝve] *s.* (*inspection*) examen, reconocimiento, enspección, estudio; (*measure*) medición agrimensura (*de un terreno*); plano (*de un terreno*); bosquejo o esbozo general (*de historia, literatura, etc.*); **— course** curso general o comprensivo; [səʳvé] *v.* examinar, inspeccionar, reconocer medir (*un terreno*), levantar un plano (*el agrimensor*).

sur·vey·or [səʳvéəʳ] *s.* agrimensor.

sur·viv·al [səʳváɪvl] *s.* supervivencia; sobreviviente; resto.

sur·vive [səʳváɪv] *c.* sobrevivir; quedar vivo, salvarse.

sur·vi·vor [səʳváɪvəʳ] *s.* sobreviviente.

sus·cep·ti·ble [səséptəbl] *adj.* susceptible; **— of proof** capaz de probarse; **— to** propenso a.

sus·pect [sʌspɛkt] *s.* sospechoso; [səspɛkt] *v.*

sospechar.

sus·pend [səspénd] *v.* suspender.

sus·pend·ers [səspéndəʳz] *s.* tirantes (*de pantalón*).

sus·pense [səspéns] *s.* (*uncertainty*) suspensión, incertidumbre; (*anxiety*) ansiedad; **to keep in —** tener en suspenso, tener en duda.

sus·pen·sion [səspénʃən] *s.* suspensión; **— bridge** puente colgante.

sus·pi·cion [səspíʃən] *s.* sospecha.

sus·pi·cious [səspíʃəs] *adj.* sospechoso; suspicaz.

sus·tain [səstén] *v.* (*prolong*) sostener; mantener; (*support*) sustentar; (*bear, endure*) aguantar; (*defend*) apoyar, defender; (*undergo*) sufrir (*un daño o pérdida*).

sus·te·nance [sʌstənəns] *s.* sustento; subsistencia; alimentos; mantenimiento.

swab [swab] *s.* escobillón.

swag·ger [swǽgəʳ] *v.* pavonearse, contonearse; fanfarronear; *s.* pavoneo, contoneo; fanfarronada.

swain [swen] *s.* galán.

swal·low [swálo] *s.* golondrina; trago; *v.* tragar; deglutir.

swam [swæm] *pret. de* **to swim.**

swamp [swamp] *s.* pantano; ciénaga; **— land** cenagal, terreno pantanoso; *v.* inundar(se); sumergir(se); **to be -ed with work** estar abrumado de trabajo.

swamp·y [swámpɪ] *adj.* pantanoso, cenagoso, fangoso.

swan [swan] *s.* cisne.

swap [swap] *v.* cambalachear, cambiar, trocar; *s.* cambalache, cambio, trueque.

swarm [swɔrm] *s.* enjambre; *v.* pulular; bullir, hervir, hormiguear.

swarth·y [swɔrðɪ] *adj.* trigueño, moreno, *Am.* prieto.

swat [swat] *v.* pegar, aporrear; aplastar de un golpe (*una mosca*); *s.* golpe.

sway [swe] *v.* mecer(se); cimbrar(se); balancearse; ladear(se), oscilar; tambalear; influir; *s.* oscilación; vaivén; balanceo; influjo, predominio; mando; predominio.

swear [swɛr] *v.* jurar; renegar, blasfemar, echar maldiciones; juramentar, tomar juramento; **to — by** jurar por; poner toda su confianza en; **to — in** juramentar; **to — off smoking** jurar no fumar más, renunciar al tabaco.

sweat [swɛt] *v.* sudar; trasudar; hacer sudar; *s.* sudor; trasudor.

sweat·er [swétəʳ] *s.* suéter; sudador, el que suda.

sweat·y [swétɪ] *adj.* sudoroso.

Swede [swid] *s.* sueco.

Swed·ish [swidɪʃ] *adj.* sueco; *s.* sueco, idioma sueco.

sweep [swip] *v.* barrer; dragar (*puertos, ríos, etc.*); extenderse; **to — down upon** caer sobre; asolar; **to — everything away** barrer con todo; **she swept into the room** entró garbosamente en la sala; *s.* barrida; extensión; soplo (*del viento*).

sweep·er [swípəʳ] *s.* barrendero; **carpet —** escoba mecánica.

sweep·ing [swípɪŋ] *s.* barrido; **-s** basura; *adj.* abarcador, que lo abarca todo, vasto; asolador; **— victory** victoria completa.

sweet [swit] *adj.* dulce; oloroso; fresco; **— butter** mantequilla sin sal; **— corn** maíz tierno; **— milk** leche fresca; **— pea** guisante de olor; **— potato** batata, *Mex. C.A.* camote, *Carib.* boniato; **to have a — tooth** ser goloso, gustarle a uno los

SU

dulces; *s.* dulce, golosina; **my** — mi vida, mi alma.

sweet·en [swítŋ] *v.* endulzar(se), dulcificar(se); suavizar.

sweet·heart [swíthɑrt] *s.* querida, novia, prometida; amante, querido, galán, novio.

sweet·meat [swítmit] *s.* confite, confitura dulce, golosina.

sweet·ness [swítnɪs] *s.* dulzura; melosidad; suavidad.

swell [swɛl] *v.* hinchar(se), henchir(se), inflar(se); dilatar(se), abultar(se); acrecentar;.*s.* hinchazón; protuberancia; oleaje; *adj.* elegante; muy bueno, excelente, magnífico; **to have a — head** creerse gran cosa; ser vanidoso.

swel·ling [swélɪŋ] *s.* hinchazón; chichón, bulto; protuberancia.

swel·ter [swéltə] *v.* sofocarse de calor.

swept [swɛpt] *pret. & p.p. de* **to sweep.**

swerve [swɝv] *v.* desviar(se); torcer; cambiar repentinamente de rumbo; *s.* desvío brusco, cambio repentino de dirección; **to make a — to the right** torcer a la derecha.

swift [swɪft] *adj.* veloz, rápido.

swift·ness [swíftnɪs] *s.* velocidad, rapidez, presteza, prontitud.

swim [swɪm] *v.* nadar; flotar; **to — across** pasar a nado, atravesar nadando; **my head is swimming** tengo vértigo, se me va la cabeza, estoy desvanecido; *s.* nadada; **— suit** traje de baño o natación.

swim·mer [swímə] *s.* nadador.

swin·dle [swíndl] *v.* estafar; *s.* estafa.

swine [swaɪn] *s.* marrano, puerco, cerdo, cochino; marranos, puercos, cerdos.

swing [swɪŋ] *v.* columpiar(se), mecer(se), balancear(se); oscilar; hacer oscilar; blandir (*un bastón, espada, etc.*); colgar; girar; hacer girar; **to — a deal** llevar a cabo un negocio; **to — around** dar vuelta, girar; **to — one's arms** girar o menear los brazos; **to — open** abrirse de pronto (*una puerta*); *s.* columpio; hamaca; balanceo; vaivén; compás, ritmo; golpe, guantada, puñetazo; **— door** puerta giratoria; **— shift** turno de trabajo desde las dieciséis hasta medianoche; **in full** — en su apogeo, en pleno movimiento; **to give someone full** — darle a alguien completa libertad de acción.

swipe [swaɪp] *v.* hurtar, sisar.

swirl [swɝl] *v.* arremolinarse; girar, dar vueltas; *s.* remolino; torbellino; vuelta, movimiento giratorio.

Swiss [swɪs] *adj. & s.* suizo.

switch [swɪtʃ] *s.* (*change*) mudanza; (*whip*) látigo, (*blow*) azote; *Méx., Andes* chicote, *Riopl.* rebenque; *Méx., Andes* fuete; latigazo; pelo postizo; cambio; **electric** — interruptor, conmutador; **railway—** aguja, cambio; **—man** guardagujas, *Andes, Riopl.* cambiavía; *Méx.* guardavía; *v.* azotar; desviar(se); cambiar(se); **to — off** cortar (*la comunicación o la corriente eléctrica*); apagar (*la luz eléctrica*); **to — on the** encender la luz.

switch·board [swítʃbɔrd] *s.* cuadro o tablero de distribución; cuadro conmutador.

swiv·el [swívl] *adj.* giratorio.

swol·len [swólən] *p.p. de* **to swell.**

swoon [swun] *v.* desvanecerse, desmayarse; *s.* desmayo.

swoop [swup] *v.* **to — down upon** caer de súbito sobre; abalanzarse sobre; acometer; **to —**

off cortar de un golpe; **to — up** agarrar, arrebatar; *s.* descenso súbito; arremetida; **at one** — de un golpe.

sword [sord] *s.* espada; **— belt** talabarte.

swore [swor] *pret. de* **to swear.**

sworn [sworn] *p.p. de* **to swear.**

swum [swʌm] *p.p. de* **to swim.**

swung [swʌŋ] *pret. & p.p. de* **to swing.**

syl·lab·i·cate [sɪlǽbəket] *v.* silabear.

syl·la·ble [síləbl] *s.* sílaba.

syl·la·bus [síləbəs] *s.* sílabo.

syl·lo·gism [sílədʒɪzəm] *s.* silogismo.

sym·bol [símbl] *s.* símbolo.

sym·bol·ic [sɪmbálɪk] *adj.* simbólico.

sym·bol·ism [símblɪzəm] *s.* simbolismo.

sym·met·ri·cal [sɪmétrɪkl] *adj.* simétrico.

sym·me·try [símɪtrɪ] *s.* simetría.

sym·pa·thet·ic [sɪmpəθ̇étɪk] *adj.* compasivo; favorablemente dispuesto; que compadece; — **towards** favorablemente dispuesto a (*o* hacia).

sym·pa·thize [símpəθaɪz] *v.* compadecer(se); condolerse.

sym·pa·thy [símpəθɪ] *s.* compasión, lástima; armonía; **to extend one's** — dar el pésame.

sym·pho·ny [símfənɪ] *s.* sinfonía; — **orchestra** orquesta sinfónica.

sym·po·si·um [sɪmpósɪəm] *s.* coloquio; simposio.

symp·tom [símptəm] *s.* síntoma.

syn·a·gogue [sínəgag] *s.* sinagoga.

syn·chro·nize [sínkənaɪz] *v.* sincronizar.

syn·di·cate [síndɪkət] *s.* sindicato; **newspaper** — sindicato periodístico; [síndɪket] *v.* sindicar, formar un sindicato; sindicarse, combinarse para formar un sindicato; vender (*un cuento, caricatura, serie de artículos, etc.*) a un sindicato.

syn·drome [síndrom] *s.* síndrome.

syn·o·nym [sínənɪm] *s.* sinónimo.

syn·on·y·mous [sɪnánəməs] *adj.* sinónimo.

syn·op·sis [sɪnápsɪs] *s.* sinopsis.

syn·tax [síntæks] *s.* sintaxis.

syn·the·sis [sínθəsɪs] *s.* síntesis.

syn·the·size [sínθəsaɪz] *v.* sintetizar.

syn·thet·ic [sɪnθétɪk] *adj.* sintético.

syr·inge [sírɪndʒ] *s.* jeringa.

syr·up = **sirup.**

sys·tem [sístəm] *s.* sistema.

sys·tem·at·ic [sɪstəmǽtɪk] *adj.* sistemático

sys·tem·ic [sɪstémɪk] *adj.* sistemático.

T:t

tab [tæb] *s.* (*flap*) lengüeta; (*bill*) cuenta.

tab·er·na·cle [tǽbənækl] *s.* tabernáculo.

ta·ble [tébl] *s.* mesa; tabla (*de materias, de multiplicar, etc.*); — **cover** tapete, cubremesa; **—land** mesa, meseta; *v.* poner sobre la mesa; formar tabla o índice; **to — a motion** dar carpetazo a una moción, aplazar la discusión de una moción.

ta·ble·cloth [téblklɔθ] *s.* mantel.

ta·ble·spoon [téblspun] *s.* cuchara grande.

ta·ble·spoon·ful [téblspunful] *s.* cucharada.

tab·let [tǽblɪt] *s.* tableta; tablilla, pastilla; comprimido; bloc de papel; lápida, placa.

ta·ble·ware [téblwɛr] *s.* vajilla, servicio de mesa.

ta·boo [tæbú] *s.* tabú.

tab·u·late [tǽbjəlet] *v.* formar tablas o listas.

tac·it [tǽsɪt] *adj.* tácito.
tac·i·turn [tǽsətɜ̃n] *adj.* taciturno, silencioso.
tack [tæk] *s.* tachuela; hilván; virada o cambio de rumbo (*de una embarcación*); amura, jarcia (*para sostener el ángulo de una vela*); **to change —** cambiar de amura, cambiar de rumbo; *v.* clavetear con tachuelas; coser, hilvanar; pegar, clavar; juntar, unir; virar, cambiar de rumbo; zigzaguear (*un barco de vela*).
tack·le [tǽkl] *s.* aparejo, equipo, enseres, avíos; agarrada (*en fútbol*); atajador (*en fútbol*); **fishing —** avíos de pescar; *v.* agarrar, asir, atajar (*en futbol*); atacar (*un problema*); acometer (*una empresa*).
tact [tækt] *s.* tacto, tino, tiento.
tact·ful [tǽktfəl] *adj.* cauto, prudente, diplomático.
tac·tics [tǽktɪks] *s.* táctica.
tact·less [tǽktlɪs] *adj.* falto de tacto o de tino; imprudente, incauto.
taf·fe·ta [tǽfɪtə] *s.* tafetán.
tag [tæg] *s.* (*label*) marbete, etiqueta; cartela; (*loose end*) pingajo, rabito, cabo; **to play —** jugar al tócame tú, jugar a la pega; *v.* pegar un marbete a, marcar; **to — after** seguir de cerca a, pisar los talones a; **to — something on** to juntar, añadir o agregar algo a.
tail [tel] *s.* (*animal*) cola, rabo; (*object*) cabo, extremo, extremidad; **— light** farol trasero, farol de cola; **— spin** barrena.
tai·lor [télə] *s.* sastre; **— shop** sastrería.
taint [tent] *s.* tacha, mancha; corrupción; *v.* manchar; corromper(se), inficionar(se).
take [tek] *v.* tomar; coger; llevar; conducir; dar (*un paseo, vuelta, paso, salto*); hacer (*un viaje*); asumir; sacar o tomar (*una fotografía*); **to — a chance** aventurarse, correr un riesgo; **to — a fancy to** caerle en gracia a uno; aficionarse a; antojársele a uno; **to — a look at** mirar a, echar una mirada a; **to — a notion to** antojársele a uno; **to — after** salir a, parecerse a; seguir el ejemplo de; **to — amiss** interpretar mal, echar a mala parte; **to — an oath** prestar juramento; **to — apart** desarmar, desmontar; **to — away** llevarse; **to — back one's words** desdecirse, retractarse; **to — back to** devolver (*algo*) a; **to — by surprise** coger desprevenido, coger de sorpresa; **to — care of** cuidar de, atender a; **to — charge of** encargarse de; **to — cold** resfriarse, acatarrarse; **to — down in writing** poner por escrito, apuntar; **to — effect** surtir efecto, dar resultado; entrar en vigencia (*una ley*); **to — exercise** hacer ejercicio; hacer gimnasia; **to — from** quitar a; sustraer de, restar de; **to — in** meter en; recibir; abarcar; embaucar; reducir, achicar (*un vestido*); **to — leave** decir adiós, despedirse; **to — off** quitar; descontar, rebajar; despegar (*un aeroplano*); remedar, parodiar (*a alguien*); **to — offense** ofenderse, darse por ofendido; **to — on a responsibility** asumir una responsabilidad; **to — out** sacar; **to — place** tener lugar, suceder, ocurrir; **to — stock** hacer inventario; **to — stock in** creer, tener confianza en; **to — the floor** tomar la palabra; **to — heart** tomar a pechos, tomar en serio; **to — to** one's heels poner pies en polvorosa; **to — to task** reprender, regañar; **to — up a matter** tratar un asunto; **to — up space** ocupar espacio; **I — it that** supongo que; *s.* toma; **take-off** despegue (*de un aeroplano*); remedo, parodia.
tak·en [tékən] *p.p. de* **to take; to be — ill** caer enfermo.

tal·cum [tǽlkəm] *s.* talco; **— powder** talco en polvo.
tale [tel] *s.* (*story*) cuento, relato, fábula; (*gossip*) chisme; **to tell -s** contar cuentos o chismes; chismear, murmurar.
tale·bear·er [télbɛrə] *s.* soplón, chismoso.
tal·ent [tǽlənt] *s.* talento.
tal·ent·ed [tǽləntɪd] *adj.* talentoso.
talk [tɔk] *v.* hablar; charlar, platicar, conversar; **to — into** inducir o persuadir a; **to — nonsense** decir tonterías, hablar disparates; **to — out of** disuadir de; **to — over** discutir; **to — up** alabar; hablar claro o recio, hablar en voz alta; *s.* charla, conversación, plática; habla; discurso; conferencia; rumor; **— of the town** comidilla, tema de murmuración.
talk·a·tive [tɔ́kətɪv] *adj.* hablador, locuaz, platicador.
talk·er [tɔ́kə] *s.* hablador; conversador; platicador; orador.
tall [tɔl] *adj.* alto; **— tale** cuento exagerado o increíble; **six feet —** seis pies de altura o de alto.
tal·low [tǽlo] *s.* sebo.
tal·low·y [tǽlowɪ] *adj.* seboso.
tal·ly [tǽlɪ] *s.* cuenta; **— sheet** plana para llevar la cuenta; *v.* llevar la cuenta; **to — up** contar, sumar; **to — with** coresponder con, concordar con.
tam·a·rind [tǽmərɪnd] *s.* tamarindo.
tame [tem] *adj.* manso; dócil; **— amusement** diversión poco animada o desabrida; *v.* amansar, domar, domeñar; domesticar; desbravar.
tam·per [tǽmpə] *v.* **to — with** meterse con, juguetear con; falsificar (*un documento*); **to — with a lock** tratar de forzar una cerradura.
tan [tæn] *v.* (*cure*) curtir, adobar (*pieles*); (*punish*) zurrar, azotar; (*sunburn*) tostar(se), requemar(se); *adj.* tostado, requemado; color de canela; bayo, amarillento; *s.* color moreno, de canela o café con leche.
tang [tæŋ] *s.* sabor u olor picante.
tangent [tǽndʒənt] *adj. & s.* tangente; **to go off at a —** salirse por la tangente.
tan·ger·ine [tǽndʒərin] *s.* naranja tangerina o mandarina.
tan·gi·ble [tǽndʒəbl] *adj.* tangible, palpable; corpóreo.
tan·gle [tǽŋgl] *v.* enredar(se), enmarañar(se); confundir(se), embrollar(se); *s.* enredo, maraña, embrollo; confusión.
tank [tæŋk] *s.* tanque; depósito; **swimming —** piscina.
tan·ner [tǽnə] *s.* curtidor.
tan·ner·y [tǽnərɪ] *s.* curtiduría, tenería.
tan·nic ac·id [tǽnɪkǽsəd] *s.* ácido tánico.
tan·ta·lize [tǽntlaɪz] *v.* molestar; hacer desesperar; exasperar.
tan·ta·lum [tǽntələm] *s.* tantalio.
tan·ta·mount [tǽntəmaʊnt] *adj.* equivalente.
tan·trum [tǽntrəm] *s.* berrinche.
tap [tæp] *s.* (*blow*) palmadita; golpecito; (*faucet*) espita, grifo, llave; **— dance** zapateado, *Andes, Ríopl.* zapateo; **—room** bar; **beer on —** cerveza del barril, cerveza de sifón; *v.* tocar, golpear ligeramente; dar una palmadita o golpecito; taladrar; extraer; **to — a tree** sangrar un árbol.
tape [tep] *s.* cinta, cintilla; **— measure** cinta para medir; **— recorder** magnetófono; grabadora; **adhesive —** tela adhesiva, esparadrapo; *v.* atar o vendar con cinta; medir con cinta.
ta·per [tépə] *s.* (*candle*) velita, candela; (*diminished*

SW

size) adelgazamiento paulatino; *v.* adelgazar, disminuir gradualmente; **to — off** ahusar(se), ir disminuyendo (*hasta rematar en punta*).

tap·es·try [tǽpɪstrɪ] *s.* tapiz, colgadura; tapicería; tela (*para forrar muebles*).

tape·worm [tépwɚm] *s.* tenia, solitaria.

tap·i·o·ca [tæpɪókǝ] *s.* tapioca.

tar [tɑr] *s.* alquitrán, brea, pez (*f.*); *Am.* chapapote; *v.* alquitranar, embrear, poner brea o alquitrán.

tar·dy [tɑ́rdɪ] *adj.* tardo, tardío; **to be — llegar** tarde o retrasado.

tar·get [tɑ́rgɪt] *s.* blanco; — **practice** tiro al blanco.

tar·iff [tǽrɪf] *s.* tarifa; arancel, impuesto.

tar·nish [tɑ́rnɪʃ] *v.* empañar(se); manchar; perder el lustre; *s.* deslustre, falta de lustre, empañamiento; mancha.

tar·ry [tǽrɪ] *v.* demorarse, tardar(se).

tart [tɑrt] *adj.* acre, agridulce; agrio; picante; — **reply** respuesta mordaz o agria; *s.* tarta, torta rellena con dulce de frutas.

tar·tar [tɑ́rtɚ] *s.* tártaro.

task [tæsk] *s.* faena, tarea, quehacer; **to take to —** reprender, regañar.

task force [tǽskfɔrs] *s.* agrupación de fuerzas militares para cierta misión.

tas·sel [tǽsl] *s.* borla.

taste [test] *v.* gustar; probar; saborear, paladear; **to — of onion** saber a cebolla; **it -s sour** sabe agrio, tiene un sabor o gusto agrio; *s.* gusto; sabor; prueba; afición; **after—** dejo; **in good —** de buen gusto; **to take a — of** probar.

taste·less [téstlɪs] *adj.* insípido; desabrido; de mal gusto.

tast·y [téstɪ] *adj.* sabroso, gustoso; de buen gusto.

tat·ter [tǽtɚ] *s.* harapo, *Carib.* hilacho.

tat·ter·ed [tǽtɚd] *adj.* roto, harapiento, andrajoso.

tat·tle [tǽtl] *v.* chismear, murmurar; *s.* habladuría, murmuración, hablilla; —**tale** chismoso, soplón.

tat·too [tætú] *s.* tatuaje; *v.* tatuar.

taught [tɔt] *pret. & p.p. de* **to teach.**

taunt [tɔnt] *v.* mofarse de, echar pullas; reprochar; *s.* mofa, pulla.

tav·ern [tǽvɚn] *s.* taberna; posada.

tax [tæks] *s.* impuesto, contribución; esfuerzo; *v.* imponer contribuciones a; tasar; abrumar; reprender, reprobar; cobrar (*un precio*); **to — one's patience** abusar de la paciencia.

tax·a·tion [tækséʃǝn] *s.* impuestos, contribuciones; imposición de contribuciones.

tax·i [tǽksɪ] *s.* taxímetro, taxi, automóvil de alquiler; *v.* ir en taxímetro; taxear (*un aeroplano*).

tax·i·cab [tǽksɪkæb] = **taxi.**

tax·i·der·my [tǽksɪdɚmɪ] *s.* taxidermia.

tax·on·o·my [tæksánǝmɪ] *s.* taxonomía.

tax·pay·er [tǽkspeɚ] *s.* contribuyente.

tea [ti] *s.* té; **linden—** tila.

teach [titʃ] *v.* enseñar; instruir.

teach·er [títʃɚ] *s.* maestro, maestra.

teach·ing [títʃɪŋ] *s.* enseñanza; instrucción; doctrina.

tea·cup [tíkʌp] *s.* taza para té.

tea·ket·tle [tíkɛtl] *s.* marmita, tetera, *Ríopl.* pava (*para el mate*).

team [tim] *s.* equipo (*de jugadores*); partido, grupo; tronco (*de caballos, mulas, etc.*); yunta (*de bueyes*): — **work** cooperación; *v.* uncir, enganchar; formar pareja; acarrear, transportar; **to — up** unirse, formar un equipo.

team·ster [tímstɚ] *s.* carretero.

tea·pot [típɑt] *s.* tetera.

tear [tɪr] *s.* lágrima; — **gas** gas lacrimógeno o lacrimante; **to burst into -s** romper a llorar; deshacerse en lágrimas.

tear [ter] *v.* rasgar(se); desgarrar, romper; **to — along** a toda velocidad; andar aprisa, correr; **to — apart** desarmar, desmontar; separar, apartar; **to — away** arrancar; irse; **to — down** demoler, derribar (*un edificio*); desarmar, desmontar (*una máquina*); **to — off in a hurry** salir corriendo, salir a la carrera; **to — one's hair** mesarse los cabellos; *s.* desgarradura, rasgadura; rasgón, rotura; prisa; **wear and — desgaste.**

tear·ful [tírfǝl] *adj.* lloroso.

tease [tiz] *v.* embromar; molestar; importunar.

tea·spoon [tíspun] *s.* cucharilla, cucharita.

tea·spoon·ful [tíspunfUl] *s.* cucharadita.

teat [tit] *s.* teta.

tech·ne·ti·um [tɛkníʃǝm] *s.* tecnecio.

tech·ni·cal [téknɪkl] *adj.* técnico.

tech·ni·cian [tɛkníʃǝn] *s.* técnico.

tech·nique [tɛkník] *s.* técnica.

tech·nol·o·gy [tɛknálǝdʒɪ] *s.* tecnología.

te·di·ous [tídɪǝs] *adj.* tedioso, pesado, aburrido, fastidioso.

te·di·ous·ness [tídɪǝsnɪs] *s.* tedio.

teem [tim] *v.* **to — with** abundar en, estar lleno de.

teen-ag·er [tínedʒɚ] *s.* joven de le edad de 13 a 19 años; *Col.* cocacolo.

teens [tinz] *s. pl.* edad de trece a diecinueve años; números de trece a diecinueve; **to be in one's —** tener de trece a diecinueve años.

teeth [tiθ] *s. pl. de* **tooth; he escaped by the skin of his —** por poco no se escapa, se escapó por milagro.

tel·e·cast [télǝkæst] *s.* teledifusión.

tel·e·gram [télǝgræm] *s.* telegrama.

tel·e·graph [télǝgræf] *s.* telégrafo; *v.* telegrafiar.

tel·e·graph·ic [tɛlǝgrǽfɪk] *adj.* telegráfico.

te·leg·ra·phy [tǝlégrǝfɪ] *s.* telegrafía.

tel·e·pa·thy [tǝlépǝθɪ] *s.* telepatía.

tel·e·phone [télǝfon] *s.* teléfono; — **booth** casilla de teléfono; — **operator** telefonista; — **receiver** receptor telefónico; *v.* telefonear, llamar por teléfono.

tel·e·scope [télǝskop] *s.* telescopio; *v.* enchufar(se), encajar(se) un objeto en otro.

tel·e·vi·sion [télǝvɪʒǝn] *s.* televisión; — **viewer** televidente.

tell [tɛl] *v.* (*recount*) decir; contar; expresar; explicar; (*identify*) adivinar; **to — on someone** delatar a alguien, contar chismes de alguien; **to — someone off** decirle a alguien cuatro verdades; **his age is beginning to —** ya comienza a notársele la edad.

tell·er [télɚ] *s.* narrador, relator; pagador o recibidor (*de un banco*); escrutador de votos.

tel·lu·ri·um [tǝlúrɪǝm] *s.* telurio.

te·mer·i·ty [tǝmérǝtɪ] *s.* temeridad.

tem·per [tɛmpɚ] *v.* templar; *s.* temple (*de un metal*); genio, temple, humor; mal genio; **to keep one's —** contenerse, dominarse; **to lose one's —** perder la calma, encolerizarse.

tem·per·a·ment [témprǝmǝnt] *s.* temperamento; disposición; temple.

tem·per·ance [témprǝns] *s.* templanza, sobriedad.

tem·per·ate [témprɪt] *adj.* templado, moderado; sobrio.

tem·per·a·ture [témprǝtʃɚ] *s.* temperatura; **to have a —** tener calentura o fiebre.

tem·pest [témpɪst] *s.* tempestad.

tem·pes·tu·ous [tɛmpɛ́stʃʊəs] *adj.* tempestuoso. borrascoso.

tem·ple [tɛ́mpl] *s.* templo; sien.

tem·po·ral [tɛ́mpərəl] *adj.* temporal.

tem·po·rar·i·ly [tɛ́mpərərəlɪ] *adv.* temporalmente.

tem·po·rar·y [tɛ́mpərɛrɪ] *adj.* temporal, transitorio, provisorio; interino.

tempt [tɛmpt] *v.* tentar; incitar; provocar; atraer.

temp·ta·tion [tɛmptéʃən] *s.* tentación.

tempt·er [tɛ́mptəʳ] *s.* tentador.

tempt·ing [tɛ́mptɪŋ] *adj.* tentador, atractivo.

ten·a·ble [tɛ́nəbl] *adj.* defendible.

te·na·cious [tɪnéʃəs] *adj.* tenaz, aferrado.

te·nac·i·ty [tɪnǽsətɪ] *s.* tenacidad; aferramiento; tesón.

ten·ant [tɛ́nənt] *s.* inquilino, arrendatario.

tend [tɛnd] *v.* cuidar, vigilar, guardar; atender; tender, inclinarse.

ten·den·cy [tɛ́ndənsɪ] *s.* tendencia; propensión.

ten·der [tɛ́ndəʳ] *adj.* tierno; delicado; sensible; **tender-hearted** de corazón tierno; *s.* oferta, ofrecimiento; ténder *(de un tren)*; lancha *(de auxilio)*; cuidador, vigilante; **legal** — moneda corriente; *v.* ofrecer.

ten·der·loin [tɛ́ndəʳlɔɪn] *s.* filete.

ten·der·ness [tɛ́ndəʳnɪs] *s.* ternura, terneza; delicadeza.

ten·don [tɛ́ndən] *s.* tendón.

ten·dril [tɛ́ndrɪl] *s.* zarcillo *(tallito de una planta trepadora)*.

ten·e·ment [tɛ́nəmənt] *s.* casa de vecindad.

ten·nis [tɛ́nɪs] *s.* tenis; — **court** cancha de tenis.

ten·or [tɛ́nəʳ] *s.* tenor; significado; — **voice** voz de tenor.

tense [tɛns] *adj.* tenso; tirante; *s.* tiempo *(del verbo)*.

ten·sion [tɛ́nʃən] *s.* tensión; tirantez.

tent [tɛnt] *s.* tienda de campaña; pabellón; *v.* acampar.

ten·ta·cle [tɛ́ntəkl] *s.* tentáculo.

ten·ta·tive [tɛ́ntətɪv] *adj.* tentativo.

ten·u·ous [tɛ́njʊəs] *adj.* tenue.

ten·ure [tɛ́njʊr] *s.* tenencia.

tep·id [tɛ́pɪd] *adj.* tibio.

term [tɜm] *s.* término; período; plazo; sesión; **-s** términos, expresiones, palabras; condiciones; **to be on good -s** estar en buenas relaciones; **not to be on speaking -s** no hablarse, no dirigirse la palabra; **to come to -s** ajustarse, ponerse de acuerdo; *v.* nombrar, llamar, denominar.

ter·mi·na·ble [tɜ́mɪnəbl] *adj.* terminable.

ter·mi·nal [tɜ́mənl] *adj.* terminal, final, último; *s.* término, fin; estación terminal; **electric** — toma de corriente; borne *(de aparato eléctrico)*.

ter·mi·nate [tɜ́mənet] *v.* terminar, acabar.

ter·mi·na·tion [tɜmənéʃən] *s.* terminación, fin; desinencia *(gramatical)*.

ter·mite [tɜ́maɪt] *s.* termita.

ter·race [tɛ́rɪs] *s.* terraplén; terraza, terrado; *v.* terraplenar.

ter·res·tri·al [tərɛ́strɪəl] *adj.* terrestre, terreno, terrenal.

ter·ri·ble [tɛ́rəbl] *adj.* terrible; **terribly** *adv.* terriblemente.

ter·ri·er [tɛ́rɪəʳ] *s.* perro de busca.

ter·ri·fic [tərɪ́fɪk] *adj.* terrífico.

ter·ri·fy [tɛ́rəfaɪ] *v.* aterrar, aterrorizar.

ter·ri·to·ry [tɛ́rətorɪ] *s.* territorio.

ter·ror [tɛ́rəʳ] *s.* terror, espanto.

ter·ror·ist [tɛ́rərɪst] *s.* terrorista.

test [tɛst] *s.* prueba, ensayo, experimento; comprobación; examen; — **tube** probeta, tubo

de ensayo; **to undergo a** — sufrir una prueba; *v.* probar, ensayar, comprobar, experimentar; poner a prueba; examinar.

tes·ta·ment [tɛ́stəmənt] *s.* testamento.

tes·ti·cle [tɛ́stɪkl] *s.* testículo.

tes·ti·fy [tɛ́stəfaɪ] *v.* atestiguar, atestar.

tes·ti·mo·ny [tɛ́stəmonɪ] *s.* testimonio.

tet·a·nus [tɛ́tənəs] *s.* tétanos.

Teu·ton·ic [tutánɪk] *adj.* teutónico.

text [tɛkst] *s.* texto.

text·book [tɛ́kstbʊk] *s.* texto, libro de texto.

tex·tile [tɛ́kstl] *adj.* textil; de tejidos; — **mill** fábrica de tejidos; *s.* tejido, materia textil.

tex·ture [tɛ́kstʃəʳ] *s.* textura, contextura; tejido.

thal·li·um [θǽlɪəm] *s.* talio.

than [ðæn] *conj.* que; **more** — **once** más de una vez; **more** — **he knows** más de lo que él sabe.

thank [θæŋk] *v.* dar gracias, agradecer; — **heaven!** ¡gracias a Dios!; — **you** gracias; **to have oneself to** — **for** tener la culpa de; ser responsable de; **-s** *s. pl.* gracias.

thank·ful [θǽŋkfəl] *adj.* agradecido; **-ly** *adv.* agradecidamente, con agradecimiento, con gratitud.

thank·ful·ness [θǽŋkfəlnɪs] *s.* gratitud, agradecimiento.

thank·less [θǽŋklɪs] *adj.* ingrato; — **task** tarea ingrata o infructuosa.

thanks·giv·ing [θæŋksgɪ́vɪŋ] *s.* acción de gracias; — **Day** día de acción de gracias.

that [ðæt] *adj.* ese, esa, aquel, aquella; — **one** ése, ésa, aquél, aquélla; *pron.* ése, eso, aquél, aquélla, aquello; *pron. rel.* que; — **is** es decir; — **of** el de, la de, lo de; — **which** el que, la que, lo que; *conj.* que; para que, a fin de que; **so** — para que; de modo que, a fin de que, de suerte que, de tal manera que; *adv.* tan; — **far** tan lejos; hasta allí; hasta allí; — **long** asi de largo; de este tamaño; tanto tiempo.

thatch [θætʃ] *s.* paja *(para techar)*; *v.* techar con paja; **-ed roof** techumbre o techo de paja.

thaw [θɔ] *v.* deshelar(se), derretir(se); volverse más tratable o amistoso; *s.* deshielo, derretimiento.

the [*delante de consonante* ðə; *delante de vocal* ðɪ] *art.* el, la; lo; los, las; *adv.* — **more** ... — **less** cuanto más ... tanto menos; mientras más ... tanto menos.

the·a·ter [θíətəʳ] *s.* teatro.

the·at·ri·cal [θɪǽtrɪkl] *adj.* teatral.

thee [ðɪ] *pron.* te.

theft [θɛft] *s.* hurto, robo.

their [ðɛr] *adj.* su (sus), de ellos, de ellas.

theirs [ðɛrz] *pron.* suyo (suya, suyos, suyas), de ellos o de ellas; el suyo (la suya, los suyos, las suyas); el (la, los, las) de ellos; **a friend of** — un amigo suyo, un amigo de ellos.

them [ðɛm] *pron.* los, las, les; ellos, ellas *(con preposición)*.

the·mat·ic [θimǽtɪk] *adj.* temático.

theme [θim] *s.* tema; ensayo; — **song** tema central.

them·selves [ðəmsɛ́lvz] *pron.* ellos mismos, ellas mismas; se *(como reflexivo)*; **to** — a si mismos; *véase* **herself.**

then [ðɛn] *adv.* entonces; en aquel tiempo; en aquella ocasión; después, luego, en seguida; *conj.* pues, en tal caso; **now** — ahora bien; **now and** — de vez en cuando, de cuando en cuando; **now** ... — ora ... ora; ya ... ya; **well** — conque, pues entonces; ahora bien.

thence [ðɛns] *adv.* desde allí, de allí; desde entonces, desde aquel tiempo; por seo, por esa razón;

TA

—**forth** de allí en adelante, desde entonces.
the·o·log·i·cal [θiəládʒɪkl] *adj.* teológico; teologal.
the·ol·o·gy [θiálədʒɪ] *s.* teología.
the·o·ret·i·cal [θiərétɪkl] *adj.* teórico.
the·o·ry [θíərɪ] *s.* teoría.
ther·a·peu·tic [θɛrəpjútɪk] *adj.* terapéutico.
ther·a·py [θérəpɪ] *s.* terapia.
there [ðɛr] *adv.* allí, allá, ahí; — **is**, — **are** hay; — followed an argument siguió una disputa.
there·a·bouts [ðɛrəbáʊts] *adv.* por allí, por ahí; aproximadamente.
there·af·ter [ðɛrǽftɚ] *adv.* después de eso, de allí en adelante.
there·by [ðɛrbáɪ] *adv.* en relación con eso; así, de ese modo; por allí cerca.
there·fore [ðɛrfor] *adv.* por eso, por consiguiente, por lo tanto.
there·in [ðɛrín] *adv.* en eso, en ello; allí dentro.
there·of [ðɛráv] *adv.* de eso, de ello.
there·on [ðɛrán] *adv.* encima; encima de (*o* sobre) él, ella, ello, etc.
there·up·on [ðɛrəpán] *adv.* luego, después, en eso, en esto; por consiguiente, por eso, por lo tanto; encima de (*o* sobre) él, ella, ello, etc.
there·with [ðɛrwíθ] *adv.* con eso, con ello, con esto; luego, en seguida.
ther·mal [θɚml] *adj.* termal.
ther·mom·e·ter [θɚmámətɚ] *s.* termómetro.
ther·mo·nu·cle·ar [θɚmonúkljɚ] *adj.* termonuclear.
ther·mos [θɚməs] (*marca de fábrica*): — **bottle** termos.
ther·mo·stat [θɚməstæt] *s.* termóstato.
these [ðiz] *adj.* estos, estas; *pron.* éstos, éstas.
the·sis [θísɪs] *s.* tesis.
they [ðe] *pron.* ellos, ellas.
thick [θɪk] *adj.* (*not thin*) espeso; grueso; (*dense*) denso; tupido; (*slow*) torpe, estúpido; — **voice** voz ronca; **one inch** — una pulgada de espesor; *adv. véase* **thickly**; **thick-headed** cabezudo. testarudo; estúpido; **thick-set** grueso, rechoncho; **thick-skinned** insensible; que no se avergüenza fácilmente; *s.* espesor; densidad, lo más denso; **the** — **of the crowd** lo más denso de la muchedumbre; **the** — **of the fight** lo más reñido del combate; **through** — **and thin** por toda suerte de penalidades.
thick·en [θíkən] *v.* espesar(se); engrosar; **the plot -s** se complica el enredo.
thick·et [θíkɪt] *s.* espesura, maleza, matorral, *Am.* manigua.
thick·ly [θíklɪ] *adv.* espesamente; densamente.
thick·ness [θíknɪs] *s.* espesor; espesura, grueso, grosor; densidad.
thief [θif] *s.* ladrón.
thieve [θiv] *v.* hurtar, robar.
thieves [θivz] *pl. de* **thief.**
thigh [θaɪ] *s.* muslo.
thim·ble [θímbl] *s.* dedal.
thin [θɪn] *adj.* (*slim*) delgado; flaco; (*sparse*) ralo; escaso; (*fine*) tenue, fino; transparente; (*weak*) débil; aguado; — **broth** caldo aguado; — **hair** pelo ralo; *v.* adelgazar(se); enflaquecer; aguar (*el caldo*); **to** — **out** ralear (*el pelo*); ralear o aclarar (*un bosque*).
thine [ðaɪn] *pron. pos.* tuyo (tuya, tuyos, tuyas); el tuyo (la tuya, los tuyos, las tuyas); *adj.* tu, tus.
thing [θɪŋ] *s.* cosa; **no such** — nada de eso; **that is the** — **to do** eso es lo que debe hacerse; eso es lo debido.
think [θɪŋk] *v.* (*cerebrate*) pensar; (*believe*) creer, juzgar; opinar; **to** — **it over** pensarlo; **to** — **of**

pensar en; pensar de; **to** — **up an excuse** urdir una excusa; **to** — **well of** tener buena opinión de; — **nothing of it** no haga Vd. caso de ello, no le dé Vd. importancia; **what do you** — **of her?** ¿qué piensa Vd. de ella?; **to my way of -ing** a mi modo de ver.
think·er [θíŋkɚ] *s.* pensador.
thin·ly [θínlɪ] *adv.* delgadamente; escasamente.
thin·ness [θínnɪs] *s.* delgadez; flacura; raleza (*del cabello*); enrarecimiento (*del aire*).
third [θɚd] *adj.* tercero; *s.* tercio, tercera parte.
thirst [θɚst] *s.* sed; anhelo, ansia; *v.* tener sed; **to** — **for** tener sed de; anhelar, ansiar.
thirst·y [θɚstɪ] *adj.* sediento; **to be** — tener sed.
this [ðɪs] *adj.* este, esta; *pron.* éste, esto.
this·tle [θísl] *s.* abrojo; cardo.
thith·er [θíðɚ] *adv.* allá, hacia allá, para allá.
tho [ðo] = **though**.
thong [θɔŋ] *s.* correa, tira de cuero, *Am.* guasca.
tho·rax [θóræks] *s.* tórax.
thorn [θɔrn] *s.* espina, púa; espino; abrojo.
thorn·y [θɔrnɪ] *adj.* espinoso; arduo, difícil.
thor·ough [θɚo] *adj.* (*finished*) completo, entero, cabal, cumplido, acabado; (*careful*) esmerado.
thor·ough·bred [θɚobrɛd] *adj.* de casta pura, de raza pura; bien nacido; *s.* animal o persona de casta; caballo de casta.
thor·ough·fare [θɚofɛr] *s.* vía pública, carretera, camino real; pasaje.
thor·ough·ly [θɚolɪ] *adj.* completamente, enteramente, cabalmente; a fondo.
those [ðoz] *adj.* esos, esas, aquellos, aquellas; *pron.* ésos, ésas, aquéllos, aquéllas; — **of** los de, las de; — **which** los que, las que; aquellos que; — **who** los que, las que, quienes.
thou [ðaʊ] *pron.* tú.
though [ðo] *conj.* aunque, si bien, bien que; aun cuando; sin embargo; **as** — como si.
thought [θɔt] *s.* (*cogitation*) pensamiento; (*idea*) idea, intención; reflexión, meditación; (*concern*) consideración; cuidado; **to be lost in** — estar abstraído; **to give it no** — no pensar en ello, no darle importancia, no hacerle caso; *pret. & p.p. de* **to think**.
thought·ful [θɔtfəl] *adj.* pensativo; considerado; atento, solícito, cuidadoso; **to be** — **of others** pensar en los demás, tener consideración o solicitud por los demás; **-ly** *adv.* con reflexión; consideradamente, con consideración o solicitud.
thought·ful·ness [θɔtfəlnɪs] *s.* consideración, atención, cuidado, solicitud.
thought·less [θɔtlɪs] *adj.* inconsiderado; descuidado; irreflexivo, atolondrado; **-ly** *adv.* inconsideradamente, sin consideración; sin reflexión; sin pensar; descuidadamente, irreflexivamente, atolondradamente.
thought·less·ness [θɔtlɪsnɪs] *s.* irreflexión, inadvertencia, descuido; atolondramiento.
thrash [θræʃ] *v.* trillar, desgranar (*las mieses*); zurrar, azotar; **to** — **around** revolcarse, agitarse, menearse; **to** — **out a matter** ventilar un asunto.
thread [θrɛd] *s.* hilo; hebra, fibra; **screw** — rosca de tornillo; *v.* ensartar, enhebrar; **to** — **a screw** roscar un tornillo; **to** — **one's way through a crowd** colarse por entre la muchedumbre.
thread·bare [θrɛdbɛr] *adj.* raído, gastado.
threat [θrɛt] *s.* amenaza; amago.
threat·en [θrɛtn] *v.* amenazar; amagar.
threat·en·ing [θrɛtnɪŋ] *adj.* amenazante, amenazador.

thresh [θrɛ] *véase* **thrash.**
thresh·old [θrɛ́ʃold] *s.* umbral, entrada.
threw [θru] *pret. de* **to throw.**
thrice [θraɪs] *adv.* tres veces.
thrift [θrɪft] *s.* economía, frugalidad.
thrift·y [θrɪ́ftɪ] *adj.* económico, frugal; próspero.
thrill [θrɪl] *v.* emocionar(se), conmover(se); estremecerse de emoción, sobreexcitarse; *s.* emoción viva, estremecimiento emotivo, sobreexcitación.
thrive [θraɪv] *v.* medrar, prosperar; florecer.
thriv·en [θrɪ́vən] *p.p. de* **to thrive.**
throat [θrot] *s.* garganta.
throb [θrɑb] *v.* latir, pulsar, palpitar; *s.* latido, palpitación.
throe [θro] *s.* agonía; congoja.
throne [θron] *s.* trono.
throng [θrɔŋ] *s.* muchedumbre, multitud, tropel, gentío; *v.* agolparse, apiñarse; atestar.
throt·tle [θrɑ́tl̩] *s.* válvula reguladora, obturador, regulador; — **lever** palanca del obturador o regulador; *v.* ahogar; estrangular; **to — down** disminuir o reducir la velocidad.
through [θru] *prep.* por; a través de; por medio de; por conducto de; por entre; *adv.* de un lado a otro; de parte a parte, a través; de cabo a baco; desde el principio hasta el fin; completamente, enteramente; **loyal — and —** leal a toda prueba; **to be wet —** estar empapado; estar mojado hasta los tuétanos; **to carry a plan —** llevar a cabo un plan; *adj.* directo, continuo; — **ticket** billete (*Am.* boleto) directo; — **train** tren rápido, tren de servicio directo; **to be — with** haber acabado con; no querer ocuparse más de.
through·out [θruáʊt] *prep. (all through)* por todo; por todas partes de; (*during*) desde el principio; hasta el fin de; — **the year** durante todo el año; *adv.* por todas partes; en todas partes; en todo, en todos respetos; desde el principio hasta el fin.
throve [θrov] *pret. de* **to thrive.**
throw [θro] *v.* tirar, arrojar, lanzar; echar; **to — away** tirar, arrojar; malgastar; **to — down** arrojar, echar por tierra, derribar; **to — in gear** engranar; **to — in the clutch** embragar; **to — off a burden** librarse o deshacerse de una carga; **to — out** echar fuera; expeler; **to — out of gear** desengranar; **to — out of work** privar de trabajo, quitar el empleo a; **to — out the clutch** desembragar; **to — overboard** echar al agua; **to — up** vomitar; *s.* tiro, tirada.
thrown [θron] *p.p. de* **to throw.**
thrush [θrʌʃ] *s.* tordo, zorzal.
thrust [θrʌst] *v.* (*push into*) meter; hincar, clavar; encajar; (*shove*) empujar; **to — a task upon someone** imponer una tarea a una persona, obligar a alguien a desempeñar un quehacer; **to — aside** echar o empujar a un lado; rechazar; **to — in** (*o* into) meter en, encafar en, intercalar en; **to — out** sacar; echar fuera; **to — someone through with a sword** atravesar a alguien de parte a parte con la espada; *pret. & p.p. de* **to thrust;** *s.* estocada, cuchillada, puñalada, lanzada; empuje, empujón o empellón; arremetida, acometida.
thud [θʌd] *s.* porrazo, golpazo, golpe sordo.
thug [θʌg] *s.* ladrón, salteador.
thumb [θʌm] *s.* pulgar; **under the — of** bajo el poder o influencia de; *v.* hojear (*con el pulgar*).
thumb·tack [θʌ́mtæk] *s.* chinche.
thump [θʌmp] *s.* golpazo, porrazo, trastazo; golpe sordo; *v.* golpear, golpetear, aporrear, dar un

porrazo.
thun·der [θʌ́ndɚ] *s.* trueno; tronido; estruendo; *v.* tronar.
thun·der·bolt [θʌ́ndɚbolt] *s.* rayo.
thun·der·ing [θʌ́ndərɪŋ] *adj.* atronador.
thun·der·ous [θʌ́ndərəs] *adj.* atronador, estruendoso.
thun·der·storm [θʌ́ndɚstɔrm] *s.* tronada, tormenta o tempestad de truenos.
Thurs·day [θɝ́zdɪ] *s.* jueves.
thus [θʌs] *adv.* así; — **far** hasta aquí, hasta ahora, hasta hoy.
thwart [θwɔrt] *v.* frustrar; estorbar; impedir.
thy [ðaɪ] *adj.* tu, tus.
thyme [taɪm] *s.* tomillo.
thy·roid [θáɪɔɪd] *s.* tiroides.
thy·self [ðaɪsɛ́lf] *pron.* tú mismo; a tí mismo; te (*como reflexivo*); *véase* **herself.**
tick [tɪk] tic tac; funda (*de colchón o almohada*); garrapata (*insecto parásito*); *v.* hacer tic tac (*como un reloj*); latir (*el corazón*); **to — off** marcar.
tick·et [tíkɪt] *s.* billete, *Am.* boleto; lista de candidatos (*de un partido*); balota (*para votar*); — **office** taquilla; despacho de boletos, *Am.* boletería.
tick·le [tíkl̩] *v.* (*touch*) cosquillear, hacer cosquillas; (*feel*) sentir o tener cosquillas; (*please*) halagar, gustarle a uno; **to be -d to death** morirse de gusto, estar muy contento; *s.* cosquilleo, cosquillas.
tick·lish [tíklɪʃ] *adj.* cosquilloso; delicado, arriesgado, difícil.
tid·bit [tídbɪt] *s.* bocado, bocadito, golosina.
tide [taɪd] *s.* marea; corriente; **Christmas —** navidades, temporada de navidad; *v.* **to — someone over a difficulty** ayudar a alguien durante una crisis o dificultad.
tide·wa·ter [táɪdwɔtɚ] *adj.* costanero.
tid·ings [táɪdɪŋz] *s. pl.* noticias, nuevas.
ti·dy [táɪdɪ] *adj.* aseado, limpio, ordenado; **a — sum** una suma considerable; *v.* asear, arreglar, poner en orden; **to — oneself up** asearse.
tie [taɪ] *v.* (*fasten*) atar, liar, ligar; *Am.* amarrar; (*unite*) enlazar, vincular; (*equal*) empatar (*en juegos, etc.*); **to — tight** amarrar bien, apretar fuerte; **to — up the traffic** obstruir el tráfico; *s.* lazo, ligadura, atadura; enlace, vínculo; corbata; empate (*en carreras, juegos, etc.*); **railway —** traviesa, *Andes, C.A., Méx.* durmiente; *Ríopl., Ch.* travesaño.
tier [tɪr] *s.* fila, hilera, ringlera.
ti·ger [táɪgɚ] *s.* tigre; — **cat** gato montés.
tight [taɪt] *adj.* (*squeezed*) apretado, ajustado, estrecho; (*sealed*) hermético; (*firm*) firme, tieso; (*stingy*) tacaño, mezquino; (*drunk*) borracho; **to be in a — spot** estar en un aprieto; **to close —** apretar, cerrar herméticamente; **to hold on —** agarrarse bien; **it fits —** está muy estrecho o ajustado.
tight·en [táɪtn̩] *v.* apretar; estrechar; estirar, poner tirante.
tight·ness [táɪtnɪs] *s.* estrechez; tirantez, tensión; mezquindad, tacañería.
tight·wad [táɪtwɑd] *s.* tacaño; cicatero.
ti·gress [táɪgrɪs] *s.* tigre hembra; *Am.* tigra.
tile [taɪl] *s.* teja; baldosa, azulejo; — **roof** tejado; *v.* tejar, cubrir con tejas; cubrir con azulejos, embaldosar.
till [tɪl] *prep.* hasta; *conj.* hasta que; *v.* cultivar, labrar, arar; *s.* gaveta o cajón para el dinero.
till·age [tíləʤ] *s.* labranza, cultivo, labor.

tilt [tɪlt] *s.* ladeo, inclinación; declive; altercación disputa; **at full** — a toda velocidad; *v.* ladear(se), inclinar(se).

tim·ber [tímbɚ] *s.* madera de construcción; maderaje; madero; viga.

time [taɪm] *s.* tiempo; hora; vez; plazo; **at -s a veces**; **at one and the same** — a la vez; **at this** — ahora, al presente; **behind** — atrasado, retrasado; **from** — **to** — de vez en cuando; **in** — a tiempo; andando el tiempo; **on** — puntual; con puntualidad; a tiempo; a la hora debida; **several -s** varias veces; **to beat** — marcar el compás; **to buy on** — comprar a plazo; **to have a good** — divertirse, pasar un buen rato; **what** — **is it?** ¿qué hora es?; *v.* cronometrar, medir el tiempo de; regular, poner en punto (*el reloj, el motor*); escoger el momento oportuno para; — **zone** zona horaria; huso horario.

time·less [táɪmles] *adj.* eterno, infinito.

time·ly [táɪmlɪ] *adj.* oportuno.

time·piece [táɪmpis] *s.* reloj; cronómetro.

time·ta·ble [táɪmtebl] *s.* itinerario, horario.

tim·id [tímɪd] *adj.* tímido.

ti·mid·i·ty [tɪmídətɪ] *s.* timidez.

tim·ing [táɪmɪŋ] *s.* medida del tiempo; cronometraje; (*pace*) selección del momento oportuno; sincronización.

tim·or·ous [tímərəs] *adj.* timorato, tímido, miedoso.

tin [tɪn] *s.* estaño; hojalata, lata; cosa de hojalata; — **can** lata; — **foil** hoja de estaño; *v.* estañar, cubrir con estaño; enlatar.

tinc·ture [tíŋktʃɚ] *s.* tintura; tinte; — **of iodine** tintura de yodo; *v.* tinturar, teñir.

tin·der [tíndɚ] *s.* yesca.

tinge [tɪndʒ] *v.* teñir; matizar; *s.* tinte, matiz; dejo, saborcillo.

tin·gle [tíŋgl] *v.* hormiguear, sentir hormigueo; **to** — **with excitement** estremecerse de entusiasmo; *s.* hormigueo, picazón, comezón.

tin·ker [tɪŋkɚ] *v.* ocuparse vanamente.

tin·kle [tíŋkl] *v.* tintinear; hacer retintín; *s.* tintineo; retintín.

tin·sel [tínsl] *s.* oropel; *adj.* de oropel.

tint [tɪnt] *s.* tinte, matiz; *v.* teñir, matizar.

ti·ny [táɪnɪ] *adj.* diminuto, menudo, chiquitico, chiquitín.

tip [tɪp] *s.* (*point*) punta, extremo, extremidad; (*money*) propina; (*hint*) noticia o aviso secreto; *v.* ladear(se), inclinar(se); dar propina (a); **to** — **a person off** dar aviso secreto a; **to** — **one's hat** tocarse el sombrero; **to** — **over** volcar(se), voltear(se).

tip·sy [típsɪ] *adj.* alumbrado, algo borracho; ladeado.

tip·toe [típto] *s.* punta del pie; **on** — de puntillas; *v.* andar de puntillas.

ti·rade [táɪred] *s.* invectiva.

tire [taɪr] *s.* llanta, neumático, goma; **flat** — llanta o goma reventada; *v.* cansar(se), fatigar(se).

tired [taɪrd] *adj.* cansado, fatigado; — **out** extenuado de fatiga, rendido.

tire·less [táɪrlɪs] *adj.* incansable, infatigable.

tire·some [táɪrsəm] *adj.* cansado, aburrido, pesado.

tis·sue [tíʃU] *s.* tejido; — **paper** papel de seda.

ti·tan·ic [taɪtǽnɪk] *adj.* titánico.

ti·ta·ni·um [taɪténɪəm] *s.* titanio.

tithe [taɪð] *s.* diezmo.

ti·tle [táɪtl] *s.* título — **holder** titulado; — **page** portada.

to [tu] *prep.* a; hasta; hacia; para; — **try** — tratar de; esforzarse por; **a quarter** — **five** las cinco

menos cuarto; **bills** — **be paid** cuentas por pagar; **frightened** — **death** muerto de susto; **from house** — **house** de casa en casa; **he has** — **go** tiene que ir; **near** — cerca de; **not** — **my knowledge** no que yo sepa; *adv.* — **and fro** de acá para allá; **to come** — volver en si.

toad [tod] *s.* sapo o escuerzo.

toast [tost] *v.* tostar(se); brindar por, beber a la salud de; *s.* tostada; brindis.

toast·er [tóstɚ] *s.* tostador.

to·bac·co [təbǽko] *s.* tabaco.

to·day [tədé] *adv.* hoy; hoy día.

toe [to] *s.* dedo del pie; punta (*de la media, del zapato, etc.*); *v.* **to** — **in** andar con la punta de los pies para dentro.

toe·nail [tónel] *s.* uña del dedo del pie.

to·geth·er [təgéðɚ] *adv.* juntamente; a un mismo tiempo, a la vez; juntos; — **with** junto con; **all** — juntos; en junto; **to call** — convocar; juntar; **to come** — juntarse, unirse; ponerse de acuerdo; **to walk** — andar juntos.

toil [tɔɪl] *v.* afanarse, trafagar atarearse; *s.* esfuerzo, trabajo, faena, fatiga.

toi·let [tɔ́ɪlɪt] *s.* retrete, excusado, común, *Am.* inodoro; — **articles** artículos de tocador; — **case** neceser; — **paper** papel de excusado, papel higiénico.

to·ken [tókən] *s.* señal, símbolo; prenda; recuerdo; prueba, muestra; ficha (*de metal*); — **payment** pago nominal.

told [told] *pret.* & *p.p. de* **to tell.**

tol·er·ance [tálərəns] *s.* tolerancia.

tol·er·ant [tálərənt] *adj.* tolerante.

tol·er·ate [táləret] *v.* tolerar.

tol·er·a·tion [taləréʃən] *s.* tolerancia.

toll [tol] *s.* doble, tañido (*de las companas*); peaje; portazgo; — **bridge** puente de peaje; — **gate** barrera de peaje; — **call** llamada por cobrar; **to pay** — pagar peaje o portazgo; *v.* tañer, doblar (*las campanas*).

to·ma·to [təméto] *s.* tomate, *Méx.* jitomate.

tomb [tum] *s.* tumba.

tomb·stone [túmston] *s.* lápida sepulcral.

tom·cat [támkœt] *s.* gato.

tome [tom] *s.* tomo.

to·mor·row [təmóro] *adv.* mañana; — **morning** mañana por la mañana; — **noon** mañana al mediodía; **day after** — pasado mañana.

ton [tʌn] *s.* tonelada.

tone [ton] *s.* (*pitch*) tono; timbre; (*sound*) sonido; *v.* dar tono a, modificar el tono de; **to** — **down** bajar de tono; suavizar; **to** — **down one's voice** moderar la voz; **to** — **in well with** armonizar con, entonar bien con; **to** — **up** subir de tono; tonificar, vigorizar.

tongs [tɔŋz] *s. pl.* tenazas.

tongue [tʌŋ] *s.* lengua; idioma; **to be tongue-tied** tener trabada la lengua.

ton·ic [tánɪk] *s.* & *adj.* tónico.

to·night [tənáɪt] *adv.* esta noche, a la noche.

ton·nage [tʌ́nɪdʒ] *s.* tonelaje.

ton·sil [tánsl] *s.* amígdala.

ton·sil·li·tis [tansláɪtɪs] *s.* amigdalitis.

too [tu] *adv.* también; demasiado; — **many** demasiados; — **much** demasiado; **it is** — **bad!** ¡es una lástima!

took [tUk] *pret. de* **to take.**

tool [tul] *s.* instrumento; herramienta; — **box** caja de herramientas.

toot [tut] *v.* tocar o sonar la bocina; pitar; tocar (*un cuerno, trompa o trompeta*); **to** — **one's own**

horn alabarse, cantar sus propias alabanzas; s.
toque o sonido (de bocina, trompeta, etc.);
silbido, pitido; pitazo (de locomotora).
tooth [tuθ] s. diente; muela; — **mark** dentellada; **to
fight — and nail** luchar a brazo partido; **to have
a sweet —** ser amigo de golosinas.
tooth·ache [túθek] s. dolor de muelas.
tooth·brush [túθbrʌʃ] s. cepillo de dientes.
toothed [tuθt] adj. dentado.
tooth·less [túθlɪs] adj. desdentado.
tooth·paste [túθpest] s. pasta para los dientes,
pasta dentífrica.
tooth·pick [túθpɪk] s. mondadientes, palillo de
dientes.
top [tɑp] s. (peak) cumbre, cima; cúspide; tope;
pináculo; remate; cabeza; (surface) superficie;
copa (de árbol); (cover) tapa, cubierta; (toy)
trompo; peonza; **at the — of his class** a la cabeza
de su clase; **at the — of one's voice** a voz en
cuello; **filled up to the —** lleno hasta el tope;
from — to bottom de arriba abajo; **from — to
toe** de pies a cabeza; **on — of** encima de, sobre;
adj. superior; más alto; —**coat** abrigo, sobretodo;
at — speed a velocidad máxima; v. coronar;
exceder; sobresalir, sobrepujar; rematar; **to —
off** rematar; terminar.
to·paz [tópæz] s. topacio.
top·er [tópɚ] s. bebedor, borrachín.
top-heav·y [tɑphévɪ] adj. más pesado arriba que
abajo.
top·ic [tápɪk] s. tema, asunto, materia, topico.
top·most [tápmost] adj. más alto; superior.
to·pog·ra·phy [təpágrəfɪ] s. topografía.
to·pon·y·my [təpánəmɪ] s. toponimia.
top·ple [tápl̩] v. echar abajo, derribar; volcar; **to —
over** venirse abajo; volcarse.
top·sy-tur·vy [tápsɪtɝ̃vɪ] adj. & adv. patas arriba;
en confusión; trastornado; enrevesado, al revés.
torch [tɔrtʃ] s. antorcha; **blow —** soplete.
tore [tor] pret. de **to tear**.
tor·ment [tɔ́rmɛnt] s. tormento; [tɔrmɛ́nt] v.
atormentar; afligir.
torn [tɔrn] p.p. de **to tear** roto, rompido, rasgado.
tor·na·do [tɔrnédo] s. tornado.
tor·pe·do [tɔrpído] s. torpedo; — **boat** torpedero;
v. torpedear.
torque [tɔrk] s. fuerza rotatoria.
tor·rent [tɔ́rənt] s. torrente.
tor·rid [tɔ́rɪd] adj. tórrido.
tor·sion [tɔ́rʃən] s. torsión.
tor·toise [tɔ́rtəs] s. tortuga.
tor·tu·ous [tɔ́rtʃʊəs] adj. tortuoso.
tor·ture [tɔ́rtʃɚ] s. tortura, tormento; v. torturar,
atormentar.
toss [tɔs] v. tirar, echar, arrojar, lanzar;
menear(se); cabecear (un buque); **to — aside**
echar a un lado; desechar; **to — up** echar para
arriba; aventar; s. tiro, tirada; meneo, sacudida.
tot [tɑt] s. chiquitín, chiquitina, chiquitico,
chiquitica, niñito, niñita, nene, nena.
to·tal [tótl̩] adj. & s. total.
to·tal·i·tar·i·an [totælətérɪən] adj. totalitario.
tot·ter [tátɚ] v. tambalear(se), bambolear(se); estar
para desplomarse.
touch [tʌtʃ] v. tocar; palpar, tentar; conmover,
enternecer; compararse con, igualar; **to — at a
port** hacer escala en un puerto; **to — off an
explosive** prender la mecha de un explosivo;
to — up retocar; s. toque; tacto, sentido del
tacto; tiento; —**stone** piedra de toque; **a — of
fever** algo de calentura; **to keep in — with**

mantener(se) en comunicación con.
touch-and-go [tʌ́tʃəndgó] adj. arriesgado.
touch·ing [tʌ́tʃɪŋ] adj. conmovedor, enternecedor.
touch·y [tʌ́tʃɪ] adj. quisquilloso, susceptible,
sensible, sensitivo.
tough [tʌf] adj. correoso; fuerte; firme; duro;
arduo, difícil; terco; empedernido, malvado.
tough·en [tʌ́fn̩] v. curtir(se); endurecer(se),
empedernir(se); hacer(se) correoso.
tough·ness [tʌ́fnɪs] s. dureza; correosidad;
flexibilidad; tenacidad; resistencia; dificultad.
tou·pee [tupé] s. peluca.
tour [tʊr] s. viaje, excursión; vuelta; jira; v. viajar
por; recorrer; hacer una jira; hacer un viaje de
turismo.
tour·ism [túrɪzəm] s. turismo.
tour·ist [túrɪst] s. turista.
tour·na·ment [tɝ̃nəmənt] s. torneo; certamen,
concurso.
tow [to] v. remolcar; s. remolque; —**boat**
remolcador; —**rope** cuerda de remolque; **to take
in —** remolcar, llevar a remolque.
to·ward [tord] prep. hacia; rumbo a; alrededor de;
para, para con; — **four o'clock** a eso de las
cuatro.
to·wards [tordz] = **toward**.
tow·el [taʊl] s. toalla.
tow·er [táʊɚ] s. torre; torreón; **bell —**
campanario; v. sobresalir, sobrepujar;
destacarse, descollar; elevarse.
tow·er·ing [táʊrɪŋ] adj. encumbrado; elevado, muy
alto; sobresaliente.
town [taʊn] s. (center) población, ciudad, pueblo,
aldea; (administration) municipio; — **hall**
ayuntamiento.
town·ship [táʊnʃɪp] s. unidad primaria de gobierno
local; sección de seis millas cuadradas (en
terrenos públicos).
tox·in [táksɪn] s. toxina.
toy [tɔɪ] s. juguete; adj. de juego, de juguete,
pequeñito; v. jugar, juguetear.
trace [tres] s. señal, indicio, vestigio; huella, rastro;
tirante (de una guarnición); v. trazar; calcar;
rastrear, seguir la huella de; rebuscar, investigar;
to — the source of remontarse al origen de,
buscar el origen de.
tra·che·a [trékɪə] s. tráquea.
tra·cho·ma [trəkomə] s. tracoma.
track [træk] s. pista, huella, rastro; pisada; vereda,
senda; vía; — **sports** deportes de pista; **race —**
pista; **railroad —** rieles, vía del tren, vía férrea o
ferrovía; **to be off the —** estar extraviado, estar
descarrilado; **to be on the —** of rastrear, ir
siguiendo la pista de; **to keep — of** llevar la
cuenta de; no perder de vista; v. rastrear, seguir
la huella de; **to — down** coger, atrapar;
descubrir; **to — in mud** traer lodo en los pies,
entrar con los pies enlodados.
tract [trækt] s. área; terreno; folleto; **digestive —**
canal digestivo.
trac·tion [trǽkʃən] s. tracción.
trac·tor [trǽktɚ] s. tractor.
trade [tred] s. (business) comercio; trato, negocio;
(swap) trueque, cambio; (occupation) oficio;
(customers) clientela, parroquianos; — **school**
escuela de artes y oficios; — **union** gremio
obrero o de obreros; v. comerciar, negociar,
traficar, tratar; trocar, cambiar; feriar, mercar.
trade·mark [trédmɑrk] s. marca de fábrica.
trad·er [trédɚ] s. mercader, comerciante,
negociante, traficante.

TI

trades·man [trédzmən] *s.* mercader, comerciante, traficante; tendero.
tra·di·tion [trədíʃən] *s.* tradición.
tra·di·tion·al [trədíʃənl] *adj.* tradicional.
traf·fic [trǽfɪk] *s.* tráfico; tráfago; tránsito; circulación; *v.* traficar, comerciar, negociar.
trag·e·dy [trǽdʒədɪ] *s.* tragedia.
trag·ic [trǽdʒɪk] *adj.* trágico.
trail [trel] *s.* *(trace)* pista, rastro, huella; *(path)* senda, sendero, trocha, vereda; cola *(de vestido)*; *v.* arrastrar(se); rastrear, seguir la pista de; andar detrás de; **to — behind** ir rezagado, rezagarse.
train [tren] *s.* *(railroad)* tren; *(dress)* cola *(de vestido)*; *(retinue)* séquito, comitiva; *v.* amaestrar(se), ejercitar(se); adiestrar(se) o adestrar(se), *Am.* entrenar(se); educar; disciplinar *(tropas)*; apuntar *(un cañón)*.
train·er [trénə·] *s.* amaestrador; *Méx., C.A., Andes, Ven., Col., Carib.* entrenador.
train·ing [trénɪŋ] *s.* adiestramiento, disciplina, *Méx., C.A., Andes, Ven., Col., Carib.*, entrenamiento; educación; **— camp** campo de entrenamiento o práctica.
trait [tret] *s.* rasgo, característica; cualidad.
trai·tor [trétə·] *s.* traidor.
tram [træm] *s.* vagoneta *(de una mina de carbón)*.
tramp [træmp] *v.* pisotear; andar a pie; vagabundear; *s.* vago, vagabundo; caminata, marcha; pisadas.
tram·ple [trǽmpl] *v.* pisar, hollar, pisotear; **to — on** pisotear, hollar; *s.* pisadas.
trance [træns] *s.* rapto, arrobamiento, enajenamiento, éxtasis; **to be in a — estar** arrobado, estar enajenado; estar distraído o ensimismado.
tran·quil [trǽŋkwɪl] *adj.* tranquilo.
tran·quil·iz·er [trǽŋkwəlaɪzə·] *s.* tranquilizador.
tran·quil·li·ty [trǽŋkwílətɪ] *s.* tranquilidad.
trans·act [trænsǽkt] *v.* tramitar, despachar, llevar a cabo.
trans·ac·tion [trænsǽkʃən] *s.* transacción, trato, negocio; trámite; negociación; **-s** actas; memorias.
trans·at·lan·tic [trænsətlǽntɪk] *adj.* transatlántico.
tran·scend [trænsénd] *v.* trascender, ir más allá de.
trans·con·ti·nen·tal [trænskɑntənéntl] *adj.* transcontinental.
tran·scribe [trænskráɪb] *v.* transcribir.
tran·script [trǽnskrɪpt] *s.* transcripción, copia.
trans·fer [trǽnsfɜ·] *s.* transferencia; traslado; traspaso; trasbordo; **— of ownership** cesión o traspaso de propiedad; **streetcar —** transferencia, contraseña, cupón de trasbordo; [trænsfɜ́·] *v.* transferir; trasbordar *(de un tren a otro)*, cambiar *(de tren, de tranvía)*; traspasar *(propiedad)*, trasladar.
trans·fer·a·ble [trænsfə·əbl] *adj.* transferible.
trans·fig·ure [trænsfígjə·] *v.* transfigurar.
trans·form [trænsfɔ́rm] *v.* transformar(se).
trans·for·ma·tion [trænsfə·méʃən] *s.* transformación.
trans·gress [trænsgrés] *v.* transgredir, violar, quebrantar *(una ley)*; pecar; **to — the bounds of** traspasar los límites de.
trans·gres·sion [trænsgréʃən] *s.* transgresión; violación de una ley; pecado.
trans·gres·sor [trænsgrésə·] *s.* transgresor.
tran·sient [trǽnʃənt] *s.* transeúnte; *adj.* transeúnte; transitorio, pasajero.
tran·sis·tor [trænzístə·] *s.* transistor.

tran·sit [trǽnsɪt] *s.* tránsito; **in — en** tránsito, de paso.
tran·si·tion [trænzíʃən] *s.* transición; tránsito, paso.
tran·si·tive [trǽnsətɪv] *adj.* transitivo.
tran·si·to·ry [trǽnsətorɪ] *adj.* transitorio, pasajero.
trans·late [trænslét] *v.* traducir, verter; trasladar.
trans·la·tion [trænsléʃən] *s.* traducción, versión; translación *(de un lugar a otro)*.
trans·la·tor [trænslétə·] *s.* traductor.
trans·lu·cent [trænslúsṇt] *adj.* translúcido; **to be —** traslucirse.
trans·mis·sion [trænsmíʃən] *s.* transmisión; caja de velocidades.
trans·mit [trænsmít] *v.* transmitir; emitir.
trans·mit·ter [trænsmítə·] *s.* transmisor; emisor.
tran·som [trǽnsəm] *s.* montante.
trans·par·ent [trænspérənt] *adj.* transparente.
trans·plant [trænsplǽnt] *v.* trasplantar.
trans·port [trǽnsport] *s.* *(moving)* transporte; acarreo; *(rapture)* éxtasis; **— plane** aeroplano de transporte; [trænspórt] *v.* transportar; acarrear; **to be -ed with joy** estar enajenado de placer.
trans·por·ta·tion [trænspə·téʃən] *s.* transportación, transporte; boleto, pasaje.
trans·pose [trænspóz] *v.* transponer.
trans·verse [trænsvɜ́s] *adj.* transverso, transversal, puesto de través.
trap [træp] *s.* trampa, lazo, red; **— door** trampa; **mouse —** ratonera; *v.* entrampar, coger con trampa; atrapar.
tra·peze [træpíz] *s.* trapecio.
trap·e·zoid [trǽpəzoɪd] *s.* trapezoide; trapecio.
trap·pings [trǽpɪŋz] *s. pl.* arreos, jaeces, guarniciones.
trash [træʃ] *s.* basura; hojarasca; cachivaches; gentuza, plebe.
trau·ma [trómə] *s.* traumatismo.
trau·mat·ic [trəmǽtɪk] *adj.* traumático.
trav·el [trǽvl] *v.* viajar; viajar por; recorrer; *s.* viaje; tráfico.
trav·el·er [trǽvlə·] *s.* viajero; **—'s check** cheque de viajero.
trav·el·ing [trǽvlɪŋ] *adj.* de viaje, para viaje; **— expenses** gastos de viaje; **— salesman** agente viajero, viajante de comercio.
trav·e·logue [trǽvəlɔg] *s.* conferencia sobre viajes.
trav·erse [trǽvə·s] *v.* atravesar, cruzar; recorrer; *s.* travesaño.
trav·es·ty [trǽvɪstɪ] *s.* parodia; *v.* parodiar, falsear.
tray [tre] *s.* bandeja; batea; *Mex.* charola.
treach·er·ous [trétʃərəs] *adj.* traicionero, traidor, alevoso.
treach·er·y [trétʃərɪ] *s.* traición, perfidia, alevosía.
tread [tred] *v.* *(trample)* pisar, hollar; pisotear; *(walk)* andar a pie, caminar; *s.* paso; pisada, huella; *Am.* pise *(de una rueda)*; **tire —** rodadura del neumático, *Am.* banda rodante.
tread·mill [trédmɪl] *s.* noria; rueda de andar.
trea·son [trízṇ] *s.* traición.
trea·son·a·ble [tríznəbl] *adj.* traidor, traicionero.
treas·ure [tréʒə·] *s.* tesoro; *v.* atesorar.
treas·ur·er [tréʒərə·] *s.* tesorero.
treas·ur·y [tréʒərɪ] *s.* tesorería; tesoro, erario; **Secretary of the Treasury** ministro de hacienda.
treat [trit] *v.* tratar; curar; convidar, invitar; *s.* obsequio, agasajo, convite; placer, gusto.
trea·tise [trítɪs] *s.* tratado.
treat·ment [trítmənt] *s.* trato; **medical —** tratamiento médico.
trea·ty [trítɪ] *s.* tratado, pacto, convenio.
treb·le [trébl] *adj.* triple; **— voice** voz atiplada;

s. tiple; v. triplicar.

tree [tri] s. árbol; **apple** — manzano; **family** — árbol genealógico; **shoe** — horma de zapato; **to be up a** — estar subido a un árbol; estar en un gran aprieto; estar perplejo.

tree·less [trílɪs] adj. pelado, sin árboles, despoblado de árboles.

tree·top [trítɑp] s. copa de árbol.

trel·lis [trélɪs] s. emparrado, enrejado.

trem·ble [trémbl] v. temblar; estremecerse; s. temblor; estremecimiento.

tre·men·dous [trɪméndəs] adj. tremendo.

trem·or [trémə·] s. temblor.

trem·u·lous [trémjələs] adj. trémulo; tembloroso.

trench [trɛntʃ] s. trinchera; zanja, foso.

trend [trɛnd] s. tendencia; rumbo, dirección.

tres·pass [tréspəs] v. invadir, traspasar; violar, infringir; pecar; **to** — **on property** meterse sin derecho en la propiedad ajena; **no -ing** prohibida la entrada; s. transgresión; pecado.

tress [trɛs] s. trenza; bucle.

tres·tle [trésl] s. caballete; puente de caballetes.

tri·al [tráɪəl] s. ensayo, prueba; tentativa; aflicción; juicio, proceso; — **flight** vuelo de prueba.

tri·an·gle [tráɪæŋgl] s. triángulo.

tri·an·gu·lar [traɪǽŋgjələ·] adj. triangular.

tribe [traɪb] s. tribu.

trib·u·la·tion [trɪbəléʃən] s. tribulación.

tri·bu·nal [trɪbjúnl] s. tribunal, juzgado.

trib·u·tar·y [tríbjətɛrɪ] adj. & s. tributario.

trib·ute [tríbjut] s. tributo; homenaje.

trich·i·no·sis [trɪkənósɪs] s. triquinosis.

trick [trɪk] s. treta; suerte; truco, artificio; maña, ardid, trampa; travesura; baza (*en el juego de naipes*); **to be up to one's old -s** hacer de las suyas; v. embaucar, trampear, hacer trampa; burlar; **to** — **oneself up** componerse, emperifollarse.

trick·er·y [tríkərɪ] s. engaños, malas mañas, astucia.

trick·le [tríkl] v. gotear; escurrir; s. goteo.

trick·y [tríkɪ] adj. tramposo, *Am.* mañero; intrincado, complicado.

tri·cy·cle [tráɪsɪkl] s. triciclo.

tried [traɪd] p.p. de **to try** & adj. probado.

tri·fle [tráɪfl] s. fruslería, friolera, nadería, nonada; bagatela; v. chancear(se), bromear; jugar, juguetear.

trig·ger [trígə·] s. gatillo (*de pistola, rifle, etc*).

trill [trɪl] v. trinar; **to** — **the r** pronunciar la erre doble; s. trino.

tril·o·gy [trílədʒɪ] s. trilogía.

trim [trɪm] v. guarnecer, adornar; atusar; recortar; podar, mondar; despabilar (*una vela*); ganarle a uno (*en el juego*); **to** — **up** adornar, componer; adj. aseado, limpio, pulcro, acicalado; s. adorno, franja, ribete, guarnición; **to be in** — **for** estar en buena salud para; estar bien entrenado para.

trim·ming [trímɪŋ] s. adorno, aderezo, guarnición; orla, ribete, franja; paliza, zurra; **-s** adornos; accesorios; recortes.

trin·i·ty [trínətɪ] s. trinidad.

trin·ket [tríŋkɪt] s. chuchería, baratija; miriñaque.

trip [trɪp] s. viaje; travesía; recorrido, jira; tropezón; v. tropezar; dar un traspié; equivocarse; hacer tropezar, hacer caer; saltar, brincar, corretear.

triph·thong [trífθɔŋ] s. triptongo.

trip·le [trípl] adj. & s. triple; v. triplicar.

trip·li·cate [trípləkət] adj. triplicado.

tri·pod [tráɪpɑd] s. trípode.

trite [traɪt] adj. trillado, trivial, vulgar.

tri·umph [tráɪəmf] s. triunfo; v. triunfar.

tri·um·phal [traɪʌ́mfl] adj. triunfal.

tri·um·phant [traɪʌ́mfənt] adj. triunfante; **-ly** adv. triunfantemente, en triunfo.

triv·i·al [trívjəl] adj. trivial, insignificante.

trod [trɑd] pret. & p.p. de **to tread**.

trod·den [trádn] p.p. de **to tread**.

trol·ley [trálɪ] s. trole; tranvía de trole; — **bus** trolebús.

trom·bone [trámbon] s. trombón.

troop [trup] s. tropa; cuadrilla.

tro·phy [trófɪ] s. trofeo.

trop·ic [trápɪk] s. trópico; — **of Cancer** trópico de Cáncer; — **of Capricorn** trópico de Capricornio; adj. tropical.

trop·i·cal [trápɪkl] adj. tropical.

trot [trɑt] v. trotar; hacer trotar; s. trote.

trou·ba·dour [trúbədor] s. trovador.

trou·ble [trʌ́bl] v. perturbar, turbar; molestar, incomodar; afligir; preocupar(se); **don't** — **to come** no se moleste Vd. en venir; s. pena, aflicción; inquietud, perturbación; dificultad; molestia; panne, avería, accidente (*a un mecanismo*); **heart** — enfermedad del corazón; **to be in** — estar en un aprieto o apuro; **it is not worth the** — no vale la pena; — **shooter** investigador de fallas o averías.

trou·ble·mak·er [trʌ́blmekə·] s. agitador, alborotador, malcontento.

trou·ble·some [trʌ́blsəm] adj. molesto, fastidioso, enfadoso, dificultoso; penoso.

trough [trɔf] s. comedero; artesa; batea; **eaves** — canal, gotera del tejado; **drinking** — abrevadero.

trou·sers [tráʊzə·z] s. pl. pantalones.

trous·seau [trúso] s. ajuar de novia.

trout [traʊt] s. trucha.

trow·el [tráʊəl] s. llana, *Am.* cuchara (*de albañil*); desplantador (*de jardín*).

tru·ant [trúənt] s. novillero, holgazán (*que se ausenta de la escuela*); **to play** — hacer novillos, *Am.* capear la escuela, *Mex.* pintar venado, *Am.* jubilarse; adj. vago, perezoso.

truce [trus] s. tregua.

truck [trʌk] s. camión; carretón; carreta; baratijas; **garden** — hortalizas, legumbres y verduras; — **garden** hortaliza, huerta de legumbres; v. acarrear, transportar en camión o carretón.

trudge [trʌdʒ] v. caminar, caminar con esfuerzo; s. caminata.

true [tru] adj. (*not false*) verdadero; cierto; verídico; fiel; (*exact*) exacto, preciso; legítimo.

tru·ly [trúlɪ] adv. (*not falsely*) verdaderamente, en verdad; en realidad; (*exactly*) exactamente, correctamente; fielmente; **very** — **yours** su seguro servidor.

trump [trʌmp] s. triunfo (*en el juego de naipes*); v. matar con un triunfo (*en el juego de naipes*); **to** — **up an excuse** forjar o inventar una excusa.

trum·pet [trʌ́mpɪt] s. trompeta; clarín; **ear** — trompetilla acústica; v. trompetear; tocar la trompeta; pregonar, divulgar.

trunk [trʌŋk] s. tronco; baúl; trompa (*de elefante*); **-s** calzones cortos (*para deportes*); — **line** línea principal.

trust [trʌst] s. (*reliance*) confianza, fe; (*credit*) crédito; (*charge*) cargo; custodia; depósito; (*firms*) trust, sindicato monopolista; v. confiar; fiar en, tener confianza en, fiarse de; esperar;

dar crédito a.

trus·tee [trʌstí] *s.* fideicomisario, depositario; **university -s** regentes universitarios; **board of -s** patronato; consejo.

trust·ful [trʌ́stfəl] *adj.* confiado.

trust·ing [trʌ́stɪŋ] *adj.* confiado.

trust·wor·thy [trʌ́stwɜ̌ðɪ] *adj.* fidedigno, digno de confianza.

trust·y [trʌ́stɪ] *adj.* fidedigno; honrado, leal; *s.* presidiario fidedigno (*a quien se le conceden ciertos privilegios*).

truth [truθ] *s.* verdad.

truth·ful [trúθfəl] *adj.* verdadero; verídico; veraz.

truth·ful·ness [trúθfəlnɪs] *s.* veracidad.

try [traɪ] *v.* probar, ensayar; hacer la prueba; poner a prueba; intentar, procurar; procesar, enjuiciar, formar causa (*a un acusado*); ver (*una causa*); **to — on a suit** probarse un traje; **to — one's luck** probar fortuna; **to — someone's patience** poner a prueba la paciencia de alguien; **to — to** tratar de, procurar, intentar; *s.* prueba, tentativa, ensayo.

try·ing [tráɪŋ] *adj.* molesto; penoso, irritante.

tub [tʌb] *s.* tina; bañera; baño; batea, cuba; *v.* lavar en tina o cuba.

tu·ba [túbə] *s.* tuba.

tube [tjub] *s.* tubo; **inner —** cámara (*de un neumático*); **radio —** lámpara o tubo de radio.

tu·ber·cu·lar [tjubɜ́kjələ·] *adj.* tuberculoso, tísico.

tu·ber·cu·lo·sis [tjubɜ̌kjəlósɪs] *s.* tuberculosis.

tuck [tʌk] *v.* alforzar, hacer o echar alforzas; **to — in** meter en; **to — in bed** arropar; **to — under one's arm** meter bajo el brazo; **to — up** arremanger, recoger; **to — up one's sleeves** arremangarse; *s.* alforza.

Tues·day [tjúzdɪ] *s.* martes.

tuft [tʌft] *s.* (*cluster*) penacho, copete; borla; (*clump*) macizo (*de plantas*).

tug [tʌg] *v.* remolcar; jalar (halar); arrastrar; trabajar con esfuerzo; **to — at** tirar de, jalar; *s.* tirón, estirón, *Am.* jalón; remolcador; **—boat** remolcador; **— of war** lucha a tirones de cuerda.

tu·i·tion [tjuíʃən] *s.* derechos de enseñanza; matrícula; *Am.* colegiatura.

tu·lip [tjúləp] *s.* tulipán.

tum·ble [tʌ́mbl] *v.* caer(se); voltear; dar volteretas; **to — down** caerse; desplomarse; **to — down** caerse; desplomarse; **to — into someone** tropezar con alguien; **to — over** volcar, tumbar, derribar; venirse abajo; *s.* caída, tumbo, vuelco, voltereta, *Am.* rodada; desorden.

tum·bler [tʌ́mblə·] *s.* vaso (*de mesa*); acróbata.

tu·mor [tjúmə·] *s.* tumor.

tu·mult [tjúmʌlt] *s.* tumulto.

tu·mul·tu·ous [tjumʌ́ltʃʊəs] *adj.* tumultuoso.

tu·na [túnə] *s.* atún (*pez*).

tune [tjun] *s.* (*melody*) tonada; (*pitch*) tono; armonía; **to be in —** estar a tono, estar afinado o templado; estar entonado; **to be out of —** estar desentonado o desafinado; desentonar; *v.* afinar, templar; armonizar; **to — in** sintonizar; **to — up the motor** poner al punto el motor.

tung·sten [tʌ́ŋstən] *s.* tungsteno.

tu·nic [tjúnɪk] *s.* túnica.

tun·nel [tʌ́nl] *s.* túnel; socavón; *v.* socavar; abrir un túnel.

tur·ban [tɜ́bən] *s.* turbante.

tur·bine [tɜ́baɪn], [tɜ·bɪn] *s.* turbina.

tur·bo·prop [tɜ́boprap] *s.* turbopropulsor.

tur·bu·lent [tɜ́bjələnt] *adj.* turbulento; revoltoso.

turf [tɜf] *s.* césped; terrón de tierra (*con césped*);

hipódromo, pista (*para carreras*).

Turk [tɜk] *s.* turco.

tur·key [tɜ́kɪ] *s.* pavo, *Méx.* guajolote (o guajalote); *C.A.* jolote, chumpe, chompipe; *Col.* pisco.

Turk·ish [tɜ́kɪʃ] *adj.* turco; *s.* turco, idioma turco.

tur·moil [tɜ́mɔɪl] *s.* alboroto; confusión.

turn [tɜn] *v.* (*rotate*) volver(se); voltear(se); girar, dar vueltas, rodar; virar; (*shape*) tornear, labrar al torno; (*become*) ponerse (*pálido, rojo, etc.*); **to — back** volver atrás; volverse, retroceder; devolver; **to — down an offer** rechazar una oferta; **to — in** entregar; recogerse, acostarse; **to — inside out** volver o volver al revés; **to — into** convertir(se) en; **to — off** apagar (*la luz*); cortar (*el agua, el gas, etc.*); **to — off the main road** salirse o desviarse de la carretera; **to — on** encender (*la luz*); abrir la llave (*del gas, del agua*); **to — on someone** volverse contra, acometer o caer sobre alguien; **to — out** apagar (*la luz*); echar, expulsar, arrojar; producir; **to — out well** salir o resultar bien; **to — over** volcar(se), voltear(se); doblar; revolver (*en la mente*); entregar; **to — over and over** dar repetidas vueltas; **to — sour** agriarse, fermentarse; **to — the corner** doblar la esquina; **to — to** acudir a; volverse a; dirigirse a; convertir(se) en; **to — to the left** doblar o torcer a la izquierda; **to — up** aparecer; **to — up one's nose at** desdeñar; hacer ascos a; **to — up one's sleeves** arremangarse; **to — upside down** trastornar; volcar; **it -s my stomach** me da asco o náusea; *s.* vuelta; revolución; giro; recodo (*del camino*); turno; virada, cambio de rumbo; **— of mind** actitud mental; **at every —** a cada paso; **to be one's —** tocarle a uno; **to do one a good —** hacerle a uno un favor; **to take -s** turnarse.

tur·nip [tɜ́nəp] *s.* nabo.

turn·o·ver [tɜ́novə·] *s.* vuelco (*de un coche*); cambio (*de empleados*); **business —** movimiento de mercancías, número de transacciones; **labor —** movimiento de obreros, cambio frecuente de trabajadores; **apple —** pastel de manzana; **— collar** cuello doblado.

turn·stile [tɜ́nstaɪl] *s.* torniquete.

turn·ta·ble [tɜ́ntebl] *s.* plato giratorio.

tur·pen·tine [tɜ́pəntaɪn] *s.* trementina; aguarrás.

tur·pi·tude [tɜ́pətjud] *s.* torpeza, vileza.

tur·quoise [tɜ́kwɔɪz] *s.* turquesa.

tur·ret [tɜ́ɪt] *s.* torrecilla; torre blindada; alminar.

tur·tle [tɜ́tl] *s.* tortuga; **—dove** tórtola.

tusk [tʌsk] *s.* colmillo.

tu·tor [tútə·] *s.* tutor, maestro particular; *v.* enseñar, instruir.

tux·e·do [tʌksído] *s.* esmoquin.

twang [twæŋ] *s.* tañido (*de una cuerda de guitarra*); nasalidad, tonillo gangoso; *v.* puntear, tañer (*una cuerda*); hablar con voz nasal, hablar con tonillo gangoso.

twang·y [twǽŋɪ] *adj.* gangoso, nasal.

tweed [twid] *s.* mezclilla de lana; **— suit** traje de mezclilla.

tweez·ers [twízə·z] *s. pl.* pinzas, tenacillas.

twice [twaɪs] *adv.* dos veces.

twig [twɪg] *s.* ramita; varita.

twi·light [twáɪlaɪt] *s.* crepúsculo; **at —** entre dos luces; *adj.* crepuscular.

twin [twɪn] *adj. & s.* gemelo, mellizo, *Méx.* cuate.

twine [twaɪn] *s.* cuerda, cordel; *v.* enroscar(se), torcer(se), retorcer(se); entrelazar.

twinge [twɪndʒ] *s.* punzada (*dolor agudo*); *v.*

punzar.

twin·kle [twíŋkl] v. titilar, parpadear, pestañear; chispear; s. titilación; parpadeo; pestañeo; guiño, guiñada; **in the — of an eye** en un abrir y cerrar de ojos.

twirl [twɝl] v. girar; dar vueltas; s. giro, vuelta; molinete, floreo.

twist [twɪst] v. (turn) torcer(se); retorcer(se); (coil) enroscar(se); s. torsión, torcedura; torzal, cordoncillo (hecho de varias hebras torcidas); curva, recodo, vuelta; rosca (de pan); **mental —** sesgo de la mente, sesgo mental.

twitch [twɪtʃ] v. crisparse, contraerse, torcerse convulsivamente (un músculo); temblar (los párpados); dar un tirón; s. temblor, ligera, convulsión, contracción nerviosa; tirón.

twit·ter [twítɚ] v. gorjear (los pájaros); temblar; agitarse; s. gorjeo; agitación, estremecimiento nervioso.

two-faced [túfest] adj. de dos caras.

two-fist·ed [túfɪstəd] adj. vigoroso; de dos puños.

two·fold [túfold] adj. doble.

two-way [túwe] adj. de dos sentidos.

type [taɪp] s. tipo; v. escribir a máquina.

type·write [táɪpraɪt] v. escribir a máquina.

type·writ·er [táɪpraɪtɚ] s. máquina de escribir.

type·writ·ing [táɪpraɪtɪŋ] s. mecanografía; trabajo de mecanógrafo.

type·writ·ten [táɪprɪtn̩] adj. escrito a máquina.

ty·phoid [táɪfɔɪd] s. tifoidea, fiebre tifoidea.

ty·phus [táɪfəs] s. tifo.

typ·i·cal [típɪkl] adj. típico.

typ·ist [táɪpɪst] s. mecanógrafo; mecanógrafa.

typ·o·graph·i·cal [taɪpográfɪkl] adj. tipográfico; **— error** error de máquina.

ty·ran·ni·cal [tɪrǽnɪkl] adj. tiránico, tirano.

tyr·an·ny [tírənɪ] s. tiranía.

ty·rant [táɪrənt] s. tirano.

U:u

u·big·ui·tous [jubíkwɪtəs] adj. ubicuo.

ud·der [ʌ́dɚ] s. ubre.

ug·li·ness [ʌ́glɪnɪs] s. fealdad; fiereza.

ug·ly [ʌ́glɪ] adj. feo; fiero; repugnante; de mal genio; desagradable.

ul·cer [ʌ́lsɚ] s. úlcera.

ul·te·ri·or [ʌltíriɚ] adj. ulterior.

ul·ti·mate [ʌ́ltəmɪt] adj. último; final; fundamental; **-ly** adv. finalmente, a la larga.

ul·tra·mod·ern [ʌltrəmádɚn] adj. ultramoderno.

ul·tra·vi·o·let [ʌltrəvaíələt] adj. ultravioleta.

um·bil·i·cal cord [ʌmbílɪk̩kɔrd] s. cordón umbilical.

um·brel·la [ʌmbrélə] s. paraguas; sombrilla.

um·pire [ʌ́mpaɪr] s. árbitro, arbitrador; v. arbitrar.

un [ʌn-] prefijo negativo equivalente a: sin, no, in-, des-.

un·a·ble [ʌnébl] adj. incapaz, inhábil; **to be — to come** no poder venir.

un·ac·cent·ed [ʌnǽksɛntəd] adj. inacentuado.

un·ac·cus·tomed [ʌnəkʌ́stəmd] adj. desacostumbrado; insólito, inusitado.

un·af·fect·ed [ʌnəféktɪd] adj. inafectado, sin afectación, natural, sincero.

un·al·ter·a·ble [ʌnɔ́ltərəbl] adj. inalterable.

u·na·nim·i·ty [junənímətɪ] s. unanimidad.

u·nan·i·mous [jʊnǽnəməs] adj. unánime.

un·armed [ʌnármd] adj. desarmado.

un·at·tached [ʌnətǽtʃt] adj. suelto; libre; (law) no embargado.

un·a·void·a·ble [ʌnəvɔ́ɪdəbl] adj. inevitable, ineludible; forzoso.

un·a·ware [ʌnəwér] adj. desprevenido; inadvertido; ignorante; incauto; **-s** adv. inesperadamente, inopinadamente; impensadamente.

un·bal·anced [ʌnbǽlənst] adj. desequilibrado; **— account** cuenta no saldada.

un·bear·a·ble [ʌnbérəbl] adj. inaguantable, insoportable.

un·be·com·ing [ʌnbɪkʌ́mɪŋ] adj. impropio; **an — dress** un vestido que no sienta bien o que cae mal.

un·be·lief [ʌnbəlíf] s. incredulidad.

un·be·liev·a·ble [ʌnbəlívəbl] adj. increible.

un·be·liev·er [ʌnbəlívɚ] s. descreído, incrédulo.

un·be·liev·ing [ʌnbəlívɪŋ] adj. descreído, incrédulo.

un·bend·ing [ʌnbéndɪŋ] adj. inflexible.

un·bi·ased [ʌnbáɪəst] adj. imparcial, libre de prejuicio.

un·bos·om [ʌnbúzəm] v. revelar, confesar, descubrir (secretos); **to — oneself** desahogarse con alguien, revelarle sus más íntimos secretos.

un·bound [ʌnbáʊnd] adj. desencuadernado, no encuadernado; suelto, desatado.

un·bro·ken [ʌnbrókən] adj. intacto, entero; indómito; ininterrumpido, continuo.

un·but·ton [ʌnbʌ́tn̩] v. desabotonar, desabrochar.

un·can·ny [ʌnkǽnɪ] adj. extraño, raro, misterioso.

un·ceas·ing [ʌnsísɪŋ] adj. incesante.

un·cer·tain [ʌnsɝ́tn̩] adj. incierto; dudoso; indeciso.

un·cer·tain·ty [ʌnsɝ́ntɪ] s. incertidumbre; falta de certeza.

un·change·a·ble [ʌntʃéndʒəbl] adj. inmutable, inalterable, invariable.

un·changed [ʌntʃéndʒd] adj. inalterado, igual.

un·char·i·ta·ble [ʌntʃǽrətəbl] adj. duro falto de caridad.

un·cle [ʌŋkl] s. tío.

un·clean [ʌnklín] adj. inmundo, sucio; impuro.

un·com·fort·a·ble [ʌnkʌ́mfɚtəbl] adj. incómodo; molesto.

un·com·mon [ʌnkámən] adj. poco común, insólito, raro.

un·com·pro·mis·ing [ʌnkámprəmaɪzɪŋ] adj. intransigente; inflexible.

un·con·cern [ʌnkənsɝ́n] s. indiferencia.

un·con·di·tion·al [ʌnkəndíʃənl] adj. incondicional, absoluto.

un·con·ge·ni·al [ʌnkəndʒínjəl] adj. que no congenia, incompatible.

un·con·quer·a·ble [ʌnkáŋkərəbl] adj. invencible, inconquistable.

un·con·quered [ʌnkáŋkɚd] adj. no conquistado, no vencido.

un·con·scious [ʌnkánʃəs] adj. inconsciente; privado.

un·con·scious·ness [ʌnkánʃəsnɪs] s. inconsciencia; insensibilidad.

un·con·sti·tu·tion·al [ʌnkánstɪtuʃənl] adj. inconstitucional.

un·con·trol·la·ble [ʌnkəntrólɘbl] adj. irrefrenable, ingobernable.

un·con·ven·tion·al [ʌnkənvénʃənl] adj. despreocupado, libre de trabas o reglas.

un·coup·le [ʌnkʌ́pl] v. desacoplar.

un·couth [ʌnkúθ] adj. rudo, tosco, inculto, grosero; desmañado.

TR

un·cov·er [ʌnkʌ́vəʰ] *v.* descubrir(se); revelar; destapar(se); desabrigar(se).

unc·tion [ʌ́ŋkʃən] *s.* unción; fervor; **Extreme Unction** Extremaunción.

unc·tu·ous [ʌ́ŋkʃəs] *adj.* untuoso.

un·cul·ti·vat·ed [ʌnkʌ́ltəvetɪd] *adj.* inculto; baldío.

un·cul·tured [ʌnkʌ́ltʃəʰd] *adj.* inculto; grosero.

un·daunt·ed [ʌndɔ́ntəd] *adj.* impávido.

un·de·cid·ed [ʌndɪsáɪdɪd] *adj.* indeciso.

un·de·ni·a·ble [ʌndɪnáɪəbl] *adj.* innegable.

un·der [ʌ́ndəʰ] *prep.* (*beneath*) bajo; debajo de; (*less*) menos de; — **age** menor de edad; — **cover** a cubierto; — **the cover of** al abrigo de, al amparo de; — **pretense of** so pretexto de; — **twelve** menos de doce; **to be** — **obligation to** deber favores a; *adv.* debajo; abajo; menos; *adj.* inferior, de abajo (*en ciertas combinaciones*); — **dose** dosis escasa o corta; — **secretary** subsecretario; — **side** lado de abajo, lado inferior; **the** — **dogs** los de abajo.

un·der·brush [ʌ́ndəʰbrʌʃ] *s.* maleza.

un·der·clothes [ʌ́ndəʰkloz] *s. pl.* ropa interior.

un·der·de·vel·oped [ʌndəʰdɪvéləpt] *adj.* subdesarrollado.

un·der·dog [ʌ́ndəʰdɔg] *s.* perdidoso, víctima.

un·der·es·ti·mate [ʌ́ndəʰéstəmet] *v.* menospreciar, apreciar en menos de lo justo; salir corto en un cálculo.

un·der·fed [ʌ́ndəʰféd] *adj.* malnutrido.

un·der·go [ʌndəʰgó] *v.* sufrir, aguantar, padecer.

un·der·gone [ʌndəʰgɔ́n] *p.p. de* **to undergo**.

un·der·grad·u·ate [ʌndəʰgrǽdʒuɪt] *s.* estudiante del bachillerato; — **course** cursos o asignaturas para el bachillerato.

un·der·ground [ʌ́ndəʰgraʊnd] *adj.* subterráneo; *s.* subterráneo; *adv.* bajo tierra; en secreto; ocultamente.

un·der·hand·ed [ʌ́ndəʰhǽndɪd] *adj.* socarrón, secreto, disimulado, clandestino.

un·der·line [ʌ́ndəʰlaɪn] *v.* subrayer.

un·der·ly·ing [ʌndəʰláɪɪŋ] *adj.* fundamental.

un·der·mine [ʌndəʰmáɪn] *v.* minar, socavar.

un·der·neath [ʌndəʰníθ] *prep.* bajo, debajo de; *adv.* debajo.

un·der·pay [ʌ́ndəʰpé] *v.* malpagar; escatimar la paga.

un·der·pin·ning [ʌ́ndəʰpɪnɪŋ] *s.* apuntalamiento.

un·der·score [ʌ́ndəʰskor] *v.* subrayar.

un·der·sell [ʌndəʰsél] *v.* malbaratar; vender a menos precio que.

un·der·shirt [ʌ́ndəʰʃɜt] *s.* camiseta.

un·der·signed [ʌndəʰsáɪnd] *s.* firmante, infrascrito; **the** — el infrascrito, los infrascritos; el que suscribe.

un·der·sized [ʌ́ndəʰsáɪzd] *adj.* achaparrado, de tamaño inferior al normal.

un·der·skirt [ʌ́ndəʰskɜt] *s.* enaguas, refajo.

un·der·staffed [ʌndəʰstǽft] *adj.* de personal insuficiente.

un·der·stand [ʌndəʰstǽnd] *v.* entender; comprender; sobrentender

un·der·stand·a·ble [ʌndəʰstǽndəbl] *adj.* comprensible.

un·der·stand·ing [ʌndəʰstǽndɪŋ] *s.* comprensión; entendimiento, inteligencia; acuerdo; *adj.* comprensivo.

un·der·stood [ʌndəʰstúd] *pret. & p.p. de* **to understand**; *adj.* entendido; convenido; sobrentendido.

un·der·stud·y [ʌ́ndəʰstʌdɪ] *s.* sobresaliente, actor suplente; *v.* servir de sobresaliente o actor suplente.

un·der·take [ʌndəʰték] *v.* emprender; tratar de, intentar; comprometerse a.

un·der·tak·en [ʌndəʰtékən] *p.p. de* **to undertake**.

un·der·tak·er [ʌ́ndəʰtekəʰ] *s.* director de funeraria; embalsamador.

un·der·tak·ing [ʌndəʰtékɪŋ] *s.* empresa.

un·der·took [ʌndəʰtúk] *pret. de* **to undertake**.

un·der·tow [ʌ́ndəʰto] *s.* resaca.

un·der·wa·ter [ʌ́ndəʰwɔtəʰ] *adj.* submarino; subacuático.

un·der·wear [ʌ́ndəʰwɛr] *s.* ropa interior.

un·der·went [ʌndəʰwént] *pret. de* **to undergo**.

un·der·world [ʌ́ndəʰwɜld] *s.* hampa, bajos fondos de la sociedad; clase criminal; — **jargon** caló.

un·der·write [ʌ́ndəʰraɪt] *v.* asegurar; subscribir.

un·de·sir·a·ble [ʌndɪzáɪrəbl] *adj.* indeseable; inconveniente.

un·did [ʌndíd] *pret. de* **to undo**.

un·dis·turbed [ʌndɪstɝ́bd] *adj.* impasible; sereno, tranquilo; intacto.

un·do [ʌndú] *v.* deshacer; desatar; desabrochar; desenredar; anular; **to** — **one's hair** soltarse el cabello.

un·do·ing [ʌndúɪŋ] *s.* destrucción; pérdida.

un·done [ʌndʌ́n] *p.p. de* **to undo**; inacabado, sin hacer; sin terminar; **it is still** — está todavía por hacer, está inacabado; **to come** — desatarse.

un·doubt·ed·ly [ʌndáʊtɪdlɪ] *adv.* indudablemente, sin duda.

un·dress [ʌndrés] *v.* desnudar(se), desvestir(se).

un·due [ʌndjú] *adj.* indebido; impropio; excesivo.

un·du·late [ʌ́ndjələt] *v.* ondular, ondear.

un·du·ly [ʌndjúlɪ] *adv.* indebidamente.

un·dy·ing [ʌndáɪɪŋ] *adj.* imperecedero, eterno.

un·earth [ʌnɝ́θ] *v.* desenterrar.

un·eas·i·ly [ʌnízlɪ] *adv.* intranquilamente, inquietamente, con inquietud; incómodamente.

un·eas·i·ness [ʌnízɪnɪs] *s.* malestar, inquietud, intranquilidad, desasosiego.

un·eas·y [ʌnízɪ] *adj.* ansioso, inquieto, intranquilo; cohibido; incómodo.

un·ed·u·cat·ed [ʌnédʒəketɪd] *adj.* inculto, indocto, falto de instrucción, ignorante.

un·em·ployed [ʌnɪmplɔ́ɪd] *adj.* desocupado, desempleado, cesante; ocioso; — **funds** fondos no invertidos o inactivos.

un·em·ploy·ment [ʌnɪmplɔ́ɪmənt] *s.* desempleo, cesantía, falta de empleo, desocupación.

un·end·ing [ʌnéndɪŋ] *adj.* inacabable, interminable.

un·e·qual [ʌníkwəl] *adj.* desigual; insuficiente, ineficaz.

un·e·quiv·o·cal [ʌnɪkwívəkl] *adj.* inequívoco.

un·err·ing [ʌnérɪŋ] *adj.* infalible.

un·es·sen·tial [ʌnɪsénʃl] *adj.* no esencial.

un·e·ven [ʌnívən] *adj.* desigual, desparejo; irregular, accidentado; — **numbers** números impares o nones.

un·e·ven·ness [ʌnívənnɪs] *s.* desigualdad; desnivel; irregularidad, escabrosidad (*del terreno*).

un·e·vent·ful [ʌnɪvéntfl] *adj.* sin novedad.

un·ex·pect·ed [ʌnɪkspéktɪd] *adj.* inesperado; **-ly** *adv.* de improviso, inesperadamente.

un·ex·pres·sive [ʌnɪksprésɪv] *adj.* sin emoción.

un·fail·ing [ʌnfélɪŋ] *adj.* que nunca falta, constante, indefectible; infalible.

un·fair [ʌnfɛr] *adj.* injusto; tramposo; **to act -ly** obrar de mala fe.

un·faith·ful [ʌnféθfl] *adj.* infiel; desleal.

un·fa·mil·iar [ʌnfəmíljəʰ] *adj.* poco familiar; desconocido; **to be** — **with** no tener conocimiento de; no estar al tanto de, ignorar; no conocer bien.

un·fas·ten [ʌnfǽsn] v. desabrochar; desatar; aflojar.

un·fa·vor·a·ble [ʌnfévrəbl] adj. desfavorable, contrario, adverso.

un·feel·ing [ʌnfílɪŋ] adj. insensible; incompasivo.

un·fin·ished [ʌnfínɪʃt] adj. inacabado, inconcluso; sin terminar, sin acabar; sin barnizar, sin pulir.

un·fit [ʌnfít] adj. incompetente, inepto, incapaz; inservible; impropio; v. incapacitar.

un·fold [ʌnfóld] v. desenvolver(se), desarrollar(se); desdoblar; revelar.

un·fore·seen [ʌnforsín] adj. imprevisto.

un·for·get·ta·ble [ʌnfɚgétəbl] adj. inolvidable.

un·for·tu·nate [ʌnfɔ́rtʃənɪt] adj. desventurado, infeliz, desgraciado, desdichado; **-ly** adv. desgraciadamente, por desgracia.

un·found·ed [ʌnfáʊndəd] adj. infundado.

un·fre·quent·ed [ʌnfríkwəntəd] adj. poco frecuentado.

un·friend·ly [ʌnfréndlɪ] adj. hostil, enemigo; poco amistoso; adv. hostilmente.

un·fruit·ful [ʌnfrútfl] adj. infructuoso.

un·furl [ʌnfɚ́l] v. desplegar.

un·fur·nished [ʌnfɚ́nɪʃt] adj. desamueblado.

un·gain·ly [ʌngénlɪ] adj. desgarbado, torpe.

un·grate·ful [ʌngrétfəl] adj. ingrato, desagradecido.

un·guard·ed [ʌngárdəd] adj. desprevenido; descuidado.

un·hap·py [ʌnhǽpɪ] adj. infeliz; desgraciado, desventurado, desdichado.

un·harmed [ʌnhármd] adj. sin daño, ileso.

un·health·y [ʌnhélθɪ] adj. malsano; insalubre; enfermizo.

un·heard-of [ʌnhɚ́dɑv] adj. inaudito; desconocido.

un·hinge [ʌnhínd3] v. desquiciar.

un·hitch [ʌnhítʃ] v. desenganchar; desatar; desacoplar.

un·ho·ly [ʌnhólɪ] adj. impío, malo.

un·hook [ʌnhúk] v. desenganchar; desabrochar.

un·hurt [ʌnhɚ́t] adj. ileso.

u·ni·form [júnəfɔrm] adj. & s. uniforme.

u·ni·for·mi·ty [junəfɔ́rmətɪ] s. uniformidad.

u·ni·fy [júnəfaɪ] v. unificar, unir.

u·ni·lat·er·al [junɪlǽtɚəl] adj. unilateral.

un·im·port·ant [ʌnɪmpɔ́rtn̩t] adj. insignificante, poco importante.

un·im·prov·a·ble [ʌnɪmprúvəbl] adj. inmejorable.

un·in·hib·i·ted [ʌnɪnhíbətəd] adj. sin inhibición.

un·ion [júnjən] s. unión; **labor —** sindicato; **— leader** jefe de un gremio obrero; **trade-union** gremio obrero; **— shop** obreros sindicados o agremiados; adj. gremial.

u·nique [juník] adj. único, singular; señero.

u·ni·son [júnəzn̩]: **in —** al unísono (en el mismo tono); al compás.

u·nit [júnɪt] s. unidad.

u·nite [junáɪt] v. unir(se).

u·ni·ty [júnətɪ] s. unidad; unión.

u·ni·ver·sal [junəvɚ́sl] adj. universal; **— joint** cruceta.

u·ni·verse [júnəvɚs] s. universo.

u·ni·ver·si·ty [junəvɚ́sətɪ] s. universidad.

un·just [ʌndʒʌ́st] adj. injusto.

un·jus·ti·fi·a·ble [ʌndʒʌ́stəfaɪəbl] adj. injustificable, injustificado.

un·kempt [ʌnkémpt] adj. desaseado, desaliñado; desgreñado.

un·kind [ʌnkáɪnd] adj. falto de bondad; descortés; cruel.

un·known [ʌnnón] adj. desconocido; no sabido;

ignoto; **— quality** incógnita; **it is —** se ignora, no se sabe, se desconoce.

un·law·ful [ʌnlɔ́fəl] adj. ilegal, ilícito.

un·leash [ʌnlíʃ] v. soltar.

un·less [ʌnlés] conj. a menos que, a no ser que.

un·li·censed [ʌnláɪsənzd] adj. sin autorización.

un·like [ʌnláɪk] adj. desemejante, distinto, diferente; prep. a diferencia de.

un·like·ly [ʌnláɪklɪ] adj. improbable, inverosímil.

un·lim·it·ed [ʌnlímɪtɪd] adj. ilimitado.

un·load [ʌnlód] v. descargar; vaciar; deshacerse de (acciones, mercancías).

un·lock [ʌnlák] v. abrir (con llave); soltar, destrabar; revelar, penetrar (secretos).

un·loose [ʌnlús] v. soltar.

un·luck·y [ʌnlʌ́kɪ] adj. (unfortunate) desdichado, desventurado, desgraciado, desafortunado; (of bad omen) aciago, de mal agüero, funesto; **an — number** un número de mala suerte.

un·man·age·a·ble [ʌnmǽnɪdʒəbl] adj. inmanejable, ingobernable, intratable, indomable.

un·manned [ʌnmǽnd] adj. desguarnecido; sin tripulación.

un·marked [ʌnmárkt] adj. sin identificación.

un·mar·ried [ʌnmǽrɪd] adj. soltero.

un·mask [ʌnmǽsk] v. desenvascar(se).

un·mer·ci·ful [ʌnmɚ́sɪfəl] adj. despiadado, inclemente.

un·mis·tak·a·ble [ʌnməstékəbl] adj. inequívoco, claro, inconfundible.

un·moved [ʌnmúvd] adj. fijo; inmutable, impasible; indiferente.

un·nat·u·ral [ʌnnǽtʃərəl] adj. afectado, artificial; anormal; **an — mother** una madre desnaturalizada.

un·nec·es·sar·y [ʌnnésəserɪ] adj. innecesario.

un·not·iced [ʌnnótɪst] adj. inadvertido.

un·o·blig·ing [ʌnəbláɪdʒɪŋ] adj. poco complaciente, descortés, descomedido.

un·ob·served [ʌnəbzɚ́vd] adj. inadvertido; sin ser visto.

un·ob·tain·a·ble [ʌnəbténəbl] adj. inobtenible, inasequible, inaccesible.

un·ob·tru·sive [ʌnəbtrusɪv] adj. discreto; sin ser visto.

un·oc·cu·pied [ʌnákjəpaɪd] adj. desocupado; vacío; desalquilado.

un·of·fi·cial [ʌnəfíʃl] adj. extraoficial.

un·or·gan·ized [ʌnɔ́rgənaɪzd] adj. sin organización; inorganizado.

un·o·rig·i·nal [ʌnərídʒənl] adj. trivial; ordinario.

un·or·tho·dox [ʌnɔ́rθədɑks] adj. heterodoxo.

un·pack [ʌnpǽk] v. desempacar; desembalar.

un·paid [ʌnpéd] adj. no pagado; sin pagar; **— bills** cuentas por pagar.

un·pleas·ant [ʌnpléznt] adj. desagradable.

un·pleas·ant·ness [ʌnpléznɪs] s. manera desagradable; desazón; desavenencia; **the — of a situation** lo desagradable de una situación; **to have an — with** tener una desavenencia con.

un·prec·e·dent·ed [ʌnprésədəntid] adj. sin precedente; inaudito.

un·pre·med·i·tat·ed [ʌnprimédətetəd] adj. impremeditado.

un·pre·pared [ʌnprɪpérd] adj. desprevenido; no preparado; no listo.

un·pre·ten·tious [ʌnprɪténʃəs] adj. modesto; sin pretenciones.

un·print·a·ble [ʌnpríntəbl] adj. que no puede imprimirse.

un·pro·duc·tive [ʌnprədʌ́ktɪv] adj. improductivo.

UN

un·pro·fes·sion·al [ʌnprəféʃənl] *adj.* no profesional.
un·prof·it·a·ble [ʌnpráfɪtəbl] *adj.* infructuoso.
un·pub·lished [ʌnpʌ́blɪʃt] *adj.* inédito, no publicado.
un·qual·i·fied [ʌnkwáləfaɪd] *adj.* incompetente; inepto.
un·quench·a·ble [ʌnkwéntʃəbl] *adj.* inapagable, inextinguible.
un·ques·tion·a·ble [ʌnkwéstʃənəbl] *adj.* indisputable, indudable; irreprochable.
un·rav·el [ʌnrǽvl] *v.* desenredar; desenmarañar; deshilachar(se); deshilar.
un·real [ʌnríəl] *adj.* irreal; ilusorio, imaginario.
un·rea·son·a·ble [ʌnrízənəbl] *adj.* desrazonable, fuera de razón; irracional.
un·rec·og·niz·a·ble [ʌnrékəgnaɪzəbl] *adj.* irreconocible, no conocible, incapaz de reconocerse; desconocido.
un·re·fined [ʌnrɪfáɪnd] *adj.* no refinado; inculto, grosero.
un·re·li·a·ble [ʌnrɪlaiəbl] *adj.* informal; indigno de confianza.
un·rest [ʌnrést] *s.* inquietud, desasosiego.
un·roll [ʌnról] *v.* desenrollar(se), desenvolver(se).
un·ru·ly [ʌnrúlɪ] *adj.* indómito; indócil; desobediente.
un·safe [ʌnséf] *adj.* inseguro, peligroso.
un·sal·a·ble [ʌnséləbl] *adj.* invendible.
un·sat·is·fac·to·ry [ʌnsætɪsfǽktrɪ] *adj.* no satisfactorio, inaceptable.
un·scru·pu·lous [ʌnskrúpjʊləs] *adj.* poco escrupuloso.
un·sea·son·a·ble [ʌnsízənəbl] *adj.* intempestivo.
un·seat [ʌnsít] *v.* destituir.
un·seen [ʌnsín] *adj.* no visto, oculto; invisible.
un·self·ish [ʌnsélfɪʃ] *adj.* desinteresado.
un·self·ish·ness [ʌnsélfɪʃnɪs] *s.* desinterés, abnegación.
un·set·tled [ʌnsétld] *adj.* (*disturbed*) desordenado, en desorden; turbio; inestable; (*uncertain*) incierto; indeciso; (*unpopulated*) deshabitado; no establecido; — bills cuentas no liquidadas, cuentas pendientes; — weather tiempo variable; an — liquid un líquido revuelto o turbio.
un·shak·en [ʌnʃékən] *adj.* inmóvil, inmovible, firme.
un·sight·ly [ʌnsáɪtlɪ] *adj.* feo, desagradable a la vista.
un·skilled [ʌnskíld] *adj.* inexperto.
un·skill·ful [ʌnskílfəl] *adj.* inhábil, desmañado, inexperto.
un·so·cia·ble [ʌnsóʃəbl] *adj.* insociable, huraño, intratable, arisco.
un·so·phis·ti·cat·ed [ʌnsəfístəketəd] *adj.* cándido, sencillo.
un·sound [ʌnsáʊnd] *adj.* erróneo, falso.
un·speak·a·ble [ʌnspíkəbl] *adj.* indecible; inefable; atroz.
un·sta·ble [ʌnstébl] *adj.* inestable.
un·stead·y [ʌnstédɪ] *adj.* inseguro, inestable; movedizo; variable, inconstante.
un·suc·cess·ful [ʌnsəksésfəl] *adj.* sin éxito, desafortunado; to be — no tener éxito.
un·suit·a·ble [ʌnsútəbl] *adj.* impropio, inapropiado; inepto; inconveniente; incongruente; incompatible.
un·sus·pect·ed [ʌnsəspéktɪd] *adj.* insospechado.
un·ten·a·ble [ʌnténəbl] *adj.* insostenible.
un·think·a·ble [ʌnθínkəbl] *adj.* impensable.
un·ti·dy [ʌntáɪdɪ] *adj.* desaliñado, desaseado; desarreglado, en desorden.
un·tie [ʌntáɪ] *v.* desatar(se); desamarrar; deshacer

(un nudo o lazo).
un·til [ʌntíl] *prep.* hasta; *conj.* hasta que.
un·time·ly [ʌntáɪmlɪ] *adj.* inoportuno; prematuro; *adv.* inoportunamente; fuera de sazón; demasiado pronto.
un·tir·ing [ʌntáɪrɪŋ] *adj.* incansable.
un·told [ʌntóld] *adj.* indecible, innumerable, incalculable, inestimable.
un·touched [ʌntʌ́ʃt] *adj.* (*unscathed*) intacto, no tocado, integro; (*impassive*) impasible, no conmovido; to leave — no tocar, dejar intacto; dejar impasible, no conmover.
un·trained [ʌntrénd] *adj.* indisciplinado, falto de disciplina; sin educación; inexperto.
un·tried [ʌntráɪd] *adj.* no probado, no ensayado, no experimentado; — law case causa todavía no vista.
un·troub·led [ʌntrʌ́bld] *adj.* sosegado, tranquilo, quieto.
un·true [ʌntrú] *adj.* falso; infiel; desleal; mentiroso.
un·truth [ʌntrúθ] *s.* falsedad; mentira.
un·tu·tored [ʌntútəd] *adj.* sin instrucción; ingenuo.
un·twist [ʌntwíst] *v.* destorcer.
un·used [ʌnjúzd] *adj.* no usado; desacostumbrado; — to no hecho a, desacostumbrado a.
un·u·su·al [ʌnjúʒʊəl] *adj.* inusitado, insólito; desusado; raro, extraño; extraordinario.
un·var·nished [ʌnvárnɪʃt] *adj.* sin barnizar; sin adornos.
un·veil [ʌnvél] *v.* quitar el velo a; revelar, descubrir.
un·war·rant·ed [ʌnwɔ́rəntəd] *adj.* no justificado.
un·war·y [ʌnwérɪ] *adj.* incauto.
un·washed [ʌnwɔ́ʃt] *adj.* no lavado, sin lavar; sucio.
un·wel·come [ʌnwélkəm] *adj.* indeseable, no deseado; mal acogido, mal recibido, mal quisto.
un·whole·some [ʌnhólsəm] *adj.* malsano; insalubre, dañino.
un·wield·y [ʌnwíldɪ] *adj.* inmanejable, difícil de manejar, embarazoso, engorroso.
un·will·ing [ʌnwílɪŋ] *adj.* renuente, maldispuesto, reacio; to be — to no querer, no estar dispuesto a; -ly *adv.* de mala gana, sin querer.
un·will·ing·ness [ʌnwílɪŋnɪs] *s.* renuencia, falta de voluntad; mala gana.
un·wise [ʌnwáɪz] *adj.* imprudente, indiscreto; necio.
un·wont·ed [ʌnwʌ́ntəd] *adj.* inusitado, inacostumbrado; inédito.
un·wor·thy [ʌnwɔ́ðɪ] *adj.* indigno.
un·wrap [ʌnrǽp] *v.* desenvolver.
un·writ·ten [ʌnrítən] *adj.* no escrito.
up [ʌp] *adv.* (*above*) arriba, hacia arriba; en lo alto; (*standing*) de pie; *adj.* levantado, derecho, erecto; (*finished*) terminado, concluido; — and down de arriba abajo; de acá para allá; -s and downs altibajos; fluctuaciones, vaivenes; — the river río arriba; — to now hasta ahora; his time is — ha expirado su tiempo; se ha cumplido su plazo; prices are — los precios han subido; that is — to queda a la discreción de Vd.; eso es cosa suya; to be — against it estar perplejo, no saber qué hacer; estar en un aprieto; to be — on the news estar al corriente (o al tanto) de las noticias); to be — to one's old tricks hacer de las suyas; to eat it — comérselo; what's —? ¿qué pasa?; *v.* levantar, alzar.
up·braid [ʌpbréd] *v.* reprender, regañar.
up·date [ʌpdét] *v.* poner al día.
up·grade [ʌpgréd] *v.* adelantar; mejorar.

up·heav·al [ʌphívl] s. trastorno.
up·held [ʌphéld] pret. & p.p. de to uphold.
up·hill [ʌphíl] adv. cuesta arriba; adj. ascendente; trabajoso, arduo.
up·hold [ʌphóld] v. sostener; apoyar.
up·hol·ster [ʌphólstɚ] v. entapizar y rellenar (muebles).
up·hol·ster·y [ʌphólstrɪ] s. tapicería.
up·keep [ʌ́pkip] s. manutención.
up·land [ʌ́plənd] s. altiplanicie, tierra alta.
up·lift [ʌ́plɪft] s. elevación; edificación (espiritual); [ʌplíft] v. elevar; edificar (espiritualmente).
up·on [əpán] prep. en, sobre, encima de; — arriving al llegar.
up·per [ʌ́pɚ] adj. superior; alto; — berth litera alta, cama alta (de un coche dormitorio); to have the — hand ejercer dominio o mando; llevar la ventaja; s. litera alta, cama alta; pala (parte superior del calzado).
up·right [ʌ́praɪt] adj. recto; derecho; vertical; justo, honrado; — piano piano vertical; s. poste; puntal; piano vertical.
up·right·ness [ʌ́praɪtnɪs] s. rectitud.
up·ris·ing [ʌpráɪzɪŋ] s. alzamiento, levantamiento; revuelta.
up·roar [ʌ́pror] s. tumulto, alboroto, bulla, gritería.
up·roar·i·ous [ʌpróriəs] adj. estruendoso, bullicioso, tumultuoso.
up·root [ʌprút] v. desarraigar, arrancar de raíz.
up·set [ʌpsét] v. (capsize) volcar, tumbar; (distress) trastornar; perturbar, turbar; desquiciar; to become — volcarse; turbarse; trastornársele a uno el estómago; pret. & p.p. de to upset; adj. indispuesto, descompuesto; desarreglado, trastornado; [ʌ́pset] s. vuelco; trastorno; desorden; indisposición.
up·shot [ʌ́pʃat] s. resultado, fin.
up·side [ʌ́psaid] s. lado o parte superior; — down al revés; patas arriba, en desorden.
up·stage [ʌpstédʒ] v. quitarle la escena a uno.
up·stairs [ʌpstérz] adv. arriba, en el piso de arriba; adj. de arriba; s. piso (o pisos) de arriba.
up·start [ʌ́pstart] s. advenedizo, principiante presuntuoso.
up-to-date [ʌ́ptədét] adj. moderno; al corriente, al tanto.
up·turn [ʌ́ptɝn] s. alza, subida (de precios); mejora.
up·ward [ʌ́pwɚd] adv. arriba, para arriba, hacia arriba; más; — of más de; adj. ascendente; hacia arriba, para arriba.
up·wards [ʌ́pwɚdz] adv. – upward.
u·ra·ni·um [juréniəm] s. uranio.
ur·ban [ɝ́bən] adj. urbano.
ur·chin [ɝ́tʃɪn] s. granuja, pilluelo; sea — erizo de mar.
u·re·thra [juríθrə] s. uretra.
urge [ɝdʒ] v. urgir, instar; exhortar; recomendar o solicitar con instancia; apremiar, incitar, estimular; s. impulso; gana, ganas; estímulo.
ur·gen·cy [ɝ́dʒənsɪ] s. urgencia; apremio.
ur·gent [ɝ́dʒənt] adj. urgente, apremiante.
u·ric [júrɪk] adj. úrico.
u·ri·nal [júrɪn̩l] s. urinario.
u·ri·nate [júrənet] v. orinar.
u·rine [júrɪn] s. orina, (los) orines.
urn [ɝn] s. urna; coffee — cafetera.
us [ʌs] pron. nos; nosotros (con preposición).
us·age [júsɪdʒ] s. usanza; uso; hard — uso constante.
use [jus] s. (application) uso; empleo; (goal) utilidad; it is of no — es inútil; no sirve; out of

— desusado, ya no usado; pasado de moda; to have no further — for ya no necesitar, ya no tener necesidad de; what is the — of it? ¿para qué sirve?; ¿qué ventaja tiene?; ¿qué objeto tiene?; [juz] v. usar; emplear; servirse de, hacer uso de; acostumbrar, soler, Am. saber; — your judgment haz lo que te parezca; to — up gastar, agotar; consumir; to be -d to estar hecho, acostumbrado o habituado a; he -d to do it solía hacerlo, lo hacía.
use·ful [júsfəl] adj. útil.
use·ful·ness [júsfəlnɪs] s. utilidad.
use·less [júslɪs] adj. inútil; inservible.
use·less·ness [júslɪsnɪs] s. inutilidad.
ush·er [ʌ́ʃɚ] s. acomodador (en un teatro o iglesia); ujier; v. conducir, llevar, acompañar; introducir.
u·su·al [júʒuəl] adj. usual; corriente, común, general; -ly adv. usualmente, generalmente, por lo general.
u·su·rer [júʒərɚ] s. usurero.
u·surp [juzɝ́p] v. usurpar.
u·su·ry [júʒərɪ] s. usura.
u·ten·sil [jutén̩sl] s. utensilio.
u·ter·us [jútərəs] s. útero.
u·til·i·tar·i·an [jutɪlətérɪən] adj. utilitario.
u·til·i·ty [jutílətɪ] s. utilidad; servicio.
u·til·ize [jútl̩aɪz] v. utilizar; aprovechar.
ut·most [ʌ́tmost] adj. (extreme) sumo, extremo; más distante; más grande, mayor; más alto; (last) último; he did his — hizo cuanto pudo; to the — hasta más no poder.
u·to·pi·a [jutópjə] s. utopía.
ut·ter [ʌ́tɚ] v. proferir; decir, expresar; to — a cry dar un grito; adj. completo, total; absoluto.
ut·ter·ance [ʌ́tərəns] s. declaración; expresión; modo de hablar.
ut·ter·most [ʌ́tɚmost] = utmost.
u·vu·la [júvjələ] s. campanilla, galillo de la garganta; úvula.
u·vu·lar [júvjʊlɚ] adj. uvular.

V : v

va·can·cy [vékənsɪ] s. vacante, empleo vacante; vacío; habitación o apartamento desocupado.
va·cant [vékənt] adj. vacante; vacío; desocupado; libre.
va·cate [véket] v. desocupar, dejar vacío; dejar vacante.
va·ca·tion [vekéʃən] s. vacación; vacaciones.
vac·ci·nate [vǽksn̩et] v. vacunar.
vac·ci·na·tion [væksnéʃən] s. vacunación.
vac·cine [vǽksin] s. vacuna.
vac·il·late [vǽslet] v. vacilar.
vac·u·um [vǽkjuəm] s. vacío; — cleaner escoba eléctrica.
vag·a·bond [vǽgəband] adj. & s. vagabundo.
va·gi·na [vədʒáɪnə] s. vagina.
va·gran·cy [végrənsɪ] s. vagancia.
va·grant [végrənt] adj. vago, vagabundo, errante; s. vago, vagabundo.
vague [veg] adj. vago.
vain [ven] adj. vano; vanidoso; in — en vano.
vain·glor·y [venglóri] s. vanagloria.
vale [vel] s. valle; cañada.
val·en·tine [vǽləntaɪn] s. tarjeta o regalo del día de San Valentín (el día de los enamorados); to my — a mi querido, a mi querida.

UN

val·et [vǽlɪt] *s.* criado, camarero; planchador de trajes.

val·iant [vǽljənt] *adj.* valiente, valeroso.

val·id [vǽlɪd] *adj.* válido; valedero.

va·lid·i·ty [vəlídətɪ] *s.* validez.

va·lise [vəlís] *s.* valija, maleta, *Méx.* velís, *Méx.* petaca.

val·ley [vǽlɪ] *s.* valle.

val·or [vǽlə] *s.* valor, ánimo, valentía.

val·or·ous [vǽlərəs] *adj.* valeroso, valiente.

val·u·a·ble [vǽljəbḷ] *adj.* valioso; precioso; preciado; -s *s. pl.* objetos de valor, hoyas, alhajas.

val·u·a·tion [væljʊéʃən] *s.* valuación, valoración; avalúo; tasa.

val·ue [vǽljʊ] *s. (price)* valor; precio; *(merit)* mérito; *(consideration)* estimación, aprecio; *v.* valorar, avaluar, valuar; apreciar, estimar.

val·ue·less [vǽljʊlɪs] *adj.* sin valor.

valve [vælv] *s.* válvula; valva *(de los moluscos)*; **safety —** válvula de seguridad.

vam·pire [vǽmpaɪr] *s.* vampiro.

van [væn] *s.* camión *(para transportar muebles)*; **—guard** vanguardia.

va·na·di·um [vənédiəm] *s.* vanadio.

van·dal [vǽndḷ] *s.* vandalo.

vane [ven] *s.* veleta; aspa *(de molino de viento)*; paleta *(de hélice)*.

van·guard [vǽngɑrd] *s.* vanguardia.

va·nil·la [vənílə] *s.* vainilla.

van·ish [vǽnɪʃ] *v.* desvanecerse, desaparecer(se).

van·i·ty [vǽnətɪ] *s.* vanidad; **— case** neceser; **— table** tocador.

van·quish [vǽnkwɪʃ] *v.* vencer.

van·tage [vǽntɪdʒ] *s.* ventaja; **point of —** lugar estratégico.

va·por [vépə] *s.* vapor; vaho.

va·por·ize [vépəaɪz] *v.* vaporizar.

var·i·a·ble [vérɪəbḷ] *adj. & s.* variable.

var·i·ance [vérɪəns] *s.* variación, cambio; desavenencia; **to be at —** estar desavenidos; no estar de acuerdo.

var·i·ant [vérɪənt] *s.* variante.

var·i·a·tion [vɛrɪéʃən] *s.* variación; variedad.

var·ied [vérɪd] *adj.* variado, vario.

var·i·e·gat·ed [vérɪgetɪd] *adj.* abigarrado.

va·ri·e·ty [vəráɪətɪ] *s.* variedad.

var·i·ous [vérɪəs] *adj.* varios; diferentes, distintos.

var·nish [vɑrnɪʃ] *s.* barniz; *v.* barnizar.

var·y [vérɪ] *v.* variar; cambiar.

vase [ves] *s.* vaso, jarrón.

Vas·e·line [vǽsəlin] *s.* vaselina.

vas·sal [vǽsḷ] *adj. & s.* vasallo.

vast [væst] *adj.* vasto; inmenso; anchuroso; **-ly** *adv.* vastamente, sumamente, muy.

vast·ness [vǽstnɪs] *s.* inmensidad.

vat [væt] *s.* tina, tanque.

vaude·ville [vódəvɪl] *s.* vodevil, función de variedades.

vault [vɔlt] *s.* bóveda; tumba; **bank —** caja fuerte; depósito; **pole —** salto con garrocha; *v.* abovedar, edificar una bóveda; dar figura de bóveda; saltar con garrocha; saltar por encima de.

vaunt [vɔnt] *v.* jactarse; ostentar, alardear; *s.* jactancia.

veal [vil] *s.* carne de ternera; **— cutlet** chuleta de ternera.

veer [vɪr] *v.* virar; *s.* virada.

veg·e·ta·ble [védʒtəbḷ] *s. (plant)* vegetal, planta; *(food)* legumbre; **-s** hortaliza, legumbres; **green**

-s verduras; *adj.* vegetal; de legumbres, de hortaliza; **— garden** hortaliza.

veg·e·tar·i·an [vɛdʒətérɪən] *s.* vegetariano.

veg·e·tate [védʒətet] *v.* vegetar.

veg·e·ta·tion [vɛdʒətéʃən] *s.* vegetación.

ve·he·mence [víəməns] *s.* vehemencia.

ve·he·ment [víəmənt] *adj.* vehemente.

ve·hi·cle [víɪkḷ] *s.* vehículo.

veil [vel] *s.* velo; *v.* velar; tapar, encubrir.

vein [ven] *s.* vena; veta, filón.

veined [vend] *adj.* veteado, jaspeado; venoso.

ve·loc·i·ty [vəlásətɪ] *s.* velocidad.

vel·vet [vélvɪt] *s.* terciopelo; velludo; *adj.* de terciopelo; aterciopelado.

vel·vet·y [vélvɪtɪ] *adj.* aterciopelado.

ven·dor [véndə] *s.* vendedor; buhonero, vendedor ambulante.

ve·neer [vənír] *s.* chapa; *v.* chapar o chapear, *Am.* enchapar.

ven·er·a·ble [vénərəbḷ] *adj.* venerable; venerando.

ven·er·ate [vénəret] *v.* venerar.

ven·er·a·tion [vɛnəréʃən] *s.* veneración.

ve·ne·re·al [vənírɪəl] *adj.* venéreo.

Ven·e·zue·lan [vɛnəzwílən] *adj. & s.* venezolano.

ven·geance [véndʒəns] *s.* venganza; **with a —** con furia; con violencia.

ven·i·son [vénəzn] *s.* venado, carne de venado.

ven·om [vénəm] *s.* veneno, ponzoña.

ven·om·ous [vénəməs] *adj.* venenoso, ponzoñoso.

vent [vɛnt] *s. (opening)* abertura; *(escape)* escape; *(utterance)* desahogo; fogón *(de arma de fuego)*; **to give — to anger** desahogar la ira, dar desahogo a la cólera; *v.* dar salida o desahogo; desahogar, descargar.

ven·ti·late [véntlet] *v.* ventilar.

ven·ti·la·tion [ventléʃən] *s.* ventilación.

ven·ti·la·tor [véntletə] *s.* ventilador.

ven·ture [véntʃə] *s.* ventura, riesgo; **business —** especulación; empresa o negocio arriesgado; *v.* aventurar, arriesgar; **to — outside** aventurarse a salir; **to — to** aventurarse a, atreverse a, osar.

ven·tur·ous [véntʃərəs] *adj.* aventurado.

ve·ran·da [vərǽndə] *s.* galería; terraza; balcón corrido.

verb [vɝb] *s.* verbo.

ver·bal [vɝbḷ] *adj.* verbal; oral.

ver·bal·ize [vɝbəlaɪz] *v.* expresar por medio de palabras.

ver·bose [vəbós] *adj.* verboso; palabrero.

ver·dict [vɝdɪkt] *s.* veredicto; fallo, decisión, sentencia; **— of "not guilty"** veredicto de inculpabilidad.

ver·dure [vɝdʒə] *s.* verdura, verdor, verde.

verge [vɝdʒ] *s.* borde, margen, orilla; **on the — of** al borde de; a punto de; *v.* **to — on** rayar en, estar al margen de; **to — toward** tender a, inclinarse a.

ver·i·fy [vérəfaɪ] *v.* verificar; comprobar.

ver·i·ly [vérɪlɪ] *adv.* en verdad.

ver·i·ta·ble [vérətəbḷ] *adj.* verdadero.

ver·mil·lion [vəmíljən] *adj.* bermejo.

ver·nac·u·lar [vənǽkjʊlə] *adj.* vernáculo; *s.* idioma corriente.

ver·sa·tile [vɝsətḷ] *adj.* hábil para muchas cosas; flexible; versátil.

verse [vɝs] *s.* verso.

versed [vɝst] *adj.* versado, experto, perito.

ver·sion [vɝʒən] *s.* versión.

ver·te·brate [vɝtəbrɪt] *adj.* vertebrado.

ver·ti·cal [vɝtɪkḷ] *adj.* vertical.

ver·y [vérɪ] *adv.* muy; **— much** muchísimo; **—**

many muchísimos; **it is — cold today** hace
mucho frío hoy; *adj.* mismo; mismísimo; mero;
the — man el mismísimo hombre; **the — thought
of** la mera idea de.
ves·pers [véspəz] *s. pl.* vísperas.
ves·sel [vésl] *s.* vasija; vaso; barco, embarcación;
blood — vaso, vena, arteria.
vest [vɛst] *s.* chaleco; *v.* conferir; **to — with
power** revestir de autoridad, conferir poder a.
ves·ti·bule [véstəbjul] *s.* vestíbulo; zaguán.
ves·tige [véstɪdʒ] *s.* vestigio.
vest·ment [véstmənt] *s.* vestidura.
vet·er·an [vétərən] *adj. & s.* veterano.
vet·er·i·nar·y [vétrənɛrɪ] *s.* veterinario o albéitar.
ve·to [víto] *s.* veto; prohibición; *v.* vedar, prohibir;
poner el veto a; negarse a aprobar.
vex [vɛks] *v.* molestar, hostigar; incomodar,
enfadar; perturbar.
vex·a·tion [vɛkséʃən] *s.* molestia, incomodidad;
enojo; vejamen.
vi·a [váɪə] *prep.* por, por la vía de.
vi·a·ble [váɪəbl] *adj.* viable.
vi·a·duct [váɪədʌkt] *s.* viaducto.
vi·al [váɪəl] *s.* frasco, redoma; **small —** ampolleta.
vi·ands [váɪəndz] *s. pl.* vianda, alimentos,
comida.
vi·brate [váɪbret] *v.* vibrar.
vi·bra·tion [vaɪbréʃən] *s.* vibración.
vi·car·i·ous [vaɪkérɪəs] *adj.* vicario.
vice [vaɪs] *s.* vicio; falta, defecto.
vice-pres·i·dent [váɪsprézədənt] *s.* vice-presidente.
vice·re·gal [vaɪsrígl] *adj.* virreinal.
vice·roy [váɪsrɔɪ] *s.* virrey.
vice ver·sa [váɪsɪvɝsə] viceversa.
vi·cin·i·ty [vəsínətɪ] *s.* vecindad; cercanía;
inmediaciones.
vi·cious [víʃəs] *adj.* vicioso; malo; maligno;
malicioso; **— dog** perro mordedor, perro bravo.
vi·cis·si·tude [vəsísətjud] *s.* vicisitud, peripecia.
vic·tim [víktɪm] *s.* victima.
vic·tim·ize [víktɪmaɪz] *v.* inmolar; engañar.
vic·tor [víktə] *s.* vencedor.
vic·to·ri·ous [vɪktórɪəs] *adj.* victorioso.
vic·to·ry [víktrɪ] *s.* victoria.
vic·tuals [vítlz] *s. pl.* vituallas, víveres.
vie [vaɪ] *v.* competir.
view [vju] *s.* (*field of vision*) vista; paisaje; (*opinion*)
parecer, opinion; (*inspection*) inspección; (*aim*)
mira, propósito; **in — of** en vista de; **to be
within —** estar al alcance de la vista; **with a —
to** con el propósito de; con la esperanza o
expectación de; con la mira puesta en; *v.* mirar;
examinar.
view·point [vjúpɔɪnt] *s.* punto de vista.
vig·il [vídʒəl] *s.* vigilia, velada; **to keep —** velar.
vig·i·lance [vídʒələns] *s.* vigilancia, desvelo.
vig·i·lant [vídʒələnt] *adj.* vigilante.
vig·or [vígə] *s.* vigor.
vig·or·ous [vígərəs] *adj.* vigoroso.
vile [vaɪl] *adj.* vil, bajo, ruin; pésimo.
vil·la [vílə] *s.* quinta, casa de campo.
vil·lage [vílɪdʒ] *s.* villa, aldea.
vil·lag·er [vílɪdʒə] *s.* aldeano.
vil·lain [vílən] *s.* vilano, malvado, bellaco.
vil·lain·ous [vílənəs] *adj.* villano, ruin, vil, bellaco.
vil·lain·y [vílənɪ] *s.* villanía, vileza.
vim [vɪm] *s.* vigor, fuerza, energía.
vin·di·cate [víndəket] *v.* vindicar, vengar.
vin·dic·tive [vɪndíktɪv] *adj.* vengativo.
vine [vaɪn] *s.* vid, parra; enredadera.
vin·e·gar [vínɪgə] *s.* vinagre.

vine·yard [vínjəd] *s.* viña, viñedo.
vin·tage [víntɪdʒ] *s.* vendimia; edad, época.
vi·o·late [váɪəlet] *v.* violar; infringir.
vi·o·la·tion [vaɪəléʃən] *s.* violación; infracción.
vi·o·lence [váɪələns] *s.* violencia.
vi·o·lent [váɪələnt] *adj.* violento.
vi·o·let [váɪəlɪt] *s.* violeta; violado, color de
violeta; *adj.* violado.
vi·o·lin [vaɪəlín] *s.* violín.
vi·o·lin·ist [vaɪəlínɪst] *s.* violinista.
vi·o·lon·cel·lo [vɪəlontʃélo] *s.* violonchelo.
vi·per [váɪpə] *s.* víbora.
vir·gin [vɝdʒɪn] *adj. & s.* virgen.
vir·gin·al [vɝdʒɪnl] *adj.* virginal.
vir·ile [vírl] *adj.* viril.
vir·tu·al [vɝtʃʊəl] *adj.* virtual; **-ly** *adv.*
virtualmente.
vir·tue [vɝtʃu] *s.* virtud.
vir·tu·ous [vɝtʃʊəs] *adj.* virtuoso.
vi·sa [vízə] *s.* visa, visado; *v.* visar, refrendar.
vis·cer·al [vísəl] *adj.* visceral.
vi·sé = visa.
vise [vaɪs] *s.* tornillo de banco.
vis·i·ble [vízəbl] *adj.* visible.
Vis·i·goth [vízəgɔθ] *s.* visigodo.
vi·sion [víʒən] *s.* visión; vista.
vi·sion·ar·y [víʒənɛrɪ] *adj.* visionario; imaginario;
s. visionario, iluso, soñador.
vis·it [vízɪt] *v.* visitar; **to — punishment upon**
mandar un castigo a, castigar a; *s.* visita.
vis·i·ta·tion [vɪzətéʃən] *s.* visitación, visita; castigo,
calamidad.
vis·i·tor [vízɪtə] *s.* visita; visitador.
vi·sor [váɪzə] *s.* visera.
vis·ta [vístə] *s.* vista, paisaje.
vis·u·al [vízjul] *adj.* visual; visible.
vis·u·al·ize [vízjʊalaɪz] *v.* representarse en la
mente.
vi·tal [váɪtl] *adj.* vital.
vi·tal·i·ty [vaɪtælətɪ] *s.* vitalidad.
vi·tal·ize [váɪtəlaɪz] *v.* vitalizar.
vi·ta·min [váɪtəmɪn] *s.* vitamina.
vi·ta·min·ized [váɪtəmənaɪzd] *adj.* vitaminado.
vi·va·cious [vaɪvéʃəs] *adj.* vivaz, vivaracho, vivo,
alegre, animado.
vi·vac·i·ty [vaɪvæsətɪ] *s.* viveza, vivacidad.
viv·id [vívɪd] *adj.* vívido, vivo; animado.
viv·i·fy [vívəfaɪ] *v.* vivificar.
vo·cab·u·lar·y [vəkæbjələrɪ] *s.* vocabulario.
vo·cal [vókl] *adj.* vocal; oral; **— cords** cuerdas
vocales; **to be —** hablar, expresarse.
vo·ca·tion [vokéʃən] *s.* vocación.
vogue [vog] *s.* boga, moda; **in —** en boga, de
moda.
voice [vɔɪs] *s.* (*vocalization*) voz; (*speech*) habla;
(*opinion*) voto; *v.* expresar, decir; **-d consonant**
consonante sonora.
voice·less [vɔɪslɪs] *adj.* mudo; sin voz; **— consonant**
consonante sorda.
void [vɔɪd] *adj.* vacío; nulo, inválido; **— of** falto de,
desprovisto de; *s.* vacío; *v.* vaciar, evacuar;
anular, invalidar.
vol·a·tile [válətl] *adj.* volátil; inconstante.
vol·can·ic [valkænɪk] *adj.* volcánico.
vol·ca·no [valkéno] *s.* volcán.
vo·li·tion [volíʃən] *s.* volición; voluntad.
vol·ley [válɪ] *s.* descarga, lluvia (*de piedras, flechas,
balas, etc.*); voleo (*de la pelota*); *v.* descargar una
lluvia de proyectiles; volear una pelota.
volt [volt] *s.* voltio.
volt·age [vóltɪdʒ] *s.* voltaje.

vol·u·ble [váljəbl] *adj.* facundo.
vol·ume [váljəm] *s.* volumen; tomo; bulto; suma, cantidad.
vo·lu·mi·nous [vəlúmənəs] *adj.* voluminoso.
vol·un·tar·y [váləntɛrɪ] *adj.* voluntario.
vol·un·teer [valəntír] *s.* voluntario; *adj.* voluntario; de voluntarios; *v.* ofrecer, dar voluntariamente; ofrecerse.
vo·lup·tu·ous [vəlʌ́ptʃʊəs] *adj.* voluptuoso.
vom·it [vámɪt] *s.* vómito; *v.* vomitar, *Méx.* deponer.
vo·ra·cious [voréʃəs] *adj.* voraz.
vor·tex [vórtɛks] *s.* vórtice; vorágine.
vote [vot] *s.* voto; votación; *v.* votar; votar por.
vot·er [vótə˞] *s.* votante, elector.
vouch [vaʊtʃ] *v.* **to — for** dar fe de; garantizar, responder de; salir fiador de.
vouch·er [váʊtʃə˞] *s.* comprobante, justificante; recibo; fiador.
vouch·safe [vaʊtʃséf] *v.* otorgar, conceder.
vow [vaʊ] *s.* voto; juramente; *v.* votar, jurar, hacer voto de.
vow·el [váʊəl] *s. & adj.* vocal.
voy·age [vɔɪɪdʒ] *s.* viaje; travesía; *v.* viajar.
vul·gar [vʌ́lgə˞] *adj.* soez, ordinario, grosero; vulgar.
vul·ner·a·ble [vʌ́nə˞əbl] *adj.* vulnerable.
vul·ture [vʌ́ltʃə˞] *s.* buitre, *Andes, Ríopl.* cóndor.
vul·va [vʌ́lvə] *s.* vulva.

W:w

wab·ble [wábl] *v.* tambalear(se), bambolear(se); vacilar; temblar; *s.* tambaleo, bamboleo; balanceo.
wad [wad] *s.* taco; bodoque; pelotilla, bolita, rollo; **— of money** rollo de billetes (*de banco*); dinero; *v.* atacar (*un arma de fuego*); rellenar; hacer una pelotilla de.
wad·dle [wádl] *v.* anadear; contonearse, zarandearse (*al andar*); *s.* anadeo; zarandeo, contoneo.
wade [wed] *v.* vadear; chapotear; andar descalzo por la orilla del agua; **to — through a book** leer con dificultad un libro.
wa·fer [wéfə˞] *s.* oblea; hostia (*consagrada*).
waft [wæft] *v.* llevar en vilo, llevar por el aire; llevar a flote; *s.* ráfaga de aire; movimiento (*de la mano*).
wag [wæg] *v.* menear; sacudir; **to — the tail** colear, menear la cola; *s.* meneo; bromista, farsante.
wage [wedʒ] *v.* hacer (*guerra*); dar (*batalla*); *s.* (*usualmente* **wages**) paga, jornal; **— earner** jornalero, obrero; trabajador; **— scale** escala de salarios (*sueldos*).
wa·ger [wédʒə˞] *s.* apuesta; *v.* apostar.
wag·gle [wǽgl] *s.* meneo rápido.
wag·on [wǽgən] *s.* carro, carreta; carretón.
wail [wel] *v.* gemir, lamentar; *s.* gemido, lamento.
waist [west] *s.* cintura; talle; blusa; **—band** pretina.
waist·coat [wéstkot] *s.* chaleco.
waist·line [wéstlaɪn] *s.* talle.
wait [wet] *v.* (*stay*) esperar, aguardar; (*serve*) servir; **to — for** esperar, aguardar; **to — on** (**upon**) servir a; atender a; **to — table** servir la mesa, servir de mozo o camarero (*en un restaurante*); *s.* espera; **to lie in — for** estar en

acecho de.
wait·er [wétə˞] *s.* mozo, camarero, sirviente, *Méx., C.A.* mesero.
wait·ing [wétɪŋ] *s.* espera; **— room** sala de espera.
wait·ress [wétrɪs] *s.* camarera, moza, *Mex.* mesera.
waive [wev] *v.* renunciar a; **to — one's right** renunciar voluntariamente a sus derechos.
waiv·er [wévə˞] *s.* renuncia.
wake [wek] *v.* despertar(se); **to — up** despertar(se); despabilarse; *s.* velatorio (*acto de velar a un muerto*), *Am.* velorio; estela (*huella que deja un barco en el agua*); **in the — of** después de, detrás de.
wake·ful [wékfəl] *adj.* desvelado, despierto; insomne.
wak·en [wékən] *v.* despertar(se); *Ríopl.* recordar (*a una persona que está dormida*).
walk [wɔk] *v.* andar, caminar, ir a pie; recorrer a pie; pasear; **to — away** irse, marcharse; **to — back home** volverse a casa (a pie); **to — down** bajar; **to — in** entrar; **to — out** salirse, irse; parar el trabajo, declararse en huelga; **to — the streets** callejear; **to — up** subir; *s.* paseo; senda, vereda; acera; paso (*del caballo*); manera de andar; **— of life** vocación; **a ten minutes' —** una caminata de diez minutos.
wall [wɔl] *s.* (*interior*) pared; (*garden*) muro; (*fort*) muralla; **execution —** paredón; **low mud —** tapia; **to drive to the —** poner entre la espada y la pared, poner en un aprieto.
wal·let [wɑ́lɪt] *s.* cartera.
wall·flow·er [wɔ́lflaʊə˞] *s.* aleli; **to be a — at a dance** comer pavo, *Andes, Méx.* planchar el asiento.
wal·lop [wɑ́ləp] *v.* pegar, zurrar, golpear; *s.* guantada, bofetón, golpazo.
wal·low [wɑ́lo] *v.* revolcarse; chapalear o chapotear (*en el agua*).
wall·pa·per [wɔ́lpepə˞] *s.* papel (de empapelar).
wal·nut [wɔ́lnət] *s.* nuez de nogal; nogal; **— tree** nogal.
waltz [wɔlts] *s.* vals; *s.* valsar, bailar el vals.
wan [wan] *adj.* pálido, enfermizo, enclenque; lánguido.
wand [wand] *s.* vara, varita; **magic —** varita de virtud.
wan·der [wándə˞] *v.* vagar, errar; **to — away** extraviarse; **to — away from** apartarse de, desviarse de; **my mind -s easily** me distraigo fácilmente.
wan·der·er [wándərə˞] *s.* vago, vagabundo.
wane [wen] *v.* menguar; decaer; *s.* mengua; diminución; **to be on the —** ir menguando o desapareciendo.
want [want] *v.* (*desire*) querer, desear; (*lack*) necesitar; *s.* falta; necesidad; escasez, carencia; **to be in —** estar necesitado.
want·ing [wántɪŋ] *adj.* falto; deficiente; necesitado.
wan·ton [wántən] *adj.* desenfrenado, libre; licencioso; inconsiderado; temerario.
war [wɔr] *s.* guerra; *v.* guerrear, hacer guerra; **to — on** guerrear con.
war·ble [wɔ́rbl] *v.* gorjear; trinar; *s.* gorjeo; trino.
war·bler [wɔ́rblə˞] *s.* cantor; pájaro gorjeador.
ward [wɔrd] *s.* pupilo, menor o huérfano (*bajo tutela*); cuadra (*de hospital, prisión, etc.*); distrito (*de una ciudad*); *v.* **to — off** resguardarse de; evitar; parar (*un golpe*).
war·den [wɔ́rdn] *s.* guardián; alcaide; **prison —** alcaide de una prisión.
ward·robe [wɔ́rdrob] *s.* (*closet*) guardarropa,

ropero, armario; (*garments*) vestuario; ropa.
ware·house [wέrhaʊs] *s.* almacén, depósito.
wares [wɛrz] *s. pl.* artículos, mercancías,
mercaderías, efectos.
war·fare [wɔ́rfɛr] *s.* guerra.
war·head [wɔ́rhɛd] *s.* punta de combate.
war·like [wɔ́rlaɪk] *adj.* guerrero, bélico.
warm [wɔrm] *adj.* (*temperature*) caliente, cálido,
caluroso; (*enthusiastic*) acalorado; (*fresh*)
reciente; — **hearted** de buen corazón; — **blooded**
apasionado; ardiente; **he is** — tiene calor; **it is**
— **today** hace calor hoy; *v.* calentar(se); **to** —
over recalentar; **to** — **up** calentar(se); acalorarse;
entusiasmarse.
warmth [wɔrmpθ] *s.* (*heat*) calor; (*friendship*)
cordialidad.
warn [wɔrn] *v.* avisar, advertir, amonestar;
prevenir, precaver.
warn·ing [wɔ́rnɪŋ] *s.* aviso, advertencia,
amonestación; escarmiento; **let that be a** — **to**
you que te sirva de escarmiento.
warp [wɔrp] *s.* urdimbre (*de un tejido*); torcedura,
deformación; comba; *v.* combar(se),
deformar(se), torcer(se); urdir (*los hilos de un*
telar).
war·rant [wɔ́rənt] *s.* (*sanction*) autorización; (*right*)
garantía, justificación; (*writ*) comprobante;
orden, mandato, citación (*ante un juez*); *v.*
autorizar; garantizar; justificar.
war·ri·or [wɔ́rɪɚ] *s.* guerrero.
war·ship [wɔ́rʃɪp] *s.* buque de guerra, acorazado.
wart [wɔrt] *s.* verruga.
war·y [wɛ́rɪ] *adj.* cauteloso, cauto, precavido,
prevenido; **to be** — **of** desconfiar de.
was [waz] *pret. de* **to be** (*primera y tercera persona*
del singular).
wash [waʃ] *v.* lavar(se); **to** — **away** deslavar(se);
to be -ed away by the waves ser arrastrado por
las olas; *s.* lavado; lavadura; lavatorio; lavazas,
agua sucia; **mouth** — enjuague o enjuagatorio;
—**bowl** lavabo, palangana, lavamanos; —**cloth**
paño para lavarse; — **dress** vestido lavable;
— **room** lavabo, lavatorio.
wash·a·ble [wáʃəbl] *adj.* lavable.
wash-and-wear [wɔ́ʃændwέr] *adj.* de lava y pon.
washed·out [wáʃtáʊt] *adj.* desteñido; agotado, sin
fuerzas.
washed-up [wɔʃtʌ́p] *adj.* fracasado.
wash·er [wáʃɚ] *s.* lavador; máquina de lavar;
arandela (*para una tuerca*); —**woman** lavandera.
wash·ing [wáʃɪŋ] *s.* lavado; ropa sucia o para
lavar; ropa lavada; — **machine** lavadora,
máquina de lavar.
wash·out [wɔʃaʊt] *s.* derrubio; fracaso.
wasp [wasp] *s.* avispa.
waste [west] *v.* gastar; desgastar; malgastar,
desperdiciar, derrochar; disipar; **to** — **away**
gastarse, consumirse; desgastarse; *s.* desperdicio;
gasto inútil; desgaste; desechos, desperdicios;
terreno baldío, desierto; *adj.* inútil, desechado;
desierto; baldío; — **of time** pérdida de tiempo;
— **basket** cesto para papeles; — **land** terreno
baldío; — **paper** papeles inútiles, papel de
desecho; **to go to** — gastarse, perderse;
malgastarse, desperdiciarse; **to lay** — asolar,
arruinar.
waste·ful [wéstfəl] *adj.* despilfarrado, gastador;
desperdiciado; ineconómico.
watch [watʃ] *v.* (*look*) mirar; observar; (*be alert*)
vigilar; velar; cuidar; — **out!** ¡cuidado!; **to** —
out for tener cuidado con; cuidar; vigilar; *s.*

reloj (*de bolsillo*); vela, vigilia; guardia;
centinela, vigilante; — **chain** cadena de reloj,
Ven., Méx. leontina; — **charm** dije; **wrist**— reloj
de pulsera; **to be on the** — tener cuidado;
estar alerta; **to keep** — **over** vigilar a.
watch·ful [wátʃfəl] *adj.* alerto, vigilante, despertio,
atento.
watch·mak·er [wátʃmekɚ] *s.* relojero.
watch·man [wátʃmən] *s.* vigilante, guardia, sereno.
watch·tow·er [wátʃtaʊɚ] *s.* atalaya, mirador.
watch·word [wátʃwɜd] *s.* contraseña, santo o seña,
consigna; lema.
wa·ter [wɔ́tɚ] *s.* agua; — **color** acuarela; color
para acuarela; — **power** fuerza hidráulica;
—**shed** vertiente; — **sports** deportes acuáticos;
— **supply** abastecimiento de agua; *v.* regar;
aguar, diluir con agua; abrevar, dar de beber
(*al ganado*); beber agua (*el ganado*); tomar agua
(*un barco, locomotora, etc.*); **my eyes** — me
lloran los ojos; **my mouth -s** se me hace agua
la boca.
wa·ter·cress [wɔ́tɚkrɛs] *s.* berro.
wa·ter·fall [wɔ́tɚfɔl] *s.* cascada, catarata, caída de
agua.
wa·ter·front [wɔ́tɚfrʌnt] *s.* terreno ribereño.
wa·ter·mel·on [wɔ́tɚmɛlən] *s.* sandía.
wa·ter·pow·er [wɔ́tɚpaʊɚ] *s.* fuerza hidráulica.
wa·ter·proof [wɔ́tɚpruf] *adj. & s.* impermeable; *v.*
hacer impermeable.
wa·ter-ski [wɔ́tɚski] *s.* esqui acuático
wa·ter·spout [wɔ́tɚspaʊt] *s.* surtidor; tromba,
manga de agua.
wa·ter·way [wɔ́tɚwe] *s.* vía de agua, río navegable,
canal.
wa·ter·y [wɔ́tɚɪ] *adj.* aguado; acuoso; mojado,
húmedo.
wave [wev] *v.* ondear; ondular; agitar; blandir (*una*
espada, bastón, etc.); **to** — **aside** apartar,
rechazar; **to** — **good-bye** hacer una seña o
ademán de despedida; **to** — **hair** ondular el
pelo; **to** — **one's hand** hacer una seña o señas
con la mano; mover la mano; *s.* onda; ola;
ondulación; — **of the hand** ademán, movimiento
de la mano; **permanent** — ondulación
permanente.
wave·length [wévlɛŋθ] *s.* longitud de onda.
wa·ver [wévɚ] *v.* oscilar; vacilar; titubear;
tambalear(se); *s.* vacilación, titubeo.
wa·vy [wévɪ] *adj.* rizado, ondulado; ondulante.
wax [wæks] *s.* cera; — **candle** vela de cera; —
paper papel encerado; *v.* encerar; pulir con cera;
hacerse, ponerse; crecer (*la luna*).
way [we] *s.* (*road*) camino; ruta; senda; (*manner*)
modo, manera; — **in** entrada; — **out** salida;
— **through** paso, pasaje; **a long** — **off** muy lejos,
a una larga distancia; **by** — **of** por, por vía de;
by — **of comparison** a modo de comparación;
by the — de paso; **in no** — de ningún modo;
on the — to camino de, rumbo a; **out of the** —
fuera del camino; apartado; a un lado;
impropio; extraordinario; **to be in a bad** —
hallarse en mal estado; **to be well under** —
estar (*un trabajo*) ya bastante avanzado; **to give**
— ceder; quebrarse; **to have one's** — hacer su
capricho, salirse con la suya; **to make** — **for**
abrir paso para.
way·far·er [wéfɛrɚ] *s.* caminante.
way·lay [welé] *v.* estar en acecho de (*alguien*);
asaltar; detener (*a una persona*).
way·side [wésaɪd] *s.* borde del camino; — **inn**
posada al borde del camino.

VO

way·ward [wéwəd] *adj. adj.* voluntarioso, desobediente.

we [wi] *pron.* nosotros, nosotras.

weak [wik] *adj.* débil; flaco; endeble; — **market** mercado flojo; **weak-minded** de voluntad débil; simple; — **tea** té claro o suave.

weak·en [wíkən] *v.* debilitar(se); desmayar, flaquear, perder ánimo.

weak·ly [wíklı] *adv.* débilmente; *adj.* enfermizo, débil, enclenque.

weak·ness [wíknis] *s.* debilidad; flaqueza.

wealth [wɛlθ] *s.* riqueza; copia, abundancia.

wealth·y [wélθı] *adj.* rico; acaudalado.

wean [win] *v.* destetar; apartar gradualmente (*de un hábito, de una amistad*).

weap·on [wépən] *s.* arma.

wear [wɛr] *v.* (*have on*) llevar, tener o traer puesto; usar; (*waste away*) gastar, desgastar; **to — away** gastar(se), degastar(se); consumir(se); **to — off** degastar(se), gastar(se); borrarse; **to — out** gastar(se); desgastar(se); consumir(se); agotar; cansar; **it -s well** es duradero; dura mucho; **as the day wore on** a medida que pasaba el día; *s.* uso, gasto; durabilidad; — **and tear** desgaste; uso; **men's** — ropa para hombres; **clothes for summer** — ropa de verano.

wea·ri·ly [wírılı] *adv.* penosamente, con cansancio, con fatiga, fatigadamente.

wea·ri·ness [wírınıs] *s.* cansancio, fatiga.

wear·ing [wɛ́rıŋ] *adj.* cansado, aburrido, fastidioso.

wea·ri·some [wírısəm] *adj.* fatigoso, molesto, fastidioso.

wea·ry [wírı] *adj.* cansado, fatigado; aburrido; *v.* cansar(se), fatigar(se).

wea·sel [wízl] *s.* comadreja.

weath·er [wéðə] *s.* tiempo; **weather-beaten** desgastado o curtido por la intemperie; — **bureau** oficina meteorológica; — **conditions** condiciones atmosféricas; —**vane** veleta; **it is fine** — hace buen tiempo; **to be under the** — estar enfermo; estar indispuesto; *v.* exponer a la intemperie; orear, secar al aire; **to — a storm** aguantar un chubasco; salir ileso de una tormenta.

weave [wiv] *v.* (*cloth*) tejer, entretejer; (*to plan*) urdir; **to — together** entretejer, entrelazar; combinar; *s.* tejido.

weav·er [wívə] *s.* tejedor.

web [wɛb] *s.* tela; membrana (*entre los dedos de los pájaros acuáticos*); **spider's** —telaraña.

wed [wɛd] *v.* casarse; casarse con; casar; *p.p. de* **to wed.**

wed·ded [wédıd] *p.p. & adj.* casado; unido; — **to an idea** aferrado a una idea.

wed·ding [wédıŋ] *s.* boda, casamiento, nupcias, enlace; — **day** día de bodas; — **trip** viaje de novios; **silver** — bodas de plata.

wedge [wɛdʒ] *s.* cuña; **entering** —cuña, entrada, medio de entrar, modo de penetrar; *v.* acuñar, meter cuñas; **to be -d between** estar encajado entre.

Wednes·day [wénzdı] *s.* miércoles.

wee [wi] *adj.* diminuto, chiquitico, pequeñito.

weed [wid] *s.* cizaña, mala hierba; *v.* desherbar (*o* desyerbar), quitar o arrancar la mala hierba; **to — a garden** desherbar un huerto; **to — out** escardar; eliminar, arrancar, entresacar.

weed·y [wídı] *adj.* herboso, lleno de malas hierbas.

week [wik] *s.* semana; —**day** día de trabajo, día laborable, día hábil; — **end** fin de semana; **a — from today** de hoy en ocho días.

week·ly [wíklı] *adj.* semanal, semanario; *adv.* semanalmente, por semana; *s.* semanario, periódico o revista semanal.

weep [wip] *v.* llorar.

weep·ing [wípıŋ] *adj.* llorón; lloroso; — **willow** sauce llorón; *s.* llanto, lloro, lágrimas.

wee·vil [wívl] *s.* gorgojo.

weigh [we] *v.* pesar; ponderar, considerar; **to — anchor** zarpar, levar el ancla; **to — down** agobiar; abrumar; **to — on one's conscience** serle a uno gravoso, pesarle a uno.

weight [wet] *s.* peso; pesa (*de reloj o medida para pesar*); carga; **paper**— pisapapeles; *v.* cargar, sobrecargar; añadir peso a; asignar un peso o valor relativo a.

weight·y [wétı] *adj.* grave, ponderoso; de mucho peso; importante.

weird [wırd] *adj.* extraño, raro, misterioso, fantástico.

wel·come [wélkəm] *s.* bienvenida; buena acogida; *adj.* grato, agradable; bien acogido, bien quisto; bien-venido; bien recibido; — **home!** ¡bienvenido!; — **rest** grato reposo o descanso; **you are** — no hay de qué, de nada (*para contestar a* "thank you"); **you are** — **here** está Vd. en su casa; **you are** — **to use it** se lo presto con todo gusto; está a su disposición; *v.* dar la bienvenida a; acoger o recibir con gusto.

weld [wɛld] *v.* soldar(se); *s.* soldadura.

wel·fare [wélfɛr] *s.* bienestar; bien; felicidad; — **work** labor social o de beneficencia.

well [wɛl] *adv.* bien; **he is** — **over fifty** tiene mucho más de cincuenta años; — **then** pues bien, ahora bien, conque; **well-being** bienestar; **well-bred** bien criado; bien educado; **well-done** bien cocido; **well-fixed** acomodado; **well-groomed** acicalado; **well-meaning** bien intencionado; **well-nigh** casi, muy cerca de; *adj.* bueno; bien de salud, sano; conveniente; — **and good** santo y muy bueno; **well-off** acomodado, adinerado; en buenas condiciones; **well-to-do** próspero, adinerado; **all is** — no hay novedad, todo va bien; **it is** — **to do it** conviene hacerlo, es conveniente hacerlo.

well [wɛl] *s.* (*shaft*) pozo; (*cistern*) cisterna; (*spring*) manantial; artesian — pozo artesiano; *v.* manar; **tears -ed up in her eyes** se le arrasaron los ojos de lágrimas.

welt [wɛlt] *s.* verdugo, verdugón, roncha.

went [wɛnt] *pret. de* **to go.**

wept [wɛpt] *pret. & p.p. de* **to weep.**

were [wɜ] *pret. de* **to be** (*en el plural y en la segunda persona del singular del indicativo; es además el imperfecto del subjuntivo*); **if I — you** si yo fuera Vd.; **there** — había, hubo.

west [wɛst] *s.* oeste, occidente, ocaso; *adj.* occidental, del oeste; **West Indies** Antillas; *adv.* hacia el oeste, al oeste; en el oeste.

west·ern [wéstən] *adj.* occidental, del oeste.

west·ern·er [wéstənə] *s.* natural del oeste, habitante del oeste, occidental.

west·ward [wéstwəd] *adv.* hacia el oeste; *adj.* occidental, oeste.

wet [wɛt] *adj.* húmedo; mojado; — **nurse** nodriza, ama de leche; *s.* humedad; antiprohibicionista (*el que favorece la venta de bebidas alcohólicas*); *v.* mojar; humedecer; *pret. & p.p. de* **to wet.**

wet·back [wétbæk] *s.* panza mojada.

wet·ness [wétnıs] *s.* humedad.

whack [hwæk] *v.* golpear, pegar; *s.* golpe; golpazo; tentativa, prueba.

whale [hwel] *s.* ballena; *v.* pescar ballenas.

wharf [hwɔrf] s. muelle, embarcadero.
what [hwɑt] pron. interr. qué; qué cosa; cuál; pron.
rel. lo que; — **for?** ¿para qué? adj. qué; —
book? ¿qué libro? — **a man!** ¡qué hombre!;
— **happy children!** ¡qué niños más (o tan)
felices!; **take** — **books you need** tome Vd. los
libros que necesite.
what·ev·er [hwɑtévɚ] pron. cualquiera cosa que, lo
que, cuanto, todo lo que; — **do you mean?**
¿qué quiere Vd. decir?; **do it,** — **happens**
hágalo suceda lo que suceda; adj. cualquiera;
any person — una persona cualquiera; **no money**
— nada de dinero.
what·so·ev·er [hwɑtsoévɚ] = **whatever.**
wheat [hwit] s. trigo; **cream of** — crema de trigo.
whee·dle [hwídl] v. engatusar.
wheel [hwil] s. (disc) rueda; rodaja; disco; (bike)
bicicleta; — **chair** silla rodante, silla de ruedas;
steering — volante (de automóvil); rueda del
timón; v. rodar; hacer rodar; girar; acarrear;
andar en bicicleta; **to** — **around** dar una vuelta;
girar sobre los talones; **to** — **the baby** pasear
al bebé en su cochecito.
wheel·bar·row [hwílbæro] s. carretilla.
wheeze [hwiz] s. resuello ruidoso.
when [hwɛn] adv. & conj. cuando; adv. interr.
¿cuándo?
whence [hwɛns] adv. de donde; de que.
when·ev·er [hwɛnévɚ] adj. & conj. cuando,
siempre que, cada vez que.
where [hwɛr] adv. donde; adonde; en donde; por
donde; —? ¿dónde?; ¿adónde?
where·a·bouts [hwérəbaʊts] s. paradero; adv.
interr. ¿dónde?
where·as [hwɛrǽz] conj. mientras que; puesto que,
visto que, considerando que.
where·by [hwɛrbáɪ] adv. por donde, por lo cual;
con lo cual.
where·fore [hwérfor] adv. por lo que; por lo cual;
por eso, por lo tanto.
where·in [hwɛrín] adv. en que; en donde; en lo
cual.
where·of [hwɛráv] adv. de que; de donde; de
quien, de quienes.
where·up·on [hwɛrəpán] adv. después de lo cual;
entonces.
where·ev·er [hwɛrévɚ] adv. dondequiera que,
adondequiera que, por dondequiera que.
where·with·al [hwérwɪðɔl] s. medios, fondos;
dinero.
whet [hwɛt] v. amolar, afilar; aguzar, estimular.
wheth·er [hwέðɚ] conj. si; ya sea que, sea que; —
we escape or not ya sea que escapemos o no;
I doubt — dudo (de) que.
which [hwɪtʃ] pron. interr. ¿cuál?; ¿cuáles?; pron.
rel. que; el cual, la cual, los cuales, las cuales;
el que, la que, los que, las que; adj. interr.
¿qué?; — **boy has it?** ¿cuál de los muchachos
lo tiene? ¿qué muchacho lo tiene?; — **way did
he go?** ¿por qué camino se fue?; ¿por dónde se
fue?; **during** — **time** tiempo durante el cual.
which·ev·er [hwɪtʃévɚ] pron. & adj. cualquiera
(que), cualesquiera (que); el que, la que, lo que; — **road
you take** cualquier camino que Vd. siga.
whiff [hwɪf] s. (waft) soplo; fumada, bocanada;
(odor) repentino olor o hedor; v. soplar; echar
bocanadas.
while [hwaɪl] s. rato; tiempo, temporada; **a short**
— un ratito; **a short** — **ago** hace poco, hace
poco rato; **to be worth** — valer la pena; conj.
mientras, mientras que; v. **to** — **away the time**

pasar el tiempo.
whilst [hwaɪlst] conj. mientras, mientras que.
whim [hwɪm] s. capricho, antojo.
whim·per [hwímpɚ] v. lloriquear, gimotear;
quejarse; s. lloriqueo, gimoteo; quejido.
whim·si·cal [hwímzɪkl] adj. caprichoso.
whine [hwaɪn] v. lloriquear; quejarse; s. gemido,
quejido.
whin·er [hwáɪnɚ] s. llorón, persona quejosa, Méx.
quejumbres; Andes quejumbroso; Riopl.
rezongón.
whip [hwɪp] v. azotar, fustigar; zurrar, dar una
paliza a, dar latigazos a; batir (crema, huevos);
vencer; **to** — **up** batir, coger o asir de repente;
hacer de prisa; s. azote, látigo, fuete; batido.
whip·ping [hwípɪŋ] s. tunda, zurra, paliza; —
cream crema para batir.
whir [hwɝ] v. zumbar; s. zumbido.
whirl [hwɝl] v. girar, dar vueltas; arremolinarse;
my head -s siento vértigo, estoy desvanecido;
s. giro, vuelta; remolino; espiral (de humo);
confusión.
whirl·pool [hwɝ́lpul] s. remolino, vorágine, vórtice.
whirl·wind [hwɝ́lwɪnd] s. remolino, torbellino.
whisk [hwɪsk] v. barrer; desempolvar (con
escobilla); batir (huevos); **to** — **away** barrer de
prisa; llevarse de prisa, arrebatar; irse de prisa,
escaparse; **to** — **something out of sight**
escamotear algo, esconder algo de prisa; s. —
broom escobilla; **with a** — **of the broom** de un
escobillazo.
whis·ker [hwískɚ] s. pelo de la barba, -s barbas;
patillas; bigotes (del gato).
whis·key [hwískɪ] s. whisky (aguardiente de maíz,
centeno, etc.).
whis·per [hwíspɚ] v. cuchichear, hablar en secreto;
soplar, decir al oído; susurrar; secretearse; **it is
-ed that** corre la voz que; dizque, dicen que; s.
cuchicheo, secreteo; susurro; murmullo; **to talk
in a** — hablar en secreto; susurrar.
whis·tle [hwɪsl] v. siblar; chiflar; pitar; **to** — **for
someone** llamar a uno con un silbido; s. silbido,
chiflido; silbato, pito.
whit [hwɪt] s. jota, pizca.
white [hwaɪt] adj. (color) blanco; (pure) puro;
inocente; (honorable) honrado, recto; —**caps**
cabrillas o palomas (olas con crestas blancas);
— **lead** albayalde; — **lie** mentirilla, mentira
venial; **white-livered** cobarde; **white-collar** de
oficina; **to show the** — **feather** mostrar cobardía,
portarse como cobarde; s. blanco; clara (del
huevo).
whit·en [hwáɪtn] v. blanquear; emblanquecer(se),
poner(se) blanco.
white·ness [hwáɪtnɪs] s. blancura; palidez; pureza.
white·wash [hwáɪtwaʃ] v. (paint) blanquear,
enjalbegar; (gloss over) encubrir, disimular
(faltas, errores); absolver (sin justicia); s.
lechada.
whith·er [hwíðɚ] adv. adonde; —? ¿adónde?
whit·ish [hwáɪtɪʃ] adj. blancuzco, blanquecino,
blanquizco.
whit·tle [hwɪtl] v. cortar, mondar, tallar; tajar,
sacar punta a (un lápiz); **to** — **down expenses**
cercenar o reducir los gastos.
whiz [hwɪz] v. zumbar; s. zumbido, silbido; **to
be** — **a** — ser un águila, ser muy listo.
who [hu] pron. rel. quien, quienes, que, el que, la
que, los que, las que; **he** — el que, quien; pron.
interr. ¿quién? ¿quiénes?; — **is it?** ¿quién es?
who·ev·er [huévɚ] pron. quienquiera que,

cualquiera que; el que.
whole [hol] *adj.* todo; entero; íntegro; **the — day** todo el día; **—hearted** sincero, cordial; **—heartedly** de todo corazón; con todo ánimo; *s.* todo, total, totalidad; **as a —** en conjunto; **on the —** en general, en conjunto.
whole·sale [hólsel] *s.* venta al por mayor, *Am.* mayoreo; **by —** al por mayor; *adj.* al por mayor; en grandes cantidades; **— dealer** comerciante al por mayor; *Am.* mayorista; **— slaughter** matanza; gran hecatombe; **— trade** comercio al por mayor, *Am.* comercio mayorista; *adv.* al por mayor, por mayor; *v.* vender al por mayor, *Am.* mayorear.
whole·some [hólsəm] *adj.* saludable, sano; salubre; **— man** hombre normalmente bueno o de buena índole.
whol·ly [hólɪ] *adv.* enteramente, completamente, totalmente.
whom [hum] *pron. pers.* a quien, a quienes; que; al que (a la que, a los que, *etc.*); al cual (a la cual, a los cuales, *etc.*); **for —** para quien; **— did you see?** ¿a quién vió Vd.?
whoop [hup] *s.* grito, chillido, alarido; respiro convulsivo (*que acompaña a la tos ferina*); *v.* gritar, vocear, echar gritos; respirar convulsivamente (*al toser*); **to — it up** armar una gritería, gritar; **whooping cough** tos ferina.
whore [hor] *s.* ramera, puta, prostituta.
whose [huz] *pron.* cuyo, cuya, cuyos, cuyas; *pron. interr.* ¿de quién?; ¿de quiénes?; **— book is this?** ¿de quién es este libro?
why [hwaɪ] *adv.* ¿por qué?; **the reason —** la razón por la que (*o* la cual); **—, of course!** ¡sí, por supuesto!; ¡claro que sí!; **—, that is not true!** ¡si eso no es verdad! *s.* porqué, causa, razón, motivo.
wick [wɪk] *s.* mecha, pabilo.
wick·ed [wíkɪd] *adj.* malvado, malo, inicuo; nefasto.
wick·ed·ness [wíkɪdnɪs] *s.* maldad, iniquidad, perversidad.
wick·er [wíkɚ] *s.* mimbre; **— chair** silla de mimbre.
wick·et [wíkɪt] *s.* postigo; ventanilla.
wide [waɪd] *adj.* ancho; amplio; vasto; extenso; **— apart** muy apartados; **wide-awake** muy despierto; alerta, vigilante; **— eyed** ojoso; **— of the mark** muy lejos del blanco; **— open** muy abierto; abierto de par en par; **far and —** por todas partes, extensamente; **to open —** abrir mucho; abrir (*la puerta*) de par en par; **two feet —** dos pies de ancho (*o* de anchura).
wide·ly [wáɪdlɪ] *adv.* ampliamente; extensamente; muy; mucho.
wid·en [wáɪdṇ] *v.* ensanchar(se), ampliar(se), dilatar(se).
wide·spread [wáɪdspréd] *adj.* muy esparcido, muy extensivo; bien difundido; extendido; general, extendido por todas partes.
wid·ow [wído] *s.* viuda.
wid·ow·er [wídəwɚ] *s.* viudo.
width [wɪdθ] *s.* ancho, anchura.
wield [wild] *v.* manejar; esgrimir (*la espada o la pluma*); ejercer (*el poder*).
wife [waɪf] *s.* esposa.
wig [wɪg] *s.* peluca.
wig·gle [wɪgl] *v.* menear(se); *s.* meneo.
wig·wam [wígwɑm] *s.* choza de los indios norteños.
wild [waɪld] *adj.* salvaje; (*animal*) feroz, fiero; indómito; montaraz; (*plant*) silvestre; *Ven.*,

Méx. cimarrón; impetuoso, desenfrenado; bullicioso; violento; loco; enojado; desatinado; ansioso; **to talk —** disparatar, desatinar; *s.* yermo, desierto, monte.
wild·cat [wáɪldkæt] *s.* gato montés; **— scheme** empresa arriesgada.
wil·der·ness [wíldɚnɪs] *s.* yermo, desierto, monte; inmensidad.
wild-eyed [wáɪldaɪd] *adj.* de ojos huraños.
wild·ness [wáɪldnɪs] *s.* salvajez; ferocidad, fiereza; locura.
wile [waɪl] *s.* ardid, engaño; astucia.
will [wɪl] *v.* (*desire*) querer, decidir; (*order*) ordenar, mandar; (*dispose of legally*) legar; *v. defect. y aux.* rigurosamente debe usarse para formar el futuro en las segundas y terceras personas: **she —** go ella irá; *en las primeras personas indica voluntad o determinación:* **I — not do it** no lo haré, no quiero hacerlo.
will [wɪl] *s.* (*wish*) voluntad; albedrío; (*legal disposition*) testamento; **free —** libre albedrío; **ill —** mala voluntad, malquerencia.
will·ful, wil·ful [wílfəl] *adj.* voluntarioso, testarudo, caprichudo; intencional.
will·ing [wílɪŋ] *adj.* bien dispuesto, deseoso, complaciente; voluntario; **-ly** *adv.* con gusto, de buena gana, de buena voluntad; voluntariamente.
will·ing·ness [wílɪŋnɪs] *s.* buena voluntad, buena gana.
wil·low [wílo] *s.* sauce; mimbrera; **weeping —** sauce llorón.
wilt [wɪlt] *v.* marchitar(se); ajar(se); desmayar; languidecer.
wi·ly [wáɪlɪ] *adj.* astuto, artero.
win [wɪn] *v.* (*achieve*) ganar; lograr, obtener; alcanzar; (*persuade*) persuadir; **to — out** ganar, triunfar; salirse con la suya; **to — over** persuadir; atraer; alcanzar o ganar el favor de.
wince [wɪns] *v.* cejar (*ante una dificultad o peligro*); encogerse (*de dolor, susto, etc.*).
winch [wɪntʃ] *s.* malacate.
wind [wɪnd] *s.* viento, aire; resuello; **— instrument** instrumento de viento; **to get — of** barruntar; tener noticia de.
wind [waɪnd] *v.* enredar; devanar, ovillar; dar cuerda a (*un reloj*); serpentear (*un camino*); dar vueltas; **to — someone around one's finger** manejar fácilmente a alguien, gobernarle; **to — up one's affairs** terminar o concluir uno sus negocios; *s.* vuelta; recodo.
wind·bag [wíndbæg] *s.* (*instrument*) fuelle; (*person*) parlanchín, hablador.
wind·fall [wíndfɔl] *s.* golpe de fortuna, ganancia repentina, herencia inesperada.
wind·ing [wáɪndɪŋ] *adj.* sinuoso, tortuoso, que da vueltas; **— staircase** escalera de caracol.
wind·mill [wíndmɪl] *s.* molino de viento.
win·dow [wíndo] *s.* ventana; **show —** escaparate, vitrina, aparador, *Am.* vidriera; **— shade** visillo, cortinilla; **— sill** antepecho, repisa de ventana.
win·dow·pane [wíndopen] *s.* cristal de ventana, vidriera.
wind·pipe [wíndpaɪp] *s.* tráquea, gaznate.
wind·shield [wíndʃild] *s.* parabrisa, guardabrisa; **— wiper** limpiaparabrisas.
wind tunnel [wíndtʌnl] *s.* túnel aerodinámico.
wind·ward [wíndwɚd] *s.* barlovento.
wind·y [wíndɪ] *adj.* airoso; ventoso; **it is —** hace aire, ventea, sopla el viento.
wine [waɪn] *s.* vino; *adj.* vinícola; **— cellar** bodega.

wing [wɪŋ] *s.* ala; bastidor (*de escenario*); **under the — of** bajo la tutela de; **to take —** levantar el vuelo.

winged, wing·ed [wɪŋd, wíŋɪd] *adj.* alado.

wing·spread [wíŋsprɛd] *s.* envergadura.

wink [wɪŋk] *v.* guiñar; pestañear, parpadear; *s.* guiño, guiñada; **I didn't sleep a —** no pegué los ojos en toda la noche.

win·ner [wínɚ] *s.* ganador; vencedor; **— of a prize** agraciado, premiado.

win·ning [wínɪŋ] *adj.* (*successful*) ganancioso; triunfante, victorioso; (*charming*) atractivo, encantador; **-s** *s. pl.* ganancias.

win·some [wínsəm] *adj.* simpático, atractivo, gracioso.

win·ter [wíntɚ] *s.* invierno; **— clothes** ropa de invierno; *v.* invernar, pasar el invierno.

win·try [wíntrɪ] *adj.* invernal, de invierno; frío, helado.

wipe [waɪp] *v.* secar; enjugar; limpiar; **to — away one's tears** limpiarse las lágrimas; **to — off** borrar; limpiar; **to — out a regiment** destruir o aniquilar un regimiento.

wire [waɪr] *s.* (*strand*) alambre; (*telegram*) telegrama; **by — por** telégrafo; **— entanglement** alambrada; **— fence** alambrado; **— netting** tela metálica, alambrado; **to pull -s** mover los hilos; *v.* poner alambrado, instalar alambrado eléctrico; atar con alambre; telegrafiar.

wire·less [wáɪrlɪs] *adj.* inalámbrico, sin hilos; **— telegraphy** radiotelegrafía; *s.* radio, radiotelegrafía; telegrafía sin hilos; radiotelefonía; radiograma.

wire tap·ping [wáɪrtæpɪŋ] *s.* secreta conexión interceptora de teléfono.

wir·y [wáɪrɪ] *adj.* de alambre; como alambre; nervudo.

wis·dom [wízdəm] *s.* sabiduría, saber; cordura; prudencia; **— tooth** muela del juicio.

wise [waɪz] *adj.* (*judicious*) sabio, cuerdo, sensato; (*prudent*) discreto, prudente; **the Three Wise Men** los Tres Reyes Magos; **to get — to** darse cuenta de; *s.* modo, manera; **in no — de** ningún modo.

wise·crack [wáɪzkræk] *s.* bufonada, dicho agudo o chocarrero, dicharacho.

wish [wɪʃ] *v.* desear, querer; **to — for** desear; anhelar; **I — it were true!** ¡ojalá (que) fuera verdad!; *s.* deseo.

wish·ful think·ing [wíʃfʊl θíŋkɪŋ] *s.* optimismo ilusorio.

wist·ful [wístfəl] *adj.* anhelante, anheloso, ansioso; tristón, melancólico.

wit [wɪt] *s.* agudeza, sal, chiste; ingenio; hombre agudo o de ingenio; **to be at one's wit's end** haber agotado todo su ingenio; **to be out of one's -s** estar fuera de sí, estar loco; **to lose one's -s** perder el juicio; **to use one's -s** valerse de su industria o ingenio.

witch [wɪtʃ] *s.* hechicera; bruja.

witch·craft [wítʃkræft] *s.* hechicería.

with [wɪð, wɪθ] *prep.* con; para con; en compañía de; **— filled — lleno** de; **ill —** enfermo de; **the one — the black hat** el del (*o* la del) sombrero negro.

with·draw [wɪðdrɔ́] *v.* retirar(se); apartar(se); separar(se); **to — a statement** retractarse.

with·draw·al [wɪðdrɔ́əl] *s.* retirada, retiro.

with·drawn [wɪðdrɔ́n] *p.p. de* **to withdraw.**

with·drew [wɪðdrú] *pret. de* **to withdraw.**

with·er [wíðɚ] *v.* marchitar(se); ajar(se); secar(se).

with·held [wɪθhéld] *pret. & p.p. de* **to withhold.**

with·hold [wɪθhóld] *v.* retener; detener; **to — one's consent** negarse a dar su consentimiento.

with·in [wɪðín] *prep.* dentro de; **— call** al alcance de la voz; **— five miles** a poco menos de cinco millas; **it is — my power** está en mi mano; *adv.* dentro, adentro.

with·out [wɪðáʊt] *prep.* sin; **— my seeing him** sin que yo le viera; *adv.* fuera, afuera.

with·stand [wɪθstǽnd] *v.* resistir; aguantar, padecer.

with·stood [wɪθstúd] *pret. & p.p. de* **to withstand.**

wit·ness [wítnɪs] *s.* testigo; testimonio; *v.* ver, presenciar; ser testigo de; atestiguar, dar fe de.

wit·ti·cism [wítəsɪzəm] *s.* ocurrencia, agudeza, dicho agudo.

wit·ty [wítɪ] *adj.* agudo, ocurrente, gracioso, divertido, chistoso; **— remark** dicho agudo, agudeza, ocurrencia.

wives [waɪvz] *s. pl. de* **wife.**

wiz·ard [wízɚd] *s.* genio, hombre de ingenio; mago, mágico.

wob·ble [wάbl] *s.* bamboleo.

woe [wo] *s.* miseria, aflicción, infortunio; **— is me!** ¡miserable de mi!

woe·ful [wófʊl] *adj.* miserable; abatido.

woke [wok] *pret. de* **wake.**

wolf [wʊlf] (*pl.* **wolves** [wʊlvz]) *s.* lobo.

wom·an [wúmən] (*pl.* **women** [wímɪn]) *s.* mujer; **— writer** escritora; **— chaser** mujeriego, faldero.

wom·an·hood [wúmənhʊd] *s.* estado de mujer; la mujer (las mujeres); integridad femenil; feminidad.

wom·an·kind [wúmənkaɪnd] *s.* la mujer, las mujeres, el sexo femenino.

wom·an·ly [wúmənlɪ] *adj.* femenil, mujeril, femenino; *adv.* femenilmente, como mujer.

womb [wum] *s.* vientre, entrañas; útero, matriz.

won [wʌn] *pret. & p.p. de* **to win.**

won·der [wʌ́ndɚ] *s.* (*marvel*) maravilla; prodigio; (*emotion*) admiración; **in —** maravillado; **no — that** no es mucho que; no es extraño que; *v.* asombrarse, maravillarse, pasmarse, admirarse; **to — at** admirarse de, maravillarse de; **I — what time it is** ¿qué hora será? **I — when he came** ¿cuándo vendría? **I should not — if** no me extrañaría que.

won·der·ful [wʌ́ndɚfəl] *adj.* maravilloso, admirable; **-ly** *adv.* maravillosamente, admirablemente, a las mil maravillas; **-ly well** sumamente bien.

won·drous [wʌ́ndrəs] *adj.* maravilloso, pasmoso, extraño.

wont [wʌnt] *adj.* acostumbrado; **to be — to** soler, acostumbrar, *C.A.* saber; *s.* costumbre, hábito, uso.

woo [wu] *v.* cortejar, enamorar, galantear.

wood [wʊd] *s.* (*material*) madera; (*stick*) palo; (*firewood*) leña; **-s** bosque; selva; **— engraving** grabado en madera; **—shed** leñera, cobertizo par leña; **fire—** leña; **piece of fire—** leño.

wood·cut [wúdkʌt] *s.* grabado en madera.

wood·cut·ter [wúdkʌtɚ] *s.* leñador.

wood·ed [wúdɪd] *adj.* arbolado, poblado de árboles.

wood·en [wúdn] *adj.* de madera, de palo; tieso.

wood·land [wúdlænd] *s.* monte, bosque, selva.

wood·man [wúdmən] *s.* (*vendor*) leñador; (*dweller*) habitante del bosque.

wood·peck·er [wúdpɛkɚ] *s.* pájaro carpintero.

wood·work [wúdwɜk] *s.* maderamen; labrado en madera; obra de carpintería.

woof [wuf] *s.* trama (*de un tejido*); tejido.

wool [wʊl] *s.* lana; *adj.* de lana; lanar; **wool-**

WH

bearing lanar; — **dress** vestido de lana.
wool·en [wúlɪn] *adj.* de lana; lanudo; — **mill** fábrica de tejidos de lana; *s.* tejido de lana; género o paño de lana.
wool·ly [wúlɪ] *adj.* lanudo; de lana.
word [wɜd] *s.* (*vocable*) palabra; vocablo, voz; (*news*) noticia, aviso; (*order*) mandato, orden; **pass**— contraseña; **by** — **of mouth** de palabra, verbalmente; *v.* expresar; redactar, formular.
word·y [wɜ́dɪ] *adj.* palabrero, verboso, ampuloso.
wore [wor] *pret. de* **to wear**.
work [wɜk] *s.* (*effort*) trabajo; (*masterpiece*) obra maestra (*task*) tarea; faena; (*employment*) empleo, ocupación; oficio; (*accomplishment*) labor; **-s** taller, fábrica; maquinaria, mecanismo; **at** — trabajando; ocupado; *v.* trabajar; funcionar; obrar; surtir efecto; manejar, manipular; resolver (*un problema*); explotar (*una mina*); hacer trabajar; **to** — **havoc** hacer estropicios, causar daño; **to** — **loose** soltarse, aflojarse; **to** — **one's way through college** sufragar los gastos universitarios con su trabajo; **to** — **one's way up** subir por sus propios esfuerzos; **to** — **out a plan** urdir un plan; **to be all -ed up** estar sobreexcitado; **it didn't** — **out** no dió resultado; **the plan -ed well** tuvo buen éxito el plan.
work·a·ble [wɜkəbl] *adj.* practicable; explotable.
work·er [wɜ́kə] *s.* trabajador; obrero; operario.
work·ing [wɜ́kɪŋ] *s.* funcionamiento, operación; cálculo (*de un problema*); explotación (*de una mina*); *adj.* obrero, trabajador; — **class** clase obrera o trabajadora; — **hours** horas de trabajo; **a hard-working man** un hombre muy trabajador.
work·ing·man [wɜ́kɪŋmæn] *s.* trabajador; obrero.
work·man [wɜ́kmən] *s.* trabajador, obrero, operario.
work·man·ship [wɜ́kmənʃɪp] *s.* hechura; trabajo; mano de obra.
work·shop [wɜ́kʃɑp] *s.* taller.
world [wɜld] *s.* mundo; **the World War** la Guerra Mundial; **world-shaking** de gran importancia.
world·ly [wɜ́ldlɪ] *adj.* mundano, mundanal, terreno, terrenal.
worm [wɜm] *s.* gusano; lombriz; **worm-eaten** comido de gusanos; carcomido, apolillado; *v.* **to** — **a secret out of someone** extraerle o sonsacarle un secreto a una persona; **to** — **oneself into** insinuarse en, meterse en.
worn [worn] *p.p. de* **to wear; worn-out** gastado, roto; rendido de fatiga.
wor·ry [wɜ́ɪ] *s.* inquietud, ansiedad, cuidado, preocupación, apuro, apuración; *v.* inquietar(se), preocupar(se), afligir(se), apurar(se).
worse [wɜs] *adj.* peor; más malo; *adv.* peor; — **and** — cada vez peor; — **than ever** peor que nunca; **from bad to** — de mal en peor; **so much the** — tanto peor; **to be** — **off** estar peor que antes; **to change for the** — empeorar(se); **to get** — empeorar(se).
wor·ship [wɜ́ʃəp] *s.* adoración, culto; veneración; *v.* adorar; reverenciar.
wor·ship·er [wɜ́ʃəpə] *s.* adorador; **the -s** los fieles.
worst [wɜst] *adj.* peor; *adv.* peor; **the** — el peor; la peor; lo peor; *v.* derrotar.
worth [wɜθ] *s.* valor, valía, mérito; precio; **ten cent's** — **of** diez centavos de; **to get one's money's** — **out of** sacar todo el provecho posible del dinero gastado en; *adj.* digno de; — **hearing** digno de oírse; **to be** — valer; **to be** — **doing** valer la pena de hacerse; **to be** — **while** valer la

pena.
worth·less [wɜ́θlɪs] *adj.* sin valor; inútil; despreciable.
wor·thy [wɜ́ðɪ] *adj.* digno; valioso, apreciable; meritorio, merecedor; *s.* benemérito, hombre ilustre.
would [wʊd] *imperf. de indic. y de subj. del verbo defect.* **will: she** — **come every day** solía venir (*o* venía) todos los días; **if you** — **do it** si lo hiciera Vd.; *expresa a veces deseo*: — **that I knew it!** ¡quién lo supiera!; ¡ojalá que yo lo supiera!; *v. aux. del condicional*: **she said she** — **go** dijo que iría.
wound [wund] *s.* herida; llaga, lesión; *v.* herir; lastimar; agraviar.
wound [waʊnd] *pret. & p.p. de* **to wind**.
wove [wov] *pret. de* **to weave**.
wo·ven [wóvən] *p.p. de* **to weave**.
wow [waʊ] *v.* entusiasmar.
wran·gle [ræŋgl] *v.* (*quarrel*) altercar, disputar; reñir; (*herd*) juntar; *Am.* rodear (*el ganado*); *s.* riña, pendencia.
wrap [ræp] *v.* envolver; enrollar, arrollar; **to** — **up** envolver(se); abrigar(se), tapar(se); **to be wrapped up in** estar envuelto en; estar absorto en; *s.* abrigo, manto.
wrap·per [ræpə] *s.* envoltura, cubierta; **woman's** — bata.
wrap·ping [ræpɪŋ] *s.* envoltura; — **paper** papel de envolver.
wrath [ræθ] *s.* ira, cólera, rabia.
wrath·ful [ræθfəl] *adj.* colérico, rabioso, iracundo.
wreath [riθ] *s.* guirnalda, corona; — **of smoke** espiral de humo.
wreathe [rið] *v.* hacer guirnaldas; adornar con guirnaldas; **-d in smiles** sonriente.
wreck [rɛk] *s.* (*destruction*) ruina; destrucción; (*shipwreck*) naufragio; (*accident*) accidente; (*wreckage*) destrozos, despojos (*de un naufragio*); *v.* arruinar; naufragar; echar a pique; destrozar, demoler; **to** — **a train** descarrilar un tren.
wrench [rɛntʃ] *v.* torcer, retorcer; arrancar, arrebatar; *s.* torcedura, torsión; tirón, arranque, *Andes, Méx., C.A.* jalón; llave de tuercas; **monkey** — llave inglesa.
wrest [rɛst] *v.* arrebatar, arrancar; usurpar.
wres·tle [rɛsl] *v.* luchar a brazo partido; luchar; *s.* lucha a brazo partido.
wres·tler [rɛslə] *s.* luchador (*a brazo partido*).
wretch [rɛtʃ] *s.* miserable, infeliz; villano.
wretch·ed [rɛ́tʃɪd] *adj.* (*miserable*) miserable; afligido; (*unfortunate*) desdichado, infeliz; (*bad*) bajo, vil; malísimo; **a** — **piece of work** un trabajo pésimo o malísimo.
wrig·gle [rɪgl] *v.* menear(se); retorcer(se); **to** — **out** of salirse de, escaparse de; escabullirse de.
wring [rɪŋ] torcer, retorcer; exprimir, estrujar; **to** — **money from someone** arrancar dinero a alguien; **to** — **out** exprimir (*la ropa*).
wrin·kle [rɪŋkl] *s.* arruga; surco; **the latest** — **in style** la última novedad; *v.* arrugar(se).
wrist [rɪst] *s.* muñeca; — **watch** reloj de pulsera.
writ [rɪt] *s.* auto, orden judicial, mandato jurídico; **the Holy Writ** la Sagrada Escritura.
write [raɪt] *v.* escribir; **to** — **back** contestar por carta; **to** — **down** apuntar, poner por escrito; **to** — **off** cancelar (*una deuda*); **to** — **out** poner por escrito; escribir por entero; **to** — **up** relatar, describir; redactar.
writ·er [ráɪtə] *s.* escritor; autor.
writhe [raɪð] *v.* retorcerse.

writ·ing [ráɪtɪŋ] *s.* escritura; escrito; composición literaria; forma o estilo literario; **hand**— letra; — **desk** escritorio; — **paper** papel de escribir; **to put in** — poner por escrito.

writ·ten [rítṇ] *p.p. de* **to write**.

wrong [rɔŋ] *adj.* (*incorrect*) falso, incorrecto; equivocado; (*wicked*) malo; injusto; mal hecho; (*improper*) inoportuno; inconveniente; **the** — **side of a fabric** el envés o el revés de un tejido; **the** — **side of the road** el lado izquierdo o contrario del camino; **that is the** — **book** ése no es el libro; **it is in the** — **place** no está en su sitio, está mal colocado; *adv.* mal; al revés; **to go** — extraviarse, descaminarse; resultar mal; *s.* mal, daño perjuicio; injusticia; agravio; **to be in the** — no tener razón, estar equivocado; **to do** — hacer mal; *v.* perjudicar; agraviar; hacer mal a.

wrote [rot] *pret. de* **to write**.

wrought [rɔt] *pret. & p.p. irr. de* **to work**; *adj.* labrado; forjado; — **iron** hierro forjado; — **silver** plata labrada; **to be wrought-up** estar sobreexcitado.

wrung [rʌŋ] *pret. & p.p. de* **to wring**.

wry [raɪ] *adj.* torcido; **to make a** — **face** hacer una mueca.

X:x

xe·non [zinɑn] *s.* xenón.

Y:y

yacht [jɑt] *s.* yate; *v.* navegar en yate.

Yan·kee [jǽŋkɪ] *adj. & s.* yanqui.

yard [jɑrd] *s.* (*measure*) yarda (*medida*); (*enclosure*) patio; cercado; terreno (*adyacente a una casa*); **back** — corral; **barn**— corral; **navy** — arsenal; **ship**— astillero.

yard·stick [jɑ́rdstɪk] *s.* yarda (*de medir*); medida (*metro, vara, etc.*); patrón, norma.

yarn [jɑrn] *s.* estambre; hilado, hilaza; cuento enredado y poco probable.

yawn [jɔn] *v.* bostezar; *s.* bostezo.

year [jɪr] *s.* año; —**book** anuario; **-'s income** renta anual; **by the** — por año; **leap** — año bisiesto.

year·ling [jírlɪŋ] *s.* primal; becerro.

year·ly [jírlɪ] *adj.* anual; *adv.* anualmente; una vez al año, cada año.

yearn [jɜn] *v.* anhelar; **to** — **for** anhelar; suspirar por.

yearn·ing [jə́nɪŋ] *s.* anhelo.

yeast [jist] *s.* levadura, fermento.

yell [jɛl] *v.* gritar, dar gritos, vociferar; *s.* grito, alarido.

yel·low [jɛ́lo] *adj.* amarillo; cobarde; — **fever** fiebre amarilla; *s.* amarillo; *v.* poner(se) amarillo.

yel·low·ish [jɛ́loɪʃ] *adj.* amarillento.

yelp [jɛlp] *v.* aullar, ladrar; *s.* aullido, ladrido.

yes [jɛs] *adv.* sí.

yes·ter·day [jɛ́stədɪ] *adv. & s.* ayer; **day before** — anteayer o antier.

yet [jɛt] *adv. & conj.* todavía, aún; con todo, sin embargo; no obstante; **as** — todavía, aún; **not** — todavía no.

yield [jild] *v.* (*surrender*) ceder; rendir; someterse; (*produce*) producir; **to** — **five percent** redituar el cinco por ciento; *s.* rendimiento, rendición; rédito.

yod [jod] *s.* yod.

yo·del [jódl] *s.* canto en que la voz fluctúa entre natural y falsete.

yo·ga [jógə] *s.* yoga.

yo·gurt [jogət] *s.* yogur.

yoke [jok] *s.* yugo; yunta (*de bueyes, mulas, etc.*); *v.* uncir; unir.

yolk [jok] *s.* yema (*de huevo*).

yon·der [jándə] *adj.* aquel, aquella, aquellos, aquellas; *adv.* allá, allí, más allá, acullá.

yore [jor]: **in days of** — antaño, en días de antaño.

you [ju] *pron. pers.* tú, usted, vosotros, ustedes; te, le, lo, la, os, las, los; **to** — a tí, a usted, a vosotros, a ustedes; te, le, les; *pron. impers.* se, uno.

young [jʌŋ] *adj.* joven; nuevo; — **leaves** hojas tiernas; — **man** joven; **her** — **ones** sus niños, sus hijitos; **the** — **people** la gente joven, los jóvenes, la juventud; *s.* jóvenes; cría, hijuelos (*de los animales*).

young·ster [jʌ́ŋstə] *s.* muchacho, niño, jovencito, chiquillo.

your [jʊr] *adj.* tu (tus), vuestro (vuestra, vuestros, vuestras), su (sus), de usted, de ustedes.

yours [jʊrz] *pron. pos.* tuyo (tuya, tuyos, tuyas); vuestro (vuestra, vuestros, vuestras); suyo (suya, suyos, suyas), de usted, de ustedes; el tuyo (la tuya, los tuyos, las tuyas); el suyo (la suya, los suyos, las suyas); el (la, los, las) de usted; el (la, los, las) de ustedes; **a friend of** — un amigo tuyo, un amigo vuestro; un amigo suyo, un amigo de usted o ustedes.

your·self [jʊrsélf] *pron.* te, se (*como reflexivo*); **to** — a tí mismo; a usted mismo; **you** — tú mismo; usted mismo; *véase* **herself**.

your·selves [jʊrsélvz] *pron.* os, se (*como reflexivo*); **to** — a vosotros mismos; a ustedes mismos; **you** — vosotros mismos; ustedes mismos.

youth [juθ] *s.* joven; juventud; jóvenes.

youth·ful [júθfəl] *adj.* joven; juvenil.

yt·tri·um [ítrɪəm] *s.* itrio.

yuc·ca [jʌ́kə] *s.* yuca.

Yule·tide [júltaɪd] *s.* Pascua de Navidad; Navidades.

Z:z

zeal [zil] *s.* celo, fervor, ardor, entusiasmo.

zeal·ot [zélət] *s.* fanático.

zeal·ous [zéləs] *adj.* celoso, ardiente, fervoroso.

ze·nith [zinɪθ] *s.* cenit, cumbre.

zeph·yr [zéfə] *s.* céfiro.

ze·ro [zíro] *s.* cero.

zest [zɛst] *s.* entusiasmo; buen sabor.

zig·zag [zígzæg] *s.* zigzag; *adj. & adv.* en zigzag; *v.* zigzaguear, culebrear, andar en zigzag, serpentear.

WO

zinc [zɪŋk] *s.* cinc (zinc).
zip code [zíp kod] *s.* sistema de cifras
norteamericano, establecido para facilitar la
entrega de cartas.
zip·per [zípə·] *s.* cierre relámpago, abrochador
corredizo o de corredera, *Am.* riqui.

zir·co·ni·um [zɪrkóniəm] *s.* circonio.
zo·di·ac [zódɪæk] *s.* zodiaco.
zone [zon] *s.* zona; *v.* dividir en zonas.
zoo [zu] *s.* jardín zoológico.
zo·o·log·i·cal [zoəládʒɪk]] *adj.* zoológico.
zo·ol·o·gy [zoáːlədʒɪ] *s.* zoología.